The Ultimate Guide
to Old-Fashioned
Country Skills

The Ultimate Guide to Old-Fashioned Country Skills

Edited by **Abigail R. Gehring**

Skyhorse Publishing

Skyhorse Publishing books may be purchased in bulk at special discounts for sales promotion, corporate gifts, fund-raising, or educational purposes. Special editions can also be created to specifications. For details, contact the Special Sales Department, Skyhorse Publishing, 307 West 36th Street, 11th Floor, New York, NY 10018 or info@skyhorsepublishing.com.

Skyhorse® and Skyhorse Publishing® are registered trademarks of Skyhorse Publishing, Inc.®, a Delaware corporation.

Visit our website at www.skyhorsepublishing.com.

10 9 8 7 6 5 4 3 2 1

Library of Congress Cataloging-in-Publication Data is available on file.

Print ISBN: 978-1-62914-216-6
Ebook ISBN: 978-1-62914-298-2

Printed in Canada

Table of Contents

Introduction

A few years back my husband befriended a man who had moved into an old farmhouse near our land in Vermont. Tired of the hustle and bustle of the city, he had come with his wife and son to lead a quieter, more sustainable life in the country. In his first year he decided to raise chickens for eggs and pigs for meat, keep a sizable garden, and start a business in town, while his wife kept a full-time job teaching school. It seemed ambitious, but he assured my husband he knew what he was doing. He didn't need books or help or advice—in fact, *he* should be the one writing books, he suggested candidly. We were saddened in the fall when he mentioned he'd lost all the meat he'd harvested because it hadn't cured properly, and not particularly surprised when, shortly afterward, he picked up and moved.

The point of this cautionary tale is that there's a great deal of value in looking back to the ways in which folks have been living off the land for centuries. Any successful homesteader will tell you he owes much of what he's accomplished to the generations who came before. Yes, modern times have brought us improvements in farm equipment, better systems to harness alternative energy, and certainly a wealth of information that's available to us anytime, anywhere. But most of the basic principles of how to grow vegetables and plant fruit trees, how to build a chicken coop or set up a camp in the wilderness, how to milk a cow or bake a pie, have not changed since our great-great-grandparents set up their homesteads. We will all make mistakes in our country-living adventures, and sometimes, even if we do everything right, things will still go wrong. But we can limit our failures by respecting the wisdom of our forefathers and mothers.

This book is a tribute to the farmers, gardeners, hunters, homemakers, carpenters, and cooks who came before us. Here you'll find a treasure trove of time-honored advice, instruction, wit, and wisdom. You'll also find some surprising reminders of eras long gone. Who knew Abercrombie & Fitch used to sell milk powder (page 281), or sold anything at all for two dollars and seventy-five cents, never mind a pack harness (page 326)? By the same token, some of the tips offered in these pages may have more entertainment value than practical application for the modern reader. For example, I cannot vouch for the effectiveness of onions stewed in brown sugar for inducing sleep (page 477), and I'm not sure I'd choose kerosene or molasses as a method for stain removal (page 487). My hope is that you'll read these pieces with open-minded curiosity and a good dose of common sense. I have enough respect for you, the reader, to trust that you'll learn from what's useful and chuckle at what's no longer practical, and not the other way around.

With gratitude to the many writers represented in these pages and to those who helped compile this work, especially faithful helpers Liam Delaney and Julia Cipriano, I present to you, *The Ultimate Guide to Old-Fashioned Country Skills*.

—Abigail R. Gehring

Cooking, Baking, and Preserving

Soups

From *Handy Household Hints and Recipes*, by Mattie Lee Wehrley, 1916

Home-Made Noodles

One egg, one-fourth teaspoonful salt, one teaspoonful baking powder, one tablespoon water, and flour to make a stiff dough. Roll out thin, let dry and cut in strips. Cook in salted, boiling water and before serving pour over croutons sautered in butter.

But if wanted for soup, add while soup is boiling a few minutes before taking up. Cold, left-over noodles may be fried in lard or drippings, and just before taking up pour over them one beaten egg. Remove from pan by inverting plate.

How To Make Good Tomato Soup

One quart can of tomatoes or fresh tomatoes in season, one pint of soup stock, ten peppercorns or a dash of red and black pepper, one small or one-half large bay leaf, four whole cloves, one slice of onion, two level teaspoonfuls of sugar and two teaspoonfuls of salt.

Cook the tomatoes and seasoning for twenty minutes, then press through a wire strainer to remove seeds and bits of seasoning. While hot, add two pinches of baking soda, as held firmly between thumb and forefinger. Soda cuts the acidity of tomatoes. Heat the butter till it bubbles in the bottom of a sauce pan, but do not let it brown. Place pan on the side of the range and mix three tablespoonfuls of flour smoothly with the hot butter. Add the strained hot tomatoes and serve very hot with croutons. If it is not convenient to use meat stock, one pint of water may be added to the tomatoes and seasoning when they first begin to cook. This makes an excellent tomato bouillon, and having no meat extracts, it will keep a long time if kept covered and in a cool place. It is always ready for quick service either as a soup or a sauce for chops or cutlets. The amount of thickening, and seasoning may be varied according to the individual taste and the purpose for which it is used.

Croutons For Soup

Croutons for soup are easily made by cutting bread into slices about half an inch thick, buttering on both sides, cutting in half-inch squares and baking in the oven until brown.

Tomato Puree

One can tomatoes, one saltspoon mace, one teaspoon salt, one saltspoon white pepper, one small onion, two teaspoons butter, two tablespoons flour.

Carrot Puree

Cook enough carrots to make one cup, when rubbed through the seive, adding the carrot puree to a cream sauce, made of two tablespoonfuls of butter and two tablespoonfuls of flour, adding one pint of milk, cook for five minutes, season to taste with salt and paprika. Sprinkle with finely chopped parsley.

Bean Soup

Use a good soup stock, add navy beans, one small onion and one cup of tomato pulp, seasoning, and boil two or three hours.

Vegetable Soup

Two pounds of brisket, two potatoes, one small cabbage, four tomatoes, one onion, one stalk leek, celery and parsley, one carrot, one-half cup butter beans, one small red pepper, one-half teacup rice, one ear corn, and salt to taste, and six quarts of water. Put beef on with water; let boil and skim, then add vegetables and cook.

More Soups, Sauces, and Veggies

From *Blue Hen's Chickens' Cook Book*, 1921

Noodle Soup

One and one-half pints of flour, two eggs, four tablespoonfuls milk, a little salt; mix into stiff dough; roll out very thin in two sheets. Lay on a cloth and dry for two hours. Fold up and cut into narrow strips; drop into boiling soup; cook twenty minutes. Enough for one chicken.

Chicken Soup

To one chicken add three pints of water; let simmer until tender; drain liquor off; add one tablespoonful of rice, two tablespoonfuls peas, parsley and noodles, butter, pepper and salt to taste; tomatoes may be used too.

Cream of Pea Soup

One pint of peas boiled and mashed through a colander; place in a saucepan one tablespoonful of butter; let it melt; then add two even tablespoonfuls of flour; stir well and then add slowly one pint of boiling water, then one quart of boiling milk, then the mashed peas.

Cook until well blended; season with salt and pepper. Serve with toasted crackers.

Tomato Soup

One quart of tomatoes; stew in one pint of water and pinch of soda. Cook on back of stove for an hour; strain through sieve, return to the fire at boiling point; stir in two tablespoonfuls of butter, mixed with a tablespoonful of flour; scant teaspoonful of salt, a little onion and red pepper; add a quart of milk or a pint of cream. Let it boil up, then serve.

Another Kind of Tomato Soup

One quart of canned tomatoes, one quart of water, one quart of milk, one small onion, two tablespoonfuls of butter, one teaspoonful of red pepper, one teaspoonful of salt, one teaspoonful of sugar.

Boil tomato and onion in one quart of water ten minutes, then add salt, pepper and sugar; press through a sieve; return to the fire; add butter and milk; let simmer for twenty minutes. Serve with croutons.

Tomato Sauce

One can of tomatoes, four tablespoonfuls of Worcestershire, two onions grated, one spoonful of butter. Cook all together ten minutes; then strain and thicken with cornstarch. This is nice with roast beef.

Fried Tomatoes With Cream Gravy

Wash and cut in halves firm and well filled tomatoes; lay in pan with skin side down; place a lump of butter over each slice; dredge with salt and pepper; fry slowly; turn and cook the other side. When done place carefully upon a heated dish. Brown the butter in the pan and add gradually two tablespoonfuls of flour and a cupful of cream or milk, stirring all the time until smooth; season with salt and pepper; pour it over tomatoes and serve.

French Fried Potatoes

Peel potatoes and cut in eight lengthwise strips, or slice very thin. Throw into iced water for an hour; drain; pat dry between the folds of a towel, or napkin, and fry to a golden brown in deep boiling fat. When tender, take from the pan with a skimmer and turn into a colander lined with tissue or brown paper, to absorb any grease that may adhere to them. Stand in the oven a few minutes, sprinkle with salt, and serve.

Stuffed Potatoes, No. 1

Wash medium sized potatoes and bake until soft. Cut potatoes almost in half, take out the potato meat; put in a bowl, half an onion (chopped) and a little parsley, butter, pepper and salt. Add enough cream to moisten potatoes; whip all together until very light; place back in their jackets, and heat in the oven; then serve.

Scalloped Potatoes with Tomatoes, No. 2

Pare potatoes, slice thin and cover bottom of earthen dish, season with salt, pepper and plenty of butter. Then cover with a layer of tomatoes; fill the dish in this way, and sprinkle plenty of bread crumbs on top. Bake till thoroughly done.

Scalloped Potatoes With Cheese, No. 3

Pare potatoes, slice thin and cover bottom of earthen dish; season with salt, pepper and plenty of butter; then add a layer of cheese; fill the dish in this way, then pour about a cupful of milk over it. Place in oven, and bake till thoroughly done.

Fried Eggplant

Peel the eggplants, slice and sprinkle a little salt over them; let them remain one-half hour; wipe the slices dry, dip them in beaten yolks of eggs, then in crumbs of crackers or bread, fry them a light brown in boiling lard. Pepper them slightly while frying. Another way is to parboil them in a little water after they are peeled, then slice, dust with flour, and fry.

Summer Squash

Unless they are extremely tender, it is best to pare them, cutting away as little as possible beside the hard outer rind; take out the ends, quarter them, and lay the pieces in cold water. Boil about an hour. Drain well, pressing out all the water; mash until soft and smooth; and season with butter, pepper and salt.

Spinach

Pick leaves from stems, and wash thoroughly. Pour over it a pint of boiling water; put on stove and cook well. Drain and chop fine; season with salt and pepper; garnish with slices of hard boiled eggs.

String Beans

Get them young and crisp, string them, break in halves and boil in water with a little salt until tender. Drain free from water, season with pepper; add butter, a spoonful or two of cream or milk, and boil a few minutes.

Lima Beans

Put a pint of beans in just enough boiling salted water to cover them, boil till tender; then drain off the water; add a cupful of cream, a little butter, pepper and salt. Simmer a few minutes, and serve.

Stuffed Tomatoes

Cut the top from soft part of tomatoes; let hang on hinge; scoop out contents, strain to get out seeds; have chopped meat well seasoned with rice that has been par-boiled, put this in tomatoes; shut down lid. Place them in a pan close together; pour the tomato juice around them. Either steam or bake one hour.

Lake Fish Salad

Take a nice large fish (one with coarse flesh is better), boil until tender and let it cool; chop, not too fine, and add some nice tender lettuce, if you can't get celery; make a dressing of three eggs, a lump of butter the size of an egg, half teaspoonful of mustard, cayenne pepper and salt to taste, four tablespoonfuls of vinegar; cook until thick.

Save out two whites of the eggs, beat light and add to dressing when cold; thin with cream. Serve on lettuce leaves.

Shrimp Salad

Break each shrimp in half and serve on lettuce leaves with this dressing: two eggs, beat whites slightly, then the yolks, and add to whites; put in one-half teaspoonful of salt, the same of sugar, two tablespoonfuls of olive oil, one-half cup of vinegar. Cook until smooth. A little mustard may be added if preferred. When cold add one-half cup of whipped cream. The cream should be added just before serving.

Tomato Salad

Pare three large tomatoes and put on the ice to get cold. Take the yolks of two hard boiled eggs, one-half a teaspoonful of salt, the same of mustard, a little red pepper and two teaspoonsfuls of olive oil or melted butter; mix all together, then add enough vinegar to make like thick cream.

When ready to serve, slice the tomatoes and pour dressing over them. Cut the whites of eggs in rings and garnish dish.

Deviled Eggs

Five hard boiled eggs, butter the size of a walnut, half a pint of milk, two teaspoonfuls of cornstarch, heaping tablespoonful grated cheese, small coffee spoonful dry mustard; take spoonful of olive oil, salt, red and black pepper; mix the yolks, mustard, olive oil and condiments together in a bowl with the back of a silver spoon; put into the chafing dish the milk; the butter with which the cornstarch has been mixed; the whites of the eggs, cut fine; a little salt.

Stir constantly until boiling hot. In the meantime let someone spread thick over slices of buttered toast the paste, over which scatter the cheese; over this pour this hot white sauce and serve.

Cheese Omelet

Take one pint of milk, one and a half teacupfuls of grated cheese, three eggs, piece of butter size of an egg, bread crumbs enough to thicken the milk.

Put the milk and bread crumbs on the fire and when just coming to a boil add cheese and butter; then take from fire and add beaten yolks of the eggs; also a little salt, cayenne pepper and a pinch of mustard; then add whites of eggs beaten to stiff froth and stir; pour into a buttered pudding dish and bake in a quick oven till brown. Serve hot.

Sauces, Salads, and Veggies

From *Handy Household Hints and Recipes*, by Mattie Lee Wehrley, 1916

Tomato Sauce

Add to half a can of tomatoes two whole cloves, pepper and salt to taste and a sprig of parsley. Stew fifteen minutes and strain through a sieve. Keep hot while you put into a saucepan a tablespoonful of butter and heat over the fire to bubbling. Add then a tablespoonful of flour; stir until smooth, pour in the strained tomatoes and stir for a minute longer.

Potatoes Au Gratin

Peel and parboil white potatoes. Slice thin and arrange in layers in a buttered pudding dish, sprinkling each layer with bits of butter and salt and pepper. Cover the top layer thickly with buttered and salted crumbs and grated cheese. Pour in carefully, not to disturb the layers, a gill (½ cup) of warm milk. Cover and set in the oven and bake for one-half hour, then uncover and brown.

Potato Cakes

Season two cupfuls of very finely mashed potato, with a half teaspoonful of pepper and a half teaspoonful of salt. Sift in one cupful of flour containing one teaspoonful of baking powder. Add enough milk to make a soft dough. Flour well, then roll one-half inch thick. Cut into potato cakes two inches square. Grease a hot gridiron very lightly, lay the cakes on it, and cook them on top of the stove or on gas that is turned low. Cover for about five minutes, until they raise and are brown on one side. Then, turn them over and brown them on the other side. When done, split them open while hot, and butter them. Serve at once.

Hashed Potatoes—Browned

Cut cold boiled potatoes into very small dice, mix with them a great tablespoonful of butter, a dash of minced onions and a tablespoonful of minced parsley. Turn into a greased frying pan, and cook long enough for the mass to brown at the bottom. Do not stir. When browned, loosen about the edges and bottom of the pan with a knife, and turn the pan upside down over a heated platter.

Candied Yams

Boil the sweet potatoes in water until done, then place in baking dish (sliced) and pour over melted butter, brown sugar and one cup of milk, and brown in oven. You can add a little nutmeg.

Chicken Salad

Cut meat from boiled fowl into dice. Do not chop meat or celery. To two cups of chicken add one cup of crisp, tender celery cut into quarter-inch lengths. Mix and season with salt and white pepper. Stir in enough French dressing to moisten salad and set on ice. Serve in lettuce-lined bowl and pour mayonnaise dressing over all.

Romaine Salad

Two heads of lettuce, one bunch of watercress, eight French radishes, two olives, eight hard boiled eggs. Cut the radishes and olives in small pieces, grate the yolks of the eggs and chop the white; add a few bits of pickle beet. Toss all up lightly and serve on the lettuce leaves with an oil or cream dressing.

Shrimp Salad

If shrimp are large, cut in half. Season well with salt and pepper, then mix well with crisp celery, chopped fine with a very little onion. Heap in salad dish, cover with a good mayonnaise and garnish with sliced hard-boiled eggs, sliced lemon, sliced beets and celery tips.

Portuguese Salad

Slice two medium-sized, firm cucumbers, one small Spanish onion, two medium-sized tomatoes, two sweet peppers and two sound apples, from which the cores have been removed. Mix in a salad bowl with four tablespoons of French dressing. Serve plain or on lettuce leaves, ice cold.

Daisy Salad

With a sharp knife cut rounds of cream or of Neufchatel cheese about a quarter of an inch thick, and lay each upon a crisp lettuce leaf. In the center of each round of cheese dispose a "heart" of finely powdered egg yolk, hard boiled and cold. (Rub it through a fine colander or put it through a vegetable press to get the powder.) Pour a French dressing on the leaf about the "daisy." Or you may simulate the

flower by omitting the powdered egg and dropping a little mayonnaise upon the cheese.

Vegetable Salad

One pint peas, one pint string beans, three heads of shredded lettuce, one bunch of parsley and one onion chopped. Boil peas and beans until tender, then mix all together with a good salad dressing.

A Tasty Cheese Spread

This can be used as a sandwich filling, spread on crackers or made into small balls and served with crisp lettuce as a salad course. It is excellent to have on hand for emergency hospitality, as it keeps for weeks, if stored in a cool place. To make it, take half a pound of American cheese, half a pound of Swiss cheese, one piece of cream cheese, one-quarter of a pound of butter, one teaspoonful of mustard, one small bunch of parsley, pepper and salt to taste and sufficient tomato catsup to moisten—about a small cupful of the catsup is what I use. Put the cheese through the meat grinder; then cream thoroughly, and add the other ingredients. Chopped nut meats or pimento may also be added if desired.

Baked Potatoes with Cheese

Here are two ways of giving zest to the regulation potato recipes: Cream cold boiled potatoes in the usual manner. Place in a dish and cover well with grated cheese. Dot with butter and brown in the oven. Select potatoes of uniform size and bake. When done cut the skin lengthwise of the potato, remove some of the inside and crowd grated cheese into the cavity. Cover the opening with white of egg and brown. Cheese souffle is an extremely dainty luncheon or supper dish. It is also used as an entree for dinner. Have ready a quarter of a pound of rich American cheese grated. Put a pint of milk into a double boiler or into a thick pan where it will not burn. Stir in a quart of stale bread crumbs. Beat until the mixture is smooth. Now add the cheese. Cook for a minute, no longer. Season with a dash of cayenne and a little salt. Remove from the fire and add the yolks of four eggs, mix lightly and stir in the well-beaten whites. Pour into a stoneware baking dish and bake ten minutes in a quick oven. Serve directly it is removed from the oven, from the dish in which it was baked.

Vegetables

From *Good Housekeeping Family Cookbook,* by Mildred Maddocks, 1906

Spinach (Swiss style)

After the spinach has been well washed and boiled with a little baking soda in the water to keep it green, put it in a strainer and squeeze out every bit of water. Now run it through the finest knife of the food chopper twice. Chop also *very fine*, a small onion or half a large one, and sauté in a tablespoon of butter, not allowing it to brown. Add half a tablespoon of flour. When blended add one cup of well flavored stock, stir until free from lumps, then mix in the spinach. Season to taste with salt and pepper, and add a tablespoon of grated cheese. Serve garnished with slices of hard-cooked eggs.

Salsify Fritters

Wash, scrape and put the salsify in cold water to prevent discoloration; cut in inch lengths, cook in boiling salted water until soft, then drain. Mash and season with butter, salt and pepper. Shape in small flat cakes, roll in flour and sauté in fresh butter, browning first one side and then the other.

Cucumber Fritters

Pare fresh, green, not too large cucumbers, cut in long, narrow pieces, and drop into ice water to crisp. Make a batter of one cup of flour sifted with half a teaspoon of salt, one teaspoon of baking powder and a pinch of cayenne, adding two whole eggs alternately with half a cup of ice water, then add a tablespoon of olive oil and the juice of a small lemon; beat in at the last moment the well beaten white of an egg and set away in the ice box until thoroughly chilled. Drain and dry the cucumbers dip them in this batter and fry brown in deep hot fat. Drain on soft paper, sprinkle with salt and mustard, or cayenne, very, very lightly if the latter spice is used, and serve very hot.

Asparagus in Aspic Jelly

Boil a large bunch of asparagus tips in salted water until tender, carefully saving the liquor in which they were cooked as the foundation for the jelly. This is made by adding to the asparagus water, a teaspoon of beef extract, half a teaspoon each of chopped celery and carrot, one bay leaf and three whole cloves; allow these ingredients to simmer for thirty minutes, and then add an ounce of gelatin that has been soaked in half a cup of cold water for ten minutes, stirring until the gelatin is dissolved. Strain the aspic through a double cloth and mold the asparagus tips with alternating layers of hardboiled eggs in an ornamental mold; this is easily accomplished by adding with a spoon only sufficient jelly to set each layer, and waiting until that is hard and firm before arranging the next in place; at serving time unmold, garnish with bunches of cress and serve with graham broad sandwiches.

Asparagus Rissoles

Roll out on the bread board half a pound of rich pie crust, and with a sharp knife cut into neat squares; have in readiness a cup of cooked asparagus tips, covered with a thick cream sauce. Arrange in the center of each square a teaspoon of the prepared asparagus, sprinkle liberally with paprika, salt and chopped parsley; then turn over the paste, the edges lapping in triangle form, and crimp the border with the tines of a silver fork. Place the rissoles, when finished, on ice for at least an hour before cooking. Fry in hot fat to a golden brown, arrange on a chop platter with a folded hemstitched napkin and garnish with crisp parsley and thin slices of lemon.

Masked Sweet Potatoes

Bake the potatoes, cut in halves lengthwise and carefully scoop out the potato. Mash well, add a little butter, pepper and salt and a little cream or milk; beat until creamy; return to the shells, heaping lightly, and place in the oven to reheat.

Candied Sweet Potatoes

Select potatoes of medium size and boil until nearly done. Peel and cut in slices. Lay these in a baking pan; melt one-half cup butter, add one-half cup sugar and stir until sugar is melted. Put one teaspoon of this on each slice and bake until brown. Potatoes should not be sliced thin.

Sweet Potato Fritters

Take one pint of mashed sweet potatoes, two eggs, half a saltspoon of salt, a cup of pastry flour and a teaspoon of baking powder, mix together with a little sweet milk and drop tablespoons of the batter into hot fat, frying a delicate brown; serve with a tomato sauce.

Potato Croquettes

Two cups of mashed white potatoes, two tablespoons of cream, a teaspoon of onion juice, a teaspoon of salt, a dash of nutmeg; yolks of two eggs, a tablespoon of chopped parsley, butter the size of a walnut, a dash of cayenne. Beat the eggs until light, and add to them the potatoes, then add all the other ingredients. Mix and turn into a small saucepan. Stir over the fire until it is thoroughly heated through. The mixture will then leave the side of the pan without sticking to it. Take from the fire, and when cool form into cylinders. Roll first in egg and then in bread crumbs and fry in boiling fat. This will make about twelve croquettes.

Potato Custards

Boil and mash six large white potatoes; add two well beaten eggs, butter, pepper, salt and one cup of hot milk; beat until very smooth and light; add a little sugar and a dash of nutmeg. Lightly fill greased custard cups and bake a delicate brown.

Potato Pyramid

Choose small round potatoes of even size, pare, drop in cold water, and let stand an hour. Drain and dry, then drop into deep fat, boiling hot, and fry to a rich golden brown. Skim out, drain on paper, then serve pyramid fashion on a napkin laid over a hot dish.

Green Peas

Soak one pint of dried green peas overnight in water to cover. In the morning place in a crock, cover with water and add one tablespoon of sugar and one teaspoon of salt. Cook for eight or nine hours, strain off the water and serve with butter or cream sauce.

Beet Fritters a la Dickens

Cut beets, after boiling, into slices an eighth of an inch thick; mince a few mushrooms with one-eighth their bulk in onions; press between two slices of beet and dip in a batter made by beating the yolk of an egg, adding a tablespoon of oil or melted butter, four of flour, and lastly the whipped white, with salt and pepper to taste; fry these fritters in very hot fat.

Squash Puff

Press dry cooked squash through a sieve; to a half-pint add two tablespoons of melted butter, quarter of a cup of milk, seasoning of salt and pepper, and two beaten egg yolks. Mix thoroughly, fold in two beaten egg whites, and turn into a buttered mold, set in a pan of hot water and bake in the oven until the center is firm. Serve turned from the mold and accompanied by a rich cream sauce made from one tablespoon each of flour and butter with a cup of scalded cream or rich milk and seasoning of salt, pepper, celery salt and mace. This can be baked in individual timbale molds if desired.

Baked Hubbard Squash

Wash a hard shelled Hubbard squash and cut into pieces large enough to handle with ease; it is impossible to make them of uniform size. Take out the seeds and pulp, being careful not to waste any of the good part. Bake like potatoes until a fork can pass through the meat easily. Serve in the shell and eat with butter and salt.

Fried Summer Squash

Wash and cut in one-half inch slices. Season with salt and pepper, dip in crumbs, then egg, then in crumbs again. Fry in fat hot enough to brown a bit of bread in sixty counts.

Stuffed Tomatoes

Select smooth, shapely fruit. Cut a slice from the top of each and scoop out the seeds and a small portion of the pulp. Fry a teaspoon of chopped onion in a tablespoon of butter, add a cup of cooked sweetbreads, cut in small pieces, half a cup of soft bread crumbs, half a cup of tomato pulp, a saltspoon of salt and a dusting of paprika. Mix well and fill the tomato shells, previously dusted with salt and pepper. Cover the tops with buttered crumbs and bake for twenty minutes in a brisk oven. Serve with Hollandaise sauce. The above proportions are ample for six tomatoes.

Tomato Fritters

To a pint of canned or stewed tomatoes add a few sprigs of celery, a slice of onion, two cloves and six peppercorns; cook ten minutes, then rub through a sieve. Melt a fourth of a cup of butter, add a fourth of a cup of flour, gradually the tomatoes, stirring constantly, and seasoning of salt, pepper and sugar as needed. Cook the mixture until quite thick, then remove from the fire and add an egg slightly beaten. Pour into a buttered shallow tin and cool. Turn onto a board dusted generously with cracker crumbs and cut into small squares or strips. Roll each piece in crumbs, then in egg and again in crumbs. Fry in deep fat. Serve as a relish with eggs or as a garnish with veal or lamb chops.

Tomatoes Parisienne

Wash and wipe firm, ripe tomatoes, and cut in halves crosswise. Heat two tablespoons of salad oil in a frying pan, lay in the tomatoes, cut surface down, and cook quickly until they are heated through but not softened. Remove to a buttered baking dish and spread the cooked surface with the following mixture: Rub six hard-boiled egg yolks to a paste with three tablespoons of melted butter, add a teaspoon each of chopped chives and of parsley, one finely-chopped shallot and four medium-sized anchovies, slightly freshened and finely minced. Sprinkle soft bread crumbs over the tomatoes and cook in a brisk oven for ten minutes. The anchovies will supply all the salt necessary for seasoning.

Tomato Cups with Corn Cream Filling

Remove the pulp from twelve ears of sweat corn, season delicately with salt and pepper, add a beaten egg, and if the pulp is dry add a tablespoon of cream to each cup of pulp. Wash and wipe a dozen tomatoes, cut a slice from the stem end and with a teaspoon remove the greater portion of the pulp; dust lightly with pepper and salt and fin with the corn, cover with bread crumbs, dot with butter and bake until the tomatoes are soft and of a rich brown color. Remove carefully to mounds of buttered toast and serve either as an entree or as the main dish at a simple family luncheon.

Escalloped Tomato and Cheese

Make a drawn butter sauce with two tablespoons each of butter and flour; cook with one cup of hot water and season with salt and pepper. Put a layer of bread crumbs in a buttered baking dish, cover with bits of tomato, then a layer of crumbs followed by grated cheese; continue until the dish is full, having a generous sprinkling of grated cheese on top. Pour over the whole the hot sauce and bake in a moderate oven until brown.

Corn Fritters

To two cups of grated sweet corn add one cup of flour sifted with one teaspoon of baking powder, two teaspoons of salt and a quarter teaspoon of paprika; add also half a cup of finely chopped

celery and the beaten to yolks of two eggs. Mix thoroughly and then fold in the stiffly whipped whites of two eggs. Drop by spoonfuls into hot fat and slowly fry to a pale brown. The fat should be about half an inch in depth in the pan—deeper than is required for sautéing, but not deep enough to cover the fritters.

Corn Soufflé

One can of corn put into a chopping machine and ground very fine. Take three eggs and whip light, separately. Add one teaspoon of melted butter. Season with pepper and salt. Stir in the yolks, beat, cut in the whites of the eggs and bake in quick oven.

Baked Beans

Soak one quart of beans overnight in water to cover. In the morning cover with water to which one-half teaspoon of soda has been added. Boil slowly until the skins begin to burst and strain off the water. Place in a bean crock and cover the beans with liquid composed of two cups of hot water, one quarter cup of molasses, one-half teaspoon of mustard and one-half teaspoon of salt, adding more hot water if necessary. Half bury one-half pound of salt pork in the top of the beans and bake for eight or nine hours.

Haricot Beans

Put a pint of washed beans in a clean five-pound flour bag and let them lie all night in a saucepan containing two quarts of cold water. The next morning simmer over a slow fire three hours; lift out the bag into a colander; untie the string and turn the beans into a frying pan with a tablespoon of butter, a gill of cream and a very little finely minced parsley; season to taste with salt and pepper and shake over the fire until hot.

Tomatoes, Corn and Onions

Butter plentifully a deep baking dish, and cover the bottom an inch deep with green corn cut from the cob. Season well with salt and pepper and butter, then put in a layer of tomatoes peeled and sliced. Season them likewise, then add a layer of sliced and soaked onions. Repeat till the dish is full, letting onions come on top. Cover with an inverted plate, and bake until nearly done—say about an hour. Then take off the plate and cook fifteen minutes longer. Sugar added to the seasoning is to many minds an improvement.

Hulled Corn

Wash two quarts of shelled corn to remove loose bits; then place in a large iron kettle with four tablespoons of saleratus, cover with cold water, let come to a boil slowly and cook about an hour. Remove the kettle from fire, drain off the water, then pour the corn, from which the hulls will already be loosened, into a large pan of water. Rub the corn between the hands to loosen the hulls; after taking off all those partly loosened put it on again in warm water, let boil about half an hour, then try to remove the rest of the hulls by rubbing as before. After all hulls are removed, wash the corn in at least half a dozen clean waters, then put on once more in warm water, and when it boils drain and add fresh water. Let the corn cook in this last water until tender, salting to taste. If the hulls do not come off readily let the corn boil an hour longer, adding a teaspoon more saleratus. This will keep for several weeks without scaling in warm weather.

Baked Corn and Beans

It is an old dish with us, yet I find few who have heard of it. It is in no sense succotash. In sweet corn time prepare a pot of Boston baked beans in the usual way. About half an hour before they are to be served take from the oven, remove the pork and thoroughly stir in the corn, which has previously been cut from the cob, then replace in the oven. Use plenty of corn. Canned corn may be used.

Baked Beans Without Pork

Soak one quart of medium pea beans overnight or twelve hours, then parboil till the skin cracks when taken up on a spoon and exposed to the cool air. Put a beef bone with marrow into the pot and fill with beans, adding two teaspoons of salt, and water to cover. Bake slowly for twelve hours, adding more water as it evaporates. Before serving take off the hard beans on top.

Cabbage Soufflé

Shred coarsely a solid, well blanched head of cabbage and cook in an abundance of salted water until tender. Drain and place in a buttered dish in layers, with a slight sprinkling of grated chosen between. To two tablespoons each of butter and flour, add a cup of rich milk, two beaten egg yolks and a saltspoon each of salt and mustard, stirring over the fire until it boils; then add the beaten whites of the eggs. Pour this over the cabbage and bake half an hour.

Cabbage with Ham

Melt a tablespoon of butter, and when hot turn in three pints of white cabbage shaved fine. Cover tightly and simmer on the back of the range until the cabbage turns yellow. Sprinkle with a teaspoon of salt, a few grains of cayenne, and a cup of minced cold boiled ham. Add one-fourth cup of white wine vinegar, stir well, cover and cook slowly for two hours.

Cauliflower Fritters

Separate cold, cooked cauliflower into flowerets, then stir into a fritter batter. Drop the mixture by small spoonfuls into hot fat, frying to a golden brown, or dip each piece separately into the batter, coat thoroughly and fry.

Brussels Sprouts

Boil one quart of sprouts in salted water till tender, drain and put in a baking dish. Dust with tablespoon (level) of flour, dot with bits of butter, pour over a cup of cream, cover with grated cheese, preferably Parmesan, and brown in a hot oven.

Brussels Sprouts with Chestnuts

Wash and trim a pound of fresh sprouts of as uniform a size as possible; plunge in boiling water when three-fourths cooked, drain; plunge in cold water and drain again; add an equal quantity of chestnuts also three-quarters cooked; moisten with half cream and half milk, season with salt and nutmeg and finish the cooking in the oven.

Carrots au Jus

Simmer in boiling salted water one quart of sliced winter carrots. Slowly cook a quarter of a cup of chopped onion in hot butter; when tender add a cup of rich brown gravy or sauce, one teaspoon of chopped parsley and the drained carrots, and simmer for fifteen minutes.

Turnips with Yellow Sauce

Pare and dice sufficient turnips to fill a quart measure. Cook in boiling water, slightly salted, until tender, drain and reserve the water as a base for the sauce. Cream two teaspoons of butter and a dessertspoon of flour, beat in the yolks of two eggs, seasoning of pepper and salt, and pour on it a pint of the turnip water. Cook for ten minutes, add the turnip dice, heat through thoroughly and serve in a hot dish.

Shaker Mashed Turnip

Pare and remove any bad spots, then boil and mash six white turnips. Drain thoroughly, add half a cup of rich cream, butter the size of an egg, and salt and pepper to taste.

Breads, Baked Goods, and Other Sweets

From *Blue Hen's Chickens' Cook Book*, 1921

Georgia Indian Cake

One cupful of milk, one tablespoonful of sugar, one egg, butter half the size of an egg, one cupful of cornmeal, one and one-half cupfuls of flour, heaping spoonful baking powder, a little salt.

Corn Bread

One overflowing pint of cornmeal, one-half pint of flour, two and one-half teaspoonfuls of baking powder, one teaspoonful of salt, two tablespoonfuls of sugar, lard size of a big walnut, one pint of milk, two eggs. Add the yolks of eggs without beating, and beat the whites stiff and add last.

Quick Muffins

Two teaspoonfuls of baking powder, one pint of milk, one teaspoonful of salt, two tablespoonfuls of sugar, a tablespoonful of lard, one egg. Warm the milk and dissolve the sugar, salt and lard in it. Mix with flour enough to make a thin batter; beat egg light, sift in baking powder with flour and add egg last. Bake in greased gem tins.

Cinnamon Buns Or Rusks

One-half pint of milk, one-half pint of water, one cake Vienna yeast dissolved in the water, one cupful of sugar, one-half cupful of butter, one teaspoonful salt and a little nutmeg. Scald milk and butter together, and cool; beat two eggs light; add to milk and butter; then add yeast, sugar, salt and nutmeg; with sufficient flour to make a sponge. When light make out not too stiff. Let rise again, then cut out, or make into rolls and bake.

Pop Overs

Two teacupfuls of sweet milk, two teacupfuls of sifted flour, one tablespoonful of melted butter, two eggs beaten, one tablespoonful of sugar. Fill hot gem pans half full. Bake twenty minutes.

Plain Loaf Bread

One pint of milk scalded, add one tablespoonful of lard and one teaspoonful each of salt and sugar. When cool, add one-half cupful of yeast or one-half cake of compressed yeast, and sufficient flour to make a thick batter. Beat thoroughly until the batter is full of air-bubbles. Cover and let stand in a warm place until morning. Early in the morning add enough flour to make a stiff dough. Knead quickly until smooth and elastic and let rise until twice its bulk. Mould into loaves, and let rise again until light. Bake in moderately quick oven three-quarters of an hour.

Sweet or White Potato Pies

One-half pound sugar, quarter pound of butter, beaten to a cream; one pound of white or sweet potatoes, boiled and mashed fine; beat potato by degrees into butter and sugar. Add three eggs beaten light, half wine glass of sherry, half wine glass of brandy, one teaspoonful of spice, quarter pint of cream.

This quantity will make three pies.

Grated Apple Pie

Six large apples grated, one cup of sugar, grated rind of one lemon, piece of butter size of a walnut, yolks of two eggs.

Use the beaten whites of eggs for the top. This makes one large pie.

Lemon Pie

Four lemons grated, remove the seeds; four eggs, two cups of sugar, one cup of molasses, tiny pinch of salt; line the pie tins with pie crust; spread layer of filling; put another layer of crust rolled very thin; then another layer of filling; finish with top crust, making three crusts.

Bake a pretty brown. Serve cold. This makes three pies.

Peach Pudding

Take a pudding dish and put a layer of bread crumbs in the bottom; then a layer of peaches, either canned or fresh fruit; then another layer of bread crumbs and another of peaches; do this until you have the quantity desired; then make a custard of one quart of milk, yolks of three eggs, two tablespoonfuls of cornstarch; sweeten to taste.

After cooked, pour over the bread crumbs and peaches and take whites and beat them stiff; spread over top and brown slightly; flavor with bitter almonds.

Queen of Puddings

One pint of bread crumbs, one quart of milk, four eggs, one cup of sugar, butter size of an egg, chocolate to taste.

Beat the whites of the eggs with a cup of sugar and spread on top after pudding is done, and put in oven to brown.

Raisin Puffs

One-half cup of sugar, one-half cup of butter, two eggs, one cup of sweet milk, two cups of flour, one cup of seeded raisins chopped fine and dredged with flour, two teaspoonfuls of baking powder sifted with flour; steam one-half hour in buttered cups. This mixture will make seven cups. Serve either with cream or lemon sauce.

Lemon Sauce:—One cup of sugar, one-half cup of butter, one egg beaten light, juice of one lemon, one-half cup of boiling water; thicken over steam.

Hot Chocolate Sauce

Put half a cupful each of sugar and water into a saucepan; let boil five minutes; then stir in slowly four ounces of Baker's chocolate melted; add half a teaspoonful of vanilla.

Let stand in a pan of hot water until ready to serve; then add half a cupful of cream or milk.

Italian Cream

One quart of rich cream whipped, whites of three eggs beaten light, one-half box of gelatine, one cup of sugar: flavor to taste; dissolve the gelatine in one-half teacup of milk; stir it into the sugar and add to it the cream which is left from whipping the cream; then stir in the whites, and lastly the cream; put in a mold on the ice.

Bavarian Cream

Whip one pint of cream to stiff froth, laying it on a sieve; boil another pint of cream or rich milk with vanilla and two tablespoonfuls of sugar until it is well flavored; then take off fire and add one-half box of gelatine soaked for an hour in one-half cup of water; when slightly cooled stir in the yolks of four eggs well beaten.

When it has become quite cool and begins to thicken, stir it without ceasing a few minutes until it is very smooth, then stir in the whipped cream lightly until it is well mixed; put in molds and place on ice.

Chocolate Blanc-Mange

One and a half ounces of gelatine in one-half pint of cold water four hours; warm one quart of milk; stir in gelatine one-half pound of sugar; let it get hot; when melted strain and add three tablespoonfuls of grated chocolate; stir continually and boil ten minutes.

Moonshine Pudding, or Pudding that Never Fails

Two tablespoonfuls of cornstarch dissolved in cold water; let come to a boil one pint of water; add to it one-half cup of sugar and a pinch of salt, and the cornstarch; remove from the fire and add to it the beaten whites of two eggs; slice three bananas and put layer of pudding and bananas alternately to top of pudding dish. Serve with following sauce:

Sauce:—Yolks of four eggs, one pint of milk, two tablespoonfuls of sugar, teaspoonful of vanilla, a pinch of salt, a few drops of rose water. Boil until thick as cream.

Chocolate Ice Cream

Three-quarters of a cake of chocolate grated and boiled until thickened in one pint of rich milk. Take off the fire; add a teaspoonful of vanilla; set aside until the next day; make a custard of the yolks of six eggs, one and a half pint of new milk and one cup of sugar, and a teaspoonful of vanilla; add one cup of sugar, one-half box of gelatine dissolved in two tablespoonfuls of water; stir in as soon as removed from the fire.

Mix the chocolate with a pint of rich cream and a heaping cup of sugar; add the custard; strain all through a rather coarse strainer and freeze.

Fairy Ice Cream

Whip a quart of cream sweetened, and flavor to taste; pack in salt and ice and let stand for three hours.

Superior Chocolate Cake

Two cupfuls of sugar, one cupful of butter, one cupful of milk, one teaspoonful of vanilla, one-half cake of chocolate melted, five eggs and three cupfuls of flour, three teaspoonfuls of yeast powder.

Icing:—One pound of pulverized sugar, water to wet it; beat slightly whites of three eggs; add sugar and then the melted half cake of chocolate. Boil until it thickens, stirring constantly; as it cools add a grated cocoanut. Flavor with vanilla.

Spice Cake

Two cupfuls of sugar, one-half cupful of butter, four eggs, one cupful of sour cream, two teaspoonfuls of cinnamon, two teaspoonfuls of allspice, one small nutmeg grated, one even teaspoonful of soda dissolved.

Orange Cake

Four eggs, one cupful of butter, two cupfuls of sugar, one cupful of milk, four cupfuls of flour (rather less), two teaspoonfuls of baking powder; flavor to taste.

Icing:—Two oranges, one-half pound of sugar, white of one egg. Boil ten minutes.

Dainty Cake

Two cupfuls of sugar, one-half cupful of butter, one cupful of milk, three cupfuls of flour; flavor. Two teaspoonfuls of baking powder; sift sugar once, sift flour four times. Very good.

Soft Gingerbread

One cupful of molasses, one cupful of butter, one cupful of brown sugar, one cupful of sour cream or buttermilk, one tablespoonful of ginger, one tablespoonful soda, three eggs, ground spices to taste; one quart sifted flour. Bake in a common baking pan in a moderate oven.

Cream Peppermints

Three cupfuls of granulated sugar to one cupful of water. Put on the stove and let boil without stirring for seven minutes. Take off and add eleven drops of oil of peppermint. Then beat until it looks cloudy and drop on oiled paper or marble.

Chocolate Caramels

Two cupfuls of sugar, two-thirds cupful of milk, butter size of an egg, one teaspoonful of cornstarch, one quarter cake of chocolate. Let it boil slowly till thick, then give it a hard beating; pour into greased tins, and when cool cut into inch squares.

Peanut Brittle

Boil one-half pound brown sugar, one-half pint New Orleans molasses, one-half teaspoonful of cream of tartar, one-half pint of water to the "hard boil" degree: then add one pint of small peanuts, and continue boiling until it cracks easily if put in cold water. Add one-quarter pound of butter and let it just boil in; remove from fire and add a large teaspoonful of bi-carbonate of soda dissolved in a little water; stir into the above mixture. As soon as it begins to rise pour it upon a marble slab, or dish, and spread thin. When cold, break into pieces. The thinner it is run the better.

More Baked Goods

From *Handy Household Hints and Recipes*, by Mattie Lee Wehrley, 1916

Brown Bread

Two cupfuls Graham flour, one-half cup white flour, one teaspoonful baking powder, one-half cup granulated sugar, one-half teaspoon of salt, one large tablespoonful of melted lard, one teaspoonful of soda, one and one-half cupfuls of sour milk.

Sift all the dry ingredients together. Stir the soda into the sour milk, and mix with other ingredients. Beat well and pour into a well-greased bread pan and bake one hour, using two radiators. The top one should not be quite as hot as the lower one.

Dinner Rolls

One cake yeast, one tablespoonful of sugar, two tablespoonfuls of lard, white of one egg, one cupful sweet milk, scalded and cooled; three cupfuls of well-sifted flour, one-half teaspoon of salt.

Dissolve yeast and sugar in the lukewarm milk. Add the white of the egg beaten to a stiff froth. Then add the lard, salt and the flour gradually. Place in a well-greased bowl and set to rise in a warm place until the bulk has doubled (about two hours).

Mould into small rolls, place in a well-greased pan and let rise again (about one-half hour).

Hints for Kitchen

From *Handy Household Hints and Recipes*, by Mattie Lee Wehrley, 1916

A basin of cold water placed in a hot oven will soon lower the temperature.

Rusty flatirons should be rubbed over with beeswax and lard, or beeswax and salt.

Tough meat may be made tender if placed in vinegar a few minutes.

To beat the whites of eggs quickly add a pinch of salt.

Dish cloths should be scalded and washed daily.

A small quantity of green sage placed in the pantry will keep out red ants.

Cold fruits require cold jars; hot fruits, hot jars.

That water for cooking should never be taken from pipes.

That a successful cook always has a good set of domestic scales.

Brooms dipped in boiling suds once a week will wear much longer.

That milk will keep sweet longer in a shallow pan than in a pitcher.

Equal parts of lime water and olive oil applied at once is a remedy for burns.

If you once use a small brush for cleaning vegetables you will never do without one.

That a coarse grater rubbed over burnt bread or cake is far better than using a knife.

That an agreeable disinfectant—ground coffee on a shovel of hot coals—will purify the air of a room almost instantly.

To restore an eiderdown quilt to its original fluffy lightness, hang it out of doors in the sunlight for several hours.

That if you would always remember to measure solids and fluids in exactly the same way success would be far more certain. No cake recipe is followed when you heap the cups or have them level full of sugar and flour and the milk half an inch below the top.

A tablespoon of turpentine boiled with white clothes will greatly aid the whitening process.

Blankets and furs put away well sprinkled with borax and done up air tight, will never be troubled with moths.

To stone raisins easily, pour boiling water over them and drain it off. This loosens them and they come out with ease.

Chloride of lime should be scattered at least once a week under the sink and in all places where sewer gas is liable to lurk.

All cake needs a moderate oven.

Keep the box of baking powder covered.

Use the common kitchen teacup for measuring.

Never let the cake dough stand any length of time before baking.

To remove chimney soot from carpets, cover with fine dry salt and brush up with stiff broom, and repeat until carpet is clean. After the first is taken up, the spots may be scrubbed hard with the salt until soot is removed.

To take out iron rust, squeeze lemon juice on spots, cover with salt and place in hot sun or iron with hot flatiron.

For burns make a thick paste of saleratus in water; cover the burn with the mixture, making the application half an inch thick.

To remove spots caused by acid on colored goods, moisten the goods and cover with saleratus before washing.

Never stir sugar and butter together in a tin basin or with an iron spoon, a wooden spoon is better than any other kind.

Be sure the oven is right before the cake is put in and then do not open the door until it has been baking at least ten minutes.

To prevent oil from spreading when painting on delicate satin or bolting cloth, mix gasoline with your oil paint. By using this medium the paint can be used very thin, giving the appearance of water coloring.

To clean mica in stoves wash in vinegar.

Chicken drippings are excellent for greasing tins.

Use vinegar to remove the smell of kerosene from tins and dishes.

A teaspoon of borax added to starch, renders the collars and cuffs much stiffer.

Pour cold water over hard boiled eggs as soon as taken from the kettle, and they will not be discolored.

If you wish to give your glass a high degree of brilliancy, add a little bluing to the water.

To remove grease stains rub well with alcohol before wetting.

A sponge saturated with camphor and placed near the bed will keep away mosquitoes at night.

Discolored enameled saucepans are easily made bright and clean by the use of powdered pumice stone.

Keep flowers fresh by putting a pinch of soda in water.

Glaze with white of egg diluted with a little water. Bake in a hot oven twenty-five minutes.

Colonial Bread (Sweet)

Three cups flour, three teaspoonfuls of baking powder, one teaspoonful of salt, two tablespoonfuls granulated sugar, one tablespoonful butter, one tablespoonful lard and three-quarters of a cup of currants or walnut meats and one and one-half cups milk. Handle lightly, let rise fifteen minutes and bake forty-five minutes. Brush over top with butter before baking. Grease pans.

Health Bread

Take three cups of rolled oats and pour over them three cupfuls of boiling water. Let them stand until luke-warm, then add one tablespoonful of shortening, three teaspoonfuls of salt, three-quarters of a cupful of molasses, one compressed yeast cake, dissolved in a quarter of a cupful of tepid water, one cupful of bran, one cupful of whole wheat flour, one small cupful of seedless raisins and about two quarts of plain white flour.

It is impossible to tell how much flour to use, but it should be mixed quite stiff. Knead well and raise over night. In the morning, knead lightly, form into loaves, lay in greased bread pans. When it has doubled in size, bake in a moderately hot oven. This quantity makes three large loaves.

Buns

Scald three cups of milk; when cool, add one cup of sugar and half a cake of yeast dissolved in a little warm water. Stir in enough flour to make the mixture a little thicker than cake batter, sprinkle with flour and set to rise over night. In the morning stir one cup of melted butter which has been creamed with one cup of chopped raisins rolled in flour. Add flour until you can handle the dough, then put it on a molding board and cut out into buns. Put these into tins and let them rise again, then bake in a moderate oven. When done, mix a little sugar and milk or white of egg and sugar and wipe over the tops of the buns before they get cold.

Corn Bread

To a cup of yellow Indian meal add two tablespoonfuls of flour, one of powdered sugar, one egg, white and yolk beaten separately; a teaspoonful of baking powder and a little salt. Stir the whole thoroughly with milk to form a thick batter, put in a buttered tin or porcelain pan and bake in a brisk oven.

Coffee Cake

One-third cup sugar, one-third cup butter, one-half teaspoon salt, one cup scalded milk, one cake compressed yeast dissolved in one-fourth cup of lukewarm water, two eggs slightly beaten; add enough flour to make a stiff batter; cover and let rise to twice its bulk. Cut down and beat thoroughly and spread evenly in two layer-cake tins. Sprinkle with nut mixture and let rise, and bake in hot oven thirty minutes.

Muffins

Cream one-third of a cupful of butter; add gradually one-fourth of a cupful of sugar and one-fourth of a teaspoonful of salt; add one egg beaten light, three-fourths of a cupful of milk, two cupfuls of sifted flour and four level teaspoonfuls of baking powder. Bake in hot buttered gem-pans about twenty-five minutes.

Quick Cinnamon Bun

Sift a quart of flour into four teaspoons baking powder and a half teaspoon salt; rub in two tablespoons shortening; add milk to just moisten. Mix, roll into a sheet, spread with butter, dust thickly with sugar, lightly with cinnamon, and sprinkle with dry, clean currants. Make into a roll, cut into two-inch lengths, stand these, cut side up, in a greased pan, and bake in moderate oven about forty minutes. Serve warm.

Ginger Snaps

Two cups New Orleans molasses, one cup lard, one teaspoonful soda, one teaspoonful cinnamon, one teaspoonful ginger. Boil; when cool add flavoring. Flour to thicken. Roll thin.

Chocolate Sauce

One square of chocolate, one tablespoonful of butter, one tablespoonful of flour, one-half cupful of milk, and a teaspoonful of vanilla. Cook the sauce in a double boiler and keep it hot until it is served.

Baked Apples

Core and peel a strip between the stem and blossom end of the apple. Place in a baking pan, fill cavity with brown sugar; add enough boiling water to cover the bottom of the pan. Bake in hot oven until the apples are tender, basting frequently with the liquor in the pan.

A Delicious Dessert

If you have part of a loaf of brown bread left, slice it up and trim off the crusted edges. Butter the pieces liberally and make sandwiches of them, using sliced bananas for a filling.

Place the sandwiches in a buttered pan, pile more bananas on the top of them and set in the oven until they are very hot. Serve either with plain cream or sweetened whipped cream. Sugar may be added if desired. These are most delicious and no one would ever suspect that this dessert was made from such homely ingredients.

Delmonico Dessert

Dissolve a package of Lemon Jell-O in a pint of boiling water. Pour half the Jell-O in mould, and when it begins to thicken press strawberries into it. Cover with shredded cocoanut. When firm cover with the rest of the Jell-O that has been kept a liquid, and make same as first layer. Put in a cold place to harden. Serve with whipped cream heaped around base and stud with strawberries.

Pie Crust

Two-thirds cup butter and lard mixed; two and one-halfs cups flour sifted once before measuring, and one tablespoonful baking powder. Mix with ice water and use a knife or spatula.

Reliable Mince Pies

One pound of currants, one pound of Sultana raisins, one pound of candied citron peel, one pound of chopped suet, one pound of chopped apples, one pound of brown sugar, one pound of seedless raisins, one-half pound of chopped almonds, one ounce of mixed spices, grated rind and juice of three lemons, grated rind and juice of three large oranges.

Chop the peel fine and put it into a large jar, then add all the other ingredients. The raisins and currants should be carefully cleaned. Mix and cover. Keep for two weeks before using. For a dozen individual mincemeat pies line gem-pans with puff pastry; put in the center two heaping teaspoonfuls of the mincemeat; cover with rounds of pastry the size of the top of the pies. Brush over with beaten egg, and bake in a hot oven for fifteen minutes.

Amber Pie

One cup of sugar, one-half cup of buttermilk, one-half cup of seeded raisins, one-half teaspoonful of cloves, one-half teaspoonful of nutmeg, one-half teaspoonful of flour, one tablespoonful of butter, the yolks of two eggs, reserving the whites for the frosting. Mix all ingredients except the egg-whites, pour into an open crust and bake until "set." Cover with a meringue made of beaten whites and a little sugar, and return to the oven long enough to brown.

Cranberry Pie

Mix one cup sugar and a tablespoon cornstarch, and one cup boiling water, and cook over boiling water until it thickens. Prepare one pint of cranberries by cutting in halves lengthwise, adding a half cup of sultana raisins, a small cup of dried currants, a teaspoon of vanilla and a little grated nutmeg; add these to the boiled syrup and fill into pans that have been lined with rich pie crust, cross-barring the top with strips of the pie crust. Bake about forty minutes.

"Cannot Fail" Pie Crust

Two tablespoonfuls shortening, one cup of flour, pinch of salt and three tablespoonfuls of cold water; mix with fork.

Banana Pie

One and one-half cups banana pulp, one and one-half cups milk, one beaten egg, one-half cup light brown sugar, one level teaspoon cinnamon, one-half level teaspoon ginger, one-half level teaspoon salt. Add the milk gradually to the banana pulp, then the beaten egg and stir the mixture into the sugar, spices, and salt mixed. Line a deep plate as for custard pie, pour in the mixture, and bake in a moderate oven until browned over the top.

Grandmother's Pumpkin Pie

To make four large pies, beat two cups of sugar into one cup of shortening until light. Grate the rind of a large lemon and squeeze out the juice, add to the eggs and sugar. Put in one teaspoon of cinnamon, a dash of nutmeg, one pint of cream and six cups of boiled and mashed pumpkin. Pour this mixture into pans lined with rich pie paste, and bake in a quick oven. The pies will truly "melt in your mouth."

Lemon Tarts

Grate two whole lemons, add two cups sugar, three well-beaten eggs, and one piece of butter half the size of an egg. Mix the ingredients thoroughly and place over the fire, stirring until it boils up, and then set away to cool. This will keep all winter, and can be used for tarts any time by making nice crust.

Angel Food

Nine large eggs (or ten small ones), one-quarter cup sifted granulated sugar, one cup sifted flour, half teaspoonful cream tartar, a pinch of salt added to eggs before beating. Sift flour four or five times; measure and set aside one cupful, then sift and measure one and one-quarter cups granulated sugar, beat whites of eggs slightly, then add cream tartar and beat until very, very stiff;

stir in sugar, then flour very lightly. Put in pan in a moderate oven at once—will bake in thirty-five to fifty minutes.

Sponge Cake

For six persons. One cup pulverized sugar, one cup flour, one-third of a cup of sweet milk, three eggs, two teaspoonfuls of baking powder. Beat whites and yolks of eggs separately and thoroughly. Add whites last. Mix, and bake in hot oven.

Cream Filling for Sponge Cake

One egg, one piece of butter (small), one-half cup of sugar, one-half cup of milk, one teaspoonful of cornstarch. Boil in pan of hot water.

Black Walnut Cake

One cup of sugar, four tablespoonfuls of butter, seven tablespoonfuls of sweet milk, one tablespoonful of cornstarch, one and one-half cups flour, three teaspoonfuls of baking powder, the whites of two eggs well beaten and one cup of chopped walnut meats. Mix the flour, cornstarch and baking powder together. Stir the sugar and butter well, add the milk, then the flour and the whites of eggs. Then put in walnut meats floured. Bake in quick oven.

Small Nut Loaf Cake

An emergency cake, easily prepared, yet delicious, which may be baked in layers, paddipans or a loaf:

One-half cup butter, one cup sugar, three eggs, one-half cup milk, one and three-quarter cups flour, four teaspoonfuls baking powder, one-half teaspoonful vanilla extract, three-quarters of a cup of broken nut meat.

Cream the butter and sugar. Sift the baking powder with the flour. Add the milk and flour to the creamed butter and sugar, as directed for white loaf. Mix thoroughly, then add a whole unbeaten egg. Mix this into the cake mixture, then add another egg and beat. Finally add the third egg and then the extract and nut meats.

Bake in the medium-sized dripping pan in a moderate oven. Frost with caramel icing. The nuts may be omitted from the cake and added to the frosting or omitted altogether. This cake is best when fresh.

Solid Chocolate Cake

Put one cupful of granulated sugar, a piece of butter the size of an egg and two squares of chocolate in a mixing pan and place on the back of the stove or over a kettle of hot water where the ingredients will melt but not boil. When they have melted stir and add the beaten yolk of one egg (reserving the white for the frosting), one cup of sour milk, a large pinch of salt and a teaspoonful of vanilla. Stir well together and add one cupful of flour, in which a level teaspoonful of soda has been sifted. Stir well, add three-quarters of a cupful of flour and bake in a slow oven.

1-2-3-4 Cake

One cup of butter, two cups of sugar, three cups of flour, two teaspoonfuls of baking powder, four eggs, three-fourths cup of milk; flavor.

Chocolate Cake

One cup sugar, one-half cup butter, one egg (beaten separately), one cup buttermilk, two cups flour, one teaspoonful cinnamon, three teaspoonfuls grated chocolate, one teaspoonful soda, one cup chopped nuts, one cup raisins. Dissolve soda and chocolate in boiling water and add last. Bake in layers with filling or in loaf tin about one hour.

Spice Cake

One and one-half cups sugar, one-half cup butter, one- half cup sour milk, two cups raisins chopped, three eggs, half a nutmeg, one teaspoonful cinnamon, cloves and saleratus; mix stiff and bake in loaf in moderate oven.

Breads and Biscuits

From *Good Housekeeping Family Cookbook,* by Mildred Maddocks, 1906

Bread

Put four tablespoons of shortening, either butter and lard mixed or one of the good fats on the market, two tablespoons of sugar and one tablespoon of salt into a bread raiser, and pour over it one quart of boiling water. Place one yeast cake in half a cup of lukewarm water and stir with a teaspoon till softened. When the water in the bread pan becomes lukewarm, pour in the yeast and stir thoroughly. Add five cups of sifted bread flour, beating it as it goes in with a wire whisk. When it becomes too thick to move with the whisk, use a slatted wooden spoon and stir thoroughly, so that the flour and wetting may become well mixed. Add flour enough to knead. When it is spongy but not dry, turn it out on a well-floured molding cloth and knead. It is the kneading that gives it the satiny smoothness and the elasticity which are invariable tests of good bread. It ought, even during this process, to begin to show bubbles in its texture. Knead them out, as much as possible. When dough is put back in the pan to rise with bubbles showing here and there, it will be full of holes and poor of taste when baked. After the kneading is finished and the dough feels as smooth as silk, wash the bread raiser and dry it, then rub well inside with butter or lard before putting the dough back again for the second raising. In the morning when well risen, cut it down. By this process I mean cutting the light spongy mass through and through half a dozen times and then turning it over and over to check fermentation for a short time. The cutting takes only a minute or two, and one can feel that if it is not attended to for half an hour, the bread will not sour. It does not hurt it at all if it has to be cut down a second time. When ready to care for it, toss on the floured molding cloth and knead again—slightly this time—till every air bubble disappears, then put it in greased pans, haring each one about half full. Cover lightly, set in a warm place and allow it to double its bulk before putting to bake.

This recipe will make four good-sized loaves. The oven, to give satisfactory results, ought to be quite hot when the bread is first put in. If you bake in a gas stove, the beat plan is to light both burners seven or eight minutes before the bread goes in. Set it on the bottom shelf, then allow it to rise to double its bulk and begin to brown very slightly. Turn out one burner and finish the baking in a cooler oven. This does away with any fear of burning; it bakes the bread perfectly and gives a much nicer crust than if the oven is very hot all the time. The management of dampers in a coal or wood stove will give the same results. According to the size of your loaves, bread will require from forty-five to sixty minutes to bake well. On taking it from the oven set the loaves on a wire stand or sieve to cool. Never wrap them steaming hot in a towel. Frequently one tastes the cloth in which bread has been wrapped, or the soap with which the cloth was washed. Besides, it shuts the steam up in the loaf, making it damp and clammy, a sure medium for the cultivation of mold. Allow the bread to become perfectly cold before putting it away in the bread box or jar, then keep it closely covered.

The first and most important "must-have" is good yeast. I have come to depend almost wholly and with the most perfect trust on compressed yeast. If your grocer keeps yeast at all, it will be fresh, the manufacturer sees to that, as the stock of each day is renewed and the old yeast cakes are taken away. Still, if you keep it yourself for a few days in a refrigerator it will not spoil. Yeast which is moist, light colored and of "reviving smell," as an old lady I know expressed it, is all right. If it gets dry, brittle, streaky and smells the opposite of "reviving," throw it away; better lose two cents than twenty cents' worth of flour, with fire and labor added. Be very careful of the heat of the water in which yeast is softened. If you have a thermometer, let the water be sixty-five to sixty-eight degrees; if you have to trust to your hand, let it be very surely no more than lukewarm.

Then the flour—it is an invariable rule to use bread flour when yeast is to be added. Bread flour will make tolerable pie or cake, but pastry flour *will not* make good bread. If, as occasionally occurs, you have flour whose nature you cannot determine, use the following test: take a handful and close the fingers tightly over it. If it remains in a soft velvety lump, even after the fingers are loosened, it is pastry flour. Bread flour will be dry and loose, it will not keep in shape.

According to the time at your disposal, allow sufficient yeast for raising. For instance, if bread is wanted made and baked in four hours, two yeast cakes would have to be allowed to the recipe I have given. There is no danger, should compressed yeast be used, of its tasting in the bread. This it called the quick-raising method. In a temperature of about sixty-eight degrees it will be ready to mold two and a half hours from the time it was set. It will be quite as good bread as that made after the slow-raising method, although I think the latter will keep moist for a longer time.

I have heard many housewives complain of bread souring. Bread sours only because of two reasons—uncleanliness in the making or the utensils, or because it was allowed to stand too long after mixing. When that occurs, the yeast has done its work completely, and the dangerous bacteria get in their work, exactly in the same way as at the point where cider changes to vinegar. I have found, too, that in hot weather milk bread will sour much more quickly than if bread is mixed with water. Then there is the question of dry bread, with a heavy feeling about it, both to the touch and to the palate. Usually this is caused either by too much flour being worked into the dough or by heavy-handed kneading. Bread, like cake, pastry, cookies and biscuit, has a point where just enough flour has been added and where no more ought to go in. This amount it is almost impossible for a recipe maker to determine, because there are so many flours, and the wetting capacities of two are hardly ever alike. It is a case of experience. A practiced hand can tell almost the instant when enough flour has gone into bread by a certain springy feeling. Then tip it out and begin kneading. It may seem moist, but it is not moist enough to stick if you intervene with well-floured fingers between the dough and the cloth. Knead quickly and lightly; a heavy hand which pounds bread instead of molding it will soon thump all the life out of it, and the bread will have the texture of cheese.

Hot Cross Buns

Beat to a cream one large cup of granulated sugar and one scant cup of butter. Add gradually three eggs beaten well and one pint of scalded milk, blood warm. Add one yeast cake softened in one-half cup of lukewarm water. Put in flour enough to make a batter as stiff as you can beat it. Beat until it blisters well. In the morning knead rapidly, but do not use over one-half cup of flour in the kneading.

Dough must be very soft. Rub over top with a little warm butter and let rise. When double in bulk cut into balls like tea biscuit. Rub each bun with a little butter and make a cross on top with a sharp knife. Let rise in pans one and one-half or two hours. Bake one-half hour.

Buttermilk Biscuits

One cup buttermilk or sour milk, one-half teaspoon soda, one-half teaspoon salt, three tablespoons lard and flour. Work the lard into the milk with the hand. Add one cup flour, sifted with soda and salt, more flour to make a dough and knead until smooth and elastic as for light bread. Roll out until one-half inch thick, cut and bake in a hot oven ten or fifteen minutes. The biscuits must be thin, almost cracker-like, and you have the real southern biscuit. It seems best to work in the lard in this way.

Steamed Brown Bread

One and one-quarter cups of Indian meal, one cup of graham meal and three-quarters cup of rye meal; one teaspoon of soda and one-half teaspoon of salt; three-quarters cup of molasses, two cups sour milk or hot water. Mix and sift dry ingredients, and return siftings to the finer part. (This sifting is to make it lighter, not to take out the coarse grains.) Add molasses, then sour milk or hot water, beat well and pour into an oiled tin with tight cover. Place to steam either in a steamer or in a tightly covered kettle partly filled with boiling water. Steam three or four hours, then dry off in the oven.

Johnnycake

Sift one-half cup each of corn meal, flour and sugar, one-half teaspoon of soda, and one-half teaspoon of salt, thoroughly together. Add one and

one-fourths cups of sour milk. Use buttermilk if you have it. Beat thoroughly, pour into cake pan and bake in a hot oven.

Date Buns

Roll light bread dough out quite thin, spread it with soft butter, and then with chopped dates. Roll the bread up and cut with a sharp knife into pieces half an inch thick, lay them in a buttered pan, let them rise until double in bulk, and bake in a hot oven.

Oatmeal Bread

Pour one quart of boiling water over two cups of oatmeal and one tablespoon of shortening; when lukewarm add one-half of a compressed yeast cake, softened in two tablespoons of lukewarm water, one cup of molasses, and one teaspoon of salt, thicken with wheat flour until as stiff as can be stirred with a spoon. Let rise overnight and in the morning mold into loaves and biscuits.

Breadsticks

Scald a cup of milk and add three tablespoons of sugar with one-half teaspoon of salt. When the right temperature (lukewarm), add a yeast cake softened in a little warm water. Too much water prevents the yeast mixing evenly. Add the stiffly beaten white of an egg and enough flour to knead. Knead well, using the palms of the hands and pushing it from you on the board with a sliding motion. When it is smooth and satiny to the touch, keeps its round shape, and does not stick to the board or hand, it is ready to be placed in a clean oiled bowl. Knead in all the flour that will be needed at this time, if not, the yeast will have no opportunity to raise it sufficiently. On the other hand, use no more than is absolutely necessary. Flours vary and

Breadsticks, Braids and
Pocketbook Rolls

for this reason no definite quantity can be given. Cover tightly in order that no crust need form. When it is double in bulk, knead again with just enough flour to keep it from sticking. Then roll with a heavy rolling pin until about a quarter of an inch thick. Cut with a medium-sized biscuit cutter.

To shape the Parker House rolls, spread each biscuit with a very thin layer of butter, then with a caseknife crease through the center, fold over and press the edges closely together. Do not butter the baking tin, and place them far enough apart to prevent their touching, even after they are raised.

Roll the biscuits between the palms until from eight to ten inches long, of uniform size and with well-rounded ends. Let them rise; bake and serve these breadsticks with soup or the salad. Brush three sticks lightly with melted butter and braid loosely. Two sticks twisted make another variation. In twisting or braiding allow plenty of room for the dough to rise, otherwise the distinctive shape will be lost. Shape others like a horseshoe, using a plain breadstick, and tie sailors' or true lovers' knots; both of these latter are effective.

"Pocketbooks" need an oblong piece of dough cut with one end pointed. Brush with melted butter and fold in thirds, leaving the pointed end on top. Press firmly together at the point. When baked they should open like a pocketbook in three crisp folds.

Rusks

Scald one cup of milk and add two tablespoons each of butter and sugar, with a half teaspoon of salt. When warm add one-half a yeast cake softened in two tablespoons of warm water. Now stir in enough flour to make a stiff batter, beat it until smooth, cover and let it rise. When risen add two eggs beaten until very light, and flour enough to handle; knead until smooth and let it rise again. Then roll out as the biscuit dough. Make into round biscuits and with a floured dull knife press through the center. When light bake them in a moderate oven. If the twice baked rusk is liked, mold into long, oblong rolls, and when baked, cut in inch slices, and dry in the oven to a golden brown.

Shaping The Rusks

Fancy Breads

Waffles and Griddle cakes

From *Good Housekeeping Family Cookbook,* by Mildred Maddocks, 1906

Waffles

Mix one pint of flour, three-fourths pint clabber (if you use buttermilk, a pint), one teaspoon salt, one tablespoon melted lard, and beat till perfectly smooth—beat hard and long, for success will depend on it. Just before you put in the irons add one level teaspoon of soda dissolved in a teaspoon of hot water. Heat the waffle iron, turn and heat on the other side, then oil thoroughly. Put a tablespoon of batter in each compartment; then cover and it will soon fill the iron. Turn at once. With a new iron oil carefully or waffles will stick.

Pumpkin Waffles

Take one cup of mashed and seasoned pumpkin, carefully drained, and add one well beaten egg, one cup of warm cream, half a yeast cake dissolved in half a cup of lukewarm water, one tablespoon of melted butter and four cups of sifted flour; thin to a rather thick batter with sweet milk; allow it to rise until light and then beat down, adding a pinch of powdered mace and ground ginger; again let it rise for twenty minutes and bake in heated waffle irons to a golden brown; dip the waffles while hot in melted butter and roll in equal parts of cinnamon and pulverized sugar.

Rye Pancakes

One pint of sour milk, one egg, three cups of rye meal, one cup of Indian meal, one-half cup of molasses, one small teaspoon of soda, small teaspoon of salt. Mix well and fry in smoking hot fat; dip the spoon first in the hot fat, then take up a piece of the dough a little larger than an English walnut, using the tip of the spoon. Shape it a little as you take it up, then drop it quickly into the fat. These require longer cooking than doughnuts. Roll, while still hot, in sugar and serve with coffee. Or serve them plain with maple syrup.

Eggs

From *Good Housekeeping Family Cookbook,* by Mildred Maddocks, 1906

Fried Eggs

Separate the yolks from the whites and put very little lard in the pan. Break the yolks and spread them all over the pan after it is hot. Season to taste and beginning at one edge, roll the yolks into a cylindrical shape and allow it to cook a few minutes. Now turn the whites into the skillet without any more lard, even though the skillet appears to be dry, spread the whites over the bottom of pan, season quickly and roll an before; let this cook in the roll. It will not burn as there is plenty of water in an egg to prevent it. The result of this method it a light, fluffy morsel.

Plain Omelet

Crack into a bowl six fresh eggs, season delicately with salt and white pepper and beat until well mixed. Drop a tablespoon of butter into a heated omelet pan, and as soon as the butter is hot, pour in the eggs and with a spatula stir all well together for three minutes. Let cook undisturbed for a moment, then fold the side next the pan handle to the center, fold the opposite side in the same manner and slip carefully to a hot dish. Serve immediately.

Eggs au Gratin

Mix together three raw egg yolks, a quarter of a cup of soft, fresh bread crumbs, two tablespoons of softened butter, one tablespoon of chopped chives, three chopped sardines, two sprigs of parsley chopped, and a light dusting of salt and pepper. Spread this mixture in the bottom of a baking dish and place in a slow oven until set; then break over it six eggs, dust them with salt and pepper and bake until done.

Eggs Vermicelli

Separate the whites and yolks of four hard cooked eggs. Chop the whites and rub the yolks through a sieve. Melt a tablespoon of butter; when bubbling, add a tablespoon of flour, gradually a cup of milk, stirring well, and salt and pepper to season. Add the whites to this sauce, spread thickly on rounds of fresh buttered toast and sprinkle the sifted yolks thickly over all.

Egg Timbales

Break open four eggs into a bowl, add half a teaspoon of salt, a saltspoon of pepper, and, if liked, a few drops of onion juice. Beat only until thoroughly blended, then add gradually a cup of rich new milk. Divide equally among six well-buttered timbale molds (common cups will serve the purpose). Stand them in a pan half filled with hot water and bake in a moderate oven about twenty minutes, or until firm to the touch. Turn out carefully on a heated platter and pour bread sauce around.

Spanish Eggs

Cut six circles of bread from a stale loaf and fry to a brown crispness in hot butter. Fry six eggs in hot olive oil, allowing one egg for each circle of bread; when the eggs are done trim the edges (a biscuit cutter is the most satisfactory implement to use when desirous of a shapely result) and lay one on each bread round, pour over a pint of Spanish sauce and serve piping hot.

Eggs and Cheese

Cut out rounds of bread an inch thick, remove a small piece in the center of each, dip in melted butter and fill the cavity with finely chopped cheese and celery. Bake fifteen minutes in a hot oven and place a poached egg in the center of each slice. Serve with toasted crackers and sliced lemon.

Luncheon Eggs with Spinach

Cook six eggs very hard; cool and cut in halves lengthwise. Take two cups of cold spinach, heat it in a few tablespoons of water, drain and rub through a colander or chop very fine. Mix with pepper, salt and butter, place it in the bottom of an earthen dish, lay the halves of eggs about on the spinach and pour over them a cream sauce, made from one cup of milk thickened and seasoned with salt, paprika and about four tablespoons of mild grated cheese. Cover with crumbs and set in the oven. Serve when slightly browned.

Pudding Sauces

From *Good Housekeeping Family Cookbook*, by Mildred Maddocks, 1906

Caramel Sauce

Butter the inside of a granite saucepan, add two ounces of unsweetened chocolate and melt over hot water; add two cups of light brown sugar and mix well; then add an ounce of butter and half a cup of rich milk. Cook until the mixture forms a soft ball when tested in cold water, then take from the fire and flavor with vanilla. Put into a sauceboat and pour while hot over each serving of ice cream. If there is delay in serving, keep hot by standing in a vessel of hot water. As this simple dressing is poured over the cold cream it immediately hardens, forming a caramel coating.

Madeira Sabayon Sauce

Put into the inner vessel of a double boiler four egg yolks and two tablespoons of powdered sugar. Have the water in the outer vessel rapidly boiling, and whip the sauce rapidly for three minutes. Pour in slowly half a cup of Madeira wine, stir for two minutes longer; take from the fire and strain over the pudding.

Pudding Sauce

Beat two eggs until very light; then add one cup of confectioners' sugar and one cup of thick cream. Beat until the whole is the consistency of whipped cream.

Hard Sauce

The hard sauce which accompanies plum pudding is seldom made exactly as it should be. First, if possible, use unsalted butter or butter from which the salt has been well washed, then add to it powdered sugar, never granulated, or what is called confectioners' sugar. Beat one cup of the butter till very creamy, then add two cups of the powdered sugar, then gradually the unbeaten whites of two eggs and the flavoring. Set it on the ice to chill. When ready to serve, put it in a cut glass dish and with the point of a teaspoon mark little scales all over the mound.

Coffee Sauce

Beat the yolks of two eggs with one-fourth cup of sugar, add half a cup of freshly made, clear, strong, black coffee and cook over hot water, stirring constantly, until it commences to thicken. When cold add a cup of whipped cream. Serve ice cream in glasses and heap the sauce over the top.

Pistachio Sauce

Whip a cup of cream until stiff and dry, add one-third cup of sugar, flavor with pistachio and tint a delicate green. Have ready half a cup of blanches and finely chopped pistachio nuts. Serve ice cream in sherbet cups, put the sauce on top and sprinkle with the chopped nuts.

Orange Foam Sauce

Beat one egg yolk until thick and lemon colored and add gradually one-half cup of powdered sugar. Beat thoroughly and add one teaspoon of orange extract.

Griddle Cake Syrup

Boil two cups of brown sugar with one cup of water until thick, clear and brown.

Vinegar

From *The Household Guide or Domestic Cyclopedia*, by Prof. B.G. Jefferis, MD, PhD, and J.L. Nochols, AM, 1905

How To Make All Kinds of Vinegar

Cider Vinegar

Vinegar making is easy enough if you have good cider and patience. Keep the barrel in a warm place, filled up to the bung, refilling as needed. When done working draw off into an old vinegar barrel, filling it not over two-thirds full. Keep the bung hole covered with a piece of screen to exclude vinegar flies. If kept in a warm place it may make good strong vinegar in less than six months' time. In an ordinary cellar it will take longer.

Vinegar for Pickles

4 quarts of vinegar; 2 cups of sugar; 3 nutmegs, grated; 2 large onions, sliced; ½ cup of grated horse-radish; 1 ounce of mustard seed; 1 ounce of celery seed; 1 ounce of salt; ½ ounce of mace, ½ ounce of black pepper; 1 ounce of allspice.

Vinegar for Sweet Pickle

6 pounds of fruit; 2 pounds of sugar; 1 quart of vinegar; 2 ounces of cassia buds or cloves.

Vinegar for Spiced Tomatoes

1 quart of vinegar; 2 ounces of sugar; 1 ounce of cloves; 1 ounce of cinnamon; 1 ounce of allspice; 1 ounce of ground black pepper.

Vinegar for Sweet Pickled Peaches and Apples

4 pounds of sugar; 1 quart of vinegar; 2 ounces of un-ground cinnamon.

To Make Vinegar Without Fruit

Inexpensive methods for making vinegar without the use of any fruit.

1. Molasses, one quart; yeast, one pint, warm rainwater, three gallons; put all into a jar or keg and tie a piece of gauze over the bung, to keep out the flies and let in the air. In hot weather set it in the sun, in cold weather by the stove or in the chimney-corner. In three weeks you will have good vinegar.

2. The cheapest mode of making good vinegar is to mix five quarts of warm rainwater with two quarts of New Orleans molasses and four quarts of yeast. In a few weeks you will have the best vinegar you ever tasted.

3. To make vinegar from acetic acid and molasses, take of acetic acid two pounds, of molasses one-half gallon, and put them into a twenty-gallon cask. Fill it up with rainwater; shake it up and let stand from one to three weeks, and you will have good vinegar. If this does not make it as sharp as you like, add a little molasses. Acetic acid is concentrated vinegar. Take one pint of this acid, and add seven times as much soft water, and you have just as good a pure white vinegar as can be made from cider, and that instantaneously.

Preservation—Canning of Vegetables and Fruits

From the National War Garden Commission Bulletin in The Housekeeper, by Laura A. Hunt, 1920

Canning of Vegetables and Fruits

The preservation of foodstuffs by canning is always effective food thrift. It enables the individual household to take advantage of summer's low prices for vegetables, even if no garden has been planted. It effects the saving of a surplus of foodstuffs that would otherwise be wasted through excess of supply over immediate consumption. It eliminates the cold storage cost that must be added to the prices of commodities bought during the winter. Of vital importance, also, is that it relieves the strain on transportation facilities of the country. All this increases the need for Home Canning and proves that this is a national obligation.

Canning Made Easy by Modern Methods

By the Single Period Cold-Pack method it is as easy to can vegetables as to can fruits and it is more useful. By the use of this method canning may be done in the kitchen or out of doors. It may be done in the individual household or by groups of families. Community canning is important in that it makes possible the use of the best equipment at small individual outlay and induces food conservation on a large scale.

Community Work

One of the best methods to follow in canning and drying operations is for several families to club together for the work. The work may be carried on at a schoolhouse, in a vacant storeroom, at the home of one of the members or at some other convenient and central location where heat and water can be made available. By joining in the purchase of equipment each participant will be in position to save money as against individual purchases and at the same time have the advantage of larger and more complete equipment. The cost is slight when thus divided and the benefits very great to all concerned.

Sterilization of Food

The scientist has proven that food decay is caused by microorganisms, classed as bacteria, yeasts and molds. Success in canning necessitates the destruction of these organisms. A temperature of 160° to 190° F will kill yeasts and molds. Bacteria are destroyed at a temperature of 212° F held for the proper length of time. The destruction of these organisms by heat is called sterilization.

Methods of Canning

There are four principal methods of home canning. These are:

1. Single Period Cold-Pack Method.
2. Fractional or Intermittent Sterilization Method.
3. Open Kettle or Hot-Pack Method.
4. Cold Water Method.

Of these methods the one recommended for home use is the Single Period Cold-Pack Method. It is much the best because of its simplicity and effectiveness and detailed instructions are given for its use. The outlines of the various methods are as follows:—

1. Single Period Cold-Pack Method: The prepared vegetables or fruits are blanched in boiling water or live steam, then quickly cold-dipped and packed at once into hot jars and sterilized in boiling water or by steam pressure. The jars are then sealed, tested for leaks and stored. Full details of this method are given on the pages following.

2. Fractional or Intermittent Sterilization Method: Vegetables are half sealed in jars and sterilized for one hour or more on each of three successive days. This method is expensive as to time, labor and fuel and discourages the home canning of vegetables.

3. Open Kettle or Hot-Pack Method: Vegetables or fruits are cooked in an open kettle and packed in jars. There is always danger of spores and bacteria being introduced on spoons or other utensils while the jars are being filled.

   "The fruit is cooked in syrup until tender, then packed in sterilized jars. The jars should be filled to overflowing, the hot rubber adjusted and the tops fastened on at once.

   To sterilize: Place clean jars and tops on a rack in a kettle of cold water, being sure that jars are completely covered by the water. Place the kettle over the fire, bring the water to the boiling point and boil 10 minutes. Dip the rubbers into boiling water. Do not remove jars from the water until you are ready to use them."

   This method should never be used in canning vegetables. Even with fruits it is not as desirable as the cold-pack.

4. Cold-water Method: Rhubarb, cranberries, gooseberries, and sour cherries, because of their acidity, are often canned by this method. The fruits are washed, put in sterilized jars, cold water is added to overflowing, and the jar is then sealed. This method is not always successful as the acid content varies with the ripeness and the locality in which the fruits are grown.

Advantages of the Single Period Cold-Pack Method

The Single Period Cold-Pack Method is a simple and sure way of canning. It ensures a good color, texture and flavor to the vegetable or fruit canned. In using this method sterilization is completed in a single period, saving time, fuel and labor. The simplicity of the method commends it. Fruits are put up in syrups. Vegetables require only salt for flavoring and water to fill the container.

Another advantage is that it is practicable to put up food in small as well as large quantities. The housewife who understands the process will find that it pays to put up even a single container. Thus, when she has a small surplus of some garden crop she should take the time necessary to place this food in a container and store it for future use. This is true household efficiency.

Single Period Cold-Pack Equipment

The Home-made Outfit: A serviceable Single Period Cold-pack canning outfit may be made of equipment found in almost any household. Any utensil large and deep enough to allow an inch of water above jars, and having a closely fitting cover, may be used for sterilizing. A wash-boiler, large lard can or new garbage pail serves the purpose when canning is to be done in large quantities. Into this utensil should be placed a wire or wooden rack to hold the jars off the bottom and to permit circulation of water underneath the jars. For lifting glass top jars use two buttonhooks or similar device. For lifting screw-top jars, suitable lifters may be bought for a small sum. A milk carrier makes a good false bottom, and if this is used the jars may be easily lifted out at the end of the sterilization period.

Commercial Hot-water Bath Outfits

These are especially desirable if one has considerable quantities of vegetables or fruits to put up. They are convenient for outdoor work, having firebox and smoke pipe all in one piece with the sterilizing vat. As with the home-made outfit, containers are immersed in boiling water.

Water Seal Outfits.—These are desirable, as the period of sterilization is shorter than in the home-made outfit and less fuel is therefore required. The outfit consists of two containers, one fitting within the other, and a cover which extends into the space between the outer and the inner container. The water jacket makes it possible for the temperature in the inner container to be raised above 212°.

Steam Pressure Outfits.—Canning is very rapid when sterilization is done in steam maintained at a pressure. There are several canners of this type. Each is provided with pressure gauge and safety valve and they carry from 5 to 30 pounds of steam pressure. This type is suitable for home or community canning.

Aluminum Pressure Outfits.—These cookers are satisfactory for canning and for general cooking. Each outfit is provided with a steam pressure gauge and safety valve.

Containers

For home use glass jars are more satisfactory for canning than tin. Tin cans are used chiefly for canning on a large scale for commercial purposes. Glass jars properly cared for will last for years. All types of jars which seal readily may be used. Jars having glass tops held in place by bails are especially easy to handle while they are hot.

Tops for Economy jars must be purchased new each year.

Containers made of white glass should be used if the product is to be offered for sale or exhibition, as blue glass detracts from the appearance of the contents.

Small-necked bottles can be used for holding fruit juices. Large-mouthed bottles can be used for jams, marmalades and jellies.

Tests for Jars and Rubbers

Jars should be tested before they are used. Some of the important tests are here given:

Glass-top Jars.—Fit top to jar. If top rocks when tapped it should not be used on that jar. The top ball should not be too tight nor too loose. If either too tight or too loose the ball should be taken off and bent until it goes into place with a light snap. All sharp edges on top and jar should be filed or scraped off.

Screw-top Jars.—Use only enameled, lacquered or vulcanized tops. Screw the top on tightly without the rubber. If thumb nail can be inserted between top and jar, the top is defective. If the edge is only slightly uneven it can be bent so that it is usable. Put on the rubber and screw on the top tightly, and then pull the rubber out. If the rubber returns to place the top does not fit properly and should not be used on that jar.

Rubbers.—Be very particular about the rubbers used. Buy new rubbers every year, as they deteriorate from one season to another. It is always well to test rubbers when buying. A good rubber will return to its original size when stretched. When pinched it does not crease. It should fit the neck of the jar snugly and be fairly wide and thick. It is cheaper to discard a doubtful rubber than to lose a jar of canned goods.

Grading

Vegetables and fruits should be sorted according to color, size and ripeness. This is called grading. It insures the best pack and uniformity of flavor and texture to the canned product, which is always desirable.

Blanching and Cold-Dipping

The most important steps in canning are the preliminary steps of blanching, cold-dipping, packing in hot, clean containers, adding hot water at once, then immediately half sealing jars and putting into the sterilizer. Spoilage of products is nearly always due to carelessness in one of these steps. Blanching is necessary with all vegetables and many fruits. It insures thorough cleansing and removes objectionable odors and flavors and excess acids. It reduces the bulk of greens and causes shrinkage of fruits, increasing the quantity which may be packed in a container, which saves storage space.

Blanching consists of plunging the vegetables or fruits into boiling water for a short time. For doing this place them in a wire basket, or a piece of cheesecloth. The blanching time varies from one to fifteen minutes, as shown in the time-table.

Spinach and other greens should not be blanched in hot water. They must be blanched in steam. To do this place them in a colander and set this into a vessel which has a tightly-fitting cover. In this vessel there should be an inch or two of water, but the water must not be allowed to touch the greens. Another method is to suspend the greens in the closed vessel above an inch or two of water. This may be done in a wire basket or cheesecloth. Allow the water to boil in the closed vessel from fifteen to twenty minutes.

When the blanching is complete remove the vegetables or fruits from the boiling water or steam and plunge them once or twice into cold water. Do not allow them to stand in the cold water. This latter process is the Cold Dip. It hardens the pulp and sets the coloring matter in the product.

Essentials for Canning

It is important to plan your work so that whatever may be needed will be ready for use. Arrange everything conveniently in advance. Preliminary provisions include:

1. A reliable alarm clock in a convenient place (set to ring when the sterilizing is done).
2. All the necessary equipment in place before beginning work.
3. Jars, tops and rubbers carefully tested.
4. Fresh, sound fruits and vegetables.
5. Reliable instructions carefully followed.
6. Absolute cleanliness.
7. If working alone, prepare only enough vegetables or fruits to fill the number of jars that the sterilizer will hold. Always blanch and cold-dip only enough product to fill one or two jars at a time. As soon as the jar is filled and the rubber and top bail adjusted the jar must be put into the hot-water bath.

8. In using the hot-water bath outfit, count the time of sterilization from the time water begins to boil. The water in the sterilizer should be at or just below the boiling point when jars are put in. With the Water Seal Outfit begin counting time when the thermometer reaches 214° F with the Steam Pressure Outfit begin counting time when the gauge reaches the number of pounds called for in directions.

Steps in the Single Period Cold-Pack Method

In canning by the Single Period Cold-Pack Method it is important that careful attention be given to each detail. Do not undertake canning until you have familiarized yourself with the various steps, which are as follows:

1. Vegetables should be canned as soon as possible after being picked; the same day is best. Early morning is the best time for gathering them. Fruits should be as fresh as possible.
2. Before starting work have on the stove the boiler or other holder in which the sterilizing is to be done, a pan of boiling water for use in blanching and a kettle of boiling water for use in filling jars of vegetables: or, if canning fruits, the syrup to be used in filling the jars. Arrange on the working table all necessary equipment, including instructions.
3. Test jars and tops. All jars, rubbers and tops should be clean and hot.
4. Wash and grade product, according to size and ripeness. (Cauliflower should be soaked 1 hour in salted water, to remove insects if any are present. Put berries into a colander and wash, by allowing cold water to flow over them, to prevent bruising.)
5. Prepare vegetable or fruit. Remove all but an inch of the tops from beets, parsnips and carrots and the strings from green beans. Pare squash, remove seeds and cut in small pieces. Large vegetables should be cut into pieces to make close pack possible. The pits should be removed from cherries, peaches and apricots.
6. Blanch in boiling water or steam as directed.
7. Cold-dip, but do not allow product to stand in cold water at this or any other stage.
8. Pack in hot jars which rest on hot cloths or stand in a pan of hot water. Fill the jars to within ¼ inch of tops. (In canning berries, to insure a close pack, put a 2 or 3 inch layer of berries on the bottom of the jar and press down gently with a wooden spoon. Continue in this manner with other layers until jar is filled. Fruits cut in half should be arranged with pit surface down.
9. Add salt and boiling water to vegetables to cover them. To fruits add hot syrup or water.
10. Place wet rubber and top on jar.
11. With bail-top jar adjust top bail only, leaving lower bail or snap free. With screw top jar screw the top on lightly, using only the thumb and little finger. (This partial sealing makes it possible for steam generated within the jar to escape, and prevents breakage.)
12. Place the jars on rack in boiler or other sterilizer. If the homemade or commercial hot water bath outfit is used enough water should be in the boiler to come at least one inch above the tops of the jars, and the water, in boiling out, should never be allowed to drop to the level of these tops. In using the hot-water bath outfit, begin to count sterilizing time when the water begins to boil. Water is at the boiling point when it is jumping or rolling all over. Water is not boiling when bubbles merely form on the bottom or when they begin to rise to the top. The water must be kept boiling all during the period of sterilization.

13. Consult time-table and at the end of the required sterilizing period remove the jars from the sterilizer. Place them on a wooden rack or on several thicknesses of cloth to prevent breakage. Complete the sealing of jars. With bail-top jars this is done by pushing the snap down, with screw top jars, by screwing cover on tightly.

14. Turn the jars upside down as a test for leakage and leave them in this position till cold. Let them cool rapidly, but be sure that no draft reaches them, as a draft will cause breakage. (If there is any doubt that a bail-top jar is perfectly sealed a simple test may be made by loosening the top bail and lifting the jar by taking hold of the top with the fingers. The internal suction should hold the top tightly in place when thus lifted. If the top comes off put on a new wet rubber and sterilize 15 minutes longer for vegetables and 5 minutes longer for fruits.) With screw-top jars try the tops while the jars are cooling, or as soon as they have cooled, and, if loose, tighten them by screwing on more closely.

15. Wash and dry each jar, label and store. If storage place is exposed to light, wrap each jar in paper, preferably brown, as light will fade the color of products canned in glass. The boxes in which jars were bought affords a good storage place.

Special Instructions for Canning Vegetables

The addition of 1 teaspoonful of salt to a jar of vegetables is for quart jars. For pint jar use ½ teaspoonful. For 2 quart jar use 2 teaspoonfuls.

Asparagus

Wash, scrape off scales and tough skin. With a string bind together enough for one jar. Blanch tough ends from 5 to 10 minutes, then turn so that the entire bundle is blanched 5 minutes longer. Cold-dip. Remove string. Pack, with tip ends up. Add 1 teaspoonful of salt and cover with boiling water. Put on rubber top and adjust top bail. Sterilize 120 minutes in hot water bath. Remove, complete seal and cool. With Steam Pressure Outfit sterilize 60 minutes at 5 to 10 pounds pressure.

Beets

Use only small ones. Wash and cut off all but an inch or two of root and leaves. Blanch 5 minutes, cold-dip and scrape off skin and stems. They may be packed in jar sliced or whole. Add 1 teaspoonful of salt and cover with boiling water. Put on rubber and top and adjust top bail. Sterilize 90 minutes in hot-water bath. Remove, complete seal and cool.

With Steam Pressure Outfit sterilize 60 minutes at 5 to 10 pounds pressure.

Cabbage and Brussels Sprouts

The method is the same as for cauliflower, except that the vegetables are not soaked in salted water. Blanch 5 to 10 minutes. Sterilize 120 minutes in hot-water bath.

With Steam Pressure Outfit sterilize 60 minutes at 5 to 10 pounds pressure.

Carrots

Select small, tender carrots. Leave an inch or two of stems, wash, blanch 5 minutes and cold-dip. Then remove skin and stems. Pack whole or in slices, add 1 teaspoonful of salt and cover with boiling water. Put on rubber and top and adjust top bail. Sterilize 90 minutes in hot-water bath. Remove, complete seal and cool.

With Steam Pressure Outfit sterilize 60 minutes at 5 to 10 pounds pressure.

Cauliflower

Wash and divide head into small pieces. Soak in salted water 1 hour, which will remove insects if any are present. Blanch 3 minutes, cold-dip and pack in jar. Add 1 teaspoonful of salt and cover with boiling water. Put on rubber and top and adjust top bail. Sterilize 60 minutes in hot-water bath. Remove, complete seal and cool.

With Steam Pressure Outfit sterilize 30 minutes at 5 to 10 pounds pressure.

Corn

Canning corn on the cob, except for exhibition purposes, is a waste of space. For home use remove the husks and silk, blanch tender ears 5 minutes, older ears 10 minutes, cold-dip, and cut from cob. Pack lightly to within ½ inch of the top of the jar, as corn swells during sterilization. Add 1 teaspoonful of salt and cover with boiling water, nut on rubber and top, adjust top bail. Sterilize 180 minutes in hot-water bath. Remove, complete seal and cool.

With Steam Pressure Outfit sterilize 90 minutes at 5 to 10 pounds pressure.

Greens

Wash until no dirt can be felt in the bottom of the pan. Blanch in steam 15 minutes. (Mineral matter is lost if blanched in water.) Cold-dip, cut in small pieces and pack or pack whole. Do not pack too tightly. Add 1 teaspoonful of salt to each jar and cover with boiling water. Put on rubber and top and adjust top bail. Sterilize 120 minutes in hot-water bath. Remove, complete seal and cool.

With Steam Pressure Outfit sterilize 60 minutes at 5 to 10 pounds pressure.

Lima Beans

Shell. Blanch 5 to 10 minutes. Cold-dip, pack in jar, add 1 teaspoonful of salt and cover with boiling water. Put on rubber and top, and adjust top bail. Sterilize 180 minutes in hot-water bath. Remove, complete seal and cool.

With Steam Pressure Outfit sterilize 60 minutes at 5 to 10 pounds pressure.

Okra

Wash and remove stems. Blanch 5 to 10 minutes, cold-dip and pack in jar. Add 1 teaspoonful of salt and cover with boiling water. Put on rubber and top, adjust top bail. Sterilize 120 minutes in hot water bath. Remove, complete seal and cool.

With Steam Pressure Outfit sterilize 60 minutes at 5 to 10 pounds pressure.

Parsnips

The method is the same as for carrots.

Peas

Those which are not fully grown are best for canning. Shell, blanch 5 to 10 minutes and cold dip. Pack in jar, add 1 teaspoonful of salt and cover with boiling water. If the jar is packed too full some of the peas will break and give a cloudy appearance to the liquid. Put on rubber and top and adjust top-bail. Sterilize 180 minutes in hot-water bath. Remove, complete seal and cool.

With Steam Pressure Outfit sterilize 60 minutes at 5 to 10 pounds pressure.

Peppers

Wash, stem and remove seeds. Blanch 5 to 10 minutes, cold-dip and pack in jar. Add 1 teaspoonful of salt. Cover with boiling water, put on rubber and top and adjust top bail. Sterilize 120 minutes in hot-water bath. Remove, complete seal and cool.

With Steam Pressure Outfit sterilize 60 minutes at 5 to 10 pounds pressure.

Pumpkin, Winter Squash

Remove seeds. Cut the pumpkin or squash into strips. Peel and remove stringy center. Slice into small pieces and boil until thick. Pack in jar and sterilize 120 minutes in hot-water bath.

With Steam Pressure Outfit sterilize 60 minutes at 5 to 10 pounds pressure.

Salsify

Wash, blanch 5 minutes, cold-dip and scrape off skin. It may be packed whole or in slices. Add 1 teaspoonful of salt, and cover with boiling water. Put on top and adjust top bail. Sterilize 90 minutes in hot-water bath. Remove, complete seal and cool.

With Steam Pressure Outfit sterilize 60 minutes at 5 to 10 pounds pressure.

String Beans

Wash and remove ends and strings and cut into small pieces if desired. Blanch from 5 to 10 minutes, depending on age. Cold-dip, pack immediately in jar, add 1 teaspoonful salt and cover with boiling water. Put on rubber and top and adjust top bail. Sterilize 120 minutes in hot-water bath. Remove, complete seal and cool.

With Steam Pressure Outfit sterilize 60 minutes at 5 to 10 pounds pressure.

Summer Squash

Pare, cut in slices or small pieces and blanch 10 minutes. Cold-dip, pack in jars, add 1 teaspoonful

of salt, cover with boiling water, put on rubber and top and adjust top bail. Sterilize 120 minutes in hot-water bath. Remove, complete seal and cool.

With Steam Pressure Outfit sterilize 60 minutes at 5 to 10 pounds pressure.

Tomatoes

Take medium-sized tomatoes. Wash them, blanch until skins are loose, cold-dip and remove the skins. Pack whole in jar, filling the spaces with tomato pulp made by cooking large and broken tomatoes until done and then straining and adding 1 teaspoonful of salt to each quart of the pulp. Put on rubber and top and adjust top bail. Sterilize 22 minutes in hot-water bath. Remove, complete seal and cool. With Steam Pressure Outfit sterilize 15 minutes at 5 to 10 pounds pressure.

Tomatoes may be cut in pieces, packed closely into jars and sterilized 25 minutes in hot-water bath. If this is clone do not add any liquid.

The Canning of Fruits

For fruits, as well as for vegetables, the Single Period Cold-Pack Method is best. With some exceptions, as shown in the table, fruits should be blanched before canning. When fruits are intended for table use, syrup should be poured over them to fill the jars. In canning fruits to be used for pie-filling or in cooking, where unsweetened fruits are desirable, boiling water is used instead of syrup. When boiling water is thus used the sterilization period in hot-water bath is thirty minutes.

Syrups

In the directions given various grades of syrup are mentioned. These syrups are made as follows:

Thin—1 part sugar to 4 parts water.

Medium—1 part sugar to 2 parts water.

Thick—1 part sugar to 1 part water.

Boil the sugar and water until all the sugar is dissolved. Use thin syrup with sweet fruits. Use medium syrup with sour fruits. Thick syrup is used in candying and preserving.

Special Instructions for Canning Fruits
Apples

Wash, pare, quarter or slice and drop into weak salt water. Blanch 1½ minutes, cold-dip, pack into jar and cover with water or thin syrup. Put on rubber and top and adjust top bail. Sterilize for 20 minutes in hot-water bath.

With Steam Pressure Outfit sterilize 8 minutes at 5 to 10 pounds pressure.

Apples shrink during sterilization and for this reason economy of space is obtained by canning them in the form of sauce instead of in quarters or slices. In canning sauce fill the jars with the hot sauce and sterilize 12 minutes in hot-water bath.

Apricots

Use only ripe fruit. Blanch 1 to 2 minutes. Wash, cut in half and remove pit. Pack in jar and cover with medium syrup. Put on rubber and top and adjust top bail. Sterilize 16 minutes in hot-water bath. Remove, complete seal. Cool and store.

With Steam Pressure Outfit sterilize 10 minutes at 5 to 10 pounds pressure.

Blackberries

Wash, pack closely and cover with medium syrup. Put on rubber and top and adjust top bail. Sterilize 16 minutes in hot-water bath. Remove, complete seal and cool.

With Steam Pressure Outfit sterilize 10 minutes at 5 to 10 pounds pressure.

For blueberries, currants, loganberries, and raspberries the method is the same as for blackberries. Sterilize 16 minutes in hot-water bath.

With Steam Pressure Outfit sterilize 10 minutes at 5 to 10 pounds pressure.

Cherries

Cherries should be pitted before being canned. Pack in jar and cover with medium syrup. Put on rubber and top and adjust top bail. Sterilize 16 minutes in hot-water bath. Remove, complete seal and cool.

With Steam Pressure Outfit sterilize 10 minutes at 5 to 10 pounds pressure.

Pears

Peel and drop into salt water to prevent discoloration. Blanch 1½ minutes. Pack in jar, whole or in quarters, and cover with thin syrup. Put on rubber and top and adjust top bail. Sterilize 20 minutes in hot-water bath. Remove, complete seal and cool. A slice of lemon may be added to the contents of each jar for flavor.

With Steam Pressure Outfit sterilize 8 minutes at 5 to 10 pounds pressure.

Peaches

Blanch in boiling water long enough to loosen skins. Cold-dip and remove skins. Cut in half and remove stones. Pack in jar and cover with thin syrup. Put on rubber and top and adjust top bail. If soft ripe, sterilize 16 minutes in hot-water bath; if flesh is very firm, 25 minutes. Remove, complete seal and cool.

Some peaches do not peel readily even if dipped in boiling water. In such cases omit dipping in boiling water and pare them.

With Steam Pressure Outfit sterilize 10 minutes at 5 to 10 pounds pressure.

Plums

Wash, pack in jar and cover with medium syrup. Put on rubber and top and adjust top bail. Sterilize 16 minutes in hot-water bath. Remove, complete seal and cool.

With Steam Pressure Outfit sterilize 10 minutes at 5 to 10 pounds pressure.

Pineapples

Pare, remove eyes, shred or cut into slices or small pieces, blanch 3 to 5 minutes, and pack in jar. Cover with medium syrup. Put on rubber and top and adjust top bail. Sterilize 30 minutes in hot-water bath. Remove, complete seal and cool.

With Steam Pressure Outfit sterilize 10 minutes at 5 to 10 pounds pressure.

Quinces

The method is the same as for apples. They may be canned with apples. Sterilize 20 minutes in hot-water bath.

With Steam Pressure Outfit sterilize 8 minutes at 5 to 10 pounds pressure.

You will find the above article to be all that is claimed for it by the manufacturer.

Miss Laura A. Hunt

Rhubarb

Wash and cut into short lengths. Cover with boiling water or thin syrup. Put on rubber and top and adjust top bail. Sterilize 20 minutes in hot-water bath. Remove, complete seal and cool.

With Steam Pressure Outfit sterilize 15 minutes at 5 to 10 pounds pressure.

Strawberries

Wash and pack closely in jar. Cover with medium syrup, put on rubber and top and adjust top bail. Sterilize 16 minutes in hot-water bath. Remove, complete seal and cool.

With Steam Pressure Outfit sterilize 10 minutes at 5 to 10 pounds pressure.

Time Table for Blanching & Sterilizing

The following time-table shows blanching time for various vegetables and fruits, and also sterilizing time, not only in the hot-water bath outfit, but also in equipment for sterilization by the water-seal method, the steam-pressure method and the aluminum steam-cooker method.

Vegetables	Blanching	Sterilizing			
		Hot-water	Water seal	Steam pressure in pounds	
				5 to 10	10 to 15
Asparagus	10 to 15	90	60	80	40
Beets	5	90	120	60	40
Brussels Sprouts	5 to 10	120	90	60	40
Cabbage	5 to 10	120	90	60	40
Cauliflower	3	60	40	30	20
Carrots	5	90	80	60	40
Corn	5 to 10	180	120	90	60
Greens	15	120	90	60	40
Lima Beans	5 to 10	180	120	60	40
Okra	5 to 10	120	90	60	40
Parsnips	5	90	80	60	40
Peppers	5 to 10	120	90	60	40
Peas	5 to 10	180	120	60	40
Pumpkin	See directions	120	90	60	40
Salsify	5	90	80	60	40
Sauerkraut		120	90	60	40
String Beans	5 to 10	120	90	60	40
Squash	See directions	120	90	60	40
Tomatoes	To loosen skins	22	18	15	10
Fruits					
Apples	1½	20	12	8	
Apricots	1 to 2	16	12	10	
Blackberries	None	16	12	10	
Blueberries	None	16	12	10	
Dewberries	None	16	12	10	
Cherries, Sweet	None	16	12	10	
Cherries, Sour	None	16	12	10	
Currants	None	16	12	10	
Gooseberries	1 to 2	16	12	10	
Oranges	1 to 2	12	8	6	
Pears	1½	20	12	8	
Peaches	To loosen skins	16 to 25	12	10	
Plums	None	16	12	10	

Pineapples	3 to 5	30	15	10	
Quinces	1½	20	12	8	
Raspberries	None	16	12	10	
Rhubarb	1 to 3	20	15	15	
Strawberries	None	16	12	10	
Fruits without sugar		30	20	12	

*Some peaches do not peel readily even if dipped in boiling water. In such cases omit dipping in boiling water and pare them.

The time given in this table is for quart jars. For pint jars deduct 5 minutes. For 2-quart jars add 30 minutes.

Homemade and Commercial Hot-Water Bath Outfits are not satisfactory for canning at high altitudes as the temperature of water in them does not reach 212° F. In such localities Water-Seal and Steam Pressure Outfits give better results, as much higher temperatures can be maintained.

The time here given is for 1 quart jars and fresh products at altitudes up to 1,000 feet above sea level. For higher altitudes increase the time 10 percent for each additional 800 feet. For example, if the time is given as 120 minutes in the table and your location is 1500 feet above sea level, the time should be made 132 minutes; for 2,000 feet, 146 minutes.

The time here given is for fresh, sound and firm vegetables. For vegetables which have been gathered over 24 hours increase the time of sterilization by adding one-fifth.

Principles of Jelly Making*

From *The Housekeeper*, by Laura A. Hunt, 1920

To be satisfactory, jelly must be made from fruit juice containing pectin and acid. Pectin is a substance in the fruit which is soluble in hot water and which, when cooked with sugar and acid, gives, after cooling, the right consistency to jelly.

Fruits to be used should be sound, just ripe or slightly under-ripe, and gathered but a short time. Wash them, remove stems and cut large fruits into pieces. With juicy fruits add just enough water to prevent burning while cooking. In using fruits which are not juicy cover them with water. Cook slowly until the fruits are soft. Strain through a bag made of flannel or two thicknesses of cheesecloth or similar material.

Test for Pectin

To determine if the juice contains pectin, boil 1 tablespoonful and cool. To this add 1 tablespoonful of grain alcohol and mix, gently rotating the glass. Allow the mixture to cool. If a solid mass—which is pectin—collects, this indicates that in making jelly one part of sugar should be used to one part of juice. If the pectin collects in two or three masses, use ⅔ to ¾ as much sugar as juice. If it collects in several small particles use ½ as much sugar as juice. If the presence of pectin is not shown as described it should be supplied by the addition of the juice of slightly under-ripe fruits, such as apples, currants, crab-apples, green grapes, green gooseberries or wild cherries.

Measure the juice and sugar. The sugar may be spread on a platter and heated. Do not let it scorch. When the juice begins to boil add the sugar. Boil rapidly. The jelly point is reached when the juice drops as one mass from the side of a spoon or when two drops run together and fall as one from the side of the spoon. Skim the juice, pour into sterilized glasses and cool as quickly as possible. Currant and green grape require 8 to 10 minutes boiling to reach the jelly point, while all other juices require from 20 to 30 minutes.

When the jelly is cold pour over the surface a layer of hot paraffin. A toothpick run around the edge while the paraffin is still hot will give a better seal. Protect the paraffin with a cover of metal or paper.

Three or more extractions of juice may be made from fruit. When the first extraction is well drained cover the pulp with water and let it simmer 30 minutes. Drain, and test juice for pectin. For the third extraction proceed in the same manner. The juice resulting from the second and third extractions may be combined. If the third extraction shows much pectin a fourth extraction may be made. The first pectin test should be saved for comparison with the others.

If the second, third or fourth extraction of juice is found thinner than the first extraction, boil it until it is as thick as the first; then add the sugar called for.

*National War Garden Commission Bulletin.

Jelly Making without Test

The test for pectin is desirable, but is not essential. In some states it is inconvenient because of the difficulty of obtaining grain alcohol. A large percentage of housewives make jelly without this test, and satisfactory results may be obtained without it if care is taken to follow directions and to use the right fruits. For the inexperienced jelly-maker the safe rule is to confine jelly-making to the fruits which are ideal for the purpose. These include currants, sour apples, crab-apples, under-ripe grapes, quinces, raspberries, blackberries, blueberries, wild cherries and green gooseberries. These contain pectin and acid in sufficient quantities.

In making jelly without the alcohol test, with the juice of currants and under-ripe grapes use 1 cup of sugar to 1 cup of juice. With raspberries, blackberries, blueberries, sour apples, crab-apples, quinces, wild cherries and green gooseberries use ¾ cup of sugar to 1 cup of juice. This applies to the first extraction of juice and to the later extractions when they have been boiled to the consistency of the first extraction.

Fruits which contain pectin but lack sufficient acid are peach, pear, quince, sweet apple and guava. With these acid may be added by the use of juice of crab-apples or under-ripe grapes.

Strawberries and cherries have acidity but lack pectin. The pectin may be supplied by the addition of the juice of crab-apples or under-ripe grapes.

Directions for Jelly Making

Wash, remove stems, and with the larger fruits cut into quarters. Put into a saucepan and cover with water. Allow to simmer until the fruit is tender. Put into a bag to drain. If desired, test juice for pectin as described. Measure juice and sugar in proportions indicated by the test for pectin or as directed under "Jelly Making Without Test." Add the sugar when the juice begins to boil. The sugar may be heated before being added. When the boiling juice reaches the jelly point skim and pour into sterilized glasses.

To Prepare Glasses for Jelly

Wash glasses and put them on a rack or folded cloth in a kettle of cold water. Heat the water gradually to the boiling point and let boil ten minutes. Remove glasses, drain and place in a pan containing a little hot water, while filling; or place them on a cloth wrung out of hot water.

To Cover Jelly Glasses. Melt paraffin and pour over the top of the jelly. Put on covers.

Apple Jelly*

Wipe the apples, remove stem and blossom ends, and cut in quarters. Put in a preserving kettle, and add cold water to come nearly to top of apples. Cover, and cook slowly until apples are soft; mash, and drain through a coarse sieve. Avoid squeezing apples, which makes jelly cloudy. Then allow juice to drip through a double thickness of cheesecloth or a jelly bag. Boil twenty minutes, and add an equal measure of heated sugar; boil five minutes, skim, test and turn into hot sterilized glasses. Put in a sunny window and let stand twenty-four hours. Cover, and keep in a cool, dry place.

To Heat Sugar. Put in a granite dish, place in oven, leaving oven door ajar, and stir occasionally.

Currant Jelly*

Currants should not be picked directly after rain. Cherry currants make the best jelly. Equal

---

*Starred recipes are not quoted from National War Garden Commission Bulletin.

proportions of red and white currants are considered desirable, and make a lighter colored jelly.

Pick over currants, but do not remove stems; wash and drain. Mash a few in the bottom of a preserving kettle, using a wooden potato masher, and continue until berries are used. Cook slowly until currants are broken and look white. Strain through a coarse strainer, then allow juice to drip through a double thickness of cheesecloth or jelly bag. Measure, heat to the boiling point and boil five minutes; add an equal measure of heated sugar, boil three minutes, skim and pour into hot sterilized glasses. Let stand twenty-four hours. Cover and keep in a cool, dry place.

Grape Jelly*

Grapes should be picked over, washed and stems removed before putting into a preserving kettle. Heat to boiling point, mash and cook twenty minutes, then proceed as for making currant jelly.

Winter Jelly Making

Fruit juices may be canned and made into jelly as wanted during the winter. Allow 1 cup of sugar to 6 cups of juice. Boil juice and sugar for 5 minutes. Pour into sterilized bottles or jars. Put into hot-water bath, with the water reaching to the neck of the containers. Allow to simmer 20 to 30 minutes. If jars are used half seal them during the simmering. Put absorbent cotton into the necks of bottles and when the bottles are taken from the bath put in corks, forcing the cotton into the neck. Corks should first be boiled and dried to prevent shrinking. They may also be boiled in paraffin to make them air-tight. After corking the bottles apply melted paraffin to the tops with a brush, to make an air-tight seal. Each bottle should be labeled and the label should specify the amount of sugar used. In making jelly from these juices during the winter follow the "Directions for Jelly Making," adding enough sugar to give the amount called for.

Fruit Butters

Fruit butters may be made from good sound fruits or the sound portions of fruits which are wormy or have been bruised. Wash, pare and remove seeds if there are any. Cover with water and cook 3 or 4 hours at a low temperature, stirring often, until the mixture is of the consistency of thick apple sauce. Add sugar to taste when the boiling is two-thirds done. Spices may be added to suit the taste when the boiling is completed. If the pulp is coarse it should be put through a wire sieve or colander. Pour the butter into sterilized jar, put on rubber and cover and adjust top bail. Put into a container having a cover and false bottom. Pour in an inch or so of water and sterilize quart jar or smaller jar 5 minutes after the steam begins to escape. Remove, push snap in place and cool.

Apple Butter with Cider

Four quarts of sweet or sterilized cider should be boiled down to 2 quarts. To this add 4 quarts of apples peeled and cut in small pieces. If the texture of the apples is coarse they should be boiled and put through a strainer before being added to the cider. Boil this mixture until the cider does not separate from the pulp. When two-thirds done, add one pound of sugar. One-half teaspoonful each of cinnamon, allspice and cloves may be added. Pour into sterilized jars and sterilize 5 minutes in steam.

Apple and pear butter may be made by following the directions for apple butter with cider, but omitting the cider.

---

*Starred recipes are not quoted from National War Garden Commission Bulletin.

Peach Butter

Dip peaches in boiling water long enough to loosen the skins. Dip in cold water, peel and stone them. Mash and cook them without adding any water. Add half as much sugar as pulp and cook until thick. Pour into sterilized jars and sterilize 5 minutes in steam.

Plum butter may be made following the directions for peach butter.

Apple Butter with Grape Juice

To every 4 quarts of strained apple sauce add 1 pint of grape juice, 1 cup of brown sugar and ¼ teaspoonful of salt. Cook slowly, stirring often, until of the desired thickness. When done, stir in 1 teaspoonful of cinnamon, pack in hot jars and sterilize 5 minutes in steam.

Dried Peach Butter

Soak dried peaches overnight. Cook slowly until tender. To each 2 pounds of dried peaches add 1 quart of canned peaches and 1¾ pounds of sugar. If a fine texture is desired, strain pulp through a colander. Cook slowly, stirring often, until thick. Pack in hot jars and sterilize 5 minutes in steam.

JAM, CONSERVES AND MARMALADES

Raspberry Jam*

Pick over the raspberries. Mash a few in the bottom of a preserving kettle, using a wooden spoon, continue until all the fruit is used. Heat slowly to boiling point, add gradually an equal measure of sugar which has been heated. Cook slowly forty-five minutes. Seal in sterilized jelly glasses.

Cranberry Conserve*

2 pints cranberries,
½ pound English walnut meats,

1 large orange,
1⅓ cupfuls water,
1 cupful Sultana raisins,
1½ pounds sugar.

Pick over and wash, cranberries, put them into saucepan with half of the water and boil until the skins break. Rub through a strainer and add the remaining water, sugar, raisins and grated rind and pulp of the orange. Bring slowly to the boiling point and allow to cook slowly for twenty-five minutes, then add the nut meats broken in small pieces and cook for five minutes longer. Divide into jars and seal.

Grape Conserve*

2 pounds grapes,
3 cupfuls sugar,
1 pound seedless raisins,
½ pound walnut meats.

Remove pulp from grapes and boil five minutes. Rub through a colander to remove seeds. Add pulp to the skins and boil it ten minutes. Add the raisins, sugar and nut meats chopped fine and boil twenty minutes, or until thick. Pour into sterilized glasses and seal.

Rhubarb Conserve*

4 pounds rhubarb,
4 pounds sugar,
1 pound seeded raisins,
2 oranges,
1 lemon.

Wash and peel stalks of rhubarb and cut in one-inch pieces. Put in kettle, add the sugar, raisins and grated rind and juice of orange and lemon. Mix, cover and let stand one-half hour. Place over fire, bring to the boiling point and let simmer forty-five

*Starred recipes are not quoted from National War Garden Commission Bulletin.

minutes, stirring occasionally. Fill jelly glasses with the mixture, cool and seal.

Spiced Grapes*

7 pounds Concord grapes,
1½ pounds brown sugar,
1½ pounds white sugar,
2 cupfuls vinegar,
1 tablespoonful cinnamon,
1 tablespoonful clove,
½ teaspoonful white pepper.

Wash grapes, remove pulp and cook until the seeds are easily removed, put through a colander. Add the pulp to the skins, add the sugar and vinegar and cook one and one-half hours or until the skins are tender. Add spices and cook ten minutes. Remove from fire and seal while hot.

Orange Marmalade*

1 dozen oranges,
6 lemons,
1 grapefruit,
sugar.

Weigh the fruit and slice it in thin slices. To each pound of fruit add one quart cold water. Let the mixture stand 24 hours. Cook slowly two hours. Weigh the cooked fruit, add an equal weight of sugar. Cook for one hour or until it stiffens. Pour into sterilized glasses and seal.

Tomato and Orange Marmalade*

3 cupfuls ripe tomatoes cut in pieces,
1 orange,
1 lemon,
½ cupful Karo.

1½ cupfuls sugar.

Wash the fruit and put through meat chopper. Combine all the ingredients and cook forty-five minutes or until mixture thickens. Pour into sterilized glasses and seal.

Pear and Ginger Marmalade (Mary Green)*

8 pounds hard pears,
Grated rind of 4 lemons,
Juice of 4 lemons,
¼ pound preserved ginger,
6 pounds sugar.

Quarter and core the pears and put through the food chopper; add lemon rind, juice and chopped ginger; mix fruit with sugar, heat gradually to boiling point and cook slowly about two hours or until thick. Pour into sterilized glasses and seal.

Spiced Prunes*

4 cupfuls cooked prunes,
½ cupful chopped cranberries,
1 cupful prune juice,
¼ cupful sugar,
Rind of ½ orange,
Juice of 1 orange,
1 teaspoonful cinnamon,
½ teaspoonful cloves.

Remove the stones from the prunes and cut them in small pieces, add the cranberries, prune juice, sugar, rind and juice of the orange and the spices. Cook twenty minutes or until thick, pour into sterilized glasses, cool and seal.

*Starred recipes are not quoted from National War Garden Commission Bulletin.

Home Drying of Vegetables and Fruits*

From *The Housekeeper,* by Laura A. Hunt, 1920

Winter buying of vegetables and fruits is costly. It means that you pay transportation, cold storage and commission merchants charges and profits. Summer is the time of lowest prices. Summer, therefore, is the time to buy for winter use.

Vegetable and fruit drying have been little practiced for a generation or more. There is no desire to detract from the importance of canning operations. Drying must not be regarded as taking the place of the preservation of vegetables and fruits in tins and glass jars. It must be viewed as an important adjunct thereto. Drying is important and economical in every home, whether on the farm, in the village, in the town, or in the city. For city dwellers it has the special advantage that little storage space is required for the dried fruit. One hundred pounds of some fresh vegetables will reduce to 10 pounds in drying without loss of food value or much of the flavor.

Drying Is Simple

A strong point in connection with vegetable and fruit drying is the ease with which it may be done. Practically all vegetables and fruits may be dried. The process is simple. The cost is slight. In every home the necessary outfit, in its simplest form, is already at hand. Effective drying may be done on plates or dishes placed in the oven, with the oven door partially open. It may be done on the back of

the kitchen stove, with these same utensils, while the oven is being used for baking. It may also be done on sheets of paper or lengths of muslin spread in the sun and protected from insects and dust.

Methods of Drying

For home drying, satisfactory results are obtained by any one of three principal methods. These are:

1. Sun Drying.
2. Drying by Artificial Heat.
3. Drying by Air-blast. (With an electric fan.)

These methods may be combined to good advantage.

Sun Drying

Sun drying has the double advantage of requiring no expense for fuel and of freedom from danger of overheating. For sun drying of vegetables and fruits the simplest form is to spread the slices or pieces on sheets of plain paper or lengths of muslin and expose them to the sun. Muslin is to be preferred if there is danger of sticking. Trays may be used instead of paper or muslin. Sun drying requires bright, hot days and a breeze. Once or twice a day the product should be turned or stirred and the dry pieces taken out. The drying product should be covered with cheesecloth tacked to a frame for

---

*National War Garden Commission Bulletin.

protection from dust and flying insects. If trays are rested on supports placed in pans of water the products will be protected from crawling insects. Care must be taken to provide protection from rain, dew and moths. During rains and just before sunset the products should be taken indoors for the purpose of protection.

Drying by Artificial Heat

Drying by artificial heat is done in the oven or on top of a cook stove or range, in trays suspended over the stove or in a specially constructed drier built at home or purchased.

Oven Drying

The simplest form of oven drying is to place small quantities of foodstuffs on plates in a slow oven. In this way leftovers and other bits of food may be saved for winter use with slight trouble and dried while the top of the stove is being used. This is especially effective for sweet corn. A few sweet potatoes, apples or peas, or even a single turnip, may be dried and saved. To keep the heat from being too great leave the oven door partially open. For oven use a simple tray may be made of galvanized wire screen of convenient size, with the edges bent up for an inch or two on each side. At each corner this tray should have a leg an inch or two in length, to hold it up from the bottom of the oven and permit circulation of air around the product.

Air Blast-Electric Fan

The use of an electric fan is an effective means of drying. Sliced vegetables or fruits are placed on trays 1 foot wide and 3 feet long. These trays are stacked and the fan placed close to one end, with the current directed along the trays, lengthwise. The number of trays to be used is regulated by the size of the fan. Drying by this process may be done in twenty-four hours or less. With sliced string beans and shredded sweet potatoes a few hours are sufficient, if the air is dry.

Some of the Details of Drying

As a general rule, vegetables or fruits, for drying, must be cut into slices or shreds, with the skin removed. In using artificial heat be careful to start at a comparatively low temperature and gradually increase. Details as to the proper scale of temperatures for various vegetables and fruits are given in the directions. To be able to gauge the heat accurately a thermometer must be used. An oven thermometer may be bought at slight cost. If the thermometer is placed in a glass of salad oil the true temperature of the oven may be obtained.

The actual time required for drying cannot be given, and the person in charge must exercise judgment on this point. A little experience will make it easy to determine when products are sufficiently dried. When first taken from the drier vegetables should be rather brittle, but not so dry as to snap or crackle, and fruits rather leathery and pliable. One method of determining whether fruit is dry enough is to squeeze a handful; if the fruit separates when the hand is opened, it is dry enough. Another way is to press a single piece; if no moisture comes to the surface the piece is sufficiently dry. Berries are dry enough if they stick to the hand but do not crush when squeezed.

Raspberries, particularly, should not be dried too hard, as this will keep them from resuming their natural shape when soaked in water for use. Material will mold if not dried enough.

Preparing Food Material for Drying

A sharp kitchen knife will serve every purpose in slicing and cutting vegetables and fruits for drying, if no other device is at hand. The thickness of the slices should be from an eighth to a quarter of an inch. Whether sliced or cut into strips, the pieces should be small so as to dry quickly. They should not, however, be so small as to make them hard to handle or to keep them from being used to advantage in preparing dishes for the table such as would be prepared from fresh products.

Food choppers, kraut slicers or rotary slicers may be used to prepare food for drying.

Vegetables and fruits for drying should be fresh, young and tender. As a general rule, vegetables will dry better if cut into small pieces with the skins removed. Berries are dried whole. Apples, quinces, peaches and pears dry better if cut into rings or quarters. Cleanliness is imperative. Knives and slicing devices must be carefully cleansed before and after use. A knife that is not bright and clean will discolor the product on which it is used, and this should be avoided.

Blanching and Cold-Dipping

Blanching is desirable for successful vegetable drying. Blanching gives more thorough cleansing, removes objectionable odors and flavors, and softens and loosens the fiber, allowing quicker and more uniform evaporation of the moisture, and gives better color. It is done by placing the vegetables in a piece of cheesecloth, a wire basket or other porous container and plunging them into boiling water. The time required for this is short and varies with different vegetables. Blanching should be followed by the cold-dip, which means plunging the vegetables into cold water for an instant after removing from the boiling water. Cold-dipping hardens the pulp and sets the coloring matter. After blanching and dipping, the surface moisture may be removed by placing the vegetables between two towels.

Danger from Insects

In addition to exercising great care to protect vegetables and fruits from insects during the drying process, precautions should be taken with the finished product to prevent the hatching of eggs that may have been deposited. One measure that is useful is to subject the dried material to a heat of 160° F for from 5 to 10 minutes before storing it away. By the application of this heat the eggs will be killed. Be careful not to apply heat long enough to damage the product.

Condition before Storing

It is important to "condition" dried products before storing them for the winter. This means that they should be placed in boxes and poured from one box to another once a day for three or four days to mix thoroughly. If any part of the material is then found to be too moist. Return to drier for a short drying. Practically all dried products should be conditioned.

Storage for Dried Products

Of importance equal to proper drying is the proper packing and storage of the finished product. With the scarcity of tins and the high prices of glass jars it is recommended that other containers be used. Those easily available are baking powder cans and similar covered tins, pasteboard boxes having tight-fitting covers, strong paper bags and patented paraffin paper boxes, which may be bought in quantities at comparatively low cost.

A paraffin container of the type used by oyster dealers for the delivery of oysters will be found inexpensive and easily handled. If using this, or a baking powder can or similar container, after filling adjust the cover closely. The cover should then be sealed. To do this paste a strip of paper around the top of the can, covering the joint between can and cover, for the purpose of excluding air. Pasteboard boxes should also be sealed in this way. Paraffin containers should be sealed by applying melted paraffin with a brush to the joint.

If a paper bag is used, the top should be twisted, doubled over and tied with a string. Moisture may be kept out of paper bags by coating them, using a brush dipped into melted paraffin. Another good precaution is to store bags within an ordinary lard pail or can or other tin vessel having a closely fitting cover.

The products should be stored in a cool, dry place, well ventilated and protected from rats, mice and insects. In sections where the air is very moist, moisture-proof containers must be used. It is good practice to use small containers so that it may not be necessary to leave the contents exposed long after opening and before using.

For convenience label all packages.

Winter Use of Dried Products

In preparing dried vegetables and fruits for use the first process is to restore the water which has been dried out of them. All dried foods require long soaking. After soaking the dried products will have a better flavor if cooked in a covered utensil at a low temperature for a long time. Dried products should be prepared and served as fresh products are prepared and served. They should be cooked in the water in which they have been soaked, as this utilizes all of the mineral salts, which would otherwise be wasted.

There can be no definite rule for the amount of water required for soaking dried products when they are to be used, as the quantity of water evaporated in the drying process varies with different vegetables and fruits. As a general rule, from 3 to 4 cups of water will be required for 1 cup of dried material.

In preparing for use, peas, beans, spinach and like vegetables should be boiled in water to which there has been added soda in the proportion of 1/8 teaspoonful of soda to 1 quart of water. This improves the color of the product.

In preparing to serve dried vegetables, season them carefully. For this purpose celery, mustard, onion, cheese and nutmeg give desirable flavoring, according to taste.

From 3 to 4 quarts of vegetables soup may be made from 4 ounces of dried soup vegetables.

Directions for Vegetable Drying

Asparagus

The edible portion should be blanched from 3 to 5 minutes, cold dipped, the stalks split lengthwise into two strips if of small or medium size or into four strips if of large size. Drying time, 4 to 8 hours. Start at temperature of 110° F and raise gradually to 140°.

The hard ends of the stalk, which are not edible, should be dried for soup stock. Blanch 10 minutes, cold dip, slice into 2 to 6 pieces, according to size, and dry as described above.

Brussels Sprouts

The drying process is the same as with cauliflower, with the addition of a pinch of soda to the blanching water.

Beets

Boil whole until more than three-fourths cooked, without removing skin. After dipping in cold water, peel and cut into ⅛ to ¼ inch slices. Drying time, two and one-half to three hours. Start at temperature of 110° F and raise gradually to 150°.

Beet Tops and Swiss Chard

Select tops of young beets or Swiss chard suitable for greens. Wash carefully, cut leaf-stalk and blade into pieces ¼ of an inch long, spread on screens and dry.

Cabbage

Take heads that are well developed. Remove all loose outside leaves. Shred or cut into strips a few inches long. Cut the core crosswise several times, and shred it for drying with the rest of the cabbage. Blanch 10 minutes, cold dip, drain, remove surface moisture. Drying time, 3 hours. Start at temperature of 110° F and raised gradually to 145°.

Carrots and Parsnips

Clean thoroughly and remove outer skin, preferably with a stiff bristle brush; or the skin may be removed by paring or scraping. Slice into thickness of ⅛ of an inch. Blanch 6 minutes, cold dip and remove surface moisture. Drying time, 2½ to 3 hours. Start at temperature of 110° F and raise gradually to 150°.

Kohl-rabi, celeriac and salsify are dried in the same way as carrots and parsnips.

Cauliflower

After cleaning, divide into small pieces. Blanch six minutes and cold dip. Drying time, three to three and one-half hours. Start at temperature of 110° F and raise to 145°. Although turning dark, while drying, cauliflower will regain part of its original color in soaking and cooking. Dried cauliflower is especially good for soups and omelets.

Celery

After washing carefully, cut into 1-inch pieces, blanch three minutes, cold-dip and remove surface moisture. Dry slowly. Drying time, three to four hours. Start at temperature of 110° F and raise to 140°.

Garden Peas

Garden peas with non-edible pod are taken when of size suitable for table use. Blanch 3 to 5 minutes, cold-dip, remove surface moisture and spread in single layers on trays. Drying time, 3 to 3½ hours. Start at temperature of 110° F, raising slowly, in about 1 or 1½ hours, to 145°, and then continue 1 and 1½ to 2 hours at 145°.

For use in soups or puree, shell mature peas, pass them through a meat grinder, spread the pulp on trays and dry.

With young and tender sugar peas use the pod also. After washing, cut into ¼ inch pieces. Blanch 6 minutes, cold-dip and remove surface moisture. Drying time, 3 to 3½ hours. Start at temperature of 110° F and raise gradually to 145°.

Green String Beans

Select only such beans as are in perfect condition for table use. Wash carefully and string. If full grown, they should be split lengthwise or cut—not snapped—into pieces ¼ to 1 inch long. If young and tender, dry them whole. Blanch 6 to 10 minutes. To set color add one-half teaspoonful of soda to each gallon of boiling water. After blanching, dip quickly into cold water, then drain thoroughly to remove surface moisture. Drying time for young beans, two hours; for those more mature, three hours. Start at temperature of 110° F and raise gradually to 145°.

Greens and Herbs

After washing carefully and removing leaves, slice, and dry in sun or by artificial heat, following directions for cabbage. If steam is not easily available, dry without blanching or cold dipping.

These directions apply to spinach, kale, dandelions and parsley.

Celery tops, mint, sage and herbs of all kinds for flavoring are treated in the same way.

Lima Beans

If lima beans are gathered when young and tender, shell them, wash, and then blanch 5 to 10 minutes, the time varying with maturity and size. Cold-dip. Remove surface moisture. Drying time, 3 to 3½ hours. Start at temperature of 110° F and raise gradually to 145°.

Okra

After washing, blanch three minutes in boiling water with one-half teaspoonful of soda to each gallon. Cold-dip. With young and tender pods dry whole; cut older pods into ¼ inch slices. Drying time, two to three hours. Start at temperature of 110° F and raise gradually to 140°.

Okra may also be dried by being strung on a string and hung over the stove. This should not be done except with young and tender pods. Heat in oven before storing.

Onions and Leeks

After washing, peeling and cutting into ⅛ and ¼ inch slices for onions, and ¼ inch strips for leeks, blanch in boiling water or steam for 5 minutes, cold-dip and remove surface moisture. Drying time, 2½ to 3 hours. Start at temperature of 110° F and raise gradually to 140°.

Peppers

Steam until skin softens; or place in biscuit pan in oven and heat until skin blisters. Peel, split in half, take out seed. Start drying at temperature of 110° F and gradually increase to 140°. Thick fleshed peppers, such as pimentos, must be dried very slowly and evenly. Small varieties of red peppers may be spread in the sun until wilted and the drying finished in a drier, or they may be entirely dried in the sun.

Another plan for drying peppers is to split them on one side, remove seed, start with air drying and finish in a drier at 140°.

Pumpkin and Summer Squash

Cut into ½ inch strips and pare. Blanch three minutes. Cold-dip, remove surface moisture and dry slowly. Drying time, three to four hours. Start at temperature of 110° F and raise to 140°. The strips may be hung on strings and dried in the kitchen above the stove.

Rhubarb

Slit the larger stems lengthwise, cut into ½ to ¾ inch lengths. Do not use the leaf. Blanch three minutes and cold-dip. Dry thoroughly. Start at temperature of 110° F and raise gradually to 140°.

Soup Mixtures

Vegetables for soup mixtures are prepared and dried separately. These are mixed as desired.

Sweet Corn

Select ears that are young and tender and freshly gathered. Blanch on cob in steam or boiling water—preferably steam—for 5 to 10 minutes to set milk. If boiling water is used, add a teaspoonful of salt to each gallon. Cold-dip, drain thoroughly, and with a sharp knife cut off in layers or cut off half the kernel and scrape off the remainder, taking care not to include the chaff. Drying time, 3 to 4 hours. Start at temperature of 110° F and raise gradually to 145°.

In using field corn it should be taken at the roasting ear period of ripeness, and the ears should be plump.

To prepare for sun-drying, corn may first be dried in the oven for 10 or 15 minutes. After sun-drying is completed the corn should again be heated in oven to 145° F to kill possible insect eggs.

Sweet Potatoes

Wash, boil until almost cooked, peel, slice or run through meat chopper, spread on trays and dry until brittle. Sliced sweet potatoes may be dried without boiling. If this is done, dipping in cold water just before drying will brighten color.

Tomatoes

Blanch long enough to loosen skin, cold-dip, peel, slice to thickness of ⅛ of an inch. Start at temperature of 110° F and gradually raise to 145°, continuing until thoroughly dried. Another method is, after peeling, to cut crosswise in center, sprinkle with sugar and dry at temperature as above until the finished product resembles dried figs.

Wax Beans

These are dried in the same manner as green string beans.

Directions for Fruit Drying

Fruit may be dried in the sun until the surface begins to wrinkle, then finished in the drier. With stone fruits, such as peaches, plums, apricots and cherries, none but fruits that are fresh, ripe and in perfect condition should be used. With apples, pears and quinces, effective thrift calls for using the sound portions of fruit that may be partially wormy or imperfect. When properly dried, fruits should be entirely free from moisture when pressed between the fingers on removal from drier. Line trays with cheesecloth or wrapping paper before spreading fruit on them.

Berries

Pick over, removing all leaves and stems, wash, if necessary, and remove, surface moisture, handling with care to prevent bruising. Spread in thin layers and dry slowly. The total drying time is four to five hours. Start at temperature of 110° F, raising to 125° in about two hours. Then raise temperature to 140° and maintain two to three hours longer.

Cherries

After washing and removing surface moisture, spread unpitted in thin layers. Drying time, two to four hours. Start at temperature of 110° F and raise gradually to 150°. If preferred, the pits may be removed, although this causes loss of juice.

Plums and Apricots

Select fruits which are ripe. Remove pits by cutting fruit open with a sharp knife. Arrange halves on trays. Start drying at temperature of 110° F and raise gradually to 145°. These fruits are usually dried with skins on.

Apples, Pears and Quinces

Pare, core and slice, dropping slices into cold water containing eight teaspoonfuls of salt to the gallon, if a light colored product is desired. Leaving them a minute or two in the salt water will prevent discoloration. (If preferred, core the whole fruit, after peeling, and slice into rings, dipping these for a minute or two into cold salted water as described above.) Remove surface moisture. Drying time, 4 to 6 hours, or until leathery and pliable. Start at temperature of 110° F and raise gradually to 150°. Pears may be steamed ten minutes after slicing and before drying. Quinces are treated in the same way as pears.

Peaches

Dip peaches into boiling water long enough to loosen skins. Then dip in cold water and peel. Cut into halves or quarters, remove stones and dry as directed for apples.

Pickling and Salting*

From *The Housekeeper,* by Laura A. Hunt, 1920

Pickling is an important branch of home preparedness for the winter months. Pickles have little food value, but they give a flavor to a meal which is liked by many. They should not be given to children.

In pickling, vegetables are usually soaked overnight in a brine made of 1 cup of salt and 1 quart of water. This brine removes the water of the vegetable and so prevents weakening of the vinegar. In the morning the brine is drained off.

Alum should not be used to make the vegetables crisp as it is harmful to the human body. A firm product is obtained if the vegetables are not cooked too long or at too high a temperature.

Spices, unless confined in a bag, give a dark color to the pickles.

Enameled, agate or porcelain-lined kettles should be used when cooking mixtures containing vinegar.

Pickles put in crocks should be well covered with vinegar to prevent molding.

Instructions for some of the most commonly used methods are given herewith.

Catsup

2 quarts ripe tomatoes,
boil and strain,
Add 2 tablespoon fills of salt,
2 cupfuls of vinegar,
⅔ cupful of sugar,
1 teaspoonful of cayenne pepper.

Boil until thick. Pour into hot sterilized bottles. Put the corks in tightly and apply hot paraffin to the tops with a brush to make an air-tight seal.

Chili Sauce

2 dozen ripe tomatoes,
6 peppers (3 to be hot),
3 onions,
¼ cupful of sugar,
2 tablespoonfuls of salt,
1 teaspoonful each of cloves, nutmeg and allspice,
1 quart of vinegar.

Simmer 1 hour. Pour into sterilized jars or bottles and seal while hot.

Chow Chow

2 pints cucumbers (1 pint to be small ones),
1 cauliflower soaked in salted water for one hour,
2 green peppers,
1 quart onions.

Chop the above in small pieces. Sprinkle 1 cup of salt over them and let stand all night. Drain well in the morning.

The sauce for Chow Chow is made as follows:

2 quarts vinegar,
¼ pound of mustard,

---

*Extract from "National War Garden Commission Bulletin."

1 tablespoonful of turmeric,

⅔ cupful of sugar,

½ cupful of flour.

Make a paste of the mustard, turmeric, sugar, flour and a little vinegar. Stir this into the warm vinegar and boil until thick. Then add the vegetables and simmer for ½ hour. Stir to prevent burning. Put in cans while hot.

Cold Tomato Relish

8 quarts firm ripe tomatoes; scald, cold-dip and then chop in small pieces.

To the chopped tomato add:

2 cupfuls chopped onion,

2 cupfuls chopped celery,

2 cupfuls sugar,

1 cupful white mustard seed,

½ cupful salt,

4 chopped peppers,

1 teaspoonful ground mace,

1 teaspoonful black pepper,

4 teaspoonfuls cinnamon,

3 pints vinegar.

Mix all together and pack in sterilized jars.

Corn Relish

1 small cabbage,

1 large onion, 6 ears of corn,

2 tablespoonfuls of salt,

2 tablespoonfuls of flour,

1½ cupfuls of brown sugar,

1 pint of vinegar,

2 hot peppers,

½ tablespoonfuls of mustard.

Steam corn 30 minutes. Cut from cob and add to the chopped cabbage, onion and peppers.

Mix the flour, sugar, mustard and salt—add the vinegar. Add mixture to the vegetables and simmer 30 minutes. Pour into sterilized jars or bottles and seal while hot.

Cucumber Pickles

Soak cucumbers in brine made of 1 cupful of salt to 2 quarts of water for a day and night. Remove from brine, rinse in cold water and drain. Cover with vinegar, add

1 tablespoonful brown sugar, some stick cinnamon, and cloves to every quart of vinegar used; bring to a boil and pack in jars. For sweet pickles use 1 cupful of sugar to 1 quart of vinegar.

Green Tomato Pickle

Take 4 quarts of green tomatoes, 4 small onions and 4 green peppers. Slice the tomatoes and onions thin. Sprinkle over them ½ cupful of salt and leave overnight in crock or enameled dish. The next morning drain off the brine. Into a separate dish put 1 quart of vinegar, 1 level tablespoonful each of black pepper, mustard seed, celery seed, cloves, allspice and cinnamon and ¾ cupful of sugar. Bring to boiling point and then add the prepared tomatoes, onions and peppers. Let simmer for 20 minutes. Fill jars and seal while hot.

Green Tomato Pickle (Another Way)

Wash and slice tomatoes. Soak in a brine of ¼ cupful of salt to 1 quart of water overnight. Drain well. Put in a crock and cover with vinegar, to which has been added stick cinnamon and 1 cupful of sugar for every quart of vinegar used. Once a day for a week pour off vinegar, heat to boiling and pour over tomatoes again. Cover top of crock with a cloth and put on cover. This cloth should be frequently washed.

Mustard Pickles

2 quarts of green tomatoes,

1 cauliflower,

2 quarts of green peppers,

2 quarts of onions.

Wash, cut in small pieces and cover with one quart of boiling water and ¼ cupful of salt. Let stand 1 hour, bring to the boiling point and drain. Mix ½ pound mustard, 1 cupful of flour, 3 cupfuls of sugar and vinegar to make a thin paste, add this paste to 2 quarts vinegar and cook until thick, stir constantly to prevent burning. Add vegetables, boil 15 minutes and seal in jars.

Piccalilli

4 quarts of green tomatoes (chopped),

1 quart of onions (chopped),

1 hot red pepper,

½ pound of sugar,

½ cupful of salt,

1½ ounces each of mustard seed, cloves and allspice,

2 cupfuls of vinegar.

Simmer 1 hour. Put into a covered crock.

Pickled Onions

Peel, wash and put in brine, using 2 cupfuls of salt to 2 quarts of water. Let stand 2 days, pour off brine. Cover with fresh brine and let stand 2 days longer. Remove from brine, wash and pack in jars, cover with hot vinegar, to which whole cloves, cinnamon and allspice have been added.

Spiced Crab-Apples

Wash, stick 3 or 4 whole cloves in each apple and cover with vinegar to which have been added stick cinnamon, and 1 cup sugar for every quart of vinegar used. Cook slowly at a low temperature until apples are tender. These may be put in jars or stone crocks.

Sweet Pickled Peaches

Wipe and stick 3 or 4 whole cloves in each peach. Put in saucepan and cover with hot vinegar, allowing 2 cupfuls of sugar to each quart of vinegar used. Cook slowly until peaches are tender. Seal in glass jars.

Table Relish

Chop:

4 quarts of cabbage,

2 quarts of tomatoes,

1 quart to be green,

6 large onions,

2 hot peppers.

Add:

2 ounces of white mustard seed,

1 ounce of celery seed,

¼ cupful of salt,

2 pounds of sugar,

2 quarts of vinegar.

Simmer 1 hour. Pour into sterilized jars or bottles and seal while hot.

Salting

The use of brine in preparing vegetables for winter use has much to commend it to the household. Preserving cabbage, string beans and greens for winter use by salting is a method which has long been used. To do this the vegetables should be washed, drained and weighed. The amount of salt needed will be one-fourth of the weight of the vegetables. Kegs or crocks make satisfactory containers. Put a layer of vegetables about an inch thick on the bottom of the container. Cover this with salt. Continue making alternate layers of vegetables and salt until the container is almost filled. The salt should be evenly distributed so that it will not be necessary to use more salt than the quantity required in proportion to the vegetables used. Cover the surface with a cloth and a board or glazed plate. Place a weight on these and set aside in a cool place. If sufficient liquor to cover the vegetables has not been extracted by the next day, pour in enough strong brine (1 pound of salt to 2 quarts of water) to cover surface around the cover. The top layer of vegetables should be kept under the brine to prevent molding. There will be some bubbling at first.

As soon as this stops set the container where it will not be disturbed until ready for use. Seal by pouring very hot paraffin on the surface.

The Use of Brine

This method is used for cucumbers, string beans, green tomatoes, beets, corn and peas, as these vegetables do not contain enough water for a good brine using only salt. Wash and put in a crock or other container within 3 or 4 inches of the top. Pour over them a brine made by adding to every 4 quarts of water used ½ pint of vinegar and ¾ cup salt. The amount of brine needed will be about ½ the volume of the material to be fermented. When fermentation is complete the container should be sealed.

To Ferment Cucumbers

Wash the cucumbers carefully. Pack them in a keg, barrel or crock, leaving space at the top for the cover. Cover them with a brine made by adding to every 4 quarts of water used ½ pint of vinegar and ¾ cup of salt. The amount of brine needed will be one-half of the volume of the material to be fermented. Place a wooden cover or glazed plate on top of the contents and press it down by weighting it with a stone or other weight, to keep the cucumbers under the brine. Fermentation will require from 8 to 10 days in warm weather and from 2 to 4 weeks in cool weather. It is complete when bubbles cease to rise when the container is lightly tapped or jarred. When this stage is reached remove any scum which may have collected, pour hot paraffin over the cover and around the weight and store in a cool place.

Green Tomatoes

The process for green tomatoes is the same as that for cucumbers.

Beets and String Beans

Remove the strings from beans. Beets should be washed thoroughly and packed whole. Spices may be used, as with cucumbers, but these may be omitted if the vegetables are to be freshened by soaking, when they are to be used.

The method is the same as with cucumbers.

Preparing For Use

To prepare these vegetables for use the brine should be drained off and the vegetables soaked in clear, cold water for several hours with one or two changes of water. They may then be cooked as fresh vegetables, with at least one change of water while cooking.

With salted vegetables it may be necessary to change the water once or twice while boiling. This is a matter of taste. Fermented vegetables should be rinsed in fresh water after removing from the container. To retain the acid flavor do not soak in water before cooking.

If cooked without soaking, fermented dandelions, spinach, kale and other greens will have a flavor similar to that of the greens in their fresh state.

Fermented corn should be soaked several hours, with three or four changes of water. During the cooking also there should be one change of water. The corn may then be used in chowder, pudding, omelet, fritters or waffles.

Salted string beans should be soaked to remove the salt and then prepared and served as fresh beans are prepared and served. Fermented string beans may be cooked without soaking and served as the fresh beans are served. Young and tender string beans may be eaten raw.

Fish

From *Good Housekeeping Family Cookbook,* by Mildred Maddocks, 1906

In selecting fish the purchaser should see that the skin and scales are bright, the eyes full and clear and the flesh firm. Beware of fish that is unusually cheap; it has probably been kept in cold storage and is far from fresh. Canned fish should be used with discretion, always removing it immediately on opening the tin and letting it stand for an hour or more before using, to absorb oxygen.

It is economical to buy a whole cod or haddock weighing three or four pounds, as the whole fish is much cheaper than when sliced and all of it can be utilized.

Try this method of preparing a cod or haddock. Clean and wipe the fish, cut off the head, cut the flesh from the backbone in two long strips. Put the head and bones over the fire in cold water and cook for one hour, to make a fish stock, as there is much gelatin in the head, and some flesh clings to the bones. Strain this stock and reserve it as a basis for a fish chowder, adding potatoes, milk, onion, salt pork and crackers according to any good chowder recipe. The fillets of fish freed from the bones may be used for baking.

Among the most delicate fish for broiling are lake or salmon trout and whitefish, which are fresh water fish from the great lakes and are in season during the winter. Broiling seems to be a simple process, yet it requires care and attention to prepare the fish without burning it. Everything should be made ready for serving before starting to broil the fish, which must be watched, turned and timed.

With a bright hot fire which broiling requires, a fish one-inch thick will cook in twelve to fifteen minutes, more time being needed for a thick fish like salmon, bluefish or shad. Use a double wire broiler well-greased with salt pork to keep the fish from breaking and sticking. Lay the fish over the fire, flesh side down, and broil it till it is a golden brown, lifting occasionally if necessary. Cook it from eight to twelve minutes, then turn onto the skin side and broil it four or five minutes. Remove to a hot platter, rub the fish with soft butter, garnish with parsley and quarters of lemon and serve. Halibut, cod, salmon steaks, bluefish, mackerel, butterfish, sea trout and shad are good fish for broiling. If cut very thick the cooking may be completed in the oven.

There are two methods of frying, one is to immerse the fish in "boiling oil" and the other to fry it in a pan with salt pork scraps; the latter is the more "tasty" the former more rapid and less likely to absorb fat if the fish is drained on brown paper. Small fish like trout, smelts, perch and pickerel are dipped whole in flour, Indian meal or egg and crumbs, and fried crisp. Cod, halibut, haddock, flounders, sole, etc, are cut in slices or fillets dipped and fried either way.

In boiling or steaming fish much is lost or wasted by absorption into the boiling water, or by evaporation. Boiling is far from an economical process, but is often convenient. A thick, solid piece of fish is required, salmon, cod, halibut and red snapper being best to boil.

Molded Fish

Butter an oval mold, lay in it a strip of boned fish, then a layer of bread crumbs seasoned with melted butter, onion juice, chopped parsley and lemon juice, pepper, salt and curry, if liked. Add more fish and crumbs till the mold is full. Moisten with one-half cup of milk or water and the whole or white of one egg, to bind the mixture together. Sprinkle buttered crumbs on top, bake for one-half hour, unmold on a platter and serve with Spanish sauce. Oysters dipped in buttered crumbs may be substituted for the seasoned crumbs, and a Hollandaise sauce used.

Baked Fillets

Each large fillet is cut into three or four small ones and dipped in flour, to which has been added a little salt and pepper. On a rack in the meat pan are placed strips of fat salt pork and sliced onion and on these are placed the fillets. On each one place a bit of butter and a slice of onion, cover and bake in a moderate oven until thoroughly cooked. (The unpardonable sin, by the way, is to serve fish in a translucent, underdone condition.) Remove the fillets carefully, rejecting the pork and onion, and serve with parsley sauce, a white sauce with chopped parsley added. Garnish with sliced hard-cooked eggs and parsley.

Baked Stuffed Fish

Prepare a stuffing with one-half cup of bread crumbs, one-fourth cup of melted butter, one-half cup of cracker crumbs, a few drops of onion juice, one-fourth teaspoon of salt, one-eighth teaspoon of pepper, one tablespoon of chopped parsley, two tablespoons of chopped pickles. Bind together with hot water. Lay one-half a boned fish on a tin sheet in a baking pan, add the stuffing in a layer, then the second strip of fish and bake for one-half hour. Serve with egg sauce.

Halibut with Lemon Sauce

Put into a saucepan containing a pint of water, one small onion minced, a teaspoon of butter, two pods of red pepper, a teaspoon of salt and one and one-half pounds of halibut cut into slices. When cooked remove fish and thicken the liquid with a tablespoon of flour or corn-starch. Break into a separate dish six eggs into which has been stirred the juice of six lemons. Add slowly, to prevent curdling, the liquor from the fish. Cook in a double boiler, stirring all the time. When thick as custard, remove from the fire and place fish in a deep platter, pouring sauce over all. Serve cold, garnished with parsley.

Haddock a la Creole

Place a filleted haddock on the rack in the meat pan. Make a thin tomato sauce of one quart of strained tomatoes, two slices of onion, two or three cloves, one-quarter cup each of flour and butter; season well with salt and pepper and pour half of it over the fish. Cook one hour in a moderate oven, basting it three or four times. When done, remove to the serving dish and pour over it the remaining tomato sauce.

Fish a la Lee

Split and bone a bluefish and place on a well-buttered sheet. Cream one-quarter cup butter, add two egg yolks and stir until well blended, then add two tablespoons each of onion, capers, pickles and parsley, finely chopped, three tablespoons lemon juice, one-half teaspoon salt, and one-quarter teaspoon pepper. Sprinkle fish with salt, spread with mixture and bake in a hot oven.

Shaker Fish and Egg

Pare six medium-sized potatoes and boil till soft with one-half pound salt fish that has been soaked twelve hours or overnight. Drain off the water. Cut the potatoes into slices and pick the fish into small pieces. Add one cup of thin cream and a piece of butter the size of an egg, and let simmer. Season with salt to taste. Slice six hard-boiled eggs on top of the fish and potato and over all pour some hot cream before serving.

Salt Cod with Tomatoes

From the center of a thick salt cod take a piece weighing about a pound, wash and soak for eighteen hours in cold water, changing the water twice. Cover with fresh cold water, heat slowly and keep at a temperature just below the simmering point for two hours and a half. Put a tablespoon of butter which has been rolled in flour, in a frying pan, add two tablespoons of chopped onion, and cook slowly until the onion is a pale yellow color. Add two cups of strained canned tomatoes, simmer for ten minutes, add the drained fish and place on the back of the range for thirty minutes. Dust lightly with pepper when it is ready for the table.

Salmon Loaf

Chop one can of fresh salmon, rejecting the skin, bones and oil. Cream four tablespoons of butter; beat four eggs, add one and one-half cups of bread crumbs, season and beat well, then add the butter and fish. Beat all together and steam one hour in a buttered mold.

Finnan Haddie on Toast

Wash two ounces of rice and cook in a double boiler with one pint of boiling water and one teaspoon of salt. When the water is absorbed add two tablespoons of butter and a little milk. Season with salt, pepper and cayenne and add a cooked finnan haddie which has been flaked. When thoroughly heated serve on toast.

Fried Sardines with Hot Mayonnaise

Free the sardines from oil and skins with boiling water. Dip in batter and deep fry in fat. For the mayonnaise, combine one tablespoon each of butter and flour with one-half cup of hot milk and a quarter teaspoon of salt. Add to this one-half tablespoon each of chopped capers, olives, pickles and parsley, one teaspoon lemon juice and quarter cup mayonnaise. Heat this, but do not let it reach the boiling point.

Rich Curry of Fish

Fry one tablespoon of chopped onion in one tablespoon of butter until brown, add one small teaspoon of curry powder, one cup of white stock, one-half cup of rich milk or thin cream, one tablespoon each of flour and butter, rubbed smooth, pepper and salt to taste. When smooth add one pound of cold flaked fish. Simmer three minutes and serve.

Escalloped Fish

Flake cold boiled fish with a silver forte. Butter a baking dish and fill it with alternate layers of fish, crumbs and sauce. Season with salt and pepper and bake till light brown. Cook scallops in the same way, using the juice with milk, to make a white sauce, and seasoning with mustard and paprika.

Creamed Fish

Flake cold boiled fish. Blend one tablespoon each of flour and butter, add one cup of hot milk. When cooked smooth, add fish, season with salt, pepper and lemon juice and serve at once.

Oysters in Shell

Select fine, fat oysters in the shell. Wash the shells carefully, open; put on each oyster on the half shell a small bit of butter, a grating of leeks, some very finely grated parsley and a sprinkle of dry cracker crumbs; a suspicion of salt and pepper. In opening see that none of the liquor of the oyster is lost, as it is needed for moisture. Make the covering very thin and bake in the shell on a flat pan in the oven for ten minutes, or until the shell takes a slight tinge of brown. Serve very hot with breadsticks.

Boston Oysters

Fill hot water pan with the strained liquor from one quart of oysters. When just boiling season with salt, pepper and butter, and when plump and curled at the edges, dip out and serve on well-browned squares of toasted graham bread.

Meats

From *Good Housekeeping Family Cookbook*, by Mildred Maddocks, 1906

The beef creature is divided down the middle of the backbone into sides or halves, which are shipped to all sections of the country. The next cut is purely local and divides into fore and hindquarters, leaving as many ribs on the forequarter as the butcher desires. A common practice, at least in the east, is to leave ten ribs on the forequarter.

The shoulder blade begins on the fifth rib and the fire ribs from the neck to the shoulder blade are called chuck; the next five, whether on hind or forequarter, are the prime ribs, and the eleventh is what is often called the tip of the sirloin, from its position, when hung up. One reason this is prized so highly is that in hanging, there is a constant tendency to force the meat juices toward this portion, making the roast juicy as well as tender.

The neck piece will furnish stews or Hamburg steak for the least expenditure. It is often used for mincemeat. From the chuck ribs, small steaks and roasts of good flavor may be obtained, while for a pot roast, choose a portion from the back of the forequarter. It will include some of the vertebræ, which will help to swell the stock kettle.

The cut sometimes called sticking piece, whose name is suggestive of its position on the underside of the neck, is very satisfactory braised or cooked in hot water with herbs and spices, and served with a tomato sauce.

Another cut called rattle rand, contains the thin, flat ends of the chuck and prime ribs, and joins the sticking piece. It is no misnomer, especially at the thin end where the rattle is plain. This is oftenest used for corning.

The hindquarter cuts are much more familiar. Here are found the most of the roasts and steaks and the economical cuts depend to some measure on local demand. An unsalable portion, in one section of the country, may be cheap, while in another it is better known, and therefore somewhat higher in price.

From the ribs toward the hips, the muscles covering the backbone are called loin. The one on the outside is the sirloin, knighted by one of England's kings. The inner muscle, dry but tender, is known as tenderloin. The tenderloin is often roasted as a fillet, larded with salt pork to supply the fat it lacks. Next come the muscles just over the hip bones called rump. If cut correctly this is tender, but is boneless and lacks the indescribable flavor the bone imparts to meat. Between the rump and the round is a wedge-shaped piece called the aitch bone. This is sometimes inexpensive, and makes an excellent roast. The price usually varies, being higher in direct ratio to the number of pounds. If the butcher will cut eight pounds, it is decidedly an economical choice.

The round is divided into upper, lower and vein cuts. The upper takes its name from the position on the butcher's block, and is the choicest; the lower is good for braising or any casserole use, while the vein is the muscle on the front part of the leg. The first three slices make very good steak, or the whole makes an economical roast.

The longer meat is hung, the tenderer becomes the fiber, but if allowed to ripen too long the meat is unhealthful. The craving for "gamey" meat is usually an acquired one and leads to digestive disorders. If beef is clear in color, firm yet springy to the touch, well-marbled or streaked with fat of a clear yellowish tinge and with a thick rim of fat on the outside, the meat will be satisfactory.

Meat should be removed from the paper as soon as it comes from the market, as the paper absorbs the juices. Wipe with a damp cheesecloth

Aitchbone, Round and Rump

Chuck Ribs and Neck Piece

Shoulder, Ribs and Sticking Piece

or bit of linen but never place fresh meat or poultry in water to soak even for five minutes, as cold water extracts the juices.

In roasting meats allow fifteen minutes to heat the piece through and ten minutes for each pound if liked rare, or if wanted well done, twelve minutes additional for each pound. For poultry, game and pork, allow fifteen minutes for each pound.

Roast Fillet of Beef

Wipe with a damp cloth, fold the thin end under, trim and skewer into shape. Lard the upper side, sprinkle with salt and pepper and dredge with flour. Put some small pieces of salt pork into a pan; when it is hot add the meat, and bake about thirty minutes in a hot oven, basting every ten minutes with the fat in the pan. Serve with brown gravy, mushroom or tomato sauce. To serve, cut the meat diagonally rather than straight across and put a little of the sauce in the center of each slice.

Chateaubriand

The Chateaubriand, which derives its name from a famous French *gourmet*, is a thick steak cut from the center of a fillet of beef. If a very large steak is desired, two slices are cut from the center of the fillet without completely separating them at one side; they are then spread open and made to appear as one steak. A tenderloin steak cut two inches thick is often substituted and sold as a Chateaubriand, but the bone and flank end must be removed, the meat turned and skewered into a round shape, then smoothed and flattened by striking with a cleaver or broad-bladed knife. Broil slowly in a well-oiled broiler from eighteen to twenty-five minutes, turning every ten seconds. Spread with softened butter or maitre d'hôtel butter, or serve with mushroom sauce, placing the sauce under the steak and the mushrooms on top.

Braised Beef

Buy about five pounds of lean beef, bottom round is good, wipe carefully and dredge thickly with flour. Brown on all sides in a frying pan in which a tablespoon of beef fat has been melted. A small onion stuck with cloves may be browned at the same time to give flavor. Place meat and onion in a wide low butter crock or jar and cover with water. Let it cook for eight or nine hours. Two hours before it is done add to the gravy one-half cup each of diced carrot and turnip, one-half teaspoon each of sage and sweet marjoram and one teaspoon of salt. Serve on a platter with gravy poured over the meat.

Meat Loaf

Buy a pound of beef from the lower round. Chop it fine and add two or three crackers, ground fine or rolled, a slice of onion and two stalks of celery, both chopped, salt, pepper and a scant quarter of a teaspoon of poultry dressing. Beat this well together and form into an egg-shaped loaf. Place this in a meat-pan, brush it over with melted butter, dredge with flour and salt and roast in a hot oven, basting occasionally, for half or three-quarters of an hour. To this may be added bits of cold steak or corned beef, chopped fine, but if cooked meat is used, add the yolk of an egg to bind it together. Make a rich brown gravy to serve with it.

Oven Stew

Buy two or three pounds of the shin of beef (from the *small* end). Have the bone broken into three or four pieces. After wiping it with a damp cloth, remove all the meat from the bone and cut into small pieces for serving. Scrape the marrow from the bone and place in a kettle and in it, brown first the meat, then the vegetables cut in cubes,— half an onion and one carrot. Now dredge well with flour and salt, adding about a tablespoon of browned flour to give color. Add one or two whole cloves, one-half cup of tomato or a little tomato catsup, then the pieces of bone. Cook in the oven in a deep iron meat-pan far three or four hours, adding potatoes, cut in cubes, one hour before serving.

Spanish Steak

Season with salt, pepper and butter, three pounds of round steak, cut two and one-half inches thick. Place in the oven in a pan with a little water, and cook thirty minutes, then cover with a layer of sliced raw onions. Cook three-quarters of an hour, then add a layer of sliced tomatoes, cook until tender, sprinkle with grated cheese and when browned serve with a gravy made from the liquor in the pan.

Spiced Beef

Cover five pounds of fresh beef with cold water. Heat very gradually. When simmering, season with salt, pepper, a few blades of mace, two dozen cloves and the same of allspice. Simmer gently until the meat is in shreds, adding more water if necessary. When done remove the spice and turn into a plain mold. Turn out on a platter and serve with slices of hard cooked egg, lemon and parsley.

Meat Ball Stew

Season a pound of Hamburg steak to taste and roll into tiny balls about the size of a walnut. Boil slowly an hour, and then add a third of a cup of rice. The meat balls keep their shape, and make a delicious stew.

Lamb Cutlets

Broil lamb chops slightly and lay in a large baking dish. Now fry together in one ounce of butter,

A Crown Roast is an attractive method of serving a Loin of Lamb.

two small onions chopped fine, one green pepper, two tomatoes and six large fresh mushrooms, add a cup of broth and season with salt and pepper, a teaspoon of curry powder and thicken with a tablespoon of flour. Pour over the chops, garnish the edges with boiled new potatoes and bake twenty minutes. Serve with boiled rice.

Rice with Lamb or Mutton

Line a buttered baking dish with a wall of rice about an inch in thickness. Fill the center with cold roast or boiled mutton, chopped small and freed from bone and gristle. Season to taste with salt and white pepper; add a little onion juice and moisten with gravy. Cover with a layer of the rice and bake, covered, in a moderate oven for half an hour. Then remove the cover, spread lightly with soft butter, and leave in the oven until delicately browned. Chicken or veal may be used in this way. Serve with cream or tomato sauce.

Mutton Cutlets a la Maintenon

Wipe six Frenched chops cut one and one-half inches thick. Split the meat on them in halves, cutting clear to the bone. Cook together till delicately browned one tablespoon of onion and one and a half tablespoons of butter; remove the onion, add half a cup of chopped mushrooms, and cook five minutes;

then add two tablespoons of flour, three tablespoons of brown stock, one teaspoon of chopped parsley, and seasoning of salt and cayenne. Spread this mixture between the chops, press them lightly together, wrap in buttered paper cases and broil over a clear fire, moving constantly, for ten minutes. Serve with espagnole sauce.

Veal Birds

Cut two pounds of thin veal steak into small squares, rejecting all bone. Season lightly with pepper and salt. Have ready a dressing of cracker crumbs, moistened with cream and well-seasoned. Place a tablespoon of the dressing in the center of each square, roll the meat and skewer in shape with a toothpick. Fry a golden brown or bake in the oven.

Roast Turkey

Insist on having the bird with the feet on, be it chicken or turkey, as the tendons may then be easily removed. Make a cut through the skin at the bend of the knee joint until the tendons are expound; insert a trussing skewer under each and pull gently with a slight twist. Cut off the feet, clean and use for soup. Pick clean of pin feathers; even if the bird has been already drawn it is safe to look for lungs and windpipe. The former are found on either side of the backbone imbedded between the ribs. Remove every trace. Make a cut at one side under the wing to remove crop and windpipe as the appearance of the roasted fowl will not then be marred.

Singe over two tablespoons of alcohol lighted in a shallow tin plate. Scrub the bird inside and out with cheesecloth dipped in warm water. Fold back the neck skin and with a sharp vegetable knife never the neck close to the body. Cook with heart and liver for gravy. Stuff with any desired dressing, using only enough in the breast to plump it well. Fold the neck skin back, bend the wings over this and fasten with skewers. When the chicken is stuffed truss the drumsticks closely and fasten securely with skewers. Remember the fewer projecting corners the more juicy and uniformly cooked will be the roasted bird.

Turkey a la Savoy

Select small pieces of cold turkey, preferably the breast; cover them with olive oil and lemon juice and place in the ice box until needed. Prepare a rich sauce, by heating in the double boiler, half a pint of cream; and when near the boiling point, season with the juice of one onion, salt, pepper and a little powdered mace. Arrange around the sides of a deep baking dish diamonds of fried bread, and fill with alternate layers of the turkey that has been carefully drained, and the cream sauce. Sprinkle the top with a little grated cheese and brown in a quick oven. Serve in the baking dish, garnished with fried parsley.

Turkey with Tomato Sauce

Mince cold turkey and prepare the sauce by stewing half a can of tomatoes, to which has been added a bay leaf, a teaspoon of sugar, a saltspoon of salt and a pinch of curry powder, for half an hour; strain and add a teaspoon of meat extract, a tablespoon of butter and a tablespoon of grated bread crumbs. Return to the fire, and stir in the turkey and a dozen button mushrooms that have been cut in two. When thoroughly heated, fill individual paper cases, cover the tops with browned bread crumbs, and serve immediately.

Turkey Dumplings

This is an old-fashioned New England dish, much esteemed by our Puritan forefathers. Make a rich shortcake dough, rolling it out on the bread board, and cut into circular pieces, about four inches in diameter; spread each piece generously with butter, and place in the center of each a tablespoon of turkey prepared as follows: chop a cup of cold turkey, not too fine; add a tablespoon of the dressing, and a stalk of minced celery, and mix well, moistening with a little giblet gravy. Fold the paste over, lapping the edges; and form into balls with the hands; arrange in a deep baking dish, and bake twenty minutes in a quick oven. Serve the dumplings with a béchamel sauce.

Soufflé a la Reine

In a double boiler, cook one tablespoon of butter with one teaspoon of flour and add slowly, stirring constantly, one cup of scalded milk; season with one-half teaspoon of salt, a little cayenne, one teaspoon of onion juice and a quarter of a teaspoon of celery salt. Remove from the fire when the sauce is slightly thickened and add one tablespoon of chopped parsley, the well beaten yolks of three eggs, one-half cup each of cold turkey and boiled ham minced fine. If preferred, one cup of minced turkey may be used in place of the combination. Stir the mixture over the fire for a moment, then set it aside to cool. When ready to bake the soufflé, beat the whites of the three eggs very stiff, fold them lightly into the turkey mixture, and fill this into buttered ramekins, making them three-quarters full. Bake in a very quick oven for about fifteen minutes, and serve immediately to prevent falling. If a baking dish is used instead of ramekins, bake a little longer.

Ducks Braised

Draw and singe a pair of ducks, wipe them inside and out with a damp cheesecloth. Line a small pen with thin slices of bacon, sprinkle the bottom with minced parsley, thyme, grated lemon peel and a little finely chopped onion. Lay the ducks in, cover with a sliced carrot, three or four whole cloves, a tablespoon of currant jelly and a cup of stock. Set over the fire and let simmer one hour, basting frequently. Slice one large turnip, fry it in hot butter, turn into the saucepan, take up the ducks and set to keep warm; let the turnip cook for ten minutes; take the slices up, arrange on the dish around the ducks, strain the gravy, thicken it with a little browned flour, pour over, and serve the ducks very hot with currant jelly and lemon sliced.

Spring Chicken

Split the chickens down the back as for broiling, lay them breast down in a baking pan, filling the depression inside the ribs with equal quantities of finely minced onion, carrot, celery and peas; season with salt and a dash of paprika, adding a generous lump of butter for each bird. Pour into the baking pan half a cup of hot water, to which has been added two tablespoons of mushroom catsup and cook in a hot oven for half an hour or until the vegetables are tender, basting frequently. Remove the vegetables and turn the chickens to brown the breasts slightly. Serve them covered with a sauce made from the same vegetables moistened with a very little hot cream. Garnish with tiny squares of fried hominy and sweet potato croquettes.

Shaker Fricasseed Chicken

Cut up the chicken as for an ordinary fricassee, put in a kettle with a perforated stand at the bottom to prevent burning, use water enough to steam and cook one hour, then add salt. When the meat is perfectly tender put it in the oven and brown thoroughly, then add rich cream to the gravy,

thickening it with a little flour and butter, and seasoning to taste. Serve in deep dishes.

Ham

Twenty-four hours before a ham is to be used scrub it thoroughly with a vegetable brush and cold, weak borax water. Then put into cold water and soak for twenty-four hours. If it is to be baked, it requires first about four hours' boiling. Use a big kettle, as the ham must be completely covered with water. Let it come to the boil very slowly. Remove the scum which rises. When it begins to boil add twelve whole cloves, twelve peppercorns, the outside stalks of one bunch of celery, two chopped onions, two cloves of garlic, one chopped carrot and turnip, two bay leaves, two blades of mace, twelve allspice berries and one quart of cider or a cup of vinegar. Never allow the ham to boil, merely to simmer slowly, that is one secret of making it tender. Allow about twenty-five minutes or half an hour to the pound. If the ham is to be used cold you can add to its tender juiciness by allowing it to stand in the pot liquor till nearly cold. Then lift it out, peel off the skin and roll it in dried bread crumbs with which three tablespoons of brown sugar have been sifted. Set it in the oven till the crumbs form a crisp brown crust. If the ham is to be baked, take it from the water, drain thoroughly, then take off the skin except around the shank, where it may be cut in vandykes with a sharp pointed knife. Cover with crumbs and stick it full of cloves, them set in a moderate oven to bake for two hours. If you prefer the ham glazed, allow it to cool as for boiled ham, then skin, wipe dry and brush all over with beaten egg. Mix one cup of sifted cracker crumbs, a dash of salt and pepper, two tablespoons of melted butter and cream enough to make the crumbs into a paste. Spread it evenly over the ham, set in a moderate oven and bake till brown, then serve hot with a brown sauce flavored with half a glass of sherry or champagne, if liked. When a baked or boiled ham goes to the table wrap about the unsightly bone a ruffle of white tissue paper, garnish with hard boiled eggs cut in quarters.

Potted Ham

To four cups of finely minced ham add a seasoning of paprika and allspice, with just enough clarified butter to make it into a paste, then press into small jars and pour over it melted butter, which will harden and preserve it as paraffin does jelly.

Scalloped Ham

Make a thin, well-seasoned white sauce and add to it cold boiled ham cut into small cubes. Pour into scallop dishes, cover with buttered crumbs and brown delicately in the oven. Garnish with rings of hard boiled white of egg and sprigs of blanched celery.

Broiled Ham

It should be cut in thin slices; put between the wires of a broiler and cook for five minutes, turning frequently, over a clear, hot fire. Serve on a hot platter with poached eggs.

Corned Tongue

Wash and trim out the roots of one or more fresh beef tongues. Put them into a stone jar, cover with brine, lay a plate over the meat and on this a stone to keep the meat under the brine. Cover securely, keep in a cold place and in a week they will be ready for use, although they will keep in the brine for several weeks in cold weather.

Brine for Corning

Put two quarts of water, three-quarters of a pound of salt, a quarter of a pound of brown sugar and a fourth of an ounce of saltpeter together into a granite saucepan and heat to boiling. Cool and strain through cheesecloth. Pour it over the meat and add a teaspoon of pepper, half a teaspoon of ginger, three bay leaves and two cloves of garlic. This amount of brine is sufficient for half a dozen tongues. Calf tongues may be corned in the same way and if desired, a piece of beef may be corned in the same brine with the tongues.

Sausage and Apples

Core four apples and slice across in one-fourth inch slices. Bake the sausages on a rack in a dripping pan. Fry the apples brown, using some of the fat extracted from the sausage. Serve on the same platter with the sausage.

Skewered Liver

Alternate small pieces of liver and bacon on skewers and bake in the oven or broil until done. This is a convenient and dainty way to serve a small amount.

Sweetbreads

Sweetbreads should be purchased as fresh as possible, and as they spoil very quickly, they should receive attention as soon as they arrive from the market. Soak in cold water an hour or longer, renewing the water an hour times to extract all the blood. Drain and let simmer in boiling salted water half an hour or until tender. Drain again, reserving the broth for subsequent cooking, and cover with cold water to keep them white and firm. When they are cooled, wipe them dry. Remove all the tubes, outside skin and fibers, taking care not to break the sweetbreads into pieces. Sprinkle with salt and pepper and put into a cold place until needed. Sweetbreads should always be parboiled in this manner, whatever the subsequent mode of preparation. It insures their thorough cooking and makes them thicker, whiter and firmer.

Lyonnaise Tripe

Clean and boil a fresh honeycomb tripe, then cut into strips about two and a half inches long and half an inch wide sufficient to make two cups. Put in a pan in the oven for a few minutes to draw out the water, then drain. Melt a tablespoon of butter, add a teaspoon of finely chopped onion, cook to a delicate brown and add the tripe, a teaspoon of finely minced parsley, a teaspoon of vinegar and salt and pepper to taste. Simmer five minutes and serve plain or on toast.

Meat and Fish Sauces

From *Good Housekeeping Family Cookbook*, by Mildred Maddocks, 1906

White Sauce

Cream one tablespoon each of flour and butter until thoroughly mixed, add to one cup of milk, cream or white stock, and cook until thickened, stirring until the flour and butter are well mixed. Season with salt and pepper.

Espagnole Sauce

Put four tablespoons of butter into a spider, and in it brown crisply one slice of carrot, one slice of onion, a bit of bay leaf, a sprig of thyme, a sprig of parsley and six peppercorns. Add five tablespoons of flour, and when well-browned add gradually one pint of brown stock, beating to a creamy smoothness with a wire whisk. Strain and season with salt and pepper.

Brown Sauce

Melt a tablespoon of butter, add a tablespoon of flour, cook, stirring continually until a light brown, then add a cup of rich gravy, meat broth or water and stir until it thickens.

Olive Brown Sauce

Cut two dozen large olives into narrow spiral strips. Melt and brown two tablespoons of butter, add two tablespoons of flour and brown again. Add gradually two cups of brown stock and stir until thick and smooth, add ten drops of onion juice, salt and pepper to taste, one tablespoon each of walnut and mushroom catsup, one tablespoon of Worcestershire sauce, and the olives, simmer for five minutes and serve with duck.

Spanish Sauce

Simmer together for ten minutes three tablespoons of vinegar, one tablespoon of chopped green pepper, a bay leaf and sprig of parsley; strain into a pint of plain white sauce, add a teaspoon of finely chopped chives and the zest of a lemon.

Tomato Sauce

Melt a fourth of a cup of butter, add a fourth of a cup of flour and gradually two cups of water, one and a half cups of stewed and strained tomatoes, half a teaspoon of Worcestershire sauce, if liked, and salt and pepper to season. A can of mushrooms may also be added if desired.

Sauce Piquante

Mix one teaspoon of onion juice, a tablespoon of Worcestershire, the juice of a small lemon, three tablespoons of olive oil and celery salt and pepper to taste. Just before nerving add a tablespoon of finely in minced parsley.

Sauce for Salmon Loaf

Heat one pint of milk and thicken with one tablespoon of cornstarch and two tablespoons of butter, rubbed together. Add the liquor from one can of salmon, one tablespoon each of tomato ketchup and Worcestershire with a pinch of cayenne. Pour over a well beaten egg, beat well and serve.

Mousseline Sauce

Beat a tablespoon of butter to a cream; add the yolks of three eggs, one at a time, then add three tablespoons of lemon juice, half a teaspoon of salt and a dash of cayenne. Cook over hot water until the sauce thickens, then add another tablespoon of butter and half a cup of sweet cream. When the sauce is hot, serve. It should be quite thick and frothy.

Sauce Béarnaise

Put half a cup of butter into a small saucepan and rub to a cream, add a fourth of a teaspoon of salt, a dash of cayenne and the yolks of two eggs, and beat well, then stir in a tablespoon of lemon juice and gradually half a cup of boiling water. Cook over hot water, stirring constantly until of a creamy consistency, add a teaspoon of finely chopped parsley and fresh tarragon and serve at once.

Sauce Trianon

Omit the parsley and tarragon and add gradually while cooking one and a half tablespoons of sherry wine.

Sauce Figaro

Omit the tarragon and add two tablespoons of tomatoes which have been stewed, strained and cooked to a pulp.

Béchamel Sauce

Cook one and one-half cups of white stock with a slice each of onion and carrot, a bay leaf, a sprig of parsley and six peppercorns, until reduced to one cop. Brown one-fourth cup of flour in one-fourth cup of butter, add the strained stock and beat until smooth. When cooked beat into it a cup of hot cream and season to taste with salt and pepper.

Egg Sauce

Melt a tablespoon of butter, add a tablespoon of flour and gradually a cup of half milk and half water, stirring constantly until it thickens. Add a teaspoon of finely minced parsley, salt and paprika to season and the finely minced yolk of a hard-cooked egg. Take from the fire, add the yolks of two eggs beaten with a tablespoon of lemon juice and serve.

Orange Sauce for Ducks

After removing the ducks from the pan add sufficient veal stock or chicken to make a pint of liquid. Add to this a tablespoon of chopped onion, a small carrot chopped, a bay leaf and a bunch of parsley, and let all simmer an hour, adding stock as the liquid evaporates. When done, strain and add the grated rind of a lemon, a seasoning of salt and a dash of cayenne. Remove from the fire and stir in a tablespoon of butter, the juice of two sour oranges, and a tablespoon of finely chopped celery. Beat three egg yolks in a warmed bowl, pour in the hot sauce, and cook in a double boiler until as thick as double cream.

Orange Marmalade Sauce

Put into a saucepan one tablespoon of butter, one tablespoon of flour, one-third of a teaspoon of salt and a slight dusting of paprika. When brown, add slowly one cup of rich brown stock and cook and stir until thick and smooth. Add, if liked, a gill of sherry and three tablespoons of Scotch marmalade, and beat hard until the marmalade is entirely and smoothly blended with the sauce. This sauce is particularly suitable to serve with quail and with grouse.

Bread Sauce

Heat one cup of milk in a double boiler, add one tablespoon of butter, one teaspoon of onion juice, salt and pepper to taste. When very hot stir in lightly half a cup of bread crumbs dried in the oven.

Hollandaise Sauce

Cream one-half cup of butter, add one teaspoon of flour, the yolks of two eggs, one saltspoon of salt, one quarter saltspoon of cayenne pepper and very gradually the juice of one-half a lemon. Pour over this one-half cup of boiling water and cook over boiling water until thickened, stirring all the time.

Entrees

From *Good Housekeeping Family Cookbook,* by Mildred Maddocks, 1906

Timbale Cases

Into a small bowl put three-fourths of a cup of flour, half a teaspoon of salt and a teaspoon of sugar. Add gradually one-half cup of milk, one beaten egg and a tablespoon of olive oil. Whip with an egg-beater until it is perfectly blended, then chill for an hour. The frying is the most difficult part of the operation. Pour the batter into a deep cup; in a shallow bowl it would soon be too low to properly cover the timbale iron. Heat the fat until hot enough to brown bread in forty counts and provide a pan with heavy absorbent paper close by. Drop the mold end of the iron into the fat long enough to become heated, remove and dip into the batter for a second. A thin film of partially cooked batter will cling, but to insure a good timbale dip again. This time no bubble or hole should marr the even coat on the iron. Dip for twelve seconds in the hot fat. Turn the iron

Timbale Ready To Be filled

upside down to drain off the fat and to keep the timbale from dropping off. Slip from the iron to the paper and dip again. For success the fat must be very hot, and the iron must be hot as well; dip the point into batter; if nothing clings it is too cold or too hot. Dip into batter, covering half the mold. When fried there will be just the right height. A fluted iron is easier for a beginner to use as there is no tendency for the fried timbale to slip off.

Cheese Fondue in Shells

Add two tablespoons of melted butter to a cup of soft bread crumbs; cover with a cup of milk and let stand about ten minutes. Add half a teaspoon of salt, a shaking of pepper, a fourth of a pound of mild cheese grated and the beaten yolks of three eggs, then fold in the whites of the eggs beaten until stiff. Turn into buttered individual timbale shells or china cups and bake in a moderate oven until the egg is set. Serve at once in the dishes.

Utensils for Making Heart-Shaped Timbales

Vegetarian Rice

Boil the rice until flaky, then mold into the shape of a loaf of bread. Cut the loaf in half and insert three tablespoons of butter and push together strain. Grate strong cheese over the top of the loaf and bake in the oven until the cheese runs and glazes the top. Serve with asparagus tips in melted butter.

Corn Soufflé

Heat one pint of milk; stir into it three-fourths of a cup of cornmeal and cook until thick and smooth. Add salt and a little butter; beat into this the well beaten yolks of four eggs and then the whites, which have been beaten separately. Pour into a baking dish and cook twenty-five minutes in a moderate oven. Serve at once.

Pigs in Blankets

Take large oysters, allowing two to be served each person, as they are too rich to serve more. Cut clear salt pork into thin slices, put it in cold water and let it come to a boil; this is to remove any strong taste or odor. After boiling place it on brown paper to drain. Wrap each oyster in a slice of pork, fastening with toothpick. Dip in beaten egg, using both yolk and white. Roll in cracker crumbs and fry in smoking hot olive oil, until brown. Use a wire croquette basket if you have one.

Sweetbread in Ramekins

Make one cup of cream sauce. Add one and a half cups of diced sweetbread and a cup of peas, either fresh or canned, turn into buttered ramekins, cover with buttered bread crumbs and bake until the crumbs are brown. Any of the mixtures suitable for creamed sweetbreads may be prepared in this way. This is a good and simple luncheon dish.

Escalloped Chicken with Green Peppers and Tomatoes

Bone the legs of the chicken and cut into neat blocks. Prepare butter sauce and mix with fowl. Take two green peppers, cut in strips, one large ripe tomato and two boiled potatoes, cut them the same as the chicken; mix all together in the sauce and simmer thirty minutes. Pour the mixture in a baking dish, cover with fine bread crumbs, butter the top and bake a nice brown. Serve with baked new potatoes.

Spanish Tamales

The following ingredients are for two dozen tamales. Three dozen ears of green corn with the husks, one chicken, two dozen Chili peppers, one quart of olives, two pounds of raisins, two cups of good lard. Salt to season sufficiently. Scrape the corn from the cob, mix with the chicken minced moderately fine, and add the other ingredients. Divide in two dozen small portions and tie up in the husks. Steam or boil until thoroughly done. This is a genuine Spanish-made tamale, as manufactured in southern California.

Deviled Crabs

To the meal of one dozen hard crabs add pepper, salt, dry mustard and Worcestershire sauce to taste. Heat two cups of fresh milk, add two tablespoons of butter, six broken crackers and some chopped parsley. Stir and cook a few minutes. Remove from fire and mix with the picked crab meat. Fill each shell, cover with cracker crumbs with a bit of butter on top. Bake in oven until brown.

Supreme of Chicken

Run through a meat chopper until chopped very fine the raw breast of a good sized chicken; beat in, one at a time, four eggs, beating the mixture after each addition until smooth; add one and a third cups of thick cream and season well with salt and pepper. Turn into buttered earthen timbale molds, half surround them with hot water, cover with buttered paper and bake about twenty minutes in a moderate oven. Serve with a sauce made of a fourth of a cup each of butter and flour, one and a half cups of chicken stock, half a cup of cream, salt and pepper to season and the yolks of two eggs.

Cheese Pie

This is a delicious accompaniment to cold sliced meat or it may well serve as the central dish for the family luncheon. Cut two-thirds of a stale five-cent baker's loaf in one-third-inch slices, and then cut the slices in halves. In a buttered shallow baking dish alternate layers of bread with layers of soft, mild cheese, cut in one-eighth-inch slices and sprinkled with salt and paprika. Beat two eggs slightly and add one cup of milk. Pour over the bread and bake until the cheese is soft, the time required being about thirty minutes.

Timbales of Halibut

Force through a meat chopper until finely chopped one and a half pounds of fresh uncooked halibut. Add a teaspoon of salt, a few grains of cayenne, half a cup of thick cream beaten until stiff and the stiffly-beaten whites of five eggs. Turn into a well-buttered mold and steam for thirty minutes, taking care to have the water surrounding it boiling steadily the entire time. Turn out, garnish with lemon and parsley and serve with egg sauce.

Ramekins of Chicken

Cut into cubes sufficient cooked chicken to make one and a half cups. Have ready a cup of

cooked and drained peas, fresh or canned, and a fourth of a cup of sliced mushrooms. Melt a fourth of a cup of butter; when hot and bubbling add a fourth of a cup of flour and gradually half a cup each of chicken stock, cream and the liquor from canned mushrooms. Season to taste with salt and paprika, add the chicken, peas and mushrooms, and when all are mixed thoroughly, place in ramekins. Cover with browned crumbs and serve.

Timbales of Liver

To a pint of young calf's liver cooked in salted water until tender, then forced through a meat chopper, add a cup of fresh crumbs moistened with a cup of chicken stock or milk, two beaten eggs, a teaspoon of finely chopped parsley, a few drops of onion juice, a tablespoon of chicken oil, bacon fat or soft butter, and salt and paprika to season highly. Mix thoroughly and turn into well-buttered earthen timbale molds. Cook in a pan of warm water in a moderate oven for about twenty-five minutes. Turn out on a warm platter and surround with mushroom sauce.

Sweetbread Timbales

Parboil and cook a pair of sweetbreads until tender. Cool and force through a meat chopper, then add four eggs, one at a time, stirring until the mixture is smooth, lastly fold in a cup of cream beaten until stiff and dry and add seasoning of salt and pepper to taste. Butter some small earthen timbale molds, put a mushroom in the bottom of each and fill two-thirds full with the mixture. Put into a pan, half surround with hot water, cover with buttered paper and bake twenty minutes in a moderate oven. Turn out and serve with green peas or stewed mushrooms.

Indian Meal Timbales

Cook two cups of cornmeal in slightly salted water for three-quarters of an hour, adding more water if necessary and boiling to the consistency of porridge. Pour into small timbale molds and set away to harden; when quite firm remove with a sharp spoon the center from each mold, leaving only a shell; unmold these, brush over with melted butter and crisp in a hot oven; then fill with any highly seasoned creamed or deviled preparation of meat, fish or game and serve inverted on a salpicon of mashed potato, garnished with sprigs of parsley and thinly sliced lemon.

Tomato Timbales

Add one-fourth teaspoon of soda to half a cup of cream and stir into two cups of cold stewed and sifted tomatoes. Add the beaten yolks of six eggs, half a teaspoon of salt, the same quantity of onion juice, a tablespoon of sugar and a dusting of paprika; lastly fold in the stiffly beaten whites of three eggs. Turn into buttered timbale molds and bake until firm. Stand the mold in hot water, which must not boil after the molds are set in the oven.

Fritter Batter

Sift together a cup of flour and a fourth of a teaspoon of salt. Beat well the yolks of two eggs, add to them gradually half a cup of milk, then stir this slowly into the flour, beating until smooth: add a tablespoon of melted butter or olive oil and stand aside an hour or longer. In cold weather several hours or overnight is preferable. When ready to use add the whites of the eggs beaten very stiff. In cold weather this batter may be kept several days.

Fig Fritters

For one dozen of these delicious fritters, take two eggs, separating the whites from the yolks, add to the yolks one cup of milk, one and one-half cups of graham flour, one tablespoon of melted butter, one-half teaspoon of salt, one cup of chopped figs and one-half cup of boiled rice stirred in; flavor with nutmeg and a little cinnamon, then stir in the beaten whites and one teaspoon of baking powder; fry in deep fat and serve with a boiled icing sauce.

Golden Ball Fritters

Put into a saucepan, a pint of water, a tablespoon of butter and half a cup of sugar. When this boils, stir into it a pint of sifted flour, stirring briskly and thoroughly. Remove from the fire, and when nearly cold, beat in four eggs, one at a time, and beating the batter between each; then add a cup of preserved ginger chopped finely, and fry brown in boiling fat. Serve with a sauce made from the ginger syrup and flavored with lemon juice.

Cranberry Fritters

Beat one egg thoroughly and stir it into one and one-half cups of milk, add one tablespoon of sugar and one cup of flour in which has been sifted one teaspoon of baking powder. When well mixed stir in one cup of thick rich cranberry sauce, and drop in spoonfuls on a hot buttered gridiron. Brown very lightly, and serve with butter and powdered sugar.

Chicken or Turkey Fritters

Separate some cold cooked chicken or turkey from the bones and cut into pieces about half an inch thick and an inch and a half long. The pieces need not necessarily be perfect in shape. Sprinkle with salt and pepper, dip into fritter batter, coating well on all sides, and fry in deep hot fat until a golden brown. Drain on brown or soft paper to absorb the grease.

Apple Fritters

Pare and core four tart apples and out in one-fourth inch slices across the apple. Sprinkle with two tablespoons of lemon juice and powdered sugar. Prepare a batter by sifting one cup of flour and one-fourth teaspoon of salt. Add two well-beaten yolks to one-half cup of milk, mix and beat into the flour, until it is a smooth batter. Add one tablespoon of melted butter or olive oil, and cut in the stiffly beaten whites of two eggs. Drain the apples carefully, dip in the batter and fry in deep fat. When cooked, drain on crushed brown paper to absorb the grease, sprinkle with powdered sugar, and serve.

Clam Fritters

Clean and pick over a quart of clams. Reserve the liquor and use it in making a fritter batter instead of milk. Put aside the soft part of the clams, finely chop the hard part, then add all to the batter, which should be quite thick. Drop by small spoonfuls in hot fat. Drain and serve as oyster fritters.

Croquettes

In making croquettes, use bread crumbs if possible, rolled or ground to the fineness of powder. Place them in on even oblong in the center of a board. Dilute one slightly beaten egg with twice the amount of cold water and place in a pie plate. Form the croquettes, roll in the crumbs, then in egg; crumbs again and set aside to fry.

Shaping a Croquette

Covering the Croquette with Egg

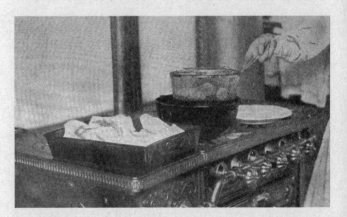

Frying Croquette

A mixture of one-third clarified suet to two-thirds of good lard is excellent for frying. Olive oil is even better but of course more expensive. Whatever fat be used heat until a bit of bread can be browned in it in forty counts. Dip the empty frying basket in the hot fat, then fill with the croquettes, taking care that there

Croquette after frying

are not enough to touch each other or the sides of the basket. When cooked drain on crushed unglazed paper. Heat the fat before attempting to fry a second batch.

Somerest Croquettes

Melt three tablespoons of butter, add one-fourth cup of flour, and pour on, gradually, while stirring constantly, two-thirds cup of milk. When the boiling point is reached, add one-half cup of grated Gruyere cheese, and the yolks of two eggs unbeaten. As soon as the cheese melts, remove from the range, fold in one cup of mild cheese, cut in very small cubes, and season with salt and cayenne. Spread in a shallow pan and cool, shape in round croquettes, dip in crumbs, egg and crumbs again, fry in deep fat and drain on brown paper.

Lentil Croquettes

Soak overnight one cup of dried lentils and half a cup of dried red beans. Drain, add two cups of water, half an onion, a stalk of celery, a small carrot sliced and two or three sprigs of parsley. Cook until soft, remove seasonings and rub through a sieve. Add one cup of soft bread crumbs, one beaten egg, salt, pepper and lemon juice to taste. Cream together two tablespoons of flour and two tablespoons of butter, pour on gradually two-thirds

of a cup of cream, bring to the boiling point and add to the lentil mixture. Mix thoroughly, cool, shape, dip in crumbs, in egg and again in crumbs, and fry in deep hot fat. Drain and serve with brown tomato sauce.

Croquettes a la Josephine

Mix thoroughly two cups of mashed sweet potatoes, four tablespoons of melted butter, four tablespoons of cream, one tablespoon of chopped parsley, one-half teaspoon of salt and a little cayenne; add the beaten yolks of two eggs to this and stir over the fire until the mixture leaves the sides of the saucepan, then set it aside to cool. Chop finely one cup of the dark meat of cold turkey, mix with it a little of the brown sauce with which it was served when roasted, and form into small balls. Surround these balls with the sweet potato mixture, about one tablespoon to each, making larger balls of uniform size. Egg and bread crumb them and fry in deep fat. Serve on a napkin garnished with parsley and accompany with a white or cream sauce flavored with a teaspoon of Worcestershire.

Sweet Potato Croquettes

Mash and sift old cooked potatoes to the amount of two cups, add two beaten egg yolks, one-half teaspoon of salt and enough cream to make them soft enough to form into croquettes, roll in crumbs, egg, and crumbs again, and fry in hot fat.

Macaroni Croquettes

Cook macaroni in boiling salted water until tender; drain, cool and cut fine. Make a thick sauce of two tablespoons of butter and four tablespoons of flour and a cup of milk, add one cup of macaroni, a heaping tablespoon of grated cheese, the beaten yolks of two eggs and salt and pepper to season.

Cool, shape, egg and crumb and fry in deep fat. Serve with tomato sauce.

Italian Croquettes

Have ready a cup of finely chopped and cooked vermicelli. Make a sauce of a fourth of a cup each of butter and flour and a cup of strained cooked tomatoes. Add a fourth of a cup of chopped mushrooms, the vermicelli, and season highly with salt and paprika. Cool, shape and fry as other croquettes.

Chupe

Cut a medium sized onion small and fry in a tablespoon of lard (this is a South American recipe— drippings may be substituted if preferred); do not let it brown; add two tomatoes cut in dice (whole tomatoes from a can may be used in lieu of fresh ones), a tablespoon of finely minced parsley and half a teaspoon of salt. Now add six potatoes pared and cut in halves, with sufficient water to cover, and cook five minutes; add two tablespoons of washed rice and simmer twenty minutes, or till rice and potatoes are done; just before serving beat one egg in a cup of milk end stir slowly into the hot ragout; remove from the fire and break in a small five-cent cream cheese.

Fried Nuts

Cold cooked farina, oatmeal or mush of any kind may be utilized. Season highly while hot with butter, salt and pepper, and when cold enough to handle shape the size of small walnuts. Dip in beaten egg, then in crushed walnuts, and fry in deep fat.

Celery Rolls

Select six rolls, cut from the top a round piece the size of a silver dollar, and scoop out the soft part;

when ready to serve, fill with the following mixture: Chop very fine sufficient celery to make a pint. Dust over a teaspoon of salt, a saltspoon of pepper, a tablespoon of grated onion, two tablespoons of tomato ketchup, four tablespoons of olive oil and one teaspoon of lemon juice. Serve very cold. The filling may be varied by the addition of a little cold chicken cut in dice, or some finely minced boiled tongue.

Hash in a New Dress

Chop fine scraps of beef or mutton, cooked or uncooked, to the amount of about a pint, season with salt and pepper, and pour on a cup of hot water. Let boil for a few minutes, thicken with a little flour, then place in shallow granite pan ready for the oven. Now take two good-sized onions, chop them fairly fine and boil until tender. Drain and spread them over hash, then make a dressing of a half-pint of bread crumbs, one egg, well beaten, two tablespoons of melted butter, salt, pepper and a little sage. Mix thoroughly and spread on top of the onion in the dish. Bake in a moderate oven twenty minutes.

Steak with Tomato

This is a good way of cooking a cheap cut of a steak. It is nicest cooked in a casserole in the oven, but, as that is very expensive when one has a gas stove, we do it usually in a tightly covered frying pan on top of the stove. One pound round steak, three-quarters can tomato, one small onion, salt, red and black pepper to taste, one-half bay leaf. Put all together in a frying pan or casserole and cook slowly three hours. Cooking fast absolutely spoils it.

Swedish Cabbage

Boil in salted water for twenty minutes a dozen good sized cabbage leaves. Drain them and fill with a mixture of one pound of raw beef chopped fine, one egg, two tablespoons of cream, one-half teaspoon of black pepper, one teaspoon of salt and chopped parsley. Rub the dish in which you mix this with a clove of garlic. Mix all together thoroughly. Roll each leaf around a tablespoon of this mixture, trim the ends neatly and tie or skewer. Lay in a dripping pan with a pint of stock or a tablespoon of butter and a pint of water, baste frequently and bake for half an hour or until tender. Remove the rolls, thicken the gravy, pour over them and serve hot.

Pork Scallop

Put a layer of cold boiled pork, chopped fine, in a buttered ramekin; season with salt, pepper and minced onion, then strew over it a layer of cracker crumbs, and moisten with milk. Add another layer of meat, and so on until the dish is filled, finishing off with a layer of the crumbs. Cover closely and bake. Ten minutes before it is done uncover and let brown. Serve with onion sauce.

Game in Potato Cases

Pare and slice five or six medium-sized potatoes, and drop into ice water for an hour's crisping; drain and cook in salted water. When done drain and shake in a current of air until dry and floury. Run through a vegetable press and whip into them a quarter cup of butter, two tablespoons of cream, beaten with two egg yolks and a light dusting of white pepper. Whip until thoroughly mixed and fluffy, then line small molds which have been brushed with butter and dusted with sifted dry bread crumbs. Melt over the fire a tablespoon of butter creamed with a tablespoon of flour, add a cup of stock, brown or white, a bay leaf, a dusting of salt and paprika, a cup of finely minced cold game, and a teaspoon of lemon juice. Simmer

for ten minutes, remove the bay leaf and fill the center of each mold; lay on a fine fat oyster, lightly parboiled, and spread a layer of potato over the top; stand in a baking pan and bake in a moderate oven for fifteen minutes. Turn from the molds and serve with mushroom sauce. These little cases make a delicious entree.

Quail Pates

These can be served hot as a second course at a formal luncheon, or they can be served cold at a theater supper, and are equally good either way. Line small pate pans with good pastry, fill with rice, adjust a top of pastry to each and bake. Remove the lid of crust and set aside, empty out the rice and remove the pastry shells from the pans. Chop fine the best of the meat, and reserve; take the bits and oddmeats left, break the bones small, cover to level with cold water and set to simmer for an hour. Make a forcemeat of the livers of the quail if at hand, if not use chicken livers, rub through a sieve, and to three tablespoons add the same quantity of chopped boiled ham, the yolks of two hard cooked eggs, a teaspoon of minced onion and a teaspoon of chopped celery. Strain the stock, season with salt and pepper and a teaspoon of Worcestershire sauce. In the bottom of each pastry shell place a morsel of finely shredded fat bacon, on this put a layer of the quail meat, next a fat plump oyster, cover with the for cement, and moisten with the stock; replace the pastry cover and set in a moderate oven for twenty minutes.

Tongue Fingers

Grate the remains of a cold tongue very fine and mix it with the yolk of an egg, a spoonful of cream and finely chopped parsley, pepper and salt. Heat it thoroughly and pour on narrow slices of well-buttered toast. Sprinkle thickly with fine bread crumbs stirred in melted butter, with a shake of red pepper, and brown quickly in a hot oven.

Kidney Relish

Split kidneys in two, remove the fat and outer skin and chop fine. Slightly brown some chopped onion in a tablespoon of butter and add a little chopped parsley, then a tablespoon of Worcestershire sauce, a sprinkling of flour, and stir in the finely chopped kidneys with salt and pepper to taste. Spread on thin slices of buttered toast, cover with a layer of bread crumbs and Parmesan cheese and place in a quick oven for fifteen minutes, then serve at once.

Yorkshireman's Delight

A Yorkshire pudding is known only as a delicious accompaniment to roast beef. Try placing good plump sausages or slices of sausage meat in a large dripping pan, pouring the batter over them, and baking in a hot oven for thirty minutes. The batter is made with two cups of flour, a teaspoon of salt, three eggs, well beaten, and two cups of milk.

Stuffed Squash

These who are in the way of procuring the small, average-sized squashes (known popularly as "individual" squashes) will find the following a palatable luncheon dish or entree. Parboil the squashes for fifteen minutes, drain, cut off a small portion of the top and remove the seeds, fill with a forcemeat, replace the covers and bake in a moderate oven an hour. To make forcemeat for five squashes brown a pint of diced stole bread in two tablespoons of butter and fry crisply brown. After cooling add a teaspoon of minced onion, two hard cooked eggs chopped fine, half a cup of blanched chopped nut meats, two tablespoons of grated cheese, half a teaspoon of salt, a dusting of paprika and two beaten egg yolks. Mix well together, slightly crushing the bread cubes.

Sweet Potato Timbales

To one cup of cooked and sifted sweet potatoes add two beaten eggs, three tablespoons of cream, two tablespoons of melted butter, one-half teaspoon of salt and a dash of white pepper. Mix thoroughly and turn into buttered timbale molds. Bake in a pan of hot water in the oven until the centers are firm. Serve turned from the molds and garnished with parsley.

Squash and Almond Croquettes

Remove the seeds from a Hubbard and bake in convenient-sized pieces, then run the pulp through a ricer. To each pint add two tablespoons of melted butter, a beaten egg, a half teaspoon of salt and half a cup of blanched, chopped and pounded almonds. Form into croquettes, egg and crumb and fry in deep fat.

Migas

Break small a pound loaf of stale bread and soak in cold water; fry a small sliced onion a light brown in two tablespoons of very hot lard; add two tomatoes cut very small and one red pepper chopped fine with some salt; squeeze the bread dry and let it stew with the onion and tomatoes for ten minutes; add a small cream cheese broken small and dish on a flat platter, laying one poached egg for each person on the top. It is both good and economical.

Puddings

From *Good Housekeeping Family Cookbook,* by Mildred Maddocks, 1906

Plum Pudding

Clean one pound of currants by washing in warm water, dry on a towel, pick them over, toss them in flour and put them in a big mixing bowl. Add one pound of raisins, stoned, slightly chopped and floured, then half a pound of brown sugar, one pound of finely chopped suet, four ounces of chopped citron, four ounces of chopped lemon peel, four ounces of chopped orange peel, one teaspoon of salt, one grated nutmeg, one teaspoon of ginger, one teaspoon of cinnamon, half a teaspoon of cloves, half a teaspoon of allspice and four ounces of split blanched almonds, one and a half pounds of flour and one and a half pounds of stale bread crumbs. Toss these dry ingredients thoroughly, then add eight well-beaten eggs, and milk enough to make a very stiff batter. One secret of success is that the batter be very well stirred. Take a square piece of strong drilling, dip it in boiling water, then rub it on one side full of flour. This forms a crust on the cloth which the water or steam cannot soak through. On the floured side lay an enameled bowl well-buttered. Turn the pudding into and cover with buttered paper. Gather the cloth together loosely, allowing one-quarter of space for the pudding to swell, set the pudding on a trivet in a kettle of boiling water, having the water come only half way up the side of the bowl, as the pudding should be steamed, not boiled. Let the water boil for six hours, keeping it replenished from the teakettle; if it stops boiling for one minute the pudding will be sticky.

Plain Plum Pudding

Four ounces of suet, four ounces of currants and raisins mixed, two tablespoons of brown sugar, two tablespoons of molasses, one egg, half a teaspoon of soda dissolved in half a cup of warm milk, and enough flour to make into a good, stiff batter. Steam two hours.

Ginger Pudding

Mix together four ounces each of bread crumbs, suet and preserved ginger, with two well-beaten eggs. Add two tablespoons of ginger syrup and steam three hours.

Date Bread and Butter Pudding

Cut half of a small loaf of white bread into thin slices, trim off the crusts, and spread each with butter and a thin layer of quince or apple jelly. Line

Plum Puddings

a buttered pudding dish with them, and spread over half a cup of cleaned dates, stoned and cut in small pieces. Then put in another layer of the spread bread, and another half cup of dates. Finish with the bread simply buttered. Cover with a custard made with one quart of milk, three eggs, half a cup of sugar and a pinch of salt. Pour it slowly over the bread, and let it stand half an hour. Bake in a moderate oven about one hour. Serve with sweet sauce or cream and sugar.

Indian Rice Pudding

To two quarts of milk add two tablespoons of uncooked rice, one-half a cup of molasses, one-fourth teaspoon of salt. Bake in a buttered dish, in a slow oven for four or five hours, stirring occasionally.

Date Suet Pudding

Stone and cut small one pound of dates. Chop six ounces of fresh beef suet and mix with it three-quarters of a pound of fine bread crumbs. Sprinkle a scant cup of sugar over the dates, and add them to the crumbs and suet. To one well-beaten egg add half a cup of milk, and stir it into half a cup of flour sifted with a level teaspoon of baking powder. Mix all well together, turn into a mold and steam three hours. Serve with lemon sauce.

Lemon Rice Pudding

Boil a cup of well washed rice in a quart of milk until very soft. Add to it while hot the beaten yolks of three eggs, the juice and grated rind of two lemons, eight tablespoons of sugar and a pinch of salt. If too thick add a little milk. It should be rather thicker than boiled custard. Turn it into a pudding dish, beat the whites of the eggs very stiff with six tablespoons of powdered sugar, spread over the top and brown delicately in a slow oven.

New England Prune Pudding

Stew one pound of prunes until soft, sweetening them to taste, and adding a few slices of orange. Arrange squares of toasted whole wheat bread, buttered and sprinkled with allspice, in the bottom and around the sides of a baking dish; then pour in the prunes boiling hot, cover the dish so that the steam may not escape, and let it cool gradually. When ready to serve, cover the top with boiled frosting garnished with squares of apple jelly.

Baked Apple Dumplings

Cut a short pie crust into five or six-inch squares. In the center of each place a pared and neatly cored apple, filling the space with sugar and cinnamon, if liked, also a clove. After wetting the edges of the pastry with white of egg, fold it over the apple, pinch and flute them to look well, and encase the apple completely. Bake from thirty to forty minutes, toward the end brushing the top with white of egg and dusting with a little sugar. Serve with hard sauce.

Cranberry Pudding

Sift together one pint of flour, half a teaspoon of salt, and three teaspoons of baking powder. Add milk to make a soft batter, stir in one cup of stiff rich cranberry sauce, and steam for one hour and a half. Serve with a cranberry sauce made as follows: Into one quart of boiling water stir one pint of granulated sugar, and cook over the fire until thoroughly dissolved. Then add one quart of sound crushed cranberries, cook for five or ten minutes, strain through a colander to remove the skins, and serve at once.

Gooseberry Soufflé

Boil one quart of fine gooseberries in just enough water to keep from burning. When soft, press through a sieve. Beat in the whites of five eggs which have been whipped to a stiff froth with half a pound of powdered sugar. Flavor with nutmeg and lemon. When very stiff whip lightly in the stiffly whipped whites of three more eggs, and set the dish in a hot oven for five minutes before serving.

Maple Shortcake

Mix and sift together two cups of flour and a level tablespoon of baking powder. Rub in one-half cup of butter and mix to a soft dough with milk. Spread the mixture evenly over two buttered pie pans, brush with melted butter and bake in a quick oven. Put together as layer cake and spread between and on top with filling.

Maple Cream Filling

Cook three-fourths of a cup of maple syrup and a tablespoon of butter until it spins a thread, then pour gradually into the stiffly beaten whites of two eggs. When the mixture is smooth, add half a cup of cream beaten until stiff and a few drops of vanilla.

Lemon Snowballs

Beat the yolks of three eggs until very light; add gradually one cup of granulated sugar, three tablespoons of water, the grated yellow rind of one lemon, two tablespoons of lemon juice, and one cup of flour in which has been sifted one level teaspoon of baking powder. Then fold in the stiffly whipped whites of the eggs, and pour the batter into fifteen little buttered cups. Steam for half an hour, then turn out, roll in powdered sugar, and serve with lemon or almond sauce.

Turnovers

One cup of brown sugar, one cup of lard, one egg, two cups of oatmeal, one cup of sour milk,

one teaspoon of soda, one teaspoon nutmeg, salt and white flour enough to roll out thin. Cut with a thin cookie cutter. Fill with jam or jelly, turn over and bake.

Stuffed Apples

Take good firm cooking apples, cut off the blossom end, scoop out the core, fill apple with chopped pecans, two teaspoons of sugar and a teaspoon of brandy. Put in a pan with a little water and bake until done, but not out of shape. Just before serving press down into the apples half a dozen brandied cherries to each apple.

Good Friday Pudding

One and one-half cups of bread crumbs and the same quantity of chopped apples; one cup of raisins and three eggs. Pot in buttered dish and steam one and one-half hours. Serve with warm sauce flavored with lemon and brandy.

Indian Pudding (Enough for five people)

Scald one quart of milk in a double boiler; while it is heating, take six tablespoons of Indian meal, and stir it up with one large cup of molasses, mixing it in the buttered baking dish, which should be a small stone jar, or an earthen pan, deep, and shaped like a flower pot. When stirred smooth, add the scalded milk, stirring well. It will look very thin, almost as if there were no meal in it. Then scatter some small bits of butter over the top, place jar in a moderate oven and bake three or four hours. When done it will be of a somewhat jelly-like consistency, with some whey and some clotted cream. Turn it out into a pretty dish and serve with plain cream.

Rice with Fruit Sauce

In a double boiler, steam one-half cup of rice in one pint of milk, season with salt. Measure one cup of raisins, boil until tender and add one-half cup of chopped citron. From the water in which the raisins were stewed make a syrup with one-half the quantity of sugar. Boil sugar and water five minutes, add two tablespoons of cornstarch and boil ten minutes, stirring constantly. Strain, add two tablespoons of butter, flavor with sherry to taste and stir half the sauce into the rice. Stir the cooked fruit and two or three sliced bananas into the rest of the sauce and pour over the pudding.

Gooseberry Pudding (boiled)

Line a pudding dish with rich biscuit crust rolled out half an inch thick. Fill with uncooked gooseberries, liberally sprinkled with brown sugar, and cover with a top crust. Pinch the edges of the crusts well together, tie over it a floured cloth, and boil for two and a half hours in water which must not cease boiling from the moment the pudding is put in until it is done. Serve with sweet sauce.

Orange Date Pudding

Place two tablespoons of grated orange rind in a measuring cup and fill the cup with mashed, stoned dates, cut in small pieces. Add two cups of grated bread crumbs, three-fourths cup of sugar and one egg beaten with one cup of milk. Let it stand a few minutes, then add one and one-fourth cups of flour, sifted with two teaspoons of baking powder. Mix all together, pour into a buttered mold and steam for two hours. Serve with orange sauce.

Bancroft Pudding

Cream four tablespoons of butter and one cup of sugar and add one well-beaten egg. Sift one and one-half cups of flour with one-half teaspoon of salt and one teaspoon of baking powder. Add one-half cup of the flour to the first mixture and beat thoroughly, then add the rest of the flour and one-half cup of milk, alternately. Finally beat one-fourth of a square of chocolate into the batter and bake thirty minutes in a moderate oven.

Marmalade Rice Cups

Pour into small timbale molds sufficient cooked rice to nearly fill them; allow them to cool and with a sharp pointed spoon scoop out the center of each (this rice may be used for rice cakes or muffins), unmold and place in a baking pan, brush over the cups with melted butter and crisp in a hot oven for ten minutes until well browned. Meanwhile prepare a rich orange marmalade by peeling six oranges, boil this rind in water for two hours, changing the water three times to remove a little of the bitter taste, cut the orange pulp in small pieces and take out the seeds, adding the cooked rind sliced in chips. Boil the weight of the oranges in sugar with a half pint of water to form a clear syrup, stir in the rind and pulp and boil for thirty minutes until rich and thick. Pour this while hot into the warm rice cups and serve accompanied by a custard sauce.

Strawberry Shortcake

To one pint of rich buttermilk add one even teaspoon of baking soda and beat well; stir in half a teaspoon of salt and enough graham flour to make a batter rather stiffer than cake batter; pat into two thin cakes and bake in a bride oven. If you object to this amount of crust lay one on top of the other to bake, with bits of butter between. Have ready a quart of strawberries sweetened and mashed. Pull the cakes apart, butter and spread the fruit between and on top. Eat with plenty of rich, sweetened cream.

Pineapple Shortcake

Sift together one quart of flour, one teaspoon of salt, three teaspoons of baking powder, add two-thirds of a cup of butter, work it lightly through, and wet it with cold milk as soft as can be handled. Roll it, spread with melted butter, and bake to a light, golden brown. Lift off the top layer, spread it with butter and put the pineapple between the two layers and on top. Whip a pint of rich cream with a tablespoon of powdered sugar and heap it over the top.

Creamy Rice Pudding

To five cups of milk in a flat baking dish add one-third cup of sugar, one-quarter cup of washed rice, two teaspoons of cinnamon and one-half teaspoon of salt. Bake eight or nine hours, stirring occasionally at first.

Bread Pudding

One cup of sour milk, two cups of bread crumbs, one cup of flour, one-half cup of butter, one cup of chopped raisins, one small cup of preserved strawberries, one cup of sugar, two eggs, one teaspoon of soda, one teaspoon of cinnamon. Mix sugar and butter to cream; soak bread in milk with soda, mix and add the other ingredients. Steam two hours. Serve with whipped cream.

Almond Pudding

Soak one cup of soft bread crumbs in three cups of cream; stir in three tablespoons of melted butter, half a pound of sweet almonds, blanched and pounded to a paste with two teaspoons of rosewater, the yolks of seven and the whites of three eggs; sweeten with half a cup of sugar, and stir over the fire until thick. Butter a pudding dish, pour in the ingredients and bake half an hour. When cold cover with a meringue made of the remaining whites and four tablespoons of sugar, and place in a cool, oven until lightly browned. Serve cold, in the dish in which it was baked, accompanied by a fruit sauce.

Ices and Frozen Desserts

From Good Housekeeping Family Cookbook, **by Mildred Maddocks, 1906**

Ices are merely fruit juices diluted with water, and sweetened. Sherbets and punches imply the use of alcoholic liquor and spices, though the former is now commonly omitted. Ices, sorbets and punches are frozen to a soft, smooth mush and usually served in the middle of the dinner before the game and salad courses.

Sherbets are punches or ices to which white of egg or gelatin is added and the freezing continued until smooth and stiff. Frappes and granites, as their names imply, are frozen to a granular mush with equal measures of salt and ice.

Ice creams may be of two kinds. So-called Philadelphia ice cream is merely a thin cream sweetened and flavored. Plain ice cream has a custard foundation to which cream, sugar and flavorings are added. In making a fruit ice cream, freeze the cream firet to a soft mush, then open the freezer, beat in the desired fruit and continue freezing.

Mousses are mixture of whipped cream, custard and gelatin which are frozen without beating or use of the dasher. They are usually packed in molds and are always buried in equal measures of salt and ice.

All mixture depends for their freezing on a simple principle. Salt dissolves readily in water. As the ice melts it loses its latent heat and the temperature of the resulting brine is much lower than that of the ice itself. Therefore it is the brine which is valuable, and the finer the ice is cracked the easier is the process of solution. Do not pour off the brine before the freezing is completed.

Provide a strong burlap or waterproof bag and a heavy wooden mallet. Ice may be crushed to a fine powder with these. One cup of coarse rock salt to three cups of finely crushed ice is the best proportion for ordinary freezing. Use a layer of ice first, then pack in the foregoing proportion, turning the freezer crank occasionally to shake and pack down the mixture. Turn slowly, especially at first, as a soft velvety cream depends in great measure upon this. After freezing, if the cream is to ripen, pour off the brine and repack with the ice and salt this time in the proportion of one cup of salt to four cups of ice.

In molding creams or ices, if for large molds, freeze rather soft; individual molds need a stiffly frozen mixture. Chill the mold thoroughly and pack solidly until it overflows. Cover with a buttered paper, press the cover down, bind tightly with a narrow strip of buttered cloth and pack deep in equal measures of ice and salt. Four or five hours will be needed. Molds which are divided in halves should have each half packed solidly; omit the buttered paper, but be sure the mold is full to overflowing, bind with the strip of buttered cloth and pack as usual.

Apple Sherbet

Boil one quart of apples in a pint of water until soft. Mash through a sieve. Add the juice of one orange and one lemon, one-half pound sugar and a quart more of water. Beat well and freeze. When of the consistency of snow, add the beaten white of one egg and finish freezing.

Ginger Ice

Boil one quart of water with two cups of sugar for twenty minutes, add one-half pint of lemon juice, one-half cup of chopped preserved ginger, and one-half cup of ginger syrup. Strain and when cold freeze as usual.

Lemon Sherbet

Juice of two lemons, one pint of sugar. Let stand a while; add one quart of milk and freeze.

Orange Ice

Put one pint of water and one and one-half cups of sugar on to boil; chip the yellow rind of three oranges, add to the syrup, boil five minutes, and stand away to cool. Peel eight nice, juicy oranges and one lemon, cut them in halves, take out the seeds and squeeze out all the juice; mix with the syrup, strain through a cloth and freeze.

Frozen Strawberry Mousse

Whip one pint of sweet double cream until thick. Fold in two cups of powdered sugar, one-half cup of finely chopped blanched almonds and one quart of strawberries slightly crushed. Turn into a pudding mold having a tube in the center. Pack in ice and salt, cover with a heavy blanket or piece of carpet, and let stand in a cool place for these or four hours. When ready to serve, turn out carefully, and fill the hollow center with sweetened berries mixed with whipped cream.

Gooseberry Ice

Stew one quart of ripe gooseberries in a very little water until soft, then press through a fine sieve. Flavor with lemon juice, and to every pint of the gooseberry juice allow one pound of loaf sugar. Stir over the fire until the sugar is dissolved, then cool, and freeze.

Prune Sherbet

Boil one pound of prunes in one cup of water until very tender, strain through a fine colander, adding a pint of sugar, the juice of one lemon and half a cup of maple syrup; return to the fire and stir constantly to prevent burning, boiling ten minutes. Remove, and when thoroughly cold add the stiffly whipped whites of two eggs; turn into the freezer, and when half frozen stir in a small cup of chopped hickory nuts. Serve in small sherbet cups, with a tablespoon of whipped cream on each portion.

Grape Fruit Sorbet

Roll and press, then cut in half, extract the meat and juice, and free from every seed. Squeeze out all the juice into a deep bowl, and allow one pound of sugar to every pint of juice (err on the side of too much, rather than not enough sugar). Stir thoroughly and pour into the freezer. Freeze like mousse, that is, "mossy," but not firm like ice cream.

Coconut Ice

Boil one-half pound of sugar and one pint of water together for five minutes, add one-half pint of coconut milk to the syrup, let it come to a boil once, then cool and freeze. This will serve five persons. To obtain a coconut with the requisite amount of milk, one must insist upon having a nut with the eyes on the surface. As the nuts age, they dry, shrinking in the process, and the eyes grow deeper. A reasonably fresh specimen should furnish a trifle more than a half pint of milk and the easiest way of extracting it is to drive a nail through the eyes, letting the milk drip through these holes into a bowl. The meat is thus left intact and ready for other uses.

Tomato Sherbet

Simmer together for twenty minutes one quart of chopped tomato, one pint of water, the juice of two lemons and the grated rind of one, two cups of sugar and half a teaspoon of ground ginger. When sufficiently cooked pass through a sieve, add four ounces of crystallized cherries and two cups of freshly grated apple. Freeze as usual, adding when nearly frozen one gloss of Maraschino and the stiffly whipped whites of two eggs.

Frozen Peaches

Dissolve two cups of granulated sugar in the juice from one can of peaches. Mash the peaches fine, place in freezer, add the juice, and finally the well-beaten whites of three eggs. Freeze as usual. This will serve ten persons.

Grape Sherbet

Boil one pint of water, one-half pound of sugar and a teaspoon of chopped lemon rind five minutes. Strain and when cool add the juice of one lemon, one-half pint of grape juice and the white of an egg. When cold, freeze. Serve in frappe glasses.

Watermelon Sherbet

Remove the edible pulp from an ice cold watermelon and rub through a fruit sieve, adding three tablespoons of red currant juice, a scant cup of confectioner's sugar and a tablespoon of gelatin that has been softened, then dissolved in a cup of warm water; turn into the freezer and when half frozen stir in a cup of meringue made by blending the whites of two eggs with four tablespoons of sugar. Freeze to the consistency of mush and serve in slender crystal sherbet glasses, sprinkled with minced candied orange peel.

Frozen Turkish Coffee

This dessert coffee extract, obtainable at reliable druggists', gives better results than the homemade product; care should be exercised in regard to the quantity used, which varies somewhat to suit the taste. Cook half a cup of sugar with half a cup of water to the soft ball stage, and pour it slowly upon the stiffly beaten whites of two eggs, beating constantly; when light and creamy, add a pint of stiffly whipped cream, a tablespoon of confectioner's sugar, a pinch of powdered cinnamon, a few drops of vanilla and about a teaspoon of coffee extract. Freeze as usual; serve in small crystal cups, garnishing each with a star of whipped cream flavored with almond extract.

Apricot Ice in Jelly Cups

Mix one pint of apricot pulp, the juice of two oranges and one lemon, the grated rind of the lemon and one pint of syrup (made by cooking for ten minutes two cups of sugar and one cup of water). Freeze in the usual way.

For the jelly cups, make a lemon jelly by softening one ounce of gelatin in one-third of a cup of cold water, add a pint of boiling water, stir until dissolved. Add a cup of sugar, and when cool the grated rind of a lemon and the juice of four. Stir in enough spinach green to give a pretty green tint. Mold in little border molds or patent Charlotte Russe molds. When firm turn out and fill the hollow centers with the ice which may be topped with a spoonful of whipped cream or sprinkled with candied mint leaves.

Mexican Ice Cream

Put a cup of granulated sugar into a smooth saucepan over the fire and stir constantly until it is melted, add a cup of English walnut meats and pour into a shallow buttered pan to harden. When perfectly cold grate or chop fine. Crumble twelve macaroons into fine crumbs, then toast in the oven a few moments. Make a custard of the yolks of two eggs, a fourth of a cup of sugar and a cup of milk, then pour over the stiffly beaten whites of two eggs and let cool. To a pint of cream add a third of a cup of sugar and beat until thoroughly mixed, add the custard and flavor with vanilla or Maraschino, then freeze. When half frozen, add the macaroon crumbs and half of the grated walnut mixture and finish freezing. Sprinkle the remaining grated walnuts over the cream at serving time.

Peanut Ice Cream

One quart of thin cream, one cup of rolled peanut meats, one cup of sugar, one tablespoon of Vanilla. Mix all together and freeze.

Macaroon Ice Cream

One pint thin cream, two-thirds cup sugar, one pint milk, one cup rolled macaroons, one tablespoon vanilla, two or three eggs, speck of salt. Make a custard of the milk, eggs, sugar and salt. Cool, add the vanilla and freeze. When nearly frozen add the macaroons, prepared by drying in the oven; they are then put through a meat chopper or rolled.

Frozen Pudding

Chop fine a cup of English walnut meats. Plump a cup of raisins by covering them with boiling water, drain after fifteen minutes and roll in granulated sugar. Beat the yolks of four eggs and half a cup of sugar until light, add two tablespoons of cornstarch dissolved in a little cold milk and gradually four cups of hot milk. Cook over hot water for fifteen minutes, stirring constantly until thickened, then occasionally. When the mixture is cold add vanilla to flavor, and freeze. When half frozen add the whites of four eggs beaten to a stiff froth with a fourth of a cup of sugar, a cup of strawberry preserves, and the prepared fruit and nuts, then freeze until stiff. At serving time garnish with whipped cream and English walnut halves.

Canton Nut Pudding

Prepare a rich, smooth custard from a scant pint of milk, two eggs and a tablespoon of sugar. When cold, add a pint of whipped cream and a scant cup of preserved ginger syrup; now pour into the freezer, and when half frozen stir in three tablespoons of chopped walnuts and a cup of thinly sliced Canton ginger. Freeze hard and serve in sherbet glasses, pouring over each portion two tablespoons of imported ginger ale.

Frozen Nut Pudding

Prepare a boiled custard by scalding a pint of milk and then adding the yolks of three eggs beaten with two tablespoons of sugar; when of the right consistency remove from the fire and stir in while hot four ounces of melted chocolate; allow

Macaroon Ice Cream with Maple Sauce

it to cool and then add a pint of whipped cream; turn into the freezer, and when half frozen pour in a cup of chopped nut meats, half a cup of candied cherries, two tablespoons of sliced preserved ginger and one tablespoon of chopped preserved citron. When frozen repack in a melon mold and serve on a large platter surrounded by burning brandy.

Biscuit Cream

Rub the yellow rind of two lemons on lumps of cot sugar, then crush the sugar to a powder, adding half a cup of confectioner's sugar, twelve grated macaroons and a pint of stiffly whipped cream; turn into the freezer and as the cream begins to stiffen, stir in half a pint of chopped Maraschino cherries together with four tablespoons of the cordial; continue freezing until very firm, then pack in individual pyramid molds.

Banana Fluff

Slice six large bananas, sprinkle with lemon juice and grated coconut and place directly on the ice to chill and ripen (for at least an hour). Mash them smooth with a wooden spoon, adding a scant cup of powdered sugar and the stiffly beaten whites of two eggs, which should be lightly folded in; now pour into the freezer, turning the crank for about four minutes, or until there is a slight resistance, when half a pint of whipped cream may be added. Freeze to the consistency of mush; serve in individual crimped paper cases lined with tiny Maple biscuits.

Maple Ice Cream

Beat the yolks of two eggs until light; add two-thirds of a cup of maple syrup and half a cup of milk. Cook over hot water, stirring constantly, until the mixture thickens; then pour over the stiffly beaten whites of two eggs and cool. When cold add a cup and a half of cream and freeze.

Pineapple Meringue

Select a medium-sized pineapple, slice and cut in small cubes. Put it in an enameled saucepan with one cup each of granulated sugar and water. Stir until the sugar is dissolved, and cook until rich and thick. Beat the yolks of six eggs until light, and pour over them three cups of scalding hot milk. Mix well, turn into a double boiler, and stir and cook until quite thick. Pour the custard into a bowl and chill on ice, then add the pineapple and syrup. Freeze quite stiff and pack in a mold. Cover closely, and pack in ice and salt. Let stand for several hours to ripen. Boil one-half cup of sugar with one-fourth cup of water until it will thread, add to it five of the egg whites whipped to a very stiff froth, and bent until cold. Turn the pudding quicker out of the mold into a very cold fireproof dish. Cover quickly with the meringue, and put in a very hot oven until slightly colored. Serve immediately.

Maple Bisque

Beat the yolks of three eggs until light; add gradually three-fourths of a cup of maple syrup, and cook standing in a pan of boiling water, stirring constantly until the mixture thickens and coats the spoon. Take from the fire and beat until cool. When it is quite cold add it slowly to two cups of cream beaten until stiff. Lastly fold in half a dozen macaroons dried in the oven and crumbled fine. Pack in ice and salt for four hours. Unmold and serve with whipped cream, sweetened to taste and flavored with vanilla. Sprinkle the cream with powdered macaroon crumbs.

Maple Ice Cream Sauce

Cook a cup of maple syrup and a tablespoon of butter until it drops thick but does not quite form a soft ball when tested in cold water. Serve hot over each portion of cream. Half a cup of chopped pecans or English walnuts is a delicious addition to the sauce. Serve with vanilla or macaroon ice cream.

Strawberry Plombiere

Wash and hull a quart of fine ripe strawberries and press through a sieve. Make a syrup with three-quarters of a pound of sugar and three-quarters of a cup of water. Add this to the strawberry pulp, cool, put it into a freezer, and turn until it begins to thicken. Then stir in one pint of whipped cream and let it remain a little longer in the freezer. Put into a mold, cover tightly, bind the edges with a strip of buttered paper, and pack in ice and salt for three hours. When ready to serve, dip the mold quickly in hot water, wipe dry, and turn out on a shallow dish. Garnish with macaroons and fine strawberries.

Iced Rice Pudding

Cover half a cup of well-washed rice with a quart of cold water, and set it over the fire. When the water begins to boil drain it off and cover the rice with one quart of milk. Cook until the rice is tender, then remove from the fire and press through a sieve. Add a pint of cream, two cups of sugar and the beaten yolks of six eggs. Return to the fire, and stir and cook for a few minutes until it begins to thicken. Add a teaspoon of vanilla and set aside to cool. When cold turn into a freezer and freeze to a stiff mush. Then stir in one-half cup of blanched chopped almonds and one cup of rich preserved peaches or strawberries, which have been drained from the syrup and beaten to a pulp.

Stir thoroughly, add a pint of whipped cream, cover and repack. Set aside for two hours or longer. Turn out and serve with compote of the fruit.

Imperatrice Frozen Pudding

Steam a scant half cup of rice in slightly salted milk; while still warm stir in two well beaten eggs, two tablespoons of powdered sugar, half a cup of seeded raisins that have been boiled for ten minutes, two teaspoons of chopped candied orange peel and a pinch of grated nutmeg; allow the mixture to cool, but not harden, and then stir in lightly a pint of stiffly whipped cream sweetened with a scant cup of sugar. Turn at once into a melon mold and pack in ice and rock salt for three hours before using. When ready to serve unmold on a cut glass platter, garnishing with glace oranges.

Frozen Orange Pudding

Prepare a rich boiled custard by slowly heating a pint of milk in the double boiler, adding two well-beaten eggs and two tablespoons of sugar; stir until it thickens well; remove from the fire and flavor with the juice of one orange and the grated yellow rind. While this is cooling, peel two oranges, and, removing pits and every particle of white skin, flake the pulp into small bits with a silver fork; sprinkle liberally with powdered a sugar and pour over, if you wish, a tablespoon of sherry. To the cold custard add a half pint of sweetened whipped cream and turn at once into the freezer, stirring in when half frozen the prepared orange pulp and a small cup of grated macaroon crumbs; continue the freezing until very stiff and then pack in a melon mold.

Macaroon Mousse

Scald one dozen macaroons in a cup of milk, and pour gradually upon the beaten yolks of three eggs, cooking over hot water until slightly thickened; when almost cold, fold into the mixture the stiffly beaten whites of three eggs, half a cup of powdered sugar, and half a pint of whipped cream. Turn into a brick mold and freeze by covering with ice and rock salt. At serving time garnish with French candied fruit arranged on a border of whipped cream.

Maple Nut Mousse

Soak two level teaspoons of gelatin in two tablespoons of cold water, and dissolve it in a cup of hot maple syrup; remove from the fire and beat until cool, then add a pint of thick cream that has been whipped with a teaspoon of powdered sugar and half a cup of finely chopped hickory nuts. Line a round mold with halved ladyfingers, holding them in place with a little fondant, filling the center with the mousse mixture; be sure that the cover is securely adjusted and bury in ice and salt for three hours. When ready to serve, unmold, covering the top with chopped nuts, and serve with a sauce.

Rice Mousse with Prunes

Cook one-fourth of a cup of rice in a cup and a half of milk, until very soft. Make a rich boiled custard with the yolks of two eggs, half a cup of sugar and half a cup of milk, adding two tablespoons of gelatin softened in a little cold water; strain this over the cooked rice and when cold, add a pint of whipped cream, twelve sifted prunes and a few drops of lemon juice. Mold in a fancy mold and pack in ice, and salt for three hours before serving, garnishing with squares of prune jelly and large stuffed prunes.

Pastry

From *Good Housekeeping Family Cookbook,* by Mildred Maddocks, 1906

Puff Paste

First, in the preparation of puff paste, choose a cool corner to work in and if possible, have plenty of cracked ice at hand. Weigh one-half pound of pastry flour and one-half pound of butter. Wash the latter in a bowl of ice water an in the illustration. Wash and knead until not a drop of water is left in the butter and it is smooth and waxy.

Now pat it into a round one-half inch thick, and place on ice. Work one tablespoon of butter into the flour and mix enough ice water with it to make a stiff dough, then knead on a floured board one minute. Cover with a clean cloth, and let it stand five minutes. Next roll the dough into an oblong sheet one-fourth inch thick and be careful to have the corners square. Pat into shape if necessary; put the butter on this and fold the free end over, striking lightly each edge to imprison the air. Fold the right side over, the left under the enclosed butter, swing the paste half around, cover and wait five minutes.

Now roll with light, even strokes into the oblong sheet, fold from the ends toward the center, forming three laps. Again cover and leave five minutes. Repeat the same process twice; remember to keep a square-cornered rectangle of paste; do not neglect the chilling or think three instead of five minutes long enough to wait.

For the last time roll, but fold in four layers, like a pocketbook. Place on ice and chill through before cutting. Shape with fluted or plain cutters into tarts and patty shells. Again chill and bake twenty-five to thirty minutes in a very hot oven. From the leftovers cut tiny buttons one-half inch in diameter to serve with clear soups. Roll out all the remnants into a thin sheet, grate hard cheese over this and cut in narrow strips three inches long. These are delicious with any soup. Serve in the shells shaved celery, stewed in cream and seasoned with pepper, salt and shredded olive, a Newburg or a shrimp wiggle; in fact, use any of the creamed entrees with your pastry. To vary a rabbit, fill the patties with hot apple sauce, then cover with the rabbit.

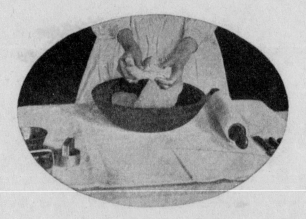

Washing the Butter for Puff-Paste

Steps in the Process of Rolling Puff-Paste

Cutting the Patties

Puff Paste After Baking

Plain Pie Crust

Place in a chopping bowl one and one-half cups of flour, one-quarter cup of butter, one-quarter cup of lard, one teaspoon of salt. With a sharp chopping knife, chop the shortening thoroughly through the flour, after which add just enough ice water to hold the mixture together (from one-quarter to one-half cup is sufficient), chopping all the time until a smooth dough is formed, which should be allowed to stand in a cold place for a day at least before using.

Shaker Pastry

Mix one quart of flour, one teaspoon of salt, one cup of fresh beef drippings, and one cup of cream, add water enough to make a dough. Roll out a bit of this mixture, spread with soft butter, sprinkle with flour, and roll up like jelly cake, cut off a portion, stand on end, heap on flour and roll out. This makes the flakes of the top crust. The lower crust is rolled out from the plain mixture.

Shaker Apple Pie

Put into the lower crust sour apples, pared, cored and cut into eighths; add a generous half pint of seeded raisins and put on the top crust. Cut it around the plate, being careful not to let it stick to the lower crust. Bake in a slow oven till the apple is thoroughly cooked and the crust is a nice brown, both top and bottom; this requires about forty minutes. While it is still hot take off the top crust and lay it carefully aside, then with a wooden knife stir the apple, removing the hard pieces, if any are left. Add sugar, cinnamon or nutmeg to taste, and a small piece of butter. Replace the top crust. Tin plates are best for the baking of these pies, but they should never be put away on the same plats in which they are baked.

Maple Custard Pie

Beat two eggs and a third of a cup of grated maple sugar, add a level tablespoon of flour and gradually two cups of milk. Turn into a deep pastry lined pan, dust slightly with cinnamon or nutmeg, and bake in a quick oven at first, to set the crust, then lower the temperature.

A New Mince Pie

The new thing about this pie is the filling, which has a different flavor from the ordinary kind because the meat in the mince is not twice cooked. Take one cup of raw beef chopped fine—this must be free from gristle and fat—mix it with three cups of tart apples, chopped fine. Add one cup of currant jelly, juice and grated rind of two oranges and one lemon, one cup of sugar, one teaspoon each of salt, cinnamon, cloves and allspice, and half a teaspoon of pepper and nutmeg. Make soft and moist with sweet cider, and add plenty of raisins, currants, citron and candied orange peel, and a very little chopped suet, if you like suet. This will make three pies, and if the three pies are not all made at once, the remainder of the mince should be canned for future use. For a winter novelty, make patties of this mincemeat, cover with a lattice crust, and, when ready to serve, pour a tablespoon of brandy over each tiny pie. Light it, and place it before each guest. Mince pie should always be served warm.

A Pumpkin Pie

Steam a small pumpkin, pared and cored, until tender, pressing through a fruit press or sieve to remove any lumps; season with a tablespoon each of ground ginger and cinnamon and stir in while still warm the yolks of two well-beaten eggs, a tablespoon of melted butter, one tablespoon of sifted wheat flour, the grated rinds of one orange, a teaspoon of salt, one cup of raisins boiled till plump and a cup of cream, or enough to form a thick batter; sweeten to taste and arrange in deep pie plates lined with rich pie crust; bake in a moderately quick oven to a golden brown.

Shaker Mince Pie

To three quarts of sour apples, pared, cored and chopped, allow one quart of beef, boiled tender and chopped fine; if very lean put in a little butter. Add a pound of seeded and a pound of seedless raisins, one cup of grape jelly, or two of grape juice, two pounds of sugar, a tablespoon of salt, and cook all together until the apple is soft. When cool add two tablespoons of cinnamon, one each of ground clove, ginger and allspice, and two grated nutmegs; the spices should be mixed together carefully before being added to the rest. If the mincemeat is not tart enough, flavor with a little boiled cider or the juice and grated rind of a lemon. More sugar or salt may be added if desired.

Date and Apple Pie

Line a pie plate with a rather rich crust, fill it with a mixture of chopped dates and apples, sprinkle over half a teaspoon of cinnamon and half a cup of sugar, cover with a top crust, and bake about half an hour in a good oven. Serve hot or cold with or without cream and sugar.

English Walnut Pie

Beat the yolks of two eggs and half a cup of sugar to a cream, odd a tablespoon of lemon juice, the juice and half the grated rind of an orange and half a cup of chopped English walnut meats. Line a deep pie plate with pastry, and when half-baked add the filling and finish baking. Cover with a meringue made of the whites of two eggs, two tablespoons of sugar and two tablespoons of chopped walnuts.

Apple and Coconut Pie

Line a deep pie plate with pastry. Pare and grate some apples, sweeten and flavor to taste, using a bit of cinnamon and either lemon juice or vanilla. Sprinkle the pastry generously with some shredded coconut, cover with the apple mixture and bake. When almost done sprinkle with coconut and do not leave in the oven long enough to brown.

Fairy Apple Pie

Core and quarter without paring, four large, tart apples, steam over hot water until tender, rub through a sieve, sweeten to taste and chill. Beat the whites of three eggs until stiff and dry. Add the apples, flavor to taste and beat again. Turn into a half-baked pastry shell and finish baking in a moderate oven. Serve hot with cream and sugar or whipped cream.

Marlborough Pie

Pare and stew some tart, juicy apples until tender, then rub through a sieve. To a cup of the hot mixture add a tablespoon of butter and a cup of sugar and stir until thoroughly blended; then add in succession the grated rind and juice of half a lemon, the yolks of two eggs beaten with half a cup of cream and, if desired, a third of a cup of wine. Line a deep pie plate with pastry, brush with white of egg and sprinkle with a third of a cup each of raisins and chopped nuts (either English walnuts or almonds). Pour in the apple mixture and bake in a moderate oven. Cover with a meringue. Brown in a very slow oven.

Squash Pie

Mix four tablespoons of sifted squash with one quart of milk. Season to taste with sugar, cinnamon, salt and ginger. Mix one teaspoon of cornstarch with two crackers rolled to a powder, moisten with one-half cup of the seasoned milk; then combine and cook all over hot water until free from raw taste. Bake in a crust as usual.

Ladylocks

Butter the lady lock irons, cut puff or plain paste into "ribbons" an inch wide, then wrap a "ribbon" about each iron lightly, winding from the small end to the large end. Let each edge merely touch the other, without overlapping. Lay the paste-covered irons on a wire frame and set in a hot oven to bake delicately brown. If desired as a course for supper or luncheon, slip them off the irons on a hot platter and fill with creamed chicken, sweetbreads, oysters, mushrooms or lobster. Serve individually with a spoonful of the white sauce which goes inside, poured around them. On top of the sauce put a sprinkling of chopped parsley or

Ladylock Irons Wound with Paste

Pastry Horns Ready to be Filled

browned bread crumbs. During shortcake season serve cold filled with strawberries, raspberries or cherries, well powdered with sugar, and garnished with whipped cream. Fill them with whipped cream, sweetened and flavored with vanilla, then pour over each a chocolate frosting. Or make the filling after any recipe for lemon pie and cover the top with a meringue, browning it delicately in a moderate oven.

Lemon Custard Pie

Beat the yolks of three eggs and one-half pound of powdered sugar to a cream, then add the unbeaten whites of two eggs and whip all together until very light. Add the grated rind and juice of three lemons and one tablespoon of butter. Cook in a double boiler until the mixture thickens, then set aside until cool. Line a pie plate (a deep one) with good paste, prick it well, and bake in a quick oven. When done, fill with the lemon custard. Beat the white of one egg with two tablespoons of powdered sugar, spread it over the top of the pie, and brown very delicately in a slow oven.

Cheese Heartlets

For these delicious little cakes, use a cream cheese, adding half a cup of powdered sugar, two tablespoons of cream and three well beaten eggs, flavor with almond and beat the mixture until smooth. Bake in small heart shaped tins, lined with puff paste.

Richmond Maids of Honor

Line small patty tins with paste, fill with the following mixture, and bake in a moderate oven twenty minutes. Mix one-fourth cream cheese (the ten-cent size) and two tablespoons sifted saltine crumbs and work with a small wooden spoon until smooth; then add one-fourth cup sugar, and one egg well beaten. Blanch one-third cup almonds, put through an almond grater, add three teaspoons of milk and pound in a mortar. Add to first mixture and beat thoroughly; then add one-fourth cup heavy cream, one teaspoon melted butter, one-half teaspoon salt and one-fourth teaspoon each grated nutmeg and almond extract. They are a bit of work, these Richmond maids of honor, but the time used in their preparation is far from wasted.

Cheese Straws

A pleasing variation of the old but always popular cheese; straws and cheese fingers, is made thus: Melt one tablespoon of butter, add one and one-half tablespoons of flour and pour on one-fourth cup of milk. Add one-fourth cup, each, of grated cheese and cheese cut in small cubes, and one egg white, unbeaten. Season with salt, paprika and cayenne. Bake pastry in finger-shaped pieces. Split

and spread with cheese mixture. Heat slightly before serving.

Pumpkin Fanchonettes

Mix one and one-half cups of stewed pumpkin very dry, with two cups of milk, one beaten egg, a half cup of brown sugar, one teaspoon of cinnamon, one-half teaspoon each of salt and ginger. Line individual tins with pastry and bake in a slow oven until brown on top.

Cranberry Pattie

Line patty pans with rich paste, and bake till done in a hot oven. When baked remove from the oven and let cool. Fill with rich jellied cranberry sauce, and spread with a meringue made with the white of one egg and half a cup of powdered sugar. Put in a cool oven until a pale straw color.

Coconut Custards

One grated coconut, one pound of sugar, one-fourth pound of butter, one cup of cream. Add the beaten whites of nine eggs, and season with essence of lemon. Bake in small shapes lined with rich puff paste.

Strawberry Pie

Line a deep pie plate with puff paste, prick it well, and bake to a delicate brown. Fill it, when cold, with fine ripe strawberries, sliced and sweetened, and pour over a cup of whipped cream which has been sweetened, flavored with lemon, and whisked lightly into the stiffly whipped whites of two eggs. Another delicious pie may be made by pouring a pint of rich custard while still warm over the strawberries in the paste. Serve very cold.

Pumpkin Patties

This delicious sweet may be appropriately served for the Thanksgiving supper and is made by paring and cubing sufficient pumpkin to make two quarts; place in a steamer with a little water and cook until tender, seasoning with a teaspoon of salt and one of mixed spices; then push through a ricer, adding half a cup to whipped cream, two tablespoons of sugar, the whites of two eggs beaten stiff, and a cup of chopped dates; blend to a cream and fill into patty shells, returning to the oven to be reheated; cap with the paste top, ornamenting the top of each with a large crystallized cherry.

Christmas Tarts

The foundation for these pastry tidbits is usually puff paste, but the following simpler paste may be used: Mix and sift together two cups of flour, two teaspoons of baking powder and a saltspoon of salt. Work in a cup of butter with the tips of the fingers. When the mixture is as fine as meal, stand it aside an hour or more to chill. Then take out half a cup and to the remainder add cold water gradually to make a stiff dough. Knead slightly, turn on a floured board and roll into a long, narrow strip. Sprinkle the dough with half of the reserved mixture and fold so as to make three layers. Turn half way round with the open end toward you, roll again into a strip, sprinkle with the remaining mixture and fold as before. Roll and fold twice more, and the pastry is ready to use. Roll into a thin sheet and cut into various shapes, as hearts, circles, strips and diamonds.

A Few of the Cakes and Pastry Waffers

Fruit Rissolettes

Put half a cup of water, a cup of sugar, a cup of seeded raisins, half a cup of chopped nuts, half a cup of tart jelly and a quarter of a cup of sliced citron together in a granite saucepan and cook until thick like preserve. Add the juice of half a lemon, take from the stove and cool. If still too thin to be firm, cook a little longer or stir until thickened. Bake the pastry and spread with this mixture.

Polish Tarts

Cut the paste into two and a half-inch squares, brush with the white of an egg, fold the corners to meet in the center, press slightly together and bake. When done put a bit of jelly or fruit cream in the center. Or fold only the two opposite corners together, bake and fill with the fruit cream.

Fruit Tarts

Bake the pastry in small patty tins and fill with the fruit creation. Cover with a meringue to which chopped nuts may be added or dust the tarts with powdered sugar for serving.

Neapolitans

Cut the pastry into strips, bake, spread with jelly or fruit cream and cover with nut icing, then put in the oven until a delicate brown. Garnish a few with half nuts or sprinkle with chopped nuts before browning.

Chocolate Pie

Line a deep pie pan with rich pie crust and bake in a quick oven. Grate one-half cup of chocolate, place in a saucepan with one cup of hot water, butter the size of an egg, one tablespoon vanilla, one cup of sugar, the beaten yolks of two eggs and two tablespoons of cornstarch (dissolved in as much water). Mix well, cook until thick, stirring constantly. Pour into the pie shell and let cool. Make a meringue of the two egg whites beaten stiff, with two tablespoons of powdered sugar, spread over the pie and slightly brown in the oven.

Mincemeat

Take two pounds of finely chopped suet, four pounds of grated bread crumbs, four pounds of currants, four pounds of raisins, five pounds of brown sugar, one and one-half pounds of candied peel, lemon, orange and citron, six pounds of apple, weighted after being chopped, two tablespoons of cinnamon, two tablespoons of cloves, one tablespoon of mace, one tablespoon of salt and two quarts of boiled cider. The ingredients are blended without being boiled; put away in jars set in a cool place this mince will keep.

Candies

From *Good Housekeeping Family Cookbook,* by Mildred Maddocks, 1906

Fondant

Boil two and one-half pounds of sugar and one-half teaspoon of cream of tartar with one and one-half cups of water until 242°F is registered on the candy thermometer. A less delicate test is that of the soft ball when tried in cold water.

Cook in a kettle with a small surface and do not attempt to cook the syrup on a damp day. Wrap a clean piece of cheesecloth around a wooden spoon, dip in hot water and wash down the sides of the candy kettle. This prevents crystallizing and should be done often. When cooked, pour gently into a large oiled platter. Hold back the last quarter cup as it is apt to crystallize the whole. Cool without disturbing until only lukewarm, then beat with two silver knives until creamy. Pour into a stone jar, cover with waxed paper and a damp cloth and let it ripen forty-eight hours before using. Fondant properly cared for will keep indefinitely.

Candies

Soft Ginger Chocolate Creams

Form fondant into tiny cones, tucking into each cone a bit of preserved ginger, well dried before using. Dip the balls into melted chocolate, one at a time, and lay on paraffin paper in a cold place until hardened.

Buttercups

Boil one cup of water, two cups of granulated sugar and a teaspoon of lemon juice until it cracks in cold water. Color a pale yellow with vegetable coloring and pour on an oiled platter to cool. Mold a cup of fondant until creamy. Roll out a portion of the yellow candy, making of it a long and narrow string about an inch and a half wide. On this lay a roll of the fondant as long as the candy and about half an inch in diameter. Wrap the candy around it, stretch all with the hands until quite small and cut in half-inch length. Any preferred flavorings can be used. A particularly pleasing combination is formed by flavoring the candy with orange extract and the fondant with banana.

Plum Pudding Bonbons

Into two cups of fondant slightly warmed mix, also slightly warmed and thoroughly dry, one tablespoon each of chopped citron, chopped candied orange peel and seeded chopped raisins, two tablespoons of currants dredged with half a teaspoon of ground cinnamon and the grated rind of a lemon, and three tablespoons of chopped nut meats; use the hands rather than a spoon. Form into small balls, dip in unsweetened chocolate melted over hot water, and place on an oiled platter to harden.

Opera Creams

Melt together slowly three-fourths cup of milk, two cups of sugar and two squares of chocolate; then boil for three or four minutes, flavor and put in a cold place. The pan should not be touched for at least an hour or until it is absolutely cold. Then beat until it becomes resistant and creamy. Drop into round bulls on paper.

Maple and Butternut Cream

Break into small pieces two pounds of "honest" maple sugar and heat in a porcelain or enameled saucepan with one pint of cream. Boil over a moderate fire to the soft ball stage. Remove from the fire, add one cup of chopped butternut meats and stir slowly until the mixture cools and begins to thicken, then pour into shallow buttered pans, score in squares and place a butternut meat on each square.

Maple Candy

Boil together for five minutes one cup of maple syrup and one cup of sugar; add one-quarter of a teaspoon of cream of tartar, two teaspoons of butter and two teaspoons of vinegar. After it has boiled until it is brittle when tried in cold water, pour it into buttered pans to cool. When cool enough to handle, pull it until it becomes hard, then cut it in pieces and allow it to stand two or three days to become "ripened."

Mexican Caramels

Put a cup of granulated sugar into a clean iron skillet and stir constantly over a slow fire until the sugar is melted, taking care it does not brown. As soon as the sugar becomes a syrup add a cup of rich milk or cream, and stir constantly until the sugar is all dissolved. Add next a cup each of granulated and of light brown sugar and boil steadily until the mixture forms a soft ball when tested in cold water. Take from the fire, add a cup of coarsely chopped nut meats and stir to a creamy consistency. Pour into a shallow pan lined with paraffin paper, spread smoothly about half an inch in thickness and mark into squares while still warm. These caramels are perfectly delicious, being both waxy and creamy. Any single kind or a mixture of several kinds of nut meats may be used. If there is any fondant at hand, pleasing variety is produced by filling the molds with a thin layer of the caramel and covering with a layer of melted fondant.

Coffee Nut Caramels

Place in a granite saucepan one cup of confectioner's sugar, half a cup of cream and a quarter of a cup of very strong coffee; stir constantly over a hot fire, until it reaches the hard ball stage, remove from the fire and stir in a cup of hickory meats. Turn out on an oiled slab or into a pan, having the paste half an inch thick, and mark into squares while warm.

Marshmallow Fudge

Cook a cup of cream and two cups of powdered sugar (pulverized), stirring gently to avoid scorching, until the mixture begins to boil. Now add one-quarter pound of chocolate, stirring, as needed, until all is melted. The mixture should boil for perhaps ten minutes, a drop being tried in cold water until soft ball stage is reached. Add an inch and a half cube of butter, and stir until well mixed. Take the fudge from the flame, and beat briskly for five or ten minutes, then pour it in a buttered fudge pan containing a half pound of cut-up marshmallows and a quarter pound of chopped pecan meats scattered through.

Chocolate Arabics

Purchase the desired number of gum drops—either the jelly sort or "jaw-breakers"—and give them a coat of chocolate. To every ounce of unsweetened chocolate, melted, add two tablespoons of milk, one or two tablespoons of sugar and the least bit of butter. Stir over the fire till smooth and, while it is warm, dip the drop into it with a fork or candy wire and place on a piece of marble. If the chocolate becomes too stiff, thin cautiously with sugar syrup. The covering entirely changes the character of the gum drops, greatly improving their flavor.

Peanut Brittle

Shell, skin and chop fine one quart of peanuts or enough to make one cup of nut meats. Place one cup of sugar in a saucepan without water and heat

gradually, stirring all the time, until the sugar is completely melted. Mix the peanuts in thoroughly, pour out on an inverted tin, unbuttered, then shape into a square with two broad knives. When the candy begins to bold its shape, mark it in small squares and continue to shape it and re-mark it until it hardens.

Butter Scotch

Two cups of light brown sugar, one cup of butter, one tablespoon of vinegar and one of water. Mix all together and boil twenty minutes. Add one-eighth of a tablespoon of baking soda, and as soon as it will crisp in cold water remove from the fire. When done pour out on a flat buttered tin and mark off in squares.

Glace Walnuts

Boil a cup of sugar, a few grains of cream of tartar and half a cup of boiling water over a hot fire. Do not stir after the boiling has begun. Remove from the fire as soon as there is a suspicion of a faint yellow tinge to the syrup, dip the halved nuts separately into the syrup, then drop onto oiled paper. Stand the syrup in a pan of hot water to keep hot during dipping.

Cookery for the Sick

From Good Housekeeping Family Cookbook, by Mildred Maddocks, 1906

Thickened Milk

Scald one cup of milk, reserving two tablespoons. Add cold milk, gradually, to one tablespoon of flour while stirring constantly to make a smooth paste. Pour into the scalded milk and stir until the mixture thickens, then cover, and cook over hot water twenty minutes. Season with salt. An inch piece of stick cinnamon may be cooked with the milk if liked, and tends to reduce a laxative condition. Thickened milk is often given in bowel troubles.

Oatmeal Gruel

Add one-fourth cup of rolled oats, tablespoon flour, one-fourth teaspoon salt, to one and one-half cups boiling water, let boil two minutes, then cook over hot water one hour. Strain, bring to boiling point, and add milk or cream if indicated.

Flour Gruel

Mix two teaspoons of flour and one saltspoon of salt and make into a smooth paste with a little cold water, then stir it into one cup of boiling water. Cook until the desired consistency is obtained. Strain; then add sugar, if preferred, and thin with a little milk.

Indian Meal Gruel

One tablespoon Indian meal, one-half tablespoon flour, one-fourth teaspoon salt, two tablespoons cold water, one and one-half cups boiling water, milk or cream. Blend the meal, flour and salt with the cold water to make a smooth paste and stir into the boiling water. Boil on back of stove one hour and a half. Dilute with milk or cream. Strain.

Cracker Gruel

One tablespoon rolled and sifted cracker, three-fourths cup milk, one-eighth teaspoon salt. Scald milk, add cracker, and cook over hot water five minutes, then add salt.

Caudle (Yeo)

Beat up an egg to a froth; add a glass of sherry and half a pint of gruel. Flavor with lemon peel, nutmeg and sugar.

Orangeade

Cut the yellow rind from one orange and pour a cup of boiling water over it. Sweeten to taste. Chill and add a teaspoon of lemon juice and the juice of the orange. Serve with shaved ice. This may be varied by using currant, grape, cranberry, apricot or grape fruit juice.

Toast Points

Cut the bread in one-fourth inch slices, trim neatly and cut in diamond shape. Dry thoroughly in the oven, then toast to a delicate brown. Toast whether served dry or as cream toast should be made in this way.

Potato Soup

To one-half cup of mashed potato add one cup of hot milk, heat in a double boiler with four drops of onion juice and one-fourth teaspoon of chopped parsley. Thicken with one-half teaspoon of flour moistened with one teaspoon of cold milk. Season with salt and red pepper if allowed. Beat thoroughly and strain.

Meat Custard

Dissolve one-half teaspoon of beef extract in a half cup of hot water, add to half a cup of hot milk and season with salt, and pepper if allowed. Pour over a beaten egg and bake in a custard cup in a pan of hot water.

Broiled Sweetbreads

Select the throat sweetbreads and soak a half hour in cold water. Place in boiling salted water with a teaspoon of vinegar. Cook without boiling twenty-five minutes. Then place in cold water. Carefully remove every trace of the pipe and membrane surrounding each lobe. They are then ready for the various dishes, but should only be heated, not again cooked. For broiling split and place in a fine wire broiler. When brown serve with lemon and toast points.

Carpentry and Woodworking

Stair Building; Poren Steps

From *Carpentry* by Ira Samuel Griffith, 1916

Stair building is an art in itself and as such belongs to millwork rather than to carpentry. However, the carpenter must know the principles of simple stair lay-out and construction for he is called upon to construct porch steps, basement and often attic stairs. In smaller communities he may also have to build the main stair. Fig. 1 illustrates three common types of stair.

In planning a stair, the first requisite is to know its rise and run, Fig. 2. The rise in this case is the vertical distance measured from the top of the first floor to the top of the second floor. The run is the horizontal span of the stair.

A good average stair for a cottage will have a rise per step of 7 inches and a run of tread of 10 inches. Variations will have to be made in both rise and tread to meet conditions, but the student may take these dimensions as starting dimensions unless otherwise directed. Steps should not be either too steep, due to excessive rise per foot, or "slow" due to extreme width of step. An old rule for determining the relation of rise to tread is: "Twice the rise plus the tread should equal 24"."

Proceed as follows: (1) Lay off on a story pole the total rise of the stair by placing the pole upright in the well hole. (2) Set a pair of dividers to 7" and step off this distance so marked. If there is a remainder, increase or diminish the divider's space and again step off the space. Continue this until a setting is obtained which gives no remainder.

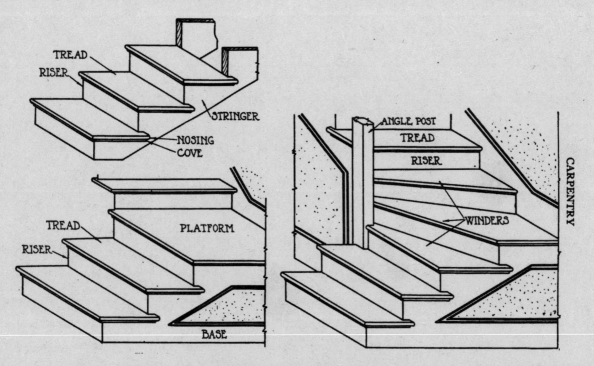

Fig. 1. Types of stairs.

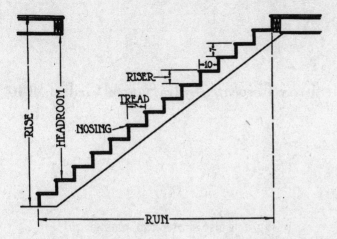

Fig. 2. Rise and run of stair.

The number of risers will be found by counting the spaces, and the rise per step by measuring one of these spaces. (3) If the run of the stair is not of exact specification (some variation is usually possible) the run per step or tread may be determined by the rule just given. If a definite total run is specified the tread must be figured. (4) Since there is always one more riser than tread, the run per step is obtained by dividing the total run in inches by the number of risers less one. The numbers thus obtained for rise and run per step are the ones to be used on the framing square in laying out the stringers.

(5) Joint one edge of each stringer straight and square and place the framing square as in Fig. 3 and

Fig. 3. Laying out string.

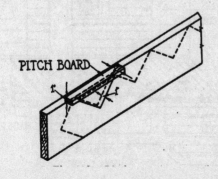

Fig. 4. Pitch board.

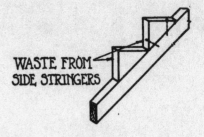

Fig. 5. Economical center stringer.

scribe along both blade and tongue. (6) Scribe the line A parallel to the 9″ run, at a distance from it equal to the rise diminished by the thickness of the proposed tread. (7) Continue to lay the square as in (5) until the required number of steps have been laid out. A pitch board might have been constructed and made use of instead of the framing square in laying out the stringers. This is nothing more than a piece of stock which serves as a template by which to lay out the rise and run of each step, Fig. 4. A cleat or fence nailed to one edge after the three edges have been planed to dimensions permits easy and accurate placing of the same.

(8) There remains the sawing out. On open stringers this is done by sawing square across the board or plank. Where the exposed ends of risers would make a bad appearance, the cuts in the stringers for risers are made mitering and the ends of the risers are mitered correspondingly. In either case the end of the riser will be flush with the exposed side of the stringer or string.

Fig. 5 illustrates an economical way of constructing a center stringer, a 2″ × 4″ having nailed to its top edge the waste cut from the side or wall stringers.

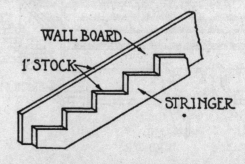

Fig. 6. Stringer for attic stair.

Porches

From *Carpentry* by Ira Samuel Griffith, 1916

Fig. 1 illustrates the manner of framing the floor of a porch. Such framework should be given a pitch downward away from the house of about 1″ in 10″ that the water may be drained.

Fig. 2 illustrates the manner of placing water table and flooring, etc. Water table is first placed, the corners being mitered and the whole furred out from the frame about a quarter of an inch to allow any dampness to escape. Porch floors should have their joints painted with lead just before being laid.

Posts and balusters are usually placed after the porch roof has been placed, the upper frame being temporarily supported by studs.

In Fig. 1 is also shown the manner of framing the bearing joists, ceiling joists and rafters for a hip roof. The various cuts are obtained in the same manner as are similar cuts on the main roof. Porch roofs are seldom given as much pitch as the main roof. They do not need as much and must, usually, be kept below the window sill line of the second story.

Fig. 2 also illustrates a common type of trim for porch cornice. Where supporting plates are long, a flitch plate girder is formed of them by the insertion between them of a stiff plate of structural steel of suitable length and width.

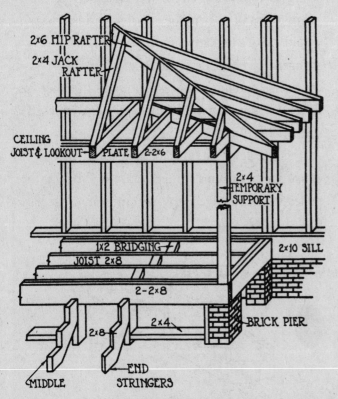

Fig. 1. Detail of porch framing.

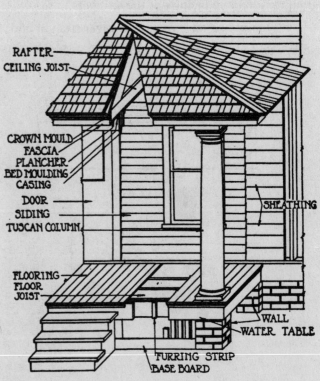

Fig. 2. Detail of porch finish.

Setting Door Jambs.—If the studs about interior door openings have been carefully selected for straightness and properly set or plumbed, the setting of the door jamb should be an easy matter. If this work has not been properly done, considerable ingenuity will be required oftentimes to get the frame set so that its edges are out of wind and the frame plumb. If a jamb should not be set plumb and out of wind, the operation of making a door fit its stops properly is a most trying one and the result usually unsatisfactory. Too much emphasis cannot be placed upon the necessity for proper placing of studs and jambs. (1) Saw off the head lugs just enough to allow the frame to be placed in the opening. (2) Cut a spacing stick of a length sufficient to reach from the floor to the under surface of the head jamb when that member is in its proper place. (3) Place the head jamb at one of its ends upon this stick and tack the jamb to the stud lightly. (4) Level the head jamb and lightly tack the second jamb, inserting wedging blocks or shingle points between the jamb and stud. A spread stick cut to hold the jambs apart properly at the base is desirable. (5) Lay a piece of finish floor against the face of each jamb and scribe along the top of this to indicate where the jambs must be cut off to fit the finish floor when it is placed. It is taken for granted that the finish floor is to be laid last. If a finish floor is not to be used, or if it is to be placed before the wall trim, the head jamb will be leveled but not located as to height, the dividers being used to scribe the feet, being set so that the proper amount will be cut off to allow the jamb to rest at the right height when cut to the scribed lines. (6) Remove the jamb and saw to the scribed lines. (7) Replace the frame and tack it at one side after plumbing it both on its face side and face edge. See that the jamb is at the right height by inserting the blocks of flooring used in scribing to length.

(8) Tack the second side-jamb close to the head. (9) Sight across the edges of these jambs and adjust the loose jamb until the frame is out of wind. Plumb its face, blocking the back. Shingles placed point to point provide easy blocking where the space is not too large. A straight-edge placed against the face of a jamb will indicate whether it has been sprung in the blocking or wedging between jamb and stud.

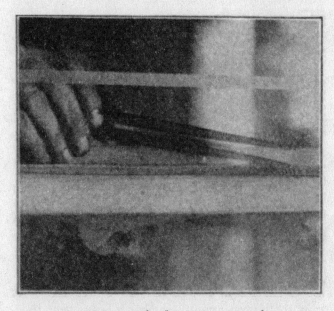

Fig. 1. Setting dividers at meeting rails.

Fig. 2. Scribing bottom of lower sash.

Hinging a Door

From *Carpentry* by Ira Samuel Griffith, 1916

The hinges most commonly used in carpentry are the kind shown as butts. Where the door stands in a vertical position, hinges in which the two parts are joined by a loose pin are generally used. By removing the pins the door may be removed without taking the screws out of the hinge. Such hinges are more easily applied than those with the fixed pin. (1) Place the door in position; keep it tight against the top and the hinge side of the frame. (2) Measure from top and bottom of the door to locate the position for the top of the higher hinge and the bottom of the lower hinge. Usually, the lower hinge is placed somewhat farther from the bottom than the higher hinge is from the top. (3) With the knife or chisel mark on both door and frame at the points just located. (4) Take out the door, place the hinge as in Fig. 3, and mark along the ends with a knife. In a similar manner mark the frame. Make certain that the openings on door and on frame are laid off so as to correspond before proceeding further. (5) Set the gauge for the depth the hinge is to be sunk and gauge both door and frame. (6) Set another gauge for width of openings and gauge both door and frame, keeping the head of the gauge against the front of the door. (7) Chisel out these gains on door and frame. (8) If loose-pin butts are used, separate the parts and fasten them in place. Use a spiral drill to make openings for the screws. To ensure the hinge is pulling tight against the side of the gain make the holes just a little nearer the back side of the screw hole of the hinge.

Fig. 1. Laying off width.

Put the door in place and insert the pins. It is a good mechanic who can make a door hang properly the first time it is put up. It is better, therefore, to insert but one or two screws in each part of a hinge until the door has been tried. (9) If the door hangs away from the frame on the hinge side, take it off; take off hinge on door or frame, or both if the crack is large; chisel the gain deeper at its front. By chiseling at the front only and feathering the cut

Fig. 2. Locating hinge position.

toward the back, the gain needs to be cut but about one-half as deep as if the whole hinge were sunk. If the door should fail to shut because the hinge edge strikes the frame too soon, the screws of the offending hinge must be loosened and a piece of heavy paper or card-board inserted along the entire edge of the gain. Fasten the screws and cut off the surplus paper with a knife. If plain butt hinges are used the operations are similar to those just described except that the whole hinge must be fastened to the door and the door held in place while fastening the hinges to the frame.

Fig. 3. Knifing hinge. Location.

Door and Window Frames

From *Carpentry* by Ira Samuel Griffith, 1916

Like other carpentry detail, window and door frames may be constructed in any one of a number of styles. Fig. 1 illustrates a satisfactory type of door frame for cottage use. The sill will be given a pitch or fall of 1″ in 12″ and will have its ends housed into the jambs. The jambs will be assembled first, being nailed together. Next, the side casings are fitted at their lower ends, cut to length and nailed. Frequently they are nailed and then cut to length. The head casing with its cap is next placed.

Fig. 2 illustrates a common type of cottage window frame. The method of procedure is not unlike that described for the door frame. The sill will be grooved on its underside to receive the top edge of the siding board and given a fall of 1″ in 10″. Jambs must be grooved to receive a parting stop as shown. Where weights are to be used each jamb

must have a pocket as detailed. The stock sawed out of the jamb may be made use of for pocket cover stock by proper manipulation. Pulleys may be placed before the jambs are assembled, at least the holes for them should be prepared.

There are a number of "tricks of the trade" in frame making. Their presentation must be left to the instructor, for the making of frames belongs to millwork and space can be spared here for general directions only.

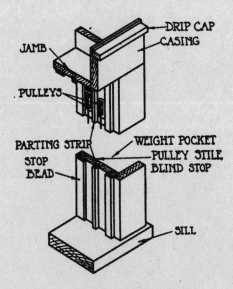

Fig. 2. Detail of window frame.

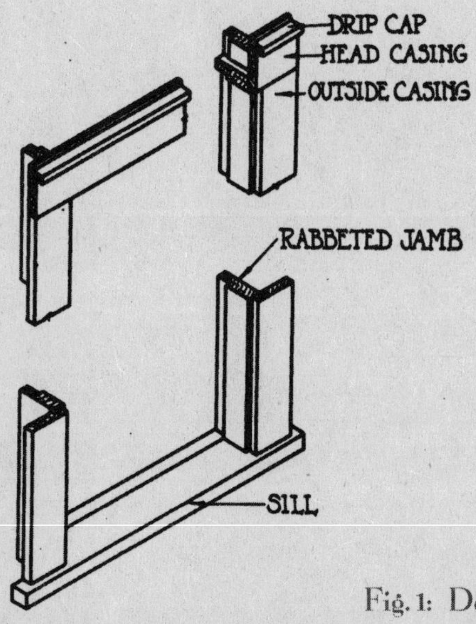

Fig. 1: Detail of door frame.

Wood and Machine Screw Sizes Tables

From *Carpentry* by Ira Samuel Griffith, 1916

The difference between consecutive sizes is .01316.

Frequently the carpenter wishes to know the diameter of hole necessary to receive the shank of a screw of a certain gauge. Should a screw gauge be accessible, he may readily determine this. Should no gauge be at hand, he may determine the size of hole by consulting the accompanying table of Wood and Machine Screw Sizes.

Example: What size bit must be selected to bore a hole for a No. 10 screw. By the table, a No. 10 screw is .18944″ in diameter. By the table of Fractional Equivalents for Decimal Values it will be seen that a 3/16″ bit must be used. The test for gauge of screw is always made over the shank just below the head.

No. of Screw Gauge	Size of Number in Decimals	No. of Screw Gauge	Size of Number in Decimals	No. of Screw Gauge	Size of Number in Decimals
000	.03152	16	.26840	34	.50528
00	.04486	17	.28156	35	.51844
0	.05784	18	.29472	36	.53160
1	.07100	19	.30788	37	.54476
2	.08416	20	.32104	38	.55792
3	.09732	21	.33420	39	.57108
4	.11048	22	.34736	40	.58424
5	.12364	23	.36052	41	.59740
6	.13680	24	.37368	42	.61056
7	.14996	25	.38864	43	.62372
8	.16312	26	.40000	44	.63688
9	.17628	27	.41316	45	.65004
10	.18944	28	.42632	46	.66320
11	.20260	29	.43948	47	.67636
12	.21576	30	.45264	48	.68952
13	.22892	31	.46580	49	.70268
14	.24208	32	.47896	50	.71584
15	.25524	33	.49212		

Strength of Materials

From *Carpentry* by Ira Samuel Griffith, 1916

Yellow pine posts

Length in ft.	Load in Tons — Size in inches					
	4×4	5×5	6×6	7×7	8×8	9×9
8	4	5	6	7	8	9
10	3	4	5	6	7	8
12	2	3	4	5	6	7
14	1	2	3	4	5	6
16	…	1	2	3	4	5
18	…	…	1	2	3	4

Hard pine beams and girders

Length In Ft.	Load in Tons — Size in Inches				
	2×6	3×6	4×6	6×6	8×8
6	1	1½	2	3	5½
8	¾	1	1½	2½	5
10	…	¾	1¼	2	4½
12	…	½	1	1½	3
14	…		½	1	2½
16	…			½	2
18	…				1

Steel I beams

Length in ft.	Load in Tons — Size in inches		
	6	8	12
10	7	14	18
12	6	12	16
14	5	10	14
16	4	8	12
18	2	6	10
20	…	4	8
22	…	2	6
24	…	…	4

Brick piers

Height in ft.	Load in Tons — Size in Inches						
	6×6	6×8	8×8	8×12	12×12	12×16	16×16
6	2	3	4	5	6	7	9
8	1½	2½	3½	4½	5½	6	8
10	1	2	3	5	5½	6	7

Stresses for Structural Timbers

From *Carpentry* by Ira Samuel Griffith, 1916

Working unit stresses used in dry locations

Species of Timber	Bending		Compression	
	Stress in extreme fibre Lbs. sq. in.	Horizontal shear stress Lbs. sq. in.	Parallel to grain "Short Columns" Lbs. sq. in.	Perpendicular to grain Lbs. sq. in.
*Fir, Douglas—				
Dense grade	1,600	100	1,200	350
Sound grade	1,300	85	900	300
Hemlock, eastern	1,000	70	700	300
Hemlock, western	1,300	75	900	300
Oak	1,400	125	900	400
Pine, eastern white	900	80	700	250
Pine, Norway	1,100	85	800	300
*Pine, southern yellow—				
Dense grade	1,600	125	1,200	350
Sound grade	1,300	85	900	300
Spruce	900	70	600	200
Tamarack	1,200	95	900	350

*NOTE: The safe working stresses given in this table are for timbers with defects limited according to the sections on defects in the rules of the Southern Pine Association for Select Structural Material. "Dense" southern yellow pine and "dense" Douglas fir should also conform to the other requirements of this rule. "Sound" southern yellow pine and "sound" Douglas fir require no additional qualifications, whereas the other species should, in addition to being graded for defects, have all pieces of exceptionally low density for the species excluded.

This table gives working unit stresses for structural timbers used in dry locations, and is compiled in the main from material furnished by the Forest Products Laboratory, Madison, Wis.

Table of brick wall contents in number of bricks
Seven bricks to each sq. ft. of wall surface

No. of sq. ft. of Wall	Thickness					
	4″	8″	12″	16″	20″	24″
1	7	15	23	30	38	45
2	15	30	45	60	75	90
3	23	45	68	90	113	135
4	30	60	90	120	150	180
5	38	75	113	150	188	225
6	45	90	135	180	225	270
7	53	105	158	210	263	315
8	60	120	180	240	300	360
9	68	135	203	270	338	405
10	75	150	225	300	375	450
20	150	300	450	600	750	900
30	225	450	675	900	1,125	1,350
40	300	600	900	1,200	1,500	1,800
50	375	750	1,125	1,500	1,875	2,250
60	450	900	1,350	1,800	2,250	2,700
70	525	1,050	1,575	2,100	2,625	3,150
80	600	1,200	1,800	2,400	3,000	3,600
90	675	1,350	2,025	2,700	3,375	4,050
100	750	1,500	2,250	3,000	3,750	4,500

Example — Determine the number of bricks in a wall 12″ × 18′ × 60′.
Solution — The wall contains a surface area of 1,080 sq. ft. By the table 100 sq. ft. contains 2,250 bricks, then 1,000 sq. ft. will contain 22,500 bricks. 80 sq. ft. will contain, by the table, 1,800 bricks, making a total of 24,300 bricks.

Fences, Gates, and Bridges

From Fences, Gates, and Bridges, edited by George A. Martin

Virginia Rail Fence

The zigzag rail fence was almost universally adopted by the settlers in the heavily timbered portions of the country, and countless thousands of miles of it still exist, though the increasing scarcity of timber has brought other styles of fencing largely into use. Properly built, of good material, on a clear, solid bed, kept free from bushes and other growth to shade it and cause it to rot, the rail fence is as cheap as any, and as effective and durable as can reasonably be desired. Good chestnut, oak, cedar, or juniper rails, or original growth heart pine, will last from fifty to a hundred years, so that material of this sort, once in hand, will serve one or two generations. This fence, ten rails high, and propped with two rails at each corner, requires twelve rails to the panel. If the fence bed is five feet wide, and the rails are eleven feet long, and are lapped about a foot at the locks, one panel will extend about eight feet in direct line. This takes seven thousand nine hundred and twenty rails, or about eight thousand rails to the mile. For a temporary fence, one that can be put up and taken down in a short time, for making stock pens and division fences, not intended to remain long in place, nothing is cheaper, or better. The bed for a fence of this kind should not be less than five feet across, to enable it to stand before the wind. The rails are best cut eleven feet long, as this makes a lock neither too long nor too short; and the forward end of each rail should come under the next one that is laid. The corners, or locks, as they are called, should also be well propped with strong, whole rails, not with pieces of rails, as is often done. The props should be set firmly on the ground about two feet from the panel, and crossed at the lock so as to hold each other, and the top course of the fence firmly in place. They thus act as braces to the fence, supporting it against the wind. Both sides of the fence should be propped. The top course of rails should be the strongest and heaviest of any, for the double purpose of weighting the fence down, and to prevent breaking of rails by persons getting upon it. The four courses of rails nearest the ground should be of the smallest pieces, to prevent making the cracks or spaces between the rails too large. They should also be straight, and of nearly even sizes at both ends. This last precaution is only necessary where small pigs have to be fenced out or in, as the case may be. The fence, after it is finished, will have the appearance of Figure 1, will be six rails high, two props at each lock, and the worm will be crooked enough to stand any wind, that will not prostrate crops, fruit trees, etc. A straighter worm than this will be easy to blow down or push over. The stability of this sort of fence depends very largely on the manner of placing the props, both as to the distance of the foot of the prop rail from the fence panel, and the way it is locked at the corner.

Fig. 1. Virginia zigzag fence complete.

Laying a Rail Fence

It is much better, both for good looks and economy, to have the corners of a rail fence on each side in line with each other. This may be accomplished by means of a very simple implement, shown in Figure 2. It consists of a small pole, eight feet long, sharpened at the lower end. A horizontal arm of a length equal to half the width of the fence from extreme outside of corners is fastened to the long pole at right angles, near the lower end. Sometimes a sapling may be found with a limb growing nearly at right angles, which will serve the purpose. Before beginning the fence, stakes are set at intervals along the middle of the line it is to occupy. To begin, the gauge, as shown in Figure 2, is set in line with the stakes, and the horizontal arm is swung outwardly at right angles to the line of fence. A stone or block to support the first corner is laid directly under the end of the horizontal arm, and the first rail laid with one end resting on the support. In the same way the next corner and all others are laid, the gauge being moved from corner to corner, set in the line of fence, and the arm swung alternately to the right and left.

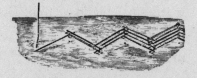

Fig. 2.

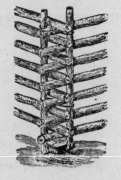

Fig. 3.　The fence begun.

Staking and Wiring

A neater and more substantial method of securing the corners of a worm fence is by vertical stakes and wires, as shown in the accompanying illustrations. When the lower three rails are laid,

Fig. 4.　Stakes in "lock."

the stakes are driven in the angles close to the rails, and secured by a band of annealed wire. The work of laying the rails proceeds, and when within one rail of the top, a second wire band is put in place. Or the upper wire may be put on above, the top rail. Annealed wire is plentiful and cheap.

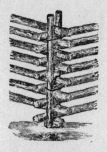

Fig. 5.　Stakes in angles.

A Fence of "Stakes and Riders"

A very common method with the "worm" or "Virginia" rail fence is to drive slanting stakes over the corner in saw-horse style, and lay the top rail into the angle thus formed. The stakes, resting on the rails and standing at angle, brace the fence firmly. But the feet of the stakes extending beyond the jagged corners formed by the ends of the rail are objectionable. This is remedied in part by putting the stakes over the middle of the panel—at considerable distance apart—and laying in them long poles horizontally. In this case the stakes should be set at such an angle as to prevent their moving sidewise along the top rail, which should be a strong one. These stakes and long riders are frequently used to raise the height of low stone walls. Figure 6 shows a fence nearly all composed of stakes and riders, which is straight and requires fewer rails than a worm fence. First, crotched stakes, formed by the forks of a branching tree limb a foot or more long, are driven a foot or so into the ground at a distance apart corresponding to the length of poles used. The bottom poles are laid into these, and two stakes, split or round poles, are

Fig. 6.　A stake and rider fence.

driven over these and the next poles laid in. Then two more stakes and another pole, and so on, as high as the fence is required. This

Fig. 7. A pole fence.

will answer for larger animals, and be strong and not expensive. For swine, and other small live-stock, the crotch stakes may be replaced by blocks or stones, and the lower poles be small and begin close to the ground.

A Pole Fence

A fence which is cheaply constructed in a timbered region, and calls for no outlay whatever, besides labor, is illustrated at figure 7. The posts are set in a straight line, having previously been bored with an inch augur to receive the pins. When they are set, the pins are driven diagonally into the posts, and the poles laid in place. It would add much to its strength, if the poles were laid so as to "break joints." A modification of this fence is sometimes made by using withes instead of pins to hold the poles in place. The withe is made of a young sapling or slender limb of beech, iron-wood, or similar tough fibrous wood, with the twigs left on. This is twisted upon itself, a strong loop made at the top, through which the butt is slipped. When in place, the butt end is tucked under the body of the withe.

Withe.

Withe in place.

Fences for Soil Liable to Heave

The main point in such a fence is either to set the posts and place a pin through them near the

bottom, so that the frost may not throw them out, or to so attach the boards that the posts may be re-driven, without splitting them, or removing the rails from the fence. The post is driven in the usual manner, when a strip of board is fastened to it by three or four spikes, depending upon the height of the fence.

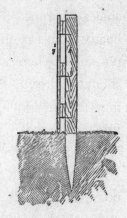

Fig. 8 End view of fence.

Fig. 9 Side view of fence.

Fig. 10 Fence with iron hooks.

A space just sufficient to insert the ends of the boards, figure 11, is left between the post and outside strip, the ends of the boards resting upon the spikes. Many miles of this fence are in use. It looks neat; besides, any portion is easily removed, making a passage to and from the field. A new post is easily put in when required, and any may be re-driven when heaved by the frost.

Where iron is cheap, a rod about three-eighths of an inch in diameter is cut in lengths of about seven and a half inches; one end is sharpened, while the opposite end, for three inches, is bent at right angles. After the boards are placed in position, the hooks should be driven in so that they will firmly grasp the boards and hold them in place.

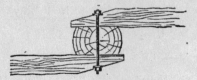

Fig. 11 Horizontal section.

A much better method is to fasten the boards temporarily in place, and then bore a half inch hole through both boards and the post, into which a common screw bolt is then inserted and the nut screwed on firmly. The two ends should, however, be put on opposite sides of the post. One bolt thus holds the ends of both boards firmly to the post, as shown in figure 11. With this style of fence, old rails or round poles may be used instead of boards.

Other Primitive Fences

In the heavily timbered parts of the country, where the settlers a few years ago were making farms by felling and burning the huge pine trees, a fence was constructed like the one shown in figure 12. Sections of trees, about four and a half feet long and often as thick, were placed in line and mortised to receive from three to five rails. This style of fence could be used by the landscape gardener with fine effect for enclosing a park or shrubbery.

In the same regions, when a farmer has pulled all the stumps from a pasture that slopes toward the highway, the stumps may be placed in line along the road with the top ends inside of the field. The gaps between where the stumps cannot be rolled close together, are filled with

Fig. 12. Log posts.

Fig. 13. Stump fence.

brushwood. A portion of this fence is shown in Figure 13.

Where other material is costly, or not to be obtained, the wicker fence, constructed of stakes and willows, is much used. In the far West it is to be seen in every town, generally built on a small embankment of earth from one to two feet deep. In this climate, with occasional repairs, it lasts from ten to fifteen years. Figure 14 shows the style of construction.

Fig. 14. Wicker fence.

Fig. 15. Brush fence.

Throughout the forest regions is found the staked brush growing on the line where the fence is constructed. Figure 15 illustrates a few rods of brush fence—such fencing being met with in our Southern States.

How A Stone Wall Should Be Built

To build a stone wall, some skill is required. The foundation should be dug out a foot deep, and the earth thrown upon each side, which serves to turn water from the wall. Large stones are bedded in the trench, and long stones placed crosswise upon them. As many whole stones as possible should be used in this

Fig. 16. Well laid wall.

place. The stones are then arranged as shown in the engraving, breaking joints, and distributing the weight equally. Any small spaces should be filled with chips broken off in dressing the larger stones, so as to make them fit snugly. As it is a work that will last a century, it is worth doing well.

Building a Stone Fence

A permanent stone fence should be built from four to five feet high, two feet wide at the base and one foot at the top, if the kind of stones available allow this construction. If a higher fence is desired, the width should be correspondingly increased. The surface of the soil along the line of the fence should be made smooth and as nearly level as possible. The height will depend upon the situation, the animals, the smoothness of the wall (whether sheep can get foot-holds to climb over), and the character of the ground along each side. If the earth foundation be rounded up previously, sloping off to an open depression or gully, less height will be needed. Such an elevation will furnish a dry base not heaved by frost like a wet one. Without this, or a drain alongside or under the wall, to keep the soil always dry, the base must be sunk deeply enough to be proof against heavy frosts, which will tilt and loosen the best laid wall on wet soil. The foundation stones should be the largest; smaller stones packed between them are necessary to firmness. The mistake is sometimes made of placing all the larger stones on the outside of the wall, filling the center with small ones. Long bind-stones placed at frequent intervals through the wall add greatly to its strength. The top

Fig. 17. Laying up a stone fence.

of the fence is most secure when covered with larger close-fitting; flat stones. The engraving shows a wooden frame and cords used as a guide in building a substantial stone fence. Two men can work together with mutual advantage on opposite sides of the stone wall.

Truck for Moving Stones

The small truck (figure 18) is not expensive, and may be made to save a great amount of hard lifting in building a stone wall. It is a low barrow, the side bars forming the handles like a wheelbarrow. It rests upon four low iron wheels. A broad plank, or two narrow ones, are laid with one end against the wall and the other resting on the ground. A groove is cut at the upper end for the wheels to rest in. The stone is loaded on the truck, moved to the place, and pushed up the plank until the wheels fall into the groove, when, by lifting on the handles, the stone is unloaded.

Fig. 18. Truck for stone.

Reinforcing a Stone Wall

A stone wall which affords ample protection against sheep and hogs, may be quite insufficient for horses and cattle. The deficiency is cheaply supplied in the manner indicated by the illustration,

Fig. 19. Stone wall reinforced.

figure 19. Round poles or rails are used, and if the work is properly performed, the fence is very effective.

A Composite Fence

The fence illustrated at figure 20 is quite common in some parts of New England. A ridge is thrown up by back-farrowing with a plow, and both that and the ditches finished by hand with a shovel. Light posts are easily driven through the soft earth, and a board fence, only three boards high, made in the usual manner. Then the stones, as they are picked up in the field, are hauled to the fence and thrown upon the ridge. This clears the field, strengthens the ridge, prevents the growth of weeds, and assists in packing the earth firmly around the bottom of the posts.

Fig. 20. Composite fence.

A Prairie Sod Fence

A sod fence, beside its other value, is a double barrier against the prairie fires which are so sweeping and destructive to new settlers, if unobstructed, for a wide strip is cleared of sods, the fence standing in the middle of it. A very convenient implement for cutting the sod is shown at figure 21. It is made of planks and scantling, the method of construction

being clearly shown. The cutting disks are four wheel-coulters from common breaking plows, all attached to an iron shaft sixteen inches apart. They are set to cut three or four inches deep. This is run three times along the line of the fence, making nine cuts, the cutters being held down by a man riding on the rear of the apparatus. Then with a breaking plow one furrow is turned directly in the line of the fence, completely inverting the sod, the team turned to the right, and a second or back furrow is inverted on top of the first. Additional furrows are cut, diminishing in width to five or six inches on the outer side, as shown in the diagram, figure 22. After the two inner sods are turned, the rest are carried by hand, wheelbarrow or a truck, (figure 18), and laid on the sod wall, care being used to "break joints" and to taper gradually to the top. If a more substantial fence is wanted, a strip thirty-two inches wide may be left as a part for the fence, the first two furrows inverted upon the uncut portion, so that their edges just touch. The sod fence is then continued to the summit just twice as thick as it would be by the process just described. After the fence is laid, a deep furrow should be run on each side, throwing the earth against the base of the fence. A very effective and cheap fence is made by laying up a sod "dyke,"

Fig. 21. Sod cutter.

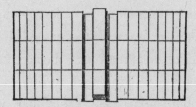

Fig. 22. The sod cut.

as above described, three feet high, then driving light stakes along the summit, and stringing two strands of barbed wire to them.

Building Board Fences

In building a board fence, always start right, and it will be little trouble to continue in the same way. Much of the board fencing erected is put together very carelessly, and the result is a very insecure protection to the field or crops. A fence-post should be set two and a half or three feet in the ground, and the earth should be packed around it as firmly as possible. For packing the soil there is nothing better than a piece of oak, about three inches square on the lower end, and about six feet long, rounded off on the upper part to fit the hands easily. Properly used, this instrument will pack the soil around a post as it was before the hole was dug. In putting on fence boards, most builders use two nails on the ends of each board, and one in the middle. Each board should have at least *three* nails at the ends, and *two* in the middle, and these nails should never be less than ten-pennies. Smaller nails will hold the boards in place for a while, but when they begin to warp, the nails are drawn out or loosened, and the boards drop off. This will rarely be the case where large nails are used, and a much stiffer fence is secured. Many fence builders do not cut off the tops of the posts evenly, but this should always be done, not only for the improvement that it makes in the looks of the fence; but also for the reason that there should always be a cap put on, and to do this, the posts must be evened. The joints should always be "broken," as is shown in the engraving, figure 23, so that in a four-board fence but two joints should come on each post. By this means more

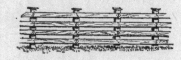

Fig. 23. Properly constructed board fence.

firmness and durability is secured, there being always two unbroken boards on each post to hold it in place, preventing sagging. On the face of the post immediately over where the rails have been nailed on, nail a flat piece of board the width of the post and extending from the upper part of the top rail to the ground.

Figure 24 shows a slight modification, which consists in setting the posts on alternate sides of the boards, securing

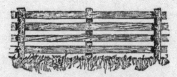

Fig. 24. A durable board fence.

additional stability. The posts are seven feet long, of well-seasoned red cedar, white oak, chestnut, or black locust, preference being accorded to order named. The boards are sixteen feet long, fastened with ten-penny steel fence nails. The posts for a space of two and a half feet from the lower end are given good coats of boiled linseed oil and pulverized charcoal, mixed to the consistency of ordinary paint, which is allowed to dry before they are set. When the materials are all ready, stretch a line eighteen inches above the ground, where it is proposed to build the fence. Dig the post holes, eight feet apart from centers, on alternate sides of the line. The posts are set with the faces inward, each half an inch from the line, to allow space for the boards. Having set the posts, the boards of the lower course are nailed on. Then, for the first length, the second board from the bottom and the top board are only eight feet long, reaching to the first post. For all the rest the boards are of the full length, sixteen feet. By this means they "break joints." After the boards are nailed on, the top of the posts are sawed off slanting, capped, if desired, and the whole thing painted. A good coat of crude petroleum, applied before painting, will help preserve the fence, and save more than its cost in the paint needed.

We see another style of board fence now and then that is rather preferable to the ordinary one;

it looks better than the old straight fence. It saves one board to each length; and by nailing on the two upper boards,

Fig. 25. A neat farm fence.

as shown in the illustration, figure 25, great extra strength is given. These boards not only act as braces, but ties also, and a fence built on well set posts, and thoroughly nailed, will never sag or get out of line until the posts rot off.

A Fence Board Holder

Figure 26 shows a contrivance for holding fence boards against the posts, at the right distances apart when nailing. A two and a half by two and a half inch piece of the desired length is taken for the upright, *a*. About its center is hinged the brace, *c*. A strap hinge, *b*, or a stout piece of leather for a hinge, will answer. Blocks or stops, *d, d, d, d,* are nailed on the upright *a*, at the required distances, according to the space between the boards on the fence. The bottom boards of the fence are nailed on first. The bottom block of the board holder rests upon the bottom board, and is held in position by the brace *c*. The boards can be placed in the holder like putting up bars, and are guided to their places on the post by the blocks, *d, d*. The boards can now be nailed on the posts, and the holding devices moved for another length. When the boards are too long, they can be pulled forward a little, and the end sawed, and pushed back to place. One man using the contrivance, can nail on nearly as many boards in a day, as two

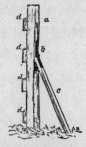

Fig. 26.

Fig. 27. Fence board holder.

persons with one to hold the boards in the old way. Figure 27 shows the manner of using the fence board holders.

Reinforcing a Board Fence

The old method of topping out a low board fence is shown at Figure 28. Since barbed wire has become plenty, it is more usual to increase the height of the fence by stringing one or two strands of that on vertical slats nailed to the tops of the posts. Yet, in cases where there are plenty of sound rails left from some old fence, or plenty of straight saplings, the old method is still a very cheap and convenient one.

Fig. 28. Strengthening a board fence.

A Southern Picket Fence

The picket fence in very general use in the Southern States, is shown in Figure 29. It will be observed that the pickets, instead of terminating in an equal-sided point, have but one slanting side, while the other is straight. Such a fence looks quite

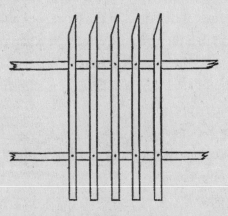

Fig. 29. Southern picket fence.

as well as one with the other style of points; and is exceedingly neat and serviceable along the line of the street, or to mark the boundary between two estates. To facilitate the sawing

Fig. 30. Bench for sawing pickets.

of the pickets, the bench or horse represented in Figure 30 is employed. This has a stop at one end, while near the other end are two upright pieces to serve as guides in sawing. The edge of one of these is far enough in the rear of the other to give the desired slope. In sawing, the saw rests against these guides, as shown by the dotted lines. In a picket fence, the point where decay commences is where the pickets cross the string pieces. Water enters between the two, and decay takes place which is unsuspected until the breaking of a picket reveals the state of affairs. The string pieces and the pickets, at least upon one side, should be painted before putting them together, and nailed while the paint is fresh.

Fences of Split Pickets

In localities where sawed timber is expensive, and split timber is readily obtained, a very neat picket fence may be made with very little outlay, by using round posts, split stringers, and rived pickets, as shown in the engraving, Figure 31. The stringers are eight to twelve feet in length, and usually one of the flat sides is sufficiently smooth for receiving the pickets. Let the stringers project a few inches beyond each post, adding strength to the fence, and should the posts decay, new ones may be driven in on either

side, and the stringers readily attached by heavy nails or spikes. With timber that splits freely, a man can drive out five or six hundred

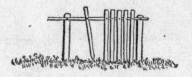

Fig. 32. Cheap fence of split timber.

pickets in a day. The construction of the fence is plainly shown in the above engraving.

Figure 32 represents a fence-made entirely of split timber, the only cash outlay being for nails. This may be made so as to turn,

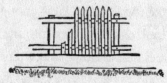

Fig. 33. Common picket fence.

not only all kinds of stock, but rabbits, etc. The pickets are sharpened and driven six or eight inches into the ground, and firmly nailed to a strong string-piece at top.

Another good substantial fence is represented by Figure 33, which, though somewhat expensive, is especially adapted for yard, orchard and vineyard enclosure. This needs no explanation. The posts should not be set further than eight feet apart; two by four inch scantlings should be used to nail to, and split palings should be nailed on with annealed steel nails.

Light Picket Fences

For enclosing poultry yards, garden and grounds, a cheap fence with pickets of lath often serves a good purpose. If not very durable, the cost of repair or renewal is light. Figure 34 shows one of this kind, which is sufficiently high for the Asiatic and other heavy and quiet fowls. The panels are

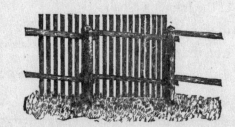

Fig. 31. A fence of split stuff.

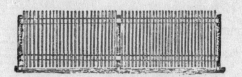

Fig. 34. Panel of picket fence.

sixteen feet long, and are composed of two pieces of ordinary six-inch

Fig. 35. Frame for making fence.

fencing, for top and bottom rails, with lath nailed across two and a half inches apart; the top ends of the lath extending ten inches above the upper edge of the top rail. Posts, three or four inches through at the top end, are large enough, and, after sharpening well, can be driven into the ground by first thrusting a crow-bar down and wrenching it back and forth. A post is necessary at the middle of each panel. Both rails of the panel should be well-nailed to the posts. These panels may be neatly and rapidly made in a frame, constructed for that purpose. This frame, shown in Figure 35, consists simply of three cross-pieces of six by six, four feet long, upon which are spiked two planks one foot wide and three feet apart, from outside to outside. Four inches from the inner edge of each plank is nailed a straight strip of inch stuff, to keep the rails of the panel in place while the lath are being nailed on. Against the projecting ends of the cross-pieces, spike two by six posts twelve inches long; on the inside of these posts nail a piece of six-inch fencing to serve as a stop for the top ends of the laths to touch when nailing them to the rails. These panels can be made in the shop or on the barn floor at odd times, and piled away for future use. Nail a wide bottom board around on the inside of the enclosure after the fence is in position.

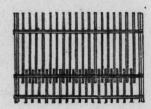

Fig. 36.

Figures 36 and 37 show lath fences high enough for all kinds of poultry. The posts in Figure 36 are eight feet apart. A horizontal bar is nailed to the posts six inches above the ground, a second one eighteen inches, and a third

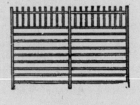

Fig. 37.

four and a half feet. To two lower strips nail laths that have been cut to half length, first driving the lower part of the laths two inches into the ground.

One advantage of this fence is, that the two strips near the bottom, being so close together, sustain pressure from dogs or outside intruders better than any other fence constructed of lath, and dispenses with a foot-wide board, so generally used.

The cheapest lath fence is made with the posts four feet apart, first sawing them in two lengthwise at a sawmill, and nailing the lath directly to the posts without the use of strips. The two upper laths have short vertical pieces fastened to them with cleat nails, and present points to prevent fowls alighting on the fence. Such a fence (Figure 37) will cost, for four feet, one-half post, three cents; twenty laths, eight cents; and the nails, three cents, per running foot, six feet high, or one-half cent per square foot.

Hand-Made Wire And Picket Fences

A very desirable and popular fence is made of pickets or slats woven into horizontal strands of plain wire. Several machines have been invented and patented for doing this work, but it can be done by hand with the aid of the bench illustrated herewith. The wire should be a little larger than that used on harvesting machines, and annealed like it. The bench, of which Figure 38 is a side view, and Figure 39 a top view, should be about sixteen feet long and have a screw at each corner for raising and lowering the holding bars. For the screws at the ends of the frame one-half to three-fourth-inch iron rod will answer. The wire is twisted close and tight to the slats, and given two or

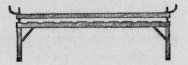

Fig. 38. Side view of bench.

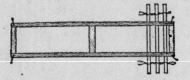

Fig. 39. Top view of bench.

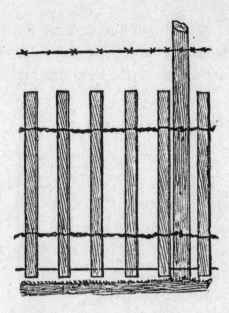

Fig. 40. Portion of the fence.

three twists between them. If the slats are of green stuff, fasten the wire to them with small staples, to prevent their slipping when they shrink. The fence is fastened to the post with common fence staples.

When this style of fence is used on one side of a pasture or highway, its effectiveness may be increased by a single strand of barbed wire stapled to the posts above the pickets, and a strand of plain wire strung along the bottom to stiffen it. The fence will then be as in Figure 40. Such a fence will last many years, and for most sections of the country is the best and cheapest combined cattle and hog fence that can be made. For a garden fence it is equal to the best picket, and at one third of the cost. By having the slats sawed about one-half-inch thick, two inches wide, and five to six feet long, it makes an excellent fence for a chicken yard, as it can be readily taken down, moved, and put up again without injuring it in the least. For situations where appearances are secondary importance, round slats are equally as good as pickets. A farmer in Wisconsin planted a few white willow trees the year that he made some fences of this kind. "When the fence began to need repairs, the willows had attained such a growth that their trimmings furnished all the material needed then and each year thereafter."

Fence of Wire and Pickets

The fence shown in Figure 41 has been introduced in some sections, and is becoming more popular

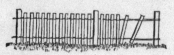

Fig. 41. Fence of wire and pickets.

every year. The posts are set ten feet apart, and are so placed that they will come on the right and left side of the fence, alternately. The pickets are split from oak, or any other hard wood, and are four or five feet long, and an inch and a half or two inches wide. When the posts are set, brace the one at the end of the line, and fasten the ends of two number nine, unannealed wires to it. Stretch the wires along to the other end of the line, and a few feet beyond the last post. One pair is to be stretched near the top of the posts and one near the ground. When the wires are stretched taut, fasten them to some, posts or other weight that will drag on the ground; the upper and lower wires should be fastened to separate weights, and these should be heavy enough to keep the wires at a great tension. Having done this, you are ready to commence building the fence. One man spreads the strands, while another places the picket between them; the other end of the picket is then raised up and placed between the upper wires, and then driven up with an axe or mallet. In inserting the pickets, the wires are to be crossed alternately, as shown in the engraving. The pickets should be dry and should be about three inches apart. It takes two persons to build this fence successfully, but it can be built more rapidly by three; one to spread the wires, one to place the picket in position, and one to drive it home. This is especially adapted, for a line or other fence which is not required to be often moved. It is fastened to the post by nailing one of the pickets to it with common fencing nails. Fences of this kind are also made with straight, round limbs of willow or other trees in place of the split pickets. Several different machines have been patented for making this style of fence.

Portable Fences of Poles or Wire

Figures 42 and 43 show styles of portable fences, which are used to some extent in the territories. The base of each is the half of

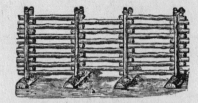

Fig. 42. Portable pole fence.

a small log, split through the center. For the fence shown in Figure 42, two augur holes are bored a few inches apart, and small poles "driven to serve as posts." Rails or round poles of the usual length are laid to the desired height, and the top of the posts tied together with wire. In situations where timber is less plentiful, a single stake is set into the base, as in Figure 43, braced, and barbed or plain wire attached by staples. Besides the advantage of being easily moved, these fences can be prepared in winter, when there is little else to do, and rapidly set in place at any time when the ground is clear of snow.

Fig. 43. Portable wire fence.

Figure 44 is a fence made of either sawed stuff, or of rails or poles, having their ends flattened and bored. An iron rod, or piece of gas-pipe, anywhere from half an inch to an inch in diameter, is run through the holes, and through a base block into the ground as far as necessary. A round stick of tough durable wood, an inch or more in diameter, will answer. The size of this rod and its strength will depend upon the amount of zigzag that is given to the lengths. If the corners are one foot on each side of a central line, the fence firmly held together by the rods, will in effect

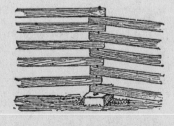

Fig. 44. Portable fence of poles or rails.

stand on a two feet wide base. Less than this would perhaps sometimes answer, and there are no sharp corners, or deep recesses for weeds and rubbish.

Portable Poultry Fences

It is often very convenient when poultry are enclosed during the growing season, to have a fence for the hen-yard which can be readily moved from place to place. The illustration, Figure 45, shows one

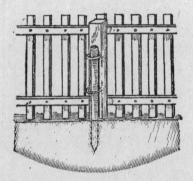

Fig. 45. Portable poultry fence.

of these. Cut the posts the same length as the pickets, and to the inner side of each attach two strong iron hoops bent into a semi-circle, one near the bottom and the other halfway up. Through these hoops drive stakes fitted to fill them closely, with sharpened points for easily entering the ground. When removing the fence the posts can be slipped off.

Turkeys, even when they have attained a considerable size, should be shut up until after the dew is off the grass, and other fowls must be confined in limited runs, while the young are small. It is quite an advantage if these runs can be changed easily, and this can be accomplished only when they are enclosed in a light movable fence. Such a fence is shown in Figure 46, on preceding page. It is made in twelve or sixteen feet sections by nailing laths to light pieces of the proper length. The upper end of the laths is sharpened; the end ones are of double thickness. The sections are placed with the end-laths intercrossing at the top, and about six inches apart at the bottom, as in cross-section, Figure 47. They are held apart by blocks, Figure 48, which rest on the upper edges of the cross-pieces and against the laths. They are held together, and to the ground, by

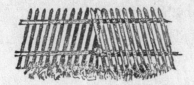

Fig. 46. Movable fence for turkeys.

Fig. 47. Cross-section of movable fence.

Fig. 48. Cross-block for fence.

stakes driven against the outer side of the end laths. As these stakes have the same angle as the laths, they hold the sections together, and also the fence in its place and down to the ground. The triangular space where the sections join is closed by a lath driven in the ground or tacked to the block between the cross-pieces. Corners must be formed of two sections inclined inward, and in the same way that sections are joined. The stakes are readily withdrawn, and the sections are so light that they are easily handled.

Making Fence Posts

There is quite an art in splitting logs into posts. Every post should have some heart wood, which lasts the longer, for two reasons: That there may be durable wood into which to drive the nails, and without it some of the posts, composed entirely of sap-wood, will rot off long before others, making the most annoying of all repairing necessary. If the log is of a size to make twelve posts, split along the lines of Figure 49, which will give each post a share of heart

Fig. 49.

wood. This will make a cross section of the posts triangular, the curved base being somewhat more than half of either side. This is a fairly well-shaped post, and much better than a square one having little or no heart wood. Although the log may be large enough to make sixteen or eighteen posts, it is better to split it the same way. It should first be cut into halves, then quarters, then twelfths. If it is attempted to split one post off the side of a half, the wood will "draw out," making the post larger at one end than the other—not a good shape, for there will be little heart wood at the small end. When the log is too large to admit of it being split in that way, each post may nevertheless be given enough heart wood by splitting along the lines, shown in Figure 50. First cut the logs into halves, then quarters, then eighths. Then split off the edge of each eighth, enough for a post—about one-fourth only of the wood, as it is all heart wood, and then halve the balance. A good post can be taken off the edge, and yet enough heart wood for the remaining two posts remain.

Fig. 50.

A Post Holder

A simple arrangement for holding a post while it is being bored or mortised, is shown in Figure 51. It consists of two long pieces of round or square timber, lying parallel upon the ground, and two shorter sticks resting upon them at right angles. The upper pieces have saddles cut out for the posts to

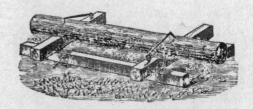

Fig. 51. A post holder.

fit into. A staple with a large iron hook or "dog," is fastened into one end of each cross-piece, as shown in the engraving. When the post is laid in position, the hooks are driven into it holding it firmly.

Driving Fence Posts by Hand

Where the soil is soft, loose, and free from stone, posts may be driven more easily and firmly than if set in holes dug for the purpose. An easy method of driving is shown in Figure 52. A wagon is loaded with posts and furnished with a stage in the rear end of the box, upon which a person can stand to give the posts the first start. Another man holds the posts upright while they are driven. When one post is driven to its place, the wagon is moved to the next place, and this operation repeated.

To drive posts, a wooden maul should be used. This is made of a section of an elm trunk or branch, eight or nine inches in diameter, Figure 53. An iron ring is driven on each end, and wedged all around, the wood at the edge being beaten down over the rings with a hammer or the poll of an axe. To prevent the posts from splitting or being battered too much, the ends of the maul should be hollowed a little, and never rounded out, and the ends of the posts should be beveled all around. The hole in the maul for the handle should be made larger on one

side, and lengthwise of the maul, and the handle spread by two wedges driven in such a way as not to split the maul.

Fig. 53. Maul for driving posts.

To Drive Posts without Splitting

Posts are very liable to split in driving, unless some precaution is used. This damage and loss can be avoided in a great measure by proper preparation of the posts before they are driven. The tops of sawed posts should have the sides cut off, as in Figure 54, or simply cut off each corner, as in Figure 56, while a round post should be shaped as in Figure 55. The part of the post removed need not be more than half an inch in thickness, but when the corners only are cut away, the chip should be thicker. In driving, it is very important to strike the post squarely on the top, and not at one corner or side. In most soils at the North, the frosts heave posts more or less each season, and they need to be driven down to the usual depth. To do this with little injury to the post, the device shown in Figure 57 may be used. It is a piece of tough hard wood scantling, *e*, eighteen inches in length, with tapering ends. It is provided with a handle, *h*, three feet in length, of quite small size, and if possible, of green timber. In using it, let one person (a boy will do) lay the bit of scantling on top of the post to be re-driven, when, with the beetle or sledge, the scantlings instead of the post is struck, thus preventing the splitting of the post. When the top of a fence is surmounted by a stringer, as in the engraving, the effect of the blow is distributed over a large space, and both stringer and post escape injury. The attendant should keep hold of the

Fig. 54.

Fig. 55.

Fig. 52. Driving fence posts.

Fig. 56.

Fig. 57. Scantling with handle in position.

handle, *h*, while the posts are being driven, and move the scantling from post to post as required.

Setting a Gate Post

No matter how strong or how well braced a gate may be, it will soon begin to sag and catch on the ground, if the gate post is not firmly planted. Sometimes, owing to the soft nature of the ground, it is almost impossible to plant the post firmly, but in such cases the work can generally be done satisfactorily by packing

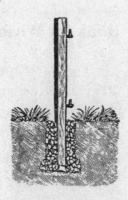

Fig. 58. A gate post set in cement.

medium-sized stones around the post, in the hole, as shown in Figure 58. If it is thought that this will not insure sufficient firmness, add good cement. Place in a layer of stones, then cement enough to imbed the next layer of stones, and so on, until the hole is full and the post planted. Do not cover up the stones with earth or disturb the post for a few days, until the cement has "set." Remember that the post must be set plumb while the work is going on, as it can never be straightened after the cement has "set." Only durable posts should be used, and this method of setting should only be followed with gate posts which are supposed to be permanent, and not with posts liable to be changed.

A still better method is shown in Figure 59. Before the post is set into the hole, a flat stone is laid

edgewise in the bottom, on the side which is to receive the greatest pressure from the foot of the post. When the post is set, and the hole half filled with earth, a second stone is placed against the post on the side to which it will be drawn by the weight of the gate. The stones receive the pressure and hold the post firmly in position.

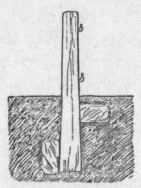

Fig. 59. Gate post braced with stones.

Fence Posts for Wet Lands

Low meadow and other marsh land is subject to heaving by the frost, and much difficulty is experienced in securing firm fences upon such ground, as the posts are drawn up by the freezing of

Fig. 60. Different methods of treating posts.

the surface. To avoid this, much may be done in the way of selecting posts that are larger at one end than the other. It will help very much to put a strong, durable pin through the bottom end of the post, or to notch it at each side, as in Figure 60, and to brace the bottom with a flat stone, driven, well into the side of the hole with the rammer. When the soil is very soft and mucky, it is best to drive the posts and to make them hold well in the ground, to spike wedge-shaped pieces to them on either side, by which they are held firmly in their places.

Live Posts

A living tree which stands in the right place, makes a very durable and substantial fence-post.

In the great treeless regions of the Mississippi Valley, where it is difficult to obtain timber for posts, it is not an unusual practice to plant trees for the purpose on street boundaries, and other places where the fence is to be permanent. White willow is well adapted for the purpose on suitable soils as it grows rapidly and bears close pruning. In situations where the soil is even moderately damp, white willow posts, four inches in diameter, cut green and set in spring, will take root and grow. The new branches soon form a bushy head, which may be cut back from time to time. It is not advisable to nail boards or drive staples directly into the tree. With a board fence, the swaying of the tree loosens the nails, and if barbed wire is stapled to the tree, the bark and wood will in time grow over them as in Figure 61. To obviate this, a stick is nailed to the tree as in Figure 62, and to this the fence is attached. A still better method is to secure the strip of wood to the tree by two or three pairs, of interlocking staples.

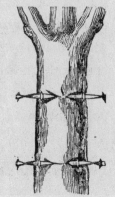

Fig. 61.

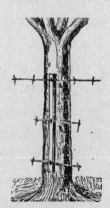

Fig. 62.

Mending a Split Post

Fence posts split from a variety of causes, and when they are in this condition they make a very insecure fence. The usual way is to merely nail an old horseshoe or two across the split part, just below the holes in the posts. This answers fairly well, but does not draw the cleft together, and horseshoes are not always on hand. A better method of doing this is shown in Figure 63. A short, stout chain is put around the top of the post, just tight enough to admit of a strong lever. The parts of the posts are then brought together by a heavy downward

pressure of the lever and held there, while a strip of good tin, such as can be cut from the bodies of tin cans, is put around and securely nailed. If the post is a heavy one and the cleft large, it is well to take the entire body of a can and double it, to give it additional strength before nailing it on. The dotted lines show where the tin is nailed.

Fig. 63. Mending a split post.

Hook for Wiring Posts

Figure 64 shows a modified cant-hook for drawing together the upper extremities of fence stakes that are to be wired, as in the engraving. The half-moon shaped iron, *a*, is riveted fast to the top end of the lever, and is to prevent the end of the lever from slipping off the stake when in use. The second iron from the top, *b*, is twenty-five inches long, with two hooks at the end, though one will do; this is to catch the stake on the opposite side of the fence. This iron is fastened in the lever by a bolt in a long mortise, in, the same way, as the hook in an ordinary cant-hook. The iron rod, *c*, has a hole in one end, and is drawn out to a point at the other—this is fastened to the lever by a bolt in a long mortise, and serves to catch in the stake or rail, and hold the stakes together, while the man adjusts the iron around the stakes. When the stakes are drawn tightly to the fence, this rod is drawn up until it strikes the stake or one of the rails, when the man can

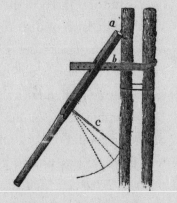

Fig. 64. A stake drawer used in wiring fences.

Fig. 65. Drawing fence posts.

let go of the "drawer," and it holds itself. The lever is four feet and three inches long, and two inches square, with the corners taken off part of the way down, the lower end being rounded for a handle, as shown in the engraving.

Drawing Fence Posts

Figure 65 shows a practicable method of drawing out fence posts by the aid of an ox team. A stout piece of timber with a large flat "foot" is placed under the chain to change the direction of the draft. Two men and a steady yoke of oxen can extract fence posts very quickly and easily by this method. A good steady team of horses will do quite as well as oxen.

Lifting Posts by Hand

A convenient and sensible implement, for taking up fence posts without the aid of a team, is shown at Figure 66. It consists of a stout pole of the size and shape of a wagon tongue. The thicker part of this pole, for about fifteen inches from the end, is shaped into a wedge. This is sheathed with a frame made of iron, half an inch thick and two and a half

Fig. 66. A convenient post lifter.

inches wide, and securely fastened with screws or bolts. The end should be pointed and slightly bent upwards. The manner of using this convenient implement is shown in the illustration.

Fig. 67. Lifting a post.

Frequently a farmer has occasion to lift posts, and has not time to wait for the construction of an iron-shod lever. Figure 67 shows a very simple, inexpensive contrivance for such cases. A spadeful of earth is taken from each side of the post, and a short, strong chain loosely fastened around the lower end of the post, as far down as it can be placed. A strong lever—a stout rail will answer the purpose—is passed through the chain, as shown in the engraving, until the end of the rail catches firm soil. By lifting at the other end of the lever the post is raised several inches, when both chain and lever are pushed down again for a second hold, which generally brings the post out. The chain is furnished with a stout hook at one end, made to fit the links, so that it can be quickly adjusted to any ordinary post.

Splicing Fence Posts

There are places, as crossing over gullies, etc., where unusually long posts are desirable, though not always easy to obtain. In such cases properly spliced posts are almost as durable as entire ones. The engraving of the front and side views, Figure 68, shows how the splice may be made to secure strength and durability. The splices should be made with a shoulder at the lower end, and well nailed together, after which one or two bands

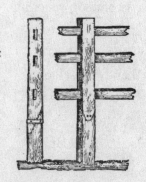

Fig. 68. Splicing fence posts.

of hoop-iron may be passed around the splice and securely fastened. The hoop-iron band is one of the most important points in a splice of this kind.

Application of Wood Preservatives

To prevent decay at the center, as well as of all that part of the post placed below ground, by use of wood preserving solutions, the following system is both novel and valuable: It is to have a hole in the center of the post, from the bottom upward, to a point that shall be above the ground when the post is in position. Then bore another hole in the side of the post with a slight inclination downward, making an opening in the center hole, as shown in Figure 69. A wooden plug, two or three inches long, should be driven snugly into the hole at the bottom of the post, in order to prevent the escape of any liquid that may be used in the operation. When the posts are set in an upright position, a preservative solution may be introduced into the hole in the side and the centre one filled with it, after which a cork plug of some kind should be inserted in the side hole, to prevent evaporation, as well as to keep out dust and insects. The solutions thus introduced will gradually be absorbed by the surrounding wood, until all parts along the entire length of the central cavity must become completely saturated. When the solutions used have been taken up by the surrounding wood, it will only be necessary to withdraw the cork or plug, and apply more, if it is thought desirable. A common watering pot with a slender spout will be a handy vessel to use in distributing the solutions.

Petroleum, creosote, corrosive sublimate, or any other of the well-known

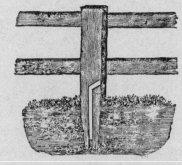

Fig. 69. Sectional view of bored piost.

wood preservatives may be used in this way. Telegraph posts might be prepared in the same way, and if the central reservoirs were kept filled with petroleum, they would last a hundred years or more. Where a large number of posts or poles are to be prepared, it would be cheaper to have the holes bored by steam or horsepower than by hand. With very open and porous wood it is quite probable that a hole bored in the side of the post and above the ground, and deep enough to hold a half pint or more of creosote or some other similar solution, would answer, but a central cavity reaching to the bottom would perhaps be best.

Wooden Gates

As board and picket fences have gradually replaced rail and other primitive fences, useful but inconvenient "bars" have begun to disappear, and tidy gates are seen. The saving in time required to take down and put up bars, rather than open and close gates, amounts to a good deal. A good wooden gate will last a long time. Gateways should be at least fourteen feet wide. All the wood used in the construction of the gate should be well-seasoned. It is best to plane all the wood-work, though this is not absolutely necessary. Cover each tenon with thick paint before it is placed in its mortise. Fasten the brace to the cross-piece with small bolts or wrought nails well clinched. Mortise the ends of the boards into the end posts, and secure them in place with wooden pins wedged at both ends, or iron bolts. The best are made of pine fence-boards six inches wide; the ends should be four by twenty-four inch scantling, although the one at the latch may be lighter. Five cross-pieces are enough. The lighter the gate in proportion to strength, the better it is. There is but one right way to brace a gate, and many wrong ones. The object of bracing is to strengthen the gate, and also to prevent its sagging. Gates sag in two ways; by the moving to the one side of the posts upon which the gates are hung, and the settling of the gates themselves. Unless braced the only thing to hold the gate square is the perfect rigidity of the tenons in the mortises; but the weight of the gate will loosen these, and allow the end of the gate opposite the hinges to sag. It is plain that a brace placed like that shown in Figure 70 will not prevent this settling down. The only opposition it can give is the resistance of the nails, and these will draw loose in the holes as readily as the tenons in the mortises. A brace set as shown at Figure 72 is not much better, as the resistance must depend upon the rigidity of the upright piece in the middle, and the bolts or nails holding it will give way enough to allow the gate to sag.

The method shown in Figure 72 is fully as faulty, while the form shown in Figure 73 is even worse. It seems strange that any one should brace a gate in these ways, but it is quite frequently seen attempted. The only right way to brace agate is shown in Figure 74. The gate may be further strengthened as shown in Figure 75. Before the gate can sag, the brace must be shortened; for as the gate settles, the points must come

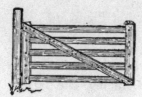

Fig. 70.

Fig. 71.

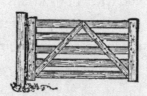

Fig. 72.

Fig. 73.

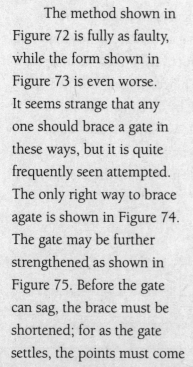

Fig. 74.

Fig. 75.

closer together, and this the brace effectually prevents.

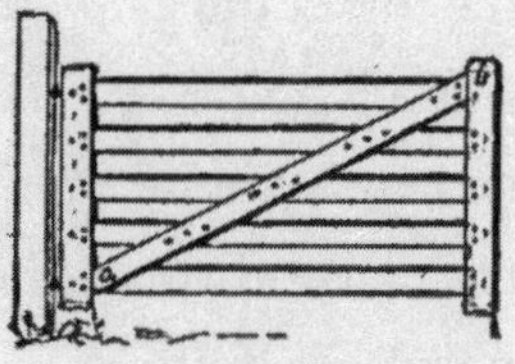

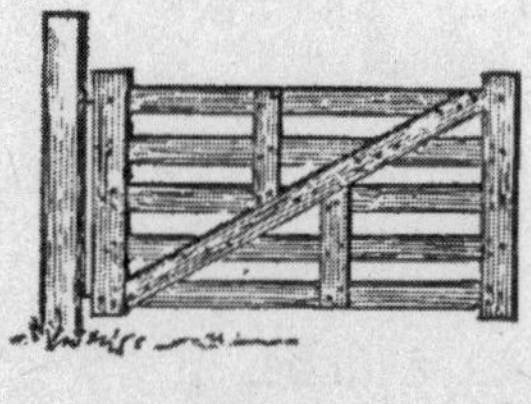

The posts should be set in such a way that they will not be pulled to one side and allow the gate to sag. The post should be put below the line of frost, or else it will be heaved out of position; three feet in the ground is none too deep. Have a large post and make a big hole for it. Be careful to set the post plumb and stamp the earth firmly in the hole—it cannot be stamped too hard. While stamping, keep walking around the post, so that the earth will be firmed on all sides. Blocks may be arranged as shown in Figure 76; but this is not really necessary, when the posts have been rightly set, although it may be advisable to take this further precaution.

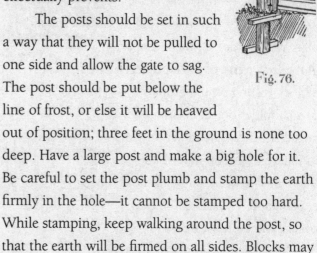

Fig. 76.

To remove the pulling weight of the gate when closed, the swinging end may rest upon a block; or a pin inserted in the end piece of the gate may rest in a slot sawed in the post, or on a shoulder of the post. Figure 77 shows one end of a combination of two plans—the iron rod from near the top of the high post holds the gate while the strain upon the post is lessened by the opposite end of the closed gate being supported on the other post.

Fig. 77.

For hanging the gate the best hinges are doubtless-those shown in Figure 78. One part passes through the end-piece of the gate, and is secured by a nut on the end. The other piece is heated and driven into the post, following the path of a small augur-hole. Next to this comes the strap hinge, which should be fastened with bolts or screws. Three easy, cheap ways of supporting the gate are shown in Figures 79, 80, and 81.

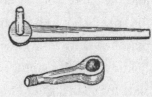

Fig. 78.

In Figure 79, a stout band of wood, or one of iron, may be used in place of the chain. And in place of the stool for the reception of the lower end of the end-piece, a block resting on the ground, or a shoulder on the post, may be substituted. The mode shown in Figure 80 is common in the West. Its construction needs no explanation. By sliding the gate back until it almost balances it may be carried around with ease. In Figure 81, the fastening, or latch, must be so arranged as to hold the lower part of the gate in position. The box of stone renders it easier to move the gate. A heavy block of wood serves the same purpose.

Fig. 79.

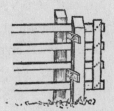

Fig. 80.

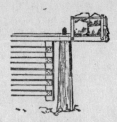

Fig. 81.

Self Closing Gates

Every self-closing gate should be provided with a drop or spring catch, a suitable bevel for it to strike against and notch to hold it. Gates opening into the garden or out upon the street, should be so hung that they will swing either way. Figure 82 shows a hinge and slide for such a gate. In opening the gate from either side, the arm of the upper hinge slides upon the iron bar, raising the gate a little as it swings around. When loosed, it slides down without help, and closes by its own weight. Figure 83 shows another form of the iron slide, suitable for a wide gate post, and more ornamental than the plain slide in Figure 82.

Fig. 82. Hinge and slide for gate.

Fig. 83.

Fig. 84.

Figure 84 shows a very good and common hanging. The upper hinge consists of a hook in the post and a corresponding eye in the hinge-stile of the gate. The lower hinge is made of two semi-circular pieces of iron, each with a shank, one of which is shown above the gate in the engraving. They are made to play one into the other. This style of hanging may be used on any ordinary kind of gate, but is especially useful for a small street gate opening into a door-yard.

There is a style of gate for foot-paths, which is not uncommon, that keeps itself always closed and latched, by means of a single upper and double lower hinge, which are to be obtained at most hardware stores. The lower hinge has two "thumbs," which are embraced by two open sockets. When the gate is opened, it swings upon one socket and its thumb, and being thrown off the center, the weight of the gate draws it back, and swinging too, it latches. A farm gate, entirely home-made, may be constructed, of which figures 85 and 86 show the gate and the hinge. The gate is braced and supported by a stay-strip, extending to the top of the upright, which forms the upper hinge, *f,* being attached to the top of the gate-post, by an oak board with a smooth hole in it. The lower hinge is separately shown at Figure 86. It consists of an oak board, *c,* an inch and a half thick, into which the upright, *e,* is mortised. In this, two sockets are cut, a foot from center to center. The sockets in this case are three inches in diameter, and

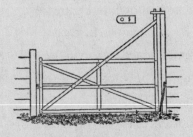

Fig. 85. Self-closing farm gate.

when the gate is in place and shut, they fit against two stakes of hardwood (locust), two and a half inches in diameter, *d*, which being curved, are nailed to the gate-post, *a*. A smooth stone, laid across in front of these

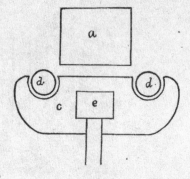

Fig. 86.   Lower hinge of gate.

stakes, takes the weight of the gate, and relieves in a measure the pressure on the top of the post. The hinges must be kept well-greased, and it is well to black-lead them also, to prevent creaking.

Rustic Gates

A picturesque rustic gate is shown in Figure 87. The fence and posts are made to correspond. Its manner of construction is clearly shown in the illustration. The vases on the top of the posts may be omitted, unless time can be taken to keep them properly watered.

A very neat, cheap, and strong rustic gate is shown in Figure 88. The large post and the two uprights of the gate are of red cedar. The horizontal bars may be of the same or other wood. The longer upright is five and a half feet long, the shorter one four and a half feet.

Fig. 87. Ornamental gate.

Fig. 88. Light rustic gate.

The ends of the former are cut down to serve as hinges, as shown in the engraving. Five holes are bored through each of the upright pieces, two inches in diameter, into which the ends of the horizontal bars are inserted and wedged securely. For the upper hinge a piece of plank is bored to receive the gate, and the other end reduced and driven into a hole in the post, or nailed securely to its top. A cedar block, into which a two-inch hole has been bored, is partially sunk in the ground to receive the lower end of the upright piece. A wooden latch is in better keeping with the gate than an iron one.

Gate Hinges of Wood

It is often convenient and economical, especially in newly settled regions, where blacksmiths and hardware stores are not at hand to supply hinges for gates, to make them of wood. The simplest and most primitive form is shown in figure 89. A post is selected having a large limb standing out nearly at right angles. A perpendicular hole in this secures the top of the rear gate standard. The foot rests in a stout short post, set against the main post. A small gimlet hole should extend outward and downward from the lowest side or point in the hole in the short post, to act as a drain, or the water collecting in it would be likely to soon rot both

Fig. 89.

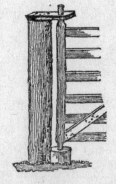

Fig. 90.

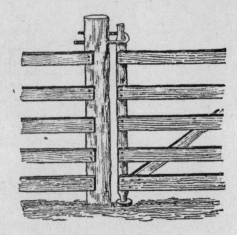

Fig. 91. A withe hinge.

Fig. 93. Socket hinges.

the standard and the short post itself. Another form is to hold the top by a strong wooden withe. A third form is illustrated in figure 90, in which the top of the standard passes, through a short piece of sawed or split plank, spiked or pinned upon the top of the post.

The form shown at figure 91 is made of a stout lithe sapling or limb of beech, hickory or other tough hard

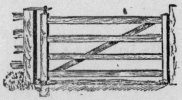

Fig. 92. Gate without hinges.

wood or, if it is attainable, a piece of iron rod.

A gate can be made without hinges by having the hanging stile somewhat longer than the front stile, and making both ends rounded. The lower one is to work in a hole in the end of a short post raised so that the soil will not readily get in, and the upper one works in a hole made in an oak piece attached to the top of the gate post. Gates of this kind can be made and hung with but little more expense than bars, and will be found far more convenient and saving of time than the latter.

Figure 93 represents a small hand-gate hung upon an iron pin driven into a hole bored in the bottom of the hinge-post, and one of similar size and material bent to a sharp angle, and fitted in the top. The lower pin rests in the sill and the upper one extends through the post to which the gate is hung.

A Good and Cheap Farm Gate

Figure 94 shows a gate of common fence boards and wire, which can be made by any farmer. The longer upright piece, seven feet long, may be made of a round stick, flattened a little on one side. The horizontal bars are of common fence

Fig. 94. Good and cheap farm gate.

boards cut to the desired length, and the shorter, vertical piece may be made of scantling, two by four inches. Three wires, either plain or barbed, are stretched at equal intervals between the upper and lower bar. A double length of wire is extended from the top of the long upright to the opposite lower corner of the gate. A stout stick is inserted between the two strands of this diagonal brace, by which it is twisted until it is sufficiently taut. If the gate should at any time begin to sag, a few turns brings it back.

Top Hinge of Farm Gate

Continual use, more or less slamming, and the action of the weather, make the gate settle somewhat, but the illustration, figure 95, shows a hinge which

Fig. 95. Top hinge of farm gate.

obviates this trouble. The upper hinge is made of a half-inch rod, about sixteen inches long, with an eye on one end, and a long screw-thread cut upon the other. This thread works in a nut, which nut has a bolt shank and nut, whereby it is firmly attached to the top bar of the gate. If the gate sags at all, it must be simply lifted off the thumbs, and the hinge given a turn or two in the nut; and the same is to be done in case of subsequent sagging. The hinge bolt must, of course, have some opportunity to move in the stile, and must be set long enough at first to allow the slack to be taken up whenever found necessary.

Strength of Bridges

Bridge building is a profession of itself, and some of the great bridges of the world are justly regarded as among the highest achievements of mechanical science and skill. But it is proposed to speak in this work only of the cheap and simple structures for spanning small streams. The measure of the strength of a bridge is that of its weakest part. Hence, the strength of a plain wooden bridge resting upon timber stringers or chords, is equivalent to the sustaining power of the timbers in the middle of the span. The longer the span, other things being equal, the less its strength. The following table shows the sustaining power of sound spruce timber, of the dimensions given, at a point midway between the supports:

A stick of timber twenty feet, between supports, will bear a load in its center only one half as great as a timber of the same dimensions, ten feet between supports. Thus four timbers six by twelve inches, in a span of sixteen feet, would bear a load of eight tons; in a twelve foot span, the same timbers would support a weight of nearly twelve tons.

Bridges for Gullies

Fig. 96. Frame for bridge.

For small gullies which cross roadways or lanes in farms, and are not the beds of constant streams, but are occasionally filled with surface water, a very simple bridge is sufficient. One like that shown in figure 96 is as good as any. The sills are sunk in a trench dug against the bank and at least to the level of the bed of the creek. The cross-sills are not mortised into them, but simply laid between them. The pressure is all from the outside, hence it will force the sills tighter against the ends, which must be sunk a little into the bed of the creek at its lowest point. The posts are mortised into the sills and plates, upon which the planks are laid. Props may be put against the lower sides of the posts to hold the bridge against the stream.

A cheap but practicable bridge is shown in figure 97. Two logs are laid across the gully, their ends resting on the banks, and to them puncheons or planks are spiked to form the bridge. Stout posts, well propped and reaching above the highest water mark, are placed against the lower side of the logs.

Length of Span.	Width and Thickness of Timber.			
	6 by 8 inches.	6 by 9 inches.	6 by 10 inches.	6 by 12 inches.
Feet.	Pounds.	Pounds.	Pounds.	Pounds.
10	2,800	2,692	4,500	6,480
12	2,400	3,042	3,750	5,400
14	2,058	2,604	3,216	4,632
16	1,800	2,280	2,808	4,050

Fig. 97. Convenient farm bridge.

If the creek rises, the bridge, being free, will be raised on the surface of the water, while the posts will prevent its being carried away. Should it not rise with the water, it opposes so little surface to the current that the posts will hold it fast.

Road Culverts

A culvert under a road is, in effect, a short bridge. The simplest form of plank culvert, resting upon stone abutments, is shown in figure 98. Such a structure is cheaply built, and serves a good purpose while the woodwork remains sound. But the planks wear out and the timbers decay, requiring frequent renewing. Where stone is abundant it is much cheaper in the end to build wholly of stone, as in figure 99. After the abutments are built, a course of flat stone, along each side, projects inward from six to ten inches, as at *a, a,* which are covered with a broad stone, *b.* Where the stream to be crossed is so narrow that a row of single stones

Fig. 98. Culvert with plank floor.

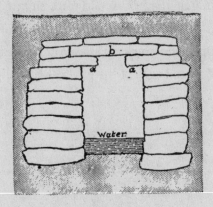

Fig. 99. Stone culvert.

is sufficient to cover the opening, a culvert like that seen in figure 100 is cheaply made. Such structures will remain serviceable for a generation, if the foundations are not undermined by the action of the water.

Where flat stones enough cannot be easily procured, culverts may be built of concrete. The abutments are first made, as in other cases; then empty barrels or sugar hogsheads, according to the capacity of the opening, are fitted in, or better still, a temporary arch is made of rough, narrow boards. The concrete of cement, sand and gravel, is then prepared and poured in, temporary supports of lumber having been fixed across each end of the culvert to keep the concrete in place until it hardens.

Small stones may be mixed with the concrete as it is poured into place, and the whole topped off with a row of them. This protection of stones on the top is valuable, in case the covering of earth is worn

Fig. 100. Cheaper stone culvert.

or wasted away at any time while it is in use. For a longer culvert a flattened arch is made of concrete, as shown in figure 101. Light timbers are laid across, the ends resting lightly on the abutments. Across the middle of these a round log is placed to support the crown of the arch. Elastic split poles are sprung over all, and upon these are nailed thin narrow boards, extending lengthwise of the culvert. The ends being temporarily protected, the concrete is mixed and poured on, as before. As soon as the concrete has

Fig. 101. Arched concrete culvert.

become thoroughly well "set," the light cross-sticks are cut in two and the temporary work removed. A cross-section, showing another form of concrete culvert, and the method of construction, are shown in figure 102. Such a culvert is more easily built than the last, but is not as strong. The best and most durable culvert is of stone, with a regular half-round arch. Such work can only be done properly by a regular mason, but in the end it is cheaper, where the stone can be obtained, than any kind of make-shift.

Fig. 102. Angular concrete culvert.

Shelters and Shanties

From *Shelters, Shacks, and Shanties* by Daniel Carter Beard, 1920

The Scout

Where birch bark is obtainable it is shingled with slabs of this bark as already described, and as shown in Fig. 17, the bark being held in place on the roof by poles laid over it and on the side by stakes being driven in the ground outside of the bark to hold it in place as in Fig. 17.

The Pioneer

Figure 18 shows the Pioneer, a tent form of shack, and figure 19 shows how the bark is placed like shingles overlapping each other so as to shed the rain. The doorway of the tent shack is made by leaning poles against forked sticks, their butts forming a semicircle in front, or rather the arc of a circle, and by bracing them against the forked stick fore and aft they add stability to the structure.

Bark Teepee

Or you may, if you choose, lash three sticks together at the top ends, spread them in the form of a tripod, then lay other sticks against them, their butts forming a circle in the form of a teepee (Fig. 20).

Commence at the bottom as you do in shingling a roof and place sections of birch bark around, others above them overlapping them, and hold them in place by resting poles against them.

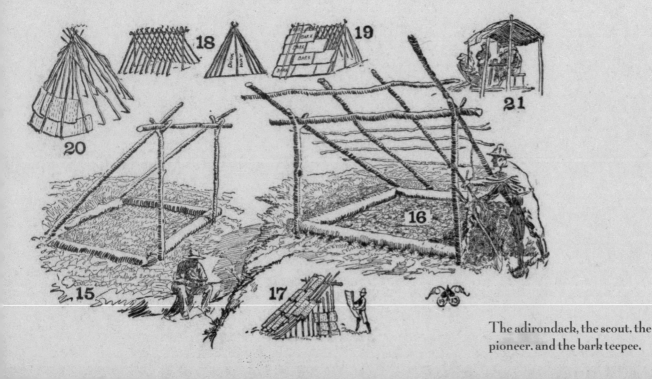

The adirondack, the scout, the pioneer, and the bark teepee.

If your camp is to be occupied for a week or so, it may be convenient to build a wick-up shelter as a dining room like the one shown in Fig. 21. This is made with six uprights, two to hold the ridge-pole and two to hold the eaves, and may be shingled over with browse or birch, elm, spruce, or other bark; shingle with the browse in the same manner as that described for the bark, beginning at the eaves and allowing each row of browse to overlap the butts of the one below it.

Apache Hogan

The White Mountain Apache builds a tent-shaped shack (Figs. 29 and 32) which is practically the same as that already described and shown in Figs. 18 and 19, the difference being that the Apache shack is not covered with birch bark, a material peculiar to the North, but the Apache uses a thatch of the rank grass to be found where his shacks are located. Today, however, the White Mountain Apache has become so degenerate and so lost to the true sense of dignity as a savage that he stoops to use corn-stalks with which to thatch the long, sloping sides of his shed-like house but by so doing he really shows good horse sense, for corn-stalks and corn leaves make good material for the purpose.

San Carlos Shack

The San Carlos Apache Indians build a dome-shaped hut by making a framework of small saplings bent in arches as the boys did in Kentucky when the writer was himself a lad, and as shown in Fig. 30. The ends of the pole are sunk into the ground in the form of a circle, while their tips are bent over and bound together thus forming a series of loops which overlap each other and give stability and support to the principal loops which

Designs adapted from indian models.

run from the ground to the top of the dome. The Indians thatch these huts with bear-grass arranged in overlapping rows and held in place with strings made of yucca leaves (Fig. 31).

Chippewa Shack

Much farther north I have seen the Chippewa Indians build a framework in practically the same manner as the San Carlos Apache, but the Chippewas covered their frame with layers of birch bark held in place by ropes stretched over it as shown in Fig. 32.

In the same locality today it would be difficult if not impossible to procure such large strips of birch bark; but the dome-shaped frame is a good one to be used in many localities and, like all other frames, it can be covered with the material at hand. It may be shingled with smaller pieces of bark, covered with brush and thatched with browse or with hay, straw, palmetto leaves, palm leaves, or rushes, or it may be plastered over with mud and made to adobe hut.

Pima Lodge

The Pima Indians make a flat-roofed lodge with slanting walls (Fig. 33) which may be adapted for our use in almost any section of the country. It can be made warm and tight for the far North and cool and airy for the arid regions of the Southwest. The framework, as you may see by referring to the diagram, is similar to the wick-ups we men made when we were boys, and which are described in the "American Boy's Handy Book," consisting of four upright posts supporting in their crotches two crosspieces over which a flat roof is made by placing poles across. But the sides of this shack are not upright but made by resting leaning poles against the eaves.

The Pontiac

The Pontiac, as here given, is my own design and invention (Fig. 36). It is supposed to be shingled with birch bark, but, as is the case with all these camps, other bark may be substituted for the birch, and, if no bark is within reach and you are near enough to civilization, tar paper makes an excellent substitute. Fig. 37 shows the framework of a Pontiac with a ridgepole, but the ridgepole is not necessary and the shack may be built without it, as shown in Figs. 36 and 39, where the rafter poles rest upon the two side-plates over which they project to form the apex of the roof. In Fig. 39, although the side-plates are drawn, the rafter or roof poles are not because the diagram is supposed to be a sort of X-ray affair to show the internal construction. The opening for smoke need not be more than half as large as it is in Fig. 39 and it may be covered up in inclement weather with a piece of bark so as to keep out the rain.

Cutting Bark

Figure 38 shows a tree felled in order to procure bark. You will note that the bark is cut round at the bottom and at the top and a slit is made connecting the two cuts as already described so that the bark may be peeled off by running a blunt instrument or a stick, whittled to the shape of a paper-cutter or dull chisel, under the edge of the bark and carefully peeling it back. If it is necessary to "tote" the bark any distance over the trail, figure 38 shows how to roll it up and how to bind the roll with cord or rope so that it may be slung on the back as the man is "toting" it in figure 36.

Building the Pontiac

To build a Pontiac, first erect the uprights E and E, figure 37, then the other two similar uprights at the rear and lay the side-plates *G* in the forks of the uprights; next erect the upright *H* and one in the rear to correspond, and across this lay the ridge-pole. Next take a couple of logs and put them at the foot of the *E* poles, or, if you want more room, further back toward where the roof poles *F* will come. Place one of these logs on top of the other as shown in Figs. 36 and 39. Keep them in place by driving sticks on each side of them. Put two more logs upon the other side of the Pontiac and then lay your roof poles or rafters up against the side-plates and over the logs as shown in diagrams 36, 37, and 39. Fig. 36 shows the roof partially shingled and the sides partially covered, so that you may better understand how it is done.

Shingling with Bark

Commence at the bottom and lay the first row with the edges overlapping for walls; for the roof you may lay one row of shingles from the bottom up to the ridge and hold them in place by resting a pole on them; then lay the next row of shingles alongside by slipping the edges under the first. When you have the two sides covered, put bark over the ridge as shown in Fig. 36. This will make a beautiful and comfortable little camp.

The pontiac of birch bark.

To Keep Out Cold

Built as here described, the cold wind might come through in the winter-time, but if you can gather a lot of Sphagnum moss from the nearest swamp and cover your roof with it and then shingle that over with another layer of birch bark, the cold wind will not come through your roof. If you treat your side walls in the same manner and heap dirt up around the edges of them, you will have a comfortable winter camp.

In the wintertime you will find it very difficult to peel the birch bark or any other kind of bark, but when the sap is flowing it is not so difficult to secure bark slabs from many varieties of trees.

The Pawnee Hogan

The Pawnee hogan is usually covered with sod or dirt, but it may be covered with bark, with canvas, or thatched with straw or with browse, as the camper may choose. Figure 42 shows the framework in the skeleton form. The rafter poles are placed wigwam fashion and should be very close together in the finished structure; so also should be the short sticks forming the side walls and the walls to the hallway or entrance. To build this hogan, first erect a circle of short forked sticks, setting their ends firmly in the ground. Inside of this, erect four longer forked sticks, then place across these four horizontal side-plates, or maybe they might be more properly called "purlins," in which case the sticks laid on the forks of the circle of small uprights will properly correspond to the side-plates of a white man's dwelling. After the circle and square

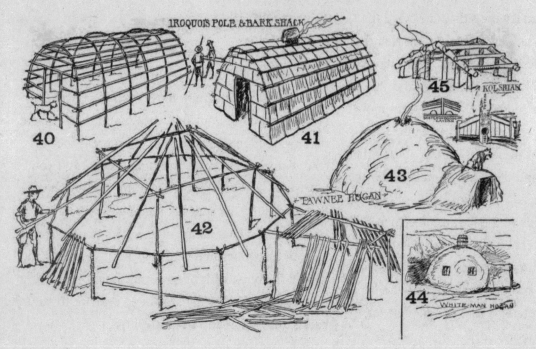

IROQUOIS POLE & BARK SHACK

40

41

42

43

45 KOLSHIAN

PAWNEE HOGAN

44 WHITE-MAN HOGAN

The iroquois, the pawnee hogan, the white man's hogan, and the kolshian.

(Fig. 42) have been erected, make your doorway with two short-forked sticks and your hallway by sticks running from the door to side-plates. In thatching your roof or in covering it with any sort of material, leave an opening at the top (Fig. 43) to act as a chimney for your centre camp-fire. If the roof is to be covered with sod or adobe, cover it first with browse, hay, straw, or rushes, making a thick mattress over the entire structure. On top of this plaster your mud or sod (Fig. 43). If you intend to use this hogan as a more or less permanent camp you can put windows in the sides to admit light and air and use a hollow log or a barrel for a chimney as shown in figure 44.

The Kolshian

The camps thus far described are supposed to be "tomahawk camps," that is, camps which may be built without the use of a lumberman's axe. The kolshian (Fig. 45) of Alaska, when built by the natives, is a large communal council-house, but I have placed it here among the "tomahawk camps" on the supposition that someone might want to build one in miniature as a novelty on their place or as a

council-room for their young scouts. The Alaskans hew all the timber out by hand, but, of course, the reader may use sawed or milled lumber. The proper entrance to a kolshian or rancheree, as Elliot calls it, is through a doorway made in the huge totem-pole at the front of the building. The roof is covered with splits or shakes held in place by poles laid across them, the sides are made of hewn planks set upright, and the front has two heavy-planks at the eaves which run down through holes in two upright planks at the corners (Fig. 45). These with the sill plank bind the upright wall planks in place.

The kolshian is undoubtedly a very ancient form of building and may be related to the houses built by the ancient cavemen of Europe. The first human house-builders are said to belong to the Cro-Magnon race who lived in caves in the winter-time, and on the walls of one of the caverns (Dordogne cavern) some Cro-Magnon budding architect made a rough sketch of one of their houses (middle sketch, Fig. 45). When you compare the house with the kolshian the resemblance is very striking, and more so when we remember that the kolshian floor is underground, indicating that it is related to or suggested by a natural cavern.

Bark and Tar Paper

To further illustrate the use of bark and tar paper, I have made the sketches shown by Figs. 46, 47, and 48. Fig. 47 is a log shack with an arched roof drawn from a photograph in my collection. To keep the interior warm not only the roof but the sides of the house as well have been shingled with bark, leaving only the ends of the logs protruding to tell of what material the house is really constructed. Figure 47 shows a fisherman's hut made with a few sticks and bark. Figure 48 shows a tar paper camp, that is, a camp where everything is covered with tar paper in place of bark. The house is made with a skeleton of poles on which the tar paper is tacked, the kitchen is an open shed with tar paper roof, and even the table is made by covering the cross sticks shown in the diagram with sheets of tar paper in place of the birch bark usually used for that purpose.

Personally I do not like tar paper; it seems to rob the camp of a true flavor of the woods; it knocks the sentiment out of it, and, except to sailors, the odor of the tar is not nearly as delightful as that of the fragrant balsam boughs. Nevertheless, tar paper is now used in all the lumber camps and is spreading farther and farther into the woods as the birch bark becomes scarce and the "tote-roads" are improved.

When one can enter the woods with an automobile, you must expect to find tar paper camps, because the paper is easily transported, easily handled, and easily applied for the purpose of the camper.

Practically any form of tent may be reproduced by tacking tar paper to sticks arranged in the proper manner, but if you make a wigwam of tar paper, do paint it red, green, or yellow, or whitewash it; do anything which will take off the civilized, funereal look of the affair.

A Sawed-Lumber Shanty

Before we proceed any further it may be best to give the plan of a workshop, a camp, an outhouse, or a shed to be made of sawed lumber, the framework of which is made of what is known as two-by-fours, that is, pieces of lumber two inches thick by four inches wide. The plans used here are from my book "The Jack of All Trades," but the dimensions may be altered to suit your convenience. The sills, which are four inches by four inches, are also supposed to be made by nailing two two-by-fours together. First stake out your foundation and see that the corners are square, that is, at right angles, and test this with a tape or ruler by measuring six feet one way and eight feet the other from a corner along the proposed sides of the house marking these points. If a ten-foot rod will reach exactly across from point to point, the corner is square and you may dig your post-holes.

Showing use of bark and tar paper.

The Foundation

You may use a foundation of stones or a series of stone piles, but if you use stones and expect your house to remain plumb where the winters are severe you must dig holes for them at least three feet deep in order to go below the frost-line. Fill these holes with broken stone, on top of which you can make your pile of stones to act as support for the sills; but the simplest method is to use posts of locust, cedar, or chestnut; or, if this is too much trouble, pack the dirt tightly, drain it well by making it slope away from the house in every direction, and lay your foundation sills on the level earth. In that case you had better use chestnut wood for the sills; spruce will rot very quickly in contact with the damp earth and pine will not last long under the same circumstances.

All through certain sections of this country there are hundreds of humble dwellings built upon "mudsills," in other words, with no foundation or floor but the bare ground.

We will suppose that you have secured some posts about two feet six inches long with good, flat ends. The better material you can obtain the trimmer and better will be the appearance of your house, but a house which will protect you and your tools may be made of the roughest lumber.

The plans here drawn will answer for the rough or fine material, but we suppose that medium material is to be used. It will be taken for granted that the reader is able to procure enough two-by-four-inch timber to supply studs, ribs, purlins, rafters, beams, and posts for the frame shown in Fig. 49. Two pieces of four-by-four-inch timber each fifteen feet long should be made for sills by nailing two-by-fours together. Add to this some tongue-and-grooved boarding or even, rough boards for sides and roof, some enthusiasm, and good American pluck and the shop is almost as good as built.

First lay the foundation, eight by fifteen feet, and then you may proceed to dig your post-holes. The outside of one of the posts should be flush or even with the outside edges of the sills and end beams of the house as shown in the diagram. If there are four posts on each of the long sides they should be equal distances apart.

Dig the holes three feet deep, allowing six inches of the posts to protrude above ground. If you drive two stakes a short distance beyond the foundation in line with your foundation lines and run a string from the top of one stake to the top of the other you can, without much trouble, get it upon a perfect level by testing it and adjusting until the string represents the level for your sill. When this is done, set your posts to correspond to the level of the string, then place your sill on top of the posts and test that with your level. If found to be correct, fill

Frame of two-by-fours milled lumber, with names of parts.

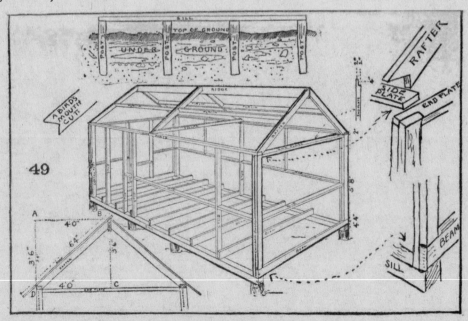

in the dirt around the posts and pack it firmly, then spike your sill to the posts and go through the same operation with opposite sets of posts and sill.

The first difficult work is now done and, with the exception of the roof, the rest only needs ordinary care.

It is supposed that you have already sawed off and prepared about nine two-by-four-inch beams, each of which is exactly eight feet long. Set these on edge from sill to sill, equal distances apart, the edges of the end beams being exactly even with the ends of the sills as in Fig. 49. See that the beams all cross the sills at right angles and toe-nail them in place. You may now neatly floor the foundation with one-inch boards; these boards must be laid lengthwise with the building and crosswise with the beams. When this is finished you will have a beautiful platform on which to work, where you will be in no danger of losing your tools, and you may use the floor as a table on which to measure and plan the sides and roof.

Ridge Plank and Rafters

It is a good idea to make your ridge plank and rafters while the floor is clear of rubbish. Lay out and mark on the floor, with a carpenter's soft pencil, a straight line four feet long (A, B, Fig. 49). At right angles to this draw another line three feet six inches long (A, D, Fig. 49). Connect these points (B, D, Fig. 49) with a straight line, then complete the figure A, B, C, D (Fig. 49). Allow two inches at the top for the ridge plank at B and two by four for the end of the side-plate at D. You then have a pattern for each rafter with a "plumb edge" at B and a "bird's mouth" at D. The plumb edge must be parallel with B, C and the two jaws of the "bird's mouth" parallel with D, C and A, D, respectively. Make six rafters of two-by-fours and one ridge plank.

The purlins and collar can be made and fitted after the roof is raised. Set your roof timber carefully to one side and clear the floor for the studs, ribs, and

plates. First prepare the end posts and make them of two-by-fours. Each post is of two pieces. There will be four outside pieces each five feet, eight inches in length, which rest on the end beams, and four inside pieces each six feet in length; this allows two inches at the top for the ends of the end plates to rest upon.

Examine the corner posts and you will see that the outside two-by-four rests upon the top side of the end beam and the side-plate rests directly upon said two-by-four. You will also observe that the inside two-by-four rests directly upon the sill, which would make the former four inches longer than the outside piece if it is extended to the side-plate; but you will also notice that there is a notch in the end plate for the outside corner piece to fit in and that the end of the end plate fits on top the inside piece of the corner posts, taking off two inches, which makes the inside piece just six feet long. This is a very simple arrangement, as may be seen by examining the diagram. Besides the corner posts, each of which we have seen is made of two pieces of two-by-fours, there are four studs for the front side, each six feet, two inches long. The short studs shown in the diagram on the rear side are unnecessary and are only shown so that they may be put in as convenient attachments for shelves and tool racks.

The first stud on the front is placed two feet from the corner post and the second one about six feet six inches from the first, to allow a space for a six-foot window; the next two studs form the door-jambs and must be far enough from the corner to allow the door to open and swing out of the way. If you make your door two and one half feet wide—a good size—you may set your last stud two feet from the corner post and leave a space of two feet six inches for the doorway. Now mark off on the floor the places where the studs will come, and cut out the flooring at these points to allow the ends of the studs to enter and rest on the sill. Next make four ribs—one long one to go beneath the window, one short one to fit between the corner post and the door stud not shown in diagram, another to fit between the door stud and window stud, and another to fit between the window stud and the first corner post (the nearest corner in the diagram). Next make your side-plate exactly fifteen feet long. Fit the frame together on the floor and nail the pieces together, toe-nailing the ribs in place. Get some help and raise the whole side frame and slip the ends of the studs into their respective slots. Make the end posts plumb and hold them in place temporarily by a board, one end of which is nailed to the top end of the post and the other to the end beam. Such a diagonal board at each end will hold the side in place until the opposite side is raised and similarly supported.

It is now a simple thing to slip the end plates in place under the side-plates until their outside edges are even with the outside of the corner posts. A long wire nail driven through the top-plates and end plates down into the posts at each corner will hold them securely. Toenail a rib between the two nearest end posts and make two window studs and three ribs for the opposite end. The framing now only needs the roof timbers to complete the skeleton of your shop. Across from side-plate to side-plate lay some loose boards for a platform, and standing on these boards let your assistant lift one end of the ridge plank while with one nail to each rafter you fasten the two end rafters onto the ridge plank, fit the jaws of the "bird's mouth" over the ends of the side-plates, and hold them temporarily in place with a "stay lath"—that is, a piece of board temporarily nailed to rafter and end plate. The other end of the ridge is now resting on the platform at the other end of the house and this may be lifted up, for the single nails will allow movement.

The rafters are nailed in place with one nail each and a stay lath fastened on to hold them in place. Test the ends with your plumb-level and when they are found to be correct nail all the rafters securely in place and stiffen the centre pair with a piece called a "collar." Add four purlins set at right angles to the rafters and take off your hat and give three cheers and do not forget to nail a green bough to your roof tree in accordance with the ancient and time-honored custom.

The sides of the house may be covered with tent-cloth, oilcloth, tin, tar paper, or the cheapest sort of lumber, and the house may be roofed with the same material; but if you can secure good lumber, use thirteen by seven eighths by nine and one quarter inch, tongue-and-grooved, one side planed so that it may be painted; you can make two sideboards out of each piece six feet six inches in length. Nail the sides on, running the boards vertically, leaving openings for windows and doors at the proper places.

If you have made a triangular edge to your ridge board, it will add to the finish and the roof may be neatly and tightly laid with the upper edge of one side protruding a couple of inches over the opposite side and thus protecting the joint from rain. Additional security is gained by nailing what are called picket strips (seven eighths by one and three quarter inches) over each place where the planks join, or the roof may be covered with sheathing boards and shingles. It is not necessary here to give the many details such as the manufacture of the door and the arrangements of the windows, as these small problems can be easily solved by examining doors and windows of similar structures.

A Sod House for the Lawn

The difference between this sod house and the ones used in the arid regions consists in the fact that the sod will be growing on the sod house, which is intended for and is an ornamental building for the lawn. Possibly one might say that the sod house is an effete product of civilization where utility is sacrificed to display; but it is pretty, and beauty is always worthwhile; besides which the same plans may be used in building.

A Real Adobe

The principal difference in construction between the one shown in Figs. 50, 53, and 57 and the one in Fig. 55 is that in the sod house the sod is held in place by chicken-coop wire, while in the ranch-house (Fig. 55) the dirt or adobe is held in place by a number of sticks.

Fig. 50 shows how the double walls are made with a space of at least a foot between them; these walls are covered with wire netting or chicken-coop wire, as shown in Fig. 53, and the space between the walls filled in with mud or dirt of any kind. The framework may be made of milled lumber, as in Fig. 50, or it may be made of saplings cut on the river bank and squared at their ends, as shown by detailed drawings between Figs. 50 and 52. The roof may be made flat, like figures 54 and 56, and covered with poles, as in Fig. 54, in which case the sod will have to be held in place by pegging other poles along the eaves as shown in the left-hand corner of Fig. 54. This will keep the sod from sliding off the roof. Or you may build a roof after the manner illustrated by Fig. 49 and Fig. 51, that is, if you want to make a neat, workmanlike house; but any of the ways shown by Fig. 52 will answer for the framework of the roof. The steep roof, however, must necessarily be either shingled or thatched or

the sod held in place by a covering of wire netting. If you are building this for your lawn, set green, growing sod up edgewise against the wire netting, after the latter has been tacked to your frame, so arranging the sod that the green grass will face the outside. If you wish to plaster the inside of your house with cement or concrete, fill in behind with mud, plaster the mud against the sod and put gravel and stones against the mud so that it will be next to the wire netting on the inside of the house over which you plaster the concrete. If you make the roof shown in Fig. 54, cover it first with hay and then dirt and sod and hold the sod down with wire netting neatly tacked over it, or cover it with gravel held in place by wire netting and spread concrete over the top as one does on a cellar floor. If the walls are kept sprinkled by the help of the garden hose, the grass will keep as green as that on your lawn, and if you have a dirt roof you may allow purple asters and goldenrod to grow upon it (Fig. 62) or plant it with garden flowers.

Thatch

If you are going to make a thatched roof, soak your thatch in water and straighten the bent straws; build the roof steep like the one shown in Fig. 57 and make a wooden needle a foot long and pointed at both ends as shown in Fig. 59; tie your thatching twine to the middle of the needle, then take your rye or wheat straw, hay, or bulrushes, gather it into bundles four inches thick and one foot wide, like those shown in Fig. 60, and lay them along next to the eaves of your house as in Fig. 58. Sew them in place by running the needle up through the wire netting to the person on the outside who in turn pushes it back to the person on the inside. Make a knot at each wisp of the thatch until one layer is finished, then let the lower ends overhang the eaves.

If in place of a simple ornament you want to make a real house of it and a pretty one at that, fill up the space between the walls with mud and plaster it on the outside with cement or concrete and you will have a cheap concrete house. The wire netting will hold the plaster or the concrete and consequently it is not necessary to make the covering of cement as thick as in ordinary buildings, for after the mud is dried upon the inside it will, with its crust of cement or plaster, be practically as good as a solid concrete wall.

Tree-Top Houses

By the natural process of evolution we have now arrived at the tree-top house. It is interesting to the writer to see the popularity of this style of an outdoor building, for, while he cannot lay claim to originating it, he was the first to publish the working drawings of a tree-house. These plans first appeared in *Harper's Round Table;* afterward he made others for the *Ladies' Home Journal* and later published them in "The Jack of All Trades."

Having occasion to travel across the continent shortly after the first plans were published, he was amused to see all along the route, here and there in back-yard fruit-trees, shade-trees, and in forest-trees, queer little shanties built by the boys, high up among the boughs.

In order to build a house one must make one's plans *to fit the tree.* If it is to be a one-tree house, spike on the trunk two quartered pieces of small log one on each side of the trunk (Figs. 91 and 92). Across these lay a couple of poles and nail them to the trunk of the tree (Fig. 91); then at right angles to these lay another pair of poles, as shown in the right-hand diagram (Fig. 91). Nail these securely in place and support the ends of the four poles by braces nailed to the trunk of the tree below. The four cross-sills will then (Fig. 95) serve as a foundation upon which to begin your work. Other joists can now be laid across these first and supported by braces running diagonally down to the trunk of the tree, as shown in Fig. 95. After the floor is laid over the joist any form of shack, from a rude, open shed to a picturesque thatch-roofed cottage, may be erected upon it. It is well to support the two middle rafters of your roof by quartered pieces of logs, as the middle rafters are supported in Fig. 95; by quartered logs shown in Fig. 92.

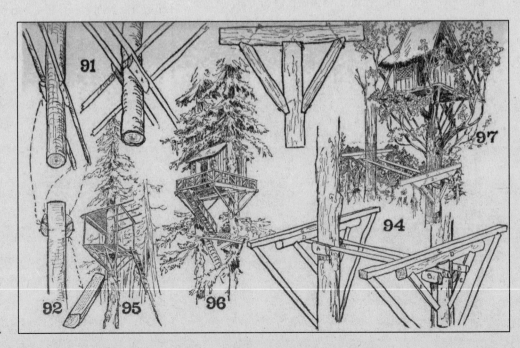

Details of tree-top houses.

If the house is a two-tree house, run your cross-sill sticks from trunk to trunk, as in figure 94; then make two T-braces, like the one in figure 94 A, of two-inch planks with braces secured by iron straps, or use heavier timber, and bolt the parts together securely (Fig. 93), or use logs and poles (Fig. 94), after which hang these T's over the ends of your two cross sticks, as in figure 94, and spike the uprights of the T's securely to the tree trunks. On top of the T you can rest a two-by-four and support the end by diagonals nailed to the tree trunk (Fig. 94) after the manner of the diagonals in Fig. 95. You will note in Fig. 95 that cleats or blocks are spiked to the tree below the end of the diagonals in order to further secure them. It is sometimes necessary in a two-tree house to allow for the movement of the tree trunks. In Florida a gentleman did this by building his tree-house on the B sills (Fig. 94) and making them movable to allow for the play of the tree trunks. Fig. 96 shows a two-tree house and Fig. 97 shows a thatch-roofed cottage built among the top branches of a single tree.

It goes without saying that in a high wind one does not want to stay long in a tree-top house; in fact, during some winds that I have experienced I would have felt much safer had I been in a cyclone cellar; but if the braces of a tree-house are securely made and the trees selected have good, heavy trunks, your tree-top house will stand all the ordinary summer blows and winter storms. One must remember that even one's own home is not secure enough to stand some of those extraordinary gales, tornadoes, and hurricanes, which occasionally visit parts of our country.

The most important thing about all this is that a tree-house is always a source of delight to the children and young people, and, furthermore, the children have over and over again proved to the satisfaction of the author that they themselves are perfectly competent to build these shacks, and not only to build them but to avoid accidents and serious falls while engaged in the work.

How to Use an Axe

The old backwoodsmen were as expert with their axes as they were with their rifles and they were just as careful in the selection of these tools as they were in the selection of their arms. Many a time I have seen them pick up a "store" axe, sight along the handle, and then cast it contemptuously aside; they demanded of their axes that the cutting edge should be exactly in line with the point in the centre of the butt end of the handle. They also kept their axes so sharp that they could whittle with them like one can with a good jack-knife; furthermore, they allowed *no one* but themselves to use their own particular axe. In my log house in the mountains of Pike County, Pa., I have a table fashioned entirely with an axe; even the ends of the boards which form the top of the table were cut off by Siley Rosencranz with his trusty axe because he had no saw.

Both General Grant and Abraham Lincoln were expert axemen, and probably a number of other Presidents were also skilful in the use of this tool; but it is not expected that the modern vacation pioneer shall be an expert, consequently a few simple rules and suggestions will be here given to guide the amateur and he must depend upon his own judgment and common sense to work out the minor problems which will beset him in the use of this tool.

Dangers

All edged tools are dangerous when in the hands of "chumps," dangerous to themselves and to anyone else who is near them. For instance, only a chump will use an axe when its head is loose and is in danger of flying off the handle; only a chump will use his *best* axe to cut roots or sticks lying flat on the ground where he is liable to strike stones and other objects and take the edge off the blade. Only a chump will leave an axe lying around on the ground for people to stumble over; if there is a stump handy at your camp and you are through using the axe, strike the blade into the top of the stump and leave the axe sticking there, where it will be safe from injury.

Remember, before chopping down a tree or before using the axe at all, to see that there is enough space above and around you to enable you to swing the axe clear (Fig. 112) without the danger of striking bushes or overhanging branches which may deflect the blade and cause accidents more or less serious.

Do not stand behind a tree as it falls (Fig. 115), for the boughs may strike those of a standing tree, causing the butt to shoot back or "kick," and many a woodsman has lost his life from the kick of a falling tree. Before chopping a tree down, select the place where it is to fall, a place where it will not be liable to lodge in another tree on its way down. Do not try to fell a tree against the wind.

Cut a notch on the side of the tree facing the direction you wish it to fall (Fig. 113) and cut it half-way through the trunk. Make the notch, or kerf, large enough to avoid pinching your axe in it. If you discover that the notch is going to be too small, cut a new notch, X (Fig. 116), some inches above your first one, then split off the piece X, Y between the

two notches, and again make the notch X, Z, and split off the piece Z, W, Y (Fig. 116), until you make room for the axe to continue your chopping. When the first kerf is finished, begin another one on the opposite side of the tree a little higher than the first one (Fig. 114). When the wood between the two notches becomes too small to support the weight of the tree, the top of the tree will begin to tremble and waver and give you plenty of time to step to one side before it falls.

If the tree (Fig. 117) is inclined in the opposite direction from which you wish it to fall, it is sometimes possible (Fig. 117) to block up the kerf on the inclined side, and then by driving the wedge over the block, force the tree to fall in the direction desired; but if the tree inclines too far this cannot be done.

There was a chestnut-tree standing close to my log house and leaning toward the building. Under ordinary circumstances felling this tree would cause it to strike the house with all the weight of its trunk and branches. When I told Siley Rosencranz I wanted that tree cut down, he sighted up the tree, took a chew of tobacco, and walked away. For several days he went through the same performance, until at last one day he brought out his trusty axe and made the chips fly. Soon the chestnut was lying prone on the ground *pointing away* from the house. What this old backwoodsman did was to wait until a strong wind had sprung up, blowing in the direction that he wanted the tree to fall, and his skilful chopping with

How to "fall" a tree and how to take off the bark.

the aid of the wind placed the tree exactly where he wished it.

Fig. 118 shows how to make the cuts on a standing tree in order to remove the bark, which is done in the same manner as that described for removing the birch bark (Fig. 38).

Railroad-Tie Shacks, Barrel Shacks, and Chimehuevis

No observing person has travelled far upon the American railroads without noticing, alongside the tracks, the queer little houses built of railroad ties by Italian laborers. These shacks are known by the name of dagoes (Fig. 136) and are made in different forms, according to the ingenuity of the builder. The simplest form is the tent-shaped shown in Fig. 136, with the ends of the ties rested together in the form of a tent and with no other support but their own weight (see the diagram to the right, Fig. 136). I would not advise children to build this style, because it might make a trap to fall in upon them with serious results, but if they use a ridge-pole like the one shown in Fig. 139 and against it rest the ties, they will do away with the danger of being caught in a deadfall trap. Of course, it is understood that the ridge-pole itself must first be secure.

Railroad ties being flat (Fig. 137), they may be built up into solid walls (Fig. 137) and make neat sides for a little house; or they may be set up on edge (Fig. 138) and secured in place by stakes driven upon each side of them; or they may be made into the form of an open Adirondack camp (Figs. 139 and 140) by resting the ties on a ridge-pole supported by a pair of "shears" at each end; the shears, as you will observe, consist of two sticks bound together near the top and then spread apart to receive the ridge-pole in the crotch.

All of these structures are usually covered with dirt and sod, and they make very comfortable little camps.

In the Southwest a simple shelter, the "Chimehuevis," is made by enclosing a room in upright poles (Fig. 141) and then surrounding it with a circle of poles supporting a log or pole roof covered with sod, making a good camp for hot weather.

Fig. 142 shows a barrel dugout. It is made by digging a place for it in the bank and, after the floor is leveled off, setting rows of barrels around the foundation, filling these barrels with sand, gravel, or dirt, then placing another row on top of the first, leaving spaces for a window and a door, after which the walls are roofed with logs and covered with sod, in the same manner as the ones previously described. The dirt is next filled around the sides, except at the window opening, as shown by Fig. 142. A barrel also does duty as a chimney.

Shacks like this are used by homesteaders, miners, trappers, and hunters; in

Railroad-tie shacks, barrel shack, and a chimehuevis.

fact, these people use any sort of material they have at hand. When a mining-camp is near by the freight wagons are constantly bringing in supplies, and these supplies are done up in packages of some kind. Boards are frequently worth more a yard than silk, or were in the olden days, and so the home builders used other material. They built themselves houses of discarded beer bottles, of kerosene cans, of packing-boxes, of any and every thing. Usually these houses were dugouts, as is the barrel one shown in Fig. 142. In the big-tree country they not infrequently made a house of a hollow stump of a large redwood, and one stone-mason hollowed out a huge boulder for his dwelling; but such shacks belong among the freak shelters. The barrel one, however, being the more practical and one that can be used almost anywhere where timber is scarce but where goods are transported in barrels, deserves a place here among our shacks, shelters, and shanties.

How to Cut and Notch Logs

You have now passed through the *grammar school* of shack making, you are older than you were when you began, you have acquired more skill and more muscle, and it is time to begin to handle the woodsman's axe, to handle it skillfully and to use it as a tool with which to fashion anything from a table to a two-story house. None of you is too young to learn to use the axe. General Grant, George Washington, Abraham Lincoln, Billy Sunday—all of them could wield an axe by the time they were eight or nine years old and do it without chopping off their toes or splitting anyone else's head open. Remember that every time you hurt yourself with an axe I have a yellow ribbon for you to wear as a "chump mark"; but, joking aside, we must now get down to serious work of preparing the logs in order to build us a little cabin of our own, a log club-house for our gang, or a log camp for our troop of scouts.

Notching Logs

To make the logs, hold together at the corners of our cabins it is necessary to lock them in some manner, and the usual way is to notch them. You may cut flat notches like those shown in Fig. 162 and this will hold the logs together, as shown by 162 E, or you may only flatten the ends, making the General Putnam joint shown in Fig. 163.

This is called after General Putnam because the log cabins at his old camp near my farm at Redding, Conn., are made in this manner. Or you may use the Pike notch which has a wedge-shaped cut on the lower log, as shown by Fig. 164 J, made to fit into a triangular notch shown by 164 H. When fitted together these logs look like the sketch marked 164 F which was drawn from a cabin built in this manner.

But the simplest notch is the rounded one shown by A, B, and C (Fig. 165). When these are locked together they will fit like those shown at Fig. 165 D.

Way up North the people dovetail the ends of the logs (Fig. 166) so that their ends fit snugly together and are also securely locked by their dovetail shape. To build a log house, place the two sill logs on the ground or on the foundation made for them, then two other logs across them, as shown in Fig. 168.

Handling the Logs

That the logs may be more easily handled they should be piled up on a skidway which is made by resting the top ends of a number of poles upon a big log or some other sort of elevation and their lower ends upon the ground. With this arrangement the logs may be rolled off without much trouble as they are used.

Chinking

A log cabin built with hardwood logs or with pitch-pine logs can seldom be made as tight as

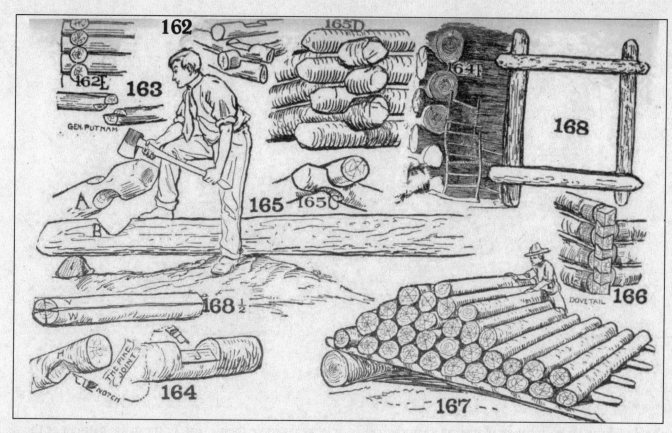

Showing how the logs are notched.

one built with the straight spruce logs of the virgin forests. The latter will lie as close as the ones shown in Fig. 162 E, while the former, on account of their unevenness, will have large cracks between them like those shown in Fig. 165 D. These cracks may be stopped up by quartering small pieces of timber (Y and W, Fig. 168½) and fitting these quartered pieces into the cracks between the logs where they are held by spikes. This is called "chinking the cabin."

To keep the cold and wind out, the cracks may be "mudded" up on the inside with clay or ordinary lime mortar.

Models

Study these diagrams carefully, then sit down on the ground with a pile of little sticks alongside of you and a sharp jack-knife in your hand and proceed to experiment by building miniature log cabins. Really, this is the best way to plan a large

cabin if you intend to erect one. From your model you can see at a glance just how to divide your cabin up into rooms, where you want to place the fireplace, windows, and doors; and I would advise you always to make a small model before building. Make the model about one foot three inches long by ten inches wide, using sticks for logs a little less than one inch in diameter—that is, one inch through or one inch thick. I have taken these dimensions or measurements from a little model that I have before me here in my studio, but, of course, you can vary them according to the plans of your cabin.

Christopher Gist

The next camp is the Christopher Gist, named after George Washington's camping friend. This camp, as you may see by Fig. 191, is built like a New Brunswick except that the side sill logs are much longer as is also the log which extends over

The stages in the evolution of a log cabin.

the doorway. Then, in place of having a wind-shield built by itself, the wind-shield in Fig. 191 is the other end of the cabin built just the same as the rear end, but it should be built of peeled logs as they are less liable to catch afire than the ones with the bark upon them. If you feel really lazy it will only be necessary to peel the bark off from the inside half of the log. Above the door at the end of the roof of the Adirondack camp part of the space is filled by logs running across, with the lower one resting upon the top of the door-jamb; this closes the shed above the wind-shield and leaves a little open yard in front wherein to build your camp-fire.

The Red Jacket

The Red Jacket continues the suggestion offered by the Christopher Gist and extends the side walls all the way across to the wind-shield, and the latter now becomes the true end of the log shack. The side walls and end wall are built up from the top of the shack to form a big, wide log chimney under which the open camp-fire is built on the ground. The Red

Jacket is roofed with bark in the same manner as the New Brunswick and Christopher Gist and occupies the important position of the missing link between the true log cabin or log house and the rude log camp of the hunter. If you will look at Fig. 184, the open-faced log camp; then Fig. 190, the camp with the wind-shield in front of it; then Fig. 191 with the wind-shield enclosed but still open at the top; then 192 where the wind-shield has turned into a fireplace with a chimney; then Figs. 271 and 273, showing the ends of the real log cabin, you will have all the steps in the growth or evolution which has produced the American log house.

The American Log Cabin

Now that we know how to make doors and door-latches, locks, bolts, and bars, we may busy ourselves with building an American log cabin. It is all well enough to build our shacks and shanties and camps of logs with the bark on them, but, when one wishes to build a log cabin, one wants a house that will last. Abraham Lincoln's log cabin is still in existence, but it was built of logs with no bark on them. There is a two-story log house still standing in Dayton, O.; it is said to have been built before the town was there; but there is no bark on the logs. Bark holds moisture and moisture creates decay by inviting fibrous and threadlike cousins of the toadstool to grow on the damp wood and work their way into its substance. The bark also shelters all sorts of boring insects and the boring insects make holes through the logs which admit the rain and in the end cause decay, so that the first thing to remember is to peel the logs of which you propose to build the cabin. There is now, or was lately, a log cabin on Hempstead Plains, L. I., near the road leading from Mineola to Manhasset; it is supposed to have been built when the first white settlers began to arrive on Long Island, but this was what was known as a "blockhouse," a small fort. In 1906 Mr. I. P. Sapington said: "I think that I am the only man now living who helped build General Grant's log cabin." Grant's house was what is popularly known in the South as a "saddle-bag" log house, or, as the old Southwestern settlers called it, a "two-pen," the pens being two enclosures with a wide passageway or gallery between them, one roof extending over both pens and the gallery.

General Grant was not afraid of work, and, like a good scout, was always willing to help a neighbor. He had a team of big horses, a gray and a bay, and the loads of cord-wood he hauled to St. Louis were so big that they are still talked of by the old settlers. In the summer of 1854 Grant started his log cabin, and all his neighbors turned in to help him build his house.

American Log House

The American log house differs from the Canadian log house principally in the shape of the roof. Our old settlers made steep gambrel roofs to shed the rain.

"Gambrel! Gambrel? Let me beg
You'll look at a horse's hinder leg;
First great angle above the hoof,
That's the gambrel, hence the gambrel roof."

The Canadians put very flat roofs on their log cabins, usually composed of logs laid over the rafters, making them strong enough to support the heavy weight of snow. The American log cabins, as a rule, are built in a milder climate, and the flat sod roof is peculiar to our Northern boundary and the hot, arid parts of our country. We build the chimneys outside of our log cabins because, as the old settlers would say, "thar's more room out thar."

One-Pen Cabin

Fig. 229 is a one-pen cabin. To build it we first snake our logs to a skid near the site of our proposed cabin (Fig. 167), from which we can roll our logs to our house as we need them. Lay out the corners and square them; notch the logs with a rounded or U-shaped notch (Fig. 165). Remember that all the logs should be two or three feet longer than the walls of the proposed building, but the notches must be the same distance apart in order to make even walls. The protruding ends of the logs may be allowed to stick out as they happen to come, no matter how irregular they may be, until the cabin is erected; then with a two-handed saw and a boy at each end they can be trimmed off evenly, thus giving a neat finish to the house.

Sills

The largest, straightest, and best logs should be saved for sills or foundations. If you are building a "mudsill," that is, a building upon the ground itself, the sill logs will be subject to dampness which will cause them to rot unless they are protected by some wood preservative.

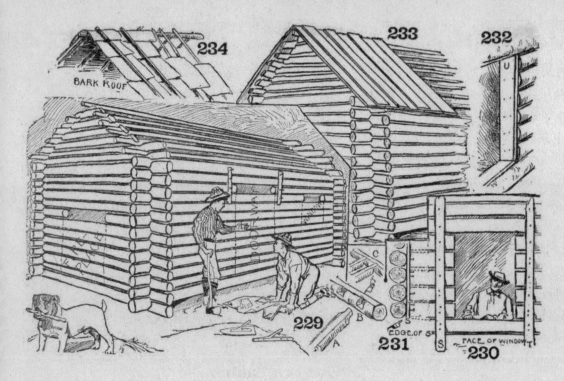

Hints and suggestions in cabin construction.

Wood Preservative

If the logs are painted with two or three coats of creosote before they are laid upon the ground, it will protect them for an indefinite time and prevent decay. Hugh P. Baker, dean of the New York State College of Forestry, writes me that—two or three applications of warm oil with a brush will be very helpful and will probably be all that the ordinary man can do. Creosote is the best preservative because of its penetrating power and the way it acts upon the fibres of wood, and in the end is cheaper than a good many other things which have been used to preserve timber. In fact, various forms of creosote are best-known preservers of organic matter. There is no advantage in using charcoal at all and I presume suggestions have been made for using it because we know that charred wood is more durable. Linseed-oil is good; ordinary white-lead paint will be better, but neither of them is as effective as creosote, and both are more expensive. You will find that carbolineum and other patent preparations are recommended very highly; they are good but expensive and the difference in price between these patent preparations and ordinary creosote is much larger than is justified by their increased value. Creosote can be procured in large or small quantities from a number of concerns. I think we have been getting it for about ten dollars per barrel of fifty or fifty-three gallons. Creosote may be purchased in large or small quantities from various manufacturing companies, such as the Barret Manufacturing Company, 17 Battery Place, New York City, and the Chattfield Manufacturing Company, Carthage, O., handle it in large quantities.

Openings

Build the pen as if it were to have no openings, either doors, windows, or fireplaces. When you reach the point where the top of the door, window, or fireplace is to be (Fig. 229) saw out a section of the log to mark the place and admit a saw when it is desired to finish the opening as shown in the diagram and continue building until you have enough logs in place to tack on cleats like those shown in Figs. 229, 230, and 231, after which the openings may be sawed out. The cleats will hold the ends of the logs in place until the boards *U* (Fig. 232) for the door-jambs, window-frames, or the framework over the fireplace can be nailed to the ends of the logs and thus hold them permanently in place. If your house is a "mudsill," wet the floor until it becomes spongy, then with the butt end of a log ram the dirt down hard until you have an even, hard floor—such a floor as some of the greatest men of this nation first crept over when they were babies. But if you want a board floor, you must necessarily have floor-joists; these are easily made of milled lumber or you may use the rustic material of which your house is built and select some straight logs for your joists. Of course, these joists must have an even top surface, which may be made by flattening the logs by scoring and hewing them. It will then be necessary to cut the ends of the joist square and smaller than the rest of the log (Fig. A, 229); the square ends must be made to fit easily into the notches made in the sill logs (B, Fig. 229) so that they will all be even and ready for the flooring (C, Fig. 229). For a house ten feet wide the joists should be half a foot in diameter, that is, half a foot through from one side to the other; for larger spans use larger logs for the joists.

Foundation

If your house is not a "mudsill" you may rest your sill logs upon posts or stone piles; in either case, in the Northern States, they should extend three feet below the ground, so as to be below frost-line and prevent the upheaval of the spring thaw from throwing your house "out of plumb."

Roofing

All the old-time log cabins were roofed with shakes, splits, clapboards, or hand-rived shingles; but today they are usually shingled with the machine-sawed shingle of commerce. You may, however, cover the roof with planks as shown by Fig. 233 or with bark weighted down with poles as shown by Fig. 234. In covering it with board or plank, nail the latter on as you would on a floor, then lay another course of boards over the cracks which show between the boards on the first course.

Gables

The gable ends of the cabin should be built up of logs with the rafters of the roof running between the logs as they are in Figs. 229 and 233, but the roof may be built, as it frequently is nowadays, of mill lumber, in which case it may be framed as shown by Figs. 49, 51, and the gable end above the logs filled in with upright poles, or planked up, or the ends may be boarded up and covered with tar paper, or the gable end may be shingled with ordinary shingles.

Steep Roof

Remember that the steeper the roof is the longer the shingles will last, because the water will run off readily and quickly on a steep surface and the shingles have an opportunity to dry quickly; besides which the snow slides off a steep roof and the driving rains do not beat under the shingles. If you are using milled lumber for the roof, erect the rafters at the gable end first, with the ridge board as shown in Fig. 49. Put the other rafters two or three feet apart.

Let your roof overhang the walls by at least seven or eight inches so as to keep the drip from the rain free of the wall. It is much easier for the architect to draw a log house than it is for a builder to erect one, for the simple reason that the draughtsman can make his logs as straight as he chooses, also that he can put the uneven places where they fit best; but except in well-forested countries the tree trunks do not grow as straight as the logs in my pictures and you must pick out the logs which will fit together. Run them alternately butt and head; that is, if you put the thick end of the log at the right-hand end of your house, with the small end at the left, put the next log with the small end at the right and thick end at the left;

otherwise, if all the thick ends are put at one side and the small ends at the other, your house will be taller at one end than at the other as is the case with some of our previous shacks and camps (Figs. 190, 191, and 192) which are purposely built that way.

If it is planned to have glass window lights, make your window openings of the proper size to fit the window-frames which come with the sashes from the factory. In any case, if the cabin is to be left unoccupied you should have heavy shutters to fit in the window opening so as to keep out trespassers.

Chinking

If your logs are uneven and leave large spaces between them, they may be chinked up by filling the spaces with mud plaster or cement, and then forcing in quartered pieces of small logs and nailing them or spiking them in position. If your logs are straight spruce logs and fit snugly, the cracks may be caulked up with swamp moss (Sphagnum), or like a boat, with oakum, or the larger spaces may be filled with flat stones and covered with mud. This mud will last from one to seven or eight years; I have some on my own log cabin that has been there even a longer time.

How to Make a Concealed Log Cabin Inside of a Modern House

It was because the writer knew that a great many folks rebelled against the conventionalities and restrictions of a modern house that he first invented and suggested the surprise den and told how to make one years ago in the *Outing* magazine. Since that article appeared the idea has been adopted by a number of people. There is a beautiful one in Toledo, Oh., where the writer was entertained during the floods, and Doctor Root, of Hartford, Conn., has even a better one in his home in that Yankee city. Fig. 308 shows a rough sketch of

a corner of Doctor Root's surprise den which he calls his "loggery."

From the outside of the house there is no indication of anything upon the inside that may not be found in any conventional dwelling, which is the proper way to build the surprise den.

Figs. 307, 309, and 310 are sketches made as suggestions to those wishing to add the surprise den to their dwelling.

To fathers and mothers having sons anywhere from twelve to thirty years of age, it is almost a necessity nowadays to give these boys a room of their own, popularly known as the "den," a retreat where they can go and sit in a chair without having fancy embroidered tidies adhere to their coat collars, where they can lean back in their chairs, if they choose, with no danger of ruining the valuable Hepplewhite or breaking the claw feet off a rare Chippendale—a place where they can relax. The greater the contrast between this room and the rest of the house, the greater will be the enjoyment derived by the boys to whom it belongs. The only two surprise dens which I have personally visited are the pride of the lives of two gentlemen who are both long past the years generally accorded to youth, but both of them are still boys in their hearts. The truth is a surprise den appeals to any man with romance in his soul; and the more grand, stately, and formal his house may be, the greater will the contrast be and the greater the surprise of this den.

If the reader's house is already built, the surprise den may be erected as an addition; it may be built as a log cabin after the manner of any of those previously described in this book, or it may be made an imitation log cabin by using slabs and nailing them on the walls in place of real whole logs. Doctor Root's surprise den, or "loggery," is made of whole logs and chinked with moss. Fig. 310 is supposed to be made of slabs, half logs, or puncheons nailed to the walls and

Suggestions for interiors of surprise dens and sketch of Dr. Root's surprise den.

ceiling and so arranged that the visitor cannot detect the deception. Personally, however, I do not like deception of any sort and would recommend that the house be made, if possible, of whole logs; but whatever way you build it, remember that it must have a generous, wide fireplace, a crane, and a good hearthstone, and that your furniture must either be made of the material to be found in the woods or selected from the antique furniture of some old farmhouse, not mahogany furniture, but Windsor chairs, three-legged stools, and deal-wood tables—such furniture as might be found in an old pioneer's home.

The principal thing to the surprise den, however, is the doorway. The outside of the door—that is, the side seen from the main part of the house—should be as formal as its surroundings and give no indication of what might be on the other side. If it opens from the most formal room in the house, so much the better. Fig. 321 shows the outside of the door of the surprise den; I do not mean by this outside of the house but a doorway facing the dining-room, library, drawing-room, or parlor. Fig. 321 shows one side of the door and Fig. 322 the other side of the same door. In this instance one side of the door is supposed to have a bronze escutcheon and a glass knob (Figs. 315 and 316). Of course, any other sort of a knob (Fig. 313) will answer our purpose, but the inside, or the surprise-den side, of the door must have a wooden latch. After some experiments I discovered that this could be easily arranged by cutting a half-round piece of hardwood (F, Fig. 312) to fit upon the square end G of the knob (Figs. 311 and 313) and be held in place with a small screw (Fig. 314). When this arrangement is made for the door and the knob put in place as it is in Figs. 315 and 316, a simple wooden latch (Fig. 317) with the catch K (Fig. 319)

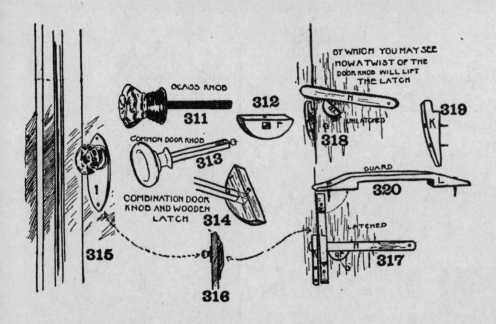

free from the noise of the children, to go over his accounts, write his private letters, or simply sit before the fire and rest his tired brain by watching the smoke go up the chimney.

Here also, over the open fire, fish, game, and chickens may be cooked, as our grandmas and granddaddies cooked them,

and the guard (Fig. 320) may be fastened upon the den side of the door as shown by *K, L,* (Fig. 317). When the door is latched the wooden piece *F* fits underneath the latch as shown by Fig. 317. When the knob is turned, it turns the half disk and lifts the latch *H* as shown in Fig. 318; this, of course, opens the door, and the visitor is struck with amazement upon being ushered into a pioneer backwoods log cabin, where after-dinner coffee may be served, where the gentlemen may retire to smoke their cigars, where the master of the house may retire,

and quaint, old-fashioned luncheons and suppers served on earthenware or tin dishes, camp style. In truth, the surprise den possesses so many charming possibilities that it is destined to be an adjunct to almost every modern home. It can be enclosed within the walls of a city house, a suburban house, or added as a wing to a country house, but in all cases the outside of the surprise den should conform in material used and general appearance to the rest of the house so as not to betray the secret.

The "surprise den." A log house inside a modern mansion.

How to Build Appropriate Gateways for Grounds Enclosing Log Houses, Game Preserves, Ranches, Big Country Estates, and Last but not Least Boy Scouts' Camp Grounds

The great danger with rustic work is the temptation, to which most builders yield, to make it too fancy and intricate in place of practical and simple. Figs. 323, 324, 325, and 326 are as ornamental as one can make them without incurring the danger of being overdone, too ornate, too fancy to be really appropriate.

Fig. 328 is a gate made of upright logs with beveled tops protected by plank acting as a roof, and a flattened log fitting across the top. The gate and fence, you may see, are of simple construction; horizontal logs for the lower part keep out small animals, upright posts and rails for the upper part keep out larger animals and at the same time do not shut out the view from the outside or the inside of the enclosure. Fig. 324 shows a roof gateway designed and made for the purpose of supplying building sites for barn swallows or other useful birds. The fence for this one is a different arrangement of logs, practical and not too fancy. Fig. 325 shows a modification of the gate shown by Fig. 323; in this one, however, in place of a plank protecting beveled edges of the upright logs, two flattened logs are spiked on like rafters to a roof, the apex being surmounted by a birdhouse. Fig. 326 shows another gateway composed of two upright logs with a cross log overhead in which holes have been excavated for the use of white-breasted swallows, bluebirds, woodpeckers, or flickers. Fig. 327 is another simple but picturesque form of gateway, where the cross log at the top has its two ends carved after the fashion of totem-poles. In place of a wooden fence a stone wall is shown. The ends of the logs (Fig. 327), which are embedded in

the earth, should first be treated with two or three coats of creosote to prevent decay; but since it is the moisture of the ground that causes the decay, if you arrange your gate-posts like those shown in the vertical section (Fig. 328), they will last practically forever. Note that the short gate-post rests upon several small stones with air spaces between them, and pointed ends of the upright logs rest upon one big stone. The gate-post is fastened to the logs by crosspieces of board running horizontally from log to the post, and these are enclosed inside the stone pier so that they are concealed from view. This arrangement allows all the water to drain from the wood, leaving it dry and thus preventing decay. Fig. 329 shows another form of gate-post of more elaborate structure, surmounted by the forked trunk of a tree; these parts are supposed to be spiked together or secured in place by hardwood pegs.

Never forget to add the birdhouse or bird shelter to every gateway you make; it is more important than the gate itself. In my other books I have described and told how to make various forms of birdhouses, including my invention of the woodpecker's house now being manufactured by many firms, including one in Germany, but the reader should make his own birdhouses. I am glad the manufacturers have taken up these ideas for the good they will *do the birds,* but the ideas were published first solely for the use of the boys in the hopes of educating them both in the conservation of bird life and in the manual training necessary to construct birdhouses.

The reader must have, no doubt, noticed that the problems in this book have become more and more difficult as we approach the end, but this is because everything grows; as we acquire skill we naturally seek more and more difficult work on which to exercise our skill. These gateways, however, are none of them too difficult for the boys to build themselves. The main problem to overcome in

Gateways for game preserves, camps, etc.

327   328

Log gate and details of same.

building the picturesque log gateway shown by Fig. 331 is not in laying up the logs or constructing the roof—the reader has already learned how to do both in the forepart of this book—but it is in so laying the logs that the slant or incline on the two outsides will be exactly the same, also in so building the sides that when you reach the top of the open way and place your first overhead log, the log will be exactly horizontal, exactly level, as it must be to carry out the plan in a workmanlike manner. Fig. 330 shows you the framework of the roof, the ridge-pole of which is a plank cut "sway-backed," that is, lower in the centre than at either end. The frame should be roofed with hand-rived shingles, or at least hand-trimmed shingles, if you use the manufactured article of commerce. This gateway is appropriate for a common post-and-rail fence or any of the log fences illustrated in the previous diagrams. Fig. 332 shows how the fence here shown is constructed: the A logs are beveled to fit in diagonally, the B and C logs are set in as shown by the dotted line in Fig. 332. A gateway like the one shown here would make a splendid and imposing one for a permanent camp, whether it be a Boy Scout, a Girl Pioneer, a private camp for boys, or simply the entrance to a large private estate.

The writer has made these diagrams so that they may be used by men or boys; the last one shows a gateway large enough to admit a "four-in-hand" stage-coach or an automobile, but the children may build it in miniature so that the opening is only large enough to admit a pedestrian.

Basic Furniture

From *The Amateur Carpenter* by Alpheus Huatt Verrill, **1915**

LIST OF NECESSARY CARPENTRY TOOLS

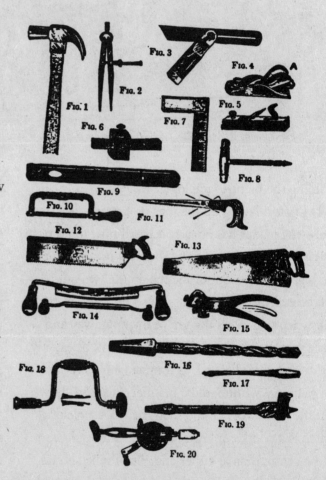

A claw-hammer	Chisels
A cross-cut saw	Gouges
A rip-saw	A steel square
Two planes	Rule or tape
A screw-driver	A level
A mallet	Sandpaper
A brad-awl	A keyhole- or compass-saw
A gimlet	A nail-set
A bit-brace	An oil-stone
Bits	Cutting-pliers
Augers	Files
A countersink	A carpenter's pencil

With these tools and an assortment of nails and screws one can make almost anything from a simple shelf to a house. There are many other useful tools which will greatly lighten your carpenter work and will add little to the expense, and among these are:

A saw-set	Dividers
A carpenter's gauge	A mitre-box
An expansion-bit	A hack-saw
Clamps	A draw-knife
A tack-hammer	An iron vise
A saw-vise	A plumb-bob and line
A bevel-square	A mitre-saw
A breast-drill	

How to Make a Workbench

In order to construct your bench you will require some 2 x 3 scantling, either rough or finished, and some 6- or 8-in. planks. Although your bench will not have to be very large or heavy, still it must be strong and solid enough to be steady, and 2-in. planks should be used. If possible obtain planks that are finished, at least on one side, for it is a hard job to plane them until after the bench is completed, and the finished boards cost very little more than the rough ones.

A good size for your bench will be 6 ft. 6 in. long by 2½ ft. in height and 32 in. wide. This will be large enough for your present use, and later on when

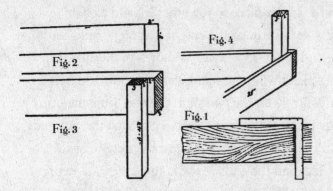

Fig. 2

Fig. 4

Fig. 3

Fig. 1

you undertake larger work you may easily build a bigger and better bench if you wish.

For the bench you will need about 30 running feet of the scantling and about 75 ft., board measure, of the planks. As the latter are to be 2 in. thick the boards will only cover about 38 sq. ft. of surface, so do not be surprised at the amount you receive.

With your ruler measure off four spaces of 2 ft. 4 in. each on the scantling, and with the square mark lines across at each space on two sides of the timber. If you have never used a square before you will have to learn how, and this is a good place to begin. Place one edge of the square along the edge of the timber, as shown in Fig. 1, with the edge at right angles across the mark you have made on the wood, as shown in the cut, and with your pencil draw a straight line across the timber from side to side. This little detail is quite important and is all too often overlooked by amateur carpenters. You may *think* you can rule a line across a piece of wood so it is at right angles to the edge and you may *think* you can saw straight, but there is no one living who *can* draw a line at right angles to another by eye alone, and mighty few people who can saw a straight line without a mark to guide them. Unless you acquire the habit of always using a square and invariably making straight right angles where boards or timbers are to join to form a square corner, you will never succeed at carpenter work. If even one board or timber is not squared up properly the whole work will be skewed and slipshod, all of which may be easily avoided by using a little care and taking a

little trouble to begin with. Get in the habit of being careful with little things and you will find that the results come out wonderfully well, but neglect the small details and you will never succeed.

Having marked off the four sections, place the timber across the saw-horses or chairs and arrange it so but one of the sections projects beyond the edge. Place your right knee on the timber above the end of the horse or chair, grasp your cross-cut saw in your right hand and starting it with short, gentle strokes across the pencil mark at an angle, begin to saw with long, steady strokes. You may laugh at such detailed directions for performing such a simple feat as sawing off a piece of scantling, but not one person in a hundred knows how to use even a saw properly. Nine times out of ten they waste strength and energy by bearing too heavily on the saw or by working with short, quick strokes until they look like a steam pump going up and down, and when the saw is nearly through the wood the outer end sags, cracks and drops down with a big splintered piece hanging to it. Remember that only on the downward stroke is any work done by the saw; draw it up smoothly without bearing on and do not bear *too* hard as you push it down. The saw will bite through the wood almost as fast with a slight pressure, or none at all, as when you bear on hard, and the cut will be much straighter and better. When the saw is a little more than halfway through the timber, place your left hand beneath the projecting end and support it slightly so it will not fall down and split the lower part of the wood.

After a little practice you will be able to follow a line very accurately and will also be able to keep your saw running true, and only one line will be required across the wood you are cutting. At first you should mark the lines on at least two sides of the timber and should watch the saw carefully to be sure it is not running off at a slant or angle. Oftentimes a saw will stick and bind when sawing rough spruce timber. If this occurs rub some ordinary laundry soap on the sides of the saw; oil will soak into the wood and will do little good, but soap will make the saw run smoothly and easily.

The four short sections having been cut off, next mark and cut two pieces each 6 ft. long and two pieces each 32 in. long. Then from your planks cut two pieces each 6 ft. 4 in. long and two shorter pieces each 28 in. long. You may now lay aside the saw for a time and busy yourself with hammer and nails in putting the framework of your bench together. To join the various pieces you will need several pounds of nails. Wire nails are the best, and those you will require should be 4 in. long, or just a trifle less, with a few 5 or 6 in. in length. Select one of the pieces of plank 6 ft. 4 in. long, and at each end measure off exactly 2 in. and draw a line at right angles to the long edge and parallel with the ends by means of the square, as shown in Fig. 2. Take one of the pieces of timber 2 ft. 4 in. in length and place it on the board with the 3-in. side down and with one edge close against the line on the plank and with the end flush and even with the edge of the plank (Fig. 3). Hold it in this position and tack it to the plank with a couple of nails. If you wish you can drive the nails almost through before placing the piece of timber, and you will probably find this the easiest method, for the timber is apt to jump about while you drive the nails, and unless you use care you will accidentally fasten it in the wrong place. After this first piece is nailed in position fasten a similar piece on the other end of the plank and then turn the plank over and drive two or three nails through the plank into the timber, using nails of the 4-in. size.

Lay the plank with the two legs aside for a few minutes and fasten two more of the 2-ft. 4-in. timbers to the other 6-ft. 4-in. plank. Now place one of the planks, with the legs, edge down on a level place and with the legs sticking up in the air, and nail one end of one of the 28-in. pieces of plank against the outer edge of the leg as shown in Fig. 4.

Nail a similar piece to the other leg and also drive a few nails through the end of the long planks into the end of the short ones as shown in the cut. The long plank will now stand without your help, resting quite firmly on the two short planks. Bring the other long plank with the legs, place it so that the free ends of the short planks bear against the outer edge of the legs and the ends of the long plank, and secure it with nails in this position. You will now have a rectangle of 2-in. planks with a leg sticking up at each corner like a low wooden fence with four posts. Mark off 6 in. from the free end of each of these projecting timbers and square a line across with the square. Across these lines nail the four remaining pieces of scantling, being very careful to have one edge straight and close to the lines you have marked, and when they are all in place the frame will be complete and will appear as in Fig. 5.

You will be surprised to find how stiff and rigid it is, provided the joints have all been made true and square, and you can turn it upside down, or rather right side up, and proceed to nail on the top.

Cut four pieces from your planks, each exactly 6 ft. 6 in. in length, and with the ends true and square. Place these on top of the frame with one end just even with the end of the framework and with the other projecting 2 in. beyond it. See that the end squares up with the end plank on the frame and with the edge of the long plank and nail it firmly in position, driving the nails along the front edge as well as across the ends. After you are accustomed to carpenter work you will be able to judge distances so well that you can drive a nail down through a board into a board or timber out of sight, but at first you will not be able to strike the spot once in a dozen times. You must therefore measure off 2 in. from the end of the plank on the upper surface where it projects beyond the frame, and then drive the nails down an inch beyond this line, thus making sure that they will enter the centre of the plank below. Nail all the top planks to the framework in this way, and then go over the nails with the nail-set and drive them down until the heads are well below the surface of the wood. Probably you know how to drive a nail, and I have taken this for granted, but even driving a nail properly requires some skill. Anyone can hammer and whack away at a nail and finally get it into the wood. It may go straight and it may go crooked, and oftentimes it will buckle and bend and turn into a "Dutchman," as boat-builders call it, and will be driven into the wood with its head bent to one side and hammered down as shown in Fig. 6. Such a thing is an eyesore and a nuisance. If the nail starts to go crooked or to bend over, pull it out and try another. If the wood is hard, knotty or cross-grained, bore a hole smaller than the nail before driving it. In most cases, however, the fault lies with the man or boy or with the hammer rather than in the wood or the nail. A crooked, chipped, loose-headed or poor hammer will usually result in crooked nails, bruised fingers and loss of temper, but even with a perfect hammer some knack is required to drive a nail properly and well. Start the nail by holding it between your finger and thumb and give it a few short taps of the hammer. As soon as it is firmly set in the wood strike hard, solid blows squarely on the head. Hold the hammer handle near the end, not near the head, and after the nail is flush with the wood give another tap to slightly sink it beneath the surface. On finished wood or delicate work this last blow should be omitted, but on rough, heavy work or unfinished wood, such as your bench, a good strong final whack will drive the head quite a bit beneath the surface of the wood.

After the top of the bench is secured in position and the nails are all set beneath the surface, go over the bench and add a few of the long nails where the lower timbers meet at the ends and where they cross the legs, and drive a few more down through the top planks into the upper ends of the legs. You do not need to fill the planks and timbers with nails or to drive them so close together that they split the wood,

but a few of the large nails will greatly strengthen the bench if placed with a little judgment.

Before your bench is complete you should nail a piece of the 2 x 3 timber along one edge, and in doing this place the timber at the further edge when the projecting end of the top is at your right hand. This little 3-in. rail along the rear of your bench will prove very useful, for without it things will be continually dropping down behind the bench and getting lost.

The bench proper is now complete, and if you have been careful to follow directions and to square up all the corners and cuts you will find that it is stiff, steady and firm. If it wiggles or tips, test the floor to see if it is truly level before you blame the bench or your work. This is easily done with your level. Set the level along the floor with the glass uppermost and see if the bubble swings back and forth and finally rests exactly in the centre of the tube at the line marked on the glass. Try the level first in one direction and then in another over the floor, and if you find the bubble ever rests at any other spot except the cross-line, you may be sure the floor is not level. In this case you will be obliged to nail a piece on the floor under the leg or legs of the bench to prevent it from tipping, but this is seldom necessary.

How to Make a Tool-Tray and a Mitre Box

In making the workbench and the shelf for your tools the work has been rather heavy and rough, but in constructing a tool-tray you may obtain excellent practice in doing really accurate and careful work, and in addition will have an opportunity of using several tools you have not before employed.

For the tray you will require some ½-in. wood, and if you wish you may use hard or fancy wood, such as walnut, mahogany, oak or cherry. A tray made of such materials will be very handsome, and

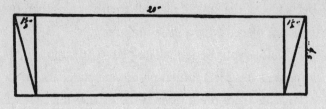

Fig. 1.

such a small quantity of lumber is required that the additional expense of using fancy wood will be very little. Even if ordinary pine or whitewood is used the finished tray may be stained and varnished and will be very attractive. Whitewood is far superior to pine for work of this sort and it is easier to get good, clear white-wood than pine and it is also cheaper. Avoid using yellow-pine or cypress for light, small work; they are both excellent woods for certain purposes, but they are apt to split unless care is used and they are harder to work than white-pine or whitewood.

The amount of material you will require for the tray will be about 10 sq. ft. of the ½-in. stuff and a piece of ⅞-in. material, 2 ft. long and 10 in. wide. If possible, obtain material of the full width, but if you cannot do this you can use boards 6 in. or more in width.

On one of the ½-in. boards measure off and mark two rectangles each 20 in. long and 5¼ in. wide and two others each 11¾ in. x 5¼ in. with the grain running lengthwise in all. Cut these out carefully, being sure to get all corners square and all sides and ends parallel. Measure off 1½ in. from each end on one edge of each of these pieces and draw a diagonal line to the opposite edge from each

of these points (Fig. 1). Saw carefully across each of these diagonal lines so that you will have four pieces all 5¼ in. wide; two of them 20 in. on one edge and 17 in. on the other and the other two 11¾ in. on one edge and 11¾ on the other. Now on the piece of ⅞ in. stuff, measure off a rectangle 19 in. x 9⅝ in. From one edge of this mark off 4½ in. and draw a straight line parallel with the edge but just 4½ in. from it. From each end of this second line measure off 1½ in. and draw a diagonal from each of these marks to the other edge, as shown in Fig. 2. Next measure off 9½ in. from the extreme ends of the rectangle, thus finding the exact centre and draw a line across from edge to edge and square with the marks that designate the edges (Fig. 2 A). Two and one-half inches above the lower, lengthwise line and 2 in. below the outer line, make a mark (Fig. 2 B), and with your square mark a line at right angles across the mark B, and extending 2 in. on either side (Fig. 2 D, D). With the 1-in. auger bore two holes through the board, centering the auger at the marks D, D, and from the edges of these holes draw a curved line as indicated, with the upper point of the curve 1 in. above the point B, and the lower part 1½ in. below B. Now from the intersection of the upper end of the diagonal marks and the line 4½ in. from the edge C, C, mark a graceful curve extending to the extreme outer edge as shown at F, F. You may have difficulty in making this curve alike on both sides of the line A, but this is readily overcome by drawing the curve for one side on a piece of stiff paper, cutting out the paper and laying it upside down, or reversed, on the opposite side of the line A. Then by tracing along the edge of the paper pattern both the curves will be identical.

In the above directions I have assumed that your ⅞ board was 10 in. in width. In case you cannot secure a board of that width you will be obliged to fasten two narrower boards together, edge to edge. In order to make a good job of this the two edges that are to join must be planed smooth, true

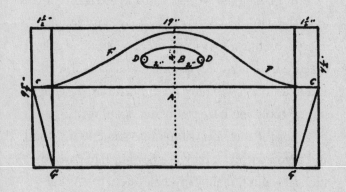

Fig. 2.

and even so they fit flush together. When this is done place them tightly edge to edge and tack two or three light cleats across the joint, and having the joint near the bottom edge, which is 16 in. long, instead of near the longer top edge. This is important, as the joint or seam if near the bottom will not matter at all, whereas if near the top it will show in the finished tray and will weaken the tray besides.

When all the marks on the piece are made as shown in Fig. 2, saw across the diagonal lines from C to G. Place the board in your bench-vise with one end uppermost and with your compass-saw cut along the line F F from C to C. With the compass-saw commence at the hole D and follow around the line to the other hole and then back along the other line to the opposite hole.

With the rasp and files smooth off the saw marks on the curved lines and finish the curved edges rounded and smooth with sandpaper. If you have sawed all the boards carefully the cut lines will be straight and smooth and free from chipped or split spots, and if you are to have a neat tray this is important. The next step is to plane off the long edges on the other four boards and take a small shaving from their sharp corners so they are slightly rounded. They should not be appreciably rounded, however, but merely smoothed. Now place one of the smaller pieces in the bench-vise with the diagonal end up and in such a position that the diagonal cut is parallel with the top of the bench. With the brad-awl or a fine drill make several holes along both ends of the larger pieces and ¼ in. from the ends. Place one of these pieces so that the end is exactly flush with the end of the piece in the vise, and with small wire nails (about 1½ in. long) inserted through the holes you have made, tack the long piece firmly to the shorter one. Place the

Fig. 3.

other short piece in the vise and fasten the other end of the long piece to it in the same way. Then place the long piece on the bench with the two end pieces sticking up and fasten the other long piece to them in the same manner. You will now have a rectangular frame 20 in. long at the top, and 17 in. long at the bottom with a top width of 12¾ in. outside and a bottom width of 9¾ in. Place this frame with the largest, or top opening, upon the bench and secure it firmly by tacking short cleats to the bench on all four sides close to the frame. Then with the block-plane cut down the edges of the frame until they are level or square across in all directions. This will be easier to understand by studying Fig. 3. As the edges of the four pieces are square and the pieces are fastened together at an angle the outer corners will be higher than those on the inside as indicated at A. Therefore these outer corners must all be planed off until the edge of your square, when placed across from side to side or from end to end, rests squarely upon the parallel surfaces of the edges as shown at B. By planing carefully and frequently trying the square you will find this an easy matter to accomplish. When this is done measure off at the upper and lower edges of the ends to find the exact centres and draw a line across from side to side. Along these lines bore several holes with a drill or awl. Now turn the frame the other side up on the smooth surface of the bench and place the centre piece, cut from ⅞-in. stuff, within it and with the ends C—G exactly in the centre of the end pieces of the frame. This is easily accomplished as you have the centre lines and holes already drilled in the ends. Insert nails through the holes, drive them into the ends of the ⅞-in. centre piece and the tray will be ready for the bottom.

For this you will have to get out a piece of ½-in. stuff 17½ in. long and 10 in. wide. If you have no wood of 10-in. width fit two pieces together as already described. Saw the piece with all ends square and true and with your ruler and square

Fig. 4.

mark a line completely around the bottom just ⅛ in. from the extreme

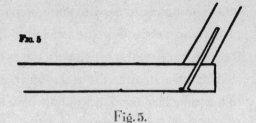

Fig. 5.

edges. Place the bottom piece in the bench-vise and with your block-plane round off all the edges, being careful not to carry the planing beyond the line marked around the edge. It is very easy to plane off the long edges with the grain, but when you come to the ends across the grain you will have to be very careful not to split or chip the corners. To avoid this, plane diagonally, rather than straight, across the grain and before planing across the ends round the corners slightly with a few strokes of the plane or a pocket knife (Fig. 4). Now clamp the centre piece, or handle, of the tray in the vise with the bottom of the tray uppermost. With the drill or awl make a number of holes around the edges of the bottom board, using care to bore them just ⅛ in. within the line you have marked

Fig. 6.

⅛ in. from the edge. Place the bottom board over the frame in the vise; move it about until the line ⅛ in. from the edge is just flush with the outer edges of the frame and drive nails through the holes up into the frame. Use nails that are not over 1¼ in. long and drive them slightly outward at an angle, as shown in Fig. 5. Across the centre of the bottom from end to end drive nails into the centre piece and your tray will be complete, save for the finishing touches. If you have used two pieces to make the centre and bottom you may now remove the cleats that held them together. With the nail-set sink all the nail-heads well below the surface of the wood and with sandpaper go over the whole tray, smoothing off all edges, corners and the surface until no rough spots or pencil marks remain. About ½ in. from each side of the centre piece and at both ends, saw straight

slits about 2½ in. deep, using care in sawing them so as not to split the wood. In these you can put your saws when carrying them about. When the wood is smoothed to your satisfaction, putty up the depressions over the nail-heads and stain, oil or varnish the entire tray. When completed it will be a handy, useful article and should appear as in Fig. 6.

Learning to Make Joints

There are a great many methods of joining two pieces of wood together, and the particular kind of joint to be used depends a great deal upon the material, the strength required, the character of the work in hand and upon the skill of the carpenter.

In former times all joints were made by hand and carpenters became very expert in making accurately fitting and beautiful joints of all kinds. Doors, windows, chests, drawers, boxes and a thousand and one other articles were made by hand with beautifully-fitted tenons, dovetails or similar joints. Nowadays nearly every kind of joint can be made far more accurately and rapidly by machinery, and there are scores of excellent carpenters who do not know how to make a good dovetail or other complicated joint.

The simplest of all methods of joining two pieces of wood is to merely nail or screw the two pieces together as shown in Fig. 1. For very rough work this serves every purpose, but the joint made in this way is clumsy and not very strong. A better way of joining two pieces of wood is by a half-and-half joint. This consists in cutting away half the material on each piece to be joined as shown in Fig. 2. This method is quite strong and if carefully done it makes a very serviceable and neat joint. This joint may be used either for pieces that join at right angles or for pieces joined with a mitre as shown in the figures. Ordinarily for mitre joints, however, it is merely necessary to nail the two pieces together edge to edge as shown in Fig. 3. A still stronger joint is the *Tenon Joint,* several forms of which are shown in Fig. 4. This is an excellent form of joint where neatness and strength are required and especially for joining the ends of timbers or for fastening uprights or cross-pieces in other timbers or scantling. It also makes an excellent joint for mitred work. For joining fine work such as furniture, drawers, cabinets, chests, etc., a form of joint known as the *Dovetail* is commonly employed. There are many varieties of dovetail joints. Most of the joints are very easy to make, but to fit a good dovetail requires great care, skill and practice. A form of dovetail which is just as neat and strong as any other is shown in Fig. 6, and this, moreover, is fairly easy to make, as it consists of holes bored in the piece *A* which are fitted over wooden pegs in the piece *B.* In making any of these so-called "mortised" joints you must use care and must work accurately if you expect good results. Before making a half-and-half joint, as shown in Fig. 2, lay off the measurements and mark the

work carefully before starting to make any cuts. The distance from *A* to *B* and from *C* to *D* should be the same as from *G* to *J* and *E* to *I.* If the two pieces to be joined are of equal dimensions the measurements will all be equal, but if the two pieces are of different sizes each piece must be marked to correspond with the dimensions of the other. The cut *B* to *E* and the cut *D* to *F* should each be one-half the thickness from *E* to *L* or from *F* to *M,* or one-half the thickness of the pieces to be joined. The cuts should all be made smooth, square and true and the surfaces to be joined (*N*) should be smooth and even. In making a mitred halved-joint a little more care must be taken, but the principle is the same as in the plain halved-joint. The cuts *A—B, C—D* should be made in the mitre-box and while *A—B* should go but halfway through the wood that from *C* to *D* should go clear through. On the piece *E* a cut at right angles to the edge *C—G* should be made half through the piece and when the two pieces are joined the junction will be scarcely visible. In making a tenon-joint as shown in Fig. 4 the cuts *A—B* and *C—D* should be equal, while *G—H* should be the same as *E—F.* There is no trouble in making this sort of joint, as it merely requires care in cutting and chiseling. In making the hole *I* it is often easiest to bore a hole through the wood first and saw from the end to this hole as indicated in Fig. 4*J,* or else bore two holes and saw from one to the other with the keyhole-saw as shown in Fig. 4 *K,* afterwards smoothing the ends square with a chisel.

To make a dovetail joint lay off the piece *A* first and cut the recesses with a fine saw and sharp chisel. Then place the piece over *B* and with a sharp pencil mark around each of the "tails" and cut corresponding recesses in the piece *B.* For common work the distance from *C* to *D* must be the same as from *E* to *F,* but if particularly good work is desired and you plan to make a "blind" joint the distance must be the same from *C* to *D* as from *G* to *H.* The one great secret in making dovetail joints is to work

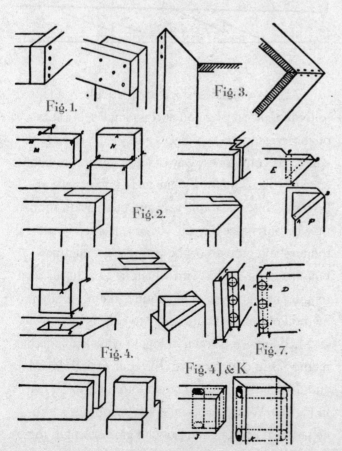

Fig. 1.

Fig. 2.

Fig. 3.

Fig. 4.

Fig. 7.

Fig. 4 J & K

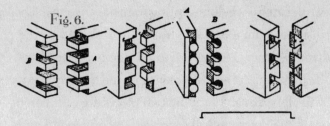

Fig. 6.

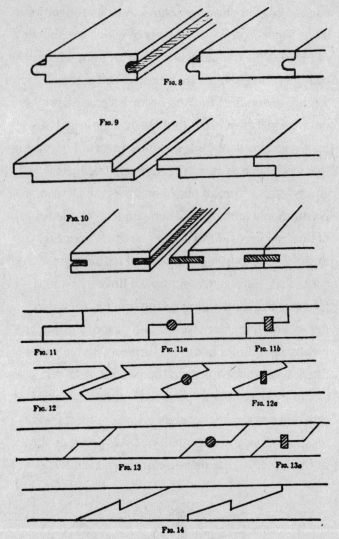

Fig. 8

Fig. 9

Fig. 10

Fig. 11   Fig. 11a   Fig. 11b

Fig. 12   Fig. 12a

Fig. 13   Fig. 13a

Fig. 14

slowly and carefully and fit the pieces from time to time as you proceed until you are sure that they fit closely and accurately together. In making the form with holes and pegs, cut away a space on A, Fig. 7, with the distance from B to C equal to the thickness of the piece D and with only a very thin portion left at D—E. Mark the distance from F to G on the piece D and draw a line parallel with the end at this distance from it, G—H. Along this line mark several points at equal distances and from these run lines to the edge as shown at I—J, K—L, M—N. Then with a twist-drill or sharp auger bore holes on each one of these lines. The holes should be of smaller diameter than the distance from I to J, etc., and the outer edge of the holes should just touch the extreme end of the piece D as shown in the figure by the dotted lines. Now place the two pieces D and A together in the position in which they are to be joined and mark the places where the holes come on the piece A. With the bit or drill bore holes half an inch deep or so into A. Make a number of smooth, round, wooden pegs that will just fit smoothly into the holes and drive them into the holes in A, fastening them securely with glue. Slip the piece D over the pegs after coating all the surfaces with glue, and drive or press the pieces firmly together. After the glue is thoroughly dry trim off the projecting pegs and smooth the edges and you will have a joint that is exceedingly strong and very neat and which is invisible from the front, or A, side. Properly this is a dowel-joint rather than a dovetail, and you will find it a great convenience to buy dowel-pin stock already made rather than to try to make perfectly true, round pegs yourself.

All the joints described are particularly adapted to joining pieces of wood at right angles, but it is often necessary to join pieces end to end or edge to edge. The commonest way of joining wood or boards edge to edge is by the *Tongue-and-Groove* method (Fig. 8). This is a simple way and boards and timber may be purchased already cut or "matched" with tongues and grooves or the young carpenter may buy matching-planes with which he can cut his own tongues and grooves as he requires them. Another method of joining boards edge to edge is by half-and-half joints as shown in Fig. 9, while still another method is to cut grooves in the edge of each board and drive a thin piece of wood into these as shown in Fig. 10. Where two timbers or scantlings are to be fastened end to end to obtain greater length there are several methods of joining which may be used. One way is to make a half-and-half joint as shown in Fig. 11, and after placing the two pieces together bore a hole through the timber and drive a peg in the hole as shown in Fig. 11a, which prevents the two pieces from pulling apart. In place of boring a hole and using a peg a square notch may be cut in each piece and a square dowel driven in as shown at Fig. 11b. A better method is to cut the timbers as shown in Fig. 12 and use either a peg or a square dowel as indicated at Fig. 12a. Still another method is shown at Figs. 13 and 13a; while by cutting the timbers as indicated in Fig. 14 the peg or dowel may be dispensed with.

In making mortised joints always try to have them fit so snugly that they must be driven together with light blows of a mallet or a piece of wood and in all light, fine work, or where the wood will not be exposed to dampness or wet, make the joints with glue. Glue, if well-made, is a great aid to the carpenter, but if poor in quality or carelessly made it is worthless and a nuisance and every amateur carpenter should know how to make and use glue properly.

Carpentry about the House

I have already told you how to put up a shelf for your workshop, and while rough and ready shelves of this sort do very for cellars, garrets, store-rooms and other out-of-the-way places, they would not serve in living-rooms, dining-rooms, kitchens or other places where shelves are frequently required. In such places shelves must be made neatly and must conform in style and finish to the rest of the room. If the room is in the Mission style the shelves should be in the same style, both in form and finish and so with every other style of room furnishings. Corner shelves are quite easy to make, as they are fitted snugly into a corner and may be easily and neatly secured in position, but even in putting up

corner shelves you should aim to make the job as neat and artistic as possible and should have them in harmony with the other fittings. As a rule shelves should be made in units, so they may be readily taken down instead of being built into a room permanently. Where screws or nails are to be driven into a plaster wall small holes should first be made and you should be careful to strike a lath or timber, for if merely driven into the plastering the support will not hold and moreover the plaster is likely to break and chip away. By using a light hammer or mallet and striking here and there on the wall, a lath or timber may usually be located by the sound, but if this cannot be done a very fine brad-awl may be run carefully into the plaster here and there until a lath is located. The very small hole made by the awl may be readily plastered or filled up, and if in paper it will not be visible.

Wherever possible attach the shelves to other woodwork. Oftentimes at least one support may be screwed to a window-frame, a corner molding, a mantel or some similar wooden object. Shelves should be fastened in such a way that the screws or nails and cleats are concealed or at least are not prominently in view.

Single shelves may be put up with ready-made iron brackets where appearances do not count for so much as utility, or brackets made of wood in conformity with the rest of the furnishings of the room may be used. Light shelves may often be hung to a wall, especially a wooden wall, with hooks, or eyes over screws, driven into the wall. Such shelves are easily removable and in many cases are superior to any other form. Where shelves are placed one

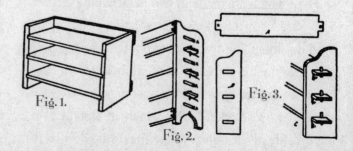

Fig. 1.

Fig. 2.

Fig. 3.

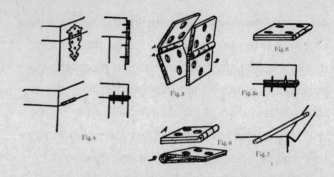

above another a very neat method is to let the ends
of the shelves set into slots or recesses in the end
pieces, which are held together either by fastening
them directly to the shelves or by tie-pieces across
the back and front edges (Fig. 1).

Shelves which may be readily taken down
and packed flat may be constructed as illustrated
in Fig. 2. In this case the ends of each shelf are
cut away as shown in A and rectangular holes of
the proper size are cut through the end pieces, B.
Through the projecting ends of the shelves wooden
wedges are thrust and thus the end pieces are kept
securely locked in position (C). Such shelves may be
hung with hooks to screws or may be fastened to the
wall through a back piece or cleat. The same method
may be followed in constructing bookshelves or
music-racks to stand on the floor but in this case
rigidity must be obtained by a cross-piece at top
and bottom which should be attached to the sides
with screws (Fig. 3). By making a bookshelf in this
way and cutting holes through the ends at frequent
intervals (A), the shelves may be adjusted at varying
distances apart to accommodate books of any size.

When shelves are protected by doors they
become cupboards, and if constructed with doors
they must be more accurately and more carefully
made than plain open shelves. Unless all joints are
carefully made and all parts squared up true, doors
will catch and bind or will sag and appear slovenly.
Care is also necessary in fitting hinges and locks.
There are a great many kinds of hinges in the world
and they vary from crude pieces of leather nailed on
the door to beautifully wrought ornamental metal
affairs. Hinges may be divided into numerous classes
some of which are made in two detachable parts.
These are known as "loose butts" and are frequently
used on doors, but for small cupboards, boxes,
etc., they are not necessary. For cupboards, chests,
boxes and other household furnishings you may
use either ornamental hinges which are fastened on
the outside of the object where they will show well

or plain metal hinges which are to be fastened on
the inside of the articles where they are out of sight.
Fig. 4 shows examples of both of these. In setting
a hinge you should take care to place it so that it
opens properly and in the direction intended by its
construction. Thus in Fig. 5 the hinge will open but
one way, as the ends of the leaves AA prevent the
hinge from swinging in the opposite direction, as
shown in B. Another style of small hinge is shown
in Fig. 6 A. In this case, if the hinge is placed as
illustrated, it will lie perfectly flat when the lid or
door is closed whereas if placed wrong side up as in
Fig. 6 B, the lid cannot close tightly and the hinge
will be bent or injured. Where the lid of a large
box or trunk is hinged some arrangement should
be made to prevent the lid from swinging too far
back and thus injuring the hinge or splitting off the
wood. Light, metal pivoted pieces may be bought
ready-made for this purpose, but strips of strong
canvas or thin leather straps fastened neatly to the
cover and the interior of the box will do just as well
(Fig. 7). Unless hinges are set perfectly parallel and
true the door or lid will not open and shut properly
and a little care in this matter will save a great deal of
future trouble and annoyance.

Where hinges of the type illustrated in Fig. 8
are used, they should be set in flush with the wooden
surface as in Fig. 8 A, for otherwise the door or lid
when closed will have an opening between itself
and the box or closet and the whole job will appear
slovenly and improperly made. Do not use hinges
that are too light or too small and if the material is

too thin or delicate to permit the use of good strong hinges, use several small ones.

In placing locks or fasteners on box covers, lids of chests or cupboard doors try to make the job as neat and workmanlike as possible. Ugly, rough locks screwed on the outside of an otherwise neat and attractive object are eyesores. Wherever possible use a concealed lock and set it into the wood by mortising, and if this cannot be done use a lock which is attached to the inside of the chest or closet out of sight. Aim to have locks, hinges and handles in harmony. A chest or cupboard with ornamental brass hinges should have lock and handles of the same general style. Sometimes a very plain box or cupboard may be made quite artistic and attractive by using fancy metal work and as a rule this ornamental hardware is easier to attach than the kind which is mortised or let into the wood and is concealed. If you keep your eyes open and look carefully at various articles of furniture, closets, cupboards, chests, etc., you will soon see how professionals handle these little items and will obtain many useful and valuable hints in this way. It is the same with other branches of carpentry; notice how others have accomplished results and try to pattern your work after them.

In every household, furniture is constantly being injured and broken and while furniture repairing is an art in itself and to mend furniture of the higher grades calls for the services of an expert, there are many occasions when one handy with carpenter's tools can mend broken chairs, tables, beds, etc., and save the expense of sending them out to a professional.

A great deal about furniture repairing may best be learned by a careful study of the furniture itself, and in a great many cases you will have to depend largely upon your own ingenuity and inventiveness in order to make strong and durable repairs that will be neat and practically invisible. As a rule do not attempt upholstery work; this is a

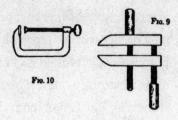

Fig. 9

Fig. 10

special trade and can be better entrusted to the hands of someone who makes a specialty of it. In a great many instances, however, the upholstery must be wholly or partially removed in order to make repairs and when this is necessary the best method to follow is to note carefully how the upholstery was put on in the first place and replace it in the same way. For the present, however, we may confine ourselves to that class of repairing which depends wholly upon carpentry work, for this is what will interest the amateur carpenter and afford an opportunity for him to exhibit his skill and ingenuity.

Perhaps the most important item in successfully repairing furniture is to have good, strong, well-prepared glue. In mending furniture the greatest dependence is placed on glued joints, which may be further reinforced by dowels, screws, etc., but nails should be used as little as possible. Many fractures of furniture are jagged, irregular and with small pieces broken off. If all these pieces are saved the fracture can usually be repaired so as to be almost invisible and very strong, but even when these are missing a good job can usually be done. All holes, cracks, uneven places and cavities left by missing chips may be filled with cement prepared by melting beeswax (cut into flakes) with crushed resin and adding dry pigment to match the wood. Use umber for walnut, Venetian red for mahogany, yellow ochre for birch, etc., and lampblack for ebony. The cement is dropped into the cavities when melted and is smoothed off when hard. If it is too brittle use more wax and if too soft more resin and only just enough color to obtain the proper shade. You will also require one or two wooden carpenter's clamps (Fig. 9), and a few small iron clamps (Fig. 10).

One of the commonest injuries to household furniture is a broken rocker to a rocking-chair. In a great many cases it is cheaper to buy a new chair or a new rocker than to repair the old one, but it is good practice and a broken rocker can be repaired so as to be as strong as new. The method to be followed is shown in Fig. 11. As the rocker is broken where the leg enters it, it is impossible to obtain a good strong joint at that spot, so the rocker is removed from the chair, the two pieces fitted together closely and the whole placed side down upon a piece of paper or cardboard.

An outline of the rocker is then traced on the card and the rocker is cut off at an angle in front of the broken spot (Fig. 11 A). The end is then cut into the form shown in Fig. 11 B, and a new piece is cut from hard wood using the cardboard pattern as a guide to replace the portion cut away as well as the broken end. This new piece is joined to the forward half with the halved-joint shown in Fig. 11 C, and is firmly glued and still further strengthened by a screw driven from the inner side and countersunk into the wood, the space over the head being filled with cement. Oftentimes a chair may be unbroken and yet be so loose and rickety in all its joints that it is unfit for use. The only thing to do in such cases is to take the chair apart, clean off all old glue and re-glue all the joints. Where the joints are very loose they may be secured by fine finishing-nails driven through them, first making holes with a drill or brad-awl, while loose joints in uprights where they

enter the seat may be expanded by driving small wedges into the lower sides as shown in Fig. 12.

Very often one or more of the posts or uprights of a chair become broken off in the holes in which they are fitted. This is a simple break to repair, although one often sees such fractures nailed or glued together in a most slovenly and slipshod manner. To repair such a break properly, first remove all particles of old glue and wood from the hole and saw off the broken end of the upright evenly. In the centre of the upright bore a straight hole for about an inch in depth and as nearly the same diameter as the end of the upright as possible (Fig. 13). Into this hole fit a round peg with the projecting end the diameter of the hole in the back of the chair and glue it firmly in both the upright and the back. Still another common break in chairs is when a piece splits out of the seat where the uprights enter (Fig. 14). To repair such a break first trim the break smooth and even and secure the upright in the hole by means of glue and a screw as in Fig. 15, and then fit two pieces of wood into the space around it as shown in Fig. 16. These pieces should be glued in position and reinforced by fine finishing nails run through both pieces and into the seat of the chair beyond. When thoroughly dry, the ends and edges should be smoothed off and finished.

Parlour chairs with light carved or ornamental backs quite frequently break where the dowels of the sides enter the rail at the top. To repair such a break (Fig. 17), remove all pieces of the old dowel and glue and bore a hole in the top of the upright. Into this fit a wooden dowel-pin, being careful to have it project far enough to reach clear through the loose piece and well into the solid back above (Fig. 18), and deepen the hole in the back sufficiently to accommodate the new dowel. Drill a small hole through the loose piece and screw it to the back as in Fig. 19, and also glue the pieces together. Place glue in the dowel-holes and drive or press the parts into place (Fig. 20). In order to hold the joints tightly together while drying,

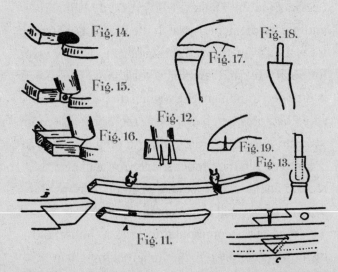

Fig. 14.   Fig. 18.   Fig. 17.   Fig. 15.   Fig. 12.   Fig. 16.   Fig. 19.   Fig. 13.   Fig. 11.

cramp the back to the uprights by strong string or light rope twisted taut with bits of stick and with pads of paper or cloth beneath the ropes to prevent scarring the varnish as shown in Fig. 21.

Chairs, tables or other furniture with round or turned legs or uprights often break in one or more places in the centre of these pieces as in Fig. 22. Such a break is very easy to repair as it is only necessary to dowel the joints together, but it is a very difficult, in fact almost impossible, job to dowel an uneven broken joint, and hence the first step is to cut off the broken post near the fracture as shown in Fig. 22 A A. The broken pieces are then glued together with not strong, but rather thin glue and are brought into close contact by tapping with a mallet or hammer. They are then set aside to dry. A hole is then bored into both ends of the sawed cuts, taking care to exactly centre the drill or bit. While the hole bored into the whole end of the post may be but an inch or so in depth, the hole in the broken piece should extend well beyond the glued fracture (Fig. 22 B). Dowels of birch or other hard wood should then be fitted in the holes glued in place and driven in tight. In using dowels you should always cut a small groove along them in order to allow the air and surplus glue in the holes to escape. If this is not done it will be very difficult to bring the dowels and joints close together and if too much force is used the compressed air and glue will frequently

split the wood. Even if this does not occur it may force the joints apart after you have set them aside to harden.

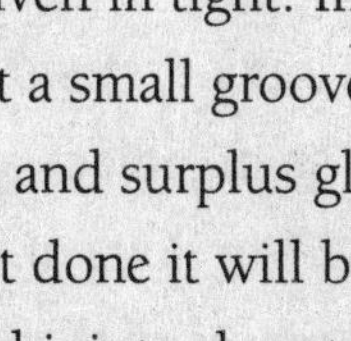

Chairs with loose, wobbly seat-frames may be strengthened by placing corner-braces of hard wood in each corner of the frame and gluing and screwing them firmly into place.

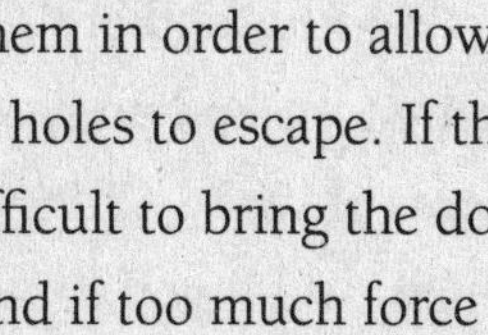

Sometimes a chair, table or other piece of furniture will be very troublesome on account of the legs being uneven. To level up chair legs or legs of furniture which rest directly on the floor, secure four small blocks of wood of exactly the same thickness and place these upon a level smooth surface. Set the chair upon three of these and with the fourth as a gauge mark around the edge of the long leg as shown in Fig. 23, and saw off the amount indicated. Where one leg is too short instead of too long a small piece of wood may be glued and nailed to the leg or the other legs may be trimmed off to correspond with the short one. Where castors are used you can level the legs in a different way. If the castors are merely screwed to the bottom of the legs with a plate, the one on the long leg may be removed, the leg cut off and the castor replaced; but if the castors are set into holes or sockets in the legs the hole must be deepened to shorten a leg or a bit of wood must be slipped in to make the castor project slightly further from the end of the leg when it is too short.

There is scarcely anything more annoying than drawers and doors that stick and bind and as such things are easily remedied there is no excuse for being troubled with them. Very often the reason that a drawer sticks is because the slides or runners or the back of the chest or bureau have warped or shrunk. When this is the case planing or cutting the drawer itself will do little good. If a drawer sticks badly, first roughen all the edges slightly with sandpaper or a file and then run the drawer in and out a few times and look it over for shiny spots and where these are seen plane or scrape off slightly. Avoid taking off any

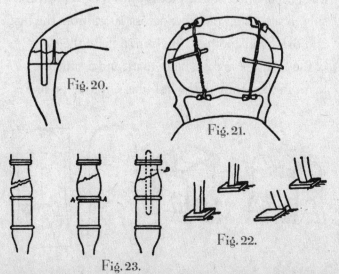

Fig. 20.

Fig. 21.

Fig. 22.

Fig. 23.

of the front edges as long as possible or the drawer will be too small and will fit loosely. If planing and smoothing here and there does not remedy the matter, remove the drawer entirely and set it upon a level surface. If all four corners do not touch the surface the drawer is out of true or "winds," and you will be obliged to bring it back into shape, which is often a difficult job. If the higher parts are planed down sufficiently to bring it into shape the drawer will be too small, but if it is out of parallel or crooked from front to back or the sides bulge, a few light blows with a hammer may rectify the trouble. Sometimes the corner joints will be found out of true or loose and this should be remedied by either taking the drawer apart and re-gluing it or perfectly square cleats may be screwed and glued in each corner to bring the angles back into true.

If the drawer, after truing up, still sticks, you should examine the runners (the wooden pieces against which the drawer slides), and see if they are parallel. They should be slightly wider apart at the back than the front and this may be determined by cutting a strip of wood the exact length of the opening of the front and sliding it back. If it binds as you push it along, or if it even touches at the rear end, the runners must be reduced at the rear. Oftentimes a runner may be loose or entirely missing or a nail-head may protrude and bind somewhere. Sometimes the sides of the article itself may be warped or bulged, and when this occurs it must be remedied by cutting or planing the runners or springing or planing the sides until the runners are straight. Sometimes one runner will be higher than the other or one end may be further up or down than the other. This can be determined by sighting along them, but this requires practice, and an easier way is to test them with a level and square. When you have all the parts smoothed and adjusted until the drawer slides out and in with a little friction, rub the edges and the runners with spermaceti wax and a linen rag. If the wax crumbles warm it slightly before

using. Common laundry or toilet soap will serve in place of the spermaceti, but is not so good.

Sometimes a drawer may be so jammed or stuck that you cannot pull it out without danger of breaking the handles or the front of the drawer. In such cases do not use chisels, screw-drivers or other tools to pry on it, but remove the back of the case or chest and while someone pulls on the handles tap the ends of the back of the drawer with a hammer or mallet, taking care to strike the end furthest in first. If the drawer still refuses to budge remove the partition between the drawers by sliding it out and if necessary remove the runners or loosen them by prying them slightly from the sides of the case.

Making a Shoe-Brush Holder and Shoe-Polishing Bench

One of the simplest things to make is a shoe brush holder and shoe-polishing bench, and, moreover, this is a most useful piece of furniture for any one's room. If you do not require a shoe-brush holder, the same design may be followed and the piece of furniture may be used to hold shoes, magazines, odds and ends, or in fact any articles that you desire to keep handy and out of sight. Select two pieces of wood 12 in. wide and 24 in. long and 1 in. thick, and if you cannot obtain pieces of this width cleat 6-in. pieces together. Four inches from one end of one of these pieces draw a light line from side to side. Draw another across 10 in. from the first and draw still another 2 in. from this. In the centre of the first line make a plain mark and a similar mark in the centre of the last line. On the first line,

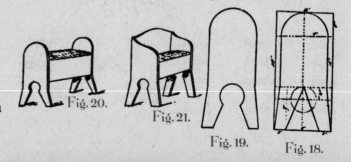

Fig. 20. Fig. 21. Fig. 19. Fig. 18.

using the mark as a centre, draw a half-circle of 4-in. radius and on the last line draw a 4-in. circle. Measure off 2 in. from either corner of the board nearest this small circle and from these marks draw lines meeting exactly in the circle at the upper edge of the circle. From the extreme ends of the large half-circle draw straight lines at right angles to the cross-lines on the board to the second cross-line and thence to the outer corners, and the board will now appear marked as in Fig. 18. With your saws and compass-saw saw off all along these marks and in this way secure a board shaped as in Fig. 19. Repeat the operation with the other 12-in. x 24-in. board, and be sure that both are exactly alike. Now get out three boards each 10 in. wide by 24 in. long and one 24 in. x 8 in. and square the ends and plane the ends and edges smooth and true. Fasten the 8-in. board to the end pieces by screws, placing the board with its lower edge on the line B (Fig. 18), and with a space of 1 in. on either side. To this board and the end pieces fasten the 10-in. boards, one on either side, thus forming an open box, and to one of these side boards hinge the third 10-in. board. See that the screws are all well countersunk and putty up the holes and finish the whole with stain and varnish or paint to suit your own taste. If the affair is to be used as a shoe-polishing bench the top may be left as a plain board, but if you wish to use it as a seat it may be fitted with a cushion or may be upholstered in leather (Fig. 20). A variation in this little piece of furniture may be made by fastening the top securely and hinging the front, or the back may be carried up beyond the rest of the bench, the ends cut in the form shown in Fig. 21 and either the top or front hinged, thus forming a neat and comfortable bench with a receptacle under the seat.

Bookshelves

Bookshelves and racks are always useful and are among the easiest of furnishings to construct.

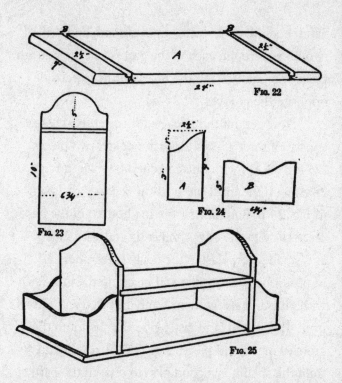

For constructing the shelf described you will require ½-in. material and you should use a wood which will appear well when finished with oil and varnish or which may be stained to imitate some fancy wood: oak, cherry, walnut, maple or other hard woods or whitewood are excellent.

The material should all be ½ in. thick and care should be used not to split or chip the wood. The principal piece is the base, A (Fig. 22), which should be 7 in. wide and as long as you wish the shelf, say 24 in. Plane ends and edges smooth and half-round and at 2½ in. from each end saw a straight line across the board about ¼ in. deep. Saw another line on the inner side of each of these and ½ in. from them and cut away the wood between the lines with a chisel, thus leaving two grooves each ¼ in. deep and ½ in. wide as in Fig. 22 B B. Next get out the two upright end pieces, each 10 in. high and 6¾ in. wide, and with the upper ends neatly rounded or sawed into an ornamental form as in Fig. 23. Five inches from the square ends of these pieces make grooves ½ in. wide by ¼ in. deep, as described for the base piece. Then get out the shelf, which should be 18½ in. long and should have the edges but *not* the ends rounded and should be 7 in. wide.

Sandpaper all these pieces until smooth and drill two holes through each of the grooves in the bottom piece and countersink the holes on the lower side opposite the grooves.

Now get out the pockets for the ends. These consist of three pieces for each pocket, two pieces 2½ in. x 4 in., with one end cut as shown in Fig. 24 A, with the third piece 6¾ in. x 3 in., as shown in Fig. 24 B. Bore holes from the bottom of the base piece close to the edges and ends and with glue and small screws fasten the pockets together and in position. Then set the end pieces in the grooves with glue and screw them firmly in place with screws from the bottom, and lastly glue the shelf into the grooves in the end pieces (Fig. 25). If you intend to stain the shelf it is a good plan to give all the parts a coat before fastening together, as in this way there will be no danger of omitting some portions or getting too much stain on others, but the grooves and the ends of the pieces to be set in them should not be stained, as the glue will adhere better to the plain natural wood.

Simple Tables, Bedside Tables, Etc.

When you have succeeded with the various simple pieces of furniture already described you will

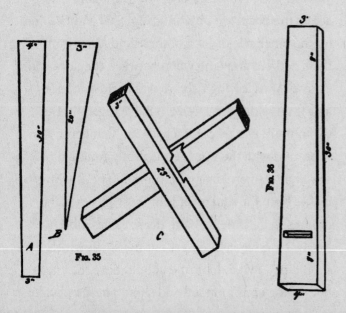

probably wish to try your skill on something more elaborate. A good article is a stand or table, and to make a plain table is not at all difficult. In this stand 1-in. stuff is used throughout, and as all lines are straight a great deal of trouble and work is obviated.

For the top you will have to cleat two pieces together, for the top will be 12 in. square and you will have difficulty in finding a good smooth-grained piece of wood of that width. Plane the two edges for the top—where the boards join—until smooth and even, and glue them firmly together. Then on one side fasten thin, neat cleats about ½ in. thick with screws, taking care to use screws that are not long enough to penetrate through the top. When the glue is thoroughly dry plane and smooth off the ends and sides until well rounded. For the legs you will require four pieces each 30 in. long and 4 in. wide at one end and 3 in. wide at the other (Fig. 35 A). When the legs are roughly sawed out clamp them together in the vise and plane all together until they are all absolutely alike. Next get out four pieces each 20 in. long and 3 in. wide and tapering to a point at one end as shown in Fig. 35 B, and plane these so all are alike while clamped together in the vise. The next pieces to get out are the cross-pieces to support the shelf. These are each 3 in. wide and 23 in. long and should be half-and-half joined in the centre (Fig. 35 C). Eight inches from the bottom (4 in. end) of each leg-piece, cut a recess 3 in. wide and ¼ in. deep (Fig. 36). On the lower side of the top draw lines from corner to corner and on each of these lines, 3½ in. from the corners, mark off spaces 3 in. long and ½ in. wide with the lines as centres, and with the chisel carefully cut out recesses ¼ in. deep as shown in Fig. 37. The bottom shelf is the next piece in order. This should be 18 in. square and on one side draw lines from corner to corner. With these lines as a guide mark lines at right angles to them (using your square for the purpose) and moving the square back and forth until the lines across the corners, measure just 3 in. When this is determined draw the lines and saw off the corners as shown in Fig. 38. Next smooth and round off all corners and edges on this piece, as well as the corner edges of the legs and the edges on the *slanting* side of the triangular pieces already described. Set the cross-piece, made by halving the two 3-in. x 3-in. pieces together, in the recesses in the lower part of the legs and place the top in position so the upper (3-in.) ends of the legs fit in the recesses made in the lower side of the top. If the top sets level and all parts fit well the next step will be to trim off a little on the inner sides of the legs so that they stand evenly on the floor.

To do this you will have to cut off a little piece of each leg, and the way to determine the amount is to place a piece of ½-in. wood on the floor close to the leg until the desired result is obtained. When this is accomplished glue the cross-pieces in their recesses and glue the tops of the legs into the places in the top and through each leg, from the outside, drive a screw into the ends of the cross-pieces. The screws may be countersunk and puttied over or round-headed screws may be used, as your fancy dictates. Set the table aside until the glue is thoroughly dry, and then turn it upside down on a flat surface. Take one of the triangular pieces and place it on the outside of a leg with the straight edge against the leg and the wide end against the lower side of the top.

You will find that if the straight edge is pressed evenly against the leg there will be a little open space between the inner edge of the end and the table top. Place a thin piece of wood or a rule along the lower side of the top and against the triangular piece and

with a pencil draw a line parallel with the top. Saw carefully along this line, and if you have done the work properly you will now find that the end of the piece fits snugly against the top with the straight edge against the leg. Repeat this operation with the other three triangular pieces and then measure off from each side of each leg at the top and also at a point a foot lower down, and mark the exact centre of each leg from side to side. Measure ¼ in. from these centres on each side and draw a line from one centre mark along the legs to the other centre. Along this line drill two or three holes and countersink the openings on the opposite sides or inside of the legs. Coat the straight edge of a triangular piece with glue, and also the end, and place it against a leg, using the two little marks ¼ in. from the centre as guides and drive screws into it from the inside of the legs. With a fine drill or bit bore a hole in each triangular piece and drive a slender, long screw through each of these into the lower side of the top. Bore a hole through each of the lower cross-braces, about 6 in. from the centre, and countersink the lower openings. Turn the table right side up, place the shelf on the cross-pieces and centre it so that the corners are equidistant from all the legs and make light marks to indicate the position. Then fasten the shelf by screws driven up through the underside of the cross-braces and your table is complete, save for finishing with stain, varnish or wax as you prefer (Fig. 39).

Having constructed this stand to your satisfaction you can turn your attention to something more difficult and elaborate. The table described in the following paragraphs may be made of any size by altering the various measurements, but the size given is very good. For this table you will require some 1½-in. square stuff for the legs and bottom pieces as well as the regular 1-in. stuff for tops, rails, etc. In making this table there are several mortised or tenon joints which will afford excellent practice at this sort of work.

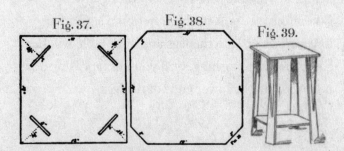

Fig. 37.   Fig. 38.   Fig. 39.

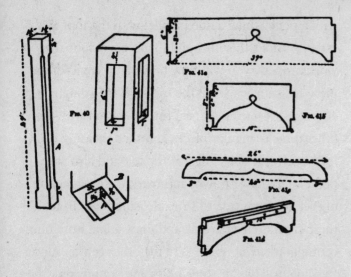

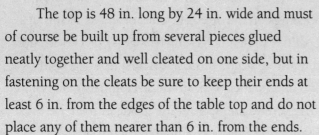

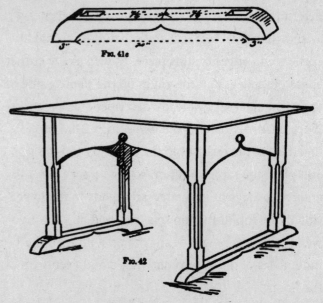

The top is 48 in. long by 24 in. wide and must of course be built up from several pieces glued neatly together and well cleated on one side, but in fastening on the cleats be sure to keep their ends at least 6 in. from the edges of the table top and do not place any of them nearer than 6 in. from the ends.

The legs should be 24 in. long and each corner of each should be chamfered for a space of 20 in., beginning the chamfers 2 in. from one end and carrying them to within 2 in. of the other (Fig. 40 A). At one end of each leg cut away for a space of ½ in. on two sides and ¼ in. on the other two sides for a depth of ½ in., thus leaving a tongue or tenon ½ in. by 1 in. and ½ in. long (Fig. 40 B). From the 1-in. material get out two pieces each 39 in. long and 8 in. wide and shaped as in Fig. 41a, and two other pieces each 15 in. long and 8 in. wide formed as in Fig. 41b. On each end of each of these pieces cut away a space at top and bottom ½ in. deep and 1 in. wide. On each leg, on two sides and at the upper end, cut recesses ½ in. deep, 1 in. wide and 6 in. long, with one end of each recess just 1 in. from the top of the legs (Fig. 40 C). Then from 1½-in. material cut two pieces 26 in. long and 3 in. wide shaped as in Fig. 41c. On each of the pieces Fig. 41a and Fig. 41b fasten pieces 1 in. square and about 10 in. long with one edge flush with the straight edge of the pieces

(Fig. 41d). Screw these cleats in position with screws through the cleats and bore other holes at right angles to them as illustrated. On the pieces Fig. 41c find the centre from end to end and from the centres measure off 7¼ in. in each direction and from these marks mark off rectangular spaces 1 in. long and ½ in. wide as indicated in Fig. 41e, and with a chisel cut these out ½ in. deep.

Coat all the tenons and recesses with glue and set the frame up as shown in Fig. 42, and set aside until thoroughly dry. When hard turn the frame bottom up, resting the upper edge on the lower side of the top, and when it is centred so that the space around the frame on the top is equal on all sides fasten the frame to the top with screws through the cleats fastened already to the side and end pieces, also placing glue between the edges of the side, the top of the legs and the lower sides of the cleats before driving the screws. Then through the lower side of the pieces at the bottom of the legs drive long screws up into the legs and your table will be complete save finishing, or if you desire, castors may be placed on the lower ends of the legs.

Boats, Bird Houses, and More Furniture

From *The American Boys' Workshop*, edited by Clarence B. Kelland, 1914

A Flat Bottom Row Boat

Here is a very simple and serviceable boat, designed for children. Before beginning actual work see that all your tools are in good condition. Next look over the drawings reproduced herewith, and get a clear idea of how you are going to do each step of the job. Plate 1 is a plan that shows every little detail and dimension, and the lad of sixteen or more will really not require any more assistance than is furnished by this print. Plate 2 is a supplementary drawing, that gives pictures, not plans, of each important stage of the construction.

You should have the two drawings close at hand as you proceed so that you can refer to them instantly. First saw out the molds, No. 1, No. 2, No. 3, and No. 4, on Sheet 1. The exact size is shown. Nail them to a plank as shown in Fig. 1 (Sheet 2). They should not rest on the plank, but should have the amount of space between as is indicated by the clearance notes printed under each one. We now tack the sideboards or side streaks on to the molds and bring them to a point at the bow or fore end. Put in the stern board and the middle bottom board. This is shown in Fig. 2 (Sheet 2). The molds are merely to aid us in shaping the boat, and nothing must be nailed to them except temporarily. Figure 5 shows how the sideboards will have to be shaved off with a plane so the bottom boards will lay flat upon them. The stem of the boat is marked Fig. 3. Its dimensions are shown clearly. Use great care in cutting it out. Figure 7 shows how the sideboards

fit into this stem piece. The boat now begins to look like the real thing. We have the sides, stern, stem, and bottom complete.

We next put in the ribs and floor timber. Figures 7 and 6 on Sheet 2 show this clearly. The seat riser is a long cleat nailed to the ribs. The floor, as in Fig. 10, consists of long cleats nailed to the floor timber. We now put on the seats and the little decking at the bow end of the boat. Next come the blocks for the oarlocks, shown very clearly in Fig. 8 (Sheet 2). Along the whole length of the boat at the top of the sideboards and stern is a strip called the fender-wale. It is shown in the drawing marked "stern view" on Sheet 1. The keel is also shown. The keel is a hard board nailed to the bottom of the bottom of the boat. It protects it when sliding on the sand of a creek bed or in shallow water.

Bill of Material

Sides.—Two boards 16′ long, 16″ wide, and ⅞″ thick.

Bottom.—*One* piece, length 14′ 4″, width 8″, thickness ⅝″.
 Two pieces, length 13′ 8″, width 7″, thickness ⅝″.
 Two pieces, length 12′, width 7″, thickness ⅝″.
 Thickness of all bottom boards is the same.

Molds.—(No. 1) one piece, length 33″, width 15″, thickness ⅞″.
 (No. 2) one piece, length 44″, width 15″, thickness ⅞″.
 (No. 3) one piece, length 43.5″, width 14.5″, thickness ⅞″.

(No. 4) one piece, length 40″, width 13.5″,
thickness ⅞″.

Thickness of all molds is the same.

Stern Board.—One piece, length 32″, width 13″,
thickness ⅞″.

Seats.—Two pieces, 15″ × 10″ × ⅝″.

Two pieces, 12″ × 7″.

Two pieces, 18″ × 10″.

One piece, 39″ × 10″.

One piece, 42″ × 10″.

All seats are the same thickness.

Deck.—One piece, 13″ × 12″ × ⅞″.

Stem.—One piece, 17″ long × 3⅝″ × 2¼″.

Oarlock Blocks.—Four pieces, 10″ × 2.5″ × 2.5″.

Ribs and Floor Timbers.—42 feet of 1″ square oak
strips.

Seat Risers.—Two strips, 14′ long × 2″ wide × ⅞″
thick.

Floor Strips.—Two pieces, 8′ long × 2″ wide × ¼″
or ½″ thick.

Two pieces, 8′ long × 2″ wide × ¼″ or ½″ thick.

Four pieces, 12′ long × 2″ wide × ¼″ or
½″ thick.

Foot Braces.—Four pieces, 8″ long × 1¾″
wide × 1″.

Two pieces, 10″ long × 1″ × 1″. All of oak.

Oarlock Block Supports.—*Four* pieces, 15″ × 2″ × 1″.
Y (Fig. 8).

Four pieces, 17″ × 2″ × ⅝″. Z (Fig. 8).

Fender-wale.—Two long strips, 16′ long × 2″ wide ×
½″ thick.

Keel—Oak board, 1″ thick, 4″ wide, and 15′ long.

Use 2-inch clout nails for nailing bottom.
Brass screws in all sizes from 1 inch long to 3 inches
long will be required. Get 10 cents' worth of each
size and fill out with more if the work demands.
The boat should receive two coats of paint
inside and three coats outside. This will take two
gallons of paint and one gallon of boiled oil for
thinning purposes. Oarlocks cost 25 cents a pair, two

pairs are required. Caulk all cracks in the bottom
with oakum.

The mark (′) means feet; the mark (″) means
inches; 2.5″ means two and a half inches.

Work very slowly and carefully. Three weeks is
good time in which to make this boat right.

A Canoe

One of the most interesting boats to build,
and one of the safest and most serviceable when
properly handled is the canoe. To construct a strong,
safe canoe is not difficult if adequate directions are
followed. It is the purpose of this chapter to tell you
in detail how to work and what materials to buy. It is
written for the average child who has only a hammer
and saw and plane to work with and but a few
dollars to spend on pleasure craft.

It will occur to you at once that the hardest
part of boat construction is the shaping. Anyone
could build a long box, but how are we going to
accomplish the graceful curving of the sides and
the neat tapering of the ends? We must build forms
or molds for this purpose, and the strips to be
bent must be pliable and softened by immersion in
boiling water or steam for hours.

The very first thing to do is to set up a heavy
plank on two strong trestles. It is marked "Z" in
Fig. 1, Plate 1. Mark the center and a line four feet
each side of the center. Then make one mold or
form like "A" and two like "B." Figure 2 shows exact
dimensions for one-half of mold "A," Fig. 3 is one-
half of "B." When you have the molds completed, set
the big one "A" on the center line of the plank and
nail it securely; the two smaller ones "B" are fastened
to the four-foot lines you have drawn. We now fasten
to each end of the plank the curved piece shown by
Fig. 5. The exact curvature of this 50-inch oak or
ash strip is indicated by the Figures. It is shaped by
being softened and bound to a form as shown for
several days. The first two long strips or gunwales

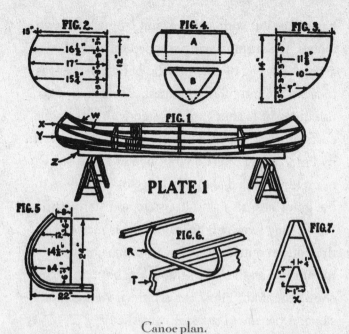

Canoe plan.

"W" are screwed to the stem and stern pieces and to the molds. Next temporarily fasten the pair "X" and the pair "Y." The work so far described is by far the most difficult to do. When complete the skeleton of the canoe will look like Fig. 1 in Plate 1. The joint and shape at the ends of those long strips is shown by Fig. 7.

The putting in of the ribs is our next concern. They should be green elm, hickory, or ash, three-eighths inch thick and one and one-half inches wide, and long enough to make the curve from gunwale to gunwale. The center or longest one is the first to be put in, as "R" in Fig. 6 shows. It goes outside of "X" and "Y" and inside the gunwales "W." The ribs are placed one inch apart and are fastened with galvanized nails. The boiling or softening of the ribs may be done by making a steam-tight box as in Fig. 2, Plate 2. The opening in the top is set over a vessel of boiling water and the ribs are placed in through the open end. In this way one burner on a gas stove may be made to keep the box full of steam. After a night's immersion in the hot vapor the ribs can be bent without fear of breaking or cracking. When the ribs are well set after being in place two days, remove "X" and "Y." Figure 3 is an iron pipe four inches in diameter, with one closed end driven into the ground at the angle indicated. It is filled with water and a bonfire built under it. Strips may be placed inside the pipe, and by maintaining a hot fire you have a fairly satisfactory apparatus for steaming the ribs.

We now remove the plank and substitute a strip two inches wide and one inch thick, and long enough to run along the bottom of the canoe, being fastened to the curved stem and stern piece. The framework of the canoe being completed, we proceed to cover it either with canvas or planking or both. The planking process is shown by Fig. 1 in Plate 2. The material used is cypress, three inches wide and one-quarter inch thick. It is shaped like the siding or clap boards used on houses and one board overlaps the other. Begin at the center and work to the sides. Clout nails are used.

They are clinched on the inner side as shown in Fig. 5. The joint used in fastening the long bottom piece to the stem and stern is shown in Fig. 4. If you wish to use canvas as a covering, observe Fig. 1 on Plate 3. The canvas should be extra heavy and may be used without the planking; that is, it may be nailed directly on the skeleton, as it appears in Fig. 1, Plate 2. Lay your wide strip of

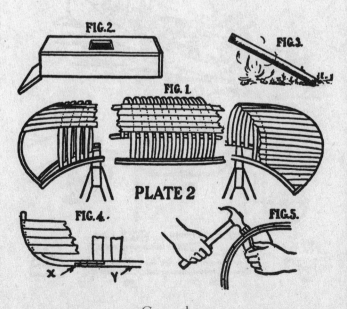

Canoe plan.

canvas on the framework and tack the center line to the center line of the canoe bottom strip. Use copper or galvanized tacks. Stretch it as you go, leaving no wrinkles or fullness. At the ends it will

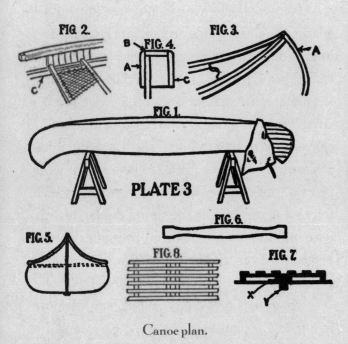

Canoe plan.

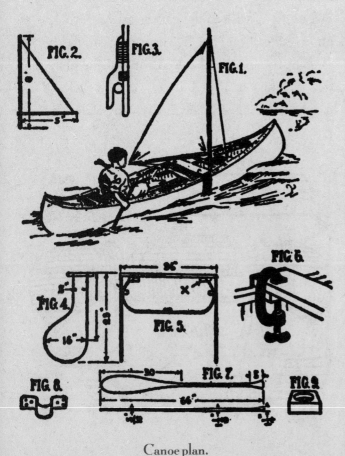

Canoe plan.

have to be cut with a shears and lapped over two inches, the surplus being snipped off and thrown away. A coating of glue may be put on the canvas to shrink it and fill up the meshes, but it is of no use unless it is afterward covered with three good coats of paint, inside and outside. The deck shown by Fig. 3, Plate 3, is now put in and a thin strip of molding nailed along the edge of the canvas to the gunwales, also an outer stem and stern strip "A." A long two-inch board or keel is nailed to the bottom outside the canvas to prevent injury to same when the boat scrapes the bottom. Figure 8 shows the floor; Fig. 7 is a sectional view of the same. A picture of the seat is marked Fig. 2; "C" is one of the inside strips to support same. Figure 6 is a brace used in the center of the boat. Notice it under the sail in the complete sketch. The boat is now entirely finished. It may be varnished on the inside to look like light oak.

Figure 4 shows size and shape of leeboards, which extend down over the sides of the boat into the water. Figure 5 is a view of same. Figure 6 shows how the leeboard device is clamped to the boat at the point "X." The whole thing, including sail, may be lifted off or added to any canoe. Figure 2 is the sail plan, Fig. 3 a homemade cleat for swinging it. The base of the mast rests in the block (Fig. 9) and passes through the strap (Fig. 8), which is made from a heavy tub hoop. This about finishes the canoe equipment. If you follow instructions you will have a good, serviceable boat. An estimate of the cost is less than $10.

Base (Temporary).—One piece, 14′ × 4″ × 2″ pine.
Stem Pieces.—Four pieces, 50″ × 1¾″ × 1″ oak.
Gunwales.—Two pieces, 16′ × 1″ × 1″ oak.
Side Strips (Temporary).—Four pieces, 16′ × 1″ × 1″ oak.
Ribs.—190′, 1½ ′ × ⅜″ ash, elm, hickory, or cypress.
Planking.—275′, 2″ × ¼″ × ⁸⁄₁₆″ cypress.
Keel.—One piece, 14′ × 3″ × 1½″ oak.

Seat Raisers.—Two pieces, 14′ × 1″ × 1″ oak.

Seats.—Ten feet, 1½″ × ½″ oak.

Thwart.—One piece, 31″ × 3″ × ⅜″ oak.

Fender-wale.—Six pieces, 16′ × 1⅛″ × 1¼″ cypress.

Deck.—Two pieces, 12″ × 6″ × ½″ cypress.

Canvas.—28″ wide by 18′ long.

Paddle, Sail, and Leeboards.—Dimensions given on
   cuts.

Paint.—Two gallons.

A Small Sailboat Combine with Flat Bottom Row Boat

The most important part of a flat-bottomed boat is the stem. This should be of good white oak. You can make it yourself, or have it cut out at a saw mill, which is easier. Next, get out the two sideboards. They should be of number one cypress, without knots or sap streaks, three-quarter-inch thick. Lay out the dimensions as shown on the plans, then saw and plane to the desired shape.

When these are done, make the molds. As they are not permanent, they can be made of old material. Be sure to leave a notch in each lower corner, or else the stringer cannot be fitted. Then make the transom, or stern board. This should be of oak.

When ready to set up, nail each sideboard to the stem with a double row of nails. Hold the mold "A" five feet from the end of the stem, bend the side boards around it, and fasten securely. Then hold mold "B" three feet from mold "A" and fasten as before. Be sure to have each mold at right angles to the center line of the boat. To fasten the sides to mold "C" and to the transom it will be necessary to fasten heavy rope around the sides, and twist it with a board in the manner shown in Fig. 2. This will bring it together, and you can fasten to mold "C" and the transom. Never drive a nail without first boring a hole for it with a bradawl. For all permanent nailing use galvanized iron boat nails. These are square cut nails.

Along the bottom of each side put in a cypress stringer seven-eighths inch thick and two inches wide, extending the full length of the boat. It will be necessary to make a few saw cuts near the stern where it bends sharply up.

The ribs are oak, ⅞″ × ⅞″ and should be screwed in eighteen inches apart.

To put on the flooring, turn the boat upside down, and plane off the sideboards and stringer so they will be flat across. Lay several strands of cotton wicking along the edge, and nail the floor boards to both sideboards and stringers. The floor boards

Plan for small sailboat.

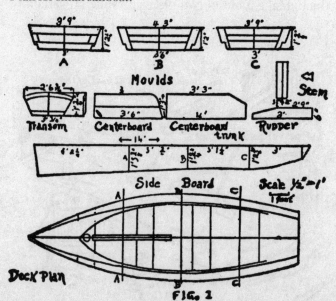

Plan for rigging a small sailboat.

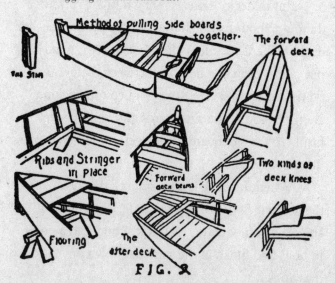

should be white pine, as clear from knots and sap streaks as possible. Cypress can be used, but it is not so good. Make as tight a joint between the boards as possible, as there is to be no caulking.

Fasten a strip of Georgia pine $\frac{7}{8}'' \times 6''$ along the outside bottom from stem to stern for a keel shoe. Be sure to get Georgia pine, and not North Carolina pine. Nail with long boat nails clinched on the inside.

Turn the boat over, and put in the seats where shown on plans one and one-half inches from the top. They should be cypress $1\frac{5}{8}'' \times 9''$.

Now the molds can be taken out. When this is done, put in a $\frac{7}{8}'' \times \frac{7}{8}''$ cypress rib, and just below the seats, extending from stem to stern.

Cut a centerboard slot where shown, two inches wide. Put a post at each end extending from the bottom of the slot as shown in Fig. 3, and nail firmly to both floor and keel shoe. The sides of the centerboard trunk should be in one piece, cypress, seven-eighths-inch thick. Before nailing them on lay two or three strands of cotton wicking where they will join the floor. Put a molding along the corner where the centerboard trunk meets the floor. It would be well to put cotton wicking underneath this, too, as the centerboard trunk is a fruitful place for leaks. The top of the centerboard trunk should be oak one-quarter inch thick.

Put in deck beams, as shown in Fig. 2. Curve them up about two inches in the center. For the side deck, make deck knees like those in Fig. 2, and put one at each seat and one between. Before putting on the deck lay several strands of cotton wicking along the top of the sideboards and nail the deck firmly to the sideboards. The deck should be cypress in strips, $\frac{7}{8}'' \times 3''$.

When the deck is laid, smooth the inside of the cockpit ready for the combing. The combing should be one-quarter-inch oak. Bring it to a point in bow, and finish in the stern as shown on drawings.

Then prepare to lay the canvas deck. Paint the deck with a heavy coat of white paint. Paint the underside of canvas the same way, and lay while paint is wet. Bring the edges over onto the sides, and nail to side boards with galvanized or copper tacks, placed close together. Nail inside edge to combing. Where edges of cloth meet on the deck, overlap, and paint thickly underneath. Do not tack to deck. Screw a two-inch half-round fender rail over joint between deck and side boards. Nail a half-inch quarter-round molding in corner between deck and combing, as shown in Fig. 3. Screw to combing four oarlock blocks, as shown in Fig. 3. They should be strengthened with brass angle irons.

For a rudder pipe use a one-inch inside diameter brass pipe. Thread each end, and screw a nut on. Before putting in, line the holes with white lead.

Make the rudder of seven-eighth-inch Georgia pine. For a rudder post use a one-inch diameter brass rod. Square upper end to fit tiller socket. Split the other end and straddle it over rudder. Rivet it with copper rivets. Bore two holes near the top and get a brass pin to fit the holes. This is to hold the rudder in. Make the tiller out of oak. A brass tiller socket such as shown in Fig. 3 can be bought for it. The centerboard should be Georgia pine one inch thick. Make it out of two pieces dowelled together,

Plan for small sailboat.

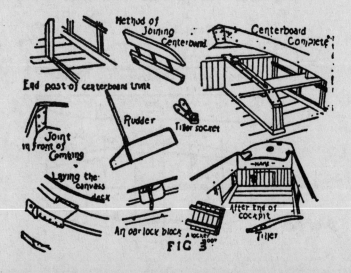

as shown in Fig. 3. Use brass rods for dowels, and be sure to bore the holes for them straight and of the same diameter as the rods. Make a five-inch slot in one corner to permit the center-board being dropped as low as possible. Fasten centerboard in with an oak pin. Fasten a brass rod to top to raise and lower it.

Make a mast hole in foremost thwart, or in forward deck. Line it with leather. Place an oak mast step on the floor directly beneath it. Make a locker at each end of boat, using beaded cypress.

Paint the whole boat with three coats of good paint. Paint the centerboard and centerboard trunk before putting them together. Use deck paint for the deck. All varnished work should be varnished with good spar varnish. Do not try to economize by using cheap varnish. It won't pay.

Obtain a mast. For the boom and sprite, get 2″ × 2″ spruce. It will be easier to round it if you get the corners cut off at the sawmill.

The easiest way to get a sail is to have it made at the sailmaker's. When giving him the dimensions, if you are having the spritsail made, be sure to give him the corner-to-corner dimension. If you are making it yourself, overlap each piece of cloth about an inch and sew with a double row of stitches. Sew a light rope around the edge, leaving a loop at the outside corner, as in drawing.

To fasten on the leg-of-mutton sail, lash it firmly to the mast hoops. Run the hilliard from the top of the sail, through a pulley at the top of the mast, and belay—that is, fasten—on a cleat near the bottom of the mast. To set the sail, insert small end of the boom into loop on corner of sail, and stretch sail as flat as possible. Fasten a rope, having a loop in one end, to the mast with a double half-hitch. Run free end of rope through slot in end of boom, through loop in other end, and fasten to boom with double half-hitch, as shown in Fig. 4.

If using the spritsail rig, lash the sail permanently to the mast. Set the same way as leg-of-mutton sail. The sprite is the spar that holds up the upper corner of the sail. This is put on the same way as the boom. The main sheet—as the rope that hauls in and lets out the mainsail is called—should be belayed or fastened on a cleat on one side, rove— that is, passed—through a pulley on the boom and belayed on the other side.

Fasten the jib to eye-bolts in stem and masthead with snap hooks. There should be two jib sheets, one on each side, led through eye-bolts, and belayed near mainsheet.

Bolt a large cleat through forward deck, and put a chock on each side of bow. Put four oarlocks on the sides, and one in the stern. Put a cleat in the stern.

A twenty-pound anchor will be about the right size.

The spritsail rig is the best for rough water and high winds, and is easy to handle, but the boat is very much under-canvased rigged this way. If you want more sail, use the leg-of-mutton sail. The mast for spritsail should be nine feet six inches high. For leg-of-mutton, it should be twice that height, but should taper very much toward the top.

The cost will, of course, vary with the locality and the fittings. The lumber, with the exception of the centerboard, rudder, and spars, will cost about eight or ten dollars. You can have the spritsail made

Plan for rigging a small sailboat.

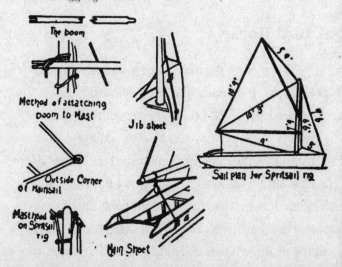

for about five. The whole boat complete would cost eighty dollars at a shipbuilders, and you can build it for less than half that sum.

Cypress

Two pieces ¾ in. × 18 in. × 14 ft.
Two pieces ⅞ in. × 2 in. × 14 ft.
Two pieces ⅞ in. × ⅞ in. × 14 ft.
One piece 1⅞ in. × 9 in. × 12 ft.
One piece ⅞ in. × 1 ft. 3 in. × 8 ft.
One piece ⅞ in × 3 in. × 12 ft.
One piece ⅞ in. × 2 in. × 1 ft. 9 in.
Four pieces ⅞ in. × 3 in. × 18 ft.

Oak

One piece 6 in. × 5 in. × 12 in.
Two pieces ⅞ in. × ⅞ in. × 14 ft.
One piece ⅞ in. × 13 in. × 2 ft. 7 in.
Two pieces ¼ in. × 6 in. × 11 ft.
One piece ¼ in. × 3½ in. × 3 ft. 9 in.
One piece 1 in. × 4 in. × 4 ft.

Georgia Pine

One piece ⅞ in. × 6 in. × 14 ft
One piece 1 in. × 7 in. × 7 ft.
One piece ⅞ in. × 6 in. × 3 ft.

White Pine

Five pieces ⅞ in. × 6 in. × 16 ft.

A Bird House

The picture illustrates a neat and serviceable bird house. It is made of three shallow boxes set at angles upon each other. The size of the boxes depends upon your own taste. For ordinary purposes eighteen inches square and six inches deep is about right for each. In designing the house it was intended as a refuge for untamed birds and so as many compartments as possible were made. Each of the shallow boxes is divided into four spaces as

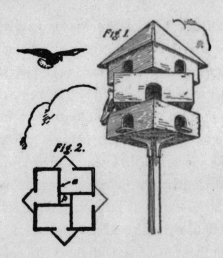

A bird house.

shown in Fig. 2. The space "*P*" is where the post comes up through the center. The perches and openings are cut out with a small circle saw. The roof is of tin or galvanized iron. It is made of four triangles lapped over each other and riveted. Two coats of steel gray paint on the outside will add to the appearance of the house and make it weather resisting.

It should be set upon a high post and made as inviting as possible for the feathered visitors. Remember that as man has encroached upon the domain of the wild creatures only three courses were open to them: either to move to remoter regions, to adapt themselves to modern conditions, or to die out altogether. The robin is one of the species that has made the best of things and tried to stay with us. It is interesting to study its habits, and this shelter will aid you in doing so. Here are some things to discover for yourself. Do the robins arrive from the South singly or in flocks? Do the sexes migrate together? How long after the arrival does nest building begin? What is their food? Is it the same in various months? All these and a dozen more lines of inquiry will make the shelter interesting.

Another Work-bench

Every craftsman should have a work-bench. It is not only a great aid in constructing things, but it is a standing invitation to work. While you are about it you might as well make a bench that will do for all time. The plan shows one that will prove strong and serviceable. Two large slide drawers provide a place for keeping your tools, while the shelf will be useful for the same purpose while a job is in progress. Figure 2 presents a side view and an end view of the completed bench. For the legs you will need four pieces of 2″ × 6″ stuff 38″ long. Fasten each pair together by means of a crosspiece of the same material, whose top edge is 12″ from the floor. Even with the top of each pair fasten a brace of like size. We now connect the pairs by putting in the lower shelf of 1″ boards.

The compartment for the drawers is now built, the joint used being like the one shown in Fig. 5. The drawers are made of 1″ stuff. Figure 4 shows the plan of construction. Make them so

A work-bench.

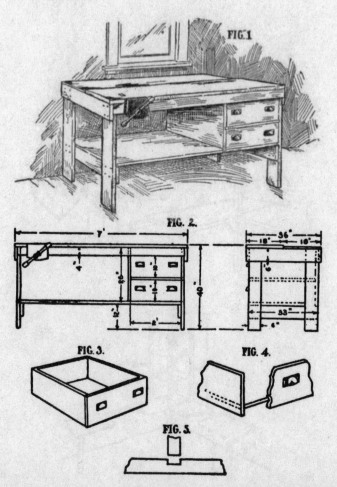

they will slide freely, permitting them to be too loose rather than too tight. The handholds may be purchased at a hardware store or a department store. Log scantlings are now nailed só as to connect the legs at the top, and next the top is put on. Our picture shows that one half of the bench has a top which is 2″ in thickness, while the other half is only 1″ thick. It will be better if it is all 2″ thick, but it will cost more. The bench vise is a simple one and may be purchased for sixty cents. A square hole is chiseled in the top of the bench near the vise end. This is to provide a stop or buffer for boards while working. Tight-fitting pegs are put into the hole for this purpose.

It is important that the bench be located where the light is good. Also see that all drafts are stopped. A nice, clean barn or the south window of an attic would be a good place for the bench. The idea, though simple, is well worth being put into practice by anyone. If you have no work-bench, you should make this one without delay.

A Smaller Work-Bench

The type of bench treated here is very common and easy to make. The Figures on the drawing show the exact size of each piece used. Figure 3 shows

A smaller work-bench.

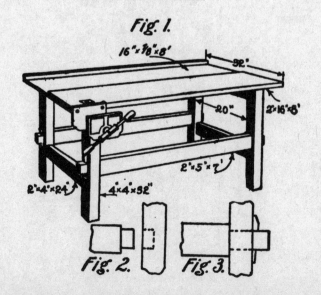

the joint used to fasten the long braces to the legs, Fig. 2 indicates how the short braces are secured. The purpose of the sketch is to give you the proper proportion to follow. You may have both of the top planks of uniform thickness if you wish, but it is not necessary.

A Work Corner

Here is a suggestion for a work corner in the barn or cellar. It may be you haven't room in your yard for a regular workshop, or possibly your parents won't let you build one; surely, however, he won't object to giving you space in the house for this. It serves a twofold purpose. By its constant presence and readiness it invites you to work, and when the decision is made it affords a good place. The first thing to do is to set up a couple of large shelves on brackets, and between the scantling tack four inch boards, which will serve as small shelves. A large box, reinforced by a double top, will do for a work bench. With a work corner like this, good, honest, beneficial occupation for the live, growing child is always assured. In the proper development of manhood, a kit of tools is just as important as a good set of books. A child working with his hands is developing his brain every second of the time.

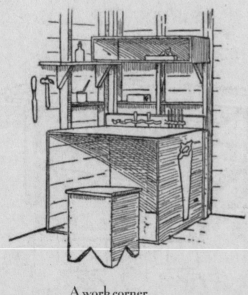

A work corner.

A Reading Corner

Here is a reading corner that suggests comfort, refinement, and the correct use of a neglected corner. If there is a corner in your room that has the light of one or more windows you could not do better than to utilize it in the manner shown by the accompanying picture.

All that you will need to build is the bench seat and the shelf arrangement, and if you wish the latter may be left out. The first thing to do is to screw a strip to the wall at such a height that its top surface will be 17″ from the floor. The strip itself

Plan for reading corner.

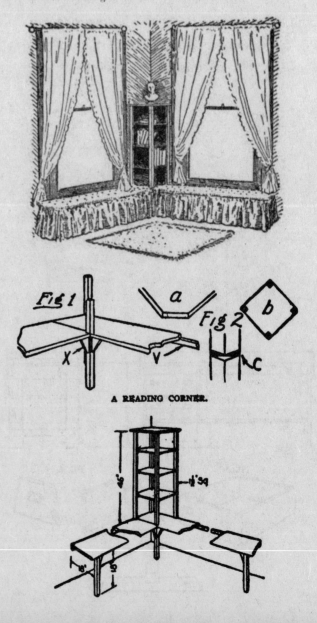

A READING CORNER.

should be 2″ × 2″ pine. The boards that form the seat should be 9″ wide. As the seat is to be 18″ wide you will need two of them to make up the width. They should be cleated together by fastening cross pieces every two feet under them with screws that are not long enough to show up on top. Put as many legs under the seat at the outer edge as you think necessary for the weight it is to bear. Space them about three feet apart.

The shelves are now made. First, make the whole thing complete and then set it on the seat, fastening in place by driving three long screws through the rear upright into the corner of the room. It should be stained and varnished to match the other wood work of the room. The seat may be upholstered and a curtain stretched from the top to the floor.

A Window Seat

Possibly you have only one window in your room, in which case the foregoing plan will be of little use to you. But here is one that will do nicely.

This serviceable window seat is easy to construct. A few minutes' study of the drawings will make clear all the necessary details and then it is up to you to do careful and painstaking work. It is

A window seat.

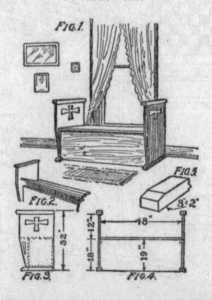

best to make it in the form of a portable bench, but the logical place to set it is as shown in the sketch. Each side piece is 32″ high and 18″ wide. Use the best wood you can get—oak, ash and maple being first choice. Yellow pine is ideal for an amateur on account of its easy working qualities, and it may be finished with shellac and stain to look rich and appropriate. The rail on the top and base of each side is 2″ thick and 3″ wide. It is screwed into place and enables you to join the several pieces that form each side neatly. These pieces are also glued. This makes a close, true fit imperative. Brush on a thin coat of liquid glue and let it dry, then apply another very thin coat and quickly join them in clamps.

The seat board rests upon cleats which are screwed to the inside of each side piece. The face of the bench consists of two 9″ boards glued and cleated together. The seat may be made in the form of a lid which raises up and the inside makes a roomy storage place. The cross-shaped opening near the top of each side may be left out altogether or may be changed to suit your own taste. When complete, go over the entire outside surface and sandpaper it thoroughly. Next dust it with a brush or vacuum cleaner and in a dust-proof room apply a thin coat of shellac. When this has dried, give it a coat of mission stain, and then polish with wax. It will wear well and prove to be a neat and valuable addition to your room.

More Bookshelves

Possibly you have not enough books to warrant you in building a sectional case, but you are sure to have enough to fill a shelf. You will find the accompanying design handsome and useful.

The first thing to do in planning this book shelf is to get two pieces of yellow pine, oak or chestnut, 4 inches wide, ⅞ of an inch thick and 22 inches long, for upright side pieces that lay flat

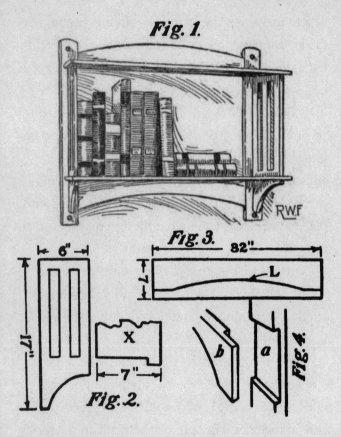

A book shelf.

conditions to do it right, and if done by amateurs the fact is noticeable at a glance. For a satiny polish use wax according to the directions on the can.

A Checker Table, Could Easily be a Chess Table

The plan herewith shows a checker table of neat and pleasing design. If you will study the top, side and end view shown by Fig. 2, you will soon have a thorough grasp of all the essentials of the plan. All the necessary dimensions are marked, and each particular part is shown in its proper relation to all the others.

We will begin work on the sides or legs. If you are using new material, we would advise you to get yellow pine. It works easily and takes a fine finish. To shape the legs you will need a brace and various sized bits, a small circle saw, a good, sharp knife and some sandpaper. First you must glue together

against the wall. We now get a piece as shown in Fig. 3 and cut it on the heavy line. It is done with a circle saw. The top piece in this Fig. 3 is the lower rail in the finished drawing. It is 5 inches wide at the ends and 4 inches wide in the center at the curve. These rails are fastened to the upright side pieces as shown in the detail sketch Fig. 4. Next shape the sides with the two long slots as in Fig. 2. This is done with the small saw. Holes are first bored to give the saw a starting point. Screws driven from the back hold the sides to the posts. The shelves are 7 inches wide and 30 inches long. The top one rests flush upon the sides and is screwed thereto. The bottom shelf is shaped at the ends as shown by "X." Its inside edge rests on the lower rail and is screwed to it. Finish hardwood by rubbing in paste filler and coating with mission stain. For pine fill with shellac and then stain. Either is made richer looking by polishing with wax. Do not put a glossy varnish on anything. It requires years of practice and special

A checker table.

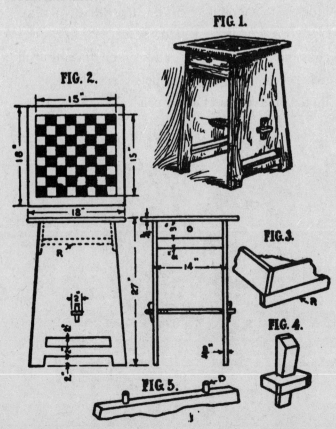

two 9″ boards to get the required width of 18″. Use liquid glue in the following manner: First put on a thin coat and permit it to dry and fill up the pores of the wood; next put on another thin coat with a brush and immediately damp the pieces together. The clamping may be done by placing the glued pieces between blocks nailed to the floor and then driving in wedges to tighten them together. You must also put something heavy on the joint so that it will not spring up. On the top of each side-piece are two wooden pegs, "D" in Fig. 5. These fit into corresponding holes in the top piece. The center brace, which extends through the legs, is toe-nailed from the inside. The wedge-shaped fastening shown in Fig. 4 is more for effect. The drawer rest near the top fits between the legs and is simply nailed into place. The detail of the drawer is pictured in Fig. 3. The piece "R" is one of the rests upon which the drawer slides. The ruling of the checker board must be accurately done in order to look right. First, make the large square, then the line from top to bottom in the center, then a line which crosses that in the center and so on. The drawer pull is a small brass knob, which may be bought for a nickel.

Finishing consists of two coats of mission stain, one day apart, and then a thorough polishing with wax, which is sold for this purpose. Altogether it makes a fine addition to a home, especially to the child's room.

Combination Bookcase and Desk

The accompanying illustration shows a combination article that you will have abundant use for. It makes a roomy bookcase for reference works and can be instantly converted into a desk for your study work. It is designed in such a simple manner that the child with only a few tools and little experience can confidently undertake to construct it. If you study the sketches you will note that every piece is shown in its proper place and every joint used is clearly pictured. Begin with Fig. 2 and you will learn the dimensions. The first thing to do is to cut out the long side pieces. The rear edge is rabbeted to receive the back pieces. Observe Fig. 6 to get this idea. You can order this done at the mill with no extra expense. If you cannot get boards 15″ wide as required, you will have to glue an 8″ and 7″ piece together to form each side. The variation in the width, as shown in Fig. 2, should be carefully marked out and sawed. Do not saw exactly on your line, as allowance must be made for the finishing to be done with plane and sandpaper. When this is done mark cross-lines for the shelves. You can sink the shelves into grooves, or put wooden cleats for them to rest on, or small angle irons. For amateur work I prefer the latter. The angles may be purchased at slight cost or made out of strap iron as thick as a book cover.

When the shelves are in place, our job will look like Fig. 4. Next comes the back, which will materially strengthen the structure. The

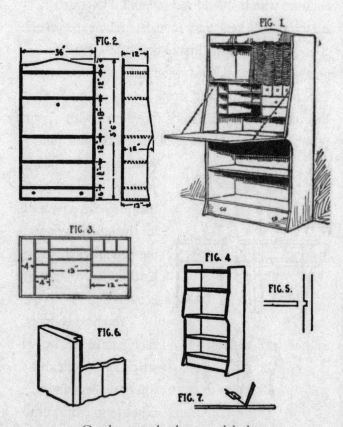

Combination bookcase and desk.

compartment box, as in Fig. 3, is entirely made before being put in place. Use quarter-inch pine for the shelves and half-inch stuff for the outer shell. All the edges are glued and 1″ brads are used to hold parts together while the glue sets. It requires a good deal of figuring to assemble the box as shown. After the outer shell is made the entire inner structure is nailed together before being slipped into it.

The drop leaf, which also serves as a writing rest, comes last. It is carefully fitted and hinged as shown in Fig. 7. Other fittings are a knob and lock and the chains. For a natural wood finish on yellow pine apply three coats of varnish, the first and second being thinned with turpentine. After the first thin coat you may stain any shade desired, applying two coats. Yellow pine finishes very nicely and will last practically as long as any hardwood.

A Writing Table

This design for a writing table has the following qualities which should recommend it to your attention. It is neat, easy to make and inexpensive.

The legs are the first to be made. Use three-quarter oak or any hard wood, or pine if you must. The measurements and shape are shown in Fig. 5. Carefully mark them out on the lumber with a pencil before cutting with saw or plane. Finish one until

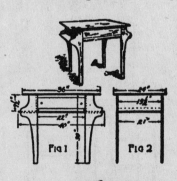

you have it as perfect as your skill will permit, then use it as a pattern for the others. When the legs are done the hardest part of the work is over.

You next connect each pair of legs by two strips, one inside the top of the legs and the other for the drawer to rest on. Figure 3 shows

A writing table.

the table when the first stage of the making is complete. Only simple shaped strips are used (leaving out the legs), and you should have no trouble in getting the legs together in the exact manner shown by the picture.

When you have this part accomplished, put on your table top.

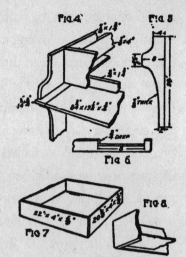

A Writing table.

Care must be taken to get the prettiest side of the boards up and to join them in a way that will show the grain off to its best advantage. A little shelf is placed on each end of the table for books to rest on.

The kind of joint you are to use so that no nails or screws will be seen is quite a feature of the work. Wherever two pieces of wood come together, use a thin coating of glue. Liquid glue is good enough. First put a thin coat on to fill up the pores of the wood, and after it has dried brush on another coat for adhesive purposes. The nails and screws used are always driven from the reverse or unseen side, and do not pierce the piece they enter clear through, but only part way. Use long slender screws and always bore a hole for each one. It takes time and patience to do it, but the best is none too good for you. Examine the stands and tables in your own home and note how the parts are held together.

A Table

Here is a useful hint on increasing the value of a table. The idea is to add a slide to the underside of the shelf. This large drawer, which is practically out of sight, makes a roomy place to store books and other material. The table itself is of simple construction and is amply described by the side and end views Figs. 2 and 3. As to material, the costlier

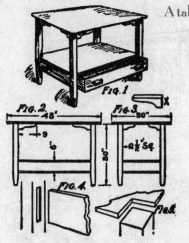

A table.

woods are always to be preferred, but pine will answer as well. The 4″ × 4″ legs taper slightly at the lower end. The first part of the work will be to glue and cleat the pieces which form the top together. The shelf pieces are glued, but not cleated. They are fitted at the corners as shown by Fig. 5. The rails are 2″ wide pieces which form the sides and back of the slide drawer compartment. They are mortised into the legs, as shown by the detail sketch Fig. 4. The brackets used are 9″ long and 3″ wide at the wide end. Dowels are used to fasten them to the legs, and screws from the underside hold them firmly to the table top. The sides and face of the slide are of 1″ stuff, the bottom is of half inch. As a finish put on a thin coat of shellac and then stain to suit taste. Wax rubbed on according to the direction on the can makes a neater and classier finish than varnish. It requires no skill to put it on, while varnish must be thoroughly rubbed and made even or it presents an ugly appearance.

A Cabinet Stand

Here is a neat and useful cabinet for books, or papers, or for curios or a collection of something not too bulky. It is made in plain mission style and will be just the thing for a beginner to try his hand at.

Your first work should be on the posts. All that you need do is to square the ends. This is not quite as easy to do as it sounds, but with great care you will be able to accomplish it. We next put in the pieces that fit on the right and left sides of the drawers. They are 1″ thick and 12″ wide, and fit between the legs. Then-length will be about 13″.

They are held in place by what is called the dowel joint. The dowel consists of wooden pegs fitted into holes bored into the two edges that come together. They are just like the pegs in a common table leaf, only they are glued tightly. After you have the sides in place let them set for a day, and in the meantime you can work on the table top and the top of the drawer section. When these are in place, you can measure and fit the drawers. The table top is fastened with dowel pins as shown in Fig. 2. In Fig. 4 "B" and "C" are small strips upon which the drawers will slide. Figure 3 shows one corner of the flat piece that fits on top of the drawers. The face of the drawers should be of 1″ material, the rest of them may be made of half-inch pine. For a neat finish brush on two coats of prepared stain a day apart and then either varnish or rub with wax. If you are careful in your work you will be more than pleased with the finished stand. It will prove ornamental and useful and will help you to keep your room neat.

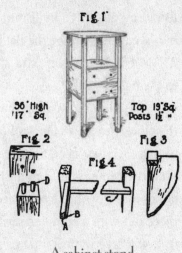

A cabinet stand.

Combination Clock and Shelf

The neat and practical article pictured here will afford a fine opportunity for the child with mechanical talent to exercise some of it. If you study the several parts that go to form it you will note that they are of simple shape and quite easy to cut out.

The first piece to give your attention to is the base. It is 22″ × 6″ and ½″ thick. Its shape is that of a simple rectangle with the corners rounded a little. Mark the curve at the four corners with the same object, say a coin or paper pattern, and do the rounding off with a knife and sandpaper. The next part we tackle will be the flat top piece, which is 24″ × 6″. Save for its extra 2″ in length it is similar to the base board.

We will now take up the part that encloses the clock. An alarm clock of ordinary size is the kind we use. We first need a piece 7″ × 5″ × ½″ thick. Find the center and from it draw a circle which tallies nicely with the clock face. Cut the circular piece out with a compass saw and fit the clock into it. It will take quite a little patient effort to do this right, but you will be well repaid for the pains you put into it, as it is the showiest part of the finished article. Now to hold the clock securely in place, we brace it on the top and bottom with pieces shaped like Fig. 4. Figure 2 shows clearly how those pieces look when in place. It is now time to build the boxlike center part shown in Fig. 2. It may be made of half-inch pine with the exception of the face piece or front. This consists of a small frame that encloses the square piece into which the clock fits.

When you have completed it, lay on the top and fasten it with small screws, remembering to always bore a small gimlet hole before inserting the screw. The hole should be just the size of the shank of the screw. The shank is that part which the thread encircles. The thread is the only part intended to bite into the wood. If you have to force hard, the screw will act as a wedge and split your work. Next comes the base board. Note the piece that runs along under it. It is about 23″ long, 2″ wide in the center and 1″ wide at the ends. Fasten it in place with glue and small nails. All that now remains to be added are the

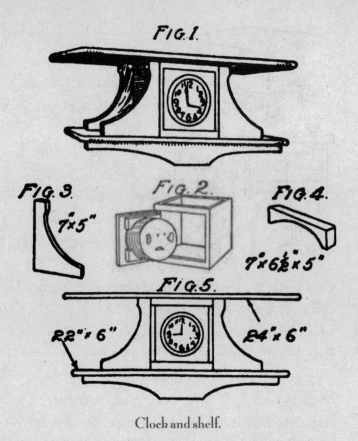

Clock and shelf.

triangular pieces shown by Fig. 3. They add much to the appearance of the clock and must be carefully shaped out. The nails that hold them in place, or perhaps it is best to insist on the slender screws, should be driven from the top and bottom flat pieces. In that way they will not be seen. Two coats of dark mission stain and one of varnish and wax will make a nice finish. If you prefer a gloss, use the varnish and wax and polish with a soft rag. If you like the rich satiny appearance usually characteristic of high grade furniture, use only the wax and after it is on a few hours rub it to a shine with felt or flannel. It will present a rich and satisfactory appearance if finished in this way.

Raising Animals

The Breeds of Sheep and Goats

From *A Study of Farm Animals* by Charles Summer Plumb, 1922

Three distinct classes or groups of sheep are recognized, depending largely upon the character of the fleece. These are fine or short, medium, and long or coarse wools. These classes are somewhat due to the sorting over of the fleeces by the wool merchant, who finds that each class serves a special purpose in his business. Another grouping is also sometimes made, consisting of the fine-wool, or Merino, class and the mutton breeds. This last arrangement, however, is more commonly referred to by shepherds than by wool dealers. There are many different breeds of sheep, some of which are but little known in America, and the following are the only ones of importance in this country.

Several different Merino families have been developed in America. They all had their origin in the sheep of Spanish breeding, but in the hands of certain men each gradually developed special features. In this way families of Merinos were established. For a great many years all sheep that had heavy folds over the body were known as Spanish Merinos. Later the people came to refer to sheep of this class that had been produced in America, as American or A-type Merinos. In time, a larger sheep, with few folds or none, developed, that produced a longer and somewhat coarser grade of wool especially suited for certain cloth manufacture. These became known as Delaine, or C-type Merinos. These sheep also produced a good grade of mutton. What are known as B-type Merinos show a moderate amount of folds, especially at neck, breast, and hind quarters. Among the Delaines are some family

branches of interest, though not widely bred, as, for example, the Dickinson and the Blacktop. Most of the Delaine improvement of importance has taken place in Ohio and western Pennsylvania.

Some of the most important features of the Merino may be considered here. These sheep produce the finest wool known, grading as XX, or X fine, or Delaine. It is so fine that over 1,500 fibers may be laid side by side within an inch space. The fleece covers the entire body, often coming down over the face to the nostrils, and covering the legs even to the toes. From sheep having folds or wrinkles over the body we should get the finest and shortest wool. The fewer folds over the body, as a rule, the larger the sheep and the longer and coarser the fleece. Average Merino wool is about 2½ inches long.

On the outside of the fleece we usually find more or less grease or oil, or yolk, as it is called, mixed with dirt. This mixture easily washes out, even in cold water. The cloth manufacturer removes this by scouring. Some fleeces in this operation lose 75 percent of their weight. Wool buyers do not like a very heavy amount of yolk, on account of this shrinkage when the wool is scoured. A common weight for a fleece is 8 or 10 pounds, but some fleeces have weighed over 40 pounds when taken from the sheep. Rams weigh at maturity 130 pounds or more, and ewes around 100 pounds. Those with folds weigh the least, while the smooth-bodied ones are larger. Merino sheep are very hardy and thrive on ordinary pasture. They run together in flocks much better than any other breed, and so are easily managed by shepherds and dogs when on great ranges or pastures. Large numbers of sheep that have Merino blood in them come into the markets, but really are of mutton parentage. They make excellent mutton, and are liked by butchers because they are neither too large nor too fat. More pure-bred flocks are found today in Ohio than in any other state, although Pennsylvania, Michigan, West Virginia, Oregon, California, and Texas have many flocks. West of the Mississippi there are large numbers of grade Merinos on the range, and without doubt they will continue popular there as long as sheep husbandry is an important industry.

The Rambouillet sheep is a breed of Merinos that has been especially developed by the French Government. In 1786 King Louis XVI of France sent a Mr. Gilbert to Spain to bring back a selection of Merinos. These were brought to one of the royal farms about 40 miles west of Paris, at a town named Rambouillet. Here on this estate the government ever since has bred the descendants of these sheep. They were introduced into America in 1840, and for many years were known as French Merinos. About 1890 the name Rambouillet came into use, and now the term French Merino is rarely used. These sheep have all the common features of the smooth-bodied Merino. It is the very largest family of this breed, however, and has been at times called the "Elephant Merino." The rams weigh about 185 pounds at maturity, though some have weighed over 250 pounds, and the ewes weigh around 150 pounds. This family is known as a mutton Merino, and the mutton

Fig. 1. Champion Rambouillet ram, 1920 Ohio state Fair. Photograph by the author.

form is an important feature. Thus one may expect a broad back and a thick leg of mutton in a good specimen of the Rambouillet.

There are two types of Rambouillet sheep, the B and C. The B type is marked with folds on neck, breast, front and rear flanks, and hind quarters, while the C type has a smooth body, with possibly one or two folds at the neck and breast. The C type represents what the more progressive Rambouillet breeders have had in mind in producing a dual-purpose sheep. The fleece of 12 months' growth should be about 3 inches long, and compact over the body, with but little yolk or dirt on the outside and grade as fine, fine-medium, or Delaine. Well-bred Rambouillet flocks shear about 10 or 12 pounds of wool per head. These sheep have grown in popularity in recent years, for they mature early, are hardy, and seem well suited to most parts of the United States where sheep husbandry thrives. On the western range and on the Pacific slope are found most of the very best and largest flocks in America. There are also numerous choice flocks in Ohio and other central western states. Rambouillet sheep have been bred to a considerable extent in northern Germany, and large numbers are now kept in South America, especially in Argentina.

The Southdown is one of the oldest breeds of sheep. Its native home is on the Southdown

Fig. 2. Southdown ram bred by King George V of England. Owner Ohio State University. Photograph by the author.

hills in Sussex country in southeast England. As a mutton sheep, the Southdown has occupied a most important place for a century or more, being still regarded the model sheep for that purpose. It has been used to help improve more breeds than any other. Southdowns were first imported into America about 1800, and since then many very excellent specimens of this breed have been imported to this country.

The Southdown has been noted for its short, neat head, which is more or less covered with wool down over the reddish-brown face. It has a short, thick neck, broad chest, wide back, thick meaty leg of mutton, and short red-brown legs. No other breed matures earlier, and it is not lacking in hardiness.

Southdowns are well suited to grazing on the better class of pastures, but are not so good for the range and poor pastures as are some others. The flesh is very fine of grain and is not inclined to be over-fat. Butchers especially admire this sheep because it kills out so well, with small amount of loss. The Southdowns, or sheep with more or less

of Southdown blood, have won more prizes in fat-stock shows where the carcasses were considered than has any other breed. At our great International Live Stock Expositions, the Southdown has usually won the grand-championship in the dressed carcass exhibit. Mature rams weigh about 180 pounds, and the ewes 135 pounds. These sheep have been criticized as being too small for the American farmer. The average fleece is short and light of weight, though of fine quality, often grading as three-eighths clothing, and this has also made the breed generally unpopular in America, although it is looked upon with much favor in Kentucky, Tennessee, and West Virginia. In spite of these criticisms, the breed commands universal respect, and many choice flocks of Southdowns are found all over the civilized world, especially among English-speaking people.

The Shropshire sheep originated from a number of different types native in and about the county of that name in western England.

In size the Shropshire sheep is medium, the mature rams weighing about 225 pounds and the ewes about 160 pounds. The head often has a covering of wool, or "cap," down to the nose, which is covered with dark brown or nearly black hair. The back is broad, the leg of mutton very good, and the body is usually deep, showing good feeding capacity. The legs are dark brown in

Fig. 3. Shropshire ram. 2nd prize. 1920 Ohio State Fair. Photograph by the author.

color like the face, and are covered with wool to the knees in front and to the ankles behind. The quality of mutton is most excellent, being second to the Southdown only. The fleece is usually about 3½ inches long, in typical specimens grading as three-eighths, and is of very good quality. A twelve months' growth from fair specimens of the breed weighs about 9 or 10 pounds, and entire flocks have averaged even more.

The good combination of size of body and weight of fleece has done much to make this breed popular with American farmers, as a great general-purpose sheep. Furthermore, the Shropshire is our most prolific breed, many ewes having twin lambs. Flocks are very common all over the so-called corn belt of the United States, especially east of the Mississippi and in Canada. The American Shropshire Sheep Association is the largest organization of its kind in the world, and has done much to promote the breed.

The Oxford Down sheep comes from the county of Oxford, in south-central England.

As stated, it is a large breed, the rams at maturity often weighing 275 pounds or more, and the ewes about 200 pounds. The color of the hair on the face, ears, and legs is a very dark brown, quite like the Shropshire. Oxfords are not so heavily wooled over the head, and often the face is rather

Fig. 5. Hampshire ewes, on farm W. J. Cherry, Ohio. Photograph by the author.

free of wool, and the ears incline to be rather smooth and large. Typical specimens have quite wide backs, fairly good legs of mutton, and deep bodies. During recent years the breed has been much improved, the flesh growing finer in quality, and the fat being laid on more smoothly. The fleece, which frequently weighs 12 pounds, is longer, more open, and coarser than that of the Shropshire and grades usually in most of the flocks of the country as quarter-blood combing.

This breed has made a favorable impression on farmers in the Middle West, where fairly early maturity, size, and heavy fleece are wanted. The ewes are quite prolific, and, though not equaling the Shropshires, make a very good showing. The Oxford may be regarded as one of the most promising breeds for future development. Recently flocks have been extensively distributed to many sheep-growing countries. There are more of these sheep on the fertile farms of Michigan, Wisconsin, Illinois, New York, and Ohio, than elsewhere in America, for they are heavy feeders and require rich pastures or forage crops in order to do their best.

The Hampshire Down sheep, like the Southdown and Oxford Down breeds, originated in southern England and under much the same conditions of climate and soil. Their ancestors were of two kinds, one with white faces and horns, and the other with dark faces and horns. Southdown blood was mingled with these two, from which cam

Fig. 4. Oxford Down ram, 2nd prize, 1920 Ohio State Fair, 1920. Photograph by the author.

the more improved Hampshire, without horns and with an almost black face, ears, and legs. William Humphrey was the most important early improver of these sheep, and, later, James Rawlence did much for them. The Hampshire is one of the largest breeds, mature rams often weighing over 250 pounds, and ewes nearly 200 pounds. The head is one of the striking features of the breed. The nostrils, lips, and face are quite black; the nose is very strong, or Roman in character; and the ears are dark, very large, and incline forward in a heavy style. Wool rarely extends much beyond the forehead. The body is large, and the form is of the usual mutton type. Hampshire sheep often seem somewhat coarse of bone and large of limb. The fleece, which grade* as three-eighths or quarter-blood, is about 4 inches long, inclines to be coarse and open, and usually does not shear much above 7 pounds with 12 months' growth.

Hampshires have long been popular for early or spring lambs, which are regarded as excellent quality. This breed of sheep has grown greatly in favor during the past few years, and large importations have been brought to the United States. On the western range lambs sired by Hampshire rams and out of ewes with some Merino blood are quite popular. Early lambs of this cross are also valued in the eastern market. This breed requires fertile pastures and plenty of feed in order to do well. Hampshires are widely distributed in North and South America, in Europe and Australia. In the United States, important flocks are kept in the northern states east of the Mississippi, especially in Pennsylvania, Kentucky, New York, and Michigan, and in the Rocky Mountain and Pacific coast states. Idaho leads.

The Dorset Horn sheep receives its name from the county of Dorset, in southern England, where it has long been bred. It is an improved form of two native, horned, white-faced breeds found in Dorset and Somerset counties. The modern Dorset

Fig. 6. A pen of Horned Dorset ewes, champions at a show of the Royal Agricultural Society of England. Photograph from *The National Stockman and Farmer*.

Horn belongs to the middle-wool class, and is of medium to large size, rams weighing about 225 pounds and ewes 165. Both sexes have horns, those of the ram at maturity being large and having spiral turns, while those of the ewes are small, and bend in a simple curve around toward the face. The head, ears, and legs have a covering of white hair, and the nostrils are of flesh color. The neck is often short, the back wide, and the body of large capacity, with a fair leg of mutton. Dorsets are popular as lambs, and for mutton, although the quality of the mutton is not of the best. The lambs feed well and lay on flesh rapidly. As wool producers, this is a breed that should do better. The fleece, which grades as three-eighths or quarter-blood, tends to be short and the weight light, ranging around 6 pounds for average animals. These sheep were first brought to America in 1885, and, while there are numerous flocks in the eastern states, more especially in Pennsylvania and New York, the breed as yet can hardly be called popular.

The Cheviot sheep comes from the Cheviot Hills in the border country between England and

Scotland. Here the land rises into grass-topped mountains, reaching nearly 4,000 feet above the sea. Grass is the universal crop, and here this breed of sheep has been raised for long beyond a century, and gradually improved during the passing years. Today the Cheviot is a medium-wool, fair-sized sheep, the rams weighing around 200 pounds at maturity, and the ewes 150 pounds. This is one of our most beautiful breeds. The head is entirely free of wool, and the face and ears are covered with white hair, on which black specks occasionally occur. The nostrils are black, the nose tends to be a bit Roman, the eye is large and prominent, and the erect ear is usually pricked up as though listening. The Cheviot inclines to be somewhat narrow of back, with a moderate depth of body and fair leg of mutton, though in recent years it has been much improved. The fleece covers the body to the back of the ears and down to the knees and hocks, the rest of the leg being covered with white hair. The fleece, which grades as three-eighths or quarter-blood combing, tends to be somewhat open and is usually about 3½ inches long and a year's growth weighs 6 or 7 pounds. The fiber inclines to be coarser than that of the Shropshire, American breeders using the latter for a standard.

Cheviots are very hardy, and in their native home on the mountains rely altogether on grass the entire year. They are active and independent, and

do not flock as do other breeds. For this reason the Cheviot has never been suited to the range country. The quality of Cheviot mutton is very superior, having very fine grain, and lacking surplus fat. In mutton carcass contests in the English and Scotch shows, this breed and its cross-breeds have always held a high place. It is not widely distributed outside of its native home, though found in the United States in New York, Ohio, Illinois, Wisconsin, and in other states of the Middle West.

The Suffolk sheep comes from the county after which it is named, in southeastern England. It belongs to the medium-wool class, and is a mutton breed of distinct merit. In the carcass contests of the Smithfield Club Show in England, it has been a leading prize winner. The head, ears, and legs of the Suffolk are distinctly black in color, giving a group of these sheep a very striking appearance. Mature rams weigh about 250 pounds and the ewes 175 pounds. The fleece is not heavy. Suffolks are not extensively bred in England, although growing in popularity and but few of them are to be found in America. In fact, they are very rare here, and are not often seen at our sheep shows, neither have they been much advertised in America.

The Tunis sheep takes its name from Tunis, in northern Africa, where it is supposed to have originated. In 1799, General Eaton, United States Consul at Tunis, received a gift of a number of these sheep, two of which survived a voyage to America. Other importations followed this one of General Eaton. These early importations were kept in the eastern and southern states, and little was done to improve them. They are peculiar in having a large, fat tail, and have often been called "Fat Tailed Sheep."

Fig. 7. Cheviot sheep on their native Scotch hills. Photograph by the author.

Fig. 8. Border Leicester ram. Photograph by the author.

In recent years, especially since about 1893, they have been bred in small flocks, in different parts of the country, but especially in Indiana, Kentucky, and New York. They are of medium size, with brown, or mottled brown and white faces, and brown legs. The tail is cut off soon after birth, as with other lambs, but the hind parts of the Tunis are somewhat heavier than corresponding parts of other breeds. The Tunis makes an excellent feeder, and lambs of this breed have met with much favor from stock buyers and the fattened lambs have sold for high prices on the market. The fleece is of excellent quality, of three-eighths grade, averaging about 3 inches long, and frequently containing red or brown fibers. But few of these sheep are to be seen, and fairs rarely make classes for them in the premium lists.

The Leicester sheep (pronounced Lester) originated in central England in the county of that name. This is a large breed, and belongs to the long, or coarse, wool class. The entire head and ears are covered with white hair, the wool not growing beyond the back of the head. The ears are large but thin, and are usually carried in an erect position. The nostrils are black, the nose is somewhat prominent, and the eye bold and attractive. The Leicester has a full, wide breast; broad, flat back; wide rump; and

Fig. 9. Cotswold ewe. champion, 1916, Ohio state Fair. Photograph by the author.

fair leg of mutton. The body form is broad rather than deep, and sometimes these sheep appear long of leg. They fatten rapidly, and the rams at maturity weigh around 250 pounds, and the ewes 175 pounds or more. As mutton producers, they are not popular, because they lay on too much fat. They require good pastures, and are not the hardiest sheep in the world.

The Leicester is the smallest of the long-wool breeds, and has a curly fleece of low quarter-blood or braid grade that does not shear very heavily, 7 to 9 pounds being about a year's growth. These unfavorable criticisms account for there being so few of them today either in America or elsewhere. Once a popular breed, this is now the least known in America of all the so-called common breeds of sheep. In northern England, in the border country, is an improved form or family known as the Border-Leicester, which is the more common type today. This differs from the English Leicester in having a more vigorous constitution, an especially lively carriage of head, and a clear white face, while the old breed has a bluish tinge to the skin of the face.

The Cotswold sheep gets its name from the fact that in early times in England these sheep were sheltered in what were called "Cots," and were pastured on the treeless hills known as "Wolds." That was in southwest England, where this breed has been kept for centuries. It is written that in 1464 King Edward IV gave permission to transport some Cotswold sheep to Spain. About 100 years or more ago, Cotswold and Leicester flocks were mixed a great deal in blood, by which crossing it is said the former was improved. These sheep were brought to America as early as 1832, and once were very popular. This is a large, long-wooled breed, larger than the Leicester, mature rams weighing from 250 to 275 pounds, and ewes 200 to 225 pounds. The head is somewhat large, and is usually white, though it may be gray or brown in tint. The nose is rather prominent, and the ears incline to be large and are carried somewhat heavily. If the forehead of the Cotswold is protected, long curly locks of wool hang down in front, often hiding the eyes. Sheep of this breed have a broad breast, wide, flat back and broad rump, and show a greater width than depth of body in the best specimens. While the Cotswold feeds very well, if on good pasture and under favorable conditions, it is not a breed suited to scant pastures. The well-fattened carcass is too large, coarse, and fat for the present demand. The fleece, which grades as low quarter-blood or braid, is coarser and the curly locks larger than with the Leicester. Good Cotswold wool is noted for its lustre, a quality much valued by the English breeders. A twelve-months' fleece is usually from 8 to 10 inches long, and weighs about 10 pounds. There are not many Cotswold flocks in the United States, and the breed is more popular in Canada than here. The demand for a smaller sheep and a different grade of wool make it difficult for this breed to become popular in America.

The Lincoln sheep comes from the county of that name on the east coast of England. This is a very old breed, and its improvement began while Bakewell was developing the New Leicester. Some Lincoln sheep were brought to America before 1800, and they have been imported in a small way ever since. This is a large breed, being somewhat larger than the Cotswold, and having much in common with the latter. The head is large, and is gray or white in color, or gray mixed with white. The wool does not cover the entire head, but a small tuft of short locks commonly extends over the forehead. The ears are large and usually have no wool on them. The body form is much like that of the Cotswold, though perhaps deeper of rib. These sheep fatten easily; but the carcasses get too heavy and have too much external fat for the present-day trade, and so the mutton is not popular. The Lincoln requires good grazing to do its best, as it is too heavy for the hill country. The Lincoln produces a fleece in long, wavy locks, which grades as low quarter-blood

Fig. 10. A group of Lincoln ewes owned by William Shier, of Michigan. Photograph from *America Sheep Breeder.*

or braid, and which is not so curly but has the same lustre as the Cotswold. A year-old fleece is usually 8 inches long, and may weigh 10 pounds or more. Lincoln sheep have grown in popularity in their native home on account of the demand for them in Argentina, where large numbers are kept. Very high prices have been paid for them in England, and in 1906 a ram sold for $7,400, the highest sum on record for the breed. In the United States, Lincolns have not gained in favor and there are very few of these sheep in this country, these being mostly in Idaho and Oregon.

The Romney Marsh sheep, also known as the Kent breed in its native home, originated in

Fig. 11. Champion Romney Marsh ram. Owner Mr. A. Matthews, New Zealand. Photograph from *American Sheep Breeder.*

southeast England, in the county of Kent, on the marshes after which the breed is named. The land here is low, rich, and moist. These sheep seem especially suited to the local conditions, as they do not suffer from foot rot as do other breeds. The head and legs are white, the back is broad, and the body is of compact form. These sheep fatten very well on rather limited areas, and make a fair grade of mutton. The fleece, which usually grades as a quarter-blood combing, weighs about 8 pounds after a year's growth, and is in good demand. Large numbers of Romney Marsh sheep are now found in Argentina, and importations to America have been made on a small scale. An association for promoting this breed was organized at Chicago in December, 1911. Since it is essentially an untried breed in America, its merits for our conditions remain to be shown. The Romney Marsh belongs to the middle-wool class, producing a fleece of low quarter-blood grade.

The Black-faced Highland sheep has long been known in the highlands of Scotland, where it grazes on the grass and heather on the highest mountains. In this breed, as in the Dorset, both sexes have horns, those of the ram being spiral and very large and showy at maturity. Highland sheep have black or mottled black and white faces, with no wool beyond the forehead. While these sheep, which are from small to medium size, produce a very fine grade of mutton on their native pastures, they are slow growers, and cannot be ranked as feeders, as we view sheep in America. Their chief value lies in their adaptability to rough, hardy conditions, enabling them to live through winters when most other breeds

would perish. The fleece, which grades as a low quarter-blood or braid, is very coarse, long, and open, falling from the body in wavy locks. Some Black-faced Highlanders have extremely coarse wool, with more or less hair about the lower thighs. In disposition they are wild and not so easily handled as other breeds. A few of these sheep have been brought to America, but they are not likely to meet with general favor.

The Angora goat derives its name from the district of Angora, in Asia. These goats were first brought to America in 1849, when the Sultan of Turkey presented some to Dr. J. B. Davis, of South Carolina. Large numbers are found today in the United States, especially in the far western and southwestern states. The Angora is smaller than the common goat, individuals usually weighing from 60 to 100 pounds. The color is pure white. The head has a pair of horns which slope backward and curve widely outward, with some twist in those of the buck, but none in the doe's. The ears are large, often six inches long or more, and droop downward slightly. The Angora makes very good mutton, but is not valued for this as much as for its fleece, commercially known as mohair. In fair specimens

Fig. 13. Toggenburg doe El Chivar's Natalie, on milking stand. This doe has a record of 2,090 pounds of milk. Photograph from the owner, Winthrop Howland of California.

Fig. 12. Angora goat king Cromwell. Photograph from *American Sheep Breeder*.

this covers the body in silky, wavy ringlets, which in a year should become about 10 inches long. The fleece ought to show a curl quite to the skin. An average weight is about 3 pounds. The better grade of goats produces a mohair that is highly valued for making certain kinds of dress goods, plushes for upholstering work, etc. Angoras have been regarded with favor by some for clearing land of underbrush. They eat the tender twigs and bark, and thus gradually kill the bushes. Goats have been used for this purpose in northern Wisconsin, Michigan, Missouri, and elsewhere.

The milk goat is common all over the world, especially in the warmer climates. It has been much improved, especially in Switzerland, Germany and southern Europe. There are many breeds, of which the Toggenburg, Saanen, Nubian and Maltese are noted as the greatest producers. The milk of the goat contains slightly more than 5 percent fat, and about 15 percent solids. It is digested very easily, and is free from tuberculosis germs, as the goat does not suffer from the disease. Goats thrive with very ordinary care, and should be kept more extensively the United States.

The Toggenburg goat has its native home in the Toggenburg valley in Switzerland. It is a medium brown in color, with a white band along down each side of the face from eyes to mouth. Toggenburgs are usually hornless, though not always, are slender and lean of body, and the does often possess udders of large capacity, many of which produce 4 or 5 quarts of milk a day. The doe El Chivars Geneva in 312 days produced 2,158 pounds of milk testing 3.37 percent fat.

The Saanen goat derives its name from the Saanen valley in Switzerland, its native home. This is a white or creamy colored goat, is regarded as hornless, though horns sometimes occur, and is usually covered with short hair, excepting along the spine, thighs and flanks, where the hair is longer. This breed is noted for milk production, and the best of them, according to Peer, give from 5 to 6 quarts of excellent milk a day. The two-year-old doe Swiss Echo produced 2,374 pounds of milk in less than 8 months, which is a remarkable.

Care and Feeding

The form of food to be fed sheep naturally depends upon the class of animals and conditions surrounding them. A fine type of roughage such as alfalfa, for example, is more easily handled in the small mouth of the sheep than is heavy, coarse material. The finer legumes and hay are, therefore, preferable to the heavier ones. It is rarely necessary to cut or chaff roughage for sheep. Roots and cabbage, however, should be sliced, for they can be fed to best advantage either alone or mixed with grain or chaffed hay. It is unnecessary to grind grain for mature sheep, for they digest entire seeds very effectively. Young lambs, on the contrary, should be fed cracked or ground feed. Where linseed cake is to be used, it will be found desirable to purchase "pea" size for sheep, for this form is palatable, is not likely to be adulterated, and does not gum up in the mouth as may happen with the meal.

The proportion of grain to roughage for sheep very naturally will depend upon conditions. When pastures are good, it is not usually necessary to feed breeding sheep grain, although in the case of nursing ewes an exception may be made. In the dry lot, when roughage and grain are used, and fattening is in progress, the weight of roughage, as a rule, exceeds that of the grain. Reports on feeding experiments, nevertheless, show plenty of examples with a contrary result. Henry and

Morrison in reporting on 17 experimental lots, including 1,180 lambs being fattened on corn,* show that where unlimited corn was fed, it required 400 pounds of grain and 436 pounds of hay to make 100 pounds of grain, while, in the case of a limited corn feed, it required but 288 pounds of grain and 655 pounds of hay for 100 pounds of gain. At the Illinois station Coffey "found that it was possible in a period of 98 days to feed 100 pounds of corn to every 86 pounds of alfalfa hay. This ration produced a prime market finish and was satisfactory in all respects except that it required close watching at times to keep the lambs from going 'off feed.'" Prof. Coffey also calls attention* to the fact that "lambs fed 100 pounds of corn to every 203 pounds of hay for a period of 98 days were graded as prime."

Feeding and caring for the lamb demand most watchful attention. As soon as it is dropped the shepherd should see that the lamb is cleaned, especially about the head. Sometimes lambs appear somewhat smothered and lacking in life, and in

Fig. 14. "Feed my lambs." John, XXI, 15. Photograph by the author.

this case the shepherd should blow gently in the mouth, and he also may move the front legs apart, and then together, alternately, to stimulate breathing. Soon after birth, the lamb should stand up, and in a few minutes it will want to mine. This operation the shepherd may assist the first time, perhaps, by helping support the lamb and guiding its mouth to one of the teats. Thereafter the lamb will probably gain strength rapidly, and nurse as desired. If the mother disowns the lamb, she should be tied in a small pen where she will be unable to interfere with her offspring's nursing. If the lamb gets badly chilled, it may be warmed by inserting all but the head in warm but not hot water, and kept there until circulation is restored, after which it should be taken out and rubbed dry and then placed with the ewe in a comfortable temperature.

The udder of the ewe should be watched carefully. Sometimes it gets caked and inflamed, and again she may produce more milk than the lamb can use. The caked udder should be bathed, with hot applications, then rubbed dry, and the milk drawn off. It may also be painted with tincture of iodine several times, but care should be taken not to blister the udder. Lambs begin to nibble at grain in ten or twelve days, and from then on their appetite for such food increases. A mixture of equal parts ground corn, oats and bran, and one tenth part linseed meal, makes an excellent feed for young lambs. Later the corn and oats may be fed unground. In the West barley or Kafir corn may replace ordinary corn, if desired. Lambs soon take to roughage of a palatable sort, like fine clover or alfalfa, or a bright leafy hay. What is known as a lamb-creep should be made in the pen, by partitioning off a space, into which the lambs can creep, in which special feed may be placed for them that cannot be reached by the ewes. When the lamb is four weeks or so old, it may be eating a quarter of a pound of grain a day, while when two months old this may be increased to three fourths of a pound daily. Lambs are often weaned when

*Feed, and Feeding. 1017.

about four or five months old. They should then be separated from the dams, and given plenty of good feed, on pasture or dry lot, as seems best. If they are to be marketed, they should be fed grain until sold and shipped.

Grouping the flock of sheep according to age and sex is important. After weaning, the ewe lambs should be fed by themselves, the ram lambs and wethers being kept by themselves for special attention and feeding. The yearling ewes also require individual attention as they come to breeding age. The ewes with lambs at foot run together, and should be by themselves; but, when the lambs are weaned, the rams are given separate pasture and shed room. The service rams are best handled by themselves. Although subject to certain oversight, they may run with the ewe flock when the ewes have no lambs at foot. This grouping of the flock is in keeping with the most careful management, but circumstances alter cases. Each shepherd must, therefore, handle his flock as best he can.

Shelter for sheep is desirable in winter, when storms prevail and snow is abundant. A common, inexpensive shed, open to the South, will serve the purpose. It is a good plan to have swinging doors, which may be hung inside overhead, and lowered in very severe weather. A wind-break of trees often furnishes excellent shelter in winter. On the hills of Scotland where hundreds of thousands of sheep roam the year round, no shelter is usually provided, excepting that found in the nooks in the valleys. On the western range many sheep perish in severe winter storms because of lack of artificial shelter. The important thing is to keep the sheep dry and protected from snow and heavy winter winds.

Exercise for sheep is essential under certain conditions. As a rule, sheep have exercise enough, but in snow-bound regions, they should, if possible, be driven out into the yards and near-by fields, and caused to exercise by eating roughage scattered

Fig. 15. The interior of a model sheep barn, showing feed racks, on the estate of Oakleigh Thorne of New York. Photograph from Mr. Thorne.

about. Prof. B. O. Severson recommends* at least twenty-five square feet of space for each mature sheep. Mature stock rams should always have plenty of exercise, and be kept in muscular, vigorous condition. Breeding ewes that have plenty of exercise in the open will drop stronger lambs than will those that are kept closely housed and not exercised. During summer, when on pasture or grazing forage crops, sheep, as a rule, get plenty of exercise; but, during the season when they are often more or less penned up, exercise should be provided.

The shearing of sheep is an important operation that requires skill and a good system of handling. Briefly described, the sheep is placed on its rump, the back resting more or less against the knees of the shearer. There are several methods used by skilled shearers to remove the fleece, of which the following is one. The shears are started in at the right front flank and the fleece is cut close to the body in a direct line to the hind flank. Then, by successive strokes, the wool is shorn over the belly, beginning at the brisket, and running the shears from the right side to the left, so that the wool here may be laid over like a blanket to the left side. Next the wool is removed from the hind legs, working

*Sheep Raising, Extension Circular 49, (1916), Penn. State College.

Fig. 16. Shearing with hand machines at the Ohio State University. Photograph by the author.

from the right to left side, cutting it away about the thighs and just over the tail head, so that the sheep may rest on a shorn rump. In doing this part, the sheep should be placed in a reclining position, so that the end of the rump may be covered with the shears.

The sheep is then placed more erect, the shearer holding it by the jaw with the left hand, while cutting the fleece upward from the brisket along the lower right side of the neck to the end of the jaw. After the fleece is removed from the lower side of the neck and over the left front leg and shoulder, the shearer removes the fleece about the head, and then in successive strokes, beginning at the top of the neck, removes the fleece to the back of the neck, and then down, from the line between the two left flanks, he runs his shears around to the middle of the back, turning the sheep meanwhile as needs be. Having removed the fleece on the left half of the neck and body, the shearer starts at the top of the neck again, and continues down as before, but on the right side, removing the fleece from the neck and body in proper order. If the job is well done, the shearer will take off his fleece, like a blanket, and spread it out as a connected whole, the inner part down, the locks together. The sides of the fleece are then turned in toward the center, and commencing with the head wool, the entire fleece is rolled up to make a neat bundle, which is tied together with

standard wool twine, no more than is necessary, just two to four times around.

Some important rules in shearing must be followed, if the work is to be done right and superior wool placed on the market. The author will assume that the fleece is clean and free of dirt, chaff, and burrs.

1 Shear on a level, smooth floor that may be kept clean.

2 Cut the wool as close to the body as possible, using the shears but once in the same place. A second cut produces short fiber, which injures the selling value of the fleece.

3 Never pull the wool or push it back with the left hand while shearing, as the skin is thus elevated and is quite likely to be cut.

4 Use as little force as possible in handling the sheep. Some are nervous and struggle, and should be handled gently. If shearing is done in warm weather, see that a struggling sheep be not exhausted and overheated. It might better be freed, as it may die if the struggle is continued.

5 Do not shear when the fleece is wet. In this condition it will mold and the fiber be weakened. Wet wool may also get stained if dung locks are present in the fleece.

6 Use only standard wool twine, such as paper or hemp. Binding twine is a positive damage. Its vegetable fibers catch in the wool and cannot be removed except by hand labor after they are woven in the cloth.

7 Leave out all dung locks and coarse belly and britch wool from the fleece, selling this separately. Thus you establish a better reputation for your wool as a dependable product. In Australia the common practice is to skirt the wool, removing the inferior, coarser parts at the neck, legs, and sides, and selling these separately. This custom has given Australian wool its fine reputation.

Fig. 17. Students trimming hoofs of sheep at Ohio State University. Photograph by the author.

Trimming the feet of sheep is frequently necessary, especially where the soil is soft and moist and free from gravel. Sheep that run on level, rich pasture, or that are kept more or less stabled, are troubled much in that the toes grow long or otherwise out of shape. The foot of the sheep is cloven, and the hoof consists of a comparatively thin upper shell and a soft under pad. With the small blade of a big, strong pocket knife one may easily trim the hoofs to a proper shape. If careful attention is given, it will require comparatively little labor to keep the feet in good shape; but, if neglected, the hoofs may grow so out of shape as to give the feet a very bad posture, quite difficult to correct. Some breeds, as the Merino, are bad in this respect.

The docking of sheep, that is cutting off the tail of the young lamb, is a very important practice.

Fig. 18. A good feed rack for sheep. Reproduced from Farmers Bulletin 810, United States Department of Agriculture.

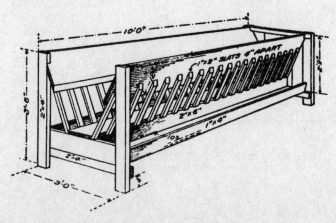

It should be removed ten days or so after birth. A very satisfactory way is to cut the tail off with the large blade of a sharp pocket knife. The lamb may be held between the legs of the operator. With the left hand the tail is raised slightly above horizontal, while at the same time with the right hand the knife blade is laid against the bare underside about an inch and a half from the body. Holding firmly to the lower part of the tail, which is then depressed, a quick upward stroke is given with the knife, which easily separates the tail, leaving it in the operator's hand. Occasionally a lamb may bleed quite a bit, but bleeding usually stops soon, and fatalities are not common. Bleeding may be stopped by tying a string tightly about the stump for an hour or so, or the wound may be seared with a red-hot iron. Lambs are also docked by other methods, as chopping off with a chisel, using a red-hot pincers, etc. The method described, however, is commonly used and is very satisfactory. The wound, after it stops bleeding, should have an antiseptic applied to it, and it should be watched to see that it heals rapidly. Tails are useless, they accumulate filth, and on the ewes interfere with breeding operations. Docked sheep are also more attractive than those with tails.

A hurdle for handling sheep is an adjustable or temporary fencing. Hurdles are universally used in Europe where sheep are grazed on forage crops or valuable pastures. Types of hurdles differ according to the section of the country. In England one can see them made in woven sections, with strong sharpened stakes at intervals, so that an area of ground may be quickly enclosed for pasturing a flock. In the sheep pens hinged, two-section paneled hurdles are a great convenience for separating out individual sheep for special purposes. Also, when of sufficient length, hurdles may be used to divide yards or pens into smaller temporary quarters. Hurdles for use in the pens need not be over thirty-six inches high, and should be constructed of light stripe of lumber,

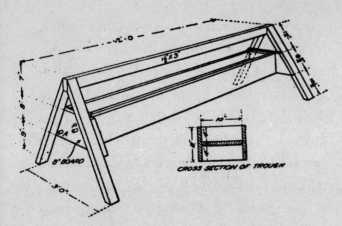

Fig. 19. A reversible movable grain trough for sheep. Reproduced from Farmers' Bulletin 810, United States Department of Agriculture.

preferably about four inches wide, and dressed down to seven eighths of an inch in thickness.

Feed racks for sheep should be so constructed that the seeds and chaff from hay or clover will not readily get into the fleece. They may have either a solid front, except a narrow space of 4 inches through which the sheep may gradually pull hay, or a slat face in its lower half, with solid board front in the upper part. A popular combination hay and grain rack is a V-form, fitting into the center of a wide feed trough, with 4-inch strips along the front to keep the grain from being spilled. Movable grain troughs are used, these being 8 or 10 inches wide, with 4-inch sidepieces, and either fastened along the sides of the pens, or with strong legs by which the trough is elevated 12 or 14 inches above the floor. Feed troughs should be cleaned out daily, and frequently washed or scalded, that they may be sweet and clean.

Pigs

From *A Study of Farm Animals* by Charles Summer Plumb, 1922

The early forms of the domestic hog were found in several countries, but more especially in Great Britain, southern Europe, and China. Large herds of swine, according to Youatt, were in existence in England prior to the Christian era. It is said that in Greece large droves were cared for by swineherds perhaps 3,000 years ago. In Italy these animals have long been valued, and the blue-skinned, thin-haired, long-legged Neapolitan hog of that country was imported into England perhaps two centuries ago to improve the Berkshire and the coarse white hogs of Great Britain. The Chinese produced a class of white pigs that American and British sailors bought on their travels and brought home, which were used to improve the native stock. Red hogs bred on the west coast of Africa were also brought to America over a century ago, and their blood mingled with our common stock. From this ancestry, after long years of careful breeding, in Great Britain and the United States, have come our present highly improved domestic breeds of swine, of which the following are of interest.

The following are some of the most important features of the Berkshire today. The color is black, with more or less white on the face, feet, and tail. When all four legs, the face, and tail are marked thus, they are termed the "six points." The head is fairly short, the nose slightly curved up or the head "dish-faced," as it is termed, and the ears are erect, pointing slightly forward. The head of the Berkshire is one of its most distinctive breed features. In size this may be classed as medium, although there are individuals of superior breeding that attain a large size. Boars often weigh 500 pounds and sows about 400. There has, nevertheless, been a feeling among corn-belt pork producers that the Berkshire lacks in size, and this has affected its popularity in face of the present-day demand for big-type hogs. The Berkshire should have a strong and fairly wide back, but it lacks the spring of rib of the Poland-China or Chester White, and neither does it have the high arch as often seen with representatives of some other breeds. The average Berkshire ham is not so round and thick as with the more distinct lard-type hog, being narrow rather than thick in the hind quarter. Good examples of the breed are neat of bone and stand

Fig. 1. A fine type of Berkshire sow, champion at Ohio State Fair. Photograph by J. C. Allen.

well on their feet. The sows farrow medium-sized litters, averaging about eight pigs.

Berkshire are fair feeders, and mature just moderately well under ordinary conditions. If not fed too much corn, they make a grade of pork that is unsurpassed. In the corn belt of America, with the feed and care given by western farmers, the Berkshire may be regarded as a lard hog; while, if fed a variety of grain, with corn only a moderate part of the ration, it makes a superior bacon. It has always been a popular breed in England, and for many years held a premier position in America, but recently it has lost much of its popularity in the great pork-producing sections of the country, due to lack of size and a tendency to slow maturity. Berkshires have their greatest hold today in the eastern United States and the South. In spite of its loss in prestige, the breed is noted for its very superior pork, and in carcass contests at the International Live Stock Exposition, and at the Smithfield Show in England, it has an unsurpassed record for winning championships.

In present color markings the Poland-China much resembles the Berkshire. The head is of medium length, and rather straight in the face; the ears, which should be somewhat thin, point forward and then break over to form what is called a lop ear. A good head lacks coarseness, and inclines to

Fig. 2. A fine type of Berkshire sow, champion at Ohio State Fair. Photograph by J. C. Allen.

be wide between the eyes, and is somewhat short, but is never dished. The body form of this breed is quite distinctly its own, the neck being short, the back wide and frequently strongly arched, and the hams highly developed. These features of head, arch of back, and thickness of hams are Poland-China characteristics. In comparatively recent years, dating perhaps with the opening of the present century, there has been a marked change of type in this breed. The tendency had been to produce a hog deficient in bone, that finished off in feeding into too small or tidy a type, while the sows were seriously criticized for under-size and small litters. This criticism resulted in a movement for improvement, out of which has come what is known as the "big-type" Poland-China, a pig of pronounced length of body, great arch of back, immense bone and great weight. In this connection, brood sows of marked increase of size and prolificacy have been developed. In the opinion of competent critics, Poland-China breeders are now going to the extreme on weight and bone, for many boars have attained weights of 600 to 700 pounds, while a few have even surpassed 1,000 pounds. Unquestionably the present-day movement has revived interest in the breed, which following the World War has undergone great popularity. This is one of the more important breeds in the American corn belt. Poland-Chinas put on fat easily, and are noted as feeders. When properly fattened, the carcass dresses out well and is popular with butchers.

The Spotted Poland-China is a type of this breed that first began to attract attention about 1912, and has since grown much in favor in the corn belt, especially Ohio, Indiana, Illinois, and Iowa. The body of the Spotted Poland-China is of large size at maturity, is covered with large black and white spots, is strong of bone and hair, and impresses one as being somewhat coarse. This type is promoted by the National Spotted Poland-China Breeders' Association. The advantages claimed for it are its size and vigor, its adaptability to the feed lot, and the superiority of the sows in producing and raising large and uniform litters.

The Duroc-Jersey is a red or sandy-colored breed of swine that no doubt obtained its special color markings from the coarse red hog brought from Africa, and from sandy or reddish English hogs, such as the Tamworth and sandy Berkshire. The present-day Duroc-Jersey is red in color, of which there are various shades, ranging from sandy or light red to a cherry color or dark red. A medium red shade is the most popular. The head has a straight face, and the ears lop over forward. The back is usually slightly arched and the ribs are well sprung. The hams do not show quite the thickness of the Poland-China, but are not to be regarded as especially deficient in this respect.

In recent years there has been developed a great movement among Duroc-Jersey breeders to produce hogs of considerable scale and bone, of the true big type, with marked length of body, strong arch of back, and superior bone. The average individual of the breed will perhaps be somewhat larger than either Poland-China or Chester White, and weights of mature boars are often given at 600 to 800 pounds, and sows at 500 to 600 pounds. In size, however, the Duroc-Jersey and Poland-China are in the same class, with more extremes to be found in the latter than the former. Duroc-Jerseys mature fairly early, and finish off in fattening at 200 to 250 pounds, at six months of age. The breed has not thus far made much of a showing in carcass test

Fig. 4. Duroc-Jersey boar. Great Orion Sensation. Grand champion National Swine Show, 1919, 1921. Owned by Ed. Kern, of Nebraska.

competition. The sows usually have large litters, this being the most prolific of the lard-type breeds. Duroc-Jerseys are extremely popular in the middle-western states where corn is abundant. In fact this breed since 1900 has had a wonderful growth in public favor, and many herds of Poland-Chinas and Berkshires have given way to the Duroc-Jersey. The breed is widely distributed over America, but is more especially prominent in Ohio, Iowa, Illinois, Nebraska, Missouri, Minnesota, Indiana, and South Dakota.

The Chester White breed of hogs gets its name from Chester county, Pennsylvania, where it has been bred for a great many years. Claims have been made that the early colonists brought over coarse white pigs to Pennsylvania. In 1820 a Captain Jeffries, of West Chester, Pennsylvania, brought some white hogs from England. Others of the same color also found their way into that section. The Chester White, as its name indicates, is white. Occasionally, small, black spots occur on the skin, but they are occasionally found in all the white breeds. The head rather resembles that of the Poland-China, in that the face is straight and the ears lopped over. The Chester White is a true lard type of hog. It is a splendid feeder, and, when well fattened, carries a very broad, arched back and has an excellent ham. The quality of bone in the legs is frequently too fine,

Fig. 3. A herd of Spotted Poland-Chinas. Photograph by the author.

and mature animals often stand badly on their feet. In recent years, in keeping with the development of the Poland-China and Duroc-Jersey, breeders of Chester Whites have emphasized scale, and the tendency has been to breed a larger, heavier-boned hog. The Chester White type, however, has not gone through so great a change as have the others, and the extremely high back and upstanding form has not been so noticeable with this breed. The usual run of mature boars will weigh around 600 pounds, and the sows 500 pounds. The sows farrow good-sized litters, the breed ranking close to the Duroc-Jersey in this respect. Sows commonly have nine pigs to the litter. The quality of pork is excellent, although inclined to have a large percent of fat. In the carcass contests at the International Live Stock Exposition, grade and cross-bred Chester Whites have made excellent records. Chester Whites are widely distributed as a breed in the North, and especially east of the Mississippi. In the South any white breed is unpopular on account of color, white hogs blistering under the sun more than red or black ones. There are many herds of Chester White hogs in Pennsylvania, Ohio, Indiana, Illinois, Missouri, Iowa, Nebraska, South Dakota, and Minnesota, and the breed is well adapted to the northern corn belt.

Fig. 5. Chester White bow, Buehler's Wonder, grand champion National Swine Show, 1921. Bred and shown by William Buehler, of Nebraska. Photograph from Mr. Buehler.

Fig. 6. A Hampshire brood sow. Bred and owned by J. Crouch & Son, Indiana. Photograph from the owners.

The Hampshire breed of swine for many years was known in America as the "Thin Rind." It is black in color, with a white belt at the shoulders which encircles the body. No one knows the fountain head of these hogs in America. In 1904 breeders of these hogs assumed that they came from Hampshire, England, and adopted that name. In view of the fact that there was an English black breed of this name in Hampshire, the author has thought the selection of this name for the American breed was unfortunate. Belted hogs have been found in different parts of Europe, and in very recent years, especially since the World War, a breed of this sort, known as the Wessex Saddle-back hog, has received much attention in England, and especially in south Hampshire. The claim is made by promoters of the Wessex that it is an old British forest breed.

For many years "Thin Rind" hogs were bred in a limited way in Kentucky, southern Indiana, and southern Illinois, and these were of the bacon type. Finally the breed was taken up by men in the corn section of Illinois, and it has gradually changed in form to a broader-backed, thicker kind, more nearly of the lard type. This transformation shows how a corn diet will change the form of an animal. Hampshire swine have straight and medium-long faces, especially with the males, and the ears vary from erect to leaning forward. The back is of medium width and the body is usually very smooth along the sides. The hams lack fullness, being more of the Berkshire type than of the Poland-China. The Hampshire is a good feeder, maturing fairly early, and producing a carcass with an excellent proportion of lean meat to fat. In carcass contests, hogs of this breed or its crosses have usually made an excellent showing, and Hampshire pigs or their grades, find great popularity with the butchers. This is not a large breed, mature boars weighing around 500 to 600 pounds, and sows 300 to 350 pounds. The sows are fairly prolific, which fact is a much-desired characteristic. Hampshires have undergone a great wave of popularity, and the breed may be classed as common, especially in Ohio, Indiana, Illinois, Iowa, Missouri, Nebraska, South Dakota, Alabama, and Georgia.

The Large Yorkshire belongs to the bacon class. As grown today, it is one of the largest breeds. Boars at maturity often weigh 700 pounds or more, and sows 500 pounds. The head inclines to be a trifle long, from an American point of view, and is sometimes slightly dished. The ears should be carried erect, but with age they usually incline forward. The body of the Large Yorkshire should show considerable length and have smooth deep sides, from which bacon may be cut to the best advantage. The back lacks the width and the ham the thickness of the lard type. The legs often appear long for the depth of body. Large Yorkshires do not mature early nor fatten and finish off so readily as do hogs of the lard type. They rather tend to continue their growth until they have attained considerable size before laying on much fat. Even then they will never fatten like our lard hogs, although they will gain as much or more in weight per day. This hog is well adapted for grazing on clover and other green feeds. The quality of the meat is of the very best. More prime bacon is made in Great Britain and Denmark from the Large Yorkshire than from any other breed, the Danes making bacon production a

Fig. 7. Large Yorkshire sow. Ohio State Lady 463. grand champion, Ohio State Fair. 1920. Photograph by J.C. Allen.

great industry. Large Yorkshire sows are noted for farrowing many pigs in a litter, this being one of the most prolific breeds. On account of its bacon, this is the leading breed in Great Britain and Denmark. In America, these hogs, though bred for many years, have never been so popular as hogs of the lard type. They are bred in sections of the North, especially in Canada, and in the northwestern states.

The Small Yorkshire, known in England as the "Small White," is of English origin. It was developed early in the nineteenth century, when certain men wished a small, very fat type of pig. This is distinctly a small breed, weighing at maturity about 200 pounds. The head is often short and extremely

Fig. 8. A Tamworth gilt at the Ohio Agricultural Experiment Station. Photograph by the author.

dished, so much so that easy feeding is impossible. In fancy specimens the head is almost distorted, the ears are erect, the neck short, back very wide, hams short and thick, and legs short. The Small Yorkshire matures early and fattens easily for its size, making a very fat type of pork. The sows are not prolific. The breed has been getting less and less common so that but few are found in America or Europe. There is no demand of commercial importance for it here or abroad, and the Royal Agricultural Society of England has recently denied it a place on its premium list.

The Tamworth is an old English breed of extreme bacon type. Its native home is central England, where it was known early in the last century. It is red or chestnut in color and of varying shades from very light to dark. In size it is large, the boars often weighing 600 pounds or more and the sows 450. The head is often undesirably long and straight. The ears at maturity are large and coarse, and lean heavily forward. The body is narrow, the depth of rib is short, the hams lack thickness, and the neck and legs are long. It does not fatten easily, and is slow to mature, but produces excellent bacon. The sows are prolific. There are few of this breed in England or America. There are a few herds in the Mississippi Valley, and the breed seems to be gaining in favor. At the National Swine Show in 1921, there was a large and fine display of Tamworths.

The Cheshire is a medium-sized, white breed of the lard type, mostly bred in New York state, the place of its origin. The breed originated about 1855, with the Large Yorkshire as an important blood line in the parentage. It resembles what the Englishman calls the Middle White, which is really a more compact, broader-backed, heavier-hammed, lardier type than the Large Yorkshire. It has a fair size, weighs well, matures early, and feeds and fattens to advantage. The sows farrow comparatively good-sized litters. This is one of the least known of American hogs.

The weight and size of the hog depend naturally on the age and breeding. In the general market, animals that weigh about 250 pounds are most satisfactory for slaughter. The average weight of the millions of hogs sold in Chicago stock yards is about 225 pounds. The market demands different hogs for different uses, however, so that all market hogs are sorted somewhat on the basis of weight, condition, and purpose. For this reason, a criticism regarding weight should take into consideration the special purpose involved. At 6 months of age 175 pounds would be a satisfactory weight, while at 12 months of age, when fairly well fed, a fat hog should weigh from 300 to 350 pounds.

Quality in hogs, as in all other animals, is of great importance. This is shown in the condition of the hair, the size of bone, and the development of the head. There should be a plentiful coat of hair that is neither very fine nor very coarse. If too fine, lack of constitutional vigor is indicated; but heavy bristles along the back, tell us surely that a coarse-grained, low grade of killing hog may be expected. The quality of the hair is an index to the quality of bone. Coarse hair naturally goes with coarse bone. Among experienced swine breeders, a bone of fair size, yet not coarse, is especially desired. The well-fattened hog requires strong bones to support the heavy body weight. A common criticism is that pigs are too small of bone and lack support of the body. For this reason, many breeders and feeders are looking for a hog that has plenty of size and bone, without coarseness. In passing judgment on animals of this class, one must be mindful to secure as much size as possible, consistent with quality. A large head for the body, with coarse thick ears, also indicates inferior quality. Many young hogs are too small and refined for their age, and never mature into animals of enough

Score card for fat hogs—lard type

Scale of Points	Perfect score	Score of hog judged
GENERAL APPEARANCE: 34 Points.		
Weight, score according to age, 175 lbs. for 6 mos.; 300 lbs. at one year	4	
Form, broad, deep, low, symmetrical, compact, standing well on feet	10	
Quality, hair fine; skin smooth; no coarseness of bone	10	
Condition, deep, firm, even covering flesh, giving smooth finish	10	
HEAD AND NECK: 7 Points.		
Snout, neither coarse nor long	1	
Face, wide between eyes; cheeks full, without wrinkles.	1	
Eyes, mild, good size, to be easily seen	1	
Ears, not coarse, of medium size, neatly attached	1	
Jowl, smooth, broad, full to shoulder	1	
Neck, thick, short, broad, full to shoulder	2	
FORE QUARTERS: 12 Points.		
Shoulders, broad, deep, full, smooth, compact on top	6	
Breast, wide, roomy	4	
Legs, straight, short, strong, wide apart, well set, pasterns upright, standing well upon toes	2	
BODY: 32 Points.		
Chest, deep, wide, large girth; flanks, well filled	3	
Back, slightly arched, very broad, thickly and evenly fleshed	9	
Sides, fairly deep, not too long, smooth, and full from ham to shoulder	8	
Belly, straight, wide trim, not paunchy	4	
Flanks, full and low	2	
HINDQUARTERS: 15 Points.		
Rump, same width as back, long, level, wide	3	
Hams, deep, wide, thick, not wrinkled, fleshed well to hock	10	
Legs, straight, short, strong, wide apart, well set; pasterns upright, strong, standing well on toes	2	
Total points	100	

Fig. 9. "The quality of the hair is an index to the quality of the bone." Photograph by the author.

feeding or breeding capacity. Excess of refinement is, therefore, to be avoided.

The food requirements for swine have been studied more extensively perhaps, than of any other farm animal. This fact is due in part to the ease with which swine may be handled and fed, and records made of growth and fattening. Exact feeding standards, however, are not generally applied in pork production. The following standards, the modified Wolff-Lehmann, as given by Henry and Morrison,[*]

_____

*Feeds and Feeding, 1917.

show the actual needs for fattening pigs, and brood sows with pigs.

A study of these standards makes clear that, as a pig increases in weight while fattening, there is a steady decline in the body requirements for dry matter, digestible crude protein, and total digestible nutrients, while the nutritive ratio steadily grows wider. Digestion experiments with breeding swine during growth show also the same decline in the need for dry matter, protein, and total nutrients. In other words, the body requirements of the pig in either growth or fattening call for a gradual lessening of the protein in the ration with an increase of carbohydrates.

The type of food best suited to the pig is of a concentrated form. The pig has a single stomach, rather limited in capacity, and, therefore, it cannot consume roughage like the cow or sheep with their compound stomachs and much greater relative capacities. It is true that hogs will do well on succulent forage crops and pastures, but even then the total amount eaten is comparatively small. The older class of hogs in winter will eat the leafy roughage of alfalfa or clover to some extent, but too much of this should not be fed. The standard grains, and mill products are best suited to the digestive tract of the hog.

The preparation of the food in swine has received considerable attention. Various experimenters have amply demonstrated that cooking the food for swine injures the digestibility of the proteins, and that better results are obtained by feeding raw rather than cooked food. Soaking grain may be advantageous, especially in the case of old corn that is hard and dry. In comparative experiments in feeding soaked whole wheat and dry whole wheat, conducted by the author at the Indiana station, and by Snyder and Burnett at the Nebraska station, a slight advantage came from soaking the grain. The grinding of grain for hogs has been somewhat advantageous. Prof. W. A.

Henry, of Wisconsin, fed ground and shelled corn in comparison for ten winters,* and found that on the average it required 501 pounds of whole corn and wheat middlings for 100 pounds of gain, and only 471 pounds of corn meal and middlings for an equal gain. Evvard, of Iowa, and King, of Indiana station, have found that no special advantage is secured by grinding corn for young pigs, but as they pass beyond 3 or 4 months of age somewhat better gains are made from ground or soaked grain. Corn-and-cob meal is not to be recommended for the pig, but, if fed, the cob should be ground fine.

Mineral food for swine is of first importance. When realize that an animal cannot live without iron in its blood, and that over 90 percent of the bony system consists of calcium and phosphorus, we must appreciate the importance of these substances in the food. For many years swine growers in the corn belt have been accustomed to placing ashes or soft coal in the pig lots. This was eaten by the pigs, but why, the farmer did not know. Prof. Henry, of Wisconsin, early in experimental swine feeding demonstrated that the bones of hogs that had been fed corn alone were deficient in ash, and broke much more easily than those of hogs fed corn and mineral matter. Since then other experiments have clearly demonstrated that minerals are an actual necessity in the diet of swine as well as of other farm animals. If hogs are fed on clover or alfalfa, with corn, they will obtain in the legumes considerable mineral matter, but where concentrates are largely relied upon for feeding, especially corn, minerals in some form are a necessity. A mixture of equal parts by weight of ground limestone, fine bone meal, and salt will make a satisfactory mineral for swine. Various kinds of mixtures are used by different feeders, many of whom also use flowers of sulphur, copperas and salt, for medicinal purposes, in addition to the other

*Feeds and Feeding, 1917

Fig. 10. Hogs on alfalfa pasture, Oregon Agricultural Experiment Station. Photograph by the author.

minerals used. For brood sows Prof. W. W. Smith recommends* a combination of 12 parts charcoal, 3 parts air-slacked lime, ground bone or ground rock phosphate, and 1 part common salt. Wood ashes in the same quantity as the lime he thinks would improve the combination. But very little salt seems to be needed by swine.

Water for swine seems to have an unusual place in the animal economy; for, besides its customary use as a drink, it is used extensively to prepare slop foods, and is also highly esteemed by the hog for bathing purposes. In cold weather hogs do not drink so heavily, excepting through slop feed, but in warm weather they need more water. Commenting on the fact that a new born pig's body consists of 80 percent water, while that of a fat hog weighing 400 pounds contains 35 percent, Prof. Evvard says.*

"The main point is that all pigs require a lot of water regardless of their own water content and we should aim to give it to them liberally. We should allow more water in summer than in winter, because of the higher temperature. Some of our sows in January drank around 4 pounds of water per head daily, whereas in April they daily drank 24 pounds. The water consumption per pound of dry matter ranged from 1.3 pound in cold winter up to 7.6 pounds in warm springtime."

*Pork Production, 1920

Pigs greatly relish a bath in warm weather, and will throw themselves down in any wet place, and wallow. They do not cool off as freely as other animals by the radiation of moisture from the pores of the skin, and so obtain relief in a wallow. Some of the more progressive swine growers supply drinking water to the stock through fountains attached to barrels holding water, and also provide shallow concrete-lined bathing pools.

The care of the sow and pigs at farrowing requires watchful attention. The sides of the pen in which the sow farrows should be provided with guards to prevent the mother from lying on her pigs. This guard may consist of a plank or a 2 × 4 piece fastened about 6 inches above the floor, and 8 or 10 inches out from the side of the pen. But very little bedding should be placed in the farrowing pen; for, if it is too thick, the small, more or less weak newly born pigs may get tangled in it, and have difficulty in getting about their mother. The dam should not be disturbed while farrowing, and the pen should be as quiet and comfortable as possible, and protected from cold drafts and dampness. Some careful herdsmen remove the pigs from the dam as fast as farrowed, and place them in barrels or baskets partly filled with straw. In cold weather a jug of warm water buried in the straw will keep the little pigs at a comfortable temperature. The young pigs should be allowed to nurse the mother every 2 or 3 hours the first day, and then after 24 hours be left with her for good. If, however, she is nervous and irritable, it may be well to keep the pigs from her 2 or 3 days, allowing them to nurse at intervals.

The sanitation of the swine quarters is of first importance. The pens should be kept free from filth and an unnecessary amount of manure, and the floors should be kept reasonably dry. One may keep swine in almost any kind of building, but a dry floor and clean conditions are equally important whatever the kind of house occupied.

The drainage about the swine quarters should be away from the buildings and yards, to promote sanitation. Unfortunately there are too many farms where the hogs are obliged to live and wallow in mud and manure, where disease germs abound. Sanitary conditions in the swine building may be improved by the free use of slacked lime sprinkled on the floors of the pens, and by freely whitewashing the walls.

The bedding of swine is customary in the northern sections of the country, especially in winter. The house or shelter should itself be comfortable, so that too much bedding will not be used. Wheat straw makes the best bedding; but, if so much is used that the pigs bury themselves in it in cold weather, when they come out to be fed they are liable to catch cold due to sudden change of temperature. Only a moderate amount of straw, therefore, should be used. In the South very little bedding is needed in winter, while in the warm season no bedding is required in the North.

Exercise for swine is regarded as a necessity. The tendency in cold weather is for the pigs to huddle close together under the straw and move about in the air as little as possible. In the latter stages of fattening, exercise is not so important, but with the breeding herd it is quite different. If the sows are to have strong, vigorous pigs, they must have enough exercise to keep them healthy and strong. Many boars are useless, because from lack of exercise they take on too much flesh and become inactive. On this subject Prof. W. W. Smith well says,* "Exercise promotes a loose, open condition of the bowels and does much to maintain a healthful functioning of the other organs of elimination, exercise contributes strength and vitality, reduces the chances of disease, costs nothing, and is an indispensable factor in the maintenance of health and breeding thrift."

In winter it is a good plan to drive the pigs about in the lots or near-by yards, scattering some corn and causing them to move about in search of it. When snow is on the ground, it is not so easy to do so; but, if the pigs live in colony houses and come to central feeding troughs, they will be compelled to move about more than they would otherwise and so will secure some exercise.

The care of pigs in hot weather has much to do with their successful development. They should be provided with shade, if possible. A woods-pasture is invaluable as a shelter from the hot sun. Portable pens or cots, that have a free circulation of air across the floor through openings on opposite sides, will furnish shade and may be fairly comfortable. A flat-roofed, low, open-sided shed in the pig lot, that costs but little for labor and material, will also furnish shade.

A wallow in warm weather gives the hog supreme satisfaction. The unsanitary character of mud wallows is to be strictly condemned, but the use of the modern concrete wallow, in which water may be kept reasonably free of filth, is to be highly commended.

Shelters and houses for swine vary greatly from a centralized building, with a series of pens, a room for feed, etc., to a colony or individual house of a single room. The centralized building should be located where drainage is good, and with feed lots and pastures conveniently connected. This house should be well lighted, so that sunshine will penetrate easily to every part. In an interesting report from 332 farmers in Kansas, 130 different dimensions of hog houses were reported. The majority of the houses reported on were from 8 to 20 feet wide and from 24 to 60 feet long, the average house being 16 by 40 feet, suitable for 10 farrowing sows. Such a house would have a central four-foot alley, with five 6 × 8 pens on each side. The windows should be placed so as to secure the

*Pork Production, 1921.

greatest amount of sunshine possible within the house. The floor may be earthen, wood, or cement. In 316 Kansas reports on the kinds of floors used, 150 reported earth, 5 earth packed over woven wire, 2 gravel, 59 wood or plank 70 cement or concrete, 2 boards over cement, 8 part earth and part cement, 8 part board and part cement, 6 part wood and 6 stone. Concrete is easily kept sanitary and rat-proof; but, unless well bedded, is inclined to cause rheumatism and pneumonia. Earth floors are cheap and are liked by hogs, but are easily rooted up, and may be very dusty or unsanitary. A movable wood floor over concrete is expensive but ideal from a health point of view. A single colony house should have a strong frame work, a roof that does not leak, and sides that are not drafty in cold weather. It should be placed on runners so that it may be easily hauled to a new location whenever desired. A house 5 feet wide and 7 feet long is of convenient dimensions. A house with a gable roof, or a two-thirds-span roof, or one with roof and sides like the letter A, is the more common. The economy "A" house advocated by Iowa Experiment Station, is very popular. It combines low cost, simple construction, and is easily adjusted for changes of temperature. Its 5′ × 7′ floor is sufficient for a good-sized sow and litter.

Fig. 13. An Iowa piggery, showing concrete foundation and outside feeding platform. Note the large amount of sunlight provided through the roof. Photograph by E. J. Hall.

Fig. 14. Hog cots and lots at Ohio Agricultural Experiment Station. Photograph by author.

Poultry

From *A Study of Farm Animals* by Charles Summer Plumb, 1922

Types and Breeds of Poultry

A classification of domestic poultry includes a number of different kinds, each consisting of a group with its types and breeds. The following is a classification commonly used.

1. Fowls and chickens.
2. Turkeys.
3. Guineas.
4. Peafowls.
5. Pheasants.
6. Ducks.
7. Geese.
8. Swans.

Fowls

The types of domestic fowls may be classified into four groups, namely:

1. Egg-laying.
2. Meat.
3. General-purpose.
4. Ornamental.

For some time poultry students have discussed these types, but more especially three, which from a practical point of view are the only ones of interest to the farmer. These three are the laying, the meat, and the general-purpose fowls. Good examples of each of these types are common all over the country. The other three types are rarely raised on the farm, being the product of the fancier, who oftentimes has his poultry outfit on a town lot. The breeds are also sometimes divided into two classes, sitters and non-sitters, according to whether or not the hens have the desire to sit on and hatch a nest of eggs.

The egg-laying type of fowl, according to Prof. H. R. Lewis,* should show a well balanced, deep, nearly rectangular body, well-developed in breast and abdomen. Great depth of body is especially desirable, but apparent depth must not be due to loose feathering, which is generally shown by an evidence of loose thigh feathers. Large capacity is essential, if a hen is to lay long and heavily. Such capacity is designated by a body that is deeper at the rear end of the keel than at the front end. The underline should be fairly straight and the back should be comparatively horizontal. Prominent breast development and evidence of a long keel are desirable qualities in a high-producing hen. The general body conformation of a heavy producer conforms very closely to a rectangle with pronounced angles rather than smooth curves. A male shows the same general characteristics as a female except that the abdomen is not so deep. Fowls of this type vary somewhat in size and weight as well as in flesh-producing capacity. The Leghorns are small, the hens weighing around 3 pounds, and do not produce much meat on the body, while the Minorcas are larger, the hens

---

*Judging Fowls for egg production. Hints to Poultrymen, vol. 8, No. 2. New Jersey Agricultural Experiment Station. 1919.

Fig. 1. The egg-laying type of fowl. Photograph from *Poultry Herald.*

Fig. 3. General-purpose type. A White Plymouth Rock. Photograph from *Poultry Herald.*

weighing about 6½ pounds, and may carry a good amount of flesh when in best condition. The fowls of this type are of European ancestry and are usually known among poultry specialists as the Mediterranean breeds.

The meat type of fowl is said to be comparable to the draft horse, beef cattle, mutton sheep, and the fat hog. It is squarely built, compact, thickly fleshed, wide of back and breast, and heavy of limb. Fowls of this type, when fat, have a carcass thickly covered with meat, and are especially valued for roasting. The hens, as a rule, are of sluggish disposition and are inferior egg-producers. The meat-type fowls sometimes weigh 10 to 12 pounds. They are of Asiatic origin, and are represented by the Brahma, Cochin, and Langshan breeds.

The general-purpose type of fowl, as might be supposed, is valued for both egg and meat production. This type is medium in size,

has considerable fullness of breast and width of back, and fattens to advantage. In egg production some general-purpose breeds have excellent records.

Standard weights vary, but 7 pounds for the hens and 9 for the cocks are satisfactory. Fowls of the general-purpose type, as a rule, belong to the American breeds, of which the Plymouth Rock, Wyandotte, and Rhode Island Red are the most common examples.

The breeds and varieties of fowls include a large number of wide difference, ranging from the tiny Bantam to the large and heavy Brahma. The breed characters of form, as applied to head, body, and legs, are rather distinct in each case. The variety characteristics are usually shown in color of feathers, though there may be other special features, such as single or rose comb. The Plymouth Rock, for example, includes six varieties; namely, (1) barred,

Fig. 2. Meat-type of fowl. Photograph from *Poultry Herald.*

Fig. 4. Barred Plymouth Rock cockerel, 1st price at Indianapolis. Photograph from *Poultry Herald,*

(2) white, (3) buff, (4) silver penciled, (5) partridge, and (6) Columbian. The following very brief descriptions of some of the leading breeds in America include the more important representatives of each.

The Plymouth Rock originated in America, and is of medium size. The head is surmounted by a single, upright red comb, and the ear lobes and wattles are also red. The neck is broad, breast full and wide, back broad, and body compact. Beak, legs, toes, and skin should be yellow in color. This breed is hardy and matures early, furnishing excellent broilers when eight to twelve weeks old. The hens are moderate layers, the eggs being of a brown color. This is a sitting breed, and the hens make excellent mothers. The mature males weigh 9½, and the females 7½ pounds. Varieties of this breed differ only in color of feathers.

The Wyandotte originated in America, and is of medium size, with a form very similar to the Plymouth Rock. These two breeds look very much alike when fowls of the same color are compared. The Wyandotte, however, should have an outline of form somewhat shorter and deeper in its lines than the Plymouth Rock. This breed has a rose comb instead of a single form, and red ear lobes and wattles. The legs are yellow. Wyandottes are excellent layers, but their eggs are of small size, brown in color. These fowls are valued for broiling and roasting, for their flesh is of fine grain and quality. The mature males have a standard weight of 8½ pounds and the females 6½ pounds. Wyandottes are extremely popular.

The Rhode Island Red derives its name from the fact that it originated in the state of Rhode Island. The American Standard of Perfection, in referring to these fowls, states that "their chief characteristics are: red color, oblong shape, compact form, and smooth surface plumage." This is a medium-sized breed, mature males weighing 8½ and the females 6½ pounds. The comb is either single or rose in form, and of medium size. The shank and feet should be yellow or reddish in color. This breed has become quite popular on account of its merit as a table fowl and for egg production. The Rhode Island Red, however, is more or less criticized for lack of uniformity in plumage color and excessive broodiness during the spring season.

The Orpington was first developed in the town of Orpington, England, from which it receives its name. There is no great difference between this breed and the general-purpose American breeds, except that the Orpington is somewhat heavier, and has skin that is white with a tendency to pink tint, and black or flesh-colored legs. The comb may be of the single or rose form. The ear lobes are red. There are three varieties, white, black, and buff. The mature males weigh 10 and the females 8 pounds. The Orpington in recent years has become very popular, ranking high for table use and for

Fig. 5. White Wyandotte cockerel. First prise at Utica. N. Y. Photograph from *Poultry Success.*

Fig. 6. White Orpington hen. Photograph from *Poultry Herald.*

Fig. 7. A vigorous White Leghorn cock at Cornell University. Eleven of his daughters averaged 197 eggs each in a year. Photograph from Dr. O. B. Kent.

Fig. 8. Minorca cockerel. Photograph from *Poultry Herald.*

egg production. Hens of this variety tend to be unreasonably broody.

The Leghorn is a breed of European origin, getting its name from Leghorn, Italy. This is distinctly an egg-laying breed. The features of importance are large, single, or rose comb, the single comb on the hens drooping to one side. The head is small, the eye of good size, ear lobes white, comb and wattles red, and beak, legs, and skin yellow. The breast is prominent, though not very wide; the back of medium width and length, the feathers snugly laid to the body, and the tail carried at an angle of about 45 degrees. The Leghorn is very hardy and one of the most active breeds of fowl, rather small of size, and famous for egg production. The females are non-sitters. There are several varieties of Leghorns, of which the white, brown, and buff are most common. Mature males weigh about 4 pounds and females 3. This is one of the most common breeds kept on American farms; in fact, it is almost universally the one that is used especially for egg production on a large scale.

The Minorca is an egg-laying, non-sitting breed, originating on the island of Minorca in the Mediterranean sea. The following is quoted from the American Standard of Perfection: "They are distinguished by long bodies, very large combs, long full wattles, large white ear lobes, dark colored legs, and pinkish-white or flesh-colored

skin. The Minorca head is carried rather high; the back is long and sloping; the tail is spread somewhat and only moderately elevated, being carried at an angle of 40 degrees from the horizontal. Their legs are firm, muscular, and set squarely under the long, powerful-looking bodies." There are both single and rose comb strains of this breed. Notable egg producers, the Minorcas rank as a close second to the Leghorns and, furthermore, they are known as the breed producing the largest egg, which is white in color.

The Light Brahma is of Asiatic origin, and has been known in America for many years. It is strictly of the meat type, and is the largest breed of fowls, the mature males weighing 12 pounds and the females 9½ pounds. The head is of medium size, with a small pea comb, medium-sized red wattles, and large red ear lobes. The breast is very broad and full, the back wide, the legs, toes, and skin yellow, and the shanks feathered. The neck, tail, and large wing feathers are black, and white striped with black, the other feathers being white. This breed is valued for roasting, but does not rate high in egg production. There is another variety called the Dark Brahma, but neither of these varieties is longer popular, and but few flocks are now kept, although they once were common.

The Cochin is also an Asiatic breed, large in size, like the Brahma, a standard weight for males being 11 pounds and for females 9½ pounds. This is a deep-bodied, massive fowl, having a loose plumage with much downy fiber underneath, which gives the entire body a fluffy appearance. The legs

Fig. 9. Light Brahma hen, Lady V. first at Chicago. Photograph from *Poultry Herald*.

are heavily feathered. These fowls are valued for roasters rather than for egg production. There are four varieties of Cochins, buff, black, white, and partridge.

The Langshan is a single-combed Asiatic breed, somewhat smaller and more active than the Brahma or Cochin, and much more popular, both for meat and for egg production. There are two varieties, the black and the white. The males weigh 9½ pounds and the females 7½ pounds, at maturity. There is much fullness of breast, and the form is compact. The legs of the black variety are bluish colored, and slightly feathered. The comb, face, wattles, and ear lobes are bright red in color.

There are many other breeds and varieties of fowls, but these are usually kept only in a small way by poultry fanciers and do not need attention here.

The bantam may be a dwarf of some of the larger breeds or a distinct breed. Bantams are kept for ornamental purposes, and have no practical value. The weights naturally vary somewhat, but 26 ounces for mature males, and 22 ounces for the females are standards. The Cochin and Brahma bantams weigh slightly more,

30 ounces for the male and 26 for the female. The bantams make very interesting pets for children.

The Turkey

The turkey is a native of America and was unknown in Europe previous to 1624. The present domesticated turkey originated from the wild stock which once was found in large numbers in this country, and is yet found to a small extent in certain parts of Pennsylvania and the southern states. According to the Standard of Perfection of the American Poultry Association, the frame of the turkey should be large, the body deep, with a broad, round, full breast that varies in prominence according to the variety." The head should be of good size, and the eyes bright and alert. The leg and shank bones should be large, straight, and well set. The carriage should be proud and erect. There are but few breeds of turkeys, and but one that may be regarded as common.

The Bronze turkey is very large, and the feathers are bronze or brown black, with shadings of color. The standard weight for an adult male is 36 pounds, and for the hen, 20 pounds. This is the most common variety raised.

The Narragansett turkey is of a metallic black color, with shadings to steel gray or approaching white. Mature cocks weigh about 30 pounds and hens 18 pounds.

The White Holland turkey, as its name indicates, has a white plumage. The beard of the male, however, is a deep black in color. Mature cocks weigh about 28 pounds and hens 18 pounds. This is not as hardy a variety as the Bronze or Narragansett, but its flesh is highly regarded, and it is the most domestic and easily controlled of all the breeds.

The Bourbon Red turkey is a native of Bourbon county, Kentucky, and is supposed to have originated from what in early days in Kentucky was known as the wild yellow turkey. The neck, breast,

Fig. 10. A Bronte turkey. Photograph from *Poultry Herald.*

Fig. 11. Pekin ducks on a Rhode Island farm. Photograph by Chas. X. Arnold.

back, body, and fluff of this breed are of a deep, brownish red. It has about the same weight as the Narragansett, the males weighing about 30 pounds and the hens 18.

The Duck

The Mallard, or common wild duck, is regarded as the parent stock, or ancestor, of all domestic ducks. This duck has a broad flat bill, small eye, good-sized head, long neck, full breast, long body, short tail, and short web-footed legs. The body has a dense covering of downy feathers, over which lies the feathery plumage. The thick plumage, which is characteristic of water fowl, is oiled by a natural secretion, which prevents water from penetrating among the feathers.

Three types of ducks are recognized: meat, egg-laying, and ornamental. Those which best supply the needs of the table for meat are most in demand.

The Pekin duck was brought to England from Pekin, China, in 1874. It is white in color and of large size, weighing 7 to 9 pounds, and is the most popular duck for table use. The bill is orange-yellow in color, while the shanks and toes are reddish orange.

The Pekin duck may be regarded as the universal favorite where duck culture is conducted on a large scale in the United States.

The Aylesbury duck is white and much resembles the Pekin. The bill is flesh-colored, and the legs and feet are pale orange. The standard weight is the same as the Pekin. These ducks are more popular in England, where they have been bred many years, than they are in America.

The Rouen duck is a breed that takes its name from a city in northern France, where it has long been bred. It is grayish in color, with dark shadings or black on head, neck, wings, and back. The bill is of greenish-yellow color, and the legs and feet orange with a green or brown shade.

The Cayuga duck originated in Cayuga County, New York. It is greenish-black in color, except some of the large wing feathers, which are brown. The bill is black, and the legs preferably black, though slate color occurs.

The Muscovy duck is a native of South America. In size it is very large, adult drakes weighing 10 pounds and females 7 pounds. The body is long and broad, and is carried nearly horizontally. The head is rather long, and large with the male, and has large crest-like feathers, which the duck often raises when excited.

Fig. 12. A "rapid growth" Pekin Duck eight weeks old. Reproduced by courtesy Cyphers Incubator Company.

Fig. 13. Toulouse geese. Photograph from *Poultry Herald*.

The head is partly bare of feathers, and the sides and top above the bill have rough wart-like coverings known as caruncles, which are red of color and rather conspicuous. The bill is pink or flesh-colored. Colored Muscovies have yellow to dark lead-colored legs, while those of the white variety are yellow. The plumage varies in color, but white or black-and-white are the favorite varieties. Ducks of this breed fly much more than others, and sometimes perch on elevated places.

The Indian Runner duck is supposed to have originated in India. It is rather small, a standard weight being about 4 pounds at maturity. The body, which is long and narrow, is carried somewhat erect, after the style of the wild penguin. The popular color is fawn or gray and white. The claim is made that the young ducks at 6 weeks of age dress into broilers weighing 2½ to 3 pounds. This duck, however, is valued chiefly for egg production, a female occasionally laying as many as 200 eggs in a year.

The Goose

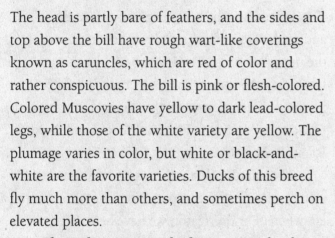

The domesticated breeds of geese have been developed from the wild breeds, but more especially the common Canadian wild goose, which is often domesticated and kept in confinement. So common is this wild goose in confinement that it is standardized in the American Poultry Association Standard of Perfection. It has a black head with white stripe, a gray body, and adults weigh from 10 to 12 pounds. There are several breeds of importance.

The Embden goose is of European origin. It is of medium size, adult ganders weighing about 20 pounds. The bill and legs are orange in color, and the plumage is white. This is a very popular breed.

The Toulouse goose gets its name from a city of that name in France. It is of large size, adults weighing about 25 pounds. The bill is pale orange and the legs a deep shade of that color. The plumage is gray, with dark shadings about the neck, back, wings, and breast. Most of our domestic flocks of commercial importance consist of these two breeds.

Indications of egg-producing capacity may be sought in several directions. In general these indications are shown in three ways:

1. In color changes due to egg production.
2. In body changes in fat and pelvic bones.
3. The period of molting.

A discussion of the above indications involves a number of special features which must be considered by themselves.

Color Changes in Hens due to Egg Production

A yellow pigment is more or less present in the hen, according to conditions. When not producing eggs, the hen lays up body fat. In the case of yellow-skinned fowls, this fat contains a yellow pigment which colors not only the body fat and skin, but also the legs, beak, eye ring, and to some extent the ear lobe. As soon as a hen begins to produce eggs, this yellow pigment fades from the body and intensifies in the yolk of the egg. So long as a hen produces eggs the pigment is diverted to the yolk, none being deposited in the body, which is now bluish-white or pink in color. When laying is discontinued, the body once more takes on the yellow color. This process of fading follows a certain well defined course, always in the following order: first, the vent; second, the eye rings; third, the beak; and last, the shanks. The kind of feed used affects the length of the fading period in the hen, because the yellow pigment is derived from the grain and green feed that the hen eats. The fowl that has had yellow corn and plenty of green feed has a larger supply of yellow pigment stored in her body than the one fed on white corn with no green feed. Further, the greater the amount of yellow pigment stored up in the body, the longer the time required for the fowl to undergo the bleaching process. With these facts in mind it is possible to select the hen that has been the continuous, consistent layer, as well as to determine those which have just begun to lay or have been poor layers.

Color Marks

The vent is the first part to lose the yellow color after egg production starts. This change is due to the fact that those parts of the body where the blood circulation is greatest fade first. A white or pink vent of a yellow-skinned bird indicates that she is laying.

The eye rings, which are in the inner edge of the eyelids, bleach out a little more slowly than the vent and, therefore, bleached or white eye rings indicate a longer production than a bleached vent.

The ear lobes on the white-lobed varieties bleach next and indicate a still longer period of production than a white vent and white eye rings.

The color of the beak is lost before that of the shanks and thus a white beak indicates that the hen has been producing eggs for a month or six weeks. The color leaves the beak, beginning at its base, and gradually disappears, leaving the front part of the upper beak last. The lower beak bleaches faster than the upper. The lower beak should be used for observation when the upper is covered with black or horn, as with Plymouth Rocks and Rhode Island Reds.

The shank color is the last to be affected, the yellow remaining in this part after it has disappeared elsewhere. For this reason we have here the surest indication of long continued production. It requires from four to five months for the shanks to bleach out after the hen begins to produce eggs. The color

Fig. 14. Rear view showing large vent and egg laying form on left, and small vent and meat form on right. Photograph from Dr. O. B. Kent.

leaves the front of the shanks first and gradually fades from the scales on the back side as the length of the laying period increases.

Body Changes due to Egg Production

The following discussion of body changes is in the order that is usually followed in culling demonstrations.

The vent of a laying hen is large, as is shown in figure 14, and it is also open, moist, and soft, while that of a non-laying fowl is small, close, dry, and puckered.

The comb of a laying hen is large, full, and bright in color, while the comb of a non-laying one is dry and comparatively hard, often covered with scale, and is pale in color.

The abdomen of a laying fowl has a fat covering that is soft and pliable, and feels much like an udder that has been partly milked. The skin is

Fig. 15. A culling demonstration. Body depth is a measure of a hen's capacity to consume a large quantity of food and consequently produce a large number of eggs. The one on the left is a deep-bodied, high producer, the one on the right a shallow, round bodied scrub. Photograph from Prof. E. L. Dakan.

also soft and velvety. The abdomen of a non-laying hen is dry and hard.

The pelvic, or pin bones of a laying hen are straight and flexible, with very little or no fat around them. They are spread far enough to permit the passage of the egg. The spread varies with the individual and the breed, and no definite measurement applies in this regard. In general, however, a laying hen will show a spread between the pin bones of at least three fingers. Practice is necessary to determine just what spread indicates that the hen is laying, keeping in mind the fact that a hen that is laying will show a greater spread of pin bones than one not laying, and that the bones of a non-laying hen are thick, stiff, and blunt, with the ends bent in.

The distance from the pelvic to keel bones of a laying hen is an important indication. A laying hen consumes more food than one that is not laying. A high egg-producer consumes more feed than a poor egg-producer. In order to consume and digest this feed the intestines of a laying hen are larger than of one not laying. When laying, the ovary and oviduct are greatly enlarged and require more room. To provide this extra space, the body increases in capacity or depth. This is noticeable by the increase in the distance from the pin bones to the end of the keel bone. The increase in size of the body cavity is secured by the dropping down of the keel bone. By measuring the distance from the pin bones to the keel bone an idea can be formed as to whether the hen is in laying condition or not. No definite measurement can be given that will fit all individual hens. As a general rule, a hen that measures less than three fingers wide of body depth, is not laying or is a poor layer, because such a hen lacks the capacity for handling a large amount of feed. The hen that shows the greater body depth may, as a rule, be selected as a good layer if in addition to this she exhibits the other marks of egg production.

The Molt Influence on Egg Production

Most hens stop laying when they begin to molt. Since the molting period covers several weeks, it is advisable to sell the hens that molt early. It is a fact no longer disputed, that a hen, in order to make a high yearly record, must be a consistent layer. The early molting hen is not a consistent layer. She takes all the fall months as a vacation for changing her plumage. The consistent layer molts late and grows her new plumage rapidly. The time of the molt is the best indication of the last year's performance. The molting period may be a guide in culling all breeds and varieties, but is of special importance with such breeds as the Orpingtons and Minorcas that do not have the yellow skin. The hen that molts early, under normal conditions, will not lay as many winter eggs as the one that molts late. Neither will the early-molting fowl begin egg production earlier in the spring than the late-molting one. No definite date can be set as to early molting. As a general rule, however, the first hens in the flock to molt should be sold, and the last to molt should be retained for breeding purposes. Hens may be caused to molt early if placed on starvation diet while laying heavily; by irregular feeding; by roosting in a house that is poorly ventilated, or in any way that tends to check egg production suddenly. Care should be taken not to let these undesirable conditions occur, otherwise a lower total egg production is quite likely to follow. If the pullets are hatched early, they will be laying early in the autumn, and thus egg production will be kept up. In an article on culling,* Professor H. C. Knandel of Pennsylvania State College touches still another side to the plumage question. He says that during the fall months the condition of the plumage is the most noticeable indication of production that applies to all breeds. The hen whose plumage appears most soiled, whose tail and wing feathers are

*The Truth about Culling. National Stockman and Farmer, Sept. 3. 1921.

Fig. 16. A hen in heavy moulting condition. Photograph from Prof. F. S. Jacoby.

badly worn, is the hen that has been laying heavily. The early-molting hen during the late fall months appears very much dressed up in her new suit, but has not produced a quantity of eggs sufficient to pay her board bill. Hence the hen that is the good producer is too busy laying eggs to stop to molt, with the result that she does not shed her feathers and get ready to engage in egg production until late in the year.

The Incubation of the Egg

The fertile egg is one that will produce a chick under proper conditions of what is called incubation. The infertile or sterile egg cannot be hatched, and so has no value in reproduction, although for food it has equal value with the fertile one. The fertility of the egg cannot be determined except by incubation. After the egg has been under the hen for five to seven days, ordinarily one may easily tell whether it is fertile or infertile. If infertile, it will appear clear and show none of the changes subsequently described.

The testing or candling of eggs is a simple process of looking through the egg with the aid of special light. One may take a piece of common cardboard, one side of which is black, in which is cut an oval hole not quite as large as an egg. If the

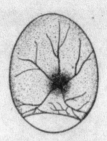

Fig. 18. The egg. Left egg dead germ; center, fertile egg on 7th day; right egg, infertile. Reproduced from Circular California Agricultural Experiment Station.

Fig. 17. A homemade egg candler. Reproduced from Farmers' Bulletin No. 1040, United States Department of Agriculture.

cardboard is held before a lighted lamp in a dark room, blackened side towards one, and an egg is held in the hole, the one that contains a chick will appear dark and opaque except at the larger end, while a sterile egg will be clear and show light. In the trade, where all eggs are examined before a light, this process is known as candling. Black lamp chimneys with holes in them are made for use in a small way; but, in the larger commercial trade, eggs are candled over sets of electric lights arranged for this purpose.

The incubation of the egg of the hen occupies a period of 21 days. The following are some of the more important changes that take place during incubation. During the first twenty-four hours the blastoderm enlarges to about a half inch in size, within which the first stages of head and some other parts appear. During the second day the heart begins to beat and the blood to flow. By the end of the third day the veins and arteries are considerably developed, and the young chick turns on its left side. On the fourth day the wing folds, and the folds forming the legs appear. The beak begins to form on the eighth day, and shows its horny shape on the twelfth. The entire shell except the air cell is occupied by the chick by the twelfth day. The feathers appear first on the eighth day, and by the thirteenth cover the body to the length of one fourth

inch. At this time the nails of the feet appear. On the fourteenth day the chick changes its position and extends lengthwise, the beak reaching the inner shell membrane. The air cell has been gradually increasing in size, and by this time is much larger. From now on, the chick increases in development to the twenty-first day. The following interesting description of the hatching process is given by Professor Lewis:*

"When ready to come out, the chick raises its head and pierces the inner shell membrane, and immediately starts breathing the air in the chamber, which causes the pulmonary circulation to become active and the embryonic circulation to cease. The head is next raised into the air chamber, and the chick deals blows upon the shell, which, when often repeated in the same place, result in fracturing it. This process is repeated until the shell is broken around about one third of the way from the large end. The chick then presses its head against the large end and its feet against the small end, and then by pushing is able to throw off the shell lid and make its exit."

The incubator is a box-like device containing a space in which eggs may be incubated by means of artificial heat. The hatching of eggs by artificial incubation has been in operation for thousands of years, especially in Egypt and China. There are various designs of incubators made, ranging in

———————————————
*Poultry Laboratory Guide, 1910.

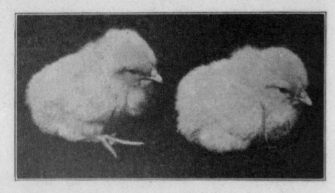

Fig. 19. A pair of vigorous day-old chicks. Photograph from Prof. F. S. Jacoby.

size from those which contain but a few eggs up to those with a capacity for thousands. Incubators in use at the present time are heated by hot air from a kerosene lamp or by a hot-water system. The hot-air type is the one in more common use. The eggs, one layer deep, are placed in movable, wire-bottomed trays. The temperature of the incubator is regulated by the automatic action of an instrument called a thermostat, which is sensitive to heat changes. This instrument is set so as to reduce or increase automatically the amount of incoming pure air. A thermometer within may be read through the glass front. Incubators should stand level, and a popular location in which to operate them is a dry cellar that will maintain a uniform temperature.

The artificial process of incubation in the incubator requires one to look carefully after the following features of importance. These are location, temperature, ventilation, and moisture, and turning and airing the eggs. The following discussion of these factors is abstracted from writings by Professor

Fig. 20. A standard incubator and lamp. Photograph from Ohio State University.

F. S. Jacoby, head of the Poultry Department at the Ohio State University.*

The location of the incubator may have a decided influence upon the number of chicks hatched. Heretofore the usual recommendation has been to locate the incubator in a cellar that maintains a more or less uniform temperature. With the improvement of the mechanical parts of the incubator, this reason for location is not so important as it used to be. The important point is pure air. The room, whether a cellar or not, should be so arranged that both the heavy gases near the floor and the light odors near the ceiling have a means of being dispelled. If the air in the room is impure, the air in the incubator will be even more so. The uniformity of temperature in a cellar is a decided help in the operation of the incubator, but it is better to have a room with a variable temperature, if the air is purer thereby. The most satisfactory results are obtained in a room having a cement or dirt floor, with a temperature of 60° to 70° F.

Temperature. The normal incubation temperature of hen eggs is 103° F. The position of the thermometer will determine the temperature at which the incubator should be operated. The thermometer may be arranged so that the bulb is in contact with the eggs or it may be hung above the eggs so that the bulb does not touch the top of the eggs. These two methods would each require a different reading to produce the correct temperature of the contents of the egg. When the bulb of the thermometer is in contact with one or two eggs and is on a level with the upper one fourth of the egg, the temperature should be 102° the first week, 103° the second week, and 104° the third week. If the thermometer is hung so that the bottom of the bulb rests on the top of the egg, the readings should be 103° the first week, 104° the second week,

*Artificial Incubation of Chickens, Bulletin 16, Vol. XV, Agricultural Extension Service, Ohio State University.

and 104.5° the third week. With the thermometer suspended just above the eggs so that the tray can be removed without striking the thermometer, the temperature should be 103° the first week, 104° the second week and 105° the third week.

The incubator thermometer should be tested at the beginning of each season by comparing the readings with those of a certified standard thermometer in warm water at 102°, 103°, 104° and 105° F, and careful note made of all variations.

Moisture and ventilation in the incubator are so closely associated that they cannot be considered separately. Nearly all incubators have some provision for supplying moisture during incubation. The use of moisture permits greater ventilation during incubation without excessive evaporation of the egg contents. The amount of ventilation will have a decided influence upon the quality and number of chicks hatched. The greatest amount of oxygen is needed from the 7th to the 20th day of incubation. The air in the incubator should always smell sweet. If it has any perceptible odor, there is not sufficient ventilation, and the eggs will not hatch as they should. The safest method of supplying moisture is by means of moisture pans located under the egg trays. The question of ventilation is automatically cared for in most incubators. Openings in the bottom, sides, or top permit fresh air to enter and impure air to pass out. If there are openings in the top of the machine, much more moisture must be supplied in the egg chamber, for there will be considerable moisture carried out of the machine with the warm air. If there are no openings in the top of the incubator, the moisture in the eggs will be conserved; but, in order to supply sufficient oxygen lo the developing embryos, there must be a system of ventilation that will circulate the air inside the incubator so that the light odors as well as the heavy gases will be dispelled and replaced with a certain amount of fresh air. As a rule, the amount of ventilation should be increased as the hatch progresses. Late hatches require more ventilation than the earlier hatches. The best guide as to the moisture requirement is the egg itself. About two thirds of the egg content should be occupied by the embryo on the nineteenth day. If too much moisture is supplied and too little ventilation allowed, the chicks will hatch with considerable irregularity and will not dry off with a soft, smooth down. If proper ventilation and moisture conditions have prevailed, the chicks will hatch out with uniformity, with a clean, soft down.

Turning and airing the eggs. Turning and airing the eggs is necessary for the production of strong, vigorous chicks. The hen on the nest turns the eggs with her feet several times a day. Turning insures an even development of the embryo and prevents any parts from adhering to the inside of the shell. The necessity for turning is apparent from the third to the eighteenth day of incubation; but, in those incubators that have automatic turning devices which permit the eggs to be turned without opening the machine, it may be desirable to turn the eggs from the second to the nineteenth day. There is no advantage in extending the time, if the machine must be opened and the egg tray removed in order to turn the eggs. Airing the eggs is a better expression than cooling, because it expresses more concisely the real value that accompanies cooling. It is the fresh oxygen that the eggs draw in as they cool that has a strengthening effect upon the embryo. The usual period for airing is from the fifth to the eighteenth day. The eggs should be turned three times a day—morning, noon, and afternoon. They should be aired once a day, preferably at noon. The length of the airing period will depend upon the development of the embryo and the temperature of the room in which the eggs are aired. It will vary from two to three minutes for eggs five days incubated early in the season, to forty-five minutes for eighteen-day eggs in the late spring or early summer. Turning by hand is undoubtedly more nearly perfect than any automatic egg turning device, and if done once a day in addition to the other turnings there will be a marked decrease in the number of crippled chicks.

Care of incubator after the hatch. Remove all shells unhatched eggs at the end of the twenty-second day. Chicks hatched after the twenty-second day will be too weak to prove worth raising.

The incubator should be thoroughly cleaned and disinfected after each hatch. Certain communicable diseases may be transmitted to the chicks through the medium of bite of egg shell and droppings, unless the trays are kept in a sanitary condition. Remove the trays and all portable parts from the interior of the machine. Scrub these as well as the inside of the machine with hot soapy water. Then drain and disinfect everything with a two percent solution of creolin or zenoleum. Replace the trays, close the door of the incubator, light the lamp, and let the machine dry out. The fumes from the disinfectant will penetrate to all parts of the machine. If burlap is used on the nursery tray, use a clean burlap for each hatch.

The foods suitable for fowls vary widely in kind and character. In fact, farm poultry will eat almost anything that has any nutritive value. So adaptable are fowls to local conditions, that, as a rule, they are fed the cheapest and most common foods grown in the region in which they are kept. Very naturally, in America corn is most commonly fed, with wheat or its by-products next in favor. In Japan, rice is the food generally used. The kind of food, however, should vary according to the age and condition of the birds, and the purpose for which they are kept. If for fattening, then a carbonaceous food is best; but, if for eggs, then that of a protein nature should be used. Protein foods recommended for fowls are meat scraps, fish meal, and milk of various forms. The common grains and cereal by-products, such as corn, wheat, oats, bran, middlings, etc., supply the necessary carbohydrates.

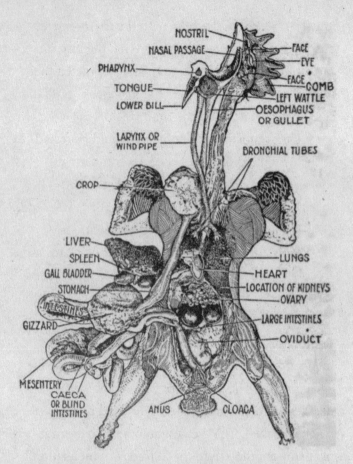

Fig. 21. Anatomical chart of a fowl. Reproduced from Poultry Manual of the G. E. Conkey Co., Cleveland.

The special preparation of feed for fowls naturally depends upon conditions. Small particles are usually preferable to large ones. Wheat and other small grains are very satisfactory. Large grains like corn are best cracked or broken. Ground or pulverized feeds, singly or in mixture, are known as mashes. Where no water is used, this food is called dry mash; with water, a wet mash. Dry mash is a favorite in some places and not in others. Clover or alfalfa hay is often thrown into the yard, the fowls readily eating the leaves and delicate parts. Young chicks require fine, easily digested food, like oatmeal, cracked wheat, finely-granulated corn, chopped vegetables, etc. Skim milk also is a valuable food for growing chickens.

Green food for fowls causes them to respond very rapidly in increased growth or egg production. When on a range of good grass no other green food

Fig. 22. Fowls eating cabbage suspended just above the head. Reproduced from the Poultry Manual.

Fig. 23. Oats sprouted in a pan. By courtesy Cypher's Incubator Company.

need be provided, but during the winter season succulent food is most desirable. Coarse vegetables are often sliced or chopped into small pieces before feeding, although entire cabbages or roots may be hung in the house or fastened to nails on the walls, from which points they will be picked to pieces. In recent years sprouted oats have been used in a small way for feed, especially for young chicks. The common plan is to make a wooden rack-like arrangement, to contain series of shallow pans. The desired amount of oats is put into a vessel and covered with warm water and let stand overnight. The surplus water is then drained off and the oats are spread over the pans to a depth of one half to three fourths of an inch. The oats should then be placed in a room, preferably a basement or cellar, having a temperature of 60 to 65 degrees. The oats should be sprinkled daily with tepid water, and, to provide drainage, the bottom of the pans should be perforated with small holes. In about ten days the sprouts will be ready to feed to the chickens, but they should be used sparingly in the first of the feeding.

Regularity in feeding fowls is essential. On many farms the poultry must forage for themselves, but under proper conditions there should be special grain feeding morning and evening. A dry mash is commonly kept in the house at all times. Other special feeds are also given early in the morning, about noon, and just before the birds go to roost. Regularity of feeding also brings the fowls into intimate touch with the poultryman, and enables

him to handle them and watch their condition to the best advantage.

Frequency of feeding fowls depends upon the age, condition, and purpose for which they are kept. Young chicks should be fed four or five times daily. The feeding of mature fowls varies among poultrymen, some feeding twice and others three times a day. If one has time to look after the stock in detail, three feeds a day for fowls in limited yards will give better results than will two. Most good poultrymen use what are called "hoppers" or "self-feeders." The hopper is a box-like arrangement containing more or less feed, from which the fowls can eat freely at any time. Scattering grain in cut straw or floor litter is a good plan, for it keeps the fowls busy and ensures slow eating, both of which habits are desirable. Some persons feed a wet mash in the middle of the day, grain being used morning and night. Some prefer one method and some another.

Fig. 24 Forced feeding of fowls in England. Photograph by courtesy of Poultry Herald.

The use of mineral foods by fowls is even more important with farm animals. Growth in proportion is really much greater with the fed fowl than the four-footed animal, while the production of eggs requires a considerable amount of mineral matter. The common supply of food does not always furnish enough of the mineral substances, and especially lime, to meet the needs of the fowl. This lack is particularly true of the laying hen. Consequently some other material must be added, and green ground or broken burned bone, granulated dry bone, and finely broken stone are commonly used, to meet this need. Ground or finely broken oyster shells have always been popular for laying hens. As to the exact needs of the body for mineral food, we do not know, but it may be assumed, as based on practice and the result secured with farm animals, that the mineral substances play a part in nutrition. Robinson, however, believes that in "good feeding of mixed rations," under range conditions young birds get all the mineral elements they require, and adult birds all they need, except for producing egg shells. He does not think grit is necessary, and since 1902 has fed none to poultry, except in the first feeds of young ducks and geese. Granulated charcoal is frequently used, being regarded as valuable for correcting sour stomach and other forms of indigestion. Some poultrymen think charcoal is a blood purifier.

Water for fowls should be clean and pure. Drinking fountains in which clean water may always be found are commendable. Fowls are rather

Fig. 25. Cheaply made drinking fountains. These are jars filled with water and turned with mouths down in pans of water. Photograph from Ohio State University.

Fig. 26. A feed hopper and covered water pan at left. Photograph from Prof. F. S. Jacoby.

frequent drinkers, and should always have plenty of clean water available. In winter, care should be taken to see that water and not ice or snow is supplied. A flock of fifty hens will use from four to six quarts of water a day in ordinary weather conditions.

Feeding rations for fowls naturally vary, some persons preferring one ration and some another. Most of these here given are easily secured or may be readily prepared, as the foods used in the combination are grown over a wide extent of country. The rations given are quoted from reports, and so differ in total amounts and in statement of weights or parts. The common method, however, is to mix up a quantity of feed, and then use as much as the flock requires.

The feeding of young chicks requires very careful attention. The following is the general course of feeding recommended by the poultry department of the Ohio State University. Milk should be the first food given. Either fine commercial chick feed or finely cracked corn and wheat should be given in the litter about five times daily, making sure the chicks have to scratch in the litter to get the grain. Plenty of exercise for the chicks is desirable. For the first week bran should be kept available in shallow pans all the time, as this is rich in mineral matter, is bulky, and serves as a mild laxative. As the chicks get older the grain feeding can gradually be reduced until only morning and evening scratch feeds are given. The following course of feeding is especially recommended for the various stages of development, using as much of the several mixtures as may be desirable.

First week

SCRATCH FEED

50 lbs, corn finely cracked

40 lbs. wheat finely cracked

10 lbs. rolled oats

MASH

Wheat bran

Milk all time

Second to eighth week

SCRATCH FEED

60 lbs. corn finely cracked

40 lbs. wheat finely cracked

MASH

20 lbs. bran

10 lbs. middlings

10 lbs. corn meal

10 lbs. ground oats

5 lbs. meat scraps or tankage*

1 lbs. bone meal

Eighth week to maturity

SCRATCH FEED

200 lbs. cracked corn

100 lbs. oats or wheat

MASH

200 lbs. bran

100 lbs. middlings

100 lbs. corn meal

100 lbs. ground oats

75 lbs. meat scrap

5 lbs. bone meal

In addition to the above, it is desirable to feed young chicks sprouted oats, cabbage, mangels, beets or green grass, each of these to be fed in finely prepared form, as may be available. When on the range such food need not be prepared. Infertile eggs from the incubator, hard boiled and chopped up, make excellent feed for young chicks and they should always be fed rather than cast aside.

Several types of poultry houses, each for a special purpose, are more or less in use in this country. These may be placed in the following classes: (a) Laying pen house, (b) fattening house, (c) brooder house, (d) colony house, (e) shelter coop. While plans and details of construction cannot be given in the limited space of this volume, some suggestions of interest and value will be found in the following pages that may be well worth careful study.

The laying pen house is designed for the purpose of keeping fowls in confinement, in groups suitable for the best results. Yards or runs limit the range of the hens. These houses are permanent of location and, as a rule, are of substantial construction. Formerly they were made with tight walls, had glass windows, and in winter the air within was kept at as comfortable a temperature as possible. Sometimes these houses were lathed and plastered. Not much attention was given to ventilation. Houses of this sort are not built as much as formerly; and, if they are, cloth screens on the front or south side replace most of the glass, pure air being regarded as a necessity. In many cases, these houses have open front windows, except in the coldest winter weather, when the cloth screens are dropped. Laying pen houses are of different styles, a common one having a simple single-pitch shed roof, with a height of 6 or 7 feet at the south, and 4 or 5 feet at the rear. It is best to have the house of a depth that will allow sunshine to reach as near the back wall as possible. A depth of 14 feet and a width of 12 to 14 feet for each pen is a satisfactory size. One should allow 5 square feet for each bird in such a house. In a house of this sort the floor should be made of concrete in order to make it rat-proof and to keep it dry. This floor may be covered with cut straw or chaff, and be used in cold weather as a scratching shed. The walls should be tight enough to prevent drafts. The roosts may be placed just above a low platform at the rear or on one side, below which are the nests. In front, plenty of window space should be provided, which should be covered with poultry wire netting, and also have cotton cloth screens, to be dropped during very cold weather. Doors of standard size are usually placed at one or both ends of the house, with wire doors in the partitions, to allow passage through the various pens. In houses containing many pens, doors are sometimes provided to give entrance from the pens into the yards.

*Use milk in place of scrap or tankage, if available.

Fig. 27. A large laying house and yards. Photograph from Prof. F. S. Jacoby.

Fig. 28. A colony house at Ohio State University. Photograph from Prof. F. S. Jacoby.

The fattening house is a small structure containing crates in which fowls are fattened, arranged along each side of a passage way. The house is of simple construction, and has superior ventilation with inferior light, as fowls are best fattened under conditions of subdued light. Fattening crates are in tiers, with feeding trays in front of each, which with other conditions provide for the least amount of labor in caring for the birds. Houses of this kind are not common on American farms, but are used especially by men who make a business of fattening fowls for market.

A brooder is a device used in connection with the incubator, and is in a sense an artificial mother. The general plan of the brooder is that of a warm box or room, heated either by a small oil stove or a coal stove. The former provides uniform warmth for from 100 to 200 chicks, and the latter for from 200 to 500. Within the brooder is what is called a "hover." A circular plate or cover of more or less diameter, according to the size of the hover, is placed about ten inches above the floor. From the rim of this plate a cloth curtain extends to the floor. Pieces of cloth are also suspended from different parts of the underside of the cover to the floor. Here and there the cloth is slit so the chicks may freely pass through and find a warm protection among the strips of cloth, comparable to being under the mother's wing. The small brooder house has but one hover, but the large houses, which are heated by coal

stoves, may have several. The temperature under the brooder should be kept as nearly 100° F as possible. A brooder house may be a simple box-like affair of one room 6 by 8 feet in size, with the hover in the back and a door and window in front. On large farms it may be of considerable size, containing a series of pens, in the end of each of which is a hover, warm air being supplied by a hot-water heating plant. The floor of the brooder should be covered with fine sand, if at all available. The brooder should have plenty of sunlight; it should be rat-proof; it should be roomy with plenty of scratching space; good ventilation should prevail; and the temperature should be easily controlled.

The colony house is a small, single-room building containing roosts and nests, and located in a yard or field. It is simple and cheap of construction, and is usually portable, so as to be easily moved from place to place. There is no one style of house; and structures are made of all kinds of material, ranging from piano boxes, at a total cost of $3 or $4 up to those made with care by a carpenter, costing $35 or $40. A fairly good type of colony house has both a door and window in front, the latter being covered with wire screening, and with a curtain to be used for cold weather protection. A small window in one end, for both ventilation and light, and a wooden floor are also desirable features. Poultrymen having houses differing widely in style of construction and lighting

Fig. 29. A handy shelter coop and run. Reproduced from "Poultry Houses."

seem to get equally good results from their fowls. Two strong arguments for the colony house are, that a flock of about the right size may be kept in a yard of suitable area; also the house may be shifted from time to time to new and clean soil conditions, thus providing good, permanent sanitation. Colony houses may be hauled into grain fields after the harvest, where the fowls secure uncommonly good forage of grain and insects.

The shelter coop is usually built for a hen and a brood of chickens. It varies much in construction. Common boxes 2 or 3 feet square, with slat or wire front; empty barrels, with a slat attachment at one end; and shelters of tent or A-shape are frequently seen. These coops should be made so as to enable the chicks to pass freely in and out, to give the hens dry and comfortable shelter, and to protect the chicks at night from rats and other vermin.

The location and construction of the poultry house require useful thought, if the most satisfactory results are to be secured. A few suggestions, therefore, which are rather general in their application, are here given.

The site of the poultry building should be where drainage is good and the soil naturally dry. Further, the elevation should be sufficient for a good circulation of air. Under damp conditions throat or lung trouble is very likely to occur. In damp soil of a clayey or loamy nature, intestinal and other parasites that affect poultry breed more freely than elsewhere. A dry location promotes clean bodies and feet, which mean the production of clean eggs.

The size of the poultry house should depend upon the number of fowls one wishes to keep. On most farms large flocks do not give as satisfactory returns as small ones. With a flock of 50, each bird should be allowed 5 square feet of room. With larger flocks not quite so much space per fowl will be required. One can obtain satisfactory returns with 100 fowls of the smaller breeds in a house with 20 by 20 feet of floor space. If fowls are crowded, good results in egg production cannot be expected.

The width of the poultry house depends upon size of the flock. Under most conditions, a house 14 or 16 feet wide is ample for each pen. One should plan to use standard lengths of timber, so that as little waste as possible will occur in sawing. Poultry houses 20 feet wide are being constructed today quite generally by farmers with large flocks, this size being economical in cost of material, and providing a maximum of space for the same.

The foundation of the poultry house should be of concrete or stone, if intended for a permanent laying house. This foundation should be deep enough in the ground not to be affected by the action of frost, and should rise 6 to 12 inches above the surface. The thickness of wall will depend on local conditions, ranging from 6 to 8 inches. Portable colony houses may be built on 4 × 4 runners. Halpin and Ocock, of Wisconsin University, recommend the use of "two small trees of some durable wood which may be flattened off on top and tapered off at both ends so as to make a satisfactory runner."

The walls of the poultry houses are built of wood, brick, concrete, or stone. The most common method is to use 2 × 4 studs nailed to 2 × 6 sills, over which matched siding is nailed horizontally. When well put together, this makes a wall free from drafts and very satisfactory. If rough boards are used, battens or strips should be tacked over any cracks. It is not desirable to place siding over the studs on the inside, for in that case rats and mice will find a

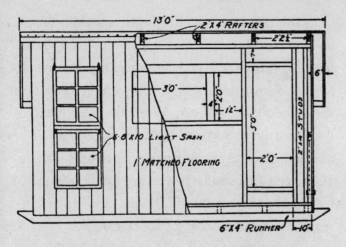

Fig. 30. Front elevation building plans of the Purdue Brooder Colony House. Reproduced from Extension Bulletin 52, Purdue University.

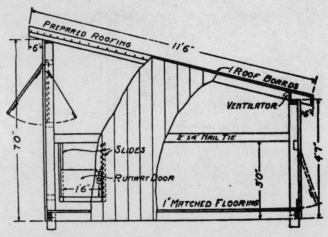

Fig. 31. End view Purdue Brooder Colony House. Reproduced from Extension Bulletin 52, Purdue University.

place for hiding. A wooden wall in winter is most satisfactory, as solid concrete or stone may be moist or frosty under some conditions. Concrete or brick walls that are partly hollow are preferable to the solid wall.

The roof of the poultry house should be strong, simple, and comparatively inexpensive. A single-span or shed roof is most common and can be built with least cost. If the house is over 14 feet wide, the usual 2 × 4 rafters should be supported. A combination roof has a double pitch, having a short pitch in front and a long one behind. This type of roof is well suited to buildings wider than 14 feet, and gives a strong construction. A two-pitch, or gable-roof, house usually has rafters of the same length, coming to a ridge in the center. This gives a high center to the pen, hence a loss of heat, so that in winter the house is likely to be cold. A ceiling is sometimes built in such a house, and attic storage room thus provided. What is called the half-monitor roof has one long sweep of rafter for perhaps two thirds the Reproduced from width of the house. Below the high point of rafter a vertical wall is dropped sufficiently to allow a line of windows. From the bottom of the window sill, a shorter length of rafter gives the necessary front pitch to the roof. There are also houses with the

fronts slanting to the ground, and others of wood that have roofs of the tent form, with no side walls in front or behind. A roof covering of rough boards and asphalt or tarred composition paper of some sort gives good satisfaction. Wooden shingles in most localities are too expensive, and in the colder sections shingle roofs are too drafty and cold in winter.

The floor of the poultry house should be of concrete in the permanent house; but, in the colony house, one of matched flooring is best. Effort should be made to keep the floor dry, and to prevent the harboring of rats or other vermin.

Fig. 32. Interior of poultry house, showing trap nests. Reproduced from Circular 37, Purdue University.

Partition material in the poultry house should usually be of wire netting. If the house is long, a close wooden or cloth partition at intervals is desirable, in order to strengthen the building, and also to prevent drafts. A house of six pens might have one solid central partition, and others of wire.

The windows of the poultry house should be adjusted to local conditions. In the southern states, glass should be unnecessary. In the colder North, an arrangement by which one sliding glass window can be arranged in connection with cloth-screened openings will give the best satisfaction. The windows should have a covering of wire screening, with curtains that are to be used only in severe weather. Some men, in fact, keep permanent open fronts in their houses, never using glass or cloth screen, and do not believe that their birds suffer from cold at any time.

Perches should be in the warmer part of the pen, free from drafts, and not high above the floor. The perches should be 12 inches apart, and not nearer the wall than 15 inches. They should be fastened together in a frame and hinged to the wall, being supported level with standards, or legs. It is a good plan to have a board platform a few inches below the perch, on which the droppings may be caught. The perches may be raised as desired, and the droppings removed. Perches of 2 × 4 pieces, on edge, with rounded corners are recommended.

The nests should be against the wall, and be 12 or 14 inches square, according to the size of fowl. Nests are sometimes placed below the dropping board, the hens entering from the back and the eggs being removed from the front by means of a hinged door. These nests have the advantage of being rather dark, as hens under such conditions rarely eat their eggs. Open nests may be fastened to the side of the pen, if desired, a common method. Trap nests are used in many houses today. The principle of this nest is that, when the hen enters, she springs a trapdoor, and so is confined until released by the poultryman. Thus he knows just what hens lay each day, and makes a record of the same. Hens laying in trap nests usually are numbered with metal leg-bands.

A dust bath in the poultry house is most important. The process of dusting is the method by which the bird keeps herself free from lice and similar pests. Many poultrymen have a corner of the pen arranged so that road dust, sifted coal ashes, or dry sand may be put there for dusting. A depth of 3 or 4 inches of dust enclosed by pieces of common 6 inch fencing boards will do. No poultry house should be without a dust bath, especially during the winter.

Fig. 33. Details of wall nests. From Extension Bulletin 57 of Purdue University.

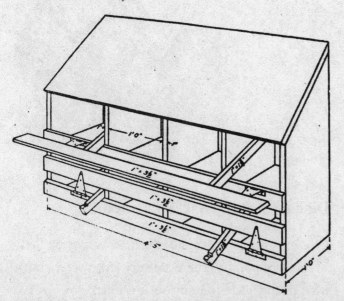

Fig. 34. A three-section trap neat, showing one section shut. Photograph from United States Dept. of Agriculture.

Practical Rules for Keeping Poultry.

From *The Household Guide or Domestic Cyclopedia* by Mrs. J.L. Nichols, 1905

1. A little glycerine applied occasionally to the combs and wattles will prevent injury by frosting.
2. A great source of contagion is the drinking troughs. Remember this if roup should make its appearance in your poultry-house.
3. In place of "tonics," drop a nail into the drinking trough and allow it to remain there. It will supply all the "tincture of iron" required.
4. If you feed whole corn, place it in the oven and parch it occasionally and feed smoking hot. The fowls appreciate it in the cold, frosty weather.
5. A little linseed or oil meal given once a week in the soft feed will promote laying. This will not come under the heading of "dosing the fowls with medicine."
6. Do not throw your table scraps into the swill barrel. Give them to the chickens.
7. One of the most important points in the keeping of ducks is to give them clean, dry quarters at night. They are very prone to leg weakness from cold, damp quarters.
8. Feed your fowls just what they will eat up clean. Fat hens or pullets are poor layers, and the latter are just what you don't want.
9. Fowls over three years old are not, as a rule, good for breeders. The males are unable to properly fertilize eggs for hatching, while the stock is usually weak. Four years is generally considered a "ripe old age" for a fowl.
10. Each hen, if properly kept, will lay from 200 to 250 eggs a year.
11. Liver and intestines are an excellent food to make hens lay.
12. Keep an abundant supply of lime where the hens can easily get at it if you desire your hens to lay well.
13. Always clean the nest well and put in fresh straw before the hen begins to set.
14. It is best in breeding to cross or mix the breeds more or less every year. It improves the flesh and general health of the fowls.
15. Pullets are better layers than old hens. Keep your stock young by disposing annually of the old broods.
16. Keep at least one rooster for every eight hens if you desire vigorous young chickens.
17. It is a good plan to change roosters every year.
18. Roosters are best at two years of age.

Fig. 1. Partridge cochins.

Diseases and their Treatments

In North America the climate is very good for all kinds of poultry. There are very few diseases but what readily yield to judicious treatment.

Most of the diseases to which fowls are subject are the results of neglect, exposure or bad diet.

How to Cure the Chicken Cholera

Symptoms.—The symptoms of chicken cholera are greenish droppings, prostration, and intense thirst. It should not be mistaken for indigestion. Cholera kills quickly, and this is a sure indication.

Remedy.—The best remedy is to add a teaspoonful of carbolic acid to a quart of water and give no other water to drink. The remedy is not a sure cure, but is one of the best. When cholera puts in an appearance, everything on the place should be thoroughly cleaned and disinfected, the remedy mentioned above being also an excellent disinfectant.

Another Good Recipe

½ pound madder.
½ pound sulphur.
2 ounces antimony.
2 ounces saltpeter.
¼ pound cayenne pepper.
Mix a tablespoonful in feed for 30 chickens.

Asthma

Symptoms.—The fowls labor for breath, opening the beak often and for quite a time, and sometimes drops of blood appearing on the beak.

Treatment.—Take the disease in hand as soon as discovered, keep the fowl warm, and give equal parts of sulphur and butter mixed in fresh lard.

Fever

Symptoms.—Restlessness, refusing to eat, drooping wings and excessive heat.

Treatment.—Mix a little castor oil with burnt butter and give a teaspoonful three times a day.

Loss of Feathers

This disease, common to confined fowls, should not be confused with the natural process of moulting. In the diseased state no new feathers come to replace the old.

Treatment.—Keep warm, and feed hemp seed and corn. Add brown sugar to the water.

Gapes

The Gapes is a very common ailment of poultry and domestic birds. More common among the young than the old.

Cause.—The disease is caused by the presence of little red worms in the wind-pipe, about the size of a small cambric needle.

Symptoms.—Gasping for breath with beak wide open, yellow beak, tongue dry and feathers ruffled on the head and neck.

Treatment.—Give a pill each morning made of equal parts of scraped garlic and horse radish, with as much cayenne pepper as will outweigh a grain of wheat; mix with fresh butter.

If a good many are affected, put from five to ten drops of turpentine to a pint of meal.

Treatment must be given in the early stages of the disease, or all remedies will fail.

Camping and Horse Packing

Camp and Trail Basics

From *Camp and Trail* by Steward Edward White, 1907

How to Determine Essentials

You may discover after your first trip that you over-packed. Avoid making that mistake a second time! When you have reached home after your trip, turn your duffle bag upside down on the floor. Separate the contents into three piles. Let pile No. 1 include those articles you have used every day—or nearly that often; let pile No. 2 comprise those you have used but once; and pile No. 3 those you have not used at all. Now, no matter how your heart may yearn over some gizmo, shut your eyes and resolutely discard the two latter piles.

Naturally, if you are strong-minded, pile No. 1 will be a synonym for your equipment. As a matter of fact you will probably not be as strong-minded as that. You will argue to yourself somewhat in this fashion:

"Yes, that is all very well; but it was only a matter of sheer chance that the Patent Dingbat is not in pile No. 1. To be sure, I did not use it on this particular trip; but in other conditions I might need it every day."

The Philosophy of Duffle

So you take it, and keep on taking it, and once in a great while you use it. Then some day you wake up to two more bits of camp philosophy which you formulate to yourself about as follows: *An article must pay in convenience or comfort for the trouble of its transportation; and substitution, even imperfect, is better than the carrying of special conveniences.* Then he hurls said Patent Dingbat into the nearest pool.

Patent Dingbats

That hits directly at the weak point of the sporting catalogues. Every once in a while an enthusiast writes me of some new and handy kink he is ready to swear by. It is indeed handy; and if one could pluck it from the nearest bush when occasion for its use arose, it would be a joy and a delight. But carrying it four hundred miles to that occasion for its use is a very different matter. The sporting catalogues are full of very handy kinks. They are good to fool with and think about, and plan over in the off season; but when you pack your duffle bag you'd better put them on a shelf.

Occasionally, but mighty seldom, you will find that something you need very much has gone into pile No. 3. Make a note of it. But do not be too hasty to write it down as part of your permanent equipment.

The wild life is not to test how much the human frame can endure—although that often enough happens—but to test how well the human wits, backed by an enduring body, can answer the question of comfort. Comfort means minimum equipment; comfort means bodily ease. The task is to balance, to reconcile these apparently opposing ideas.

The Logic of Woodcraft

A man is skillful at woodcraft just in proportion as he approaches this balance. Knowing the wilderness, he can be comfortable when a less experienced man would endure hardships. Conversely, if a man endures hardships where a woodsman could be comfortable, it argues not his toughness, but his ignorance or foolishness, which is exactly the case with our blatant friend of the drawing-room reputation.

Concerning Hats

Stetson Hat the Best

Long experience by men practically concerned seems to prove that a rather heavy felt hat is the best for all around use. Even in hot sun it seems to be the most satisfactory, as, with proper ventilation, it turns the sun's rays better even than light straw. Witness the Arizona cowboy on his desert ranges. You will want a good hat, the best in material that money can buy. A cheap article sags in the brim, tears in the crown, and wets through like blotting paper the first time it rains. I have found the Stetson, of the five to seven dollar grade, the most satisfactory. If it is intended for woods travel where you are likely to encounter much brush, get it of medium brim. In those circumstances I find it handy to buy a size smaller than usual, and then to rip out the sweat band. The friction of the felt directly against the forehead and the hair will hold it on in spite of pretty sharp tugs by thorns and wind. In the mountains or on the plains, you can indulge in a wider and stiffer brim. Two buckskin thongs sewn on either side and to tie under the "back hair" will hold it on, even against a head wind. A test will show you how this can be. A leather band and buckle—or miniature cinch and latigos—gives added security. I generally cut ample holes for ventilation. In case of too many mosquitoes I stuff my handkerchief in the crown.

Kerchiefs

About your neck you will want to wear a kerchief. This is to keep out dust, and to prevent your neck from becoming reddened and chapped. It, too, should be of the best quality. The poorer grades go to pieces soon, and their colors are not fast. Get it big enough. At night you will make a cap of it to sleep in; and if ever you happen to be caught without extra clothes where it is very cold, you will find that the kerchief tied around your middle, and next the skin, will help surprisingly.

Coats

A coat is useless absolutely. A sweater is better as far as warmth goes; a waistcoat beats it for pockets. You will not wear it during the day; it wads up too much to be of much use at night. Even your trousers rolled up make a better temporary pillow. Leave it home; and you will neither regret it nor miss it.

Sweaters

For warmth, as I have said, you will have your sweater. In this case, too, I would impress the desirability of purchasing the best you can buy. And let it be a heavy one, of gray or a neutral brown.

Buckskin Shirts

But to my mind the best extra garment is a good ample buckskin shirt. It is less bulky than the sweater, of less weight, and much warmer, especially in a wind, while for getting through brush noiselessly it cannot be improved upon. I do not know where you can buy one; but in any case get it ample in length and breadth, and without the fringe. The latter used to possess some significance beside ornamentation, for in case of need the wilderness hunter could cut from it thongs and strings as he needed them. Nowadays a man in a fringed buckskin shirt is generally a fake built to deceive tourists. On the other hand a plain woods-manlike garment, worn loose and belted at the waist, looks always at once comfortable and appropriate. Be sure that the skins of which it is made are smoke tanned. The smoke tanned article will dry soft, while the ordinary skin is hardening to almost the consistency of rawhide. Good buckskins are difficult to get hold of—and it will take five to make you a good shirt—but for this use they last practically, forever.

Overshirts

Of course such a garment is distinctly an extra or outside garment. You would find it too warm for ordinary wear. The outer shirt of your daily habit is best made of rather a light weight of gray flannel. Most new campers indulge in a very thick navy blue shirt, mainly, I believe, because it contrasts picturesquely with a bandana around the neck. Such a shirt almost always crocks, is sure to fade, shows dirt, and is altogether too hot. A lighter weight furnishes all the protection you need to your underclothes and turns sun quite as well. Gray is a neutral color, and seems less often than any other to shame you to the wash soap. A great many wear an ordinary cotton work shirt, relying for warmth on the underclothes. There is no great objection to this, except that flannel is better should you get rained on.

Under-clothes

The true point of comfort is, however, your underwear. It should be of wool. I know that a great deal has been printed against it, and a great many hygienic principles are invoked to prove that linen, cotton, or silk are better. But experience with all of them merely leads back to the starting point.

If one were certain never to sweat freely, and never to get wet, the theories might hold. But once let linen or cotton or silk undergarments get thoroughly moistened, the first chilly little wind is your undoing. You will shiver and shake before the hottest fire, and nothing short of a complete change and a rub-down will do you any good.

Now, of course in the wilderness you expect to undergo extremes of temperature, and occasionally to pass unprotected through a rainstorm or a stream. Then you will discover that wool dries quickly; that even when damp it soon warms comfortably to the body. I have waded all day in early spring freshet water with no positive discomfort except for the cold ring around my legs which marked the surface of the water.

Wear Woolen Underclothes Always

And if you are wise, you will wear full long-sleeved woolen undershirts even on a summer trip. If it is a real trip, you are going to sweat anyway, no matter how you strip down to the work. And sooner or later the sun will dip behind a cloud or a hill; or a cool breezelet will wander to you resting on the slope; or the inevitable chill of evening will come out from the thickets to greet you—and you will be very glad of your woolen underwear.

A great many people go to the opposite extreme. They seem to think that because they are to live in the open air, they will probably freeze. As a consequence of this delusion, they purchase underclothes an inch thick. This is foolishness, not only because such a weight is unnecessary and unhealthful, but also—even if it were merely a question of warmth—because one suit of thick garments is not nearly so warm as two suits of thin. Whenever the weather turns very cold on you, just put on the extra undershirt over the one you are wearing, and you will be surprised to discover how much warmth two gauze tissues—with the minute air space between them—can give. Therefore, though you must not fail to get full length woolen underclothes, you need not buy them of great weight. The thinnest Jaeger is about right.

Trousers

Moleskin and Khaki

The matter of trousers is an important one; for unless you are possessed of abundant means of transportation, those you have on will be all you will take. I used to include an extra pair, but got over it. Even when trout fishing I found that by the time I had finished standing around the fire cooking, or yarning, I might have to change the underdrawers, but the trousers themselves had dried well enough. And patches are not too difficult a maneuver.

The almost universal wear in the West is the copper-riveted blue canvas overall. They are very good in that they wear well. Otherwise they are stiff and noisy in the brush. Kersey is excellent where much wading is to be done or much rainy weather encountered—in fact it is the favorite "driving" trousers with rivermen—but like all woven woolen materials it "picks out" in bad brush. Corduroy I would not have as a gift. It is very noisy, and each raindrop that hits it spreads at once to the size of a silver dollar. I verily believe an able pair of corduroys can, when feeling good, soak up ten pounds of water. Good moleskin dries well, and until it begins to give out is soft and tough. But it is like the one-hoss shay: when it starts to go, it does the job up completely in a few days. The difficulty is to guess when that moment is due to arrive. Anything but the best quality is worthless. Khaki has lately come into popularity. It wears remarkably well, dries quickly, and is excellent in all but one particular: it shows every spot of dirt. A pair of khakis three days along on the trail look as though they had been out a year. The new green khaki is a little better. Buckskin

is all right until you get it wet, then you have—temporarily—enough material to make three pairs and one for the boy.

The best trousers I know of is a combination of the latter two materials. I bought a pair of the ordinary khaki army riding breeches, and had a tailor cover them completely—fore, aft, and sideways—with some good smoke-tanned buckskin I happened to have. It took a skin and a half. These I have worn now for three seasons, in all kinds of country, in all kinds of weather, and they are today as good as when I constructed them. In still hunting they are noiseless; horseback they do not chafe; in cold weather they are warm, and the hot sun they turn. The khaki holds the stretch of buckskin when wet—as they have been for a week at a time. Up to date the smoke tan has dried them soft. Altogether they are the most satisfactory garment of this kind I have experimented with.

Socks

The Ideal Footwear

Get heavy woolen lumberman's socks, and wear them in and out of season. They are not one whit hotter on the feet than the thinnest you can buy, for the impervious leather of the shoe is really what keeps in the animal heat—the sock has little to do with it. You will find the soft thick wool an excellent cushion for a long tramp; and with proper care to avoid wrinkles, you will never become tender-footed nor chafed. At first it seems ridiculous to draw on such thick and apparently hot socks when the sun peeping over the rim of the desert promises you a scorching day. Nothing but actual experience will convince you; but I am sure that if you will give the matter a fair test, you will come inevitably to my conclusion.

If a man were limited to a choice between moccasins and shoes, it would be very difficult to

"Mountain on mountain towering high, and a valley in between."

decide wisely which he should take. Each has its manifest advantages over the other, and neither can entirely take the place of the other.

The ideal footwear should give security, be easy on the feet, wear well, and give absolute protection. These qualities I have named approximately in the order of their importance.

Security of Footing

Security of footing depends on the nature of the ground over which you are traveling. Hobnails only will hold you on a slope covered with pine needles, for instance; both leather and buckskin there become as slippery as glass. In case of smooth rocks, however, your hobnails are positively dangerous, as they slide from under you with all the vicious force and suddenness of unaccustomed skates. Clean leather is much better, and buckskin is the best of all. Often in hunting deer along the ledges of the deep box canons I, with my moccasins, have walked confidently up slants of smooth rock on which my hobnailed companion was actually forced to his hands and knees. Undoubtedly also a man carrying a pack through mixed forest is surer of his footing

and less liable to turned ankles in moccasins than in boots. My experience has been that with the single exception mentioned, I have felt securer in the buckskin.

Wear

The matter of wear is not so important. It would seem at first glance that the one thin layer of buckskin would wear out before the several thick layers of a shoe's sole. Such is not always the case. A good deal depends on the sort of ground you cover. If you wet moccasins, and then walk down hill with them over granite shale, you can get holes to order. Boots wear rapidly in the same circumstances. On the other hand I have on at this moment a pair of mooseskin moccasins purchased three years ago at a Hudson's Bay Company's post, which have seen two summers' off and on service in the Sierras. Barring extraordinary conditions, I should say that each in its proper use, a pair of boots and a pair of moccasins would last about the same length of time. The moccasin, however, has this advantage: it can be readily patched, and even a half dozen extra pairs take up little room in the pack.

Waterproofing

Absolute protection must remain a tentative term. No footwear I have succeeded in discovering gives absolute protection. Where there is much work to be done in the water, I think boots are the warmest and most comfortable, though no leather is perfectly waterproof. Moccasins then become slimpsy, stretched, and loathsome. So likewise moccasins are not much good in damp snow, though in dry snow they are unexcelled.

In my own practice I wear boots on a horseback trip, and carry moccasins in my pack for general walking. In the woods I pack four pair of moccasins. In a canoe, moccasins of course.

You will see many advertisements of waterproof leather boots. No such thing is made. Some with good care will exclude water for a while, if you stay in it but a few minutes at a time, but sooner or later as the fibers become loosened the water will penetrate. In the case of the show window exhibit of the shoe standing in a pan of water, pressure of the foot and ground against the leather is lacking, which of course makes all the difference. This porosity is really desirable. A shoe wholly waterproof would retain and condense the perspiration to such an extent that the feet would be as wet at the end of the day. Such is the case with rubber boots. All you want is a leather that will permit you to splash through a marsh, a pool, or a little stream, and will not seek to emulate blotting paper in its haste to become saturated.

You will have your choice of three kinds of moccasin—the oil-tanned shoe pac, the deerhide, and the moosehide.

Shoe Pacs

The shoe pac is about as waterproof as the average waterproof shoe, and would be the best for all purposes were it not for the fact that its very imperviosity renders it too hot. In addition continuous wear affects the oil in the tanning process to produce rather an evil odor. The shoe pacs are very useful, however, and where I carry but two pairs of moccasins, one is of the oil tan. Shoe pacs can be purchased of any sporting goods dealer.

Moccasins

The deerhide moccasin, in spite of its thinner texture, wears about as well as the moosehide, is less bulky to carry, but stretches more when wet and is not as easy on the feet. I use either sort as I happen to get hold of them. Genuine buckskin or moose is rather scarce. Commercial moccasins with the porcupine quills and "Souvenir of Mackinaw" on them are made by machinery out of sheepskin. They are absolutely useless, and last about long enough to get out of sight of the shop. A great majority of the moccasins sold as sportsman's supplies are likewise very bogus. My own wear I have always purchased of Hudson's Bay posts. Undoubtedly many reliable firms carry them; but I happen to know by personal experience that the Putman Boot Company of Minneapolis have the real thing.

Slickers

Horseback in a rainy country is, however, a different matter. There transportation is not on your back, but another's; and sitting a horse is not violent exercise. Some people like a poncho. I have always found its lower edge cold, clumsy, and wet, much inclined to blow about, and apt to soak your knees and the seat of your saddle. The cowboy slicker cannot be improved upon. It is different in build from the ordinary oil-skin. Call for a "pommel slicker," and be sure it is apparently about two sizes too large for you. Thus you will cover your legs.

Should you be forced to walk, a belt around your waist will always enable you to tuck it up like a comic opera kind. It is sure ludicrous to view, but that does not matter.

Matches

Matches, knife, and a compass are the three indispensables. By way of ignition you will take a decided step backward from present-day civilization in that you will pin your faith to the old sulphur "eight-day" matches of your fathers. This for several reasons. In the first place they come in blocks, unseparated, which are easily carried without danger of rubbing one against the other. In the second place, they take up about a third the room the same number of wooden matches would require. In the third place, they are easier to light in a wind, for they do not flash up and out, but persist. And finally, if wet they can be spread out and dried in the sun, which is the most important of all. So buy you a nickel's worth of sulphur matches.

Match Safes

The main supply you will pack in some sort of waterproof receptacle. I read a story recently in which a man was recognized as a true woodsman because he carried his matches in a bottle. He must have had good luck. The cardinal principle of packing is never to carry any glassware. Ninety and nine days it may pass safely, but the hundredth will smash it as sure as some people's shooting. And then you have jam, or chili powder, or syrup, or whiskey, all over the place—or else no matches. Any good screw top can—or better still, two telescoping tubes—is infinitely better.

The day's supply you will put in your pocket. A portion can go in a small waterproof match safe; but as it is a tremendous nuisance to be opening

such a contrivance every time you want a smoke, I should advise you to stick a block in your waistcoat pocket, where you can get at them easily. If you are going a-wading, and pockets are precarious, you will find your hat band handy.

The waterproof pocket safe is numerous on the market. A ten-gauge brass shell will just chamber a twelve-gauge. Put your matches in the twelve-gauge, and telescope the ten over it. Abercrombie & Fitch, of New York, make a screw top safe of rubber, which has the great advantage of floating if dropped, but it is too bulky and the edges are too sharp. The Marble safe, made by the Marble Axe Company, is ingenious and certainly waterproof; but if it gets bent in the slightest degree, it jams, and you can no longer screw it shut. Therefore I consider it useless for this reason. A very convenient and cheap emergency contrivance is the flint and steel pocket cigar lighter to be had at most cigar stores. With it as a reserve you are sure of a fire no matter how wet the catastrophe.

Knives

Your knife should be a medium size two-bladed affair, of the best quality. Do not get it too large and heavy. You can skin and quarter a deer with an ordinary jackknife. Avoid the "kit" knives. They are mighty handy contraptions. I owned one with two blades, a thoroughly practicable can opener, an awl or punch, a combined reamer, nail pull and screwdriver, and a corkscrew. It was a delight for as long as it lasted. The trouble with such knives is that they are too round, so that sooner or later they are absolutely certain to roll out of your pocket and be lost. It makes no difference how your pockets are constructed, nor how careful you are, that result is inevitable. Then you will feel badly—and go back to your old flat two-bladed implement that you simply cannot lose.

Sheath Knives

A butcher knife of good make is one of the best and cheapest of sheath knives. The common mistake among amateur hunters is that of buying too heavy a knife with too thick a blade. Unless you expect to indulge in hand to hand conflicts, or cut brush, such a weapon is excessive. I myself have carried for the last seven years a rather thin and broad blade made by the Marble Axe Company on the butcher knife pattern. This company advertises in its catalogue a knife as used by myself. They are mistaken. The knife I mean is a longer bladed affair, called a "kitchen or camp knife." It is a most excellent piece of steel, holds an edge well, and is useful alike as a camp and hunting knife. The fact that I have killed some thirty-four wild boars with it shows that it is not to be despised as a weapon.

Duffle Bags

Now all these things of which we have mention must be transported. The duffle bag is the usual receptacle for them. It should be of some heavy material, waterproofed, and should not be too large. A good one is of pantasote, with double top to tie. One of these went the length of a rapids, and was fished out without having shipped a drop. On a horseback trip, however, such a contrivance is at once unnecessary and difficult to pack. It is too long and stiff to go easily in the kyacks, and does not agree well with the bedding on top.

This is really no great matter. The heavy kyacks, and the tarpaulin over everything, furnish all needed protection against wet and abrasion. A bag of some thinner and more pliable material is quite as good. Brown denim, unbleached cotton, or even a clean flour sack, are entirely adequate. You will find it handy to have them built with puckering strings.

The strings so employed will not get lost, and can be used as a loop to hang the outfit from a branch when in camp.

Toilet Articles

A similar but smaller bag is useful to be reserved entirely as a toilet bag. Tar soap in a square—not round—celluloid case is the most cleansing. A heavy rubber band will hold the square case together. The tooth brush should also have its case. Tooth wash comes in glass, which is taboo; tooth powder is sure sooner or later to leak out. I like best any tooth soap which is sold in handy flat tin boxes, and cannot spill. If you are sensible you will not be tenderfoot enough to go in for the discomfort of a new beard. Razors can be kept from rusting by wrapping them in a square of surgeon's oiled silk. Have your towel of brown crash—never of any white material. The latter is so closely woven that dirt gets into the very fiber of it, and cannot be washed out. Crash, however, is of looser texture, softens quickly, and does not show every speck of dust. If you have the room for it, a rough towel, while not absolutely necessary, is nevertheless a great luxury.

Shape of Tent

The proper shape for a tent is a matter of some discussion. Undoubtedly the lean-to is the ideal shelter so far as warmth goes. You build your fire in front, the slanting wall reflects the heat down and you sleep warm even in winter weather. In practice, however, the lean-to is not always an undiluted joy. Flies can get in for one thing, and a heavy rainstorm can suck around the corner for another. In these circumstances four walls are highly desirable.

On the other hand a cold snap makes a wall tent into a cold storage vault. Tent stoves are

Method of tightening rope.

little devils. They are either red hot or stone cold, and even when doing their best, there is always a northwest corner that declines to be thawed out. A man feels the need of a camp fire, properly constructed.

"A" Tent the Best

For three seasons I have come gradually to thinking that an A or wedge tent is about the proper thing. In event of that rainstorm or those flies its advantages are obvious. When a cold snap comes along, you simply pull up the stakes along one side, tie the loops of that wall to the same stakes that hold down the other wall—and there is your lean-to all ready for the fire.

When you get your tent made, have them insert grommets in each peak. Through these you will run a light line. By tying each end of the line to a tree or sapling, staking out the four corners of your tent, and then tightening the line by wedging under it (and outside the tent, of course) a forked pole, your tent is up in a jiffy. Where you cannot find two trees handily placed, poles crossed make good supports front and rear. The line passes over them and to a stake in the ground. These are quick pitches for a brief stop. By such methods an A tent is erected as quickly as a "pyramid," a miner's, or any of the others. In permanent camp, you will cut poles and do a shipshape job.

Tarpaulins

Uses of the Tarpaulin

Often, however, you will not need to burden yourself with even as light a tent as I have described. This is especially true on horseback trips in the mountains. There you will carry a tarpaulin. This is a strip of canvas or pantasote 6 × 16 or 17 feet. During the daytime it is folded and used to protect the top packs from dust, wet, and abrasion. At night you spread it, make your bed on one half of it, and fold the other half over the outside. This arrangement will fend quite a shower. In case of continued or heavy rain, you stretch a pack rope between two trees or crossed poles, and suspend the tarp over it tent wise, tying down the corners by means of lead ropes. Two tarps make a commodious tent. If you happen to be alone, a saddle blanket will supplement the tarp to give some sort of protection to your feet, and, provided it is stretched tightly, will shed quite a downpour.

The tarp, as I have said, should measure 6 × 16. If of canvas, do not get it too heavy, as then it will be stiff and hard to handle. About 10-ounce duck is the proper thing. After you have bought it, lay it out on the floor folded once, as it will be when

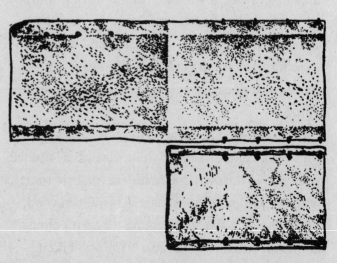

Tarpaulin, open and folded.

you have made your bed in it. To the lower half and on both edges, as it lies there, sew a half dozen snap hooks. To the upper canvas, but about six inches in from the edge, sew corresponding rings for the snap hooks. Thus on a cold night you can bundle yourself in without leaving cracks along the edges to admit the chilly air.

Blankets

A six or seven pound blanket of the best quality is heavy enough. The gray army blanket, to be purchased sometimes at the military stores, is good, as is also the "three-point" blanket issued by the Hudson's Bay Company. The cost is from $6 to $8. One is enough. You will find that another suit of underwear is as warm as an extra blanket, and much easier to carry. Sleeping bags I do not care for. They cannot be drawn closely to the body, and the resulting air space is difficult to warm up. A blanket you can hug close to you, thus retaining all the animal heat. Beside which a sleeping bag is heavier and more of a bother to keep well aired. If you like the thing occasionally, a few horse blanket pins will make one of your blanket.

To Sleep Warm

It is the purpose of this chapter to deal with equipments rather than with methods. There are a great many very competent treatises telling you how to build your fire, pitch your tent, and all the rest of it. I have never seen described the woodsman's method of using a blanket, however. Lie flat on your back. Spread the blanket over you. Now raise your legs rigid from the hip, the blanket of course draping over them. In two swift motions tuck first one edge under your legs from right to left, then the second edge under from left to right, and over the first edge. Lower your legs,

wrap up your shoulders, and go to sleep. If you roll over, one edge will unwind but the other will tighten.

Quilts

In the forest your rubber and woolen blankets will comprise your bed. You will soften it with pine needles or balsam. On a horseback trip, however, it is desirable to carry also an ordinary comforter, or quilt, or "sogun." You use it under you. Folded once, so as to afford two thicknesses, it goes far toward softening granite country. By way of a gentle hint, if you will spread your saddle blankets *beneath* your tarp, they will help a lot, and you will get none of the horsey aroma.

Pillows

A pillow can be made out of a little bag of muslin or cotton or denim. In it you stuff an extra shirt, or your sweater, or some such matter. A very small "goose hair" pillow may be thrust between the folds of your blanket when you have a pack horse. It will not be large enough all by itself, but with a sweater or a pair of trousers beneath it will be soft and easy to a tired head. Have its cover of brown denim.

Pails

On a pack trip a pail is a necessity which is not recognized in the forest, where you can dip your cup or kettle direct into the stream. Most packers carry a galvanized affair, which they turn upside down on top of the pack. There it rattles and bangs against every overhead obstruction on the trail, and ends by being battered to leakiness. A bucket made of heavy brown duck, with a wire hoop hemmed in by way of rim, and a light rope for handle carries just as much water, holds it as well, and has the great advantage of collapsing flat.

Wash Basins and Wash Tubs

A wash basin built on the same principle is often a veritable godsend, and a man can even carry a similar contrivance big enough for a washtub without adding appreciably to the bulk or weight of his animal's pack. Crushed flat, all three take up in thickness about the space of one layer of blanket, and the weight of the lot is just a pound and a half.

Collapsible canvas bucket and wash basin.

Hatchets

If you carry an axe at all, do not try to compromise on a light one. I never use such an implement in the woods. A light hatchet is every bit as good for the purpose of fire-wood, and better when it is a question of tent poles or pegs. Read Nessmuk's *Woodcraft* on this subject. The Marble Safety Axe is the best, both because of the excellent steel used in its manufacture, and because of the ease of its transportation. I generally carry mine in my hip pocket. Get the metal handle and heaviest weight. I have traveled a considerable part of the Canadian forests with no other implement of the sort.

Folding lantern.

Axes

On a horseback trip in the mountains, however, this will not suffice. Often and often you will be called on to clear trail, to cut timber for trail construction or to make a footing over some ultra-tempestuous streamlet. You might peck away until further orders with your little hatchet without much

luck. Then you need an axe—not a "half axe," nor a "three-quarter axe"—but a full five-pound weapon with an edge you could shave with. And you should know how to use it. "Chewing a log in two" is a slow and unsatisfactory business.

To keep this edge you will carry a file and a water whetstone. Use your hatchet as much as possible, take care of how and what you chop, and do not wait until the axe gets really dull before having recourse to your file and stone. It is a long distance to a grind-stone. Wes Thompson expressed the situation well. He watched the Kid's efforts for a moment in silence.

"Kid," said he sorrowfully at last, "you'll have to make your choice. Either you do *all the chopping or none of it.*"

Repairs

Needle, thread, a waxed end, and a piece of buckskin for strings and patches completes the ordinary camp outfit. Your repair kit needs additions when applied to mountain trips, but that question will come up under another heading.

A Good Two-Man Outfit

Get for a two-man outfit two tin cups with the handles riveted, not soldered. They will drop into the aluminum coffee pot. Omit the soup bowls. Buy good steel knives and forks with blackwood or horn handles. Let the forks be four-tined, if possible. Omit the teaspoons. Do not make the mistake of tin dessert spoons. Purchase a half dozen of white metal. All these things will go inside the aluminum coffee pot, which will nest in the two aluminum kettles. Over the top you invert four aluminum plates and a small tin milk pan for bread mixing and dish washing. The latter should be of a size to fit accurately over the top of the larger kettle. This combination will tuck away in a canvas case about nine inches in diameter and nine high. You will want a medium-size steel fry pan, with handle of the same piece of metal—not riveted. The latter comes off. The outfit as modified will weigh but a pound more than the other, and is infinitely handier.

Luxuries

However closely you confine yourself to the bare necessities, be sure to include one luxury. This is not so much to eat as for the purpose of moral support. I remember one trip in the Black Hills on which our commissary consisted quite simply of oatmeal, tea, salt, and sugar, and a single can of peaches. Of course there was game. Now if we had found ourselves confined to meat, mush, oatmeal pones, and tea, we should, after a little, have felt ourselves reduced to dull monotony, and after a little more we should have begun to long mightily for the fleshpots of Deadwood. But that can of peaches lurked in the back of our minds. By its presence *we were not* reduced to meat, mush, oatmeal pones, and tea.

Occasionally we would discuss gravely the advisability of opening it, but I do not believe any one of us down deep in his heart meant it in sober earnest. What was the mere tickling of the palate compared with the destruction of a symbol.

Take Your Pet Luxury

Somewhat similarly I was once on a trip with an Englishman who, when we outfitted, insisted on marmalade. In vain we pointed out the fact that glass always broke. Finally we compromised on one jar, which we wrapped in the dish towel and packed in the coffee pot. For five weeks that unopened jar of marmalade traveled with us, and the Englishman was content. Then it got broken—as they always do. From that time on our friend uttered his daily growl

or lament over the lack of marmalade. And, mind you, he had already gone five weeks without tasting a spoonful!

So include in the list your pet luxury. Tell yourself that you will eat it just at the psychological moment. It is a great comfort. But to our list:

Bacon is the stand-by. Get the very best you can buy, and the leanest. In a walking trip cut off the rind in order to reduce the weight.

Ham is a pleasant variety if you have room for it.

Cereals

Flour.—Personally I like the whole wheat best. It bakes easier than the white, has more taste, and mixes with other things quite as well. It comes in 10-pound sacks, which makes it handy to carry.

Pancake Flour, either buckwheat or not, makes flapjacks, of course, but also bakes into excellent loaves, and is a fine base for camp cake.

Boston Brown Bread Flour is self-rising, on the principle of the flapjack flour. It makes genuine brown bread, toothsome quick biscuits with shortening, and a glorious boiled or steamed pudding. If your outfitter does not know of it tell him it is made at San José, California.

Cornmeal.—Get the yellow. It makes good Johnny cake, puddings, fried mush, and unleavened corn pone, all of which are palatable, nourishing, and easy to make. If you have a dog with you, it is the easiest ration for between-meat seasons. A quarter cup swells up into an abundant meal for the average-sized canine.

Hominy.—The coarse sort makes a good variety.

Tapioca.—Utterly unsatisfactory over an open fire. Don't take it.

Rice, the Ideal Stand-by

Rice.—I think rice is about the best stand-by of all. In the first place, ten pounds of rice will go farther than ten pounds of any other food; a half cup, which weighs small for its bulk, boils up into a half kettleful, a quantity ample for four people. In the second place, it contains a great percentage of nutriment, and is good stuff to travel on. In the third place, it is of that sort of palatability of which one does not tire. In the fourth place it can be served in a variety of ways: boiled plain; boiled with raisins; boiled with rolled oats; boiled, then fried made into baked puddings; baked in gems or loaves; mixed with flap-jacks. Never omit it from your list

Buy Only the Best Brands

Baking Powder.—Do not buy an unknown brand at a country store; you will find it bad for your insides after a very short use. Royal and Price's are both good.

Tea and Coffee.—Even confirmed coffee drinkers drop away from their allegiance after being out a short time. Tea seems to wear better in the woods. Personally, I never take coffee at all, unless for the benefit of some other member of the party.

Potatoes are generally out of the question, although you can often stick a small sack in your kyacks. They are very grateful when you can carry them. A desiccated article is on the market. Soaked up it takes on somewhat the consistency of rather watery mashed potatoes. It is not bad.

Onions are a luxury; but, like the potatoes, can sometimes be taken, and add largely to flavor.

Saccharine Tablets

Sugar.—My experience is, that one eats a great deal more sweets out of doors than at home. I suppose one uses up more fuel. In any case I have many a time run out of sugar, and only rarely brought any home. Saxin, crystallose and saccharine are all excellent to relieve the weight in this respect. They come as tablets, each a little larger than the

When you quit the trail for a day's rest.

head of a pin. A tablet represents the sweetening power of a lump of sugar. Dropped in the tea, two of them will sweeten quite as well as two heaping spoonfuls and you could never tell the difference. A man could carry in his waistcoat pocket vials containing the equivalent of twenty-five pounds of sugar. Their advantage in lightening a back load is obvious.

Fats.—Lard is the poorest and least wholesome. Cottolene is better. Olive oil is best. The latter can be carried in a screw-top tin. Less of it need be used than of the others. It gives a delicious flavor to anything fried in it.

Mush.—Rolled oats are good, but do not agree with some people. Cream of Wheat and

Germea are more digestible. Personally I prefer to take my cereal in the form of biscuits. It "sticks to the ribs" better. Three-quarters of a cup of cereal will make a full supply of mush for three people, leaving room for mighty little else. On the other hand, a full cup of the same cereal will make six biscuits—two apiece for our three people. In other words, the biscuits allow one to eat a third more cereal in half the bulk.

Fruits

Dried Fruit.—This is another class of food almost to be classed as condensed. It is easily carried, is light, and when cooked swells considerably. Raisins lead the list, as they cook in well with any of the flour stuffs and rice, and are excellent to eat raw as a lunch. Dried figs come next. I do not mean the layer figs, but those dried round like prunes. They can be stewed, eaten raw, or cooked in puddings. Dried apples are good stewed, or soaked and fried in a little sugar. Prunes are available, raw or cooked. Peaches and apricots I do not care for, but they complete the list.

A Good Remedy for a Chill

Salt and Pepper.—A little cayenne in hot water is better than whiskey for a chill.

Cinnamon.—Excellent to sprinkle on apples, rice, and puddings. A flavoring to camp cake. One small box will last a season.

Milk.—Some people like the sticky sweetened Borden milk. I think it very sickish and should much prefer to go without. The different brands of evaporated creams are palatable, but too bulky and heavy for ordinary methods of transportation. A can or so may sometimes be included, however. Abercrombie & Fitch offer a milk powder. They claim that a spoonful in water "produces a sweet whole-some milk." It may be wholesome; it certainly is sweet—but as for being milk! I should like to see the cow that would acknowledge it.

Syrup.—Mighty good on flapjacks and bread, and sometimes to be carried when animals are many. The easiest to get that tastes like anything is the "Log Cabin" maple syrup. It comes in a can of a handy shape.

Altitude's Influence on Cooking

Beans.—Another rich stand-by; rich in sustenance, light in weight, and compressed in bulk. Useless to carry in the mountains, where, as a friend expressed it, "all does not boil that bubbles." Unless you have all day and unlimited firewood they will not cook in a high altitude. Lima beans are easier cooked. A few chilis are nice to add to the pot by way of variety.

Pilot Bread or Hardtack.—If you use it at all— which of course must be in small quantities for emergencies—be sure to get the coarsest. It comes in several grades, and the finer crumble. The coarse, however, breaks no finer than the size of a dollar, and so is edible no matter how badly smashed. With raisins it makes a good lunch.

Butter, like milk, is a luxury I do without on a long trip. The lack is never felt after a day or two. I believe you can get it in air-tight cans.

Macaroni is bulky, but a single package goes a long way, and is both palatable and nutritious. Break it into pieces an inch or so long and stow it in a grub bag.

The Hiker's Kit

From *The Boy Scout's Hike Book,* by Edward Cave, 1920

Only a few years ago, prior to the Spanish-American war, to be more definite, if one wanted a pack-sack, or boots, moccasins, blankets or clothing for use on a hunting or a fishing trip in the woods, one likely as not got them from Port Arthur or Duluth or Marquette. And one had a lumberman's outfit, nothing else. I sometimes think the sportsmen would be better off today, at least as to their duffle, were they still in a large measure dependent upon the same source of supply. For lumbermen's duffle is made for service, whereas much that is sold to sportsmen today seems to me chiefly intended to be ornamental.

The Boy Scouts, of course, do not give their camping duffle anything like the wear and tear that the sportsman gives his. For the main part, their camping trips are comparatively tame, and the regular Scout uniform, common shoes, cheap blankets, and ordinary tents will do. There are two

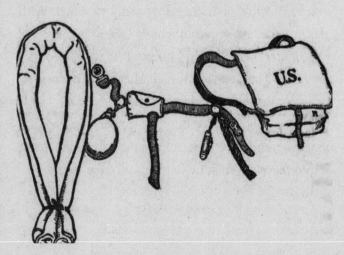

The scout's hiking kit, with blanket-roll separate from the pack-sack to show how it should be rolled.

things, however, that the Scout should give special attention to—his pack-sack and his bed.

Haversack and Knapsack.—A haversack is a bag with a single shoulder strap, made to carry at the side; a knapsack has two shoulder straps and is carried on the back, high up on the shoulder blades. Neither is well adapted for carrying the hiker's kit, and in fact both are sadly out of date.

Both of these bags were developed for the use of soldiers. The Century Dictionary says that "originally the military knapsack was meant for carrying food, but it has gradually become appropriated to a totally different purpose, as the transportation of clothes and the like, and food is carried in the haversack." This being the fact, the name should be discarded, for "knapsack" means "food sack." However, in this country the knapsack was discarded some years ago, and our infantry soldier carries all his equipment, except his rifle, in one complete highly developed harness, with everything except ammunition, canteen, and first-aid pouch strapped in one compact roll, called the pack. And civilian hikers carry theirs in what is commonly called a pack-sack.

The best pack-sack made is one originated and patented by Poirier in Duluth, Minn., about twenty-five years ago. The North is the real home of the pack-sack, which is the white woodsman's improvement on the tumpline of the Northern Indians. With the latter, the Indian carries anything, from a backload of flour to a miscellaneous bundle folded ingeniously in pack-cloth, tent or blankets,

Some packs.
From left to right, the poirier, prospector's, grain-bag, rucksack, and pack-basket.

puckered at the ends, with the tumpline serving for drawstrings, and tied in the middle with the loose ends of the line. The tumpline, of course, is simply the carrier, the pack-cloth, tent or blankets serving in lieu of a sack.

The Tumpline Pack.—To make the bundle as above described, the Indian first lays his pack-cloth on the ground, and piles his duffle on the middle of it. Next he takes the leather tumpline (which is some fifteen feet long and about two inches wide for a foot in the middle where it goes across the wearer's head but otherwise little more than a heavy thong), and lays it with the headpiece at one end, and the two ends across the pack-cloth, one on each side the duffle and a foot or so from the edge. The ends of the cloth are now folded over the two end pieces of the tumpline and the duffle rolled up in the cloth, making a roll with the head piece out at one side and a tip-end of the tumpline sticking out each end of the bundle. To complete the job the Indian pulls up the ends of the tumpline, so puckering the folded-in ends of the pack-cloth and securing sufficient line to knot each end to the carrying loop, carry to the middle of the pack, twist once around the other end of the line, pass around the middle of the pack and tie.

The manner of carrying this pack is shown in an accompanying illustration, which also shows how any bag or bundle, or several of them, can be carried on top, without being fastened there. The headpiece goes across the top of the packer's head, toward the

forehead. And take my word for it, one needs to get well used to this mode of packing before one attempts anything approaching a heavy load.

This method of packing, clever though it is, imposes too much hardship upon white men, and it is only used by them on short canoe carries or portages. Many of the Indians, too, have largely given it up, using in its stead the white man's pack-sack. It has one excellent feature, however; in fording a swift stream or crossing on a log or in walking on treacherous ice, the packer has no fear of being drowned by his pack; for it is not strapped on him. The feature is retained in the Poirier pack above mentioned, by means of a headstrap, which is separate from the shoulder straps, and is shown hanging down in the illustration. Naturally it is intended that under such circumstances this pack is to be carried by the headstrap alone. For heavy packing over portages, however, both shoulder straps and headstrap are used, other duffle being piled up on top of the pack.

The Poirier Pack-Sack.—The Poirier pack is a simple flat bag, made in four sizes, the largest 30 × 30 inches, and the smallest 18 by 18 inches. The shoulder straps lead from a common center near the top of the front of the sack, and attach to the two lower corners, a buckle in each strap (not shown in the illustration) provides for adjustment to fit the wearer. I fancy that when Poirier first brought out his pack the fit of the shoulder straps must have made a great hit. Formerly the soldier's knapsack had been the pattern after which pack-sacks were made, and of all the bunglesome contraptions, the old-fashioned army knapsack was about the worst. Whereas the shoulder straps of the Poirier pack-sack started from a common or "single-fire" center, between the shoulder-blades, like a pair of suspenders, those of the army knapsack went straight across the shoulders, starting from opposite corners of the bag. In early times they crossed the wearer's breast. Thus with the Poirier type of pack,

More packs.
Left to right, the boy scout's pack, modified knapsack, turkey, pack-harness pack, and tumpline pack.

the straps hugged the wearer "where he could stand it," while the army type of knapsack hung its weight close to the points of his shoulders. You will readily understand the difference if you place the point of your shoulder under the butt of a heavy pole and lift it, then shift the weight closer to your neck. Before going further, I want to say that the pack worn by our infantry soldiers today is a highly developed affair and beyond criticism. Also that I believe the Swiss chamois hunters were the first, in modern times at least, to use the single-point suspension in connection with a pack.

Another good feature of the Poirier pack (the patent has expired and it is manufactured by various concerns) is the cut of the flap, and the three long straps that hold it down. These straps enable the pack-sack tripper to make his pack-sack large or small, according to the contents; therefore a snug pack is always assured. With the large sizes—too large for a boy—the blanket, poncho and tent-cloth go inside, folded against the packer's back, to make the pack ride easy. With the child's size it is carried in the conventional roll, over the shoulder, or strapped in a bundle on the top of the pack.

Boy Scouts living in Minnesota or the Upper Peninsula of Michigan, where these packs are common, cannot do better than use them. I would recommend them for every Scout if it were not that I have worked out an excellent substitute, costing only half as much, which I will describe further along in this chapter.

The Prospector's Pack.—The pack shown in the second position, which I call the prospector's pack, is one I have used for heavy packing, and like very much. I consider it superior to any pack made in the way it hugs the back, if well loaded and properly hung. But it is in some respects inferior to the Poirier pack. It is a homemade affair, consisting of a simple flat bag of heavy brown canvas in dimensions 24 × 36 inches, with canvas loops or "keepers" to hold the straps, and two 5 ½-foot straps. I first had only the four canvas straploops on the back of the bag, but later made an improvement by putting two similar loops on the other side close to the bottom. By running the straps through these, they were secured against any possibility of slipping out of position, which formerly they had done, unless the corners of the bag were well filled, especially when taking the pack off or putting it on. I think a further improvement would be to rivet each strap to the bag on the bottom.

The blanket, rolled in the tent-cloth, five feet long, goes in this bag in the form of a letter U, the poncho or stretcher is folded and tucked down flat and smooth on the front side, or that which will be next the packer's back, and kit, grub etc., go in the middle of the blanket-roll U. Lastly, the upstanding ends of this are bent over together, one overlapping the other, and the top of the bag is folded down and secured by a strap passed vertically around the pack. I have used the same method of loading in connection with the Poirier pack-sack, and like it. It gives you a pack much easier to pack and unpack, that is more flat and rides better than if loaded with the blanket and the tent-cloth folded.

The Grain-Bag Pack.—The third pack illustrated is the easiest to procure and the quickest made that I know of. And it is much used by men in the Northwest as an emergency pack-sack, or to serve where a regulation pack-sack is not had. I have used such a pack repeatedly, when the question of how to carry a back-load seemed perplexing—until

I got hold of a grain-bag and a halter strap. The regular two-bushel cotton bag is what you want, not the clumsy "feed-bag" of burlap. Get a couple of walnuts, corn-cobs, or stones of similar size, and put one in each corner of the bag. Next, pile in your duffle, filling the bag half or two-thirds full. Tie the top of the bag upon itself, with a single knot now, tie your halter strap around the neck of the bag below this big knot, using also a single knot, tied in the center of the strap. Last, tie each end of the strap around a corner of the bottom of the bag, behind the walnut or stone, using a single knot as before. To adjust the straps, take up or let out through the knots tied to the corners.

The Rucksack.—The fourth illustration shows the Swiss rucksack, which means literally back-sack. It is primarily a mountaineer's pack, and the shoulder straps start from a common center, as in the Poirier pack-sack. There are several different models, the one most commonly used being a single bag in size about 16 × 20 inches, closing at the top with a drawstring, the puckered opening being covered with a flap that buckles down. The model shown (rather imperfectly) in the illustration, is 18 × 22 inches, but a much larger bag when opened to its full capacity, the bag having a number of gores which can be let out by loosening a strap. The pockets on the back are handy for carrying camera, maps, etc. It is not, however, as practical an everyday pack as the Poirier type, and it costs three times as much; perhaps because it is a "fancy" bag.

The Pack-Basket.—The last illustration in this row shows the Eastern pack-basket, which is much used by guides and sportsmen in the Adirondacks and Maine, and to some extent in the Maritime provinces of Canada. It is mostly used for a grub-pack, on canoe trips, but has nothing to recommend it for use on the trail. And the Poirier type of pack-sack double discounts it at its own game—portaging.

The first picture in the second row showing different packs, illustrates my adaptation of the soldier's *haversack* (no longer used in the army and to be obtained for 75 cents from any dealer in condemned military supplies) as a pack-sack. This I will describe at length further along in this chapter.

Other Pack Bags.—Next is an Eastern modification of the antiquated knapsack. This bag is carried by a canvas yoke, which fits the wearer better than the straps of a knapsack. Adjustable straps extend from the shoulder yoke to the bottom corners of the bag. A better pack-sack, also essentially Eastern, is the one named for "Nessmuk" or George R. Sears, author of a little book entitled "Woodcraft" which for many years was the only reliable handbook on camping and woodcraft. The "Nessmuk" pack-sack (erroneously called a "pack," since a pack is a pack only when it is packed), looks somewhat like the pack-sack previously mentioned, except for having a single point of suspension. The boxed sides, however, taper in at the top, and the top is puckered under the flap with a drawstring. The original Nessmuk pack-sack, I believe, did not have the shoulder straps meeting at a common center at the top of the bag.

The third illustration in this row shows the woodsman's "turkey," which is made with a grain-bag or a feed-bag and a short piece of rope. A small potato, a short section of corn-cob, or something of the like, is put in one corner of the bag, and one end of the rope tied behind it. Then the contents of the bag are piled in, and the bag is tied at the top with the other end of the rope. It makes a fairly comfortable one-shoulder pack, and is a trick worth knowing. The neck of the bag goes over the shoulder, so there need be no fear of the rope.

The last pack, made with a tumpline, has already been described. That immediately preceding it represents a duffle-bag or a pack done up in a tent, poncho, or blankets, carried with a pack-harness. This harness consists of two straps which go around the bag or bundle horizontally, and the carrying straps, which preferably should start at the top from a common center but in the Eastern manufactured article usually are attached, as illustrated, to the same sort of canvas yoke as is used on the pack mentioned above as a modification of the knapsack.

You now have a brief outline of the practical pack equipment used in the United States and Canada, with the exception of the pack I recommend for Boy Scouts, those of the soldiers, and a few mongrels that need not be discussed. I should like to describe the soldiers' pack as used in this country, it is so neat, practical, and interesting—I almost said unique. But I have not the space, and such a description would be of no practical value to the Scout, since the government does not allow anyone but a soldier to have the new army pack. Besides, it contains a number of features a Scout would not want. So now for the details of my Scout's pack-sack.

The Haversack Pack-Sack.—I first described this pony pack-sack (as I then called it) in the June, 1911 number of *Recreation*, of which I was then the editor. And as that year the Boy Scout movement was sweeping over the country, and there was no practical Boy Scout pack-sack, many Scout Masters followed my suggestion. I am glad to say I have had many testimonials as to the satisfaction the little rig has given. Among the Scouts of my own troop, No. 1 of Mamaroneck, N.Y., it is voted the best equipment we have.

To begin with, I wanted a small pack-sack, suitable for carrying camera and lunch on an ordinary day's hike, yet large enough, if necessary, to carry the necessaries for a trip of two or three days away from any point of grub supply. I bought an ordinary soldier's condemned haversack, with a single shoulder strap, the haversack being made to carry at the hip. I unhooked the strap from the two D rings at

Front view of scout's pack.

the upper corners of the bag, and thought to cut it in two and make shoulder straps of it. (This I have since done with another haversack, and is done by the Scouts in my troop). But I wanted to make sure to have a broad strap over the shoulders, where the weight would come, so used the old haversack strap for one shoulder strap, and got some leather and cut another one for the other shoulder. I got four iron D rings and four short pieces of leather strap, and secured a D ring to each lower corner of the front (back if you like, but I call it front because it is the side that goes forward) of the bag with rivets and stitching. The other two D rings I secured in the same fashion to the top of the bag, using, however, a 4 × 6-inch piece of sole leather as a reinforcement inside the bag and placing the rings in the center instead of at the corners. I then riveted and sewed my shoulder straps to these upper rings, and, using the brass hooks, four in all, from my haversack strap, adjusted my straps and hooked them to the lower D rings. I would have used a single ring at the top, attaching both straps to it, as on the Poirier type of pack-sack (see illustration) but did not have one and was in a hurry. Anyhow, I intended to put on a single ring later. This, however, I did not do until recently; and in the meantime, because of being not properly made in the first place, this bag, which I made simply for my own use, has been the cause of other bags also being made with the two-point suspension, instead of the proper single-point secured by using one large ring. While satisfactory enough for my own use, boys who borrowed this bag found that the straps were apt to slip off their shoulders if the bag were loaded lightly. To prevent this they crossed the straps at the top. And then when I would go to shoulder my pack I would find I couldn't get into it.

This bag, of course, is only large enough to carry cooking kit and grub, but no duffle. To get around this, I riveted on the five blanket straps, using one rivet to each, and reinforcing on the inside of the bag with a bit of strap. These straps are twenty inches long; be sure you do not make yours shorter. When the bag is used for a day's trip and no tenting is carried, they are rolled up, each in a neat little roll held by the buckle.

Tent-cloth and stretcher or tick will be described in the chapter on Tents and Tent Making. Your blanket should always be a double one, and of wool. Do not use a cheap, shoddy blanket; they are both uncomfortable and unhygienic, it being impossible to keep them dry.

The Blanket Roll.—To make up your blanket-roll, for strapping around the pack as shown in the illustration, first spread out your stretcher, or if using a combination tent (which you will find described in the chapter on Tents and Tent Making), spread that. Fold one end over so your cloth is five feet wide. Make a mark with a soft pencil and you will always know where to fold. If using stretcher and tarpaulin tent, now spread your tent on the stretcher, same size or smaller. Next, shake out your double blanket and fold it first the *long* way once, then fold this long strip on itself twice, or making three such folds in all, one on top of the other, in dimensions 3 × 5 feet. Lay this on the tent-cloth, and last of all spread on top your sweater and your pillow-bag, containing towel, handkerchiefs, clean socks, etc., which cannot go in the pack-sack. Now start on one of the long sides and roll, and roll tight. Do not include the stretcher or tent-cloth, whichever happens to be on the bottom. When your blanket is half rolled, pull the roll back to the edge of your outside canvas, and roll again, this time rolling in the canvas also. Make it tight; use your knees to help you. When you get within a foot of the edge of your canvas, stop and fold in half of it; then complete the roll, stopping when the folded edge of the canvas is almost underneath. Now bend the two ends up forming a U, with the folded edge of the canvas on the bottom or outside of the bend; see drawing. This will cause it to hold snug and neat. Strap your roll in place around the bag, and, if the bag is loaded, as it

should be before the blanket-roll is strapped on, you are ready to hike.

As to the contents of the pack-sack, for the present I shall simply give a suggestion, in the form of a list, followed with a few explanatory notes. In the next chapter, however, I will give further attention to this subject.

The best mess-kit I have been able to secure for Boy Scouts consists of the following:

Frying-pan, stamped steel, 7¾ inches in diameter at top; handle cut off and fitted described below.

Bread-pan, retinned stamped steel, 7¼ inches diameter at top, 5¾ inches at bottom, 3 inches deep; detachable bale.

Cooking pot, retinned stamped steel, 5½ inches diameter, 3½ inches deep; bail handle and cover.

Tin plate, 7¾ inches diameter.

Tin cup, 3 × 3 inches, straight sides, holds ¾ pint.

Cooking knife, 4¾-inch blade, butcher pattern; serves all purposes.

Table fork, teaspoon and tablespoon.

The Mess-Kit.—The frying-pan I bought for 10 cents. I cut the patent "cold" handle off with a hacksaw, and with a hammer, pliers and a vise as tools, bent the edges of the remaining 3½-inch stub around to the underside, forming a half-round base in which, after drilling three holes, I riveted a 2 ½-inch section of ¾-inch thin iron pipe. In this I push any convenient round stick, when commencing cooking operations, thus having a long cold handle, and I am not bothered with an awkward frying-pan handle in my pack. Almost every troop of Boy Scouts includes at least one person who has a breast-drill and can drill the holes for these rivets. Not having rivets handy, I cut off some wire nails, and for washers used some from worn-out automobile spark plugs. The piece of pipe also came from the scrap-box, having formerly served as a conduit for ignition wires on one of my cars.

A practical mess-kit for scouts.

1. Frying-pans; 2. Bread-pans; 3. Pot; 4. Cup; 5. Plate; 6. Provision bags; 7. Provision cans; 8. Butter jar; 9. Lard tin; 10. Milk bottle; 11. Salt shaker; 12. Bread pan bail; 13. Knife-sheath; 14. Ditty-kit; 15. Dish-towel.

The bread-pan is called by dealers in household supplies a pudding dish, and can be duplicated in light tin for 10 cents. It will pay any troop, however, to order their mess-kits all at one time, through one dealer, and get retinned stamped (and of course seamless) steel. The cost for bread pans should not be more than 15 cents.

The cooking-pot is one listed in catalogues as a sauce-pot, and is hard to obtain in this size. If a number are ordered at once, as above suggested, they should not cost more than 35 cents each. This and the bread-pan should be obtained from a concern dealing in hotel and restaurant supplies; your local dealer can get them if you insist. Do not accept cheap kitchen tinware.

Cup, anywhere for 5 cents; same for plate.

Forks and spoons can be bought by the dozen, and will average 2½ cents each for a good quality. And a serviceable cooking (butcher) knife will cost 25 cents.

Thus for a dollar you can get together a mess-kit that is in every way superior to anything on the market. It will "nest" all in one little bag, or if you like you can carry it as follows: Put knife, fork, and spoons, each in a leather sheath, in the pockets at the sides of the pack-sack, and the plate in the pocket of the flap. Frying-pan in the

frying-pan pocket that buttons (cut out the buttons) inside the bag; the bread-pan and the cooking-pot, the latter nested in the

The ditty-kit.

former and with a bag containing dishrag, soap, and dishtowel inside, down in the pack, bottom side in the hollow of the frying-pan in its bag and top side to fit in the hollow of the plate when the flap is buckled down. To make sure these nest as described, pack other things around and below them. And in order that the bottom of the frying-pan may not get too hard against your back, insulate it with your spare shirt, if on an extra-shirt hike, or your towel if not.

The other contents of the bag consist of a ditty-kit, a first-aid can, and the food containers. The first is made as shown in an accompanying illustration, size to suit individual notions, and preferably of some strong goods such as brown denim or khaki. The contents are placed in the pockets, the flaps folded over, and the whole rolled up until closed by the flap, then secured with the straps. This is a rough and ready duplicate of the traveler's toilet roll, and contains toilet articles, needle and thread, waterproof match-safe (loaded), spool of adhesive plaster, extra first-aid supplies, and other things, such as you might carry in your pockets.

The First-Aid Can.—The first-aid can is a combination tin-and-cardboard mailing case 5½ inches long by 2¼ inches in diameter, costing 15 cents if you get it at retail from your druggist, or perhaps five cents if procured in dozen lots from a supply house. Like the other cans mentioned here and in the next chapter, it may be substituted by a baking-powder can. Personally, I like the screw top and the fact that this type of can does not rattle or dent. It contains 1 roller bandage, a triangular bandage, 2 antiseptic compresses of sublimated gauze, assorted safety-pins, and a glass vial of tincture of iodine with rubber stopper. If hiking in a snake country it is well, though not so necessary as is generally believed outside of snake country, to carry in addition a hypodermic syringe and the antidotes that go with it, a solution of potassium permanganate and another of strychnine. For directions for using these, consult your Scout Master. In passing, I may say that among the natives of real snake country, carrying a hypodermic is practiced to about the same degree that the carrying of a compass is practiced by the bushmen of the Canadian wilderness, which is to say that nobody but a tenderfoot or a stranger carries one.

Bread-pan with bail attached.

The tin cup goes in the pack on top, where you can get it easily. Same applies to the pocket camera, if you have one. The 3¼ × 4¼ size I find the most satisfactory, after trying many different ones. A good place to carry a map is in the pocket of the flap of the bag, along with the plate. There are, of course, a few extras which are desirable but not necessary. They all add to the load, and I think it best that they be distributed around among the party.

What It Weighs.—These things I have mentioned, together with the grub (see next chapter), Scout axe and knife (and canteen, according to circumstances) on your belt, complete your load. And it is a real load, as you will soon find. In fact, it may be that you haven't the necessary physique to tote it. There are plenty of Scouts who haven't. So in the chapter on Special Equipment I will tell how to make a trek cart that will carry the camping equipment of the average patrol, and which at least will be welcome aid to the smaller fellows.

The weight of the pack is as follows:

Pack-sack	2¼ lbs.
Tent-cloth	3¼ lbs.
Stretcher	1½ lbs.
Blanket	5 lbs.
Pillow-bag (including towel, handkerchiefs, and socks)	¾ lbs.
Mess-kit	2½ lbs.
Ditty-kit	1 lbs.
First-aid can	¼ lbs.
Grub-containers	1 lbs.
Grub (liberal, for 2 days)	4 lbs.
Miscellaneous extras (including sweater)	1½ lbs.
Total	23 lbs.

Grub

From *The Boy Scout's Hike Book,* by Edward Cave, 1920

For the most part, hikes made by Boy Scouts do not compel the carrying of desiccated foods and the abstinence from fresh butter and yeast bread that falls to the lot of sportsmen making long trips in the wilderness. On the average overnight hike, there is no reason for going without bread and butter. And, indeed, they generally are to be met with along the way on longer hikes, for the long hike of the Scout is pretty apt to pass a good many farmhouses. And if my experience serves me right, the bread and butter one gets on the farm are worth going out of one's way for. Also eggs and milk—yes, and I'll include ice-cream. I've never tasted better ice-cream than I used to get from a certain Iowa farmer's wife in return for turning the freezer. You can get fresh vegetables and fruit in season; potatoes, onions, and the like at any time and the pies!

The Handy Grub Supply.—There is no reason in the world why a Scout should travel on short rations, even if he is so loaded down with duffle he can't carry but a little grub. But here's a pointer: The bigger your party the less chance you have with the farmer's wife. Better split up and forage by twos. And remember that there is nobody so independent as the American (or Canadian) farmer, and that good nature will get you more favors than anything else will. I have many a time been denied opportunity to purchase food—perhaps on account of my looks—by farmer women who not only relented but provided bountifully when we got acquainted. Having been raised a farm boy I perhaps have some advantage at this sort of diplomacy; but "what

man has done Scout can do" certainly applies here, because a Boy Scout only has to look hungry, being pretty generally known to be honest. And it's easy to look hungry, isn't it?

All things considered, I hesitate to suggest a grub list for the overnight or two-days' hike. The sensible thing is first of all to consult the home larder. Next, your appetite. Generally I take a survey of the ice-box and the pantry, and pick out what prepared food I want. Then I add what is necessary in the way of such staples as flour, cornmeal, tea (the woodsman's drink always), bacon, eggs, Crisco (an excellent substitute for lard), baking powder, etc. Finally, after taking stock of what I have accumulated, I make out a list of the things that are lacking, and get them. It is seldom I have to make any purchases.

The Wilderness Near Home.—To get a real taste of the life of the woodsman, or bushman as he is called in the British colonies, you will of course want to go for several days away from "civilization." You can do this, perhaps, without going far. I live in a town of 5,000 inhabitants, twenty miles from the heart of New York City, and I can find plenty of woods seclusion between here and the great city, where but for the sound of an occasional automobile siren or a train whistle I might easily imagine myself a thousand miles away. The wood-thrush that so many rave about having heard in far places, sings his beautiful bell-like melody in the trees fifty yards from my window, and the white-throated sparrow, or Canada bird, that is so much a part of the Northern wilderness, stops here on his migrations and stirs me with his high-pitched cascade of song. In fact, the only thing I lack to bring a most satisfying imitation of the wilderness within a half hour's hike of where I am writing is the fir trees. And without them—well, I'm spoiled. But you can do it and perhaps not miss the fir trees at all, and again you may have all you want of them.

For a little trip into some such quiet corner, where you may "hide out" and sense something of the charm that lays hold of the wilderness traveler and enslaves him for life, the following list of pack-sack tripper's sure-enough staples is suggested:

For Individual Scout, Three Days, Seven Meals
(Any time of year, any location, no allowance for fish, game, wild fruits or nuts.)

Flour	1¾ lbs.
Cornmeal (yellow)	1¼ lbs.
Rice	6 oz.
Bacon (lean)	1 lb.
Lard (or crisco)	4 oz.
Sugar	¾ lb.
Coffee (ground)	4 oz.
Tea	½ oz.
Baking powder	2-oz.
Evaporated cream	7 oz. (fluid)
Salt	4 oz.

That appears like pretty "dry fodder," doesn't it? But remember, the lone timber-cruiser or prospector hiking far beyond the edge of things is compelled to go light, and if you want to emulate him, you must not turn up your nose at his grub list. Especially when it is remembered that you haven't the muscle nor the room in your pack for carrying what he *could* carry. And please note that you have almost six pounds of grub.

Now suppose we see what sort of a three days' bill of fare we can get out of this. To begin with, you will eat your breakfast before leaving home, and will get your supper at home the day you return.

That means three dinners, two suppers and two breakfasts to get.

FIRST DAY	
Dinner	*Supper*
Hoe Cake	Boiled rice and milk, with sugar
Fried bacon	
Hot biscuits	"Dough gods"
Coffee	Tea
SECOND DAY	
Breakfast	*Dinner*
Fried rice	Corn dodgers
Flapjacks, with Syrup	Broiled bacon
	Hot biscuits
Coffee	Coffee
Supper	
Corn meal mush and milk, with sugar	
Corn batter cakes, with syrup	
Tea	
THIRD DAY	
Breakfast	*Dinner*
Fried mush, with sugar	Boiled rice
Broiled bacon	Fried bacon
Hot biscuits	Biscuit loaf
Coffee	Coffee

Not so bad, is it, for results from such an unpromising little grub list? Sure, you probably will have some grub left over after some of your meals. But I have no way of knowing what your eating capacity is, or how hard a day's work you will do. I have simply struck a safe average. Many a trailer goes longer with less variety, although it must be admitted the practical man on the trail generally eats as well as he can, and nowadays is getting into the way of carrying desiccated and dried foods. But let us see how our menu is prepared.

Before you go afield, take your 3 × 3-inch tin cup, which holds ¾ pint, and with a file scratch on it inside and outside marks which will enable you to use it as a measure. A mark 1 inch from the bottom will be the ¼-pint mark, a mark 2 inches from the bottom the ½-pint mark. Make these marks carefully and thoroughly, so you can always be guided by them. Now for the recipes:

Hot Biscuits.—Make sure to have a steady, hot fire that will have burned down to coals when your biscuits are ready to bake. Take ⅔ cupful (half pint) of flour, 1 level teaspoonful baking-powder, ¼ teaspoonful salt, 1 teaspoonful cold Crisco (or lard), and with your tablespoon mix well in the bread pan. Add water to which sufficient evaporated cream has been added to make a half milk, half water solution, and mix as rapidly as possible, until you have a fairly stiff dough. Tilt the pan and expose the bottom, on which dust some flour, flop dough back on this and dust flour on top. Turn your plate upside down, dust well with flour and rub some on your hands. Turn the loaf out on this improvised bread-board and quickly but not too roughly flatten it with your hands to ¾-inch thickness. "Flour" the top of the ½-pound baking-powder tin you carry your ground coffee in, and with it stamp out your biscuits. Lastly, after another dusting with flour, gently but firmly take them one at a time, and—put them in the hot ashes to bake. No pan, no reflector or oven. Just rake away the ashes a bit and put your biscuits down in a neat little row, and then rake the hot ashes around them—not on top of them. And when they have risen get your coffee pail or preferably your frying-pan going *over* them, making your coffee or your hoe cake and incidentally reflecting the heat down on top of them. No, they won't be dirty, at least not enough to hurt. You can blow the ashes off them when you fish them out. Try them with a sliver of wood; when no dough adheres, spear them with your fork. Hot? Not at *that* end of the fire by the time they

Baking with bread-pan and frying-pan.

are done. A fire follows its fuel, and if you are a good camper, the last fuel you put on was at the other end, where you are going to heat your dishwater.

Hoe Cake.—Take ½ pint of cornmeal (if you have a pretty good appetite), and in your bread-pan mix in with it ⅓ teaspoonful of salt and ½ tablespoonful of melted Crisco (or lard). Mix well, pressing the grease into the meal with your tablespoon. Add warm water sufficient to make a thick batter, stirring well. Have the frying-pan clean, grease with Crisco and a bit of rag, and heat pan. Spread a *thin* batter in the pan, and cook over a steady, moderately hot fire that has burned down to coals. Turn the cake as you would a flapjack, when the bubbles in it have burst, meantime shaking the pan occasionally to keep the cake from sticking.

Fried Bacon.—Just *fry* it; if you don't know how, your qualifications as a Scout should worry you.

Coffee.—For each cupful you expect to drink, put into your cooking pot a *short* (about three-quarters full) cup of water. Put on the lid and bring water to a boil. Take it off and put in a tablespoonful of ground coffee for each cup of water. Put back on the fire where it will get sufficient heat to bring it to a boil in half a minute. As soon as it boils, remove and "settle" it by pouring in enough cold water to make up for what was left out in the first place—half a cup if you are making two cupfuls. And your Mocha and Java being worth the name, you should have good coffee.

Boiled Rice.—Take a little more than half of your rice and wash it in cold water, using your bread-pan. Have your cooking-pot three quarters full of salted water, boiling hard, and dump in your rice. Let boil for about twenty minutes, but not too hard (half an hour if boiling gently), and stir occasionally. Strain off the water and set the pot to one side or hang it up high over the fire, with the lid off. By the time you are ready to eat, the rice will have swelled considerably, and dried nicely; you probably will have twice as much as you can eat.

This being the case, do not eat out of the pot, but serve what you want on your plate; the balance is to be fried in the morning.

"Dough Gods."—Take ⅔ cupful of flour, 1 small teaspoonful of baking-powder, ¼ teaspoonful of salt, and 1 slice of fat bacon, minced fine as possible. Mix thoroughly in your bread-pan and add water slowly, stirring and working with your cooking-spoon till you have a fairly stiff dough. Flour the loaf top and bottom, flour your hands and pat the dough out into a couple of big cakes about half an inch thick. Bake in the ashes, same as the biscuits. Or, as your frying-pan is not working, warm and grease it, and put in one of your cakes. Place over a steady slow fire (hot coals, not blazes), and shake occasionally so the cake will not stick to the pan. When it is brown on the bottom, slide it out on your plate, previously greased, and stand it up on its edge beside the fire, so the heat will bake it on top. Now attend to the other one the same way, except you can use the frying-pan to stand it up at the side of the fire. Turn your "dough gods" around as it becomes necessary so they will bake evenly on both sides. When they get enough "backbone," you can take them out of the pans and prop them, so they lean with their tops toward the fire. Have them close, and provide a good steady bed of coals, not too hot.

This "bread" is somewhat similar to biscuit loaf. It is the old way of baking with bacon instead of rendered grease or lard, used by men who carried nothing they could do without, and whose only food staples were flour, bacon, baking-powder and salt.

Fried Rice.—Made with the boiled rice left over from the last meal. Simply cut into cakes and fry.

Tea.—Boil a cupful of water (in your cup if necessary), and when boiling put in ½ teaspoonful of tea. Take off the fire and let stand for five minutes to steep.

Flapjacks.—Take ⅔ cupful of flour, 1 small teaspoonful (not quite level full) of baking powder, ¼ teaspoonful of salt and mix well in the bread-pan, adding cold water and stirring well until you have an even batter. Grease frying-pan, heat it, and cover the bottom with batter about an eighth of an inch deep. Bake over hot fire, shaking the pan occasionally to keep the "jack" from sticking. When the air bubbles have about all burst, "flip" your cake upside down, and cook the other side. Place on plate close to fire and cook the rest of your batter. Be ready to eat as soon as the last one is done; for "the older they are the tougher they be."

Syrup.—Put 6 teaspoonfuls of sugar in your cup, add enough boiling water (from that for the coffee) to just cover it, set in the coals and stir till the sugar is dissolved, then let simmer (boil gently) for five minutes. Pour out in your plate to cool. If you have too much for your flapjacks, leave some in the cup to sweeten the coffee.

Corn Dodgers.—Take ⅔ cupful of cornmeal, ¼ teaspoonful of salt, and ⅓ cupful of warm (not too hot) water. Mix into a stiff dough, and then with your hands roll this into the dodgers, which are about the size of pork sausages. Get the frying-pan *hot*, grease it, and put in your dodgers. Fry them brown, then turn them out into the bread-pan previously greased and warmed. Set this among the coals and invert the frying-pan over it. Rake coals around and over the bottom of the frying-pan. The dodgers should be well baked in about fifteen minutes, depending upon your fire.

Broiled Bacon.—Use a long-handled green-stick fork, turn the slices frequently, and remove when they begin to brown.

Cornmeal Mush.—Mix in your bread-pan ¾ cupful of meal with 1 teaspoonful of salt. Have 3 ½ cupfuls of water in your cooking-pot and bring it to a hard boil. Add *cold* water to the meal to make a soft batter, mixing well. Now with your tablespoon dip the batter into the boiling water a little at a time, so as not to stop it boiling. Stir well, to prevent lumps forming, and after about ten minutes put the cover on and hang the pot up where it will cook slowly with no danger of scorching. Stir once in a while, and if necessary thin with boiling water. Cooking should be complete in an hour. Pour what you don't eat into the frying-pan, previously greased, to stand overnight and "set" for frying.

Cross-section view of bean-hole and dutch oven.

Corn Batter Cakes.—Take ⅔ cupful of cornmeal, ⅓ cupful of flour, 1 small teaspoonful of baking-powder, 1 teaspoonful of sugar, 1 small teaspoonful of salt, mix, add cold water gradually and stir to a thick batter. Fry like flapjacks.

Fried Mush.—Cut the cold mush into narrow slices, and fry over a hot fire, using plenty of Crisco.

Biscuit Loaf.—This is prepared same as biscuits, except the loaf is not flattened or rolled in any way. Be sure to rub the Crisco or lard "shortening" thoroughly into the flour, leaving no lumps. Bake in one loaf, using the frying-pan to start with, and leaning the loaf against a clean, flat stone when it is baked enough to stand on end. Follow baking instructions given for dough gods.

Now you have a solid foundation on which to build a good reputation for camp cooking. By adding to the above list such other staples as dried beans, split peas, barley, and dried fruit, and using not only the recipes given, but as many more as you can find, you can have quite a surprisingly elaborate menu. And this all with staple grub.

Why Carry Water?—You will of course prefer to add a little more weight and bulk to your pack and spend less time cooking. And you *can* have butter. You will want to carry eggs, and canned goods, butter, a fresh steak, fresh fruit and even potatoes on occasion. Go ahead; you're doing the eating—and the packing. I merely want to casually remark that the equivalent in fresh and canned grub of your six pounds of the dry variety will weigh—oh, say ten or twelve pounds at least. And the excess weight will be almost all water and refuse. For example, just think of the water in a couple of cans of corn—more than half by actual weight. And a can of corn weighs 2¼ lbs. That means 1⅓ lbs. of water to every can. Fresh beef, eggs, potatoes, canned beans, contain more than one half water, and fresh fruit, canned soups and fruit still more. Do you want to lug a pail of water all the way from home, or can you get along with the water you can obtain at your camp-site? I think you will do best to go pretty "dry"; flour, cornmeal, rice, and bacon contain less than half as much water. And there's that 19-pound pack besides the grub, you know.

As a Scout, you of course know how to broil or fry meat, boil or fry eggs, boil, bake, or fry potatoes. You now have a standard list of staples and recipes as a guide, and I shall discuss cooking—beans, sure; they take so much time to cook—in several subsequent chapters. I therefore shall conclude this one by telling you how to pack your grub.

Your Food Containers.—First make or get some little provision bags, assorted sizes, say two large, three medium and two small, of "balloon silk" (No. 1 Egyptian sailcloth, or "spinnaker duck"), with paraffin ironed into it, the largest to hold a quart of flour, and leave room for tying securely, the smallest to hold a couple of ounces of baking-powder. (If you use self-raising flour you will save yourself the bother of fussing with baking-powder and salt.) Cornmeal, sugar, bacon, rice, beans, split peas, dried fruit, tea, etc., go in these bags. Next, three or four of the screw-top mailing cases described for carrying the first-aid kit (see preceding chapter), assorted sizes, or some baking-powder tins with tight-fitting lids. These are for ground coffee and such other provisions as require to be "corked up," such as desiccated eggs, desiccated potatoes or the like, if you have them, raisins, etc. Along with these

I sometimes carry "pemmican," which I make by chopping up chipped beef. If convenient, for your lard get a small can of the friction-top (pry-up lid) kind. I use one 2 × 2 inches that formerly contained automobile tire "gum." Also (from the druggist, 5 cents), a 2-oz screw-top ointment jar for butter, and a 4-oz., screw-top glass (called a "tall round jar") for evaporated milk or cream. Lastly, a wooden salt shaker and a piece of cheesecloth the size of a table napkin, edges hemmed, to wrap up bread or biscuits in. The salt shaker is "muzzled" by unscrewing the top, covering the holes with a wad cut from a bit of tent-cloth, and screwing it on again. Finally, mark each container so you will know it at a glance.

As "a workman is known by his tools," so a good hiker is known by his outfit. Have everything right, at least for your own comfort and satisfaction. And to top off with, get all the skill you can in handling a cooking fire. For suggestions, see the following chapters. Learn that a good cook is known by his fire, and like A. B. Frost's dog Carlo, you will be hard to beat.

Tents And Tent Making

From *The Boy Scout's Hike Book,* by Edward Cave, 1920

By no means do you need a conventional closed tent for camping out on hikes. If you camp in thick woods where fir trees are plenty, a simple tarpaulin of waterproofed sheeting or light sailcloth, 7 × 9 feet in dimensions, will serve as a waterproof roof, pitched as a lean-to, or as a wedge or A-tent, big enough for two or three Scouts. And if desired you can thatch the sides of your lean-to or the rear of your wedge tent with fir browse. With your choice of these two shelters your comfort is comparatively secure. You have but to use good judgment in pitching your camp—and sometimes a powerful mosquito and fly "dope." Your bed you will also make of browse.

But fir trees are far from abundant these days, more's the pity. And there are conditions and times—insect times, for example—when a closed tent is desirable even for an overnight camp. Hay or ferns are not good substitutes for fir browse unless dry, and they never are dry if cut the same day.

Scouting For Shelter.—First of all, you will of course take stock of the local conditions affecting your hiking. It may be, if you are not in the "fir tree belt," your patrol or troop can rig up a shanty or a cabin or get the use of an abandoned lumber camp (beware of vermin; use the stable or cook house in preference to the bunkhouse) or some isolated hay barn for sleeping in on overnight hikes. And you may be able to use an abundance of thoroughly "cured" hay for your beds. I've slept in a hay barn, shed or stack more than once in preference to making camp. But a point I must admit is, I have never struck a match in any such shelter; it would not be safe, and it would not be fair to the owner of the building and the hay. Camping without a camp-fire being almost as unsatisfactory as going "swimming" in a puddle, and there being so much satisfaction in having your shelter and your bed along with you, wherever you go, you will be almost certain to be interested in this chapter.

First of all, I want to urge you to be slow to adopt the tenting ideas of other campers. You can easily make a whole series of unfortunate mistakes, for the reason that so many campers get into the way of showing off by making fancied improvements. Tent making offers so much opportunity for "expressing" individual ideas that the beginner is easily bewildered by the confusion of tents. And in the end, if you go far enough along the trail, you will agree that there is only one way to do a thing right. Furthermore, you will have learned that a substitute, once you have it, is generally used. Let me give you an example:

The Substitute Tent.—Some years ago I was going to make a light 9 × 9 tent, and decided upon

Camping with a phillips combination tent-bed.

the pyramid or miner's type. The tent was wanted for making overnight canoe trips on the Hudson River, which near New York City is a much travelled highway. Our camps were made under the Palisades, on the New Jersey shore, on a narrow beach where no seclusion from other campers could be had, and a closed tent was required. It was also necessary to carry the tent pole, the Inter-State Park regulations forbidding cutting poles. I selected the pyramid form because it could be put up by one man in less than five minutes, with but four tent pegs and one jointed pole, and on account of its shape, which promised me indifference to wind and rain. A very good friend, the most practical sportsman, in many respects, I have ever known, told me how he had elaborated the miner's tent by adding an open doorway and an awning and using two jointed poles (*inside* the tent, not outside as in the trail tent used in the West) instead of one, to support it, and of course two poles for the awning. It was, in short, a combination of the Yalden octagonal canoe tent and the pyramid tent. And so, instead of a pyramid tent, with my wife's assistance I made a tent like this one "invented" by my friend.

Since the first time I set it up I have never liked the features of this tent—the Yalden door and awning—that do not belong to the original miner's pattern. I long ago discarded the awning poles and cut one of the two jointed tent poles down to serve as a single jointed pole, as in the usual miner's tent, thereby eliminating not only one pole, but part of another besides. The awning—it is a courtesy to call it such—if spread, pulls the tent out of shape (we were very fortunate in cutting and fitting and our tent when pitched was found to "set" equally as well as did that of my friend) and flaps and shakes in the wind in a very annoying fashion. I now almost invariably roll it up above the doorway, except if rain is expected, when I peg it down close to the ground, leaving just enough room to slip in and out of the tent under it.

I have been using this tent in this fashion for five years, and I dare say I shall continue to until I wear it out—unless some day I get desperate and cut the awning down and make a drop curtain of it. The point I want to make is the "fancy" tents are not apt to give satisfaction. You want simplicity, and have no more use for a complicated tent than for an "improved" axe.

Some Tent History.—Again, it is possible to be fooled by some fancied "new idea." A certain "new" tent made its appearance in the tent catalogues three or four years ago, and is listed in one of them as a recent invention. It is, however, nothing more than a copy of a tent Nessmuk, in his book "Woodcraft," published in 1888, tells of making, and of which he says, "It was a partial success," and furthermore, that it was made "on the same principle" as "the old Down East 'coal cabin,' which embodied the principle of the Indian camp." This supposedly modern tent, instead of being an improvement on the designs of ten and twenty years ago, you see is in reality one of the many *discarded* by the man who, "after more than fifty years devoted to woodcraft," gave the campers of America their first good manual—today a classic—in which he told them that for a summer camp for going light—he never went any other way—he had "finally come to prefer the simple lean-to or shed roof," which was "only a sheet of strong cotton cloth 9 × 7 feet," waterproofed with lime and alum.

Nessmuk told the campers no more about tents than what other skillful woodsmen knew as well as he did. The 7 × 9 tarpaulin was the best *roof* for a woodsman travelling as Nessmuk did. And it still is.

But the average camper is by no means a woodsman. Nor is the Boy Scout. The idea of sleeping out "in" a tent that is nothing but a roof pitched shed-roof fashion, is not attractive to many. They want to be housed in, and the mysteries of the night shut out. Candidly, I myself like to be well housed, under certain circumstances, such as when unavoidably camping where mosquitos or black flies are bad, or when the rain is coming down in sheets on the exposed knoll where I have camped to get away from them. If camping in the Southwest, in the country of the much touted but none the less to be avoided hydrophobia skunk and the sidewinder rattlesnake, I surely would shut myself in at night. There are many things to consider, in recommending a tent for use in all parts of the country, by all kinds of people.

Making a Choice.—Out of all the different designs of tents, so many of which are attractive to you, how are you to know which is best for you? Perhaps you have been trying to work it out with paper patterns, as suggested by Mr. H. J. Holden, is his article "Tent Making Made Easy," in your manual, supposing you are a member of the Boy Scouts of America. If so, I want to say first that it is an excellent plan, and secondly that in my judgment he obviously had in mind tents for general use, instead of exclusively for hiking. Lastly, the best all-around tent that can be made with a rectangle of cloth was left out entirely. Nevertheless, I am sure the article has been of much value to the Scouts, not so much for the detailed instructions given as for the suggestions conveyed, as to how a simple rectangle of sheeting can be made into a number of different tents.

The Best Hikers' Tents.—For my own use on hikes I have two different tents, both of which I made myself. Neither one is an original design of mine. I simply followed well-known tent-making principles and made them to suit myself. Both are, I think, especially well adapted for the use of Boy Scouts. One is a 7½ × 12 tarpaulin of No. 1 Egyptian sailcloth ("balloon silk," or "spinnaker duck," inexpensive and easily obtained), fitted with grommets for pitching in any of three or four different ways, and most often pitched in

what one of my Scouts called "pyramiddle" style, explaining that it was "like half a pyramid tent split in the middle." This is my "rain and mosquito" tent, and while primarily a one-man tent for use with a stretcher bed of generous proportions, it will comfortably accommodate two sleeping on ticks or browse. The proportions are different from any I have seen, and I think better. The other is a combination of stretcher-tick and tent, with a 7½ × 8½ roof, can be pitched in a number of different ways, and although different from any other tent is the result of evolution, not invention. As I am responsible for the features that distinguish it, I am glad to say there is nothing "fancy" about it. Neither of these tents is manufactured, so you will have to turn tent-maker to get one. But that should not bother a Scout. And in the end, there's a lot of satisfaction in having camping equipment you yourself have made.

The Tarpaulin Tent.—To make the 7½ × 12 tarpaulin tent, get either four yards of heavy unbleached cotton sheeting 90 inches wide, or 12 yards of 30-inch No. 1 Egyptian sailcloth ("balloon silk"). If the former, hem all around with a ¾-inch hem. If the latter, cut into three 12-foot pieces, sew these together with a *lap seam*, arid hem all around. Always hem on the same side. If you cannot operate a sewing-machine, you doubtless

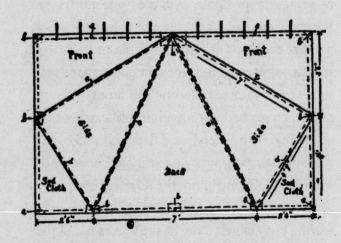

Fig. 1.   Plan of the tarpaulin tent.

will have a better tent than otherwise; for whoever does the work for you will sew a straighter seam than you could anyhow. It takes practice, and your tent is done before you can acquire skill. If, however, you are going to do the work yourself, sew your stretcher-tick (see sketches) first, for practice. Make it of 4 yards of yard-wide heavy unbleached sheeting.

To strengthen your tent and as a guarantee that it will set well and will not pull out of shape, you should now reinforce it by sewing ½-inch tape with a double row of stitching, along the four lines *c* Fig. 1, running from the point of the grommet hole which will be the peak, *a*, to those which will be the four corners of the tent when it is pitched as in Fig. 2. These with the outside hems—and the lap seams if made of balloon silk—will also give it strength to withstand pitching as a shed or as a wedge tent. To get them on properly, you will need to spread your tent on the floor, inside up, mark the lines off with a pencil, a chalk-line and a yard-stick before attempting to sew with the machine. Next, mark the places for the grommets, *a* and *b*, Fig. 1, and reinforce these on the inside with small squares of cotton, say 3 × 3 inches. That at *a* should be 4 × 6 inches. Be sure that *a* is placed on the proper edge so your outside lap seams will overlap downward from it, so they will shed rain.

The "Sickening Details."—Now get a dozen ½-inch galvanized grommet rings from some awning maker; or, if necessary, get a hardware dealer to procure some for you. Ordinary iron rings would rust and rot your tent. To sew these in, first cut a small cross in the hem of your tent where the pencil mark is, insert the ring between the goods, and bind with No. 25 linen thread waxed with a bit of shoe-maker's wax. Work it all around, buttonhole fashion, sewing with a double thread. Do not insert grommets at the places marked *d*, as that would result in a couple of holes which would spoil your tent-cloth for pitching in more than one way.

Instead, sew a 2-inch loop of double tape at these places. You will seldom use them. Sew grommets at the places marked *e*.

Get five yards of braided (not cable laid) window-sash cord, and cut off 7 pieces 10 inches long. Double each of these and tie with a single knot, forming a loop. Push these loops through the grommet rings marked *b*, from the inside; you will note the knot is too large to pull through the hole, and the stiffness of the cord keeps the loop open so there is no danger of it coming out of the hole unless purposely pulled out. You now have your peg-loops. To complete your tent, except water-proofing, take the rest of your sash-cord and make your tent-rope, as follows: Push one end of the cord through the grommet *a* from the outside and tie a bowline knot inside, having a 3-inch loop. Take a piece of tough-grained hardwood such as elm—I have used the remnants from making tool handles—and shape to ⅜ by ½ by 2-inch dimensions, and in it on the ½-inch side bore two ⅛-inch holes, each ⅜ inch from an end of the wood, making them 1 inch apart. This is your tent-rope slide.

The "Tarp" Tent in Use.—Now, except for water-proofing, and possibly dyeing, the former of which I shall discuss at the end of this chapter, your tent is ready to set up. I have shown in Fig. 2 how to pitch it in the semi-pyramid form, which provides a tent which may be closed to keep out rain or insects, or opened to receive the heat of the camp-fire. This latter feature is very desirable, not only to secure comfort on cold nights, but as a means to drying out in wet weather. The broad, sloping back wall of the tent reflects the heat of the fire upon you and your bed; not so well as does the roof of the lean-to, but quite satisfactorily. When closed up, the tent is very snug, and because of its steep tapering sides it behaves well in a hard blow and sheds rain easily. When set up, the two triangles marked "sod cloth" in Fig. 1 are turned in. It is not necessary to use a pole if a tree is convenient; simply throw the tent-rope

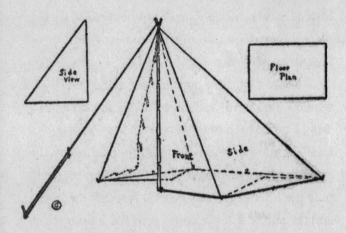

Fig. 2.   Plan of tarpaulin tent erected.

over a limb and make fast. If a tree cannot be used and it is desired to have the camp-fire close in front, to get the full benefit of the heat, use two tent-ropes, carrying each to one side of the fire. No guy ropes are used, it is only necessary to drive six tent-pegs, and if you have your pole and your pegs the tent can be put up in two minutes—if the ground isn't too rocky. The floor length of 7 feet is necessary, because of the pitch of the roof, to accommodate a stretcher of proper proportions.

To Keep out Mosquitoes.—My tent is made of balloon silk, so called, cost $2.65 (for the goods), and weighs 3¼ pounds. It is made positively mosquito and gnat proof only by stretching inside it a smaller tent of cheesecloth, suspended from the same point and tied down all around with tapes to my stretcher. This inner cheesecloth tent is troublesome to make, but it is worth a dozen times the bother. It is a replica of the tent itself, except for being a foot narrower and having a foot more height. It is sewed shut in front and must be entered at the bottom. You have to get inside it before making it fast anywhere. It works well with a stretcher, but easiest without, when you can weight it with four poles, taken inside it with you. Hem the bottom with cotton, and reinforce it with tape on the lines of draft.

As for camping in a place that might produce such sanguinary visitors as hydrophobia skunks,

etc., I would recommend a sure-enough *closed* tent, of any good type, having a ground cloth sewed in and a pucker-string door and a good, tall doorsill. Such a tent would require a couple of windows, well up in the peak and screened with strong close-woven netting.

Other Shelters with the "Tarp."—This tent-cloth, being a simple flat sheet, can of course be pitched in a number of different ways, forming an open camp. The best of these is shown on the right in Fig. 3. This is a shed tent large enough for two, providing 5 × 7 floor space, the roof being 7 × 7½ and the front 5½ feet high. The side walls are complete except for a 1½-foot triangle. Note that a 2½-foot triangle is turned under at each bade corner. Weight these with a pole and they need not be pegged. A corresponding triangle of unused cloth at the front is shown folded around the supporting pole. It should be rolled around the pole. Tie a bit of cord through the grommet *b* (see Fig. 1) and around the pole, then roll until the grommet *e* is reached. Tie sash-cord through the three grommets *e* and *a* and around the ridge pole.

The sketch in the center shows a simple wedge tent with open ends, floor 6 × 7½; height at peak 5½ feet. That on the left shows how to utilize part of the tent-cloth as a poncho for the bed, to keep down the ground dampness, and the balance for a lean-to roof. Poncho 4½ × 7½; roof 7½ × 7½; height 4 feet. The wedge is a good rainy-day shelter for several Scouts. If the rain drives in at one end, hang a poncho there. The sheds are best for cool weather. Build your fire about six feet from the front, and have a good reflector for it. More about this in other chapters.

Fig. 3.   Other ways to pitch the "tarp".

The Phillips

Tent.—My other hiking tent is ordinary and old-fashioned enough, the tent part of it being like Nessmuk's favorite, "only a sheet of strong cotton cloth," of nearly the same proportions, being 7½ × 8½ instead of "9 × 7 feet." But attached to it, in fact an integral part of it, is an 18-inch wall with a clothes pocket

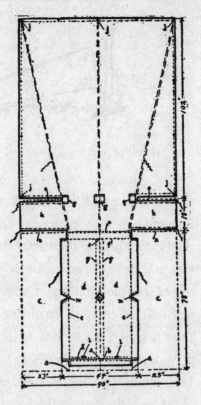

Fig. 4.   Plan of the phillips combination tent-bed.

Two views of phillips tent pitched with tick and ridge-pole. In *a* the flaps are up, swing. How they may be turned back; *b* shows them pegged down for the night.

and a stretcher-tick. It is therefore tent, wardrobe, and bed all in one; complicated yet simple. It can be pitched in a half dozen different ways on the ground and the bed made either a stretcher or a tick filled with dry leaves, dry grass or ferns or browse. And it can be slung between a couple of trees and the bed used as a hammock. The several sketches show how it works, and the diagram, Fig. 4, gives the dimensions. With this and the instructions for making the other tent before you, a few particulars should be all you will require in addition.

Get 5½ yards of the heaviest unbleached cotton sheeting, 90 inches wide. Spread on the floor and make a 6-inch cut at *a, a,* (*for a double bed*), a 26-inch cut at *n, n,* and a 23-inch cut at *0, 0.* Fold the flaps *c, c* over on *d, d,* and sew together, *but not to d, d.* Sew through both thicknesses along the lines *e, e, q, q,* and *f,* making the *e, e* seams 3 inches from the edge of the doubled goods, seams *q, q* 3 inches apart, and the *f* seam same distance from the end. Sew both

thicknesses together along the line *p,* and hem at same time. Now fold up the four thicknesses at the bottom and sew at *b,* making a hem at the same time. Cut the four corners as shown in diagram, cut out notches *m, m* and the square hole *r,* and hem and bind these seven places, using tape where necessary. To bind the notched corners, cut a strong piece of chalk-line cord and bind it in the corner under the goods, using waxed linen thread to bind with, as in binding grommets. Before turning the goods over so the seam in the center of the stretcher is underneath, cut the *bottom* sheet along the line *k,* including *s,* and as close as possible to the seam *b.* Hem this, bind the corners, cut and work buttonholes at *l, l,* sew buttons on the top section to button in these. Cut the bottom sheet at *s.* at the head of stretcher, hem and bind corners.

Now your stretcher-tick is finished—for two. For a single occupant, make the stretcher 30 inches wide, and of course with no "pole hole" in the center. Now turn the goods over.

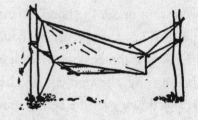

Phillips combination tent-bed slung as a covered hammock; the bed is a stretcher, made by lashing the poles.

To complete the tent, hem the wardrobe flaps *h, h,* bind corners, attach tapes at ends, sew ½-inch tape along

Phillip tent pitched as a lean-to, with stretcher for single occupant.

the lines *i, i,* and down the center, attach the pole loops *g, g, g,* hem outside of roof of tent, and bind in the grommets. Those marked *j* are necessary; the others will enable you to peg down snugly against wind and rain.

Tarp Tent a Raincoat.—So your tent making is done! In mentioning these tents in other chapters, the first is referred to as the "tarpaulin" tent, because when taken down it becomes a simple flat "tarp," folding more compactly than any "made up" tent and useful in many ways. Waterproof it with turpentine and paraffin, following the instructions I give you, and as a tent it will never leak (unless torn or burned by sparks), and I will tell you how to make an excellent raincoat of it also—better than you will believe. For a big long raincoat (too big for any but a big boy) fold your tarpaulin tent once, making a doubled sheet, 6 × 7½. Hold it by the doubled 6-foot side, put it on in the same manner as instructed to put on a blanket, using the tent-rope to girt it about your waist. If you want to carry a pack, let the hood drop around your hips, shoulder your pack, and then pull the hood up over the pack and shoulders. If you have not left the "skirt" too long there will be all the room you want under the hood, no matter how big your pack is. For average use, it should be folded twice, to 3¾ × 6 dimensions. Hold it long way vertical, belt it snugly around you and have it so the hood hangs down over the belt all around, and it will not "soak through" at the waist. Pull the collar up around your head, tie a piece of rope around your neck, fold the collar down, and the hood or cape will "stay put" without holding. The cape will fall to your waist in front, giving you plenty of arm room if you want to work. To keep the arms dry, fold them under the cape.

Phillips tent as a lean-to with double stretcher.

Phillips tent guyed to a tree, with tick for two.

The second tent also is adaptable for use as a raincoat, when waterproofed. Run a cord through the bottom hem of the stretcher, fold over on the tent and tie to the grommets at the other end, or top of tent roof; fold again, to 4¼ × 7½ dimensions and four thicknesses. To distinguish this tent, I have named it the Phillips tent, after W. S. Phillips, a Western sportsman and one time prospector, from whom I got the idea of using a single length of 90-inch sheeting for both tent and ground cloth. Making a stretcher by folding over the two outside thirds of the ground cloth (making a 30-inch stretcher), and sewing it as I have described, and making a wardrobe pocket to put my clothes in at night where they would be dry occurred to me as a logical thing to do, and turned out to be very satisfactory, to me at least. The tent can be used for one, two (with the 44-inch stretcher), or even three, but in the latter event, the bed must serve as a tick. The stretcher when made for one is so wide there is never any difficulty about the blanket sliding off at night, no matter how you use it; although if you know how to "roll" in a blanket you will never have this to bother you, no matter how narrow your cot. To fill the ticks of the stretcher if made for two, use a stick to push the "stuffing" in. I think you will generally prefer to use the stretchers.

Waterproofing.—To waterproof your tent-cloth and stretcher, and do a good job of it, I advise the turpentine and paraffin formula, as given in the "Official Handbook of the Boy Scouts of America," and which is a reprint of an article I wrote for *Recreation.* Take a cake of paraffin (weight, 1 lb., price 10 cents), shave fine and put in a gallon of turpentine, which you should have in a metal pail. Place the pail in a larger pail or a boiler or tub of *scalding* water. Do not take the turpentine near fire, as it is inflammable. The hot water will heat the turpentine, and the hot turpentine will dissolve the paraffin. This is not advised by Kephart or Breck, but is the best way. Stir thoroughly, and renew your supply of hot water if necessary. When paraffin is all dissolved, pile your tent into a tub and pour the waterproofing solution over it. Work the tent all over carefully with your hands, so that every fiber gets well saturated. You must be quick, for the paraffin begins to thicken as it cools, there being more of it than the turpentine will "take up." And work out of doors, in a breeze if you possibly can, as the fumes of the turpentine will almost surely make you sick if you try it in a room. When you have the tent thoroughly saturated, hang it up to drip and dry, but do not wring. It will take it a day, maybe more than a day. Meantime, waterproof your stretcher, *but not your provision bags*, with the left-over turpentine and paraffin mixture.

The tent will look rather dirty after it dries, if you have used enough paraffin, but it will be all right except for the odor, after it has been out in the sun for a day. The turpentine odor will be rather offensive at first, but you will not mind it after a few days.

Some use gasoline instead of turpentine, but this is dangerous. Better pay the extra cost of the turpentine and not run the risk of a bad accident. Furthermore, if you use gasoline you have nothing but paraffin to *waterproof* your tent; the gasoline all evaporates and only the paraffin remains. Turpentine, on the other hand, considerably assists in rendering the cloth waterproof, and it stays with it indefinitely. A tent "paraffined" in this way is never stiff and greasy, like the ordinary "balloon silk" tents made by the tent makers. And it turns the water just as well; better in the long run, because it does not crack, as they do.

. Now that you have been to so much trouble to get a tent that is *right*—which no "dog" tent or other ready-made arrangement is—take care of it as zealously as you guard your axe. When you build your camp-fire, remember that "what goes up has got to come down" applies to sparks. Don't let some chump pile a lot of dead brush on the fire and send a shower of sparks aloft to come down on your tent and bum holes in it.

Have a Good Bed.—To conclude, I want to tell you that among hunters the raw tenderfoot who gives no promise of ever graduating from his class is known by his willingness to sleep on the ground. My favorite camp bed is the best that money will buy, a pneumatic mattress and a pneumatic pillow, both of which I inflate by "lung power." And I am not ashamed of it, and have plenty of good company. The man who sneers at such a bed invariably has never slept on one. We do not go to the woods to rough it, but as Nessmuk said, to smooth it: "We get it rough enough at home; in towns and cities, in shops and offices, stores, banks—anywhere that we may be placed—with the necessity always present of being on time and up to our work; of providing for dependent ones; of keeping up, catching up, or getting left." But, alas! My pet bed weighs too much to go on hiking trips. And so I tote a stretcher-tick. But, take my word for it, I make it comfortable before I turn in. This generally means that it is rigged as a cot, with good strong stakes to support it mid-ships, and these guyed out so I may "flounce" about to the full extent of a real flapjack nightmare without danger of coming down. Have a good bed! Someday you'll agree with me that it is half of camping.

Making Camp

From *The Boy Scout's Hike Book,* by Edward Cave, 1920

Now that I have helped you pick out your outfit, suppose we take a little overnight hike. Say we leave home on a Friday evening, after school, rather early in the month of March. Starting the season in typical boy fashion by being a little previous, you may think, until I tell you where we are. This is the only hike I can make with you. The next one, in the next chapter, you will have to make alone. After that will come a patrol hike, and last a troop hike. You will notice I am devoting a chapter to each season of the year, and each hike is made in a different part of the country. This is in order that I may get close to *your* hiking in at least one chapter. We live in such a big country that camping conditions vary greatly. So to start off with, thus early in the season, I am going to take if for granted that you live in Florida.

A short trip as a starter, say not more than three miles. And at that we have stopped a couple of times for a short rest. Now, it a few minutes after five o'clock, we are come to our camp-ground, a bit

warm, apprehensive of mosquitoes, and in a hurry to get camp made before dark. It is a flat country, is Florida, taken by the large. And we are on the flat East coast, in the prairie country of the upper Indian River. But what a place to see and hear the wildfowl! Too bad, indeed, that we did not come earlier in the year, before they started northward.

Choosing a Camp-Site.—For our camp-site we have chosen a knoll of "hummock" land that strives bravely to be a promontory in a country of no promontories by shouldering close to a little fresh-water lake, of which there are thousands on these prairies. On our knoll there is a scattering growth of pine and live oak trees, and surrounding it on all except the lake side, a fringe of palmettoes. The coarse prairie grass and the scrub palmettoes grow waist high. We might almost as well have left the tent at home, for it is no trick at all to thatch a lean-to with the broad palmetto fans. But—the mosquitoes!

These countless shallow lakes and ponds of the prairies, so attractive to the wildfowl and so pleasant to be about in late fall and winter, in this semi-tropical climate, are bound to breed mosquitoes *all the year round*. And by the middle of March they begin to get pestiferous. We've got to keep them out, or we'll not get much sleep. We have wisely selected our camping ground on this knoll, where we are sure of dry ground and a breeze. The latter, of course, will perhaps keep the mosquitoes away; but we are to have a good time, and not taking any chances. Now to make camp.

A good camp-site. Two lean-to tents and a fly between them, making an ideal fair-weather camp.

Dividing Camp Duties.—First we will rustle some firewood and a couple of forked poles for the tent. Dead pine limbs furnish all we want of the former, but we have to hunt industriously for our crotched tent poles. What are you staring about? *Two* poles? Why, yes—for our wedge tent. I'm not letting you start out with a real hiking tent. I brought a "made up" tent, such as you might buy, to give you a chance to try it before deciding you want to go to the trouble of making a tarpaulin or a Phillips tent. As I was saying, poles are scarce; there's no underbrush and mighty few saplings out here on this knoll. Burned off by a grass fire? No, it's prairie country, that's all; trees don't grow profusely on this kind of soil; too much sea sand in it. You rustle some firewood and I'll get the poles. Select dead limbs that are not lying on the ground, if you find plenty.

Here we are! A couple of live oak saplings, trimmed long, the branches above the fork of each will make tent-pegs and the like. When you have to lug wood, bring the tree with you. Now, while I am cutting these and working up your firewood, take the tent and go and collect a big bundle of that moss (long moss) hanging from the live oaks; don't be afraid of getting too much. We want it for our bed. Eke it out with pine straw if you find it slow work getting it.

How to Make a Fire.—Everything ready? Now to make camp. First we'll light our fire, and while it is burning down to coals we will pitch the tent, make our bed, and prepare our grub for cooking. Right here in this little clear patch of sand is the place for it. First we select three small sticks cut from a dead branch that has not lain on the ground, and whittle them in the form of "rosettes," as in *a*, Fig. 1, leaving the shavings attached. These we stick in the ground as shown at *b*, making a sort of tripod, with the shavings sloping downward. Now a few dry splinters made by splitting up a couple of dry sticks the size of your thumb are stacked around the tripod, as at *c*. On one side I have a bunch of

dry twigs of lead-pencil size, and on the other some larger split wood. Split wood burns better than round. To strike my match, I squat *facing*

Fig. 1.   How to build a fire.

the wind, strike the match and hold in my cupped hands with the stem up and the head down and pointed into the hollow of my hands, toward the wind. Fire goes up, so a match when struck should be held vertical, *if there is no wind*. As there is a breeze, the match is held with the head pointed toward it when it is struck; in this way whatever breeze strikes it before I can get my hands cupped around it will blow the blaze up the stem, not away from it. When my match is blazing nicely I hold it down, still guarding it carefully, and quickly touch it to the shavings of the tripod of rosettes. As they also are slanting upward, and not smothered with too much other wood, I have a blaze in a jiffy.

One at a time I add the twigs, building the fire up gradually and standing every stick on end, leaning on the burning cone. The big sticks come last, added from time to time so not to smother the blaze; and finally they all are blazing merrily. And you have seen the regular woods-man's way of lighting a fire.

But what a small fire, you say?

Plenty big enough. For a cooking fire for one or two you should not stack up more wood than you could shelter with your hat if you were to pile it up and put the hat on the point of the cone. You don't need a big fire, and besides, it would be so hot you could not get near it.

Cutting Tent-Pegs—With the fire started, we will pitch the tent and make our bed. A few clips with the belt axe and the nine pegs are ready. Notice how long they are; two of them are in reality stakes a foot and a half long, and the rest are a foot long at least. Always cut your tent-pegs long and they never will be too short. In this sandy soil eighteen inches is not too long for the guy stakes and corner pegs. And always chop a stick on an angle of about 45 degrees, never across the grain at a right angle.

Now for a look at the ground; we want a smooth level spot free from long grass, and we must clean it up, pound down the lumps and fill the hollows before the tent goes up. If we were to make our bed on the long grass, hoping to derive some advantage from it, the hummocks of grass roots would before morning worry us as much as so many stones, and the grass would be damp. Four poles laid to make a rectangle 4 × 7 feet, and staked on the outside so they will stay put, give us the frame for our bed. This must be staked out before the tent goes up, as driving the stakes afterward is not feasible—unless it is raining, when "you drive them when it clears." For the same reason a stretcher bed must be made before the tent is pitched over it, unless using a big tent.

Pitching a Wedge Tent.—The two crotched poles are already cut the proper length, because I know it is just 5 feet 3 inches from the tips of the fingers of one of my hands to the heel of the other hand when I spread my arms out at full reach. And the height of our tent is 5 feet. So up goes the tent. And while we are about it, just notice how much work there is to it. It keeps two fellows busy to put a wedge or A-tent up properly in five minutes, and it is an awkward job at that. First we drive the guy stakes, placing them well out fore and aft, say so they will be ten or twelve feet from the tent. Next we make the tent rope fast to the rear stake, run it through the large grommet at the aft of the tent ridge, and through a similar grommet in the cheesecloth tent inside, knot it, carry it forward, measure, knot, pass through the fore grommets and carry it out to the stake in front. Then we lay the tent over on one side of our bed and peg out that side, so arranging the peg loops on the pegs that they will be in proper position when the tent is erected. The crotched poles are now laid in position engaging the

tent rope at front and back of the tent, and the tent rope tightened to what is thought suitable tension to hold the tent erect. Now if you were alone you would stand at the center of the bottom of your tent, grasp it at the ridge with both hands, and haul it up "on its feet." There being two of us, each will take hold of a pole, and, having raised the tent will peg his corner down. Lastly, the tent rope must be tightened, adjustments made and the remaining three pegs driven. And our tent is up—less a small matter of driving ten more pegs, seven of which we will not bother with, one at each corner, one in the middle of each side, and one at the back being enough to hold.

No time to admire our camp now. While you lay some palmetto fans on the floor, distribute the moss, spread our ponchos and lay out the blankets, I will be getting supper started.

You want to watch, you say?

All right. Let me have your cooking pot; I'm going down to the lake for water. I'll help you spread the blankets when I come back.

The Odor of Fried Bacon.—Bed made, now we're ready to put the finishing touch to the camp. All it needs is the odor of—what? Why *bacon*, of course, fried sure as you live—and it will be welcome *where* you live, too, or I miss my guess. When Kipling wrote "Who hath smelt wood smoke at twilight," he hadn't been carrying a pack. The wood smoke smell is all right, but the bacon smell makes *my* mouth water.

Lake water all right for coffee? Sure. If you want a drink of water there's some in my canteen.

Now you see I didn't build any rack over my fire, to be burned down, perhaps, before I was ready to use it. Not much fire there? More than you think. I put some split sticks of green oak on it when you weren't looking. I have a couple of the full-round ones here, two feet long, hewed flat on one side, to serve as bed-sticks to set my pots and pans on. I'd rather use stones, as the wood will smoke a little, but

I haven't seen any stones big enough or of the right shape. See, I put them so they are about six inches apart *on top* at one end and two at the other. I had to trim them a little on the inside so they would not crowd the coals too much. Notice I throw out the butt-ends of firewood that have not burned; they are in the way, and they smoke. Now I have a long "forest range," with the wide end pouted toward the breeze. This will serve our purposes tonight, and in the morning we will make another. The reason for having the "trench" face the breeze is that otherwise the bed-sticks would serve as a wind-shield, whereas now they give the fire a draught. See the coals brighten up? On goes the second cooking pot, with water for the potatoes.

I brought the supper grub, you that for breakfast. This simplifies cooking and does not disturb your pack tonight. Coffee water's beginning to steam already. I brought a couple of things in the concentrated line, to introduce you to it. If you stay a camper, and I know you will, you'll "wear out" a lot of this sort of grub, as a guide of mine once said. Here in this little friction-top can which I could put in the pocket of my coat I have our potatoes. They're evaporated, and equal to about six times their weight of the fresh article. I'm a potato "fiend," and this evaporating business makes me happy. I've 12½ cents worth of potatoes, or 8 ounces, enough for a meal for both of us. They look like Saratoga chips, don't they? Into the pot they go. I let them simmer awhile till they swell up, then strain off some of the water and stew them. Wait till you try them.

Coffee water's boiling? Well, take the pothook there and set it back where it will keep hot. We are going to have concentrated coffee, too.

A Difference in Soups.—Here goes for soup; no, not the evaporated kind, but that which comes in the plebeian tin can. I'm not ashamed to say I've a small

Hiker's pot-hook.

can of ox-tail for each of us. We might get along with a couple of "beef cubes," each weighing about a quarter of an ounce, and coating 3 cents and good for a cup of beef tea, but I prefer to *eat* something. There's no sense in going light to the extent of taking concentrated nourishment in place of a square meal on a little two-meal hike like this. That bread-pan up at the narrow end of the range has some water in it that must be about hot enough by this time. Watch me juggle it with my detachable bail. See the three holes in it under the rim, two on one side and one on the other? I just hook this jointed bail in them, so, and I've got the pan. It won't tip, either, because of the three points of suspension; ordinarily a shallow pan is very tippy when carried by the rim. You can rig your bread-pan the same way. I'll just add a little of the water for the coffee, and pour in the soup. No, don't use a knife to open a can; use your axe. Cut a cross in the top and pry up the jagged corners.

Cold Grub from Home.—Now we'll be getting out the cold victuals: cream cheese and lettuce sandwiches, wrapped in damp cheesecloth and done up in paper. (I brought them in the cooking pot, in my pack-sack.) Also, four good juicy jam sandwiches, wrapped in oiled paper. That is the package I put in *your* cooking pot when you said there was nothing in it but your cup.

Here is my concentrated coffee. I carry enough for six cups in this tiny friction-top can. I just put a teaspoonful in each of our cups and fill with hot water. It dissolves almost immediately, and all we have to do is add sugar and cream. It is excellent coffee, too.

For sugar I always use the real thing. The substitutes, saccharine and crystalose, are mere sweeteners, having no food value. Sugar is good for you. Milk I carry in a small screw-top glass, the glass generally in a tin-and-cardboard mailing case. I do not use ordinary condensed milk, but the evaporated kind. My bottle holding 4 fluid ounces contains plenty for both of us for two meals.

While I've been talking away, I've had the bacon frying. I haven't said anything because it has been so much fun to see you wiggling your nose like a rabbit just at the good promising aroma of it. Now I'll build up the fire a bit, as I shall put the dishwater on as soon as the coffee-water pail is empty. What do you think of a bed of live oak coals as a cooking fire?

Well—we're ready! "Go to it," as they say in the bush.

The Hiker's Appetite.—Those stars indicate the passing of time with nothing said. That is the way we eat on the trail. Meal-time is eating time; if a fellow wants to talk, he can do that afterward. "Everybody's chewing it," and any interruption results in a growl. If you ever eat in a lumber camp with the crew, you will see man eat his level best, if not his prettiest. Hard work in the outdoors develops that kind of appetite. And as I have remarked before in this book, hiking with a pack is hard work.

Dusk has come and we have not noticed it, the fire, having been built up, furnishing our light. I'll get out my folding candle-lantern.

Funny there aren't any mosquitoes, you say?

Well, yes, although to tell the truth there is a surprising absence of the pests in Florida, everything considered. Northern folk who know what the topography of the state is, cannot understand that it is not "eaten up" by mosquitoes. Not being interested in mosquitoes, I have not inquired into the reasons why their status here is not better. It is good enough for me, as the cheesecloth tent inside the other one doubtless suggested to you. They drive me wild. And I detest smearing myself up with dope, while I've never yet seen the smudge that did much good.

Around the Camp-Fire.—With the dishes washed and put away, and our beds made up, we can lounge awhile. If we only had a tarpaulin tent we could open it up in front and enjoy the camp-fire, for there is a suggestion of dampness in the air. Just think of having pine knots to burn and no shed tent to sit under! Yes, and that reminds me to tell you that although this beautiful wedge tent we have provides floor space of only $4\frac{1}{3} \times 7\frac{1}{3}$, and is only 5 feet high, giving it the same "accommodations," practically, as my "tarp" tent, it weighs exactly twice as much, in balloon silk and costs $9.85!

Notice how still it is? A little earlier in the year we would hear all kinds of wild-fowl trading back and forth; for this is a great winter resort for them. And they are all night-owls. Now if we could be out on the marsh we might encounter around the ponds or lakes such other night prowlers as the otter, the wildcat, the raccoon, the alligator, the mink, and of course the possum and the rabbit. They are all about here, plenty of them; for this is real wilderness. But they keep discreetly hidden one and all, in the tall marsh grass and the water, and one needs rubber boots and day-light to even find their tracks. We would be lucky to see a couple of the few half-wild cattle that are the only "civilized" tenants of the prairies.

Hiking Alone

From *The Boy Scout's Hike Book,* by Edward Cave, 1920

It is a good thing for anyone to be entirely alone in the outdoors once in a while, and take stock of philosophy and other character resources. In fact, the stock may be found so low it would be embarrassing to be otherwise than alone. And under any circumstances the experience is refreshing, to say the least. Whether or not one gathers new reserve of confidence and energy, as one is pretty apt to, there is an overpowering feeling of getting well *rinsed*.

Now I suspect you are thinking of the long "lone" trips Daniel Boone made, and wondering how he survived feeling entirely washed away! The best thing for *you* is to try it on yourself. I mean for you to make a hike "by your lonesome."

And that immediately is a horse of another color. Hadn't thought of doing a thing like that, had you? Don't exactly like the idea, do you? Afraid?

A Woodcraft Camp.—You were tempted to bring no tent-cloth, knowing you would find abundant white spruce saplings with which you could make a lean-to. Finally you compromised and brought a poncho. And now you set to work to make a lean-to with it. Instead of building a frame in the usual way or stretching the poncho by means of a series of short guy ropes tied to a supporting rope between two trees—a good stunt, by the way—you select a couple of small spruces that stand out by themselves on the edge of the open knoll where you have stopped, and are the right distance apart. You lop off the branches on the side of each that faces the other and stretch your shelter between them, in the form of a shed roof, pegged to the ground at the back. This not only furnishes you tent poles already placed, but the ends of your tent are already thatched and you have sufficient browse for your bed without going a step for it. A neat trick, you think, but there is a neater one still, which you will learn in due time if you follow woods ways.

It doesn't take long to make such a camp. Picking the browse—it should be done by hand, as there is a tendency to lop off *branches* instead of browse if you use a sheath knife or a belt axe—and shingling the bed constitute the larger part of it. You lay four poles on the ground, forming the boundaries of your bed, and wherever necessary stake them against rolling outward. Then, starting at the head of the prospective bed, you lay a row of the spruce fans, butts down, concave bend of stem up, tips overlapping the head pole. Row after row is added in the same orderly manner until you reach the foot. Then you start at the top and shingle another layer. A poncho spread on top would save your blankets

Going it alone.

How to browse a bed.

somewhat, and keep down dampness, but why quibble, with bough beds so scarce these days!

Camp Chores.—There is a spring you know about that needs digging out, and you think you will trench the lean-to. So you get out your "digger." And between this work and scouting for likely bass coves, making a forest range and working up firewood, noon comes before you realize it.

Lonely? No, not yet. Been too busy—and happy.

After dinner you get out your tackle and rig up, and for a half hour practice casting for accuracy, using a tournament weight instead of a lure. It is well to get your hand in, for you will be at a disadvantage in fishing from the shore—but, hold on! Why fish from the shore, even if there isn't a boat on the lake? You were going to wade, of course, but that amounts to almost the same thing. Now, a raft——

Building a Raft.—Where is the Scout who does not know enough about pioneering to build a raft? A raft is in order, and what with cutting the necessary poles, and lashing them with wild-grapevines, fishing time will come and you will not get your swim. No matter, you'll get it first thing in the morning. Willow is selected because of its buoyancy and there being a good thicket of the sand-bar variety close to camp. It is nearly valueless and you feel no qualms about cutting it. Luckily you find a couple of 5-inch trees which give you four good 6-foot logs. Dry wood would have been better. With some smaller poles lashed across them, and a couple of pieces of board picked up on the lake shore nailed (with old nails found in the boards) on top to furnish a smooth footing for bare feet, you have a good raft. But how it sinks when you get aboard! Not very buoyant after all. Logs are too small. But it will serve. And with your rod taken down and slung over your shoulder with a cord, you push out, using your pole in a manner that, to see you, would make an Illinois River duck hunter's "pusher" fall overboard, but getting there just the same. And you

anchor successfully, sixty or seventy feet out from a likely cove, by pushing the pole down between the logs of your raft and ramming it into the mud. Now for action!

"Whizz!" goes the reel, and your lure, a salt pork imitation of a minnow, on a Seward "weedless" hook with a spinner on the shank and a weight on the trailer, plops into a little bay at the edge of the wild rice and rushes.

The Gamest Fish That Swims.—"Splash! Slam!" Gee! Something doing in a hurry. Got one right off the bat. You struck the hook home with a strong twitch of the rod the instant you felt he had the lure, for he would detect the hook in short order and eject it. Up out of the water he goes, in a desperate attempt to throw the hook out. "Splash!" Letting a bass swim away with the bait and turn it around in his mouth and swallow it may be all right for the fisherman who baits with live minnows. But your way demands a fight from the first tug. You grind away on the multiplier, and don't let Mr. Bass get any slack line, not even when he jumps. Once again be jumps and shakes his head. He's a small-mouth for sure. Now you can see him in the water, darting from side to side, fighting his little best. How green he looks. And how you have to watch out now to prevent him from making you feel green, by darting under the raft. Let him get one hitch around that anchor pole, and—good night!

But that must not happen with the very first fish on a new rod. Gently but firmly you wear him down, then you slip the net into the water behind him, let him drop back into it, and with a lift he is yours. Yes, he's a small-mouth, "inch for inch and pound for pound the gamest fish that swims."

Mercifully—and prudently—you dispatch him while still holding him in the net, with the hook in his mouth. Keeping fish alive on a stringer is, next to taking more than can be used, the worst fool thing an angler can do; yet thousands persist in it and call it "keeping them." Who wants to eat fish, flesh or fowl that *died*, as such fish do die, slowly and painfully. A rap on the head with the axe handle does it. Then he is strung on a cord and slipped into the water, to trail from the raft. He weighs but little over a pound, but he pulled like a two-pounder. Another like him, and you'll have to quit, as you must not take more than you can eat for supper. You soon get him.

Time to Eat Again.—For your supper fire you have cut and split an armful from a white ash windfall. It is dry, hard, and will burn down to good lasting coals. Burn just about as well if it were green. Chops and splits easily, yet you're glad you have a new straight 20-inch handle in your Scout axe. You sure can *chop* with it. But wait till you get a new head, a good one, of the proper wedge shape.

Your dinner was in reality a cold lunch, with only coffee to appease a rather strong desire for something hot. Now to eat!

Supper

Barley soup

Broiled small-mouth black bass

Macaroni and cheese

Baked potatoes

Raspberries and cream

Fresh bread and butter

Tea

That is the prospect. And a long evening to prepare and eat it. Broiling is simple enough. You brought a wire broiler along for the purpose, and you know enough to grease the broiler so it won't stick to the fish, which of course you split in halves, removing the spine. The berries are to be had for the picking, big, luscious red fellows such as Michigan's sandy

A camper's crane, or dingle-stick.

soil produces, all you want of them right in camp. You figured on them too, and instead of any kind of dessert brought extra supplies of sugar and evaporated cream.

The macaroni and cheese is the only problem. But first you put the potatoes to baking, in the hot ashes—not embers—at one end of the fire. You have both your pot and your bread-pan on the fire, the former at the wide end hanging low from a dingle-stick, or camper's crane, and the latter sitting on the bed-sticks. When the former comes to a boil, you put in a teaspoonful of salt, and get out your little bag of macaroni. You have about a quarter of a pint, broken into short pieces. Nothing to do but dump it in the water and let it boil for about thirty minutes, so far as you can remember. "Well, here goes," you say aloud, and that is one more worry disposed of.

Dressing Fish.—Then you go get your fish, which you left at the raft. To dress them—what on earth makes you think that you can eat both of them?—you straddle a log, and commence by scaling the largest one. You hold him by the head, tail toward you, and with your fish knife scrape toward you; around the fins and gills you scrape at right angles, using the point of the knife. Both sides scraped, you sever head, belly fins and side fins with three deft cuts, and when the head is removed the entrails come with it. You next cut out the vent, flop your fish, and cut deep down on each side his dorsal, and yank that out too. No need to do it, as you'd get the fin when you split him; but it's force of habit. Now you wash him, scrape off the slime that remains, wipe him dry with your "fish towel," split him in halves and remove his spine, and he is ready.

And he's enough, being larger than the first one caught.

A wind-break is desirable sometimes, especially for baking.

Horse Packing

From *Camp and Trail* by Steward Edward White, 1907

You will find the Mexican or cowboy saddle the only really handy riding saddle. I am fully aware of the merits of the McClellan and army saddles, but they lack what seems to me one absolute essential, and that is the pommel or horn. By wrapping your rope about the latter you can lead reluctant horses, pull firewood to camp, extract bogged animals, and rope shy stock. Without it you are practically helpless in such circumstances. The only advantage claimed for the army saddle is its lightness. The difference in weight between it and the cowboy saddle need not be so marked as is ordinarily the case. A stock saddle, used daily in roping heavy cows, weighs quite properly from thirty-five to fifty pounds. The same saddle, of lighter leather throughout, made by a conscientious man, need weigh but twenty-five or thirty, and will still be strong and durable enough for all ordinary use. My own weighs but twenty-five pounds, and has seen some very hard service.

Sawbuck saddle.

Riding saddle.

Stirrups

The stirrup leathers are best double, and should be laced, never buckled. In fact the logic of a wilderness saddle should be that it can be mended in any part with thongs. The stirrups themselves should have light hood tapaderos, or coverings. They will help in tearing through brush, will protect your toes, and will keep your feet dry in case of rain. I prefer the round rather than the square skirts.

Cinches

In a cow country you will hear many and heated discussions over the relative merits of the single broad cinch crossing rather far back; and the double cinches, one just behind the shoulder and the other on the curve of the belly. The double cinch is universally used by Wyoming and Arizona cowmen; and the "center fire" by Californians and Mexicans—and both with equally heated partisanship. Certainly as it would be difficult to say which are the better horsemen, so it would be unwise to attempt here a dogmatic settlement of the controversy.

How to Attach the Cinch

For ordinary mountain travel, however, I think there can be no doubt that the double cinch is the better. It is less likely to slip forward or back on steep hills; it need not be so tightly cinched as the "center fire," and can be adjusted, according to which you draw the tighter, for up or down hill. The front cinch should be made of hair. I have found that the usual cord

Proper way of arranging straps and holster and saddle.

cinches are apt to wear sores just back of the shoulder. Web-bring makes a good back cinch. The handiest rig for attaching them is that used by the Texan and Wyoming cowmen. It is a heavy oiled latigo strap, punched with buckle holes,

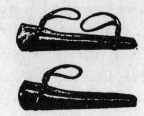

Saddle holder— usual arrangement of straps.

passing through a cinch ring supplied with a large buckle tongue. You can reach over and pull it up a hole or so without dismounting. It differs from an ordinary buckle only in that, in case the rig breaks, the strap can still be fastened like an ordinary latigo in the diamond knot.

Saddle bags and Saddle Blankets

On the right-hand side of your pommel will be a strap and buckle for your riata. A pair of detachable leather saddle bags are handy. The saddle blanket should be thick and of first quality; and should be surmounted by a "corona" to prevent wrinkling under the slight movement of the saddle.

Quirts

A heavy quirt is indispensable, both for your own mount, if he prove refractory, but also for the persuasion of the pack horse.

Sling Shorts

When with a large outfit, however, I always carry a pea shooter or sling shot. With it a man can spot a straying animal at considerable distance, generally much to the truant's astonishment. After a little it will rarely be necessary to shoot; a mere snapping of the rubbers will bring every horse into line.

Bridles

The handiest and best rig for a riding bridle can be made out of an ordinary halter. Have your harness maker fasten a snap hook to either side and just above the corners of the horse's mouth. When you start in the morning you snap your bit and reins to the hooks. When you arrive in the evening you simply unsnap the bit, and leave the halter on.

Scabbards

There remains only your rifle to attend to. The usual scabbard is invariably slung too far forward. I always move the sling strap as near the mouth of the scabbard as it will go. The other sling strap I detach from the scabbard and hang loop wise from the back latigo-ring. Then I thrust the muzzle of the scabbarded rifle between the stirrup leathers and through this loop, hang the forward sling strap over the pommell—and there I am! The advantage is that I can remove rifle and scabbard without un-buckling any straps. The gun should hang on the left side of the horse so that after dismounting you need not walk around him to get it. A little experiment will show you how near the horizontal you can sling it without danger of its jarring out.

Pack outfits

So much for your own riding horse. The pack outfit consists of the pack saddle, with the apparatus to keep it firm; its padding; the kyacks, or alforjas— sacks to sling on either side; and the lash rope and cinch with which to throw the hitches.

Pack saddles

The almost invariable type of pack saddle is the sawbuck. If it is bought with especial reference to the animal it is to be used on, it is undoubtedly the best. But nothing will more quickly gouge a hole in a horse's back than a saddle too narrow or too wide for his especial anatomy. A saddle of this sort bolted together can be taken apart for easier transportation by baggage or express.

Under side of pack saddles.

Another and very good type of pack rig is that made from an old riding saddle. The stirrup rigging is removed, and an upright spike bolted strongly to the cantle. The loops of the kyacks are to be hung over the horn and this spike. Such a saddle is apt to be easy on a horse's back, but is after

Shape of collar pad— for pack saddles.

all merely a make-shift for a properly constructed sawbuck.

Padding and Rigging the Pack Saddle

Pads

We will assume that you are possessed of a good sawbuck saddle of the right size for your pack animal. It will have the double cinch rig. To the under surfaces tack firmly two ordinary collar-pads by way of softening. Beneath them you will use two blankets, each as heavy as the one you place under your riding saddle. This abundance is necessary because a pack "rides dead"—that is, does not favor the horse as does a living rider. By way of warning, however, too much is almost as bad as too little.

Breasting and Breeching

The almost universal saddle rigging in use the West over is a breast strap of webbing fastened at

the forward points of the saddle, and a breech strap fastened to the back points of the saddle, with guy lines running from the top to prevent its falling too far down the horse's legs. This, with the double cinch, works fairly well. Its main trouble is that the breech strap is apt to work up under the horse's tail, and the breast strap is likely to shut off his wind at the throat.

The Britten Pack Rig

Mr. Ernest Britten, a mountaineer in the Sierras, has, however, invented a rig which in the nicety of its compensations, and the accuracy of its adjustments is perfection.

Every one becomes a convert, and hastens to alter his own outfit.

The breasting is a strap (*a*) running from the point of the saddle to a padded ring in the middle of the chest. Thence another strap (*b*) runs to the point of the saddle on the other side, where it buckles. A third strap (*c*) in the shape of a loop goes between the fore legs and around the front cinch.

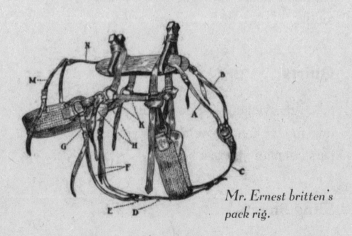

Mr. Ernest britten's pack rig.

The breeching is somewhat more complicated. I think, however, with a few rivets, The Britten straps, and buckles you will be able to alter your own saddle in half an hour.

The back cinch you remove. A short strap (*d*), riveted to the middle of the front cinch, passes back six inches to a ring (*e*). This ring will rest on the middle of the belly. From the ring two other straps (*ff*) ascend diagonally to the buckles (*g*) in the ends

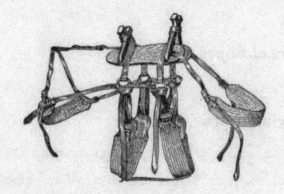

Ordinary and inferior pack rig usually employed.

of the breeching. From the ends of the breeching other straps (*h*) attach to what would be the back cinch ring (*k*). That constitutes the breeching rig. It is held up by a long strap (*m*) passing from one side to the other over the horse's rump through a ring on top. The ring is attached to the saddle by a short strap (*n*).

Such a rig prevents the breeching from riding up or dropping down; it gives the horse all his wind going uphill, but holds firmly going down; when

one part loosens, the other tightens; and the saddle cinch, except to keep the saddle from turning, is practically useless and can be left comparatively loose. I cannot too strongly recommend you, both for your horse's comfort and your own, to adopt this rigging.

Kyacks

The kyacks, as I have said, are two sacks to be slung one on each side of the horse. They are provided with loops by which to hang them over the sawbucks of the saddle, and a long strap passes from the outside of one across the saddle to a buckle on the outside of the other.

Undoubtedly the best are those made of rawhide. They weigh very little, will stand all sorts of hard usage, hold the pack rope well, are so stiff that they well protect the contents, and are so hard that miscellaneous sharp-cornered utensils may be packed in them without fear of injury either to them or the animal. They are made by lacing wet hides, hair out, neatly and squarely over one of the wooden boxes built to pack two five gallon oil cans. A round

Nearing a crest and in sight of game.

hardwood stick is sewn along the top on one side—to this the sling straps are to be attached. After the hide has dried hard, the wooden box is removed.

Only one possible objection can be urged against rawhide kyacks; if you are traveling much by railroad, they are exceedingly awkward to ship. For that purpose they are better made of canvas.

Canvas Kyacks

Many canvas kyacks are on the market, and most of them are worthless. It is astonishing how many knocks they are called on to receive and how soon the abrasion of rocks and trees will begin to wear them through. Avoid those made of light material. Avoid also those made in imitation of the rawhide with a stick along the top of one side to take the sling straps. In no time the ends of that stick will punch through. The best sort are constructed of OO canvas. The top is made of a half-inch rope sewn firmly to the hem all around. The sling straps are long, and riveted firmly. The ends are reinforced with leather. Such kyacks will give you good service and last you a long time. When you wish to express them, you pack your saddle and saddle blankets in one, telescope the other over it, and tie up the bundle with the lash rope.

Lash Rope

The lash rope is important, for you will have to handle it much, and a three months' trip with a poor one would lose you your immortal soul. Most articles on the subject advise thirty-three feet. That is long enough for the diamond hitch and for other hitches with a very small top pack, but it will not do for many valuable hitches on a bulky pack. Forty feet is nearer the ticket. The best is a manila half inch or five-eighth inch. If you boil it before starting out, you will find it soft to handle. The boiling does not impair its strength. Parenthetically: do not become over-enthusiastic and boil your riata, or you will

make it aggravatingly kinky. Cotton rope is all right, but apt to be stiff. I once used a linen rope; it proved to be soft, strong, and held well, but I have never been able to find another.

Picket Ropes and Hobbles

Picket ropes

So you have your horses ready for their burdens. Picket ropes should be of half-inch rope and about 50 feet long. The bell for the bell horse should be a loud one, with distinctive note not easily blended with natural sounds, and attached to a broad strap with safety buckle.

Hobbles

Hobbles are of two patterns. Both consist of heavy leather straps to buckle around either front leg and connected by two links and a swivel. In one the strap passes first through the ring to which the links are attached, and then to the buckle. The other buckles first, and then the end is carried through the ring. You will find the first mentioned a decided nuisance, especially on a wet or frosty morning, for the leather tends to atrophy in a certain position from which numbed fingers have more than a little difficulty in dislodging it.
The latter, however, are comparatively easy to undo.

Hobbles should be lined. I have experimented with various materials, including the much lauded sheepskin with the wool on. The latter when wet chafes as much as

Natural cinch hook of oak.

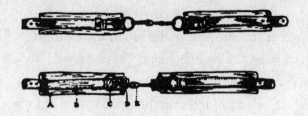

A–Wash Leather.
B–Heavy Leather.
C–Steel Ring.
D–Buckle.
Hobbles—Wrong (upper) and right sort.

raw leather, and when frozen is about as valuable as a wood rasp. The best lining is a piece of soft wash leather at least two inches wider than the hobble straps.

How to Attach Hobbles

With most horses it is sufficient to strap a pair of these around the forelegs and above the fetlocks. A gentle animal can be trusted with them fastened below.

But many horses by dint of practice or plain native cussedness can hop along with hobbles nearly as fast as they could foot-free, and a lot too fast for you to catch them single handed. Such an animal is an unmitigated bother. Of course if there is good staking you can picket him out; but quite likely he is unused to the picket rope, or the feed is scant.

Side Lines

In that case it may be that side lines—which are simply hobbles by which a hind foot and a fore foot are shackled—may work. I have had pretty good success by fastening a short heavy chain to one fore leg. As long as the animal fed quietly, he was all right, but an attempt at galloping or trotting swung the chain sufficiently to rap him sharply across the shins.

Very good hobbles can be made from a single strand unraveled from a large rope, doubled once to make a loop for one leg, twisted strongly, the two ends brought around the other leg and then thrust through the fibers. This is the sort used generally by cowboys. They are soft and easily carried, but soon wear out.

Jam Hitch

1. *The Jam Hitch.*—All hitches possess one thing in common—the rope passes around the horse and through the cinch hook. The first pull is to tighten that cinch. Afterward other maneuvers are attempted. Now ordinarily the packer pulls tight his cinch, and then in the further throwing of the hitch he depends on holding his slack. It is a very difficult thing to do. With the jam hitch, however, the necessity is obviated.

The beauty of it is that the rope renders freely one way—the way you are pulling—but will not give a hair the other—the direction of loosening. So you may heave up the cinch as tightly as you please, then drop the rope and go on about your packing perfectly sure that nothing is going to slip back on you.

The jam hitch.

The rope passes once around the shank of the hook, and then through the jaw (see diagram). Be sure to get it around the shank and not the curve. Simplicity itself; and yet I have seen very few packers who know of it.

The Diamond Hitch

2. *The Diamond Hitch.*—I suppose the diamond in one form or another is more used than any other. Its merit is its adaptability to different shapes and

sizes of package—in fact it is the only hitch good for aparejo packing—its great flattening power, and the fact that it rivets the pack to the horse's sides. If you are to learn but one hitch, this will be the best for you, although certain others, as I shall explain under their proper captions, are better adapted to certain circumstances.

The diamond hitch is also much discussed. I have heard more arguments over it than over the Japanese war or original sin.

"That thing a diamond hitch!" shrieks a son of the foothills to a son of the alkali. "Go to! Looks more like a game of cat's cradle. Now *this* is the real way to throw a diamond."

Colorado Versus Arizona

Certain pacifically inclined individuals have attempted to quell the trouble by a differentiation of nomenclature. Thus one can throw a number of diamond hitches, provided one is catholically minded—such as the "Colorado diamond," the "Arizona diamond," and others. The attempt at peace has failed.

"Oh, yes," says the son of the alkali as he watches the attempts of the son of the foothills. "That's the *Colorado* diamond," as one would say that is a *paste* jewel.

The joke of it is that the results are about the same. Most of the variation consists in the manner of throwing. It is as though the discussion were whether the trigger should be pulled with the fore, middle, or both fingers. After all, the bullet would go anyway.

I describe here the single diamond, as thrown in the Sierra Nevadas, and the double diamond as used by government freight packers in many parts of the Rockies. The former is a handy one-man hitch. The latter can be used by one man, but is easier with two.

The Single Diamond

Throw the pack cinch (*a*) over the top of the pack, retaining the loose end of the rope. If your horse is bad, reach under him with a stick to draw the cinch within reach of your hand until you hold it and the loose end both on the same side of the animal. Hook it through the hook (*a*, Fig. II) and

A downward journey.

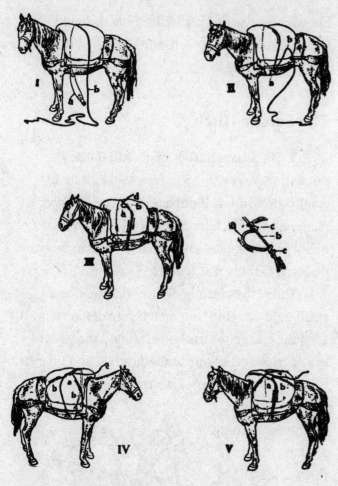

The single diamond.

When you have done this, go around the other side. There take up the slack on b-b, Fig. IV. With all there is in you pull the loose end (c, Fig. IV) in the direction of the horse's body, toward his head. Brace your foot against the kyacks. It will sag the whole hitch toward the front of the pack, but don't mind that: the defect will be remedied in a moment.

Next, still holding the slack (Fig. V), carry the loose end around the bottom of the alforjas and under the original main pack rope (c). Now pull again along the direction of the horse's body, but this time toward his tail. The strain will bend the pack rope (c), heretofore straight across, back to form the diamond. It will likewise drag back to its original position amidships in the pack the entire hitch, which, you will remember, was drawn too far forward by your previous pull toward the horse's head. Thus the last pull tightens the entire pack, clamps it down, secures it immovably, which is the main recommendation and beautiful feature of the diamond hitch.

The Double Diamond

The double diamond is a much more complicated affair. Begin by throwing the cinch under, not over the horse. Let it lie there. Lay the end of the rope a lengthwise of the horse across one side the top of the pack (Fig. 1). Experience will teach you just how big to leave loop b. Throw loop b over top of pack (Fig. 2). Reverse loop a (Fig. 2) by turning it from left to right (Fig. 3). Pass loop a around front and back of kyack, and end of rope d over rope c, and under rope d.

Pass around the horse and hook the cinch hook in loop (e).

This forms another loop (a, Fig. 4), which must be extended to the proper size and passed around the kyack on the other side (Fig. 5). Now tighten the cinch, pull up the slack, giving strong heaves where the hitch pulls forward or back along the left of the

bring up along the pack. Thrust the bight (a, Fig. III) of the loose rope under the rope (b); the back over and again under to form a loop. The points (c-c) at which the loose rope goes around the pack rope can be made wide apart or close together, according to the size of the diamond required (Fig. V). With a soft top-pack requiring flattening, the diamond should be large; with heavy side pack, smaller.

Now go around to the other side of the animal. Pass the loose end (d, Fig. III) back, under the alforjas, forward and through the loop from below as shown by the arrows of direction in Fig. IV.

You are now ready to begin tightening. First pull your cinch tight by means of what was the loose end (b) in Fig. II. Place one foot against the animal and heave, good and plenty. Take up the slack by running over both ends of the loop (c-c, Fig. III).

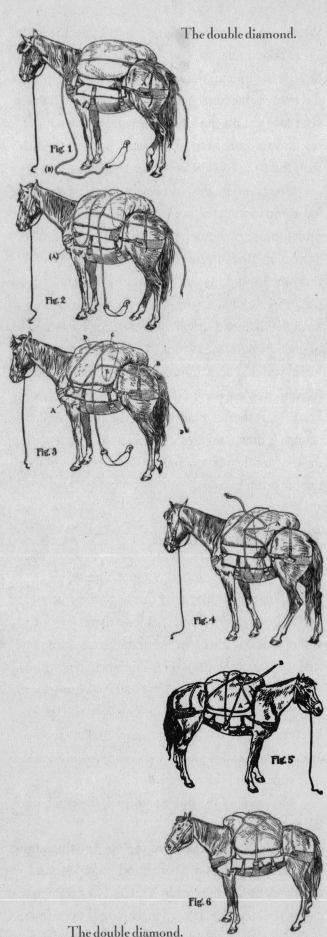

The double diamond.

Fig. 1

Fig. 2

Fig. 3

Fig. 4

Fig. 5

Fig. 6

The double diamond.

horse, ending with a last tightener at the end (*b*, Fig. 5). The end is then carried back under the kyack and fastened.

The Square Hitch

3. *The Square Hitch* is easily and quickly thrown, and is a very good fair-weather lash. In conjunction with half hitches, as later explained, it makes a good hitch for a bucking horse. For a very bulky pack it is excellent in that it binds in so many places. It is thrown as follows:

Throw the cinch hook over the pack, and cinch tight with the jam hitch before described. Lead the end across the horse, around the back of kyack on the other side, underneath it, and up over at *a*. The end here passes beneath at *b*. You will find that you can, when you cinch up at first, throw a loose loop over the pack comprising the bight *bed*, so as to leave your loose end at *d*. Then place the loop *bed* around the kyack. A moment's study of the diagram will show you what I mean, and will also convince you that much is gained by not having to pass rope (*a*) underneath at *b*. Now pull hard on loose end at *d* taking care to exert your power lengthwise of the horse.

The square hitch.

Pass the line under the alforjas toward the rear, up over the pack and under the original rope at *c*. Pull on the loose end, this time exerting the power toward the rear. You cannot put too much strength into the three tightening pulls: (1) in cinching through the cinch hook; (2) the pull forward; (3) the pull back. On them depends the stability of your pack. Double back the loose end and fasten it. This is a very quick hitch.

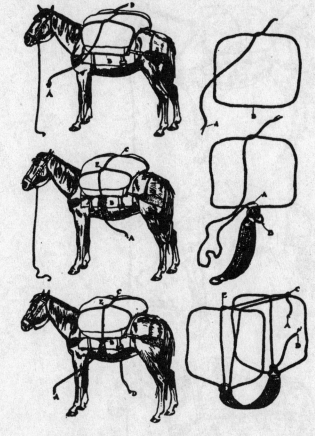

The Bucking Hitch

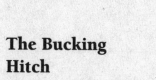

The bucking hitch.

4. *The Bucking Hitch* is good to tie things down on a bad horse, but it is otherwise useless to take so much trouble.

Pass the pack rope around the kyacks on one side, and over itself. This forms a half hitch, below which hangs the cinch. Lead the pack rope over the top of the pack, around the other kyack, and through to form another half hitch. Cinch up, and throw either the single diamond or the square hitch. The combination will clamp the kyacks as firmly as anything can.

The Miner's Hitch

5. *The Miner's Hitch.*—This hitch is very much on the same principle, but is valuable when you happen to be provided with only a short rope, or a cinch with two rings, instead of a ring and a hook.

Take your rope—with the cinch unattached—by the middle and throw it across the pack. Make a half hitch over either kyack. These half hitches, instead of running around the sides of the kyacks, as in the last hitch, should run around the top, bottom, and ends (see diagram). Thrust bight (*b*) through

The miner's hitch.

cinch ring, and end (*a*) through the bight. Do the same thing on the other side. Make fast end *a* at *c*, and end *d* at *e*, cinching up strongly on the bights that come through the cinch rings.

The Lone Packer Hitch

6. *The Lone Packer or Basco Hitch.*—This is a valuable hitch when the kyacks are heavy or knobby, because the last pull lifts them away from the horse's sides. It requires at least forty feet of rope. I use it a great deal.

Cinch up with the jam hitch as usual. Throw the end of the rope across the horse, under the forward end of the kyack on the far side, beneath it and up over the rear end of the kyack. The rope in all other hitches binds against the bottom of the kyacks; but in this it should pass between the kyack and the horse's side (Fig. 1). Now bring a bight in loose end (*a*) forward *over* rope (*c*), and thrust it

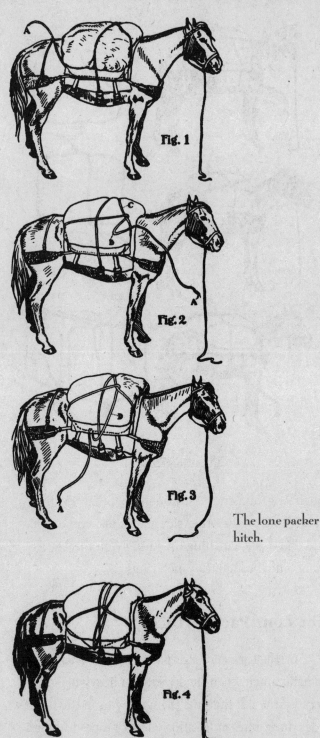

Fig. 1

Fig. 2

Fig. 3

The lone packer hitch.

Fig. 4

Fig. 5

The lone packer hitch.

through *under* rope (*c*) from front to back (Fig. 2). Be sure to get this right. Hold bight (*b*) with left hand where it is, and with the other slide end (*a*) down along rope (*c*) until beneath the kyacks (Fig. 3). Seize rope at *d* and pull hard directly back; then pull cinchwise on *a*. The first pull tightens the pack; the second lifts the kyacks. Carry end (*a*) across the pack and repeat on the other side. Fasten finally anywhere on top. Fig. 4 shows one side completed, with rope thrown across ready for the other side. Fig. 5 is a view from above of the hitch, completed except for the fastening of end (*a*).

A Modification

In case you have eggs or glassware to pack, spread your tarp on the horse twice as long as usual. Cinch up with the jam hitch, lay your eggs, etc., atop the rope; fold back the canvas to cover the whole, and then throw the lone packer, placing one rope each side the package.

The Squaw Hitch

7. *The Squaw Hitch.*—Often it may happen that you find yourself possessed of a rope and a horse, but nothing else. It is quite possible to pack your equipment with only these simple auxiliaries.

Lay your tarp on the ground fully spread. On half of it pack your effects, striving always to keep them as flat and smooth as possible. Fold the other half of the canvas to cover the pack. Lay this thick mattress-like affair across the

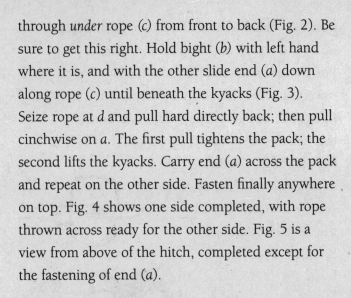

Fig. 1   Fig. 2

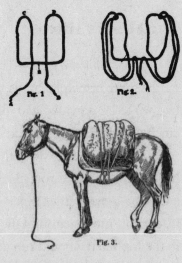

Fig. 3

The squaw hitch.

horse's bare back, and proceed to throw the squaw hitch as follows:

Throw a double bight across the top of the pack (Fig. 1). Pass end *a* under the horse and through loop *c*; and end *b* under the horse and through loop (*d*). Take both *a* and *b* directly back under the horse again, in the opposite direction, of course, and pass both through loop (*e*). Now cinch up on the two ends and fasten.

Sling no. 1.

Sling

8. *Sling No. 1.*—When you possess no kyacks, but have some sort of pack saddle, it is necessary to improvise a sling.

Fasten the middle of your rope by means of two half hitches to the front of the pack saddle (Fig. 1). Throw the ends (*b, b*) crossed as shown in Fig. 2. Place the box or sack in bight (*a*), passing the rope around the outside and the ends, as in Fig. 3. The end of the sack should be just even with the front of the pack saddle. If you bring it too far forward the front of the sling will sag. Pass the end (*b*) underneath the sack or burden, across its middle, and over the top of the saddle. When the other side is similarly laden, the ends (*b,b*) may be tied together at the top; or if they are long enough, may be fastened at *c* (Fig. 4).

Another Sling

9. *Sling No. 2.*—Another sling is sometimes handy for long bundles and is made as follows:

Sling no. 2.

Fasten the rope by the middle as explained in the last. Fasten ends (*b, b*) to the rear horn or to each other (see diagram). Leave the bights of the rope (*a, a*) of sufficient length so they can be looped around the burden and over the horns. This sling is useful only on a regular pack saddle, while the other really does not need the rear pommel at all, as the ropes can be crossed without it.

The Saddle Hitch

10. *The Saddle Hitch.*—There remains now the possibility, or let us hope probability, that you may someday wish to pack a deer on your riding saddle, or perhaps bring in a sack of grain or some such matter.

Throw the rope across the seat of the saddle, leaving long ends on both sides. Lay your deer aboard, crosswise. Thrust a bight (*a*) of one end through your cinch ring, and pass the loop thus formed around the deer's neck (Fig. 1). Repeat on the other side, bringing the loop there about his haunch. Cinch up the two ends of the rope, and tie them on top.

The saddle hitch.

The great point in throwing any hitch is to keep the rope taut. To do this, pay no attention to your free end, but clamp down firmly the fast end with your left hand until the right has made the next turn. Remember this; it is important. The least slip back of the slack you have gained is going to loosen that pack by ever so little; and then you can rely on the swing and knocks of the day's journey to do the rest. The horse rubs under a limb or against a big rock; the loosened rope scrapes off the top of the pack; something flops or rattles or falls—immediately that cayuse arches his back, lowers his head, and begins to buck.

How to Pack Fragile Stuff

It is marvelous to what height the bowed back will send small articles catapult-wise into the air. First go the tarpaulin and blankets; then the duffle bags; then one by one the contents of the alforjas; finally, after they have been sufficiently lightened, the alforjas themselves in an abandoned parabola of debauched delight. In the meantime that horse, and all the others, has been running frantically all over the rough mountains, through the rocks, ravines, brush and forest trees. You have ridden recklessly trying to round them up, sweating, swearing, praying to the Red Gods that none of those indispensable animals is going to get lame

The result of not getting the hitch on snug.

in this insane hippodrome. Finally between you, you have succeeded in collecting and tying to trees all the culprits. Then you have to trail inch by inch along the track of the cyclone, picking up from where they have fallen, rolled, or been trampled, the contents of that pack down to the smallest. It will take you the rest of the day; and then you'll miss some. Oh, it pays to get your hitch on snug!

Kinds of Canoes

Practicable canoes are made of birch bark stretched over light frames; of cedar; of basswood; of canvas, and of canvas cover over stiff frames.

Illustrating how to pack eggs or glassware.

The Birch Bark

Advantages and Disadvantages

The birch bark canoe has several unassailable advantages. It is light; it carries a greater weight in proportion to its length than any other; it is very easily mended. On the other hand it is not nearly so fast as a wooden canoe of sweeter lines; does not bear transportation so well; is more easily punctured; and does not handle so readily in a heavy wind. These advantages and disadvantages, as you can see, balance against one another. If it tends to veer in a heavy wind more than the wooden canoe, it is lighter on portage. If more fragile, it is very easily mended. If it is not quite so fast, it carries more duffle. Altogether, it is a very satisfactory all-around craft in which I have paddled many hundreds of miles, and with which I have never been seriously dissatisfied. If I were to repeat some long explorations in the absolute wilds of Canada I should choose a birch canoe, if only for the reason that no matter how badly I might smash it, the materials are always at hand for repairs. A strip of bark from the nearest birch tree; a wad of gum from the next spruce; some spruce roots; a little lard and a knife will mend a canoe stove beautifully.

Selection of a Birch Bark

In selecting a birch bark canoe the most important thing to look after is to see that the bottom is all one piece without projecting knots or mended cracks. Many canoes have bottoms made of two pieces. These when grounded almost invariably spring a leak at the seam, for the simple reason that it takes very little to scrape off the slightly projecting gum. On the other hand, a bottom of one good piece of bark will stand an extraordinary amount of raking and bumping without being any the worse. If in addition you can get hold of one made of the winter cut of bark, the outside shell will be as good as possible. Try to purchase a new canoe. Should this be impossible, look well to the *watap*, or roots, used in the sewing, that they are not frayed or burst. The frames should lie so close together as fairly to touch. Such a canoe, "two fathoms," will carry two men and four hundred pounds besides. It will weigh about fifty to seventy pounds, and should cost new from six to eight dollars.

Cedar end Basswood

A wooden canoe, of some sort, is perhaps better for all smooth and open-water sailing, and all short trips nearer home. It will stand a great deal of jamming about, but is very difficult to mend if ever you do punch a hole in it. You will need to buy a longer craft than when getting a birch. The latter will run from twelve to fourteen feet. A wood canoe of that length would float gun-whale awash at half you would wish to carry. Seventeen or eighteen feet is small enough for two men, although I have cruised in smaller. Cedar is the lighter material—and the more expensive—but splits too readily. Basswood is heavier, but is cheaper and tougher.

Paddles

The Indian paddle is a very long and very narrow blade, just as long as the height of its wielder. For use in swift and somewhat shallow water, where often the paddle must be thrust violently against the bottom or a rock, this form is undoubtedly the best. In more open, or smoother water, however, the broader and shorter blade is better, though even in the latter case it is well to select one of medium length. Otherwise you will find yourself, in a heavy sea, sometimes reaching rather frantically down toward the water. Whatever its length, attach it to the thwart nearest you by a light strong line. Then if you should go overboard you will retain control of your craft. I once swam over a mile before I was able to overtake a light canoe carried forward by a lively wind.

Knapsacks

The harness for packs is varied enough, but the principle remains simple. A light pack will hang well enough from the shoulders, but when any weight is to be negotiated you must call into play the powerful muscles lying along the neck. Therefore, in general, an ordinary knapsack will answer very well for packs up to say thirty pounds. Get the straps broad and soft; see that they are both sewed and riveted.

Tumplines

How to Carry Packs

When, however, your pack mounts to above thirty pounds you will need some sort of strap to pass across the top of your head. This is known as a tumpline, and consists of a band of leather to cross the head, and two long thongs to secure the pack. The blanket or similar cloth is spread, the thongs laid lengthwise about a foot from either edge, and the blanket folded inward and across the thongs.

The things to be carried are laid on the end of the blanket toward the head piece. The other end of the blanket, from the folds of which the ends of the thongs are protruding, is then laid up over the pile. The ends of the thongs are then pulled tight, tied together, and passed around the middle of the pack. To carry this outfit with any degree of comfort, be sure to get it low, fairly in the small of the back or even just above the hips. A compact and heavy article, such as a sack of flour, is a much simpler matter. The thongs are tied together at a suitable distance. One side of the loop thus formed goes around your head, and the other around the sack of flour. It will not slip.

Pack Harnesses

By far the best and most comfortable pack outfit I have used is a combination of the shoulder and the head methods. It consists of shoulder harness like that used on knapsacks, with two long straps and buckles to pass around and secure any load. A tumpline is attached to the top of the knapsack straps. I have carried in this contrivance over a hundred pounds without discomfort. Suitable adjustment of the headstrap will permit you to relieve alternately your neck and shoulders. Heavy or rather compact articles can be included in the straps, while the bulkier affairs will rest very well on top of the pack. It is made by Abercrombie & Fitch, and costs two dollars and seventy-five cents.

Tumplines.

Exploration

From *The Boy Scout's Hike Book*, by Edward Cave, 1920

Daniel boone, America's greatest scout and pioneer hero, was a surveyor, and because of that fact was of inestimable service to his country where, had he not possessed his small knowledge of civil engineering, he might have lived and died in comparative obscurity. He was not only able to lead parties into the wilderness, but could make accurate maps, and so preserve in concrete form the information obtained on his trips. He not only knew how to measure the width of a stream or a lake as the Boy Scout manuals describe, but he could *survey*. His maps, rough though they were, never were based on guesswork. Instruments? He doubtless never carried them on his exploring trips; but he knew the tricks of the profession.

Measuring Distances with a Wheel.—When I was a boy my father used to talk about the great Livingstone and about "Chinese" Gordon. The former was my favorite, although the redoubtable Gordon was the most praised by my father, who was always a soldier at heart. I got to reading the big "histories" that fired my father's imagination, and liked best the books by Livingstone. A feature about

In the land of "been-there".

them that interested me greatly was the accuracy with which he described everything. Finally, I found among other things that he had used a counter on one of the wheels of an ox-cart and so measured the distances he travelled. That set me to measuring distances in a similar way. I tied a bit of white rag around one of the wheels of the buggy and by counting the number of times it went around as I walked the horse, measured the distance from our front gate to the house. We always had said it was "a quarter of a mile," but I found that it was in fact only 380 yards, or 60 yards less than estimated.

I became interested, and my father, who had employed surveyors, showed me how to measure distances with a right-angled triangle, which he made for me of planed lath (Fig. 1). He mounted it on the end of a 4-foot section of a broken fork handle, by means of a screw, and when he had sharpened the staff stuck it in the ground; see Figure 2. He explained to me that the proportions of this triangle, 12 × 12 × 17 inches, would always make a true right-angled isosceles triangle. You may forget the name, as I did, but remember the dimensions.

Fig. 1. How to make a right angle isosceles triangle.

Using A "Settler's Jackstaff."— If you wish to measure the distance of an air line across a river, lake,

Fig. 2. The "settler's jackstaff".

impassable swamp or other place where you cannot go, set up such a "settler's jackstaff," as he called it, as at *a*, Figure 3. Put a pin in the point of the corner *z*, and another 4 inches from it toward *x*. Sight along these pins from ✕ to *z* and train them on the inaccessible point *c*. Now, without moving the triangle sight over two pins similarly placed, from ✕ to *y*; this will give you the bearing of a right angle, and you should have a companion set up stakes, as indicated by 1, 2, 3, to carry it out. Pull up your jackstaff, plant a stake with a red flag of some sort in the hole left by the staff, and proceed along the line of stakes 1, 2, 3, When you reach a point where the line *y z* of your triangle will sight exactly at the inaccessible point *c*, as shown at *b* you have but to measure the distance from *a* to *b*. The distance from *a* to *c* will be exactly the same. If you want to know how far it is from *b* to *c*, it is to the distance from *b* to *a* as 17 is to 12; figure it out, it's easy.

Now, to measure the distance to other inaccessible points, as *n*, *p*, *s*, Figure 4, take the *x z* right-angle bearing of each from your base line *a b* and plant a stake, then proceed along the base line until, with the jackstaff set up and the right angle *y x* aligned on the base line, the line *y z* of your jackstaff triangle is sighted at each of these inaccessible points. See diagram. The distance from *m* to *n* is the same as from *m* to *o*, and so on. Thus from a base line on one side of a lake you can plot the other side, as shown, the intermediate shore line of course being sketched in on your map by guesswork. By taking lots of pains you can plot every bit of it.

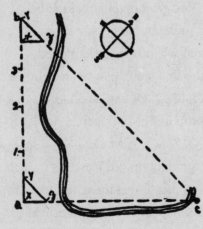

Fig. 3.   Range finding by the right angle system.

Of course there are better systems, but I am giving this one as I believe it will help you to understand others to follow, as it helped me.

Making a Surveying Outfit.—By far the most popular system of quick

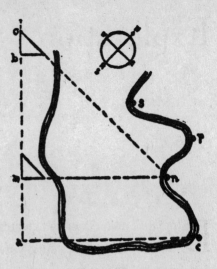

Fig. 4.   Finding the range of other points to map the lake.

and simple surveying in this country is called "plane tabling," and gets its name from the use of a plane table. To make a serviceable plane table, get a small drawing board, not less than 12 ✕ 17, and preferably 24 ✕ 24, if you can get it. Turn this face downward and find the exact center. Now get an ordinary camera tripod, made of wood and having a *wide* top, 4 or 5 inches in diameter if you can get it. Procure a view camera screw-socket and countersink and fasten it securely in the exact center of the underside of the drawing board. You need a socket for a view camera, because they are the strongest; any camera dealer can obtain one for you. Get a carpenter's small plumb and some cord to make a plumb line.

Next you need a straight yardstick, for an alidade. Not the cheap article given away as an advertisement but one of hardwood. If you can get one with a ruling edge so much the better. For intersection work with the plane table this yardstick requires only the addition of a couple of sights. By making one of these a "peep" sight, however, you can also do traversing.

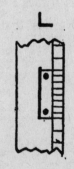

Fig. 5.   How to make the knife-blade sight and mount on the alidade.

For the "knife-blade" sight, cut a piece of right-angled brass to 1 inch long, by ¼ inch each other dimension. Drill holes and mount on the 15-inch mark, so the vertical section is in the center of the rule and in precise alignment with it. For the peep 1 × 11¼ inches and cut a ½ × ½-inch hole squarely in it, leaving ¼ inch of brass on three sides and ½ inch on the other. Bend up to a right angle so when the ½-inch base is secured on the yardstick the hole in the vertical section will be exactly ½ × ½ inch with its bottom margin formed by the base. Mount on the 30-inch mark, and cut off the remaining 6 inches. Now you have an alidade which, although not up to a surveyor's telescope will serve your purposes. It is not like any other alidade I know of, but I have found it practical, and it has the advantage that it will stand handling.

Fig. 6.   How make the peep sight of the alidade.

Surveying By Intersection.—To plot an irregularly fenced field such as is indicated in Figure 7 by the line 1, 2, 3. etc., to 12, by intersection, proceed as follows:

Set tripod at *a*, fasten plane table on it, with a piece of drawing paper thereon, held by thumb tacks. Make a mark for *a* on the paper, and another 3 inches from it for *b*, and draw the base line through them. Now measure off 150 yards, with a tape or by pacing it off, in a straight line from *a* in the direction you want the base line to run. Plant a stake there; it represents *b* on your plane table. Place your alidade on the table so the scale is along the line from *a* to *b* on your paper, and the peep sight toward you. Sight through the peep and over the knife-blade at the stake *b*. A red flag on the stake will help. When the sights are aligned your pencil line *a b* will also point straight from you to the stake. Tighten the thumb-screw so the table cannot be moved.

Now your assistant goes to where the fence starts at 1, turns and goes out to the corner 2. Don't move the table. Sight the alidade at him, peep sight to your eye, across the top of the table, the scale side resting on the mark *a*. Draw the line from *a* to 2. You cannot tell how far away he is, so carry the line out indefinitely. Continue in this manner until your assistant is at 12. He should plant a stake exactly where he stands at each point.

Take your plumb and hold it as near as you can so it hangs directly below the mark *a* on your map. (Directly under the tripod is good enough; I hang the plumb on the thumb-screw.) Mark the spot on the ground. Move the tripod and drive a flag stake in this marked spot.

Range Finding Lines.—Go to the stake at *b* and erect the table. Swing table around, and with the alidade train it so the line *b a* on your map runs directly toward the stake you left behind you at *a*. The mark *b* on your map should be directly above the hole where the stake *b* was planted. Tighten the thumbscrew so the table will not turn.

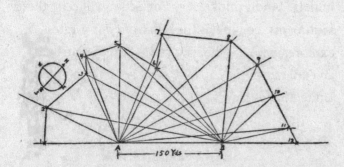

Fig. 7.   Surveying by intersection.

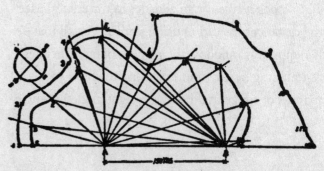

Fig. 8.   Surveying two lines from one base line.

Signal your assistant to start back over the course he has staked. When he stops at 11, sight the alidade at him, peep sight at your eye and scale side against the mark *b* on your map. Draw the line *b* 11. Continue until your assistant has gathered all his stakes and you have drawn your last line, *b* 2.

Draw the line of the fence from 1 around to 12. Now, as your scale is 50 yards to 1 inch, if you will measure off the distances between the points 1, 2, 3, etc, you will find the total length of the fence is 587 yards 1½ feet.

The Best Compass.—Surveying with compass, protractor and tape is both laborious and complicated. They teach it to the Scouts in England, having them trundle a measuring wheel. I think the use of the stadia, so much practiced in this country, far superior. If interested in compass surveying, get a civil engineer to show you a real surveyor's box compass, with a floating dial, a hair sight and a throw-off lever to raise the needle off the pivot when it is not in use. Set your heart on that sort of compass, and when you get it, get it big, not less than 3 inches in diameter. Meantime, I advise you to bone up on geometry, as the indications are that you're going to be a civil engineer.

Sketching.—For sketching, use quadrille ruled paper pads, and to obtain a fairly accurate skeleton by following the intersection or two-point system (so named because the angles from one base line point intersect those of the other at the point of aim with the alidade) I have described, pace off a base line, and use your sketching pad as a plane table and a pocket rule for an alidade. In traversing, pace the distances instead of using stadia rods; all that is required is to follow the plane-tabling principles as to taking bearings and marking them on your maps. For range finding by the right-angled triangle principle, if you ever wish to use it draw a 3 × 3 × 4½ inch triangle on a sheet of sketching paper, and sight it by placing your pocket rule (folded) along the line to be sighted. You will have some difficulty improvising a support for your pad in using it as a plane table; that will give you a chance to exercise your resourcefulness. But don't overtax yourself and these principles by trying too difficult a job of surveying. Stick to fairly level country and leave steep mountains and deep gorges to the fellows who can sign C. E. after their names.

Peary on Amateur Exploration.—Surveying, of course, is by no means all of amateur exploration. By far the biggest thing about it, I think, is the fact that it leads you into all sorts of interesting corners right around home that you never have imagined existed. That is the really worthwhile thing: to know one's own stamping ground. Commander (now Rear-Admiral) Robert E. Peary said to me on the day he sailed on his successful North Pole expedition: "I have no sympathy for the tourist, who travels guidebook in hand, searching out everything that is old; who has seen the midnight sun yet cannot point out the North Star. I do not honor the man who has climbed the Pyramids and yet has never been over the hills in sight of his own door-yard. I believe in the man who likes to get off the beaten track and steer his own course, just as I have more regard for the boy who has climbed a bee-tree that nobody else ever suspected was a bee-tree than for the boy who has climbed the Statue of Liberty and defaced the good bronze with his initials." And I think every Boy Scout will echo these sentiments, coming as they do from our greatest explorer, who, by the way, started on his career as an explorer in the capacity of a civil engineer in the United States Navy.

Woodcraft

From *The Boy Scout's Hike Book*, by Edward Cave, 1920

I think woodcraft in the highest sense is more an instinct than an art. I have known intelligent men who had been in the woods most of their lives yet were but poor woodsmen. To excel in it one must have aptitude and knack, just as in horsemanship, bicycle riding or shooting. I do not call it woodcraft to exercise ordinary horse sense about things in the woods, although paradoxically that is what it amounts to. There is a cunning that distinguishes your real wood-craftsman, and it is difficult to describe. Some say the characteristic that marks every good woodsman is his power of observation. Perhaps it is. But to me he seems more *wild* than anything else. I don't mean a wild man in any of the ordinary senses, of which at least two opposites will occur to you. I mean wild in the sense that to me he seems to fit into the woods as a part of them. This may be an odd fancy. Nevertheless, I think many Boy Scouts will agree with me that a deer or a wild turkey, any game animal or bird, looks distinctly wild, from its protective coloration to its furtive movements and its lithe symmetry, not excluding even bruin in his fur overcoat, and that it is quite possible to conceive of a man having similar qualities.

Where Observation Fails.—A black spruce swamp, few and far between nowadays, is perhaps the most difficult to find one's way through of all the tangles of the North; though I've seen some cedar swamps that were bad enough. In the South the rhododendron laurel thickets (in the Appalachian Mountains), and the canebrakes are in their way equally puzzling at times. We will suppose that an uncommonly observing woodsman for some good reason has on a gray day entered any one of these three innocent looking man-traps, and finds himself without a compass and with the sun obscured by clouds. Now what? Where does his power of observation come to the fore now? Every black spruce tree or every rhododendron shrub looks just

The drumless drummer.

How to build and thatch a brush shelter after the plan of the old indian camp.

How to build and thatch a brush lean-to.

like the next one; as for the cane—"they ain't no diffrunce, nohow," as the lost darky said.

It is commonly known that most men when lost travel in a circle. I've done some circling myself, and so has Mr. Kephart, according to his letters. Very few men with much experience in the woods can truthfully say they have never been "turned around." The Indians of the North, and not a few white men brought up in the bush, practice diligently to overcome this peculiar tendency to "go round and round"; and they succeed. An old friend of mine, Mr. Thomas Reynolds, for many years in the employ of the Hudson's Bay Company in Canada, told me that in forty years in the bush he never knew of an Indian or a white bushman carrying a compass.

But what has come of our woodsman? He cannot climb up a rhododendron or the canes to get an outlook, nor will it do him much good to climb one of the small black spruce trees, for all the other trees are just about the same size as the biggest one he can find, and he could not get high enough in its top to see over them. Perhaps be has practiced at walking in a straight line. But has he ever practiced it in the rhododendrons or the cane or in a black spruce swamp? It is not likely; generally a man picks a safer place. So how is he going to get out? Which way shall he go? Bless me! I don't know. Nor do I know how observation or reasoning from cause to effect is going to aid him. But I do hope for his own sake and the sake of his family that there is something in the theory that there is something in the theory that there is such a thing as a man having

an inborn sense of direction, and that he has it good and plenty.

Getting There Without a Compass.—I have been badly mixed in a fog while coon hunting at night in the Mississippi River bottoms, and in a combination of snowstorm and spruce swamp in Quebec—aye, and in the heart of New York City, momentarily, on emerging from the subway. So I know from experience that this instinct of direction which some possess to a greater degree than common is by no means Infallible. But I maintain that it does exist, and moreover that it is good company.

Practical Observation.—Next, let everything that is out of the ordinary be your signal to stop, look, listen. Practice concentration; that is to say, form a habit of paying close attention to a few things. If looking for a spring, for example, let that be your search, and pay particular attention to nothing else but unusual things. It is by the unusual things that we recall a place in the woods where we have been before. And naturally, the more you know about the woods the more unusual things you will observe. Then if you get turned around and cross your own trail, as you probably will, instead of seeing trees that "all look alike," you will find yourself saying, "Why, there is that same peculiar tree again; I must have walked in a circle."

One time my mother, coming on foot from the country post-office and making a short cut through the bush, noticed tome young pigs rushing across her path. She knew they belonged to a neighbor and were in the habit of going home at night to be fed. But it was too early in the afternoon for them to be going home. It was evident to her that something had alarmed them. To many another less observant the pigs would have been merely running through the woods, for reasons known only to young pigs. She was reading a newspaper as she walked along, but the incident distracted her interest in it and she commenced to fold it up, meantime looking about

Making a lean-to of corn-stalks on a frame of poles.

her, when lo! A big Canada lynx that had crept up to her sprang away in alarm at the flourish and rattle of the paper. He had been after the pigs, and it may be, though rather doubtful, that he thought he saw better game. He squatted in the path and glared at her, and even screamed at her. But she rattled her newspaper and waved it at him some more, and thus scared him off.

The Lay of the Land.—Thus from one thing to another you will progress, and soon from noticing unusual rocks, trees, sounds and the like, you will find yourself graduating to the class who do not bother particularly with small details, but are guided by the lay of the land. This in almost any woodland or forest, save a swamp or wide flat, should be your best ally in finding your way about. A woodsman going into strange country, no matter how wild, takes account of the direction the streams flow, and from that knows how the ridges, hills, or mountains must run. In the mountains he knows the trails are bound to follow the course of least resistance, and a brief survey from some lookout serves to tell him where to find them, if any exist. He does not intend to go hunting those trails; he determines where they are and goes to them. Of if following one that is obliterated most of the way, and is not spotted, perhaps running in open country, he keeps going, taking the course which he knows it naturally runs, and has the satisfaction of cutting into it once in a while where unmistakable evidence of it remains.

Some Precautions.—It is not reasonable to expect that Boy Scouts will take the same hazards as hunters do, or go alone into what may prove dangerous country. But it is well to give some rules to be observed by a party of Scouts camping in wild forested country, so no member of the party may go astray.

On making camp, four trails should be blazed toward camp from the four points of the compass. These should extend out as far as there is any probability of any one straying, and each be blazed in some distinguishing way. This will not be a very big job, and will always be a guide back to camp when found. Let the entire party ascend some high point, if possible, near the camp, where a good outlook may be had. In some sections of the country this may not be practicable, but if not make an attempt to get an outlook from a tree, to which every Scout should climb and make a thorough observation. A map of the surrounding country should be made, if you have not already a satisfactory topographic map, and each member should copy it and carry his copy with him. With reference to this map, be sure that from it you fix in your mind, and in a notebook, the compass direction from camp of every prominent landmark. Pay particular attention to the streams and the ridges separating them. Then when you go from camp in a given direction, count the streams and the ridges you cross, and *do not forget the count*. If there is any chance of forgetting, check each off in your notebook. If instead of crossing streams you stay on the ridges, keep track of the heads of the ravines. Each stream, each ridge, each ravine, gulch or arroya, is an infallible sign-post if you do not neglect to keep count of them. With this information, some attention to the compass, the wind, any prominent landmarks, and being convinced in your own mind that water always flows downhill, you ought to feel no concern about finding your way back to camp. As a further safeguard, however, I suggest that there be a rule against any member leaving camp alone, especially if there is probability of a storm, and that if for any reason whatever this rule be broken, the Scout must leave word in camp as to the time he leaves and where going. He should then keep careful track of how long he is out and as nearly as possible how far he goes. And, of course, he should never leave camp without his pack-sack, containing compass, map, first-aid can, waterproof match-box filled with vesta matches, rabbit wire (for snares), fish-line with split-shot sinkers and hooks, and emergency rations; which latter may be whatever he sees fit to carry. In canebrake or thicket country he should have a hunting horn. Other precautions may occur to you; there are plenty of them; so many, indeed, that by the time you got through with them it might be time to go home.

Crossed sticks held by a stone: take the other trail.

What to do when lost? *Sit down*

If You Get Lost—That is the very first thing, even if you have to hunt a dry place to sit upon. It is time to think things over, mostly to think them over backward.

Sit right where you are, and calmly think. Think where you have been and what you have done, and think of the instructions you read in the

The chopped stem of a bent-over bush points the way from camp. To back-trail, look for the "pale" bushes, easily seen because the under sides of the leaves are unusually pale.

chapter on Emergencies in this book, on what to do when lost.

I believe the most fruitful cause of getting lost, where a party are in the woods together, is the fact that when two or more are together one generally leads the way and the others are inclined to pay small heed to where they are going. There are pleasant things to talk and think about, and Bill is acting as guide. The party in general do not observe closely, and consequently do not acquire a good knowledge of their surroundings. Let one of those trailing the trusted Bill get separated from the party and he will be yelling and whistling for help in short order. If he is not heard he may get rattled, and then there are rough times ahead for him. If the party get lost it is because Bill has not been attending to business. "Don't talk to the motor man."

No matter if you are the last fellow in the line, and the crowd is making as much noise as a brass band, keep your eyes open and know where you go. Then if you fall behind and miss your way, you can always back-track to camp. And remember in this connection that it is often the case that "the longest way around is the shortest way home." Don't attempt the unknown short-cut but go back by the known long way. Don't forget!

Emergencies

From *The Boy Scout's Hike Book,* by Edward Cave, 1920

The greatest hiking emergency is to be badly lost. Other risks pale into insignificance before it, even the risk of being mistaken for a deer by some fool hunter. Not that the danger is greater, but on account of the scare that goes with a real, grown-up case of being badly lost I don't think anything could be more terrible than to literally run one's self to death in a panic.

A chopped foot, a broken bone, sunstroke, poisoning (toadstool, snake, gila monster, tarantula, ivy, or just plain ptomaine), a combination of deep water and acute indigestion, all sorts of calamities can happen to a Boy Scout. A belligerent papa bovine or a contentious "wood pussy" may furnish excitement, lots of it and easy as you please. There are plenty of possibilities; one could string out a catalogue extending all the way from the runaway horse on the next block, out into the woods, and around the back way home to the mad dog under the veranda. To prescribe a course of action for each would require a book in itself. And you wouldn't buy the book! There is one cardinal rule, however, which would properly be the first to observe in practically every emergency, and there is plenty of room for it here, and in your memory: *Keep cool!*

Lost and Alone.—To return to the subject of getting lost: a point to be borne in mind is that in the case of almost any other mishap you are pretty sure to have at least one other Scout with you. Somebody is within call, somebody will come along, or if not you can probably go for help. In the case of a water accident there is often the chance of rescue; or if not, the worst may be mercifully quick in arriving. But if you are seriously lost!

As I have said, it will be pretty ugly if you are *badly* lost (There is a way to get lost neatly and with credit to yourself.) A crazy man lived for years with a farmer neighbor of ours who found him lost in the bush, demented from his experience. He was *badly* lost He was not so far away from a settlement, but he was lost with a vengeance. And his panic robbed him for life of his reason. Another man to the same situation but nevertheless not *badly* lost might have fared far better, doubtless would have.

To take up the subject where it was dropped in the chapter on Woodcraft, if you find you are lost you will be scared a little, to say the least *Sit down!* You are apt to get more scared. And that is a bad business. Remember it is panic that kills men lost in the woods. *Sit down!* Next, if at all late in the day, begin to think about making a bivouac for the night right where you are, or in the beat place close by. Nothing very serious has happened. You have not suddenly been transported to some other planet.

Getting a move on.

If you sit down for a while and quietly look about you, you may even find that you are sitting right spank in the middle of the trail back to camp. It his happened more than once. True, the sun may be looking down at you out of the northwestern sky, and the little demons of panic may be hammering hard to be released from your brain to race through your veins. But it is a cinch that if you remain seated long enough the sun will go down, and you haven't seen anything in the papers about him giving up his regular setting place in the west sou'-west. In the meantime, as I said, you will probably spy some familiar object, or if not may realize that you can easily retrace your steps to the last unusual place or object you passed. And you are apt to tell yourself out loud what a chump you were for starting to get rattled.

What to Do.—If after a good rest you still are at sea, seek the nearest high point to secure an outlook. I've heard of a man lost for some hours in the cane who finally climbed a little basket-oak tree to which in his circling around he kept returning. And there within a few rods was his camp! Failing to see your way out, get busy making a comfortable camp and give any signals agreed upon. The proper signal to be given with a firearm when lost is one shot and then after a short pause (time enough to reload a shotgun) two shots in quick succession. This signal should be repeated at regular intervals, and is bound to attract attention if heard. It should also be used in case of accident. Smoke signals, if practicable, are best made with damp leaves or grass or rotten wood, put on a hot fire. The signals should be similar to those made with a gun, three separate columns of smoke or three big puffs from one fire, made by holding a blanket or a coat over the smudge and lifting it, meaning "I am lost," or, "There has been an accident" Three blasts on the horn should mean the same. If your companions in camp are properly posted and hear or see your signals they will reply by repeating your signal, after which a

single shot fired at regular intervals or a single, steady column of smoke will guide you to camp. You had better let them come and find you, and remember that a Scout does not mind ridicule.

Case of the caddis fly.

Prepare for the Worst.—To be seriously lost in wild country is a calamity to be met with the utmost fortitude and good sense. Calmness should govern one's every action, if possible. Opportunities to kill bird or beast for food should be taken advantage of, for you do not know how badly you may need food before you find your way out or are rescued. I have mentioned the carrying of fish-line and hooks, and rabbit wire. You should know how to find bait for your hooks. The big white grubs found in a rotten log or stump will generally attract fish if skilfully offered. Also the larva of the stone fly, both the larva and the pupa of the caddis fly, the larva of the dragon fly, and the helgramite, dobson, or clipper. The value of the angle worm you well know, but it is not apt to be found when wanted. The larvae of the stone fly are found under stones or sticks, hanging on for dear life. The "caddies" are found in their case, on the bottom of streams, on the gravel and on the sides of stones or under them. Trout eat them case and all, but it is best to pull the larva (grub) or pupa (worm) out and thread it on the hook. The larva of the dragon fly is found in swampy places and stagnant pond holes, sometimes under the surface, or, it may be, on the marsh vegetation above the water.

Larva (left) and pupa of the caddis fly.

Larva of the dragon fly.

The helgramite.

The helgramite is found by turning over stones in the shallows of the stream; be quick, and take him from behind, or he'll pinch your fingers. Snails, grasshoppers, and of course minnows and meadow frogs, are also good bait.

To snare rabbits, make your snare as shown in the illustration and set in a rabbit path or runway at night. Trim a small standing sapling (4), fasten a piece of the soft brass wire to the end, twist around a short trigger-stick (2), and make a noose (1). Cut a nearby sapling off, or drive a stake, and notch (3), hook the trigger-stick (2) in this notch, holding the sapling bent down. Fasten the noose erect in the split stick (5). A good way is to make a little lane of brush ending against a log or tree, place the loop or noose in this, and bait with some white-wood twigs or other food which rabbits like. Put one or two twigs in the lane, and the rest against the tree beyond the noose. You

How to make a lost man's rabbit snare.

may not approve of snaring rabbits, nor do I; but sportsmanship must step aside when a human life is at stake.

Save Your Resource.—Save your matches and your strength. If you are pretty sure you are only a short distance from the trail or from familiar ground, as you must be, the thing to do is to first of all make familiar the place where you are. Blaze a conspicuous tree on four sides, and write or bum any message you think of on these blazes. Don't use a cipher, as others besides your companions may have to search for you. Then start out with this for a central point and circle around it but don't lose it. There's no need to lose it; if you do you are too rattled to trust yourself to travel and should slop! Just camp right there and wait for help. If, however, you find you can trust yourself, make several circles, each one larger, going *very slowly*, stopping frequently to look

and listen, as if hunting a deer instead of your camp. Now you will remember why you should always notice particularly the unusual things and disregard the usual. For you will realize that an ordinary deer, with its protective coloration, is very hard to distinguish in the woods if standing perfectly still. How much easier to see a pure white one (there are such, called albinos), or even to see one running. But the ordinary rocks and trees are neutral, all seemingly just alike, and all most emphatically still. It is only the unusual things that can possibly mean anything to you, and the "sign" you are looking for is as hard to see as a deer standing still.

Failing to get on familiar ground by circling, and of course being uncertain as to your location, having found no familiar landmarks in sight from your lookout (if one was climbed), you had best camp and wait. However, if you are bound to make a try at getting somewhere you must set out to travel in a straight line. The place to use a compass is in camp, in a fog or a snowstorm, in a swamp or a cane-brake and nowhere else; but get out your compass.

We must not forget that for some utterly amazing reason the sun is in the northwest. If it were night and you could see the stars the Big Dipper would be off on a tear in the southeast, no doubt. Travelling by starline, except in open country, by the way, is feasible only in fiction. "All stars look alike" when you look at them through a canopy of thick treetops, even when the limbs are bare.

Travelling by the Compass.—Get out your compass (which you should never carry near knife or axe, or it will be demagnetized), set it down and let the needle "freeze." Twist it around so the north point is under the point of the needle—unless using a floating-dial compass, which is better—and take a good earnest look at what it tells you.

That compass is right. If you had two compasses, which is an excellent idea, you could prove it. Don't laugh; no less an old-timer than

Emerson Hough says a lost man needs two compasses. Remember that it always points north. (Don't quibble about the magnetic pole.) It always points north, whether the streams flow uphill and the sun has gone visiting, or not.

North, south, east or west, you are not sure which way to go. Perhaps you came southwest from camp, then turned west, then northwest; that might place you directly west of camp. But you think you have circled; in fact you have circled good and plenty. But it is a certainty that you are not east of camp, isn't it? That eliminates half of the question. Shall you head north, south or east, or in any intermediate direction? That is up to you. If you have any sense of direction now is the time to trot it out I am taking for granted that the lay of the land tells you nothing; that it is flat anyhow, and you don't believe there is a stream within a hundred miles— except the one from which you just got a drink, which of course doesn't count, being a little stranger. Woodsmen are apt to follow downstream when lost, but you wouldn't follow that stream for a million, because it goes in the wrong direction.

Remember your map-making instruction, and sight over your compass at some distant tree. Now go straight to that tree. If you have to detour, pick out a tree behind you for a mark before you start. Arriving at your tree, look back and locate the tree you left, turn your back squarely to it and, looking ahead in the same direction, pick out another tree and go to it. Keep this up; if going to a tree without any deviation you can pick out another in line beyond it as you approach it. Check up once in a while with your compass.

Making Detours.—A lake, marsh or bend in a river may interfere with you in travelling by the compass, making a long detour necessary. (Put away your compass as soon as landmarks appear.) Before starting around, pick out a landmark, preferably a prominent hill, or if there is none, then a conspicuous growth of trees, beyond lake, marsh or

river bend, in line with the direction you wish to go, and let that be your guide in getting back on your line. In going around you may have to cross ravines, circle bayous, goodness knows what. Perhaps you may not get back on your line; indeed, you may find your line would lead you in impossible places. Very well; just make the proper allowance and take up a new line that will cut into your original line at some certain point, bead your course for there, and then once more take up your original course. Hold to your determination to keep to that one direction and that one line until you "get somewhere," and you will do it. If you keep going in one direction and compensate properly for any deviations, you are bound to. When contours disappear, use the compass.

Remember that little streams run to big ones, and that big ones generally have names and appear on maps; also that lakes do not fall out of the sky over night, but generally have names and appear on maps too. Furthermore, that roads, trails or portages have a habit of going to rivers and lakes, at least in a lumber region. By circling your newly discovered lake—unless it be a young Superior—or by going up or down a large stream, you are pretty sure to come to one of these roads, if you haven't already come across an old "snake trail" leading to the site of the one-time skidway right alongside of one. If it is a "driving" stream down which the lumbermen have run logs in times past you will find their dim trails along its banks.

By this time you should know where you are, at least approximately. But it is by no means a time for taking anything for granted; if, for that matter, you ever should when alone in strange forest. Now, if ever, it is time for you to recall Daniel Boone's advice, "Be sure you are right and then go ahead." You have come in a straight line and left a message behind you. Also you have blazed your trail. Don't neglect every precaution just because you have found a strange tote road.

Strange Roads and Trails.—On a tote road, the corduroy logs in the low places or on the bridges will be worn the most on the aide away from the logging camp. On a logging road, just the reverse. A tote road is used for hauling supplies to the camp, consequently the wear of sleigh runners and wagon wheels comes on the side of the corduroy logs that is away from camp. The logging road is used for hauling logs to sawmill or roll way, away from the camp, so the corduroy is worn most on the side toward the camp. In country where there are game trails, they will be found to run together at an angle in the direction leading to water, for obvious reasons. In the South the cattle trails run together in the same way. Any trail in wild country that has been used by man is almost sure to have been blazed. An old blazed trail is very difficult to follow, particularly if the man who spotted it cut through the bark, as in that case the sap exudes and heals the wound. But in the case of a trail so deeply worn as to be discovered "on the ground" it can be followed without the aid of the blazes. All you need to find them for is to learn from them which way the trail leads, and what sort of man made them.

A trapper's line will lead you nowhere to your advantage. You will know it from its meanderings. A lumberman's line, if found, generally will be fresh or eke accompanied by a logging road; for cruisers are not addicted to spotting trails except as a guide for the loggers. Such a trail will lead away from tote road, lake, river or skidway, to the site of a prospective logging job. The blazes will be on the side of the trees away from where the timber is to be cut, or has been cut. Surveyor's lines invariably run straight; detours are made by right angles. They are spotted "fore and aft, "or each tree on both sides, two blares on an aide.

Sit Down!—To conclude this long dissertation on a subject which I have said can be dismissed by two words, I will say that in looking through Mr. Kephart's book I find he gives credit to those same two words for getting him out of his difficulty the first time he was lost. And it is a pleasure to know he got them from my old friend S. D. Barnes, of Arkansas; who he would have found, by the way, had be taken the trouble to look, has quite a conspicuous bump of locality on his manly brow. I am happy to have such illustrious accompaniment:

SIT DOWN! That is what to do if you get lost

Forest Fires.—Other emergencies may arise, as the result of fire, storm or flood. Here the order of the day is very different. In the case of a bad bush fire, the last safe-guard attempted is back-firing, or building a fire in advance of the oncoming forest fire, to burn a strip of intervening forest across which it is hoped the real conflagration will not jump. In most cases a camping party has ample warning of the approach of a fire to make their escape; it is those who remain to fight the flames that take the risk. Nowadays the forests are so valuable that no bad forest fire breaks oat, either in this country or in Canada, without there being a force of fire wardens, forest rangers, or even soldiers, quickly on the scene to fight it. And of course they will have charge. Inasmuch as this is the case, and there are serious penalties for starting a fire, Boy Scouts should hesitate to start a back-fire. It is their place to first get to a place of safety and report the fire if it starts near them; then to join in the fight if wanted.

Needless to say, it is *criminal carelessness* to permit camp-fire to set fire to the forest, and no camp-fire or cooking fire should ever be left behind to burn itself out. Douse your fire thoroughly, and then take a pole chopped to the form of a paddle and dig the ground up where the fire has been, and

Tree blazes. Left, trail from camp: center, trail turns right: right, trail to camp.

drench this. A camp-fire may burn down deep in the duff of the forest floor and smolder for days, to eventually bunt into flame and start a disastrous conflagration.

Sand or dirt thrown on a surface fire will do much toward extinguishing it. And of course every Scout knows how to beat out a fire with evergreen branches. A back-fire must always be started to the windward of a stream, a road, or a long strip raked clean of dry leaves and trash and spread with fresh earth or sand. This strip needs to be long enough to stop the approaching fire, and the ends must be watched or the back-fire may execute a flank movement. It is in the dense forests where there is considerable down timber and thick ground cover that fires are bad. I have known such a fire, fanned by a fairly high wind, to not only bum nearly every tree in its path, and the duff right down to the underlying sandy soil, but to set fire to farm buildings half a mile away. It is astounding to see the large pieces of burning bark and other debris that will rise from such a fire and borne on the heated air sail long distances, and start new fires. I will never forget the fire which started one August Sunday, in a timberland near our home, showered us all afternoon with burning brands, which we only prevented from burning us out by the hardest kind of effort Barns were burned on both sides of us, with horses and cattle, and one man. It was caused by carelessness on the part of a man who had been burning brush. Again, I have seen a bad forest fire caused by a careless smoker throwing away a burning match.

What to do if cornered by fire? Hunt a hole or get out on the water. Under an overhanging bank of a stream is a good place. You may even have time to do some tunneling. But if you do, 'ware cave-ins. If exposed, thank your stars if you are wearing woolen clothing, and if you can manage to, get well drenched before the fire comes. Keep down. Heat rises, and so docs smoke. Get where there are not so many trees. Perhaps you can work around to windward. Don't underestimate the danger. A very insipid little fire can burn you to death or suffocate you.

Wind Storms.—I have never been mixed up at dose hand with a bad windstorm, my nearest approach being an experience in the woods in southern Illinois not far from St Louis, the evening the cyclone devastated that city. A couple of trees came down around us, where my brother and I were camped in our wagon, and there were a few branches blown about, but I do not recall that we thought much of it at the time, except that it was a wild storm. There really is not much to be done in the case of a windstorm, because if bad, it is pretty apt to take matters in its own charge. It is wise precaution never to pitch your tent under large trees that may fall on it if blown down. A dead tree is especially to be avoided. Watch out sharply for falling limbs. When deer hunting in the Adirondacks once, a companion camped us in a deserted lumber shanty close under a leaning dead tree. I was afraid of it, and he confessed it was not a very reassuring situation, and so at the expense of some effort, for we had a couple of doer to carry, we moved to another shanty. A couple of weeks afterward we were told by letter by the lumber boss that the leaning stub had smashed in the shanty roof "and busted the stove."

Floods.—Floods not infrequently take toll of inexperienced or careless campers who make their camp in some narrow valley close to a stream. A cloudburst comes, or a dam bursts, upstream, usually in the middle of the night, it seems, and—you know the rest. Keep up out of reach. A gorge is no place to camp anyhow; nor is a low island or bottom land close to any stream that can possibly flood you out If you have ever seen a bad flood you won't hanker for the adventure either. Aside from being chased up on a levee by Father Mississippi one spring morning with my tent bearing a neat, brown high-water mark, I have nothing to record in the way of experience. But I have seen plenty of evidence of what a cloudburst will do, and reiterate, camp high!

As a Scout you are prepared for accidents, having had or being in position to receive special instruction in first aid and life saving. Your Official Manual gives you good directions, and unless you are a lone Scout or a member of a patrol with no Scout Master, these instructions have been or will be supplemented by others by men competent to teach you. Personally, I think the methods of breaking "death grips" taught the Y. M. C. A. members by George H. Corsan, are very good indeed, as is also his system of teaching the crawl stroke, and I advise you not to miss a chance to become acquainted with them.

Coolness and good common sense will stand you in good stead in any emergency. You must depend upon your own judgment, largely, except in rendering first aid, when technical principles must rule. Take account of your capabilities and limitations, do your best, but do not attempt the foolhardy.

Observation

From *The Boy Scout's Hike Book,* by Edward Cave, 1920

The "eagle eyes" of Indians, old-time scouts, woodsmen, plainsmen, mountain men, have been celebrated time without end. One might think, if inversely one did not think, that these men were born with telescopic eyes. On the other hand, Mr. Kephart might tell us they were not born with better eyes than common, that they merely cultivated their wonderful eyesight, through uncommon interest in things difficult to see. For my part, I think they had mighty good eyes to begin with, and trained them well.

The Eyes of Old-Time Scouts.—The only old-time scouts whose eyes I have noticed particularly have been Captain Wm. F. Drannan, who was chief of scouts under General Crook when, as he told me, "Buffalo Bill,—not the original Buffalo Bill,* but Cody—was a boy," and Captain Jack Crawford. I would say the eyes of both were especially interesting, and easily enough suggestive of the intense eyes of an eagle or a hawk, particularly those of Captain Drannan. I have often noticed that the eyes of noted hunters—and by that I mean hunters who are their own guides—especially those who have spent much time in "big" country and been accustomed to long vistas, have a distinctly different quality or expression from those of other men. It is a different expression from that of the expert long-range military rifle shot, too, if my observation amounts to anything. But I would not attempt to tell

Seen and unseen. He whistled to attract their attention.

by looking at the eyes of different boys which could see the sharpest. For even the eyes of an Indian boy among them would not have developed the hawk-like intenseness that in later years would mark him as keen sighted. In short, extra good scouting eyesight is largely acquired, but the fellow who develops it to the highest degree is the one who had extra good eyes to begin with.

Seeing "By Deduction."—For the same reason that you should pay attention to the unusual things to avoid losing your way in a strange country, you should look for the unusual things to develop your eyesight. A woodsman or a plainsman often in fact "sees by deduction." To illustrate, if he sees something unusual and cannot make it out, his brain instantly sets to work to help, and perhaps he shortly sees very clearly what the thing is. You can prove this to your satisfaction easily enough. It gives you a peculiar feeling to see what has been but a vague blur take form when the brain turns on a little more eye-strength.

One afternoon, while hunting wild turkeys in southern Missouri, I was sitting very still with my

*Hon. Wm. Mathewson, still living, at Wichita, Kansas.

back to a tree when I heard a slight noise behind me on my right, as of something walking in the dry leaves. Craning my neck ever so slowly, I got a glimpse of a movement just over the bulge of the ridge, at the base of a tree, about fifty feet away. It was close to dusk, and I had reason to believe what I had seen was the back of a turkey. With straining eyes and aching neck I watched the place intently for some minutes, not daring to move, as, if it was a turkey I was in a bad position to get a shot if it took alarm. There was another movement, just a fleeting glimpse of something dark, and another rustle of leaves. It was very like the action of a turkey scratching for acorns. I kept on looking out of the tail of my right eye, and my! How my neck did ache. More movements. But by this time I was pretty sure it was not a turkey, because a turkey would certainly have stopped feeding to raise its head to reconnoiter. And as it turned out it was not, but a very different "bird" with four feet, a couple of white stripes on its back and a bad (smelling) reputation. Rest assured I didn't disturb him at his grubbing.

Practice for the Eyes.—Similarly, a Scout who is awake will know many things he sees but imperfectly. And all the time his eyesight will be growing more keen from the practice. It is concentration that docs it; concentration upon the unusual, the out-of-place. Movement, naturally, will attract his attention the most quickly. At first this will have to be pronounced, but in time a very slight movement will be noticed.

It is excellent practice and good fun to find a comfortable scat, keep perfectly still and watch. At first nothing will seem to be stirring. That is because you have been about Wait and by and by the Hidden Things about you will resume their activities. You may be surprised to suddenly perceive you have company that you never suspected to be in the neighborhood. Keep still. They will all lie low or silently slip away unseen if you do not. It is fun to play at being a stump, and you will be surprised to

find that the wild creatures' eyes are not nearly so good as you supposed. You will find that very few of them will discover you with their eyes if you do not move. Some may scent you, but otherwise you will be pretty well hidden if you sit down almost anywhere. Deer are not sharp-sighted, but when it comes to smelling! To "hide" yourself without concealment, select a background similar in color to your clothing. This will not be difficult if you are wearing your uniform. Colored hatband, tie or neck kerchief should be removed. And remember that to be still means just that and nothing less.

Playing Stump.—Once while sitting still by a trout stream, I had an amusing adventure with a mink. For some time I could see him loping about in the shallows, in his nervous and seemingly aimless way. I did not expect he would come near me, but finally he vanished, to reappear on the driftwood pile upon which I was sitting, wet and sleek and vicious looking, almost within my reach. He sat up and looked right at me, seeming not sure whether he was looking at a man or had been eating too much fish. I said "Hello! Brother Mink," and he gave such a jump that be actually fell into the brook. Had I tried to stalk him, when I first saw him, be surely would have noticed the first movement I made and slipped away.

Hunters and nature students quite naturally get to be good observers, and see very many interesting things in nature besides what they see of the animal life. But a Boy Scout can see more in a given locality, if he sets himself to doing his best, because he is interested in everything. A sink in a limestone ridge, a red sky in the east at sunset, a wolf track in a washout, a pebble turned damp side up—he notices all sorts of things, usual and unusual, because so many things tell him so much, in the fascinating game of "reading sign."

Studying Tracks.—Learn to distinguish the tracks of whatever wild animals there may be in the section where you make your hikes, and to read sign for yourself. Putting two and two together will explain many problems. If not blessed with the

Tame tracks.

opportunity to study tracks of large game, which you most likely will not be, turn your attention to what you have, even field mice, chipmunks, and the like. And do not despise the practice to be had from tracking domestic animals and people. Some of the best and most important trailing ever done has been that of following the tracks of horses and men. And, by the way, do not be led by the drawings in your Scout manual to believe that the hind feet of a horse are larger than his front ones. Any blacksmith will prove to you that this is not true of the average horse. The front ones are the larger; or at least they make the larger track. The hind track is longer, but narrower.

Dry tracking is naturally the most difficult. If you can follow a dry trail in the woods or fields you are a wonder. Get out early, before the dew or the frost is off the grass; your chances are much better then. Grass trailing is easy if the grass is high or wet with dew. The grass will be found to be bent in the direction the trail runs, if following a newly made trail. A runway, as of deer or other animals, will of course require closer scrutiny, and if animals have passed and repassed on it during the night, may

puzzle you well. As your chief object and practically your only hope will be to learn what animal or animals have passed, hunt a damp or wet place and figure it out. In the case of hoofed animals the tracks of the males may be said to be generally less pointed than those of the females, to spread wider, and to "stagger" more.

On wet ground you will easily recognize the difference between the fresh walking, trotting and running tracks of any heavy animal, not alone by the manner in which they are placed, but by the amount of impress made. If it is not raining but the ground is wet, absence of water in deep hoof tracks is sure indication that they have been but recently made. Droppings are known to be fresh, of course, if warm.

Bird Tracks.—Of the birds, the ground runners—the quail and grouse of different species and the wild turkey—largely non-migratory, will be about the only ones whose tracks will interest you, and then only in the snow. The quail never hops like a robin or other upland birds of its class, and its dainty tracks will be easily known, being about the size of those of a pigeon. Scatter feed in likely places in severe weather, and provide shelters of brush or cornshocks. The quail are getting pitifully scarce, and we have no better bird. The ruffed grouse will not take feed so provided, except mast (acorns and beech-nuts), and winter-green; it is useless to provide them grain. The track is sure to be recognized by a Scout living where these birds are to

Tracks unmistakably wild. The deer was walking; when it came to the bear's track it got the bear's scent, and went away "on the jump."

An example of bad judgment in selecting a camp-site.

be found. The same may be said of the blue grouse, age hen, sharp-tail grouse, and the prairie chicken. Of the two latter, the sharp-tail, has feathered legs and feet, while the prairie hen has not.

Hearing Things.—Hearing plays a part in observation that is of more importance than you might think. An experienced duck hunter can tell the species of a flock of ducks almost as far as he can see them, by their flight; but it takes a past master to know them at night by the sound of their wings, and maybe a murmuring call or two floating down out of the black mystery of the sky. And that reminds me that night is the time of times to hear things worthwhile in the wilds. The "voices of the night" will give you many a thrill. Have you ever beard a toad ay when caught by a snake? Do you know the squall of a 'coon, the bark of a fox, the hunting caterwaul of a lynx, the whistle of a deer? Have you ever heard a cat bird *sing*—not mew, but sing, at night, in a way most entrancing to hear, surpassing by far the best efforts of the celebrated hermit thrush? Do you know the meaning of the stealthy movements you hear? Can you hear a porcupine gnawing a hemlock top—or if you hear it at all do you pass over it merely as "some noise?" Have you heard the gray wolves' saturnalia, or the alligators' "fight bellow"? Does the distant barking of a farm dog or the neigh of a horse tell you anything in particular? Or are you like the man of whom the poet said:

"A primrose by a river's brim
A yellow primrose is to him."

To come right to the point, observation in its highest sense means the harmonious exercise of all the faculties keyed up to concert pitch. It means to be awake in every fiber to the challenge which Nature gives us, and know what is going on about us. To know by sight, sound, and scent all we can, and then some; which latter may apply to anything, from discrimination in choosing a campsite to prognosticating a mild winter. And it is decidedly worthwhile; in my opinion the really big feature of what we call "scouting."

A Trek Cart.—The matter of a trek cart is one not to put aside without serious consideration. If you are blessed with good roads, do not live in the heart of a big city, and the suburban trolley means little or nothing to you, and particularly if you are not up to carrying a twenty-pound pack, you had better get interested in making a cart—unless your troop or patrol already have one. Troop No. x in Port Chester, N. Y., near neighbors of ours, have one which they made that I think is an excellent model. The illustrations accompanying this chapter will give you a good idea of what it is like. Their Scout Master, Mr. A. G. Clark, tells me they use it mostly for overnight hikes and are able to pile into it all the equipment one of their patrols have use for. The body is of cypress, 6 feet 3 inches long by 30 inches wide, has an oak spreader with iron braces at each end, on the bottom, and rests cm an oak bed-piece mounted on a steel axle. The wheels are of hickory, and of course were bought "ready-made," the bows are hickory and were obtained from a delivery wagon that had passed its stage of usefulness. The pole is attached with a bolt hinge, and in camp serves both as a prop for the cart and as the bottom section of a jointed flagstaff. The canvas is waterproofed, and lettered in dark green (well done, by a Scout) and the cart is painted olive drab.

The port chester trek cart.

Traction is by ropes tied to the front spreader.

Detail view of the trek cart.

The tread of this cart is too narrow for use on any but the[1] best roads, such as we have in this section, and I recommend the standard 56-inch tread, or 60 inches if in the South; Even if the highways are generally good, you will need the standard tread as soon as you come to a back lane or woods road—unless such lane or road has been used only by sleighs, when wheeling will likely enough be out of the question anyhow.

Such a cart will transport grub, tents, and folding cots, and prove a blessing to small Scouts.

The Horseback Outfit—Horseback? You can't beat It Best of course, if you are going to browse along and "eat off the country" rather than herd a pack animal or two, because you can travel if your horse is your ship. Having your horse, you doubtless have your saddle. If not, let me recommend the McClellan. I know that if you live in some parts of the West you will follow your own inclinations and get a swell-fork stock saddle. If your pony or horse is well set up, well and good, for you doubtless are not much of a load for him. But you don't need that horn, nor the weight. A stock saddle is made for work, the heaviest kind of it. Why go buggy riding in a lumber wagon? The cavalry saddle will carry you and your outfit, and it will save your mount. You may not be able to snake wood with it, and you may feel more secure wedged in between the high cantle and the swelled fork of the Mexican saddle, but I still think the light, cool McClellan will better suit your horse.

The same tent, stretcher, and blanket will serve, and everything else except the pack-sack and the heavy-soled shoes. Add a pommel slicker. And to

your horse outfit (having saddle, saddle blanket, halter, and bridle), add 30 feet of strong, tight, ¾-inch hemp rope (for picket), a 4-foot section of hobble rope (unwound from heavy rope), 8 belt-lacing thongs, or whangs, grain-bag for oats, and a curry-comb.

Your tent and slicker will serve in lieu of saddle-bags. Roll stretcher-tick and extra clothing in the slicker, and tie across the pommel; tie the ends down with whangs. Make a yard-long roll of blanket, grub and utensils, all in the tent- cloth, and big around as a stovepipe; sling behind the cantle, strap, and tie the ends down to the spider-straps with whangs. When you carry oats (you can buy them almost anywhere in the country, so will not need to carry them far), divide them equally in the bag, which tie in the middle with a whang, throw the bag across the pommel and tie. Oats will not be needed if the grazing is good, of course; but don't forget your horse. Four quarts a day is about right.

Break your horse or pony to picket by the pastern of one of his front feet. Instead of by the halter, as he will be much less likely to throw himself. Use the bowline knot, and wrap the loop around the pastern well with a neat strip of some strong woolen cloth, in lieu of a bobble cuff. If the horse has never been picketed before, protect the pasterns of his hind feet with burlap, so if he does become entangled with the picket rope he will not burn himself, at least not seriously, in his struggles before you can quiet him. The reason for picketing him by a fore pastern instead of by the head is that the picket rope then is always on the ground, and much less likely to catch his hind feet. Of course a horse cannot be picketed in brush or among trees, rocks or stumps, and hobbling becomes necessary. Do not tic him short to stand all night as at a hitching post, or he will become stiff. Besides, he must feed. Take the soft unwound hobble rope and with it tie his forelegs together above the fetlocks, 10 inches apart and no more, as follows:

Pass the rope around one leg and bring the ends together, cross and twist tight for 10 inches; pass the ends in opposite directions around the other leg, and push them through the twisted strands as in making a splice. Turn him loose and watch the rascal hop. Put the bell on him if in the woods, and be sure the pasture is good, or you may find be has hopped some miles toward home when you turn out in the morning.

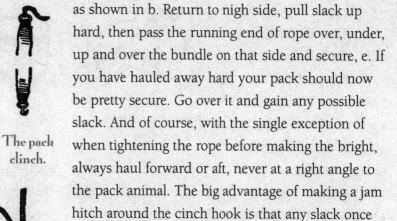

The pack clinch.

How the jam hitch is made.

Pack-Horse Transportation.— There is nothing intricate about the "diamond hitch" that you so often see mentioned as being "mysterious." The various diamond hitches and others are simple enough. But you do have to use judgment in throwing any hitch, as you will easily understand when I explain some of them, or as you fully realize if you do know the art. Yes, packing is an art; an art for the handy rather than the brainy.

The Cross-Tree Hitch.—Attach the hitch-rope to the ring of the pack-cinch, and throw the cinch across the top of the pack and let hang down to ground. Reach under and catch the cinch, bring up and engage hook, using the jam hitch, as shown. Cinch up by pulling down on the standing rope and taking up the slack by pulling up the running, or loose, end. If not using the jam hitch you would simply pull upon the running end and would have to hold the slack gained. Make a bight with the running end and pass under the standing rope. Go around to the off side of the animal, enlarge the bight, reverse it and loop over and under your pack

as shown in b. Return to nigh side, pull slack up hard, then pass the running end of rope over, under, up and over the bundle on that side and secure, e. If you have hauled away hard your pack should now be pretty secure. Go over it and gain any possible slack. And of course, with the single exception of when tightening the rope before making the bright, always haul forward or aft, never at a right angle to the pack animal. The big advantage of making a jam hitch around the cinch hook is that any slack once gained never gets away from you. Two can pack better than one.

The Single Diamond Hitch.—The single diamond hitch is started in exactly the same manner as the cross-tree hitch. When you come to making the bight, make it small, and take two turns around the standing rope with it. Go around to the off side and carry the running rope to the rear, under the pack, forward, and pull snug but not taut; carry up, over, and down through the bight to the position shown at *b*. Now return to the nigh side, and haul away forward, throwing your weight on the rope and bracing your foot against the pack. Carry the running rope under the pack and to the rear, bring up over and pass under the standing rope around which the bight was wrapped, in the opening of the bight. Haul away to the rear, and make fast. Tighten up all around if any slack can be gained; if properly handled in the first place, of course, not any can. You will now observe your bight and the standing rope around which it is wrapped form a diamond. It is this diamond which automatically takes or gives in all directions, so maintaining a uniform degree of

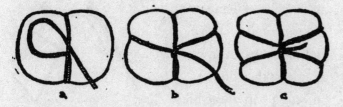

The cross-tree hitch, top view of the pack. Running rope not tied at c.

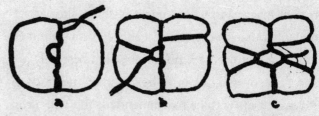

The single diamond hitch, top view; running rope not tied at c.

tightness on all four sides of the pack, that has made this hitch famous.

Only practice, and lots of it, will make you a good packer. There are great many things to learn, not the least of

How the single diamond hitch secures the pack on a horse.

which is how to keep your pack animal from getting a sore back. To get the hang of these hitches, it is by no means necessary to have a pack animal and an outfit, as described. You can make a pack of your blanket and with your tent rope for both hitch rope and cinch (a bowline knot for the cinch-hook) can pack it on anything that will furnish a suitable back.

Canoe Cruising.—Canoe cruising is not exactly hiking. Still, not a few boys who read this book will wish to make scouting trips in canoes or rowboats. And for my part, I know of no pleasanter way to make a trip than in a canoe. You can be so comfortable, the going is so smooth, and generally so interesting. Carries are sometimes difficult, but there are such things as fair winds and favoring currents to make up. Dangerous? When I used to canoe on the Hudson River I had an all-cedar decked cruiser that I could sit in and paddle when it was completely swamped. As for swamping it, I had to do that by main force, for the little boat was as steady as a church and rode everything in the way of a wave the Hudson had, as sedately as a black duck. I used to put much of my kit and duffle in the watertight compartments fore and aft, and as the hatches were small this entailed small packages. Lately I have owned an open canvas covered paddler, and had more leeway as to what I might wish to take with me. Of course, every canoeist should be a swimmer.

For a cruise with no carries, or at best only a short one or two, the grub-box used by the Hudson River cruisers is to be recommended. You will have to make yours if you want one, as they are not on the market. An accompanying illustration shows

Some canoe cruising adjuncts to the hiker's kit.

fairly well what it is like. The legs are detachable, the lid props up, and with an extra board carried for the purpose laid in its place, becomes a good table. Instead of in one of these I carried my grub in a round tin flour-can. My blue-flame kerosene stove went in another, together with a flask of alcohol for priming. These stoves were used because of the scarcity of firewood, not because they were by any means a joy forever. If you ever use one, build a wind-shield for it, if you expect to cook anything with it when the wind blows. A cylinder of tin or sheet brass, just the right height, to slip on it around the burner and inside the supporting arms of the grate, is a good thing.

You can carry a good big tent in a canoe, and I do not know of a better all-around design than the so-called canoe tent. It is similar to the tarpaulin tent described in an earlier chapter, but has a wall at the back. If you are using an open canoe and are husky enough to wrestle it, learn how to carry it on the paddles, Indian fashion.

Pioneering.—Building bridges or rafts, and other so-called pioneering activities, will be among the most interesting of the big things to be tackled on your hikes. All necessarily will have to be of a nature to be quickly gotten out of the way; for the hiker makes a flying camp and is up and away. The plodding jobs must wait; or at least they do not become a part of the hike. For a 20-foot bridge that can be built in an hour

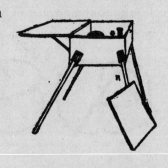

Canoeists' combination grub-box and table.

by a couple of patrols who are handy, I think that
originated by Troop No. I of Port Chester,

N.Y., is a very good example. Its construction
will readily be understood from the accompanying
illustrations. I have seen this bridge built, with poles
that were already cut, in an incredibly short time;
but no trestles had to be erected. Different forms of
trestles will appeal to different Scouts. The design
which I suggest is a good .strong one, though perhaps
taking longer to make than some others. These
trestles are not used by the Port Chester Scouts.

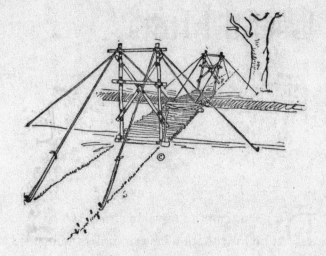

Fig. 1.   A scouts' suspension bridge.

Useful Hints

From *The Boy Scout's Hike Book*, by Edward Cave, 1920

Do not attempt to travel in strange woods at night without a lantern, unless compelled to, and then only if on a road. On the plains or the prairie, far from any light or mountain spur to guide you, you will be as badly off unless the stars are out; darkness obliterates all the contours and, as the saying is, "everything looks the same."

If wearing a hat, take it off to listen. Or if you must keep it on, pin the brim up at the sides or fold it in on your bead. The brim causes a current of air past your ears that may interfere with hearing a very faint sound.

In the springtime, after the fall and winter rains, is an excellent time to look for Indian arrow- and lance-heads. Erosion, the enemy of agriculture, is the friend of the relic hunter.

If you get drenched by a shower and are too far from camp or other headquarters, take off all your clothes, wring them out and dress again, and you'll be the better off for it.

Before diving in deep water for the purpose of search, spend *several minutes* breathing deeply and forcibly, to produce the effect upon your lungs that will enable you to stay under water much longer than you normally could. If you begin to feel dizzy from this deep breathing you will know your lungs are sufficiently overcharged.

If fly-fishing for trout early in the spring, when they do not take flies readily, try the midge flies, which are tied on the smallest hooks, Nos. 12 and 14. The standard size hook for trout is No. 8.

A red sky in the morning is a sign of bad weather or a big wind; gray sky, fine weather. At sunset, a pale yellow sky promises rain or snow, a bright yellow, wind. When the outlines and colors of the clouds are soft, look for fair weather, but if the cloud forms are dearly outlined and their colors gaudy, watch for rain, and perhaps strong wind. When you take a last look at the sky at night before turning in, if you see high upper clouds moving in a different direction from the lower clouds, expect the wind to change. If no lower clouds are seen, note the direction of the wind; if blowing in a different direction from that in which the clouds are drifting, it will change.

Waterproof match-boxes of hard rubber and having a screw top are to be purchased in the best sporting goods stores, but are rather high priced, if you consider only the material in them. But the service they render makes up for this. Before getting one of these I used a couple of brass shotgun shells, 10 and 12 gauge respectively, the latter telescoped in the former. In fact I still use them some of the time, for old sake's sake. If you haven't such a match-box I have been told you can waterproof your matches by dipping them in shellac and spreading them to dry. You would need a rough surface to ignite a match so waterproofed, but could carry them anywhere and need not worry about them. I have not tried this trick with shellac. With liquid glue the matches

A hitler's cellar.

would not burn. Perhaps I did not allow them to dry sufficiently before trying them.

A folding pocket camera case makes an excellent receptacle for carrying notebook, map, sketching pad, pencils, drinking cup, etc. Leave the strap off, cut two slits in the back near the top, and slip it on the belt. Secondhand cases are sometimes to be had cheap in camera stores. I have carried one when my pack was crowded.

Use wood ashes and a damp cloth to scour your cooking utensils. Sand is not nearly so good and scratches your tinware.

Get aluminum instead of re-tinned steel cooking utensils if you can. But do not have an aluminum cup or teaspoon, as the aluminum alloy is such a good heat conductor that you will be forever burning your mouth.

The best head-net to ward off mosquitoes and black flies, which are often a great nuisance in the woods, is made of Brussels silk veiling (net) of fine mesh. This material is strong, and this is necessary, as there is plenty of opportunity to tear it going through the woods. The best color is black. Make the diameter of the net sufficient to go over your hat, and have it long enough to tie with a draw-string under the collar of your shirt. A stiff hat brim is necessary to keep the net away from your face and neck, or the pests will get to you, sure.

Even with a good head-net as above described, you will need a good mosquito dope. That prescribed by Nessmuk in his little classic, "Woodcraft," is a good one, and is made as follows: Take 3 oz. pine tar, 2 oz. castor or olive oil (I prefer the latter, on account of its less offensive odor), and 1 oz. pennyroyal, simmer together over a slow fire, and bottle for use. A good trick I learned from Doctor Breck is to carry your pocket supply in a bicycle oil-can. Rub the stuff (for stuff it is, and no mistake) on wrists, hands, face, neck and ears— don't forget the ears, and behind them. And leave it on, so you get a good mahogany colored enamel finish. The amount given will be enough for a patrol of eight Scouts for a week if you are wise and neglect to wash. Dirty? No, clean. The dope is clean, and no dirt can get through it if you put enough on. What do you need the dope for if you are wearing a head-net? Why, for protection when you take the net off, as you will, not only to eat your meals but to get relief from wearing it. You cannot mop the perspiration off your face when wearing a veil, and you will want to. And here another difficulty arises—dope vs. handkerchief! Use a big blue bandana that you do not object to getting stained. A head-net which Doctor Breck gave me was half Brussels silk net and half (the back half) ordinary black bobbinet of the best quality. The Brussels net (his idea, I believe) was intact when the cotton stuff was picked full of holes by the brush. Here is a good tip: Don't make your net larger than the diameter of your hat brim.

To get dry wood when everything, apparently, is soaking wet, find a sound stump or log, or even a partly rotten one, and chop into it; you'll be pretty sure to find dry wood inside. Standing dead wood, of course, is best.

The ordinary Scout axe will stand a lot of service if properly handled. However, some Scouts may wish for something better, and for their benefit I will say that the reward is worth the hunt. The best axe I have been able to get is a tomahawk, shaped somewhat like the famous Hudson's Bay Company axe. It was made by a concern in El Dorado, Penn., and cost a dollar for the head alone. The advice of

The scout's auger. Size ¼ inch detachable handle. Indispensable for pioneering.

any woodsman will be to have the best axe you can get, "hang" it properly, and take elaborate care of it. The proper way to carry a belt axe, by the way, is with the edge to the rear, and as the most convenient place is behind the left hip (for a right-handed person) all manufactured axe-sheaths or muzzles are wrongly made.

The best cure I have found for ivy poisoning is made by boiling a dime's worth of cardamom seeds (capsules with seeds in them) in a pint of water (for a bad case) and applying the "tea" thus mode as a lotion when cold. I have been poisoned quite a number of times, once severely, when a boy, and have tried numerous remedies. The more frequent the application the quicker the remedy. A friend of mine was quail hunting in Kentucky and got poisoned with poison sumac, used this remedy and found it good. Poison ivy is known from Virginia creeper by the fact that its leaves are in dusters of three, while those of the harmless and beautiful creeper are in fives. Poison-sumac is identified by its white berries; otherwise it looks much like other sumacs and colors beautifully in the fall.

Be careful of stepping on loose stones, especially on a hillside. A round one may roll under you some day and stand you on the back of your neck, as one did to me.

Leather straps, such as skate straps, pack-sack straps, belts and axe sheaths, should be oiled occasionally with neat's foot-oil to prevent dry-rot. I did not realize the importance of this until a good gun-case was beyond saving; now I have a wide-mouth brown bottle of the oil always at hand. Apply to suitcases, handbags, thermos bottle cases or anything leather of value. For that matter, it is a shame to allow even a little strap to be ruined by neglect.

The standard rope used for lariats is cable-laid (twisted, not braided) manila, ⅜-inch in diameter, stretched to eliminate tendency to kink. Make an eye splice at one end, preferably around a brass hondo

but not necessarily. Finish the other end with the Matthew Walker knot.

Pine pitch will help you in getting a stubborn fire to burn.

Common mud is good for bee-sting, but tincture of Iodine k better. The latter is good for any insect bite; and in fact I consider it the best germicide for a Scout to carry. The Japanese soldiers carried it in crystal form in their last war, but the crystals dissolve very slowly.

Take a yard of "rapid flow" rubber tubing, to be obtained in drugstores, and either an empty "bottle-neck" rifle shell or the brass screw-socket of a gas tip, and you can make a good flexible blow-pipe with which fire making under difficulties will be made easier. Flatten the base or large end of the brass cylinder (if a shell, first cut the base of!) so the opening is less than 1/32 inch by about 5/3 inch. Insert other end in the tube. And there you are. Stewart Edward White mentions using such an instrument, but larger, given him by a Mr. Robert Logan, who called it an "inspirator." It certainly "inspires" a fire to bum. Hold the nozzle well down under your fire and blow steadily and strongly in the other end of the tubing. I have had one of these blow-pipes ever since Mr. White first described his, and often make good use of it, though I carry it only when there is prospect of having to bum wet wood.

The horse that loves sugar is easiest caught.

Punch a jagged hole in the side of a tin can, large enough to push a candle through. Insert a short piece of candle and light it. Set

Flexible blow pipe.

with the bottom of the can to windward, and you will have a well reflected light that will not blow out. To carry it, rig a wire bail fore and aft.

To mount a horse that may be "bad," stand at his left shoulder, facing backward, pull his bead around toward that shoulder by the cheek-strap of the bridle or by taking a short hold of the rein on that side, turn the stirrup around toward you and insert the foot (left, of course), grasp the horn or pommel of the saddle with the *right* hand, and swing on. If the horse does not start forward you will find it awkward; practice it anyhow. If he does jump forward or to one side, you will land in the saddle. Learn to vault on and you will not be bothered by a horse that won't "stand."

An opened umbrella makes a fair substitute for a canoe sail with which to take advantage of a fair wind.

Kneel on the bottom of a canoe in rough water.

The hour hand of a watch makes two circuits of the dial while the sun goes once around the earth; therefore, while the hand of the watch travels 90 decrees of its circle, say from 9 to 12, the sun covers only 45 degrees. That is why if you point the hour hand of your watch at the sun, the point midway between it and the figure 12 is south; providing, of course, that is it not exactly 12 o'clock, or close to it. South of the Equator the sun is due *north* at noon; one would have to point the figure 12 on the watch dial at the sun, and then the point on the dial midway between the hour hand and the figure 12 would be north.

A hot stone makes a good substitute for a hot-water bottle, which is something one does not carry on hikes. Scouts who eat unwisely may be glad to know this trick some night when they get a touch of abdominal cramp. Or fill a canteen with hot water.

The infantry soldier's old-fashioned entrenching tool, which can be had for 65 cents from dealers in condemned military supplies, is a very handy tool for Boy Scouts. You can both dig and chop with it and it hangs on the belt in a strong scabbard. I have had one for a long time, and made a lot of use of it

The sanitary precautions of the fixed camp should apply on the hike as well. A latrine need not be dug, but waste matter of any kind should

The scout's "digger".

be decently buried. Use the Scout's "digger" just described.

A carborundum instrument hone is the best all-around knife sharpener you can get hold of. Good for the axe, too. The best way to keep an axe sharp is to be mighty careful not to dull it.

A flannel sweat-band for the hat instead of the conventional one of imitation leather, is considered preferable by some old hikers. Until you get used to it, however, it is apt to be disagreeably itchy to the forehead.

No matter what virtues may be ascribed to it in "cowboy" stories, which are seldom written by persons who really know anything about cowboys, a hair rope, or rope made of horse-hair, is, or rather was, never used as a lariat. It is too light and flimsy. It has, or had, a certain reputation for keeping rattlesnakes away from a man sleeping on the ground, if laid in a single coil around his position, but in fact its value for this is about the same as the practice of carrying a hone chestnut to keep away rheumatism.

A candle may come in handy in kindling a fire some rainy day. It will provide a constant flame that will make an impression where a match would fail. The camper's folding candle lantern, by the way, is a blessing.

The best maps are to be obtained from the Director of the U. S. Geological Survey, Washington, D. C. Write asking for a "key" map of the state or states you are interested in. This will cost you nothing, and from it you will select the maps you want, ordering them by the names as given on the key map. They will cost you 5 or 6 cents each, *in coin*. Unfortunately, the map you want generally is not yet made.

Take a 5 ½-foot section of the tip of an ordinary 15-cent bamboo fishing pole, and with some stiff copper wire and some waxed thread you can make an excellent bait-casting rod. Copy after some "regular" bait-casting rod, or if you cannot do this, get a fishing tackle catalogue and copy from an illustration. Make the guides and the "top" (for the line) of the wire, whipped on with the waxed thread. Fasten

The soldier's flying-pan. Can be bought second-hand for fifteen cents.

the reel securely on the rod with strong soft copper or brass wire. Wind the butt with cord to make a large enough hand grasp. This is a freshwater bass, pickerel or wall-eyed pike rod.

To open a water blister, sterilize a needle, and thread with a short bit of white thread. Pass the needle through the blister and leave a short bit of thread in the bole so made to act as a drain. Remove the thread when the blister is drained.

If you suspect the presence of a deer or other wild animal in some thicket or other cover, and desire to get a look at it, draw lots for the best place, and having done this let the fortunate one stand to leeward and near what seems the logical place for the animal to emerge. Then let the other Scout go around to windward. If you are both very quiet the animal will take alarm on getting the scent of the Scout to windward and doubtless attempt to quietly sneak out. If watching for a deer you must be very alert to see it. Naturally it will take the best way out and will not go toward the place where the scent comes from. If, however, the Scout to windward is noisy and attempts to drive the deer to you, he will most likely succeed in driving it out in some other direction.

Wear a pair of old "kid" gloves with the fingers cut off to protect your hands from black flies; suede is the best, because soft. Dope them well. Make sure to have long shirt sleeves, and fasten them snugly. I have found good elastic bands a big help, and prefer to have the shirt sleeves sewed up right down to the cuff, so I can just manage to get my hands through. Button, fold over and secure with a good fiat rubber band.

Don't sleep in damp blankets; or rather, don't let them stay damp, but dry them before night for you'll have to sleep in them, damp or dry. Damp blankets are bad medicine.

To sleep warm if you have to bivouac in cold weather, and have a good full-grown axe and know how to use it first build a good big fire on the place where you want to make your bed. When this has burned down, say in an hour, rake it to one side, clear away embers and ashes, and make your bed on the warm, dry ground where the fire has been. Build two slow fires, one on each side of you; or have a big rock or a thicket for a windbreak and build a fire beside this, not behind it, but out where the wind will hit it. The warm air from the fire will eddy around behind your windbreak, if you have chosen your location wisely and have the fire in the right place.

Look for butternut (white walnut) trees at the bottom of a hill.

If you cannot see the Big Dipper in the sky at night, which you know appears to revolve around the North Star once in 34 hours, remember that opposite the Big Dipper on the other side of the North Star and the same distance from it is a big irregular W of stars, known as Cassiopeia's Chair. There are six stars, five of which are bright. An imaginary line drawn from the bottom of the most acute of the two triangles of the W and bisecting it will lead nearly straight to the North Star. Familiarize yourself with this constellation and you will be the better equipped to follow a star line.

In prairie country, if you have no wood, hunt for cattle chips to make your fire. I can't tell you how the old-time plainsmen managed to make

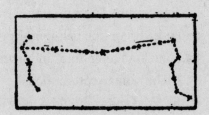

The compass in the sky. Left, Cassiopeia's chair; center, north star; right, big dipper.

a fire with buffalo chips on a rainy day, unless they carried a reserve supply of them. More likely they carried kindling. And that is not a bad hint for you. A stick or two of pine in your pack will not burden you, and will go a long way in getting less suitable material to burn.

Buckle spurs with the buckle on the inside of the instep, not the outside, if you want to wear them cowboy fashion.

The best ski and snowshoe bows are necessarily made of split wood.

If travelling in a country of no bridges and you come to a stream or river, be sure to cross before you make camp. Otherwise the water may rise or a storm come up and prevent you from going on the next day.

In fording a deep, swift stream, be sure you carry your pack so it will fly off if you fall, or it may drown you. Two or three Scouts together, carrying a pole, can wade a stream that would sweep a lone Scout off his feet. The heaviest Scout and heaviest end of the pole belong upstream, and all should walk abreast.

A few acetic acid crystals put in the coffee pail will render coffee made from alkali water fit to drink, providing the water is not too strongly impregnated with the hydrates.

In the Pacific Coast country a chinook (a warm wind in the spring) may have the same effect upon a stream as a cloudburst. Don't camp on the near side, and be sure you are above possible high water; the driftwood is your guide.

If using more than one pack animal, let one carry the grub and cooking utensils, so you will have but that one to unpack to get your supper started. As for dinner or lunch, good packers seldom eat during the middle of the day if travelling, or at best take only a snack.

Plainsmen use sods to make a fireplace, especially if cooking with cattle chips. Dig a square hole 10 inches deep and have a shallow trench leading off from it. Cover this trench with sods, making a flue. It should slope downward to the fire-hole, which should be deeper than it.

You can make a good shelter for the night with cordwood or with a cornshock. Don't despise material already cut for you.

To make lemonade capsules, get some 1-ounce gelatin capsules, and your sugar and lemons. Squeeze the lemons out over the sugar, and let stand till dry. Pulverize and put up in the capsules. A capsule will make a cupful. A gentleman by the name of Barnard who has done a great deal of hiking told me this about a year ago, and it is one of the best tricks I know.

The first "tent" I ever had was a tepee made with poles and sods. It was a good one, too, after I found out how to get a draught in it so the smoke would go out the smoke-hole and rigged a couple of smoke-flaps made of some old carpet. I had to make holes around the bottom by taking out a sod here and there, to let the air in. Then I made a wind-wall inside by hanging some of the carpet from the poles; this kept the draught from annoying me and shot it up along the roof, and out the smoke-hole with the heated air from the fire. I don't advise you to attempt a similar tepee, but I know you can make an excellent lean-to with poles and sods. Use *heavy* poles—and put it up to stay, with its back to the direction from which the prevailing winds will blow. The grass will grow on it and you'll have a "soddy." Such a little house with the little prairie sunflowers growing all over it will make a never-to-be-forgotten rendezvous.

To dip clean water, put cup or pail well down under the surface and raise quickly. The upward rush of the water will carry off floating "dirt" in the water on or near the surface and you will have the clean water from below.

To "roll" in a blanket, lie down with it spread across you; raise your legs with the knees stiff and with your hands alternately "flip" each side of the blanket under you, one of top of the other. Lower feet, raise on heels and shoulders and tuck under your hips. Now if you roll one way or the other, you will always have your blanket around you. Some believe that if you he faces downward you will not sleep so cold. I am sure I can't say; but I sleep that way a good deal.

Warm an axe before chopping in very cold weather, or it may chip. Chopping keeps it warm. Choppers use their mittened hands to produce the desired warmth when necessary. Not so necessary if you have the right axe.

Hunt a hollow for a bivouac in cold weather. But remember that the wind will blow up a ravine or draw, and that low ground may be damp ground—generally is damp ground. An ideal place would be a little mound in a thicket in a closed-in hollow. A high hill, bluff or cliff nearby will cause a draught.

In mountain climbing remember that the grass is often more treacherous than the steepest "slide." Small Hungarian hob-nails are the best. Some like screw-hobs, like the calks the river drivers use, but blunt instead of pointed. They have a square head and are put in with a wrench. A few well scattered are much better than too many.

Land a canoe by bringing it broadside on to the shore, if possible. Beware of rough rocks. Step into a canoe right over the keel; never in fact ever step anywhere else in it.

A stretcher will be cold on a cold night unless you put a folded blanket under you.

An ordinary canvas duffle bag with the top tied like a grain bag, makes a moth-proof storage place for woolen blankets and the like when at home. That is how I keep all my woolen camp duffle.

Moths will destroy the feathers of artificial flies.

Don't soak a gut leader (for fishing) over night; too much dampness rots it. Soak till soft, then stretch straight on the wall between two pins.

A fire-jack made of light steel, $\frac{1}{8} \times \frac{1}{4}$ inch, made to fold up, is good patrol equipment if a cart or

other conveyance is used. Make it 8 × 20 inches, with 3 crosspieces, and legs to fold. When you have the steel, all you need is a breasts drill, a bit and some rivets. See diagram.

A patrol fire-jack: folds flat.

To get a drink with your hat, use the top of it; don't be a chump and dip the water in it. Double it, with the rim in your hand, and drink out of the point of the crushed-in crown.

You cannot place too much importance upon getting good water. The Indian and the old-timer first find water, then camp; the tenderfoot camps first then hunts water.

Pitch your tent on a bit of ground having natural drainage if you can, so you will not need to ditch it.

Find your campsite at least an hour before dark, unless pressed hard for time; take more time if necessary.

When the low mists over a lake or a river clear quickly in the morning dear weather may be expected.

Carry quinine if in a malarial country. Carry a cathartic if out for a couple of days or more.

Don't ever carry a loaded gun in a carriage, wagon or boat. And never point a gun at anyone, even if you are absolutely sure that it is not loaded. Do not permit anyone who persists in playing the fool to remain in your company. I have known a number of boys and men to be badly shot due to improper handling of guns, some of than friends of mine.

A lantern will warm a closed tent considerably, and a charcoal fire in a galvanized bucket with holes cut in the sides near the bottom and a lid on top, will be found a blessing on a rainy day. Scatter the embers of the fire and you will have charcoal. If you wish to make it purposely, burn willow.

It is a good stunt to make your stretcher narrower in the middle than at the ends. The poles will bend with your weight even when guyed out.

Transplanting a seedling. A good scouting service.

If you have provided for this your stretcher will be taut when loaded. A piece of heavy unbleached sheeting 45 inches wide and $6 feet long will make you a good stretcher and also be handy for a variety of purposes. Hem 1½ inches deep on the long sides, and sew in grommets, about a dozen on each side. With a piece of sash-cord you can lace this sheet about a frame of poles, and of course will draw the edges closest in the center, where the greatest bend of the side poles comes. Lace on one side, around one of the poles, so you will not lie on the rope. I like a pole at head and foot of a stretcher, but you can do without them, especially if your bed sags. For my part, I want a bed that lies straight.

Never toss away a burning match. *Put it out!* Of all the fools there are, he is the biggest who tosses burning matches.

It is fun to transplant a seedling once in a while. I often have done it. If you find a little tree that hasn't any show where it is growing, change it to a better place. But be sure you know how to transplant and that you have water. The water is necessary to settle the earth so the air will not get to the roots. Too much air, dead seedling.

Every hiker accumulates about twice as big an outfit as he needs. Someday, for an experiment get out all the things you think you want to carry and pile them all up together. It will appall you, if you are so fortunate as to be able to satisfy even half of your desires. Too much! Cut it down to the things you cannot do without.

If you live in the West, it is a good thing to know that a strong tea made with the leaves of sage brush cures mountain fever. You cannot drink too much of it, for it is fierce stuff to swallow and you will quit the minute you begin to feel better.

Heat a number of round rocks the size of croquet balls, enough to more than fill a galvanized water pail, and dump in a hole in the ground the size of the pail, but half a foot deeper. Fill the interstices with smaller hot stones. Invert the pail over the hot stones, and bank around with earth. You've got a fireless heating stove that will keep a 9 × 9 wall tent warm all night.

The best hiker's coat, when you wear one, is a mackinaw reefer.

Mercurial ointment is the best rust preventive I know of. I use it in my guns.

Every fellow who ever amounts to anything as a runner, runs "on his toes." He adds "knows how" to natural ability. Don't be a flatfoot—at anything.

Hunting, Fishing, and Trapping

Hunting and Fishing Basics

From *Buzzacott's Masterpieces; or, The Complete Hunters', Trappers', and Campers' Library of Valuable Information* by "Bozzacott," 1913

To carry the camp stuff most easily, back-loads should be so made up that the softest parts should rest upon the shoulders and neck, and when adjusted and supported by a strap that passes across the forehead, boxes and cumbrous articles may be packed on top; by this method fifty pounds may be carried with comparative ease. Fishing rods, paddles, axes, etc., should be tied together in bundles in two places at least, and when shouldered, boots, kettles, and the like, may be slung over their upper ends. Where a canoe or boat is to be carried, lash the paddles lengthwise one foot apart across the bars or thwarts amidships, turn the canoe upside-down, rest one end upon a convenient projecting branch of a tree at such a height that you can easily pass under, and then thrusting in your head so that the paddles will rest upon the shoulders, raise and balance it, and proceed on the journey. If the canoe is too heavy for one person, it should be shouldered by two men, one at each end, and carried right side up. There is a knack in walking, too, which should be acquired, namely: always run your eye along the trail at least a rod in advance, so that you may not only see soft places, rocks, roots, and other obstructions, but calculate to a nicety just where your steps are to be made. This practice will prevent stumbling; it also enables one to discern a blind trail easily, and teaches him to observe any strange signs which might otherwise pass unnoticed.

Basic Tips for Stalking Animals

One is—they take care that the ground behind them, or trees, buildings, etc., are of the same color as their clothes.

And the other is—if an enemy or a deer is seen looking for them, they remain perfectly still, without moving so long as he is there.

If wearing dark clothes get among dark bushes, shadows of trees or rocks, shade of dark ground. If light clothing, choose the ground beyond the shade or shadows. Keep perfectly still, and creep or crawl when every opportunity affords; watch and wait for your chance to sneak up a few yards or so at a time. If you can get closer by a circuitous route take it—if the wind is not in your way; only never show yourself on the sky line. If you are observed don't move or blink—keep still, and you will reassure them. To dodge or disappear would be suspicious. If they are watching you remain quiet, and they will think your head or body part is a stump or rock. In peering over a hill or rock raise your head inch by inch; lower it the same way. Never raise or lower it suddenly.

When hiding behind a big stone or mound, etc., they don't look over the top, but round the side of it.

When stalking one should wear moccasins and walk lightly on the ball of the foot, keeping the heels off the ground, so as to be shod with silence. In looking over an object remember any quick or sudden movement of the head on the skyline would be very liable to attract attention, even at a considerable distance.

At night keep as much as possible in low ground, ditches, etc., so that you are down in the dark, so that anything that comes near will be visible to you outlined against the stars on higher ground.

Remember always that to stalk a wild animal you must keep down wind of him, even if the wind is so slight as to be merely a faint stir.

Before starting to stalk you should be sure which way the wind is blowing, and work up against it. To find this out you should wet your thumb all around with your tongue, and then hold it up and see which side feels coldest, or you can throw some light dust, or dry grass or leaves in the air and see which way they drift.

How to find Direction

If you have not a compass the sun will tell you by day where the north is, and the moon and the stars by night.

At six o'clock in the morning the sun is due east, at nine o'clock he is southeast, at noon he is south, at three o'clock in the afternoon he is southwest, and at six o'clock he is due west. In winter he will have set long before six o'clock but he will not have reached due west when he is set.

Finding the North

To find the south at any time of day by the sun—hold your watch flat, face upwards, so that the sun shines on it. Turn it round till the hour hand points at the sun. Then, without moving the watch, lay the edge of a piece of paper or a pencil across the face of the watch so that it rests on the center of the dial and points out half-way between the figure XII and the hour hand. The line given by that pencil will be the true south and north line.

Decent Tips for Predicting Weather by Observing Animals

When mules or horses frequently bray, snort or sneeze, you may expect weather changes.

When bats are astir early or late fine weather is indicated.

When bulls lead the cows to pasture and are restless to get out, look for rain. If the cows lead, moderate sign. When they sniff the air and crowd together, expect a storm.

When goats, sheep or cows reluctantly leave the pasture expect rain.

Cattle—sheep—eat greedily before a storm; sparingly before a thaw. Feed up hill in wet weather, downhill in dry weather.

Observe which way a hedgehog builds a nest— if it faces North, South, East or West.

For the winds will blow, and the storms do go
The contrary way, I'll have you know.

Pigs squealing, running about with hay or straw in their mouth, foretells storm, rain or change.

When ducks and chickens are restless, pick and prune at their feathers, look out for rain.

When fowls roll in dirt or sand, rain at hand.

When roosters crow as they go to bed, change of weather.

When birds fly high and sing long, sign of fair weather.

There is a greater tendency to rain when the moon is in the quarter after full moon, especially with the moon in Perigee.

Northerly winds are prevalent in the last quarter.

Southerly winds are prevalent in the first quarter.

When the Rain precedes the Wind,
Topsail sheets and the Helm mind:
But when the Wind precedes the Rain,
Hoist your Topsails up again.

Mountain winds blow up mountain during the day and down at night.

More tips on predicting weather

When poplar, cottonwood, maple and willow leaves show their under sides, rain will follow.

If on the trees the leaves still hold.
The coming winter will be cold.

For **early blossoms** bear little fruit; late blossoms plenty.

Plenty acorns or berries, plenty winter.

Trembling aspen leaves in calm weather, change is coming.

Scales of Pine Cones open in dry weather, close in wet.

Corn or Indian Fodder, when dry and crisp, dry weather.

When damp and limp, look for rain.

Corn Husks, thick or thin, betoken cold accordingly.

Dandelion Blossoms close before a storm or change.

Corns, old wounds or sores itch before rain.

Rheumatic pains increase or decrease likewise.

Nervous, irritable persons, are likewise affected by changes.

Salt and soap dishes sweat before rain.

Fires burn bright or dull, according to the weather.

Smells are more offensive before rain; less afterward.

When pigs and critters play in mud there is no fear of a flood.

Rooks tremble at approach of rain or change.

Crows, ravens, jack-daws calling late indicate storms: calling early, fair weather.

When Plover pipe and shrill and fly high, good weather.

When woodpeckers get busy, expect rain.

If **owls hoot** at night, good weather to come.

When robins rest high and call, good sign; if silent and restless and rest low, bad weather is to come.

When the smoke of the camp-fire hangs low and does not ascend, expect rain or sudden change.

When the smoke ascends straight up, fine weather,

When animals venture not to roam,
But hug the spots about their home,
'Tis a sign that weather changes are near:
But when they travel, and to distance go—
They know 'twon't neither rain nor snow.

What the Bible Says about Weather Signs

"When ye see the south wind blow, ye say there will be heat; and it cometh to pass."—St. Luke 12:55.

"When ye see a cloud rise up from the west, straitway ye say there cometh a shower, and so it is."—St. Luke 12:54.

"When it is evening ye say it will be fair weather, for the sky is red; and in the morning it will be foul weather, for the sky is red and lowering."—St. Matthew 16:2-3.

In Job 37:27-35, we are told of the signs by spreading of the clouds, as laid down in this Book, and of the fact that cattle judge by the vapor, air or noise of approaching storms.

Pale evening sunset indicates rain.

When birds fly low, look out for wind or rain.

When birds fly high it is a sign of fair weather: when insects bevy abroad and fly high also.

When snipe drum and strut, dry air, good weather.

When starlings and crows gather together, wet weather.

When swallows fly low and near the water, rain.

When swans or geese fly against the wind, strong winds from the direction they fly.

Wild geese or swans going to water, fine weather.

Unusual silence before thunder or rain means a storm.

Thunder in the morning, wind: at noon, rain: at evening, tempest changes. After much thunder expect much rain.

Comb clouds, in the form of hen-scratches or mares-tails, indicate strong winds.

Salmon or fish-like clouds, ark shape—in east or west—strong winds. North or south, fine and moderate.

Look for changes in the weather at changes of the moon.

When birds they play in flocks together, good weather.

Magpies, one alone, weather's bad; two together, weather's good.

Owls scream in bad weather or at night; change.

Lightning Signs. With north wind, west rain. North and southwest, wind and rain; otherwise fair.

Winds of The Day—wrestle and fight longer and stronger than those of the night.

Rain before wind, indicates bad weather; wind before rain, fair weather.

West winds are favorable to wet weather or showers.

East winds, cold and wet together.

South winds, bring heat and thunderstorms.

But North winds blow them back again.

Northwest winds, bring the finest weather.

But when the winds are in the east, it's fine for neither man nor beast.

Mackerel sky, neither wet nor dry; changeable.

Low clouds indicate rain: **high clouds,** moderate winds.

No clouds, fair weather; **all clouds,** storm or change.

When birds fly high, fine weather sends insects out; and they rarely fly high except in light weather.

Clear signs at sunrise or sunset—clear day, or vice versa.

Rain before seven, quits before eleven.

When atmosphere is clear and unclouded, when distant objects seem near, skies cloudless, stars very bright watch out for changes; especially when owls hoot, crows caw, birds and insects fly low, flies and ants bestir themselves to hunt food—expect rain.

Changes in the weather at mid-day are usually of duration.

Sudden changes of temperature, change of the weather.

As one reads faces, so can weather signs be read by their signs.

List of Different Kinds of Deer Tracks

The appearance of a deer's track upon bare ground varies much, and a trail may in a quarter of a mile run through a dozen or more variations. All appearances may, however, be included under the following heads, and the great majority of tracks you will see will correspond exactly with the description of the class:

1st. Distinct impressions of the whole hoof.

2nd. Faint impressions of only the points of the hoof.

3rd. A slight rim of dirt or dust thrown up by the sharp edge of the hoof.

4th. Slight scrapes upon hard ground, recognizable only by the change of color, being made by a faint grinding of the finest particles of the surface without any impression.

5th. Mere touches or spots showing only a faint change in the shade of the color. There is scarcely

Antlers and horns of the elk.

A month's growth of antlers—up to the shedding season. The last picture in this illustration shows the condition of coat in spring when summer hair is coming in and winter hair is being shed.

any air so dry that the ground during the night will not absorb a trace of moisture. The least disturbance of the top particles of such soil, even without grinding them over each other, will make a difference in the shade of the color, which will be visible under some point of view though invisible from others, depending upon the direction of the light.

6th. Crushing or grinding of the surface of friable rocks, and mere scrapes or scratches on harder rock or frozen ground.

7th. Depressions in moss, grass, dead leaves, etc.

8th. Dead leaves, sticks, etc., kicked or brushed aside or overturned, or broken or bent, etc.

9th. A plain bending or separating of the spears of grass or weeds. This is generally caused by the feet treading down the stalks at the bottom and not as the next (No. 10) is.

10th. A bending of the spears of grass or weeds, etc., by the legs of the passing animal. In this case the bend itself of the spears is hardly noticeable except by the change in the shade of light cast by them. In such case a faint streak of differently shaded color will be found running through the grass or weeds, visible only from some directions.

11th. Change of color from brushing dew, rain-drops, or frost from grass, weeds, etc.

12th. Upturning of the under surfaces (generally moist) of stones, leaves, etc.

These twelve classes include about all you will need to study. There are, of course, some others, but generally so accidental and rare that you had better skip such places and seek the trail farther on, such as the under surface of dry leaves pressed against wet ones beneath but not upturned. It will not be worthwhile to spend time on a trail in looking for such signs.

Building a Blind

If there is an abundance of drift wood along the water's edge make a blind out of it. If the shores are free from shrubs dig a hole in the sand large enough to hold one or two shooters, make the opening no longer than is absolutely necessary. It may be made less conspicuous by partly covering with boards, throwing sand over this improvised roof to hide the boards from view. Wear clothing the same color as the surrounding shrubbery or background. Brown clothing for sand bars is best. Above all else, avoid wearing a black hat or coat, as the birds are extremely wary of black objects. For ordinary shooting put out at least two dozen decoys, placing them about seventy-five feet from the blind and scattering them in uneven positions. Then get into the blind and await the game.

Duck shooting is neither an art nor a science; it is a combination of both, made possible only by practice. Neither does it follow that because a man may be a good trap-shot at clay or live birds he will be a good wing shot in the blind. There are few "straight-away" shots from the blinds and many cross shots, with an exceedingly swift target. It is the fast cross shots and the quick, startled rises that puzzle the beginner.

Taking off the Hides

Small animals should be cased, or opened, by peeling the skin off from the hind quarters. Make a cut from front to hind legs and strip it off like skinning a rabbit. Cut off around the legs and remove the skin clean from the bones, with the knife keeping all fat and flesh on the body proper. If slippery use a dry rag around the bony parts, or a split stick. Tie a loop cord or wire to fasten the hind legs upon so as to hold secure, fastening it to the hut or a tree. Skin clear back to nose, cutting loose eyes and ear cartilage. To skin them open cut from breast to the lower jaw—be careful to cut in a straight line—follow with the knife on the inside of fore and hind legs clear to the toes and claws, which should be left on all fur pelts, peeling the hide off, using the knife to keep it free from fat or flesh as much as possible. Do not draw the skin too far away from the body—just enough to handle the knife freely—to bend it. Let the knife blade point toward the carcass or body not toward the skin, **but away from it,** so as to avoid cutting the skin or gashing it. The cleaner the skin is taken off the better it is, and the least fleshing will have to be done. With care and practice one will soon learn the knack. I have often skinned as high as two or three hundred animals in a day and on scaling voyages (South Shetland seal) have averaged that many for days.

On one voyage we captured as high as 5,000 seals in one season. The price we received for them in the **London market averaging $20 each**. In these cases no fleshing was necessary so cleanly were they removed before salting and packing. All these were cased open.

"BUZZA COTT."
Head Sealer.
Record—Voyage of the sealing Schooners fleet of Williams & Haven. New London. Conn.

Stretching and Curing Small Skins

The market value of a skin is greatly affected by the care taken in removing it from the animal, and in drying it. The common way is to tack the skin to the barn door and let it remain stretched until quite dry. The trapper in the woods having no such convenience as the barn door at hand, is obliged to resort to other methods. One plan is to dry the skin on a hoop. A skin to be dried in this manner must not be ripped down the belly, but it is cut from the lower jaw of the animal to just below the forelegs; the lips, eyes, and ears being cut around, the skin is stripped off, leaving the fur side inward. The hoop consists of a branch of hickory or other elastic wood, an inch through at the butt. This is bent and pushed into the skin, which is drawn tight, and fastened in place by notches in the bow, drawing the skin of the lip into these notches. A much neater way, and one generally preferred, is to use stretchers of thin wood. As these have to be carried by the trapper, they are made of light wood and very thin. They are three-sixteenths of an inch thick, twenty inches long, six inches wide at the larger end, and slightly tapering. They are rounded to a blunt point at the lower end, and the edges chamfered. The skin is drawn over the board, and secured with tacks. Skins stretched by either of these methods should not be dried in the sun nor by a fire, but in a cool place where they will be sheltered from the rain.

No salt or other preservative is used upon skins intended for the market.

Dressing and Tanning Skins and Furs

There are various ways of dressing skins, but some are easier and better than others. Several of the recipes given below have been advertised and hawked about the country at five dollars each.

We will commence with what is called oil-dressing, and, to begin at the beginning, the directions would be, "first catch your deer." As soon as the hide is taken off from the deer's back it should be grained; to do this, provide yourself with a beam eight inches through, and six feet long; put two legs in one end, and let the other rest on the ground, so that it will stand at a steep slant. The beam must be of hard wood, shaved smooth, without a ridge in it.

Provide yourself with a knife. One made for the purpose is best, but you may make a very good one by taking an old shaving knife and grinding it square across the edge, until it has a face about a sixteenth of an inch across. Then whet the corners smooth, so that they will not cut the skin. A piece of a scythe, with a handle at each end, makes a good fleshing knife.

Now sit down, with the highest end of the beam against your belly, and lay on the skin, hair side down, and proceed to take off all the flesh and fat, and every unequal substance before you turn the hair side up. Then commence to grain, with the neck of the skin next to you, and shove against the hair, having a firm hold of the knife, and shoving with some strength, when off will go a streak of the grain, and so proceed until it is all off. This is the way to grain a green hide just taken from the animal.

To grain a dry hide, first put it in a tub or barrel of warm water, and let it lie for twenty-four hours, and then add to each half barrel of water a pint of good slaked lime, and let it stand twenty-four hours more; then proceed as with a fresh skin.

When the work is properly done, the skin will be as clear as glass, with no streak of grain or other uneven substance left; unless it is in this condition, it will not dress well.

Now, in order to dress one buck skin, take eight quarts of fresh rain water and warm it, and put in one pint of soft soap. Put in the skin while the liquid is warm, and work it with the hands, or punch it with a stick, until the soapsuds is quite worked into it, say twenty-four hours. Then take it out and pass it between two sticks, or pass it through a good wringing machine. Then pull it until it is dry, in the hot sun, or before a hot fire. Next stretch it out to its full size, and spread on some soft grease, or any animal oil, until it is well oiled through. Then heat up the suds again, and apply half as much more soap, and put in the skin again and work it well for a time, and let it lie twenty-four hours longer. Then take it out and pull it dry as before. For all doe skins, and for yearling bucks, this will be enough, but old buck skins must go in once more, and when pulled dry again they will be as soft as velvet.

The best grease to use is butter, which is the greatest softener in the world, and a less quantity will answer than of any other grease.

When the skin is dressed and pulled dry, you may apply ochre to make it yellow, or hang it up in a smoke-house and smoke it with a smudge of rotten water elm, which will make it a beautiful reddish yellow.

Another process is to let the skin lie in clear water until the hair will slip off, and then grain it on the beam. This is a very good way. I have practiced it, and found the leather as tough as that of the green hide.

Take the brains out of the head of a deer, or of a hog, tie them up in a cloth, and put them into a gallon of water, and boil for an hour; then squeeze the cloth so as to press through as much as you can; let it stand until you can barely hold your hand in it without scalding; then put in the grained skin, working it continually for two or three minutes; then take it out, wring it, and pull it dry. If not soft enough, heat up and put in again; then work it and dry it as before. No doubt it will be done by this time, but if it is still a little hard, apply a small amount of butter, and work it in thoroughly, and then smoke, as before directed. This is the Indian dressing. There is no doubt that the first recipe—the oil dressing—is the best of all.

Tanning.—The first thing to be done preparatory to tanning a hide or skin is to soak it, as no hide can be tanned unless it has been soaked and properly broken on a fleshing beam. Soak in soft water, and, unless the hides have been salted, add a little salt to the water. Green hides should remain in until thoroughly well soaked, say from ten to twelve hours, according to thickness; dry hides from two to six days. All hard or unbroken spots must be softened after soaking. To remove the hair or wool, immerse the hide or skin in a liquor composed of ten gallons of cold, soft water, eight quarts of slaked lime, and eight quarts of hard wood ashes. Let it soak from two to six days, or until the hair or wool slips off easily.

If it is desired to keep the wool or hair clean, instead of using the liquor take equal parts of slaked lime and hard wood ashes, and make into a thin paste, with water. Spread this on the flesh side, and then roll up the skin, flesh side in, and place it in a tub or barrel, barely covering it with water. Let it soak from one to ten days, or until the hair or wool can be easily removed; then take the hides from the soak, and scrape off the hair and flesh with a fleshing knife.

The hides, by being soaked in the lime liquor, are raised too much to be submitted to the tanning liquor. They must first be reduced to their original thickness, by being entirely freed from the lime. This is done by what is termed "bating."

A bate is made of ten gallons of cold, soft water, one-half bushel of wheat bran, and a quarter of a pound of sulphuric acid. It should be prepared a day or two before using, in order that the bran may ferment. By using lukewarm instead of cold water, the process will be hastened. Put the hide into this bate, and let it remain until it is reduced to its natural thickness and is as soft as a green hide. Then remove it and rinse it in soft water, and work it out, at least once, over the fleshing beam. For a thick hide, a second rinsing and working will be necessary.

Tanning Liquor.—For light hides, add one-half bushel of wheat bran to ten gallons of soft, warm water, stirring it in. Let it stand in a warm room until it ferments, then add seven pounds of salt, and stir it until it dissolves, then add slowly, and stir in, two and a half pounds of sulphuric acid. Into this liquor put the hide, and handle it until it is perfectly saturated.

This tan will impart no color to the leather, but will act as a mordant for setting a variety of bark or vegetable colors. This tan liquor, when properly prepared, has a sour, pungent taste, sharper than the keenest vinegar, but is not so strong as to injure the tongue or hands. This is the test for the strength of the liquor. If it becomes much reduced below this test, while the hides are in it, it must be strengthened. To do this, remove the hides; then skim off the bran, which is now worthless, and add to the old liquor fermented bran, salt and acid, as before. Light hides should remain in the tan liquor from four to twelve hours. Then rinse them in soft water, two or three times, pushing out all the tan from the fur or hair. All tanned skins should he thoroughly rinsed before applying the liquid stuffing, which is composed in the following manner:

Take one-third leached lye and two-thirds tanner's or neat's foot oil, beat together, and apply with a stiff brush. Give calf skins two coats, furs one light coat, and deer skins two coats, one on each side. Hang them in the shade to dry. When half dry, take them on the beam over some yielding substance, and by pushing the edge of the flesh

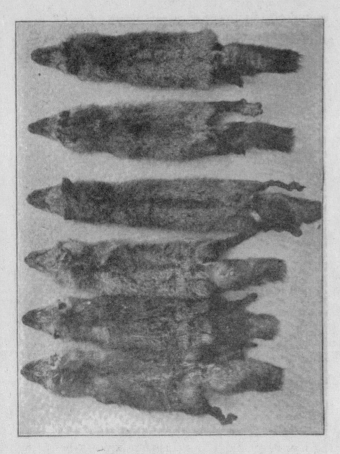

Fine furs, the right and wrong methods of dressing them.

knife stoutly over the leather in all directions, it will become soft and pliable.

In treating a calf skin, when the liquid is nearly dried in, apply a thorough coat of water-proof stuffing.

All hides and skins when drying are like full cloth. When wet they contract or pull up, and have to be stretched. To do this, take the hide after the liquid stuffing is dried in, dampen it, and place it on the fleshing beam over some yielding substance like a sheep skin. Then use the flesh knife (a circular knife, like the cook's chopping knife). By pushing the edge stoutly in all directions over the leather, it will become stretched, and be made fit for the various uses to which it is to be put.

The following is a simple way to dress deer skins. First have them grained, as already directed. Then, into a two-gallon stone pot, put two quarts of rain water, one ounce sulphuric acid and one gill of salt.

Put in the hide, work it well for two or three minutes, wring it out, pull it dry, and smoke it.

To Dress Fox Skins

Commence to skin the fox by ripping down the back of each hind leg until the slits meet at the crotch. Don't rip up the belly, but skin the body whole. Skin the tail by putting a split stick over the bone of the tail, between the hide and the body. Hold it tight, so that it will scrape the bone of the tail, and then pull this out of the hide. Draw the hide over a board, made ready of a width from end to end, and when it is dry slip it off and turn it fur side out; then it is ready to sell.

Beaver Skins

Rip the skin as you would that of a sheep. Stretch it to its full size in all directions, and nail it on a board to dry. It may be dressed by a mixture of equal parts of rock salt and alum dissolved in water, with coarse flour stirred in to make it about as thick as cream. Spread this on about half an inch thick, and when dry scrape it off. If this is not enough, put it on a second time.

To make it into furs, pluck out the long hairs.

Otter Skins

Skin him nearly the same as the fox, only that the tail must be ripped up, and when the hide is turned down to the four legs, they must be skinned out carefully. Slip the skin over a board that will not fit it so tightly as to injure the fur. Stretch out the tail, and hold it in place by tacking it with small nails around the edges. If it is a real black fellow, that shines like a crow, probably you will get eight or ten dollars for him. It may be dressed in the same manner as a beaver skin.

Mink Skins

The same directions in all respects as for the foregoing save that after the paste gets dry it should

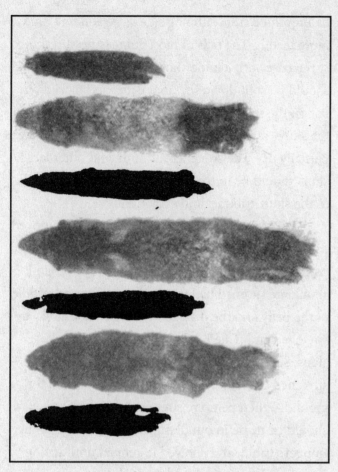

Silver fox and marten pelts.

be scraped off with the bowl of a spoon, taking care to keep the skin stretched tightly, so that the astringent matter will not shrink it too much.

The skin may be dressed as soft as velvet, and the alum and salt will set the hair securely.

During the warm, summer months the mink is nearly stripped of his fur, the skin is thin, and the butts of the hair stick nearly through, making the pelt black.

The skin is in its prime from mid-winter until about the middle of May.

Muskrat Skins

These skins are very tender, and the flesh is very tough, so that they will not bear fleshing until they have laid for at least six hours in the tan liquor described above for light deer skins. After this it should be fleshed over the flesh side of a sheep skin, with the circular fleshing knife. The fur may be

enlivened by being rubbed with a mixture of equal parts of scorched bran and clean white sand.

Raccoon Skins

These should be nailed on a board to dry, and smeared with a paste made of equal parts of alum and salt dissolved in a weak solution of sulphuric acid, say 2 ounces of alum, 2 ounces of salt, 1 drachm of sulphuric acid, 1 pint of water, and a little wheat bran. When nearly dry, scrape it off with a spoon, and work the skin very soft.

This may be done by rolling up the skin, instead of nailing it on a board; or it may be put in the tan liquor recommended for light deer hides.

Bear Skins

Tan in the same manner in all respects as the Raccoon skins.

More about Preparing Pelts

Many industrious trappers lose much hard-earned money in carelessly prepared peltries. All pelts should be removed from animals when first captured, except in severe weather in the north, where animals may be kept frozen for weeks without injuring the fur. Skins should be well stretched and cleaned of all loose flesh when green; they should not be scraped too severely, however, as in so doing the fibre is often injured. They must be dried away from the camp fire, in the shade or open air. Pelts dried under a hot sun soon become very hard and dry, and are liable to tear, particularly those from thin-skinned animals, such as the fox, lynx, wild-cat, muskrat, etc. Fatty skins, like those of the bear, raccoon, seal and skunk, can be exposed to the sun without injury; the heat draws the fat to the surface, and it is then easily removed. Alum, salt and saltpetre are often applied to green pelts by amateurs, but it causes shrinkage, and also prevents quick, soft soaking and easy currying when first handled by the tanner.

Furred animals are trapped in cold weather, and no preservatives are necessary in drying the skins. The blood should never be washed from the flesh side of a pelt, as water injures the skin and causes decomposition. The skins of most animals should be drawn over stretchers, with flesh side out, and edges tacked in position. Of the class treated thus, mention might be made of the otter, fox, fisher, marten, mink and muskrat. The skin of the muskrat should be stretched over a shingle, with sides slanted on thin end, and corners rounded.

The animals mentioned should be skinned as follows: Cut the skin through around the ankles; then place a small, sharp knife in the incisions, and open the skins down the inside of the hind legs to the cauda. This amount of cutting will enable the skin to be pulled over the head of the animal without tearing, and to come off in bag-like shape. The tails are drawn out by placing the fleshy part between two sticks, with a slight notch in each; they will thus be prevented from slipping sideways, and will draw more readily. The tails of most animals need starting at the base with a knife. Tails of the otter and skunk should be split down the underside, and tacked out flat on the stretcher. The feet are generally left on fox skins, and the fur side turned out when they are partially dry. The stretcher for mink and other large skins should be in three pieces, to facilitate removal, as the skins contract and stick tightly.

The skins of several furred animals are removed differently from those described. Those of the bear, panther, wolf, wolverine, lynx, badger, beaver and skunk are skinned flatly, by cutting down the middle of the belly and the inside of the legs. Such skins are stretched and nailed on any flat surface. Very large skins, such as the moose, caribou, elk and deer, are stretched on pegs driven through their sides in the ground. When pelts are stretched and dried, they should be made in bundles, placed in the top of the trapper's cabin, and allowed to remain until spring. Early in the season a mixture of salt, saltpetre and alum is used for the largest skins.

Fishing Bait

From *Fisherman's Lures and Game-Fish Food* by Louis Rhead, 1920

The Hellgrammite

The most active and prolonged wriggler of all live baits is the hellgrammite, an exceedingly effective bass bait. Because of the extreme toughness of the larva, its constant wriggle and continued life after being hooked, it is much sought by the angler. Large perch and chub cannot resist it. Pickerel have been known to take it, but other baits for that fish are superior. Wall-eyed pike, big catfish, and eels will take it, but trout will not touch it. I have tried it in pools where large brown trout abide near where bass lie, and the bass have always responded to it.

The hellgrammite is the aquatic larva of a fly, the horned corydalus (*Corydalus cornutus*), somewhat resembling and closely allied to the dragonfly. It is supposed to exist for several years in the larval state under loose rocks on or just below the water-line of rivers and other waters of low temperature. Here its life is spent in devouring other smaller insect larvæ, and during this period it is most suitable for baiting purposes. But this repulsive-looking, yet harmless, creature is used as bait in all three stages of its life. First in its larval—*creeper* stage; then in the dormant *pupa* stage, and last after the final change into the adult *flying* insect. The corydalus is a large, fierce-looking insect with four gauzy wings which, when at rest, lie flat over the body, which is a cinnamon color on the belly, dark brown at the sides, and dull black at the head and thorax. It begins its flight after dusk and, like the creeper, is entirely nocturnal in its habits. I have never seen it in flight during the daytime in New York regions. This fine, large insect is very abundant on Montana streams, where it is used extensively by anglers who hook them alive to fish at the surface for the big rainbows. These big rainbows run up to fourteen pounds' weight, and they are so adroit in nipping the insect from the hook that several experts requested me to make an

Rainbow-trout
salmo iridens.

artificial from specimens sent me in "spirits," which I did, and named it the "Winged Hellgrammite." Its body measures over two inches in length, the wings extending half an inch beyond the tail, and with the two long black horns at the head the entire insect measures three and three-quarter inches long.

The artificial hellgrammite creeper differs somewhat in having a row of short-pointed feelers along each side of the abdomen. The belly is grayish cream-color, the back dark brown with black shiny head and thorax. The artificial of this creeper has been found exceedingly good in many swift and still waters for large or small-mouth bass and wall-eye. A smaller and decidedly different species, the artificial of which I have named the "Trout Hellgrammite," because I found it frequently in the stomachs of brook-trout in widely different localities, is described in detail elsewhere along with the other creepers that trout take as food. The hellgrammite creeper is very easily captured and may be kept a considerable time in damp grass and rotten wood at low temperature.

The Crawfish

In placing the crawfish second in value as a bait, I do so because it is equally effective in swift streams and in placid lakes over almost the entire continent of North America. Indeed wherever bass abide, a five, medium-sized, light brown crawfish is resistless in any condition of weather or season. This fresh-water crustacean is very prolific in all brooks and streams of a low temperature, and frequently in lakes. Its habit is mostly nocturnal, and it burrows holes in the pebbly sand as a protection from its enemies. Its abode can easily be identified by the little mound of fresh sand beside its hole, and if we are quick in our movements we can scrape them out a few inches down, wait a few minutes for the water to run clear and capture them. It requires practice to do it with success, for they are nimbleness

personified, running equally fast backward or forward. Indeed, their capture, like any other bait, is quite a difficult undertaking, filling up the off days or early hours when bass are not in a biting humor.

While the crawfish is an expert swimmer, it rarely leaves the bottom to swim in mid-water or near the surface, but crawls slowly in search of food among the stones and sand. It feeds mostly on small fish, dead or alive, and. like marine crustaceans, is very pugnacious, with frequent combats among its own kind or with other creatures it happens to meet. It is rarely seen by day, and little is really known of its natural habits except in confinement As a bait, its best qualities are the lively kicking movement and hardihood after being hooked, and the prolonged time it takes while swimming downward from the surface after the cast. Bass will dash after it on its journey down, and it is generally perfectly aware of them, so, on reaching the bottom, it will instantly crawl under a stone out of reach. The amateur soon learns that it is best to keep this nimble bait swimming free from the bottom. It swims along entirely with its tail, the numerous legs being used only to balance the body, and it is for that reason I have, after many trials, succeeded in making the artificial with a disjointed tail to move up and down from the body, giving a lifelike appearance to the lure if played property in working the angler's rod-tip. In its natural environment the crawfish grows rapidly, casting its shell several times in one season. When very young, it is pale yellow in color, growing a darker brown with age. For my own part I prefer this bait to be light cinnamon color, not over two inches long with the tail stretched. Many anglers consider a four-inch dark colored crawfish is most effective in either lake or stream.

The Cricket

Next after the crawfish I consider the cricket third in value, because it is eagerly taken by all game-fish, both in lake or stream. Its jumping propensities in meadows through which meanders a trout stream lead to sure disaster, for all kinds of fish congregate in certain fruitful places to await these leaps of death. So soon as the cricket alights on the surface, it kicks and spins rapidly around, making its way to shore. But its landing-place is invariably down the gullet of trout or chub; indeed any fish will take it that happens to be in sight. If properly hooked it makes a most effective live bait by reason of the continued rumpus made at the surface. The cricket never sinks, alive or dead, and especially in placid water is an easy prey, due to its frantic efforts to get back on land, which are so very obvious that fish cannot fail to see them quite a distance away.

Large, full-grown specimens are not common until late in the fall after the trout season closes, and for that reason they are not so popular for trout as for bass. Sometimes they come out during July. When they do, I consider them superior to any other bait (except minnows) for brown trout during the daytime. My artificial cricket made in three different sizes of cork bodies was highly successful with brown trout as early as June 3, of last year. This is one of the few instances where the artificial is of greater service than the natural bait, as it is also more durable, for the cricket, when hooked, is very tender, and is easily flipped off, besides being repeatedly nipped from the hook by the fish. A very few casts will find this bait limp and almost lifeless. For trout fishing the smallest size is much the beat. Bass seem to prefer a good big size, running up to the surface after it as they do after a fly. In Lake George I caught bass on crickets in water thirty feet deep. The most fruitful hunting-ground for crickets is under corn shucks and piles of decaying weeds or other vegetation. If the reader will carefully examine the representation of the artificial cricket he will consider it, as I do, the best imitation of all my nature lures. It looks still more natural when placed in the water. After a little practice the vibrant rod-tip can be skillfully made to give the lure all the actions of the natural insect, with a result that is exceedingly interesting both in the manner it is made to act and the way trout are seen to take it.

The Lamprey

This most excellent bass bait is another of limited service. Bass and chub seem to be the only fish that take it with any degree of certainty. Its peculiar wriggle while swimming is its best point, for it is an awful pesky live bait to get snagged on the bottom. We are obliged to keep the live lamprey on the move all the time or good-bye to our tackle. The lamprey-eel (often known as the "lamper") belongs to a very low order of animals, having no bony skeleton, no gills, ribs, or limbs, and being a naked eel-shaped creature with a sucker mouth, the lips of which are fringed with fine hairs. It inhabits the fresh cold waters of rivers and brooks, and gets its living by attaching itself to other fishes, feeding on them by scraping off the flesh with its rasp-like teeth. Adults attain to a weight of several pounds and two feet in length.

This creature is the only one I would never think of breeding or transplanting for food purposes, indeed its destruction and extinction from our streams would be a most desirable thing. Like the common eel it is nocturnal in its habits, moving about the deeper parts of the bed of rivers in sluggish places which are haunted by suckers and other coarse fish. It is only the very young that is used for bait, the best size being about five inches long. These are usually found in black muddy sand close to the shore of slow-moving backwaters of rivers, and a shovel is all that is necessary to capture them. Dig deep, best under several inches of water, and throw the mud upon the dry bank, then search through it with the hands for the wrigglers. They are more slippery and agile than the eel, and of all live bait the most difficult to impale on the hook. A dead

Various creatures that game-fish (Darwin from living specimens).

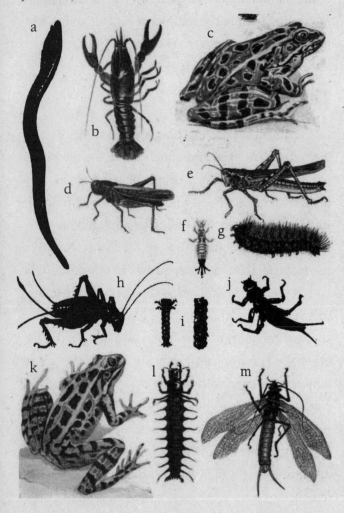

a) Young lamper-eel; b) Adult crawfish; c) Green leopard-frog; d) June grasshopper; e) Common red-legged grasshopper; f) Nymph-creeper; g) Brown hairy caterpillar; h) Cricket; i) Caddis-creeper and case; j) Trout-hellgrammite creeper; k) Brown pickerel-frog; l) Bass-hellgrammite creeper; m) Base winged hellgrammite.

one is no attraction to the bass; its wriggle only is the attraction.

By the time this is in print I shall have perfected a floating lamprey; at present my artificial, while very natural in appearance, is the only non-floating bait I have made. It wriggles all right, but must be kept moving or it sinks to the bottom, with the same difficulty to recover as the natural bait. I shall work on this bait till I succeed in producing a lamprey that wriggles and at the same time floats in suspension

about mid-water or near the bottom, according to where it is fastened on the leader. In many rivers the lamprey as a bait is most attractive to bass, and if the artificial is made as I think it ought, it will be one of the best baits for bass fisherman to use.

The Green and Brown Frogs

I do not place the frog so far down on the list because of its being inferior to the others as an effective bait, but by reason of its limited availability. The frog is not always, everywhere effective. In certain waters it is supreme, either for bass, pickerel, pike, or muskellunge. Large chub, perch, wall-eyed pike take the frog, at times. I have often fished brown-trout waters with frogs caught on the banks of the stream, but failed every time, though I have ocular proof of trout taking frogs. I witnessed a big captive brown trout gobble four fair-sized green frogs in less than as many minutes, in one case tearing the limbs from the body; a second after, the body vanished likewise. There are certain special waters in which the frog, green or brown, is an irresistible bait for bass and pike.

In the temperate zone, east or west, there are a large number of species of astonishing variety as to size, shape, and color. The most abundant, covering a wider range, is the black-spotted, green leopard-frog; also the brown, banded pickerel frog; it is to these two kinds I have devoted much time in the last several years in developing a perfect artificial imitation so as to give the angler a worthy substitute for the live frog. In all my long fishing career I do not know of a more painful or cruel pastime than casting out a live frog hooked by the lips. If not taken by the fish in the first few casts, the frog turns over on its back, swells up like a rubber ball, and is then worse than useless. In that condition some anglers take it from the hook, give it a short respite by hooking a new one. A far more effective way to fish a frog is to just drop it on the water, sit still and wait while froggie wends its own path without restraint till it happens to meet its doom in the shape of a savage fish on the lookout for just such a gastronomic tidbit as the bass considers it to be.

The ideal frog water is a weedy, shallow lake, and although very prolific, they are never abundant where game-fish abide. Being both a land and water creature they live in constant danger of being devoured, not only by fish, but by reptiles, birds, and animals which take the frog as part of their diet, from the smallest tadpole to the big bullfrog. Along the riverside an observing angler will find many more frogs than he would imagine, particularly about grassy slopes and shallow backwaters. I have noticed that their color is similar to their environment. You observe most often the brown frog near rocky, stony shores, and the green frog mostly abide among the green weeds and grasses of both lakes and streams.

This fact is well to remember in the choice of color to use for bait, for the reason that fish naturally are more apt to prefer a bait similar to their daily diet. Between the two species, brown or green, there seems to be no preference; one is just as effective as the other, but I do think if brown is common in a certain locality, it is wisdom to use that color, natural or artificial. The habits of the frog are so well known it is not necessary to give details. My artificial is unsuitable for trolling. Like the natural frog it should be cast lightly in open spaces between weeds and lilypads, or just made to skip along the surface of open water. In a running stream frogs do not often swim across, but when they do, they strike rapidly along with the water flow. They are most effective when cast at the sides where the water is fairly deep and are visible to the fish lying below in the middle of the stream.

Fishing Knots and Kinks

From *Kinks: A Book of 250 Helpful Hints for Hunters, Anglers and Outers*
edited by Harry N. Katz, 1917

A Hook they can't Swallow

By I. E. Catterton

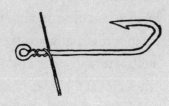

How many of you have had trouble in removing your hook from the mouth of a fish after you have caught him, simply because he had swallowed the hook too deeply? Now if you will get a small piece of wire and twist it tightly around the shank of your hook, letting the ends project about an inch, you will have no such trouble. The wire prevents the fish from swallowing the hook. Do not place the wire too far down on the shank nor yet too far back. Use your own judgment in this and regulate your distance according to the size and length of the hook you are using.

A Hinge Fire Rack

By Geo. K. Parker

The accompanying simple kink is a great help on a camping trip of any kind. It is easy to carry and will save many a turned-over coffee pot or frying pan. You take three 8-inch strap hinges and just put a stove bolt through the middle hole and you've got

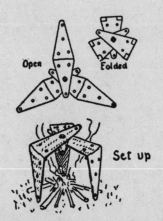

the dandiest little fire rack ever made. When not in use it can be folded and carried in coat or grip.

A Simple Rod Holder

By Wm. Herwig

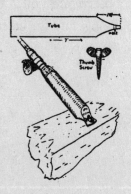

Desiring a rod holder for trolling, still-fishing and the like, I set about to make one. In a plumbing shop I found a piece of tubing that just slipped easily over the butt of my rod. This I purchased for the enormous cost of five cents. Next I cut off the tube to about seven inches in length and proceeded to pinch or flatten one end with a few blows from a hammer. In this flattened end I bored a hole large enough to accommodate an ordinary thumb screw. Now all I have to do is to screw my bit of tube tight to the edge of the boat or pier, stick in my rod and I am all set. Where it is not desired to screw the tube tight, a bit of string may be run through the screw hole in the tube and tied to the boat. I find it best to have the tubing of such a diameter as to allow the rod handle a little play.

An Antproof Bread Box

By Frank E. Wilder

One of the most disagreeable experiences of camp life is to come home after a long fish or hunt, to the little log cabin for a good supper and find that red ants or cockroaches have beaten you to it by several hours. You say to yourself, "There is no use trying to keep food from hungry red ants; what more can a man do than to put his food into a good bread box?"

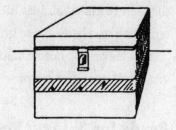

Fly-paper.

Here is what he can do to prevent those unpleasant raids on his food supply which keep his wife from being with him: Buy five cents' worth of fly paper. Take a sheet and cut it lengthwise in strips. Cover the back of one strip with paste (a mixture of flour and water can be used) and place it horizontally on the side of your food container, as in the diagram. Continue to paste on the strips in the same manner until you have completely encircled your container with fly paper. Now no bug that walks can get into your bread box and spoil that big meal you and your wife are going to have after a day in the open.

CARTRIDGE BELTS

By A. W. Stevens

Do you prefer to carry your cartridges in a belt, but refrain from doing so because they slip out and are lost? A strip of rather thick leather sewed on the belt a short distance above the loops will help hold

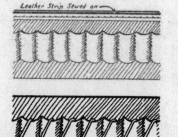

the cartridges in. This is not an absolute insurance against loss, but it helps.

To carry cartridges in a belt made for cartridges of a larger size, lace a leather thong or thick string through the loops. If there is still too much room, lace back again so as to cross the strings.

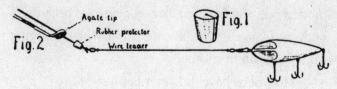

Keeping Agate Tip from Chipping or Breaking

By C. L. Creutz

During August, when on a fishing trip in Wisconsin, I had the misfortune of breaking the agate tip on a Heddon casting rod. I always use a wire leader in casting, as it is very much easier to change "plugs" if the bass are not "looking 'em over" as they should. After a cast I retrieved the lure too closely to the tip, causing it to break the agate. Luckily, I had another tip with me and had an inspiration to keep this one intact. Found in my tackle box (for some reason or other placed there several years ago) an Eberhard Faber rubber pencil eraser. Then the thought struck me, "Why not make a protector for the tip?" No sooner said than done. Took the eraser and with a knife cut it into about six or seven "protectors" looking something like Figure 1. Took a small nail and poked a hole through from top to bottom of "protector." Drew my line through it and fastened line to leader as in Fig. 2. Had no more trouble and did not even have to watch the leader when I retrieved the lure, as the moment the rubber protector struck the tip I had to quit winding her up. Intend to have a couple of erasers in my tackle box for emergency cases in the future.

A Kink on Fish Transportation

By George Raveling

Have you ever taken a trip to some isolated lake, fished for a couple of days and captured a fine mess of the finny beauties and on the morning of departure turned them all back out of your live box into the lake on account of not being able to procure ice, and a pail to carry them in, or because both were too cumbersome to handle while changing from one train to another?

Most of us have, however badly we have wanted to take just a mess home to our family or a couple to pass along to some doubting Thomas who seemed skeptical about our tales (tales, mind you, not tails), of what we caught. Here is how I succeeded in taking a nice little bunch home without being cumbersome and without ice on a warm June day, although the location of the fishing waters made it necessary to travel all day and make five changes en route.

First the fish were gutted and gilled and washed clean inside and out. Then the insides were stuffed with green cottonwood leaves and more leaves spread upon several thicknesses of paper upon which the fish were placed, and another layer of leaves over the fish. Then the bundle was rolled up, being careful to overlap the ends, and several more papers wrapped around the outside.

The package, upon being unwrapped after the journey, disclosed the fish in as fine shape as when they left the lake; and let me tell you, they look real tempting in a bed of nice green leaves.

If leaves are not available, good clean slough grass will serve the purpose just as well.

Beads for Salmon Eggs
By E. S. Brooks

It is unlawful to use salmon eggs for bait in Oregon, but there is nothing said about amber beads. So I take a small vial, full it with small amber beads the size of salmon eggs, put in some water and cork it up. I attach my triple hook with a small rubber band around one hook, fasten it to the neck of the vial with a few turns of a fine fish line, and there you are.

It works equally well with a good, fat grasshopper or grampus, but in that case I do not put any water in the vial, as they are surface baits. The glass being invisible in the water, the redsides go for the bait to beat three of a kind.

Caring for Fishing Gear, Casting Tips, and More

From *Streamcraft* by George Parker Holden, 1919

Some Tips on Caring for Your Fish Rod

Never leave your rod lying on the ground for length of time, and never leave it in the bottom of a boat, an invitation for it to be stepped on. Above all do not leave it lying out over-night, or standing up against a tree or the side of the tent in camp. Do not leave it out overnight at all—take it indoors; and keep it out of the water when fishing. After use, carefully straighten out any joints that may have become bent from unusual stress, dry it with a soft cloth, and apply a little thin oil, like "Three-in-One," both to rod and the steel guides. Never put it away in a damp bag. When the rod is disjointed even the individual joints should not stand on end and lean against a support. And when assembled and it is resting horizontally, see to it that its support is equally and well distributed throughout its entire length.

While the rod is unused for a long time, as during the Winter months, the very best method of storage is to joint up the rod and hang it by its tip; and whether a little warped or simply to keep it true it is a good plan to attach a weight—a flatiron for instance—to the butt. If space for this procedure be not available, hang up at least the jointed top- and middle-joints in this way; or suspend each individual joint from its end. And they should be hung in a place neither too damp nor too dry. A continuous exposure to dampness will warp any rod, and an excessively dry atmosphere will so shrink the wood as to loosen the ferrules.

Rods kept on grooved forms or so transported should not have the retaining-tapes tied too tightly around the joints. You can achieve a very serviceable and inexpensive carrying-case by means of a piece of ordinary galvanized leader pipe painted with green enamel. A wooden plug supplies the bottom and you can make a cap of sole-leather for the other end (or resort to the harness-maker) and attach a leather handle at the middle.

If there is a very pronounced set or warp in any of the joints, the hanging treatment alone is not effective; before applying it over, correct the defective joint by bending it strongly in the opposite direction at the points needing treatment, between little wooden pegs thrust into holes in a board, or between partly-driven wire nails the sides of which are padded with a good thickness of cardboard. Leave it thus for a time, but do not neglect to inspect it occasionally. Another method is to secure the larger end of the joint between the jaws of your vise, so that the joint will extend horizontally in front of your workbench, and attach a light weight to the unsupported end, and so leave it for a season. This by the way is a handy method of making accurate comparisons as to the relative rigidity of joints or of rods, by measuring the extent of the vertical deflection produced by a definite weight. Or you may support the warped joint at both ends, in such a manner as will prevent its turning on its axis, and hang a weight from the middle. For the very worst cases of "the bends" the only way is to remove wrappings, mountings, and varnish and then to remedy the condition after carefully heating the wood over a lamp or gas flame.

Rods are often set by the strain of playing and holding an extra big fish, though in the aggregate most of them are required to do much more work in luring than in landing the quarry. The use of the Wells detachable grip or handgrasp is a very important factor in preserving rods from set, permitting as it does intermittent change in the direction of chief strain throughout the day's, week's, or season's casting and fishing. Another advantage of the independent handle is that the permanent grasp will interfere with bunching the joints of a number of rods when packing them for transportation. The slender tops especially are liable to become bent where the handle prevents these joints from lying snugly alongside of buttjoints.

Any loosened windings or ferrules or chipped or cut places in the varnish should receive prompt attention; and after a season of long-continued and frequent use the whole rod should have a light rubbing-down with rotten-stone and water and then receive a thin new coat of the best quality of spar varnish. Wood ashes or powdered chalk mixed with linseed oil, Sapolio, or Dutch Cleanser will clean up tarnished German-silver ferrules or other metal parts; but you don't want them too bright.

A rod that is too limber or "whippy" to suit the taste of its owner may be stiffened materially by judicious amputation at the end of the joints; a half-inch to an inch removed from one or more joint-ends will make a great difference in the action. The best place to operate at first is at the small end of the middle-joint and large end of the top. In many instances the small end of the butt does not need attention, and the butt end of the middle-joint should never be touched.

To repair a smashed joint (it generally is the top), cut and file the broken ends to a bevel at least an inch long; glue, wind solid with silk, and

varnish. If practicable place a guide at the splice. An emergency repair may be made by splicing the fracture with birch-bark or a split reed from the streamside, and adhesive tape may be used for the binding.

To prevent the joints of your rod from sticking together at the ferrules so tightly as to make it difficult to disjoint them after use, lubricate the male or inner ferrule before assembly with a little mutton-tallow or vaseline. Or you can make use of some of your own natural oil by wiping the center ferrule against the hair at the back of your head; you should have some left there, but if absolutely bald you may resort to the side of your nose. Despite such precaution, if the joints persist in sticking after some unusually protracted period of the rod's assembly, and after a judicious degree of force has not availed to separate them, then try again after heating the female or outer ferrule gently and only at the offending point and then *allowing it to cool*; for this you may use a candle-or even a match-flame. In disjointing rods, do so preferably with a straight, steady pull—don't jerk; and—especially if a slight twisting strain is employed, at all—be sure that each hand has hold upon the *ferrule-ends*—that neither grasps the wood near the connecting joint. Before resorting to the heating process you can avail yourself of the assistance of a friend, who grasps your hands when they have thus been placed; then you pull together.

The remedy for the contrary condition of loose-fitting ferrules is the application of beeswax to the center ferrule.

In open country carry the rod, balanced, with butt ahead, but never carry an assembled rod any great distance through the woods; take it down even if you do not unstring it. In carrying a short distance through the woods or brush, wind the line spirally about the rod, hook the fly to a reel-band, and reel up the line taut. Have the rod pointing straight ahead of you, getting it through the openings tip first, the butt and yourself following. Similarly, in climbing a fence or crawling under, put the rod ahead.

Rigging the Rod.—To properly string a three-joint rod, proceed as follows: Pick up the butt-joint with handgrasp and seat the reel so that it will come underneath the rod, with handle to the right, when the line-guides are also down, and so that the line will render from the lower side of the reel-spool straight to the first or bottom guide. Draw from the reel about fifteen feet of line, and lay down the butt-joint. Next joint the top- to the middle-joint; thread the line through the remaining guides; and then—and not till then—joint the combined smaller joints to the butt. When taking down the rod you generally may reverse the process, yet discretion sometimes prompts one first to disjoint the top—when cramped for free space about the rod-tip. Attach leader and flies.

For fastening the line to the loop at the end of the leader we prefer the simple jam-knot reinforced by a knot in the end of the line, as shown in Fig. 1. It is a secure fix and yet the leader is readily detached. Fig. 2 shows another method, which makes it safe without the knot in the end of the reel-line and also has the advantage that the projecting end points toward the fly. Fig. 3 illustrates yet another good way. With some the stevedore knot is the choice; and occasionally an angler will be encountered who whips a gut loop to the end of his reel-line, or who prefers to fasten line to leader by the single fisherman's-knot (see Fig. 21), cheerfully sacrificing a bit of line now and then for the sake of having leader and line practically continuous. Again, you may whip a loop with fine silk in the end of the reel-line itself, and then varnish it.

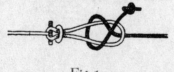

Fig. 1.

Fig. 2.

Fig. 3.

The arrangements shown in Figures 1, 2, and 3, for

Stevedore knot.

attaching the reel-line to the leader, are likewise applicable for the attachment of a dropper-fly straight snell to a dropper-loop in the leader. While not more than two flies for lake fishing and only one for the stream or any dry-fly work is preferable, there are many good anglers who like to fish with three flies on the cast when fishing with wet flies. One objection to multiple flies is well illustrated in the predicament of an angler who through hooking a two-pound chub on his stretcher-fly risked the loss of the three-pound trout at the same time fast to the hand-fly. Flies should be fastened to the leader about forty inches apart. The bottom dropper- or bobber-fly, next the reel-line (also called hand-fly), should have the longer snell or connecting piece of gut which suspends the fly; and it should be the larger or largest fly, as the cast will alight better when the end fly—stretcher-, tail- or point-fly—is a small one. The middle dropper-fly snell may be four or five inches long when tied.

There are numerous plans for attachment of a dropper-fly. Do not tie any dropper-fly loops in your leader after the manner shown in Fig. 4, because this method does not give a direct pull and therefore one strand of gut is likely to cut another (A). This form of loop tends also to hang parallel with the leader, thus favoring the fly's fouling—snell's winding around—the leader instead

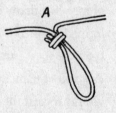

Fig. 4.

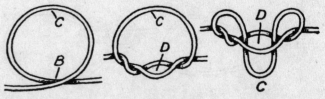

Fig. 5, 6, and 7.

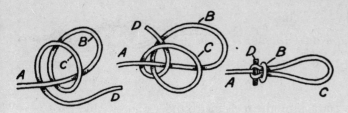

Fig. 8, 9, and 10.

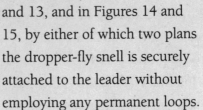

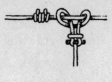

Fig. 11.

of standing out free of it. These objections are obviated by the arrangement illustrated in Figures 5, 6, and 7. Make a simple loop in leader (Fig. 5), roll the gut at B between thumb and finger (Fig. 6), and next invert the loop C through the strands at D (Fig. 7).

Neither should the loop in the end of the leader for the attachment of the line be constructed in the faulty way noted above. The best way is that shown in Figures 8, 9, and 10.

A double loop (B and C) is made in the gut A, as seen in Fig. 8; next pass the D end of gut between these loops (Fig. 9); then pull loop C through loop B (Fig. 10). Not a few anglers resort to the reliable bowline knot.

Junctions between loop and loop unquestionably are the most convenient arrangement of any, but many experts do not like any kind of looped connections—multiple loops least of all—because they enmesh air bubbles which make the cast too conspicuous and scare off the fish. Such would regard the methods noted above (Figures 1, 2, and 3), of connecting a straight, loopless gut snell with a leader loop, as a compromise. Another such compromise is the simple trick of hanging the looped snell of a dropper-fly against a knot in the leader, shown in Fig. 11. Arrangements more favored by the particular angler are shown in Figures 12

and 13, and in Figures 14 and 15, by either of which two plans the dropper-fly snell is securely attached to the leader without employing any permanent loops.

Referring now to Fig. 14, when traction is made at A and B the slip-noose is pulled tight, upsets itself, and turns the end of the snell over that is caught within it (Fig. 15).

The snell of a fly should be of the same thickness as that of the part of the leader to which it is attached; if it is much lighter in weight this favors the fouling of the snell around the leader.

Some anglers like to make up a *number of complete casts* for wet-fly fishing, each carrying either two or three flies, and to change the whole cast, leader and all, instead of changing individual flies. In making up such permanent casts a neat stunt is to form the dropper snells from extended portions of the strands of the leader itself, when tying up the leader.

Because the snell of any well-made fly will become weakened at its point of attachment to the fly before the fly itself will be unfit for use, eyed flies are preferred to snelled flies by the majority of experienced anglers. For securing the hook end of a dropper-fly snell to an eyed fly or the end of the

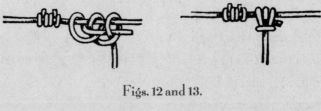

Figs. 12 and 13.

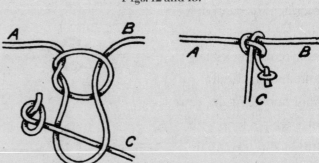

Bowline knot.   Figs. 14 and 15.

leader to the stretcher-fly, Major
Turtle's knot is reliable. Figures
16, 17, and 18 clearly illustrate
the maneuver as applied to a
bare hook. The only objection
is that in passing the fly itself
through the loop (Fig. 17) it is
liable to get mussed up. This
may be obviated by employing
the simple jamknot (like Fig. 1,
showing attachment of line to

Figs. 16, 17, and 18.
Major turle's knot.

leader, but minus the knot in end), but as this is
of dubious security here we prefer the very nice
figure of-eight device. This knot is formed as shown
in Fig. 19, the loop A is then slipped over the eye of
the hook and the whole drawn taut from the side B
(Fig. 20).

Leaders for fly-fishing generally are made
either six or nine feet in length, and tapered, using
at least three sizes of gut. For bait-fishing, a level
leader from one to three feet long will meet the
requirements. The fineness of a fly leader will be
governed largely by the sizes of flies that you are to
fish with; Refina gut usually is fine enough for the
terminal lengths.

For fastening the strands together the single
fisherman's knot is simple and neat. The detail is
shown in Fig. 21. The ends passed twice around
the main strands make the double fisherman's-knot.
After both knots have been pulled tight, pull them
up close against each other and cut off the surplus
ends. These ends may be cut closer with safety if
first turned in by an additional hitch, as seen in
Fig. 22. It will readily be understood that if one of
these turned-in or
turned-back ends
is left sufficiently
long it may serve
as the *snell for a
dropper-fly*. This
is the "snell stunt"

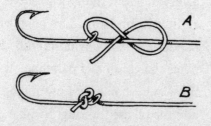

Figs. 19 and 20.

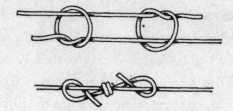

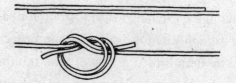

Figs. 21 and 22. Single fisherman's-knot.

Figs. 23 and 24. Single water-knot.

Figs. 25, 26, and 27.

that we referred to in a previous paragraph. Another
and a very easy way of connecting leader strands is
by lapping the lengths and then making a simple
knot (single water-knot) which includes both, as
in Figures 23 and 24. By passing the strands twice
through the loop the double water-knot is formed.
Yet another excellent method is one noted recently
by Mr. A. H. Chaytor of England, in *Forest and
Stream*, the details of which are made sufficiently
explicit by the illustrations, Figures 25, 26, and 27.

After leaders are tied up they should be soaked
again, then stretched between pins or brads and so
dried, after which they may be rolled into large coils
and put away till used.

When making or repairing casts and changing
flies on the stream, a most useful article is a pair of

tiny blunt-pointed scissors that may be carried in the shirt pocket. Have them secured by a cord.

Hook and Fly Sizes.—The most useful sizes of artificial flies for trout fishing are numbers 10, 12, and 14—the 12 in most brands being the best for all-round use—according to the American system of indicating hook sizes. Larger flies than these are used late in the evening, for large trout, for bass, and for salmon. Confusion arises from the fact that the modern British system of "new numbers" denominates the smallest midge fly as 000, the two next larger being 00 and 0. Then follow numbers 1, 2, 3, etc., the larger numbers denoting the larger flies. By the prevalent American plan—old numbers—the smallest size, corresponding to the British 000, is numbered 17; 16 is the next larger size, as the flies grow larger the numbers getting smaller. The corresponding English new sizes for the numbers 10, 12, and 14 flies that we illustrate are numbers 5, 3, and 1 respectively. (Number 14 pictures a dry fly.) In the plate showing the sizes of hooks, numbers 5 and 6—the larger of the series of smaller hooks—are Limerick bend, while the others are Sneck bend; all of this series are down-eyed, upturned-shank Pennells.

When it comes to larger hooks, used principally for salmon flies and for bait-fishing for bass, pickerel, and pike, the sizes and numbers run as indicated in the series of the larger hooks shown. Numbers 1, 2, 3, and 4 picture down-eyed Pennell Limericks; numbers 1/0 to 4/0 are Sproat hooks. The number 2 Sproat is a very popular hook for bass. We will reserve discussion of further hook details for the chapter on "The Angler's Flies.'

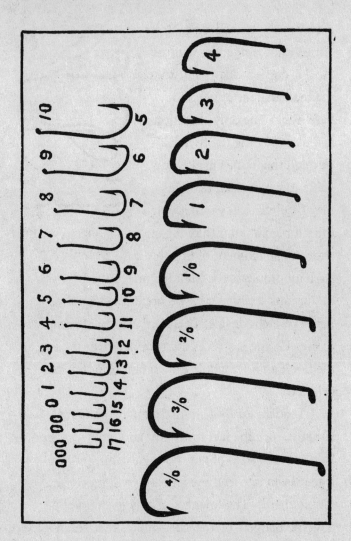

Hook and fly sizes and numbers.

"This reference to the subject of flies calls to mind a specimen of the curious advice sometimes thrust upon the novice by those who would pose as experts, writing in the sportsmen's magazines. Imagine that most dainty and precise result of the fly-tier's art, a dry fly, so carefully fashioned as to its radiating hackle and upstanding wings, carried *pressed flat* between two layers of oiled felt! The suggestion of Dr. Harry Gove of New Brunswick is a very different thing from subjecting flies to this continued pressure. Says he, place a few pieces of paraffine wax in a wide-mouthed bottle and add twice the volume of paraffine oil. Place the bottle in hot water, shaking it now and again until the wax and the oil are thoroughly mixed together. Now immerse the flies in it for a few minutes, then take

No. 10   No. 12   No. 14

them out and press them gently between two folds of cloth to remove superfluous oil. They will not require another application for a lengthy period.

If you do not possess one of the costly but convenient English aluminum fly boxes, divided into little compartments each with its individual transparent and spring-hinged lid, you can carry eyed artificials loosely in any small commercial hinged tin-box that is not too shallow. This is a very popular method with many of great practical experience. Or you can plait a piece of paper and place this in the box, and stick the flies through the tops of the folds.

Also you may manufacture a more elaborate handy receptacle out of a box an inch or more deep crystallized ginger confection comes in from the fancy grocer's, or out of some styles of hinged tin cigarette-boxes. This arrangement, as we will now describe and picture, permits of carrying dry flies without mashing them and in such a way that inspection of and selection.

From the stock is greatly facilitated. Narrow strips of zinc are placed crosswise on a pad made from the felt of an old soft hat, and each is riveted to the box cover by three small brass escutcheonpins. Another, removable pad which is riveted to a zinc base-plate, fits easily into the bottom of the box. Place the transverse strips on one pad opposite the spaces between strips on the other, and vary the widths of both strips and spaces for the accommodation of flies of different sizes. Upright pieces of zinc at the ends of the removable section strike the inside of the cover and keep the two pads apart when the box is closed. Give the felt occasional doses of turpentine applied by means of a

Homemade fly-box.

glass medicine dropper; this will keep the box moth proof. (A good general plan for the safe storage of flies is to keep them in a tightly-stoppered wide-mouthed bottle or preserving-jar.) Thrust through a slit in the felt at the right end of the removable pad is a small pair of tweezers such as any drug store supplies. The ear-spoon end was cut off and the shank filed down to make a bodkin for cleaning out obstructed hook-eyes.

Between the removable pad and the box bottom there is abundant room for a number of wet flies, eyed or snelled, in envelopes and for a few extra leaders.

The points of the dry-fly hooks are inserted under the edge of the zinc strips and between them and the felt underneath; they do not penetrate the felt. In placing a fly in position, turn it edgewise, pass it under a strip, and then turn it so that the fly stands erect. Reverse the process in removing the fly.

Even better than the zinc are strips of sheet celluloid or of oiled or shellaced cardboard which are sewn to the felt pad by their lower edges, and their ends caught by a thin leather binding which extends all around the borders of the pad.

The inside of the box may be given an application or two of white enamel paint and the outside treated similarly in green, brown, or black.

The novice should heed the caution not to attempt at first to get out any great length of line, but to concentrate his efforts upon clean-cut work; and he must learn that a harmonious balance of line weight and of rod weight or stiffness is absolutely essential to proper and successful casting of the artificial fly. A heavy line is necessary to bring out the action of a stiffish rod, but the same line will impede or kill the action of a rod that is too light or whippy to handle it. Lines most commonly used are graded from D, the heaviest, through E, F, and G, to H, the lightest of these five sizes. In most cases a five-ounce rod should carry an E enameled line, whether level or tapered, and anything over six ounces a D line.

A. Shipley's *Dictionary of Flies; Trout Fly-Fishing in America*, by Charles Z. Southard; and *The Salmon Fisher*, by Charles Hallock. To this we might add *The Ouananiche and its Canadian Environment*, by E. T. D. Chambers. For the literary side of the subject the reader is referred to the writings of Dr. van Dyke and to the catalog of, books in the chapter on "Fishing in Books," in his *Fisherman's Luck*.

"The styles of fly-casting which the angler should at least know about whether or not he becomes familiar with all, are: the overhead or overhand; underhand or side; switch or Spey; loop or grasshopper; wind or steeple; flip or snap; and the dry-fly. Of bait-casting—"spinning," as the English term it—he should know about the ordinary cast, strip-casting, and casting in the Greenwood-Lake style, with the long bait rod; and then he can essay casting from the quadruple-multiplying reel, with the short rod, Kalamazoo style. If upon practical acquaintance with the foregoing his ambition is not yet quenched, he can further try out all these with the *left hand*.

The overhead cast is the parental or fundamental style of fly-casting, all others being but variations designed to meet special conditions of weather or water or other obstacles. The rod is brought back very little beyond the shoulder and,

after a slight pause, line and fly (or flies) are shot out by action chiefly of the forearm and *wrist*, the elbow being close to the body. We have never seen the more important points that should be observed better summarized than by Mr. Samuel G. Camp, in the following words: Remember "to hold the rod with the thumb extended along the upper surface of the hand-grasp; not to carry the rod too *far back* in the back-cast [butt-joint barely beyond the vertical, or back of the ear—remember that the tip is carried back much farther by the pull of the line]; not to delay the back-cast too long, and to start it *forcefully* [mark that]; to start the forward-cast when the line first begins to pull on the rod, and to *start it rather easily* and *finish strongly*; and, finally, not to allow the rod to go too far down toward the water at the end of the forward-cast [it should stop considerably short of horizontal]."

The wrist action is an important factor throughout the whole process; it is emphasized in picking the fly off the water and then blends with the forearm motion in making the back-cast, and it is sharply in evidence at the finish of the forward-cast. In wrist action lies the secret of "making the rod do its full work." When once you have caught the knack of utilizing this element to its full value you will note as a revelation with what slight effort and

No. 1. Starting the back-cut. (End of the "fifth phase.")

No. 2. About u far back of vertical as lower part of rod should go. (Fly clear of water and end of line has started backward.)

No. 3. Nearing end of forward-cast. (End of line traveling forward. Note double curve in rod.)

No. 4. Cast completed. (Fly just dropping to water.)

how smoothly the cast is delivered. The *correct timing of the back-cast* and other fine points are acquired instinctively, only by practice. As one lengthens the cast, the back-cast pause must be lengthened correspondingly. A point that helped the writer much is to endeavor to throw the line straight *up in the air* when lifting the fly from the water, instead of *thinking* of throwing it behind you. Too low a back-cast, caused by *carrying the rod too far back over the shoulder,* and the failure to start the back-cast *suddenly* enough are the common errors of the novice. A quick twist of the wrist from left to right, in effecting the back-cast, seems both to facilitate it and minimize the chance of the line striking the rod or coming back into the rodster's face, especially when it is breezy.

(The accompanying illustrations of the overhead fly-cast are from photos of that veteran angler, the late Lou S. Darling, taken by Edward Cave.)

In a communication to *Forest and Stream*, Warren Coleman writes interestingly of a "previously undescribed movement of the rod in fly-casting" Says he, "In my analysis of the act, the completed cast consists not of three, but of four phases: (1) The back-cast; (2) the pause; (3) *an advancement of the whole rod*; and then, (4) the forward-cast." He claims this third phase to be vital to the proper execution of the cast of moderate distance and longer, and describes the movement as consisting of an "advance of the whole rod, including the butt, for the purpose of 'feeling out' the tension of the line as it swings back, in order to find the exact moment at which the forward-cast should be made." It is very well understood that there is such an exact point, when the line is going out behind, at which the forward movement must be begun if one is to achieve a perfect result.

We are inclined to believe that Mr. Coleman's observation is correct; also that his third phase corresponds to Mr. Camp's instruction above, to start the forward-cast "rather easily." Farther, we think that there is yet one more—a fifth (first in order of time)—distinct phase included in the act of casting. This likewise consists in "feeling out the line," but just preceding the back-cast. The rod is drawn in toward the caster to straighten and tauten the line or to bring the fly to the surface preliminary to the quick snap of the wrist which jerks it off the water.

Please note that Mr. Camp defines that "psychological moment" when to begin the forward-cast as the time "when the line first begins to pull on the rod," and *not* when it has *straightened out behind*—the time-honored injunction that one hitherto has invariably encountered. We have taken the pains to emphasize this here because the following paragraph in Mr. Camp's excellent treatise, *The Fine Art of Fishing*, is of especial interest to the present writer since it confirms his own observations of expert fly-casters on the stream, under favoring conditions of light that permitted every inch of the rod and line to be seen; and it is the first time that he has noted such confirmation in print.

"I have suggested," says Mr. Camp, "waiting for the line to straighten out behind the caster in the back-cast, that is before beginning the forward-cast. Instantaneous photographs of expert casters, however, show that in actual practice the line does not entirely straighten out in the rear before the forward-cast is started; that, in fact, there is a considerable loop at the end of the line which *straightens out just after* the caster begins the forward-cast. [See illustration, "Expert dry-fly caster at work." It is from a pencil portrait, by Louis Rhead, of that accomplished angler G. M. L. La Branche. He is shown as having started the forward-cast; note the end of the line.] The theory of this is quite plain. If, when casting a rather long line, you wait until the line becomes quite straight behind you, you wait just long enough for the line to lose its life. The forward-cast, then, should be started when the line, having passed to the rear of the caster, first begins to *pull appreciably on the rod.* But do not start the forward-cast too quickly, because this is likely to snap off the end fly."

The two-handed style of casting is preferred, we are not now referring to the use of two hands *on the rod*, as in casting with the double-grasp salmon-rod, but to that method in which the caster, taking the line in his left hand between the reel and the first guide, pays out and retrieves it with this hand when casting, fishing the flies, or playing a fish. (See again the picture of Mr. La Branche in action.)

Expert dry-fly caster at work
(From original drawing by Louis Rhead).

In making the fishing cast, the ensuing back-cast, and in striking a fish be sure to hold the left hand rigid, close to the body, or else hook a finger of the rod-hand over the line to hold it firmly. The loop of line, retained between the reel and the bottom guide, should never be too long, else it is liable to become fouled. On the forward-cast the loop, thus under the guidance and control of the left hand, may be shot out through the guides; such shooting of the line not only adding to the length of the cast with little fuss, but flies so delivered will land gently, especially if the line be *retarded ever so slightly* at the last moment before the flies drop. In single-handed manipulation of the tackle the same result is accomplished by raising the rod-point a little. Another and more generally known wrinkle of value in aiding this feathery alighting of the flies upon the surface of the water, is to aim at a point a few feet above the water instead of directly at the surface, in making the forward-cast.

Accuracy in casting is developed gradually by making it a point to aim at some definite spot on the water. By constant observation of this practice a complete coordination of eye, brain, and rod-arm may ultimately be acquired that results in the flies acting in a marvelously obedient fashion.

In making the *side or underhand* cast, the rod travels parallel with the water, in the back-cast, and but little higher than the rodster's waist. The rod-hand is kept low, with its back toward the water, and the line travels only three or four feet above the water. The forward-cast must be started quickly to keep the line out of the water on the back-cast. This cast is very useful under bridges, overhanging branches, or other obstructions.

The *switch or the Spey* casts are resorted to when there is an obstruction behind the angler that prevents the usual back-cast. Many writers consider them identical, but our understanding of the matter is that the flies are not lifted from the water preliminary to making the switch cast; they are drawn slowly toward the caster on the surface of the water. After being so moved a short distance, with the rod carried a little to the *right* and back coincidently until it is nearly vertical, and after a pause that allows the flies to *stop moving*, the rod is then brought straight forward and down, which rolls a loop of line out over the water; as the cast is extended the loop enlarges. (Switching the line in this way is sometimes employed to lift the flies off the water preliminary to the regular overhead cast. It obviates the noisier "rip" of the fly and leader through the water, incident to the customary back-cast, when there is a long line out.) Observe that, contrary to the technique of the ordinary cast, the line in the switch cast is *retrieved slowly* and thrown

forward quickly. In this cast as sometimes made both hands are brought into use on the rod, the left hand steadying the butt as a fulcrum.

The ensuing description of the cast named from the Scotch river Spey is Louis Rhead's. I have read at the very least a half-dozen different and altogether diverse ones. "It is necessary to fish downstream. We are looking down the river with a rocky cliff behind us; our rod-point is rather low, pointing toward the fly, and our line is extended downstream. Suppose our rod-point is at A; we raise and withdraw it smartly, following the curve shown, to B, when our *line will be off the water*; then we depress it to C again and raise it to D, by which time the fly and a portion of the line will be *touching the water almost at our feet*; then we switch the rod forward sharply from D to E, and the line follows round in a curve, leaves the water and rolls out downstream in front of us. The progress of the rod-point from A to D must be steady and rather quick than slow; but from D to E it can hardly be too quick."

The *loop or "grasshopper"* cast is distinct from the above, and often is unwittingly produced while casting a moderate length of line, when the intent was to straighten out the line in the air, in the

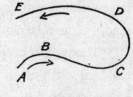

Curve followed by rod-tip in spey cast.

forward-cast, before the flies dropped. *The cause of this is bringing the rod too far forward in the forward-cast.* It is intentionally made use of in fishing when casting an unusually long line, to cause the flies to alight quietly. The line is doubled back behind the leader as it hits the water, the force of the cast sending the leader upward and onward in a slow

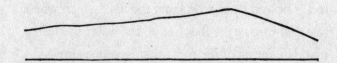

Line extended in air above water and flies dropping wholly by gravity.

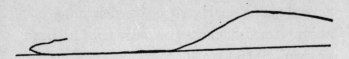

Line slapping water before flies alight (loop cast).

curve that drops the flies on the water some distance ahead. The caster may aim to have the loop strike some definite object as a rock or log, beyond which it is intended that the flies shall alight.

This is the style of cast also and of necessity employed in *tournament distance casting*, the record being 135 feet or more for a single-handed rod. Special, very heavy lines are used, greased with graphite, and about thirty feet of this distance represents slack line shot out through the guides. It has been demonstrated that the most effective tournament lines are made with a long front taper, a moderately short heavy belly, a quick back taper and with a small level back-line to facilitate shooting the line. In tournament work the line is not carried on the rod on a fishing reel, but is unwound from a large wooden tournament reel that lies on the casting platform near the caster's feet.

The *wind or steeple* cast employs the usual back-cast, only the flies are sent as straight up in the air as possible; and the line is then driven forward by a strong outward and downward *chopping* motion, which brings the rod closer to the water than at the finish of the regular overhead cast. Plenty of strength with quick, snappy wrist action is required for successful execution.

The *flip or snap* cast is used with a short line, under overhanging branches where free casting is an impossibility. The hook, at the end of leader and line withdrawn about as long as the rod, is grasped between the left thumb and forefinger. The rod is bowed by drawing taut the line, which when released throws the flies out on the water by the unaided spring of the rod—that is, it does unless the hook unfortunately sinks itself into the careless angler's finger instead. The cast may be lengthened a bit if a little slack line is held by the forefinger of the rod-hand, between the reel and the first guide.

In *casting the dry fly*, a single fly is orthodox, and is so dressed that it will *float upon the surface of the water*. Buoyancy is further promoted by the occasional application of white paraffine oil or ordinary kerosene thereto, and also by greasing the leader and some twenty or thirty feet of the reel-line (with mutton-tallow), so that they will not sink and drag the fly under.

(Theodore Gordon did not grease his *leader*, but preferred to have this part of his tackle to lie just under the surface.) In addition, several false casts, between the actual fishing casts, are made by switching the fly backward and forward through the air, to keep it dry. If you will carefully watch an expert while he thus is carrying his line in the air, you will note that his back- and forward-casts differ from those movements of the fishing cast in that they are less extended and are uniform and continuous—there is no definite pause; also that he inclines the rod to the right, in making the backward movement, so that the line is less likely to strike the rod. All the while his wrist is working his rod-hand smoothly backward and forward, the hand itself is swinging in a little circle from right to left—opposite to the direction of a clock's hands.

The cast is made up or up and across the stream, and especially over quiet pools and still reaches of water, and the fly is not drawn through or over the water, but is allowed to take its course with the current as it floats naturally upon the surface. If the fly does not alight with its wings standing upright—"cocked"—retrieve it immediately and cast again. The slight retarding of the line by the left hand just before the fly drops, as noted under discussion of the overhead cast, almost invariably *insures too the cocking of the fly*, and especially if used in connection with a high forward-cast.

The commonest method of *casting bait with the long rod* is by means of a side cast following a preliminary back *swing*. During the back-cast, of whatever character, no attempt is made to keep the heavier baits in the air; they are allowed to rest on the water a moment before being impelled forward, and some slack line having been held in the left hand or laid in coils in the boat, this is taken up through the guides as the bait shoots forward. There are various local modifications of this general technique. An enameled or some other form of waterproof line preferably is used, and it must be flexible and not kinky. In this style of casting it is of even more importance than in fly-casting, that the slack line shall not be inclined to spring into small coils, as enamel-dressed lines are likely to do when they have been left on the fishing reel for a considerable time prior to use. We repeat that a good rubbing-down with mutton-tallow or linseed oil before putting such lines away in large loose coils, and previous to renewed use, will promote flexibility. The long rod may be used with baits of suitable weight for casting directly from the reel, and the lightest baits may be cast like a fly.

In the *strip* cast, the left hand manipulates the line in something of the same manner employed in two-handed fly-casting. It is especially applicable when fishing from a boat. The reel and line are rigged as for fly-fishing—reel underneath rod and handle to the right. Sometimes a short gut leader is used, or one of fine wire if pickerel or pike may be encountered. The heaviest baits are used only with the short bait-casting rod.

Have about six feet of line beyond the rod-tip, and then strip an additional twenty feet or more from the reel and lay it neatly coiled in the bottom of the boat, so the line will not foul during the cast. Carry the rod to the right and a little backward—if

preparing to cast from right to left—pointing it slightly in the direction of the water, and then give it a smart swing forward, across the body, and a little upward. Just immediately before the rod points in the direction it is desired to cast, release the hold of the left hand on the line sufficiently to allow it to run out between the fingers, but retain enough control of the line so that it will not feed to the first line-guide faster than it will run through, else a tangle will result. The line is retrieved by stripping it through the guides at moderate speed with the left hand, in a series of short, sharp jerks. During this process always hold the rod-point well down in order to minimize the angular bend of the line, and consequently its friction, at the tip-guide.

The *Greenwood-Lake style* of casting with the long bait rod is one modification of the foregoing. The bait is cast forward as above, some more line stripped from the reel, and part of this additional slack is *taken up in the subsequent back-cast*, wherein the bait is allowed to rest upon the water behind the caster for an instant; then it is brought forward for the final or fishing cast with the line *pulling taut in the left hand* which grasps it; and as the bait thus shoots forward again, as much *more slack* as possible is carried out through the guides, thus considerably increasing the length of the cast. The fishing cast is made with the casting-arm fully extended and with

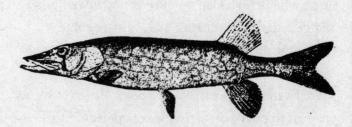

Pickerel (*esox reticulatus*).

Wet and dry flies on the water.

Pike (*esox lucius*).

a swing of the whole body from right to left, in the direction that it is intended to land the bait.

A modification of strip-casting is sometimes employed in boat fishing with the *short casting-rod*, but one having the reel below the hand. The rodster generally is seated, and the overhead cast is used exactly as soon to be described, except that instead of casting from and also retrieving the line by means of the multiplying-reel, the line runs out from coils laid in the bottom of the boat and is then retrieved by the left hand, in the short jerks characteristic of all strip casts. The reel may be single-action and the click is on. The line is held until the end of the swing, and subsequently rendered and controlled, between the first and second fingers of the rod-hand.

"*Bait-casting*"—has come to be understood to mean the casting of artificial bait directly from the reel and by means of a short rod, as distinguished from casting the lighter natural or artificial baits with a long rod. The method originated in the West and has had a rapid growth in popularity. It is applicable either to lake or stream. The writer well recalls the advent of the first exponent of this style of fishing in Ulster County, New York, about the year 1898, and the excitement he caused by the many big bass that he caught in the then novel manner in local lakes. The baits used—generally some of the innumerable varieties of artificial lures, whether wooden minnows or otherwise, and generically designated "plug"—have some of them as many as five gangs of three hooks each! Many if not most—and whether for "topwater" or "underwater" use—carry nine hooks. However we are glad to note that a recent development in this class of baits is a line of miniature wooden minnows carrying only a double or even a single hook and designed for use with the long rod; they are called in the trade "fly-rod wigglers."

The most insatiable bait-casting addicts are known as "plug fans" or "pluggers." If the plug fisherman finds himself in the way of attempting to invest in and try out every variety of bass lure that is advertised in the sportsmen's magazines as a "sure killer," his path surely will lead either to bankruptcy or to the insane asylum. The following equipment of this class is sufficient: An underwater bait of the wooden-minnow type, say with green back and white belly; a red and white small "Tango" minnow; a surface bait of the revolving-head type, colored white, or yellow with gold spots; a "Baby Crab Wiggler"; some large bucktail-flies and an assortment of other interchangeable bass flies of different colors, which can be attached to a small spoon and used with or without pork-rind strips, as noted in the chapter on "Flies." The last, and lighter, baits require weighting in order to cast them with the short rod, and a "coin" sinker placed a little ahead of the fly and against a split-shot serves the purpose nicely. These remarks apply also to the phantom minnow.

The casting itself is as complex as fly-casting and hence quite as productive of pleasure as the satisfactory accomplishment of any bit of involved technique. But however enthusiastic the reader may become over this mode of angling, it is hoped that he will restrict the armament on whatever types of "dreadnaught" or "submarine" he shall particularly affect, to the use of *three single hooks at most* (the legal limit in some waters), or better yet, to one.

The cast is made either by a side or overhead movement. The former is the easier to learn and drops the lure with less splash; the latter is more accurate and with it a longer stretch of water may be covered. Eighty or ninety feet is only a moderate cast for one who is proficient. The standard line for this game is a small hard-braided undressed-silk one, though some prefer the soft-braided finish. A line of twelve pounds breaking strength is very popular. The smaller the line, the less friction and weight, consequently the longer the cast that it is possible to make. For tournament work a very light line is used (often the domestic size A sewing silk) and a stronger, short piece—trace—is attached to the one-half or three-quarter ounce casting-weight to take the initial strain. The *reel used is a quadruple-multiplier*—making four turns of the spool to one of the handle—designed for this especial purpose; it has a wide spool. Meek's "Simplex," the "South Bend" anti-backlash, the "Redifor," the "Talbot," Hasting's "Good Luck," the Benjamin "Thumezy," the "Worth," and Meisselbach's "Takapart" and "Tripart" are among the very best of moderate-priced reels of this class. Some are obtainable in free-spool designs, in which the gears are unmeshed in casting, permitting the spool to revolve while the balanced-handle remains stationary. They also are made to automatically spool the line evenly, and again there are luxurious creations that embody all these various refinements. The "anti-backlash" patterns are a boon for night fishing. The common nondescript cheap reel would not last an hour at this work. Be sure that the *reel click is off* before casting.

In making the *overhead* cast the bait is reeled to within a foot of the rod's tip. The rod—not over six feet long, and five being the most popular—is first held at arm's length, pointing in the direction of the contemplated cast, with reel uppermost and thumb holding the line tight against the top side of the spool; then it is raised by gradually bending the elbow straight back over the shoulder as far as you can comfortably reach; though in distance casting rod and arm are carried back more to the side of and away from the body, as pictured. Also in making long casts, the body bends backward, the weight being on the right foot, which is behind. (In tournament *fly-casting* the right foot is advanced, for a right-handed caster, and as the body sways in making the back-cast the toe is raised but the heel remains planted.) In tournament work some raise the left foot from the ground and have the left hand extended and raised, like a shotputter's. The forward-cast is started with a smooth, deliberate, half-pushing motion that should be steadily accelerated, and finished with a strong, sharp forward and inward turn of the wrist, so that

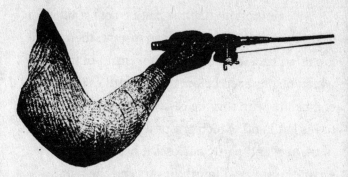

Position of arm and hand at beginning of a long overhead cast.

At end of overhead cast. Note reel position.

the line runs from the reel with the latter *on end, in the position of handlebar uppermost*. So held, the spool will spin most freely. The body is poised on the left foot, in front, at the end of the forward-cast, and in distance efforts the right may then be off the ground. In casting for accuracy, many right-handed casters place the right foot foremost.

Until the moment of releasing the line—which is just about as the rod-tip is above the caster's head—and permitting the momentum imparted to the plug to carry the line out through the guides, the thumb of the rod-hand is kept firmly pressed against the spool of the reel. The thumb's pressure is then lessened slightly but not wholly removed, a continuous gentle pressure being necessary to prevent the reel from over-running—running faster than the line is running out through the guides—and causing a backlash and its accompanying snarl.

As with fly-casting, better results are attained when actually fishing, by deliberation and a considerable wrist action which permit the spring of the rod to supply much of the impetus. With more force anti speed put into the effort increased thumb pressure becomes necessary, which, in turn, retards the line. Yet a full-arm swing is required with a stiff rod.

It is important that the bait be *not permitted to lie dead on the water* even for an instant, therefore it is started back by a drawing movement of the rod which begins even before the bait strikes the water; coincident with this the caster is passing the rod to his left hand, which grasps it just in advance of the reel and partly encloses it between the second, third, and fourth fingers and the palm, while its thumb and forefinger guide the line from side to side so that it will spool evenly on the reel, the cranking of which has already been started with the right hand.

It makes a sight of difference whether the line *is* let go at exactly the right moment; a too tardy release will result in the bait striking the water at the feet of the caster. The even winding of the line on the spool in reeling in is a very important factor of smooth, successful casting; without due attention thereto a backlash is a foregone conclusion. The great knack of the whole business is in this and in learning so to "thumb the reel" that its speed is at all times properly adjusted to that of the outrunning line. Backlashes are less liable to occur in casting from a full reel. Keep the rod-point low when reeling, to reduce friction at the tip-guide. Some believe in reeling in the bait very slowly; others in rapid movement or in mixing it up.

In making the *underhand or side* cast, the rod is held below the waist-line, is swung rearward at arm's length, and then forward and slightly upward with a steady, sweeping movement, to the point where the released line will shoot the bait in the desired direction. The other details remain the same.

At the Beginning of the Open Season.—A prime factor in the appeal that trouting makes to the angler is that the quarry, whose name is a perfect synonym for gameness, is the wariest fish that swims. In early April—until the young maple leaves are half out, as Nessmuk says—natural bait will be found more successful than the artificial fly. (The expression "live bait" is restricted to bait-fish by most anglers.) Trout are then lying quietly along shore, at medium depth, and avoid the swift water. The best way to take them is with well-cleaned angleworms or with white grubs, the latter being Nessmuk's preference. From toward the latter part of May—"apple-blossom time"—till pretty well along in July, and sometimes even right up to the beginning of the close season, is the fly-fisherman's Elysian period. Most success then is generally had from the rapids or riffles, or just at the foot of rifts; though the largest trout are oftenest caught in pools—"holes" of whatever size—at any time, the "whoppers" monopolizing the deepest and coolest places; but there may be a pair, male and female, "at home" in one choice spot.

Upon occasion large trout will go foraging at night, chasing minnows up into the shallows. As the sun becomes hotter the fish again take to the deeper pools and to spring-holes or pools at the junction of some inflowing smaller and colder stream.

We recently enjoyed the opportunity of studying an amusing demonstration of trout traits. A small spring feeder brook which joined the main stream just below camp served as our refrigerator and drinking supply. We had partially dammed this at one point and deepened the hole above. Where it cut in under the bank, near a projecting small rock, a baby trout about two inches long had settled himself. (Young fish are called "fry" until they attain a length of several inches, when they are "fingerlings.") Whenever a pail of water was dipped, upstream he would dart for some ten feet, only to return to his original position shortly after things had quieted down. When upon occasion a still smaller troutlet would come too near his preempted abode, the first would dart at him savagely and butt him away. "Little Jimmy" could be found at this exact spot at any time during the two weeks we were in camp. "Big Jim," who lived near a large rock in the main stream a little above camp—ah! that is another story, and not yet concluded we trust.

Natural Bait, its Collection and Cultivation.— Natural bait also is more successful when the water is fouled (roily) after a heavy rain, especially worms— sometimes grasshoppers—and used with a sinker. The best method of cleansing or scouring angle- worms (facetiously, "garden hackles") is to keep them in moss in an earthen-ware crock or flower-pot, in a cool place. The best moss is that having long roots, and such may be found on rocks where water is trickling through it. Large slabs of this may be peeled off the rocks, so cohesive is it. It should then be thoroughly washed and wrung out in water before receiving the worms. A teaspoonful of milk may be spread over it occasionally and a little sprinkling of water. Every few days remove any dead worms. In a week or less the worms have become toughened and very clear, almost transparent from having lost their earth. An English correspondent of *Forest and Stream* says that for fifteen years he has used in lieu of moss, a wad of dampened—*old lace curtain!* He dents a hollow in the top into which he deposits his freshly- dug worms, which cleanse themselves beautifully in their passage through the coarse mesh of the fabric. First wash out all the starch from the lace, then squeeze up tight, loosen up by shaking, and then place in a waterproof worm-bag.

When carrying worms to and at the water don't put them in a box and dump dirt on top of them; put in the soil first, worms on top and let them find their own way into it.

Worms may be bred in a worm-box, which should be at least three or four feet square and of nearly the same depth. In one corner of the bottom cut a small hole for a drain and cover this with a double thickness of wire mosquito-screen tacked firmly in place. Sink the box where it will not receive the full direct force of the sun's rays, but a touch of sunshine at sometime during the day is beneficial. The side of a barn is a good place, where the earth is damp; but it must have suitable protection from the rain so as not to become water-soaked. Sink the box two-thirds of its depth. Put in about six inches of good garden loam and then a couple of good- sized pieces of sod. Continue with alternate layers of loam and sod till the box is nearly filled, with loam at the top.

The best time to collect your worms is after a rain. Select only the liveliest, healthiest looking ones, and of course unmutilated. About an ordinary tin- canful will be enough to put in the box. About every two weeks replace the old sod and loam with fresh. The best feed for the worms, says "R. P. L."—who notes all these interesting details in a letter to *Forest and Stream*—is coffee-grounds mixed with corn- meal. (There was another detail, a most delicious one, concerning *male and female* worms, that Mr. Li—no! we will say no more; we forbear because of his many good works.) When feeding, dig little wells here and there into the earth and place in them some of the mixture. The worms will learn to find the places in short order. They should be fed once a day, and a couple of fistfuls is enough for a feeding. To "call up" the worms dash a couple of dippers of water on the surface; and this should be done once in a while to keep the earth moist. You can start this breeder in the Spring, or not later than June, and a couple of these boxes will supply an abundance of worms even in August, when they are as scarce as hen's teeth.

Other forms of natural bait, for fresh-water generally, include minnows and other small fish, crawfish, hellgramites, the pupæ of the dragon-fly, shrimp, snails, grasshoppers, crickets, June-bugs and other beetles, small frogs, field-mice, bluebottle- flies or a few similar, abundant species of other large land flies having two flat wings, and their larvæ (maggots), some of the larger water flies, as May-flies or drakes, also the stone-flies and their larvæ; salmon eggs, fish eyes (pectoral fins are used for artificial "flies"), meat (pork-rind also is used not as a natural bait, but to simulate a minnow), and vegetables. (A strip cut from a larger fish's side and white belly, near the tail and including a portion thereof, or the "throat-latch" of a pickerel, make good casting substitutes for the minnow.) Nessmuk's white grubs doubtless were the large ones found often in rotting stumps and logs, or dug from the soil.

Minnows and worms usually are fished downstream or across and down, with or without a shot sinker, and allowed to run with the current; unless bottom-fishing in still water, when a sizable sinker is used and perhaps a float or bobber. Worms are tucked on the hook by catching the point just underneath the skin at several places and leaving quite a bit of both ends to wriggle. This is the available method of fishing in small brooks or parts of a stream that run through a tangled overgrowth of vegetation which prevents casting. The bait is worked with the aid of the current into all the likely nooks and crannies, which often hide surprisingly good fish that remain unmolested for the most part because of their inaccessibility to the less venturesome and persistent anglers.

The smallest frogs are used and hooked through both lips, same as a minnow, unless still-fishing, when the latter may be hooked crosswise amidships, just underneath the dorsal fin, but not so deeply as seriously to injure it. Remember that the cardinal rule in still-fishing for bass with the minnow, to await the second run before striking, does not apply to similar angling for trout, which if you are to succeed in hooking them, must be given but little time. The bass grabs the minnow, makes a preliminary run with it, pauses to swallow the bait, and then is off again on his way, but the trouts exhibit no such methodical deliberation. Small grasshoppers are best, and the hook is inserted under the collar-joint just back of the head, and thrust through the length of the body to the tail, or else crosswise through the shoulders; crickets similarly. Or these fragile insects may be tied to the hook with fine thread, and we think that Mr. Froggie, if used at all, is also thus best fastened around the waist to the hook. Frogs are a late-season bait.

Crickets are found under stones, especially flat ones, after mid-August when the nights begin to get cool, and particularly on hills having a Western exposure, and they may be fed on pieces of peeled apple or on sliced tomato while in captivity. Make a cricket cage out of a cigar-box by cutting a window in the cover

Umbrella minnow net, open and folded.

Wire minnow trap.

and screening it with wire mosquito-net. A little screw-eye turned across a slot in the edge makes a handy lock. At one end of the box cut a hole about an inch in diameter and close this door with a cork secured by a string.

Minnows may be caught on the minutest of hooks, attached to a line of common black sewing-thread, and baited with small bits of worm, or a little ball of flour-dough mixed with absorbent cotton to hold it together. Minnow seines and "umbrella" nets also are used. Best of all is a minnow trap—collapsible or telescopic for portability—sunk in mid-water in a shallow spot, near or under the bank, and baited with bread crumbs.

A trap of the general style of the one pictured may be constructed in a few minutes from galvanized wire netting, of not larger mesh than quarter-inch. You transport it in the flat and set it up simply by lacing the edges together with wire or cord. The main piece measures 20 by 31 inches; this makes a cylinder 20 inches long by about 10 inches in diameter. The funnel end in the flat, is of the shape shown, having a 6½-inch radius and a 2-inch hole. The other end may be a circular piece of 10 inches in diameter. Anchor with a stone attached to the bottom by a short piece of heavy cord; and a small wooden buoy secured to the upper side may mark its location. Point the funnel end downstream. For lake use you may make it with a funnel entrance at each end. To remove your catch partly unlace at the end.

Making a portable minnow trap. Pattern for funnel end.

Upon occasion minnows may be scooped up by sweeping through a school with a fine-meshed landing-net, most successfully in the shallows at night, by aid of a flashlight; or they may be captured singly by stunning them by hitting with another, good-sized stone the one under which they have darted to hide.

It has been stated that fifteen to twenty minnows, from two to two and one-half inches long, can be kept alive all day in a corked quart bottle of water by changing the water occasionally. If the fish are biting well it will be necessary to fill up the bottle only when replacing the water spilled in taking out a fresh bait.

For night fishing especially it is not necessary to preserve the minnow alive, in casting, and the large hook used may first be passed through the gills and then inserted lengthwise of the body, entering near the tail with the point directed toward the head, and in such a manner as to curve the body and cause the bait to revolve or spin when drawn through the water. (The natural minnows preserved in formalin solution, tablespoonful to a pint of water, are not bad emergency casting-bait, and are purchasable in various sizes, by the bottle. They are sometimes used on an Archer spinner.)

An easy way *to catch grasshoppers* is to scare them into the water and then pick them from the surface; or go into a corn-field, scaring them from the grass onto the corn, and reach around and grab them off the further side of the corn-blades to where they retreat to hide from you; their shadows will show through the leaves on your side, revealing their location.

Grasshoppers—the yellow-bellied field fellows about one and one-quarter inches long—being one of the best of all-round baits for trout, bass, and the smaller fish—pan-fish—as well, during late July, all of August, and even well into mild October, Mr. George Gilbert's ingenious method of catching them wholesale as revealed in *Forest and Stream*, is worthy of extended publicity. (Special attention of Dr. van Dyke.) Two bait hunters, armed with a well-dampened piece of cheese-cloth a yard wide and three yards long, seek a level space where the grass is not too high. Such a favorable spot is often located, in midsummer, alongside a road or in a field clearing, that is swarming with grasshoppers. Each person holds the net at one end, so that it is spread out evenly and sets vertically between them. Make the "drive" against the wind if a palpable breeze, at a good jog for about fifty paces, with the lower edge of net just clearing the top of the grass. The hoppers, alarmed, rise from the grass and will lodge against the net and cling there because of the dampness. Then, at a signal, come together quickly, before the "belly" has had a chance to get out of the net, and wad the net into a loose ball. Sit down, unroll the net a little at a time and pick out your captives. Under favorable conditions, as on a hot August day and in a meadow recently cut over, you may net three hundred in a single haul.

Store them in a tin box that is watertight at bottom and sides, but is provided with a number of fine air holes near the corners, and with a two-inch slot at one end of the top, about three-eighths of an inch wide and closing with a sliding door. Keep the box out of the hot sun. For wading, carry a supply in one of the boxes, having a slide in the cover, in which several brands of "cube-cut" or "grain-cut" tobaccos are packed in.

Devices sometimes employed to get the bait where it is wanted or to render it more effective, are floating it downstream on a chip or leaf, or feeding it to the fish before angling for them—a practice akin to salt-water "chumming." The same thing is sometimes done at night, within the glare on the water, at a likely spot, of a fire built at the water's edge. A very foxy stunt is to drop a fly on a patch of floating foam—which collects insects—and allow it to rest there till it sinks through. Other forms of decoying fish are sometimes resorted to when food is sorely needed in camp, as placing some minnows in a large corked bottle, the cork having a small hole through it, and suspending it in mid-water. Maggots falling from flyblown meat hung over a fish hole will likewise entice fish. A blind may be made of branches, to hide behind, in the vicinity of some especially promising hole affording no natural shelter from which to stalk it; this should be constructed the day before fishing.

Other Trout Habits.—Further data in reference to the habits of trout are that the principal feeding times are from five to ten A. M. and five to eight P. M. They rarely rise at night after the steam begins to come up like smoke from the water, or in the early morning till it has cleared away. After a hard rain or in misty weather they are all-day feeders. The observation that the largest trout are not great surface feeders applies more particularly to the native Eastern brook trout (*Salvelinus fontinalis*) than to the brown or German trout (*Salmo fario*).[1] Trout are

more agile in rapids than in shallow water or pools, and must be struck quicker—indeed they frequently hook themselves in swift water, before the angler has time to strike; but irrespective of this the large trout themselves often strike more deliberately than do small ones. Southard says they rarely rise to the artificial fly a second time the same day [if pricked]; which means that they do—sometimes.

The swift-water trout is likely to be lighter colored and slimmer than the denizen of the dark, deep, shaded pool, which often is chunky and of very dark color—this referring to the same species in the same stream. Under certain conditions spotted trout (*fontinalis*) may spend a good part of their existence, like salmon, in salt water—*sea-trout* (but the steelhead trout of the West is a sea-going rainbow); they then grow heavy very quickly and change coloration, losing their spots. In lakes and ponds all trout and bass are largely ground feeders because they find most of their food near the bottom. Other interesting observations, by Mr. Southard (*Trout Fly-Fishing in America*), are as follows:

Rise most readily to artificial fly when they have been and are feeding and almost gorged. [Apparently regard the surface fly as a delicacy or sort of dessert—see further explanation ahead, in discussing "bulging" trout.]

Large "rolling" fish taken only on sunken fly.

Use larger flies in early Spring, numbers 4 to 6, when the fishes' sight is poor.

September (when open season) one of the best times for fly-fishing both in lakes and streams—just before spawning.

It is understood that the dry fly is cast up across stream and allowed to drift down with the current uninfluenced by the angler, and cocked, with wings erect; and that four or five false casts are made into the air before permitting it to alight each time. Blowing upon the fly occasionally also assists in keeping hackle and wings in shape. While the fly is traveling downstream the left hand is employed in

Brown trout, 20 inches. Dried skin mounted flat on birch-bark panel, nipigon indian style, in camp by the author day after it was caught, and eaten.

[1] Eggs originally introduced into America from Germany, by von Behr in 1882, the first hatching being in 1883.

gathering in the slack, to keep the line measurably taut in anticipation of the rise of a fish, and the strike of the rodster which should instantly follow it. The great obstacle to the fly's floating down on the current in a lifelike manner, insurmountable at times, is the "drag," caused by the wind or current catching the loop of the line between the rod-tip and the cast and drawing the fly under. The only way to combat it is to get directly below the spot where you want to cast and to cast straight upstream into the wind, or to lay the line directly downstream—"drifting" it—so that the fly will keep ahead of the line. In casting across, a drag may be partially ameliorated by paying out some slack line so soon as the fly has dropped.

Especially in dry-fly fishing there is every advantage in keeping the *rod-point high at the end of the forward-cast*—

The fly thrown well up into the air drops altogether by gravity, and thus the fatal error of slapping it down on the water is wholly obviated;

There is more speed, hence certainty, in striking the fish;

In casting directly downstream, the lowering of the rod after the fly has alighted permits the fly to remain longer on the water before being pulled under by the current.

Upstream Fishing.—As trout habitually lie poised or resting with their heads pointing against the current, upstream, whether or not on the immediate lookout for food floating down, it often is good generalship, especially in fishing the smaller streams having a quick fall, and all the more so when the water is low and clear, to fish *up the stream* and thus approach your quarry from below and beneath, regardless of whether you are fishing wet or dry, "worming it," or even if fishing with the minnow. By this plan not only are the fish less liable to see you, but also there is less chance of pulling the hook out of their mouths in striking, and any muddying of the water or loosening of gravel in wading will not disturb fish in the unfished water above. If using the minnow the bait may be cast up and across into the deeper water, and having completed the arc which brings it to the line limit below the fisherman, it may then be drawn up to him against the current, along the shallower side of the stream, in a series of twitches.

As upstream work is largely short-line fishing—the arm reaching out to the uttermost in making the cast and the rod being held high and the flies drawn lightly over the surface of the water directly toward the caster with a slow, quivering, and upward and backward movement—it is here that the ideal of "no part of the tackle on the water except the flies" may appreciably be realized. In this way trout occasionally are stalked and taken at the end of not

By courtesy of forest ant stream
"The smaller, rapid streams that are full of rocks and small pools".

over ten feet of line. But this does not succeed in broad, shallow, quiet, and open water.

Trout Habits; Lures and their Use

When it comes to the manipulation of the wet fly after it has been cast, "fishing the fly," our real expert customarily does not draw it against the current, but after casting it up and across the stream, draws it diagonally across  and down, on or just under the surface generally, and recovers it with the back-cast before it comes to a stop by the straightening of the line. The fly should most always be played deliberately over or through the water, *not quickly*; it should remain a *perceptible time*, and longer on still water. A good plan is to pause after it alights—draw a short distance—pause—draw again—pause—then make the back-cast. Flies are best played upon the surface by an upward and backward movement of the rod, under the surface by a side and upward movement.

It is better to use but one fly in stream fishing and two for lake fishing, and when using two the dropper or bob may just touch the water occasionally, the tail or bottom fly then being under. Flies should be attached to the leader not less than three feet apart. Mr. Southard commends fishing with the fly from four to six inches underneath the surface in calm water without a ripple; also the plan of making a few false casts even in wet-fly fishing, placing the fly *within an inch or two of the surface* before landing it quietly, when fish are rising to the surface.

Striking the Fish.—The following advice is pertinent with regard to the attempt at hooking or striking the fish, when fishing with the fly. It must be done very quickly in clear water with a snappy rise; quickly in roily water with an ordinary rise; slowly when a slow rise. The greater the slack in the line the greater must be the force of the strike; less force

is required on than under the surface; less force in swift than in still water. A slack line and low rod-point when fishing with the wet fly means that the fly is submerged. We repeat that large fish generally rise deliberately, often quietly sucking in the lure rather than "striking" it, and that they then should be struck deliberately by the rodster, especially if the fish itself is clearly seen in rising. The best general rule for striking is that you must not wait to *feel* anything but should twitch your wrist the instant you *see* any disturbance of the water in the vicinity of your fly. The novice needs also to be cautioned that *when using very fine leaders,* as *often employed in dry-fly angling, the "strike" should consist of hardly more than a tightening on the line*, else the tackle is likely to part; even an old hand may find himself reminded of this after a moment of excitement in the presence of an exceptionally heavy rise following a prolonged period of unfruitful casting.

Playing and Landing the Fish.—Ordinarily the fish when hooked is then "played"—alternately allowed to run and being reeled in a bit, or anon held steady on the taut line and spring of the rod—until when exhausted he is finally reeled in short, brought to the surface where he lies over on his side, when he is quietly netted, the landing-net being cautiously submerged well clear of him and brought *slowly* up underneath—no hasty "side-swiping" movements. If an unusually large fish is hooked in a stiff current, the angler sometimes may go ashore and endeavor to get below him, before completing the capture. It is this practise of playing which admits of landing a fish on the fine tackle that so often is essential to hooking him in the first place. Sir Walter Scott has pictured it neatly in some verses on salmon fishing in his favorite Tweed—

> Till watchful eye and cautious hand
> Have led his wasted strength to land.

This is all right for open water. Again, having hooked a goodly fish close to cover in a deep hole, or in heavy rapids from whence he cannot be led into quieter water, or when on a long line, it may be imperative for any chance of saving the prize to "snub" him, to "give him the butt" at once, that is to raise the rod quickly, causing it to arch strongly, and to net him soon as possible without yielding an inch, even at the risk of a smash-up.

When without a net the only alternative is to lead your captive to the nearest accessible sufficiently shallow spot and to beach him. Fish are never lifted clear of the water on a light rod and line such as is correct for fly-fishing, so that the unsupported direct weight of the fish falls on the tackle.

No trout under full seven inches long or bass under ten inches should be creeled (these minimum legal lengths should be marked on your rod butt or net handle); and all fish that you decide to keep should be killed at once, either by hitting them over the head, by severing the vertebræ with a thrust of your knife-blade just back of the head, or by putting your thumb in the mouth and bending the head back and breaking the neck. This not only is merciful to the fish but preserves its flesh in better condition.

Not the least of the beauties of fishing with the artificial fly is that the quarry, not gorging the bait, is not hooked in a vital part, but lightly, through the lip. The angler should therefore see to it that this advantage is not spoiled by careless handling in the case of surplus and undersized fish that it is intended to return uninjured to the water. Such fish should always be handled with wet and not dry hands, to avoid rubbing off the natural protective slimy coating on the skin of the fish. Once this is damaged the fish becomes the prey of parasites and disease that shortly kill it. Instead of grabbing the captive by the gills and squeezing him while he struggles, the hook often can be freed without lifting him entirely from the water or from the net and without touching him with the hands at all.

Dapping or Dibbing.—Upon occasion a large trout may be caught from where he lies quietly in a deep hole, by "dapping" for him. This is often resorted to in some difficultly accessible shaded jungle spot late in the season. It necessitates an approach close enough so that the bait, whether natural or artificial, at the end of but a few feet of line and hanging downward from the rod which generally is projected from cover of the bank, is steadily lowered right in front of the fish's nose. If he is observed to be lying near the surface, a suitable natural bait such as a grasshopper or the dry fly may be used. As he is allowed no quarter when hooked but, as the inelegant phrase of the vernacular has it, is "hossed out," stout tackle is essential. This is the small boy's regular plan of campaign, with a "wum."

General Observations.—When you start fishing begin to ascertain by experiment which method is best for the present occasion—flies on surface and in constant motion or slightly submerged and given a few deliberate jerks between appreciable pauses, at each cast, and fishing the rapids or the swift- or still-water pools. The flies should be allowed not only to follow the natural trend of the current and eddies, as would a derelict insect, but should be cast also just at the outside edge of the swifter water. The submerged fly is indicated for flooded, discolored, rough or broken water. Dark hackles are good for cold, windy days. Toward evening on dark days try the Coachman, Quaker, Grizzly King, Seth Green, Silver Doctor.

Trout lie along the bank and both above and below rocks in the current out in the stream, in wait for food floating down; above, in the quiet space under the rock, between the dividing waters, is a favorite spot for brown trout. Sometimes it will happen in a stream that you will catch mostly brown trout on flies and in the pools, and mostly natives in the riffles and on minnows; or in a large pool, brown at one point and native at another; or some analogous phenomena.

Fish all large pools first from below, and then work toward the upper end; thus you can land fish

"Fish all large pools first from below." (No "sportsman angler" this, but a typical "real expert.")

Photo by R.Lionel De Lisser

from the lower end of the pool without spoiling your chances for other and perhaps larger fish at the upper end.

Keep quiet, as screened as possible, and the sun to your front or side, never behind you, else the shadow of self, rod, and line will frighten the fish. Tread lightly along the bank, and slide rather than step, in wading, to avoid vibration. Aim to have the leader—they call it a trace or foot-line, across the water—*straighten out in the air and the flies to alight gently as may be at each cast*; nothing is of greater importance than this. It is well also to keep the reel-line itself off the water *as much as possible*, which means the avoidance of unnecessary long casts. The angler never lived who could cast any length of line and have only his flies and leader touch the water; such instruction is but a sample of some of the outrageously impractical stuff that has been written to the confusion of the novice. A proficient caster does however get out an amazing amount of line at the same time succeeding in having his flies and leader drop *before* the line rests on the water; this is something quite different. A short cast is one from twenty to thirty feet; thirty to forty feet is a medium cast; and forty to fifty feet is a long cast for actual fishing; and many more fish are caught with casts under than over forty feet.

Body Materials.—Aside from the hook, which forms the foundation or skeleton upon which the artificial fly is built up, appropriate materials are required for imitating the body, wings, legs, and tail—caudal stylets—of the naturals. For the first, peacock herl from the bronze-green plumes of that bird, herl from dyed ostrich feathers, and various shades of chenille, silk-floss, and of crewel and other wools[2] are used. In some brands the colors are shaded from dark to light in the hanks, so that you can select any tint desired. Mohair or pig's wool, harness felt, silver and gold tinsel and fine wire, and raffia—a tough grass stocked by wholesale florists— also are commonly used body materials. Raffia bodies are quite durable, especially if varnished; raffia also keeps its color when wet, and wool better than silk, which darkens considerably. Strips split from straw, from dried corn husks or blades of grass have been utilized. (*Emergency flies* may be constructed of flower petals, birch bark, and bits of clothing, etc.) Horsehair makes a good ribbing, also winding for extended bodies, and the white may be dyed. Quill from the most delicate feathers is used to wind the very slender bodies of *quill-flies* or "quills,"

[2] Henry Hesse. 399 Sixth Avenue, New York, is headquarters for crewel and other yarns.

which steadily are growing in popularity. For this purpose the stripped peacock herl of an eye-feather, natural color, bleached, or dyed, is most highly prized, its half dark and half light coloration giving a very natural ribbed effect. Quill-flies take their names from the color of the hackle, thus, Ginger Quill, Red Quill, etc. Quill has been also selected for making extended bodies.

Some anglers are very partial to these detached or elongated bodies, which curve upward from the shank of the hook where it meets the bend, but I believe that in the experience of most who have used them they have been disappointing. If the fly-tier desires to make any of the artificials with extended bodies, the *drakes—which include the March browns—should be so constructed*, as the tail-ends of these naturals are cocked up most emphatically. The March or large-brown category includes the March Brown, Turkey Brown, August Dun (drake), and Great Red Spinner—that is, these are varying forms of the same insect (not of the same individual insect) as it appears at different periods. A particularly suitable material for making these bodies, because of its color, translucency, softness, and flexibility, is delicate strips of crude rubber manipulated after the method of the late H. G. McClelland, a lamented contributor to the London *Fishing Gazette*, which will be detailed later on. And strips of vulcanized rubber cut from a very thin sheet and put upon the stretch have been utilized for covering colored bodies to impart a more natural appearance.

Wings.—But including the fashioning of the whole fly—body, wings, legs, and tail—there is scarcely a beast or bird of the field, or bird of the air or of the water, that does not pay tribute to the fly-tier. The quaint old poet Gay has put this prettily into verse:

To furnish the little animal, provide
All the gay hues that wait on female pride;
Let nature guide thee—sometimes golden wire

The shining bellies of the fly require;
The peacock's plumes thy tackle must not fail,
Nor the dear purchase of the sable's tail.
Each gaudy bird some slender tribute brings
And lends the glowing insect proper wings.
Silks of all colors must their aid impart.
And every fur promotes the fisher's art;
So the gay lady with extensive care
Borrows the pride of land, of sea, of air;
Furs, pearls, and plumes the glittering thing
    displays;
Dazzles our eyes and easy hearts betrays.

Turkey tail-feathers, the plumes or breast-and wing-feathers of the swan, domestic goose, duck, and pigeon, the guinea-hen, wood duck, gray and brown mallards, heron, woodcock, quail, grouse or partridge, blue-jay, kingfisher, seagull, and starling are mostly in demand for wings. Feathers from *waterfowl* generally are preferred, but nearly all the varieties needed are obtainable from domestic hens, turkeys, pigeons, and ducks. On some flies whole small breast-feathers or the tips of small wing-feathers (as from the sparrow) are used for wings instead of strips cut out from the side web of the wing-feathers; and, again, the tips of small hackle-feathers are occasionally employed, especially for spinners.

For a *transparent substance* at once suitably delicate and durable, recourse is had to the scales of shad, pike, or herring, and to the splitting of certain quills, as that from the root of a crow's feather, to obtain their inner membrane; soaking in hot water facilitates this. As scales and quill will take a stain some extraordinarily fine results can be produced; manipulation of these materials in tying the fly is aided by softening the wing-ends in warm water. "Cello-silk," a product used for surgical dressings, much finer than the thinnest sheet celluloid, offers most interesting possibilities; it will stand sterilizing, that is boiling in water. (We wonder if anyone has

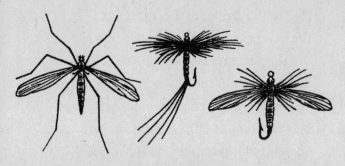

Natural and artificial spinners (middle fly represents a spent gnat).

experimented with tinted bond paper or genuine vellum, perhaps colored or mottled with a fine brush and the thinnest of oil colors and then dipped in collodion, marine glue, paraffine, linseed oil, or varnished!) Mr. McClelland has pointed out that newspaper print can plainly be seen through the wing-feather of a starling laid over it, and S. Howarth, quoting this, comments that no other feathers are so suitable for the wings of many small duns and spinners, number 12 or smaller.

In *handling fish-scales*, first sort them, discarding those too small or imperfect for use, and then separate the remainder into three classes, first and second selection and what is left. The largest and best formed will go into the A-1 class. They are readily sorted by picking up a mass of them with the left hand from a shallow dish of water in which they have been soaking (just water enough to cover them well), separating them by sliding between the thumb and fingers, and then by picking them up one by one with thumb-forceps and laying them down on a sheet of paper to dry. They will curl up in drying without pressure, but are easily flattened just before use by wetting them again and then re-drying between sheets of blotting-paper, with a weight on them, or by ironing them between cloths.

Harrington Keene even separated the delicate inner portion from the outer and hornier part of the scale and used that. (The late John Harrington Keene, noted American angling author, was born in England, his father being Queen Victoria's

professional fisherman in Windsor Great Park.) Python scales have been used.

We illustrate a pike's scale in its natural shape, and indicate by the dotted lines how to cut and trim it with scissors for use as a pair of flat wings. And by superimposing one pair upon another you may make double wings. Cut away the outer two-thirds of the central part, but leave a bit projecting from the angle between the wings at the root of the scale, to bind onto the back of the hook shank in order to fasten them with added security. The winding-thread passes over this little tag and the shank and between and under the wings; three or four turns of the thread are also taken over the point of the wing-V in front of the wings, in finishing. The writer ties these flies most successfully by first catching in the hackle by its tip, then the tail-whisks (if any), next winding the body, after which the hackle is wound and the wings put on last. The second sketch shows how a pair of upright wings may be cut from a shad-scale for a dry fly. They fold together along the median line.

Pike-scale flat wings.

Shad-scale upright wings.

Gauze wings are made from the most delicate fine-meshed gauze, stretched flat and glued over an opening cut in a stiff pasteboard frame. The outline of the wings to be cut out is then traced with a camel's-hair pencil, and veining may likewise be simulated, or imitated and the gauze reinforced by interweaving fine hackle or herl quills. One or more applications of a thin solution of varnish, marine glue, or of pure rubber dissolved in chloroform is then made to fill, stiffen, and waterproof the gauze.

Hackles.—True hackles, the long slender feathers with fine quill and stiff, readily-separating web, from high upon the necks of gamecocks preferably, are utilized for making legs, and a few fibers of hackle or other feather simulate the tail or caudal stylets. Horns or feelers may likewise be formed, and these latter sometimes with horsehair. Other than true hackles are sometimes used, notably saddle-feathers. Even the hackle-feathers of wildfowl, gamecocks, and bantams have more "pep" in them than do the hackles of the common barnyard rooster, and that is why they are preferred—they stand out better. They also are more lustrous. As the reader shortly will note, the rich brown (chestnut) hackles, the color of those obtained from the Rhode Island Red breed of poultry, are most in demand. The cochy-bonddhu hackle, brown-tipped with a black center, is another particularly useful variety.

The following notes are from McClelland: Hackles are obtained in all shades from ordinary fowls; blue from Andalusians; white, cream, and yellow from Leghorns and Dorkings; buff from Cochins. They are best collected early and late in the year. Feathers from the cock are generally used, but some ginger and black ones from hens. Other sources of supply are the wren's tail, black plover toppings, the jungle-cock, and various game birds from which come honey duns, blue duns, stone duns, yellow duns, and excellent red ones from the grouse. From the partridge, speckled brown; from the snipe, golden. The dotterel supplies light duns and the starling, black. The darkest and glossiest red-brown from gamecocks are called "dark red game." The palest and most yellowish of the foxy reds are called "ginger." "Dun" means a dingy brown or mouse color. Of the combinations, "badger" is one with a black or dark dun center and a white or creamy edge. "Honey duns" or "brassy duns" have a dark dun center and a honey yellow edge. The "furnace" has a black center and edge with dark red between; in a "white furnace" the white replaces the red, etc. A "grizzled" hackle is one in which light and dark are evenly mixed.

1.—Fasten hook in vise, at the bend, as shown. Wax about a fifteen-inch length of tying-thread.

(The McClelland recipe for wax is equal parts of resin and turpentine, mixed by placing the container

Steps 1 and 2.

in boiling water; then pour into collapsible tube. J. Harrington Keene's formula has been printed as follows: Burgundy pitch, 480 grains; light resin, 240 grains; mutton-tallow, 96 grains. First melt pitch and resin together, then mix tallow in thoroughly; pour into a dish of water and pull like candy, then lay on a piece of greased glass to cool. Cut into small pieces and roll in paraffine paper. Keep a small working bit in a folded piece of old kid glove. But in the third edition of Keene's *Fly-Fishing and Fly-Tying*, 1898, the formula is given thus: white resin, four ounces; fresh lard, one-half ounce; white wax, one-quarter ounce. Melt resin, add wax and lard, let simmer for quarter of an hour, then pour into cold water and pull, etc.)

2.—Starting just a little space behind the eye— to leave room for the hackle—catch end of thread under ("thread" means your tying-silk) and take four or five turns around the shank, winding away from you and making close turns toward the bend of the hook. Cut off close short end of thread.

The tying-silk must be wound *as tightly as it will stand* without parting, and a handy arrangement for catching and holding taut the thread at any time you wish to drop it is the following: Between the legs of a common wooden clothespin jam a piece of rubber from the front side of which you cut out a V-shaped piece, and then further make a cut into the angle of the notch to correspond with the leg of a Y. Bore a hole in the front of your workbench which will take the clothespin snugly, and into which you insert it head first. Or it may lie on top of a table, projecting a little beyond the edge, to which it is clamped under the end of the vise. When you want to relinquish the thread temporarily catch it in this rubber slit. No knots are made in the tying-thread—excepting possibly a single half-hitch the better to hold the work at some critical stage—until it is permanently secured when the fly is completed; it is "carried along" with the progressive manipulations of the other parts of the fly all the way to the finish.

A dry fly in the Halford pattern (split-winged) differs mainly from a wet fly in the *style of the wings*; its wings are *double*—there are four, two on each side, one superimposed upon the other; they curve or flare out, having their convex surfaces facing each other and toward the body of the fly; and they are set *upright* (cocked-winged) or inclined a little forward, toward the head of the fly (eye-end of the hook).

3.—If you make the wings from strips taken from a feather of the first shape pictured, you may cut them from both sides of the same feather, a pair of strips for each double-wing from each side; but if from a feather of the second shape shown—the shape of the long wing-feathers most widely used—you must get your strips from corresponding sides of matching right and left wing-feathers; for one fly-wing must have a curve and flare exactly *corresponding* to the other, not the same

Clothespin thread-holder.

but just the *opposite*; and the wings must be of equal length.

In cutting out strips, one-eighth of an inch will be about the right width for a number 10 or 12 fly. Separate them from rest of feather web with the point of a penknife blade carried edge first from the quill outward and upward between the fibers; or you can use the bodkin point. Now scissor them free at base, close to the quill. The proper distance for the wings to extend above the body (shank of the hook) in order to attain a well-proportioned fly is exactly the *overall length of the hook to which the fly is tied*.

4.—Cut four strips of wing-feather for wings and pair them, exactly overlapping; pick them up between left thumb and forefinger; place them in position on back of hook, a pair of the lower ends projecting a little below the shank on each side of the hook, where the tying-thread stopped; secure with a few turns of the thread in front of the wings.

(Follow corresponding maneuver for attachment of a single or double pair of shad-scale wings, but first catch in hackle butt under the wings. In making especially the first of these turns throw the tying-thread over the feathers loosely and *do not pull tight* until the end is carried well over, away from you, and around shank; then pull snugly directly *down*. Otherwise you are likely to twist the feathers over toward the far side of the shank. To further offset this twisting

Shad-scale upright-winged dun, tied by author.

Step 3. Cutting wings'.

Step 4.

Steps 5 and 6.

Steps 8 and 9.

of the wings around shank before they are firmly secured, hold them *twisted a little toward you* as you are pulling this first loop of the thread taut.)

5.—With right thumb and forefinger (or middle-finger) turn back toward hook, point the ends which project below the shank and then hold them with the corresponding left fingers; catch with a couple of turns of the thread *behind* the wings. Tension on ends as you fold them back pulls upper ends of wings *forward*, and the turns behind also pull them into and hold them in position wanted. (The curved-end dental thumb-forceps is helpful here, and long fore-finger- and thumb-nails are an asset for this as for other manipulations. Many tiers cut off these projecting wing-ends, without thus turning them back, but this construction is not nearly so durable.)

6.—With scissors cut off at a bevel the turned-back wing-ends (dotted line in illustration), and catch them in with thread.

7.—Strip the down from the butt of a hackle-feather. With two or three more turns of thread secure the hackle at the cleaned butt end, placed on

Step 7.

top of shank with quill lying between the wings, the tip directed away from the hook and with the outer (darker and glossier) side of hackle facing you; that is, the hackle may stand on edge (perpendicular plane), and in working away from you this brings the bright side to the front, or toward eye of hook. Carry thread in long spirals down to where shank joins bend of hook.

8.—Lay four fibers of hackle (some say two or three and others use five or six) or other selected feather fibers on top of shank where it joins the bend, and overlapping shank about a quarter of an inch; catch these tail-stylets with a couple of turns of thread; carry an additional turn *behind fibers to cock them up.* (The exact place of attachment of the tail-whisks, which marks the extent of the body, is a point opposite to midway between the barb and point of the hook.)

9.—Lay on piece of body material similarly and secure end; cut off surplus short end (in making full bodies wind two strands at once and loop it around thread to catch it in at the start); carry thread in long spirals back to wings and with the next turn *pressing against back of wings, pull wings up and well forward to desired position;* make the next turn in front of the wings, then two oblique (X) turns around shank and *between* wings, thus making their position more secure and *spreading* them slightly.

10.—Wind body material around shank up to wings, and by *forcing it up against back of wings further brace them in their upright-forward set;* secure with thread; cut off surplus body material.

11.—Catch the point of the hackle with pliers and wind it on, *on edge*, and with a slight twisting manipulation, first to the left then to the right to cause the fibers to stand out nicely, watching the upper fibers toward hook shank to see that they are not wound under and releasing them when required with the bodkin point; make most turns of hackle in front of wings, two *between* if you wish to further spread them, and maybe one behind. Secure end of hackle with a few turns of thread, perhaps adding a half-hitch; cut off surplus.

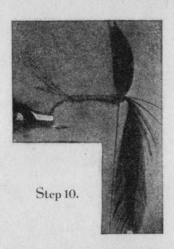

Step 10.

Step 11.

Step 12.

(Many prefer the hackle entirely in front of the wings; it is *not laid back* toward the bend of the hook, but is allowed to stand out in all directions as it naturally will.)

12.—Fasten thread with three half-hitches just behind eye of hook, or better, with an invisible knot of three or four close turns, working toward the eye and over the end which you have doubled back and laid under these coils parallel with shank, as shown in the illustration (A winds over and secures B). Hold loop of thread taut over point of bodkin and pull end of thread till loop hugs needle; withdraw bodkin, give a final firm and steady pull to make all secure and cut thread off close with a sharp penknife, being careful not to cut the hackle. With bodkin pick out any fibers remaining caught under turns of hackle or of thread. (Some tiers split the hackle through its quill and use a half-hackle to

mitigate this difficulty; but this seems rather adding an unnecessary difficulty. A much simpler stunt is to strip the fibers from one half of the feather.)

Put a drop of white shellac from the small end of a toothpick, or a similar sliver of wood, on end of winding to further secure and to waterproof it. (A good plan is to keep a little varnish in a corked vial, and to have a toothpick inserted into bottom of cork.) Spar varnish does not dry so quickly as shellac, but is better protection. In either case avoid obstructing the eye of the hook. And—eureka! Your fly is finished.

A friend in a rare moment of supreme confidence ('tis thus, one by one, that most of these little kinks are acquired) has revealed to me his "lazy-man's trick" for facilitating the tying of the invisible finishing-knot at the head of the fly. He folds a little strip of stiff paper, cuts a tiny nick at the middle of the fold, and first passing the tying-thread through this hole, then places the hole over the eye of the hook, the paper thus serving as a retractor to hold the hackle and wings back out of the way. Rather neat, isn't it?

The *wings of a standard wet fly* are made of a single pair of feathers or strips; they are dressed flat—lie close to the body of the fly, extend just to the bend of the hook, and usually they are not spread or flared out from the body, and are set with their concave surfaces together. Or a single-feather wing, as that from a mallard's breast, may be used with the concave surface looking toward the back of the hook.

A wet fly may sometimes be put together by tying body and hackle before setting the wings, and by making reversed or turned-back wings. Thus you would start it as shown in Fig. 1, catching in the tail and body material.

Then you lay the butt end of your feather (or feathers) to serve for wings, on the back of the hook, turn back—to lie alongside the quill—the lower part of web, and wind over all this (which thus makes body padding) first with thread (Fig. 2) and then with the body material. The feather would now lie with tip directed away from hook and with concave surface looking up. If two whole feathers, feather tips, or strips are used the concave surfaces may look up and a little out at this stage.

Next you start the hackle as illustrated by Fig. 3, perhaps catching it in by the tip.

In winding the hackle you will stroke the fibers back toward the bend of the hook after each turn, and you will remember that you wind away from you and that the brighter side of hackle must always face toward the head of the fly. Make the last turns, at the shoulders, more bushy than the rest; and after

Fig. 3.

Fig. 4.

all the hackle is wound on hold it well back by the paper retractor or by thumb and forefinger of left hand while you take a couple of turns of the thread or a half-hitch to keep it so. When the legs are completed your work will now look like Fig. 4.

It remains but to turn back your wing wings into place, to hold the same there by few half-hitches, and to apply the finishing touches (Fig. 5). If the wings are not thus reversed but are secured at once in their permanent position, you have a "straight-wing" fly.

It will be seen after looking over the list below that Dr. Gove is about right in stating that these *eighteen shades are most characteristic of trout insect food*, and that you will note that most of them are subdued and not decided colors: dark red, ginger-dun, claret, yellow, gray,

Fig. 1.

Fig. 2.

Fig. 5.

orange, black, olive, purple, red-brown, amber-red, green-brown, lead color, yellow-dun, mulberry, white, yellow-green, and blue. You also may note that the above shades may be well represented in comparatively but few sterling fly patterns, as in

Black Gnat, Brown and Gray Hackles, Beaverkill, Cahill, Coachman, Cow-dung, the duns including Whirling Dun and Hare's Ear, Queen and King of the Water, the drakes including March Brown, Bluebottle, Montreal, Red Spinner.

Camp Cookery

From *The Tramp's Handbook* by Harry Roberts, 1903

Boiling and stewing are the methods most generally useful to the tramp, and many a pleasant meal has been cooked in nothing more elaborate than an old meat tin. But, for general use, a pan with a swing handle should be provided. A useful shape is that illustrated. This pan or service-kettle is sold at the Army and Navy Stores, fitted with tea-kettle, frying-pan, gridiron, three dishes, three plates, three basins, three cups, three condiment boxes, vessels for butter, sugar and tea, three knives, three forks, and three spoons, all packing within the boiler. The whole canteen is sold for £ 1, 16s. 6d.

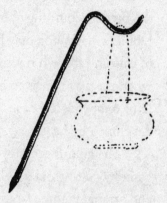

Kettle-hook.

A pan or kettle is easily heated over an open fire either by resting it on stones arranged to carry it, by suspending it over the fire from the iron hook or kekauviskoe saster, by supporting it at the end of a long pole as in the illustration, or by making the fire in a sort of trench and resting the kettle on the two sides.

Roasting may be performed by piercing the bird or joint with a pointed stick and holding it to the fire until cooked; or a rod of green wood may transfix it, the rod being supported over the fire by a forked prop placed at either end; or the joint may be suspended by the fire by means of the kettle prop. Frying is performed exactly as over the kitchen fire of houses—the essential points being to have plenty of fat in the pan, and to have that fat "boiling" before placing therein the object to be fried.

In grilling, as in roasting, it is usually desirable to subject the meat to a great heat at first, so that the outer layer of albumen may be at once coagulated and the inner juices thus retained. Therefore a clear, hot fire is required. The gridiron should be held about four inches from the fire until it becomes hot, when it should be smeared with fat, and the meal or fish placed on it. It should then be held about two or three inches from the fire for a couple of minutes, at the end of the first minute the meat being turned so as to expose its other surface to the heat.

Then the gridiron should be withdrawn to about six or eight inches from the fire until the meat is cooked, the meat being reversed every two or

Pole used as kettle-hook.

The "grip" broiler.

three minutes. A thick steak takes about twenty minutes, a small fish about eight. A steak should be about three-quarters of an inch thick, and, previous to being cooked, should be sprinkled with pepper, but not with salt. A very useful gridiron is the Grip broiler sold at 2s. 6d. by the Enterprise Hardware Co., 86 Dale Street, Liverpool. It is a double grid, and is made of polished sheet steel. Its perforations being set up inwards, it prevents loss of gravy into the fire. By frequently turning this gridiron, the gravy is well and evenly distributed, so that it serves as a self-acting baster. It is also useful for toasting bread.

A simple gridiron is easily made from a piece of stout wire bent as shown in the illustration.

Hoe-cakes and other products of the griddle-plate may be cooked equally well in a strong iron frying-pan, one with a looped handle which can be suspended from the kettle-prop being preferable.

Bread, cakes, meat or fish may be baked nearly as well by means of a camp fire as by means of a scientific oven. The simplest way is to build up a big wood fire and so get a considerable heap of ashes. These should be swept aside, and the cake or meat placed on the heated ground, the ashes being again raked over it and the fire continued above. A more elaborate oven may be made by inverting an old iron frying-pan or similar vessel over the object to be baked, and replacing the fire over and around the pan; or a sheet of iron may rest on four stones placed at its corners, the cake being underneath it, and the fire over and around it.

A very useful appliance is a sort of iron grille about two feet square, provided at each corner with a leg two inches long. The grille should be made up of stout transverse bars about half an inch apart. It is a useful base on which to build a fire, and under it baking operations of all kinds may be performed. If necessary, the space under it can at any time be made deeper by excavation. As an alternative to this, a sort of perforated iron box with a close-fitting cover may be used. In this can be placed a cake, bird or joint which it is desired to bake, the whole box being buried in the ashes or earth, and the fire kept burning above. Again, a joint, bird, rabbit or hedgehog may be embedded in a casing of clay and thrown bodily into the fire till cooked, when the clay case is to be broken abroad and the joint removed, full of its own juice and the aromas developed by heat.

The gold-digger's oven is made in a sloping bank by cutting out a right-angled triangular prism and arranging three large flat stones as shown in the illustration. The lower horizontal stone does not reach to the back of the excavation, being entirely supported by the two sides; the higher horizontal stone is supported by the back and the two sides of the cutting, but does not reach so far forward as does the lower stone. The front stone rests on the ground, and leans against the lower horizontal stone, but does not quite come into contact with the higher one. A going fire is placed on the ground, and when all is hot the bread or cake is placed on the lower stone.

The Bedouin oven is made by digging a hole in the ground and lining its sides and bottom with stones, a large flat stone having also been obtained of such a size as nearly, but not quite, to cover the opening when required. A big fire is then made in and above the hole, the covering stone being also heated, though not covering the hole. When the stone walls have become intensely hot the fire is raked out of the hole, fragrant or innocuous leaves are thrown in, the joint wrapped in its skin or in wet paper is also placed in the hole, the top stone is replaced, and a roaring fire is kept going above till the cooking is complete.

A wire gridiron.

A few rough general rules as to the time required to cook meats by various methods may be useful to the utter novice. They are stated but as rough guides, to be modified according to circumstances, but these modifications are only to be learnt by experience. Most meats and poultry require to be boiled about a quarter of an hour for each pound weight; that is to say, a piece of mutton weighing four pounds requires to be boiled for about an hour. Most fish requires boiling for about eight minutes for each pound weight. Potatoes and most other vegetables must be boiled for about twenty minutes or half an hour. In roasting, frying, grilling, or boiling meat, unless the joint be very large, it is necessary to expose it first to a high temperature in order to seal in the juices by coagulating the outer layer of albumen. It should then, especially in the case of roasting, be subjected to a somewhat lower degree of heat. Meat that is being roasted should be basted with its own fat or with made gravy every ten minutes. The time required for roasting is, according to thickness, from fifteen to twenty minutes for every pound weight, and fifteen minutes over.

Should it be wished to extract the juices from meat, as in the preparation of soup or stew, the meat or bird should be broken or cut into small pieces and placed in cold water, which is gradually to be brought to boiling point.

Trapping

From *Science of Trapping* by Elmer Harry Kreps, 1909

To properly set a steel trap on dry land one should dig a "nest" for the trap, deep enough to allow the covering to be flush with the surroundings and just a little larger than, and of the same shape as the trap when set. This hollow should be lined with dry leaves or moss and the trap placed therein. To make the trap rest solidly so that there is no danger of it being tipped over also to make the jaws set level, the spring should be twisted around towards the jaw which is held down by the trigger or "dog". The trap should then be covered with some light, dry material in keeping with the surroundings, a few dead leaves or a sheet of paper being used first to prevent the covering from rolling under the pan and in that way prevent the trap from springing. Instead of doing this some trappers place a bunch of cotton or dry moss under the pan but I do not think this advisable.

In all cases when setting traps at dens, on trails or at the entrances of enclosures, the trap should be so placed that the jaws will be lengthwise of the animal's approach so that it will step between the jaws and not over one of them. If the setting is reversed the rising jaw will sometimes throw the animal's foot out of the trap.

There are various good methods of fastening and the proper one to use depends on the nature of the surrounding and the species of animal that one is setting for. Water animals should be drowned as quickly as possible after they are caught and in order to secure this result the "sliding pole" is used. This is simply an inclined pole leading into deep water and of a size that will enable the ring of the trap chain to travel easily its entire length. The most common way of using the sliding pole is to thrust the small end into the bed of the stream and fasten the other end securely to the bank. The pole should have a few branches near the small end to prevent the ring from sliding off. All water animals when caught in traps plunge into deep water immediately and the ring of the trap chain sliding down the pole makes it impossible for the captured animal to again regain the shore. In order to make this outfit more certain when setting for large animals such as otters and beavers, a stone of six or eight pounds should be tied firmly to the chain but not near enough to the trap to interfere with the action of the swivel.

In trapping for muskrats and mink, the usual practice is to simply stake the trap the length of the chain into the deepest water available, the weight of the trap being sufficient to hold the animal under water.

Trap set in correct position at entrance of den.

For land animals the trap may be fastened to a "clog." This is simply a chunk of wood, a pole, brush or stone, the object being to hamper the animal in its movements and prevent it from getting a dead pull on the trap and chain. In fastening to the clog the staple may be used or the chain may be dropped through the ring so as to form a loop which is slipped over the clog, a few snags being left stand to prevent the chain from being drawn over the end. When setting for bears the ring is slipped over the clog,—a pole,—and fastened with a spike or wedge. Some trappers prefer to use a pronged iron drag and this is especially desirable when trapping for the more cunning animals such as the fox, coyote and wolf as the drag may be covered without leaving much sign. A stone may be used in the same manner by securing with wire to the end of the chain.

For the animals mentioned the traps are sometimes staked down solidly, the stake being driven out of sight, but this gives the animal a dead pull and they will sometimes escape.

Such of the fur-bearers as are likely to escape by gnawing or twisting off a foot may sometimes be held securely by the use of the "spring pole" or better still, the "balance pole." The spring pole is a small springy sapling, trimmed of its branches and planted firmly in the ground. The trap is fastened to the small end which is drawn down and held in that position by being hooked lightly under a crotched stake or a link of the chain may be hooked to a headless nail driven in the side of the stake. In theory this device works nicely but in practice it is not found to be perfect as the wood will lose its "spring" if kept bent for some time, especially in freezing weather. The balance pole is more faithful in its action. It is simply a long slender pole fastened in a crotch or tied to the side of a sapling, the trap being secured to the small end. It is so balanced that the weight of the butt will not only lift the trap but the captured animal as well. It is fastened down in

The balance pole.

the same way as the spring pole and is released by the struggles of the animal.

In order to keep steel traps in perfect working order, they should have a certain amount of attention. Repairs will be necessary at times and before the trapping season commences one should look them all over and see that they are in good condition. The triggers should be so adjusted that the pan will set level. All parts should work freely and the trap should neither spring too easily nor too hard. Rust on traps is not desirable and may be prevented to a great extent by boiling the traps occasionally in a solution of evergreen boughs, maple, willow or oak bark or walnut hulls. This will give the traps a blue-black color and they will not rust for a considerable length of time. New traps will not take the color very well but they should be boiled just the same to remove the oil and also the varnish with which some manufacturers coat their traps. Some trappers smoke their traps before setting believing that the odor of the smoke will smother that of the metal. This, however, is not in my opinion a good idea, as clean iron has no odor and the smell of smoke enables the animal to locate the trap, thus having just the opposite of the effect desired.

Others again grease or oil the traps, which is also bad for the same reason, and another thing worth considering is the fact that a greased trap does not have as good a grip as one which has not been so treated. For my own part I would rather have my traps red with rust than to have them oiled, and if it is necessary to oil the joints of a stiff working trap, use some oil having practically no odor, never strong smelling substances such as kerosene.

As before mentioned, steel traps are made in various sizes so that they may be used for all animals, from the smallest to the largest.

The No. 0 is the smallest size and is intended for such small animals as the pocket gopher, the rat and the weasel. If the spring is of fair strength as it is in the higher grades they may also be used for muskrat and marten. They are used extensively by the marten trappers of the Rocky Mountain region.

The No. 1 is known as the muskrat trap and is the best size for this animal. It is also used for mink, skunk, opossum and marten.

The No. 1½ is a very popular trap as its size and strength adapt it for general use. It is known as the mink trap, but the tendency among trappers is to use the 1½ for larger game and the No. 1 for mink. It is the best size for skunk, and if the spring is of fair strength, it will hold the fox, coon, fisher and lynx as well as all smaller animals.

The No. 2, which is the smallest size of the double spring style is known as the fox trap. It is also the best size for coon and is sometimes used for otter especially in the North, but in my opinion it is too small for regular use on otter.

Next in order is the No. 3 which has been named the otter trap, and it is the proper size to use for this animal. It is also used for catching the coyote, beaver, wild cat and lynx and is a very popular trap in the more remote sections of the country.

The No. 4 trap was originally intended for the capture of the beaver and is the proper size for that animal. The higher grades of this are also used to a great extent for trapping the timber wolf, also for otter and coyote.

The best trap for wolves, however, is the 4½ which was designed especially for trapping these animals. It is considerably heavier than the No. 4 and is fitted with a longer chain and a pronged drag. This size is also used for taking the cougar or mountain lion.

The bear traps are known as the No. 50, the No. 5 and the No. 6. The No. 50 is the smallest but is sufficiently strong for the black bear. For those who prefer a larger trap for this animal, the No. 5 will prove satisfactory, and it will also hold the grizzly, but is rather small for that animal. The size best adapted to the capture of the larger varieties of bears is the No. 6, which will hold almost any living animal.

The Skunk

The skunk makes its den in the ground, usually along a gravelly hillside, and it sometimes makes use of the den of the woodchuck. In thickly settled countries where the dens have been destroyed by hunters, they often make their homes under barns and out-buildings, and even under dwelling houses, much to the discomfort of the inmates.

The skunk is a nocturnal animal, searching for food only at night and remaining in its den during the day. During the cold part of the winter, they remain in their dens, coming out only on warm nights, until after the middle of February, when their mating season commences, and the males travel, at this time in almost all kinds of weather.

The young are born in April and May, and there are usually from four to ten in a litter, though occasionally there will be a larger number.

Their food consists mostly of insects, grubs, young birds and eggs, and when they have an opportunity to do so, they will kill and eat poultry, etc. They are also fond of carrion, and even the flesh of their own kind.

The skunk.

The most common method of trapping the skunk is to set the trap in the entrance of the den, without bait, but where there are many dens, or where the dens are hard to find, it is best to use bait. In setting the trap in a den, it should be set just inside the entrance, unless the mouth of the den is small, when it should be set just outside. The trap should be set with the jaws lengthwise of the hole, so that the skunk steps between the jaws, and not over them, as by stepping over the jaw the foot is likely to be thrown out of the trap, by the jaw, as the trap springs. This rule also applies to all traps set in dens or enclosures of any kind. The common way of fastening is to stake the trap or fasten to a clog, but the balance pole is better.

No great care is necessary in covering the trap, as the skunk is not suspicious, but it is always best to use care, especially in setting baited traps, as one never knows what animal may come along. On one occasion I caught a fox in a trap set for skunk.

It is a good idea also, when trapping at dens, to put a small scrap of bait inside of the den, as many skunks that are traveling about, only look in and turn away, and if the trap is set inside, will not be caught. If, however, there is a small bait inside the den, the skunk will attempt to get it, and will be caught in the trap.

Traps set for skunk should be visited every day, as otherwise the captured animals are likely to escape. They seem to struggle more on dark stormy nights, and during such weather, one should get around to his traps as early as possible in the morning.

Sometimes one can find a well-defined trail leading away from the mouth of the den. In such a case, several traps may be set in the trail, thus doubling or tripling the chance for a catch.

When good dens cannot be found, dig a hole under an old stump, and place a bait inside, setting the trap directly in front of the hole and cover with dry dirt. Sprinkle some scent about, on the stump and ground; use care in setting as you are likely to catch a fox, providing the trap is carefully set and covered, and the stake driven out of sight. For bait use tainted meat of almost any kind.

Another good way is to find a spot of sandy ground, and set the trap in a small hole, covering with sand. Cut the bait into small pieces and scatter it all around the trap, also, if you have it, sprinkle some scent around. The trap may be fastened to a brush drag, and the brush set up to look as though it were growing there.

If you can find a tree or stump with two spreading roots, set the trap between these roots and fasten the bait on the side of the tree, about ten inches above the trap.

Still another way is to make a small pen of old, rotten wood, stones or stakes, setting the trap in the entrance, and placing the bait in the pen beyond the trap.

Any natural enclosure, such as a hollow log, a hole in the bank, or in a wall or pile of stones, makes a good place in which to set a trap.

Skunks may also be taken in box traps, deadfalls and snares, and they seldom become scented when caught in such traps.

For bait, the following are all good: muskrat, skunk, chicken, birds of any kind, rabbit, squirrel, mice, rotten eggs or fish—tainted bait is always to be preferred for skunks, fresh bait being second choice.

To make a good decoy, take one-half dozen rotten eggs, and the scent of one skunk, and mix thoroughly. A mixture of the male and female scent is probably best. Many of the decoys recommended for the fox are also good for skunk. The scent of the skunk itself, is one of the very best to use.

Most trappers object to having the scent of skunks on their clothing and for this reason I give the following methods for killing the captured animals, so that they will not throw their scent. If the trap is staked, or fastened to a clog, cut a club about four or five feet long, and approach the animal very slowly, using care not to make any quick movements. If the skunk raises its tail, as though it intended to throw its scent, stop, and stand perfectly still until it drops its tail again, when you can go nearer. In this way if you are careful, you can easily get within striking distance, when you should deliver a good smashing blow across the back. If the back is broken, the muscles which operate the scent glands will be paralyzed, and there will be absolutely no danger of getting a charge of perfumery.

Some trappers fasten their traps to the end of a ten or twelve foot pole, and by approaching carefully, can pick up the pole, when by going slowly, the skunk may be led to the nearest water where it may be drowned. Lead the skunk into shallow water, gradually working it into deeper, holding its head under until nearly drowned, then let it have a little air,—just a breath, and push it under again, keeping it there until its struggles cease. If the animal is caught by a front foot, it may be carried to the water, as a skunk can seldom throw its scent if lifted off the ground, and not allowed to touch anything with the hind feet or tail.

Another method is to cut the animal's throat with a small, very sharp, pointed knife blade, attached to the end of a ten foot jointed pole. Approach the animal carefully and place the point of the knife against the side of the animal's neck, just over the jugular vein. Push steadily against the knife; as soon as the blood flows freely, move away and allow the animal to die.

Perhaps the quickest method is to shoot the skunk in the center of the back, with a 22 caliber rifle or pistol. This breaks the back killing the animal almost instantly, and there will be no scent whatever.

If the trap is fastened to a balance pole you can kill the animal by a blow across the back. Never shoot them in the head, or strike the head with a club, as they are certain to throw their scent if killed in this way.

If the fur of the skunk has become scented, I use the following method for removing the scent: Build a fire and throw an armful of evergreen boughs on it so as to make a dense smoke. Hold the scented animal in the smoke for about five minutes, using care to keep it away from the fire or the heat will curl the hair. After the skunk is skinned hang the skin in an airy place for a few days, when there will be practically no smell left.

Before skinning or handling the skunk, rub your hands with some kind of grease. After the animal is skinned, wash your hands well, using soap and hot water; there will be no scent remaining on the hands. Benzine or gasoline will also remove the scent from the hands or clothing. Cider vinegar is also said to be good. If the clothing is buried overnight in damp ground, the scent will usually draw out.

The Mink

The mink has a long, slender body, a small head, and rather short legs. The tail is usually about

The mink.

eight inches long and is quite bushy. The fur is thick, fine and glossy, and the color varies from a very light brown to very dark. The usual color is dark brown, the fur on the tail being darker than that on the body.

The mating season commences about the last week in February and ends about the middle of March. The young are born in April, there being from four to six in a litter.

The mink is not an amphibious animal, but it is found only along the streams and water-courses, from which it obtains a large part of its food. It is a great rambler, traveling long distances along the streams and lakes, and always following the same route. When on these trips it explores the drifts and log-jams, holes in the bank, hollow logs, etc., which habit is taken advantage of by the trapper.

The fur of the mink is at its best during the months of November, December and January in the north; while in the extreme south, they are only number one during December and January. In February, the fur commences to fade, and they are not worth so much. The dark colored skins command the best prices.

The food of the mink consists of fish, frogs, birds, squirrels, mice, rabbits, muskrats, etc., all of which are good for bait. They are also very fond of poultry.

The traps most used for mink are the Nos. 1 and 1½. The webbed jaw and the double jaw traps are especially desirable for mink, as when caught in these traps, they cannot escape by gnawing off the foot.

There are probably more methods used in trapping the mink than in trapping any other animal. In localities where they take bait well, the usual plan is to set the trap in the entrance to a natural or artificial enclosure, on the bank of the stream, placing a bait on the inside of the enclosure. The trap should be nested down, and covered with some light material in keeping with the surroundings. The trap may be fastened to a light clog or a balance pole, or if very close to the water, to a sliding pole. The bait should be strictly fresh. Some good scent may be used if desired. Hollow logs and holes in drifts and under stumps make good places for sets. Some trappers do not set in an enclosure, but hang the bait about eighteen inches above the trap. I do not, however, consider this a satisfactory method. When an artificial enclosure is used, it should be roofed over with bark, or evergreen boughs to protect that trap from the snow.

For fall trapping, many prefer to set traps in the water. The following method is one of the best for a water set: find a steep bank where the water is shallow, and runs smoothly and rapidly, make a hole in the bank, on a level with the water, making the hole about ten inches deep and about four inches in diameter. Put a piece of fresh bait back in the hole, fastening with a small stick, and set the trap in the water at the mouth of the hole. Stake the trap the full length of the chain into the water and cover with mud or water-soaked leaves.

Along the streams where little sand-bars lead out into the water select a place on one of these bars, where the water is only an inch or two in depth, set the trap under the water, close to the edge of the stream. Fix a small fish on the point of the stick, out in the stream a foot from the trap, pushing the stick down until the bait rests partly under water. Stake the trap so that the catch will drown. This is a very successful set and requires but little time and trouble to make.

In some localities the mink do not take bait well, in which case, blind sets—traps without bait must be depended upon. In the fall while the water is still open, find a high bank where the water leads off fairly deep, leaving only a very narrow strip of shallow water, at the foot of the bank. Set the trap in the edge of the water and stake full length of the chain into the stream. Place a couple of water-soaked leaves on the trap, and drop a few pinches of mud on them to hold them in place. The steep bank on one side and the deep water on the other will guide the mink into the trap. If, however, the shallow water extends out some distance from the bank, take a chunk of water-soaked wood, and stand it in the water, just beyond the trap, leaving the top rest against the bank. This will leave only a narrow passage over the trap, and you may be pretty sure of catching your mink. A similar set should be made on the opposite side of the stream, if conditions are favorable. This is a very good method for use in the south.

After streams are frozen, a different plan must be adopted. In such cases if you can find a jam or

Mink set under log.
X X shows positions of traps.

drift extending across the stream, find an opening, leading through this drift, close to the bank, and set the trap in this opening, covering with fine, drift dirt. In case you cannot find a suitable passage, make one and stop up all other holes. A little scent of the right kind may be used here to good advantage.

The illustration shows two traps set under an old log, spanning the stream. The log protects the traps from rain or snow, and a glance at the cut will show that it would be practically impossible for a mink to pass along the stream without being caught. The same set is good for the raccoon. If the stream is frozen, fill the opening under the log with old, dead brush, so that there is no chance for the mink to pass, except over the traps.

Another good method for the wary mink is as follows: find a high, steep bank along the stream; if it overhangs, so much the better, and about two feet above the water, make a hole about four inches in diameter, and a foot or more deep. Leave the dirt that you dig out, rest directly in front of the hole, and set the trap in this dirt, covering with same. Pack dry moss around the jaws and cover the trap first with a sheet of paper, finishing with a thin layer of dirt Put some good mink scent in the hole; the musk of the mink itself is best for this set. If the traps can be visited every day, it is a good plan to stake the trap, so that the mink will roll around over the ground, and the next one will be more easily caught.

Where mink travel around a lake, go to the outlet and lay a hollow log across the stream, just where the water leaves the lake. Set a trap in this log, covering with fine, rotten wood, and every mink that travels around the lake, will attempt to run through the log, and will be caught. If you cannot find a hollow log near at hand, build a covered passage-way of poles and chunks, and set your trap in this passage.

Scents are much used and there are some few which have proved attractive. Fish oil is one of the most common scents for mink and other animals. It is made by taking fish of almost any kind, cutting them into small pieces, and putting in a wide mouthed bottle. Let stand in a warm place, loosely covered, until the fish are thoroughly rotted, and in a liquid state; this scent may be used alone or combined with others.

If a female mink can be caught, during the mating season, remove the generative organs, and place them in a bottle, adding about two ounces of fish oil and all of the mink musk you can get. This is undoubtedly the best scent ever devised. It should be used without bait.

The White Weasel

The ermine of Europe is a species of weasel, and the American white weasel is sometimes called the ermine, its fur being used to imitate the fur of that animal.

The change of color in the fur of this animal is not understood by naturalists. It occurs only in the most northern portions of its range and it is not known whether the animal really sheds its brown summer coat when the cold weather approaches or whether the fur bleaches, but it is certain that the change occurs in some way, the fur becoming white in the fall and changing to brown again in spring.

The smallest variety of the weasel is found in northwestern Canada and Alaska and with it the black tip of the tail so characteristic of the weasel is missing. Very large weasels are secured in the northern part of Maine, but it is said that the finest skins are obtained in Nova Scotia and Newfoundland.

The weasel from many sections have a peculiar, sulphury yellow cast to the fur, especially on the hind-quarters, and of many of these stained skins only the black tip of the tail is of value. What causes the stain is not known, neither is there any known method for removing it. One fur buyer states that about seven out of every ten skins received, show this yellow stain and are of little value.

The weasel is one of the most blood-thirsty of animals and is very courageous. It is a terror to rats, mice, rabbits, partridges and poultry. It will kill for the love of slaughter, even when not hungry, and I have known a single animal to kill more than thirty chickens in a night, sucking only a little of the blood from each.

On one occasion I knew a farmer who had turned a drove of fair-sized pigs into a pasture, and one day, hearing a wild squealing over along the pasture fence, went to investigate. He found the entire drove of porkers running along the fence and squealing from terror, and following them was a little brown weasel.

Curiosity is highly developed in the weasel. Many times I have seen them in my camp at night and if I remained perfectly quiet they would approach to within a few feet and stand upright on their hind legs to get a good view. At the least movement, however, they would disappear only to return a minute later.

As before mentioned the weasel is a blood-thirsty creature, and when it

The white weasel.

finds some food that is to its liking it can scarcely be driven away. On various occasions I have found them attempting to remove the bait from my traps and such times I would adjust the trap so as to be very easily sprung, and then step aside and wait for the animal to be caught.

The weasel has a sharp eye and a keen nose. While trapping in the North I would always keep on hand a supply of snared rabbits for use as bait, and often weasels would come into the camp at night, attracted by the bait, and it is interesting to note how quickly they could scent out the freshest rabbit in the pile and by biting into its ears would attempt to drag it away. Quite often they were able to move a fair sized rabbit I usually kept a trap setting in my camp and in this way in one season caught fifteen weasels in one camp.

I have never learned anything regarding the breeding habits of the weasel, but judging from the large numbers of these animals found in favorable localities, I would say that they are very prolific.

For trapping this animal I recommend the No. 1½ trap and prefer a trap that is loosely hinged and springs easily, such as the Victor. Any trap will hold a weasel but when caught in the smaller sizes they quite often double up about the jaws, and when they die and freeze in that position it is difficult to remove them from the trap. With the 1½ they are always caught over the body and there is little trouble from that source. As the animal is so very light in weight it is necessary that the trap springs very easily. There are various styles of rat traps on the market which make excellent weasel traps, but as one never knows what animal may happen along, I prefer to use the steel trap.

My method of setting is to place the trap inside of a small enclosure of chunks of wood, bark, sticks or whatever is most convenient. No covering is needed but when setting on the snow I make a bed of evergreen boughs for the trap to rest on. Rotten wood will answer just as well. I fasten the bait with a stick just back of the trap so that the weasel will be obliged to stand on the trap when attempting to remove the bait, for it should be remembered that they will never eat any food where they find it if able to move it away. Fasten the trap securely for some larger animal is likely to be caught. I do not place the traps far apart, where tracks are seen in fair numbers, and I drag a fresh killed rabbit from set to set, splitting it open with a knife so as to leave a bloody trail. Any weasel that strikes the trail is sure to follow it.

For bait I prefer rabbit to anything else as it contains more blood than other baits and fresh blood is the only scent that I know of which will attract the weasel.

The Marten

In size the marten is about the same as the mink of the North and East, being somewhat lighter in the body, but the longer fur causes it to appear fully as large. It has longer legs than the mink, and the feet are larger and heavily furred. The tail is thick and bushy, the ears and eyes, large and the muzzle is more pointed than that of the mink. The fur is very

The marten.

fine and soft, the color varying from a rich yellow to almost black. The fur of the tail is darker than that of the body, and the face lighter. The ears, on the edges, are greyish white and there is always a yellow or orange spot on the throat.

In the more southern portions of their range, the martens are quite pale. The finest and darkest skins come from Labrador and the country east and south of Hudson Bay, also from northern British Columbia and the Interior of Alaska and the Yukon province. The marten is strictly an animal of the woods, being found only in the heavily timbered country. Their favorite haunts are in the rough, broken country, where the timber is of various kinds. They feed on rabbits, squirrels, mice, birds and eggs and probably have no trouble in obtaining a sufficient amount of food, but unlike the mink and the weasel, they never kill more than is needed to supply their wants.

The young are usually born in April, and there are from three to five at a birth. Just where they make their dens I cannot say. Some writers say they live in hollow trees, while others assert that they live in holes in the rocks or ground. I should say that the latter idea is most likely to be correct, at least as regards the marten of the far north, as in that part of the country, hollow trees are few and far between. One peculiarity regarding the martens is the fact that they occasionally disappear from a locality in which they were formerly numerous. The common supposition is that they migrate to new feeding grounds when food becomes scarce.

The marten travels mostly in the gullies and depressions on the mountains and hills. As they usually follow the same route, when one sees their tracks in such a place, he can be reasonably sure, if he sets his trap there, that he will make a catch. They are not shy or suspicious and are easily caught. In many ways, marten trapping is the most pleasant as well as the most profitable kind of trapping. As they are found only in the timbered country, the trapper does not feel the storms like he would in an open country. They are easily caught, light to carry and easily skinned. Moreover, they are a very valuable fur and if one is in a good locality, he will make a large catch in a season. They usually become prime about the 15th of October and remain in good condition until the last of March.

In countries where the snow does not fall too deep, the traps are set in small enclosures, the same as for the mink. If there is snow on the ground, I set my traps as follows. With my snowshoes, I tramp the snow down solid, at the foot of a tree, and build a small pen of stakes, or chunks split from an old stump. The stakes or chunks are arranged so as to form the sides of the pen, and the sides are placed about six or seven inches apart, the tree forming the back of the pen. I roof the pen with evergreen boughs, to protect the trap from the falling snow. It is a good idea to leave a couple of boughs hanging down over the mouth of the pen so as to hide the bait from the birds, and also to prevent the rabbits from entering the pen. I set the trap on a bed of boughs, just inside of the pen, and cover lightly with tips of evergreen. The bait is placed on a stick behind the trap. I fasten the trap to a toggle, but if only marten is expected, the trap may be fastened in almost any way, as they seldom escape. It is also a good idea to bend a small twig and place it under the

A marten set.

pan of the trap, to prevent it from being sprung by birds, squirrels and weasels.

For bait, rabbit, partridge, squirrel, fish, small birds or meat of almost any kind is good. The Indians sometimes smoke-cure salmon, pickerel, or white fish for marten bait, and other trappers use putrefied salmon roe, but the majority prefer to use fresh bait. Some trappers advise dragging a piece of fresh, bloody meat along the line, to lead the marten to the trap.

Another very good method is the following: Find a small spruce about three inches in diameter, and cut the tree about two feet above the snow, leaving the top of the stump V shape.

Draw the tree forward and lay it over the stump, so that the butt of the tree will be three or three and a half feet above the snow. Now, about a foot back from the end, flatten off a place for the trap and set the trap on the pole. Tie the trap fast with a light string and loop the chain around the tree. Split the butt of the tree, and fasten the bait in the split. This is a very good set, possessing advantages over most methods. The birds cannot eat the bait, the trap is not bothered by weasels or rabbits, the marten must stand on the trap when trying to get the bait, and when caught, falls off the pole and cannot get back.

In the mountains, where the snow falls deep, the traps are set on the trees, five or six feet above the snow. The most common way is to make two cuts in the tree with an axe and drive in two wooden pegs, about five inches apart. Set the trap and place it on the pegs, one peg passing through the bow of the spring, the other between the jaws and the bottom of the trap. Draw the chain around the tree and staple solidly. The bait is pinned to the tree, about a foot above the trap. A bunch of boughs may be placed over the bait to hide it from the birds.

If desired, a notch may be cut in the tree and a trap set in the notch. The notch should be about four inches deep and about twelve inches from top to bottom. Cut the bottom smooth so the trap will set solid, and fasten the bait in the top of the notch. Staple the trap to the tree. If desired, you can lean a pole against the tree for the marten to run up on, but this is not necessary.

The trapper should always be on the lookout for places in which the trap may be set without much labor. Sometimes a tree can be found with a hollow in one side, and this makes a good place for a set. Lean a pole against the tree, with one end resting in the hollow, set a trap on the pole and place a bait in the cavity above the trap. At other times a cavity may be made in the side of a rotten stub and a trap set in the same way. The traps recommended for marten are the No. 1 of any make, but the No. 0 Newhouse is much used. If there are fishers, lynx and other large animals about, it is best to use a No. 1½ trap. Deadfalls are also used and they may be built on the ground or snow, or on the top of a stump, or the side of a tree. The track of the marten resembles that of the mink, except that it is a trifle larger and the footprint wider in proportion to the length. The toes do not make as clear a print as do those of the mink, the feet being more heavily furred.

The Fisher

In general appearance, the fisher resembles both the marten and the wolverine, but is larger than the former and smaller than the latter. Compared with the marten, the ears are smaller and more rounded, the tail longer and the animal is far more stoutly built. An average, full size fisher will measure two feet from the nose to the root of the tail and will weigh from ten to fifteen pounds. The tail is peculiar, and is the most valuable part of the skin. It measures, usually, about sixteen inches in length, is heavily furred, thick at the base, and tapers to a point. The color of the fur varies, some specimens being very pale and others almost black. The general

The fisher.

as it feeds largely on the berries of the mountain ash, and in seasons when these berries are plentiful, the fisher does not take bait well. At such times the Indian trappers will often use a bunch of mountain ash berries for bait.

They are found most plentiful on the higher ground, where the land is fairly well timbered, and the surface of the country is very ragged. They are great travelers and follow the wooded ravines whenever possible. Like all other animals of a rambling nature, each individual has its regular route of travel, and when you see a track, especially in a ravine, you may be sure that the animal will come that way again. The fur becomes prime about the first of November, and remains in good condition until the first of April, or sometimes longer. They are not very prolific, there being only from two to four in a litter. The young are usually born in April.

Usually, the fisher is easily trapped and will enter the trap as readily as the marten, but there are "off seasons" when food is plenty and the animals are rather shy. On such occasions I have seen them refuse to cross my trail in the snow. In most cases, however, they will jump into the trail and follow it to the trap. When trapped, the animal struggles violently and if the leg is broken, is likely to twist off the foot and escape. It will also chew up everything within reach and the traps must be well fastened. The use of a balance pole is advised, but where, for any reason, it cannot be used, the traps should be fastened to a heavy log. The most common method for trapping the fisher is by setting a trap in a pen of stakes or a natural enclosure, the same as recommended for marten, but the pen should be larger. It should be two feet high, wide at the top and just wide enough for the trap at the bottom.

The bait should be placed on a stick in the back of the pen and the trap should be covered with some light material. The pen should be roofed with evergreen boughs, to protect the trap from the snow.

color is a yellowish grey on the face, head and neck, light brown on the back, dark brown on the hind-quarters and the tail and legs, a brownish black. The under-parts are darker than the back. The fur is fairly fine and soft, though not nearly as fine as that of the marten.

For its size, the fisher is an exceedingly powerful animal, and is rather hard to hold in a trap, as it will struggle as long as life lasts. The animal possesses a musk, having a peculiar, rank odor, which it ejects when alarmed. The food of the fisher consists principally of rabbits, partridges and other small animals and birds, but it will scarcely refuse anything in the line of flesh, occasionally eating mink, weasel, etc., out of traps. It also preys on raccoons in the parts of its range where those animals are found, and sometimes kills and eats the porcupine. Neither is it a strictly carnivorous animal,

It is the custom among the Indian trappers to make the trap pen of green wood, splitting it and placing the stakes so that the split side will be inward. The object in this is to enable the animal to more easily locate the bait, for sometimes when the fisher scents the bait but cannot find it at once, he moves on. If, however, the pen presents a bright interior, it attracts the animal's attention and leads to an investigation. This method is used generally, but should not be employed when setting for the more wary animals.

For trapping the fisher, I recommend the No. 1½ traps of all makes, also the No. 2 Victor and Oneida Jump traps. Mr. Charles Carner, a noted trapper of California, uses the following method. Find somewhere on the fisher's route of travel, a small bushy evergreen tree with limbs coming down to the ground, cut away a few of the limbs, on one side, so as to make a sort of enclosure. The limbs that are cut away should be stuck in at the sides and back to make the pen tighter. The bait should be tied to the stem of the tree and the trap set a short distance in front of the bait, so as to catch the animal by the fore foot. The trap is fastened securely to the butt of the tree. Mr. Carner recommends the use of the following scent: fish oil, oil of anise, assafoetida and muskrat musk, thoroughly mixed. He saturates a rabbit with the scent and draws it from trap to trap, and on the last trap uses the rabbit for bait. This scent is also used by some other noted trappers.

I have also caught fishers by building a pen on an old log, lying with one end above the ground. I would make some splits in the log with my axe, drive in a few stakes and weave evergreen boughs among the stakes, roofing the pen with boughs. The trap should be set the same as in the first method and should be stapled to the top of the log, so that when the animal jumps off on either side, he cannot get his front feet or the trap down to the ground. The above methods are all very good, but if a particularly shy animal refuses to enter the pen, try setting in a natural enclosure, and if this fails, try the following method:

Under some thick evergreen tree, scrape up a cone shaped pile of snow, making it two feet high and pack the snow solid. Have the trap fastened to a clog and bury the clog in the snow. In the very top of the mound, hollow out a place for the trap and line this place with evergreen tips. Set the trap in this nest, cover it with a piece of paper, and brush a half inch of snow lightly over the paper. For bait, use a whole partridge or rabbit and hang it by a string from a limb of the tree, so that it hangs about two and a half feet above the trap.

Brush your tracks shut with a bunch of boughs and when looking at the trap do not go too close. This method is very good for the shy ones but is too much trouble to use as a regular set, when putting out a long line of traps. The best places in which to set for fishers is in the timbered ravines, especially where two ravines join. Other good places are at the ends of lakes, the points of swamps, and in narrow strips of timber connecting larger bodies.

The Otter

The otter is an aquatic animal, living in and near the streams and lakes, and getting its living from them. It has a long body, short, stout legs, and webbed feet; the tail is long, thick at the base, and tapering to a point. The neck is thick, the head comparatively small, with small ears, set well down on the sides of the head. The far is of two kinds, the under fur being fine, soft and wavy, and of a light silvery color; while the outer fur or guard hairs, are longer, coarser, and usually straight, the color varying from brown to almost black. The fur of the tail and under parts is shorter and stiffer than that on the back, sides and neck; that on the under parts having a silvery tint. Otters frequently measure three and one-half feet in length and weigh from fifteen to twenty-five pounds. The skin, when stretched,

The otter.

will often measure five feet from tip to tip, and sometimes even more.

The food of the otter consists principally of fish, trout being their favorite food; but they also feed on muskrats, clams, frogs, and the smaller animal life, found in the beds of streams and lakes.

They capture muskrats by entering their houses and their holes in the banks.

Otters usually make burrows in the banks of streams, lining the nest with leaves and grass. The entrances to these burrows are under the water and it is my belief that they inhabit them only during the breeding season. The young are born in April and May and there are from two to four in a litter.

The otter is a great traveler, following the lakes and water courses, sometimes going a distance of one hundred miles on a single trip. Apparently he is always in a great hurry to reach a certain place, some lake or pond, at which, having reached, he may remain for several months, and again he may leave immediately after his arrival.

Otters sometimes have slides on the banks of streams, down which they slide into the water, apparently for pastime. They also have landing places on the banks of streams and on logs projecting into the water, where they go to roll in the grass and leaves, or to lie in the sun. These places are seldom visited in the fall, but in the spring they will land at almost every place as they come along.

In traveling, they usually follow the center of the stream, as they are more at home in the water than on land. In winter they travel under the ice, wherever the water is deep enough to allow of their passage. The otter's legs being very short, he has a peculiar method of traveling on the ice or snow. He throws himself forward, sliding on his belly, and by repeating the move in rapid succession, is enabled to get along at a surprising rate of speed.

Wherever there is a sharp bend in the stream, the otter will make a short cut across the point, and if the stream is traveled much, you will find a well-defined trail in such a place. Where two streams lie close together, they sometimes have a trail from one stream to another. Also wherever a long point of land projects into a lake, they are likely to have a trail across the point.

The best traps for otter are the numbers 2½, 3 and 3½ Newhouse; the Nos. 3 and 4 Hawley & Norton; and the No. 14 Oneida jump, also the "Seminole" pattern, Blake & Lamb.

The point to keep in mind when trapping for otter, is that they are very shy of the scent of man; more so perhaps than any other animal, and unless great care is observed, are likely to be frightened entirely out of the locality in which you are trapping. This human scent theory is disputed by some trappers, but I speak from my own experience, and from the experience of many expert trappers with whom I am acquainted. If one will use a little judgment he will readily understand why human scent is alarming to many wild animals. Man is the natural enemy of all wild animal life, and all wild creatures realize this fact. Now you will see that any indications of the presence of man, puts the animal on its guard; especially is this the case in the wilderness where the animals are not accustomed to seeing the tracks of man wherever they go. When an animal finds human scent, he has positive proof that man has been in that vicinity.

Footprints and other human signs, if there is no scent, are not so alarming, as they are likely to be mistaken for signs made by some wild animal. Although the animals of the wilderness are more afraid of human scent than those found in the settled countries, they are just as easily trapped. The more wary animals found in settled parts, are always looking for danger because of the continued presence of man in their locality, but on the other hand, they are not likely to be frightened by human scent because it is a common thing to them.

As mentioned before the otter is to visit the beavers, if there are any about, so if you know of a family of beavers, go to that place and if you can find an old beaver dam, on the stream somewhere, below where the beavers are located, make a break in the center of this dam, so that all of the water will flow through this opening, and set the trap in the water, in the upper end of this passage. Narrow down the passage to about eight inches, by driving a few old stakes on each side of the trap. The trap may be staked, but it is better, if the water is deep enough, to use a sliding pole, so that the captured animal will drown. No covering is needed on the trap, but after it is set, the entire setting should be drenched with water, to remove the human scent. This is an excellent set and will remain in working order until late in the fall, as the water immediately above the break in the dam will not freeze until long after other water is closed by ice. Even in the coldest weather this set may be kept from freezing by roofing it over with evergreen boughs, and banking it well with snow.

Find a narrow place in the stream, where the water flows smoothly, and narrow up the stream by placing a bunch of old dead brush in each side,

leaving a passage of about eight inches in the middle. Lay a few stones among the brush to keep them in place. Set the trap in the opening, and splash water over the brush and banks. The trap may be staked but it is better to fasten to a clog. Cut a small sapling of such a size that the ring of the chain will just pass over the butt of the sapling. Slip the ring over the clog and fasten it by splitting the butt and drive a wedge in the split, or by driving a staple over the ring. The clog may be placed on the upper side of the brush, used to block the stream, and the top may be tied to the shore, so that it will not be carried away by high water. In very small streams, a narrow passage may be made by simply placing a few stones in either side, leaving a narrow passage in the middle, in which to set the trap.

When you can find a sharp bend in the stream with a trail across the point, set the trap in the water, at the end of the trail. Use same care as advised for the other sets.

For spring trapping this method is excellent: if you can find one of the otter's landing places on the bank, prepare the place for setting in the fall in the following manner: Make a nest for the trap in the center of the trail and fill the nest with grass and leaves. Lay a bunch of dead brush or a chunk of rotten wood on each side of the trail, so as to leave only a narrow passage and cut a clog and lay it in place. The otters seldom visit these places in the fall, so there is no danger of frightening them. In the spring, before the snow is all gone, go and set your trap in the place prepared, covering with the leaves and grass, and attach to the clog, covering the entire setting with a little snow. As the snow melts, it takes with it all of the scent and signs, leaving the trap ready for the first otter that comes along.

If you do not find the landing places until after the snow is gone, set the traps just the same, washing the scent away by sprinkling with water, or set the traps in the water where the otter climbs up the bank.

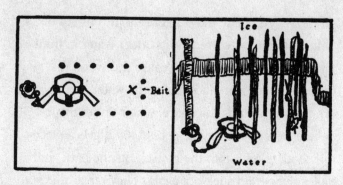

Otter trap set under ice.

Another very good method for spring trapping is to set the trap in the edge of the water, where the bank bluffs a little, sticking up a few fresh cut, green sticks behind the trap, and at the sides. Post a piece of the dried oil castor of the beaver on a stick, behind the trap, and about ten inches high. The ordinary beaver castor is also good. The oil castor is very attractive to the otter, and the green sticks are also attractive, as the otter mistakes them for beaver cutting. Always fasten the trap so the animal will drown, as you are likely to catch a beaver in this set.

One of the best methods of trapping otter in winter, after the streams are closed with ice, is as follows: Find a long pool of still water, where yon are sure the otter will be traveling under the ice, and at either end of this pool, where the water is about ten inches deep, cut a hole through the ice, make a pen of dead sticks in the water, making the pen about nine inches wide, by twelve or fifteen inches deep. Now take a fish and fasten it to a stick, in the back of the pen, and set the trap in the entrance, staking it securely. Drive the stake about ten inches in front of the pen, and directly in front of the trap. The object in this is to cause the otter, in entering, to twist his body, in which act, he will put his foot down in the trap. Throw some snow in the hole, so it will freeze over. The bait should be renewed once a week. In case you cannot get fish for bait, use the head of a rabbit, the breast of a partridge, or a piece of muskrat. The bait should be skinned.

The Beaver

The beaver is an amphibious animal, resembling the muskrat in appearance but much larger. It has the same thick, heavy body, short neck and scaly tail. The hind feet are large and strong and the toes are connected by a web; the front feet are small. The tail is "paddle shaped," four or five inches wide and about ten inches long. When full grown, the beaver will weigh from forty to fifty pounds, although occasionally a much larger one is found. The under fur is very fine and soft, and is mixed with longer and coarser hairs called "guard hairs". The prevailing color is a rich, reddish brown, on the back and sides, and ashy beneath.

The food of the beaver consists mostly of bark, of such woods as poplar, birch, willow and cottonwood, as well as the roots of the water lily. In the south they also eat corn.

Beavers build houses of sticks, stones, and mud, similar in shape to the houses of the muskrat, locating usually in the edge of a pond or lake, but

The beaver.

often making a large pond to suit their requirements, by building a dam across the stream. Even when their houses are built on a lake or pond, they always build a dam across the outlet, so as to raise the water two or three feet.

The dams are built of the same material as the houses. Sometimes there are one or two small dams found below the main dam, and they are so well made that they will last for many years, and are so tight that the water usually drips evenly over the top.

The houses are also very well made, the walls being several feet in thickness. There are usually two entrances, both under water. The size and general shape of the house depends on the number of beavers inhabiting it. The house of a full family of beavers will usually measure about twelve feet in diameter at the water line, but will sometimes be even larger, and the height is about six or seven feet. When there are only two or three beavers, the house is much smaller, and more pointed on the top.

A full family consists of from six to eight members. There are usually two old beavers, two or three two year olds, and two or three young. The reason for this is that the young beavers remain two years with the parents, and as it requires several years for them to grow their full size, there are always three sizes in a family. When they have reached the age of two years, they start out and make a house of their own, the beavers born the spring before, becoming the medium size, and a new litter taking their place. By autumn, the beavers that have left the main family have their house and dam completed and a store of food laid up for winter.

Many of the beavers travel about through the summer, following the streams, and return to their homes early in the fall. Sometimes, if they are late in getting back they will have to work day and night, in order to get sufficient food gathered for winter, before the ice comes. This food consists of saplings and small trees, which they gnaw off about a foot above the ground, drag into the edge

of the water, where they are out up into pieces of different lengths, stored away, under water in front of the house. Just how they cause this wood to sink, remaining in place under the water, is a mystery. The beaver spends the entire winter under the ice. When he feels hungry he goes out and gets a piece of wood, takes it into the house, eats the bark, and takes the peeled stick out again. They repair the house and dam each fall and they also make holes in the bank under water, to which they can retreat in case the house is disturbed, or when they hear a noise on the ice.

The best traps for beavers are the Nos. 2½, 3, 3½ and 4 Newhouse, the No. 4 Victor, the No. 4 Oneida Jump, and Blake & Lamb.

The following methods of trapping are for use in open water, in either the fall or spring. The first method given is usually considered best:

Find a place where the bank bluffs a little and the water is of good depth. Make a little pocket in the bank, several inches deep, and set the trap in the water directly in front of this pocket, where the pan of the trap will be about two inches under water. Take a piece of beaver castor and fasten it to the bank with a stick, about fourteen inches above the water, and as far back in the pocket as possible. If you are using some other scent instead of beaver castor, just dip a small stick in the scent and fasten

Trap set for beaver—sliding pole.

it to the bank. Fasten the trap so that the beaver will drown; the sliding pole is best. Be sure to use a dead pole or stake, as if a green pole is used the other beavers may carry it away, trap and all. This is a very good method for spring and fall, or at any time when there is open water:

Set the trap under water at the foot of a steep bank, and fasten a couple of green poplar or cottonwood sticks on the bank, directly over the trap, so that the beaver will step into the trap in trying to reach them. Have the fresh cut ends of the sticks showing plainly, and make your set near the house or dam so that the beavers are sure to see it. Fasten trap so that the captured animal will be sure to drown. No covering is needed on traps when they are set under water.

Look for the beaver's slides or trails where he drags his food into the water, and if the water is deep enough to drown him, set the trap under about two inches of water, just where he lands on the bank. This set is all right in the fall, when the beaver is laying in his food for the winter, but is not much good in the spring. Some trappers set the trap a foot or more from the shore, where the water is about six inches deep, as by so doing the beaver is caught by the hind foot, and is not so likely to escape. When using a set of this kind, it is best to use a number 3½ or 4 trap, as the No. 3 is too small for the beaver's hind foot.

Beavers usually have a slide or trail over the center of the dam, and this makes a very good place to set a trap. Set the trap under water on the upper side of the dam, just where the trail leads over. Be sure to fasten the trap so that the animal will drown, as if it is not drowned, it is almost certain to escape, and even if it does not, the others will be frightened and you will have a hard time to get them.

Go close to the beaver's house where the ice is thin, and by cutting small holes in the ice, find a place where the water is about twelve inches deep. Having found such a place, enlarge the hole until it is about sixteen by twenty inches in size, making a pen the same size as the hole, by shoving down dead sticks about four inches apart. If the bottom is very hard, you will have to freeze the sticks to the ice, to hold them in place. This may be done by throwing snow in the water, and packing it around the sticks and against the edge of the ice. When the pen is completed, cut a piece of green poplar about 1½ or 2 inches thick and two or three feet long, and fasten it to a stake by one end—the poplar being placed at a right angle to the stake. This green poplar is for bait, and the stake should be driven down in one corner of the pen so that the bait is within two or three inches from the bottom, and close along one side of the pen, extending a foot or more beyond the entrance.

The trap should be staked and set well inside of the pen, and quite close to the bait, so that the jaw of the trap will just clear the bait. This set will be readily understood by referring to the cut. If the bottom is of thin mud, as is often the case, you will have to make a bed for the trap, by sinking a bunch of evergreen boughs inside of the pen. It is also best to fasten the bait near the entrance to prevent the beaver from swinging it around. When the set is completed, cover the hole with evergreen boughs, bank it with snow, to keep it from freezing.

It is best to let this set go for about a week before looking at it. The beavers will be frightened

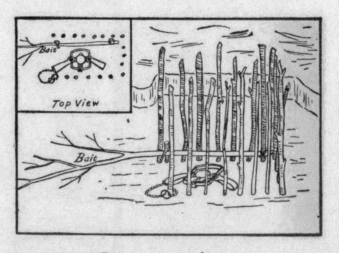

Beaver trap set under ice.

and will not approach the set for a few days, but finally one of them musters up courage enough to try to pull the bait out of the pen. When he finds it fast, he cuts it off at the entrance of the pen, takes it to the house to eat it; this sharpens his appetite, makes him more courageous, and he finally ventures into the pen for the balance of the bait. In attempting to cut the bait, he places one front foot on the bait and the other one in the trap. When using this set you should use three or four sets at each house.

Another good ice method is as follows: Find the proper depth of water, about fourteen inches, and make a pen of dead sticks, arranging them in the form of a half-circle. Now take some green poplar and shove them down firmly into the bottom, about six inches apart, close up to the stakes, on the inside of the pen. These bait sticks must be long enough to reach above the ice, so that they will freeze fast at the top. Stake the trap and set it in the center of the enclosure, with the pan about nine inches from the center bait. Throw some snow in the hole so that it will freeze, and hold the bait sticks securely.

The following method is one of the best for use in deep water: Cut a dead pole about four inches in diameter and six or seven feet long. Flatten the pole at one end, looping the trap chain around the pole, then set the trap on the end of the pole and tie it with a string to hold it in place. Now, cut an oblong hole in the ice, and place the pole in the water in an inclined position so that the trap is about twelve inches below the ice. Pack wet snow around the pole to hold it in place, fasten two sticks of green poplar in the ice over the trap, one on either side. In attempting to cut the bait, the beaver will put his foot in the trap.

The Muskrat

The muskrat is a nocturnal animal, but is sometimes seen in the day time. Their food consists of grass and roots, fruit, grain and vegetables. They will also eat clams, sometimes, when food is scarce. They thrive best in sluggish streams and ponds, bordered with grass and flags, the roots of which are their chief support and from the tops of which they construct their houses. These structures are dome shaped, and can rise up to a height of five feet from the water. The entrances are at the bottom, underwater, so that the inside of the house is not exposed to the open air. From six to ten muskrats are sometimes found in one house. Hundreds of these dwellings can be counted from a single point in many large marshes.

The muskrats found on the streams do not build houses, but live in holes in the bank, the entrances of which are underwater. The muskrat is found throughout the greater part of the United States and Canada. They are especially numerous in the marshes on the coast of Delaware and Maryland. This muskrat ground is owned by private parties, who lease the ground to the trappers for a certain

The muskrat.

length of time, the trapper catching all the animals he can in that length of time. Muskrats are also very plentiful in some parts of Western Canada. These animals are very prolific, bringing forth from six to nine at a birth and three litters in a season. They have many enemies, such as the fox, mink, otter and owl, but their greatest enemy is man.

Muskrats are trapped in the fall, winter and spring, but they are not prime until mid-winter, and some are not fully prime until the first of March. Nevertheless, they are more easily caught in the fall, and as the skins bring a fair price, the most trapping is done at this time, that is, for "bank rats,"—those living in holes in the banks. Where the muskrats live in houses, they are trapped mostly after the ice has formed.

In the far North the skins are in good condition until the first of June, while in the extreme South they should not be trapped after the first of April. The muskrats found in settled districts are larger and better furred than those of the wilderness. Also, those found East of the Mississippi River are larger than those of the West.

When trapping for these animals, the traps should always be staked full length of chain into deep water, so that the captured animal will drown, as otherwise they are almost certain to twist off the foot and escape, unless they are caught by a hind foot. Many trappers set their traps several inches under water, as by so doing they catch the rat by a hind foot, and there is very little danger of them escaping. Some stake their traps the length of the chain into deep water, and drive another stake about a foot beyond. The muskrat, when caught, winds the chain around the outer stake and is thus prevented from reaching the bank. Others prefer to tie a stone on the end of the chain, and lay the stone in deep water.

The traps most used are the Nos. 1 and 1½, but the No. 0 is also used sometimes. The Victor trap is a great favorite, as it does not have as strong a spring as the higher priced traps, and is not so likely to break the animal's leg. The single spring Oneida Jump traps are also fine traps for muskrats.

One of the most common methods of trapping the muskrat is to find their slides on the bank and set the trap at the foot of the slide under about two and a half or three inches of water. No covering is needed.

If you can find a log with one end lying in the water, examine same and if there are muskrat droppings on the log, cut a notch for the trap, so that it will be just underwater when set in the notch. The chain may be stapled to the log.

Another good way is to find their holes in the bank and set a trap in the entrance, staking into deep water.

If the water is still and there is much grass in the water, look around and you will find their feeding beds,—beds of grass which appear to be floating on the water. Set traps on these beds, underwater.

If you know there are muskrats about and you cannot find any of the places described above, select a steep bank, and set the trap under two or three inches of water at the foot of the bank. Pin a piece of bait to the bank about ten inches above the trap.

Where muskrats are found in large numbers as in a pond or slough, proceed as follows: Get a board about twelve inches wide and sixteen feet long and nail strips across it, arranging them in pairs, just far enough apart to let a trap set between. A board of this size will hold six or eight traps. The traps may be stapled to the edge of the board and some small pieces of bait scattered the entire length. The traps should be covered with dirt or dead grass. Attach a rope to one end of the board and anchor it in the water where the muskrats are sure to find it.

To trap muskrats in their houses in winter, cut a hole in the side of the house, and set the trap inside, on the bed. Fasten the trap to a stick outside of the house and close the opening tight, so the diving hole will not freeze. I have had best success at this kind of trapping by using a small trap, No. 0, and a good length of chain, as it gives the rat more chance to drown. The traps should be visited evening and morning.

In the spring, when the ice has just commenced to melt, you will find small piles of grass roots projecting above the ice. Move this aside and you will find a hole in the ice, with a feed bed directly in under it. Set a trap on this bed and cover the hole.

The best baits for muskrats are sweet apple, parsnips, carrot, pumpkin, corn and the flesh of the muskrat. While they do not eat the meat, they will go to smell at it, which is all that is needed. Muskrat musk, beaver castor and catnip are all attractive to the muskrat.

The Fox

The Silver or Black fox is the most beautiful and most valuable of all the foxes. It is found in the high, northern latitudes of both continents. In this country, it is found as far south as the northern tier of states. They are most abundant in the interior of Alaska, the Northwest Territories, Ontario, Northern Quebec, Labrador and Newfoundland.

The red fox.

At the London fur sales, specimens have been sold at over one thousand dollars each, but the average price is probably about two hundred dollars. Wherever the Silver fox is found, the Cross or Patch fox is found also, and they also range somewhat farther south. They are always found in greater numbers than the Silver variety.

The Red fox is the most common and is distributed over a larger territory than the other varieties. They range from the northern timber line, to well down in the Southern States. They are probably most abundant in the Eastern provinces of Canada and the England States, but they are found in fair numbers in parts of New York, Pennsylvania, West Virginia, Tennessee, Arkansas, Missouri, Michigan and the larger part of Canada and Alaska.

The Gray fox is one of the least valuable, and is most abundant in the Southern States. In the East they range as far north as Connecticut. In some places they have supplanted the Red species, and in other places the grays have disappeared and the reds have taken their place.

The fox, as well as the wolf and coyote, belongs to the dog family, which is second, only to man in intelligence. The different species are all practically the same size, but the same varieties vary in size in different localities. The average weight is from nine to ten pounds. In general appearance they somewhat resemble the dog, being rather light of build, considering their height. The ears are erect and pointed, the tail thick and bushy, and the muzzle small and pointed. The fur varies in the different species, being coarse and rather short on the Gray, while that of the Silver fox is extremely fine and soft.

The mating season comes in February, and the young are born usually in April, there being from four to nine in a litter. They make dens in the sand hills and in rocky districts, den in the rocks.

Except during the breeding season they spend very little time in the dens, but lie during the day in some clump of brush or weeds, or often on top of a stump or log. In mountainous sections they lie during the day, somewhere on the mountain side and come down into the valleys at night in search of food.

The fox is not strictly a carnivorous animal. When food is scarce they often feed on apples and other fruits, but their regular food is flesh. They are fond of partridge, rabbits, mice, skunk, muskrat or opossum flesh, carrion of almost all kinds, fish, eggs, poultry, and often they come around the camps and gather up the scraps, bread, bacon rinds etc. If they are given time and not disturbed they become quite bold in coming to such places for food and the trappers sometime take advantage of this peculiarity by baiting them awhile before setting the trap.

The fox in the North becomes prime in the beginning of November and remains in good condition until the middle of March, when the fur begins to take on a rubbed and woolly appearance. In the South they do not become prime until the last of November or the beginning of December and go out of prime in February. Most of the foxes are trapped in the fall before the ground freezes too hard for dry sets, and of course, many of them are not prime.

The traps recommended for the fox, for dry land use are the Nos. 2 and 3 Oneida Jump and Blake & Lamb, the 1½ Newhouse and Hawley & Norton and the No. 2 Victor. For water and snow trapping, the Nos. 3 and 4 Oneida Jump and Blake & Lamb, and the 21½ and 31½ Newhouse will be found most desirable.

In places where there are springs and small streams, there is no better method than the old water set, which is made as follows: It is best to find a spring which does not freeze, but for early fall trapping a brook will do. The rise and fall of the water in small streams sometimes makes trouble, and a spring or small pond gives best results. The spring should be at least four feet in diameter and should be prepared for the set in the summer, but if care is used, may be fixed up during the trapping season. A moss covered stone, or a sod (according to surroundings) should be placed about a foot and a half from shore, and should rise about two or three inches above the water. This is the bait sod.

The trap is set halfway between the sod and the shore, and the jaws, springs and chain should be covered with mud, or whatever is found in the bottom of the spring.

The pan of the trap should just be covered with water. Now take a nice piece of moss or sod and place it on the pan of the trap, so that it will rise an inch above the water. When properly placed, this sod will look natural, and will apparently be a safe stepping place for the fox. The pan should be so adjusted that it will not spring too easily. A small piece of bait and also some scent should be placed on the larger sod.

In making this set you should wade up the outlet of the spring, and stand in the water while making the set. Do not touch the bank or any of the surroundings. The trap should be fitted with a chain about three feet in length, with a two prong drag attached, but most trappers simply wire a stone of eight or ten pounds weight to the end of the chain. The drag, whatever is used, should be buried in the bed of the spring.

Water set for fox.

I recommend the flesh of the muskrat, skunk, opossum or house-cat for bait, and it should be allowed to taint by remaining about a week in a glass jar. This method was first used by William Schofield, a famous fox trapper of the Eastern states. Two men have been known to catch over one hundred foxes in a season with this method, besides considerable other furs taken in the same traps, for the method is good for many other animals besides the fox.

One trapper recommends setting the trap in exactly the same manner, except that the bait sod is omitted, and the bait, a bird, is fastened by means of a stick thrust in the bottom of the spring. The stick must be entirely out of sight, and the bird, apparently, floating in the water. Both of these methods are very good, and are especially recommended for the novice, as they are the easiest and surest methods to start on.

Look for fox tracks in old stock trails, foot paths, old roads in the woods, openings under fences, etc., and having first cleaned the traps by boiling or washing, find a narrow place in the trail and dig out a nest for the trap. Make this nest so that when the trap is set in, the jaws will lie lengthwise of the trail. Line this nest with dry grass or leaves, and having attached the trap to some sort of a drag, set it and place it in the place prepared. Fill in all around the outside of the jaws with dry dirt, and cover the springs. Now lay a piece of clean paper over the trap and cover all with about one-fourth inch of dirt, making it look like the other parts of the trail as much as possible. The chain and drag must be carefully concealed.

It is best to have a basket or piece of canvas in which to place the dirt while making the set and to carry away what is not needed. Do not spit near the trap, and do not leave any signs of your presence. It is not necessary to wear gloves, but the hands should be kept clean. This is an excellent method, especially for the old, sly animals.

The following directions are almost the same as you will get when you buy a method at from $1.00 to $5.00 or more. "Prepare your bait about a week before you want to set the traps, by cutting into pieces about half the size of an egg, and placing in a clean jar to become tainted. Put a little bit of scent on each bait before placing in jar. There are different ways for preparing the traps; most trappers prefer to boil them in hemlock boughs, or lay them overnight in running water. Wear clean gloves when handling the traps and carry them in a clean basket. Now find an old stump or a rock along some hillside, and dig a hole under it making the hole four or five inches in diameter and ten or twelve inches deep. Stake the trap solid, driving stake out of sight, and set the trap about ten inches in front of the hole. Cover the trap first with a piece of clean paper and finish by about one-fourth inch of dirt dug out of the hole. It should look as if some animal had dug the hole and scratched the dirt out in front. Use a small shovel made for the purpose, or a sharpened stick to dig the hole, and keep your gloves on all the time. Do not walk around, but stand in the same spot until the set is complete. Now put a piece of bait in the back of the hole, using a sharpened stick to handle the bait and put just a little scent by the side of the hole. When you catch a fox, kill him without drawing blood, and set the trap back in the same place. Your chances for catching another fox are doubled. Skunks, coons and other animals will also be caught in these sets."

The following method is a good one to use in settled countries, as it is not so likely to catch dogs and other animals, as other methods are. Find an ant-hill, a small, pointed knoll, an old rotten stump, a moss covered rock, or an old log with one end off the ground. Set the trap on the highest point, covering carefully, so that it looks just like it did before the trap was set. Place a fair sized bait, such as a skunk or muskrat about eight feet away from the trap. The fox is always suspicious of a bait, especially a large one, and will always get on the highest point to look at it before going close. Of course, there must be no other place for him to get up on near the bait. In the winter, traps may be set on muskrat houses, and bait placed on the ice. I think it best to set the traps several days before placing the baits, as in that way the human and other scents have a chance to pass away. When baiting, go just close enough to throw the bait into place.

The first method given is the one used by the Canadian Indians, for taking the silver fox in the great northern wilderness. Out on the ice on some frozen lake, or on any open, windswept piece of ground, make a cone-shaped mound of snow, beating it solid, so that it will not drift away. The trap should be fastened to a clog, and the clog buried in the mound. Make the mound about two feet high, and make a hollow in the top for the trap to set in. The hollow should be lined with cat-tail down, or some other dry material, and the trap set in the hollow and covered first with a sheet of white notepaper, finishing with a half inch or more of loose snow. Do not handle this snow with your hands, for if you do it will be certain to freeze on the trap. The best way is to take a bunch of evergreen boughs, and brush the snow up over the mound so that it sifts lightly over the trap. The covering on the trap should be a little lower than the top of the mound so that the wind will not uncover the trap. The bait is cut into small pieces and stuck into the sides of the mound.

After the trap is set it will only require a short time for the wind to drift your tracks shut and remove all traces of human presence, and the trap will remain in working order as long as the cold weather lasts. If water rises on the ice it will not reach your trap, and if there is a snow storm, the first wind will blow the loose snow off the mound, leaving just a little over the trap. When looking at the traps you should not go nearer than fifty yards, and do not turn off your route, but walk straight by.

This is a splendid method for use in the far north where the snow never melts or freezes during the winter months.

For use in the settled countries I have been very successful with this method. Find where foxes travel on old wood roads, and with your traps clean, drags attached, go and break a trail in the snow by walking back and forth on the road, and set the traps in this broken trail without bait. The traps should be set and covered, as in the other method, and the chain and clog pushed under the snow at the side of the trail. Do not let it appear that you have stopped at all, and when looking at the traps you can follow the trail and step right over the traps. In settled localities, the fox will follow the trail because the walking is better, but in the wilderness where the track of a man is seldom seen, they not only refuse to follow the trail, but often will not even cross it.

I believe that scent is more used for fox-trapping than for trapping any other animal. Some of the best trappers, however, do not use any scent at all, but I believe that if the right kind is used, that it is a great help. One of the best scents known for dry land or water sets is prepared as follows: Remove the fat from one or two skunks, chop it fine, and take a sufficient quantity to almost fill an ordinary pickle bottle. Take two mice; cut them up and add to the fat and let the bottle stand in the sun until the mixture is thoroughly decomposed; then add the scent of two skunks and five or six muskrats. The bottle must be kept covered so the flies will not blow it, but it must not be tightly corked. Different trappers have different ways of preparing this scent, but I think this way is the best.

Another very good one is made by allowing the flesh of a muskrat to rot in a bottle, and adding about four ounces of strained honey and one-half ounce of essence of musk.

Pure fish oil is attractive to the fox, and is used by some very good trappers. We believe that one of the most successful scents, especially for winter use, is made by taking the generative organs of the female fox when in heat and preserving it in alcohol. The urine of the fox is also good, but in using these two scents, no bait should be used.

The brine from mackerel or other fish is claimed to be a good scent for foxes, but if there are any porcupines or snow-shoe rabbits about, it will make plenty of trouble as the salt is very attractive to these animals.

The Raccoon

The common raccoon is the one of principal interest to the trapper and fur dealer. The body is short and stout, like that of the badger. Its head resembles that of the fox. Its tail is ten or twelve inches long, thick and bushy. The feet are bare and the toes long. The general color is grey, the tips of the hairs being darker. Occasionally a very dark one is found, in some cases being almost black. The tail is ringed with black and a black band crosses the eyes. The raccoon is a nocturnal animal, is omnivorous and hibernates during cold weather, coming out in search of food only on warm nights.

This food consists of green corn, grapes and other fruits, fish, frogs, clams, birds and their eggs and they are also fond of poultry. In search of food, they travel mostly along the streams and in early fall, in the corn fields.

They den in hollow trees, having an entrance at a considerable distance from the ground. In mountainous districts, they also den in holes among the rocks.

The young are born in April and May and from two to six are brought forth at a time. Their mating season is generally about the last of February and the beginning of March, and at this time the males travel considerably, crawling into a hollow tree wherever daylight overtakes them.

In the North they become prime about November 1st; the season being later in the South.

The raccoon.

They remain in good condition until late in the spring. The fur is used mostly for coats and robes.

The nature and habits of the raccoon, like all other animals differs considerably in different localities. In most sections they are very easily trapped, but those found in some parts of the Pacific Coast are said to be quite cunning. Any of the articles of food mentioned above will make good bait; fresh fish however, being preferred. The traps to use are the No. 1½ Newhouse or Hawley & Norton, the No. 2 Victor, and the Nos. 2 and 3 Oneida Jump and Blake & Lamb traps. The trap should be fastened to a clog, and in some cases an iron drag could be used to advantage, as the coon will get fastened up on the first brush he comes to.

The most common method is to set the trap in the entrance of a pen of stakes, at the edge of the water where the animals travel. The trap may be set dry or underwater, as preferred, and the bait should be placed in the back of the pen.

Another very good method, much used in the South, is to fasten a piece of bright tin or a piece of a white dish on the pan of the trap and set the trap under about two inches of water, near the bank. No bait is used, but a little scent may be used on the bank to good advantage.

The Southern Trappers sometimes find a tree, stump or rock in the edge of the water, and set the trap in the water, just where the coon will walk, when passing around the obstruction. A fence made of brush will answer the same purpose.

Where the bank is steep and the water is shallow, dig a six inch hole, straight into the bank at the edge of the water. Fasten some bait in the back of the hole and set the trap in the water, directly in front of the hole.

Where coons are visiting a corn field, find where they go through the fence and you will sometimes find a well beaten trail. Set the trap in the trail, covered, and fasten to a clog.

If you find a log lying across the stream and there are signs of coons about, cut a notch in the top of the log and set the trap in the notch, covering with rotten wood or moss. You are likely to catch a fox in a set of this kind.

When a den tree can be found, cut a pole five or six feet long and six inches thick; lean it against the tree and set the trap on the pole. Cover the trap lightly with moss and staple to the tree.

Any natural enclosure along a stream, such as a hollow log or a hole under a stump, makes a good place to set a trap. When trapping for foxes with water sets, many coons will be caught in the traps.

One of the best scents for coon is made as follows: To a pint of fish oil, add twenty or thirty drops of oil of anise and two ounces of strained honey. Pure fish oil is used by some trappers and beaver castor, muskrat musk and oil of anise are also good.

The Badger

The badger is an animal of peculiar build, having a heavy, broad body, at times appearing almost, flat, as when it crouches close to the ground, and the legs are short and stout. The feet are furnished with long, strong claws, adapted for digging. The tail is short, the ears short and round, the eyes small and black. A full grown specimen will measure about two feet or more from the end of the nose to the base of the tail.

The color is a grizzly, yellowish grey, being darker on the back. A white line traverses the face, head and neck, bordered with black, which latter marking extends around the eyes. The sides of the face and the throat are white, and there is a black patch in front of each ear. The legs and feet are black. The back and sides of the body are mottled somewhat by narrow streaks of darker fur.

The badger.

The fur, or more properly speaking, the hair, is long and appears to be parted on the back as it hangs off to either side from a line down the center of the back. Each separate hair shows a number of colors and it is this which gives the animal the peculiar grizzled appearance. Although the animal is, as before stated, of a heavy build, the casual observer would scarcely credit the animal with the great strength which it really possesses because of the apparently soft and flabby body. However, the strength of the animal is surprising. They are slow moving creatures and were it not for their strength and powers of digging, they would have difficulty in procuring a sufficient amount of food.

They feed on the small burrowing animals mainly, such as the prairie dog, the gopher and the pouched rat, and they are enabled to capture many of these animals by digging them out of the dens. They also eat mice and reptiles and the eggs and young of ground-nesting birds.

Being such an expert digger, the badger makes a deep den. The entrance to the den is wide and surrounded by a mound of earth. In addition to the main den the animal has a number of others nearby, so that one would scarcely know which of them is the main burrow. They are hibernating animals and remain in the dens during the cold portion of the winter.

The animal is of a rather timid nature, and when alarmed seeks safety in the den if possible, but when surprised far from the den, will hide wherever possible and failing to find cover will flatten down close to the ground and by remaining very quiet, will try to escape notice. However, when pursued, and finding escape impossible, they will fight desperately.

The young are born in early spring, there being as a rule three or four in a litter.

The fur of the badger is used for making brushes of various kinds, its peculiar texture making it especially desirable for this purpose. It is not used for wearing apparel.

The No. 3 trap is the proper size use for this animal, and only the stronger ones should be used. They are caught and held occasionally in smaller and weaker traps, yet such cases are exceptional.

As the animal is not a valuable one and is not found in large numbers in any one locality, they are not much sought by the trappers and the most of the skins which reach the market are from the animals caught in traps set for other game. The wolf and coyote trappers catch them occasionally, as they may be captured by any of the methods used for those animals.

Perhaps the best way in which to capture the badger is to set the trap at the entrance to the main burrow, that is, the one showing the most use. The trap should be set just outside of the entrance and should be securely staked, using a long stake driven out of sight in the ground. The jaws of the trap should be parallel with the passage, so that the badger will step between the jaws, and not over them. It should be bedded down so that the covering will be flush with the surroundings.

Traps may also be set with bait. On the plains, material for enclosures cannot be found but the traps may be set between clumps of sage brush or cactus, placing the bait behind the trap, the setting being so arranged that the badger will be obliged to walk over the trap in order to reach the bait. The trap should be securely staked in all cases. For bait, rabbit, sage hen, prairie dog or almost any kind of fresh meat may be used.

Household Hints and Home Remedies

The Value of Laundry Work–Purifiers

From *Approved Methods for Home Laundering* by Mary Beals Vail, 1906

The one great privilege of rich and poor alike is the possession of clean clothes. Water is free, soap is cheap, and sunshine and fresh air are everywhere. For centuries we have been training ourselves to like the "feel" of clean, smooth garments, the odor of freshly laundered linen, and the appearance of clothes clean and uniform in color, free from wrinkles, and straight as to threads of material. We may not have known that this very cleanliness is the strongest supporter of good health, but it is. The skin is made more active by the fresh clothing, which, in turn, absorbs the impurities thrown off by the skin. Moreover, clean, boiled clothes never carry disease germs.

In discussing any subject, we must first learn of the materials to be handled. With the knowledge of these, intelligent work and satisfactory results are sure to follow. In our special subject, HOME LAUNDERING, the information side will be discussed under the several heads: *Purifiers, Soil, Fabrics, and Laundry Aids*.

Sun, air, and water—Nature's purifiers—stand first and are indispensable. The sun's rays have wonderful properties, direct and indirect, in the form of heat. Nothing can compare with them. Many forms of minute plant life, molds, and certain bacteria, will not grow in the sunshine; and sun and air, together with moisture, break up harmful compounds, rendering them harmless. Moist heat at boiling temperature or higher kills all life if kept at that temperature long enough. The lower the form of life, the longer will it withstand heat. So, in order that clothes may be sterile, that is, free from life, they must be boiled at least ten minutes, and preferably twenty. Dry heat kept at a higher temperature for a longer time acts in the same way, but if not controlled, it may injure the fabric. Ironing applies heat for so short a time that it cannot be depended on to purify clothes.

Air, being one-fifth oxygen, aids in the breaking up of harmful compounds and, when in motion, scatters dirt.

Water is our chief dirt carrier. When in motion, water holds in suspension particles of dirt, which float away. Much of the soil of clothes may be dissolved in water, or, by the aid of soap, an emulsion is formed and the dirt is carried off.

Primitive methods of washing depended almost entirely upon flowing water to cleanse clothes, and washing in streams is still the method of cleansing used among people of simple habits today, a flat stone, upon which to rub or pound the clothes, being the only aid, unless soap is used.

More depends upon the kind of water we have for laundry work than upon anything else. Soft water is best, but it may absorb many things in its journey from the clouds. After air and roofs are washed, rainwater may be stored for use, but if we get water from a stream or lake, it may bring with it particles of plants or soil. These may be strained out, or the water may be allowed to settle, the clear water being then carefully poured off. Water which has soaked into the ground and appeared again in stream, lake, spring, or well, may have absorbed some mineral matter that may make it undesirable for laundry purposes.

The most common mineral found in water is lime, which makes water hard. Temporary hardness of water is most common. It is due to a soluble lime compound which will combine with soap to form a greasy scum. To overcome this difficulty water should be boiled. In case the hardness is not removable by boiling, it is called permanently hard water. To overcome this, add lime water or weak carbonated alkali before boiling. In softening water with an alkali, only as much as is necessary to do the work is desirable. More acts upon clothing and hands, weakening fabric and skin. The larger the amount and the greater the strength of the alkali, the worse the effect.

The *alkalies* commonly known and used in the household are:

AMMONIA, a gas dissolved in water, and mild in its action if diluted; it readily evaporates if heated. It is comparatively expensive.

BORAX, a powder, mild and expensive.

SAL SODA, OR CARBONATED ALKALI, a crystal or powder, stronger and cheaper than borax.

POTASH OR LYE, a liquid or solid, strong but little used in modern times. It is derived from wool ashes by a process of leeching; is used in making "soft soap."

CAUSTIC POTASH AND CAUSTIC SODA are very strong and not expensive, but are rarely known in the household. One or the other is almost invariably used in the manufacture of laundry soaps.

SOAP, a very essential purifier, is discussed in a separate chapter.

RUBBING, POUNDING AND RINSING are valuable mechanical aids in purifying clothes.

Removing Stains

From *The Household Guide or Domestic Cyclopedia* by Mrs. J.L. Nichols, 1905

Grease Spots.—Cold rainwater and soap will remove machine grease from washable fabrics.

Stains from Acids can be removed by spirits of hartshorn, diluted. Repeat, if necessary.

Iron Rust.—Dip the rusty spots in a solution of tartaric or citric acid; or wet the spots and rub on hard, white soap; expose it to the heat; or apply lemon juice and salt, and expose it to the sun.

To Take Out Scorch.—Lay the article scorched where the bright sunshine will fall upon it. It is said it will remove the spot, and leave it white as snow.

Mildewed Linen.—This may be restored by soaping the spots; while wet, covering them with fine chalk scraped to powder, and well rubbed in.

To Remove Mildew.—Remove mildew by dipping in sour buttermilk and laying in the sun.

Coffee Stains.—Pour on them a small stream of boiling water before putting the article in the wash.

Grass Stains.—Wash the stained places in clean, cold, soft water, without soap, before the garment is otherwise wet.

Tea Stains.—Clear, boiling water will remove tea stains and many fruit stains. Pour the water through the stain, and thus prevent its spreading over the fabric.

Medicine Stains.—These may be removed from silver spoons by rubbing them with a rag dipped in sulphuric acid, and washing it off with soap suds.

Fruit Stains.—Freezing will take out all old fruit stains, and scalding with boiling water will remove those that have never been through the wash.

Ink Stains.—Ink stains may sometimes be taken out by smearing with hot tallow, left on when the stained articles go to the wash.

Ink in Cotton, Silk and Woolen Goods.—Saturate the spots with spirits of turpentine, and let it remain several hours; then rub it between the hands. It will crumple away without injuring either the color or the texture of the article.

To Remove Paint Stains on Windows.—It frequently happens that painters splash the plate or other glass windows when they are painting the sills. When this is the case, melt some soda in very hot water and wash them with it, using a soft flannel. It will entirely remove the paint.

To Remove Grease from Coat Collars.—Wash with a sponge moistened with hartshorn and water.

To Clean Wall-Paper.—Tie a soft cloth over a broom, and sweep down the walls carefully.

Stains on the Hands.—A few drops of oil vitriol (sulphuric acid) in water, will take the stains of fruit, dark dyes, stove blacking, etc. from the hands without injuring them. Care must, however, be taken not to drop it upon the clothes. It will remove the color from woolen, and eat holes in cotton fabrics. To remove ink or fruit stains from the fingers, take cream of tartar, half an ounce; powdered salt of sorrel, half an ounce; mix. This is what is sold for salts of lemon.

Removing Grease from Silk.—Apply a little magnesia to the wrong side, and the spots will disappear.

To Clean Furs.—Shake and whip them well; then brush; boil some flax seed; dip a rag in the water and wipe them slightly. This makes them look nearly as good as new.

To Preserve Furs.—First, hang them out in the sun for a day or two; then give them a good beating and shaking up, to be sure no moth is in them already. Then wrap up a lump of camphor in a rag, and place in each; then wrap up each in a sound newspaper and paste together, so there is no hole or crevice through which a moth can gain entrance.

To Clean Velvet.—Wet a cloth and put it over a hot flat-iron, and a dry one over that; then draw the velvet across it, brushing it at the same time with a soft brush, and it will look as nice as new.

Wrinkled Silk.—Wrinkled silk may be rendered nearly as beautiful as when new, by sponging the surface with a weak solution of gum-arabic or white glue; then iron on the wrong side.

To Make Cloth Water-Proof.—In a pail of soft water put half a pound of sugar of lead, half a pound of alum; stir this at intervals until it becomes cool; then pour it into another pail and put the garment therein, and let it be in for twenty-four hours, and then hang it up to dry without wringing it.

To Color Kid Gloves.—Put a handful of logwood into a bowl, cover with alcohol, and let it soak until it looks strong—one day, perhaps. Put one glove on the hand, dip a small woolen cloth or sponge into the liquid, wet the glove all over, rub it dry and hard until it shines, and it will be a nice purple. Repeat the process, and it will be black.

Washing Kid Gloves.—First, see that your hands are clean, then put on your gloves and wash them as though you were washing your hands, in a basin of spirits of turpentine. This method is used in Paris. The gloves should be hung in the air, or some dry place, to carry away the smell of turpentine.

Grease spots in cloth may be taken out by applying a solution of salt in alcohol.

Paint on Clothing.—Soak in kerosene a while before washing; also paint brushes. If on the hands, dampen with it and it will wash off easily.

Inkstains on a white surface should be wet with milk and rubbed with salt, allowing it to remain on for some time. Two or three applications may be found necessary.

Alcohol for Grass Stains.–It is claimed that alcohol will immediately remove grass stains from any white material.

Grease Spots on Velvet.—Grease spots on velvet or cloth can be removed by dropping a little turpentine over the place, and rubbing it dry with a piece of clean flannel. Continue this until the grease has vanished. If the nap of the velvet has become flattened, raise it by damping the wrong side, stretching it out, and ironing it on the wrong side. This is best done by standing the iron on end and passing the velvet over it.

Removing Paint from Woolen Goods.—Turpentine will remove paint from woolen goods and silk fabrics. Saturate the spot with spirits of turpentine and allow it to remain for hours. Rub the cloth between the fingers and the paint will crumble off without injuring the goods.

Grease Spots on Wall Paper.—A great many folks are very often annoyed at finding grease spots on the pretty wall paper adorning their rooms. A good way to remove these spots is to put powdered French chalk, wetted with cold water, over the places, and let it remain for twelve hours or more. When you brush off the chalk, if the grease spots have not disappeared, put on more chalk, place a piece of coarse brown paper or blotting paper on this, and press for a few minutes with a warm iron.

Or apply a little powdered pipe clay only dampened enough to make it stick, and brush the dried powder off later. The ugly grease spots will be gone.

Wall paper that has become bruised or torn off in small patches, and cannot be matched, may be repaired with ordinary children's paints. Mix the colors till you get as nearly as possible the desired shade, and lightly touch up the broken places, and at the distance of a foot or two the disfigurement will be quite unnoticed.

Scratches of Matches.—If matches have been scratched on bare walls by careless hands, cut a lemon in two, rub the marks off with the cut end, wash the acid off with clear water, and when dry rub with a little whiting till the faintest mark is removed.

Special Instructions for Taking Out Stains

From Approved Methods for Home Laundering by Mary Beals Vail, 1906

BLOOD—If fresh or recently dried, soak in cold or tepid water, rub out; when stain is brown and nearly gone, use soap and warm water. If very dry, soak and wash out; use Javelle water or peroxide of hydrogen.

BRASS—Rub with rancid lard or butter before washing. Warm white wine vinegar is a solvent for brass or copper, but must not be used on colored goods.

COCOA—Wash in cold water first, then rinse and pour boiling water through it. If resistant, try a bleaching agent.

COFFEE—Pour boiling water through it from a height. If resistant, try a bleaching agent.

FRUIT—Alcohol softens and dissolves many fruit stains. If the alcohol is warmed over hot water it will be more efficient; later, use boiling water poured from a height. If resistant, try sulphur fumes, dilute muriatic acid, or a bleaching agent.

GRASS—Alcohol will dissolve the green coloring matter of plants and is recommended when the material cannot be washed.

GREASE or OIL—Wash with cold water and soap first, and use solvents after drying, if necessary. Axle grease, rub with lard and let it stand to soften, then wash out. For fabrics that cannot be washed, the material may be treated with gasoline. Rub always toward the centre of the stain, and have several folds of clean cloth under the spot. Use always by daylight and in a draft. Ether is better than gasoline and is used in the same way. Powdered chalk or blotting paper may be used to absorb the oil. Kerosene will evaporate. Vaseline stains should be soaked in kerosene before washing. Chloroform, or preferably carbona, is a better solvent than gasoline, and with either there is no danger of flame or explosion.

INK—Place stained portion in sweet or sour milk and allow it to stand several days. Change milk, wash out in clear water, and try again, if necessary. Unless you know the character of the ink, it is hard to know what to recommend. Try peroxide of hydrogen and dilute ammonia if the stain is fresh, lemon and salt, acid oxalate of potash, known as salts of lemon, or oxalic acid, and lastly Javelle water.

Red Ink—Wash with cold water or water and ammonia. If it does not come out, use Javelle water.

IRON RUST—Lemon juice, salt, and hot sunshine may dissolve the stain, but more often muriatic acid is necessary. Oxalic acid may be tried, acid oxalate of potash, known as salts of lemon, or oxalic acid and dilute muriatic acid. If available, ox-gall will remove iron stain.

MEDICINE—Alcohol usually dissolves medicines. For iodine, use hyposulphite of soda or chloroform.

MILDEW is really a plant, a mold growing on the fibre. It shows itself in warm weather when clothes are kept damp for a day or two. If fresh it may be removed, but if old it will not come out. Wet in strong soap suds, cover with a paste of soap and powdered chalk, or chalk and salt, and put in the strong sunlight for hours. If it does not yield to these, Javelle water or bleaching agents may be used, but the fibre is liable to suffer.

MILK OR CREAM—Wash out with cold water, and later use soap and cold water.

MUCOUS, as in handkerchiefs, should be washed in ammonia and water before using soap. In case of a heavy cold it is best to soak all handkerchiefs in a strong solution of boracic acid for several hours.

PAINT OR TAR—If fresh and washable, use soap and water; if not washable, use gasoline. If dry and washable, soften with lard or oil and then use soap and water; if not washable, soften and wash in gasoline. If color is delicate, soften with oil and rub out with ether or chloroform. The most effectual remedy for dry paint or varnish is amyl acetate or resin spirits; soften stain with one of them and wash out with gasoline.

PERSPIRATION—Use strong soap solution and let the garment lie in the sunshine. The perspiration under the arms is different from that of the rest of the body and requires an acid to neutralize it. Use diluted muriatic acid.

SUGAR OR GUM—Dissolve with warm water if washable; with diluted alcohol if not washable.

TEA—Rub out in cold water first, then pour boiling water through it. Glycerine may be used to soak the stain.

WAX—Cover the spot, both sides, with brown or blotting paper and apply a warm (not hot) iron. It may be dissolved by hot alcohol.

WINE—For red wine, cover with a layer of salt while fresh, then use boiling water. Moist salt and sunshine may be used if it does not come out easily. For white wine, wash first with cold water, then with soap and water.

How to Clean Brass

From *The Household Guide or Domestic Cyclopedia* by Mrs. J.L. Nichols, 1905

First rub over with a little lemon-juice, and then dry thoroughly; then place the article in paraffin, and let it soak for three or four hours. Take it out, and while wet rub thoroughly with emery powder. The ordinary knife powder will do. Use a piece of old flannel, or new, if you have no scraps of anything else. When clean rub the article well with a clean duster, so as to remove all the powder, and then finish off with a leather. Of course the rubbing in of the powder takes time, but the result is perfection.

Rust may be removed from steel by rubbing the article with kerosene oil and leaving it for twenty-four hours. Then rub thoroughly with a mixture of kerosene and fine emery powder.

How to Make all Kinds of Furniture Washes and Remove Stains, Bruises, Moths, etc.

From *The Household Guide or Domestic Cyclopedia* by Mrs. J.L. Nichols, 1905

W. W. Wickle's Furniture Polish

1½ qts. raw linseed oil,
½ qt. boiled linseed oil,
1 qt. turpentine,
3 ozs. beeswax.

Furniture Polish

Equal quantities of common wax, white wax and white soap, in the proportion of one ounce of each, to a pint of water. Cut the above ingredients fine, and dissolve over a fire until well mingled. Bottle and label.

A good temporary wash is kerosene oil.

To Remove Stains, Spots and Mildew from Furniture

Take ½ pint of 98 percent alcohol,
¼ ounce of pulverized resin,
¼ ounce gum shellac.

Add ½ pint of linseed oil. Shake well, and apply with a brush or sponge. Sweet oil will remove finger marks from varnished furniture, and kerosene from oiled furniture.

To Take Bruises Out of Furniture

Wet the part with warm water, double a piece of brown paper five or six times, soak it and lay it on the place; apply on that a hot flat-iron till the moisture is evaporated. If the bruises be not gone, repeat the process. After two or three applications, the dent or bruise will be raised level with the surface.

A Polish For New Furniture

1 pint of alcohol.
1 ounce shellac.
1¼ ounces copal.
1 ounce dragon's blood.

Mix and dissolve. Apply with sponge or soft brush.

A Polish For Wood Or Leather

1 pint alcohol.
3¼ sticks scaling wax.

Dissolve by heating it, and apply warm with sponge.

N. B.—The sealing wax should be the color of the leather, black, red or blue.

To Remove Moths From Furniture

Moths may be exterminated or driven from upholstered work, by sprinkling this with benzine. The benzine is put into a small watering pot, such as is used for sprinkling house plants; it does not spot the most delicate silk, and the unpleasant odor passes off in an hour or two into the air.

Care must be used not to carry on this work near a fire or flame, as the vapor of benzine is very inflammable. It is said that a little spirits of turpentine added to the water with which the floor is washed will prevent the ravages of moths.

To Clean Mirrors, Window Glass, etc.

Take a soft sponge, wash it well in clean water and squeeze it as dry as possible; dip it into some spirits of wine and rub over the glass; then have some powdered blue tied up in a rag, dust it over your glass, and rub it lightly and quickly with a soft cloth; afterwards finish with a silk handkerchief.

To Remove Stains In Tables

Wash the surface with vinegar; the stains will then be removed by rubbing them with a rag dipped in spirits of salts. To repolish, proceed as you would with new work. If the work be not stained, wash the surface with clean spirits of turpentine and repolish it with furniture oil.

To Take Smoke Stains From Walls

An easy and sure way to remove smoke stains from common plain ceilings is to mix wood ashes with the whitewash just before applying. A pint of ashes to a small pail of whitewash is sufficient, but a little more or less will do no harm.

Furniture Polish

A simple furniture polish for common use is made by mixing two tablespoonfuls of sweet or linseed oil with a tablespoonful of turpentine. Rub on with a piece of flannel and polish with a dry piece.

How to make Oil Finished Furniture Look New

Many good housekeepers are often at a great loss in knowing how to keep varnished furniture, and the kind generally known as "oil finished," looking fresh and new without going to the expense of having it re-varnished or gone over by a finisher. Here is a never-failing polish; after thoroughly dusting the article and cleaning off whatever specks may be on it, she should mix and apply the following: take one teaspoonful of pure cider vinegar and add to it one gill of pure raw linseed oil. Shake thoroughly until mixed. Apply with a soft woolen rag, rubbing gently. It is only necessary to dampen the rag with the mixture and not to thoroughly wet it. It soon dries and leaves the article with a bright, new face. This preparation has the advantage of not gumming, but giving a fresh look to every article of furniture it is applied to.

How to Stain a Floor

Take one-third turpentine and two-thirds boiled linseed oil, with a little japan dryer added. Buy a can of burned sienna, and blend it thoroughly with this mixture. This gives a rich reddish brown. Mix the paint quite thin, so that it will run readily. Lay it on with a good-sized brush stroking the brush the way of the grain of the wood. Put on several coats, allowing each one to become perfectly dry. Lastly, give the floor a good coat of varnish, and when thoroughly dry it will be found as satisfactory as a stained floor can be and easily kept clean.

The Care of Hardwood Floors

Parquetry Floors.—The parquetry inlaid floors are much more easily cared for, as well as more durable, when polished with wax than any other preparation.

In laying a new floor the best paste filler should be thoroughly applied by one who understands his business and then floor wax applied with a flannel cloth without the use of varnish, shellac or hard oil. It requires a heavy-weight floor brush to give a polish, but persistence and perseverance will give better results and less liability to scratching than any other method. This method has been in use in the old country many years.

Plain Oak.—A plain oak floor can be treated in the same manner.

To clean a floor never use soap and water, the dirt can be removed with turpentine or the use of some of the patent "restorers" furnished by the manufacturers of hard-wood floors. Apply the turpentine or restorer with a woolen cloth and plenty of elbow grease, then use the wax. A thin coating of wax should be rubbed over the entire surface of the floor with a woolen cloth and then polished with the brush. The brush should be moved in straight lines first one way and then the other.

To Give the Finishing Touch.—Place a clean flannel cloth under the brush and rub the floor with this.

In an ordinary room that has very hard use, once a month is often enough to polish a floor. In bedrooms or where the floor is almost entirely covered with rugs once in every three months is sufficient.

How to Take Measures for Patterns

From *The Household Guide or Domestic Cyclopedia* by Mrs. J.L. Nichols, 1905

Dresses, Coats, Vests, Pants and Shirts

To Measure for a Lady's Basque or any Garment requiring a Bust Measure to be taken:—Put the measure around the body, over the dress, close under the arms, drawing it closely—not too tight.

To Measure for a Lady's Skirt or Overskirt:—Put the measure around the waist, over the dress.

To Measure for a Lady's Sleeve:—Put the measure around the muscular part of the upper arm, about an inch below the lower part of the arm's-eye, drawing the tape closely—not too tight.

Take the measure for Misses' and Little Girls' Patterns the same as for Ladies'. In ordering, give the ages also.

To Measure for a Boy's Coat or Vest:—Put the measure around the body, under the jacket, close under the arms, drawing it closely—not too tight.

To Measure for a Boy's Overcoat:—Measure about the breast over the garment the coat is to be worn over.

To Measure for Trousers:—Put the measure around the body, over the trousers at the waist, drawing it closely—not too tight.

To Measure for a Shirt:—For the size of the neck, measure the exact size where the collar encircles it, and allow one inch—thus, if the exact size be fourteen inches, use a pattern marked fifteen inches. In other words, give the size of the collar the shirt is to be worn with. For the breast, put the measure around the body, under the jacket or coat, close under the arms, drawing it closely—not too tight.

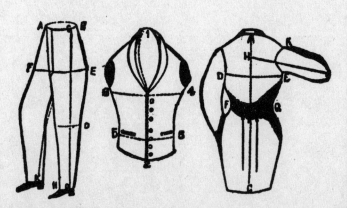

How to take the Measure for a Suit of Clothes

Take these Measures over the Vest: Inches.

From 1 at center of back of neck, round the inside edge of the collar, to height required from top button.
From top button to 2 for length in front.
From 3 to 4 round breast.
From 5 to 6 round waist.

Measure for Pants

From A to B round waist.
From C to D, top to bottom.
From center to fork, close up, down to K, for length of leg inside, the leg straight down.
F to G round the seat.

L round the knee.
From H to I round bottom.

Take these Measures outside the Coat:

From A to B.
Continuing on to C for full length.
From H to I for elbow joint.
Continuing on to K for length of sleeve.

Take these Measures under the Coat:

From D to E round the breast.
From F to G round the waist.

For an Overcoat

Take the last two measures over the undercoat: the others same as above.

How to Destroy all Kinds of House Insects

From *The Household Guide or Domestic Cyclopedia* by Mrs. J.L. Nichols, 1905

1. Insects do not grow by imperceptible increase in size as a bird or a cat. All insects pass through several changes from the egg to the perfect state. The horrid caterpillar that crawls in our path today will soon be seen flitting among the flowers in the form of a beautiful butterfly.
2. To destroy house pests successfully, the history of the insect, from the egg to the perfect state, must be well known. The successful housekeeper must always be a close observer and a careful student in order to keep her house free from noxious insects.

How to Avoid Fleas

1. There are no human fleas in North America. The dog and the cat flea are the only species that annoy us.
2. The eggs of the flea are very small, white and oblong, and are laid on the dog or cat, and, being sticky, adhere to the hair until they are ready to hatch, when they fall to the ground. They hatch in about a week, and in less than two weeks attain their growth. They then pass through a pupal stage, and in two weeks more the perfect flea appears. They flourish best in sandy soil.
3. Remedy. Put olive oil on the dog or cat or both, as the case may be, and rub it into the hair thoroughly and after a few hours wash out with warm water and soap.
4. Dalmation Insect Powder rubbed into the hair and sprinkled around the dog's kennel or the cat's sleeping place is also a good remedy.

How to Exterminate the Carpet Bug

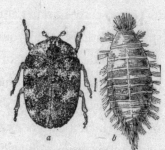

The Carpet Bug (Anthienus Scrophulanæ) or Buffalo Bug, as it is sometimes called, was first noticed in the city of Buffalo, New York.

The grub which does the damage is about one-fourth of an inch in length. It is covered with hair as shown in the above illustration a, b. It spins no cocoon like the caterpillar, but when full grown the skin splits on the back and shows the insect. A few weeks later the skin bursts again, and the perfect little bug, as shown in a, appears. It is marked with red, black and white spots and is less than one-eighth of an inch in length.

Remedy. When once in a carpet it is a very difficult insect to destroy. In some houses carpets cannot be used, as they are eaten as fast as they can be put down. Tallowed paper placed around the edges of the carpet is a very good preventive.

When a carpet is cut as if with scissors following the seams in the floor, the simplest and safest remedy is to pour benzine in very small quantities along the seams; also running a hot flat iron over along the seams of the carpet is very destructive to both the insect and the eggs. Sprinkling the paper with benzine before the carpet is tacked down is an excellent precaution. Pour half a pint of turpentine into your hot-water pail, and scrub the boards with your long-handled brush, and add another half-pint when you mop it all up. Then no buffalo moths will attack the carpets you have prepared floors for.

How to Destroy Clothes Moths

One of the greatest enemies of the homemaker is the clothes moth. It is very small and makes its way through the smallest crevices. The female moth finds its way in early summer among the clothes and furs, suitable for food for its young, and there deposits about fifty or more eggs. In about a week the eggs hatch and the young worms begin to eat upon the cloth upon which the eggs were laid. It spins a sort of case which it lengthens and enlarges. Not content with eating and making a house for itself upon the cloth upon which it lives, it cuts its way in various directions through the cloth and drags its case after it. As the weather gets warmer the little worm closes its case at the ends and in three weeks the perfect moth will make its appearance.

Remedy. Beat the garments well early in the spring and occasionally during the summer. It is better to keep the articles in a large paper bag. Occasional airing is good.

For clothes packed in boxes or trunks, put a little oil of cedar on a piece of paper and roll up and wrap with other paper to avoid soiling the garments, and put several of these rolls into each box or trunk. Carbolic acid, turpentine or benzine is equally good, used in the same manner.

Black pepper, a piece of camphor gum, or a handful of snuff wrapped up with the clothes is excellent.

Caution. Camphor should never be used in keeping seal skin, as it takes the color out of the fur.

A close closet lined with tar paper is the best for furs. It is also excellent for clothes.

The Common Moth

In May the clothes-moth begins to fly about our rooms. It is a small, light, buff-colored "miller," dainty and beautiful on close inspection. Its highest mission seems to be to teach us to set our affections only upon incorruptible treasures which "moth and rust cannot destroy." But it is necessary to keep a sharp lookout for the safety of our furs and flannels, and we must wage war upon it. In the first place, we must carefully put away everything we can, upon which it will lay its eggs. If we pack away our furs and flannels early in May, before the moth has begun to lay its eggs, and leave them in boxes and bags so tight that the flying moth cannot squeeze in, no further precaution is necessary. Clean paper bags are recommended for this purpose—those used for flour and meal bags. They should be without holes or opening anywhere. These bags, when filled and closed firmly, may be put away on closet shelves or in loose boxes, without danger to their contents, so far as moths are concerned, without need of camphor or other strong odors to drive the moths away. Furs are usually sold in boxes in which they may be kept. Beat them well when you finally put them away for the season. If you delay putting them away until June, examine the furs well, and shake and beat them thoroughly, in order that any moth eggs that may possibly have been laid in them may be thoroughly removed or killed. Furs sealed up early in May need no camphor or tobacco or other preventive. Muff and tippet boxes should be tied up securely in bags, or made safe by mending holes and pasting a strip of paper around the juncture of the cover with the box below, so as to close all openings. Woolen garments must not hang in closets through the summer, in parts of the country where moths abound. They should be packed away in tight trunks or boxes, or sealed up in bags. Woolen blankets must be well shaken and carefully put away, unless they are in daily use. Early in June the larvae of the moth begin their ravages, and then, unless you dwell in places where moths are not found, look sharp, or you will find some precious thing, that you have forgotten— some good coat unused for a few weeks, or the woolen cover of a neglected piano—already riddled by the voracious moths. It is their nature to eat until they have grown strong enough to retire from the eating business, and go into the chrysalis condition.

How to Keep Furs from Moths

Moths will avoid light and sunshine. Before packing away furs, sun them several hours in the open air, then tie them tightly in a linen, cotton or paper bag, which is whole. A little snuff placed in the bottom is a good thing.

If moths are already at work, fumigate with sulphur placed on live coals. Close the room in which the furs are placed, and be careful not to inhale the fumes. Fumigating rooms after scarlet fever or other contagious diseases is said to destroy all the disease germs.

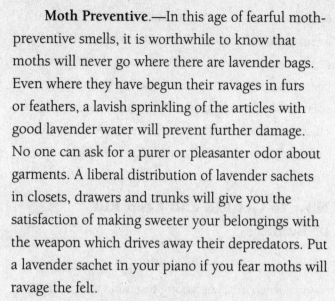

Moth Preventive.—In this age of fearful moth-preventive smells, it is worthwhile to know that moths will never go where there are lavender bags. Even where they have begun their ravages in furs or feathers, a lavish sprinkling of the articles with good lavender water will prevent further damage. No one can ask for a purer or pleasanter odor about garments. A liberal distribution of lavender sachets in closets, drawers and trunks will give you the satisfaction of making sweeter your belongings with the weapon which drives away their depredators. Put a lavender sachet in your piano if you fear moths will ravage the felt.

Another Infallible Remedy is compounded of the following sweet-smelling things: Lavender, thyme, rose, cedar shavings, powdered sassafras, cassia, and lignea in about equal quantities, with a few drops of attar of roses thrown upon the whole.

Tansy Leaves, spread freely among woolens and furs, are a protection against moths.

Turpentine is an excellent preventive against moths, although naphtha is preferable, the odor leaving much sooner; it will drive ants and cockroaches away if sprinkled about the shelves and cupboards.

Whole Cloves are now used to exterminate moths, and some say they are much better than tobacco, camphor, or cedar shavings.

The Best Preventive of moths is care. Cedar chests, camphor, and pepper avail nothing if a garment is laid away with the egg of the moth in it. If it is, in season, shut up in paper or cloth so that no millers can possibly reach it, there will be no need of pungent odors. Benzine is the best remedy if the moths have stolen a march and are ravaging carpets or furniture. Pour it freely upon any carpet or upholstered furniture and it will not stain.

The Buffalo Moths, the most destructive of all household foes, try equal quantities of borax, camphor, and saltpetre, mixed. Wash the floor with a strong solution of it, and scatter it under the edge of the carpet and in your closets and drawers. The beetle that lays the eggs comes early in February and then the fight must begin. Naphtha is considered an efficient remedy, but it must be repeatedly used in order to destroy each successive generation.

How to Get Rid and Keep Rid of Bedbugs

1. The eggs of the bedbug are white in color and oval in shape. The young resemble the parents, and it takes about eleven weeks to get its full growth. Like reptiles, they can live many years without food. Mr. Goeze, of Germany, has kept them six years in a bottle without a particle of nourishment of any kind.
2. Keeping the bedding and bedstead perfectly clean is the best preventive.
3. Remedy.—Pour hot water into the crevices and then apply benzine to the different parts of the bedstead.
4. Unpurified petroleum mixed with a little water is also a sure remedy. Corrosive sublimate is a very good, but a very poisonous cure.

How to Exterminate Spiders

Take a small common kerosene lamp and light it, and late in the afternoon or early in the evening look over the corners and places where spiders are commonly found, and when one is seen hold the lamp chimney directly beneath it, and it will fall at once into the chimney and be instantly destroyed. It is not difficult in this way to destroy all the spiders in the house in a few evenings. It avoids killing them by sweeping them down, and staining the walls or carpet. Early in the evening is the best time.

How to Preserve Books from Book Moths

The little Bristle Tail or Silver Fish has a little, long, slender body covered with a delicate silver scale; it has no wings and passes through no changes. It feeds on the paste of the binding of books, devours leaves, eats off the labels in Museums and is generally destructive to both books and papers.

Books are also eaten by the larva of a little bug that produces a ticking sound like a watch—it is called the "Death Watch," as it is usually heard in the night ticking like a watch.

Remedy. A little rag saturated with benzine or carbolic acid placed along the back of the shelves will clear the library of all insects. Inject Powder sprinkled over the books will destroy the little "Silver Fish" insect instantly.

Mixture for Destroying Flies

1 pint infusion of quassia,
4 ounces brown sugar,
2 ounces ground pepper.

To be well mixed together, and put in small shallow dishes when required.

How to Keep Out Mosquitoes

If a bottle of the oil of pennyroyal is left uncorked in a room at night, not a mosquito, or any other blood-sucker, will be found there in the morning.

A Domestic Remedy for Destroying Flies

½ tablespoonful black pepper, in powder,
1 teaspoonful brown sugar,
1 tablespoonful cream.

Mix them well together, and place them in the room on a plate, where the flies are troublesome, and they will soon disappear.

To Banish the Flies

The following is vouched for: Take one ounce of camphor gum, one ounce of corrosive sublimate, one pint of oil of turpentine; grind the sublimate thoroughly, put into a strong bottle and add the camphor gum. Pour on the turpentine and shake occasionally. It should be fit for use in 36 hours. Heat a piece of iron and drop a few drops on it in the stable and till flies will leave. Flies may be driven out of the house by dropping a few drops on a hot stove-lid. Practiced every other day will, it is said, soon drive out all flies.

A Cure for Bee and Wasp Stings, Spider Bites, etc.

Apply ammonia or common soda and water. If there is much inflammation and redness, apply a solution of borax and warm water. Apply with a rag saturated with the solution.

A New Way of Trapping Ants

1. Ants are very difficult pests to expel from the house. There have been many recipes and experiments tried, but without any satisfactory results.

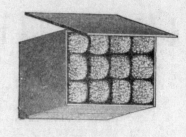

2. The ants that infest our houses live only in rotten wood, either in the decayed sills of the house or in rotten timbers and old fences nearby. It is best to remove all such hiding places if possible.
3. Remedy.—Ants are very fond of sugar, and anything containing it will attract them. Sweeten a pan of water to a thin syrup, and then dip a large sponge into it, and wring it out. Place the sponge where the ants can get at it; it will soon be filled through and through with ants, then take it up carefully and plunge it into boiling water, and again set it by saturating it with the thin syrup. A few days' trial will, for a long time, exterminate the annoying pests.
4. A trap more simple but not so effectual is a plate covered with a thin layer of lard and placed where the ants can easily get at it. This trap is more to destroy the little yellow ant than the larger species.

How to Destroy Ants

Boiling water, kerosene, or a solution of fresh insect powder in water, poured into the hill, will destroy the inhabitants at once. Where the nests are outside of the house this is a sure remedy.

Household Hints

From *Handy Household Hints and Recipes* by Mattie Lee Wehrley, 1916

Leather chairs and leather bindings can be brightened by being rubbed with a cloth which has been dipped in white of an egg.

Mix cold starch with soapy water instead of clear, cold water, and the result will be more satisfactory.

What Salt Will Do

A damp cloth dipped in salt will remove egg stains from silver, or tea stains from china dishes.

Salt under bread and cake in oven will prevent scorching on bottom.

Salt is excellent for removing dirt from wash bowls.

Hints for Kitchen

A basin of cold water placed in a hot oven will soon lower the temperature.

Rusty flatirons should be rubbed over with beeswax and lard, or beeswax and salt.

Tough meat may be made tender if placed in vinegar a few minutes.

To beat the whites of eggs quickly add a pinch of salt.

Dish cloths should be scalded and washed daily.

A small quantity of green sage placed in the pantry will keep out red ants.

Cold fruits require cold jars; hot fruits, hot jars.

That water for cooking should never be taken from pipes.

That a successful cook always has a good set of domestic scales.

Brooms dipped in boiling suds once a week will wear much longer.

That milk will keep sweet longer in a shallow pan than in a pitcher.

Equal parts of lime water and olive oil applied at once is a remedy for burns.

If you once use a small brush for cleaning vegetables you will never do without one.

That a coarse grater rubbed over burnt bread or cake is far better than using a knife.

That an agreeable disinfectant—ground coffee on a shovel of hot coals—will purify the air of a room almost instantly.

To restore an eiderdown quilt to its original fluffy lightness, hang it out of doors in the sunlight for several hours.

That if you would always remember to measure solids and fluids in exactly the same way success would be far more certain. No cake recipe is followed when you heap the cups or have them level full of sugar and flour and the milk half an inch below the top.

A tablespoon of turpentine boiled with white clothes will greatly aid the whitening process.

Blankets and furs put away well sprinkled with borax and done up air tight, will never be troubled with moths.

To stone raisins easily, pour boiling water over them and drain it off. This loosens them and they come out with ease.

Chloride of lime should be scattered at least once a week under the sink and in all places where sewer gas is liable to lurk.

All cake needs a moderate oven.

Keep the box of baking powder covered.

Use the common kitchen teacup for measuring.

Never let the cake dough stand any length of time before baking.

To remove chimney soot from carpets, cover with fine dry salt and brush up with stiff broom, and repeat until carpet is clean. After the first is taken up, the spots may be scrubbed hard with the salt until soot is removed.

To take out iron rust, squeeze lemon juice on spots, cover with salt and place in hot sun or iron with hot flatiron.

For burns make a thick paste of saleratus in water; cover the burn with the mixture, making the application half an inch thick.

To remove spots caused by acid on colored goods, moisten the goods and cover with saleratus before washing.

Never stir sugar and butter together in a tin basin or with an iron spoon, a wooden spoon is better than any other kind.

Be sure the oven is right before the cake is put in and then do not open the door until it has been baking at least ten minutes.

To prevent oil from spreading when painting on delicate satin or bolting cloth, mix gasoline with your oil paint. By using this medium the paint can be used very thin, giving the appearance of water coloring.

To clean mica in stoves, wash in vinegar.

Chicken drippings are excellent for greasing tins.

Use vinegar to remove the smell of kerosene from tins and dishes.

A teaspoon of borax added to starch, renders the collars and cuffs much stiffer.

Pour cold water over hard boiled eggs as soon as taken from the kettle, and they will not be discolored.

If you wish to give your glass a high degree of brilliancy, add a little bluing to the water.

To remove grease stains rub well with alcohol before wetting.

A sponge saturated with camphor and placed near the bed will keep away mosquitoes at night.

Discolored enameled saucepans are easily made bright and clean by the use of powdered pumice stone.

Keep flowers fresh by putting a pinch of soda in water.

Help for Sore Throat

Boil about thirty leaves of common sage in half a pint of vinegar for half an hour. When cold add one tablespoonful of honey. Use as a gargle diluted with a little warm water.

For a Burn

If applied quickly, the white of an egg will relieve the stinging pain from a burn and prevent inflammation.

Use equal parts of linseed oil and limewater.

Cramps in Stomach

A few drops of oil or essence of peppermint is good for cramps in the stomach and bowels and for diarrhea. It should be taken in a little sweetened water.

Cough Medicine

Jamaica rum, honey, linseed oil—equal parts.

Farmers' Department

From *Mrs. Owens' Cook Book and Useful Household Hints*,
by Frances Emugene Owens, 1884

CUTTING UP MEATS. DISEASES OF ANIMALS.
ROAD-MAKING. MISCELLANEOUS.

Cutting Up Meats

Give diagrams showing the manner of cutting up meats at the present day for home consumption. Packers have a different method. On the quarter of beef the figures are made to correspond with the like parts in the beef on foot. It is the same with the porker.

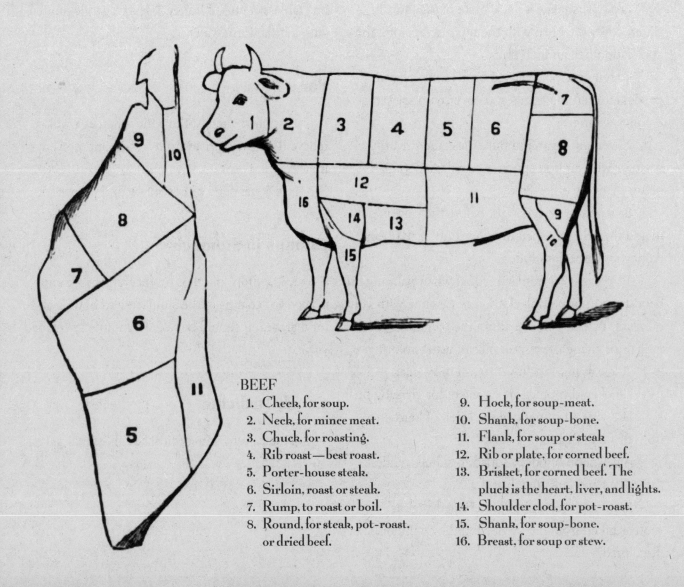

BEEF

1. Cheek, for soup.
2. Neck, for mince meat.
3. Chuck, for roasting.
4. Rib roast—best roast.
5. Porter-house steak.
6. Sirloin, roast or steak.
7. Rump, to roast or boil.
8. Round, for steak, pot-roast, or dried beef.
9. Hock, for soup-meat.
10. Shank, for soup-bone.
11. Flank, for soup or steak
12. Rib or plate, for corned beef.
13. Brisket, for corned beef. The pluck is the heart, liver, and lights.
14. Shoulder clod, for pot-roast.
15. Shank, for soup-bone.
16. Breast, for soup or stew.

Miscellaneous

From Mrs. Owens' Cook Book and Useful Household Hints, by Frances Emugene Owens

Paint For Kitchen Floor

Three pints oil, 1 pint dryer, 3 pounds white lead. 5 pounds yellow ochre; add a little turpentine.

Shellac For Floor

Allow 5 ounces shellac to a quart of alcohol. Use as soon as dissolved. After a floor is painted or stained (and dried), apply the shellac with a brush; let dry and apply again. Two or three applications, which are very easily made, will brighten up a room wonderfully, and it will require nothing but wiping with a damp cloth to keep it bright for many months. Any homemaker can do both the painting and applying the coats of shellac.

Cleaning Silver

One-half ounce prepared chalk, 2 ounces alcohol, 2 ounces aqua ammonia. Apply with cotton flannel, and rub with chamois-skin. Wash silver in very hot, clear water, and wipe dry with a soft towel, and you will have no need for silver soap, or any other preparation.

Cleaning Brass Or Copper
C. D. Hicks, Racine, Wis

One pint alcohol, 1 ounce oxalic acid, 2 papers Me. Eagle Tripoli, 1 star candle. Shave the candle into the other mixture, and let stand until dissolved. Then it is ready for use. Shake before using. Apply the mixture, and when dry rub off with a woolen cloth. The same mixture without the candle excellent for cleaning glass.

Furniture Polish

Raw linseed oil, 4 ounces; balsam of fir, 2 drachms; acetic ether, 2 drachms. Dissolve the balsam in 4 ounces alcohol; then mix all together. To use, shake well and apply with a soft cloth. But very little is needed on the cloth.

Polish For Old Or Marred Furniture

One ounce kerosene. 1 ounce shellac, ½ ounce linseed oil, ½ ounce turpentine. Keep corked, shake, and apply with a soft sponge.

Roaches

Equal parts of borax and white sugar will drive away roaches or Croton bugs.

Moths

Put salt under the edges of carpets when tacked down.

Bed-Bug Poison
Mrs. R. W Louis Chicago

Six ounces corrosive sublimate, 6 ounces camphor gum, 1 pt. spirits turpentine; shake well, mix; let stand a day. Shake before using.

Crockery Cement

To mend broken china, glass, marble, or common crockery, mix fresh-slaked lime with white of egg until it becomes a sticky paste. Apply to the edges, and in 3 days it will be firm.

Liquid Glue

Best white glue, 16 ounces; white lead, dry, 4 ounces; rain water, 1 quart; alcohol, 4 ounces. With constant stirring dissolve the glue and lead in the water, by means of a water bath. Add the alcohol, and continue the heat for a few minutes. Pour into bottles while still hot.

Cleaning House

From *Mrs. Owens' Cook Book and Useful Household Hints*, by Frances Emugene Owens, 1884

The melancholy days that come,
    The saddest of the year.
When scrubbing-brushes, mops, and brooms
    Art flying far and near,—
When carpets, curtains, rugs, and beds
    Are stretched on fence and line,
And everything is upside down—
    O, sad, unhappy time.

At this cheerful time of year, a few hints to the newly initiated may prove helpful. They are not written for the veterans in the service, although such may possibly be benefited somewhat by glancing at them. It is a good plan to regulate and renovate all bureau-drawers and closets before the general siege then have the wishing and ironing finished and put away. Wash up everything that is soiled. Bake enough bread, cookies, and cake to last several days. Roil a large ham, if possible, and bake a big pot of beans. These, with preserved fruits, will make a good meal with hot tea or coffee.

The general rule to begin at the garret and finish with the cellar is a good one in the main. But sometimes, with a large house and insufficient help, the cellar gets but an indifferent cleaning if left till all hands are tired out. It is, in reality, the most important part of the whole house. There can be no health, with foul, disease-breeding gases escaping into the living rooms above, to be breathed into the system. Malarial diseases are often traced to a cellar of decayed vegetables. Typhus and typhoid fevers, cutting down whole families, can be traced directly to the fearful emanations from a filthy cellar.

After removing all rubbish from each nook and corner, and giving it a thorough airing, give it a good coat of white-wash, yellowed with copperas. Wash the windows and steps.

Next, go to the upper story and begin in good earnest the cleaning and putting things to rights after an accumulated disorder of six months or a year. Even with constant watch-care, things will get out of place, and house-renovating is just as sure to be a necessity, as is the cleaning necessary to health.

First and foremost, let in the air. Give things a systematic sorting over, putting articles of a kind together in boxes or sacks, and labeling them. Sweep the ceiling and walls down. Wash the windows and the floor. Wipe up dry. If there are any signs of moths, make sure that there is no fire or light in the room, and sprinkle benzine plentifully around the cracks and crevices. Have but little in the dish you use. Exercise great caution in its use. It will be death to the moths. The odor is disagreeable, but of short duration. Wash the steps down, and you are ready for the chambers.

A good step-ladder is one of the indispensables in every house. Be careful, however, and see that it stands securely before ascending it. I have a lady acquaintance who fell from one that stood insecurely, and has been made almost helpless for life, from the effects of the fall.

Before beginning the general cleaning, take everything from the walls. Dust and wipe off and put into the closets, which are already cleaned. Shut the doors. Take one room at a time. Move everything out; take up the carpet. Have it folded and carried right out into the yard and spread upon the grass, or hung on the line. After it is beaten well on the wrong side with whips or canes, sweep it very particularly on the right side, with a good, firm broom. Do not sweep against the pile in velvet or Brussels.

Sweep the bare floor, and get the dirt up before opening the windows. If sawdust can be gotten, dampen it and sprinkle the floor with it. Wash hard-finished walls, and wipe dry. Paper walls should be wiped off with a broom wrapped in old flannel. Change the cloth for a clean one when it gets soiled. Of course, a wall-brush with an extension handle is the best of anything for this purpose, but the broom is a good substitute.

Next, wash the windows; then the woodwork. Put ammonia in each pail of water to soften it, and half the labor is saved. Change the water often. Use strong suds for the floor, and change the water often, Wash but a square yard at a time and wipe it dry.

Take the next room the same way. By the time that is cleaned, the first one will be ready for the carpet to go down. Sprinkle salt entirely around the room under the edge of the carpet. It is a very sure preventive of moths. If kalsomining has to be done, of course the labor of house-cleaning is greatly increased. A good recipe will be found for kalsomine in this chapter, which, if closely followed, will give excellent results. For those who prefer white-wash. I give also the famous "White House" recipe.

It is poor economy to try to put down a carpet alone. The better it is put down, the better it will wear. I think it pays to hire a man who makes carpet-laying his business, they furnish their own tacks, which alone is quite an item, and it is much more satisfactory when done. Laying a heavy carpet is a piece of work that no woman ought ever to attempt. Many persons still use straw under their carpets, and it is certainly clean and sweet. In cities and towns it is more customary to use the regular carpet-lining paper, which is heavy and durable. For stairs be sure and use either padding or lining, and have the carpet a yard extra in length to allow you to change its position occasionally, and so save the wear where the edges of the steps come.

Replacing the furniture in the room is comparatively easy. The pieces should be well dusted and polished. If not convenient to polish the same day, it can be done any other day. A good recipe for polish will be found in this chapter. For cleaning marble I have found sapolio to be very good.

Broken marble may be mended by the use of the crockery cement given further on in this chapter. I knew of a broken tomb-stone being mended with this simple preparation that has stood the wind and feather of many years.

Dining-room floors are better uncarpeted in families having young children. In fact, they are better in summer, in any family. Have the floor stained or painted, and it is always easy to keep it clean and sweet. If carpeted, have a crumb-cloth that can be taken up and shaken at will, and thus protect the main carpet.

When the kitchen is reached by the attacking party, gather up all of the lamp-burners and put into strong soda-water and boil up in some convenient vessel. Into a boiler, put all of the baking-tins, dripping-pans, waffle-irons, gem-irons, etc., and boil them 15 or 20 minutes in suds or soda-water. If you use either of the washing preparations given in the "Laundry" chapter, put some of it in the water. The fluid is excellent for this purpose. Don't scour your life away on tinware. Wash clean, wipe dry, and let that suffice.

While the tins and pans are cleaning themselves in the boiler, get the pantry ready to place them back. Use enameled cloth for shelves, instead of paper. It costs but little, and is so easily cleaned that it pays a good interest on the investment. Clean the walls either by washing, kalsomining, or white-washing.

See that the sinks and drains are thoroughly disinfected. Copperas is the cheapest, and one of the very best for this purpose. Make a solution of it in water and sprinkle in the places needing it, besides putting a small vessel containing it in the same places.

When the stoves are put away, rub each length of pipe with kerosene, wrap a paper around it and number it; so that it can be put up in the fall according to the numbering. The kerosene will keep it from rusting.

Be sure and clean the soot out of the stove-pipe holes in the chimneys before they are covered foe the summer.

Have the doors and windows screened after the cleaning is done. Put mats and scrapers at the doors.

If it is a possible thing, do your cleaning on bright, sunny days. Polish the grates about the last thing, using recipe given farther on.

Look bed-steads over in March. Apply Persian insect powder, or the poison mentioned in the latter part of this chapter. Even after the general house-cleaning, they should be looked after once a week. Bed-bugs can never get the mastery if fought in this manner.

When winter clothes are put away for the summer, examine carefully, shake well, and wrap each article in paper and tie up securely. I always put my furs and fur-trimmed cloak in an old linen pillow-case and baste it up, being sure there are no holes through which the moth-miller can crawl to lay her eggs. Blankets can be wrapped in old sheets or large papers.

A Home-Made Carpet

Paste the floor of the room over with newspapers. Over this, paste wall paper of a pattern to look like carped or oil-cloth. Put down as smoothly as possible, match it nicely where the widths come together. Use good flour paste. Then size anti varnish it. Dark glue and common furniture varnish may be used. Place a rug here and there, and your room is carpeted.

To Save Stair Carpets

Stair carpets should always have a slip of paper, or a padding made of cheap cotton batting, tacked in a cheap muslin part under them, at and over the edge of every stair, which is the part where they wear first. The strips should be within an inch or two as long as the carpet is wide and about four or five inches in breadth. A piece of old carpet answers better than paper if you have it. This plan will keep a stair carpet in good condition for a much longer time than without it.

Lining Stair Carpets
Mrs. Clarissa O. Keeler, Baltimore, Maryland.

A stair carpet lined with new cotton will almost never wear out. It saves the strain, especially if moved occasionally so that the wear does not come all the time in the same place.

Patching Carpets

Take pieces of cloth and paste over the holes with a paste made of gum tragacanth and water.

Sweeping Carpets

Use coarse wet salt for sweeping both matting and carpeting. It keeps the dust down and brightens the carpet.

Carpet-Cleaner

Dampen sawdust with water, and sprinkle ammonia on it and use on a carpet. It will brighten it very much.

Ink Stains

Can be removed from a carpet by freely pouring milk on the place, and leaving it to soak in for a time, then rub it so as to remove all ink, and scoop up remaining milk with a spoon; repeat the process with more milk, if necessary; then wash it off completely with clean cold water, and wipe it dry with cloths. If this is done when the ink is wet, the milk takes all stain out of woolen material instantly; but when it has dried, a little time is required.

Another method: As soon as the ink is spilled, put on salt, and cover well. Remove as fast as it becomes colored, and put on fresh. Continue this till the salt is white, sweep well, and no trace of ink will remain. Cornmeal used similarly on coal oil spots on carpets, will remove every particle, even if a large quantity has been spilled.

Grease Spots

Grease may be removed from a white floor by making a common hasty pudding of corn-meal and laying it on the spot until cold.

To remove grease from wall paper pulverize a common clay pipe, mix it with water into a stiff paste, laying it on very carefully, letting it remain overnight. Then lightly brush it off.

Systematic Housework

From *Putnam's Household Handbook*, by Mae Savell Croy, 1916

Organization

Organization is as necessary in the household as in the office or factory. The hub of the home is the kitchen and to get efficiency in that sphere there must be system. The foundation of system is laid by the architect who plans the house, and if the cupboards, sink and drains, and other conveniences be planned wisely with a view to economy of labor half the work is already done. Alas, however, most kitchens are planned with a range on one side of the kitchen and cupboards, sink, and drains scattered around almost anywhere without regard to convenience.

If there is not enough drainage space near the sink, a table on castors which can be rolled to the sink is a good substitute. A large tray on which sets a wire drain will take the place of the regular drainboard. If this table be long and narrow so that it can be rolled through the door into the pantry or dining-room, numerous steps will be saved in putting away the dishes. If the baseboard has been left out from the doors between kitchen, pantry, and dining-room, so much the better.

The placing of the icebox is very important. This is provided for in the average modern house today by an addition in the form of a small porch, or a special place in the pantry, but if no space has been set aside for it, it should be as near the working table as possible. While the kitchen is a hot place for a refrigerator, it is better to have it there than to put it on an exposed porch for the rain to swell and crack the box.

The range is an item which is not always given the thought it deserves. High ovens and broilers and glass doors do splendid duty in comparison with the old oven to which one must stoop and the method of opening the doors to look at cakes and bringing them out a sad fallen lump. Ranges come in almost every conceivable style and at practically any price and it is not at all necessary to pay a high price to get a well-planned range. The price is based on the finish rather than on the arrangement. For one who docs much broiling there are to be had broilers so built in that the meat can be turned without opening the door.

If one is fortunate enough to have a tiled kitchen, the task of keeping it clean is reduced to a minimum, but this is very expensive and the next best thing is to paint the kitchen with a glossy enamel paint which can be easily washed. Paper is a very inferior finish for a kitchen, for the walls will not remain fresh longer than a few weeks even with the best of care. Grease and dust are sure to settle. Linoleum makes a splendid floor covering and a good grade is not expensive in the long run. A cheap linoleum soon loses its pattern and is an eyesore when this has happened.

One can hardly have too much cupboard room in the kitchen and pantry and all cupboards should have doors in order to save the contents from having to be constantly dusted. It is to be hoped that a broom closet has been planned to hide from view the brooms, carpet sweeper, and unsightly dusting cloths. A pot closet is a delight to the one who takes pride in a neat kitchen and it should have good strong hooks on which to hang the pots. If agate or enamel pots are set one inside another they soon become chipped or cracked.

To plan the housework systematically with regard to hours is to reduce the work materially. As much of breakfast as is practical should be prepared the night before. With regard to cooked cereals, this is advisable only with a coal stove or fireless cooker, but it is to be hoped that one or the other of these is in use. After breakfast, the dining table should be cleared, the dishes rinsed and stacked in the dish pan, and water poured over them. While the dining-room is being swept and dusted the dishes are soaking. The glassware and silver and delicate pieces of china should be washed and put out of the way before beginning with the heavier dishes and pots. In the water in which the silver and glassware have been washed may be washed the pots and pans. If the stove is cleaned next, there is left only the soaking dishes, and the labor is almost finished. To wash dishes in very hot soapy water and place them in a wire drain means the avoidance of drying them, for if the water is hot and soapy they will be sweet and clean after draining dry and they will have a luster equal to any polish to be given with a cloth. By the time the cupboards are straightened and the kitchen floor swept, the dishes will be dry and can be carried in the drainer to the pantry, and the kitchen work is ended—for the time being anyway.

For the floor covering and the walls to harmonize displays interest and taste, and any effort spent to make the kitchen attractive will not be lost. A window box with blossoming flowers adds a charming note, and care should be taken to select plants that are suited to the exposure. For instance, if the window be on the north, a box filled with rich soil, kept moderately damp, will yield a splendid harvest of lilies of the valley or pansies. And what more pleasing sight than to have these little heads nodding at you while paring the homely yet nutritious tubers for dinner. If the kitchen window has a southern exposure there is a great variety of choice in flowers and even roses can be grown to advantage in a window box.

Windows should be opened in the bedrooms upon rising and by the time the kitchen work is finished they will be thoroughly aired. If the rooms are thoroughly cleaned once each week, with a general dusting daily, the work will be light. It pays not to let a room get too dirty. After tending to the bedrooms the halls should be gone over with a carpet sweeper, and next the attention should be given to the bathroom. Bathrooms cannot be kept too clean. Let us hope they are tiled to begin with, but if not, it is not difficult to keep them clean if they are given systematic attention. A long-handled mop dipped into a pail of water to which a little ammonia has been added is a very easy way of caring for a bathroom floor. By rubbing this over the floor regularly each morning and giving the floor a thorough scouring once a week, the bathroom in an average family will be kept in good condition. Of course the basins and tubs should have a daily scouring, using some good cleansing powder which does not contain too much alkali. The mirror should be kept polished and soiled towels should never be left in sight.

Laundry work can be made much easier by a little thought ahead of time. To put the clothes in soak in *cold*, soapy water the night before facilitates the work. If hot water is used any stains that may happen to be in the clothes will set and many of them can never be removed. Soap should not be rubbed on the clothes as the alkali in most soaps is too strong for many delicate fabrics if rubbed into the weave.

In the Kitchen

If *dishes* are washed in hot soapy water and rinsed in clear, cold water they will not have to be dried. Unless the water is very dear, they will be streaked when dry and will lack the polish that they should have.

A tablespoonful of ammonia added to the *dish water* will take the place of soap.

Cut glass should be washed in hot soapsuds and not dried but left to drain. After the air has dried it, rub briskly with a Turkish towel as this fabric leaves no lint and gets down into the cuts better than ordinary toweling.

To *clean pans* that have been scorched by food adhering to them, sprinkle dry baking soda in them and allow them to stand for a while. They can then be readily and quickly cleaned.

A *wooden tub* or bowl for *washing dishes* will spare the dishes from the chipping which they so often get from a metal pan or basin.

A few accessories to the kitchen, which will soon become necessities after having been used, are a *rubber dish mop*, a *rubber hose* for rinsing dishes, and a strong wire basket *dish drainer*. The mop will mean a great deal in the care of the hands, as will also the hose. The dish drainer should have protruding wires in the center that the dishes may stand up and not be permitted to touch, or they will not dry readily. Care should be taken to secure a drainer that is large enough for all the dishes or there will be constant annoyance at having to use so much care in stacking them.

Boil water in very *dirty pots* to which washing soda has been added instead of scraping them. This will not only save the pots but will be very much easier than scouring them.

Aluminum utensils need special care. They should not be allowed to stand with soda or soapy water in them nor should they be washed with a strong brown soap. For regular washing hot water and a neutral soap are advised. Any necessary soaking should be done with clear water. To remove discolorations, steel wool with neutral soap is advisable. Boiling in clear water to which a spoonful of vinegar has been added is also effective. Oxalic acid cannot be endorsed. It is a dangerous poison.

Tissue paper which ordinarily is consigned to the wastebasket will prove to be very useful if kept in the kitchen for the purpose of wiping the grease from pots and pans and for any other use where cloths would be used. This will mean a great saving in washing dish towels.

Cotton crêpe cut into one-yard lengths makes very serviceable *dish towels*. These require no hemming and do not need to be ironed. They give a fine polish to glassware, are non-linty, and have the added advantage of being very inexpensive.

A roll of *paper toweling* placed near the kitchen sink is a great labor and time saver. This can be used for cleaning the sink, scraping refuse from plates, for covering food, putting up lunches, and in countless other ways. Much of the disagreeable task of washing hand towels and dish towels will be spared and they are quite inexpensive if purchased in quantity.

Old window shades can be utilized for roller towels and kitchen towels if they are soaked and boiled clean, thus taking out the dressing. They can also be dyed and utilized for window curtains and for making up into rag rugs.

A handy little *dish washer for the milk bottle* which is too narrow for the hand and cloth is made from the wire handle of a grape basket, if it is straightened out, and the hook left on one end.

An iron sink may be kept free from rust and grease by wiping daily with a soft paper wet with kerosene.

The chief concern of *a porcelain sink* is not to mar the surface of the enamel. Soap and water, with a little kerosene, will keep it immaculate.

A little kerosene poured down *the kitchen sink* at night is a precaution against *water bugs*.

Two thirds boracic acid mixed with one third powdered sugar sprinkled around the baseboard, shelves, and other places which *roaches and water bugs* frequent will cause their death. This mixture is poisonous to them.

To dean steel on oven doors, it should be rubbed briskly while the steel is warm with a soft cloth dipped in vinegar.

To clean a rusty gas oven, saturate a woolen cloth with linseed oil and rub over the entire oven until the rust disappears. Next rub thoroughly.

Windows and Mirrors

A rag dipped in paraffin will *clean windows* perfectly and give a brightness impossible to obtain with water. Tissue paper, or any soft paper, makes a good polisher, leaving no lint.

Chamois cloth makes an excellent *window cleaner*, and is not expensive as it lasts such a long time.

Use no soap on *window* glass. Instead, use old muslin and clean soft water. A cotton cloth dipped in a little alcohol will add brilliancy to the final rub.

Never use linen to *clean mirrors or windows* as it sheds lint and often causes streaks.

The addition of a little kerosene for *washing windows* gives a brilliant polish. It is especially good in winter as the oil prevents the water from drying before the cloth can be brought into play.

Silver and Other Metals

Table salt rubbed on egg stains on *silver* will cleanse them.

Silver should be washed in a bowl or basin by itself. If touched with a greasy cloth it will have to be washed over again. It should always be well rinsed in order to retain the polish.

Common lump starch can be used with very gratifying results for *cleaning silver*. It should be

rubbed on with a damp cloth, left to stand for a few minutes, and rubbed dry with cheesecloth.

Many housekeepers are annoyed to find their *silver* tarnished, although they have carefully polished it before putting it away. Try putting a piece of camphor ice away with it and you will find it free from tarnish.

An easy way of cleaning *silver* that is not badly tarnished is to put it in an aluminum pan filled with boiling salt water and leave it there to boil for a few minutes. It can then be easily polished by rubbing with a piece of chamois cloth.

Rub oil upon *iron vessels* and the *iron* top of *stoves* and let stand for a few minutes; then cover with powdered alum. The stove or vessel will keep almost like new.

There is nothing equal to kerosene for *removing rust from iron*. A stove cleaned with ordinary stove blacking moistened with kerosene will look like new. Before storing stove pipe away for the summer rub it well with kerosene, stuff the ends with paper to keep out moisture, and the pipe will be entirely without rust when fall comes. Any metal article that is badly rusted should be immersed in kerosene and allowed to remain until the rust has softened, then wiped with a soft cloth and polished with whiting, sand soap, or bath brick, according to the finish of the metal.

To remove *rust* from a knife, plunge the blade into an onion and leave it there for an hour or so. Then polish it in the usual way.

Copper and *brass* vessels are brightened by using vinegar and salt in the water when washing.

To remove tobacco stains from copper or brass ashtrays apply a little denatured alcohol with a brush.

To clean zinc, cut a thick slice of lemon and rub the stained spots on the zinc with it. Let it remain for an hour, then wipe off the acid. The zinc will be as clean and as bright as when new.

An excellent method for cleaning *zinc* is to wash with hot soapy water, afterwards polishing with flannel dampened with kerosene.

Kerosene is splendid for cleaning *tin*. It leaves a beautiful polish.

A *sewing machine* may be cleaned by moistening all of the bearings and metal parts with kerosene, running the machine rapidly for a few minutes, and then thoroughly wiping off all the liquid with a soft cloth.

Gasoline will *remove rust from nickel*.

Woodwork and Marble

Annoying *match marks* can be removed from white *paint* by rubbing with a cut lemon. To prevent future marring, smear the spot lightly with Vaseline. After a few attempts to repeat the scratching on the greasy surface, the most persistent offender will finally desist.

To take white *marks* from a polished *wood* surface dampen a clean piece of chamois or flannel with essence of peppermint or cedar oil. This will take away marks caused by hot water and marks made by hot dishes, and will not injure the most highly polished surface.

Soot on *woodwork* can be removed by the use of kerosene.

Vinegar used in *removing paint from glass* will be very effective.

Water in which onions have been boiled, if rubbed over *picture frames* will keep the frames free from *fly specks*.

If the white of an egg is applied with a small camel's hair paint brush to *fly specks on gilt frames*, then rubbed gently with a soft cloth, the specks will disappear.

To clean white paint, boil two or three onions well, and the water they are boiled in will cleanse painted woodwork effectively. No soap will be needed; all the dirt will disappear, leaving the paint clean and glossy.

For cleaning varnished woodwork, scour with bran.

A few drops of oxalic add on *unpainted boards* will lessen the task of scrubbing wonderfully.

Warm water and a neutral soap should be used on *enameled surfaces*. A little kerosene added to the water acts like a charm. Immediate drying with a soft cloth is essential, following the grain when possible. Where spots or stains occur, a little ammonia should be used instead of kerosene. This calls for quick treatment, however, and the ammoniated water should be rinsed off, or the paint as well as the stain will be removed.

Where *too much alkali* has been used on *painted or enameled surfaces*, sweet oil applied at once will neutralize any bad effect.

To clean varnished surfaces use kerosene and water, or a weak solution of soap powder, ammonia, or soda; dry thoroughly; retouch with a thin varnish or shellac.

Five cents' worth of coarse sandpaper will last a long time for rubbing *stone steps or window sills* to remove marks. After rubbing they should simply be dusted with a cloth or duster. They will stay white much longer by using this method of cleaning than by using water. Gloves should always be worn while doing this rough work.

Stains on *marble* can be removed by making a paste of benzene and powdered soapstone and spreading it over the marble and leaving it overnight. It should be washed off with warm water. It may be necessary to give more than one application.

There is nothing better than kerosene for removing *paint spots from porcelain or glassware*.

One of the disagreeable things connected with *cleaning the bathroom* is washing out the *tub* after it has been cleaned with any of the various powders on the market. If an ordinary bath spray is attached to the faucet every bit of powder will be removed in a very few seconds.

To clean a white sink, bathtub, washbowls, and toilet bowls, use a soft cloth moistened with turpentine and wipe dry with another soft cloth. If rust appears in the sink, use kerosene.

The Floors

Paraffin oil, which can be purchased at any drug store for about twenty-five cents per quart, is excellent for waterproofing kitchen *floors*. It should be applied cold with a soft rag. It dries easily. A quart of oil is sufficient for a medium-sized kitchen.

Melted candle grease and turpentine in equal parts make an excellent *floor polish*.

A mop dipped into a pail of water to which ammonia has been added and rubbed over *linoleum* will keep the floor clean and heavy cleaning will not have to be done so often. Care should be taken not to let water get under the edges of the linoleum as this will cause it to swell and stand up in welts. Cleansing powders used on linoleum tend to turn it gray.

Wash *linoleum* and oilcloth with lukewarm water, then polish it with a soft woolen cloth which has been dipped in milk.

To make *floor-cleaning* easier, take a piece of two-inch board large enough to set a pail upon. Bore holes one and one half inch from each corner and insert castors. The pail can then be pushed from place to place with the foot and save a great deal of unnecessary lifting.

Substitute kerosene for soap in cleaning *shellacked floors*. Use the liquid in the proportion of one cupful to each pail of water. Do not have the water more than lukewarm, wash the floor with a well moistened soft cloth, and polish with a floor mop. The colors of oilcloth and linoleum will be wonderfully freshened if rubbed with a piece of flannel dipped in kerosene.

To remove spots of *paint from hardwood floors* apply kerosene, rub briskly, and follow by rubbing the floor with a soft cloth wrung from lukewarm water.

If *cork floor covering is waxed, shellacked, or varnished*, the cork will not only last longer but

grease will be prevented from soaking in. Milk is sometimes used on cork and linoleum coverings but an oil-mop is less expensive and just as effective.

Curtains, Carpets, Draperies, etc.

Draperies hung out on the line when the wind is blowing will be freed from all *dust* and the necessity for beating and shaking is done away with.

A dingy *carpet* can be brightened by using a mop wrung out of tepid water which has had a little ammonia put into it. Turpentine, too, is a good medium for brightening dark colors.

A weak solution of alum will revive the colors of a faded *carpet* after a thorough sweeping.

Salt sprinkled over *carpets* before sweeping preserves the colors and keeps away moths.

To remove ink stains from carpets pour salt on the spot immediately. Put on a second application of salt when the ink has soaked into the first application. When the salt ceases to become discolored, wash the stain with tepid water, without soap. The stains cannot be successfully removed after they have dried in.

Ink spots on carpet may be removed by washing with sweet milk and sprinkling with cornmeal. This should be left on overnight and upon sweeping up next morning the colors will remain bright.

Sheets should be turned each way, paying no attention to the top or bottom and they will wear much longer, as the strain will be distributed.

Fold the sheet back over the tops of the *blankets* and the blankets will keep clean much longer.

A piece of thin muslin sewed to the *blanket*, reaching about eight inches, will protect the blankets wonderfully and dispense with cleaning bills.

Furniture

To wash furniture boil one half cake of Castile soap in one gallon of water. When cold, add one ounce of linseed oil. Wash the wood with this cold mixture. Leather couches can be washed with it and when dry the leather can be oiled. Olive oil can be substituted for linseed oil.

An excellent *furniture polish* is made of equal parts of kerosene, turpentine, and vinegar.

To remove ink stains from mahogany furniture put a few drops of spirits of nitre into a teaspoonful of water; touch the spot with a feather dipped in the fluid and the ink will disappear.

If *polished oak, cherry, or walnut pieces* are given a thorough, monthly cleaning they will retain their luster indefinitely. First dust with a slightly dampened cloth and then wash quickly with tepid soapsuds made with mild white soap. Clean a small part at a time, dry immediately, and polish with a piece of old flannel slightly moistened with a few drops of kerosene. *Polished mahogany* requires the same periodical cleaning. Dust it first with a dry cloth, wipe quickly with a piece of flannel wrung out of cold water, and rub with a piece of dry flannel until the luster is restored.

Dull-finish oak furniture, such as Flemish, fumed, or Mission, will retain its original appearance if all dust is carefully wiped away once a month with a piece of old flannel wrung dry out of tepid water. In the summer months, this dusting should be followed by wiping with a piece of flannel very lightly moistened with turpentine. In the winter follow the first dusting with a quick washing with naphtha soapsuds. Use hot water and a mild white soap, and add one tablespoonful of naphtha to each gallon of water. Do the washing with a piece of chamois skin. Wash a small part at a time, wipe dry with flannel, rubbing until the wood feels hot. Use a good furniture polish on the wood occasionally.

Enameled iron beds should be first dusted and then washed with tepid suds, then dried and polished with a solution composed of half a pint of sweet oil and alcohol and one tablespoonful of thin white varnish. *A brass bed* should not be washed but cleaned by rubbing with a piece of chamois cloth, slightly dampened. Obstinate spots can be removed with a light application of prepared chalk.

Delicate colored enameled furniture should never be washed with soap and water but should be cleaned with sifted whiting applied with a slightly moistened cloth, and then wiped off with a piece of old flannel wrung out of clear, cold water, and polished with a piece of silk.

Antique furniture should be carefully dusted and wiped with a slightly dampened cloth. It should then be washed with warm soapsuds, using a mild soap, adding a tablespoonful of naphtha to each gallon of water. A small part should be washed at a time and should be dried at once with a piece of flannel wrung from hot borax water and rubbed with a piece of chamois skin until the wood feels hot. The best prepared piano polish should then be applied with a piece of soft flannel.

Natural finish willow or wicker furniture should be thoroughly washed with warm soapsuds containing enough borax to make the water soft. The reeds should be scrubbed with an ordinary scrubbing brush and wiped off with a dry cloth and set in the sun until all dampness has disappeared.

Ten Health Commandments

From *Putnam's Household Handbook*, by Mae Savell Croy, 1916

1. Ascertain and maintain your proper weight.
2. Eat plain, digestible food.
3. Breathe deeply through the nose. Stand, walk, and sit erect.
4. Sleep outdoors if possible, if not, at least in a room with open windows.
5. Learn to rest until you are really rested.
6. Avoid patent medicines and all alcoholic drinks.
7. Wear porous clothing and keep away from people with colds or other illnesses unless it is absolutely necessary to be near them.
8. Exercise in the open air whenever possible—but exercise somewhere anyway.
9. Eat an apple a day.
10. Forget to worry about anything that might concern you.

General

From *Putnam's Household Handbook*, by Mae Savell Croy, 1916

The *yolk of an egg and salt* is very beneficial for *toothache* or a pain in the face. Mix the salt with the egg until about the consistency of mustard and use the same as a mustard plaster. This remedy is also good for *snake bite*.

Hiccoughs can be cured by taking a mouthful of water, pressing inward the tragus (the little protection in front of the orifice of the ear), and then swallowing the water. This has never been known to fail.

To dislodge a *fishbone*, try sucking a lemon and swallowing the juice slowly. The citric acid in the lemon will dissolve the bone and it will slip harmlessly down the throat.

Gum Arabic applied to a *burn* will stop the pain immediately as it shuts off the air.

The *skin of a boiled egg* is a most effective remedy for a *boil*. Peel the skin off carefully and apply to the boil. It will draw off the matter and remove soreness in a few hours.

An alcohol rub given a patient who has to lie in bed will *prevent bed sores*.

Sitting on stone will oftentimes cause *hemorrhoids*.

The weakest part of the spine is the back of the neck. When in *danger of sunstroke* see that the back of the neck is well protected.

The juice of half a lemon in a glass of water taken before breakfast will prevent *biliousness*.

Stew spring *onions* in coarse brown sugar and take a teaspoonful at night. This will not only *produce sleep* but is very healthful.

Exercising at night until physically tired is excellent as a cure for *insomnia*.

A glass of *warm milk* upon retiring will bring sleep.

A hot water bottle at the base of one's spine will *rest the nerves and often produce sleepiness*.

Few persons think to *read advertisements to invalids*, yet invalids are as interested as anyone else in keeping up with current inventions and ideas.

Lettuce is good for the *nerves*.

Beets and turnips contain *iron*.

Tomatoes are good for the *liver*, as they stimulate it.

Celery is good for *rheumatism*.

Spinach is good for the *bowels*.

Carrots clear the *complexion*.

Asparagus is excellent for the *kidneys*.

For those who suffer with *cold feet* there is nothing that will prove a greater comfort than *a sand bag*. Sand bags are particularly good *for neuralgia of the face* as they retain the heat a long time and may be made as small and light as desired. The sand should be placed in a tightly woven bag and this bag placed in still another bag.

A teaspoonful of salt to a pint of warm water rubbed into *weak ankles* strengthens them.

In bathing the feet of an invalid, draw the wet cloth across the sole always in the same direction *and the feet will not be tickled*.

The first thing to do for a *sprained ankle* is to plunge it into hot water and keep it there—as hot as can be borne, adding more hot water from time to time to keep the temperature high. The heat will tend to loosen up the ankle tissues and help them to assume their natural positions. After soaking the ankle for an hour, bind it with flannel cloths wrung out of hot water (almost boiling) and cover with dry flannels.

For tired and perspiring feel, dissolve Epsom salts in the bath water.

A strong salt water bath is very restful for *tired feet*.

When *hot cloths* are necessary in time of illness, a colander is a labor-saving device. Place the colander with the hot cloths over a kettle that is half full of boiling water. Cover colander closely and keep the kettle on the back of the range. In this way the change of cloths is quickly and easily made.

In cases of illness *where hot compresses* are needed there is always the danger of burning one's hands when attempting to wring hot cloths out of boiling water. To avoid this *use a potato ricer*.

The sick-room should be kept immaculately clean and should have a constant supply of *fresh air*.

Windows should be opened in a sick-room every two hours in cold weather and left to stand open a short while only for fear the patient will get chilled.

A small quantity of *carbolic acid* poured into a very hot vessel will drive out *flies and purify the air*.

Burn *vinegar* in the sick-room to *purify the air*.

To ventilate the room at night and not soil expensive curtains, make bags of muslin and slip the curtains in them, pinning the bag to the top of the curtain.

A shield to use before the window on a cold night, which will still permit the air to enter, is made of a piece of heavy canvas or duck. The shield should hook to the window at both top and bottom. This will keep out the heavy winds and yet permit sufficient air.

An *electric fan* in the sick-room is a comfort in winter as well as in summer. It will warm a cold room as effectively as it will cool a warm one. Place the fan in front of the radiator and start it. Within a very short time the air in the room will have been circulated through the coils of the radiator. The room will be comfortable in only a fraction of the time required for the radiation alone.

Six or eight glasses of *water* should be taken into the system daily.

In case of fainting lay the patient on his back and loosen the clothing. The head should not be as high as the rest of the body in order that the blood may rush to the head. Provide all the air possible. If the patient does not revive, sprinkle water on the face and give a teaspoonful of aromatic spirits of ammonia in a large glass of water.

Hysterics should be treated as simply as fainting.

If food gets lodged in the throat it can sometimes be worked out by pressing on the outside of the throat and working it up with the fingers.

A little *bicarbonate of soda* in water for bathing will cool a *fevered patient*.

A *pinch of salt added to olive oil* will rid it of the unpleasant taste and will make it agreeable to even the most exacting.

When a *dim light* is required, put finely powdered salt on the candle till it reaches the black part of the wick. It will give a mild light all through the night.

Disinfectants

Sunshine is the best *disinfectant* ever yet discovered. *Clothes* damp from perspiration should be dried in the sunshine, and all bedding should be put out in the sun regularly on cleaning days.

Sal soda as a disinfectant is invaluable. Metals should be wiped with a solution of sal soda and water; clothing should be washed with this solution, and it is good for bathing a patient, though the solution should be weak for this purpose.

A vessel of cold water setting in the room absorbs *unhealthy gases*. The water should not be used for drinking purposes.

Extreme *heat* is a disinfectant.

A room can be thoroughly disinfected by *burning sulfur*. Close the windows and doors and stop up the keyholes. Two pounds of sulfur is sufficient for a room twelve by twenty feet.

Clothing should be washed after being worn during contagious diseases, in water to which has been added a little carbolic add.

In burning *disinfectants*, they should be put in a dish which stands in another dish containing water.

Food and Drink

All *water* should be boiled before allowing invalids to drink.

A *safe drink for thirsty invalids* is made with a teaspoonful of pearl barley, an ounce of sugar, and a quart of boiling water. Add part of the peeling of a lemon and let stand twelve hours.

Currant jelly or cranberry juice mixed with water makes a pleasant *drink* for an invalid.

Retain water in which green vegetables are cooked for *broths* for invalids. Beat up an egg in it for bouillon. This gives the body salt, potassium and nourishment.

To *remove the fat from broth or soup* intended for a delicate stomach, it is not necessary to allow it to become cold as is usually done. Instead, place a fine wire sieve on ice until it is thoroughly chilled and pour the liquid through this. The fat will stick to the cold wire and the broth will be ready for use.

A glass of *buttermilk* before retiring and another upon rising in the morning will help greatly in getting rid of a coated tongue, or other symptoms of a *disordered stomach*. It is also excellent for clearing a muddy complexion and if a quart a day can be taken a decided change will be noticed in the complexion

after a few weeks. This is a very simple and a very effective remedy for ailments which often call for drugs.

A glass of *buttermilk* at night will induce *sleep*.

Coddled eggs are very healthful and there is no danger of them ever becoming too hard. Let a kettle of water come to a fast boil, pour this boiling water over a pail of eggs, and cover with a lid and let stand until ready to use. They will not harden to more than a creamy consistency.

Raw meat is not palatable to an invalid and when it is ordered, it is best to make sandwiches by grating it very fine and mixing with pepper and salt before spreading on the slices of bread.

When a *glass tube* is necessary for the patient who cannot sit up to drink from a cup, *a stick of macaroni* will serve admirably if the other is not at hand.

Colds

Powdered *borax* snuffed up the nose will dry out a *cold in the head*.

Alum dissolved in water makes a very effective gargle for a *sore throat*.

To cure a cold without the aid of *fresh air* is almost impossible. Sunshine and fresh air alone will go far toward curing a cold that is not too deep seated.

A ten-minute leg and arm *exercise*, and a hot lemonade preceded by quinine will cure almost anyone of a *cold*.

Quinine followed by a drink of *hot whisky and water* is excellent for a *cold*.

In doctoring a cold, care should be taken to keep the *bowels* moving freely. If the system is in good condition a cold is not likely to be contracted.

Alternate *gargles of peroxide and Listerine* are recommended for a *sore throat*. Peroxide tends to dry up sore places but used alone is very rough for a naturally dry throat.

Keep the *feet warm* at night and you win avoid many *colds*.

A little turpentine on a piece of woolen cloth is beneficial for a *sore throat*.

Cold plunges are splendid preventatives of *colds,* but if the constitution cannot stand the shock, it is well to take a tepid bath and let the cold water run in gradually until the water is very cool. Many colds are contracted by taking hot baths just before going out.

An *alcohol rub* is recommended for a pain in the side or neck which is caused from *cold in a muscle.*

An *alcohol rub after a bath* is almost a sure preventative of *colds*.

A teaspoonful of garlic juice on a little sugar will generally ward off a *cold*.

Poisons

To prevent *accidents* from bottles containing *poison*, tie a tiny little bell to the neck of the bottle or paste a piece of sandpaper securely to the top of the cork, the rough side out. One can easily detect the rough surface and thereby know the contents.

Keep all bottles of *poison* labeled in large letters.

A very simple and effective *cure for poisoning from sumac* or from poison oak is obtained from boracic acid. Bring a solution of the acid to the boiling point. Wring woolen cloths out of it and lay upon the affected parts as hot as it can be borne, covering with another woolen cloth to keep in the heat. When cool repeat this process and keep up for twenty minutes. After two hours repeat again. The heat does not bum the patient as might be expected but stops both the burning and the itching.

A small flashlight kept in the bathroom medicine cabinet will often *prevent the wrong bottle being taken at night.*

When cattle have eaten laurel their lives can often be saved by administering strong coffee. Strain and while warm turn it down their throats if they will not drink it.

The Teeth

To remove tartar from the teeth: Wind a piece of absorbent cotton on an orange stick and dip in lemon juice and then in pumice stone. This should be applied vigorously to the tartar spots.

Old-fashioned cider is one of the very best of *tooth washes*.

Lemon juice will remove tartar, but it should be thoroughly removed afterward by rinsing with tepid water, as acids are injurious to the teeth if allowed to remain on.

In times of illness when there is *danger of using powders and pastes in connection with medicines*, prepared chalk is recommended as being perfectly safe.

The fastidious man or woman who does not care to run the risk of *unpleasant odors in the mouth* will find the following a very satisfactory preventive:

Boric acid, 1 drachm Hydrogen peroxide, 2 fluid ounces Glycerine, 1 fluid ounce Rose water, 3 fluid ounces. Mix, dissolve, and filter.

The teeth should always be cleaned thoroughly before retiring at night.

The Skin

Garlic eaters have good skins, for garlic is excellent in treating eruptions of all sorts.

Tissue paper should be kept on the toilet table. It is good for thoroughly *drying the skin and for rubbing off cold cream* when applied to the face.

The Hair

Half a cupful of salt and flour in equal proportions rubbed through the bristles of a *hairbrush* will make it as *clean* as new. Shake the mixture out well before using the brush.

Hairbrushes and combs should be cleaned by washing in water to which ammonia has been added.

Merely dip the bristles of the brush up and down in the solution.

Kerosene oil is very good for rubbing into the *roots* of the *hair*. It should be left on overnight.

Vaseline rubbed into the scalp will prevent the *hair from falling out* and will give a new growth of hair. White Vaseline should be used for light hair and the reddish-tinted Vaseline for dark hair.

Hot curling irons should never be used on the hair. Each time they are used the hair is injured, if not some of it actually burned off. If the hair is rolled into tight curls at night and then rolled into a little knot and a hairpin stuck through it, it will have a naturally curly appearance. Care should be taken not to put it up too tight as it does not take much to pull out the roots. Kid curlers also are desirable, but many of the metal curlers are very injurious as they cut the hair.

A very beneficial *treatment for the hair* is to walk out doors without a hat on during warm damp weather or when the dew is falling. This is good for both complexion and hair. The damp air is a beautifier and if the feet and body are well protected there will be no danger of taking cold.

For *oily hair*, beat the white of an egg as stiff as possible and rub it into the hair until it is wet all over. Allow this to dry when the egg will brush out like a fine white powder and leave the hair fluffy and bright.

One of the very best of preparations for retaining the *tint of auburn hair* is a solution of 5 cents worth of salts of tartar diluted in a pint of warm water. This should be rubbed into the hair until a good lather is worked up, and left on the hair for about half an hour before rinsing in clear water. This is very cleansing and will bring out what auburn tints there are in the hair.

After *washing the hair* a good way to thoroughly rinse it is to fill a common tin flower sprinkling can with water and suspend on a nail or hook above the head over the bathtub. The water comes with just enough force to rinse and the sprinkler can be filled as often as necessary.

A hair shampoo which will leave the hair soft and silky is made by dissolving one-half ounce of carbonate of ammonia and one ounce of borax in one quart of water; then add two ounces of glycerine in three quarts of New England rum and one quart of bay rum. Moisten the hair with this liquid; shampoo with the hands until a light lather is formed; then wash off with plenty of water.

To rid the scalp of dandruff requires daily care. Take four ounces of glycerine, five ounces of tincture of cantharides, four ounces of bay rum, and two ounces of water. This should be applied once a day and rubbed well into the scalp.

As a hair wash: Dip the hair in a basin of warm water. Rub the juice of a lemon into the scalp, rinse thoroughly and dry with a soft towel. The lemon juice removes dirt and grease, leaving the hair soft and glossy.

Gray hair should always be shampooed with a soap that is pure white. A tinted soap will leave the hair yellow. Castile soap is recommended.

A rubber bathing cap for dusting and other housework will protect the hair much better than a cloth one. For wear when working with gasoline or kerosene it is invaluable.

The hair should be frequently ventilated in order to keep the scalp healthy. A sun-bath is very important to keep the hair in good condition. This should be given at least once a week.

In applying tonics to the scalp the hair should be parted in strands and the tonic applied directly to the head with a piece of absorbent cotton. The ends of the hair should then be shaken vigorously in order to send a quick current of air through it.

Tar soap should not be used on *light hair*. In order to bring out the light tints, a pure white soap, preferably Castile, should be used. Tar soap, or other dark soaps can be used to advantage on *dark hair*.

The following lotion is excellent *for use on soggy hair:*

- ¼ oz. powdered bicarbonate of soda
- ¼ oz. powdered borate of soda
- 1 oz. eau de cologne
- 2 oz. alcohol
- ⅛ oz. distilled water.

This should be well shaken and applied to the hair every night and massaged well into the scalp. This is to be used only for those whose scalp and hair are in a moist condition.

A simple and effective hair invigorator is composed of two pints of bay rum, one pint of alcohol, one ounce castor oil, one-half ounce carbonated ammonia, and one ounce of tincture of cantharides. These ingredients should be well mixed and if applied consistently will not only prevent the hair from falling out but will prompt its growth.

Miscellaneous Hints

From *Putnam's Household Handbook*, by Mae Savell Croy, 1916

Coarse salt will *drive fleas away*, but care should be taken not to get it around plants as it will destroy them.

To wipe the screens with kerosene will keep out the little *mosquitoes* that work their way through the netting. To keep them vanquished, this should be done every day or two.

Gum camphor laid among books on the shelves will *keep the mice away*.

Cayenne pepper sprinkled around places where *mice* frequent will keep them away.

When the refrigerator is kept in a cold entry and the door is left open for exposure in order to avoid an ice bill, it is well to fit a wire screen into the door to keep out *mice*.

Pour a little *turpentine* in the corners of wardrobes, trunks, and chiffoniers and the *moths* will not molest the articles stored therein.

If *eyeglass lenses* are rubbed with a little *soap* and then polished, there will be no moisture deposited on them when going from a cold to a warm atmosphere.

When a *door sticks at the top*, rub it over with a little *yellow soap* and the annoyance will cease.

Laundry

From *Putnam's Household Handbook*, by Mae Savell Croy, 1916

The alkalies commonly known and used in the household are:

Ammonia, a gas dissolved in water, and mild in its action if diluted; it readily evaporates if heated. It is comparatively expensive.

Borax, a powder, mild and expensive.

Sal Soda, or Carbonated Alkali, a crystal or powder, stronger and cheaper than borax.

Potash, or Lye, a liquid or solid, strong but little used in modern times. It is derived from wood ashes by a process of leeching; is used in making "soft soap."

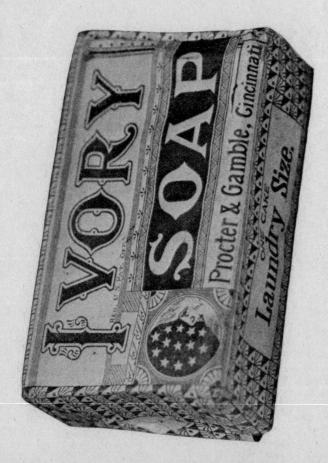

Woolens

Woolen material will easily shrink if carelessly handled. A "neutral" soap must be used, and if a soap claims to wash without shrinking, it does so only because you follow carefully the directions that come with the soap. Strong soaps or alkalies, except the milder ones—borax and ammonia—weaken the fiber and make it more liable to shrink. The rubbing on of soap of any kind is not desirable, because you must get it out and it may require the rubbing of the material, which tends more than anything else to mat the wool and shrink the garment. Hot water and then cold must not be used, because heating expands the fibers, and as they lie so close together, they may interlock; then, when the cold contracts the fibers, they cannot unlock. As a consequence, the material shrinks. Extremes of temperature, then, are to be avoided.

Shake the dust out of the flannel. Make warm suds with Ivory Soap solution. Have it so the hands can very comfortably be held in the water. If the garment is quite soiled, add half a tablespoonful of household ammonia for each gallon of water, and let the garment soak for ten minutes. Draw the garment through the hands, work it up and down, and squeeze it, but do not rub soap on it or rub it on the board. Put through the wringer, turn the garment wrong side out and put it through a second suds the same temperature as the first. If any soiled spot does not yield to this treatment, lay it upon the table or other smooth surface, hold it straight, and rub it briskly with a small brush. If necessary, use a little soap solution on the brush. Rinse the garment quickly through several waters of the same temperature as the first water. Rinse flannel until the water is clear. Put it through the wringer or squeeze the water out; do not twist it. Shake it or hang it out to dry where it is warm—not where it is so hot that the garment will steam, or where it is cold. Guard against extremes of temperature. Stretch the garment into shape as it dries. This is especially true of ribbed underwear, which also does not need to be ironed. Press flannel when nearly dry, on the wrong side, until perfectly dry, using a moderately warm iron. Never have the iron so hot that the flannel will steam, and press, rather than rub it. Closely twisted and woven wool will shrink less than loosely woven materials.

Silks

Silk fiber is smooth and shiny, and for best results requires the same treatment in the laundry as wool. If rubbed hard, the fiber is broken and the shiny effect lost. It should never be boiled.

Wash silk carefully in warm water, with Ivory Soap solution in it. Soak twenty minutes if necessary, and take fresh suds for the washing. Do not rub silk except with a soft nail brush over a smooth surface. Rinse in several warm waters until the last water is clear. Place between dry towels and put through wringer loosely adjusted, or squeeze water from it and hang to dry where you can watch it. When nearly dry, iron with a moderately hot iron, until perfectly dry. If the iron is hot the silk will be stiff. A thin muslin spread over the silk before ironing may give letter results when material is thin. If silk is colored, it will lie better to try a sample, and to set it as you would colored cottons, with salt or vinegar.

For white silk use one teaspoonful methylated spirits to one pint of water for rinsing.

For yellowed handkerchiefs or other fine linen, soak in cold water to which a little ammonia has been added. Then cut a large lemon into slices, including the rind, and boil it in a pan. When at the boiling point put in the handkerchiefs and boil them 20 minutes.

*General Principles of Stain Removal

"The removal of stains is a necessary feature of the laundering and general care of clothing and other household textiles. Most stains may be removed easily at home, provided reliable methods are known and a few simple precautions are taken.

Too much emphasis cannot be laid on the importance of applying the stain removers while the stain is still fresh, for usually it is much more difficult to remove an old stain than a fresh one. Changes in the character of the stain, brought about by drying, exposure to air, washing, ironing, or in other ways, often make it necessary to use chemicals in removing old stains, whereas in many cases much simpler methods are successful if the stains are treated when fresh."

The nature of a stain should be known, if possible, before its removal is attempted, since this determines the treatment to be adopted. Moreover, if an unsuitable stain remover is used, the stain may be "set" so that its removal becomes difficult or even impossible.

The kind of fabric upon which the stain occurs also should be known. The method of treatment adopted depends as much upon the nature, color, weave, finish and weight of the fabric as upon the kind of stain. Cotton and linen are destroyed by strong acids and attacked to some extent even by weaker ones. Concentrated acids, therefore, should never be used in removing stains from these

---

*Farmers Bulletin 861. "Removal of Stains from Clothing and Other Textiles."

fabrics, and when dilute acids are used they should be neutralized afterwards with a suitable alkali or removed by thorough rinsing; otherwise the acid may become concentrated on drying and destroy the tillers. Generally speaking, alkalis do not attack cotton or linen fabrics to the extent that acids do. However, long-continued or repeated exposure to alkalis, especially in hot solution, weakens the fibers.

Wool and silk, being more delicate than cotton and linen, require more careful treatment. The use of very hot water must be avoided, since it turns both wool and silk yellow, shrinks wool, and weakens silk and injures its finish. These materials also will not stand much rubbing, as this felts together the wool fibers and results in a shrinkage or thickening of the material, while the silk fabrics, as a rule, are too delicate to stand much rubbing without breaking or separating the filers. Both wool and silk are dissolved by strong alkalis and are injured even by washing soda or strongly alkaline soap. The only alkalis which should be used in laundering or removing stains from wool and silk are the milder ones like borax or dilute solutions of ammonia. Acids, with the exception of nitric which weakens and turns the fibers yellow, do not attack wool and silk readily.

In general it is more difficult to remove stains from wool and silk than from cotton or linen. In removing stains from materials made from two or more kinds of fibers, such as silk and cotton mixtures, the effects of the stain removers upon all of the fibers should be considered. No chemical should be used which would injure the most delicate fibers present.

It is also much more difficult to remove stains from colored than from white materials, for the reason that most of the bleaching agents which must be used to remove persistent stains are likely to destroy the color of the material as well.

Methods for Treatment of Stains in General Laundering

Ordinary laundering for removing stains, should be done as follows: First, soak the stained portion in cold or lukewarm water, rubbing the stain with a neutral soap if necessary. Follow this by thorough rinsing in clean water, after which the article may be laundered as usual. Use this method only for cotton and linen (white or fast colors) and the so-called wash silks and washable woolens. If the materials are delicate, sponge them.

Sponging

Sponging is applicable to all fabrics, but especially to delicate materials or colors which ordinary laundering might injure. Spread the stained article on a flat surface in a good light, and beneath the stain put a cloth folded into several thicknesses, or clean, white blotting paper, to absorb the superfluous liquid. Change the pad for a fresh one as soon as it becomes soiled. Sponge with a clean, soft lintless cloth (preferably of the same material as that stained) and renew it as frequently as may be necessary. Lay the stained material with the wrong side up and apply the water to the back, so that the foreign substances can be washed from the fibers onto the pad without having to pass through the material.

Removal of Stains

Stain	Reagent	Method of Removing
Tea Coffee	Boiling water	Spread stained part over a bowl and pour boiling water on it from a height, so as to strike stain with force. Use Javelle water as a last resort. Use glycerine to remove stain from coffee and cream.
Cocoa Chocolate	Cold water or Borax & tepid water (Soap sets the stain)	Sprinkle with borax and soak in water.
Milk Cream	Cold water	Wash in cold water; then follow with soap and water.
Medicine Grass	Alcohol 1. Molasses 2. Alcohol 3. Ammonia & water 4. Kerosene or butter	Soak in alcohol. 1. Soak in molasses, follow with warm water. 2. Wash in alcohol. 3. Wash in ammonia water. Not to be used on delicate colors. 4. Rub in kerosene or butter, followed by soap and water.
Orange	Cream of tartar	Rub with moistened cream of tartar.
Mildew	1. Lemon juice 2. Paste (1) tablespoonful starch, juice of 1 lemon, Salt	1. Put on lemon juice and place in direct sunlight. 2. Cover spot with paste, and let stand 48 hours. Repeat if necessary.
Iron Rust	1. Lemon juice and salt 2. Hydrochloric acid	1. Sprinkle stain with salt. Moisten with lemon juice, and lay in sun. 2. Stretch stain over a bowl containing 1 quart water and 1 teaspoonful borax. Apply acid, drop by drop, until stain brightens, then dip at once into water in a bowl. Repeat if necessary.
Blood	1. Cold water & Fels Naptha soap 2. Paste of raw starch	1. Wash in cold water; rub with soap, and soak in warm water. 2. If thick goods, make a paste of raw starch, and apply several times.
Fruit	1. Boiling water 2. Javelle water	1. Spread stain over bowl, and pour boiling water through it from a height. 2. Use Javelle water and boiling water in equal quantities. Let soak a few minutes. Rinse in boiling water.
Ink	1. Milk 2. Oxalic acid 3. Salt and lemon juice. 4. Javelle water. 5. For carpets and rugs, salt or cornmeal	1. If stain is fresh, place in milk; if milk is discolored, add fresh milk, and allow stain to lie in it until milk sours. Wash in tepid water. 2. Place stain over bowl, sprinkle with acid, and pour boiling water through it. When stain is removed, wash in water containing ammonia. 3. Cover with salt and lemon juice. 4. Soak a few minutes only in Javelle water; rinse in clear water, and keep repeating. Rinse carefully. 5. As soon as accident occurs, throw a handful or so of salt or cornmeal on the stain, and brush

		out discolored salt or meal with a whisk broom, adding more as long as there is any ink to absorb.
Paint Varnish	1. Benzine Turpentine 2. Chloroform Naptha 3. Olive oil and chloroform	1. Rub with benzine or turpentine. For a dry stain, soften with vaseline before rubbing with benzine or turpentine. 2. For delicate colors use chloroform or naphtha. 3. For old stains, cover with oil and rub with chloroform.
Perspiration	Soap solution—Wash with soap and suds and place in sunshine.	
Mucus	Ammonia and soap	Soak in ammonia water, then wash with soap.
Mid	Baking soda	Dampen a cloth, dip in soda, and rub on spots.
Scorch	Soap solution and sun on white goods, hot water and ivory soap.	Dip in soap solution, and expose to sunlight for a few hours. Rub.
Grease	On woolen and colored goods, hot iron and blotter. Solvents for Grease: Gasoline Benzine Naptha Alcohol Ether Chloroform (The most expensive; good for delicate silks) Magnesia for silks. On floors: Cold water.	Put a blotter or unglazed brown paper under stain as it is stretched over ironing board. Pass hot iron back and forth over stain until grease melts and is absorbed by the blotter beneath. These solvents must all be used with caution—never used in closed room, near a fire or lamp. Dissolve 1 teaspoonful salt in 4 tablespoonful alcohol—for silk. Rub on magnesia; brush off when dry. Pour cold water on at once before it has time to sink in to the wood. The grease then hardens, and it can be scraped up with a knife.
Wagon Grease Wheel Grease	Eucalyptus oil lard	Rub on, stand a short time, then wash in turpentine, or with warm, soapy water.
Pitch Tar Machine Oil	Cold water & borax	Rub moistened borax on stain, rubbing from outside of stain to center; then wash in cold water.
Ice Cream Soda	Gasoline Chloroform	Sponge with lukewarm water; rub gently with flannel.

Gardening

Lawns, Hedges, and Trees

From Garden Guide: The Amateur Gardeners' Handbook, edited by A.T. De La Mare, 1920

Planting and Care of Osage Hedges

The first requisite for a hedge of any kind is to secure thrifty plants of uniform size. Osage Orange plants are raised from seeds by nurserymen, and when of the right size, should be taken up in autumn and "heeled in." The ground, which it is proposed to occupy by the hedge, should be broken up in autumn and then re-plowed in spring, unless it is a raw prairie sod, which should be broken a year before the hedge is planted. It is a very usual, but very bad practice, to plow a ridge with a back-furrow, as shown in figure 106. This leaves an unplowed strip of hard soil directly under the line upon which the hedge is to stand. When harrowed, it appears very fair on the surface, but it is useless to expect young plants to thrive on such a bed of hard soil, and its result will be as seen in figure 107. The first growth is feeble, irregular, and many vacant spots appear. The land should be plowed as in figure 108. When the sod is rotted, the land should be harrowed lengthwise of the furrows, and the dead furrow left in the first plowing closed by twice turning back the ridge. There is then a deep, mellow, well-drained bed for the plants in which the roots have room to grow and gather ample nutrition. Figure 109 shows the effect of this kind of cultivation. As a barrier against stock, or a windbreak, it is best to plant in double rows, each row being set opposite the spaces in the other, thus:

It is highly desirable that the hedge should be in true, uniform rows, either straight or in regular

Fig. 106. Badly plowed ground.

Fig. 107. Hedge plant on hard ridge.

Fig. 108. Properly plowed ground.

Fig. 109. Hedge plant in mellow soil.

curves. This can be done only by setting closely to a line. Osage Orange plants may be raised from seed, but as this is a difficult operation, it is usually best to buy young plants from a reliable nurseryman. They are best cut down to about six inches high, and the roots partially trimmed. It is an advantage to "puddle" the roots, which is done by dipping them in a mixture composed of one-half earth and half fresh manure from the cow stable, wet to, the consistency of a thin paste. There are various methods of setting the plants. Some use a trowel with a blade about ten inches long; others a dibble, and a larger number than either of the others, a spade. For setting long lines, in situations where appearances are of secondary importance, young Osage plants are set very rapidly by running a furrow where the rows are to stand, laying the plants with their roots spread on the mellow soil, one side of the furrow. A furrow is next turned upon the roots, and the plants which may have been disarranged are restored by hand. A tread of the foot will consolidate the earth around each plant. Unless the subsoil is naturally very porous, the ground must be thoroughly under-drained. A line of tiles should be laid six or eight feet from the line of the hedge. The ground for four or five feet on either side of the hedge should be kept thoroughly cultivated the first three or four years after planting. This cultivation is to be done early each season and cease the first of July, to give the new wood a chance to ripen. The plants should be permitted to grow the first year undisturbed. The following spring, the hedge should be cut off close to the ground with a scythe or mowing machine, and all vacancies where plants have died out or been thrown out by frost, should be filled. The ground on both sides of the ridge is to be kept well cultivated. Figure 110 shows the difference in root growth in cultivated and uncultivated ground.

A thick growth of young shoots will appear, and these are to be cut back to four inches high in the middle of the summer and again in September. The object is to obtain a dense growth close to the ground. The third year the pruning is to be repeated, only the shoots must be left four to six inches above the last previous cutting. The lateral shoots which are near the ground, are to be left undisturbed.

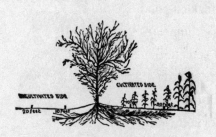

Fig. 110. Effect of cultivation.

The trimming should be such as to leave the hedge broad at the base, with a regular slope to the summit like a double-span roof.

Another method is to permit the hedge to grow untrimmed for four or five years. It is then plashed, or laid over sidewise. This is done by cutting the plants about half through on one side with a sharp axe, and bending them over as shown in figure 111. The hedge is first headed back and trimmed up to reduce the top. In a short time new shoots will spring from the stubs and stems, making a dense growth of interlacing stems and branches. Another method of laying a hedge is to dig away a few inches of earth on one side of each plant to loosen the roots, then lay the plant over to the desired angle and fasten it there. The earth is then replaced around the roots, treaded down firmly. We believe that a patent is claimed for this process, but its validity is seriously questioned.

It is essential that hedges, whether planted for ornament or utility, shall be kept in shape by trimming every year. It is less labor to trim a hedge three times during the year, when the branches are small and soft, than once when the branches have made a full season's growth. If the hedge is trimmed once in June and again in August, it will be kept in good shape, and the labor will be less than if the trimming was put off until spring. In August the branches can be cut with shears or a sharp corn knife. The foliage on them will aid in their burning, when they have dried a few days in the sun. The thorns are not so hard as in the spring. The brush will be less, and on account of their pliability and greater weight, will pack into the heap much better. If trimmed in August, the hedge will not make any considerable growth during the fall. August

Fig. 111. Hedge "plashed."

trimming does not injure the hedge, rather helps it, as it tends to ripen the wood, preventing a late autumn growth to be injured by the winter. The loss of sap is less than when the trimming is done in the early spring, as then the wounds are larger, and do not heal before the sap flows. Do not neglect to burn the brush as soon as it has dried sufficiently. If allowed to remain on the ground, it will harbor mice and other vermin. Trim the hedge in August and burn the brush. The trimming should be done in such a manner as to expose the greater amount of foliage to the direct action of the light, air, rain and dew. This is attained by keeping the sides at every trimming in the form of sloping walls from the broad base to the summit like a double-span roof. They are sometimes trimmed with vertical sides and broad, flat top, but this is not a favorable plan for permanency. The lower leaves and stems die out leaving an unsightly open bottom of naked stems, with a broad roof of foliage above. Such trimming and its results have done much to bring hedges into disrepute.

Hedges for the South

The Osage Orange is a native of the Southwestern States, and flourishes on good soil anywhere in the South. Yet there are certain succulent plants which grow so rapidly in the South, and require so little care that they are very successfully employed for hedges in the Gulf States. One of these if the *Yucca Gloriosa*, or Spanish Bayonet. Its natural habit of growth is to produce a dense mass of leaves on a long stem. But by cutting back the growth of the stiff, armed leaves is produced low, down, and a hedge of this soon becomes an impassable barrier. Large panicles of beautiful white blossoms are produced at the summit, making such a hedge very ornamental during the flowering season. Various species of cactus are also employed in the Southwest for hedges. Some of the

Middle-Western States may be seen a hedge like figure 112. At some distance from the highway,

Fig. 112. Cactus hedge.

a field had been enclosed with the tree cactus, which only grows from four to ten feet high. The plants that were in the line of the fence were left growing, and those cleared from the field were woven into a formidable barrier to anything larger than a rabbit. While no two rods in this fence are alike, its general appearance is like that shown in the engraving.

Ornamental hedges and screens

Hedges and screens for ornamental purposes alone do not come strictly within the scope of this work, but we will briefly mention a few desirable plants for the purpose. The Japan Quince, *Cydonia Japonica*, of which figures 113 and 114 show a branch, flower and fruit, is one of the best deciduous plants for an ornamental hedge. It will grow in almost any soil; if left to itself it forms a dense, strong bush, but it may be clipped or trained into any desired form. Its leaves are of dark glossy green, they come early in spring and remain until late in autumn. This is one of the earliest shrubs to bloom in spring; its flowers are generally intense scarlet, though there are varieties with white, rose-colored, or salmon-colored flowers. A hedge of this plant is not only highly ornamental, but its abundant thorns make a good barrier. Privet, *Ligustrum vulgare*, makes a very neat screen, but will not bear severe cutting back, and is therefore suitable only for grounds of sufficient extent to admit of its being allowed to make unrestrained

Fig. 113. Branch of Japan Quince.

growth. The common Barberry, *Berberis vulgaris*, also makes an exceedingly pretty screen in time, but it is of slow growth. The Buffalo Berry, *Sheperdid argentea*, has been tried for hedges, but for some reason it has never attained any popularity. In the Southern States, the Cherokee rose has been found quite successful for the purpose, and nothing in the shape of a hedge can exceed, in striking effect, one of these in full bloom. For evergreen screens nothing is better than the hemlock, *Tsuga Canadensis*. The Norway spruce is of rapid growth and bears cutting well. The arbor vitæ, *Thuja occidentalis*, is also very successfully employed for the purpose.

Fig. 114. Fruit and flower.

Planning the Home Grounds

If one's place is but a small area of so many dozen square yards, it is great fun to do one's own planning, and little can go wrong.

Should the place be more pretentious, running to one or two acres, it might be money in one's pocket to consult a landscape gardener, or an experienced nurseryman or designer. There are several excellent books, too, that can be referred to, and from which valuable information can be got on the laying out of home grounds. One of these is "Cridland's Practical Landscape Gardening."

The first considerations in the composition of a garden or the grounds about one's place are privacy, variety, shelter, balance.

The planning and arrangement of the features of a garden or of the grounds about the house should be as carefully considered as the choice and placing of the furniture in one's home, or the choosing of a suit of clothes, or a dress to wear. The same idea holds, namely, the planning of a suitable, agreeable, comfortable composition. The garden has been called the outdoor drawing-room.

The arrangement of the drives and the grading of the lawns, the drainage when necessary, and the arrangement of the buildings and outhouses should all be preconceived and settled in an orderly, economical manner. As far as possible there should be no mistake about the main, permanent features. The minor features may be changed quite a great deal in the coming years and almost surely will, as new ideas and points of view assert themselves. This changing of the minor features is a part of the recreation of gardening. Thus one may considerably alter the contour of a shrubbery border, or may indeed eliminate it altogether. The same holds good of flower beds and borders, which are easily altered, removed or added to; but with large trees or the heavier groups of shrubs the expense of removal and shifting prohibits this being done except out of dire necessity.

Where one has the choice of building one's house or choosing its location, the best aspect for it is where the front porch faces; another good position is facing due south. In any case, as everybody likes abundant sunshine or ought to see to it that the windows and living rooms face in the direction of abundant light. These places that are hidden beneath a dense canopy or half a forest of trees may suit, and do suit, some folks, but they are terribly depressing to the great majority of us, besides being, one should imagine, not conducive to health. Light, air, and freedom, are good watchwords for the builder and planner.

Character can be given to an entrance by simply having two ornamental pillars built there, with possibly an iron arch over them. If this is planted with creeping vines and is supported at the sides with groups of evergreens, it adds wonderful dignity and seeming value to the property.

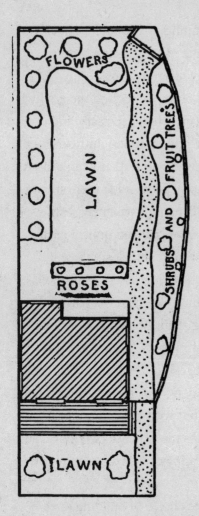

Actual layout of a backyard garden fenced on lot 30 x 100 ft. Standard apple, plum and pear trees were planted around the divisional fences. They did not unduly shade the hardy flowers. The smooth gravel path terminated in an arbor over which roses, ivy and clematis grew. Rhododendrons, evergreens, hardy heaths, viburnums, etc., with bulbs between were used on the right hand border. There was a sun parlor at the back of the house. The garden lay due south.

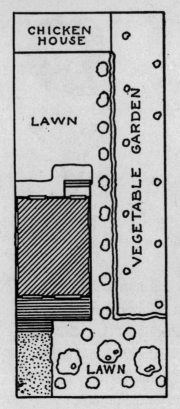

Suburban lot fenced, on 40 x 100 ft. A low hedge divided off the vegetable garden. Fruit trees and bushes were lined by the side of this while pillar. Roses, dwarf roses, neat shrubs and beds of flowers were elsewhere well disposed. The vegetable plot was a model of good cropping, containing tomatoes, corn, beans, beets, celery, carrots, spinach, herbs and salads. Raspberries lined the fences. This ran east and west.

While winding paths or drives are graceful, they should not be made meaninglessly, but are in order where the ground slopes a little or dips, or where irregularity exists. Certainly these can always be added or made in order to get the curved line. Even in small places, as our plans show, the swinging line of beauty can be had. Straight paths may, however, be more convenient, and can still be tasteful and harmonious. They are undoubtedly neat.

No book can tell the reader exactly what may be the best arrangement for his garden or property. Every garden should have a character of its own, and generally does, unless in the case of the very smallest, where nearly all opportunity for variety is extinguished; yet it is remarkable what can be done on a quarter or an eighth of an acre. We have often seen plots of 30 ft. x 100 ft. Laid out with much variety and taste, and which were full of interest.

It is all too true that thousands of gardens and grounds all around our American homes are bore to desolation. The democratic idea and feeling against planting of hedges and the lining off of one's property makes for deadly uniformity. The arguments that unhedged or unfenced grounds would be contrary to the best artistic conception and treatment of a city or suburb as a whole, ought not to be allowed to sway the property owner from making the most and the best of his own place. There is a school of landscape gardeners and city planners who seem to set their face against this, encouraging the open community type of home grounds. The latter will never get us anywhere as a nation of garden lovers, and almost entirely precludes the practice of the finer gardening. We plead rather to see places nicely hedged or railed off, so that stray dogs and unceremonious persons may be kept at a proper distance, but most of all for the sake of the enjoyment and encouragement of that quiet privacy without which the true pleasures of gardening cannot be attained.

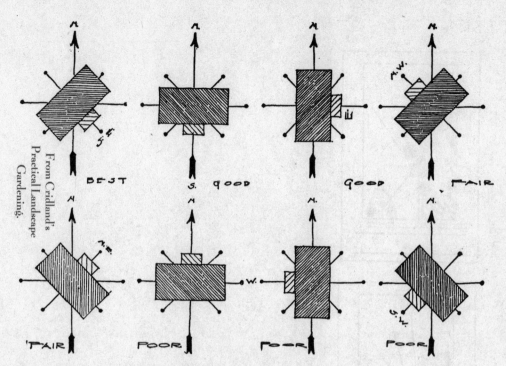

From Cridland's Practical Landscape Gardening.

BEST   GOOD   GOOD   FAIR

FAIR   POOR   POOR   POOR

Facing south-east is the best exposure of the house in relation to the sun.

Which is the best—to have a big, bare lawn and a few trees, or an odd group of shrubs here and there, or the trimly hedged and fenced grounds, with lower borders, specimen trees and shrubs beds and belts of roses, arches of roses and other climbers, water basins, an arbor or rose house where tea or ice-cream may be partaken in the sunny summer days, or where in some shady corner we can enjoy a siesta or a book in the open air?

Haven't you seen many working men's house just like this—gaunt and bare, no neat hedges no neat lawns, not even a geranium or a canna in sight?

The fact is we do not make half enough use of the grounds about our homes; they are left blank in most instances. We warmly urge the planting of light screen belts of trees and hedges around the property, which need not be so dense as to prevent a neighbor or passerby from enjoying glimpses of your garden. Regel's rivet, California broad-leaved privet, golden privet, hemlock, arbor vitæ, austrian pine, white pine, norway spruce, rambler roses, ivy, ampelopsis, plane trees, berberis thunbergii, are among the easily grown subjects that are useful in such screen belts, and most of which can be increased on one's own

place at little expense if the suggestions given in another part of this book are carried out.

The initial expense of planting the outer parts and main features of the grounds or garden need not be large. By the exercise of a little patience one can grow-on a good many things for future developments. Poplars should only be used sparingly. They grow fast, it is true, and for that reason are often employed, and in some places are elegant and pleasant enough, but generally they are "messy," losing their leaves early, and their roots often choke up drains. The almost constant rustling of their leaves and other aspects of the trees are disagreeable to many people.

Make provision for a good space of lawn, and treat the lawn well. Water in motion, as in fountains, is often desirable but is a secondary consideration, just as the number and amount of flower beds or borders is, as also the introduction of rock gardens, arbors and such like. The thing of prime importance is to have the main features properly planned at the outset—the garage, the barn, the poultry run, the kitchen or vegetable garden, and the other parts of the place such as have been already spoken of, also

Reproduced from Cornell bulletin 361.

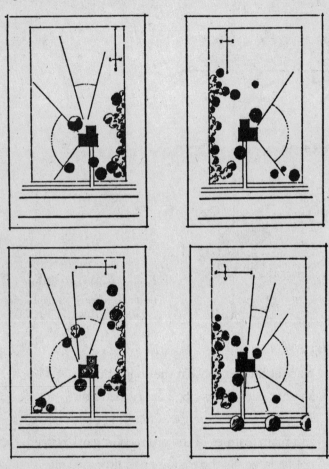

Fig. A. *Planting plan to insure best effect of shade, outlook, protection, and privacy on a lot facing north.*
Fig. B. *Planting plan to insure best effect of shade, outlook, protection, and privacy on a lot facing north.*
Fig. C. *Planting plan to insure best effect of shade, outlook, protection and privacy on a lot facing east.*
Fig. D. *Planting plan to insure best effect of shade, outlook, protection and privacy on a lot facing west.*

the grading and terracing (if any), are among the first matters that require attention. Minor undulations or changes of the surface can he left for a future day. It is not, we repeat, necessary to have a cut and dried plan from the beginning; far better to let it grow with your knowledge of the place. What may be called the adventitious, luxurious or additional features will, practically speaking, take care of themselves. You will gradually come to find out the most appropriate spot for this or that. Do not be in a hurry; allow the place to grow up. It will suit your pocket better and furnish endless recreation and pleasure. It will keep your mind happy and active. You will be interested and learning all the while. This is true gardening, and the meaning and the reward of gardening and garden making.

Some pains should be taken to have clean, well-made paths. Take out 6 in. or 8 in. of soil and fill with clinkers, rough ashes or stones, finishing off with smaller stones, bound or rolled in with a little soil. For a strong, permanent road, concrete may be employed. If a cement surface is objected to, gravel can be strewn over before the cement sets, and be rolled in. Grass paths are comfortable and beautiful.

Is this not a superb setting for a home?

Brick is also good. It is well also to have a tile or slate or wooden edging to the paths, as this makes for neatness and easy up-keep.

You will find that by walking around your district or other districts, your walks are as a book; at every turn you will gain some experiences or suggestions that may be modified or adopted with profit on your own grounds.

Lastly, there is no place so unpromising that it cannot, by dint of knowledge, skill, effort and some small financial expenditure, be made a beautiful or trimly garden.

Seed Mixtures

No one variety of lawn grass is the beat. In order to get results we must not depend on one grass alone, but must so mix our varieties that a thick turf is formed not only quickly, but permanently. Some grasses live but a year, and require an annual resowing. Cheap mixtures contain some of these. It is interesting to know that the roots of some grasses go deeper than others; for this reason good mixtures utilize the whole top-soil most advantageously. Reputable seedsmen can be depended upon to supply proper mixtures for various purposes. Go to them, tell them your soil conditions, and they will give you the proper mixture.

Kentucky blue grass is no doubt the most used. It does not make a good sod the first year, but improves in subsequent years. It succeeds admirably on the limestone soils. In midsummer, it is apt to become somewhat brown. Canada blue grass is useful for dry and clayey soils and seems able to resist drought. Many of the Fescues are extremely valuable. The Fine-leaved Sheep's Fescue has the narrowest blades. The Hard Fescue is useful in forming a dense mat and stands drought. Besides these, the Creeping, the Sheep's and the Meadow Fescues all form sods, and are useful for mixtures.

A lattice screen, supported at the base by a wall. Between the chinks of the stones and in a channel along the top, suitable plants are grown.

For immediate results, but not lasting, a little Italian rye grass can be used. The Rye grass is an annual and will give a good appearance the first year. Oats sown upon a new lawn not only help the appearance but shade the tender perennial grasses and allow them to get a good start. Red Top seems to succeed even on slightly acid soils, and forms a dense mat. The sweet vernal grass is odorous and gives a softness to the lawn. Wood Meadow and Rough Stalked meadow grass both succeed well in the shade. White Clover is also useful in mixtures; it forms a dense ground cover and thrives in most soils and climates. A quart, which is a little over half a pound, should be used for every three hundred square feet of surface. The Clover is to be sown separately, as the seed is heavier.

When and How to Sow

Grass may be sown as soon as the snow has gone and the ground warmed slightly. It is an advantage to get it well started before the trees begin to shade the soil, perhaps as early as April. If sown later, especially in midsummer, the hot sun will make it difficult for the grass to start. The soil will need careful and thorough watering. Grass seed may also be sown in the autumn, from mid-August to October, with good results. If a day just before a rain can be chosen it will be found that the grass will be up in a few days. If no rain is in sight, give a thorough sprinkling of water, but not with force, else the seed will be washed out. If it

Some flower gardens are so situated that it becomes necessary to run a lattice-work fence around them. A dainty, ornamental fence like the above, if painted white, is very suitable.

is windy, the seed will scatter badly, and will not come up evenly.

When large areas are to be sown it is best to divide the lawn into approximately ten-foot squares and treat each separately, else it will be difficult to sow uniformly. To cover the seeds, the areas should then be raked in two directions, after which the lawn should be thoroughly rolled. This will compact the soil so that the seeds are in contact with the soil particles.

An effective disposition of a lawn.

There is a tendency here to overdo through too heavy a planting. This arrangement entails much labor to keep in condition.

Care of the Lawn

The yearly care of the lawn consists first of a slight mulch of thoroughly rotted manure in the winter. This not only protects the grass from the cold, but supplies plant food as well. In the spring, when growth first starts, the coarser material should be removed and the lawn given a dressing of bonemeal. An application of nitrate of soda, which is best applied in solution (one oz. to two gallons of water), will give the lawn a good start. To renovate the lawn, seed can usually be sown about one-half as thickly as for new lawns.

Frequently bad spots are found. These are often due to the fact that in grading some large stone has been left in the soil which cuts off the supply of water from below. At other times the soil becoming a little sour, causes the bare spot. Dig up such an area deeply and remove the stones. Place in fresh soil, a little lime and decayed manure. It is advisable to give an extra heavy seeding also.

Exterminating the Weeds

Many of the objectionable weeds on new lawns are annuals, and they may be entirely eradicated in one year if they are prevented from seeding. Many other weeds, such as docks, dandelions and Canadian thistles, are perennials, and are provided with underground fleshy roots which must be dug deeply and pulled up. Cutting them just below the surface aggravates the situation, because three or four shoots start in place of one.

Hedges and Fences

Hedges of Privet, Berberis, Siberian Dogwood, Box, Yew, Ilex, Buckthorn, Cratægus Oxyacantha, Hemlock, Arbor Vitæ and Norway spruce—Location—Soil—Fences with Climbers

Much has been said of late regarding the wholesale manner in which fashion has dictated that every sort

When this property of one acre was purchased there was not a tree or a plant on the place. The frontage on the main road is 120ft. on a side road some 400ft. The ground rises splendidly from the main road: the house was placed 200ft. from that road. Judicious planting has made these home grounds "a thing of beauty and a joy forever." From the very first plantings of very small stock the attractiveness of the place has improved from year to year.

of fence and boundary should be removed. The word "garden" carries with it the meaning of enclosure. We in America are getting more and more away from having even our own dooryards to ourselves. Often we cannot tell where our province leaves off and the next begins. Marauders have full sweep. There is something home-like about an enclosure with some degree of privacy. Because the city is abolishing every means for such privacy we wish at times to be by ourselves, and the country is chosen. Hedges or boundaries need not be emphasized, but let us not

Ungainly and displeasing. The grass is unkempt; the shrubs in front are wild growths that have sprung up of their own accord, yet the situation is ideal for gardening.

fear to put up some little shrubbery to shield us from the public gaze, and let us enclose parts of our own domain by a low hedge. Formidable fences are not advocated, but private areas bounded by hedges are always interesting.

Low hedges of the graceful Ligustrum regelianuin (Regel's Privet) are very handsome; or Berberis thunbergii, with its red berries and fall coloring; or the Siberian dogwood (Cornus alba sibirica). For an evergreen hedge, nothing has been used more than Box. This is not hardy in all parts of the north, and is a very slow grower. For starting the hedge old plants may be broken apart and set out. The dwarf Japanese Yew (Taxus cuspidata var. brevifolia) is very hardy but has hardly become known as yet in American gardens. Ilex crenata microphylla can also be used.

Taller hedges are best made of the Ibota (Ligustrum Ibota), common Privet (Ligustrum vulgare), or the California Privet (Ligustrum ovalifolium). The California Privet is seen at its best in the Eastern coastal states, from Maine south, and succeeds admirably from the very edge of the beach up to ten miles inland, where it is one of the best materials to use, but in many inland northern localities it freezes to the ground every few years so that the character of the hedge is destroyed. The Golden Privet is very bright and cheery, but hard to buy. The Buckthorn (Rhamnus cathartica) is a useful

Rough, neglected surroundings—no planting attempted. no lawn, no shrubs, no flowers. How much the dwellers miss.

Privet put to good use and charming city street arrangement.

and not easily penetrable hedge. Cratægus crus-galli and oxyacantha are also useful. They will require close pruning when small to induce branches at the base of the plants. Cratægus crus-galli, on account of its dangerous needle-like thorns, should not be set out where there is a sidewalk. Hedges of hemlock, arbor vitæ, and Norway spruce are substantial when the taller ones are wanted. The hemlock is the finest, since each plant merges into the next admirably.

A common blunder with hedges is to locate them too near walks so that they are injured by the constant brushing against them by the passersby.

The soil should be prepared deeply and well as for ordinary shrub planting. The practice is not advised of placing two rows of shrubs for a hedge. The hedge can be kept cleaner of weeds and its growth is more symmetrical by planting only one row. It is advisable in setting a hedge to set the plants so that they touch at planting time. This means that the smaller plants, as Barberry, will be planted sue to eight inches, and Privets ten to twelve inches apart. The soil must be thoroughly firmed around the plants at setting.

For pruning hedges, see chapter on pruning.

Board or picket fences are employed between the smaller suburban yards. These can be covered with rambler roses, honeysuckle in variety, or other climbers. By proper pruning and thinning these will not get too heavy or cumbersome, and can readily be held back if the fence requires to be painted. Iron fences and galvanized or alumina plated fences are also used, the latter being strong and durable. Or again, a soil bank can be thrown up and be planted with trees and shrubs. The consideration of brick and stone walls hardly comes within the scope of this book.

Hemlock hedge. Tsuga canadensis. Imposing, yet the greenery is soft and pleasing.

Trees for Shade and Shelter Upon the Lawn

The trees each of us would choose for our lawn decoration would most probably be those for which we have a personal liking. From childhood, we reverence a certain type of tree either because of fruits it bears, its shape or its fall colors. Nothing compares with the American elm for restful beauty; especially so are the forms which are vase-shaped and with foliage to the soil. The tulip tree makes a strong appeal; the foliage is glossy bright green above and pale below, and the tight bark of older trees is beautiful. What is more effective than a huge red or black oak with its strong and often crooked branches, which so often grow out at right angles to the trunk? Such a tree is in mind which takes up as much room as the little Dutch house beneath it. Specimen beeches, which are branched to the soil, though usually very formal in shape, are yet graceful. All persons progressive enough to read garden

The oriental plane.   Platanus orientalis.

Much used in street planting and best employed where the houses stand 60 to 80 feet apart across the street.

books, of course, would never spoil the beauty of the lawn trees by removing the lower limbs. This especially applies to the beech. It is peculiar, but many persons have not realized that if they prune off the limbs of a young tree it is very difficult ever to get new branches to start out from below again. The white birch is graceful and dainty, but it is being attacked by a borer to such an extent that it is best not to advise planting it. To this brief list might be added a host of others according to personal preference.

Besides the larger trees, there are a great number of very useful smaller growing trees. There are many crab apples which are most excellent; one of the prettiest, with double pink flowers, is Bechtel's crab. A very handsome variety of Japanese crab, it has deep red buds which on opening become white or a blush pink. The beauty of this tree in bloom is overpowering. Many of the thorn apples are handsome. They require a great deal of water and should not be planted where they can rob the perennials.

A tree known but little and valued because of its very superior autumn tints, is the Sorrel tree (Oxydendron). For autumn effect, the maples are excellent, as is also the sweet gum.

One must avoid great spots of vivid color in trees, for too great an abundance of purple plums and beeches, Japanese maples and variegated yellow forms are going to destroy the dignified beauty of your garden.

Evergreen

We must now say a word about the evergreens. They are ever beautiful and ever graceful as well as evergreen. To no other trees does the injunction to let the lower limbs grow apply so much as to the evergreens. How different are our tastes! In the evergreens some of us enjoy the informal, look-as-though-they-were-weather-beaten sorts. We enjoy

American arbor vitæ thuya occidentalis filiformis. Highly decorative, standing singly at any appropriate point.

The Colorado blue spruce

There are more delicate and softer appearing evergreens, it is true, but even so the blue spruce has a place all its own as a sturdy, hardy and beautifully colored specimen tree.

pines which have had some accident when young and have four or five trunks instead of one. We admire the Austrian pine at any stage of its growth; the pitch pine when it becomes old and picturesque, with its sturdy short branches, and persistent globular cones, and the long, heavy foliage of the red pine. Others will much prefer the conical firs and spruces. The greatest beauty is seen in a perfect specimen of Norway or Oriental spruce, branching to the soil and hung with huge cones; or perhaps the blue-green or grayish-green foliage of the silver fir (Abies concolor) is a great attraction, for this is one of the most beautiful trees of this type. The latter is prettier than the Colorado blue spruce, which some think is over planted; it is a trifle bright and has such stiff foliage that, in the minds of many, it does not compare with the softer and more graceful foliage of the silver fir.

Among smaller growing evergreen trees we have the Japanese cypresses or Retinisporas, the foliage of which is graceful and the habits charming. The Arbor vitæs, especially the Chinese species, are very handsome. For mass planting, the hemlock is admirable; the foliage is most dainty; the trees merge into one another very nicely. Because of the interesting bristly appearing cones and the soft foliage, the Douglas fir is to be admired. The Rocky Mountain forms are hardy, but the Coastal plain form is not in the east. The Irish juniper is most slender and vertical, but it is an inferior tree because the winter snows spread the branches and often break them or ruin the shape of the tree. It would seem well to tie the trees up a little before winter. The pyramidal forms of Juniperus virginiana are superior to the Irish juniper. They are a substitute for the popular cypress effects seen in France.

Planting Trees

The best method of ascertaining how to plant a tree properly is to observe the carefully prepared sketches. More can be seen in these pictures than can be expressed in words. The main object is to have a hole large enough for the roots, and to get the trees just a little deeper than they stood in the nursery. An important necessity for newly set trees is a support. The wind whips the tree about and the young roots are easily loosened. Stakes should be set deeply and be a real support; or the tree may be supported by wires, taking care that these wires are in contact with rubber packing on the branches so that they are not girdled; pieces of old rubber hose may be used for this purpose.

Shrubs

(Take our advice and pick out a few varieties that no one in your town has; don't limit yourself to what everyone sees everywhere. Hydrangeas, snowballs, common lilacs, etc. If you are thinking of going into shrubs, get a catalog from a reliable dealer and study it carefully for its illustrations and letterpress. Bear in mind that the cheapest is not always the best; also that the larger plants are naturally dearer than the smaller ones. Where nearly every shrub is so beautiful it is a comparatively easy matter to select two or three out of the ordinary.)

For the garden, whether large or small, some shrubs are necessary. They not only furnish a good foliage background, but some are very beautiful for their flowers, which are not only decorative in a landscape way, but are highly useful for cutting. They are the proper sort of plants for hedges and for screening unsightly objects.

In establishing a new planting of shrubs give the soil good, deep preparation and spade in a liberal supply of stable manure and bonemeal. Let the planting be done either in spring or fall. In the spring shrubs should be set out as early as the soil can be worked. After the growing season begins they are somewhat weakened by not being in the soil; besides, they should be well established before the hot weather arrives. Many gardeners prefer to plant in the fall because often there is less work which is urgent at that time of the year. All such stock should be given ample time in which to have an opportunity to get their roots established before permanent freezing and should be thereby protected during the winter by a good mulching of

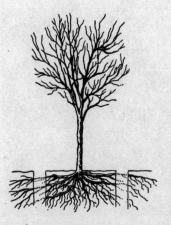

This tree is correctly planted, each root well spread, and neither too deep nor too high. The dotted lines show where to dig if it is required to transplant it.

manure. For an immediate effect the shrubs should be planted almost twice as closely as they are to stand permanently. It is, therefore, advised to plant only part of your place the first year and plant it thickly. By the time you are ready to plant the other part you can draw upon the first planted beds for your stock. Gardens, unlike houses, can be changed and rearranged easily. Shrubs rarely suffer from transplanting if done at the right time and watered thoroughly.

The proper time for pruning is very important.

Wrong method of planting.

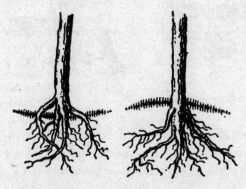

In the left-hand picture the tree is obviously placed too high, and its roots are also cramped. In the other case the soil is mounded up too much, thus shedding off the water.

Certain of the Best Shrubs

For general screen planting few shrubs compare with the lilac. It is exceedingly hardy and the flower is always a favorite. If the good varieties of lilacs are used, the individual blooms will be important. The only way to grow good, large blooms is to keep all the suckers from the base of the plant removed; plants so treated will resemble trees.

Here is a selection of good varieties of Syringa vulgaris, the garden lilac, flowering in late May: Single—Marie Le Gray, white; Charles X, rosy lilac; Frau Bertha Dammann, white; Ludwig Spaeth, deep purple-red; Gloire des Moulins, rosy lilac; Alba grandiflora, white. Double—Mme. Lemoine, white; Miss Ellen Willmot, white; La Tour d'Auvergne, violet-purple; Mme. Gasimir-Perier,

A planting diagram of the National Rose Society.

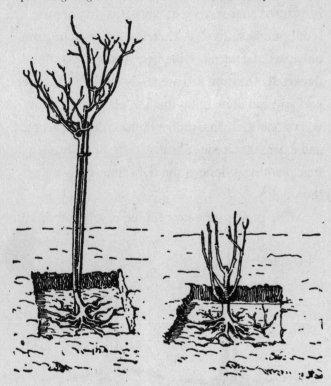

The whitened parts of the stem indicate the depth to which a standard and a dwarf rose should be planted; that is, the same depth as they were when in the nursery.

creamy white; President Grévy (semi-double), bluish lavender; Antoine Buchner, light pink. Van Houttei's Spiræa, also known as bridal wreath, is unrivaled for prolificacy and grace of bloom. While the long sprays of white blossoms are soon shattered by the rains and the plant does not give a very permanent flower effect, yet, with its beautiful green foliage and bushy growth, when properly pruned, it remains a most satisfactory shrub.

For the early spring display there is nothing so cheery as the bright yellow flowers of the golden bell (forsythia), of which there are several forms; the one known as suspensa is most effective when planted at the top of a wall or rock ledge and allowed to grow down. Even after flowering the foliage retains a good color. The upright forms need to be massed, as individuals are not graceful.

A popular summer-flowering hardy shrub is the hydrangea Paniculata grandiflora. It has handsome dark green foliage and bears in great profusion immense panicles of white flowers, which gradually change to rose and bronze. The shrub should be severely pruned in early spring.

The snowball (Viburnum opulus sterile) is one of the best of flowering shrubs, bearing clusters of handsome globular pure white flowers in May.

Bush or shrub honeysuckles (Loniceras) are attractive shrubs of upright habit and very desirable for mass and border planting. They produce showy flowers which are often followed by bright-colored berries.

No shrubbery is complete without a specimen or two of the Japanese maple (Acer palmatum), of which there are several forms. They are beautiful little trees or shrubs of graceful habit, their delicately cut leaves of various shades of color being especially attractive in spring and autumn.

Excellent beds or borders are arranged, using tall shrubs, such as red bud (Cercis) and hawthorns at the back, with mock orange (Philadelpuhs coronarius) and wiegela at the midground and edged with Deutzia gracilis or Spiræa thunbergii; or for lower beds, the use of Berberis vulgaris at back with Berberis Thunbergii and Mahonia in the foreground.

For a bed remaining attractive during the winter use a few Kerria japonicas, which have green twigs, or Cornus alba sibirica, with its red twigs, both of which retain their color all winter.

Grouping of splræa van houttei and viburnum plicatum (snowball).

There is a large group of shrubs with beautiful foliage. None equals the graceful horizontal branching of Regel's privet. The flowers are not very conspicuous, being white, but they are followed by attractive black berries. The dainty narrow, minute foliage of the Spiræa thunbergii is excellent; the tiny white flowers coming in early May add an extra charm. In the region of central New York the tips of branches winter-kill, so that they need to be dressed a little in the spring.

Certain shrubs are fascinating because of peculiar flowers, seeds and bark. The sweet shrub, Calycanthus floridus, or, as it is also called, the strawberry shrub, is very interesting; the twigs are aromatic all winter and the leather-petaled, dull red flowers are very individual in fragrance. Picked today they have one fragrance, perhaps that of strawberries; tomorrow, the fragrance is more like that of apples. Closely resembling C. floridus is C. lævigatus, but the flowers of the latter are not so sweet. The winged spindle-tree (Euonymus alata) bears peculiar corky angles on the twigs, and a funny little orange fruit inside of a hard red husk.

Shrubs with Edible Berries

Shrubs which, though ornamental, produce berries which are good to eat, are interesting not only to you, but to the birds they attract. Many persons do not know that barberries make a very good jam, especially palatable served with the Thanksgiving turkey or wild game, being appropriate as well as tasty. Goumi, or Elæagnus longipes, produces an elongated red berry in June or July which is excellent picked from the plant and eaten. The Vacciniums, blueberry or huckleberry, besides being ornamental, are, as we all know, of an excellent flavor. Elderberries to some tastes make a pie superior even to huckleberries. The red-fruited variety should not be eaten. The nannyberry (Viburnum Lentago) bears a black fruit very freely. It has somewhat the flavor

of bananas. Besides, there are the blackberries, the raspberries and the currants, species which are often ornamental.

Broad-Leaved Evergreen Shrubs

There are a number of interesting evergreen shrubs. None are so popular as the rhododendrons, which should have a soil free from lime. If you live in a limestone region, before you attempt to grow them dig out the beds to a depth of three feet, filling in with good wood-soil or leaf-mold. Provide good drainage by putting a layer of ashes at bottom of the trench. The secret of success with rhododendrons is to keep the roots cool and moist. In winter they should be deeply mulched with leaves. In summer, they must have an abundance of water. In some rhododendron plantations a "syringe" of water plays upon the beds continually. They like shade usually, but often by a proper choice of plants, plantations may be successful even in the sun. In winter a framework of burlap gives the protection from the wind. They should always be massed, for rhododendrons, unless in beds by themselves, are either apt to receive too much fussy care or none

Mixed but effective planting of iris, peonies, rhododendrons and Juniperus stricta on top of terrace. Lombardy poplars are seen in the background at rear of house.

A garden scene in summer.

In this bosky dingle are shrubs of many kinds and tall umbrageous trees. The bananas are grouped for the season only; likewise the yuccas; filamentosa is the hardiest of the yuccas.

at all. The best early varieties are Roseum elegans, an old rose colored variety, and Everestianum, a lavender, both flowering in late May. Then in early June we have Album elegans, a large white; Mrs. C. S. Sargent, a pink; Caractacus, a red; purpureum, a purple; and Lady Grey Egerton, a silvery gray lavender.

There are a number of azaleas which are most brilliant, the best being Azalea pontica and A. mollis, in the various colors, and Azalea amœna, which is a superb claret pink.

A shrub which has proved perfectly hardy is the Japanese holly (Ilex crenata, var. microphylla); it grows about four feet tall and is excellent. The American holly is hard to transplant but seems hardy as far north as Cape Cod. The leaves should be removed and plants transplanted in the spring. The Mountain laurel (Kalmia latifolia), is, perhaps, the best evergreen shrub grown; it succeeds a little easier than rhododendrons and without protection of the tops retains a good appearance all through the winter. The Mahonia, or Oregon grape (Mahonia aquifolium), is an excellent shrub; it succeeds perfectly if planted so that leaves are shaded from winter sun. It surely looks fresh, green and glossy in midwinter.

Ground Cover and Low Growing Shrubs

Oftentimes one wishes a ground cover of very low shrubbery in the shade, and few plants are as valuable as Pachysandra terminalis for this purpose. Vinca minor is also useful; but the leaves are not so large. The common juniper (Juniperus communis adpressa) is also valuable; it requires sun. All of these three plants are evergreen. Several excellent low deciduous shrubs for ground cover in the sunshine are the aromatic dwarf sumach (Rhus aromatica) and yellow root (Xanthorrhiza apiifolia), which spreads rapidly by underground stems; it does not thrive in limestone soils. Sweet fern (Myrica asplenifolia) will thrive on the driest, sunniest slopes; memorial rose (Rosa Wichuraiana) is excellent, bearing numerous white flowers in late June or July; English ivy; and Euonymous radicans var. vegeta may also be used. The English ivy, though very beautiful, is often rather tender; it enjoys a moist soil and shade in winter.

Bushes for Wet Places

When planting grounds it is often desired to obtain shrubs for planting in wet places, some that will attract either by their flowers, berries or other features.

There is a shrub which always comes to mind when this subject is thought of, Clethra alnifolia, because of the profusion and fragrance of its flowers. It blooms in midsummer or later, the bush is usually covered with panicles of white flowers of peculiar fragrance. In its wild state it is usually found on the banks of streams, or otherwise near water, so that it is well suited when planted in similar positions. There is another native Clethra, the C. acuminata, but the alnifolia is the best for the purpose.

The white fringe, Chionanthus virginica, is at home in a wet place. It is wild in situations which are almost under water at times. This has white flowers, too, but they come early in spring with the leaves, and because of the fringe-like appearance of the flowers the shrubs are called old man's beard in some portions of the south.

Another shrub of great merit is the Magnolia glauca, the one of our swamps and low grounds, which is almost evergreen, and famous everywhere for the fragrance of its flowers. It is often found side by side with the white fringe. Both of these, though often listed as shrubs, grow to the size of a small tree in time, if kept to one shoot when young.

The bayberry, Myrica cerifera, is a good wet position shrub, delighting in damp ground, although it can be found growing wild on light gravelly soil. When grown in groups where one plant shelters the other they are somewhat evergreen in character. The flowers are greenish white and small, making no display to attract, but the berries when ripe are covered with a white, waxy substance, making their clusters conspicuous and attractive.

Found in similar situations to the above mentioned shrubs is the Azalea viscosa, a species renowned for the fragrance of its blooms. The flowers are pure white, expanding in July and August. It is one of the most admired of azaleas, yet not at all common in cultivation.

In Vacciniums (Blueberries), a good one for wet ground, is V. corymbosum. It delights in such situations. In spring it presents to view beautiful clusters of white flowers. Edible, dark colored berries follow; later on, with the approach of autumn, the foliage becomes of a lovely orange bronze color. It is then foremost of all the foliage shrubs famous for their autumnal display of color.

The sheep laurel (Kalmia angustifolia) with its purplish pink flowers may also be used; as also the Chamædaphne, the Andromeda and Ledum.

These shrubs would give one a good start in planting a wet place, but they do not exhaust the list; many more could be added.

Rose walk at a country home.

This arbor is covered with prairie roses, vars. Baltimore belle and queen of prairie.

Soils

The soil best suited for roses is usually considered to be a medium heavy clay loam, especially for hybrid perpetuals, briers and climbers. The hybrid teas and teas prefer a lighter soil. The hybrid perpetuals, hybrid teas and teas require perfect drainage.

Width of Beds

Roses are best planted in beds. If they are to be worked from both sides, five or six feet is wide enough and three feet is the proper width for beds against the walls. Beds that are too wide necessitate stepping in them when picking the blooms or when cultivating. Narrow beds are poor because of the intrusion of grass roots upon the nourishment which would otherwise go to the roses. If possible it is

A rustic pergola.

Such pergolas can be made of peeled oak or pine, or of any durable branches one can get—but never birch; that won't last beyond a season. A variety of vines can be trained here.

best to reserve the rose beds for roses alone and not attempt growing any other plants in these beds.

Preparation of Soil

Dr. Huey has said that it is much better to put a fifteen-cent rose bush in a fifty-cent hole than to put a fifty-cent rose bush in a fifteen-cent hole. The preparation of the beds should take place in the fall in order that the soil may have an opportunity to settle.

All rose beds should be dug eighteen inches or two feet deep. The subsoil should be loosened and thoroughly manured, then fill in to over half the depth with manured top-soil over which spread a good layer of compost. By compost we mean soil which has been thoroughly enriched by manure (one barrow of manure to three of soil) and bonemeal; this should be allowed to become thoroughly incorporated with the soil, piling alternate layers of soil and manure and allowing to remain for a few months or a year. When the bed is finished it should be two or three inches above the normal level.

The main secret of successful rose growing lies in the proper preparation of the bed.

Time to Plant

Spring is the best time to plant the hybrid teas and teas. If the beds have been carefully prepared the previous fall, the soil will get into good condition quickly. The nursery stored plants can be set out as soon as land can be worked. The pot-grown stock, if it is not crowded, can well be kept till May. These latter plants are growing and there is no necessity for giving a check by planting in open ground sooner. If the stock is frosted when received, cover the whole plant with soil until the frost is drawn out. The plants are often rather dry when received; the bark is shriveled and the roots brittle. If the whole plant is either buried in soil or placed in water before planting, it will be greatly benefited. In planting budded or grafted roses remove all buds which may be present upon the stock below the soil and prune the broken roots. All tops should be severely cut back so that each bears three to four eyes; this is especially necessary and should not be neglected. The roots should be spread naturally and in the case of budded plants, so placed that the point budded is two or three inches below the surface of the soil. It is absolutely necessary to plant very firmly; the soil

Showing the difference in foliage between a sucker "B" and a good strong shoot "A."
A—Typical rose leaf with five leaflets. B—Typical leaf of a "sucker" or brier with nine leaflets.

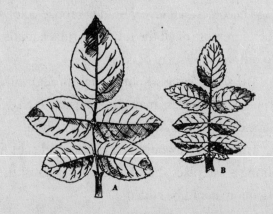

must be filled in about the roots most carefully and made solid. The hole should not be entirely filled, but the plant should be watered, after which dry soil is placed on top to prevent baking.

Summer Treatment

Keep the soil continually cultivated to retain as much moisture as possible; the stirring need not be deep, otherwise roots are injured. A mulch of lawn clippings is beneficial. Each time a new supply is ready the other will have been dried and worked into the soil. After every rain the soil should be loosened. A good syringing of water every day from the start of the season will go a long way toward keeping the insects off. The time for syringing is morning or evening. At midday it is rather injurious to the foliage. All through the summer, watch for suckers; they usually have more leaflets—five to seven, the garden varieties having but three to five. They should not be broken off but cut down to the roots. (See cut).

Cutting Roses

If the roses are cut properly many varieties will continue to bloom until autumn. The bud should be cut so that five-leaf foliage is left upon the stem. Refer to the sketch below. If the rose stem is cut at C there is only a three-leaf remaining upon the stem; such cuts rarely give such good flower stems. Cut at any B there are five-leaves left

Showing where to cut a rose to obtain more flowers. See paragraph above "cutting roses."

and flower buds will start growth very soon. Cut at any A other flower stems develop slowly, if at all. Cut roses then to a five-leaf.

Rose Insects

The rose plant louse or aphis is one of the commonest pests; it appears on the young growths and reproduces with great rapidity, soon covering the plants. The tips of branches are stunted and the buds only produce deformed flowers. The daily syringe advocated elsewhere will do much to lessen the attacks, for the insects will be washed off the plants. Whale oil soap (one pound to ten gallons of water), or some reliable nicotine preparation will surely kill them.

There are several rose slugs. In each case they are worms which skeletonize the leaves and even attack the plant when the leaves first unfold. Arsenate of lead (one pound arsenate of lead to twenty-five gallons of water) is effective, but even water will check them if applied with force. Hellebore is good dusted on the leaves; it should first be diluted to half its weight with flour or plaster.

The leaf hoppers can be controlled by spraying with tobacco extract on underside of leaves. The rose leaf roller can be controlled with arsenate of lead. There is also the rose scale, which can easily be washed from the canes with corrosive sublimate or on a large scale sprayed with lime sulfur, or the canes burned.

The rose beetle is especially prevalent on sandy soils. It appears in early summer, feeding on leaves and flowers. Hand picking is really necessary. They should be dropped into kerosene. The larvæ feed on roots of rose plants. Some persons have lessened the injury from rose bugs by allowing chickens to have the run of the rose beds for several hours a day in May, when the larvæ are coming out of the ground.

Bed of the pink tea rose Lady Ashtown and other rose beds on lawn with Yew hedge behind. The statuary adds finish, dignity and interest.

Screen for the side or back of a house. Grape vines may be used, but they must be kept free of insects and other "crawly things." Ampelopsis, Clematis or Wichuraiana roses also can be recommended.

Rose Diseases

Mildew causes a powdery effect upon leaves. It is especially prevalent upon the crimson ramblers and moss roses. It appears when the nights are cool and days are hot and sultry, and disfigures the plant, but does not affect the next year's crop of flowers. Powdered sulfur upon the leaves is used as a control.

Black spot is the most serious disease of the American beauty and other hybrid perpetuals. It is confined to the foliage and appears in midsummer. It looks like a black or purple spot one-quarter inch in diameter; the blotches more evident on the upper surface. When the patches are examined they will be found to have a fine mycelium growing on them which causes premature defoliation. The leaves should always be removed if possible.

Spray with Bordeaux mixture (3-5-50), or other copper fungicides.

Leaf-scroch, when severe, causes the infected areas of the leaf to drop out. The canes are also attacked. The wild roses, too, are infested. The best control is to use copper fungicides.

Rose rust is especially prevalent on hardy varieties. It has summer spores and winter spores and attacks canes as well as leaves. The best preventive is the removal and burning of all rusted canes.

Rose canker appears as a warty growth on the canes; excrescences on wood. It can only be cut out when found. It is caused by a fungus.

Kinds of Garden Roses

Most of the roses mentioned in the following pages are favorites in the north; many other varieties can be tried in less severe climates—which refers also to the northern part of the Pacific coast.

BRIER ROSES. There is a huge group of shrubby or brier roses. On the whole, they are hardy and grow under adverse conditions. Some of them will be useful for making a hedge. If a rose garden is to be made, plan it in the winter and make preparations to surround it with a row of briers.

Rambler rose-covered Summer House
Such a structure as is shown here can be made by the man of the house or a local handy man with tools.

No rose is hardier, freer-blooming and more disease-resistant than the Japanese rugged rose, or Rosa rugosa. Bearing single and double, crimson, pink or white flowers, it is the first one to place in the hedge. There are a number of rugosa hybrids which are admirable.

Of charming fragrance and exquisite colors are the Penzance hybrids. Lord Penzance, a hybridizer of roses, used the standard garden varieties of roses and crossed them with the sweet brier. The result is a wonderful group of roses with apple-scented leaves and delicate pinkish orange, salmon and rose-pink single flowers.

We must not pass over the early yellow roses, two of which are of great importance. The earliest and lighter yellow rose seen in every old-fashioned garden is the Persian yellow and a few days or weeks later the golden yellow variety, which is slightly tinged with red on some of the center petals, is Harrison's yellow. The foliage of this latter rose is charming; it is a pity that these two roses bloom but once a year. Another fine brier well worthy of selection is the Prairie brier, Rosa setigera, and as it has a tendency to climb, should be given some sort of a trellis or fence. It blooms late and bears huge pink single flowers in large trusses.

CLIMBING ROSES. While we are speaking of a trellis for the Prairie rose, let us also say a word for the climbing roses. They can well be planted around our little garden or they can be trained on poles, or on the porches. The old crimson rambler is disliked by many people because it gets buggy and mildewed. Instead, plant Excelsa, which is the hardiest and most brilliant crimson climber we have. The finest light pink is without doubt the Dorothy Perkins; its clean foliage, dainty buds and abundance of bloom are highly admired. Tausendschön, or thousand beauties, is indeed another peerless pink; the individual flowers are large and stand out prominently in the trusses; the color, which is deep pink upon opening, changing later to white, is exquisite. A beautiful climbing rose, with clusters of single deep crimson flowers, is hiawatha.

A large-flowering variety, and one on which the flowers are produced very profusely, is the Christine Wright. The blooms are in small clusters and are of a clear wild-rose pink. The plants are sometimes not great climbers, but they are effective, at least at the base of the pillar. Dr. W. Van Fleet is a leader in the hardy climbing class—a sturdy, rapid grower, with healthy, deep green foliage and bearing a great profusion of large flowers, the long, pointed buds opening a delicate flesh-pink color.

The yellows are rather too tender to be really climbers. Aglaia is beautiful, being deep golden yellow in bud. Gardenia is the finest yellow climber and succeeds nicely in central Ohio. The flowers are like gardenias and the foliage is glossy, firm and brilliant. The pretty glossy foliage of many of these roses has been derived from the memorial rose (R. Wichuraiana). The memorial rose is very useful as a ground cover, being unexcelled for covering waste land, and trespassing upon steep banks can be successfully prevented by planting this rose.

THE TEA ROSES. The Teas really are perpetual blooming; they have exquisite colors and thick, leathery petals; besides this, their buds are pointed, but they are tender and should receive good protection. The snow-white Maman Cochet is large, fragrant and productive; the color becomes a trifle pink in the fall. The buds of Lady Hillingdon, deep apricot-yellow in color, are certainly irresistible for cutting. Marie Van Houtte, whose color can be described either as a pink shaded cream white or *vice versa*, is also charming.

THE HYBRID TEAS. In the hybrid teas are combined some of the hardiness of the Hybrid Perpetual as well as the more or less perpetual blooming quality, and the richness of coloring and beauty of form of the teas. The array of good varieties is almost endless. Among the pinks the first that deserves to be recognized is Jonkheer J. L. Mock, that beautiful rose, the outside of the petals of which are much lighter in color. The flowers are very fragrant and the stem erect and strong. The killarney brilliant is much superior to the pink killarney, but it is rather more single than the other pink varieties; although it opens quickly it remains for some time before shattering and is remarkable for its freedom of bloom. We cannot pass Lady Alice Stanley without recognition. The color is a lovely coral-rose, the inside a little lighter. The flowers are nearly perfect in form, color, fragrance and size. The popular Caroline Testout, which is used extensively upon the streets of Portland, Oregon, is a superb bedding variety. Other fine pink varieties are Mrs. A. R. Waddell, Souvenir du President Carnot, Mrs. George Shawyer, Lady Ashtown, Dean Hole, La France.

The most superb lemon white variety is, no doubt, Kaiserin Augusta Victoria; it is constantly in bloom and has a superior elegance which makes it the best white hybrid tea.

In reds we have, first, Gruss an Teplitz, a velvety rich glowing crimson and very sweet. It is never out of bloom from spring until frost. A dazzling color is displayed by the variety Chateau de Clos Vougeot; it is not a strong grower but a continual bloomer. Laurent Carle is much lighter

than the other red varieties mentioned; it is a carmine and intensely fragrant. Etoile de France bears a very double, cup-formed flower of deep crimson. Other good reds are Lieutenant Chaure and Mary Countess of Ilchester.

Among the salmony or coppery shades, sunburst is one of the most successfully grown. It is superior to Mrs. Aaron Ward in color and form. Another is Ophelia, a more decided pink salmon than Sunburst, and a variety which has been received throughout the rose world with enthusiasm. Mrs. Arthur Robert Waddell is free flowering; though rather small, it is a superb salmon rose with a golden sheen.

It is difficult to know where to place some roses, such as the incomparable Mme. Edouard Herriot, the "Daily Mail" rose, which is described by its introducer, Pernet-Ducher, as "coral red, shaded at the base with yellow." Another has described the color as appearing like "sunshine upon a copper-red metal." It is a splendid variety and worthy of

The sort of garden we all delight in. Baby Dorothy rose and baby Tausendschön roses are massed around the sundial.

acquaintance. One variety, a rich yellow, suffused carmine, commands the attention of all; it is Marquise de Sinety, a semi-double and very fragrant.

THE HYBRID PERPETUALS. The word "perpetual" in the title of this group is a misnomer; they are not perpetual. They have resulted from a cross between the tea, a perpetual rose and the various groups of very hardy roses, so that they are hardy, but not in many cases do they bloom a second time. They are the vigorous varieties for general use. It is difficult to say of this class of roses: "Here is a list of the best twelve." Someone will surely remark: "Why, he does not even know the best variety of them all." Nevertheless, we all agree that Frau Karl Druschki is the finest white. The buds are handsome and it seems to bloom for a longer season than most. If you leave out Clio from your planting you would miss a very beautiful flesh pink. Another, and a free bloomer, is Mrs. R. G. Sharman-Crawford. A bright cherry red, a fine and rather new rose, which is always successful, is Gloire de Chedane Guinoisseau; perhaps an improvement upon Ulrich Brunner. Prince Camille de Rohan and Hugh Dickson are both deep velvety crimsons. Paul Neyron is the largest deep pink variety, frequently criticized for being too coarse and large. The Jack rose, or, as it is called in the catalogs, General Jacqueminot, does well everywhere; it is a brilliant scarlet crimson. Another excellent strong grower and a deep scarlet is J. B. Clark. A very sweet and perfectly formed crimson carmine is the variety Captain Hayward. Mme. Masson is a hybrid perpetual which produces blooms at intervals during summer and fall. It is a sweet-scented crimson. Captain Christy bears a full flower which is tinted white and pale blush. Magna Charta is always admired for its vigor of growth and its bright, rosy pink flowers, which possess great substance.

PERNETIANA. A group of roses of recent interest has been developed by crossing Harrison's yellow with other types. The result is a group of yellowish roses known as pernetiana roses, from their introducer, Pernet. Two deep yellow varieties of great beauty are Soleil d'Or and Rayon d'Or.

MOSS ROSE. The moss rose, with its bud encircled by a delicate mossy covering, holds a strong attraction for all. It is surprising that the interesting variety, Hat of Napoleon, is not more planted. In France it is called Chapeau de Napoleon. It is mossier than others. The large, pure white buds of Blanche Moreau are classical examples of the moss rose. The pink crested moss and the bright red Henry Martin are also splendid varieties.

Flowers

From *Garden Guide: The Amateur Gardeners' Handbook*, edited by A. T. De La Mare, 1920

Combinations of Perennials

A planting of delicate pink hollyhocks, in front of which we place a good clump of white phlox, is to be much commended. Similarly, the phlox will combine nicely with delphinium.

A bed of peonies, in which have been planted some Lilium speciosum, rubrum and album, is good; the peonies will have finished flowering before the lilies begin.

Huge beds of German iris of one variety are shown by themselves, but since they are out of bloom before July 1st it is well to have something to maintain the beauty. A few attractive shrubs are then useful. Especially decorative are Viburnum

Long borders of hardy flowers growing freely and in great luxuriance. The arch in the garden wall focuses the view. No straight trim edges, yet there is abundant room to walk. These borders run right up to the dwelling house.

Opulus and some of the honeysuckles which produce ornamental berries.

Coreopsis lanceolata and a deep violet blue delphinium make an excellent contrast.

Another yellow and blue combination is Speedwell (Veronica spicata) with evening primrose (Enothera missouriensis). The slender spikes of the Speedwell contrast nicely with the large, brilliant yellow flowers of the evening primrose.

Probably no flower of the autumn is so graceful and welcome as the lovely Japanese anemone. Excellent white and pink varieties are available. As they make no effect till mid-September they are best combined with a tall, ornamental grass which will give a good background.

The large group of perennial asters, or Michælmas daisies, should not be forgotten; they are the charm of the real late fall garden. Planted at the rear of borders they make an excellent foliage background for the earlier flowering plants. Especially noteworthy is the Aster ptarmicoides, a very erect, strong-growing white species which blooms a trifle earlier than some of the others. A truly beautiful light blue is the beauty of Colwall and a good pink is A. Novi-Belgii St. Egwin. A very late species, five to six feet tall, is A. tataricus; it possesses excellent clean foliage and bluish violet flowers. One of the largest flowering sorts is A. grandiflorus.

The larkspurs and onkshoods (Aconitum) are planted to advantage in conjunction with Madonna lilies (Lilium candidum). Spring bulbs are often

Does not this charming border planting make you feel like having one of your own?

combined with a few Adonis amurensis, a very pretty little yellow-flowering plant with finely cut leaves.

Under trees where grass will not grow, plant some Ajuga reptans. Vinca minor, called variously myrtle and periwinkle, is very useful as it spreads rapidly, is evergreen and bears pretty blue flowers.

In every home yard there is a certain small area, between perhaps the walk and the wall, which it would be advantageous to have filled nicely with plants; such an area is nicely planted to Bishop's weed (Ægepodium). This plant has green and white variegated leaves and thrives in any soil. It is rapid growing, but only attains a height of twelve inches.

Excellent contrast combinations can be had by the intense blue Anchusa italica and the yellow Marguerite (Anthemis tinctoria), placing the Anchusa at the back.

Another good combination is that of German iris, among which is planted the summer hyacinth (hyacinthus, or Galtonia candicans), with its long spikes of white bells and its broad leaves. The bulbs of the summer hyacinth are placed in the soil in the spring; when they bloom the iris will have finished its blooming but will furnish a foliage base.

An effective use of the blue Aquilegia, or Columbine, is to place a number of these plants at the base of a yellow rose; for example Harrison's yellow, or Persian yellow.

Considerations for a Perennial Border

We have a great many classes of perennials, some of which are so wild and aggressive that they should only be planted among the shrubbery. We have others which are very dainty and tender and whose growth must be carefully watched and their special needs for protection attended to. We must scatter plants through the length of the border which will bloom throughout the season. We should, furthermore, attempt to get good color combinations. The heights to which the plants will grow should be known, otherwise the taller ones may be in front and the more dwarf ones in the

Bringing the flower garden up to the house.
Note also the brick path and other architectural features.

background. It is always well in an informal border to let the back line be somewhat broken; plants at some points are a little shorter.

Situation of Border

Choose a southern exposure where it is not in too close proximity to large tree roots. It should be somewhat protected from the direct force of the wind, otherwise fragile flowers will not be very lasting. Most perennials enjoy a medium light loam.

Preparation of Soil

As with annuals, but perhaps more so with perennials, the soil for borders should be deeply and thoroughly prepared; two to three feet is none too deep, for plants must remain in one place for a long time. In the case of peonies it is detrimental to move them often and it is frequently two years, and in some soils three years, after moving a peony plant before it blooms normally. Manure and a complete fertilizer should be well worked into a new border. All perennial borders profit by an application of bonemeal, hardwood ashes and sheep manure every year or two. Perennial borders which have been flowering year after year and to which much manure has continually been added, become somewhat sour and an application of slaked lime every two years is very beneficial. Many of the perennials do not attain their proper maturity before the winter when they have been excessively fertilized and forced into continued sappy growth. They then suffer from cold. All soils for borders should be loose, so that they can be easily kept stirred. Soils are made light or loosened by manure,

sand or fine coal ashes. Clay soils surely need some such treatment.

Planting

A rule which has been given in setting perennials is to put them a trifle closer than half their height. For example, Columbine grows two feet tall; for good clumps place young plants one foot apart. This rule will not apply in subsequent years, for as the plants grow they must be thinned out. A good liberal planting is always the better plan.

Plants should usually be set a little deeper than they were when growing in the nursery. Care must be exercised not to bury them too deeply, however, for some perennials, as violets and German iris, are almost surface creepers. In placing the perennials in the soil, spread the roots symmetrically; do not wad them and cram them into a little hole.

Spring Planting

The planting of perennials is best done in spring when the tops are just about to start into growth. There is danger in planting when the soil is too moist, especially in clayey soils, which if they become caked are difficult to pulverize during the whole growing season.

A mixed border of hardy flowers.

Autumn Planting

In the autumn most perennials can be transplanted successfully if set out in time so that their roots get established before cold weather. If perennials must be moved in full growth they should always be cut back; especially is this the case when much soil is removed from the roots. All newly set stock should be watered. There is usually less work in autumn than in the spring, hence this season is often preferred for planting.

Cultivation

Through the growing season the surface soil should be loosened so that air may enter in order to encourage root action, as well as to conserve the moisture, and keep the weeds in check. Under the heading of "Lawns" we have mentioned the value of lawn clippings as a summer mulch to conserve moisture. We very strongly recommend well decayed stable manure and leaf mold, where these are obtainable.

Watering

Watering, although beneficial, is less necessary if the soil is always kept loose. In dry seasons water may be applied, using plenty at one time. Little drippings of water are bad for all plants, for such a method of watering only destroys the surface looseness. Syringing the foliage is beneficial; in many cases it serves to keep insects in check if done vigorously. Wherever possible, water pipes should be laid with faucets at regular intervals for use in the garden.

Staking

Many of the perennials will become tall and some support will be necessary. Do not make it conspicuous. Paint the stake green and tie with green cord or raffia, but do not use an old mop handle nor tie with brilliant calico. A light, but long stake placed at the center of the plant is effective. Twiggy branches of trees may also be used. In that case scarcely any tying is needed. Let the stakes be placed early; when the plants have made a great growth they cannot be effectively supported, so that a natural appearance is lost. The whole beauty of a garden is frequently marred by the absence of stakes or a poor method of staking.

Sowing

Many annuals, such as petunia, phlox, verbena, ornamental tobacco, China asters, snapdragon, cosmos, sweet alyssum, pansy, annual larkspur, salpiglossis, scarlet sage, swan river daisy and torenia, benefit by being sown indoors in order to give them a growing start before placing in open soil.

March is the best time to sow. This necessitates procuring a good loam in the autumn and storing it in the basement. The soil need not be rich, but it should be loose, which can be accomplished by the addition of well-rotted manure, or if this is not available, sifted coal ashes or sand will be useful. This soil should not be allowed to become dry in the basement, but should be moistened every month or oftener, according to its condition. It must not be kept too wet, otherwise it will sour badly.

Seed must always be sown thinly; thick sowing is a general cause of failure with annuals. Some seeds, as petunia, verbena, ornamental tobacco, salpiglossis and portulaca, are very minute, and should not be covered with soil. A newspaper and a pane of glass placed over the pot or box will retain the moisture and keep the sunlight from the seed. When the seed is not covered, the soil should be thoroughly watered before sowing. Larger seeds are best sown in rows and should be covered with soil about three times their diameter. To keep out the light and prevent the pots from drying, the use of newspaper over the pots is excellent. As soon as the seedlings get above the soil, they should be given the best light conditions, otherwise they will become very spindling and weak. Good light and rather cool conditions indoors, together with thorough but not too frequent watering, should produce stocky plants.

Excepting such as mignonette, sweet sultan, love-in-a-mist, heliotrope, and the poppy-like plants, as eschscholtzia, argemone and papaver, most annuals can be successfully transplanted. When seeds of these latter are sown they are best placed in very small pots, using only two or three seeds in a pot.

Preparation of Soil

The soil should not merely be loosened by a rake, but if good flowers are wanted, thorough preparation should be given and decayed manure added. After many of the annuals have grown two or three leaves tall, they will benefit by being pinched back; in other words, the main shoot should be cut out. This will cause the plants to become branchy and bear three times as many flowers. Especially successful is pinching such plants as stock, nemophila, butterfly flower, petunia, baby's breath, annual chrysanthemums, clarkia, cosmos, godetia, salpiglossis, swan river daisy and calliopsis.

Combinations of Annuals

It is hardly ever advisable to buy mixed colors of flowers; it is much better to buy packages of good separate colors and mix them. Nothing is prettier than huge masses of one color. Bicolor or variegated flowers are to be avoided, because they often give a dull appearance as seen in beds.

Let us make a few recommendations for combinations of annuals or ways in which they give the best effects:

In making beds for annuals they should not be too wide; if against a fence, four or five feet,

Foxgloves (Digitalis) are hardy biennials; they seed and reproduce themselves freely.

and if in the open, six or seven feet, is sufficient; otherwise, they cannot be handled easily either for picking the flowers or for cultivating and weeding. Few annuals can be sown so that they are exactly the proper distance apart when they bloom. They must, therefore, be thinned. According to the variety they all need from six to eighteen inches between plants. Poppy beds are always too thickly planted, for poppy seed is very fine and difficult to sow properly. They must be thinned if the poppies are to attain their proper development.

A bed of blue bachelor's buttons can be nicely edged with sweet alyssum or candytuft, both of the latter being white. The bachelor's buttons will furnish a constant supply of cut flowers.

Snapdragon, of which a delicate pink variety, perhaps, is chosen, will be excellent combined with dusty miller.

Another bed will be showy, composed of California poppies planted in front of the taller pot marigolds. This will be in tones of orange-yellow.

Entire beds, perhaps five by ten feet, of verbenas, planted 12 inches apart each way, will prove very effective.

Grow a fine lot of young Drummondii phlox plants, a white variety, and after filling a bed with them placed eight inches apart, plant bulbs of the pink variety America gladiolus between the plants.

Into your bed of pansies transplant a few of the dainty blue Browallia demissa; this will cast a very light and airy effect over the whole bed.

On some narrow strip, where there is little room, try Godetia rosamond with its satiny pink flowers by itself. You will be rewarded by a very pretty display.

A huge bed of Nicotiana sylvestris, the ornamental tobacco, near a porch where you can get the great fragrance in the evening, is very satisfactory. The Nicotiana self-sows and it will be necessary to keep these in check.

In a hot, sunbeaten, dry place, sow the portulaca or sunplant. The metallic seeds self-sow and the plant will come up year after year. This is the old-fashioned "seven sisters" plant which some persons fancy bears seven colored blooms on one plant.

In some pots, to be placed on posts or on a wall, plant a few of the trailing lobelias (Lobelia erinus) or a few nasturtiums.

In a corner where you want something out of the ordinary, plant a few seeds of the giant spider plant (Cleome). The flowers are rosy crimson, and possess long filaments and pistils followed by long, slender seed pods. They are strong, attractive, but a trifle weedy.

Edge a bed of cannas or other tall plants with fountain grass (Pennisetum).

To combine with bouquets, grow a little clump of cloud grass (Agrostis nebulosa).

For the sweet pea bouquets do not neglect planting some baby's breath (Gypsophila elegans). This will look well grown in a bed with annual larkspurs or with stocks. Baby's breath must be planted several times during the season if a continuous supply is needed.

Some persons admire small hedges of summer cypress, or kochia, but this plant turns a very bad bluish-crimson color in autumn—a color which harmonizes with nothing.

When the season does not prove too moist, or when planted upon sandy soils, the dwarf or cupid sweet peas are excellent. They bear rather long stems and very good flowers.

No annual flower blooms for so long a time as the petunia. If the colors can be selected before setting the plants into the bed, the results will be better. It will be unnecessary to combine them with anything else, as they are all-sufficient, and are as useful for beds two feet square as for huge borders a hundred feet long and four wide.

Where a dainty blue edging plant is wanted, use Swan River daisy, (Brachycome), placing the plants about six inches apart.

If you must neglect your garden, but want a good show of color, try huge beds of zinnias or marigolds.

If you wonder what to use for edging any bed, decide to use sweet alyssum; it is a most adaptable border plant. When it appears to be nearly through blooming, cut it back and it will start up again.

Biennials

This is a class of plants which lives but two years. The seed can be sown in the summer or early autumn one year; the young plants form a rosette of leaves but do not bloom until the following year, after which they usually die. One of our commonest garden plants is a biennial, namely, foxglove. Many other plants are best treated as biennials, as, for example, some campanulas, hollyhocks, anchusa and sweet William, all of which decline after two years. There are few plants to rival the foxglove; it possesses such excellent foliage that nothing need ever be planted at its base; besides, the stately spires of inverted glove fingers are most attractive.

Hedge of Ipomœas, or morning glories. Sow out of doors at the end of May.

China "comet" asters. To be had in all sorts of types and a multiplicity of colors.

Biennials are best protected for the winter by pulling the leaves together and packing straw between them, in which case they seem to stand the cold nicely. If poorly protected the center of the plant decays, leaving it hollow; the stems then do not become strong enough to bear the truss of bloom; at the same time the excellent foliage is entirely gone. This is too often the case with the beautiful Canterbury bells (Campanula Medium), which should not be too thickly covered but properly handled.

The Asters

Asters as they are recognized today are what have resulted from the development and improvement of the China aster. The real asters are small, daisy-like flowers, resembling the single-flowered China aster and known in England as Michælmas daisies.

There are all sorts of types of China asters, all of which have been improved from one single-flowered sort. They are annuals, easy of culture, and with their profusion of bloom and color make a brilliant garden display, particularly in the autumn. The best types to grow are the branching, with long, strong stems; the crego, hohenzollern, end comet, all of which are flat-flowered; the king, which has long needle-like petals, and the ball-like sorts, as Victorias, Truffaut,

and peony-flowered perfection. There are early, medium and late kinds. The later flowering sorts are most successful with the home gardener.

The seeds of the earlier varieties may be started in the hotbed or window in March. For late summer and autumn flowers sowings may be made in the open ground in April or May. Vigorous growth is encouraged by two transplantings. When the seedlings are large enough to handle, transfer to flats or beds. Transplant again when the plants are three or four inches high, setting them where they are to bloom, twelve to fifteen inches apart; the branching sorts need more room to develop. Do not let the plants get a check in any way due to want of water, or cramping of root system. A rich, well prepared soil suits them best. Wood ashes or slaked lime incorporated with the soil will do much to prevent root and stem diseases to which asters are liable.

The Cannas

These handsome subjects mark a wonderful development by the plant breeder. At first the cannas were only prized as foliage plants; the petals were narrow and the flower was very unattractive. Now we have an excellent series of wonderful cannas with superbly colored gigantic flowers, all of which are of easy culture and great value for the garden, where

Cannas are easy to grow and well repay the slight labor required.

they are planted in formal beds or mixed in the perennial border.

Starting Cannas

In March the roots, which have been stored during the winter, are best cut up so that there are one to three buds or eyes on each piece. They can then be planted in boxes of sand or sandy soil and placed in a light window. If the season is late and the plants get rather large, they should be placed in pots; those four inches high are generally large enough.

Cannas are tender and should not be planted in the open ground before all danger of frost is past. There is no advantage in planting too early, for they do not make good growth till the ground becomes thoroughly warm.

Preparing Canna Bed

Spread a wheelbarrow load of well-rotted manure over each square yard of soil and dig deeply: the soil should be loosened to a depth of fifteen to eighteen inches. The deeper the digging the better will the bed absorb water. Large-leaved plants always require lots of water. Careful attention must be given to the question of the planting of varieties of

harmonious colors as well as of the proper heights. We give herewith a list of select varieties:

Eureka, white, 4½ ft. high; sensation, pink, 3 ft.; City of Portland, pink, 3½ ft. King Humbert, red, 4½ to 5 ft.; meteor, red, 5 ft.; firebird, red, 4 ft.; fiery cross, red, 4 ft.; favorite, yellow and variegated, 4½ ft.; Panama, yellow and variegated, 3 ft.; San Diego, yellow and variegated, 4 ft.

A supplementary list of equally fine varieties contains the following: Wyoming, reddish bronze leaves and ochre colored flowers, tall and good; Richard Wallace, soft creamy primrose trusses and green foliage, effective and desirable: compact habit; Venus, deep pink flowers, dark green foliage, sturdy grower; Souv. de Anthony Crozy, brilliant scarlet and gold, flowers large, a free bloomer and dwarf; J. D. Eisele, rich orange scarlet, 5 ft., one of the very best; Rosea gigantea, immense flowers of a deep old rose color; one of the finest and most beautiful; Mrs. Alfred Conard, salmon pink, large and fine; Feurnur, intense orange, 5 ft., a good canna; Gustav Gumpper, the best golden yellow. Others of prime excellence comprise Florence Vaughan, tall growing, flowers rich yellow and scarlet; Mme. Crozy, dwarf, brilliant scarlet with gold center; Prof. Myers, dark foliage, crimson flowers; gladiator, resembles Florence Vaughan, or vice-versa, but not so tall and has more

Even as a foliage plant, without flowers, the canna is beautiful.

red splashes on the yellow; Win. Saunders, reddish foliage and scarlet trusses; Queen Charlotte, matures early, flowers crimson with yellow edge; Jean Fiscot, one of the dwarfest, flowers crimson; Reubens medium grower, dark foliage and crimson flowers.

For the sake of its handsome shining green foliage, and its general stateliness, canna gigantea is recommended. It is very handsome next to the walls of one's house.

Cannas usually spread a little and, as they are large growing, should be planted at least eighteen inches apart. The orchid-flowering varieties require from twenty to twenty-two inches between the plants. In planting firm the roots well and cover with four to five inches of soil.

Cannas from Seed

Because of the extreme hardness of the shells. Canna seeds should be soaked for a few days before planting. The seeds are also frequently nicked with a file or sharp knife. Sow half an inch deep in a sandy loam in a box or pot and place in a hotbed or some other warm location. When large enough to handle pot off singly and keep under glass until the open beds are ready to receive them.

DIGGING AND STORING. When the tops are killed by the frost the roots can be dug in the morning, and if the day is sunny they can be left to dry. They must be stored where they can be kept warm, for if they are cold and damp they decay. They may either be buried in sand or soil, although sand is preferable. If a greenhouse is available the roots may be stored under the benches. It is really unnecessary to wait until the tops die down, for the beds may be wanted to plant with bulbs, in which case let the cannas grow as long as possible and then dig them.

Coleus

For grouping on lawns, ribboning and carpet bedding, the coleus is one of the most useful and attractive of ornamental plants. It is a tender perennial, grows from a foot to two feet high, and the colors and variegations of its foliage are rich and beautiful. Using shallow pots or pans, sow the seed in March or April in good, mellow soil, covering lightly with earth; maintain an even temperature and do not allow the soil to become dry. When the weather is settled and warm, transfer the seedlings to the open ground, preferably in a sheltered situation. Under favorable conditions, they will attain perfection the first season.

As a border for beds of flowering plants, coleus stands without a rival, and, by judicious pinching out of the tips of the shoots, the plants can be maintained at any desired height, conforming to the size of the other plants in the bed, while still retaining their beautiful color effects. The coleus always does best when planted out in the full sunlight, yet, at the same time, it is a plant that can be recommended for partially shaded situations as well.

The Dahlia

There is little question why the dahlia has gained in popularity. The newer varieties win our admiration as soon as we see them. Should you insist that the dahlia is very formal and stiff we should answer that the ones to which you refer are perhaps stiff because they were carefully bred for regularity and symmetry, and you would look upon them as triumphs of the breeder's art if you knew that the modern varieties have been evolved from several wild Mexican species. Near Mexico City, at an altitude of one thousand to two thousand feet above that of the city, we find the wild forms on the sides of the deep ravines in partial shade. It is hot in the daytime, but really gets cold at night. How nicely this explains why our varieties bloom best in the cooler days of autumn.

It was at the end of the eighteenth century before the dahlia reached Europe and soon after

Duplex Form of dahlia

The dahlia it essentially the poor man's flower and most nobly does it respond, in its innumerable types, to its really trivial needs.

three varieties were known. Soon doubles were produced. The flat ones were first very popular; then the ball-shaped blossoms of the show type were greatly in evidence. Between 1830 and 1860 the interest in dahlias became intense, and great premiums were paid for good varieties. Then in 1870 followed varieties which were flatter, less formal and delicately colored. In 1872 a new species, dahlia Jaurezii, was introduced. This is the progenitor of the cactus dahlias, a type universally admired at present because of its graceful form and delicate coloring. The cactus types are combined with the singles to produce the peony-flowered forms from which have been eliminated the weak stems, resulting in an exalted form, and well-shaped blooms of matchless colors borne upon wonderfully strong plants. The large-flowered singles are having a great wave of popularity now, for they are often beautifully colored. In 1899 there was a pretty type produced in France in which there is a row of smaller and much more slender petals, of a different color, surrounding the central disk of an otherwise

single flower. This type has been termed the Collarette dahlia.

Cultivation

The dahlia is typically fall blooming and succeeds in any location where killing frosts do not come too early. If the plants are not seriously checked in their growth by frosts, they will usually bloom very nicely in most parts of New York State, New England and the Central West. The soils best adapted to dahlias are those which are somewhat sandy, but they will grow on heavy clay. The regions which are influenced more or less by the ocean, that is, where cool nights are prevalent, are perhaps the most noted for dahlia growing, especially Long Island, New Jersey, Rhode Island, Maryland and Massachusetts in the east, and without a doubt the best dahlias we have ever seen were in British Columbia, Northern California, Washington and Oregon. Heavy soils may be lightened by coal ashes, sand, and coarse manure. Sandy and lighter soils will benefit by manure or clay to make them more moisture-retaining. Nitrogenous fertilizers are rarely applied because they cause too great vegetative growth and a retarding of the flowering period.

Starting the Tubers

The tubers should be started about April 1st in a warm, light room, merely placing them in a

Hedge of dahlias surrounding a typical home in Victoria, B. G.

shallow box of sand or light soil. When the young shoots begin to show, they should be so cut that one or two eyes are allowed to remain on each piece; the eyes start from the collar (see Contents plant Propagation).

Time and Distance of Planting

They may be planted late in April or May, according to the season. It is better to set them out late than too early. As the dahlia makes a large plant it should be given plenty of room; even four feet by four feet is not too much if the variety is a large one. Planted much closer the plants are difficult to tend. The tubers should be placed about four inches deep, planting them flat or in such a position that the growing point is faced up toward the surface of the soil. Firm the roots well.

Supporting

The average root will make several shoots. Allow them to grow until they make the first set of leaves; by that time the strongest can be selected and the others cut away below the surface of the soil. Sometimes two shoots may be allowed to grow, but never more; as a rule one shoot is sufficient. Tie the shoot to a stake when about a foot high and do not neglect tying as the plant develops, for this is very important. To cause the plants to branch at any certain height, the tip is pinched out; this causes lateral shoots to start.

For Attaining Large Flowers

If the soil is carefully and diligently cultivated there will be little need for watering, which is detrimental unless consistently practiced. Thorough watering should be given each time and at regular intervals; otherwise plants will be checked and flowers will suffer.

In order that each individual flower may be as large as possible, especially in the case of the show and fancy types, which produce a great many flowers of medium size, it is best to disbud the main branches leaving only the terminal bud. It is often best to allow only six or eight branches. The singles, collarettes and pompons are rarely pruned or disbudded, the idea being to get plants with as many flowers as possible. The cactus varieties are apt to have their weak neck habit intensified by excessive pruning and disbudding, so that they should be cautiously disbudded, removing only part of the buds.

Flowers are best cut in the morning or evening and any foliage not wanted should be removed. The stems should then be placed in water up to the base of the flowers and removed to a cool place. Hard-stemmed varieties are best placed in hot water and allowed to remain until the water cools, when they should be removed to fresh cold water. Under no circumstances attempt to ship for exhibition without the pre-cooling.

Storage

When the autumn killing frosts arrive, perhaps in mid-October, and the foliage is killed, take up the plants at once and allow them to dry a little in the sun. Cut off the stems so that a stub of three inches is left. Then place them in a cellar where temperature will surely remain above freezing, about forty to forty-five degrees F. They may best be placed with the stems down on shelves and covered with soil or sand. When storing large tubers it may not be necessary to cover them; merely place them in a heap on shelf or floor, keeping the stems to outside. Do not let them get dried out; if they shrivel, sprinkle a little water over them. If kept too moist they will soon mildew.

The Raising of dahlias from Seed

This is fascinating work, particularly the single forms. Of these, if the seed is sown in a frame or greenhouse in March, the plants will come into bloom in July; they will also flower if the seed is sown where it is to remain, the same as most of the annuals. The seed of the double dahlias should be sown in February or March, and the plants grown on the same as if from cuttings. With good care they will come into flower early in September, when the pleasure commences. The certainty of getting something good and the possibility of getting a flower worthy a name, possibly better than any of the existing forms or varieties, makes this branch of floriculture of extreme interest.

The young seedlings should be set close together, not more than two feet apart; when they come into flower weed out such as are not desirable to keep. Another reason for close planting is that except for the single varieties, the plants do not attain in their first season as large growth as if from tubers.

Chrysanthemums and Daisies

The word chrysanthemum has been derived from the Greek *chrysos*, gold, and *anthemon*, flower.

It is very interesting to see just how many plants are really chrysanthemums. The wild ox-eye daisy, the Shasta daisy, the Pyrethrum (from which insect powder is made), the Feverfew of our grandmother's garden, the Marguerite, or Paris daisy of the florist, as well as the monster decorative blooms of the expert culturist indoors, are all chrysanthemums.

Some of the chrysanthemums, or 'mums, as the gardener affectionately calls them, are annuals. In the case of most of the annual species the blooms resemble huge daisies. They are white or some shade of yellow, and often, as in the case of Chrysanthemum carinatum, they have a maroon or red ring of color at the center. The annual types can be sown in April, in the open ground, where they should be thinned to eight inches, or, if large plants are wanted, pinch them back when several leaves are tall and place them twelve inches apart.

A cluster of hardy chrysanthemums propagated by cuttings or by division of the root, and also of great interest to grow from seed.

A rich, sandy loam suits them best and they surely love the sun.

They bloom profusely throughout the summer and early fall. The species known as golden feather (Chrysanthemum præaltum var. aureum) should be sown indoors in March and though really a perennial, it is treated as an annual. It is used as a yellow-leaved border plant.

An excellent characteristic of some perennial chrysanthemums is that they reproduce themselves so nicely by the production of suckers or underground stems. One of the species which multiplies itself in this manner is the feverfew (Chrysanthemum parthenium). It is a very old plant, but it certainly bears an interesting little tufted white and yellow flower in clusters which, coming in June, is well worthy of a place in the garden. It self-sows its seed, but rarely becomes a nuisance.

Two white daisy-like species are well worth cultivating. The first is the shasta daisy (Chrysanthemum maximum), a gigantic white field daisy of very vigorous growth, producing flowers from June throughout the summer. They have very good keeping qualities and are effective in the border or as a cut flower. Another species, a shrubby daisy (Chrysanthemum nipponicum), blooms in the fall and produces its flowers on the stems from the old shoots of the previous year.

The class known as the hardy chrysanthemums and which resemble the indoor varieties are of two types, the button-like varieties or pompons, and the aster-like or large-flowering varieties. Most of the varieties are hardy if protected in the winter by dry leaves. They enjoy constant cultivation and a rich soil which has been deeply prepared. They are best planted in the spring and advice is frequently given that all old plants should be divided up and reset each year, for they exhaust the soil. Good seed is now available of this type and they may be grown successfully by this method.

As soon as the plants have grown four inches tall, especially if few plants are available, and a good display is wished, they should be pinched. This will cause them to branch freely, each shoot bearing a number of buds. From the very start in growth the plants must be staked. The greatest fault with this group is that they all fall down near blooming time, and the whole beauty of the plant is destroyed unless carefully staked. The shoots can easily be tied to stakes if the stakes are once in place. If the very largest flowers rather than the greatest quantity of bloom are wanted, feed with liquid manure when buds begin to show and remove many of the smaller buds on each stem. Chrysanthemum blooms will be much better if a covering is placed over them during the cold fall rains or on the nights of frosts.

The Delphiniums (Larkspurs)

The charming and immensely popular delphinium, which is better known, perhaps, by its common name, larkspur, is well adapted for beds and borders. There are both perennial and annual sorts. For variety and beauty of blossoms, few other plants can equal the perennial delphiniums, especially the improved English or hybrid kinds. Growing to a height of three to six feet, they bear on their erect stems long, graceful spikes of magnificent flowers, ranging in color from pure white through all shades of blue, while the clean, curiously cut foliage shows off to advantage. If the stems are cut off close to the ground when the flowers begin to wither, second and third crops will follow and the season of blooming is thus prolonged until late fall.

Delphiniums are easily cultivated. They succeed best in deeply dug, loamy soil, enriched with fine manure, but any well-fertilized soil will give good results. Seed sown in the hotbed or indoors in February will produce plants which should begin to bloom in the garden about the middle of June. When seed is sown in the open ground flowers may not come until the second season. As soon as the weather is favorable for transplanting, set the young plants from two to two and one-half feet apart in the bed. Apply a little bonemeal to the soil around the plants during the summer, and in very dry weather give them a copious supply of water. Dusting the crowns with coal ashes before winter sets in will protect them from insects. Among the good varieties are: belladonna, turquoise blue; Chinense, gentian blue; formosum, deep blue with white center; moerheimi, pure white. There are many others with larger flowers.

The annual larkspurs bear spikes of handsome flowers and their fine colors are strikingly effective in the bed or shrubbery border. They grow two to three feet high and in a sunny situation bloom all summer. Seed should be sown in the open ground in April.

The Geraniums

An ideal plant for pots and bedding, the geranium has always been a great favorite in both house and garden, and well deserves its commanding place among the most attractive and satisfactory of old-fashioned flowers. In every section of the country it is popular as a bedding plant and its magnificent trusses of single, semi-double or double flowers, surmounting a wealth of bright green, healthy foliage, furnish a decorative feature which never fails to gain the highest admiration. It is of vigorous habit and a profuse and continuous bloomer, the colors comprising a great number of shades and combinations, with pure white, rose, salmon pink, scarlet and crimson predominating. For many years the geranium has periodically gained acquisitions of wonderful novelties from both European and American introducers, with the result that today it carries a longer list of varieties than most other plants in cultivation. Among the interesting and beautiful types are the cactus-flowering, the ivy-leaved, the scented-leaved and those bearing variegated foliage.

Geraniums may be propagated by sowing seeds in a hotbed, but for ordinary garden purposes the method of raising plants from cuttings is generally preferred. The best time to take cuttings is when the plants have ceased flowering and they may be successfully struck in a propagating house or a frame, using pure loam mixed with sand and lightly pressed into small pots well drained with potsherds. Side shoots which have not flowered, cut close to the stem, are considered the best cuttings. They should not be placed in the pots before the wound has dried up. When the pots are filled give them a gentle watering and keep them in a temperature of fifty to fifty-five degrees. Nipping off the top buds will induce symmetrical and bushy growth. Another way to increase by cuttings is to place the cuttings in shallow

The geranium well deserves its commanding place among the most satisfactory of old-fashioned flowers.

pans and then give them the usual treatment. In the garden bed the soil should be thoroughly pulverized at the time of digging and mixed with well-rotted manure. Transplanting may be done as soon as the weather has become warm and settled. Established plants cut down in the fall are transferred to pots and held during the winter in a temperature of about forty-five degrees.

Among the best varieties are S. A. Nutt, scarlet; Beaute Poitevine, orange rose; Mrs. Lawrence, salmon pink; Mme. Jaulin, peach pink; Mrs. E. G. Hill, orange and white; la favorite, dbl. white; Alphonse Ricard, orange scarlet; Jean Oberle, soft flesh color with pink center; Mme. Buchner, snow white; and Dina Scalarandis, blush.

The Gladiolus

Here we have a regal flower stately enough for the finest mansion, as well as a democratic flower charming for the cottage window and home garden. Each year finds new uses for the gladiolus, which now holds first place among the summer blooming bulbs. First, because of the great range of color; secondly, because of wonderful keeping qualities, each spike keeping over a week; thirdly, because of its easy cultivation, primarily the same as that for potatoes; and, fourthly, by the proper choice of established varieties they can be commended because of their cheapness. This flower is extensively utilized for all kinds of decorative work. Large vases or baskets of the stately flower spikes fill a place quite distinct from any other flower. As a garden subject the gladiolus is unexcelled for furnishing a long season of bloom, extending from mid-July until frost, either in a bed, in which case the plants should be very close, or in clumps in the herbaceous border.

The best soil for the gladiolus is a medium loam. It appreciates good fertility, but seems sensitive to any manure in contact with the bulbs.

Manure is good if applied in the autumn previous to planting. The best fertilizer for general use is one that would be called a potato fertilizer, rich in potash and phosphoric acid, both chemicals being useful in the proper formation of good bulbs. Bonemeal is also extensively used. Liquid manure, when the buds are forming, seems beneficial.

There should be given space in every garden for a planting of gladioli.

Gladioli are not hardy, except some varieties of lemoinei, and even these require protection in New York State. Planting should be deferred until all danger of frost is past. A well-planned succession in planting is advisable. The depth to plant is determined by the character of the soil. In the lightest soil seven or eight inches is not too deep, but in heavy clay four or five inches would be a sufficient depth. There are two reasons why the bulbs should be planted as deep as the character of the soil will permit: first, the gladiolus is moisture-loving, and in deep planting its roots are in the cooler moist soil; secondly, the soil acts as a support, no other support for the stems being necessary ordinarily. Commercially, the bulbs, or as they are more properly called, the corms, are usually planted in rows, often two rows, about six inches apart, in the furrow.

Upon the approach of frost the corms are dug, but the stems are not removed. They are then stored in an airy placed to dry thoroughly. After several weeks the last year's exhausted corms and the old stems may be removed and the stock cleaned. The best storage temperature is from 40 to 45 deg., and in a rather dry atmosphere. If the corms become heated they start prematurely; if too humid they rot or start into growth. A shallow tray three or four inches deep insures the corms against heating.

Propagation

(1) By seeds. By this method new varieties are obtained, but the standard varieties, being hybrids, do not come true when started from seed. (2) By cormels, or "spawn" (the small, hard-shelled little cormels borne upon the old ones). These, if planted (preferably in a 3 in. flat) during the spring following the season in which they were produced, will bloom one or two years later, or usually one year sooner than from seed. (3) By the annual renewal of corms of which there are from one to six, produced above the old corm each year.

The Iris

Could the real beauty of the coloring of the iris be expressed in words, such a description would be a masterpiece. The word "iris" has come from the Greek for rainbow. It is the colors of the rainbow we deal with in growing iris. When the form of the iris bloom is considered we realize that it is most dainty and elegant and surpassed by few other flowers. The fragrance of many varieties is so dainty that it vies with that of any rose. The adaptability to varying conditions, such as excessive moisture, continued drought, extended freezing and almost perfect

Year after year these irises give prodigal returns for minimum care.

baking, is remarkable. The rapid reproduction of most varieties is an important point in its favor. Because of all of these favorable attributes we commend the various forms of this incomparable flower.

We shall mention only the forms of easiest growth. They will be sufficient until one realizes the true range of excellence which is found in the roll of its one hundred and forty species; then you will grow Californian iris from seed, you will erect frames especially for the proper drying of your Oncocyclus iris and no amount of labor will be too much if the new variety can only be made to bloom for you. That is for the future.

To appreciate the iris one should have a little idea of what its parts are. The flower consists normally of three petals which stand upright, and three which droop more or less; these are well named, respectively, the standards and the falls. Inside of the standards are noticed three petal-like parts; these are actually lobes of the pistil, the female parts of the flower; it is a most peculiar formation, especially when we know that the little fringed pocket at the apex of each is really the stigma or part which receives the pollen. The two-forked tip of the pistil is called the crest. Just beneath the pistil is a stamen, the male part of the flower. If we look

at a German iris we will find a very heavy beard on the base of the fall, while the Japanese and Siberian irises do not have this tuft of hairs. In some irises the standards are very small, often smaller than the crests of the pistil. Many times the standards, though large, do not stand upright at all.

There is a notion that irises are all water loving; this is not true. Two irises only can be planted in the water; these are the common Blue Flag (Iris versicolor), our little wild iris, and the yellow European iris (Iris pseudacorus). These two irises may well be used in water gardens, but they will succeed perfectly in ordinary garden soil. The wild iris is hardly as beautiful as some of the others that might be grown, but the yellow European iris has luxuriant foliage and large, clear yellow flowers, and deserves wider popularity.

The Japanese iris (I. Kaempferi) and the Siberian iris (I. sibirica) thrive very nicely at the edges of pools; they will not grow with their crowns submerged, however. The flower of the Japanese iris differs from the others in being flat, the standards not being upright. There are several forms of the flower; some have six petals and others, because the standards are much abbreviated, are called

Typical German Iris Bloom.

The wonderful Japanese Iris (I. lævigata. or I. Kaempferi), colonized. While enjoying a moist, open situation this Iris does well in a variety of soils and positions.

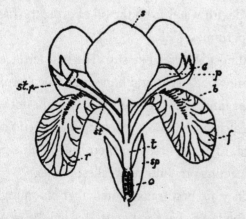

s, standard, p, pistil; c, crest of pistil; st. p, stigmatic pocket; st, stamen; f, fall; t, tube; sp, spathe valve: o, ovary; r, reticulation; b, beard.

three-petaled iris. The flowers are very large. They enjoy good fertility and a constant stirring of the soil, which should never bake over the roots. The Japanese iris likes to be flooded when in bloom, but at no other time. They bloom later than the other sorts and varieties can be selected which bloom from mid-June till nearly the end of July.

The Siberian iris, with its blue or white flowers and grass-like foliage, is indeed a beautiful garden subject. The spikes are also effective in vase arrangements. The white variety, snow queen, with its golden blotch on the falls, is excellent, as are also the intense blue orientalis varieties. Neither the Japanese nor the Siberian iris is insistent upon being planted in moist soil.

Under "bulbs" we have given a discussion of the Spanish and English irises.

Perhaps no group is so easily grown, requiring as little care as does the German iris group. They are very hardy and stand all sorts of adverse conditions, growing in the parched soil under the eaves of houses, thriving where children tramp the soil to the hardness of a cement pavement, blooming under trees choked by grass, and still give flowers as pretty as an orchid. They should always be planted quite on the surface of the soil, not deeply, and are best placed in bold groups. So rapid is the multiplication

Iris border backed with shrubs in a semi-wild, garden.

that if a fine variety costs a dollar it usually produces so rapidly that the same plant will give five or ten dollars-worth of stock for another year. The dwarf varieties of German iris are known as pumila hybrids. When the tall varieties were crossed with the dwarf varieties an intermediate group resulted, known as intermediate or interregna varieties. The blooms are large and most exquisite in color. The range of colors in German iris is extraordinary, varying from pure white to deepest yellow, purple and violet and including delicate lavender, blue and even approaching pink. The Pumila varieties are the earliest to bloom in this group, usually in early May. They are followed by the Intermediate, then last, the tall, a few of which open in late May or early June.

It is interesting to know that Iris florentina, the old-fashioned sweet, early-blooming, pale lavender-white species, is the orris-root of commerce and believed to be the original of the *Fleur-de-lis*, or French national floral emblem. The belles of ancient Greece grew it both for flowers and root, and the growing of this root is a leading industry of northern Italy. The rhizomes are dug in the summer and peeled to remove the outer bark. The separate joints are laid aside to dry until the end of two years, when they will have acquired a delicate fragrance of violets. The root pieces, which have a white appearance, are brought to the market by perfumers who powder them for dentifrices or sachet powders, or when distilled with water from the oil of orris, the basis of many perfumes.

Almost all irises like sun. The best fertilizers for them are wood-ashes and bonemeal. The German iris likes lime; the Japanese iris is thought not to like a calcium soil. Most irises are sensitive to active manure. After the first year there will be little need for protecting any but the weakest plants.

They are best transplanted after blooming, when the leaves have matured; this will be in August or September, not much later, for roots should become established before freezing. The spring is considered a poor time to move them. When iris clumps begin to choke themselves out by covering the ground so that young shoots have difficulty in establishing roots, they should be broken up and set in another place. Due to the prolificacy of German iris this will be necessary every third year.

The Marigold

There is something captivating even about the name marigold, and all the plants bear yellow or golden flowers. Most of us, after all, love the gold.

They can be had in heights from cushion-like dwarf (Tagetes pumila) of the French type, and the coarser, taller Scotch marigold or Pot marigold, to the three and one-half foot of the robust African ones. Like the zinnias, they bloom profusely and for many weeks. They all love a sunny position and do reasonably well in light soil, albeit, a fairly fertile one. Seed can be sown in May where the plants are to grow, or seedlings may be raised in hot frames in boxes to be transplanted at the latter end of April.

The Pansy

Favorites with all, pansies are rarely omitted from the flower garden, be it large or small. Everybody loves the pansy. The reason is that the rich, velvety substance and brilliant colors of the flowers make it so radiantly beautiful and attractive. Nothing is more effective in spring and summer than a design or bed composed of a good selection of pansies in full bloom; the dainty flowers also make charming table decorations. Hybridization and scientific culture have produced many wonderful strains, as shown in the lists annually presented to the public by the various seed firms. For instance, we now have the giant Trimardeau pansies, the ruffled pansies, the mottled pansies, the butterfly pansies and a hundred and one other sorts, all bearing flowers of a more or less gorgeous character.

Pansies are rarely omitted from a flower garden, be it large or small.

Pansy seedlings may be propagated in spring for summer blooming, or in the autumn for early spring use. Select beds sheltered from cutting winds, with the soil rich, cool and moist, but well drained. For outdoor bedding in the early spring sow the seed in August in drills, covering one-sixteenth to one-eighth inch deep. When the seedlings are large enough to handle, thin out or transplant to stand eight or nine inches apart. Cultivate and keep the ground free from weeds, and apply water freely in dry weather. Protect the young plants during the winter with straw or other light litter; they are sometimes carried over in coldframes. In extremely hot weather temporary shade should be provided, as the rays of the midday sun tend to injure the colors of the blooms.

The Petunia

This most pleasing annual may be fittingly described as everybody's flower. It succeeds everywhere, even under unfavorable conditions, and no garden, however small, is complete without it. Given a sunny location, it can always be depended upon to furnish blooms in abundance from early summer until late autumn. It grows twelve to eighteen inches in height, produces single or double flowers of many exquisite shades and colorings, and makes a grand show in beds, borders, window boxes

Single petunias.
Petunias succeed everywhere, even under unfavorable conditions, and no garden is complete without them.

or vases. In recent years new and beautiful strains have been added to the petunias list, the blossoms being of exceptionally large size and in many cases finely ruffled or fringed. Seed is best started in March or April in a hotbed or in a box placed in a sunny window of the house. Set out the young plants, when ready, one foot apart each way. The weaker seedlings should not be thrown out, as they often bear the finest double flowers. In sheltered positions the petunias will sometimes seed itself and come up the following season.

The Peony

Like many other plants intensely interesting because of their charming blooms, the peony first came to the attention of the world as a medicinal plant. It was named after Paeon, a mythological doctor, for the roots of the species officinalis have been used in the making of a broth.

Peonies are easy to grow; they are permanent and when once established are impatient of being moved. They are perfectly hardy wherever apples can be grown and can easily be protected in the colder regions. They bear large and showy flowers, of a great range of colors; some are delicately scented. The plants are so free from insects that they prove themselves to be ideal for cut blooms or landscape flowers.

There are a number of interesting species of the peony. The most seen is the Chinese peony (Pæonia albiflora). This is the standard peony of which we have so many matchless varieties. The plant of the narrow-leaved or fennel-leaved peony (P. tenuifolia) is very beautiful, but the blooms last a short time. It blooms in May, the pretty scarlet flowers nestling among the dainty dissected foliage. At about the same season the shrubby or hardy tree peonies (P. Moutan) open their enormous glossy single or double flowers. The shrubby peony grows very slowly. It should be planted where it is sheltered from the wind. Closely following in season are the European peonies (P. officinalis). These are the old-fashioned crimson peonies of the garden; they produce very satiny-petaled blooms, which possess a not unpleasant soapy odor.

The last groups to bloom are the albiflora varieties. These often begin to bloom in New York State for Memorial Day. For a succession of varieties to bloom, the Rev. C. S. Harrison, who might

Mons. Jules Elie.
Be sure to include this one in your collection.

Peonies are glorious in a massed bed, equally striking when brought into the home, with their long stems and massive flowers.

be called the Chaplain of American Gardeners, recommends the varieties P. umbellata rosea, l'Esperance, Edulis Superba, Monsieur Dupont, Richardson's Rubra Superba, Henry Woodward, Richardson's Grandiflora. Mr. Harrison, speaking further of prolonging the blooming of the peony, says: "There is also a system by which the blooming of a single variety can be prolonged. Take a row, say of Festiva maxima; wait until the ground has frozen solid; leave the end of the row uncovered. Then, farther on, put on mulching and increase the depth until, at the other end, it is a foot to eighteen inches deep; leave this on. The covering keeps the frost in; then the plant will take some time to push up through the mulching. You can apply this system to the later varieties and so lengthen the flowering season considerably."

A word may be necessary to explain the method of doubling in the peony. The normal or single flower is composed of *petals* (we shall call all the petals, *guard petals* in this case); *stamens*, or the male part of the flower (these are yellow at the tip and bear pollen); and the *pistil*, each section of which we call a *carpel* (this is often red and bears the seed). In doubling, the stamens become wider and wider until they resemble the petals; then we call them *petaloids*. In the same way the seed-bearing power is lost by

the female parts, changing to resemble petals at the center of the flower.

The following are the types recognized by the American Peony Society:

1. *Single*. There are a few broad petals, the center being filled with stamens.
2. *Anemone-flowered*. The stamens are a trifle widened, closely resembles the Japanese.
3. *Japanese*. In this type doubling has just begun; the filaments of the stamens have widened; the anthers are also much developed. The guard petals, the petals at the base of the flower, are the same as in the single varieties.
4. *Bomb*. The petaloids, or the transformed stamens, have become still wider and thickly set; the petals approach the guards in form, but are still distinguishable from each other.
5. *Semi-double*. Several rows of large petals and some with petaloids in all stages of transformation. A loose bloom.
6. *Crown*. When the carpels, the parts of the pistil, transform into petals they may form a different center from the guard petals and petaloids, giving the appearance of a small rose in the center of the flower.
7. *Semi rose*.
8. *Rose*. A fully double form. The stamens and carpels are both transformed. It is really a developed Bomb, for in this case the petaloids are merely wider and indistinguishable from the guard petals.

The following is a list of best varieties for home grounds:

- Festiva maxima. White, center carmine; medium early.
- Couronne d'Or. A late-blooming, semi-double white.
- Monsieur Jules Elie. An early silvery pink.

- GRANDIFLORA. Late, bright flesh pink.
- DUCHESSE DE NEMOURS. Deep pink, early; a fine double.
- EDULIS SUPERBA. An early dark pink.
- FELIX CROUSSE. Midseason; a brilliant red.
- JEANNE D'ARC. Large, soft pink; midseason.
- AVALANCHE. Milk white, creamy center.
- EUGENE VERDIER. Salmon pink, changing to clear pink.
- MARIE LEMOINE. A very late sulfur white.
- MODESTE GUERIN. Bright rose pink; midseason.
- MME. DUCEL. Silvery pink, flushed salmon; vigorous dwarf; midseason.
- MME. VERNEVILLE. Rosy white, with sulfur white guard petals.
- BARONESS SCHRÖDER. Flesh changing to white; vigorous: excellent.
- LIVINGSTONE. Fine late flower of silvery pink.
- MONSIEUR DUPONT. Ivory white with lively carmine border on central petals.
- LA TULIPE. Semi-double; almost white; mid-season.
- DELACHIE. Dark red; semi-double; mid-season.

Planting and Cultivation

The soil should preferably be heavy rather than light; a clay loam is excellent if it can be worked deeply. The peony is a gross feeder and enjoys a good mulch of well-rotted manure in the winter. The time for planting is August or September, right after the plant has completed its growth. If transferred in the spring many of the feeding roots will be torn from the plants. The roots of the peony are thick, almost no fibrous roots being formed; instead very fine, delicate feeding roots start from the main roots.

The plants should be planted at least three feet apart and the crowns should be buried three inches below the surface, and if planted too deeply, the plants will not flower freely. If they are planted too shallow the winter frosts will heave them from the soil.

The stalks should be cut off a few inches above the soil just before winter. A winter mulch of from four to six inches of well decayed manure will also prevent heaving and winter injury. When the plants have finished blooming, the cultivation must not be neglected since they must make a good growth and mature their foliage, else the crop of bloom for the next year will suffer. Every five years the peony should be divided and replanted, unless the plants stand far enough apart to allow root development. It takes two or three years for a commercial three- to five-eyed root to throw characteristic blooms.

Types of Peonies
S.—Single. showing (g), guard petals; (s), stamens; (c), carpels or lobes of pistil.
J.—Japanese type: stamens wider than in Single.
B.—Bomb type. The stamens become narrow petals, called petaloids.
SD.—Semi-double. Many petaloids are quite wide and are mixed among the stamens.
C.—Crown. The stamens are wider and petal-like. The carpels, which before have remained unchanged, are now petal-like.
R.—Rose. In this type there is an entire transformation of that bloom.

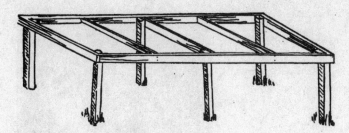

Rack for supporting peonies. Also used as a tomato support.

Preserving the Blooms

Preserve the blooms after bringing into the house by stabbing or slitting the stems below the water line.

Disbudding

The albiflora varieties produce many buds in a cluster; if the best size blooms are preferred, all but the main or crown bud should be removed while they are yet small. Some weaker growing varieties are especially benefited by this practice. Single varieties are not disbudded.

Staking

Certain very floriferous varieties will need some sort of support. One of the best and most permanent methods is to build a rack of wood over the peony border and train the young shoots inside of this rack. For individual plants there is no better way than to use a barrel hoop supported on three uprights.

Diseases

There are several diseases which attack the leaves, buds and stems. They are easily kept in check by spraying with Bordeaux mixture when the plants first start into growth in the spring. Besides this, the diseased parts and all stems should be burned each fall, for only by careful sanitation can the trouble be lessened.

The Poppy • Papaver

The poppy should be given a place in every garden, it is so graceful and delicate and beautiful. The Shirley poppy is rightly considered the finest of the annuals. There is nothing more fairy-like than a bed of these grand single poppies, with their long, slender stems surmounted by silken blooms of the most charming tints. As cut flowers in the house they are most attractive and will last for several days if gathered before expanding. There are many more splendid strains of annual poppies, notably the double peony-flowered, the fringed varieties and the dainty yellow-petaled California.

The hardy perennial Oriental poppy, with its gorgeous dark scarlet flowers, blotched black at the base of each petal, makes a highly pleasing show about the beginning of June. The stately Iceland poppy (P. nudicaule), also a hardy perennial, with light green, fern-like foliage, bears a wealth of brilliant flowers on slim stems. These poppies will bloom the first year from seeds.

Seeds of annuals should be sown early in the spring, scattered not too thickly and covered with a light sprinkling of soil. Thin out to five or six inches apart. They do not bear transplanting. When sown in the spring Oriental poppy plants die down in July and August, but reappear in the fall, when they should be removed to their permanent quarters.

Sweet Peas

It would appear from the foregoing that the answer to the question of where to plant sweet peas is "everywhere," but the fact remains that sweet peas, to give a measure of pleasure, require much care. They should be planted on a well-drained soil only, or one in which the excessive rains of spring will not cause water to stand around the roots and start mildew. They endure little shade, for the plants should make a sturdy growth. In the shade the growth is weak and spindly and but few flowers are produced.

Place peas, then, in the open, giving them all available light and air, although a little shade from midday suns of June and July is, of course, beneficial. Hot weather causes short stems on peas and the best hay and grain weather ends them.

Preparation of the Soil

This is an important point. Peas like the cool soil and attempt to strike down deeply. Dig a trench two or three feet deep, break up and turn over the subsoil. Do not use if for top soil if it is poor. Put in a liberal amount of stable manure and work in a heavy dressing of bonemeal. This preparation should be made in the fall and the bed left all winter. When working over in the spring give a good, liberal coating of well decayed manure or some fertilizer. If the soil is deficient in lime, dust the surface with fresh lime in fall or winter, using it as soon as slaked. As early as the ground can be prepared in the spring, dig a trench or furrow five to six inches deep and six inches wide. Sow the seed on the bottom and cover with two inches of soil. As the vines grow up, fill in the soil until level with the garden surface. Sweet pea specialists advise using a liberal quantity of seed, enough to make sure of securing a good stand, and when well started, thin the plants out to two to five inches apart. Sweet peas are often sown in double rows five inches apart in the trench, with trellis or other support placed between.

Sowing Seeds in Pots

In order to gain a month in season sweet peas may be sown in three-inch pots in February and placed in a coldframe. But they are generally sown a month before wanted for outdoor planting and a smaller pot is used. Four seeds are sown in each pot. The frame should be thoroughly cleaned and dusted with soot or lime. They can stand quite a lot

The sweet pea—perhaps the most dainty of all flowering annuals.

of cold, but do not have them wet at the same time. Transplant outdoors when possible; this is usually about mid-April. Normally, the seed should be sown in open ground as early as March. As soon as the soil is warm enough the seeds will germinate.

Fall Sowing

For the autumn sowing of sweet peas, a piece of soil should be selected which will warm quickly in the spring. Spade it up to good depth, two to three feet, but use no manure. Make a trench two inches deep and sow the seed thickly and cover with loose soil. When the seedlings have germinated and freezing weather has begun, cover with four inches of coarse litter or straw, which must be removed in the early spring after heavy frosts are past. The seed should be sown so that the shoots are just at the surface of the soil when winter sets in; therefore, sow in late October or early in November, according to latitude.

Summer Treatment

Give frequent cultivation and when the plants are nicely budded work bonemeal into the soil along the rows. If conditions are very hot and dry

Roses on arches and sweet peas on trellises between.
On either side are rose beds in the lawn. Iris beds in the
foreground.

give the plants frequent syringings, which will keep down the red spider, and will not allow aphis a chance to multiply.

Staking

Perhaps no method is so successful as the use of brush. Stretching string from pole to pole is an easy way. Such cord can be easily removed when the peas are through blooming. Coarse poultry yard netting is rather useful for supporting the vines, but has two objections: it must be cleaned each year, and it is thought to become heated a little too much, causing the sweet pea vines to dry prematurely.

Gathering the Flowers

The flowers should be kept closely picked during the blossoming season, as the vines cease to bloom when the seed pods are allowed to set.

Preparation of Beds for Bulbs

Nearly all bulbs succeed especially well on the sandier loams, but will even grow on nearly pure sand or heavy clay. The heavy clay soils are easily loosened by the addition of sand or coal ashes. Manure used at all must be so thoroughly incorporated with the soil that it impossible for any of it to be in contact with the roots or bulbs, both of which appear to be very sensitive to manure. Bonemeal, spread over the soil at planting, is excellent. Leaf mold is ideal for mixing with the soil if it is obtainable.

Time of Planting

Some bulbs do not stand the cold; they are planted in spring and must be dug before winter each year. Examples of such bulbs are: gladiolus, summer hyacinth (Galtonia candicans), montbretia, tigridia, tuberose, zephyranthes, Tuberous begonia, canna, dahlia. Most other bulbs should be planted in the autumn. It is best to plant them as soon as they can be obtained from the dealer. If they remain out of the soil too long much of the nourishment is evaporated. Especially susceptible to deterioration due to deferred planting are crocus, lilies, snowdrops and fritillaria. This will bring the greater share of bulb planting in October.

Planting Bulbs

The rule for depth of planting is that they should be planted twice their diameter deep in the soil. This does not always apply, for it is usually better to get them a little deeper. The useful chart given on the following page shows the depth to plant. It is advisable in planting choice sorts to set them on a layer of one or two inches of sand. This will insure good drainage and keep bulbs from decaying.

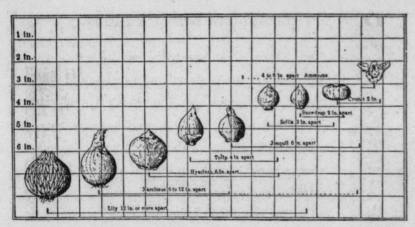

This diagram shows approximately how deep and how far apart to plant the different kinds of hardy bulbs in light soil. In heavy soil plant an inch to an inch and a half nearer the surface.

List of Ferns With Cultivation Tips

- ADIANTUM PEDATUM (Maidenhair). Prefers a well-drained, light soil. It is of a poor color when grown in the sun.
- ASPIDIUM. (See *Dryopteris*).
- ASPLENIUM: ACROSTICHOIDES. Moisture loving; some shade. Endures sunlight if cool.
- ANGUSTIFOLIUM. Avoid the removal of old fronds. New crop springs up and weakens the plant.
- ASPLENIUM FILIX-FŒOWNA (Lady Fern). Good, rich loam, moist. Excellent, well-formed fronds, which are very variable.
- PINNATIPIDIJM. A small evergreen fern found in depth of glens. Useful for planting between stones.
- PLATYNEURON (Ebony Spleenwort).
- TRICHOMANES. A rock garden plant.
- CAMPTOSORUS RHIZOHPYLUS (Walking Fern). Prefers dry ledges.
- CHEILANTHS LANOSA. Pefers deep shade.
- TOMENTOSA. Prefers less shade more moisture.
- FENDLERI.
- CYSTOPTERIS BULBIFERA. Plant in shade upon a moist bank.
- FRAOILIS. Fronds die curly in August.

- DENNSTÆDTIA (Dick-Sonia) PUNCTILOBULA (Hay-oceutod Feni). Heavy growth. Grow for cutting for summer.
- DRYOPTERIS (Aspidium) BOOTTII. Does not need winter shade.
- CRISTATA, var.
- CLINTONIANUM. Swampy ground.
- FILIX-MAS (Male fern). Rich soil; deep shade.
- GOLDIEANA. Cool, rich soil. Good in acid soil or leaf mold. Large, heavy growth.
- MARGINALE. When transplanted in full leaf the plants rarely survive. Like a rich, moist soil and deep shade.
- NOVEBORACENSIS. Not good for cutting. Easily transplanted.
- SPINULOSA, var. INTERMEDIA (*Spinulose Shield Fern*) Good in wet, and under trees as well.
- THEIYPTERIS. Partial shade in marshes.
- LYGODIUM PALMATUM (The Climbing Fern; Hartford Fern). This fern is difficult to establish. It is moisture loving.

Moisture loving plants bordering the water.

- ONOCLEA SENSIBILIS (Sensitive Fern). Wet ditches and rich, moist soil; partial shade.
- STRUNTHIOPTERIS (Ostrich Fern). Burns in full sunshine.
- OSMUNDA CINNAMOMEA (Cinnamon Fern). Moist, rich.
- CLAYTONIANA (Interrupted Fern). Move while dormant.
- REGALIS. Peaty; branching; edges of brooks.
- POLYPODIUM VULGARE. (*Common polypody*). Can be planted up the ledges of gorges.

Water Lilies

A lily pond of tank, its surface covered with the charming flowers of its aquatic plants, is regarded as an indispensable acquisition in any well arranged garden, for it furnishes a decorative effect as unique as it is handsome. The culture of new kinds of water lilies has made great progress in recent years, and there are now to be had a large number of varieties which produce flowers of unusual beauty, ranging in color from pure white to red, rote, pink, crimson and blue.

Flagstone path through bog-garden and semi-wild garden. Good use can be made of gunneras spiræas, Japanese irises, Knot-grass, Giant Reed and similar plants.

William Tricker, of Arlington, N. J., who specializes in water lilies, says: "These are universally grown, at least where horticulture is one of the fine arts. They are indigenous to all parts of the world, but in no part can all species and varieties be grown to equal such as is possible in our own clime. Here, in a well-appointed garden, or in our public parks and gardens, can be seen our own native species, the European and the many hybrids, the Japan and Egyptian lotus, the Mexican species, the African, Zanzibar and Australian species and hybrids which are various shades of blue, also specimens from tropical India, where the flowers open at night shielded from the burning rays of the sun, and last but not least, the giant Victorias from South America, V. regia from the region of the Amazon and V. Trickeri from Argentina, the tributaries of live Parana river.

"Water lilies are as indispensable as hardy perennial and other decorative plants. Associated with ornamental sub-tropical plants, they lend a moat pleasing and charming effect to the landscape. They are also valuable as cut flowers, especially the tender varieties, both day and night bloomers. The day bloomers furnish superb flowers on long stems in red, white and blue colors. The night blooming varieties possess a charm distinct from all others, the rotors varying from pure white to pink with shades of red, carmine arid crimson, which are very brilliant under artificial light. They are of simple culture, requiring a moderately rich soil, water and sunshine. The hardy varieties should be planted in May in this latitude, and on until the middle of August. The tender water lilies should lie planted about live first of June, when warm, settled weather is assured. Keep the pond filled with water to supply loss by evaporation, but springs and running streams must be avoided as they lower the temperature of the water to a dangerous degree."

Most seed houses will supply plants and complete cultural directions on application.

Rock Gardens

From *Garden Guide: The Amateur Gardeners' Handbook*, edited by A. T. De La Mare, 1920

Construction

The amount of construction necessary will vary according to what is at hand to begin with. Let us suppose that we have a rocky bank which may even be a sort of supporting wall; perhaps we have a small brook whose sides we would like to plant, or we may have to construct the garden from the start.

The first case, that of a rocky bank or wall, is the simplest to manage. It may be necessary to use a wedge to open up some of the cracks so that they become larger: these should be filled with a rather rich, not too light, soil consisting of good loam and one-fourth manure. It is advisable to have all the crevices open into areas of soil. This we cannot do upon natural rock banks. With these natural rock gardens we must take a chance as to the depth of the crack and soil.

In planting a brookside, boulders and rocks will be available usually. The problem here is to build up the rocks informally and with soil between them. Many an innocent summer brook is a bad marauder in the spring. Confute your efforts to the areas above the flood and perhaps sow a few annuals near the water. Do not spend too much energy arranging the rocks nicely in the basin of the brook. The water will no doubt destroy all your efforts.

When we must construct an entirely new rockery, the problem is greater. It should run nearly north and south; this will provide various exposures for different plants. Above all things, avoid any cut stone, brick or anything artificial. Statuary is never at home in a rock garden. If the garden must lie made from flat land, the best thing to do is to dig out a little valley, running it very irregularly. The soil removed can be used to build up on the sides, so that the little vale appears deeper than it is. Shrubs can be planted about the mound on the outside. It must be added that there is danger in having a wet hole instead of a beautiful rock garden if the created valley has poor drainage. This building up of the soil must be done in a very irregular way and care should lie taken that the top soil is saved from the land which will he covered, for it will again be needed to cover the subsoil laid bare.

When the soil has been removed the rocks can be placed. They should never be arranged in correct tiers, nor should the direction of the strata in the rock be seriously changed. The sketch shows the strata of the rocks naturally arranged and provided with a dip which will catch the moisture. Leave plenty of soil space between the rocks and plan little pockets to catch the water. Provide drainage by the use of a quantity of ashes or fine gravel in the center of the mound. The rocks get very hot and some plants may dry readily. If a little water can be provided it should be conducted to the top and allowed to seep down through the crevices. In winter a protection of straw and decayed manure over the plants will be beneficial. It is best not to remove this protection too early. Neglect it a bit. Evergreen brunches are excellent for those covering plants which do not die down each year.

Material for Rock Garden

The rock garden is essentially a wild feature and a great deal of native material should be used. No variegated or freak horticultural varieties should be introduced. Even fancy and well-bred varieties are better when absent. We refer to dressy varieties as the Mme. Chereau German iris or, in fact, anything of this sort. It is well to grow in the rockery the interesting little plants which need special attention to be seen properly.

Bulbs are excellent. Snowdrops, narcissus, scillas, fritillarias and crocuses are all quite necessary.

Large trees should be avoided and some trees especially: for example, hawthorns and elms require much water and should never be planted. The smaller evergreens: junipers and arbor vitæs. Broad-leaved evergreens: yucca and cacti are excellent.

If the rock area is extensive and a very quick result is wished, the use of annuals is excellent. Dr. Southwick has used annuals most effectively

This picture shows a closer, more intimate view of a rock garden. In this instance it is employed most fittingly as an ornamental feature between the inner flower garden and outer semi-wild parts.

Diagram to show in a general way, placing of the boulders or large stones in the making of rock garden. A shelving arrangement is adopted, leaving spaces, called pockets, between the stones. These should be arranged so as to catch the rain. At the same time the water must pass readily away through drainage channels.

in his "Garden of the Heart" in Central Park, N. Y. The otherwise objectionable colors of petunias are there very cheery. Lobelia erinus is indispensable. California poppies, either the golden, the crimson or the white ones, are very pretty. Baby's breath (Gypsophila muralis, the pink, or elegans, the white) adds a graceful touch. The ornamental grasses look well combined in various places with the various blooming perennials. The annual larkspurs and lupines are both good blue subjects. Portulacas, sanvitalias, bouncing bet (Saponaria ocymoides) and nemophila are of just the proper habit for the rockery. Speaking of rock gardens in California, even as far south as Los Angeles, a writer in a paper there says: "Those rock gardens are positively alluring, for if one but follows a bank having a turn in direction of but a quarter circle he may find at one end the Edelweiss of the European Alps, and at the other, through gradual transitional plant zones, cacti from the desert sands. Next to the alpines is often brought in fern dells with trickling streams and waterfalls."

Plants for Window Boxes

From *Garden Guide: The Amateur Gardeners' Handbook*, edited by A.T. De La Mare, 1920

For Shady Situations

- Tuberous begonias
- Begonia semperflorens
- Fuchsias
- Cobæa scandens
- Vinca
- Foliage geraniums
- Crotons
- Funkia yariegata
- Ferns
- Palms
- English ivy
- Trailing euonymus
- Wandering Jew
- *For winter Effect*
- Box (Buxus)
- Dwarf Thuya
- Dwarf Retinispora
- Irish Juniper
- Hemlock, small plants
- White Pine, small plants
- English Ivy
- Trailing Euonymus
- For Sunny Situations
- Geraniums, tall
- Ivy geranium
- Petunia
- Ageratum Houstonianum

For Sunny Situations

- Cobæa scandens
- Phlox Drummondii

- Nasturtiums
- Verbena
- Lobelia erinus
- Coleus
- Lantana
- Cigar Plants (Cuphea)
- German Ivy, or Wandering Jew
- Portulaca
- Mesembryanthemum
- Sweet Alyssum

Dracæna indivisa is always useful in the porch box. When its usefulness in the box is over it may be potted and kept all winter.

The excellent clear colors of verbenas are always admirable when used alone or in combination. They flower profusely and continue fresh in appearance.

Entrance porch and window box. Ampelopais veitchii is well and freely used.

The nasturtium is incomparable for filling urns or for porch decoration. For a northern exposure the Tuberous begonia is excellent. The colors of the single as well as the double varieties are very effective. They should always have the best soil available.

The best vine for trailing over the edge and extending downward for five or six feet is the German ivy. If this has grown into quite a jungle when procured from the florist, cut it back and let it start out gracefully. Vinca, or periwinkle, a variegated green and white vine of exceeding long growth, is everybody's favorite. It stands adverse conditions. Cobæa scandens will trail down or climb up. Creeping Jenny (Lysimachia nummularia) succeeds admirably in shade and, furthermore, in some sections of the country it can be gathered from the wild. Kenilworth ivy (Linaria cymbalaria), a neat, nearly hardy, lavender-flowered trailer, can be tried, also Asparagus sprengeri, a plant popular with the florist and very useful in the window box.

Trailing plants of less rampant growth include: Lobelia erinus (not the compacta variety); the flowering habit is unexcelled. Another blue is the ageratum, which, like lobelia, is always in bloom, and it is fragrant. The trailing varieties of coleus

Paneled window box showing bracket sup- ports, also side brackets above, for plants.

Self-watering window box.
This shows body of box, false bottom, (B) Above water chamber or reservoir (W) and two sponges (S) by which the water passes up to the soil. The water supply is replenished through a tube in the right-hand back corner (T).

have a good habit, but the colors are much mixed. Verbenas and petunias are useful by themselves as well as the front margin of the box.

A little plant useful for the more personal porch boxes is the forget-me-not. It is not very permanent but will bloom when many of the other plants have only started growth. When it finishes blooming it may be dug up. The remaining plants will, no doubt, keep up the foliage and flower effect.

For the green and more formal window box, plants of aucubas can be procured from the florist. In winter the plants are useful on enclosed porches.

All boxes should be raised a little above the base or sill on which they rest; otherwise both box and sill quickly rot. The self-watering type prevents dripping, but even they require attention on hot days, especially when in sunny positions.

Nothing better bespeaks home joys, grace and comforts than a well-filled window box.

Vegetable Gardening

From *Garden Guide: The Amateur Gardeners' Handbook*, edited by A. T. De La Mare, 1920

The Vegetable Garden info and Tips

When the spring comes everybody thinks, or ought to think, about gardens. Professor L. H. Bailey says: "The nature-desire may be perpetual and constant, but, the garden-desire returns with every new springtime." The possibilities of the garden are very great, and the home or kitchen garden has become a national and economic necessity as an adjunct to every home with a plot of round, no matter how small. A bountiful provision of clean, newly gathered produce, secured within a few yards of the kitchen door, tends to diminish burdensome grocery and meat bills; and as they are not subject to deterioration in transportation and by exposure on the markets, home-grown vegetables are always crisp and tender and retain their characteristic flavor.

While the home gardener should never be satisfied with anything but abundant crops of the best quality, let him also bear in mind that the garden should be an expression of orderly arrangement. No garden can do its best without intelligent care. A well thought out scheme must be followed if complete success is to be achieved. Have the plot properly laid out before beginning its development. Mark on the plan the location and quantity of each vegetable to be grown and the dates for sowing and setting. Companion and succession crops should be indicated. With the ground thus planned for utility, the crops may be so arranged that there will be a continuous supply of fresh and superior vegetables for the family table.

In some instances, a vegetable garden is objected to on the ground that it interferes with the beauty of the surrounding effects. But the latter can be made to fit in with the general scheme. A well-planned and neatly-kept vegetable garden need never detract from the general appearance of the place; usually it is a decidedly attractive feature; it lends an air of simplicity and "hominess" which flowers alone cannot furnish. On a "dollars and cents" basis alone, the vegetable garden is, or can almost always be made, a paying factor. Even where that side of the matter is to be disputed there is no question that to get the very best quality of vegetables you must grow your own.

The commercial grower must be guided in his choice of varieties by the market demands, and by the factor of big yields, even though the varieties which meet these requirements may not be those of the best table quality. The home gardener, on the

An amateur's vegetable garden. All the space utilized and everything growing luxuriantly.

other hand, may select varieties which satisfy his own personal taste. Furthermore, there are many vegetables which, to be had at their very best, must be gathered only a few hours before they are used. As an old saying has it: "The pot should be boiling before you pick your corn."

As a healthful recreation, nothing surpasses the cultivation of culinary vegetables. It never gets monotonous, for the work changes from day to day, and every day brings its own problems. The work involved may be made as mild or as strenuous as is desired. If one fears that not enough exercise is to be had with a hoe, a few hours' "trenching" with a spade will give him as big an appetite for his dinner as anything he can find to do.

It is not necessary to hesitate about having a vegetable garden because such a location as you may have available is not naturally the most ideal for the purpose. The plot of ground which cannot, with intelligent preparation, be made to grow successfully practically every one of the garden vegetables is by all means the exception and not the general rule. At the same time it pays well to take advantage of any favorable natural conditions that may be at

hand. The best soil is what is termed a "sandy loam," that is, a good clay soil in which there is enough material of a sand-like character to keep it friable and workable at all times of the year, while moisture is retained by it for a long time. If you have only a heavy clay soil, it can be improved by adding sand, wood ashes, sifted coal ashes, lime and humus. If the soil is light and sandy, heavy loam or muck added to it will improve it, and humus will also be very beneficial.

Drainage is one of the most important factors. If your garden spot is low and wet, by all means put in a drain tile at the first opportunity. Deep spading, and in extreme cases, loosening up the subsoil with agricultural blasting powder, will tend to overcome this difficulty.

If the garden can be located in a spot where it is protected from prevailing winter and spring winds, the earliness of the crops will be advanced very noticeably. A good, thick hedge of hemlock, spruce, or privet to the north and west of the garden, if it is not naturally sheltered, may be made to serve the double purpose of providing a wind shield, and of screening it from other parts of the place.

Small vegetable garden on suburban lot with neat wire fence on left and wooden pathway.

Digging, Manuring and Preparing the Soil

With the soil adequately enriched and thoroughly prepared, success is half won before you begin. Insufficient preparation, no matter how good your seeds may be, will remain a drag and a handicap throughout the entire season. The soil is the sole source of nourishment for the tremendous development plants will have to make through the comparatively few weeks of the growing season. All their food is absorbed in the form of a weak solution. We have already spoken of the necessity for thorough drainage. The soil must also be well pulverized. It pays, therefore, to take time to prepare, just as thoroughly as you possibly can, your garden soil, no matter how impatient you may be to get at the more interesting tasks of seed sowing and planting.

If your garden plot is sufficiently large for a horse or team to turn in, plowing will be much cheaper and on the whole much more satisfactory. Unless your soil is very light and sandy, it will pay to plow as deeply as possible without digging up the subsoil. If possible, plow or spade up in late fall, leaving the soil in ridges, harrowing in spring. If not able to do this, then plow early in the spring. If the garden has to be dug by spade, you will have to watch carefully to see that the job is done thoroughly. It is hard, slow work and nothing is to be gained by trying to skimp it. The garden that is dug shallow, left lumpy or merely fine on the surface, cannot give good results. Dig at least ten to twelve inches deep. Manure should be spread evenly over the ground before spading. It is usually best to throw the first row or furrow of soil out entirely, and then put the manure from the next strip on the bottom of the furrow dug out, proceeding in this manner across the piece.

When planting or sowing is to be done the whole plot should be raked over. It may be that only a small part of it will be wanted for immediate use for the hardiest seeds or plants, but if it is all given the same treatment the moisture will be conserved. It pays to take a good deal of care and time to get all trash and stones raked up and removed before you think of getting the surface ready for planting.

For practical results the enriching of your garden can be accomplished in no better way than by the application of all the manure you can conveniently get. It should be well-rotted and not green and lumpy. Horse and cattle manure mixed that has been kept under cover and has thoroughly fermented but not "fire-fanged" or burned out, is the best. If you can get enough of this to spread it three or four inches deep all over your garden, you will have the foundation for big crops.

Chicken manure is particularly powerful, but should have been kept so that it is fine and dry, and not stuck together in a pasty mass. If you have only a small quantity, it is wise to keep it just for use in hills and for transplanting rather than to spread it over the whole garden. Sheep manure, like chicken manure, is very high in nitrogen, and should be used in the same way. Within recent years it has been possible to purchase cattle, horse and sheep manure in standardized, prepared forms which are dry and convenient to handle. Where yard manure cannot be conveniently obtained, these can be used.

Because it has been increasingly difficult to get manures in sufficient quantities, commercial fertilizers have come more into use. As it is more convenient, the small gardener usually buys his fertilizer in the form of a completely mixed preparation.

It will be well to have on hand, however, a small quantity each of fine ground bone, guano or dried blood. These are all quick acting fertilizers which can be used in hills or drills. You can also use all the wood ashes you can get. Dustings of lime are also helpful. Commercial "humus" or prepared decayed vegetable matter is inexpensive and will prove very beneficial. It is often advertised.

Sowing and Transplanting

The operations of planting and transplanting are two at which the gardener must become expert as soon as possible. The first step is to have a thoroughly prepared seed bed or planting surface. Have the soil thoroughly pulverized. It may then be left until ready for use. Just before you sow or plant, the surface should again be gone over with an iron rake. Make it as smooth and line as you possibly can.

Directions for Sowing

It is best to buy seed from a good, reliable seed house rather than to depend upon what you may find at the local hardware or grocery store. Small seeds such as lettuce, radish and onions may be merely raked into the surface; medium size seeds, such as beets, spinach and parsnips, from one-quarter to one-half inch and the comparatively large seeds, such as cabbage, carrots and pumpkins, about, one-half inch deep. In showery weather the seeds should be covered more lightly than in normal conditions, in a very light soil, or in hot, dry weather, cover more deeply. In extra early sowings of peas, put the seeds in a little deeper but not much.

Lettuce, beets, onions. carrots, peas and wire netting support for peas. This garden is a model of flood keeping.

As a general guide, sow onions, (also plant onion sets) smooth peas, early beets, radishes, spinach, turnips and cabbage just as soon as the ground can be worked in the spring. When peach and pear trees are in bloom, the medium hardy seeds, including beets, carrots kohl-rabi, lettuce, wrinkled peas, parsnips, salsify, tomatoes, Swiss chard may be sown and also lettuce, cauliflowers, beets and onion plants from the coldframes may be set out.

When the apple trees are in blossom, now the tenderest seeds—beans, sweet corn, cucumbers, okra, melons, pumpkins and squash.

After all danger from late frost is past, set out growing plants of tomatoes, peppers, egg plants, pole beans, melons, sweet corn and okra.

Poor germination results ore often due to the fact that seeds are loosely covered in the soil. They should be well firmed and covered. Firming can generally be done well enough with the back of the hoe or rake.

For neatness make every row straight, using your garden line and reel frequently. Tag every row as soon as it is sown or planted, marking on the date as well as the name of the variety. You will thus be able to keep track of the time required for the different varieties to nature, which will be of great value to you in succeeding years.

Transplanting

Transplanting should be done preferably during showery weather, or in the late afternoon, and the plants will take hold more quickly. If they are shaded in some way for a few days, especially if the weather is windy and sunny, all the better. An irrigation system is of the greatest benefit, in transplanting or planting, as the work can be done at any time with an almost positive certainty of success. In all transplanting the soil ought to be pressed firmly.

Seeds may be sown directly in the soil, but usually it is better to sow in "flats" or seed pans, which can be moved about from one sash to another and handled more conveniently in transplanting. Small seeds should he barely covered from sight, while larger ones should be covered to the depth mentioned a few paragraphs bock. It is important to press the seed firmly into the soil when sowing. Label each variety carefully and water with a fine spray so as to not wash out the seeds.

As soon as the little seedlings are up it will be necessary to give some fresh air every day or two to keep them healthy and vigorous, the temperature bring kept at from 60 to 75 deg. according to the things being grown. As soon as the first two or three true leaves appear, the seedlings should be transplanted, either into other "flats" or into the frames, setting them from two to three inches apart each way so they will have plenty of room.

During this season watering should be done only on bright mornings so that the soil will have a chance to dry off before night, as this will lessen the danger of "damping off." Avoid over-watering, as the soil dries out very slowly when the sashes have to be kept on most of the time.

Tomatoes, peppers and eggplants should be transplanted a second time, preferably to pots, before being set outdoors. If they have been given plenty of room at the first shift in the frames or lists, they can be put into three and a half or four inch pots, and be in bud and blossom when set into the garden.

It is very important that all plants, whether hardy or tender, should be "hardened off" carefully before being moved from the frames to the open garden. To do this, leave them uncovered all the time for several days and nights before you set them out, putting on the sashes only if frost threatens. Should plants inadvertently get touched by frost, watering them with ice-cold water in the morning and keeping them shaded from the sun will often enable them to recover when they might otherwise be lost.

Watering—Irrigating

Within the last few years there have been developed several systems for applying water artificially. Any gardener who has a water supply with thirty pounds pressure available can get his own rain whenever he wants it by installing an irrigation system, at a very slight cost.

The type that has been most widely used consists of horizontal piping supported a few feet above the surface of the garden and perforated at regular intervals. These pipes can be turned by a handle and a valve turns the water on or off as needed. A single line of pipe will water a strip of ground twenty-five feet wide on either side, or a total of fifty feet.

Another system which is slightly more expensive and applies the water more rapidly, has adjustable circular sprays placed every twenty five or thirty feet along the line of pipe. It also does excellent work.

Watering with a hose by hand is not to be compared with water applied by a modern irrigating system. The soil can be soaked evenly and to as great a depth as desired, the water being put on whenever and wherever wanted by simply turning a valve and occasionally turning the pipe. For very small gardens a portable system of both types can be had.

General Principles of Cultivation

Late afternoon or evening is the best time for watering vegetables. If a hand hose is used, wet the ground thoroughly by letting the spray rise in the air and fall in a fine shower. To produce a similar result hold the sprinkling can as high as possible.

What is "cultivation?" Why do we do it and what does it accomplish? We cultivate to keep down weeds that might rob the growing crop of sunlight, air and nourishment; to conserve the moisture in the soil; to keep the soil open and aerated, and to pulverize the soil or break up its particles and thus assist the chemical and bacteriological changes in the soil. Cultivation brings these results. It also creates what is called "a soil mulch," i. e., a layer of dry soil on the surface which checks the loss of moisture from the lower layers to the surface where it evaporates rapidly.

The cultivation work required on any crop will depend largely on whether or not you get the first hoeing and weeding done just as soon as it is possible to do it, or let it go for a few days or a week later.

Within a week or ten days the soil between the rows will have begun to form a crust again, and new crop of weed seedlings may have sprouted. This means another hoeing promptly. We do not think that it is any exaggeration to say that eighty percent of the work in taking care of gardens is due to the fact that these hoeings and hand weedings are allowed to go for several days after they should have been attended to. The tedious task of hand weeding may be lessened considerably by using one of the small hand weeders.

Cultivation should be kept up frequently enough to maintain a dust mulch at all times. Cultivation with a wheel hoe should be kept up as long as it is possible to get between the rows. Then you should substitute for it a double or slide hoe. The types with runners or wheel to guide the blade and hold it even do much better and easier work. By all means, provide yourself with one.

Rotation of Crops

Garden rotation—that is, changing the location of vegetable plantings each season—is of much importance and should be carried out as far as possible. An excellent plan to follow is to raise surface crops one year on a plot where root crops were grown the year before.

Insects and Diseases

There are a number of insects which are almost certain to put in appearance every season. One important thing in combating insects and diseases is to be prepared to ward off attack. In cases where preventive measures are not possible, be prepared to act immediately if trouble appears. Owing to the large number of remedies, cures and poisons which the gardener sees advertised or hears about, he is likely to get the idea that the question of plant pests is such a complicated one that no simple and systematic measures are possible. As a matter of fact, warfare with plant troubles, while it is always serious enough, is by no means as complicated as at first appears. The first step to take and the most important thing to know is what kind of enemy you are fighting in any particular case. While their

A vegetable garden for supplying a large household. Here, and in the smaller gardens depicted on other pages. Cleanliness and careful cultivation are pre-eminent. Observe the handsome pergola around the exterior.

number is legion, they can be classified into three or four groups (as spoken of in a chapter on insect pests and fungous diseases), against each of which the same weapons are effective.

Harvesting and Storing

There are thousands of amateur gardeners who leave enough fruit and vegetables on or in the ground at the end of the season to make all the difference between profit and loss on their season's operations. Learn to utilize everything you grow. Every head of cabbage that splits, every ear of corn, or handful of beans that gets too old to use, every root that is left to freeze in the ground, is just so much waste. While many things can be successfully stored through the winter, or a large part of it, others must be canned. The usual mistake is to try to do all the canning in a rush at the end of the season. The prejudice against canned things is largely due to the fact that they are not canned until they are already old and tough. (See chapter on fruits and vegetables for winter.)

In storing vegetables, a few things need an exceptionally dry and warm place, such as a corner of the attic near the chimney. The storage room must be perfectly clean. Get it ready early. Some folks like to provide containers to hold the different fruits or vegetables and so make them easy to handle. Some vegetables demand a free circulation of air about them, while others must be kept barely moist by some packing material. Ordinary cracker boxes and slatted vegetable or onion crates, each of which holds about a bushel, level full, are cheap, clean and convenient, and can be obtained at any grocery store. The boxes are also excellent for keeping apples and other fruit, and for packing root crops such as parsnips, salsify, turnips, beets, carrots and winter radishes in sand or sphagnum moss, and also for packing celery for winter. Slatted crates axe good for onions, squash, cabbage, and for handling tomatoes, melons, eggplant and so forth, which can be kept for some weeks in a cool place. Directions for storing and harvesting the individual crops are given in paragraphs that follow, but the fuller general information is given in this paragraph on storage. *See also Storage Cellar Diagram and accompanying notes.*

Plant-by-plant Growing Guide

From *Garden Guide: The Amateur Gardeners' Handbook*, edited by A.T. De La Mare, 1920

Asparagus

This excellent vegetable may be grown from seed, but as it does not come into full bearing until the third or fourth year from sowing it is more satisfactory to purchase two-year-old roots. A hundred or two asparagus plants, well cared for, will supply the home table. Select well-drained soil in which to plant this crop, preferably one a little sandy. Dig out trenches about eighteen inches deep and three feet apart. Tread into these six inches or so of manure, and cover this with good soil to within six inches of the surface. On this prepared bed, during the late autumn or early spring, set the roots a foot apart, spreading them out evenly. Fill the trench only two-thirds or so at first, and work the rest of the soil in until it is level as the plants develop. Beans, beets, carrots, lettuce, can be grown between the rows of asparagus during the first part of the season. As the shoots or growths develop in the spring, a few of the largest may be cut, but only for a few weeks the first year. Cultivate thoroughly, however, to get as vigorous a

Refugee wax beans.

growth of plants as possible. Cease cutting when the shoots become tough or stringy (about June 24 in the latitude of New York) and allow the tops to grow, removing and burning them in the late fall. Then cultivate the soil and apply manure or fertilizer. This is to throw strength into the crown for the early spring growth, as the succulent roots act as storehouses of plant food.

Beans

Always select a warm and fertile soil if available. Avoid nitrogenous manures or fertilizers near the seeds. As beans will not withstand cold weather, it is quite useless to plant before the ground is reasonably warm. Bush beans are planted in rows 24 to 30 in. apart, 1½ to 2 in. deep; thin out to 3 or 4 in. between each bean. Good results are obtained by planting in double rows 5 to 6 in. apart. As the plants develop hill them slightly.

Cultivate the soil frequently, but never while the foliage is wet, as hoeing when the vines are moist spreads disease and often results in a failure of the crop. Pick the pods before they attain full size; they are then tender and almost stringless. For a continuous supply make successive sowings every ten days or two weeks.

Hot bed cold frame open seed bed asparagus rhubarb or herbs

The dwarf limas are only partly dwarf, and should be given more space than the green and wax beans. Put the seed in edgewise with the eye down,

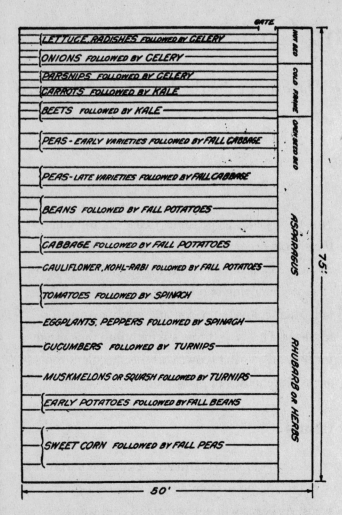

GATE

LETTUCE, RADISHES FOLLOWED BY CELERY	HOT BED
ONIONS FOLLOWED BY CELERY	
PARSNIPS FOLLOWED BY CELERY	COLD FRAME
CARROTS FOLLOWED BY KALE	
BEETS FOLLOWED BY KALE	
PEAS - EARLY VARIETIES FOLLOWED BY FALL CABBAGE	ONION SEED BED
PEAS - LATE VARIETIES FOLLOWED BY FALL CABBAGE	
BEANS FOLLOWED BY FALL POTATOES	ASPARAGUS
CABBAGE FOLLOWED BY FALL POTATOES	
CAULIFLOWER, KOHL-RABI FOLLOWED BY FALL POTATOES	
TOMATOES FOLLOWED BY SPINACH	
EGGPLANTS, PEPPERS FOLLOWED BY SPINACH	
CUCUMBERS FOLLOWED BY TURNIPS	RHUBARB OR HERBS
MUSKMELONS OR SQUASH FOLLOWED BY TURNIPS	
EARLY POTATOES FOLLOWED BY FALL BEANS	
SWEET CORN FOLLOWED BY FALL PEAS	

75'

50'

Plan for the cropping of a southern garden 50ft. By 75ft. From U. S. farmers' bulletin 647.

and if possible, avoid planting within two or three days of rain.

Pole or running beans are usually planted in specially prepared hills 3 to 4 ft. apart, and supported on rough poles or stakes with cross pieces. A better way is to grow them in rows, and support them on a continuous trellis. For a long bearing season keep all pods picked off as fast as they are large enough. Many varieties, however, are good as shell beans after they mature.

Pole limas should not be planted until the ground is thoroughly warm. Set the seed, eye downward, in hills 4 to 5 ft. apart. In each hill place 8 to 10 beans, 1½ to 2 in. deep, and when the plants are established thin to 4 or 5. Many gardeners now use the bush lima instead of

the pole; they are just as satisfactory and require no support.

Beets

Beets thrive in well enriched, moist soil. Sow the seed 1 in. deep in drills 12 to 15 in. apart, and thin out early to 4 in. The thinnings from the crop make excellent greens. As with all the root crops, especially when planted early in the season, growth will be

Egyptian beets.

greatly stimulated by a slight application of nitrate of soda. Make two or three sowings between April and the latter part of June when the crop for fall use and winter storage is put in.

Cabbage

Use deep and very rich soil which is not lacking in lime, and in addition to this, put manure or fertilizer in the hills or rows. Cover the seed ¼ to ½ in. deep. The early varieties may be set as close as 16 in. or 18 in., the rows being 30 to 36 in. apart. For late varieties leave 18 to 24 in. between plants. Plants started under glass are set out early in April, and seeds planted at the same time will give plants for a succession crop. Plants for the late crop are started in the latter part of May or early during the first half of June. As a rule, the earlier the better. One of the most important points in growing strong plants for transplanting is to thin them out to several inches apart as soon as they are well started; also keep them thoroughly cultivated at all stages of growth. A slight hilling up as they develop is desirable. Two or three light applications of nitrate of soda given a week or so after transplanting, and again in from

Cabbage—fresh and tempting.

"heads" or curds must be protected from the sun soon after they begin to form by tying the leaves together over them. The "heads" remain in the best of condition for only a few days and should be examined frequently when about ready to prevent "going by."

Celeriac—Celery

Celeriac is a turnip-rooted form of celery used for cooking. Its cultivation is similar to that for celery, but it does not need banking or blanching. Sow about ¼ in. deep in drills 18 in. apart and thin out to 6 to 8 in.

The first requirement in growing good celery is a good supply of water. The soil can hardly be made too rich. Early cabbage and early beets, peas, lettuce, etc., are usually out of the way in time to put in the celery, so that the same ground can be used, but an additional dressing of fertilizer should be given. For early use set out strong plants in April or May, putting the rows 3 to 4 ft. apart, and the plants 6 in. in the row. Where irrigation is available the plants are sometimes grown in beds, being placed 8 to 10 in. apart each way; many more sorts may be grown in the same area but they never are as heavy as those grown in rows. The early crop is blanched where it grows, either by backing up with soil which is drawn in carefully about the stalks to hold them in an upright position as they develop, or through a more convenient means; that is, celery blanchers of various types which are now obtainable. For late fall and winter use, the seed is sown one-eighth of an inch deep in April and the plants set out in June or July. Stronger plants can be obtained by transplanting from the seed-bed to give the plants several inches apart each way. This makes them stocky and develops a fibrous root system which will give quicker and better results than if they are set out in the garden. When raised in a frame, sow your seed in a shaded position. In transplanting,

ten to fourteen days, will help wonderfully in giving the crop a strong start. Very palatable "greens" can be obtained by leaving the stalks of early cabbage in the ground to produce "sucker growths." Keep a sharp lookout for insect pests. During the growing season the plants may be troubled by a destructive green worm, which can be controlled by a weak spray of arsenate of lead early in their growth, but just before the heads begin to form it is safer to use a non-poisonous remedy; Slug Shot is very effectual as a destroyer of these troublesome pests; apply it when the plants are moist from dew.

Cauliflower

This crop is handled in much the same way as cabbage, with the following additional cultural requirements. The plants are more tender and should not be set out until a week or so after the first planting of cabbage. Cauliflower is a very gross feeder and even larger quantities of manure and fertilizer can be applied with advantage. An abundance of water is also of the greatest importance. To be kept white and tender the

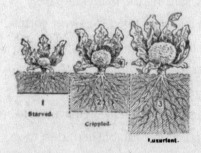

1 Starved.   2 Crippled.   3 Luxuriant.

Cauliflower—proving that shallow cultivation cripples all plants. Deep cultivation is essential to healthy, luxuriant growth.

water thoroughly and shade from the midday sun for a few days. Be careful not to get any soil over the hearts of the plants. Give clean culture and one or two top dressings of nitrate of soda as the plants develop, and throw enough soil up to them to hold the stalks upright. The celery

Golden celery.

crop should never be worked or handled while the foliage is wet as this will tend to augment any disease there may be. Blanching is accomplished by taking up the plants with such soil as adheres to the roots, and packing them close together and upright in a trench 12 to 15 in. wide, and deep enough so that the tops of the leaves come about on the level of the soil. As cold, freezing weather approaches, the trench is covered with mulch or with boards; a portion of the crop left for winter use may be transferred to boxes and stored in the cellar. See winter care of celery.

Chicory—Chinese Cabbage—Collards

Sown in spring one-half inch deep in rows 18 in. apart and thinned to 6 in. apart, the chicory (or Witloof) plant yields long, parsnip-like roots by fall, when they are dug and shorn of leaves to within 1¼ in. of the neck. The roots are then replanted 1½ to 2 in. apart in trenches and covered with 8 in. of fine soil. Here they produce an abundance of blanched leaves which make a splendid winter salad; they can also be cooked as greens.

Chinese, or celery cabbage (Pe-Tsai) is a very desirable vegetable, a native of China, is easily and rapidly grown in good garden soil. It requires

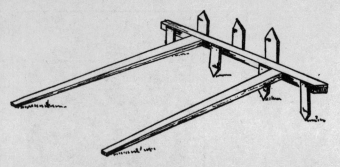

Handy device for marking off rows in the vegetable garden.

about the same treatment as cabbage, but as it has a tendency to run to seed in the hot summer months, sowing should be deferred until July or early August. Cover seed ¼ to ½ in. in rows 24 to 30 in. apart, and thin the young plants to 18 to 20 in. The heads, which are easily blanched, resemble well-grown cos lettuce. They make a very palatable dish when cooked like spinach or cabbage, or they can be used raw as a salad.

Collards are of tall growth and produce a loose cluster of leaves. The variety known as Georgia, which endures extreme heat, is largely grown in the southern states and used as a substitute for cabbage, the leaves being tender and of fine flavor. Sow seed in rows 24 to 30 in. apart and cover to depth of ½ in., allowing the plants to stand 18 to 24 in. apart in the row.

Cucumbers

For melons a light, warm soil is preferable, but they will succeed in almost any garden soil, provided there is good drainage. When all danger of frost is past sow the seed about ½ in deep in hills 4 ft. apart each way. Much earlier crops and better results may be had, by starting the plants in paper pots in cold frames as recommended for sweet corn. It is well, however, to use larger pots—say, 4 in. square. Fill each about half full with a compost of light soil and old, thoroughly rotted manure. Thin out to three or four plants, and after they have been set out long enough to become established, thin to

Emerald melon.

two plants to a hill. Keep the soil between the plants well cultivated until the vines cover it. In setting out started plants, the hills or rows should be enriched with well-rotted manure or guano or blood and bone, the same as when planting seeds. A method of ensuring a good standing from seed is to soak half of the seed you have to plant overnight in warm water, dry it off in fine dust or land plaster, and mix with the rest, planting two together, covering some preferably a little deeper than others. The advantage of this is that whatever the conditions that follow planting may be, enough of the seeds to make a good stand are pretty certain to come through. If the vines are wanted to continue bearing for a long time, pick off fruits as they mature, whether they are needed or not. For late use and for pickling, a second planting may be made the latter part of June.

The greatest difficulty in succeeding with melons and other cucurbits or vine crops is to protect them from the striped yellow beetle, the melon louse and the black wilt. In order to make sure of a crop, give a general purpose spraying every ten days or two weeks, using a soapy-nicotine spray. As it is essential to cover the underside of the leaves as well as the surface, an angle nozzle should be used and a sprayer sufficiently strong to produce a good mist.

Eggplant.

Where such a sprayer is not available, dry spraying or dusting may be substituted, keeping the plants well covered from early growth.

Eggplant

The eggplant is another vegetable which revels in the richest soil and an abundance of moisture. General culture is the same as that recommended for tomatoes, except that the plants do not have to be staked up or pruned. The plants should be grown in pots and for best results repotted once or twice so that they are in three and a half or fours when set outdoors, which should not be until after tomatoes are planted. If the hotbed or coldframe is used for propagation, sow the seed one-half inch deep and transplant once or twice before transferring the plants to their permanent place in the garden. Set the plants 2 ft. apart in rows 2½ to 3 ft. apart. The most dangerous enemy to be encountered in growing eggplants is the striped potato bug. Arsenate of lead paste may be used, but if a few plants are grown, hand picking (knocking the beetles off with a small stick or paddle into a pan half full of kerosene and water) will prove effective and will give little trouble, as the beetles are killed *before* they eat.

Endive—Horse Radish

Endive is another salad grown mostly for fall use. Sow the same as lettuce in June or July, and thin to about 12 in. It requires blanching to be ready for use. The individual heads may be tied up loosely with raffia, or two 6 or 8 in. boards temporarily nailed together in an inverted V shape may be

Kohl-rabi, white vienna.

placed over the row, blanching a section at a time. Do not work crop when the leaves are wet.

While only a small quantity of horseradish may be needed for home use, a few plants may be grown as easily as not. Instead of seeds, sets or small pieces of roots are planted. They are perfectly hardy, and can be taken up in fall or early spring, just as wanted. Two dozen roots will give an ample supply for a small family. Its chief cultural requirements are plenty of moisture and a deep, rich soil. Set plants 12 to 15 in. apart in rows 24 to 30 in. apart.

Lettuce

While lettuce can be grown from early spring until late in the season (and with the use of frames the year around), success with it will depend very largely upon using the right type for the particular season or conditions under which each successive crop is to be grown. The number of varieties in general culture is so great that it is rather confusing, but if the gardener gets the several distinct types fixed in his mind, he can make his selection intelligently. All varieties can be classed in general in two groups: the loose-leaf and the headed. The former are the easier to grow, but as a general rule, the latter are considered of better quality, although that is mostly a matter of taste. The loose-leaf type is suitable for growing under glass, being for this purpose much less subject to the dreaded rot, which quickly destroys head lettuce under glass, and

also for growing outdoors in spring, early summer and fall. With irrigation it can be grown easily throughout the summer months, but in dry weather runs quickly to seed. The head types of lettuce may be considered in three sections: the butter head, the cabbage head and the tub. Of these, the loose-leaf is suitable for spring and fall use. The hard or crisp heading sorts take longer to mature but form heads which resist the heat and are slower to run to seed, and are good for mid-summer growth; they are not suitable for forcing. The cos type, most varieties of which have to be tied up to blanch thoroughly, is quite distinct in appearance and flavor from the other types, but is easily grown and should be given a place in most gardens, even in small gardens, for variety. It is suitable for use during mid-summer and early fall. To be of the best quality, lettuce must be quickly grown. It requires an abundance of moisture and a high percentage of available nitrogen in the fertilizer or manure. Well-rotted horse manure is particularly adapted to the growing of this crop. The best method of growing lettuce in the garden for ordinary family use is to sow the seed thinly ⅛ to ¼ in. deep in rows 12 to 15 in. apart. A mistake often made in sowing the seed in drills in the open is to let the plants stand too thickly. Thin them out as soon as they are well started to 6 or 8 in. in the row, or even more in rich soil under irrigation. To have a succession of crops around the year start plants in January or February for setting out into the frames, and make a small sowing every two weeks or so thereafter, changing the type you use according to the changing seasons. Partial shading during the hot summer months will help to improve the quality of the lettuce.

Melons

Melons are delicious in the hot summer days, and quite easy to grow. Make a little mound about 2 ft. in diameter, slightly above the surrounding

Tender lettuce.

ground and, in its center, plant four or five seeds, about 6 in. apart and 2 in. deep. Two seeds may be put in each hole, but finally thin out to four plants on each hill. When these have made growth, about 2 ft. long, pinch out the top. This will accelerate

Muskmelon.

lateral growth, and on these you will soon see the young female or fruit blossoms, which develop with amazing rapidity. A piece of glass, slate or shingle put under each fruit will keep them off the ground and assist in hastening the maturity of fine, well-netted specimens. When the fruit will leave the vine without being forced, it is ripe and ready for the table. In northern locations where the seasons are short, it is always a good plan to start at least part of the crop early in paper pots or in frames. Heavy soil should be avoided, if possible. If it must be used, add plenty of sand and leaf mold to the soil in the hill when preparing it, and raise the hill slightly; keep it flat but bring it a couple of inches above the ground level. Should any fungous diseases develop a spraying with arsenate of lead will usually be effective. Among good varieties are honey dew, rocky ford, emerald gem, hackensack; but there are many others. Sometimes a local variety is the very best to plant; watch your neighbors and adopt any variety which shows improvement, or some special worthy feature. Never plant melons near melons, gourds or squash, as they cross-fertilize and become worthless.

Onions

Onions are used in all stages of development, from seedlings as big as a pencil, eaten raw, to the mature, dried bulb. They may be grown from seed, from prickers (seedlings started under glass and set out later in the garden), sets (which are

very small bulbs of standard varieties, grown small especially for this purpose), or from the perennial multiplier, the potato or Egyptian onion. The last three propagate themselves by multiplying, either at the roots or at the top of the seed stalks, the cluster of bulblets being divided up and set out for the following crop. They may be planted either in early spring or in late fall.

Onions from seed yield very heavily in rich soil, but the preparation of the seed-bed must be of the best as the seed is fine. Sow ½ in. deep in drills 1 ft. apart and cover firmly; eight to twelve seeds are drilled in to the inch of row. Thin to 2 or 3 in. The young onions thus pulled out are most appetizing eaten raw with a dip of salt. In addition to rich and very thoroughly prepared soil, the most important thing in growing onion seed is to keep ahead of the weeds. The plants when they first come up are very small, not much bigger than blades of grass, and the whole crop may very easily be lost through neglect in this regard. Go through it with the wheel hoe and also by hand within a week or ten days after they break ground. Continued clean culture and occasional light applications of nitrate of soda will keep the crop developing vigorously until mid-summer. Lime in the soil and soot sprinkled along the rows will tend to mitigate the damage done by the onion maggot. The most certain remedy for the maggot, however, is a poison spray or bait for the flies, which can be applied only with a strong pressure sprayer. When the plants get too large to go through them with the wheel hoe, the slide or scuffle hoe should be used, the kind with guides or runners in front of the blades, which hold it at an even depth, making the work easier and lessening the danger of injury to the bulbs. As soon as the tops die down, the bulbs should be pulled and laid in windows and raked over every day or two until thoroughly dried; then they may be taken and the tops cut off, spread out on a floor or in an open shed, or packed in slatted onion crates, which hold

Onions are indispensable. Those thinned out from the rows make a dandy breakfast relish.

Making provision for winter.

about a bushel apiece, to dry off thoroughly before being packed away for the winter.

For transplanting, to get large bulbs, the seeds should be started under glass in February or early March, and transplanted in April or early May, setting the plants about 3 in. apart. Seed should be sown very thinly in flats, with rows 3 or 4 in. apart. Keep them as near the glass as possible, and transfer them to the coldframes as soon as it is safe, so as to get hardy, stocky plants. In transplanting the roots are trimmed back to within three-quarters of an inch or so, and half of the tops removed, when they can be handled readily, and practically none will drop out if the work is properly done. Sets planted early in the spring by pushing the bulbs down into ground until they are slightly covered will make a quick growth, and give onions ready for use before those from "prickers" or seed sown in the open. Rich soil and two or three hoeings is all that will be required.

Potatoes

Of all field and garden products the potato is the most valuable. On the menu of at least one meal every day in the year the humble spud appears as the leading vegetable.

In preparing seed potatoes for planting, much attention should be paid to the eyes or buds, these being the vegetative parts of the tuber. They are clustered mainly at the flower or seed end. The other end, called the stem end, usually has only one or two eyes. A test of the producing capacity of the

eyes, carried out by the Monmouth County (N. J.) Farm Demonstration Office, showed that, calculated on the acre basis, the flower or seed ends had an advantage in yield of eighty percent over the stem ends, and twenty percent over the middle eyes, while the latter produced fifty percent more than the stem ends. It is advisable then, for the home garden, to reject the stem ends unless you have ample room. In case they are used, a good eye from the middle of the tuber should be included in the piece to be planted. Too many eyes make for foliage, but not for potatoes.

The potato should be cut so that two strong eyes are left on each piece. Penetrate as deeply into the tuber as possible, as the plant in its early stages of development depends largely upon the mother potato for its sustenance. Some gardeners favor the use of small whole potatoes for seeds, but those of medium size, cut to two good eyes, are generally preferred. The blossom ends are the first to start growth and yield the earliest crop.

To get extra early results select clean, medium sized potatoes of an early variety, and cut in quarters or halves, pushing the pieces down into a flat of sand till they are nearly covered and as close together as they will go. If these are kept in a sunny place, protected from frost and watered, the roots will make a vigorous growth, while the tops will remain very short and stocky, so they will be only

2 to 4 in. in length when they are ready to set out. An astonishing growth will result during the first two or three weeks.

A well-enriched sandy loam is best suited to the raising of potatoes, though they may be successfully grown in any good, well-drained garden soil. Prepare the ground in the same way as for general crops. Planting should begin as early in the spring as the ground can be worked. Late or main crop potatoes are planted in May or early June. The row or trench method is decidedly the best and most economical for the ordinary home garden. Dig a trench 5 to 7 in. deep. Apply a good dressing of well-rotted stable manure or fertilizer. Cover with two inches of soil, upon which set the seed potatoes 12 to 15 in. apart. Then finally cover with soil to a depth of 3 to 4 in. The distance between the rows should be 2½ to 3 ft. Work up the soil about the plants when they have made a good growth. To keep the ground clear of weeds and at the same time conserve the moisture, cultivation should be maintained throughout the growing season. The hand hoe is the most convenient tool to use in this operation.

When the vines die off, the potatoes are ready for harvesting, which should be done in fine, dry weather, and completed before the advent of frost or very cold weather. Cold rains cause potatoes to become sodden and of inferior quality. Potatoes soon become green and unsuitable for table use if they are allowed to lie exposed to the sun after digging. Store them in a darkened, dry, well-ventilated, frost-proof cellar that has a relatively low and even temperature.

To make sure of success it will be necessary to protect the potato plants from early and late blight and the Colorado beetle, known as the potato bug. Saving the vines means saving the potatoes. Every ten days or two weeks after the foliage has well developed, spray with Paris Green or Bordeaux mixture, to which arsenate of lead has been added; this combination spray, while combating insect pests, is effective as a preventive of disease. Careful watch

Potato tuber, considerably reduced.

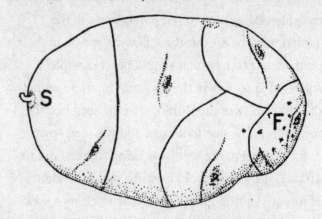

S, stem end, or end to which it was attached to the parent plant the previous season. F, the so-called flowering or growing end; here there are usually too many buds or eyes—several of these had better be scooped out before planting. The lines show how this particular tuber may be cut up for planting, but the eyes vary in each and every tuber.

must be kept for all insect troubles, and particularly for the aphis, which, unchecked, will ruin a crop in less than a week. Use a nicotine solution for aphis.

Rhubarb

One of the most valuable of our garden products requires a minimum of care for a maximum of yield.

Six to a dozen plants will supply a medium sized family. The soil should be made very rich and dug as deep as possible. Crowns taken from old established clumps are usually used for planting. Put them 3 to 4 ft. apart each way. The crowns themselves should be planted quite shallow, being covered with about 4 in. of soil. Plants set out in the spring will bear quite abundantly the following season; or

Scarlet globe radish.

young plants sown from seed in the spring, and transplanted in June to temporary rows in the garden, may be set out the following spring in their permanent place, which should be, if possible, a sheltered spot, where they will not interfere with the cultivation of other things. In the seed bed the rows should be one foot apart and the seed sown ½ to 1 in. deep, the seedlings being thinned out to 10 to 12 in. Rhubarb, like asparagus, stores much of its early spring plant food in the thick root stalks over winter. Therefore, manuring or fertilizing in the fall will help the following crop. Dressings of nitrate of soda in spring also produce splendid results, but be careful to keep it off the leaves. To bring one or two stools into early bearing, cover at opening of spring with 4 or 5 in. manure. Set anything around the plants which will keep the heat in; a melon frame is ideal. Do not neglect to remove all seed-bearing stalks as quickly as they form.

Spinach—Squash

As with lettuce and some other crops, success with spinach depends largely on choosing a variety suitable for the season for which it is wanted. For spring use, winter spinach is sown the previous fall and carried over with a mulching of hay, straw or dried litter. In spring, two or three succession plantings can be made to maintain the supply until summer. Sow about ½ in. deep in row 12 to 18 in. apart, and thin to 4 in.

New Zealand spinach is a distinct type, its greatest charm being the fact that it resists heat and grows luxuriantly during hot weather. It is of branching habit, spreading 3 or 4 ft., and thrives in any rood garden soil. The seed is very hard and should be soaked in tepid water for several hours to aid germination. When the ground has become warm in May, sow in rows about 3 ft. apart, covering the seed one inch and thinning to 12 in. in the row. Another method—and a good one—is to sow

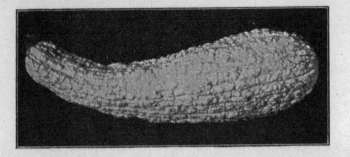

Crookneck squash.

in hills 2 ft. apart, leaving 2 or 3 plants in each hill. Pick off the thick, succulent leaves and tender shoots, preserving the main stems; the plants will immediately start out into new growth, yielding delicious greens until frost.

Squash should be planted or started in frames, as recommended for the melons and melons already discussed. For earliest use, plant a few bills of scalloped or crookneck type of summer variety. These may be had in the bush form, thus taking up comparatively little space. There are a few varieties, such as fordhook and delicate, which will serve for both summer and winter use. Bush varieties may be planted in hills 4 or 5 ft. apart each way, while for running sorts the hills should be 7 to 8 ft. apart to allow for proper development. Cover the seed ½ to 1 in. deep. Put 8 or 10 seeds in each hill and thin to 2 or 3 of the strongest plants. If the plants are kept well dusted with tobacco or wood ashes during the early stages of growth, it will help to discourage the appearance of the insects likely to attack them. Success of the late or winter varieties may be made much more certain by starting them in paper pots in frames and setting out. The first sign of the deadly squash borer is likely to be a slight wilting of the leaves on a hot, bright day. Make a thorough examination at once at the base of the stem, and if you find a small hole from which a gummy, yellowish matter has exuded, slit the thin cavity lengthwise until you find the intruder. Then cover the joints of the stem with a little soil; new roots will form and the plant will go on growing.

Tomatoes

As soon as danger from late frost is over, set out the strongest, stockiest plants you can find, even if you have to pay several cents more apiece for them. A half handful or so of bone or guano in each hill will produce a strong start. However, a little chicken manure, or a well-rotted compost may be used for this purpose. Set the plants deep, even if you cover several inches of stem, as new roots will be formed all the way up, and you will be better prepared, therefore, for dry weather. For garden culture the plants should be supported by 4 to 5 ft. stakes, a trellis, or the specially prepared circular tomato supports now available. Set them from 18 in. to 2 ft. apart in rows 3 to 4 ft. apart. As soon as the plants reach the tops of the stakes, nip off the terminal buds. This strengthens the vine and gives more nourishment to the fruit. Two dozen plants or so, if they are well cared for, will provide an abundance of fruit for the average family. If you intend to can for winter supply, fifty plants is none too many for a family of five or six persons. To get the earliest and the smoothest fruits, keep the vines tied up to stakes

Tomatoes trained to a fence.

or trellis with raffia, strips of cloth, or soft twine, as they grow. Train each plant to not more than 3 or 4 stems by pinching off the side shoots which appear in the axils of the leaves. Avoid injuring the flowering or fruit buds. An intensive method of culture is to set plants 16 in. apart in a double row 18 in. apart, leaving a space of 3 ft. between the rows. The plants are pruned to single stems and trained to stakes 4 to 5 ft. long. By this method the fruits which do set will have more nourishment and more sunshine than if the vines are allowed to grow bushy and sprawl on the ground. Remove all suckers from the base of the plant. The newly set plants must be protected from cutworms with paper collars or poison baits, but strong, pot-grown plants are likely to defy them, as they are too large and tough to be eaten through readily. By the proper choice of early and late varieties a succession of good tomatoes may be had. Just before danger of frost pick all the mature fruits and pack them in straw in a coldframe to ripen up. In this way they may be had for several weeks after frost. A green tomato is excellent for pickles and preserves or it can be ripened in the cellar. It is highly advantageous to start tomatoes from seed in a coldframe or in a box placed in the sunny window of the house. A small packet of seed will yield all the plants you require for transplanting, and there will be some left to fill up gaps. Sow in March, broadcast or in drills 5 in. apart, covering ½ in. deep. In order to secure strong, vigorous plants, transplant once or twice before planting in the open ground. If potato bugs appear on the tomato plants pick them off by hand. Light sprayings of Bordeaux mixture should prevent leaf-blight and leaf-curl. Fruits showing signs of rot on the blossom end must be removed as soon as discovered.

Depths For Planting

A good rule to follow in planting a fruit tree is to set it deep enough so that it will stand up firmly without artificial support. In sandy soil deeper planting may safely be practiced, while on heavy or wet soils shallow planting is recommended. As a general rule, six inches is quite deep enough for all small fruits, and eight inches for apple, pear, plum, peach and cherry trees.

Dwarf trees can safely be planted to the depth they have been previously grown in the nursery, but not deep enough to afford any possibility of the scion or graft taking root in the soil, otherwise your dwarf tree will cease to be such, as the rooting scion will cause a very strong growth. Undue vigor in fruit trees should be checked by root pruning.

Having chosen a location, proceed at once thoroughly to cultivate the ground, using a subsoil plough, or digging as deeply as possible; then cover the whole with a liberal dressing of well-rotted farmyard manure, and a liberal sprinkling of bonemeal, and dig over again. In this plant your fruit trees. Should your soil be a rich loam it will be well adapted for the small fruits as well as cherries and apples, but heavy or clayey soils will produce fine pears, while sandy soil will grow luscious peaches. A careful study of conditions previous to planting will save a large amount of inconvenience, labor, expense and regret later on. Apple and pear trees take about six years to come into bearing, but after that the crop increases annually. Pruning will accelerate fruit production to a large extent and providing a good selection of varieties has been made, it is possible to have apples nearly every month in the year, the proper facilities being available for winter storage. Good cultivation is beneficial to the growth of fruit in general and liberal treatment will increase results.

Apples

These do best in a rich, loamy, well-drained soil, in a position preferably facing the east or southeast. This situation protects the trees from north and west winds and retards blooming in spring, thereby often preventing the destruction of the blossom by late spring frosts and the consequent failure of the crop. In planting, select a three-year-old tree, which can be procured at any reliable nursery, and insist on this being true to name, because a mistake at this point means years of disappointment. Do not make the common mistake of planting your tree in a small hole or planting too deeply, but be liberal in all your treatment and your tree will respond accordingly. Prune all broken and damaged roots, and after spreading the remaining roots evenly in the hole, cover with fine earth and give the tree a slight shake. Allow the earth to sift down among the fine roots, then put on more soil and tread in firmly, finish filling the hole, and put on a generous mulching to keep the soil about the tree moist, for upon this mulching often depends the life of the tree. After the tree is firmly planted, prune in the head to five or six branches and reduce these to half their original length. Attach a label to the tree and it is ready to take a permanent place in the garden.

During its first season of growth all superfluous shoots should be cut out, keeping in mind the future form of the mature tree. The second season, the previous year's growth should be cut back about half, and after this the tree will usually need only thinning out the center and such shoots as cross each other, to secure abundance of light and sunshine. The shoots which come out of the stem should be rubbed off as they appear. This treatment applies to standards, which should be planted at least twenty-five feet apart, but in a small garden, trees known as pyramids, cordons, and espaliers may be grown with success. These can be purchased in that form and are used for covering arches or for growing against buildings, walls or fences. They have the advantage of producing fruit quicker than standards and in taking less space in which to grow, a consideration where room is limited. Pyramids could be planted in a row ten feet apart, cordons three feet apart against a wall or to form an arch over a walk, and espaliers along each side of a walk or against a wall or building, thus making the most of restricted space. Their pruning is more severe and may be done in July and in spring, the production of fruit bearing spurs being the end in view.

The prevention of San José scale is necessary to success, and a spraying with any good insecticide sold for that purpose must be given while the trees are dormant in spring; lime and sulfur mixture treatment is very good. Then the familiar codling moth has to be dealt with. arsenate of lead, three pounds to fifty gallons of water, sprayed through a fine nozzle, has proved the very best treatment for this pest, but many egg clusters can be gathered from the trees if carefully scrutinized while pruning. The trees should be sprayed as soon as possible after the blossoms fall, the object being to get some of the insecticide into the calyx before it closes up tight, or the fruit turns downward. Avoid spraying the poison on the fruit.

Typical half standard apple tree suitable for the amateur's garden.

Another spraying is necessary for fungous growth on the fruit. This should be done with arsenate of lead as soon as possible after the woolly down begins to come off the young fruit. No particular time can be stated, as in different localities the season varies, but by taking notice of the condition of the fruit, no mistake can be made. If green or black aphis appear on the growth of the young trees, spraying with what is known as "Black Leaf 40" is the best remedy. It is a preparation of nicotine in a concentrated form, and should be used according to directions supplied with each can.

Apples are seldom propagated except in nurseries, where large quantities are raised from seed and the many varieties in demand are then grafted on these seedlings while they are quite small. Grafting is sometimes practiced in gardens for introducing a new variety on an old or objectionable kind.

In giving a list of varieties, due attention has been paid to sorts designed to keep the family supplied for a greater part of the year. In almost every locality, there are varieties which do particularly well, and which are general favorites; because of this fact, it is always well before planting, to inquire from some of the older settlers, whom you know raise good fruit, what special variety succeeds best with them. The following list, however, covers a wide range, and the varieties named are adaptable for general planting. Make a selection for early, medium and late.

- EARLY HARVEST. Fruit pale yellow tender and good. Bears early. Late July and August.
- RED ASTRACHAN. Fruit largely covered with light and dark red. A good early, and bears young. August and September.
- SWEET BOUGH. Fruit greenish yellow. The best early culinary variety. August and September.
- YELLOW TRANSPARENT. Fruit clear yellow; tender, juicy, with a pleasant flavor. July and August.

- DUCHESS OF OLDENBURGH. Fruit red striped, crop, tender, juicy, aromatic. A good culinary variety. Late August and September.
- GRAVENSTEIN. Fruit yellow striped, good size, attractive appearance, excellent quality. September to November.
- TOLMAN SWEET. Fruit pale yellow, decidedly sweet. A good dessert apple. November to January.
- MAIDEN'S BLUSH. Fruit lemon yellow with crimson cheek; very attractive. September to November.
- SUTTON BEAUTY. Fruit attractive, red. Fine grained, crisp. A good dessert apple. November to March.
- RHODE ISLAND GREENING. Fruit green. The very best culinary apple. October to March.
- BALDWIN. Fruit red. The well-known winter apple. October to May.
- NORTHERN SPY. Fruit splashed with red; very crisp; of fine flavor. December to June.

- WAGENER. Fruit red, large, subacid. An apple of superior excellence. October to March.
- SIBERIAN CRAB. The crab apple furnishes a most delightful jelly; none better. It is also ornamental and might be planted where non-fruiting trees are planted now. Other crab apples are golden beauty, hyslop, Martha and transcendent. September and October.
- JONATHAN. Fruit brilliant red; very highly flavored, juicy, fine grained. October to March.
- McINTOSH. Fruit bright deep red; flesh white; juicy, with slight acid flavor. September to January.
- STARK. Fruit large, round, greenish yellow, with red stripes; flesh yellow, mildly acid. November to January.
- WILLIAMS. Fruit rich dark red; large, with tender crisp white flesh. July to August.

Evolution of the espalier trained tree.

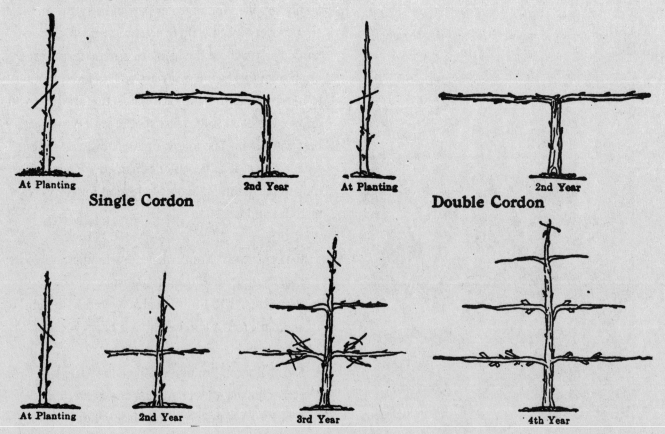

Single Cordon   **Double Cordon**

At Planting   2nd Year   At Planting   2nd Year

At Planting   2nd Year   3rd Year   4th Year

Prune as shown: remove weak growths. In June, pinch back all side growths to the fourth leaf to hasten the formation of fruit-bearing spurs.

Growing and Training Cordon and Espalier Fruit Trees

[Growing fruit trees in these shapes is an endless source of delight to the gardener and we recommend giving the art a trial if only commenced with a few trees, their first cost being but a trifle and the reward great.]

Cordons and espaliers are not difficult to train and, by following the diagrams shown on opposite page, nicely grown specimens can soon be obtained. Sometimes a young tree can be bent down to form a single cordon, thereby saving a season's growth, but a double cordon would have to be formed the first year as shown in the diagram.

A single galvanized wire, anchored firmly at each end and drawn tight, standing one foot above the ground, is necessary to support the cordon, the height being a matter of choice, as the tree can be started at any height desired. Should the young tree make very strong growths, these should be shortened back in spring and carefully watched and tied to ensure a straight branch when new growth commences.

All side growth should be pinched back in June or July, leaving three or four leaves; these will form the fruiting spurs later. The spurs should not be allowed to crowd or weak growth will result. The trees can be allowed to reach each other and are easily kept within a restricted space. They come into bearing early and produce fine fruit.

An espalier is an amplified cordon, the treatment being identical in the first stage. Branches at equal distances up the stem look best, and three good growths must be encouraged at the first pruning, two for lateral branches, and one for a continuation of the main stem; these should be tied and kept straight, as the future appearance of the tree depends upon it.

The third year spurs will begin to form on the lowest branches, these should be treated the same as those on the cordons. Fine fruit will reward the labor bestowed upon them.

Upright or oblique cordons consist of a single stem, allowed to grow slowly by cutting back a portion of the matured growth each year in order to encourage the formation of fruiting spurs at close intervals all up the stem. The side shoots should be treated same as for single or double horizontal cordons, but a straight leading shoot must always be assured for the continual development of the tree.

These may be planted two feet apart, against a fence, building, or wall, or to cover an arch in the fruit garden.

Espaliers may be trained on ordinary garden stakes. 4 to 5 ft. high, placed one foot apart; or, iron rods may be used, or an ordinary piece of wire fence, in fact any material that will keep the young growths in the proper position during training.

Currants

Currants are used principally for culinary purposes, and unless wanted for preserves, a few plants will generally be sufficient for ordinary use. The red and white varieties are the ones usually grown, but some like the black, and a few of these should be included. The reds are the most popular, but they all make delicious jelly; the black particularly so. Served on the table freshly picked, the white and red, mixed, make an appetizing dessert.

Any soil of a medium-rich nature will grow good currants, and they are not particular as to situation. They prefer a light, open space preferably to one that is shaded by trees. They may be planted in spring or fall, and must be attended to in the matter of pruning to ensure a good crop of fruit annually. All young shoots should be pruned back about half, and only a few left to form the bush, care being taken annually to remove all young growth which springs from the base of the bushes, otherwise

Standard (or tree) red currant.

This form of bush has special merits, being ornamental as well as utilitarian.

they will get too thick and small fruit will result. Standards are in every way preferable as they can be more easily pruned and the fruit is kept up out of the dirt, a great advantage on sandy soils.

If planted four feet apart, they will soon grow up and fill the space between each plant. As currants admit of hard pruning, they may be used for bordering garden walks, or planted against fences to utilize space, where this is a consideration.

The currant worm is one of the worst pests we have to deal with. Powdered hellebore dusted on the plants is a good remedy, but they should be watched for carefully as soon as the foliage appears, and kept destroyed until the foliage becomes hard. Ordinary road dust, air slaked lime, or any fine dust, has been used successfully in destroying the currant worm, but it should be applied quite early in the morning, or late in the evening when the foliage is damp with dew; it is then very evenly distributed and most effective. There is some danger in using a liquid insecticide because the fruit is small and it is almost impossible to wash off all traces of poison.

Pruning currant shoots

1. Twig should be cut back to bud m shown in Fig. 3. No. 2 shows torn snag.

Currants are usually propagated from cuttings made of the ripened shoots, and root quite freely if put in during the fall. The best varieties are:

- FAY'S PROLIFIC. Red, sweet, large and very productive.
- CHERRY. Large and very prolific.
- POMONA. A new variety; keeps long after getting ripe.
- CHAMPION. Black, berries large, of good quality Boskoop.
- GRANT.
- BAR-LE-DUC, WHITE GRAPE. Black.

Peaches

To those in the warmer parts of the country where the winters are not too severe, a few peach trees will add much to the revenue of the garden, and who does not like peaches? They can be served in so many appetizing ways. The peach is not a long-lived tree, and will not produce profitably for more than five or six years. After the fruit begins to get small, new trees had much better be planted.

Peaches thrive in a light, well-drained soil and preference should be given to a northern aspect, as this tends to retard the date of flowering and prevent a total loss of the crop which would result if subjected to a freezing temperature while the trees are in bloom. At best peaches are a precarious crop unless well protected from cutting winds. During winter, if the temperature falls to ten degrees below zero, the blossom buds will generally be killed although in a dormant state, and no fruit can be expected under such conditions. Peach trees come into bearing early, and for this reason young plants should be selected for planting and careful attention given to pruning to get the tree into shape.

Early fall is the best time to plant, as the trees have a chance to get rooted a little before the ground becomes severely frozen. The roots being very fine, the trees should be planted as near the surface as consistent with firm and secure planting, and a stake put at each tree, if necessary, to prevent its moving. Peaches like the ground around them cultivated, and much better fruit will result.

They require little pruning except to cut back strong growths, and to thin out if the branches become too crowded. Dwarf standards are preferable, but in small gardens trees can be trained against a building or on a fence. Under this method of culture they produce fine fruit, and ripening is assured in unfavorable seasons.

A spraying with arsenate of lead will check any tendency of fungous growth if done while the leaves are quite small; if done after the fruit gains size the woolly down which covers it holds the spraying solution and may cause some disfigurement. Aphids usually attack the young leaves and if planted against a wall frequent severe syringing with force enough to dislodge the insects will keep them in check. A solution of nicotine may be used effectively against this black aphis, but is almost sure to leave a stain on the fruit and should not be applied in any case after the fruit is half grown.

Early varieties are the best to plant as the season is none too long for the maturing of the fruit.

New varieties are raised from seed and their perpetuation is secured by budding. This is done when the stock is quite small and usually close down to the ground.

The best kinds are those which are known to do well in particular localities, but those named are known to be generally good, and can be safely recommended, and are all freestone varieties:

- ALEXANDER. Medium size, white flesh, rich flavor. July.
- BELLE OF GEORGIA. Large, showy, red cheek; flesh white, firm and sweet. August.
- EARLY CRAWFORD. Large, yellow, of good quality. Early September.
- HALE'S EARLY. Melting and rich flavor. August.
- ELBERTA. Large, yellow with red cheek; of fine quality. September.
- CHAMPION. Very large, white flesh; very productive. August.

Pears

Successful pear culture is only practicable where the condition of the soil permits a free growth of wood. The trees may be planted closer together than in the case of apples, because the tendency of the pear tree is to grow tall rather than to spread out. Where an apple orchard is planted, pear trees may be planted between the rows until the apple trees require the room, when they should be cut out rather than encroach upon the room allowed for the apple trees. Pears come into bearing much quicker than apples, and the trees never assume large proportions. It is well to bear this in mind when planting, but a small pear tree will produce liberally, and a careful selection of varieties will give a long season of fruit. Pears delight in a heavy soil, and as they bloom early in the season a sheltered position should be selected where some protection may be had from a windbreak of tall evergreens or group of buildings, or from the natural formation of the place chosen, such as the shelter afforded by a hill. The tree should be planted on the eastern slope when many are to be grown, but in the small garden pyramids or espaliers should be used. These give the best results, yielding a large amount of fruit in a restricted space. Pears respond to good cultivation and will stand closer pruning than apples. The tall growing varieties should have the heads cut hard to prevent the trees reaching too great a height, which makes the gathering of the fruit difficult. It is good policy, therefore, to keep the trees low and bushy. Pears make spurs freely, and in pruning, this fact should be held in mind. Encourage a free, open, branching habit, and prune to clothe the branches with fruit-bearing spurs, cutting out all superfluous growth at the spring pruning.

Probably the worst enemy of the pear is rust and fungus, an attack of which causes the fruit to grow deformed and unsightly. A frequent spraying with arsenate of lead, three pounds to fifty gallons of water, will keep the foliage and fruit in good condition. This should be applied immediately after the blossoms fall, and again about three weeks later, and should any sign of fungus growth appear later, another spraying should be given to insure good looking fruit and a clean, healthy growth to the trees.

Pears are usually grafted, and trees can be purchased much more cheaply than they can be grown to a fruiting age.

The following tried and popular varieties will prove a valuable addition to the garden:

- CLAPP'S FAVORITE. Large, pale yellow; flesh fine, juicy and buttery. August.
- BARTLETT. A very popular variety; large, shapely, melting; luscious flavor. September.
- SECKEL. Fruit small but very sweet and melting. One of the best.
- KIEFFER. Large; golden yellow when ripe; juicy, with Quince flavor. October and November.
- SHELDON. Large, russet and red; aromatic flavor; rich and delicious. October and November.
- BEURRE d'ANJOU. Large and handsome; flesh melting, extra fine. November.

Pears should be gathered as soon as the seeds are black, and stored in a dry, airy room until fit for use.

Plums

No garden is complete without a few plums, so useful for table and culinary purposes. The Japanese plums are wonderful bearers, and produce annually large quantities of fruit. Their abundance makes it necessary to thin out the fruit to prevent rotting in clusters on the branches. Plums are not particular as to soil, as their roots spread so much nearer the surface than apples or pears, and any fairly good loamy soil that is well-drained will produce fine fruit, but cultivating around the trees is very beneficial. Plant early in the fall; be liberal with the spade, make large holes, spread the roots out evenly, and plant firmly.

Plums should not be pruned except for conserving the shape of the trees, particularly the Japanese varieties, which usually grow very strong the first season, and pruning back is a temptation, but if pruned they only produce another strong growth. If left alone they will form fruit buds all along these strong growths and so check excessive vigor. Plums are the earliest fruits to flower, and a sheltered position should be given them, or plant them on a northern exposure where the buds will be retarded until danger of freezing is past. Spraying, to be effective, should be done very early, and again as soon as the blossoms fall, because the fruit is eaten without removing the skin. Plums intended for the table should be allowed to ripen fully on the tree, but for preserving and culinary purposes they may be gathered earlier. Should plums insist on making a strong, rank growth, the best remedy is root pruning. Lift the trees in the fall and shorten back all strong roots, keeping the roots exposed as short a time as is possible to complete the work. Some plums can be raised successfully from seed, the Greengage being one of these; but they are usually budded or grafted on the wild plum stock.

The curculio is the worst pest we have to deal with, and the only way to fight this insect is to gather up all the fruit which falls prematurely and burn it, as in these fallen fruit the larvæ remain until full grown, when they eat their way out and enter the ground, where they change into the pupa state. The full grown beetle emerges in about four weeks and hides under the bark of the tree or some other protection until spring business opens up.

Another insect which sometimes causes trouble is aphis. Spraying with a nicotine solution will destroy this pest, or the tops of the young infested growths can be cut off.

Some of the very choicest plums for eating are:

- OULLIN'S GOLDEN GAGE. Large, delicious flavor. August.
- TRANSPARENT GAGE. Very large, round, juicy and rich. July.
- GREENGAGE. Medium size, round, green, rich. August.
- COE'S GOLDEN DROP. Very large, golden yellow, rich flavor. September.
- VICTORIA. Large, oval, red. Useful for every purpose. August.
- MAGNUM BONUM. Large red. Good culinary variety. September.
- For culinary purposes: ABUNDANCE, BURBANK, RED JUNE, SATSUMA and WICKSON.

Raspberries

The popular raspberry is always welcome in the home, and only when freshly gathered has it that lovely flavor peculiar to this fruit and which makes it so desirable in the home garden. Raspberries must be handled with the greatest care or the fruit will become bruised and soon ferment. Small baskets should be used when picking, to prevent excessive weight, which invariably crushes the tender berries, and they soon become unfit for use.

The plants are not particular about the kind of soil they grow in nor the location. They grow best in a good, rich, well drained, loamy, cultivated garden soil, and should be planted in rows two feet apart and four feet between the rows. They are best tied to a wire trellis for support and to facilitate ease in gathering the fruit.

The young growths which spring from the base of the plants, should be thinned out to four or five, and after the season's fruit is over, the old fruited wood should be cut out close to the ground, and the young shoots given every chance to ripen before winter sets in, when they may be tied together in bunches of five or six canes and left in this way until spring, when they must be tied to the wires and trimmed evenly along the top to make them look nest.

Raspberries are not subject to much trouble from insects or diseases.

They are propagated by division of the roots or from cuttings, which should be taken from the ripened shoots and inserted in the ground in September, and will commence to grow the following spring.

There are red, yellow and black raspberries, but the red varieties are the most popular. A few well tried varieties follow:

- CUTHBERT. Red, large and sweet; the most popular of all Raspberries.
- BRANDYWINE. A large, bright red berry; a good cropper.
- GOLDEN QUEEN. Large, amber color; fine quality.
- CUMBERLAND. Very large, black, glossy berries, juicy and sweet.

Strawberries

No garden is complete without strawberries, and as they are so easily grown, no garden should be without them. What is nicer than a dish of strawberries picked fresh from your own garden? Strawberries like a rich soil and well repay a very liberal application of fertilizer. The best time to plant a bed is in September, when the young plants are just ready. Select an open piece of ground away from tail trees or shrubs; dig in a liberal dressing of well-rotted farmyard manure, with a sprinkling of bonemeal, and in this plant your strawberries one foot apart in the rows and two feel between the rows.

After the first hard frost throw over them some light protection—straw, old hay or anything that will not be liable to pack down on the plants too tightly. The object of this covering is not to keep the plants from the cold, but to protect them from the sun, which causes more failures than the cold. This covering should be removed after spring opens up, but not too early, as a little growth may have already started, and if exposed to a late frost may cause much injury. The plants which will have become loose by the action of the frost, should be gone over and firmly pressed into place, the beds lightly forked to prevent the growth of weeds, and when they are

Good sized strawberries.

in bloom, some straw or salt hay should be placed around and between the plants to prevent the soil from splashing on the ripe fruit.

To lengthen the season of fruiting, the first blossoms may be picked from some of the plants, and these will fruit about three weeks later. Strawberries are sexual and bi-sexual, that it to say, in some the flowers have pollen and seed organs, in others only one set of these. To insure fruiting it is necessary to plant some of each kind, unless the bi-sexual varieties alone are selected. A bed once planted is good for at least three years, when it should be renewed. If at all possible start a new bed one year before the old bed is to be destroyed.

All runners should be cut away annually as soon as the fruiting season is past, unless some are wanted to make a new bed, in which case the strongest plants should be left until wanted and the runner should be stopped at the first strong plant to accelerate rooting.

Strawberries, fortunately, are not troubled with many insect pests or fungous diseases, and their propagation by runners is very simple, as they root freely of their own accord and can be cut off and planted where they are to remain.

There are many fine varieties and their selection is largely a matter of preference. The following are bi-sexual and are all good, tested sorts:

- *Early.*—CLYDE, MARSHALL, BEDERWOOD.
- *Mid-season.*—ABINGTON, MCKINLEY, SHARPLESS, NICK OHMER.
- *Late.*—COMMONWEALTH, GANDY, BRANDYWINE.
- *Autumn or Perpetual.*—AMERICUS, PROGRESSIVE. These have small fruit and very little of it. To give results they must have extra care.

Fertilizing

From *Garden Guide: The Amateur Gardeners' Handbook*, edited by A.T. De La Mare, 1920

Sources of Fertilizers

There are three main sources from which fertilizers can be obtained: animal manures, green manures, and commercial fertilizers.

Animal Manures

Animal manures of all kinds are what are called complete fertilizers; this means that they supply all the essential elements of plant growth; properly saved and composted so that the straw material that is used in bedding the animals is well decayed, they are as good as anything which can be supplied. Since the advent of automobiles, however, stable manure is getting scarce and difficult to obtain.

Green Manures

Green manures are so named because they are plants of various kinds that are grown upon the soil, preferably when no other crop could occupy it, and are spaded or plowed under in a green condition.

Any kind of plant will make green manure, but the preference is always given to those of the legume family. The blossoms of plants of this family are, almost all of them, pea-like in character. All of the peas, beans, and clovers are legumes. Remarkable characteristics of these plants are the knots or tubercles on the roots. Bacteria live in these tubercles and store up in them the nitrogen existing in the form of gas in the air. None of the other plants but those of the legume family take nitrogen from the air and store it in the soil. If any other green plants, such as rye, rape, kale or turnips are used for green manure they simply return back to the soil what they have taken from it. Even then they are of great benefit as they help, like manure does, to bind the particles of sandy soils together and make clay soils friable. They also furnish organic matter which, in turn, makes humus that is of great value in holding the moisture in the soil.

Commercial Fertilizers

Commercial fertilizers are so called because they are bought and sold and gathered together from all parts of the earth. The dung of sea birds that had collected on some of the rocky coasts and islands of South America was one of the earliest forms of commercial fertilizers. It is called guano. Another was the bones of animals that were collected in the desert places of the world and brought home and ground into fine dust. Three of the important sources of the present day, are the phosphate rocks of Tennessee, Florida, and South Carolina; the nitrate beds of Chili, and the potash mines of Germany. The slaughter houses and the garbage collected in the large cities also add their quota to the commercial fertilizer groups. Other materials, such as the meal from cotton seed, after the oil has been pressed out; the bones and other portions of fish after the oil has been removed; the sulfate of ammonia that is a by-product in the manufacture of coke, all help to increase the fertilizer supply. There is also being manufactured at the present time calcium nitrate, which is nitrogen that is taken from the air (by means of electricity) and combined with lime.

These materials are all used and are apportioned and mixed so as to supply varying proportions of the main food requirements of plants. Commercial fertilizers are sold under the inspection of the state chemists. They are sold according to the amounts of nitrogen (ammonia), phosphoric acid and potash which they contain. The dealers have found that it pays to make up special brands for special crops containing such varying amounts of the three important elements as may seem to be of special benefit to the crop to be grown. They are, therefore, put up in bags and labeled with special reference to the crop they are suited to.

The manuring of any crop must always be with reference to the fertility of the piece of land being; used. If the soil is almost devoid of organic matter nothing much but trees and shrubs will grow upon it and these make but poor growth. If plenty of water can at all times be supplied, commercial fertilizers will give good results where the humus content of the soil is low, but under ordinary conditions the commercial fertilizers do beat where there is an abundance of organic matter It is always advisable, when possible, to use all three of the different kinds of fertilizers.

The most expensive element in fertilizers is the nitrogen. For this reason do not buy cheap or low priced fertilizers. Crops like early potatoes, cabbage, lettuce, beets, tomatoes, sugar corn, spinach, eggplant, peppers, melons, melons and squash should be fertilized with a fertilizer that contains at least five percent of nitrogen, seven or eight percent of phosphoric acid and five or six percent of potash. For beans and root crops and all fruit trees or bushes, use fertilizers containing two percent of nitrogen, eight percent of phosphoric acid and four or five percent. Potash will be found good.

Any of these commercial fertilizers can tie supplied at the rate of two ounces to the square yard of land before planting the crop. The material should be well mixed in with the soil. If the land is quite poor, and has had no other manure, the same amount can be scattered over the soil around the plants when they are half grown, and hoed or cultivated in.

Bonemeal

Raw animal bonemeal is a good fertilizer. It contains both nitrogen and phosphoric acid and can be used at the rate of a quarter-pound to the square yard. This is a good fertilizer to keep on hand as it does not lose its value by being stored. It is quite dry and if kept in a dry place, it will not get into hard lumps like some of the other fertilizer ingredients. It is somewhat slower in its action than a fertilizer made up to analyze the same from acid phosphate and nitrate of soda.

Nitrate of Soda

Nitrate of soda is valuable to use alone, or it can be mixed with its equal weight of acid phosphate and used on any crops where tenderness of leaf is desirable. It should be used as a top dressing at the rate of one ounce to the square yard in the early spring, and again when the plants are half grown.

Most of these fertilizers, either the made up brands, or the separate ingredients can be purchased at the seed stores in large cities and at general stores in the country towns.

Poultry Manure

Poultry manure can be used effectively in the garden. It is a complete fertilizer, but for crops like potatoes, turnips, beets, onions, and beans, it is well to use some acid phosphate with it. Poultry manure should be kept dry so that it can be scattered over the soil at the rate of one pound to the square yard. Acid phosphate can be mixed with it at the rate of twelve pounds to the hundred of poultry manure, or applied directly to the soil along with the poultry manure at the rate of two ounces to the square yard.

Lime

Calcium or lime is quite valuable in gardens where green manures are used considerably. It will also be of much benefit on vacant building lots or fields intended to be used for gardens. Lime can now be obtained from the same dealers as the fertilizers, either in the form of ground lime-stone or hydrated (slaked) lime. Both of these forms are convenient to apply. The hydrated lime is quicklime that has been slaked by the action of steam. It is quick in its effort and should be used at the rate of half a pound to the square yard of freshly plowed or dug soil. The ground limestone should be used in the same way but at the rate of one pound to the square yard. Lime is used to "sweeten" soil. For instance, some soils become too rich owing to over-heavy manuring. In such case, the manuring should stop for a season but a coating of lime should be given instead. The lime itself is not a fertilizer; it unlocks other plant food that is in the soil, making it available for the roots. Lime ought not to be applied along with manure (dung), but be forked in early in the spring. It has the property of making clay more open or friable, and conversely, of firming a sandy soil. It neutralizes the acids that are in soils. It is good for all vegetable soils.

Miscellaneous

There are some other manures on the market that are handled more especially by seedsmen and others who supply greenhouse men. These are the dried cattle, hog and sheep manures that are collected in cattle pens and cars. They are quite valuable in promoting plant growth and may be used at the rate of half a pound to the square yard. The rates of application given here are moderate and safe. Commercial fertilizers should always be carefully weighed and not guessed at, not only for the sake of economy but for the fact that some of the highly concentrated kinds may do more harm than good if applied injudiciously. When applying as a top dressing, avoid spilling the fertilizers on the leaves of the plants.

Humus as a Fertilizer

Humus is the name given by gardeners to decomposing vegetable matter. In many ways it is like dung. This matter may comprise lawn mowings, leaves from deciduous trees, and all the odds and ends of vegetative growth that one cleans up or gets from the garden. Too often this material is bundled out of sight or pitched away as useless. It is a gold mine. Have a place for it and accumulate all you can. Turn it over once or twice to facilitate rotting. Every spring, spread it on the soil and dig it in or keep it in reserve for particular purposes. If the humus heap has had lime applied, it will be still better. Whatever has not been thoroughly decomposed can be held back. Humus darkens soil and dark soil absorbs the warmth of the sun. Humus holds moisture, therefore is liked by the roots. It opens up a stiff soil and aerates it. Moreover it furnishes an essential medium for the bacteria that teem in all fertile soils and which manufacture food for the use of the plants. It is invaluable, and many derelict soils could be made to yield crops if humus and dung were applied. It is especially valuable on sandy soils.

Where and How to Use Fertilizers

The animal manures from the stable, those from the horse, cow and pig, can be spread on the land and plowed under for the coarser feeding crops, such as cabbage, corn, melons, squash, etc. Ten or twelve pounds to each square yard would be a fair dressing of these manures. Stable manure should never be put directly on land upon which parsnips, carrots or salsify are to be planted. It will invariably induce them to form prongy, inferior roots. These crops should go on land that was manured the season previously or else be fertilized with commercial fertilizer. The green manures can be sown on pieces of land which would otherwise lay bare in winter. Rye is the latest crop of these that is worthwhile to plant; this can be sown after the final crops come off, just before freezing weather. The clovers and vetch must be sown earlier. Frequently, this is done at the last cultivation that is given to the later summer crops; such as tomatoes and sugar corn. Any plants that are planted for green manures should be plowed or spaded into the soil early in the season while they are soft and succulent for much of the value of the green manures is in the decayed vegetable matter it supplies to the soil. The process of decay is very much more rapid if the material is turned under when the plant is quite tender. This is especially true of rye. If the rye gets tall and woody it will not decay rapidly enough to be of any benefit to the crop following it.

Commercial fertilizers should always be applied just a little before planting or shortly after the crop gets started. The elements they contain are very soluble in water and the nitrogen is quite easily leached out through the drainage. On account of this solubility, care should always be observed in applying them. Only a very slight amount should come in contact with the germinating seeds so it is always best to thoroughly mix them with the soil. The fertilizing of the garden with commercial fertilizers is not so complex a proposition as it often appears to the novice. The confusion in the matter has come about largely through there being such a multitude of brands with such varying percentages of nitrogen, phosphoric acid and potash. There are a few essentials that must be known about commercial fertilizers; after these are understood the real is easy.

Manufacturers of fertilizers use as a basis for most of their goods the phosphate rock which has been dissolved by being mixed with sulfuric acid. To this is added tankage, nitrate of soda, muriate or sulfate of potash, dried garbage, or any other material that has high fertilizing value. It is then all ground and mixed by machinery, after which it is analyzed by the chemist.

All fertilizer manufacturers have certain brands that are put out for some special purpose, such as "special corn grower," or "potato fertilizer," or "special truck crop grower." The name is not important but the percentage of nitrogen, phosphoric acid and potash is very much so.

Pruning

From *Garden Guide: The Amateur Gardeners' Handbook*, edited by A.T. De La Mare, 1920

What Pruning Includes

Besides the general removal of large branches, pruning includes the process of pinching, or removing undeveloped eyes to check growth in a certain direction; trimming, shortening top and roots at transplanting; topping, removing the leader or a flower stalk to retain the energy in the plant rather than in making a strong leader or seeds; suckering, the removing of shoots at base of plant to throw the strength into the plant itself. This would include the cutting of shoots from the stock in grafted plants; disbudding, removing of small buds at sides of main ones to throw the food into the perfect production of the larger flower; ringing, the cutting out of a narrow ring of bark from a branch of a tree (in the case of fruit the result is the production of a large specimen due to the fact that the food is all kept at the place beyond the ring); root-pruning, the cutting of roots at planting time so that they may be symmetrical and have clean, undecayed surfaces, but the top must always be shortened proportionately when this is done; sprouting, the cutting out of all sterile, unfruitful branches, which are usually called water sprouts.

Roses

If we observe rose bushes, we will be able to see that they bloom from what were the strong shoots the previous season, and that these shoots become weaker when another shoot begins to grow lower down. Therefore, there is an annual renewal of wood, and this is why pruning is necessary. Most roses must be pruned severely at planting. Some climbers are ruined from the start by too little pruning. In order to keep the bushes opened nicely, the cut must always be made to an outside bud. Take care not to leave stubs above a bud either; the tips always die back and may die back farther than preferred.

Briers and Roses for Landscape Effect

Those roses which are to be seen in mass and with which a profusion of bloom is to be preferred to a few slightly larger blooms, should be pruned but little. The main work is to improve the shape of the bush and cut out the very oldest wood. Wood which has flowered year after year should be cut out from the base of the plant so that the younger shoots may be given a chance. Prune in March.

Climbing and Polyantha Roses

Little pruning is necessary in spring except to cut out any branches which have been killed. The old wood can usually be gradually removed year after year. All new canes should be carefully tied up. Prune in March.

Hybrid Perpetuals

Various soils and climates cause the hybrid perpetuals to be either very tall bushes or, in other

Pruning a dwarf rose.

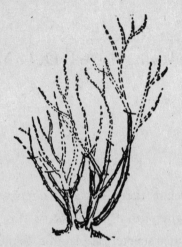

The dotted lines show the growth or stems that are to be cut away. As a rule amateur gardeners are too much afraid to prune hard. "The weaker the growth the harder the pruning," is a fairly safe rule to follow.

localities, only to attain a height of three feet. The varieties differ greatly in height and amount of pruning needed. The weakest shoots should be pruned the most severely; in the same way the strongest varieties need the least pruning. Never leave a weak shoot. Care must be exercised that all shoots are not pruned to the same height. Prune early in spring for main pruning because the shoots are apt to freeze back if done in fall or winter. The canes of the strongest varieties, which may be eight or nine feet long, should be shortened a third in autumn to prevent the injurious whipping by the autumn winds.

Shrubs

There are essentially two classes of shrubs—the spring and the summer blooming ones. Those which bloom in the spring have their flower buds all formed on the bushes by the previous autumn; they are usually near the top of the plant. Any pruning in late winter or early spring causes a removal of these flowers.

The most pernicious habit is the one which so many enthusiastic gardeners have of pruning

Pruning shrubs.

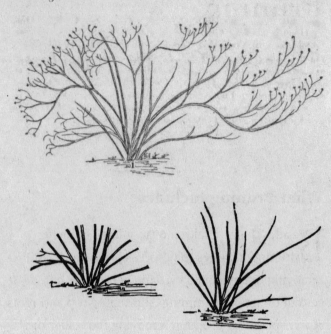

1. An unpruned example. 2. Pruned so that all the branches are of equal length. This is improper but all too commonly practiced. 3. Growths thinned out and shortened. This is the correct method. It is the same shrub in each case.

everything in the spring, and not only that, but making the graceful barberries, spiræas and mock pranges into formal, stiff shapes, due entirely to cutting their bushes with shoots all the same length.

Many spiræas and golden bells never bloom well, while the hydrangea blooms perfectly, merely because every one prunes in the early spring, which is not at all the proper time for, say, golden bells, but exactly proper for hydrangeas. Spring blooming shrubs must be headed in a trifle after flowering, which will cause the production of flowering wood for another year.

Hedges

A hedge, in order to give the best light conditions to the lower branches, should be broad at the bottom and narrower at the top. It is best not to be flat on top, for snow quickly lodges in this sort of hedge and spreads it so that the true beauty is spoiled. Hedges should be trimmed before growth starts in the spring and again lightly in late summer or fall. The young growth is best kept its proper length before it grows very long, otherwise the cut ends of the branches are large and over conspicuous.

Fruit Trees

In pruning fruit trees for home grounds, there should be an effort to keep them always low headed and open. This means that from the start the branches should be encouraged to grow out from the main trunk. Avoid allowing the branches to start so that a crotch is formed and have them

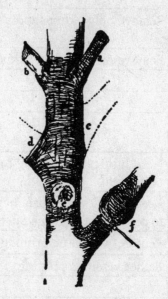

Pruning a limb

(a) Branch cut off too long. (b) The branch (a) after several years, has died back but cannot heal. (c) Branch cut properly. (d) Branch which is cut so that a little pocket is left in which water can settle and cause decay. (e) A wound healing properly. (f) Branch being strangled by a wire-tie.

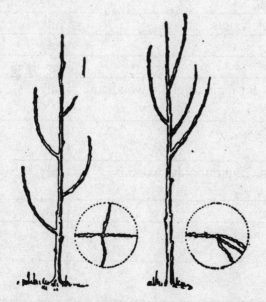

Young trees pruned.

One at the left pruned properly, the head started low and branches well distributed. One at right—head too high, branches form a crotch and tree is not balanced.

distributed around the tree so that when they bear fruit there will be a natural balance. As the years pass, less pruning is necessary on fruit trees, except to keep the center open so that some light can get in to color the fruit. Dead or crowded branches must be removed. Any appearance of disease is better cut out than any treatment that can be given it. A tree once in good bearing condition seldom needs extensive pruning.

Directions for Pruners

Below is given a list of some seventy-five of those plants in general use, with directions how and when to prune. By following the directions given the amateur gardener will be able to show good and satisfactory results.

Name	How to Prune	When
Akebia Amorpha frutescens	Give only a little pruning.	July
Apple	Requires pruning each year. For home garden, apple tree heads should be low so that the fruit may be readily picked. Keep the tree open in center by removing all branches which interfere, those which cross or shade each other.	Feb.-Mar.
Azalea Ghent and mollis	Remove old wood.	July

Berberis Thunbergii vulgaris	Remove only oldest shoots to retain form.	July
Blackberries	Remove old canes after fruiting; tip back in spring to 6 ft. or 8 ft.	
Celastrus		July
Cerasus, Ornamental		July
Cercis canadensis japonica		July
Cherry, Sour	Need little pruning except to remove branches which are crossed or broken.	Feb.-Mar.
Cherry, Sweet	Keep head low because they have tendency to grow tall, and also to prevent the damage often caused by sun and wind.	Feb.-Mar.
Chionanthus virginica	Requires very little pruning.	July
Clematis	Rather vigorous pruning.	Jan.-Mar.
Colutea Arborescens		Jan.-Mar.
Crat Ægus Oxyacantha		July
Currants	Canes bear two or three times; cut out few oldest canes each year, otherwise fruit becomes small.	Feb.-Mar. Late summer
Deutzias	Unless overly long, do not cut back shoots.	July
Dogwood		July
Dwarf Horse Chestnut		Jan.-Mar.
Elæagnus Longipes	Needs to be looked over each year for removal of old wood and straggling branches.	July
Exochorda Grandiflora (See Pearl Bush)	Cut back just after flowering.	
Flowering Currant (Ribes aureum)	Encourage vigorous young growth. Trim out older wood.	July
Flowering Plum		July
Forsythias	Thin out branches and trim back others immediately after flowering.	
Fringe Tree (See Chionanthus)		
Golden Bell (See Forsythia)		
Golden Chain (See Laburnum)		
Gooseberries	Remove oldest shoots annually. In July or August cut each back a bit; it causes more fruit buds to form.	Late summer
Grapes	Persons who have inherited tangles of grape vines should exercise care in pruning the first year. Do not remove too much at the start, otherwise no grapes will be produced. When possible, all immature canes should be pruned back to a single eye if the vines are very large, but two eyes may be left if the vines are quite small. When the grapes have nicely set we seem to think that they are benefited by cutting off the tips of each bearing cane two leaves away from each bunch. The canes usually branch in this case, and they may be cut back a little	Jan.-Mar.

	even then. Should one acquire or have to buy new vines, it is well to have a definite simple system of training. Grapes at planting and the year after should have the vines cut back two to three eyes. Then head back to 20 to 24 in. long. Several systems of training are good. Munson System. Claimed to be the easiest for the amateur. Kniffin System. Good if wind is not too strong; simple. Single trunk is carried to the upper of two wires and two canes are taken out at an eye for each wire. Each year all the canes are removed except a shoot from each; spurs are chosen from the trunk. A vine may carry 40 buds usually. The fruit canes are produced on shoots of previous year's growth. Chautauqua System. Two short, permanent branches are established at the lower wire; two or three canes are left on each arm and tied up to upper wire; these canes are renewed each year from buds at their base. When arms get too old, new ones are easily established.	
Hibiscus syriacus (See Rose of Sharon)		
Honeysuckles	The climbers and the bush honeysuckles, except spring flowering standishii and fragrantissima, which should be pruned in July.	Jan.-Mar.
Hydrangea	Hydrangeas bloom upon wood produced the current season from older wood. They must, therefore, not be cut down wholly to the ground, otherwise they bloom poorly.	Jan.-Mar.
Hydrangea paniculata	These shrubs should be large because they are old; they should not be allowed to get into a monstrous size when young; their beauty is entirely spoiled by such treatment. If one does not admire the flower stalks, they are best pruned in Nov.	Jan.-Mar.
Indian Currant		Jan.-Mar.
Japanese Quinces		July
Kerria japonica		Jan.-Mar.
Laburnum vulgare	Shorten any straggling shoots after flowering.	July
Ligustrums		Jan.-Mar.
Lilac	Prune out old wood if specimen flowers are preferred, also prune out all the sprouts from the base.	July
Magnolias	Require only that old wood shall be removed. Tar over all scars.	July
Mahonia aquifolia	Require only that old wood shall be removed.	July
Matrimony Vine		Jan.-Mar.
Mountain Laurel	Requires only that old wood should be removed.	
Neviusia alabambnsis		July
Pæonia Moutan		July
Pavia (See Dwarf Chestnut)		
Peach	The peach bears on shoots of previous year. The tree must, therefore, never be headed back; whole branches should be removed when pruning. Heading in does cause production of new wood, but method advised is better.	Feb.-Mar.

Pear	Low heads, keeping them open if possible. Keep all branches free from water sprouts.	Feb.-Mar.
Pearl Bush		July
Philadelphus		Jan.-Mar.
Plum	Moderate pruning to remove old branches and new ones if tree becomes overloaded.	Feb.-Mar.
Privet (See Hedges)		
Prunus Double flowering almond Dwf. dbl. flowering almond P. tomentosa P. triloba		July.
Quinces	Head very low. Cut back ends of branches. Fruit borne on wood of current season.	Feb.-Mar.
Raspberries, black	Bear on wood which grew previous year.	After fruiting
Raspberries, red	Remove old canes after fruiting, leaving young canes. Do not head back as with blackberries, or black raspberries; suckers start too freely. Early spring clip back ends of shoots so that ends are 30-36 in. long or do not prune if trained on trellis.	July-Mar.
Red Bud		July
Rhododendrons	Remove oldest wood; remove seed pods.	July
Rhodotypos kerrioides		July
Ribes (See Blackberries and Raspberries)		
Rose of Sharon		Jan.-Mar.
Snowball (Viburnum Opulus sterilis)	This is naturally a badly shaped shrub; prune to improve form.	July
Snowberry		Jan.-Mar.
Spiræa Van Houttei	Remove old wood; shear off old seed capsules. Cut away half the branches that have bloomed.	July
Spiræa Thunbergii	In the north the tips freeze; they need a little spring pruning. Main pruning after flowering.	July
Spiræas (summer-blooming)	Thin them out in winter. Cut back shoots that have flowered.	Jan.-Mar.
Staphylea trifoliata	Require only that old wood shall be removed.	July
Tamarix	Prune hard back.	Jan.-Mar.
Varnish Tree (See Kœlreuteria)		

Viburnum	Includes hoble bush, arrowwood, snowball.	July
Weigela (diervilla)	Cut out old wood. Remove seed vessels.	July
Wistaria		July
Witch Hazel		July

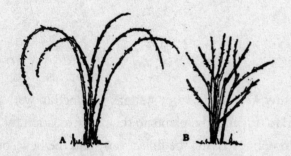

Pruning raspberry canes.
Remove all the old canes in winter as shown at A. Canes of black raspberries. when growing. can be tipped to produce laterals as at B. These will fruit the following year.

Transplanting

From Garden Guide: The Amateur Gardeners' Handbook, edited by A.T. De La Mare, 1920

Basic Principles

There are certain basic principles common to all the different kinds or classes of transplanting. These may be listed as follows:

1. Keep the roots from drying out.
2. Injure the feeding root system as little as possible.
3. Balance unavoidable root disturbance and reduction of the absorption area by reducing the transpiring (leaf) area of the plant.
4. Prepare the soil thoroughly; firm it securely around the newly set place and do not let it dry out while the plant is getting established in its new location.

These rules apply, with very slight modifications, to transplanting activities of all kinds. This should be kept in mind as we discuss the detailed methods of handling different classes of plants, even though each rule may not be specifically referred to in each case. On the other hand, if they are strictly adhered to and conscientiously followed, there is almost no limit to the extent to which successful transplanting can be carried. As an instance, the writer recalls the moving of some shrubs—lilac, mock orange, spiræa, etc., on the occasion of the purchase of a suburban property in mid-spring, just when the plants were in bloom. It seemed almost ridiculous to try to transplant them, but the attempt was made. Moreover, as a result of wetting the ground thoroughly before digging the shrubs, keeping the root systems wrapped in wet burlap, rushing the plants to their new location by automobile, having the holes ready and the new soil moist, and keeping the earth from drying out at any time thereafter, the attempt was entirely successful. The plants were established with little if any check; indeed some of them did not show so much as a wilted blossom after twelve hours in their new location. Of course, success of that sort means lots of care and effort, but it is good to know what can be I accomplished when the need arises and one is willing to take trouble.

Transplanting Seedlings

The first transplanting of vegetable or flower seedlings started in a pot, pan or flat is termed "pricking out," and should be done as soon as the first pair of true leaves appear. Before this the seedlings are likely to be too delicate to handle; if left much longer in crowded rows they are likely to become spindly and weak.

Several hours before pricking out, wet the soil in the flat and that into which the plants are to go; they are more easily removed from moist soil, more of which will cling to the root hairs. Lift out small bunches of the seedlings with a small stick or trowel—a small, diamond-shaped mason's trowel is excellent—separate them gently with the fingers, holding them by the leaves, and reset them an inch or so apart each way. Make a hole for each plant with a small dibble or skewer, let the seedling stand about as deep as it was before, and press the soil well around the roots with the fingers. When all are planted, the flat or bed may be gently sprinkled until the soil is quite moist, and then slightly shaded if the sun is hot and shines full upon it.

Whenever possible, it is desirable to transplant such seedlings a second time before setting them out in their permanent locations. This shift should be done when their leaves begin to overlap, and should leave them about four inches apart each way. In the case of eggplant, which suffers if its roots are much disturbed, or any plants for which special care is desired, this second shift should be into small pots or old berry boxes. The latter and the various kinds of paper pots can later be set directly in the field or garden without removing the plants which will soon send their roots out through the cracks or through the paper as it rots away. When pots are not used, this second transplanting usually injures the root system more or less, so it is well to pinch off about half the leaf surface of each seedling as it is set out.

Whenever cabbage, tomato, pepper or other plants that are attacked by cutworms are set outdoors, it is well to wrap a paper collar around the stem of each one. This should extend about an inch above and an inch below the surface of the ground. Another type of cutworm preventer is a disc of tough paper (tarred roofing paper is good) slit to the center and slipped around the stem of the plant close to the ground. An additional precaution that is especially worthwhile in the case of lettuce is to cover each newly set out plant with an old berry box or some kind of commercial plant protector or shade. This will tend to prevent severe wilting and a resulting check; but whatever is used, be sure to provide for ventilation through or under it.

Transplanting to the Open Ground

Whether you have raised your plants from seed or have bought pot grown stock from a nurseryman or plantsman, the details of setting out both vegetables and ornamentals are the same. In the small garden it is usually possible to arrange or wait for conditions that are just about right. A damp, cloudy day is best, especially if there is good chance of a rainstorm before long. Otherwise, wait until the cool of the evening so that the plants may have the night in which to get over the shock of being moved—for it is a shock—and then, if the next day is clear and hot, shade them slightly.

In planting strawberries it is customary to trim the roots off evenly about six inches long, as well as part of the tops. This gives a thick, uniform bunch of fibrous roots that are easily handled and quickly inserted into an opening made in the soil with a thrust of spade. This is good practice with any fibrous-rooted plant that stands transplanting well, but there are many sorts with which the less root disturbance, the better. In moving these, prepare the hole, invert the pot, bolding the stem of the plant between the first two fingers, tap the rim of the pot against any hard object and place the root ball in the hole with the slightest possible loss of soil; then fill the hole with water and let it soak in before replacing the soil. The final step is to leave a slight depression around the plant so that surface water will run in toward the roots rather than away from them, as it would from a mounded up surface. If the soil is heavy and tends to bake, sprinkle a little loose, dry earth around the plant as a mulch to prevent excessive evaporation.

In this connection, a hint in regard to packing growing plants for shipment may not be out of place. If they are to go any distance and be out of the soil for any considerable time, do not soak the soil or try to keep it wet during the trip. On the contrary, have it only normally moist, wrap the plants (singly or in small bundles) snugly in slightly moistened newspaper, tie each package and pack all together in a papa or burlap lined basket. Later, when you have set them all out, and not until then, give the plants a good drink. This method gives them much less of a shock than the commoner one of soaking them first, then having them often dry out in transit and suffer all the more by contrast.

After setting out plants, as with all growing crops, water copiously *when they need* and cultivate between times. *Do not* sprinkle lightly every little while, as the plants do not absorb moisture through the leaves and a shallow wetting of the soil only attracts the roots up toward the surface, where the first real drought often kills some of them.

Transplanting Shrubs and Small Trees

As far as general transplanting methods are concerned, these two classes of plants may be considered together. As with practically all plants other than herbaceous, they are generally moved while dormant, although, as noted above, success may result from spring or summer moving if sufficient care is given. For evergreens, the former practice of transplanting only in August and early September is still recommended by some, but the dormant system, especially that involving the frozen ball of roots, is quite in common use.

The success with which shrubs are moved depends largely upon their root systems; nursery grown stock that has been transplanted at least once has a more bushy, compact root system than wild field grown specimens, and is therefore more satisfactorily transplanted. Likewise, plants with a shallow, spreading root habit are easier to handle than tap-rooted or fleshy-rooted sorts, such as the walnuts, hickories, magnolias, etc. Taking first the ordinary dormant system, the essential steps are about as follows:

Upon receipt of plants from the nursery, leave them wrapped unless a delay of several days must elapse before they are set out; in this case unpack and heel them in, in a somewhat shaded place where the roots will keep moist.

At planting time cut off clean all injured roots and trim back any excessively long ones.

Have the hole big enough to take the root system without crowding. Straighten the roots out as naturally as possible when the plant is placed in the hole.

Let the tree or shrub set about an inch deeper than it set before except in the case of a hedge, when the plants should be set four to six inches deeper in order to develop a thick, much branched base.

Fill in first with the top soil taken from the hole; then add the bottom soil mixed with manure if possible; finish off with more top soil if any is left.

Firm the soil thoroughly, working it in among the small roots. Water the plant well before filling the hole completely.

Cut back the top to balance the root pruning and also to shape the head of the shrub or tree.

When all is finished, mulch with loose soil, coarse manure, or other litter. If severe drought ensues, water well every few days.

In the case of trees taken from the semi-shade of a nursery and set out in early spring, a wrapping of straw around the trunks for the first season may prevent destructive sunburn and bark cracking as a result of the intense, bright sunlight.

When moved any time except in winter, broad-leaved evergreens should have a good part of their leaves stripped off to check evaporation, and thus aid the plants in getting settled. This is not necessary if the plants are moved with a frozen ball of earth.

Transplanting Fruit Trees

This operation is practically the same as that described for shrubs except that as fruits are rarely moved when large, the dormant, early spring or late fall method is the one most commonly used. It is at these times that fruit trees are shipped from the nurseries. The pruning of newly set fruit trees is generally more severe than that of shrubs or ornamentals as it is usually desirable to determine the form and arrangement of the head at this time. This means cutting back the main stem, removing all the side branches but three or four symmetrically arranged around it so that they will not develop weak crotches, and cut these back to a length of six inches or so. Peaches, according to one system of training, are cut back to a single, branchless stem or "whip" when planted.

Another important point in planting fruit trees is their correct alignment. Of course this is more important in a large orchard than in the home fruit garden, but even here straight, evenly spaced rows make a good appearance; moreover they permit the most economical use of the space. The place where each tree should stand must therefore be accurately located either by sighting through a transit or farm level, or by careful measuring, then the tree must be set right there. One of the best ways to assure this result is to use a planting board. This is a plank about five feet long and a few inches wide with three notches cut into it along one side—one near either end and one in the middle. When the spot for each tree is located and marked with a stake, the board is placed with the center notch against the first stake and two other pins are stuck in the ground where the other notches are. The board and the central peg are then removed and the hole is dug without removing the two guide stakes. When it is deep enough, the board placed back against the two pegs, the tree is placed in the hole with its trunk in the center notch just where the locating peg originally stood. By keeping the tree in this position until the hole is filled, it is assured of its exact place.

In some parts of the country transplanted fruit trees have to be protected against the depredations of field mice, rabbits, etc., that gnaw the bark off the trunks. This is best done by encircling each tree with a guard or protector of thin wood veneer, wire netting or stiff building paper, although there are various old recipes for whitewashes and evil-smelling mixtures of mud, manures, carbolic acid, etc., designed to repel attacking rodents.

Fall Planting Opportunities

Many people have a curious notion that the spring is the only natural planting time. The truth is that experience has shown that fall is one of the best seasons for the gardener to set out trees and shrubs. For one thing, work presses less heavily in the autumn. There are fewer things to do in the flower and vegetable gardens, with the result that more time is left to devote to the care of the trees and shrubbery, without which no suburban or country home is complete. The nurserymen are less rushed in the fall and can therefore give more careful attention to the orders which they receive. All things considered, there is no better time to transplant most ornamental trees and shrubs, as well as raspberries, blackberries, currants, and many of the fruit trees.

There are some exceptions. Most of the trees which have stone fruits, such as both the edible and ornamental peaches and cherries, are better left until spring in the colder section of the country, although they are planted to some extent in the fall. There are ornamentals too, with soft, fleshy roots, such as the magnolias, which shouldn't be planted during this season. The average nurseryman will frankly tell which trees are not suitable for fall setting.

When shrubs and trees are set out in the fall, they make growth quickly in the spring and often are much farther along at the end of the season than when planting is left until the spring months, particularly if the spring is a late one, so that planting has to be delayed. One other point in favor of fall planting might be mentioned, although it applies especially to perennial plants. At this time the garden maker has a lively recollection of the appearance which the different plants have made when in bloom, and is therefore able to choose those which he would like for his own garden much more intelligently than he could four or five months later when his remembrance of the past summer's experiences will have become dulled.

Some writers have asserted that the fall is not a good time to set out evergreens, but on the other hand, some of the most expert nurserymen and garden makers declare that the results from fall setting are fully as good, if not better. In a year of heavy rainfall, the planting of evergreens can be done with perfect safety. In seasons of drought, of course, no plants can be put in with assurance unless a large amount of moisture is available to be applied artificially.

One reason why so much difficulty is found in transplanting evergreens of any kind, from the woods or the fields to the garden, is because of the damage which is unavoidably done to the root system. Plants growing wild make very long roots which must be broken off in getting them out of the ground. Nursery planted stock, on the other hand, is usually shifted so often that the roots are short and bunched in a solid mass close to the base of the plant. This greatly facilitates transplanting without giving the trees or shrubs a setback, and is the principal reason why nursery grown stock is preferable for transplanting to that which is found growing wild.

Operations Resembling Transplanting

Not greatly different from transplanting is the division method of propagation of herbaceous perennials discussed elsewhere. In this, the clump or crown of iris, rhubarb, phlox, etc., is dug up, cut into several pieces with a sharp spade or knife— being sure that each piece carries an eye—then each piece is replanted in newly enriched and well-prepared soil.

There is also "heeling in," which might be called a transplanting into temporary quarters when it is necessary to delay setting some plants for a while. To do this, dig a wide but shallow trench with one end gently sloping; against this lay a row of the plants. Sprinkle some soil over their roots, then lay another overlapping layer on them shingle fashion. Continue in this way until all have been packed in, compactly but with their roots completely covered with soil. Fruit trees, shrubs, berry bushes, etc., can be kept this way all winter if they arrive too late in the fall to be set out; or for several weeks in the spring if delivered before satisfactory conditions for planting appear. Of course the soil in and on top of the trench must be kept moist in very dry weather.

Finally, we may consider sodding, which is practically the transplanting of grass. The main object in doing this well is, of course, to get a strip of strong sod of uniform width and thickness. Success will depend largely upon having a good turf underlain with a good clean soil free from stone, to cut from. Strips a foot wide and any desired length are first cut with a grass edger or path trimmer. One man then cuts the strip loose; by sliding a spade or regular sodding tool under it, while a second man rolls the strip tightly toward him. As a rule pieces two and a half to three feet long are most convenient to handle. As in all transplanting, the soil should be slightly moist for best results. The ground to be sodded should be carefully prepared and the soil fined and made perfectly smooth and slightly higher than would seem necessary. Next, lay the strips of sod, putting them together tightly and adding or removing soil beneath wherever this is necessary to produce a smooth surface. Fill any cracks or breaks with fine soil, and when a considerable area is sodded, go over it and pound it down firmly with the back of a flat-bladed spade. A heavy tamper may also be used or a lawn roller, provided the latter is not permitted to move or loosen the sod. When thoroughly firmed, water the new grass plot well, soak it in fact, and keep op a program of rolling, watering and cutting as required until it is well established. Bare spots should be treated to a dusting of grass seed.

Here again we find of moat importance the fundamental suggestions or precautions back of all transplanting: Disturb the roots as little as possible (that is, cut the sod as deep as you can conveniently handle it). Do not expose the roots to the sun and drying wind a moment longer than absolutely necessary. Firm the sod thoroughly after transplanting (in this cue by beating with a spade). Water promptly and abundantly whenever necessary, and refrain from sprinkling in between. Trim bock the top growth to balance the unavoidable injury to the feeding root system (by having the grass cut short before cutting the sod and keeping it trimmed after it is in place).

Cold Weather Preparations

From *Garden Guide: The Amateur Gardeners' Handbook*, edited by A.T. De La Mare, 1920

Leaf Coverings

It is usually better to wait until the ground is a little frozen before applying the winter mulch. It prevents a premature start in spring, due to a slight heating caused by fermentation. Perennials which retain their leaves through the winter, as well as biennials and sweet William, heuchera and many others, are best covered with straw or leaves, but not manure, which often disfigures the foliage due to its decay. An excellent method, however, is to cover the beds with evergreen boughs and then place leaves upon these, in which case the leaves are prevented from matting. Leaves which mat together badly, as elm, maple, and other trees which drop their foliage early, are not as valuable as oak. Coverings which are too thick cause a premature

Straw or reed mats.

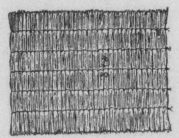 

It is a fairly easy matter to manufacture a good, stout reed mat or straw mat for protective purposes. A ball of stout cord and the necessary material for the mat; a little dexterity in binding these into bundles and in twisting the cord, as shown in the drawing, is all that are necessary. These mats can be put to a dozen good uses. Supplied also by the seedhouses.

Another form of winter protection.

The ordinary coldframe, especially if covered with mats in hard weather, is sufficient shelter for all that class of plants which are spoken of as "doubtfully hardy." Parsley can be wintered here: Violets can be grown and flowered in deep frames: tender roses and shrubs for placing out of doors in summer can find a place.

start in the spring, resulting in crippled growth because of the late frosts.

Unless the perennials are diseased the tops may remain during the winter; breaking or cutting them off often exposes the growing points.

Protecting Lilies

For protecting lilies a mound of ashes, placed over the crown, is frequently advised. The tiger, the Canada, the coral, the handsome, the thunbergian, and the Turk's cap can be successfully protected in this manner. We have had occasion before to mention the protection of eremurus, which consists of using a deep box filled with leaves and left over the plants till rather late in the season, otherwise the young shoots will be injured in the spring.

Windbreaks for Trees and Shrubs

For many trees and shrubs, a windbreak will be the proper sort of shelter from the drying winds of winter. Trees are apt to be injured in winter by the loss of water by evaporation from the twigs; this cannot be supplied by the frozen roots, and the plant dies. Temporary fences may be erected of boards or cornstalks which will give the required break to the full sweep of the wind. Such protection is placed on the south side of broad-leaved evergreens to shield them from the winter sun. The branches of either deciduous or evergreen trees should be tied up when the trees are somewhat columnar and are susceptible to breaking by wind or snow. This is especially necessary with Irish juniper.

Tender plants and newly set trees, evergreens and others, are successfully protected by tying them together and covering with hemlock boughs. Other trees and shrubs are covered deeply so that the roots do not freeze, in which case many are encouraged to grow under adverse conditions.

It is the alternate freezing and thawing of the trunk and branches of fruit trees that causes them to crack open on the south side. Low heading is the only precaution.

Conditions That Suggest Frost

1. Weather comes in "waves," hence an abnormally warm spell during the frost season is liable to be followed by a sudden drop in temperature.
2. A clear sky permits increased radiation and improves the chances of frost.
3. The passing of a storm is usually followed by "clearing and colder," which often means a frost.
4. A still, clear air with a steadily falling temperature in the late afternoon is a good sign of frost.
5. Frosts are more likely to occur in the open country and in small villages than in and near large cities; they occur on lowlands and in "pockets" and valleys sooner than on hillsides; they are less frequent near bodies of water than away from lakes, the ocean, etc.; northern, western, eastern and southern slopes are frosty in decreasing order as given; sandy, well drained, and dark colored soils are less liable to frost than heavy clays and wet, poorly tilled, light colored types.

To Ward off Frost

Since frosts accompany dry, clear, still air and the radiation of heat from the ground and plants, the following methods of preventing them can be employed in the small garden according to the means at hand: (1) Heating of the air by means of smudge fires, orchard heaters, etc.; (2) the moistening of the air by means of sprays; (3) a combination of (1) and (2), such as the discharge of waste steam into the air; (4) ventilation, or the stirring of the atmosphere, to prevent the settling of layers of cold air on the plants; (5) irrigation by the furrow or flooding system; (6) the covering of tender plants with cloths, paper, a mulch, etc.; (7) the spraying of the plants themselves both to prevent the formation of frost and to help thaw out hardy plants that may have been touched overnight.

Fall Treatment of Plants with Reference to Frost

VEGETABLES.—Perennials, such as asparagus, horseradish, Jerusalem artichoke and strawberries axe entirely hardy. It is, however, well to mulch them after the ground freezes, partially to prevent alternate thawing and freezing, which tend to heave them out of the ground, and partially to add plant food to be dug in the spring.

Annuals may be put into four groups with relation to their ability to withstand frost, as follows:

1. *Entirely hardy.* Those marked a may be sown or planted in late fall for early spring use. The rest may be left in the garden to be harvested as

needed. For convenience it is well to mulch the root crops to make digging easier: corn, Brussels sprouts, corn salad (a), kale, leek, parsnips, salsify, witloof chicory (a), spinach (may be handled both ways)

2. *Hardy*. These will stand a light freeze but should be harvested before the ground *freezes* solid. In the case of frosted lettuce, thaw out slowly in ice water and use at once. carrots, lettuce, onions, peas, and rutabagas.

3. *Fairly hardy*. These will stand a light frost and do their best in cool weather: beets, cabbage, cardoon, cauliflower. celery, celery cabbage (Pe-tsai), kohl-rabi, potatoes radishes, Swiss chard.

4. Practically all other vegetables need warm weather in which to make good growth, and protection from even the lightest frost.

FLOWERS: Perennials are, of course, hardy as to root, even though their tops may be killed down. The following, however, continue to bloom well after the first frost: chrysanthemum, gaillardia grandiflora, Antirrhinum majus, Coreopsis lanceolata, and Lathyrus latifolius.

Annual sorts growing from bulbs that are hardy and that therefore can be planted in the fall for spring blooming, include: lilies, crown imperial, hyacinth, lily of the valley, narcissus, scilla, and tulips.

Narcissus for best results should be dug after flowering and allowed to ripen before being replanted in the fall.

Plants with tender bulbs which should be dug after frost has killed or blackened the tops but before the ground freezes, include the following: begonia (Tuberous), caladium, dahlia, gladiolus, tritoma, and tuberose.

Of non-bulbous annuals which are not expected to last more than one season, there are some that continue to bloom even after a mild frost. Among these are aster, cosmos, sweet alyssum, clarkia, marigold, pansy, ten-weeks stock, etc.

Greenhouses and Cold Frames

From *Garden Guide: The Amateur Gardeners' Handbook*, edited by A. T. De La Mare, 1920

Advantages of a Greenhouse

We merely wish to call attention in this place to the advantages of such a house. A succession of flowers can be had during the winter at small cost, either by lifting the geraniums from outdoors in the autumn and potting them up, as well as Salvias and some other summer flowering plants, or by sowing little batches of seeds, or planting bulbs and bringing these on gradually. We all know how difficult it is to make a success of Dutch bulbs in the ordinary dwelling house, owing to the dryness of the atmosphere and the fluctuation of temperatures. In a greenhouse these conditions can be regulated to suit the plants.

Frames and Their Uses

The garden without its quota of frames is like an automobile without tires; you may run it, but it is hard and slow work to get anywhere with it. Frames, properly managed, will accelerate and supplement the garden throughout the year. The frames (which you can build yourself with little trouble if you do not care to buy them) and the sash are not expensive. With reasonable care and if kept well painted, they will last indefinitely. The writer has a sash which has been in continuous use for over twenty-two years. Concrete frames are growing in popularity, as they can be built at little additional expense and will last practically forever. They are tighter and warmer than wooden frames, and they

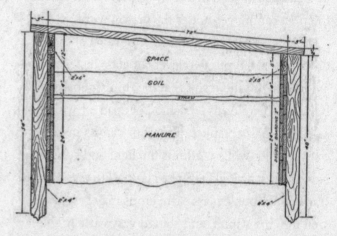

Section of a hotbed frame with details of measurements. Reproduced from a Cornell bulletin.

do not warp or settle, so that the sash always fits them tightly, a very important point.

Standard size sash covers a space 3 by 6 ft., and the frames to support it are made to correspond. In building of wood it is better to use 2-in. planks, although inch boards are often employed. In building a wooden frame, after ascertaining the correct size to fit the particular sash you are buying, put in posts of 3 by 4 in. stuff with the inside corner planed down for an inch or so, to avoid a sharp edge. There should be a drop of about from 3 to 4 in. from the back to the front. If you can get boards or planks 6 and 9 in. wide and 6 or 12 ft. long, practically no cutting will have to be done in building the frame. Let the sides come down well below the ground as the soil inside should be a few inches below the general ground level. After it is finished, a layer of gravel or roofing slate on the outside, or banking up with soil, nearly to the top,

Small forcing frame.

will greatly increase its efficiency in keeping out cold. Concrete frames should be made 4 to 6 in. thick and sunk well below the ground level so that the frost cannot get under the mason work.

At least part of your sash should be of the double glazed type. Two layers of glass instead of one are used, with the result that the thin air space left between them forms a cushion of dead air which is as effective as a blanket of wool or canvas in keeping out the cold, while it admits the light and sunshine as readily as a single layer of glass. With a good tight frame and double glass sash, crops may be grown well into the winter, and started very early in the Spring, without any other protection.

With single glass sash, wooden shutters or burlap mats are used as an extra covering in cold weather. If these are employed in addition to double glass sash, half hardy crops like lettuce can be carried through very severe weather without any artificial heat at all, and the frames will be ready for use in the spring as early as they may be wanted, without having to wait for them to thaw out

Hotbeds are made one to two feet deeper than for coldframes, to allow for the layer of manure put in to furnish the heat.

Location

Generally it is best to locate with southern exposure and with a protection of trees or fence at north. Three feet should be allowed back of frame to the fence to allow for working facilities. Do not put the frame where the spring rains may drain into it. Good drainage is especially important in winter as well as in Spring.

Preparation of Bed

During winter, deep the snow out by a covering of boards. In the middle of March, or six or eight weeks before plants can be safely put out of doors, if the bed has been constructed as directed, two feet of fresh manure is placed in the frames. Nothing but fresh manure will suffice, horse manure being best, which has been piled and turned several times to bring to a uniform temperature. As placed in frames, the manure should gradually be stamped rather firmly. To ensure more uniform heating, a layer of straw is used to cover the manure. Soil which has been stored in basement is then spread over to a depth of four inches. The soil should be rather sandy and should consist of good loam, leaf mold, sand and some well decayed manure. Put on the sashes and, as Mrs. Rion, in "Let's Make a Flower Garden," says: "Let her bile." It will steam tremendously for four or five days, then it gets down to regular business of more or less even heat. There are nice thermometers to be had to take the bed's temperature; find out when its fever has dropped below ninety degrees; then you know it is time to go ahead and plant.

Another sort of hotbed may be constructed by placing a coldframe upon a heap of manure which in

One of the king construction co.'S double-glazed frames, a very valuable type.

the colder regions should be a foot and a half thick when packed rather firmly. Hotbeds can be easily heated by running a pipe from the heating plant of the house into the frame which can be located near the house.

Management of Hotbeds and Coldframes

Radish, lettuce, cabbage tomato, cauliflower, aster, pansy, scarlet sage, verbena, and such seeds, are planted in rows, several inches apart. The ventilation of the frame must be carefully attended to and if moisture condenses on the glass the sash should be lifted a trifle on the side away from the prevailing wind. Sashes should be capable of being raised at any angle. Much damage can be done by leaving the frame closed tightly on sunny days, for the crops are easily burned.

The watering should be done on sunny mornings. When the plants have produced their

A well-sheltered line of coldframes facing due south. How invaluable they are.

third leaf they should be transplanted, according to their various needs. Lettuce will, perhaps, be matured in the frames and will need to stand eight inches apart, while tomatoes may be set out three inches apart and transplanted again. On really cold nights the hotbeds should be covered with some sort of mat, either of straw or padded cloth.

Pests and Diseases

From *Garden Guide: The Amateur Gardeners' Handbook*, edited by A.T. De La Mare, 1920

Insect Pests—Arranged by Host Plants

Apple

Leaf-Crumpler: **Case Bearers: Bud-Moths**: Several kinds pass the winter as small caterpillars and feed upon the unfolding leaves, occasionally doing considerable damage. Spray with lead arsenate as soon as trees begin to look green; repeat a week later.

Canker Worms: Small looping caterpillars feed upon the leaves during May, and when disturbed, spin down on silken threads. Spray foliage with lead arsenate before blossom buds open, and again soon after the petals fall. In unsprayed orchards sticky bands of tree-tanglefoot should be placed around the trees late in October, and kept sticky until January 1st, and again kept sticky from April 1st to June 1st.

Canker Worms.

Tent Caterpillar: Forms nests at the forks of the branches during the month of May and devour the leaves. Spray with lead arsenate just before blossoms open and again after they fall. Egg-masses may be clipped off and burned during winter, and the nests may be removed with a cone-shaped brush.

Tent caterpillar.

Codling Moth or Apple Worm: Larva burrows inside the fruit, particularly around the core. Spray with lead arsenate soon after blossoms fall and repeat three to four weeks later. Both foliage and fruit should be kept well covered with spray until fruit is nearly grown.

Lesser Apple Worm: Feeds on the surface of fruit that is nearly mature, often injuring it in storage. Spray as for codling moth.

Gipsy Moth: Occurs in the United States only in Southeastern New England. Brownish, hairy caterpillars defoliate the trees in May and June. Spray foliage with lead arsenate, using 5 to 10 pounds of the paste in 50 gallons of water. From August to May, seek for egg clusters and destroy them *in situ* by soaking with creosote. Band trees with tree tanglefoot.

Leaf-roller: Green Fruit Worms: Palmer Worm: Caterpillars feed upon leaves and partly grown fruit, often seriously injuring it. Spray with lead arsenate as for codling moth.

Tussock Moths: Tufted caterpillars of several species feed upon the leaves the latter half of summer. The white-marked tussock moth and the hickory tussock moth are usually the most abundant and therefore the chief offenders. Spray with lead arsenate as for codling moth.

Codling moth or apple worm.

Gipsy moth.

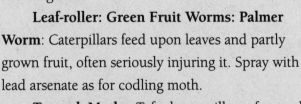

Red-humped Caterpillar: **Yellow-necked Caterpillar**: Feed in clusters on ends of branches, often stripping young trees in August and September. Gather by hand and destroy, or spray the foliage with lead arsenate.

Fall Web-worm: **Brown-tail Moth**: See Pear.

Curculios: Grubs of both apple and plum curculios infest the fruit, making it gnarled and ill-shaped. Spray twice after blossoms fall, and remove infested fruit in thinning.

Apple Maggot or Railroad Worm: Small, legless white maggots burrow in the flesh of the ripening fruit of sweet and sub-acid varieties, especially those ripening early in the season. Will greatly injure fruit in storage unless kept at a low temperature. Keep trees sprayed with lead arsenate as for codling moth. Destroy all infested fruit.

Round-headed Borer: **Flat-headed Borer**: Grubs tunnel in the trunk near the ground. Dig out the borers wherever saw-dust appears. Apply a mixture of lime-sulfur and lead arsenate to the trunks.

Round-headed borer.

Leaf- blister Mite: See Pear.

Red Spider: Clover Mite: Injure the leaves, especially in dry seasons, by feeding on the surface, causing them to turn yellow or rusty in color. Eggs of clover mite are often abundant on tree trunks through the winter and are orange red in color; they are killed by the lime-sulfur spray in early spring. For summer treatment, spray leaves with kerosene emulsion or nicotine solution.

Apple Red-Bugs: Two species of red leaf-bugs suck the sap, causing the leaves to become distorted and the fruit to be irregular with depressed spots usually most abundant near blossom end. Spray with nicotine solution (1 pint in so

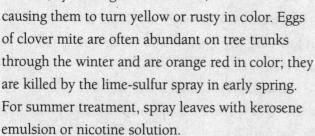

Apple red-bugs.

gallons water) either separately or in combination with lead arsenate, lime-sulfur or Bordeaux mixture.

Tarnished Plant Bugs: Suck the sap from the fruit, dimples developing from the punctures. Spray with nicotine solution as or red bugs.

Leaf Hoppers: Whitish insects sucking sap from the underside of the leaves, causing a whitish spotting or mottling on upper surface. Spray with nicotine solution as for red bugs.

Woolly Apple Aphids: A white, woolly or cottony mass on bark represents a colony of this aphid, which sucks the sap, forming swellings or galls on the twigs. It clusters in wounds and prevents healing. It also forms galls on the roots, and often the smaller roots decay. Plant only clean or fumigated stock. Apply tobacco dust liberally and work into the soil around trees. Spray with kerosene emulsion to kill aphids on twigs.

Rosy and Green Aphids: Rosy aphids attack the fruit clusters which fail to develop, and also the leaves, causing them to curl. The green aphids usually attack only the leaves of terminal shoots and water sprouts, causing them to curl, thus checking the growth. Spray with nicotine solution as for red bugs.

Rosy and green aphids.

Oyster-shell Scale: Scurfy Scale: Both occur on the bark and are elongated or pear-shaped shells, the former about the same color as the bark; the latter, light gray or whitish. The insect under the shell sucks sap from the twigs. Spray with nicotine solution, soap and water, or kerosene emulsion about the second week in June.

Oyster-shell scale.

San José Scale: See Scale Peach. Illus.

Ash

Oyster-shell-Scale: See Apple.

Asparagus

Asparagus Beetles: Both adults and larvæ of the common asparagus beetle, and the twelve-spotted asparagus beetle feed upon the leaves, often injuring new plantations. Cut everything clean during the cutting season; later spray with lead arsenate. New plantations should be sprayed when the beetles first appear.

Common asparagus beetle.

Asters

Blister Beetles: The black is the most common; it feeds upon the flowers. Daily hunting and shaking the beetles into a pan of kerosene will quickly clear them. Some cover after that with mosquito netting.

Aster blister beetle.

Barley

Army Worm: See Grass.

Bean

Weevil: Adults lay eggs in the pods in the field and keep on breeding in the dried seed, finally ruining it for planting or for food. Fumigating for 36 hours with carbon disulphide, using about two fluid ounces in a shallow dish on top of the seed in a tightly-covered barrel, will kill the weevils without injuring the beans for food or for planting. Mixing the beans with an equal weight of air-slaked lime will prevent damage. If to be used for food only, the beans may be heated in the oven to kill weevils, but if the temperature approaches 150° F. the vitality of the seeds is endangered.

Bean weevil.

Green Clover Worm: Occasionally slender, green, wriggling caterpillars riddle the leaves in July.

Dust string beans with a fine powder. Beans to be shelled may be sprayed with lead arsenate.

Aphids: Black aphids on leaves and new shoots sucking the sap. Spray with nicotine solution.

Beet-swiss chard

Leaf-Miner: A small fly lays eggs in the leaves and the maggots tunnel or mine between the upper and lower leaf surfaces. Destroy all infested leaves and practice late fall plowing. Destroy all plants of the weed known as "lambs' quarters" in which this insect breeds.

Leaf-Miner

Leaf-miner.

Birch

Tussock Moths: See Apple, Hickory and Horse Chestnut.

Birch Leaf Skeletonizer: Small yellowish larvæ feed on both sides of the leaves in late summer, often stripping the trees. Spray in July with lead arsenate.

Bronze Birch Borer: The grub makes a spiral tunnel just under the bark of upper main branches, ridges showing on the outside. Often kills trees. Cut and burn infested trees before May 1st.

Blackberry

Blackberry Sawfly: Larvæ feed upon leaves in June and July. Spray with lead arsenate about June 15th.

Blackberry Crown Borer: Grub tunnels in larger roots and at base of stem. No remedy except to dig out and destroy.

Red-necked Cane Borer: Grub tunnels in stalks, forming galls or swellings often three inches long. Cut and burn all infested canes in winter or early spring.

Box

Leaf-miner: A small two-winged fly lays eggs in the leaf and the larvæ tunnel between the upper and lower surfaces. Destroy infested leaves. Fumigate the plants with hydrocyanic acid gas.

Oyster-shell Scale: See Apple.

Cabbage-cauliflower

Cabbage Worm: Velvety green worms feed on leaves throughout the season. Spray unheaded plants with lead arsenate. Use insect powder or hellebore on headed plants.

Cabbage worm.

Cabbage Looper: Smooth looping caterpillars feed preceding the late summer, and often tunnel into the cabbage head. Spray as for cabbage worm.

Cabbage looper.

Cabbage Maggot: Tunnels in the stem and main root of early set plants, near the surface of the ground, checking growth and often killing the plants. Place tarred paper discs around stems when plants are set. Practice crop rotation.

Cabbage maggot.

Cabbage Aphis: Clustered underneath the leaves, this insect sucks the sap, often causing much injury. Under-spray with nicotine or kerosene emulsion.

Carnation

Aphid or Green Fly: Sucks the sap from stems, leaves and buds. Spray with nicotine solution, soap and water, or fumigate with tobacco.

Celery

Celery Caterpillar: Devours the leaves of celery, fennel, parsnip,

Celery Caterpillar

Celery caterpillar.

parsley and carrot. Hand picking is usually the best remedy. Parsnip and carrot may be sprayed with lead arsenate.

Cherry

Cherry or Pear Slug: Eats on upper surface of leaf. Spray with hellebore or lead arsenate.

Canker Worms: See Apple.

Cherry Maggots or Fruit Flies: Larvæ of two species infest ripening fruit. Sprinkle foliage in early June with sweetened lead arsenate to kill the adults.

Cherry or pear slug.

Cherry Aphids: A brown aphid on underside of leaves, sucking sap and curling the leaves. Spray with nicotine solution, kerosene emulsion or soap and water.

Chestnut-chinquapin

Canker Worms: See Apple.

Nut Weevils: Long-nosed snout beetles lay eggs in developing fruit and the grub infest the nuts. Destroy all infested nuts. Fumigate nuts with carbon disulphide as for beans.

Weeviled chestnut.

Two-lined Chestnut Borer: Slender, flat-headed grubs tunnel under bark of chestnut and oak trees. Badly infested trees should be burned or the bark removed before insects mature and spread to other trees.

Chrysanthemum

Aphis or Black Fly: Sucks the sap from the tender leaves and flower stems. Plants should be sprayed with or dipped into nicotine solution or soap and water. Fumigate with tobacco. A steady stream of water from your hose will often prove effective.

Cineraria

Aphis or Green Fly: Sucks sap from new leaves and stems. Treat as for preceding.

Columbine

Columbine Leaf-miner: A two-winged fly lays eggs on the leaves and the maggots tunnel between the upper and lower surfaces. Destroy the leaves first infested and cultivate the ground around the plants.

Corn

Cut Worms: See Tomato.
Army Worm: See Grass.
Corn Ear Worm: Eats the immature kernels at tip of ear. Dust with sulfur and powdered lead arsenate, equal parts.

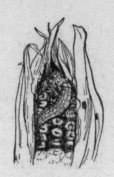

Corn ear worm.

Cranberry

Fireworm or Black-headed Cranberry Worm: Small, pale green, black-headed caterpillars web the leaves and new shoots together and feed inside the nest. Spray with lead arsenate to kill the caterpillars. Flood the bog for three days to kill the pupæ.

Yellow-headed Cranberry Worm: Small, green, yellow-headed caterpillars injure plants in same manner as the preceding. Spray with lead arsenate. Keep bogs flooded until about May 20.

Cranberry Fruit-worm: Pale green larvæ infest the berries. Flood the bog for about two weeks as soon as the fruit has been harvested. Destroy all infested berries.

Cucumber

Striped Cucumber Beetle: Eats the leaves of young plants. Larvæ tunnel in main root or stem just underground, sometimes killing the plant. Dust plants heavily with

Striped cucumber beetle.

land plaster or dry lead arsenate. Cover plants with screens.

Melon Aphid: See Melon.

Currant

Currant Worm: Eats leaves in May. Spray with lead arsenate or fresh hellebore. Dampen leaves, then sprinkle with air slaked lime.

Currant worm.

Currant Stem Girdler: Adults girdle new tips after laying eggs in them. Clip off and burn these tips at any time of the year.

Currant Borers: Larvæ of two species—one a moth and the other a beetle—burrow in the pith of the stems, causing the leaves to droop and finally killing the canes. Destroy infested canes in May.

Four-lined Leaf-bug: An active bug, striped lengthwise with black and yellow, sucking sap from the terminal leaves. Spray with nicotine solution.

Scurfy Scale: A light gray, pear-shaped scale on bark sucking the sap. Spray second week in June with kerosene emulsion or nicotine solution.

San José Scale: See Peach.

Currant Aphid: Yellowish green aphids sucking sap from the underside of the leaves causing them to curl. Underspray with nicotine solution or kerosene emulsion.

Cyclamen

Leaf-Mite: Transparent microscopic mites cause leaves to curl; plants do not blossom. Syringe under leaf surface strongly with water. Spray with, or dip the plants in, nicotine solution (1 part to 400).

Dahlia

Tarnished Plant Bug: Sucks the sap from the stems and developing buds, causing them to drop off. Spray with nicotine solution.

Stalk borer.

Stalk Borer: Larva burrows up and down inside the main stem, the upper portion usually wilting and dying. Slit the stem lengthwise with care and kill the borer.

Dogwood

Sawflies: The larvæ of several kinds feed upon the different kinds of dogwoods. Spray with hellebore or lead arsenate.

Egg-plant

Flea-Beetle: See potato.
Colorado Potato Beetle: See Potato.

Elm

Spiny Elm Caterpillar: Black spiny caterpillars in clusters strip certain branches of elm, willow and poplar. Remove cluster and destroy while caterpillars are small, or spray with lead arsenate.

Elm Leaf Beetle: In May the adults eat holes through the leaves, and in June and July the grubs eat the green tissue from the under surface. Spray under surface of leaves with lead arsenate about June 1st to kill the newly hatched grubs.

Elm leaf beetle.

Canker worms: see Apple.
White-marked Tussock Moth: See Horse Chestnut.
Leopard Moth: Larvæ make deep tunnels under the bark, often girdling the branches, which later break off. Small trees may be examined, and the borers killed by injecting carbon disulphide and closing the openings, or by inserting a wire.
Elm Scale: Oval, brown, soft scales, with white marginal fringe, occur in the crevices of the bark of the trunk and larger branches. Spray with kerosene emulsion.

White Elm Scale: A whitish, pear-shaped scale on twigs. Spray about June 10, with kerosene emulsion.
Elm Woolly Aphids: Several species curl the leaves, or form in cottony masses on the bark. Spray with kerosene emulsion.

Euonymus

Euonymus Scale: Various species of Euonymus are injured by this scale, which has narrow white shells in the male, and pear-shaped gray or brown shells in the female. Cut and burn the worst infested twigs. Spray in June with kerosene emulsion to kill the young.

Euonytnus scale.

Fern

Woolly Bears: Several light brown hairy caterpillars devour the fronds in late summer. Spray with lead arsenate.
Hemispherical Scale: Brown, oval, convex scales on fronds of plants under glass. Apply soap and water or nicotine solution as a dip or spray.

Geranium

Greenhouse leaf-tyer: Small, green wriggling caterpillars feed upon the leaves of plants under glass. Spray with lead arsenate.
White Fly: See Tomato.

Gooseberry

Currant Worm: Larvæ devour foliage Apply hellebore or lead arsenate early in May.
Yellow Currant Fruit Fly: Small maggots infest the berries, which color prematurely and drop. Destroy infested fruit.
Gooseberry Fruit Worm: Greenish larvæ feed inside the berries. Destroy infested fruit.

Grape

Grape Plume Moth: Green spiny caterpillars web together the leaves of new shoots. Crush by pinching the nests.

Grape Vine Flea Beetle: Adults and larvæ devour the leaves. Spray with lead arsenate.

Rose Chafer: Long-legged, brown beetles appear about the middle of June and feed upon the leaves, flowers and newly set fruit, often doing great damage. Spray heavily with lead arsenate just before blossoms open and, if necessary, again after fruit has set.

Rose chafer.

Grape Root Worm: Adults eat chainlike holes in leaves in July, and grubs eat roots, often causing great injury. Spray foliage with lead arsenate.

Grape Berry Moth: Larvæ feed inside the berry. Spray with lead arsenate after fruit sets, and repeat twice at intervals of ten days. Place paper bags over the clusters soon after the fruit sets.

Sphinx and other Caterpillars: Several kinds of horn worms, as well as other caterpillars, feed on the leaves. Spray with lead arsenate or practice hand-picking.

Grape berry moth.

Grape Phylloxera: Sucks sap from leaves and roots, forming galls, causing serious injury to European varieties. Graft on stocks of native species.

Grape Leaf-Hopper: Small yellow red-marked leaf-hoppers sucks sap from underside of the leaves. Spray with nicotine solution.

Grass

White Grubs: These are the larvæ of June beetles and when nearly mature and abundant in the soil cause much damage, especially in dry seasons, by eating off the roots of grass, corn, potatoes, strawberries, etc. Plow in fall to expose insects. Harrow very thoroughly before planting.

White grub.

Army-worm: Occasionally, brown, striped caterpillars are so abundant as to strip the leaves and heads from grass and grain during July; they move like armies from one field to another, sometimes doing great damage. Use poisoned bran mash. Plow deep furrows across the line of march, with the steep side barring their progress. Sprinkle worms with kerosene. Spray strips of grass or grain with lead arsenate to protect the fields beyond.

Army worm.

Fall Army-worm: Attacks lawns and millet in September, like preceding, but does not migrate in such large numbers. Same remedies apply. Plow in late fall.

Hickory

Walnut Caterpillar: See Walnut.

Fall Web-worm: See Pear.

Hickory Borer: Larvæ tunnel in solid wood of trunk. The burrows may be found by the sawdust ejected. Inject carbon disulphide into the burrow and close the entrance.

Hickory Tussock Moth: White and black hairy caterpillars feed upon the leaves in late summer. Spray with lead arsenate.

Hickory Bark Beetle: Small black beetles breed under the bark, and the galleries soon girdle the tree. The adults emerge through small round "shot-holes" in the bark. Beetles also feed at base of leaves, causing them to break off and fall in midsummer. Badly infested trees should be removed before May, and either burned or else the bark removed. Spray healthy trees about June 1st with strong lead arsenate with nicotine solution added.

Nut Weevils: Larvæ infest the fruit or nuts. See Chestnut.

Hickory Gall Aphid: Curious galls on the leaf stems often cause the leaves to fall in midsummer. Galls contain large numbers of aphids. Spray with nicotine solution just as new growth starts in spring.

Hop

Hop Aphid: Green aphids sucking sap from the under leaf-surface. Spray with kerosene emulsion.

Horse chestnut

White-marked tussock moth.

White-marked Tussock Moth: Black and yellow, red-headed, hairy caterpillars, each bearing four upright tufts of white hairs, devour the leaves. Spray with lead arsenate.

Iris

Iris Root Borer: A larva tunnels in the root stocks, injuring many plants. Destroy infested root stocks. Burn over iris beds in winter to destroy the eggs.

Juniper

Juniper Web-worm: Small brown caterpillars feed upon the leaves which they web together. Spray with lead arsenate.

Larch

Larch Sawfly: Larvæ defoliate trees in midsummer. Spray with lead arsenate.

Woolly Aphid: White cottony tufts on bark and at the leaf whorls. Spray with kerosene emulsion.

Lettuce

Aphid or Green Fly: Sucks sap from the leaves. Spray with soap and water or fumigate beds with tobacco.

Lilac

Lilac Borer: A white larva tunnels in the twigs. Cut and burn infested twigs.

Oyster-shell Scale: See Apple.

San José Scale: See Peach.

Lily

Stalk Borer: See dahlia.

Aphid: Yellow aphids with red markings suck the sap from under side of leaves. Spray with nicotine solution.

Linden

Canker Worm: See Apple.

White-marked Tussock Moth: See Apple and Horse Chestnut.

Linden Borer: White larvæ tunnel in wood at base of tree. Dig out borer or inject carbon disulphide.

Locust

Locust Borer: Larvæ tunnel in solid wood of trunk. Inject carbon disulphide into the burrows and close the entrance.

Maple

White-marked Tussock Moth: See Horse Chestnut.

Other Tussock Moths: See Apple.

Canker-worms: See Apple.

Maple Borer: Larvæ make spiral tunnels just under the bark of trunk or larger branches. Examine the trees in September; the burrows may be located by the sawdust thrown out. Inject carbon disulphide and close the entrance.

Woolly Maple Leaf Scale: White cottony masses of wax containing females and eggs occur on the

Maple borer.

underside of the leaves of sugar maples in Midsummer; the insects suck the sap and cause the leaves to fall prematurely. Males and larvæ are found in the crevices of the bark where the latter pass the winter in white cases. Spray dormant trees with nicotine solution and soap. Burn infested leaves as they drop.

Woolly maple scale.

Cottony Maple Scale: On red and silver maples, large, oval, brown scales pass the winter on the bark of the branches and in summer develop conspicuous cotton-like tufts of white wax nearly half an inch in length. Spray with miscible oils.

Terrapin Scale: Small, reddish brown oval scales occur on small twigs of red and silver maples, sometimes killing them. Spray with kerosene emulsion.

Oyster-shell Scale: See Apple.

Maple Aphids: Green aphids are common on under surface of leaves of Norway and sycamore maples in June. Spray with nicotine solution or kerosene emulsion.

Marguerite

Marguerite Fly or Leaf Miner: A maggot tunnels between upper and lower surface layers of the leaves. Spray with nicotine solution every ten or twelve days.

Melon

Striped Cucumber Beetle: See Cucumber.

Melon Aphid: Sucks the sap from the underside of the leaves, curling them and causing much damage if abundant. Under spray the leaves with nicotine solution.

Millet

Fall Army Worm: See Grass.

Nasturtium

Aphid: Brown aphids cluster on stems and leaves, sucking the sap. Spray with nicotine solution.

Oak

Canker Worm: See Apple.

Brown-tail Moth: See Pear.

Orange Striped Oak-worm: Black and orange striped caterpillars feed upon the leaves late in the season. Spray with lead arsenate.

Oats

Army Worm: See Grass.

Onion

Maggot: Infests the bulb of the young and growing plant. Practice crop rotation.

Thrips or White Blast: Very small insects feed upon the surface of the leaves, causing a whitish appearance. Burn all tops and refuse; burn over the grass land around the field to kill over-wintering insects. Spray with nicotine solution.

Thrips or white blast.

Peony

Rote Chafer: Feeds on blossoms of white varieties. See Grape.

Palm

Scales: Various white and brown scales infest the species of palms found in green houses. Apply nicotine solution or soap and water as a spray or as a dip.

Pea

Pea Weevil: The adult lays eggs in the pods in the field, and the larvæ develop in the dried seeds and the emerging beetles leave round holes. Fumigate with carbon disulphide or cover with air-slaked lime. See bean.

Green Pea Aphid: Sucks the sap from stems and leaves in June, often causing great injury, when abundant. Early varieties may mature a crop before being greatly injured. Spray with nicotine solution and soap.

Peach

Peach Sawfly: Larvæ feed upon leaves in June and July. Spray with lead arsenate.

Peach Borer: Larvæ tunnel under bark at base of trunk. Dig them out in May and again in September. Paint trunks with lead arsenate and lime-sulfur from just below the surface to a foot from the ground.

Peach sawfly.

Fruit Bark Beetle or Shot Hole Borer: Small black beetles tunnel just under the bark, girdling the tree, and emerging through small "shot holes." Burn infested trees and keep others thrifty.

Plum Curculio: See Plum.

San José Scale: Small circular shells containing insects which suck the sap from twigs, leaves and fruit. On fruit a red spot surrounds each insect. Spray dormant trees with lime-sulfur.

Black and Green Aphids: Suck sap from leaves and shoots. Spray with nicotine solution.

San José scale.

Pear

Pear or Cherry Slug: See Cherry.

Brown-tail Moth: Occurs only in Eastern New England. Brown, hairy caterpillars hibernate in nests on twigs and feed on leaves in May and June. Cut and

Brown-tail moth.

burn winter nests. Spray with lead arsenate as soon as blossoms fall, and again in August.

Codling Moth: See Apple.

Fall Web-worm: Brown, hairy caterpillars feed in webs or nests at ends of branches the latter part of summer. Clip off and burn nests when small. Spray with lead arsenate.

Leaf Blister Mite: Forms galls or blisters on unfolding leaves, causing many leaves to fall in July. Blisters turn red, and later brown. Spray dormant trees in late fall or early spring with lime-sulfur.

Pear Psylla: Jumping plant lice suck sap from leaves and shoots, causing many leaves to fall in July. Spray with lime-sulfur in spring just before buds open. Spray infested trees with nicotine solution in July to clean up the fruit.

San José Scale: See Peach.

Pear Thrips: A very small insect that feeds upon the fruit buds, destroying them. Spray with nicotine solution just as buds open and again after blossoms fall.

False Tarnished Plant Bug: Punctures the small and developing fruit, causing it to become irregular and knotty. Spray with nicotine solution and soap.

Phlox

Red Spider: Injures leaves, causing them to turn yellow. Spray with kerosene emulsion or with soap and nicotine solution.

Pine

Sawflies: The larvæ of several native and imported species feed upon the leaves. Spray with lead arsenate.

White Pine Weevil: Larvæ tunnel under the bark of the leader, causing it to wilt and die in Midsummer. Ornamental trees may be protected by spraying leaders about May 1st with lead arsenate or lime-sulfur. Jarring the beetles into a net once a week during May will greatly reduce the damage.

Infested leaders should be cut and destroyed before the adults emerge.

Pine Bark Aphid: Aphids with cottony wax secretion form white patches on bark, sucking the sap. Spray with kerosene emulsion.

Pine Leaf Scale: White, pear-shaped shells on leaves contain insects sucking the sap. Occasionally kill small trees. Spray with nicotine solution or kerosene emulsion about the second week in June.

Plum

Plum curculio: Grub infests the growing fruit, causing it to fall. Jar the trees once a week, for six weeks after trees bloom; catch the beetles on sheets and destroy them. Also spray during the same period with lead arsenate.

Plum curculio.

Fruit Bark Beetle or Shot-hole Borer: See Peach.

Plum aphids: Suck sap from under side of leaves. Spray with nicotine solution and soap.

San José Scale: See Peach.

Poplar

Poplar Tent-maker: Larvæ feed on leaves and fold them together near ends of branches, forming nests. Spray with lead arsenate.

Spiny Elm Caterpillar: See Elm.

Tussock Moths: See Apple, Hickory and Horse Chestnut.

Poplar Borer: Larvæ make large galleries in wood of trunk. Dig out or inject carbon disulphide into the burrow and close the opening.

Poplar and Willow Curculio: Larvæ tunnel in smaller trunk and branches. Destroy badly infested trees. Cut out borers: inject carbon disulphide.

Oyster-shell Scale: See Apple.

Poppy

Aphids: Black aphids suck the sap from stems and leaves. Spray with nicotine solution.

Potato

NOTE—Potatoes require vigilant watching. Watch your crop for three particular enemies: The flea beetles and adult Colorado beetles may appear soon after the leaves show above ground and should be given attention. Larvæ of the Colorado beetle do not appear until about the first of June. About July 1st watch for aphids and spray to eradicate the incipient colonies before the aphids spread over the whole field. Unless promptly checked the aphids will ruin your entire crop in a few days.

Flea Beetle: Small, black, jumping beetles eat holes through the leaves. Spray both upper and under surfaces heavily with lead arsenate.

Colorado Potato Beetle: Both adult and larvæ devour the leaves. Spray or dust with lead arsenate.

Three-Lined Potato Beetle: Larvæ feed upon the leaves and carry their black excrement on their backs. Spray with lead arsenate.

Colorado potato beetle.

Potato Aphid: Green aphids appearing in large numbers suck the sap from the shoots and under side of the leaves, causing much damage. Spray with soap and nicotine solution.

Potato aphid.

Privet

Privet or Lilac Borer: Larvæ tunnel in the stems. Remove and destroy infested stems.

Quince

Round-headed Borer: See Apple.

Quince Curculio: Adults feed upon, and the grubs feed inside, the growing fruit, causing it to be knotty. Jar the trees as for plum curculio. Spray with lead arsenate.

Aphid: See Apple.

Radish

Maggot: See Cabbage.

Aphid: See Turnip.

Raspberry

Raspberry Sawfly: Larvæ feed upon the leaves. Spray with lead arsenate or hellebore.

Cane Borer: Larvæ tunnel inside the canes. Cut and burn infested canes.

Rhododendron

Rhododendron Lace Bug: Sucks the sap from the under surface of the leaves, leaving brown spots of excrement. Spray with nicotine solution or kerosene emulsion.

Rose

Rose Slug or Sawfly: Eats away the green tissues of the leaves, only the network remaining. Spray with lead arsenate, hellebore, or nicotine solution.

Rose Chafer: See Grape.

Rose Leaf-Hopper: Whitish, jumping and flying insects which suck the sap from the underside of the leaves. Spray with nicotine solution.

Rose Aphid or Green Fly: Sucks the sap from the tender leaves and shoots. Dip the shoots in, or spray with nicotine solution.

Rose Scale: Whitish, circular shells on the stems contain insects which suck the sap. Cut and burn the worst infested stems. Spray with nicotine solution.

Rye

Army Worm: See Grass.

Wheat Midge: See Wheat.

Snapdragon

Leaf-Mite: Causes leaves to curl and plants do not blossom. Spray with nicotine solution.

Snowball

Aphids: Suck sap from the leaves, causing them to curl. Dip in, or spray with nicotine solution.

Spiræa

Aphids: Suck the sap from the new shoots. Use nicotine solution as a spray or dip.

Spruce

Spruce Bud Moth: Larvæ feed on leaves of terminal shoots of the branches, often causing much damage. Spray with lead arsenate.

Spruce Gall Aphid: Forms galls at the base of the new growth on Norway and other spruces. Spray in late fall or early spring with nicotine solution and soap or kerosene emulsion.

Squash-pumpkin

Squash-vine Borer: Larvæ tunnel in the stem near its base, causing decay. Cut slits lengthwise in the stem and kill the borers. Cover the joints of the vine with earth and new roots will be formed to support the plant. Grow a few early plants for traps, and when well infested, destroy them. Plant the main crop rather late.

Squash-vine borer.

Squash Lady-Beetle: Adults and larvæ feed upon the leaves. Spray with lead arsenate.

Striped Cucumber Beetle: See Cucumber.

Squash Bug or Stink Bug: A brown bug, three-fourths of an inch in length, which sucks the sap from the underside of the leaves, causing them to wilt and die. Underspray with kerosene emulsion to kill the young. The old bugs and the egg clusters may be gathered by hand.

Squash lady-beetle.

Strawberry

Strawberry Sawfly: Larvæ devour the leaves. Spray with lead arsenate or hellebore.

Strawberry Flea-Beetle: Eats round holes through the leaves. Spray with lead arsenate.

Strawberry Leaf-Roller: Larvæ roll leaf and feed inside. Spray with lead arsenate. In bad infestations burn over fields as soon as crop is harvested.

Squash bug or stink bug.

Strawberry Weevil: The females of this small snout beetle cut off the blossom buds of staminate varieties when ovipositing. Plant pistillate varieties in part. Spray with lead arsenate.

Strawberry Crown Borer: Grub feeds in the crown of the plant. Practice crop rotation. Burn over infested field in fall.

Strawberry White-fly: Sucks sap from the underside of the leaves. Underspray with soap and nicotine solution.

Strawberry Root Aphid: Sucks sap from leaves and roots, killing plants. Spray with nicotine solution. Set clean plants on land not infested.

Sweet potato

Tortoise Shell Beetles: Feed upon leaves. Spray with lead arsenate.

Tobacco

Flea Beetle: Eats holes through the leaves. Spray upper and under leaf-surfaces heavily with lead arsenate.

Cut Worms: See Tomato.

Tobacco or Tomato Horn Worms: Large green caterpillars with horn on the tail devour the leaves. Practice hand picking. Spray with lead arsenate.

Horn worm affects both tomato and tobacco.

Tomato

Cut Worms: Eat off the stems of the plants near the ground; certain species climb the plants and eat the leaves. Scatter poisoned bran mash around the field just at night so that the cut worms may have a chance to get it before it dries.

The cut worm, a general pest.

Flea Beetle: See Potato or Tobacco.

Stalk Borer: See dahlia.

Tomato or Tobacco Horn-worms: See Tobacco.

Greenhouse White-Fly: Immature insects suck the sap from the under sides of the leaves. Underspray with soap and water. Fumigate greenhouses and frames with hydrocyanic acid gas.

Tulip tree

Tulip Tree Scale: Large, brown, hemispherical scales on bark of lower branches, sucking the sap. Spray with lime-sulfur in fall or winter.

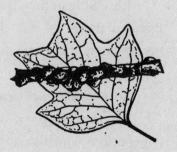

Tulip tree scale.

Turnip

Cut Worms: See Tomato.

Cabbage Root Maggot: See Cabbage.

Turnip Aphid: Green aphids on underside of leaves sucking the sap. Underspray with soap and water or nicotine solution.

Violet

Violet Sawfly: Larvæ devour leaves. Spray with lead arsenate or hellebore.

Eel-worms: Infest the roots, forming galls. Plant in new soil or sterilize old soil by steam. Add plenty of air-slaked lime to the soil.

Walnut

Walnut Caterpillar: Clusters of black caterpillars covered with whitish hairs strip the branches and finally the tree in August. Spray with lead arsenate. Clip off twigs when caterpillars are small, and kill by crushing.

Walnut Weevil or Curcullo: Adults feed at base of leaf stems; larvæ tunnel in new shoots and infest the fruit of Persian and Japanese Walnuts. Spray with lead arsenate.

Wheat

Army Worm: See Grass.

Hessian Fly: Maggots burrow in sheath of a leaf at base of stem, causing the stalks to turn yellow and die. Plant rather late, say about September 1st.

Wheat Midge: The fly lays eggs on the chaff and the maggots feed upon the developing kernels, so that the heads ripen early and produce no grain. Burn stubble before plowing. Plow infested fields deeply in the fall.

Green Bug or Aphid: Green aphids suck the sap from leaves. Destroy in early fall all volunteer wheat and oats. Practice crop rotation.

Willow

Spiny Elm Caterpillar: See Elm.

Poplar Tent Maker: See Poplar.

Poplar and Willow Curculio: See Poplar.

Oyster-shell Scale: See Apple.

Aphids: Large reddish aphids congregate on twigs in fall, and suck the sap. Spray with kerosene emulsion or nicotine solution.

We wish to add just a few words in regard to the enemies treated in this and the proceeding chapter. The main method for controlling them is to prevent them by the strictest sanitation. All diseased or insect-infested parts must be burned such stock must never be planted in your clean garden or allowed to remain there if it has already started. Land which is known to be infested with various pests must be avoided.

A sucking insect—note the formidable beak used to pierce plants and extract juices.

Keep down weeds which harbor diseases and insects. A method which must not be scorned is hand picking when possible. Anything which contributes toward the best culture of

Head of biting insect—note jaws, large compound eyes, and the feelers near jaws and eyes.

the plant will be found a control for the enemies as well. If you have questions as to just how to control any of the various maladies, consult your seedsman, florist or nurseryman, but do not lose time—insects and diseases work quickly.

The gardener should become familiar with the ways of the insects, for some are valuable and should be admired. Those who have read Sir John Lubbock, Faber or Maeterlinck realize that the insect world is quite as romantic as our own.

Plants become yellow not only as a result of insect injury or disease, but also when they get too much water or too little or when the soil is too poor or too rich. Be sure of the cause before you try to cure the trouble.

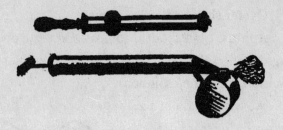

The upper figure shows an ordinary brass garden syringe. Be sure to buy a good article to begin with: it pays. The lower figure shows a brass vaporizing sprayer. This is just what is needed for applying liquid insecticides and fungicide.

Concerning the Control of Diseases

All methods of controlling plant diseases are based upon one of four principles: exclusion, eradication, protection and immunization. *Exclusion* is a matter of preventing the introduction of disease producing fungi, bacteria and the like into a given country or locality. This is most commonly attempted by legislation, exclusion laws and quarantines. *Eradication* refers to the removal of a pathogene from an area when once it has gained a foothold, and involves many operations, such as sorting out and destroying diseased seed, plants and plant parts, soil sterilization, crop rotation and seed disinfection. This principle may be applied in the control of a large number of diseases. In practicing *protection* methods we work from the standpoint of a plant and place some barrier between it and the parasites which attack it. In the operation of spraying which is a protective measure, we place a layer of poison called a fungicide on the leaves of a plant and when the fungus comes in contact with the poison it is killed. The addition of certain substances to the soil to prevent organisms from attacking the roots of plants, as in the liming of soil to prevent club root of cabbage, may be classed as a protective measure. *Immunization* involves the selection or breeding of varieties or strains which are resistant to certain diseases. In some few instances the application of this principle is practical and not a few resistant varieties have been developed in recent years, as,

for example, cabbage is immune to yellows and beans are immune to anthracnose.

The More Common Diseases of Garden Crops

Apple

Bitter rot (*Glomerella cingulata*). Causes a rot of the fruit, which at first is brown in color; later small pink masses appear on its surface. Finally the whole fruit rots and then shrivels into a mummy, which sometimes clings to the tree. Cankers also form on the limbs. They should be removed in the winter and burned. Spray with Bordeaux mixture (4-4-50) once before buds open and afterwards according to the weather.

Black rot or New York Apple tree canker (*Physalaspora Cydoniae*). Fruit is rotted and covered with black pimples and shrinks to a mummy; leaves are often spotted and cankers develop upon the limbs. Remove cankers or cankered limbs. Spray foliage with Bordeaux (4-4-50) about the middle of July and again two weeks later.

Blister canker (*Nummerlana discreta*). Cankers are formed on the limbs or body and at first are dull brown in color, later becoming darker. When the canker enlarges the bark blisters and comes off. Finally the small, raised, nailhead fruit bodies of the fungus are formed on the surface of the wood. Cut out small cankers. If large, remove the diseased limb.

Brown rot (*Sclerotinia cinerea*). See Plum.

Fire blight (*Bacillus Amylovorus*). See Pear.

Powdery mildew (*Podosphaera leucotricha*). The leaves become covered with a white or grayish powdery-like mildew which usually affects their growth where infection is severe. Twigs also are attacked. In the latter part of the season minute black bodies may be seen on this whitish overgrowth. Spray with a mixture prepared by adding 3 pounds of copperas (iron sulfate) to

50 gallons of 1-50 lime-sulfur solution. About four sprayings are recommended during the season.

Rust (*Gymnosporangium Juniperi-virginianae*). One stage occurs on the red Cedar as Cedar apples which are brown gall-like growths and produce yellow gelatinous horns in Spring; the other stage occurs on apple leaves and fruits. The spots on the apple leaves are at first small and yellow, but later they become orange colored on the upper side of the leaf; small pimples develop on the spots while on the lower surface minute cuplike structures are formed, the edges of which are split in a star-like manner. Severe infections cause the entire leaf to turn yellow and fall. To control this disease eradicate the Red Cedars within a radius of at least one mile. Spraying is not very effective, but lime-sulfur 1-40 may be used; spray the new leaves as they unfold.

Scab (*Venturia inaequalis*). Occurs on the leaves and fruit. It shows first on the under, later on the upper, surface of the leaves as circular, olive green, superficial patches which later turn darker. The leaf under the spot may become convex or puffed. When infection is severe the entire leaf may be involved. On the fruit, the spot is at first olive green and later has a dark center with a white papery margin. This is one of the most serious of apple diseases. Spray with lime-sulfur (1-40). (1) When the buds show green; (2) Just before the blossoms open; (3) When the petals fall; (4) Two or three weeks after the petals fall.

Sooty blotch or Fly speck (*Leptothyrium pomi*). Irregular, superficial, sooty blotches which may be rubbed off the apple skin, or minute fly specks thickly crowded in spots over the surface of the fruit. The treatment for apple scab will easily control this disease.

Stippen. Known also as "bitter pit;" a disease not due to an organism, but is said to be due to the improper distribution of water to the fruit. It may be recognized by the depressions on the surface of the fruit which are caused by the development of brown, corky areas in the flesh of the apple. Good cultural practices, as proper drainage, cultivation and pruning should be followed. Uniformity in the water supply during the growing season reduces losses from this disease to a minimum.

Asparagus

Rust (*Puccinia asparagi*). Attacks the green tops which develop after the shoots have been cut. It may be recognized by the final dying of the tops and the small red or black colored pustules formed on the stems and needles. In severe infections the tops turn yellow and the needles fall from the stems. Toward the end of the season the black or winter stage develops. To control this disease, obtain rust-resistant strains.

Aster

Leaf rust (*Coleosporium Sonchi-arvensis*). May be recognized by the orange-colored pustules or *sori* which develop chiefly on the underside of the leaves. Spray with Bordeaux mixture, before the rust appears.

Bean

Anthracnose (*Colletotrichium lindemuthianum*). A very serious fungous disease. It is distinguished by the circular and sunken black spots on both the pods and seed which may at certain times contain pink, gelatinous pustules on their surfaces. The leaf veins on the underside of the leaves and the stems also may be affected. The disease is carried over winter on the seed, hence, use clean seed obtained by selecting pods free from these spots. Spraying with Bordeaux (5-5-50) will also reduce the amount of disease. Resistant strains of some varieties like Red Kidney are now to be obtained.

Blight (*Bacterium phaseoli*). A bacterial disease. Shows at first as large brownish areas on the leaves with yellowish, water-soaked margins. Later these spots become darker in color and dry. The pods also develop water-soaked spots which are circular or irregular in shape often with red margins, and not sunken as in the case of anthracnose. As with anthracnose the seed which becomes infected from the pod carries the organism over the winter. No satisfactory method of control is known except the use of disease-free seed. Resistant varieties have not yet been developed.

Beet

Leaf spot (*Cercospora beticola*). Very common fungous disease. Appears first as round, brownish spots with red to purplish borders. Later, after the spots enlarge, they become ashen and papery in the center, which finally drops out and leaves holes in the leaf. When severe, these spots may coalesce and destroy the entire leaf. Burn the diseased leaves. Spray with Bordeaux mixture (5-5-50) when the plants are about six weeks old. Make later sprayings about 10 days apart.

Root rot (*Phoma betae*). Causes a black dry rot on stored roots. Small, pimple-like structures are formed on the surface of the diseased area. Also large circular spots are produced on the leaves. Spray with Bordeaux mixture and remove all diseased leaves before placing the beets in storage.

Scab (*Actinomyces chromagenus*). Known by the circular scabs with raised margins and depressed centers which form on the roots. Same as scab on potatoes, which see. Do not grow beets if potato scab is known to be present in the soil, or where beets have been previously affected with this disease.

Blackberry

Anthracnose. See Raspberry.
Leaf spot (*Septoria Rubi*). Spots appear on the leaves first as small whitish or brownish areas. When very numerous on a leaf, they may cause it to dry up. Spray with Bordeaux mixture.
Orange rust. See Raspberry.

Cabbage

Black leg (*Phoma lingam*). Affects the leaves, stems and roots. The leaves are spotted, but not seriously injured. The chief injury is caused by a rotting of the stem and root which turn black; the leaves then wilt and the plant dies. Disinfect the seed as for black rot.

Black rot (*Bacterium campestre*). Affects also cauliflower, kale, Rape, kohl-rabi, Brussels sprouts, radish, turnip and other members of the mustard family. The leaves show at the edges large dead areas, in which the veins are black. The entire leaf soon yellows and falls from the plant. The blackening of the veins, easily seen on holding a diseased leaf up to the light, is diagnostic of this disease. On splitting a diseased stalk, a blackening of the sap tubes is apparent. The bacteria live over in the soil and on the seed. Soak the seed 15 minutes in corrosive sublimate solution 4 ounces to 30 gallons of water, then dry in the shade.

Club root (*Plasmodiophora brassicae*). A serious disease caused by a slime mould, which produces enormous swellings of both the main and lateral roots. These swellings or clubs are irregular and unsightly in appearance. In hot, dry weather, wilting of the tops of affected plants frequently occurs. The organism lives in the soil. Practice crop rotation, set healthy plants, apply 2 to 3 tons of lime per acre to infested soil at least one year before planting again to cabbage.

Yellows (*Fusarium conglutinans*). Its appearance is much the same as that of black rot, but the darkening of the veins begins at the base of the stem and works outward, while in black rot it does just the opposite, starting at the edge of the leaf and working toward the base. Use seed of a resistant variety.

Carnation

Fusarium Stem rot (*Fusarium sp.*). Affects the stem causing a dry rot near the base. A slow dying of the top takes place. Change the location of plants each year, and in the greenhouse use fresh or sterilized soil. Avoid overwatering.

Leaf spot (*Septoria Dianthi*). Shows small circular grayish spots on the leaves and stem. Spray about once a week with blue vitriol (copper sulfate) 1 pound to 20 gallons of water.

Rhizoctonia Stem rot (*Corticium vagum var. Solani*). Rot takes place at or just below the surface of the soil and causes the plant to suddenly wilt. Observe the same precautions as controlling of Fusarium stem rot. Do not set plants too deep.

Rust (*Uromyces Caryophyllinus*). Appears first as a small elongated blister like structure which later ruptures and exposes deep brown powdery masses. Present on both the stems and leaves. Avoid an excess of moisture in the greenhouse and spray with blue vitriol, 1 pound to 20 gallons of water.

Celery

Early blight (*Cercospora Apii*). Spots appear first as pale yellow areas, irregular and somewhat angular in outline. Later they turn brown and finally the center becomes an ashen gray. May destroy the entire plant. Spray with Bordeaux mixture (5-5-50). Beginning when the plants are first set, make about 6 applications during the season.

Cherry

Late blight (*Septoria Petroselini var Apii*). Affects flowers, which turn brown and wither, and fruit, which at first is rotted; then small, light brown pustules are produced on its surface. Finally the fruit becomes a hard, wrinkled mummy, which either hangs on the tree or falls to the ground. Spray with lime-sulfur (1-50) or dust with 90 parts of sulfur to 10 parts of arsenate of lead, first when the blossoms show white but before they open, later when the calyx is being shed, and finally about 2 to 3 weeks before fruit begins to ripen.

Leaf curl (*Exoascus Cerasi*). The leaves become crinkled and turn reddish in color. On their lower surface appears a whitish coating. They fall prematurely. The diseased leaves appear only on abnormal outgrowths from affected twigs called witches' rooms. Prune out the diseased twigs.

Leaf spot or Shot hole (*Coccomyces hiemalis*). Spots appear on the leaves which at first mere discolorations, soon become dark red or purple in color; finally the center drops out leaving a "shothole," or the leaf turns yellow and falls. Plow under old leaves and spray with lime-sulfur (1-40) or Bordeaux mixture (5-5-50); or dust with sulfur 90 parts and arsenate of lead 10 parts. Make first application when calyx is shedding; repeat 10 days later and again after picking. Do not use Bordeaux on sweet cherries.

Powdery mildew (*Podosphaera Oxyacanthae*). Leaves and twigs of young shoots are covered with patches of white mildew which spreads finally over the whole leaf or twig. Small black spherical bodies develop on the surface of this mildew. Dust with sulfur or spray with lime-sulfur (1 to 50).

Cranberry

Gall (*Synchytrium Vaccinii*). Small, reddish galls are formed on the young stems, leaves, and sometimes, on the flowers and fruit. They are in color. Burn the bog over in the autumn and keep it dry during winter.

Hypertrophy (*Exobasidium Oxycocci*). The buds in the leaf axils grow out into shoots which bear swollen, enlarged leaves of a pinkish color. No remedy is known.

Scald (*Guignardia Vaccinii*). Appears on berries, first as watery areas which enlarge and soften the whole berry which turns brown; several spots may develop on one berry. Finally the affected berries become scalded in appearance. Sometimes black dots appear on them. Spray with Bordeaux mixture (5-5-50) to which a resin fish oil sticker is added.

Cucumber, Melon and Squash

Anthracnose (*Coletotrichum Lagenarium*) causes circular brownish spots on leaves and elongated light brown spots on stems. The spots on the fruits are sunken and have small pinkish gelatinous masses on their surfaces. Spray frequently with Bordeaux mixture (5-5-50).

Downy Mildew (*Peronoplasmopara cubensis*). At first small yellowish angular spots are produced on the leaves. These enlarge and may involve the entire leaf which finally dies. In moist weather a white downy growth may be seen on the underside of the leaf. Spray the vines every 10 days with Bordeaux mixture (5-5-50).

Wilt (*Bacillus tracheiphilus*). Causes a wilting of a leaf and finally of the entire vine, which dies. Keep vines free of bugs and striped beetles which spread the bacteria. Pull and burn diseased vines.

Currant

Leaf spot (*Mycosphaerella Grossulariae*). Appears as small brown spots on the upper and lower sides of the leaf. As these spots, which often run together, enlarge, the centers become whitish and small black pimples arise on their surfaces. Leaves turn yellow and fall prematurely. Spray with lime-sulfur (1-50) or dust with a mixture of ground sulfur 90 parts and powdered lead arsenate 10 parts, as follows: When the first leaves appear and every two weeks following.

Anthracnose (*Pseudopeziza Ribis*). Appears as numerous small brown circular spots on the upper surface of the leaves, and also on the berries. When severe the leaves turn yellow and fall. On the leaf stems small, slightly sunken spots may be seen. Spray with Bordeaux mixture (5-5-50) or lime-sulfur (1-40) first, when the leaves are unfolding and subsequently at intervals of from 10 days to two weeks. Spray more frequently in moist weather.

Egg plant

Leaf spot (*Phomopsis vexans*). Large, irregular patches, gray or brown in color, on which small black pimples subsequently form, are produced upon the leaves. Similarly appearing sunken spots or cankers are produced upon fruit and stalks. Plant only disease-free seed or treat seed with corrosive sublimate (1 to 1,000) for 10 minutes. Wash in running water 15 minutes and plant at once. Do not plant on land which grew diseased egg plants last season.

Gooseberry

Anthracnose. See Currant.

Leaf spots See Currant.

Powdery mildew (*Sphaerotheca Morsuvae*). This disease may be recognized by the powdery white patches occurring on leaves, stems and fruit. These patches finally turn brown as they run together. Sometimes diseased berries are deformed and may crack open Spray with lime sulfur (1-40) when the buds open, and later at intervals of 10 days until four or more sprayings have been made.

Grape

Anthracnose (*Gloeosporium ampelophagum*). Small spots with raised borders and depressed centers are formed on the shoots and tendrils. These enlarge in the long direction of the shoots and later the center becomes more depressed and grayish. Small dark brown spots appear on the berries with a red border; as they enlarge they become depressed, but remain circular. Cut out and burn diseased wood. Spray dormant vines with lime-sulfur (1-9). Spray the vines with Bordeaux mixture (5-5-50) first, when the shoots are about 12 inches long, second, just before the flower buds open, and third, just after the blossoms fall. Follow with two more sprayings about 10 days apart.

Black rot (*Guignardia Bidwellii*). Shows on berries at first as small blanched areas. As the spots increase in size their surfaces become sunken and contain numerous small, black pimples. Usually the entire grape is diseased and dries into a hard, shriveled mummy. Reddish brown spots appear on the leaves. Spray with Bordeaux mixture (5-5-50) as for anthracnose; destroy mummies; make applications of spray just before rains.

Downy mildew (*Plasmopara viticola*). Appears first on upper side of leaves as small yellowish spots, indefinite in outline. As these enlarge they turn brown and become dry and brittle. On the lower side of the spot a downy white growth, noticeable especially in moist weather, appears. Other parts of the vines are similarly attacked. Plow under old fallen leaves in the Spring. Make 5 or 6 applications of Bordeaux mixture (5-5-50) beginning just before the blossoms open.

Powdery mildew (*Uncinula necator*). Powdery white patches are produced on both upper and lower surfaces of the leaves. Finally on these white patches small black pimple-like bodies develop. Severe attacks cause dwarfing of the vines. Dust the diseased plants with sulfur from one to six times during the season.

Lettuce

Drop (*Sclerotinia Libertiana*). Causes wilting of the plants which drop to the ground. White cotton-like growths appear on the underside of the leaves. Later small, hard, black bodies are formed. Remove and burn all diseased plants. Greenhouse beds may be disinfected with formaldehyde. Very difficult to control especially in field-grown lettuce.

Gray mold (*Botrytis sp.*). Seldom serious in the field. The edges of the outer leaves are first wilted, the wilted patches becoming covered with grayish, downy fuzz. The whole leaf may be affected and die, the disease working slowly toward the center of the head. Avoid high temperature, excessive moisture and poor ventilation.

Lilac

Mildew (*Microsphaera Alni*). White powdery patches form on the leaves. Later in the season these become a grayish white and bear minute black spherical bodies. Dust with sulfur.

Lily

Blight (*Botrytis sp.*). Yellowish brown spots appear on the leaves and buds early in the Spring. Later these enlarge and become covered with a light brown dusty mold, which destroys the leaves and blossoms. Remove infected plants and burn.

Melon

See Cucumber.

Onion

Blight or Downy mildew (*Peronospora Schleideniana*). At first patches of fuzzy down cover the affected leaves; these spots are soon blanched and in a short time the leaves are entirely wilted over. Spray with Bordeaux mixture. Not easily controlled.

Neck rot (*Botrytis Allii*). Causes a rotting of the onion bulb at the neck, accompanied by a grayish fuzz and hard black bodies. The disease occurs in the field but is particularly severe in storage. Remove and destroy diseased plants. Store bulbs in a cool, dry, well ventilated place. Dry thoroughly before storing.

Smut (*Urocystis Cepulae*) Attacks young seedlings but not onions grown from sets. Shows on the seedling leaves as elongated opaque spots, which finally rupture and expose a black powdery mass. Drill in formalin (1 pint to 16 gallons) with the seed at the rate of 200 gallons per acre.

Pea

Leaf spots (*Ascochyta Pisi*). Small, circular spots with dark borders and lighter centers, bearing small, black pimple-like bodies, form on the leaves. Similar spots are found upon the pods and stems, which also, are attacked. Avoid use of diseased seed.

Peach

Brown rot (See Cherry). Dust with sulfur and arsenate of lead. Use a 90-10 mixture.

Leaf curl (*Exoascus deformans*). At first the new leaves swell and wrinkle, the leaf-blade puckering along the midrib. At this time the leaf is peculiarly colored with red and yellow tints. Later the upper portions of the affected leaf turn whitish and assume a velvety appearance. Spray in the fall or the early spring before the buds swell, with lime-sulfur (1-15). Cover every bud.

Yellows (Cause unknown). May be recognized by the yellowish color of the foliage and the premature development of the fruit. The appearance of an excessive number of slender yellowish shoots occurs in advanced stages of the disease. Destroy affected trees. Do not drag them through the orchard.

Scab (*Cladosporium Carpophilum*). Olivaceous to black, scabby patches on the fruit and twigs. When severe the spots run together. The fruit is often distorted and the skin may crack open. Spray with self boiled lime-sulfur (8-8-50) four to five weeks after the petals fall, and again three weeks later, or better, dust with sulfur and arsenate of lead, as for brown rot.

Pear

Fire blight (*Bacillus amylovorus*). The blossoms, young fruit and twigs appear as if burned, but affected leaves remain attached to the twigs. Cankers are formed on the larger limbs, and in the spring milky drops filled with bacteria exude from them. Cut out the cankers in the fall and early spring and disinfect the wound with corrosive sublimate (1-

1000). Later paint over wounds with coal tar. During the summer, remove diseased spurs and twigs as fast as they appear and disinfect cut surfaces with corrosive sublimate.

Leaf spot (*Mycosphaerella sentina*). Small angular spots with definite dark colored margins and grayish white centers are found on the leaves. Spray with lime-sulfur (1-50) just after the petals fall, two weeks later, and again in another two weeks.

Scab (*Venturia Pyrina*). See Apple scab.

Peony

Blight (*Botrylis Paeoniae*). Causes a rotting off of young shoots early in Spring. Brownish spots with target board markings form on the leaves. In moist weather a grayish fuss may be observed upon these diseased portions. The same disease blasts the buds. Sometimes small black bodies are produced on the rotted stems. Remove and burn the diseased parts. Spray with Bordeaux mixture.

Plum

Black knot (*Plowrightia morbosa*). Knots from ½ in to several inches in length are produced on the young twigs. At first olivaceous in color, they later turn to a coal black. Frequently the twigs on which knots form are bent back upon themselves. Remove and burn the knots in the fall or early winter.

Brown rot. See Cherry.

Shot hole (*Coccomyces prumophorae*). See Cherry.

Potato

Blight (*Phytophthora infestans*). Spots, black in the center and with a water-soaked margin, begin to develop, usually at the tip or margin of the leaves. Under moist conditions a white frost-like down encircles the diseased portion. Soon the whole plant dies. At this time an offensive odor is developed.

Spray with Bordeaux mixture (5-5-50) when the plants are about 6 in. high. Follow with other sprayings about 10 days apart. Spray just ahead of rain periods if possible.

Rhizoctonia stem rot (*Corticium vagum*). Small, brownish black bodies which may be easily removed from the skin, form on the surface of the tubers. The sprouts often rot before they get through the ground. The stem near the ground is also attacked and often rotted. Plants grown from such seed produce many little potatoes. Treat the seed with corrosive sublimate (4 ounces to 30 gallons) for 1½ hours.

Scab (*Actinomyces scabies*). Rough scabs on the surfaces of the potato. Usually the margin is raised and the center depressed. Avoid the addition of lime or wood ashes to the soil. Treat seed with corrosive sublimate solution. (4 ounces to 30 gallons of water), for 1½ hours.

Raspberry

Anthracnose (*Plectodiscella veneta*). Affects principally the canes, which at first show small, purplish elliptical spots. Later these become larger and somewhat sunken and the centers turn a grayish white. Sometimes these spots run together and large areas of the stems become diseased. Remove diseased canes. Set only plants free from the disease. Spray with Bordeaux mixture (4-4-50).

Orange rust (*Gymnoconia interstitialis*). A bright orange colored rust covering the underside of the leaves which become dwarfed and rolled. Dig up and destroy diseased plants.

Leaf spot. See Blackberry.

Rose

Black spot (*Diplocarpon rosae*). Circular or oval black patches with indefinite margins on the upper side of the leaves. Often whole leaves become covered when these spots run together. Affected leaves turn yellow and fall prematurely. Spray with ammoniacal copper carbonate or dust with sulfur.

Powdery mildew (*Sphaerotheca pannosa*). Powdery patches on the leaves and sometimes on the young shoots. Dust with sulfur.

Squash. See Cucumber.

Strawberry

Leaf spot (*Mycosphaerella Fragariae*). Small red to purplish spots which, as they enlarge, become grayish white and papery in the center with a purplish border. Remove the diseased leaves before setting plants and spray with Bordeaux mixture (4-4-50). Mow leaves after fruiting and burn over the patch.

Sweet Potato

Black rot (*Sphaeronema fimbriatum*). Dark brown to black patches on the surface of the potatoes indicate rotted portions beneath. The affected parts are dry and black. Avoid diseased sets and plant in soil that is not infested. Practice crop rotation.

Soft rot (*Rhizopus nigricans*). The potatoes become soft and wrinkled; after a while, a moldy growth develops on their surface. This later takes on a gray to blackish appearance. Store in a cool, dry, well ventilated cellar and from time to time remove all diseased potatoes.

Tomato

Blossom end rot. (Cause unknown.) A black, dry rot which occurs at the blossom end. Greatly influenced by the soil moisture. Increase the water holding capacity of the soil by proper cultivation, irrigation and addition of organic matter.

Leaf spot (*Septoria Lycopersici*). Small numerous circular spots with definite margins on the leaves. Small, black, pimple-like structures develop toward their centers. Spray thoroughly with fish oil soap-Bordeaux, especially the lower surfaces. Remove diseased leaves.

Tulip

Blight (*Botrytis parasitica.*). Grow on the dormant bulbs as small black bodies about the size of pinheads. Causes a spotting of the leaves and flowers and finally blights them. When the stem is rotted through, the plant falls over. A grayish fuzz may be seen on affected parts in moist weather. Select clean bulbs to set out in the fall and in the spring remove and destroy any diseased plants which may appear.

Garden Tools

From Garden Guide: The Amateur Gardeners' Handbook, edited by A.T. De La Mare, 1920

The presence of a garden always carries with it the need for some tools. The first tools needed, perhaps, are a spade, fork, rake, trowel for transplanting, hoe, sickle for trimming grass, and a watering can. In all of these tools nothing is more important than their strength. Strong unions of the steel to the wood are important, for it is here that the tool breaks most quickly. All the tools that are meant to be sharp should be kept so, or else their work cannot be done efficiently. The spading fork is especially useful in digging up borders and about trees, as it does not cut off roots. If a half-moon turf cutter is not available, the spade is indispensable for edging beds. Large and small hoes are both useful, the large one for general use, and the small one for working about in small places. The Dutch or English scuffle hoe is most useful for loosening the surface of the soil and cutting off weeds. A small hand cultivator is now on the market having prongs which are easily removed or of which the cutting angle may be changed.

Hotbed thermometer.

Two lawn beaters or levelers and a garden roller.

Light ladder used for gathering fruit.

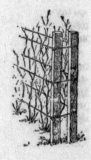

End posts and wires or strings pea or bean supports.

Hand spading pork—buy a good one.

An easy method of sawing posts off level.

A broad-wheeled barrow.

B

A

Garden steps.
A sickle. sometimes used instead of shears.

Dibbles. The small ones are safest unless the soil is loose and spongy.

Frame barrow for leaves, grass or similar material.

Shows a device for hoisting a barrel up steps or incline.

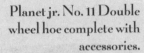

Planet jr. No. 11 Double wheel hoe complete with accessories.

Many will feel that a wheel hoe is a very useful accessory tool; it will certainly come in handy, and can be used for hoeing, cultivating, furrowing, hilling up or raking. Combination seed drills and wheel hoes are also very serviceable. For the larger vegetable garden the seed drill is most useful. With a seed drill the furrow can be opened, the seed sown, covered, the soil compacted over the row and the next row marked.

A wheelbarrow will surely be wanted; a good type is shown in the sketch. Some wheelbarrows are poorly balanced and are difficult to handle in the garden.

Shelves and temporary storage box for fruit.

Small dibbles of different sizes for making holes are popular with many but they should be used with caution in heavy soils that are likely to be compacted by their use. Often a narrow bladed trowel is a safer and more efficient tool.

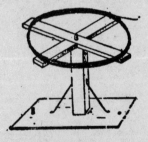

Device for winding cord or wire. A modification of this can be used for winding hose-pipe.

A little frame against a basement window.

Pruning shears which are procured at ridiculously low prices are never worth anything. They are not sharp and injure the plants because in attempting to cut a branch, it is pinched and crushed. Good steel shears should be chosen fitted with strong springs which will cause them to open after cutting. The larger hedge and grass shears should also have these springs, otherwise they are a nuisance.

Long-spouted watering can.

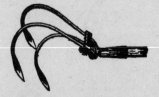

Three-pronged hand cultivator.

Approved form of asparagus Knife.

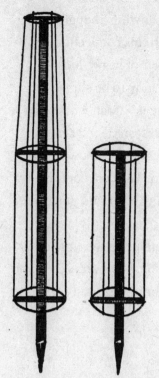

Tall and short supports for beans or other climbing plants.

A tree guard.

For the lawn we need as well as the standard ball-bearing lawn mower, a narrower one for trimming the edges; if you have much lawn you will appreciate the value of this machine for trimming to the very edge. A wooden leaf rake or one of those with bent wire teeth will enable you to keep the lawn neat without tearing the turf as usually occurs when the ordinary steel rake is used.

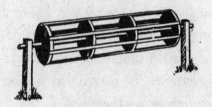
Roller for cloth or paper shade.

Showing how simply a shade or protecting cover can be unrolled.

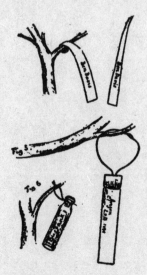

Two pairs are really necessary—one for light and one for heavy work.

Labels for fruit trees.

The top two are of thin stripes of copper or tin; the largest one is of wood, while a third is shown in a sealed bottle.

Hand trowel—the best obtainable is none too good.

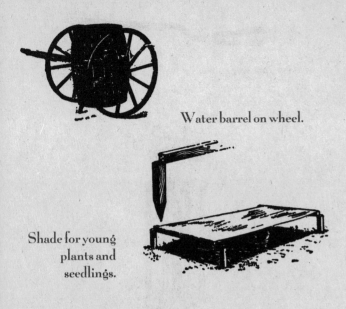

Water barrel on wheel.

Shade for young plants and seedlings.

Pruning saw.

are as good as anything bought for the purpose. In this connection, too, keep a stout pair of heavy, loose-fitting boots handy to be slipped on whenever there is garden work to be done. Low shoes, sneakers, etc., may seem more suitable for hot weather, but avoid them. They are continually filling up with pebbles and gravel and in wet weather, in the early morning, or when you are using the hose they are no protection whatever. When you garden dress for it; it pays.

To keep the rows straight in the vegetable garden, a good stout garden line is necessary.

For cutting glass to be used in the hotbeds a glass cutter should be at hand. Very cheap steel ones can be bought, as well as better ones with diamond points. It is a rather simple matter to cut glass if a flat surface is available. The main object is to get a deep, even cut entirely across the glass.

Gloves are needed when pruning roses and other thorny plants. Perhaps old discarded ones

Scuffle hoes of different patterns.

Games and Toys

Games

From *A Handbook of Games and Programs for Church, School, and Home*
by William Ralph La Porte, 1922

Get-Acquainted Games

Ice Breakers

One of the most important things upon which the success of any social gathering depends is the way in which the guests are received, introduced, and made to feel at ease. A person cheerfully received feels happier, and enters into everything far better for the rest of the evening. This depends not only upon the game played after everyone has arrived, but also upon what the first ones shall do until the others come. A good way to accomplish this is to ask in the invitations that each person bring a joke or riddle. These furnish laughter for any number of people.

Animals:

Pin name of an animal on each guest's back. The first one guessing what he is by questioning others, who in turn try to mystify him, is the winner.

Neighbors:

Formation, single or double circles. One person in center points to one in circle, asking name of neighbor on right side. If not answered before ten counts, person caught goes to center. Neighbors change when told, avoiding former neighbors. (May be in double circle, one partner behind other; outer circle numbers exchange places frequently, necessitating constant watchfulness on part of numbers of inner circle.)

Yes or No:

Give each person ten beans and have him engage in conversation without saying "Yes" or "No." Each time he uses either word he must surrender one bean to his partner in conversation. See who can win the most beans in a given time.

Active Social Games

Social programs are usually more refreshing and enjoyable when at least part of the evening is devoted to games for the group, involving more or less moving about. Mild physical activity in a social atmosphere is very stimulating.

Care should be taken not to overdo the active games. It will be found advisable to introduce occasional quiet games to offset the others. When handling crowds that are overboisterous use special care not to give too many active games that might lead to rowdyism and rough actions.

Catch of Fish:

Two teams, equal in number, start at opposite ends of room, and move toward center. Players of one team clasp hands and try to encircle players of opposite team. Players caught in circle are caught fish, and drop out of game, or join opponents. Fish that reach opposite end of room without being caught then become the net, and game goes on until all players of one side or the other are caught. (See also "Humming Birds and Snake.")

Curtain Ball:

Players of two teams stand on opposite sides of a high curtain, and toss or bat the ball back and forth, the object being to prevent the ball falling to the floor. One point is scored every time a team fails to return a ball. The excitement is increased by the uncertainty of the point at which the ball will appear. For social occasions toy balloons make the safest and most exciting balls. Several of these may be kept going at once.

Fox (Slap Jack):

Form circle. One player—fox—stays outside of circle and taps shoulder of player. Fox runs to left and one tapped to right, around circle. Object—for each to try and get back to position of one tapped. One left out is fox.

Among the many variations of this game is one in which the circle holds hands, and a couple, holding hands, takes place of fox. Couple run around circle and strike clasped hands of some couple, who immediately run in opposite direction, as above described. (For social purposes, substitute walking for running.)

Have You Seen My Sheep?

Player goes around circle asking, "Have you seen my sheep?" Another player asks, "What was he like?" First player describes the dress and general appearance of someone in circle. Second player guesses who is described. If he guesses right, he chases that player around the circle, trying to tag him before he can get back to his place again. If tagged, the person described becomes the questioner; otherwise "player two" becomes questioner.

Sculptor:

One player is called a sculptor. While he is looking at the others they dare not move, and are to remain in a fixed position like statues. The sculptor turns his head and counts seven. During the count the players may move; but when the sculptor turns around, if anyone is moving he is sent back to the starting point and must start over again. The object is to get to the other end of the room without being caught by the sculptor. The last one across the room becomes "It."

Still Pond. No More Moving:

One player is blindfolded and placed in the center of a group of players. The blind one counts out loud as rapidly as he can, up to ten, during which time the players are to rush away from him as far as they can get. As soon as he reaches ten, he cries, "Still pond, no more moving," and the players must stand perfectly still. Three steps are allowed the players, which they may use at any time to avoid being caught. After a player is caught and identified, he in turn is blindfolded and becomes "it."

Wolf and Sheepfold (Cat and Rat):

Players form circle with lamb (one player) in the center of the circle and wolf (another player) outside the circle. Wolf tries to break through the clasped hands of the circle. If he succeeds, the players on the other side of the circle must let the lamb out of the circle, and then clasp hands tightly, preventing the wolf from escaping. If the wolf again breaks through the clasped hands, the lamb is again admitted to the circle, the object being to prevent the wolf from catching the lamb. When lamb is caught he becomes the wolf, and another lamb is chosen.

Quiet Social Games

Games of the quiet type may be made very interesting, especially for small groups. As a rule, it is inadvisable to build up the entire program from quiet games, but, rather, to plan a fair mixture of mildly active and quiet games.

Animal Alphabet:

Two sides; person from each side names animal beginning with letter "a." Alternate in turn until a player cannot think of any more "a" animals. That side gives up a player to other side. Begin again with "b," etc. Time limit. Side having more players wins.

Beast, Bird, Fish:

Players are seated in a circle. One player stands in the center with a soft ball made by crushing paper or knotting up a handkerchief. This is thrown at one of the players by the one in the center, who says quickly, "Beast, bird, or fish," then repeats one of these classes and immediately counts ten. The player designated must name some beast, bird, or fish, according to the class last named by the thrower, before the latter has finished counting ten. Failing to do so, he changes places with thrower.

Cross Questions and Crooked Answers:

Boys given funny questions by boy, and girls given funny answers by a girl. Line up facing each other and read questions and answers.

Hickey Pickey Hokey Pokey:

Players seated in circle. "It" in center points finger at some player and says "Hickey Pickey Hokey Pokey." Player must call out name of his next-door neighbor on right before "it" finishes word or exchange places with him. Seats should be changed often so players will learn names of several others.

Huntsman:

All leave room while leader hides given object, then re-enter. When object is seen person takes a seat without disclosing its location to others. Continue until all are seated. First one is new leader.

Scandal:

Players sit in long line or circle. First turning to second, whispers rapidly some remark. Second whispers it exactly as he heard it, to third player, and so on until the line is finished. The last player then whispers it to the first player, and first player repeats his original remark to the company, and follows it with the form in which it just reached him.

Statues:

Players choose what position they will assume and become as still and as silent as statues. One player is "Judge." It is his business to try to make the statues laugh. All who laugh pay forfeits, but the one who keeps his face grave longest becomes "Judge."

Teakettle:

One player is sent from room. Remainder of group decide upon a word with more than one meaning, such as "can." The other player is then called in and asks questions of the group. The answers should all contain the hidden word, but the word "teakettle" should be used in place of the word. The one whose answer reveals the word becomes "It" for next time.

Quaker Meeting:

The player who is "It" goes to each person and says, "Brethren, this is a very solemn occasion." He says it in a comical manner, trying to make them laugh. Any who laugh must pay a forfeit, or the first one he makes laugh must change places with him.

Questions:

Players sit in circle, with "It" in center. "It" goes about asking questions of various players. The question must be answered, not by the one addressed, but by the player on his right. Any player answering a question addressed to him, or failing to answer one addressed to player on his left, changes with questioner.

Competitive Social Games

Competitive games have a distinct place in the social program, and it is possible to arrange a very attractive evening's entertainment on a competitive basis. This may be in the form of the so-called "Fake" or "Indoor Athletic Meet," or under some other striking head. If desired, the competitive games may be made merely a part of the evening's entertainment.

Experience has demonstrated that an easy way to handle a large crowd is on the competitive basis, with the group divided preferably into two separate teams, arranged on opposite sides of the room, with captains to select representatives for various games, and yell leaders to stir up enthusiasm. If possible, see that every member of each team takes part in at least one game. Make the competition exciting and comical.

For convenience, the events suggested are listed under the headings of "Dashes," "Obstacle Races," and "Field Events."

Hopping Water:

Hop 20 feet with glass of water in the right hand.

Elopement:

Couple from each group given suitcase containing both boy's and girl's hat and coat. Each must don these; run to goal; take them off; return them to suitcase and run back to starting point. Next couple repeats operation, etc.

Hobble Hurdle:

Hobble contestants with sacks or rope. Barriers of pasteboard or other light material placed across room. Contestants jump or wiggle length of course.

Walk the Chalk Line:

Player walks along irregular chalk line or string laid on floor while looking through large end of opera glasses. Score according to distance walked before losing balance or before stepping off line.

Playground Games

The informal playground games have a very definite educational influence in stimulating keener observation, getting quicker reactions, quickening the sense perceptions, and the imagination, and in developing agility and skill. Their social value is incalculable, and they are worthy of far wider use in recreational programs.

Most of them emphasize the primitive instincts or hunting, chasing, fleeing, and capture. Some are highly competitive, others less so. In most cases their formation is of the circle or line type.

Black and White:

Players divided into two teams, equal in number, and standing in parallel rows. A disk, black on one side and white on the other, is twirled. If white side comes up, the white team may tag the black. The blacks are safe if they can stoop before being tagged. Any player tagged drops out of game. If the black side of disk comes up, the blacks tag the whites. Team wins that puts out all opponents. Keep players alert by frequent twirling of disk. (Or, instead of stooping, players may run to specified goal. Those caught may join opponents instead of dropping out.)

Cap Tag:

One person is "It." One person holds cap in hand. The "It" runs after him and if the latter is tagged, he becomes "It." Person having cap may throw it to the other players if he is in danger and "It" then chases person holding cap. If cap is dropped, person dropping it becomes "It." A game called "Poisoned Handkerchief" is played in same way. Circle is formed, and "It" is in the center trying to tag person with the handkerchief.

Hill Dill:

Two parallel boundary lines are drawn from 30–50 feet apart; one player is chosen to be "It" and stands in the center. The other players stand in two equal groups beyond the boundary lines, one group on each side. The center player calls out, "Hill, Dill! come over the Hill!" The other players then change goals and as they run across the open space the one in the center tries to tag them. Any who are tagged, assist him in tagging the others.

Snatch the Handkerchief:

Parallel lines are marked about fifty feet apart. Half way between lines on a stick is placed a handkerchief. Players divide, each side taking its place behind own line. At signal, player on right of each line runs to get handkerchief. One getting it is pursued by opponent. If caught, the one with the handkerchief is opponent's prisoner. If not caught, the opponent is prisoner. Side having most prisoners wins.

Handmade Toys

From Home-made Toys for Girls and Boys by A. Neely Hall, 1915

The **Paper Pinwheel** shown in Fig. 1 is one of the best whirlers ever devised. A slight forward thrust of the stick handle upon which it is mounted starts it in motion, and when you run with the stick extended in front of you it whirls at a merry speed.

A piece of paper 8 or 10 inches square is needed for the pinwheel. Fold this piece of paper diagonally from corner to corner, both ways. Then open the paper, and with a pair of scissors cut along the diagonal creases, from the corners to within ½ inch of the center (Fig. 2). Next, fold corners *A, B, C,* and *D* over to the center, as shown in Fig. 3, run a pin through the corners and through the center of the sheet of paper, drive the point of this pin into the end of the stick handle, and the pinwheel will be completed.

The **Pinion-Wheel Windmill** in Fig. 4 may be made of cardboard or tin. A circular piece 10 or 12 inches in diameter is required. After marking out the outer edge with a compass, describe an inner circle about 1 inch inside of it; then draw two lines through the center at right angles to each other, and another pair at an angle of 45 degrees to these. These lines are shown by the heavy radial lines in Fig. 5.

One-half inch from each of these lines draw a parallel line, as indicated by dotted lines in Fig. 5. The next thing to do is to cut out the disk, and cut along the heavy lines just as far as the lines are shown in the diagram (Fig. 5), and then to bend up the blades thus separated, to an angle of about 45 degrees,

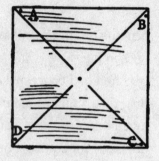

Fig. 2. Diagram for Paper Pinwheel.

Fig. 3. How the Paper Pinwheel is Folded.

Fig. 1. The paper pinwheel is the simplest pinwheel to make.

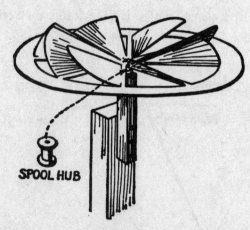

SPOOL HUB

Fig. 4. A Pinion-Wheel Windmill.

Fig. 5. Diagram
for Pinion-Wheel
Windmill.

bending on the second set of radial lines (dotted lines in Fig. 5).

You had better make a cardboard pinion-wheel first, then a tin one afterwards, as cardboard is so much easier to cut. A pair of heavy shears will be necessary for cutting a tin wheel, and a cold chisel for separating the edges of the blades.

To Mount the Pinion-Wheel drive a long nail through the center, through the hole in a spool, and into the end of a stick. Then nail the stick to a post or a fence top.

How to Make a Malay. Figure 18 shows a detail of the completed kite, Fig. 19 the completed framework, and Figs. 20, 21, and 22 the details for preparing the frame sticks.

The Sticks. This kite has a vertical stick and a bow-stick, each of which should be 40 inches long, about ¾ inch wide, and ⅜ inch thick, for a kite of medium size. In the cutting of the sticks lies half the secret of making a kite that will fly successfully.

Drive a small nail or large tack into each end of the two sticks, to fasten the framing-string to

(Figs. 20 and 21), and notch the side edges of the bow-stick near each end for the attachment of the bow-string (Figs. 21 and 22). The amount to bend the bow-stick is important. For a kite with a bow 40 inches long the distance between the string and stick should be 6 inches (Fig. 21). Use a strong twine for the bow-string, and tie it securely to the notched ends.

Framing the Sticks. Fasten the bow-stick at its exact center to the vertical stick, placing it 4 inches down from the top of the vertical stick, as indicated in Fig. 19. Drive a couple of brads through the two sticks to hold them together, and then reinforce the connection by wrapping the joint with strong linen thread, crossing the thread in the manner shown.

When the two sticks have been joined, connect their ends with the framing-string. Stretch this string from stick to stick, and tie securely to the end nails. Instead of the end nails, the sticks may be notched to receive the framing-string, but the nails are more satisfactory because the string can be tied fast to them and will not slip.

Covering the Frame-work. The strong light-weight brown wrapping-paper now so generally used makes an excellent covering for the framework. A few sheets can be purchased at a near-by store for the purpose. You will likely have to paste together two or more sheets to make one large enough. The paper should be placed on the outer face of the bow-stick, and should be allowed a little fullness instead of being stretched tight as on hexagonal tail kites.

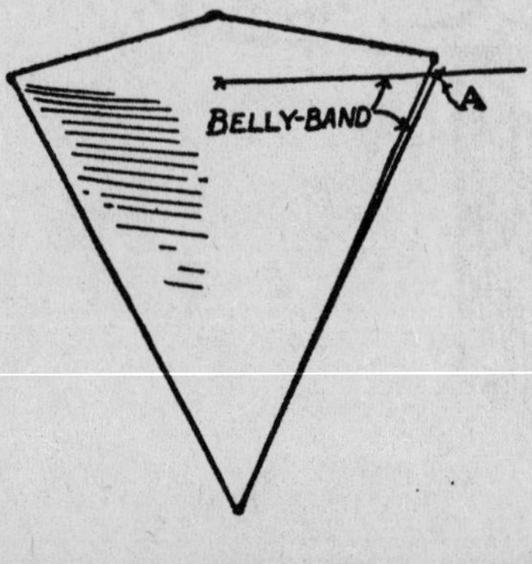

Fig. 18. Completed
Malay Kite with
Belly Band Attached.

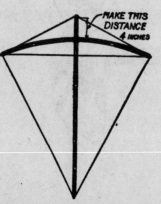

Fig. 19. Framework of
Malay Kite.

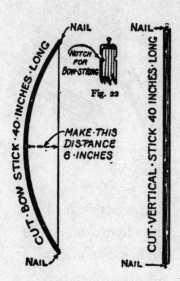

Fig. 20. Detail of Vertical Stick.
Fig. 21. Detail of Bow-Stick.
Fig. 22. Detail of End of Bow-Stick.

Lap the edges of the paper over the framing-string in the ordinary way of covering a kite.

Attach the Bridle at the intersection of the bow-stick and vertical stick, and at the lower end of the vertical stick (Fig. 18), and make it of the right length so when held over to one side it will reach to the end of the bow, as indicated in Fig. 18. Tie the flying line securely at the point *A* (Fig. 18) ; then the kite will be ready for its maiden flight.

Flying-Line. The kind of cord which a mason uses for his plumb-lines is splendid for flying the Malay kite. If you cannot get some balls of this, be certain that what you do get can be relied upon, because it is provoking to lose a kite which you have taken a great deal of pains in marking, through the breaking of the flying line.

The Box-Kite. Of the more pretentious kites, none is as popular as the rectangular box-kite.

Box-kites may be purchased ready-made in a number of sizes, but they are not cheap, and it will pay any boy to take the time necessary to make one. While their construction requires considerable more work than the single-plane type of kite, it is not difficult.

Figures 23 and 24 show a kite of scientifically developed proportions. Pine, spruce, and whitewood are the best materials for

The Kite Sticks, though any strong, light-weight wood of straight grain may be used if easier

to obtain. If you live near a lumber yard or planing-mill, possibly you can get strips of just the size you require from the waste heap, for the mere asking, or for a few cents get them ripped out of a board. If not, you will find it easy enough to cut them yourself with a sharp rip-saw.

Fig. 23. Raising the Box-Kite.

The Side Frames. Cut the four horizontal sticks ⅜ inch thick and ⅜ inch wide, by 36 inches long (*A*, Fig. 25), and the four upright connecting sticks (*B*, Fig. 25) ¼ inch thick, ½ inch wide, and 10 inches long. Tack the upright sticks to the horizontal ones 6 inches from the ends of the latter, as shown in Fig. 25, using slender brads for the purpose, and clinching the projecting ends. In fastening these sticks, be careful to set sticks *B* at right angles to sticks *A*.

After fastening together the side-frame sticks as shown in Fig. 25, lay them aside until you have prepared.

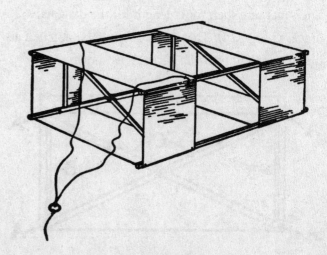

Fig. 24 The Box-Kite.

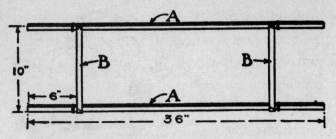

Fig. 25. Make Two Side Frames like this.

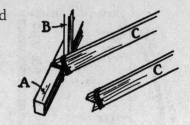

Fig. 27. Detail of Diagonal Braces.

Fig. 27, and they should be a trifle long so they will be slightly bow-shaped when put in place. In this way the frames will keep the cloth or paper bands stretched tight.

The Covering for the End Cells. A light-weight muslin or tough paper should be used for this material. Cheesecloth will do if you give it a coat of thin varnish to fill up the pores and make it air-tight, after it has been put on. The light-weight brown wrapping-paper now so commonly used is good covering material.

The cell bands for the kite illustrated should be 10 inches wide and 5 feet 9 inches long. If of cloth, they should be hemmed along each edge to prevent raveling and to make a firm edge. If of paper, the edges should be folded over a light framing-cord and pasted. Sew together the ends of the cloth bands, or paste the ends of the paper bands, lapping them so the measurement around the inside will be exactly 5 feet 8 inches, the proper measurement around the sticks of the finished kite.

Assembling the Kite. Slip the bands over the side frames, spread the frames to their fullest extent, and hold them in this position by means of sticks sprung in temporarily between upright sticks *B*. Then measure the proper length for the diagonal braces *C* (Fig. 26). These sticks should be notched at their ends to fit over the sticks *A*, as shown in

The notched ends of the diagonals should be *lashed* with thread to keep them from splitting. Lashings of thread around the frame sticks *A*, as shown in Figs. 25 and 27, will keep the ends of the braces from slipping away from the uprights *B*, which is the proper position for them. Bind the braces together at their centers with thread, as shown in Figs. 24 and 26. Coat the lashings with glue after winding them, and the thread will hold its position better. The cloth or paper bands should be fastened to each horizontal frame stick with two tacks placed near the edges of the bands.

There are several methods of **Attaching the Bridle**, but that shown in Fig. 24 is generally considered the most satisfactory. Of course, the kite is flown other side up, with the bridle underneath. The three-point attachment has cords fastened at the two outer corners of one cell, and a third cord to the center of the outer edge of the other cell; and the four-point attachment has cords attached at the four outer corners of the kite. The ends of the bridle should be brought together and tied at a distance of about 3 feet from the kite. It is a good plan to connect the ends to a fancy-work ring.

A Home-Made Toy Motor-Boat

The toy motor-boat shown in Figs. 48 and 49 is propelled by a tin propeller run by a rubber-band motor. A handful of rubber-bands will cost only a few cents, and the rest of the working material can be picked up at home.

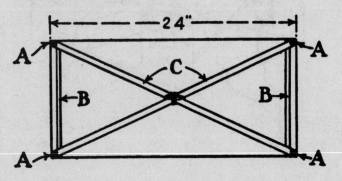

Fig. 26. Cross-Section of the Box-Kite.

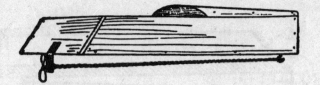

Fig. 49. The Completed Motor-Boat.

Prepare the Bottom of the Hull out of a piece of wood 1 inch thick, making it of the shape and dimensions shown in Fig. 51. Be careful to curve the side edges the same. Use a

Fig. 50. Stern, with Motor in Place.

saw for cutting out the piece, then smooth up the edges with a plane and sandpaper. The stern should be sawed off on a bevel as shown in Fig. 52.

The Sides of the hull (B, Figs. 52 and 53) are thin strips 2½ inches wide. Nail one to one edge of the bottom block, then saw off the bow end on a line with the bow of the bottom block, and the stern end on the same slant as the bevel cut on the stern of the bottom block. With one piece in position, nail on

Fig. 51. Diagram of Hull.

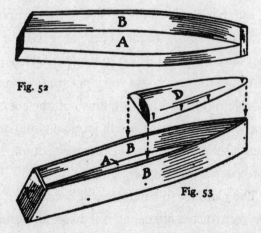

Fig. 52

Fig. 53

Figs. 52 and 53. How the Hull, Sides, Stern and Deck Pieces are Assembled.

the second side and trim off its ends. If you have any difficulty in making a neat joint between the bow ends of sides B, take a piece of tin from a can, bend it around the bow, and tack it in place as shown in Fig. 48. The stern piece (C, Figs. 53 and 54) should be cut next, to fit the slanted ends of the sides.

The Deck (D) extends from the bow almost to the center of the boat. Its top surface should taper in its length and curve from side to side. The piece may be whittled or planed to this shape. Fasten it with brads to the top edges of the sides of the boat.

To Complete the Boat, go over the work carefully, trim off all projecting edges, drive nail heads beneath the surfaces, putty nail holes and cracks, and give the wood two coats of paint of whatever color you want to have the motor-boat.

The Propeller (E, Fig. 54) is cut from the side of a tin can. Cut a piece 3 inches long and ¾ inch

Fig 48. Launching the Toy Motor-Boat.

wide, round its ends, and with the point of a nail pierce a hole through it each side of the center of the length of the piece (Fig. 55). To finish the propeller, it is only necessary to take hold of the two ends and twist the piece into the shape shown in Fig. 56.

The Propeller-Shaft requires a short piece of wire with one end bent into a hook (*F*, Fig. 56). Stick the straight end of this shaft through one hole in the propeller, and the hooked end through the other hole, then twist the hooked end over on to the main part of the shaft, as shown in Fig. 57. Make a tight twist so the propeller will be held perfectly rigid on the shaft.

The Bearing Plate *G* (Figs. 54 and 58) supports the propeller. Cut it out of a piece of tin 1½ inches wide by 3 inches long, bend it in half crosswise to give it stiffness, and then bend it lengthwise to the angle shown so it will fit over the slanted stern of the boat. Punch two holes through the upper end for nailing the plate to the stern, and a hole at the lower end for the propeller-shaft to run through.

For a Thrust Bearing, slip a couple of beads over the propeller-shaft, between the propeller and bearing plate *G*. Probably you can find glass beads in your mother's button bag.

After slipping the beads on to the shaft, and sticking the shaft through the hole in bearing plate *G*, bend the end of the shaft into a hook; then screw a small screw-hook into the bottom of the hull, at the bow end (*I*, Fig. 54), and you will be ready for

The Rubber-Band Motor. Rubber-bands about 1½ inches in length are best for the purpose. Loop these together end to end (Fig. 60) to form a strand that will reach from hook *I* to the hook on the propeller-shaft; then form three more strands of this same length, and slip the end loops of all four strands over the hooks.

To Wind the Motor, give the propeller about one hundred turns with your finger; then, keep hold of the propeller until you launch the boat.

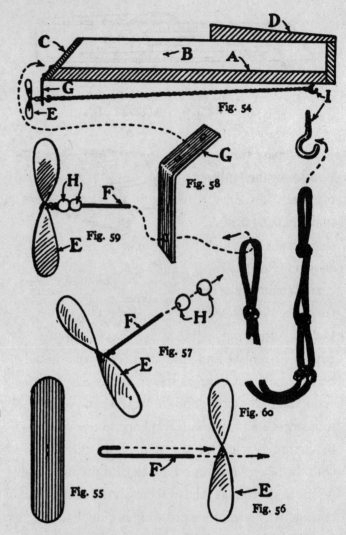

Fig. 54. Longitudinal Section of Assembled Motor-Boat.
Figs. 55-59. Details of Propeller.
Fig. 60. Rubber-Band Motor.

There are many ways of elaborating upon the design and construction of this toy motor-boat, but, having given the necessary instructions for building a simple model, I am going to leave further development for you to work out. Here is an opportunity for you to use your ingenuity. Devise an adjustable rudder, add a keel, finish off the cockpit with a coaming, install a headlight made from a pocket flashlight—in fact, see just how complete a motor-boat model you can build.

The Cars for this railway will have their trucks constructed alike, and it is a simple matter to transform a car from one style into another. Figure 79 shows a top view of a truck. For the bed of this

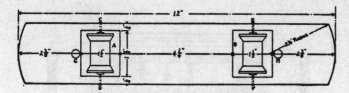

Fig. 79. A Top View of Car Truck.

cut a three-eighths-inch board twelve inches long by two and one-quarter inches wide, and, after rounding the ends as shown in the drawing, cut a mortise at *A* and *B* two and three-eighths inches from either end. Procure two one and one-half inch spools for wheels, and drive a wooden peg through the hole in each, cutting off the ends so they project a little beyond the hole, as shown in Fig. 80. Then bore four holes in the edges of the truck-bed with a gimlet at *C*, *D*, *E*, and *F* (see drawing), and, after setting the spools in mortises *A* and *B*, pivot them in place with small finishing nails driven into the wooden pegs. These nails should fit loosely in the gimlet holes. In order to drive them into the exact centers of the spools, it is best to locate these points upon the ends of the pegs before placing the spools in the frame. A quarter-inch hole should be bored in the top of the truck-bed at *G* and *H* (Fig. 79) in which to fasten the two uprights *I* and *J* (see Fig. 81). Make the uprights four inches long and whittle a peg upon the lower ends to fit holes *G* and H (see Fig. 82). Bore a hole with a gimlet in the top of each and run a piece of heavy wire from one to the other, bending it as shown in Fig. 81.

Fig. 80. Spool Wheels.

Fasten *K* between *I* and *J*, as shown. Place a small brass ring upon the wire before you fasten it in place. A small hook should be screwed into one end of the truck and a screw-eye into the other end, for couplings, should you wish to hitch two or more cars together.

A Gondola Car, such as shown in Fig. 83, should have its truck made similar to Fig. 79, with the exception that it should be two inches shorter, in order that cigar-box strips can be used for the side pieces. Cut the strips an inch and one-half high and fasten them to the bed of the car with brads. This car may be used as a trailer.

The car shown in Fig. 81 is a rather crude affair, but with a little more work may be transformed into a better looking car—**A Street Car** such as is shown in Figs. 84 and 85 being an example of what can be made. The sides, ends, and roof of this car are made of cardboard. Figure 86 shows a cross-section taken through the center of the car. The two side pieces *A* should be prepared first, as shown in Fig. 87. With a ruler and lead-pencil draw in the windows about as shown in the drawing, using double lines to indicate the sash. Then, with a sharp knife, cut out the center of each just inside of the inner line. These windows may be left open or may be covered on the inside with tissue-paper. If tissue-paper is used, oil it to make it more transparent. When the two sides have been prepared, bend each along the dotted lines (see Fig. 87) and tack one to each side of your car truck as shown in Fig. 86. When properly bent, the distance between the upper part of the sides should be two and three-quarters inches. Cut the two inner ends of the car the shape of Fig. 88, using

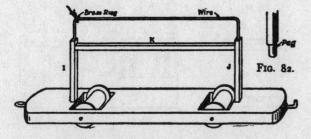

Fig. 81. The Completed Car Truck.

FIG. 82.

Fig. 83. A Gondola Car.

a compass with a radius of two and one-half inches with which to describe the curve at the top. Draw in the panels and sash lines as you did those upon the side pieces, being careful to get them on the same level, and cut out the door and window openings. Fasten these end pieces between the sides with glue, and also tack them to the uprights of the car (*I* and *J*, Fig. 81), which will come just inside of them. The roof is made in two sections (*B* and *C*, Fig. 86). For *B* cut a piece of cardboard twelve and one-quarter by three and three-quarter inches (Fig. 89), draw the curved end with a compass, using the radius shown on the drawing, and slit the corners as indicated by the dotted lines. When this piece has thus been prepared, remove the wire from the top of the truck (see Fig. 81). Bend the cardboard over the sides and ends of the car, and lap corners *D* and *E* over *F* and *G*, and *H* and *I* over *J* and *K*, tacking them with thread to hold them in place. To fasten this part of the roof to the top of the car, cut a number of small strips of linen, and glue them to the under side of the roof and to the inside face of the sides and ends of the car (see Fig. 86). The upper portion of the roof *C* should be made out of a piece of cardboard bent into the shape of Fig. 90, and cut at the ends so the upper portion of *C* projects a little beyond its sides. Draw the ventilation lights upon the sides of *C* as shown on the drawings, and then fasten the piece upon the top of *B* with strips of linen in the same manner as you fastened *B* in place. *C* should now have the same curve to its top as *B*. Cut and glue a piece of cardboard in each end of *C* to complete the roof. The shape of this piece is shown in Fig. 91. The outer ends of the car should be made as shown in Fig. 92, and tacked around the ends of the wooden truck platform, and also fastened to the under side of the roof with strips of linen. The window openings may be cut in each end, but it will make a stronger car if they are simply drawn upon it. Cut four cardboard steps similar to Fig. 93 and tack them to the sides of the front and rear platforms. When

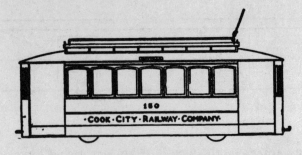

Fig. 84. Side View.

the car has been put together, replace the wire in the tops of uprights *I* and *J* (Fig. 81), running the ends through the roof (see Fig. 84). Paint the sides and ends of the car yellow with brown trimmings, and paint the roof a light gray. Water colors can be used for the purpose. Letter the name of your car-line upon the sides and the number

Fig. 85. End View.

of the car upon each end and side. The route should be lettered upon strips of cardboard with pins run

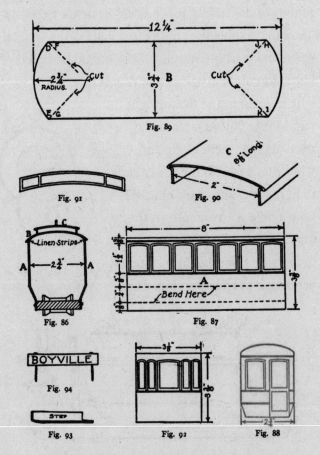

Figs. 86–94. Details of Toy Street Car.

through them as shown in Fig. 94, these strips to stick in the roof of the car (see Figs. 84 and 85).

Having seen how the car is made, you will find it a simple matter to make designs for

Other Cars, using the same scheme for the trucks, and altering the patterns for the sides, ends, and roof, to suit the design.

Nothing has, as yet, been said about the

Operation of the Railway. The car or cars are placed between the wooden tracks, and the trolley (or cord attached to the ring on top of the car) is tied to the trolley-line as in the illustration. Upon starting your engine, water-motor, or whatever motive-power you have, the car will run from one end of the track to the other. When it has reached the support of the trolley-line, it will stop long enough for the cord trolley to pass around the wooden wheel, and then run in the opposite direction until the other support is reached. It will thus be seen that the trolley hangs to the upper part of the cable, or trolley-line, in running one way, and to the lower part on the return run. In changing the direction of the run, the ring to which the trolley is attached slides to the other end of the car.

A **Station** such as is illustrated in Fig. 95 is made out of cardboard and mounted upon a seven-eighths-inch board large enough to form a railway platform. After cutting out the side and end pieces, with door and window openings placed as shown in the illustration, fasten them together with strips of linen glued in the corners. Make the roof low and extend it over the platform upon each side and over the gable-ends, as shown in the illustration. Paint the sides of the depot the

regulation depot red, and the roof a shingle or slate color. Paint the door and window-sash black, letter the name of the station upon the gable-ends, and with a ruler and lead-pencil rule off the boards upon the sides, and the slate or shingles upon the roof. As this is a typical railway station, two may be made of the same pattern, one for either end of your car line.

Home-Made Toy Elevators

The elevator shown in Fig. 96 is a unique mechanical toy well worth one's making. Release the little car at the top floor, and it will descend to the ground floor, and then return to the starting point, without you having to touch it a second time. A magical elevator? Perhaps so. A little mechanical device performs the trick.

The more stories there are the more fun there is in operating the elevator. This is why I have adapted the scheme to

A Toy Office Building. Six stories are shown in Fig. 96, but you can make a modern sky-scraper with as many stories as you like. A packing-case 3 feet 6 inches long, stood on end, was used for the model. Another box or two can be added to the top for additional stories. Besides the box, or boxes, get enough box boards for floors and partitions.

Make the Floors in two pieces (*A* and *B*, Fig. 98), so the opening for the elevator shaft can be cut out of the end of one piece in the manner shown. This opening should be about 5 inches square. Mark out and cut the boards for all of the floors at one time, and be careful to get the shaft opening the same in each floor. Cut the notch *C* in board *A* about 1 inch square.

Fasten the floor boards in place with nails driven through the sides of the box.

The Partitions, a pattern for which is shown in Fig. 99, can be made quicker by omitting the doorway, but this is easy to cut by sawing along the

Fig. 95. The Railway Depot.

sides and then splitting out the piece between the saw cuts.

The Elevator Car should be built up of cigar-box wood, as shown in Figs. 101 and 102. The front portion (*D*) should be about 3 inches wide, 2½ inches deep, and 4 inches high, and the rear portion (*E*) should be of the same width, 2 inches deep, and 2½ inches high. Fasten these upon the base piece *F* as shown.

The Elevator Guides. Bore the holes *G* through the top and bottom of the car, close to the sides, for guide wires *H* to run through (Figs. 101 and 102). These holes may be bored with a screw-eye if you haven't a gimlet or drill. Bell-wire, or almost any wire that you have on hand, will do for the guides. Fasten two screw-eyes into the under side of the top of the shaft, the same distance apart as holes *G*, and in the proper position so they will come exactly over them (*I*, Fig. 100). Use the car for determining these measurements. Then bore two holes through the bottom of the shaft directly below the screw-eyes (*J*, Fig. 100). Attach the wire to one

screw-eye, run it down through holes *G* in the car, through one of the holes *J*, then across to and up through the other hole *J*, up through the other set of holes *G* in the car, and attach to the second screw-eye *I*.

The Cables. The elevator is lifted by means of VW cord *L* (Figs. 97 and 101). Fasten this cord to a tack driven into the top of the car, then run it up and over spool *M* (Figs. 97 and 101), over spool *N* (Fig. 97), and tie to weight *K*,

The Counter-balance. A bottle, filled with sand to make it weigh more than twice as much as the car, should be used for this. Screw a small screw-eye into the cork to tie the cord to.

The counter-balance runs up and down in

The Smoke-Stack, which is fastened to the back of the building (Fig. 97). Make the stack of cardboard mailing-tubes, joining them end to end with bands of paper pasted around them. Fasten the stack to the back of the building with wire straps, and brace the top as shown in Fig. 96, but leave it unattached until you have adjusted

The Overhead Pulleys, or *sheaves*. These are spools. You will see by looking at Fig. 100 that spool *M* turns on the axle *O*, and the ends of this axle are cut to fit snugly in screw-eyes *I*. Fasten pulley spool *N* in the smoke-stack by means of a

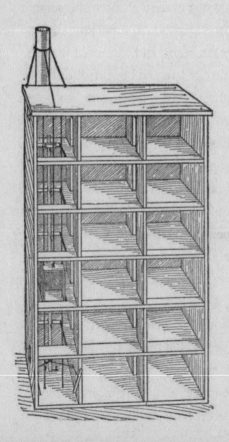

Fig. 96. A Toy Office Building with Elevator.

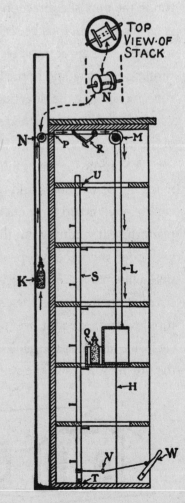

Fig. 97.

wooden axle pushed through holes pierced in the side of the stack, as is shown in the small drawing above, Fig. 97. Bore a hole through the back of the building for the cable cord *L* to run through (*P*, Figs. 97 and 100), and cut another through the smoke-stack.

How the Car Operates. When the weight and cord have been adjusted and the smoke-stack erected, the elevator will run from the ground floor up to the roof of its own accord, because the counter-balance is much heavier than the car. To make it descend it is necessary to add weight to the car, to make it enough heavier than the counter-balance so it will drop of its own accord. This is done with a

Ballast consisting of a bottle of sand or salt of twice the combined weight of counter-balance *K* and the car. After filling the bottle, cork it up, and screw a screw-eye into the cork. Then screw the eye of a 2-inch hook-and-eye into the roof of the building, directly over the center of box *E* of the elevator (*R*, Figs. 97 and 101), and attach one end of a rubber-band to the hook and tack the other end to the top of the elevator-shaft (Fig. 101).

With the hook and rubber-band properly adjusted, this is what happens when the car ascends to the top of the shaft. The bottom of the rear portion of the car strikes bottle *Q*, lifts it enough to release the end of the hook (*R*), and the rubber-band springs the hook out of the way (Fig. 97). The bottle remains upon the rear portion of the car, and its weight carries the car to the bottom of the shaft.

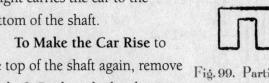

Fig. 98. Floors.

Fig. 99. Partitions.

To Make the Car Rise to the top of the shaft again, remove bottle *Q*. Replace the bottle upon the end of hook *R*, and it will be in position for the next trip downwards. Cut the holes *Y* and *Z* (Fig. 100) through the out-side wall of the shaft for hand holes through which to reach bottle *Q* and hook *R*.

Figures 97, 100, and 103 show

The Clog-Dancer (Fig. 109) is an easily made loose-jointed doll. His dancing-stage is a shingle or piece of stiff cardboard held on the edge of a chair beneath your knee. He is held by means of the string attached to his head, so that his feet rest lightly upon the stage, and he is made to jig by tapping the outer end of the stage with the free hand. With a little

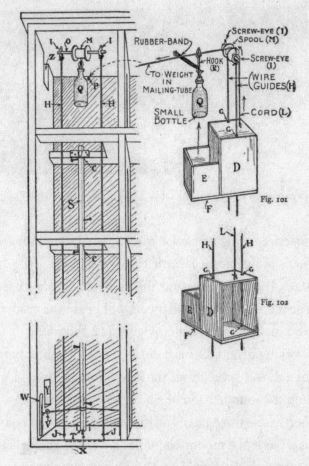

Fig. 100. Front View of Elevator Shaft.
Figs. 101 and 102. Elevator Car Details.

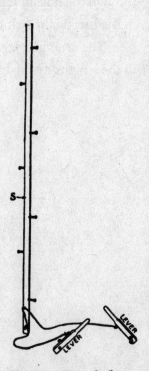

Fig. 103. Detail of Brake and Controlling Levers.

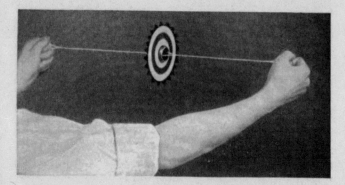

Fig. 108. The Buzz-saw whizzes when you twist the Cord.

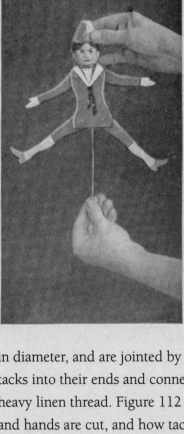

Fig. 110. Pull the string and Jack jumps comically.

practice the figure can be made to go through the steps of the most eccentric clog-dancer.

The more grotesque the dancer's appearance is, the more amusing his dancing will be, so the cruder you make him the better. Figure 112 shows the working details for his construction. The center part of a thread-spool forms the *head,* and a spool-end and the rounded end of a broom-handle form the *hat.* These three pieces are nailed together. The *body* is a piece of a broom-handle, and a spool-end nailed to it forms the *shoulders.* Drive a nail into the end of the body, tie a string to this, and run the string up through the hole in the head, and out through a hole in the hat; tie the string to a fancy-work ring.

The *arms* and *legs* are made of sticks whittled to the lengths marked in Fig. 112, and about ¼ inch

in diameter, and are jointed by driving tacks into their ends and connecting these with heavy linen thread. Figure 112 shows how the feet and hands are cut, and how tacks are driven into them for the thread connections. Paint the clog-dancer's body, arms, and legs white, his head, hands,

Fig. 109. The Eccentric Clog-dancer is a Circus in himself.

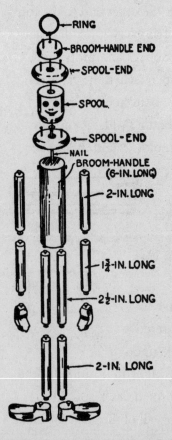

RING
BROOM-HANDLE END
SPOOL-END
SPOOL
SPOOL-END
NAIL
BROOM-HANDLE (6-IN. LONG)
2-IN. LONG
1¾-IN. LONG
2½-IN. LONG
2-IN. LONG

Fig. 112. Details of Body of the Clog-Dancer shown in Fig. 109.

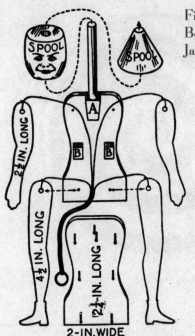

Fig. 113. Details of Body of the Jumping Jack shown in Fig. 110.

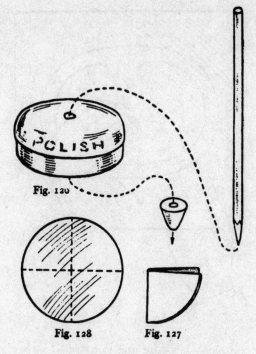

Fig. 126–128. Details of Shoe-Polish Can Top.

and feet black, and mark his eyes, nose, and mouth upon his face in white.

A Spool Top. The top is made from a half of a spool and a short piece of lead-pencil. Saw a spool into halves, and then taper one half from its beveled end to the center. Sharpen the piece of pencil to a point, and push it through the spool until its point projects just a trifle. Spin the spool top in the same way as the clock wheel tops.

A Spinning Top Race-Track. By drawing a track upon a piece of cardboard, as shown in Fig. 129, with an opening on the inside, great fun may be had by starting any one of the small tops just described, with the exception of the balance-wheel top, in the center of the space inside of the track, and tilting the cardboard so as to cause the top to spin through the opening on to the track, and around the track. There is a trick in keeping the top from running off the track that can be acquired only with practice.

A Shoe-Polish Can Top. This is a sure-enough good looking top, and it spins as well as it looks. It is made of a pencil, a cone-shaped piece cut from a spool, and an empty shoe-polish can.

The dotted line in Fig. 126 indicates how the end of the pencil sticks through a hole in the shoe-polish can, then through the cone-shaped piece of spool. The hole through the can must be located in the exact center, so the top will balance properly. To find the center, place the box bottom down upon a piece of paper, and with a pencil draw a line around it. Cut the paper along the center, and you will have a piece the shape and size of the can bottom. Fold the piece in half, then in half again the other way (Fig. 127), open it up, and the inter-section of the two folds, indicated by dotted lines in Fig. 128, will be the exact center. With the center located, place the piece of paper first upon the bottom, then upon the top of the can, and punch a hole through the center of it and the can, with the point of a large nail. Increase the size of the hole enough to admit the pencil.

To spin the top, hold the upper part of the pencil between your hands, with the palms together, and slide your hands back and forth, first slowly, then rapidly. Release it so as to cause it to drop squarely upon its point upon a level wooden surface.

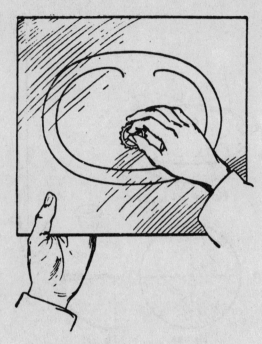

Fig. 129. A Spinning Top Race-Track.

Fig. 131. Diagram of Spiral for Spiral Top.

The steadiness of this top's spinning will depend entirely upon the accuracy with which you cut the center hole for the pencil.

A Spiral Top. The top in Fig. 130 presents a curious appearance while spinning, the spiral design upon it seeming to change its form as the top revolves.

The only difference between the construction of this top and the shoepolish can top is in the substitution of the spiral disk for the polish can. A pencil and cone-shaped piece of spool are required as in the case of the other top.

Fig. 130. A Spiral Top.

The spiral design for the disk, shown in Fig. 131, is large enough so you can make a tracing of it on a piece of transparent paper, and then trace it off upon a piece of cardboard. Fill in alternate rings with black ink or water-color, in the way shown, then cut out the disk, pierce a hole through its exact center to fit over the pencil end, and glue the under side to the top of the

cone-shaped piece of spool. Spin this top in the same way as the shoe-polish can top is spun.

A Home-Made Doll-House

Here is nothing more interesting to build than a doll-house, and the construction is within the ability of the average girl. If brother is willing to lend a hand with the carpenter work so much the better. Sister can attend to the finishing and furnishing, which are important parts of the work that she can do more handily than a boy can. But there is no reason why either a girl or boy cannot undertake a doll-house like that shown in Figs. 220 and 221, and carry the work to a successful completion, by carefully following the instructions and diagrams in this chapter.

The Building Material. The doll-house in the photographs was built of packing cases. You can buy these at a dry-goods store at 15 or 20 cents apiece.

The Floor Plans are shown in Figs. 222, 223, and 224. Your boxes may make it necessary to alter the dimensions given, but that will be simple to do. Patterns for

The Partitions are shown in Figs. 225 and 226. In cutting the second-floor partitions (Fig. 226), miter one edge of *E* and *F* to allow for the bedroom door opening, shown upon the plan, and miter the edges of *G* to fit between them above the door. The mitering is shown in the drawings (Fig. 226).

Besides cutting a stair opening in the second floor, make an opening three by five inches in the second and third floors for

The Elevator-Shaft Care must be taken to have these openings exactly over one another. Make the opening in the second floor six by eight inches in the place indicated upon the plan. This will allow for the elevator shaft and stairway. No stairway has been built to the third story, as the elevator serves the purpose, and one would take up too much of the ball-room space.

The Side Walls should measure nineteen inches wide by twenty-four inches high, and the other two walls thirty inches wide by twenty-four inches high. That portion of

The Rear Wall enclosing the kitchen and bath-room is hinged to open (see Fig. 222), and

The Front Wall is made in two sections, each hinged to a strip of wood an inch and one-half wide nailed to the two edges of the house, as shown in Fig. 220.

The Windows are four by five inches, so four-by-five camera plates can be used for the glass.

The Roof had best be made in two sections, each measuring twenty-eight inches long by twenty-

Fig. 221. Interior view of doll-house.

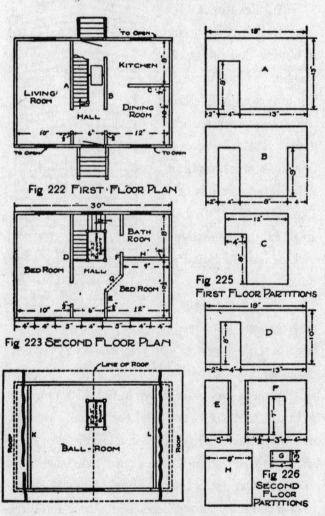

Fig 222 FIRST FLOOR PLAN

Fig 223 SECOND FLOOR PLAN

Fig 225 FIRST FLOOR PARTITIONS

Fig 226 SECOND FLOOR PARTITIONS

Fig. 222–226. Plans of Doll-House and Patterns for Partitions.

Fig. 220. The home-made doll-house.

four inches wide. Fasten the boards together with battens on the under side and, after mitering the upper edge of each, nail them to the house so that the ridge is fifteen inches above the third floor. Then nail a board nineteen inches long by ten inches wide in the peak of the roof (D in Fig. 228), and a narrow strip three inches from each side wall (K and L in Fig. 224). These cut off the triangular shape of the ball-room and give it a better appearance.

The Chimney is a solid block of wood with narrow strips nailed to all sides near the top (Fig. 227). Make it eight or ten inches long, and cut off the bottom to fit the slant of the roof. Paint the block red, and mark off the mortar joints in white.

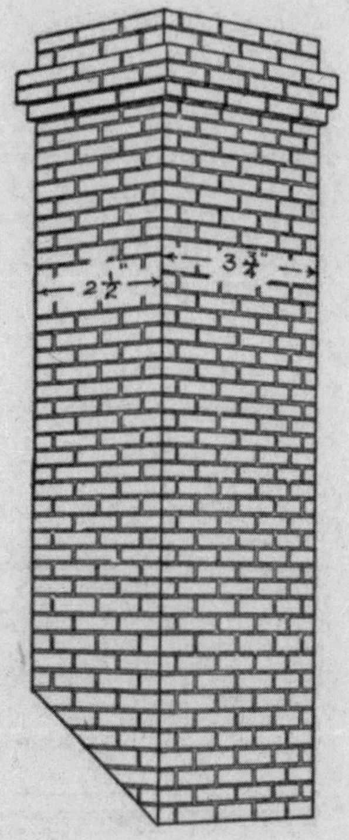

An Elevator is something which is found in but few doll-houses. It was built in this house, thinking it might please the young mistress, and it proved such a success that the scheme has been worked out carefully in Figs. 228, 229, 230, 231, and 232, that you may include it in the house you build.

The cutting of the elevator-shaft has already been described. For material, procure two small pulleys such as is shown in Fig. 230, four feet of brass chain, six feet of No. 12 wire, half a dozen double-pointed tacks or very small screw-eyes, a short piece of lead pipe, and a cigar-box. Make

The Car out of the cigar-box, cutting it down to two and one-quarter inches wide, three and three-quarters inches deep, and seven inches high (see Fig. 231). Place two of the double-pointed tacks or screw-eyes in each side of the car for the guide-wires to run through and another in the center of the top from which to attach the brass chain.

The Guide-Wires are made of very heavy wire that will not bend easily. Cut two of a length to reach

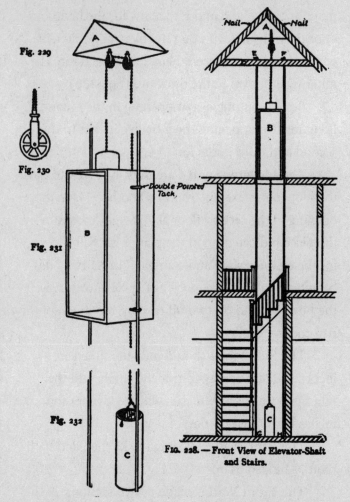

Fig. 227. The Chimney.

Fig. 228. Front View of Elevator-Shaft and Stairs.
Fig. 229-232. Details of the elevator.

from the first floor to the ball-room ceiling, and after running them through the tacks in the sides of the car, stick their ends into small holes bored at E, F, G, and H (Fig. 228). The upper holes should be bored through the ball-room ceiling, while the lower ones need be bored but part way through the first floor. Care must be taken to have these holes in the correct position, so the elevator will run up and down upon the wires without striking the sides of the shaft. The easiest way of fastening the wires in place is to run the upper ends through the holes, until the lower ends can be set into their sockets, and then drive two double-pointed tacks over the top of each wire, as shown at E and F in Fig. 228.

Now run the elevator up to the top of the shaft, and mark upon the ceiling where the screw-eye in the top of the car strikes. At this point bore a hole through the ceiling and two inches back of it bore another hole, through which to run the weight-chain. When this has been done, cut a short block of wood to fit the peak of the roof and

Screw the Pulleys into it two inches apart (Fig. 229). Fit the block in the peak of the roof, centering the front pulley over the top of the car as nearly as possible, and drive a couple of nails through the roof boards into it to hold it in place temporarily. Then

Attach the Chain to the tack in the top of the car, slip a piece of lead pipe about an inch long over the chain, allowing it to set on the top of the car to make the latter heavier (Fig. 231), and run the chain up through the first hole in the ceiling, over the pulleys, and down through the second hole. To the end of the chain attach a piece of lead pipe for

The Counter-balance (*C*, Fig. 232). This should be just heavy enough to make a perfect balance between it and the car, which can be obtained by whittling off the end of the pipe until the weight of the two is the same. Make the chain of sufficient length so the weight will rest upon the first floor when the car is at the third floor. You can now tell whether or not the pulleys are in the right positions. When they have been adjusted properly, nail the block firmly in place.

The Gable-Ends. The front gable-end consists of four pieces (*A, B, C,* and *D,* in Fig. 233), the dimensions for the cutting of which are given in the illustration. After preparing these, nail *A, B,* and *C* in their proper positions in the gable of the roof, and trim the edges of *D,* if they need it, to fit between. To prevent the movable section from pushing in too far, it will be necessary to nail a narrow strip of wood to the roof and third floor, just inside of it. The rear gable is made in one piece, and is fastened in place permanently.

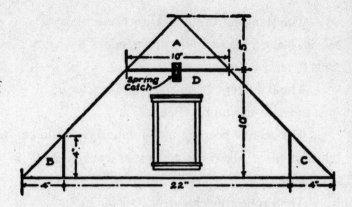

Fig. 233. The Front Gable-End.

The movable gable and all hinged portions should have

Spring-Catches with which to shut up and lock the house (see the illustrations).

The Stairway is shown in Fig. 228, and the details for its construction will be found in Figs. 234, 235, 236, 237. This stairway is made in two parts, with a platform between. Cut a block of wood the shape and size shown in Fig. 234 for the platform, with notches at *A* and *B* for the tops of the lower stringers to fit in. Then

Prepare Two Stringers of thirteen steps similar to Fig. 235, and two stringers of five steps similar to Fig. 236, laying off the steps by means of a cardboard pattern, or *pitch-board*, of the size shown in Fig. 237. After cutting out these pieces, fasten the tops of the lower stringers in the notches *A* and *B* in the platform, and nail the platform in its proper position in the corner of the hall. When this has been done, nail the bottoms of the upper stringers (*E* in Fig. 236) to the sides of the platform at *C* and *D* (Fig. 234), and set the tops in notches cut in the edge of the second floor.

The Treads and Risers of the steps—the horizontal and vertical boards—should be cut out of cigar-box wood.

Cut

The Newel-Posts out of short square blocks, and

The Hand-Rails out of strips of cigar-box wood. Make a groove in the under side of the hand-rails to receive the ends of

The Balusters, or spindles. Toothpicks are of just the right size for balusters.

The delicate portions of the stairways should be glued in place. Make slits in the stair treads to stick the bottoms of the balusters in.

The Front Steps are clearly shown in Fig. 220. Make the solid balustrades out of pieces of box board, and the step treads and risers out of cigar-box wood. Prepare the rear steps in the same way.

Cut the Window Openings in the places indicated upon the plans (Figs. 222 to 224) and the

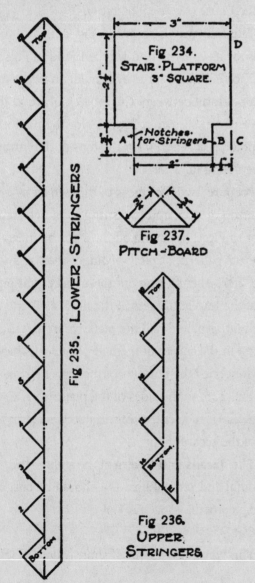

Fig. 234-237. Details of Stairs.

photographs. First bore holes in the four corners of each window space; then saw from hole to hole with a compass-saw.

Old camera plates are excellent material for

The Window Glass. Fasten the glass in the openings with small brads in the same way that glass is fastened in picture-frames, and putty it in the same way that window glass is puttied, to hold it firm.

The Front and Rear Doors can be painted upon the front of the house. Openings are not necessary.

The Outside Trimmings. Strips of cigar-box wood should be cut up for the outside door and window casings, and be tacked around the openings as shown in Fig. 220. Nail a molding or a plain strip of wood to the front edge of the third floor, as shown in Fig. 220.

Castors will make it easier to move the doll-house about. Cut four blocks of wood, fasten a castor to each, and nail one block inside each corner of the foundation frame.

The Interior Woodwork. Cigar-boxes make excellent hardwood floors. Fit the pieces close together and fasten with small brads.

Make the door and window casings, picture-moldings, and base-boards out of strips of cigar-box wood.

After completing the carpenter work of the house,

Set the Nail-Heads,—that is, drive them below the surface of the wood,—putty these holes and all cracks and other defective places, and sandpaper rough surfaces.

Paint the House a cream color, with white trimmings and a green roof. Stripe the foundation walls to indicate courses of stone work. Paint the front door a mahogany color, with panels indicated upon it, and make the rear door white. The painting of the chimney has already been described.

The inside walls may be oiled, or painted with white enamel or any other color desired.

Furnishing the Home-Made Doll-House

With the carpenter work of a doll-house completed, the finishing of the inside,—wall papering and painting,—and selecting of furnishings for the various rooms, remain to be done. This requires as much care as the building of the house, and while any boy can do the work, the help of a sister will perhaps simplify matters and give to the rooms a daintier appearance.

The Walls and Ceiling of the kitchen and bath-room should be painted with white lead or white enamel. For the other rooms select paper having a small design, such as is to be found on most ceiling papers. If you have ever watched the paper-hanger at work, you have noticed he puts on the ceiling first, allowing the paper to run down the walls a little way all around instead of trimming it off. Then he hangs the wall paper, and if there is no border to cover the joints of the ceiling and wall papers he carries the wall paper up to the ceiling. Use flour paste to stick on the paper, and a cloth or photograph-print roller to smooth out the wrinkles. The dining-room should have a wainscot of dark paper below the chair-rail, and a paper with little or no figure upon it above.

All Hardwood Floors, the stairs, door and window casings, baseboards, and picture moldings should be varnished thoroughly or given several coats of boiled linseed-oil.

All floors, with the exception of the kitchen, bath-room, and hardwood floors, should be fitted with

Carpets. If you do not happen to have suitable scraps on hand, they can be procured at almost any furnishing store where they make up carpets. Select pieces with as small patterns as possible. The floors of the bath-room and kitchen should be covered with oilcloth.

Rugs for the hardwood floors may be made out of scraps of carpet.

Window-Shades may be made for each window out of linen, and tacked to the top casing so that the bottom of the curtain reaches just above the center of the opening. Each window should also have

Lace Curtains made out of scraps of lace. They should either be tacked above the windows or hung upon poles made out of No. 12 wire, cut in lengths to fit the windows. Screw small brass hooks into the top window-casings for the poles to hang upon.

Handsome Portières for the doorways can be made with beads and with the small hollow straws sold for use in kindergartens. For the

Bead Portières, cut threads as long as the height of the door and string the beads upon them, alternating the colors in such a way as to produce patterns. Then tie the strings together to a piece of wire the width of the doorway, and fasten the wire in the opening. The

Straw Portières are made similarly.

From magazine illustrations you can select

Suitable Pictures for each room, but if you are handy with brush and pencil you may prefer to make the pictures yourself. These may be mounted upon cardboard and have their edges bound with passe-partout paper to give the effect of frames, or frames may be cut out of cardboard and pasted to them. Hang the pictures to the picture molding with thread.

A Cosey-Corner may be fitted up in the ball-room by fastening a strip of a cigar-box in one corner an inch and one-half above the floor for the seat, and hanging draperies on each side of it. Pillows may be made for it out of scraps of silk stuffed with cotton.

A doll-house properly proportioned in every detail, including the selection of its furniture, is pleasing to look at, and is to be desired much more than some of the specimens to be found in the stores. These very often have parlor chairs larger than the mantel, beds that either fill two-thirds of the bedroom space or are so small they are hidden from view by the chairs, and other furniture accordingly, all having been selected without any thought as to size or fitness.

Care must be taken, in buying the furniture, to have the pieces suitable to the rooms. It will no doubt require more time than to purchase the first sets you come across, but when you have completed the selections, the result will be a much better appearing doll-house.

By carefully searching the toy-shops you are almost certain of finding what you want for the various rooms, as about everything imaginable in furniture has been manufactured. Porcelain bath-tubs, wash-basins with real faucets and running water, gilt furniture, chandeliers, and such articles are tempting to buy. But it is rather expensive to fit up a house in this way, for, though each piece may not amount to very much, they count up very quickly.

A Home-Made Toy Stable

The stable illustrated in Figs. 238 and 239 is designed in keeping with the doll-house in Chapter XIII. It is shown in the background of the photograph of this doll-house (Fig. 220). If you prefer a garage instead of this stable, you may omit the stalls, and make one or two large windows in the rear wall in place of the small high windows shown. The building's construction is very simple. The dimensions are: width, twenty-four inches; depth, twelve inches; and height, twenty-two inches. The barn contains five stalls on the ground floor and a hay-loft above.

To build the stable according to the drawings, a box ten by twelve by twenty-four inches should be procured for

The First Story. If you have a box of different proportions it will be a simple matter to make such alterations in the details as it will require.

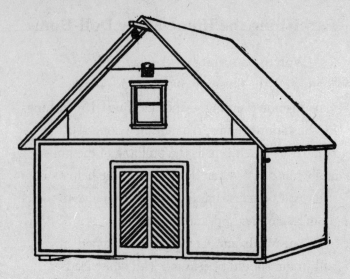

Fig. 238. Exterior of Stable.

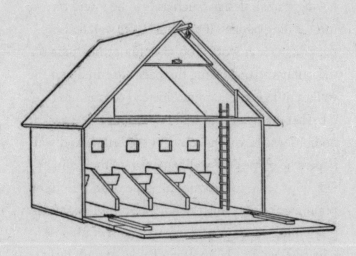

Fig. 239. Interior of Stable.

The Roof is made in two sections, each fifteen by eighteen inches, and is fastened to the top of the box so that the peak is twenty-two inches above the bottom.

The Gable-End is made in four pieces, as shown in Fig. 240, A, B, and C, to be nailed in place, and D to be movable as in the case of the doll-house. Make a three-by-five-inch window in the center of D and fasten the glass in place with strips. Strips should be nailed to the roof just inside of the movable section to prevent the latter from setting in too far, and a spring catch fastened to C and D as shown, to hold the movable section in place.

Figure 241 gives the patterns and measurements for

The Stall Partitions, four of which should be cut out and fastened to the floor of the stable four inches apart, or so they will divide the inside width into five equal stalls.

The Feed-Troughs are made out of two strips of cigar-boxes fitted between the stalls, as shown in Figs. 239 and 241, and are fastened in place by means of brads and glue. Above the stalls cut

Small Windows an inch and one-half square in the rear wall. These are the ventilating windows for the stalls, and may be left open.

Figure 242 shows the construction of

A Ladder to the hay-loft. This is made out of two sticks twelve inches long, with strips of cigar-boxes two inches long glued to them half an inch apart, as shown in the drawing. Cut away a section of the hay-loft floor two inches square and stick the end of the ladder up through the opening, fastening the uprights to the edge of the floor (see Fig. 242).

A stick about three inches long, with a very small pulley attached near the end, should be fastened in the peak of the roof for a

Feed-Hoist (see Fig. 238).

The first story has

A Drop-Front, as shown in Figs. 238 and 239. This is made from the box-cover. Fasten the boards together with battens placed upon the inside, and hinge it to the bottom of the stable. Nail two cleats to the under side of the floor (see Fig. 238) to lift it off the ground just enough to allow the front to drop without springing its hinges.

When the front is down it forms an incline upon which to run the horses into the stable. For this reason it is not advisable to cut an opening in it, but merely

Represent a Stable Door on the outside (see Fig. 238). This is done with paint and a fine brush. First paint a green panel in the center of the front, and then mark off a couple of panels within this space with black paint, and stripe them diagonally to represent beaded-boards.

With strips of wood half an inch wide make

A Simple Trim around the door, the sides of the stable, and around the gable, as shown in the illustration.

When the carpenter work has been finished,

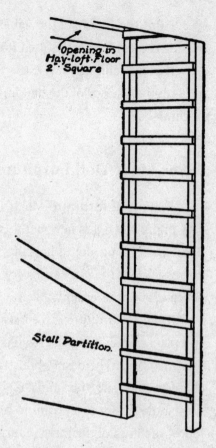

Fig. 242. Ladder to Hay-Loft.

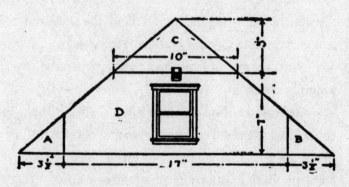

Fig. 240. Front Gable-End.

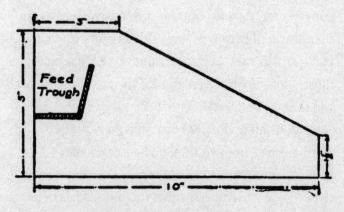

Fig. 241. Stall Partitions.

Paint the Inside of the stable white, and the outside the same colors as used for the doll-house.

If you Prefer a Garage, use your ingenuity to fit up the interior of the building as you think it ought to be.

Home-Made Doll Furniture

The metal furniture which you can buy is very pretty when it is new, but this new appearance does not last long after it has come into a youngster's possession, for the pieces are very slender and delicate, and thus easily broken.

Wooden furniture is the most durable kind, and plain and simple pieces will generally outlast the fancy ones. The designs illustrated in this chapter make very substantial pieces, as there are no spindle legs or fancy arms to break off. They follow the lines of the mission furniture, that simple style used in the early American mission schools, and which is to-day being extensively made in handsome pieces for the furnishings of modern homes. You will find the

Miniature Mission Furniture, illustrated and described in this chapter, simple to make and something which is easy to sell, for there is nothing like it at present upon the market.

Cigar-boxes furnish the nicest material for making this furniture, and the various parts can be cut to the right shape and size with

A Scroll-Saw. Procure small brads and glue with which to fasten the pieces together.

To Prepare the Cigar-Boxes for use, place them in a tub of boiling water and let them remain there until the paper labels readily pull off. Do not use a knife in removing the paper, as it is likely to roughen the wood. The paper will come off by allowing it to soak long enough. When the boxes are clean, set them in the sun to dry, after binding the covers to the backs to prevent them from warping. Pull the boxes apart when they are thoroughly dry, and throw out

such pieces as have printing upon them, for these would spoil the appearance of the furniture if used.

In order to simplify the matter of cutting the parts that make the furniture, the curved pieces have been drawn out carefully, so that they can be laid off upon the strips of cigar-boxes without any trouble, by the process of

Enlarging by Squares. These drawings are shown one-quarter of their full size (half their width and half their height). To enlarge them procure a piece of cardboard nine by thirteen inches, or a little larger than twice the size of the drawing each way, and divide it into squares just twice the size of those on the following page. That will make sixteen squares in the width of the cardboard and twenty-four in the length, each half an inch square. In order to get the squares spaced equally, it is best to lay off the points first with a ruler along the top, bottom, and two sides of the sheet of cardboard, and then connect the points with the ruler and a sharp lead-pencil. Then number the squares as in the illustration, using the figures along the sides and letters across the top and bottom of the sheet.

With the sheet of cardboard thus prepared it is a simple matter to

Reproduce the Drawings of Figs. 259 to 266 by locating the points of the curves and corners of the pieces, as shown in the illustrations, in corresponding positions in the squares on your cardboard sheet. The curves may be drawn in by eye, after locating them with reference to their surrounding squares, but the surest way of enlarging them accurately is by laying off the points where the curve strikes each horizontal and vertical line in the illustration, upon the enlarged drawing. These points can then be connected with a curved line.

Make all of the lines heavy so they can be distinguished from your guide lines, and after carefully going over the drawing, comparing it with the original pattern to see that no mistake has been

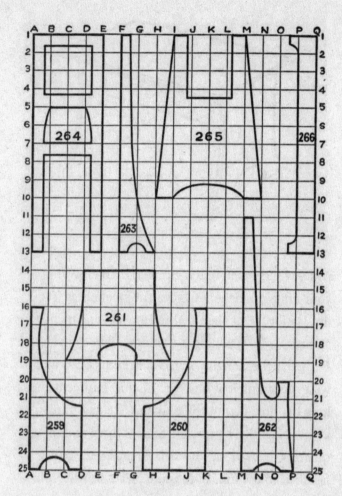

Figs. 259–266. Patterns for Furniture.

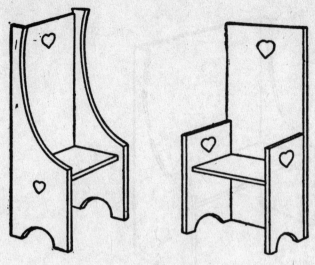

Fig. 267–268 Chairs.

made in locating the points in enlarging, cut the various pieces apart. These will give you

The Patterns with which to mark out the pieces on the wood.

We will first note the construction of

The Chairs shown in Figs. 267 and 268. These are four and one-half inches high, two inches wide, and an inch and one-half deep. Cut the back for the chair in Fig. 267 four and three-eighths inches high and an inch and three-quarters wide, the sides by the pattern in Fig. 259 and the seat an inch and one-quarter by an inch and three-quarters. With the pieces cut out, fasten them together with brads and glue, placing the seat between the arms and back so that it is an inch and one-half above the base.

Cut the back for the other chair (Fig. 268) four and one-half inches high by two inches wide, the seat an inch and a quarter by an inch and three-

quarters, and the sides an inch and three-eighths wide by two and one-half high. To get the curve in the bottom edge of the side pieces, use the pattern in Fig. 259.

The Settee (Fig. 269) should have its sides cut by the pattern of Fig. 260. Make the back piece three and three-quarters inches wide and three and one-quarter inches high, and the seat three and three-quarters inches by an inch and one-half. Fasten the seat against the back an inch and one-half above the base.

Tables for the living-room, dining-room, bedroom, ball-room, and nursery of a doll-house may be patterned after the designs of Figs. 270 and 271. These should be two and one-half inches high to be of proper proportion for the chairs.

The pieces necessary to make Fig. 270 are a top two inches square, two sides an inch and one-half wide by two and one-half inches high, and a shelf an inch and one-quarter square. Fasten the pieces together as in the illustration, placing the shelf between the side pieces an inch from the bottom.

The other design (Fig. 271) will do nicely for

A Dining-Room Table, or table for the center of the living-room. The top of this should be five inches long and three inches wide. Cut the side pieces by the pattern in Fig. 261 and, after fastening

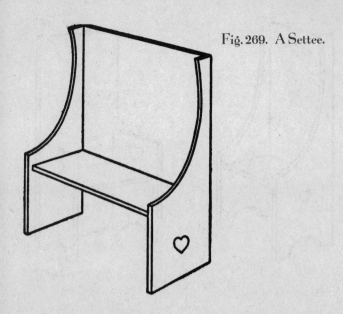

Fig. 269. A Settee.

Fig. 271. Another Design.

them to the under side of the table-top four inches apart, brace them with a strip three and three-quarters inches long by half an inch wide, as shown in Fig. 271.

A Side-Board similar to Fig. 272 should be made for the dining-room. The pattern for the side pieces is shown in Fig. 262. After sawing these out, cut a piece seven inches long by three inches wide for the back and fasten the side pieces to the edges of it. The location of the shelves can be obtained best by referring to Fig. 272 and the pattern in Fig. 262. Cut the bottom shelf (*A* in Fig. 272) three inches long by an inch and one-quarter wide and fasten it to the side pieces half an inch above the base (line 24 on pattern, Fig. 262). Make shelf *B* three by one inches and place it at line 22. *C* should be three and three-quarters inches long by an inch and one-half

wide, with a small notch cut near each end with your knife, to make it fit over the side pieces (see illustration). Cut shelf *D* three inches long by half an inch wide, fastening it in place at line No. 17, *E* three inches long by seven-sixteenths of an inch wide, fastening it at line No. 15, and *F* three inches long by three-eighths of an inch wide, fastening it at line No. 13. The top shelf (*G*) is three and three-quarters inches long and half an inch wide and is fastened to the tops of the side pieces as shown in the drawing.

The lower portion of the side-board is inclosed with two doors two inches high by an inch and one-half wide. Small pieces of cloth may be used for hinges, but it is better to use pins, running them through the shelf above and below (*A* and *C*, Fig. 272) into the doors. Stick the pins near the edge of the doors and see that they are straight, so the doors will open easily. A small mirror attached to the back between shelves *C* and *D* will complete this piece of furniture.

A Mirror in a frame should be made for the

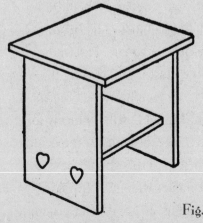

Fig. 270. A Table.

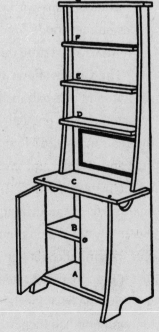

Fig. 272. A Side-Board.

living-room of the doll-house. A neat and suitable design for one of these will be seen in Fig. 273. For its construction cut two sides by means of the pattern in Fig. 263, a piece five inches long by three inches wide for the back, and a strip three inches long by three-eighths of an inch wide for a shelf. Fasten the sides to the edges of the back piece, and the shelf between the sides about three-quarters of an inch above the base. Now procure a mirror such as you can buy in a toy-shop for five or ten cents (or a piece of a broken mirror cut down to the right size will do very nicely), and attach it to the center of the back.

The Grandfather's Clock (Fig. 274) makes an effective piece of furniture for the hall or living-room, and is easily made. Figure 264 shows the pattern for the front of this clock. The back is made the same, with the omission of the square opening cut in the front frame for the clock-face. Cut a block of wood two by two by three-quarters inches to fit between the frames at the top. After nailing the pieces together, procure a face from a toy watch, and fasten it in the opening made for it in the front frame. A button suspended by means of a piece of thread from a tack placed in the bottom of the block forms the pendulum.

It will be unnecessary to give any suggestions for **Kitchen Furniture,** such as chairs and tables, for these can also be made out of cigar-box wood similar to the designs illustrated in this chapter, with perhaps a few modifications which will make them simpler.

Now for the making of some pieces of bedroom furniture. You will find in Figs. 275 and 276 two designs that are easily carried out, one or both of which may be used for

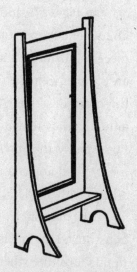

Fig. 273. A Mirror.

The Beds of a doll-house. To make Fig. 275, cut the head and foot by means of the pattern in Fig. 265, and cut the two sides by means of the pattern in Fig. 266. After preparing these pieces and fastening them together as shown in the illustration (Fig. 275), cut a few strips a quarter of an inch wide for slats and fasten them between the sides of the bed. It is advisable to fasten these in place to prevent them from being lost.

The side pieces for the other bed (Fig. 276) are cut out with the same pattern (Fig. 266). Make the head and foot

Fig 274. A Grandfather's Clock.

pieces three by four and one-half inches, cutting a piece two by an inch and one-quarter out of the top of each as shown in the drawing (Fig. 276), and using the pattern of the other bed for cutting the curve in the bottom edge. Nail the pieces together in their proper places, after which cut some slats and fasten them in the bottom.

The Dresser (Fig. 277) is made somewhat similar to the side-board. Cut the sides by the same pattern (Fig. 262) and fasten them to the edges of the back piece, which should be six and one-half inches high by three inches wide. Cut shelf A three by one and one-quarter inches, B and C three by one and one-eighth, D three by one and three-sixteenths, and E and F one-half by one and one-quarter inches.

Fig. 275. A Bed.

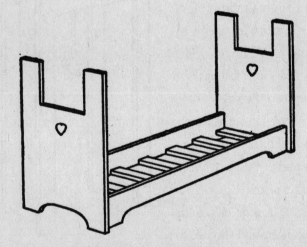

Fig. 276. Another Design.

an inch in diameter, in holes made in the sides with a gimlet (see illustration). This forms the towel-rack. Hang a small drapery over the lower portion of the stand.

Finishing. When the pieces of furniture have been completed, they should be rubbed down with emery-paper to remove the rough edges, and also any rough places that may have been caused by soaking the boxes in water. Then give the wood several coats of linseed-oil.

Fig. 277. A Dresser.

This makes a beautiful finish for this kind of wood, which may be improved by adding a coat of wax. The little hearts may be painted upon the pieces as shown in the illustration, with a small brush and red paint, or may be cut out of red paper and glued to the wood.

If desired, the bedroom furniture may be painted with white enamel.

Other Cigar-Box Furniture

Fasten shelf *A* between the sides at line No. 24 (see Fig. 262), *B* at line No. 23, *C* at line No. 22, *D* at line No. 21, and notch the ends of *E* and *F* to fit over the side pieces at line No. 20.

Drawers to fit the lower shelves of the dresser may be made out of small strips of cigar-boxes or pieces of cardboard, glued together. A small mirror fastened in the position shown in the drawing will complete the work upon this piece of furniture.

A Wash-Stand can be made for the bathroom and each of the bedrooms similar to Fig. 278. The sides for this should be five inches high by an inch and one-quarter wide, and the shelves one by three inches. Fasten the lower shelf three-quarters of an inch above the base, and the top shelf at a height of two and one-half inches. When the stand has been put together, fit a round stick, about an eighth of

In Figs. 279 and 282 will be found some pieces of furniture that are simpler to make than those just described, and although they may not be so pretty, they present a very good appearance when neatly made.

The author constructed many pieces of this furniture when a boy, and found them

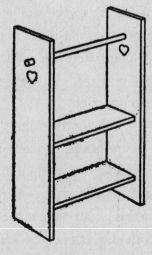

Fig. 278. A Wash-Stand.

Fig. 279. A Doll's Folding-Bed.

The Dresser shown in Fig. 282 is made out of a box the same size as the larger one used for the folding-bed. Saw the sides of the box in half, crosswise, and remove the upper half and the end piece. Then nail the end across the tops of the remaining halves of the sides. When this has been done, divide up the lower portion of the box into compartments as shown in the drawing (Fig. 283). This should have a small drapery hung over it. The upper portion of the dresser should have a mirror attached to it, and some lace draped over the top and sides will add greatly to its appearance.

All you will have to do in making

A Wardrobe will be to fasten some small hooks inside of a cigar-box, attach the cover with a strip of linen—the same way it was attached before you soaked it off—and hang a mirror on the front.

These pieces of furniture were designed for separate sets, and would not do for doll-houses the size of those in the preceding chapters, unless the boxes were cut down to smaller proportions.

suitable as presents, and something that was always easy to sell.

The cost of making a set amounts to but a few cents, cigar-boxes being the principal material. They are also very quickly made, as the boxes require but little cutting.

For the construction of

A Folding-Bed, such as is shown in Figs. 279 and 280, select two cigar-boxes, one of which will fit inside the other. The smaller box should be a little shorter than the inside opening of the larger box. After removing the paper from each, place the smaller box inside the larger one, as shown in Fig. 279, so that the bottom of the inner box is flush with the edge of the outer box. Then drive a brad through both boxes on each side, about three-quarters of an inch from the end as shown at *A* (Fig. 279). These brads should run through the outer box into the bottom of the inner box, and should be driven in carefully so as not to split the wood. The inner box should now fold down as shown in Fig. 280, moving upon the brad pivots. Purchase a five or ten cent mirror and fasten it to the front of the bed, after which cut two wooden feet similar to Fig. 281 and glue the pegs on the ends of these in gimlet holes made above the mirror. Finish the wood the same as described for the other cigar-box furniture.

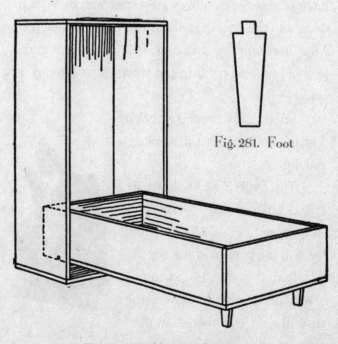

Fig. 281. Foot

Fig. 280. Folding-Bed (open).

The Round Center Table and Dining Table

The Round Center-Table (Fig. 292) should have a base built up of four strips as shown in Fig. 296. Cut the circular top 5 inches in diameter. A saucer may be used with which to mark this out.

Select a long flat box for

The Dining-Table shown in Fig. 293, and after making four built-up legs as shown in Fig. 297 fasten them into the four corners of the box table top with brads and glue.

In making the little

Square-Seated Chair (Fig. 294), cut the seat about 2 inches wide by 2¼ inches deep, the front legs 2⅛ inches high by ⅜ inch wide, and the back legs 4½ inches high by ⅜ inch wide. Brace the legs and back with crosspieces, and you will have a very firm and artistic dining-room chair.

Select a box about 9 inches by 5 inches by 2¼ inches in size for making

The Doll's Cradle shown in Fig. 295. Cut the two rockers by the pattern in Fig. 298 and fasten them to the bottom of the box 1 inch from the ends. Use the rim of a breakfast plate in drawing the arc of the rockers; then draw the rounded ends, being careful to get

Fig. 282. Dresser Completed.

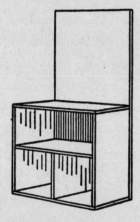

Fig. 283. A Doll's Dresser.

Fig. 289. A Jack-in-the-box.

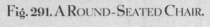

Fig. 291. A Round-Seated Chair.

Fig. 292. A Round Center-Table.

Fig. 295. A Doll's Cradle.

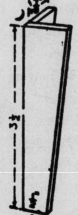

Fig. 296. Pedestal of Center-Table.

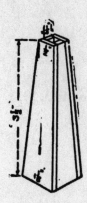

Fig. 297. Leg of Dining-Table.

them alike. Saw out the rockers very particularly so as not to split off the ends. Fasten the pieces to the cradle box with brads driven through the box bottom into their top vedge.

After the cigar-box toys have been made, rub down the wood with fine sandpaper. Then drive all nail-heads below the surface, fill up the holes with putty stained to match the wood

Fig. 298. Pattern for Cradle Rockers.

as nearly as possible, and finish with two coats of boiled linseed-oil. Apply the oil with a rag, then wipe off all surplus oil with a dry cloth.

Kites

From *The American Boys' Workshop* edited by Clarence B. Kelland, 1914

A Large Plane Kite

Kite flying, although the oldest form of scientific amusement, seems to be entering a new era of development. Perhaps it is because of the intense interest which attaches to anything in the way of aerial navigation, accentuated by the late successes of aviators both here and abroad. At any rate, new kite models are appearing every day, and not only boys, but men whose names are high on the scroll of fame are the inventors.

The wood used for the framework was straight grained laths planed on all sides. For the main beams of the front section and the top and bottom of the rear section the laths were ripped in two; for the uprights and connecting pieces they were cut in three pieces lengthwise. Begin by making the main section, Fig. 3, which is composed of three planes. Eight sticks two feet long are used for uprights, and six sticks four feet long for the main beams. They are nailed together with small brads. The corner joint is shown at Fig. 2. The two ends are made first, using two sticks two feet long and two fourteen inches long. Connect these by the four four-foot beams. This gives the framework for the top and bottom planes. Then halfway between the two the middle one is built in. Now sixteen inches from the ends of each plane the uprights are fastened. This is clearly shown by the diagram, Fig. 3. The wire skids shown in the picture to protect the kite in running to fly it or in landing should be put in now. For the rear section we use six pieces fifty-seven and one-half inches long, four pieces two feet long, and six pieces fourteen inches long. As laths are only forty-eight inches long, they will have to be spliced by overlapping and nailing. The back end should be framed first as in the case of the main section. The dimensions are given and the manner of joining is the same as for the part already described. When this rear section is built it must be attached to the front section. When they have been joined, each cell or square is braced with fine wire fastened from corner to corner. For a covering use strong muslin. It is laced and sewed on, first the middle planes and then the outside. The bridle cord is fastened to the ends of the middle cord. Where the strings come together should be a distance of three feet from the frame. For flying the kite strong fish-line is required. You will be repaid many fold for the labor of making it when you see it up in the air like a real aeroplane and feel the mighty tug at the cord. The kite, though large, is simple, serviceable, and efficient.

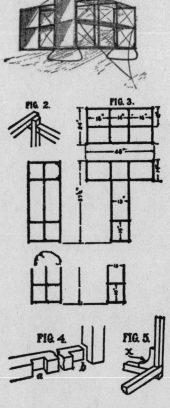

Plan for plane kite.

A Man-Lifting Kite

Of late years so much experimenting with kites has been done by earnest investigators that new types and models appear almost every day. In reality, nearly all of those models are closely related to the common type of flat paper kite known to every boy in the world. However, more skill has been used in keeping down the weight and increasing the pulling power, and in some instances kites have been made so strong that they would lift a man off the ground. In this article is described one of those giant models with tremendous lifting power. Only three sticks are used, but these must be of the best quality. Spruce is a good wood on account of its being light and tough, but no doubt you will be able to find as good material, if you can't get spruce. Be sure your sticks are straight grained and a trifle heavier in the middle than at the ends. Material one-half inch square is good, but I have a leaning for pieces one and one-half inches wide and one-half inch thick. The latter are heavier, and that, for a beginner, is one bad disadvantage. Where the sticks cross each other they may be fastened together with two brads or by tying with thread. The long single stick is bowed by stretching a stout cord from end to end, as is shown in Fig. 2. The belly band, or bridle cord, as it is called by the wise ones, is put in as indicated by Fig. 1. The tying should be done at a distance of about ten inches from the points. The kite is covered with fine meshed cloth. Light muslin, drilling, or Japanese silk are used a good deal for this purpose, but I would advise you to get the first mentioned, as it is the cheapest. The kite has no tail, as the bow effect makes it unnecessary. In putting on the cloth leave it full enough to permit of bellying out. The cord used to fly the kite must, of course, be heavy in proportion to the rest of it. I do not say that one of the kites will lift a heavy man off the ground, but I have seen three or four on a single line do so.

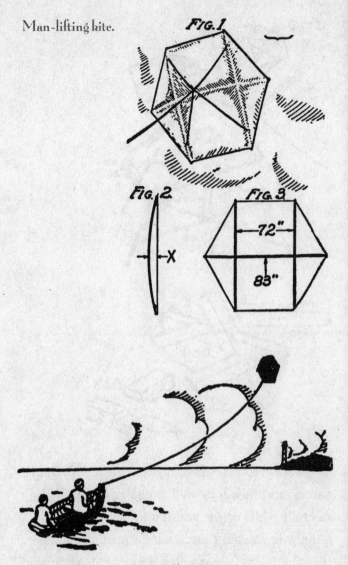

Man-lifting kite.

Fig. 1

Fig. 2 —X

Fig. 3 72" 83"

Kite hauling boat.

Some day when you go rowing put one of those big fellows up and tie the end of the line to the bow of the boat. If there is any kind of a stiff breeze it will pull you along, but, of course, getting back is a different thing. It may be tried on an ice-boat and will no doubt be able to send you gliding along. You should put some kind of reel on your boat. A simple one can be made by placing a spool between two upright posts.

A Box Kite

Here is a box kite that is framed in quite a new way. It is not as strong as the regular four-sided frame, but it has the advantage of lightness, and is

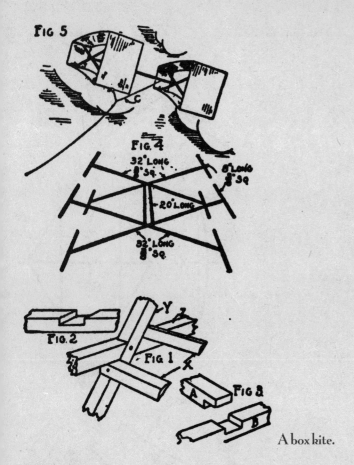

A box kite.

twenty-inch pieces. Spruce or pine are the choice of materials, but anything will do in a pinch. Lightness and toughness are the qualities to look for. The sticks would be better to be one-quarter inch square, but of the lighter woods they may be one-half inch square. Figure 2 shows the notch cut in each long stick where they join each other to make the X-shaped end. The cross-sticks on the ends of the thirty-two-inch pieces are also notched as shown in the detail Fig. 3. Glue all joints and also secure them with small brads. The covering is of light muslin. When it is lashed on it will materially strengthen the frame. There is no certain way of attaching a bridle cord other than to be sure that "C" is longer than the other string so that the kite will tilt slightly upward. Rub linseed oil on the sticks and it will preserve them against splits and warping.

A Tubular Kite

Here is something quite new and different in the kite line. The type of kite shown here has been tested and found effective. The first thing to make is a rectangular frame 36 × 6". It is made of quarter-inch spruce or any tough wood. The pieces are fastened together with small brads taken from a cigar box. In the center of this rectangle place another stick forty inches long. Now you want a light hoop for each end. The kind your mother uses for fancy work will be just the thing. They can be purchased for a nickel a pair. The cross-pieces, slightly bowed, are next tacked on. The joints may be reinforced by wrapping with waxed thread. The covering may be either cloth or paper. Make a tube of Japanese silk by sewing the edges of a piece one yard long and a trifle over a half yard wide together. Slip it over the rings before you put the cross-pieces on. It should fit tightly. The ends a few inches back are not sewed until the thirty-six-inch cross-pieces are on. The pieces mentioned are secured in place, then the tube may be finished to the ends and fastened to the

so constructed that the strength is where the strain comes most. It will fly well, but must be handled carefully while on the ground. To have success in kite flying you must understand something about the principles of aeronautics. A kite or an aeroplane floats on the same principle that a boat does. The air is a medium that has density and weight just like water, but, of course, not so great. The planes or flat surfaces of this kite rest upon the air and are supported by it. The ascent of a kite of this type is due to the tilting upward of the fore part of it. If it were held parallel to the earth it would not go up. In the upper air there are strata or layers. Some have more density than others, and when the plane strikes one of those it may be easily pulled up this hill of air just as you would pull a sled up a more solid incline.

The central cut shows the framework of this kite so clearly that a lengthy explanation would be quite superfluous. In the detail drawings you may see how the joining is done. In Fig. 1 "Y" and "Z" are the thirty-two-inch sticks, "X" represents the

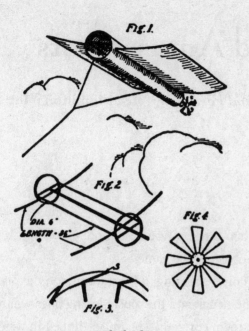

A tubular kite.

Kite Parachute

Kite flying in itself is great fun, but when you can add something to the simple pleasure of seeing your kite soar high above your head and tug at the string you hold in your fingers, you will find a fresh delight in the pastime. Of course, you have seen balloon ascensions and parachute drops. Well, why not add the parachute feature to your kite? It can be done very easily if you will study the following directions:

Get a piece of tissue paper or cloth shaped like Fig. 3. Tie a cord twenty inches long to each corner and bring them together at the lower ends, at which point a light weight, such as a piece of corncob, is tied. Pierce the center of the cloth with a pin and bend it over the string as shown in Fig. 2. When the wind has carried the parachute to a good height a slight jerk will release it.

hoops by stitching through holes punched in the hoops or bored with a gimlet. The side wings are too simple to need any explanation. The bridle cord is attached to the central stick. The string used for it may be passed through the cloth by using a needle. The purpose of a bridle cord is to give the kite a tilt. The fore end must be the highest always. An angle of 45 degrees is right for this kite. The long center stick is also used as a bearing for the propeller in the rear. The propeller is made of a light pine block four inches in diameter and a half inch thick. Slant cuts to the depth of an inch are made with a saw as shown in Fig. 3. Into these cuts blades made of basket wood or cardboard are glued. Bore a gimlet hole in the wooden disk and for a shaft use a nail that fits loosely and is tightly imbedded in the long stick. The kite is now ready for a trial.

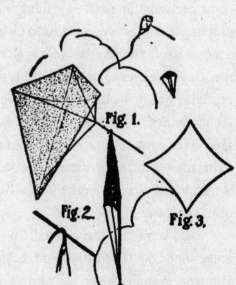

Kite parachute.

Miscellaneous Games and Amusements

From *Home Games and Parties*, by Mrs. Hamilton Mott, 1898

Game of the Five Senses

All the guests are seated around a large table, and the master or mistress of ceremonies informs them that their five senses are to be tested and prizes given to those who can prove theirs to be the keenest.

First comes the test of sight or observation. All are blindfolded, and a number of articles are thrown haphazard upon the table,—gloves, handkerchiefs, penwipers; anything and everything will serve the purpose. The bandages are then to be lifted for only a moment, after which the order is given to pull them over the eyes again. The table is swept clean of all the things, the bandages are removed, and each guest is provided with pencil and paper and must write a list of the articles noticed during the momentary glimpse permitted. The one whose list is the longest receives a prize for the best sight or quickest power of observation.

Next comes the test of smell. The bandages are resumed, and in turn, vinegar, cologne, kerosene, lavender water, bay rum, orris-root, smelling salts, oranges, camphor, paregoric, and apples are presented to the noses of the company, who may write down the names without looking on, making the list more legible when the bandages are removed.

In testing the taste, allspice, raw oatmeal, horseradish, chocolate—almost anything may be offered that is not too unpalatable. It is well to have many familiar things, and only a puzzling one now and then, since pleasure, and not perplexity, is the chief object of the game.

For the hearing, different notes on the piano may be struck and the music-loving ones will readily name them correctly. The finger dipped in water and passed around the rim of a glass makes familiar music. The ringing of a silver and of a brass bell, the tinkle of ice in a glass of ordinary water and the dull click it makes in a glass of sparkling mineral water, the sound of metal on metal, of glass on glass, and wood against wood—these and numberless others are easily provided if musical instruments are not within reach.

The sense of feeling may be tested by passing quickly from hand to hand a variety of things that cause a little surprise and so put one off guard. A glove filled with wet sand gives one an uncanny feeling if grasped unexpectedly; a harmless bit of cotton wool following after this is almost as unpleasant, and a bristling brush for cleaning lamp chimneys is a most puzzling object when held but for an instant before being claimed by one's neighbor. Even a raw potato and a handful of gelatine are puzzling objects to name, when deprived of those invaluable auxiliaries, our eyes, for all the tests are made while the company is blindfolded.

The prizes need be but the merest trifles.

A Penny for Your Thoughts

Have you ever studied a coin to see how many symbols it represents? By following the directions given below you will find that you will be the means of giving a pleasant time to one or any number of friends, as "A Penny for Your Thoughts" is a game in which both young and old may participate.

Get enough tally cards for each guest, on the top of which write, "A Penny for Your Thoughts." Attach a ribbon to each card with a small pencil at the end, and have holes put through enough pennies to string one on each tally, in order that everybody may have one to study out by himself.

The questions given below are to be written on the cards, leaving enough space for the answers. Of course, an allotted time is given in which the answers may be written, and when time is called the one having the greatest number correct is the recipient of the prize.

Questions and answers will be given below, but the one giving the party, of course, withholds the answers until the close of the game.

1 Can you find a messenger? One cent (sent).
2 Mode of ancient punishment? Stripes.
3 Means of inflicting it? Lashes.
4 A piece of armor? Shield.
5 A devoted young man? Bow (beau).
6 A South American fruit? 1 Date.
7 A place of worship? Temple.
8 Portion of a hill? Brow.
9 Spring flowers? Tulips.
10 Three weapons? Arrows.
11 The first American settler? Indian.
12 Emblem of victory? Laurel wreath.
13 An animal? Hair (hare).
14 Two sides of a vote? Eyes and nose (ayes and noes).
15 An emblem of royalty? Crown.
16 One way of expressing matrimony? United State.
17 Youth and old age? Youth 18—98 Old age.
18 Part of a river? Mouth.
19 Something found in a school? Pupil.
20 Part of a stove? Lid (eyelid).
21 Plenty of assurance? Cheek.
22 The cry of victory? Won (one).
23 Implements of writing? Quills.

A Cobweb Party

Imagine the rooms, halls, and stairs of a house all tangled in a web of strong twine, the guests struggling, twisting, tripping, and weaving themselves together in their endeavors to unravel the meshes, while all are laughing at the sight,—that is a "Cobweb party."

It is startling to find familiar rooms in such a haze of gray twine. The staircases appear to be pitfalls; the dressing-rooms, traps. Every one warns every one else. When all have worked their way to the hostess, they are told to draw lots from trays of numbered cards; one tray for women, another for the men. Each is given at the same time a little stick, on which to wind the string which fate has sent. The men's strings, perhaps, start at the hall table; the women's, at the rug by the door.

There are cards at the beginnings of the strings, with numbers corresponding to those which have been drawn. After one has found the right twine, one is to wind it up, following whithersoever it leads. The library doorway may be an almost impassable web, yet, incredibly soon the balls are all wound. Many strings lead to prizes; dainty trifles of some sort. Others have spiders at their ends, made of larch cones and wire.

A New Auction Sale

A new version of the "Auction Party" has been found to be very amusing. The invitation reads thus:—

An Auction Sale.
  No check nor money need yon bring;
    A draught might give yon cold;

> We're only doing this for fun,
>> The buyer here is sold.

A little bag, containing fifty beans, is given to each person as he or she enters the parlor. This is the highest amount one can bid. Each guest also receives a catalogue consisting of the following lots:—

1 A Trilby Souvenir.	17 A Dainty Mouthpiece.
2 One Cent.	18 The Tie That Binds.
3 A Souvenir of Greece.	19 A Literary Cut.
4 A Pair of Kids.	20 A Sharper.
5 The Fortune-Teller.	21 Satsuma Tray.
6 The Latest Racket.	22 Before the Deluge.
7 An Aid to Reflection.	23 Sèvres China.
8 The Missing Link.	24 A Good Match.
9 A Bunch of Dates.	25 A Man's Delight.
10 A Pointer.	26 Oliver Twist.
11 Love *vs.* Wealth.	27 A Study in Astronomy.
12 Aztec Pottery (rare).	28 The Family Pet.
13 Rank and File.	29 Black Beauty.
14 The Lost Chord.	30 A Diamond Pin.
15 On Guard.	
16 Measure for Measure.	

The articles are to be packed in boxes, wrapped in paper, and tied with ribbons the color of the decorations, and then carefully numbered. They should be of trifling cost. The fun depends largely upon having a witty auctioneer, who can produce lively bidding. Below is given the list of the articles corresponding to the titles:—

1 Silver Heart.	7 Small Mirror.
2 Cologne.	8 Sleeve-Links.
3 Vaseline Box.	9 Calendar.
4 Kid Hair-Curlers.	10 Emery.
5 White and Gold Daisy.	11 Little Scales.
6 Tennis Racket.	12 Bowl.
	13 Onion and Nail-File.
14 Piece of String.	23 China Plate.
15 Watch-Guard.	24 Match-Box.
16 A Tape-Measure.	25 Pipe.
17 Silver Spoon.	26 Silver-Twisted Pin.
18 Necktie.	27 Gold Crescent.
19 Paper-Cutter.	28 A Cat.
20 Knife.	29 A Black Doll.
21 China Tray.	30 A Dime and Pin.
22 Noah's Ark.	

A Moonshine Party

Consult the almanac for a moonlight evening. Decorate your rooms with the moonflower, or if you live in the country perhaps you can get some of the herbs called moonwort, sometimes known as honesty.

Provide each one of your guests with a blank card and pencil, and give them fifteen minutes in which to record as long a list as they can make of the poems, songs, stories, and other literature in which the moon is given a prominent part. The authors' names also should be given.

At the end of the allotted time let several or all of the company be called upon to read from the cards. To the one who has the best list give an almanac or calendar in the form of a dainty booklet, with the moon's phases illustrated in gilt. Give a toy lantern for the booby prize. Some one can look over the lists and award the prizes while there is music, which should be appropriate to the occasion. The hostess may call upon one or two of her guests to relate the story or legend which is noted on their cards, and which promises, from the subject, to be short and entertaining.

This idea may be utilized for a session of a literary society by elaborating the programme with more music and other exercises. The members should respond to the roll-call with a quotation about the moon. One member might have a biographical paper about Doctor Moon, of Brighton, who gave light to the blind by the present convenient system of raised print. There should be a short scientific talk explaining a lunar eclipse, the tides, or the phenomenon of the harvest moon. Assign this to some one who will be careful not to be too prosy, and who will illustrate it with large, plain diagrams. The last literary number should be something humorous, in which the moon shall have a prominent part.

A Flower-Guessing Evening

For this entertainment the hostess provides white cards, similar in size to dance programmes, tied with dainty ribbons, and having numbered questions written upon them. The guests are expected to guess the answers, which are the names of flowers, both wild and cultivated. This "Flower-Guessing Game," seemingly difficult at first, after being thoroughly explained becomes deeply interesting and enjoyable. When the cards have been collected the hostess counts the correct answers on each card.

Below is a list which may serve for a party unless something original is preferred:—

1 My first wears my second on her foot. Lady's slipper.
2 A Roman numeral. IV (Ivy).
3 The hour before my English cousin's tea. Four-o'clock.
4 Good marketings. Butter and Eggs.
5 A very gay and ferocious animal. Dandelion.
6 My first is often sought for my second. Marigold.
7 A young man's farewell to his sweetheart "Forget-me-not."
8 Her reply to him. "Sweet William."
9 The gentler sex of the Friend persuasion. Quaker Ladies.
10 Its own doctor. Self-heal.
11 My first is as sharp as needles, my second is as soft as down. Thistledown.
12 My first is a country in Asia, my second is the name of a prominent New York family. China Aster.
13 My first is the name of a bird, my second is worn by cavalrymen. Larkspur.
14 A church official. Elder.
15 A very precise lady. Primrose.
16 A tattered songster. Ragged Robin.
17 My first is sly but cannot wear my second. Fox-glove.
18 The color of a horse. Sorrel.
19 A craze in Holland in the seventeenth century. Tulip.
20 My first is an implement of war, my second is a place where money is coined. Spearmint.
21 A disrespectful name for a physician. Dock.
22 Fragrant letters. Sweet Peas.
23 My first is a white wood, my second is the name of a yellowish Rhenish wine. Hollyhock.
24 What the father said to his son in the morning. "Johnny-jump-up!"
25 My first is a facial expression of pleasure, my second a woodsman's means of livelihood. Smilax.
26 An animal of the jungle is my first, my second is the name of a tall, fair lady. Tiger Lily.
27 My first is made in a dairy, but is seldom served in my second. Buttercup.
28 My first wears my second on his head. Cox-comb.
29 A close companion. Stick-tight.
30 A fashionable evening shade for dresses. Heliotrope.

Game of Characteristics

A most interesting way in which to spend an evening is by playing "Characteristics" a game which may be made attractive to any number of people. A leader must be chosen to read aloud a list of certain "characteristics" of noted people. From these "characteristics," which must aim to be descriptive, and from their initials, the assembled company must try to discover who the celebrities are. The mode of operation of the game is as follows: Provide each player with a pencil and a card, upon one side of which is written a list of the "characteristics" of certain noted people, leaving blank spaces opposite for the names of the persons described. Immediately after the distribution of these cards the game may be explained, and the announcement made that half an hour will be given for the unraveling of the mysterious words to the left of the card. If desired, partners may be selected. The giving of prizes should be optional. The following list of "characteristics" will doubtless suggest many others to intending hostesses:

Literary

Happy Children Appear	H. C. Andersen
Explains Asia	Edwin Arnold
England's Bright Bard	E. B. Browning
Riotous Blustering	Robert Browning
Rustic Bard	Robert Burns
Terrible Complainer	Thomas Carlyle
Tragic Career	Thomas Chatterton
Shakespeare's Truest Critic	S. T. Coleridge
Weird Concocter	Wilkie Collins
Wofully Crazed	William Cowper
Comical Delineator	Charles Dickens
A Clever Doctor	A. Conan Doyle
Recognized Wisdom Everywhere	R. W. Emerson
Recounting Horrors	R. Haggard
Our Well-known Humorist	O. W. Holmes
Touching Humanity	Thomas Hood
Wonderfully Interesting	Washington Irving
Charming Levity	Charles Lamb
Truthful Negro Portraits	Thomas N. Page
Wonderful Historic Person	W. H. Prescott
Winsome Stories	Walter Scott

Wonderful Sapience	William Shakespeare
Perished by Sea	P. B. Shelley
Her Books Sell	H. B. Stowe
Rebuked Society	Robert Southey
Beguiling Traveler	Bayard Taylor
Arthur's Troubadour	A. Tennyson
What Magical Talent	W. M. Thackeray
Makes Travesties	Mark Twain
Charming, Delightful Writer	C. D. Warner
Neat Parlor Writer	N. P. Willis
Wrote Wondrously	William Wordsworth

Historical

Naturally Belligerent	Napoleon Bonaparte
Came Confidently	Christopher Columbus
Opposed Cavaliers	Oliver Cromwell
Ever Elegant	Edward Everett
Brilliancy's Forerunner	Benjamin Franklin
Protested Hotly	Patrick Henry
Receivers' Earnest Love	Robert E. Lee
Always Loyal	Abraham Lincoln
Marvellous Light	Martin Luther
War's Triumphant Soldier	W. T. Sherman
Declamatory Weightiness	Daniel Webster
Noted Words	Noah Webster
Great Warrior	George Washington

Miscellaneous

Perfectly Tremendous Boaster	P. T. Barnum
Pride (of) Boston	Phillips Brooks
Best Broadcloth	Beau Brummel
Famed for Charms	Frances F. Cleveland
Well-Earned Glory	William E. Gladstone
Thoroughly Honest	Thomas Hughes
Rabid Iconoclast	Robert Ingersoll
Hamlet's Interpreter	Henry Irving
Feminine Nobility	Florence Nightingale
Prancing Roughly	Paul Revere
He Made Search	EL M. Stanley

Progressive Conversation

For a Progressive Conversation party cards are provided with topics or questions for each lady. When the bell rings, each man finds his partner and converses on the topic assigned till the time is up, when he passes to the lady above; and so on, till he has conversed with every lady. The balloting then begins, the ladies voting for the man they found most entertaining, the men for the lady. The largest number of votes call for the first prize.

A Pop-Corn Party

Much of the success of a pop-corn party depends upon having everything as informal as possible. Instead of using fine stationery for the invitations, and indulging in the conventional polite phrases, take corn-colored paper and ask your friends "To meet Mr. C. Cobb." Here is a description of a delightful pop-corn party, which shows how to have a good time:—

"All the girls were dressed in bright woolen gowns, and the men in their business suits. In the dressing-room each girl was presented with an addition to her toilette in the shape of a necklace of pop-corn sewed upon satin ribbon, each necklace having a distinct color. Upon entering the parlors we found all the men adorned with watch-chains to correspond. We were speedily invited into the dining-room, where a bright open fire was burning, and were told that this time the girls were to do 'the popping.' And they did, while ghost stories were told, songs were sung, and conundrums given and guessed. As the corn was popped it was given to the hostess, who, in a corn-colored crépon gown, presently invited all the men to take partners. This they did by selecting the girls whose necklaces in color matched their watch-chains.

"And then we sat down to a veritable feast of corn at a table which had been entirely arranged in corn-color, and upon which were served salted, sugared, and buttered pop-corn, pop-corn balls, lemon jelly-cake, lemon sponge-cake, lemonade hot and cold, lemon ice cream, lemon water ice and lemon jelly. After our delicious supper we returned to the parlor and were handed cards with pencils attached. Our hostess then rang a bell and called order, and when order reigned she requested us to write eight nouns beginning with corn, and the name of a general beginning in the same way. In ten minutes she rang the bell again and collected the lists. The best one read, 'Cornflower, cornstarch, cornice, cornet, cornea, corner, corn-cake, cornucopia, General Cornwallis.' The maker of this list received a pretty corn-colored paper lamp-shade as a prize; and the girl who only had two words on her list received the booby prize—a corn-colored paper dunce-cap, which she was compelled to wear the rest of the evening."

A Peanut Hunt

If written invitations are issued for a peanut party, have two peanut shells painted in water colors on one corner of the paper.

The hostess provides herself with a quantity of peanuts, and conceals them in every imaginable spot in the rooms where she is to entertain her guests,—behind pictures, under mats, among the flowers, everywhere there are peanuts. After the guests have all arrived, a small bag is handed to each one, and the company are told that whoever first fills his or her bag with peanuts wins the prize of the evening.

Then begins the merry hunting—here, there, and everywhere—for peanuts. A pretty way is to have the bags made of silk, with a ribbon or cord and tassel at the top, and a fanciful design of peanuts on one side; they are then preserved as dainty souvenirs.

A Bundle Party

For those who like guessing games a bundle party offers a chance for fun in plenty. After all the guests have arrived they are taken to a room where, reposing upon a table, they find a collection of packages of various shapes and many sizes, each one distinctly numbered. To each guest there is handed a slip of blank paper and a lead pencil; then the hostess makes the following explanation: "There are thirty bundles upon this table; each bundle is numbered. Each one of you may handle any or all of the bundles as long and as much as you please, provided that you do not open them nor tear the wrappers. When you have used your sense of touch to your entire satisfaction you must write down the name of the article that you think is in the bundle, and number your guess as the bundle is numbered. Should you find a package, on the contents of which you cannot decide definitely, put its number on your list and make a dash after it. When you have examined all the bundles and recorded your guesses I will open each package and hold the contents up to your view. You will then consult your lists, and those who have hit on the article will hold up their right hands, and I will mark opposite each girl's name the numbers that she guesses correctly. To the one whose name has the most numbers attached will be given a prize."

When all the bundles have been examined and the guesses recorded, the hostess takes up a bundle, announces its number, and after giving time to examine the lists, she opens the package and holds its contents up to view. When she has credited the number to those who have raised their right hands she asks each unsuccessful guesser to read out the name of the article assigned to that particular number. Suppose that the first bundle contains a peacock feather; only a few persons will be likely to hit on the right article, while the other guesses may be very wide of the mark, so that the reading will afford much amusement.

It is possible to vary this "Bundle Party" by making of it an auction sale instead of a guessing contest, and this entertainment may prove quite as enjoyable as those already described. To do this it is necessary to appoint one of the elders of the company auctioneer, and it is well in doing this to select a person who has ready wit and is an easy speaker. Provide the auctioneer with a mallet, and place on a wooden table in front of him an assortment of bundles and parcels of varying sizes and shapes. To each guest must be given, on arrival, a small bag, box, or basket containing either fifty or one hundred beans. If there are many parcels and a limited number of guests it will be better to give each guest one hundred beans, as they will then have plenty of currency for their purchases. The only point to be especially observed is that each guest must receive the same number of beans, so that there may be no advantage given any individual. The auctioneer, after the guesses have been registered and before the parcels have been opened, will hold the packages up for bids from the assembled guests, the package in each case being awarded to the highest bidder. The opening of the parcels later will add greatly to the merriment and amusement of the guests, who will then discover how wise or how foolish their bids have been.

A Good Geography Game

Every bright boy or girl likes a game that exercises the wits. Here is a capital one for a rainy day or a long evening:—

A leader is chosen, and every player has pencil and paper. The leader then selects a word, "Republican," for instance, and each player writes all the geographical names he can think of, beginning with R, the first letter of the word.

Three minutes is usually allowed for each letter, though a longer or shorter time may be fixed, if desired. When the leader calls "Time," every one should stop writing.

The leader then reads his column of names, and as he calls a word, all others who have it say "Yes," drawing a line through it. If all have the word, that is the end of it; but in case some have failed to write it, then the fortunate ones who have it, write after the word the number of those who did not. When the leader has finished, the player at his left reads his remaining words, writing numbers after them as before. Of course, he will get at least one on every word, since the leader failed to have any of them. If the next player has any words left, he reads them, getting at least two on each; the next then reads his, and so on through the company. Then each player adds the numbers at the right of his words, setting down the total.

Now, all being ready for the second letter, the leader calls, "Begin", and all proceed to write words which commenced with E. When the leader calls "Time," the one at his left begins to read, counting just as before. Each letter in the word is treated in the same way, and when the last is finished, each player adds his points, and the one who has the most wins the game. The company may be divided, so that half shall combine against the other half. Then, instead of an individual, it is a side that wins.

The game will revive geographical knowledge, for whenever a name is challenged, the writer must tell something about it, and in what part of the world it may be found. One of the chief advantages of the game is that it may be played by any number—the more, the merrier.

How to Give a Calico Party

A big barn makes the best setting for a Calico party, sheaves of grain and pyramids of pumpkins decking the floors, stalks of corn hanging from the rafters, and weird Jack-o'-lanterns grinning in dark corners.

Cut and fold the calico the size of note paper, and have the invitations printed on the face of the sheet. Fashion the envelopes of the same calico stiffened. Calico may include lawns, ginghams, sateens, and curtain calico, and the bizarre air of the costumes lifts the party out of the ordinary.

In various parts of this book there will be found games suited to just such occasions.

A Heart Party

The old-time donkey party has suggested a new form of evening entertainment, namely, a "Heart Party." A large heart made of red flannel cloth is pinned upon a sheet hung from a door. In the centre of the heart there is sewed a small circle of white. Arrows of white cloth with pins placed therein are given to the guests, each arrow bearing a number, the number corresponding to a list whereon the names and numbers of the guests are placed. The point of the game, of course, is to see which person, when blindfolded, will pin the arrow nearest to the central spot of white. Four prizes may be offered— one each for the lady and gentleman coming the nearest to the centre, and one each to those coming the farthest from the bull's-eye. Appropriate prizes would be a heart-shaped pincushion, a heart-shaped photograph frame, a silver heart-shaped pin, and a heart-shaped box of bonbons. A good booby prize would be a Brownie holding a tiny heart, with an arrow inscribed "Try, try again."

Who Is It?

Photographs of famous people, labeled with names that do not belong to them, may be handed about among a company of persons for correction. What seems at first glance to be a simple act of adjustment, calls for considerable study and a good memory. The portraits of Wagner, Beethoven, Paderewski, Rubinstein, Ole Bull, Whittier, Queen Victoria, Emperor William of Germany, Gladstone, Shakespeare, Milton, Dickens, Tennyson, Scott,

Burns, Longfellow, Washington, Lafayette, Napoleon, and others should be chosen.

A Valentine Party

Cupid's target, an oracle of fortune to be tested at a valentine party, should be set up either in a spacious room, from which all the furniture has been removed, or in a cleared barn, if the festivities are held in the country. The wooden frame should be heart-shaped, and the centre of white muslin. It should be painted with a three-inch border of green; a second three-inch row of black; a third of yellow; a fourth blue; fifth red. These simulate a succession of hearts, one inside the other. A less expensive frame may be made of card, or heavy pulp board, covered with cheap white cloth, and then painted. Each arrow should be decorated with a bit of colored ribbon, a different color for each, and the bows decorated either to match or of a contrasting color.

As the guests arrive the ladies choose their arrows, and the gentlemen bows; the bows and arrows which match designate the partners for the evening. There is always a charm in the expectation of a chance partner, and each guest accepts his or her fate gracefully.

The room in which the target is set up should be lighted gayly with Chinese lanterns, and the target fastened securely in place at one end of the room. When ready to begin, the lanterns are lit, and the merry fortune-seekers proceed, equipped with bows and arrows, to learn their fate, each guest having been provided with a fate-card of two rhymed lines prepared by the hostess. These cards are carefully consulted after each shot. The cards, with their couplets of prophecy, read as follows:—

Love and riches wait, I ween,
Him or her who hits the green.

Arrow flits the yellow by:
You'll be married ere you die.

Should your arrow pierce the blue,
Love is on the wing for yon.

Loveless, weeping little maid,
If her arrow pierces red.

She who passes one and all,
Lovers many at her call.

He who passes one and all,
His chance to wed is very small.

When the shooting is over, the guests are invited into another room, where a little page presides over Saint Valentine's magic wheel, and gifts dispatched from Fun-land serve to minister balm to disappointed archers.

Saint Valentine's wheel must be light in weight, of medium size, and balanced on a pole through the hub, so that it will turn readily. The tire and the spoke should be wound with ribbon. A variety of color adds to its enchantment. Should economy be a consideration, strips of cheesecloth will do. Two little boys, one on each side of the pole upon which the wheel revolves, guard it. They may be dressed in blue and silver gauze, with girdles of roses, gilt bows and arrows, and silver wings. Saint Valentine presides at the wheel, dressed as King of Hearts, in a red coat, red and white striped stockings, blue knee-breeches, cut in points and covered with hearts, a large satin collar in the shape of two hearts, a red cap, hanging sleeves, and **scepter** all covered with hearts. On each spoke of the wheel are small cards numbered. As Saint Valentine revolves the wheel swiftly, each guest in turn seizes a card, souvenirs having been prepared corresponding in number to the cards. The favors should be as much alike as possible, and of course of a character that will be reminiscent of Saint Valentine.

After the souvenirs have been distributed the refreshments should be served. They may be either simple or elaborate, but the color scheme of both table and refreshments should be rose-colored and white. The sandwiches may be cut heart-shaped, and the cakes iced in rose-color or white. Kisses, lady-fingers tied together with rose colored ribbons, and rose-colored bonbons in heart-shaped boxes, should be everywhere.

Impersonations

A device not too much used to prove a novelty in most homes, is the designating of each guest as he arrives with the name of some noted character. A card with the name upon it is pinned on the shoulder; this is referred to by the others in conversation, but is not examined by the wearer. From the remarks addressed to him he is to guess whether he is personating Buffalo Bill, Mr. Cleveland, Chauncey M. Depew, or possibly some local celebrity, being expected to wear the card until he is successful.

Book Reviewing

An entertaining game, called "Book Reviewing," is similar to the old-fashioned game of "Consequences," and is played as follows: Each guest writes an author's name on a slip of paper, which is folded over and passed to the one who sits next to her, who writes the title of a book; the paper is again folded and passed to another, who writes a criticism upon it. Of course, as many slips are made use of as there are participants in the game. When these papers are read the jumble of authors, books, and reviews is most amusing.

A few actual samples are here given: Author, "Samuel Johnson;" book, "Alice in Wonderland;"

criticism, "Never since the days when Homer hawked his 'Iliad' through the streets of Greece has any literary work so carried the world by storm. We sincerely doubt if in the ages to come anything will exceed it." Author, "Rider Haggard;" book, "Dictionary;" criticism, "The tone is weak, the characters impossible, and the plot exceedingly unnatural. There is really hardly a readable page in the whole book."

Buzz

A lively game is "Buzz!" The guests are seated around the dining-table. The one at the head of the table begins by saying "One," the next "Two," and so on; only the seventh person and every multiple of seven must remember to say "Buzz" instead; if they fail to do this they drop out of the ring, and the next begins with "One" again. The sport of the game is to remember "seven" or the multiple, viz.: fourteen, twenty-one, twenty-eight, thirty-five, and so on. The one who holds out the longest is to receive a prize; the first to fall out of the ring is awarded the booby prize.

Personally Conducted Excursions

Here is an entertainment requiring rather unusual preparations; still, the novelty of the affair is worth the trouble and expense. Have your invitations worded thus:—

Dear Sir: [or, Dear Madam:]

I am making up a party for a winter tour in the United States. It will be very select, and I should like the pleasure of numbering you among the tourists. It will be perfectly safe for you to come alone, as I shall have an unlimited number of chaperons on hand.

I have had large experience in all modern modes of travel, having frequently gone on extended trips on the trolley lines. Being a linguist of no mean ability

670 The Ultimate Guide to Old-Fashioned Country Skills

I can act as interpreter to any form of the "United States" language.

The expense will be slight.

The porter has agreed to be paid only in his own coin, and has magnanimously offered to give as good as the guests may send.

The cars are well lighted, evenly heated by furnace, and built for use.

The train will start from my home on, _____ _____ at 8:30 P. M.

Meals are included.

The itinerary includes stops at most of the leading cities and points of interest in the United States.

The accompanying coupon will entitle you to a ticket and all the privileges of the party. Present it at the ticket-office on the evening of the start.

Yours respectfully,

_____

Guests are supposed to go to such a party in travelling costumes. Upon entering the hall they find a screened corner, with the conventional ticket-window where tickets are issued. The hostess stands nearby, ready to hand the wraps over to the baggage-master. The parlor has been transformed into a waiting-room, and there is a gatekeeper to restrain the passengers from entering the sitting-room, or parlor-car. The tickets are of the regulation length, and printed on green paper, as follows:

Funville, Frolictown, and Featherbrain Railway

Special Excursion Ticket

Rules and Conditions

This ticket is not transferable, reversible, nor salable. It must be signed by the person to whom it is assigned.

The company will not be responsible for cattle killed by the carelessness of passengers who throw sandwiches out of the window.

Doctors are not provided, but if you have the grip it can be checked by the baggage-master.

The porter is a pirate who deserves no quarter.

If the ventilation is not sufficient tell your wife.

Yon are prohibited in this State from standing on the platform.

The conductor will not punch this ticket.

The stations at which this train stops are:

1 Where all have bean. [Boston.]

2 The greatest engineering feat. [Wheeling.]

3 An improvement on the ship which grounded on Mount Ararat. [Newark.]

4 A military defense, and a Paris dressmaker. [Fort Worth]

5 A city whose end and aim is "go." [Chicago.]

6 Our board of city fathers, also a precipice. [Council Bluffs.]

7 An accident which results in a ducking. [Fall River.]

8 An exclamation, an appeal to maternity, a laugh. [Omaha.]

9 An opera encore. [Sing Sing.]

10 Named for the King of France who reigned from 1226 to 1270 A. D. [Louisville]

11 A deceased farmer who was twice dictator of Rome. [Cincinnati.]

12 Named for an ancient city whose downfall, after a long siege avenged the abduction of a woman. [Troy.]

13 A place for the lingerers. [Tarrytown.]

14 Named for the father of our country. [Washington.]

15 A high place, and what all children love. [Mount Desert.]

16 A superlative, and rushing waters. [Grand Rapids.]

17 A girl's nickname, and relations by blood or marriage. [Nankin.]

18 A purely American product, and a continuous structure. [Cornwall.]

19 A girl's name, and a Roman garment. [Saratoga.]

Attached to each ticket there is a lead pencil, and blank spaces are left in which answers are to be written. Of course, in the original tickets the answers are not given. Promptly at eight-thirty the passengers, who have by that time assembled, are allowed to pass through the gate into the sitting-room, and take seats in the parlor-car; then when all are seated a whistle is blown, the conductor calls "All aboard," a bell is rung, and the party is supposed to have started.

At the proper time the conductor calls out that the train has stopped, and the company repair to the parlor, to listen to music while the train crew determine which passenger has guessed the greatest number of places on the route; the reward being a miniature travelling-bag. Then refreshments are served.

Misquoted Quotations

Misquoted quotations afford mental occupation for lovers of poetry. Write out on slips of paper certain much-read verses from "Maud Muller," "The Psalm of Life," Tennyson's "Maud," Shakespeare's plays, Dickens's or Thackeray's novels, etc. Change a few words, or even a whole line, and see who can recall exactly the original language.

Who Painted It?

A congenial employment for people whose thoughts turn to art is to recall in a stated time the names and painters of familiar masterpieces. Copies of these, numbered (prints or cheap photographs answer every purpose), should be displayed about the room as if it were an art exhibition. Cards and pencils should be provided for noting guesses. Millet's "Angelus," Munkacsy's "Christ Before Pilate," Raphael's "Sistine Madonna," Murillo's "Immaculate Conception," Rubens's "Descent from the Cross," Lepage's "Joan of Arc," Paul Potter's "Bull," Millais' "Princes in the Tower," may be included in a list of famous works.

Telegrams

The game of "Telegrams" may be played by asking each one of your guests, in turn, to suggest the initial letters that shall compose the words of the message. Here is an example, one made use of at an impromptu gathering. The letters furnished were C. T. M. M. W. B. H. C. P. T. S. T. D., and the message one person made from them was: "Come Thanksgiving morning. Mother will be here. Come prepared to stay to dinner."

Crambo

A New version of the old game of "Crambo," which Webster defines as a word given, to which another finds a rhyme, is the following: One writes a question, folds the paper over, as in the game of "Book Reviewing" and passes it on. The next adds a noun, folds again, and again passes it to his neighbor, who must write a rhyme in which the question is answered, always weaving in the noun.

An example given at one party will suffice to illustrate:—

The question was: "Where are you going, my pretty maid?"

The noun written after the first folding was "Gumdrops," and here is the rhyme:

"A maiden chanced on a sunny day
To cross the field where I raked the hay,
Her cheeks were rosy, her hair was brown
And she looked a queen in her russet gown,—
'Where are you going?' I asked the lass.
'To buy some gumdrops, please let me pass.'
So I stood aside and she went her way,
But I often think of that sunny day,
And that queenly girl with her hair of brown,
Who charmed me so in her russet gown,"

The author of the above never had claimed to be a rhymester.

A Literary Salad

A pretty use for quotations is to twist pieces of different shades of green tissue paper into the shape of lettuce leaves, and place them in a salad bowl—having previously pasted upon each a short quotation, written distinctly on white paper—and pass them about as a salad, inviting each partaker thereof to guess the name of the author whose quotation adorns the lettuce leaf which he has chosen.

A Book-Title Hunt

At "A Book-Title Hunt" the guests will find the parlor filled with the queerest collection of miscellaneous articles that ever was seen in so dainty a room. Tables, the mantel, the top of the piano, the window curtains and portières—every available spot may bear some article that certainly does not belong there; upon the walls there may appear photographs, engravings, and cards with parts of magazine advertisements pasted upon them, apparently arranged haphazard, with no regard to harmony of subject or color.

It will be bewildering at first, but that there is method in this apparent madness will be shown by the fact that some of the articles about the room are placed in little groups, while others stand by themselves, each group or separate article bearing a number, as does each of the pictures upon the walls. Each guest is furnished with a pencil and two or three sheets of paper held together at the top by a silken thread. Down the left-hand side of each sheet are the figures 1, 2, 8, 4, 5, 6, etc., covering the number of titles that are to be hunted for.

When all the guests have arrived the hostess strikes a bell, and the "hunt" begins. But where are the books? Looking on one of the tables for some favorite volume one may perhaps see a slender crystal vase holding a flower of saffron hue, while nearby is carelessly laid a string of tiny brass bells.

Pinned to a curtain there may be a half-length portrait of General Grant.

A few moments suffice for every one to catch the spirit of the game, and merry groups are soon wandering from table to mantel, thence to another table, stopping on the way to examine the mystic symbols on the walls. Every now and then a little scream of delight will indicate that a fair hunter has solved some mystery.

At one party a puzzled group collected about a card on the mantel on which were pasted the tails of a horse, a dog, and a bird, all cut from advertisements; not quite so baffling a problem was a child's toy, a small gray cottage, to which some ingenious hand had contrived to add seven artificial points. The top of the piano had upon it the most incongruous collection of things possible: a china plate, upon which were placed some small pieces of bright coal; the crown of an old straw hat; a pile of ragged oak leaves; a doll dressed in red and gray, and a tiny pastry-board, upon which rested two small bits of well-kneaded dough.

A limit of time had been fixed before the game began, and when it had expired, one of the gentlemen of the party called out from a complete list, famished by the hostess, first the number, and then the title of the book belonging to it. The guests checked off the right titles they had discovered upon their lists, and upon comparing notes the one who had guessed the largest number of titles correctly received the first prize, a handsome copy of "Unfamiliar Japan," while the booby—the lowest on the list—became the proud possessor of "Mother Goose," bound in linen.

One list of guesses bore these names:

1 "A Yellow Aster."
2 "The Bells."
3 "Half a Hero."
4 "Terminations."
5 "House of the Seven Gables."

6 "Black Diamonds."

7 "The Crown of Straw."

8 "Torn Leaves."

9 "In Scarlet and Grey."

10 "Dodo."

The game may be played like progressive euchre by dividing the company into groups of four or six, having a certain number of articles on each table, and allowing only a certain limit of time before group number one moves on to table number two, stopping when each group has visited every table.

Rainy-Day Diversions

It was the mother of quite a large family who declared, "I can bring up a whole family with a pair of scissors and a mucilage bottle," and she was not very far from right. Bright days, as a rule, take care of themselves; there are so many pleasant spoils to be enjoyed out of doors. But the tug-of-war comes with rainy weather. Then something new and interesting must be planned to occupy the children's time and attention, and for boys and girls of varying ages there are many varieties of pleasant and instructive occupations to be enjoyed with scissors and paste.

Little girls from eight to twelve may give a "Reception to Royalty," by collecting pictures of kings and queens, emperors and empresses, princes and princesses of various royal courts. While cutting them out carefully, and preparing them so that they may stand alone, mamma may tell them the story of their royal lives and something about the country and people where they live. The "standers" are made by pasting a strip of moderately thick paper or pasteboard an inch wide, perhaps, full length at the back of the picture. Let the pasteboard broaden at the heel; cut it an inch beyond the toe. When partly dry, bend at the heel to form a right angle. The figures will then stand quite firmly, and may be moved from place to place.

When a sufficient number of people are made ready for the reception, then the blue-room furniture at the White House (stationers sell these pictures at a penny or two a sheet) may be cut out in the same way, and, with the necessary formalities of presentation, the reception may go on. Little girls who have a taste for millinery, dress-making, or doll-dressing may cut out all sorts of hats, bonnets, and garments, and arrange for a spring or fall opening.

Boys of the same age may purchase an endless variety of soldiers. Army and navy officers, artillery companies, army wagons, ambulances, etc., also pictures of famous war generals and their staff officers; in fact, a complete set of classified pictures may be secured for representing an army. These, cut out carefully and strengthened with "standers," as described above, furnish material for many a well-fought battle. The instruments of slaughter, a couple of bean-blowers manipulated by two small boys. Brigadier-generals both valorous and famous, fallen heroes carried off the field in ambulances, horses and men falling on every side, the quick return to life of entire companies, and the rapid "setting up" preparatory to a new encounter, are all interesting to small boys. Fences, trees, rocks, hills, horses, tents, and the pleasant bivouac scene may all be played by preparing the required pictures. Boys who have a taste for animals and birds may prepare extensive "Zoos."

Ring Games and Frolics

From *Home Games and Parties*, by Mrs. Hamilton Mott, 1898

Children never tire of ring games. They like the simple ones best—those that do not tax the memory to any great extent. They prefer something with a catching swing in the rhythm, carrying the same words through many verses, with just enough verbal change to indicate the progress of the game.

The Game of Flowers

The game of flowers is simple and sweet. It is played similar to "London Bridge." Two children stand opposite each other and raise their joined hands. Those forming the ring pass under, while all keep saying or singing, suiting the action to the words they sing:—

> "We're looking about for a daffodil,
>   A daffodil, a daffodil:
> We're looking about for a daffodil;
>   We've found one here."

At the word "here" the raised arms come down and enclose the head of the child who happens at that moment to be passing underneath their hands. Then all sing:

> "We find one here, we find one here;
>   We're looking about for a daffodil,
>   And find one here."

"Daffodil" now takes the place of one of the children who caught him or her, then calls out, "Buttercup."

The children all understand that buttercup, instead of daffodil, is the word, so they make the lines:

> "We're looking about for a buttercup,
>   A buttercup, a buttercup," etc.

The leader may hold a bouquet and give to each child the flower chosen.

The next child, "Buttercup," being duly "found," takes the place of "Daffodil," and the child who has held that place goes into the ring. The newcomer calls out the name of some flower, like bright bluebell, daisy flower, or mignonette, and substituting that word they sing as before. Each child tries to be ready with the name of some favorite flower, and the game may close when each child flower has been "found."

Fox

A game in which the children can run is always a favorite. "Fox" is another ring play, so easy that the smaller children can play it without help. One of the child "foxes" stays outside the ring and slyly slaps the shoulder of one of the children. "Fox" runs to the left, the child to the right. They meet, pass each other going at full speed around the ring. The one who gets back to the "den" (the place in the ring where the child was standing) may hold that place, and the other must be the fox and try a race with some other child.

Magic Bridge

The magic bridge is another popular game. The children; join hands and form in a ring. If the number is large there should be four "bridges" at the quarter points of the ring, these being numbered one, two, three, and four,—one opposite three and two opposite four. The bridges are formed by two children who raise their joined hands for the others to pass under. The pianist leads with a bright, familiar air, and the children all follow the tune, singing tra-la-la, tra-la-la, as they dance and skip along, keeping step to the music. They go one or more times around in a circle, then the leader indicates where a "bridge" is to be made. Two children raise their joined hands, and the two children standing opposite in the ring cross the centre of the circle. All the others following after, pass under the "bridge." Then, turning to right and left respectively, the two lines follow the path of the circle as formed first, meet, join hands again, and a new circle is formed. Another "bridge" appears as if by magic, and the children opposite it lead again through it, the while keeping the merry measure with song and dance. This is one of the prettiest of dancing games, which it is not necessary to "know how" to do; they learn it as they go.

Jingle Bells

"Jingle Bells" is another frolic which pleases the little ones. Let mamma or the hostess harness up the children for a "team". They have a string of small bells around their necks, and a cambric or tarlatan rope is used for the "tackle"—the children taking hold of it by twos, except the last in line, who acts as "driver." The pianist plays the well-known college glee, "Jingle bells, jingle bells, jingle all the way," and the children trot away at a merry pace. The leaders hurry on, making devious turns to right and left, supposedly through snowdrifts and over high hills

and down in deep valleys. The children sing the chorus, and the trip proves so delightful that they are never ready to stop until a long journey has been made.

The above games may all be successfully played by a large party of children.

Jack Frost

Little folk delight much in games of action. Jack Frost understands children pretty well, so he gives them plenty of lively exercise when he comes along. The leader need not describe the game beforehand to the players, but all may form in a large ring, and the children be divided into groups of ten. To each ten an adult should be assigned, who can assist the little people should they need help in understanding the game as it progresses. Let each group face the centre of the room, where the leader stands, and place each number one at the left end of each section.

The leader claps her hands together and calls out, "Where is Jack Frost?" A boy dressed (or not) to represent his icy kingship, runs around the ring and swings a wand touching number one of each section on the right hand. Each number one turns to the left and says to number two, "Jack Frost came this way." Number two asks, "What did he do?" Number one replies, "He nipped my right hand, oh!" Immediately number one shakes the right hand violently. Number two turns to number three and says, "Jack Frost came this way." Number three inquires, "What did he do?" Number two replies, "He nipped my right hand, oh!" Number two begins to shake violently its frost-bitten hand and number one continues the shaking. This goes on in the same way until number ten is reached. By that time everybody in the room is shaking a frosty right hand, which must be kept still shaking while Jack Frost again goes flying around the room and touches the left hand of each number one. Then, as before, number two is told by number one that Jack Frost came this way, and that he nipped his or her left hand. Then, by the same process, word is carried by repeated questions and answers and hand-shaking to number ten, until everybody in the room is shaking two frostbitten hands.

Jack Frost again flies around and nips the right foot of each number one, and a right foot is added to the shaking members. Then later a left foot; then two feet together; and the children are all shaking their hands and hopping up and down upon both feet. Then the right ear is nipped, and the hand-shaking and jumping go on with the head turned down upon the right shoulder. The left ear falls a victim, and the head turns upon the left shoulder. The last round inquires, "Has Jack Frost bitten you enough?" The reply is affirmative, and the heads jerks assent. It must be understood that at no moment during the entire game do the players cease from shaking each part of the body that has been nipped with frost

Shakers

Shakers is a game which children of all ages enjoy. A ring is formed, including the whole company. The leader explains the game somewhat, and begins singing, adapting the words to the descending musical scale:—

"I put my right hand in" (toward the centre of ring),
"I put my right hand out" (turn body square about
    and thrust arm out),
"I give my right hand shake, shake, shake" (suit
    action to words),
"And I turn myself about" (turn square about to
    face centre of ring).

Then the action song goes on;—

I put my left hand in,
I put my left hand out,
I give my left hand shake, shake, shake," etc.

Succeeding verses change as follows: "I put my two hands in," then "my right foot," "my left foot," "my two feet" (jumping), one after the other. This is a pleasant go-to-bed game for small children.

Children are also delighted with action that represents different kinds of labor. They are naturally imitative, and the leader needs but to start the different movements and the little people will at once join in. Take the different movements of the haymaker, for instance. He swings the scythe, he tosses the hay in spreading, he rakes it, he sits down to rest, he eats his lunch, he drinks cool milk, he takes a noon nap, he wakes up, pitches the hay upon the cart, he calls haw, haw, haw! Gee, gee, gee! To the oxen, he swings a whip, and when the loads are all in he claps his hands for joy. Each motion the children can imitate, and they do this, keeping time to music.

A Bean-Bag Contest

An exhilarating game of bean-bags may be played indoors, as there is no tossing nor throwing. First there should be a dozen red and a dozen blue bean-bags made. Each bag should be made of strong material, and in size ten inches long by seven wide, and be filled about half full of beans. Among a company of boys and girls two leaders and an umpire should be chosen. The leaders should choose sides, and the ones chosen should take their places behind the leaders, all facing the same direction, so as to form two columns of players—the dozen blue bags placed on a chair in front of the leader of the "blues," and the red bags placed in front of the leader of the "reds." There should be the same number of children in each column, and at the lower ends of the columns should be placed chairs on which to receive the bags. When the last bag has passed down to the end of the column the players should right-about-face, so that the ones at the foot of the lines may become leaders in sending the bags back to the place of starting. There are five orders:—

Pass bags with right hand. Pass bags with left hand. Pass bags with both hands over the head. Pass bags with right hand over the left shoulder. Pass bags with left hand over the right shoulder.

Before beginning the contest a few trial orders should be given, so that each player shall fully understand the game, as one dull player will lose the game for the most active side. When only one hand is used in passing bags the other hand should be placed on chest or hip, so that the umpire can see that there is no unfairness. When the twelve bags have been the length of the columns and back to the chair from which they were taken the leader shouts "out," and scores a round for the "blues" or "reds," whichever it may be. The side that reports the most "outs" is, of course, the winning side, and each player should be decorated with a buttonhole bouquet. As the game is exhilarating, cooling refreshments should be served. The bags may be filled with peanuts, and opened when time for refreshments comes, if the game is played out-of-doors.

Home Parties for Children

From *Home Games and Parties*, by Mrs. Hamilton Mott, 1898

In the number of guests children's parties may range from two to two hundred. The invitations should always be sent out in the name of the child for whom the party is given, and the delight of sending and receiving the invitations is increased a hundred-fold if tiny note paper be used for their inscription. Children's parties should be held not later in the day than 4 P.M., and should continue for either two or three hours. Three to six are the ideal hours for such an entertainment, as the little guests then reach home in time for bed.

What to Give the Little Ones to Eat

The party itself, in the minds of children, is invariably the supper, and especially that part of it which consists of ice cream. From the following list of dishes, which are available for children's suppers, menus which are attractive and hygienic may be readily compiled: Bouillon, hot and cold; oyster stew, creamed chicken, cold chicken, chicken croquettes, rice croquettes, finger rolls, thin slices of bread and butter, chicken sandwiches; chocolate and vanilla ice cream, lemon and orange water ice, orange and lemon jelly, charlotte russe, sugar cookies, lady fingers, sponge-cake, cup-cake, and small chocolate cakes.

The soups should be served if possible in fancy bouillon cups with an accompaniment of crackers. Creamed chicken should be served in fancy paper patty cases. Bread should be sliced very thin, evenly buttered, and then out into fancy shapes, circles, and diamonds. Sandwiches should be rolled or cut into the same fancy shapes. Ice cream is especially welcome when served in individual forms. Home-made desserts, such as blanc mange and jelly, are also most attractive if made in little individual forms. Cakes should be small and generously iced. Chocolate is the drink *par excellence*, especially when served in after-dinner coffee-cups. If fruit is served at all it should be very ripe and sweet. Candies should be of the simplest kind, those containing nuts, figs, dates, raisins, etc., being avoided. Nothing gives a child more pleasure than the old-fashioned paper motto candies.

The Table for the Little Guests

The arrangement of the table must receive special attention. Great success is obtained by using four or more small tables arranged as a hollow square. The children are then readily waited upon, and more easily kept in order should the party include any especially mischievous boys. Flowers may be dispensed with, unless *boutonnières* and small bouquets are distributed at each place. When this is done, and tiny guest cards with "Brownie" decorations used, the little folks' delight is much increased. High chairs must be provided for the smallest guests, unless low tabled are used for these mites; in which case small chairs, bibs, mugs, and spoons are also in order. If fruit is to be eaten, allow it to be used as decoration, serving each variety by itself on low flat dishes ornamented with natural leaves. The candies and cakes also should appear on the table, as they add greatly to its decorative effect The sandwiches and bread and butter should be served lavishly on a number of small dishes, so as to permit one dish to be available to every four guests.

The Popular "Spider-Web" Party

Next after the supper in order of importance, but before it in point of time, comes the entertainment provided. If any special form has been arranged the invitations should so announce it—"Spider Web," "Punch and Judy," "Candy Pull," "Soap Bubble," or "Fish Pond" being written in the lower left-hand corner of the invitation. For a "Spider-Web Party" quite elaborate preparations are needed. From the central chandelier of the parlor should depend a large brown spider, whose back is sufficiently hollowed to contain a gilded spool, about which should be wound the ends of innumerable tinsel cords, the lines of cords interlaced and wound about so as to make a gigantic web which will stretch through two or three rooms and even up a staircase, always ending behind some chair, picture, couch, or table, and always having at the end an inexpensive gift of a toy or a box of candy.

Amusement with Soap Bubbles

For a "Punch and Judy" show an entertainer is usually provided. A "Candy Pull" must; be given in a kitchen, and for this molasses, sugar, and butter must be provided in large quantities. Several bright saucepans and a clear fire are necessary, as well as two or three grown people to superintend the actual candy cooking. Plenty of aprons must also be at hand, and unlimited good nature.

For a "Soap-Bubble Party" a long, narrow table should be covered with a trebly-folded blanket, over which should be placed a sheet. As many small basins—paper maché are best—must be supplied

as there are children, and several extra clay pipes to allow for breakage. The suds may be prepared the day before from Castile soap. If a little glycerine be added the bubbles will gain in tenacity and brilliancy. Care must be taken to keep the fluid tightly corked until it is needed. Prizes may be awarded for the longest, the shortest, the greatest number at one blow, the largest and the smallest bubbles blown. The pipes, of course, which may be decorated with ribbon, should be carried home as souvenirs.

Fun at a Fish Pond

A "FISH POND" is a large tub or clothes-basket in which are various small packages so tied that a loop is left in each. A fishing rod with a good-sized hook is provided, and each child given a certain number of opportunities to capture the gifts.

Where Merriment is Plentiful

A "DONKEY PARTY" is, of course, well known; an "Elephant Party" is of the same kind, where the attempt is made when blindfolded to properly place the trunk, and a "Nose Party" is one where the attempt to locate the nose on a huge face is made. These parties afford great merriment, and if prizes are offered for the nearest and the furthest attempts, special incentives for proficiency and consolation for inaptness are provided. Magic-lantern exhibitions are always appreciated, as are the efforts of a prestidigitateur.

A Juvenile Auction

An "Auction Sale" gives great fun to its participants. Each child is provided with a small basket or bag containing fifty dried beans. A large basket containing parcels of every shape and size is brought in, and an older person selected as auctioneer. These packages may contain things of value and of no value, of use and of no use, but in every case their identity must be hidden by their wrappings. The auctioneer, who has no knowledge of the contents of the parcels, must proceed to describe with great imagination the articles for sale, trying to guess from the shape what the articles may be. The children bid their beans for the parcels, each bean representing one cent, each article being sold at auction to the highest bidder.

Good Old-Fashioned Games

For those children who simply love games the old-fashioned party is revived. Two older persons are needed to successfully manage such an affair, both being persons who can sing, and one able to play the piano. "Going to Jerusalem" is a great favorite. A row of chairs numbering one less than the number of participants in the game is arranged with the backs alternating. The children are then seated, the extra child standing at one end as leader. The pianist plays a gay tune, to which the children march around the chairs. The pianist then stops suddenly in the middle of a phrase, and every one, including the leader, scrambles for a chair, the person left over being out of the game. A chair is then removed and the march continues, a person and a chair being removed with each tune. When there are but two contestants and one chair the struggle is exciting and amusing. The person who gains the chair has succeeded in getting to "Jerusalem."

Another well-known game is "Stage Coach," which may be varied by a "Mother Goose" story, in which the children are given the names of various characters in "Mother Goose," the narrative concerning them requiring the same recognition of characters as in "Stage Coach,"—"Mother Goose flew away" being the synonym for "the stage coach broke down." "Oats, Peas, Beans," is an old-fashioned but very enjoyable game. "Miss Jennie Jones" and "Here

We Go Bound the Mulberry Bush" are much alike, but sufficiently different to prove very entertaining. The old game of "Can You Dance Lobi?" is very mirth-inspiring. "Drop the Handkerchief," "Puss in the Corner," "Pass the Slipper," and "Who's Got the Button?" are great fun. "Pillows and Keys" is a famous old game. "Clap-in, Clap-out" is another enjoyable one.

For Little Ones over Ten Years

Where the guests are all over ten years of age a progressive party is much appreciated. Tables seating six should be provided, also tally cards, which should be similarly decorated in groups of three with ribbon. Pink, blue, red, yellow, purple, and white are good colors to use in each case, the three persons who play together being designated by having the same colors. "Lotto" and "Authors," or other like games, may be played at alternating tables, the points being counted according to a system carefully explained to the children. The winners should progress from table to table, the three children progressing the greatest number of times, and the three progressing the least, securing prizes. This amusement must not be attempted with children younger than ten, as, in the first place, it does not furnish entertainment to minds younger than that, and further, great disquiet and dispute will follow the prize awarding. For children younger than that the "Caucus Race" principle must be observed—"everybody must win and all must have prizes."

A Simple Patty-Pan Party

One little girl of nine did so want to have a real birthday party, but when people live in the country it is not always easy to plan and prepare for company. Nannie's mamma, however, finally hit on a plan which is worth telling and worth copying. Down she went to the village store and bought a dozen and a half bright tin patty-pans, nine tin cups, and some tiny note paper and envelopes, and that same day Nannie wrote eight invitations as follows:

MY DEAR FRIEND: Next Tuesday is my birthday. I am nine. Come over and play with me at my party at three o'clock in the afternoon. Be sure and come early.   Your friend,
                                                    Nannie.

P. S.—Wear your every-day dress and apron.

Promptly at three o'clock the next Tuesday eight little girls in clean aprons arrived and sat solemnly down in the parlor. Then Nannie's mamma told them that the party was to be in the kitchen, and some one suggested "Candy Pull."

That magic word hurried them out to the kitchen; and there on the table were nine groups of things, each one consisting of a bowl, a tin cup, a soup-plate, a crimped patty-pan, a tablespoon, a teaspoon, and a doll spoon and fork. On a smaller table nearby stood sugar, eggs, and other ingredients, while a brisk fire burned in the range.

"Now," said Nannie's mamma, "we will all go to work and make our own cakes and custards for tea, and see how well we can do it. I want each little girl to have something nice to take home to show her mother what a good housekeeper she can be. No one knows, until she tries, how much fun it is to cook."

The children were delighted at the prospect, and examined their groups of dishes. Then each child was given half a cup of sugar in the bowl, and a lump of butter, and was taught how to beat them together well; then the yolk of an egg was added, the white being put in the soup-plate to be whipped light with a fork later. Then a little flour, two tablespoonfuls of sweet milk, and two doll spoonfuls of baking powder after the rest of a teacupful of flour had been stirred in. When it came to beating the whites the little arms grew tired, and it seemed as if those whites never would stand alone, but at last

they were added to the batter, which was whisked with a tablespoon until it bubbled. In order to have each cake different a tablespoonful of grated **coconut** for one, the same of chocolate for another, some currants, pounded almonds, chopped raisins, and citron and lemon peel, spices, lemon juice, and pink coloring and vanilla were arranged.

When all were ready a teaspoonful of batter was put in each buttered patty-pan, all set in a large pan and put in the oven. Mamma attended to the baking, and very soon each little girl had two pretty, crinkled cakes for her very own.

Then came the boiled custard, with a cup of milk put on to heat in the tin cup, an egg and two tablespoonfuls of sugar beaten together, meanwhile the boiling milk poured on the mixture and well stirred before putting back in the tin cup to thicken. While the custard and cakes were cooling the children ran out to the garden and gathered jonquils and violets for the table, which they helped Nannie's mamma to arrange with her pretty china dishes.

When the flowers were all arranged and everything looked lovely, a surprise came in the shape of a beautiful birthday cake with nine candles around the edge and one "to grow on" in the middle. Also several dishes of candies, nuts, preserves, and sandwiches appeared. By that time the custard was cool enough to flavor, and all sat down to enjoy themselves, which they did most heartily.

After tea, when the candles had been blown out, the big cake cut and tasted, and going-home time had come, each little girl's own private opinion was that the dear little cake, which she was about to carry home to her mother in a new patty-pan, was the best part of the party.

An Open-Air Party for Little Folk

Fairyland becomes a reality to children when reveling with many playfellows in the freedom of an "outdoor party." Manners are not so narrowly scanned out under the wide blue sky as in a drawing-room, and, in common with other frolicsome young animals, children seem to rejoice in their liberty as in something for which God and Nature intended them. The holiday feeling which the wee folk bring with them in their merry little hearts, the brightening effect of the fresh perfumed air, and the excitement of each other's society, make any great effort for their amusement unnecessary.

In the joy of receiving an invitation to a "pound party," the children will be glad of the opportunity to give pleasure suggested in the words, "A pound package solicited, to be given to the poor." The tender young hearts will be quick to feel sympathy for the privation and suffering of the unfortunate, and it is a sweet lesson to learn early in life that when pleasure comes to us in any form we are to "pass it on" that some other may be gladdened also. Pounds of tea, sugar, coffee, rice, prunes, crackers— though costing but a trifle—will carry pleasure and perhaps needed relief to some poor homes.

It will add to the fun if you can get a little donkey, caparisoned in true Spanish style with worsted tassels, red, blue, and yellow galore, bearing a large pannier on each side, into which the parcels may be dropped. If the animal be left to wander about the lawn, and the children have to chase him a little in order to make their contributions, the fun will be the greater. If, by accident, any of Jack's antics should dislodge a package or two, the catastrophe will probably be received with peals of laughter and the contents not greatly injured. Donkeys are usually docile little animals, and may be had for hire in many country towns. Besides, it is probable that a ride on donkey-back may be a novelty to some of the children. The little ones will exchange eager confidences about what their particular packages contain, and the sense of importance in playing the rôle of benefactor may be a new pleasure.

To dispose of the little souvenirs they may play a new game called "Bubbles and Bundles." The little gifts must be previously prepared, each one placed in a box or made into a bundle, and tied up as prettily as possible in colored tissue papers, with ribbons to match. Some may be grotesque to excite curiosity, and others artistic. A little practice will soon reveal the wonderful possibilities of tissue paper to make most dainty and charming trifles.

These bundles are suspended by ribbons on a strong cord, or clothes-line suspended from tree to tree, in a manner remotely to suggest a cobweb. The children are provided with pretty terra-cotta soap-bubble pipes, tied with ribbons, and a huge bowl of soapsuds is brought upon the scene. A tablespoonful of glycerine added to the suds will prevent the bubbles from breaking easily. Two persons at a time take turns in blowing. The bubbles must be thrown off the pipes into the air, and the children get under them and try to blow them against the packages that they wish for their own. If the bubble hits the bundle, the latter is awarded as a prize, and when a child has secured one he does not try again. It has all the mysterious charm of a game of chance without its objectionable features.

To distinguish between the gifts appropriate for the boys and those for the girls, it may be determined to wrap those for the former in scarlet, yellow, and green, while the others may be pink, blue, white, and lilac. The souvenirs may be as simple and inexpensive as those in a "grab-bag" at a fair,—children are easily pleased,—or they may be as fine as means may permit or taste dictate.

Little tables set out under the trees, prettily decorated with daisies and buttercups, will enable the children to "play tea-party" after an ideal fashion. A sensible menu that will leave no unpleasant after-effects may consist of chicken sandwiches, milk or cocoa, ice cream in flower moulds, sponge-cake, lady-fingers, and plain bonbons. The costume mottoes never fail to create a little flutter of excitement and fun, for the boys like the noise and the girls enjoy the "dressing up."

Lawn Parties and Outdoor Fêtes

From *Home Games and Parties*, by Mrs. Hamilton Mott, 1898

During the summer and early autumn months country towns and villages are, as a rule, full of city visitors and boarders. How to entertain them is a matter of special interest to hostesses and their young friends. As a help in that direction this chapter offers a variety of novel suggestions.

Whatever kind of fête is decided upon, it is worth while to make it distinctive in type by suitable costumes, decoration, and menu. Visitors are to be depended upon for help in this direction. Usually, little expense need be incurred.

The degree of elaboration must depend upon the size and location of grounds, and the particular kind of serving intended. If tables are set, menu, cards, and plate souvenirs of rustic type should be used, also centrepieces representing the idea of the fête. If a picnic lunching is preferred, let the costumes and general decorating serve that purpose.

A Mother Goose Frolic

Children are always delighted with a costume party, and the Mother Goose family is to them an enjoyable company. So, the hostess who would wish to please the little people, could do no better than to invite them to a lawn party, with the request that each shall come as one of Mother Goose's children. The hostess, or the little girl whom she may choose, should serve as Mother Goose, and receive the company. The costumes required are so simple that no great skill or expense is necessary in preparing them. A well illustrated copy of the book would give helpful hints about what to wear.

A lawn furnished with swings, and with hoops to trundle, also games,—croquet, battledore and shuttlecock, ball, etc.,—would insure for the children a happy time. Yet, as pertinent to the Mother Goose idea, a "gooseberry" tree is suggested as a vehicle of conveyance for bonbons and gifts. This tree should stand apart from the others, and may well be not over eight feet tall. Upon it toys, sugar animals, fishes, birds, etc., are hung, just like a Christmas-tree. Each should be labeled, not for the children by name, but for the character they assume, thus: Sheep for Bo-peep; Fish for Simple Simon; Baby for Rock-a-bye; Spider for Miss Muffit, etc. A merry dance around the tree, and the singing of Mother Goose songs, should precede the picking of these unique "gooseberries" from the tree.

For plate souvenirs large sugar plums, with rhymes from "Mother Goose," each suited to the character chosen, pasted upon one side, are pretty; and a handsome pyramidal centrepiece may be made by stacking gooseberry tarts to form the required shape, then daintily decorating the same with flowers, the pedestal being covered wholly with roses. Tarts and roses are to be distributed later.

Rustic Pastime for Girls

The holiday costumes of peasants in all European countries are picturesque. Many of them, especially the Swiss, French, Italian, and Alsatian, are very pretty. They are particularly suitable for out-of-door fêtes, and a company of pleasure-seekers could hardly choose more fittingly for enjoying a summer afternoon than to prepare for a peasants' party with the idea of representing as many different countries as possible.

Games, dancing upon the lawn, and other sports, may be enjoyed in imitation of the joyous fêtes so famous among Europeans.

There is another popular suggestion—that of a dairy-maid party. This, too, is pretty for costuming—the broad Gainsborough hat, fan waist, velvet bodice, full and rather short skirt, with low shoes and colored stockings, being generally worn on holidays. The floor of the dairy house, or the big barn, is cleared, and by lantern light, and with the music of rustic fiddlers, old-time "figures" are recalled and games of other days revived. Then milk, cream, cakes, cheese, curds, whey, ices, and berries are handed about, the company sitting the while upon milking-stools—a most pastoral type of serving.

Then, again, there is the corn roast in its season, just when the field corn is "in the milk." The evening is best for this. Companies ride to the roast, if they choose, in hay wagons. A glowing hard-wood fire greets the guests: they spear the corn ears with long, sharpened poles, then kneel down before the fire to roast them. Blankets are spread upon mounds of newly-mown hay for seats, and the corn, when roasted golden-brown, is served.

Dancing upon the lawn by moonlight, with Chinese lanterns among the trees, and the firelight sending forth cheery rays, is a scene to tempt a band of happy young people.

Duties of the Matrons

The absence of conventionality, while it may be, and is, one of the pleasantest features of country and seaside life, places upon mothers and chaperones a double duty and care. In preparing for lawn parties, at which, by the way, there should be matrons,—indeed, there is greater need of this than in home society, where everybody is well known,—the older friends may do much to assist in matters of costuming, entertaining, refreshment-serving, and introduction. The ideal pleasure party is one in which children, young people, and adults all have a happy part.

Guests at mountain and seaside hotels are not always the kind of companions parents would choose for their children and young friends, yet a kindly courtesy demands that no one shall be excluded from the general merry-making. It, therefore, requires a deal of tact on the part of the older people to protect the younger members. The presence of the "grownups" is the best protection.

A Gypsy Camp

A "Gypsy Camp" is a pretty and attractive affair, and easily managed, even where there are but few trees in the grounds. Invitations written upon cards cut from the inner peeling of birch bark, if such can be obtained, are most suitable, and may read something after this style: "The Shonshone gypsies will camp at Blank's Grove. One hour after the sunset gun, meet us, wearing the costume of your tribe."

By this card the people invited understand that they are to join the company wearing the dress of their respective tribes. As many different tribes as possible should be represented, and from as many different countries. There can be little difficulty in this age of pictorial literature in finding pictures or paintings to give models for the required costumes. They differ very little among the semi-barbaric tribes (and those are the types most picturesque for representation) from the costumes of the peasantry, being rather more showy in color, and more profusely ornamented with beads, buckles, and bracelets.

The conventional gypsy costume generally worn by European tribes consists of the white blouse waist, with a bright-colored corset bodice, which is really neither more nor less than an ordinary corset worn upon the outside of the dress, laced at the back with bright red cord; bright colored, and full gathered, or plaited skirt; low shoes, with stockings to match the dress; broad-brimmed hat, with broad ribbon streamers, but more often an orange or red handkerchief tied over the head. Strings of beads of every variety of colored glass and coral are massed about the neck and waist. They also hang from the shoulders with the ends caught by bracelets above the elbow or at the waist, and are sometimes looped from shoulder to shoulder. Many varieties of colors are combined, so that, even with the same style of dress, their costumes are wholly different in effect.

The men wear high-crowned hats, with long feathers or plumes; blouses in bright showy stripes; long waistcoats of contrasting color; long dark stockings; full trousers and low buckled shoes; fancy-colored necktie and handkerchief make up costumes both suitable and attractive.

To Prepare the Lawn

It is a pretty idea to set up a goodly number of tents and booths. The tents, of course, should have canvas roofs, the sides being left uncovered. Booths, which look picturesque and pretty, are easily made thus:—

Set firmly in the sod, in a circle, a half-dozen posts, say eight feet high, with another post a little longer, and one foot, at least, taller, in the centre of these. Connect their tops with the centre post by narrow boards; also connect the outer posts with each other in a similar way. Then form a network of ropes sufficiently close to hold up the fresh green boughs, which, being heaped upon it, form the roof of the booth. Wind the posts with ivies and greens; then ornament them with flowers or bright bits of red, orange, and blue bunting. Hang Chinese lanterns between the posts, and the structure will be complete. It will be pretty enough to remain all summer, with now and then a fresh covering of greens. A large booth of this kind, set in the centre of the grounds, with a camp-fire built near at hand, over which a gypsy kettle (nearly every farmhouse can furnish one) is hung, with blankets spread about among rustic seats, makes a very good representation of a genuine gypsy camp.

Chinese lanterns, plenty of them, should be hung in the tents and among the trees. There should be music, also. The nearest imitation of gipsy music is given by playing upon combs, Jews'-harps, and violins, accompanied by clappers or "bones," tambourine, and drums. The mouth harmonica also is good. The weird and seemingly tuneless music of the gypsy cannot be closely imitated. The rhythm of it is strongly marked, and those who do not play keep the time by clapping their hands, striking their knees, and joining in a guttural tone, emphasized at each rhythmic beat. A gypsy dance upon the lawn would be suited to the hour. Songs, merry choruses, and bright stories should abound.

The Question of Refreshments

Served in gipsy style the refreshments may consist of coffee (supposedly cooked in the steaming kettle hanging above the fire), tropical fruits, such as oranges, lemons, bananas, nuts, raisins, etc. Cool drinks should be brought around in large pails, and dipped there from into tin or earthen mugs. Plates, napkins, and all other signs of a more civilized serving should be dispensed with as far as possible. A large company may be thus served with very little effort.

Fortune-telling belongs to gypsy life, though the more intelligent tribes of to-day make little use of it. Mysterious oracles, "whose glib tongues spin mirthfully the thread of fortune," ought to have a place.

Sometimes fêtes of this kind are arranged for the purpose of assisting some charity, or for establishing a magazine and book club. Then young girls in costume sell oranges, peanuts, candies, etc., and pretty Italian gypsy girls play the tambourine and sing songs for the help of the treasury.

The novelty and brightness of this rural scene, especially under the light of an August or September moon, cannot fail to delight a company of merry young people.

Some Other Out-Door Fêtes

With July comes the Fourth, always suggestive of the Red, White, and Blue—bunting, flags, and fireworks; and whatever kind of celebration is decided upon, whether boating, picnicking, or an "at-home" fête, the national emblem and colors must rule the day. The colors of no nation lend themselves so beautifully and so gracefully to decoration as do those of America, and in whatever fête given out-of-doors our national colors should in some manner take part.

A Haymakers' Picnic for July

It is the month, too, of hay-making, and a "haymakers' picnic" furnishes a novelty with which city people, especially, are delighted. The young people braid yards of clover, daisy, and buttercup blossoms for decorating the big hay wagon. Wheels, stakes, and shaft, and the broad hay frame are all wound, festooned, and wreathed. The oxen, too, are dressed in a flower-bedecked yoke, their horns tied with ribbons, and a broad floral saddle placed upon their backs.

Girls wear broad-brimmed hats, gingham dresses, strong boots, and long leather gloves to protect the hands while haying, and men wear linen "jumpers," their trousers tucked into high top boots; also leather gloves.

Hampers are packed with a generous lunch, and the haymakers ride away in their gala wagon to the field which, if possible, should border a lake or pond surrounded by plenty of shade. There the haying goes on, not with modern methods, but after the more pastoral type, the men swinging scythes, and the girls spreading the grass, then raking it ready for making the load.

Luncheon is served at high noon, the hayers sitting upon mounds of newly-mown hay. The conventional "noon hour" is extended, so that sailing, rowing, fishing, or berry picking may be enjoyed, after which a hay load of convenient size is prepared, and they all ride homeward, haymaker fashion, on the top of the load.

A "Fish Fry" for August

Dog days and showery weather make the fish hungry; and, in the opinion of many folk, there is no sort of a holiday that quite equals an all-day fishing picnic. The party starts off in the cool of the early morning for a drive of a dozen miles to some pond or lake. They camp upon the shore and start a glowing fire. Then all take boats for fishing, with a right earnest purpose of catching enough shiners, trout, or perch for dinner.

"If the day is right
And the big fish bite,"

there's little danger of failure; yet the fortunes of the day are safest in the hands of experienced fishermen, such as usually frequent fishing grounds. They know the haunts of the fish, and are sure to bring them in. They can dress them in a trice, and no *chef*, though he may be a thousand times French, can produce such crisp, dainty, delicious morsels as will those same queer old fishermen, with nothing at hand but a long-handled fry pan, a bit of salt pork, a dish of Indian meal, and a wood fire whose very smoke seems to add the crowning flavor.

For side dishes take field corn, with the husks on, also potatoes and green apples; bury them either in white sand of the beach, or in clean ashes, then build above them a glowing fire, and after an hour's cooking they come forth "fit to set before a king."

For the Warm September Days

City people who linger during the warm September days to watch the ripening fruit, and bringing in of the yellow corn and grain, must enjoy right heartily an "apple bee" or "husking," arranged in exact imitation of the old-fashioned pattern of fifty years or more ago.

It is not difficult to find in ancient chests and attics well-preserved costumes of that period. Arrayed in these, the young people often begin the "bee" by gathering the orchard apples with their own hands during the afternoon; then in the evening young men come, armed with "Jacks" for paring the fruit, and maidens equip themselves with apple knives for "quartering and coring" it; also long slim needles for stringing the prepared pieces. After stringing the fruit they hang it in festoons along drying bars suspended from the ceiling of the old-fashioned kitchen. Then underneath these they dance the "figures" of "ye old time," and revive the games and frolics of that day. Refreshments should not vary much from the old-time menu,—doughnuts and cheese, pumpkin pie, popped corn, home-made molasses candy, and sweet, new cider.

A "husking," which follows the fashion of our grandparents' day, takes place on the big barn floor where corn "stooks" bank the outer walls, the center being reserved for the yellow mound of husked ears, to which all contribute a share. Milking stools are set for seating the huskers. As fast as the "stooks" are husked they are removed, and the corn is carried to the bin by basketfuls. Searching for ears of red corn furnishes a deal of merriment. By these the sweethearts for the evening are chosen, duplicate ears in the order of finding deciding the choice. When the corn is all husked, and the floor cleared, and the primitive style of serving such old-time goodies as mince and pumpkin pies, apple turnovers, fruit, nut and honey cakes, with coffee and cider has been enjoyed, then under the lantern light, the clean, soft hay sifting down from the overhanging beams and rafters, many songs, legends, and stories fill the hour; or, to the music of fiddle, fife, and snare-drum, the barn-floor dance goes on.

The Best Picnic Luncheon

The luncheon is one of the most enjoyable features of picnicking, and the following hints may prove helpful in preparing and packing the same, so that, when served, it may tempt both the eye and the appetite.

Meats for sandwiches should be boiled the day before; then, after the removal of bone, skin, and gristle, they should be put in packing tins, heavily weighted, and set in a cool place over night. Cut in thin slices.

Bread one day old is best, and a sharp knife is needed for cutting it into thin slices not over three inches square. These, buttered slightly, may be daintily filled with ham, salad, sardines, tongue, or whatever one likes. Then cut pieces of confectioners' paper just large enough to cover the sandwiches neatly. Place them side by side, closely packed, and they will preserve their shape without breaking. The paper is not to be removed until they are served.

Cakes must also be one day old, and, for picnic use, a little extra flour in stirring, and an extra five or ten minutes in baking, will insure a firmer crust. Frosting, if put on hot, does not crackle and fall off. Cookies are more desirable than loaf cake, as are, also, cup and gem cakes. Jelly and cream confections are seldom good for picnic serving.

Pies made of jellies, fruits, or sweets are best cooked turnover fashion, the pastry covering the filling entirely. Lay them in paper covers for convenient serving.

Lemon, orange, strawberry, raspberry, or currant juices should be extracted, then sweetened, and, when the sugar is well dissolved, bottled. Drinks can then be prepared by adding two tablespoonfuls of the liquid to a tumbler of ice water. All these juices combined make a delicious drink.

Strong coffee or tea may also be prepared and served in the same way. Bright tin mugs are more convenient than tumblers, and there is no danger of breakage.

Hampers, with several trays, are very desirable for packing. Ordinary lunch baskets cause difficulty. White confectioners' paper should be used for lining the basket, and for separating the different kinds of food; also, for covering neatly individual pieces. Cookies and crackers must be put in tight boxes. Plates are too heavy, but bright, new biscuit tins— the square shapes are best—are useful in packing, and with fringed napkins laid inside, they serve well for salvers in handing the food around. Paper napkins are best.

Whatever is to be eaten last should be packed at the bottom of the hamper, and that to be served first, at the top. Fruit, pickles, olives, and cheese must not be forgotten.

A Wild-Rose Party

The invitations should be sent out during the latter days of May or early days in June, the invitation card, of heavy white paper, being decorated with a spray of wild roses.

When the guests assemble upon the lawn each one should be handed either bouquet or *boutonnière* of wild roses, the gentlemen being permitted to select partners, and all to arrange themselves comfortably in close proximity to the hostess, who for this occasion is given the seat of honor, close beside a rustic table covered with wild roses. Each lady is handed a long strip of rose-colored paper, and each gentleman a pencil, and the party begins in earnest. The hostess reads aloud the following questions, the answers to which are to be found in the names of flowers, and written in order on the slips provided; and, as two heads are better than one, the gentlemen may hold many consultations with their partners before they write down the answers which, between them, they have guessed.

The hostess begins the story in this wise: "This is a floral love story taken from the leaves of a bud's journal; her name was Violet."

1 What was her nationality and appearance? [An American Beauty.]

2 What was his disposition and name? [Sweet William.]

3 What was his object in matrimony? [He wished to Marigold.]

4 How did he offer himself? [He Aster.]

5 To whom did she refer him? [Poppy.]

6 What did her father ask concerning William's prospects? [Anemone—any money.]

7 How long had Violet been out in society? [Four seasons.]

8 By whom were they married? [Jack-in-the-pulpit.]

9 How many attended the ceremony? [Phlox.]

10 Who were the bridesmaids? [Wild Rose and Lily-of-the-Valley.]

11 What was the color of their gowns? [Heliotrope and Pink.]

12 What did the bride wear on her head? [Bridal Wreath.]

13 What did she resemble? [Maid in a Mist.]

14 What did the bridegroom wear for the last time? [Bachelor's Buttons.]

15 What did he resemble? [A Night-blooming
Cereus—Knight blooming serious.]

16 How was the house decorated for the reception?
[With Blue Flags and Yellow Flags.]

17 What did they throw after the carriage?
[A Lady's Slipper.]

18 Where did they go on their wedding trip?
[Magnolia.]

19 What animals did they see on visiting a menagerie?
[A Dandelion and great Solomon's Seal.]

20 What two presents did they take to her parents?
[A Dutchman's Pipe, and Yellow Jacket.]

21 What did they take to her good little brother?
[Trumpet-vine.]

22 At what hour did he awaken them blowing it?
[Four-o'clock.]

23 How long did he keep it going?
[Until Deadly Nightshade.]

24 What happened when they took it from him?
[He did Balsam—bawl some.]

25 Whom did they engage as cook?
[Black-eyed Susan.]

26 Who was her young man? [Ragged Robin.]

27 For what was a plumber called in?
[A House-leek.]

28 When Sweet William left home on business what
were his parting words? [Forget me-not.]

29 What did she reply? [Speedwell.]

30 What happened when she saw him returning?
[A Yellow Rose—a yell arose.]

31 How did she salute him? [With Tulips.]

32 What bonbons did he bring her?
[Buttercups and Marshmallows.]

33 How did Violet rule her husband?
[With a Goldenrod.]

34 Was their happiness enduring? [Everlasting.]

When all have finished, the papers are
collected and prizes are given to the two who have
guessed the most answers correctly, and, of course,
to the two who have been least clever in guessing.

Flower stick-pins, sunflower pincushions, vases,
or a box of buttercups and marshmallow bonbons
make suitable prizes. The prize for the couple who
have been least successful may be a huge bouquet
of roses, or a bonbon box filled with rose-colored
"April-fool" candies. Then refreshments may be
served upon small tables covered with snowy
cloths and lavishly decorated with viands of a rosy
hue. A delightful afternoon party may thus be
brought to an end.

It is difficult to imagine anything which
can be made more charming than the wild- rose
luncheon here described. The season is the one of
the year which lends itself most readily to outdoor
entertainments, and the prolific growth of roses
during June suggests at once the suitable flower for
the decorations.

A "Farmer's Supper"

Very attractive is the idea of a "farmer's
supper." Though it may be utilized for indoor use,
it is prettier on the lawn. It may be given by those
who have ample grounds, with conveniences for
entertaining large companies, or, picnic fashion, by
a company of young people, each person bringing
contributions for the table; or, if desired, it can be
arranged for in a hall or vestry, when members of
Young People's Benevolent Societies wish to raise
money to carry on their charitable work.

The "supper" calls together, in rustic costume,
the various characters belonging to farm life. The
farmer and farmer's wife, with their sons and
daughters, receive the company, and give a supper,
to which all are invited—dairy men and dairy
women; haymakers—men who swing the scythe,
and maids who "spread the fallen grass;" boys who
tend the sheep, and little "Bo-peeps" who lose
them; plow-boys wearing gloves and whips, and
berry pickers bringing their "pails heaped high
and red"; gardeners and flower girls; hunters and

fisher lads; market girls with baskets of eggs or fruit or vegetables, all come in costume suited to their station and work. The village lawyer, doctor, deacon, and squire may also be added to the list, with the neighborhood rhymester and wit, and the singer of local songs.

The costumes may well be copied from English or continental farm life, or perhaps the American type of a generation ago, since the farmer and his family of to-day wear little or nothing to mark by their dress the nature of their life and work.

Tables spread upon the lawn should be furnished wholly with the fruits of the farm and dairy, the special dishes, such as boiled dinner, baked beans and brown-bread, not omitted. The farmer offers to his guests bread from his fields of corn, rye, and wheat; butter, cheese, milk, cream, and curds from his dairy; berries and fruits from his fields and orchards; flowers and fresh vegetables from his gardens; fish captured (perhaps) from his meadow brooks; poultry and meats fed by sweet pasturage and grains, and sugar from his own fair maple orchard.

Where the size of the grounds permits, various games, such as quoits, ball, and croquet, etc., foot and jumping races, also swinging, tilting, and dancing upon the lawn may be enjoyed. If indoors, such old-time games as hunt the slipper, stagecoach, and their like can be revived. Choruses, songs, and recitations of the pastoral type, with tableaux and pantomime representing scenes in farm life, may well be offered as a part of the entertainment.

A Midsummer Ice Party

How many housekeepers have received with dismay the news that some intimate friend is visiting a neighbor's in sultry, summer weather, knowing that the intelligence means to them the necessity of giving a dinner to the visiting friend and her hosts, and asking some people to meet her—and this when

the thermometer is most at home in the nineties, and even thoughts of food and dining produce acute discomfort?

However, it is possible to give a formal dinner, which will delight all concerned, even on a sultry August evening, and such a one is the ice party now to be described.

Limit the diners to eight in number, if possible, unless your dining-room will seat more than this with amplest elbow-space. Name seven o'clock as the hour for dinner, and suggest in your informal notes of invitation that evening dress, like oysters, be limited to the months with an "r", whereupon your male guests will call you blessed.

Cover the table with the snowiest of linen cloths, and use for a centrepiece a frosted- glass bowl of white, or so-called Christmas roses. At each cover place a guest-card of pure white pasteboard sprinkled with diamond dust, in imitation of frost, and having tied to it, with a frosted ribbon, a *boutonnière* or a bunch of the white roses. Use only white bonbons, in glass dishes for candies, and candles with white frosted shades for illumination.

The dinner must be of the simplest kind. Little-neck clams, served on the half shell, in beds of cracked ice, with celery as a relish, will make an acceptable first course. Omit soups, unless you wish to serve iced bouillon, which but few people like. Cold salmon, cold trout, or any other fish served cold with mayonnaise dressing will be found delicious and appetizing. Your meat course, which should follow, will be the only one in which hot dishes are to be served: "French" lamb chops, Bermuda potatoes, and green peas. Guava jelly should accompany the chops. Lettuce with French dressing, salted wafers and Neuchatel cheese should be served in the salad course. Vanilla ice cream, moulded into snowballs, and ornamented with a sprig of holly or evergreen, if either can be secured, with frosted fancy cakes, angel's food, or any other cake with white icing, will make a delicious and simple dessert Iced or hot coffee—whichever is preferred—should be provided, and bonbons.

A Fern Lunch Party

A cool and pretty entertainment for the late summer is a fern party, which is especially within the reach of all out-of-town residents. Gather from the woods as many ferns as you can, the largest to the smallest—each has its particular mission in the scheme of decoration. In sending out your invitations paste neatly at the top of the card a tiny fern of delicate pattern.

On the day of your entertainment, if the exterior of your house will lend itself to the plan, mass ferns generously upon the piazza; have them follow the railing, let them be arranged in shady corners on the porch, and, of course, meet the eye in the hall. In the dressing-rooms, over the white linen covers on the dressing-tables, lay the ferns so they will completely cover them, and decorate the mirrors, fireplaces, and mantels. Exquisite effects can be obtained at the windows with the soft lace curtains. In the drawing-room bank the mantelpieces, and at one end tie a large green satin bow, made of feather-edge ribbon. Tie bunches of ferns on the lampshades. You will find that the green of ferns will blend with almost any shade of silk, but, of course, all strikingly inharmonious colors should be removed from the room.

When the guests enter the dining-room the effect should be that of going into a fernery. Bank the mantel like that in the drawing-room. In the corners have large boxes filled with ferns, and arrange them to run up as high as possible, which can be done by the aid of tacks and fine green cord. Have the table laid with a fine white damask cloth, fern pattern, if possible, and at the two diagonal corners arrange gracefully loose bunches of the larger ferns tied with large bows of ribbon. The linen centrepiece should be embroidered in a fern design, and on it place a

big glass bowl filled with the choicest specimens of the delicate plant. Set each plate on a mat of ferns, which can be easily made by covering a stiff foundation with them. The white candles should have green paper shades, and the *entries* should, whenever permissible, be garnished with bits of green.

For favors get small glass bowls and ornament them with narrow green ribbons, Line with moss and fill with earth, and then plant in them tiny specimens of maiden-hair fern. This will make a novel and welcome souvenir.

Old-Fashioned Barn Parties

To insure the success of a barn party a moonlight night should be selected. The barn chosen should be large, the floor space ample, and the decorations lavish. They may consist of green boughs, vines, and golden-rod, and a number of American flags. The two large opposite doors should be thrown wide open for free circulation of air. The floor should then be cleared, swept, and washed. High up over one door a large flag may be draped, and wires stretched across from beam to beam, away from direct draughts, upon which Japanese lanterns may be hung, care being taken that none are allowed to come in contact with the bunting in case of one's taking fire. Chairs also should be provided, and a rope stretched across one side of the open space, on the farther side of which place a table. On this table place a large bowl of soapsuds, into which a spoonful of glycerine has been put, and by its side place half as many pipes as there are to be guests. Prepare half as many cards also as there are to be guests, and write across the full length of each card the name of an agricultural implement, as a hay-rake, hay-cutter, pitchfork, hoe, spade, scythe, sickle, mower, plow, reaper, binder, seeder. Each card should be numbered at the top and bear a question concerning the implement named on it;

besides which the number and a query concerning it should be written at the back upon the lower half. Questions like the following will answer:—

1 What is the true mission of a harrow?
2 Can you tell a harrowing tale?
3 What is a hoe used for?
4 What is a good receipt for hoe cake?

The cards should then be cut in halves.

When the guests arrive a numbered half is given to each young woman, and each half upon which a query is written is given to a young man, who proceeds to match it, retaining as his partner the young woman whose card completes his own. When all have found their partners, the hostess, who is constituted "judge" for the evening, calls out, "Number One," and the young woman who holds this number is escorted to a seat in the middle of the floor, her partner putting to her the question upon his half of the card. She then demands of him an answer to number two. These must be answered in the hearing of the others, and for each failure to do this a forfeit must be paid. When all have participated it is put to vote as to who gave the brightest answer, the winner being granted a first trial at the soap-bubble contest which ensues.

Taking her place by the table on one side of the rope, she selects pipe number one; her partner places himself opposite her on the other side of the rope, and she then proceeds to make the largest bubble possible without breaking it. When this is accomplished she wafts it into the air as high as possible toward her partner, who tries by blowing it in the opposite direction to prevent it from crossing the rope to his side. Should he prevent it from bursting on his side of the rope one point is scored for himself and partner and another turn is allowed. If, however, the bubble crosses over to his side one point is given to the next player, who immediately takes her place at the bowl with her partner

opposite. When all have participated, a large bunch of old-fashioned flowers is presented to the young woman who formed the largest bubble, another to the man who won the most points, and another to the one who won the least, and so on.

Refreshments may be served from tables spread out under the trees, upon the branches of which are hung bright lanterns.

A Corn Husking

Late in October when the corn has matured and been stacked in the barn, informal invitations may be sent out to all the neighboring young people to attend a husking bee.

Previous to the evening mentioned the ears of corn are stripped from the stems and formed into two huge piles upon the barn floor. Lanterns should be hung here and there upon the beams to give the necessary light, and stools provided for the workers. The company, on arrival, is divided equally, one half being assigned to one pile, the other half to pile number two, and the contest begins, each division striving to finish its pile first. The husks must be entirely removed from each ear, and whoever first discloses to view a red ear is considered especially fortunate, as the first red ear shown is supposed to bring good luck to its possessor.

After all the ears have been husked the winner of the red ear is escorted in state to the house, where a warm fire (always an open one, if possible) and a supper are waiting.

Decorate the walls of the room in which the supper is to be served with as much green as can be procured at this season of the year. Procure a dozen pumpkins, remove the pulp, cutting a hole at the top of the shell; cut also four stars in the sides of each pumpkin, cover with light yellow paper, and place candles inside. These lanterns, being set in various convenient spots about the room, and lighted just before the supper is served, shed a corn-colored glow over the room. Have the table spread with a snowy cloth. In the centre place a tall vase filled with any late autumn yellow flowers, dahlias, chrysanthemums, or marigolds; place a candle at each end of the table screened by yellow crêpe paper shades. The refreshments may consist of egg and lemon butter sandwiches, cornbread, chicken salad, sponge-cake, gold-cake, lemon ice cream, and lemon water ice, cup custards, honey in the comb, lemonade and coffee.

An Apple-Paring Bee

The guests assemble around the blazing open fire. Two large baskets of apples are brought in. A row of dishes is placed upon the hearth in front of the fire, and a short distance above the dishes is stretched a wire, to which apples are to be fastened in a row to roast. Next, knives are distributed, and each one attempts to slide his or her knife safely round and round an apple taken from the basket without breaking the paring. This being accomplished, each one privately gives to his or her paring the name of a favored one, stands in the middle of the room, takes the paring by one end, twirls it three times around the head from right to left, and drops it over the left shoulder to the floor, repeating:

"I pare this pippin round and round again,
My sweetheart's name to flourish in the plain;
I fling the unbroken paring o'er my head,
My sweetheart's letter on the ground is read."

The paring is supposed immediately to assume the form of the first initial of the favored one's name. Again, an apple seed is cut in halves, each half named and stuck upon the closed eyelids. It is rarely that either one remains on long. If both drop at the same time then it is reasonable to suppose that the experimenter will go unloved to his or her grave.

Should one, however, remain longer than the other, that one will prove constant through life. While all this has been going on, the apples growing tender and juicy before the fire drop one by one into the dishes placed beneath. It is then that pitchers of cream are brought in with small bowls and spoons, and the evening closes with roasted apples and cream.

Old-Time Spelling Match

The fact that a spelling bee is to form a part of an evening's entertainment need not be indicated upon the programme, it being a part of the fun to catch people unawares.

After the arrival of the guests the choice of a "teacher" and two leaders is effected by ballot. The two leaders then stand out at the end of the room opposite each other, and each chooses alternately one of the company at a time, to represent his side, until all have taken their places in two lines.

The teacher, who is supplied with a book, then gives out a word to the person at the end of the line at her right. If the word is correctly spelled, the next word is given out to the person at the end of the opposite side at her left. If this person fails to spell this word correctly she must immediately leave the line, and the same word is put to number two on the opposite side. If the word is correctly spelled she is privileged to choose one person from the opposite line to step over to the foot of her own line. Another word is then given to the opposite opponent, and so on down the lines. It often happens that two equally proficient spellers are pitted against each other for some time, when the contest becomes very exciting.

It is a good plan, lest the contest become wearisome, to limit the time for the last participant. If at the end of six minutes the winner has not failed on any word given, he or she becomes director of the revels that follow, and must be implicitly obeyed for the rest of the evening. The first duty is to announce a "recess," and having been previously instructed, he or she leads the way to an adjoining room, where upon a table, in a pile, lie boxes of various shapes and kinds, neatly tied. These are distributed among the young women, after which it is announced that each box contains a small school luncheon, and that a young man accompanies each. Then comes a distribution of the young men in the same way that the boxes were distributed, and each young woman shares her luncheon with her partner. Should the box contain an apple, a sandwich, and a cake, these must be halved.

After "recess" follow games, or music, or recitations, as the winner of the contest wills.

A Jolly Mother Goose Party

For a Mother Goose Party send out the following invitations:

> Reunion of the Goose Family.
> Mother Goose
> At Home
> _____   _____
> from eight to eleven o'clock.
> _____

With this card may be enclosed another, upon which may be written:

> Please come costumed as one of the
> goslings, and bring an original verse
> explaining your mishaps.

As, for example, Old Mother Hubbard might write:—

> "I'd been giving a tea—
> All the ladies were there:
> And that must explain
> Why my cupboard was bare."

Or the "Old Man Dressed all in Leather" might ask:—

> "Why do I dress in leather?
> The reason I'll unfold:
> One day I dressed in cassimere
> And caught a dreadful cold."

Secure a large pan such as bread is mixed in, and cover it with a large sheet of light brown wrapping-paper. Cut the paper an inch and a half larger than the pan, cut a hole in the middle large enough to admit a man's hand, and secure the paper around the outside edges of the pan with mucilage.

This "Jack Horner" pie graces the head of the table later.

The servant who admits the guests receives from them the envelope containing their verses, and places them, still sealed, in the pie.

Mother Goose may stand conveniently near the entrance to the drawing-room, and should greet the guests by name if possible.

During the evening a slip of paper is handed to each guest with the name of one of the Mother Goose characters upon it. The hostess retains a list of these, and calls each, in turn, to repeat within the space of one minute the familiar verse relative to this character. Failing to do this, a forfeit must be paid. The one who is most prompt in responding correctly may receive as a pledge a goose-quill pen, and the one who fails, a copy of "Mother Goose." Just before refreshments are served the "Goose Drill" may be participated in to the time of a march, and the couples proceed to the refreshment-room, where they are served to:—

(1) Shared by the Walrus and Carpenter.
(2) A King's dish.
(3) A Queen's lunch.
(4) Taffy's spoils.
(5) The golden eggs.

(6) Fragments from the "old woman's broom."

(7) What the baker made.

(8) Sample of the Pieman's ware.

(9) Jack-a-dandy's delight.

(10) What the ships brought.

The numbered list of refreshments may be printed upon small cards, which may be retained as souvenirs of the occasion. The guests order what they choose. The key, which is retained by the hostess, is as follows:—

No. 1—Oysters.

No. 2—Bird pie.

No. 3—Bread and honey.

No. 4—Beef sandwiches.

No. 5—Egg sandwiches.

No. 6—Cheese-straws.

No. 7—Rolls.

No. 8—Washington cake-pie.

No. 9—Plum cake.

No. 10—Apples and comfits.

After refreshments have been partaken of, each guest in turn reaches into the depths of the "Jack Horner" pie and removes a plum—one of the sealed envelopes—and reads aloud the verses contained therein.

Halloween Romps and Frolics

From *Home Games and Parties*, by Mrs. Hamilton Mott, 1898

What Hallow's Eve, or Halloween, as it is popularly called, means, or how it came by its extravagant and fantastic customs, is unknown. It is the vigil of Hallowmas or All Saints' Day, yet it has no Christian meaning, but, on the contrary, is essentially paganistic. Authorities agree in placing it under pagan festivals, and absolutely separate it from any Christian anniversary. The most ancient of Halloween customs was the building of a huge bonfire by each household; on that night spirits were supposed to walk the earth, strange dreams foretold prosperity or adversity, lovers were tested by various charms, future marriages were arranged, and the wilder the superstition the more current its belief.

In modern times Halloween has always been enjoyable because of the popular superstitions attaching to it as a night when any supernatural story might be believed, any charm tested, any frolic permitted,—a night when imagination might run riot, and any ceremony, however extravagant, be indulged in.

We are all of us the better for an occasional frolic, and Halloween, with its quaint customs and mystic tricks, affords opportunity for much innocent merriment.

Arrangements for a Party

When one has decided on a Halloween frolic, and the invitations have been arranged and sent, many problems confront the hostess, each requiring more thought than the ordinary party.

The matter requiring most thought is, perhaps, the decoration of the rooms. The Halloween arrangements which are too elaborate miss their point. An ideal place in which to hold such a party is the large, old-fashioned country barn, with the sweet-smelling mows above, and the soft light of many lanterns hung from the rafters. With the barn party, however, the almost indispensable wood fire must, of necessity, be outside. In the majority of cases the party should meet in the house, within a few rooms, and the old-fashioned pumpkin or squash be the chief dependence.

Let all the light that is used, either indoors or out, come from pumpkin lanterns. The smaller ones, hollowed out and with grotesque faces cut in the rind, should be fastened with wire around ordinary gas-burners, while one huge pumpkin, with a lamp looking out from the grinning face, and apples, nuts, and oranges piled around it, will make a sufficiently striking centrepiece for the supper-table. To add weirdness and quaintness to the Jack-o'-lanterns, when the pulp has been removed and a large incision made for the face, stretch over the opening a grim mask of colored paper, with nose, eyes, and mouth cut as you would in a pumpkin, and glue it fast over the incision. Use a different color for each pumpkin. These many colored faces are more effective in a dark room than the ordinary Jack-o'-lantern. Candles placed inside should not be lighted until the guests arrive.

For the rest, bunches of wheat or grasses over pictures and in vases, ears of ripened corn, and festoons of brilliant cranberries strung upon a thread, will give a suggestion of the country to the scene. Wherever possible, have a roaring, crackling, open fire.

How to Entertain the Guests

Any innocent joke, perpetrated in a spirit of friendly mischief, will befit the night. The idea of the olden time centred around the pairing of lad and lass; hence the chestnuts were put before the fire to test the future of those whose names they bore,—if they burned steadily, the courtship would go well; if they popped apart, the course of true love would not run smooth. Hand-glasses, with apples beside them, should be placed here and there, so that the modern Eve may eat her apple and wait for Adam to peep over her shoulder.

Greater pleasure, however, will be found in the games which all may play. The tab of water with floating apples which must be lifted out by the teeth alone, and the fork suspended from the ceiling, with its lighted candle at one end and the apple from which a bite is to be taken at the other, will cause much merriment. The search for the ring in flour is also much enjoyed. The flour containing a ring is packed upon a large platter. The guests each cut off a slice with a knife, and the one uncovering the ring must pick it up with his teeth.

Lead, melted in large iron spoons, may be dropped in water, and fortunes told from the shapes which it assumes.

Great amusement may be had by placing two hickory-nuts, about three inches apart, on the hearth in front of an open fire. One is supposed to represent the girl who places it there, and the other, her as yet undeclared but mentally chosen lover. Should the nuts burn brightly, a happy marriage will result. Should the nut named after

the man jump toward the nut named after the girl, she may expect a proposal before the next new moon.

Hunting for the Hidden Wedding-Ring

Hunting for the wedding-ring is another test which creates great sport. A ring, a thimble, and a nickel should be hid somewhere in the room; to the one who finds the ring his or her marriage is assured; the thimble, he or she will live a life of single blessedness; the nickel promises wealth.

The weal or woe test is made by trying to toss an apple through a horseshoe which is suspended in a doorway at a convenient height. Each fortune-seeker tries to throw an apple through the shoe; if successful, happiness is his or hers.

The old tricks of swinging a wedding-ring over a goblet and slowly repeating the alphabet— the letter which is said as the ring touches the glass being the initial of the future husband's or sweetheart's name,—walking around the house at midnight, and going downstairs backward to meet one's fate, are familiar to all. If lover or sweetheart does not appear at the foot of the steps, or round the corner of the house, then drink salt water before retiring, and lover or sweetheart will appear in your dreams, according to tradition, with a cup of cold water; should you awake before you drink,

> "Lover is fled!
> And you'll never wed."

Divining by the Cake with Candles

Much sport may be had at supper-time by having a large cake in the centre of the table with as many candles around it as there are guests, each candle a different color. The cake is passed last. The guests each take a candle and a piece of cake, choosing whatever color pleases their fancy. As they do so some one reads:

> He who takes the candle blue,
> Will find his sweetheart ever true.
>
> The pink the sweetest of them all,
> Will wed a fellow six feet tall.
>
> Alas, for yellow, bright to see,
> Your lover e'er will jealous be.
>
> Happy she who orange takes;
> Now begin your wedding cakes.
>
> Hopeless, homeless bachelor he,
> if white candle his should be.

The hostess may evolve some other pleasant and clever couplets to finish the list. The candles come in play later, when each tries his or her fate. All candles lighted, each holds his at arm's length, and blows three times; should the candle go out the first time, he will be married that year; if the second, in two years; if the third, in three years.

Supper may be served between the games and fate-charms, or afterward, and may consist of salads, sandwiches, biscuits, olives, cakes, nuts, apples, and coffee.

Invitations for a Brownie Party

For children from seven to ten years a new and helpful turn to Halloween may be given by sending out the following invitation on Brownie note paper:

> THE BROWNIE CLAN
> Will met at the home of _____
> on Halloween
> October thirty-first, from seven o'clock till nine
>
> *Your presence is requested.*

On the opposite page place the following verses, with the request that they be memorized before the party:—

BROWNIE SONG

> We all are Brownies, every one,
>   We have a Hidden wand,
> And twining round it are the words:
>   "We love to lend a hand."

CHORUS

> A helping hand is all we have;
>   And that we gladly give,
> Hurrah! hurrah! for Brownies all
>   Wherever they may live.
>
> We Brownies dearly love a joke,
>   We are a merry band,
> But most of all and best of all,
>   We love to lend a hand !

CHORUS

Mysterious Work of the Brownies

With a suggestion or two from the older folk the children will speedily catch the spirit of the occasion. While impatiently waiting for the evening in question, the mysterious work of a Brownie hand will be manifest. The lessons will be learned before the usual time, unasked errands will be run, the baby will be kept entertained, and the once disordered room will be found tidy. On entering the Brownie precincts on October 31, the children are mysteriously led, the boys into one room, the girls into another, whence they emerge in Brownie costume,—pointed caps of brown felt with a tassel dropping to one side, and moccasins of the felt, with long, pointed toes. These slippers may be put on over the shoes, and so will deaden the footfalls, as well as make the figure picturesque. If more elaborate costuming is desired, the drawings of

Mr. Palmer Cox may be used as models, and the familiar Dude, Chinaman, Indian, and Policeman figure in the revels.

Brownies Ready for Fun

In the centre of the room into which the children go for refreshments may be a huge pumpkin, hollowed out and filled with bundles of all sizes and shapes. As the children stand in charmed curiosity the hostess explains that these are Brownie gifts for a needy family in the neighborhood, and then proposes that the band carry and leave them at the door, and that, before they go, they sing the song on their invitations. A circle is formed, and the children dance and sing the Brownie song: "We all are Brownies, every one," etc., to some familiar tune, then bundles will be grasped in eager hands, and the Brownie band will steal forth. A mysterious walk, much hushed laughter, a loud knock at the door, and a hurried scamper—and the Brownies are again at headquarters, ready for fun and frolic. Many of the jokes and games suggested are appropriate for children, and may be carried through with zest until it is time for the band to disperse. As the Brownies lay aside their caps and take up their more usual headgear, inside each may be hidden a small present—a Brownie penwiper, a box of pencils, or any one of the trifles dear to childish hearts—to carry home as mementos of an evening which will always be proof to them that there may be not only fun and frolic, but thoughtfulness for others, in Halloween parties.

A Fairy Folk Frolic

For another sort of revel transform a room into a fairy grotto, thus: Cover the side walls with green cambric,—not too dark nor too smoothly placed. Loop the same in easy festoons to cover the upper wall. Then among these festoons fasten trailing vines and small tree branches. Upon the cambric covering the side walls make rough, free charcoal sketches of rocks, recesses, caverns, and smaller grottoes. Intermingled with and covering the sharper outlines, place with judicious taste small trees, branches, and vines, liberally decorated with spangles, shining pendants, and baubles. Arrange also glittering draperies of fabrics, known as cloth of gold and silver, with silver and gold fringes. Stars, diamond and heart- shaped figures cut from gilt, amber, and silver paper should be added. These decorations may be pinned lightly to the cambric. Place a few lamps with chimneys of red, blue, and yellow glass, and, under their soft tinted light the scene is indeed beautiful.

The parlors can be similarly arranged if desired, otherwise the rooms should be cleared, the carpet covered 'with white cloth, and the general decorations may well consist of bright colored tarletans and flowers. In the centre of the room suspend a bright-colored hoop, to which gay ribbons, not less than three yards long, should be fastened at equidistant points. With these, each claiming a color to match their costume, the children perform the fairy frolic, the changes of which are similar to the May-pole dance, except the final braiding of the May pole. These same ribbons may be used later in the scarf revel,—a beautiful *mélange* of music, color, and motion.

Fairy costumes for little girls are of tarletan or tulle, liberally ornamented with glittering fringes and spangles. The queen ought to wear a crown and elaborately fashioned dress; the wee godmother a somber costume, brown bonnet, and spectacles.

Arranging a Scotch Halloween

This idea will be particularly appropriate, as Scotland is the home of Halloween. Request that the dressing of the ladies be especially simple, and that each one may wear a white apron, kerchief, and small cap, and that the men appear either in Highland plaid and kilts, or in golf costume with Tam-o'-Shanters. Request, also, that those invited use Scotch words and idioms. If this has been asked on the invitations the guests will have an astonishing number of mystifying words at their tongues' end. In this day of the "Bonnie Brier Bush" there are few intelligent people who may not easily master several phrases. Sing Scotch songs,—some of the more familiar ones being used as a chorus. During refreshments have bagpipes played, if a piper be available, and provide that the pipes may be in a separate room from the guests. Later in the evening draw around the open fire, and have a story which is essentially Scotch, told by a good story-teller.

Recitations of Scotch poems, and readings from Scotch authors, may also be given, and add to the pleasure and knowledge of the guests. Burns' poem of "Halloween" is especially appropriate, and "Tam o' Shanter" will help to produce the sensation of thrilling excitement, which is the true Halloween spirit. And, of course, the evening must close with all the guests' voices raised in singing "Should auld acquaintance be forgot?"

Helps in Arranging Tableaux

From *Home Games and Parties*, by Mrs. Hamilton Mott, 1898

Unvarying rules for successful tableaux are as hard to give as unvarying rules for cakes. They both need large dashes of judgment; yet there are some suggestions which should be followed accurately if you desire to devote an evening to this form of entertainment.

What the Manager Needs

To begin with, to be a successful manager of an affair of this sort, beauty and age must be overlooked entirely, and the eye must be trained to quick recognition of a type, and be able to use such a one intelligently. The promoter of this form of entertainment must steel his heart and gird on the armor of patience, for he will need but little of the former and much of the latter. The work being usually made more difficult by suggestions, it will require wonderful dexterity on the part of the leader to steer successfully his little company around the shoals of rivalry into the smiling port of content. Of course, the beauty of her set may insist upon posing for the principal roles; regardless of the fact that her Anglo-Saxon profile does not suit the part in the least, and pretty Mrs. Young Wife, who tips the scales at a hundred and sixty, may shed many tears if not allowed to impersonate Psyche. These are the thorns in the path of the manager, and only one with rare tact can escape their sting.

Arranging the Stage

To get to the actual working details, the first thing to do is to select your room. One that connects by folding doors with the one to serve as auditorium is the best to choose. Let the whole space occupied by the doors be filled in with black gauze stretched across the opening, and the foot and top lights placed behind it. This arrangement produces the effect of a thin mist, light enough to be easily seen through, and yet softening the rugged outlines and bringing out the points of the picture at the back with a clearness that is wonderful. This gauze is one of the most important features in tableaux, and should no sooner be disregarded than the arrangement of the stage. Of course, it is to be understood that reference is made only to such an entertainment as can be given in either a city drawing-room or the spacious rooms of a country mansion. Very few people, no matter how much they may enjoy theatricals and tableaux, can afford to set apart a room or hall for such purposes, consequently preparations of the sort described below must be made whenever any such festivities are contemplated.

Your stage must, of course, be raised above the audience. It should be not less than fifteen feet in depth, with as much space behind it as can be spared, and ten feet in width. To represent banks or other elevations there must be movable benches or platforms. Frames for the living pictures must be secured. As all pictures are not the same size, several frames must be arranged. Some may be hired. A simple one can be made by using moulding by the foot, bordered all round by cloth of some subdued tone. Portières may serve as curtains, yet there may be possibly some homes where these hangings are not used; in which case the folding doors must screen the actors from the spectators, and each frame be provided with a separate bit of gauze, instead of the one large piece in the doorway doing duty for all. Once let the stage, the gauze, and the lights be arranged, and the main trouble is over.

When the work of selecting the persons who are to represent these living pictures begins, the manager must look first for that much-needed quality—grace. Grace goes farther than any other attribute to suggest beauty, and it must be kept in mind that it is a work of art which is to be represented, lest mere prettiness deceive by its superficial attractiveness. In everyday life a woman is deemed plain if afflicted with a poor complexion, but in tableaux this defect does not signify, and should not be considered.

Not Color, but Form

Some faces can assume more than one type by a different arrangement of hair, costume, and light The death mask of Shakespeare reveals this peculiarity, for in one view we discover the German, in another the French, and in a third the Greek. Some have even said they detected a trace of the African. Be that as it may, many faces are capable of taking on more than one type, and such are the best subjects for tableaux. The color of hair or eyes does not have the bearing on the artistic representation that form does. A dark person may be less suitable for picturing the Southern and Eastern races than many fair-skinned children of a Northern clime. Color is a much more manageable quality in tableaux than form, yet even this can be apparently changed if a little artistic knowledge is brought to bear upon thè operation. A gown of unrelieved black will cause some faces to appear thin, while the same person, in a white gown, owing to the reflected lights which destroy the shadows, will look quite plump.

Strong colors, such as black, dark red, and blue, should be used where the type is fine, lacking a subtlety of modeling, giving the impression of imperfect finish. If the finish is finer than the type, the use of lace, the glint of satin, and the reflection of transparent white give the face the very opposite quality of severe line.

Colors by Lamplight

Great care should be taken in the selection of colors, as many that appear warm and lovely in the daytime are quite the reverse by lamp or gas light. Especially is this true of many purples, that are hideous browns under the glare of the gas. Likewise, some pinks become yellow, some blues green. Be sure, if you choose any one of these colors, that they will appear the same when you wish to use them before the footlights.

Do not forget that size is only a relative matter. To represent height or weight, judicious contrasts serve even a better purpose than actual proportions. A woman not more than five feet high can be made to look very tall if she carries her head well, and no one would think her tiny unless placed beside other and larger women. As the single figure in a picture attired in ruffs and jewels she would appear commanding.

People look taller on the stage than in a room, owing, undoubtedly, to their being on a higher level and appearing larger, as figures seen against the sky always do. Sharp lights and shadows are rare magicians, causing a perfectly proportioned man or woman to appear absolutely attenuated, while an over-stout person becomes just delightfully plump and round.

Elaborate Subjects

Having gone over the mechanical workings of *les tableaux vivants*, the next thing to do is to choose the most beautiful and effective pictures to represent. At Osborne, the Queen's residence on the Isle of Wight, among other subjects "The Four Seasons" and "Taking the Veil" were given. The former is somewhat hackneyed, as there never were yet tableaux given by amateurs who did not claim that subject for their own. However, it is a pretty picture, and capable of much originality of thought in the costuming and arrangement. At Osborne the Princess Patricia, youngest daughter of the Duke of Connaught, represented Spring in a thin gauzy gown, with an overturned basket of violets and daffodils in her lap. The youth of the Princess made her the most worthy embodiment of the infant season that could be chosen. One of the ladies-in-waiting impersonated Summer in pink satin profusely adorned with roses, while Princess Beatrice, the Queen's favorite daughter, looked the very embodiment of Autumn in a sheeny gown combining the dead-leaf tones and ruddier hues of frost-touched foliage, elaborately draped and festooned with autumn leaves, a coronet of which she wore on her fair hair. Winter, in white furs and powdered hair, was represented by another lady-in-waiting.

"Taking the Veil" is another elaborate subject. There must be black-robed nuns, priests, and acolytes. The novice, attired in white, kneels at an altar rail, and the others are grouped effectively about.

Simplicity is Effective

Romantic subjects are legion, and always form pleasing pictures. If you do not care to go to the trouble of arranging elaborate scenes, every-day subjects may be chosen: something simple and heartfelt, which will be certain to appeal to the audience. Among these may be mentioned the gypsy fortune-teller holding the palm of a shy young girl, while her lover looks on from the background as if trying to hear if he has anything to do with the future that the old hag is pretending to read from the lines in the little hand. The Italian mother holding her baby up to place flowers on the shrine of the Virgin is another lovely tableau, and the young girl bidding adieu to a gay young cavalier is a picture full of grace and spirit.

All of these are easy to manage. Of the more elaborate, nothing could be more thoroughly artistic than a series of pictures from the works of Shakespeare. The heroes and heroines of the great bard lend themselves readily to this style of entertainment. For instance, Othello telling of his triumphs and his troubles to Des-demona and her aged father; the aged King Lear and his daughters; the sleepwalking scene, and the witches' incantation from Macbeth; the wooing of Katharine in King Henry V., and a picture of that other Katharine, the shrew, so greatly in contrast to the gentle French princess.

There are hundreds of them ready to be chosen, but none more attractive than the representation of "Ophelia at the Brook." Let the hair of Ophelia be very dark and her face pale; the figure tall, slender, and graceful. A woman with some dramatic talent or a ready intuition of what is required of her should be chosen for this part. The brook can be formed of gauze stretched over a mirror. Surround it by water plants, vines, ivy,—anything that will give it the appearance of a real brook. All of these can be hired at a florist's if the entertainers are city residents; if not, the woods, even in winter, will furnish sufficient green to answer the purpose. A bough of pine near the foreground can be introduced by tacking it to a screen. Ophelia, in a flowing gown of white, stands gazing into the brook, the right hand uplifted, grasping the bough, while in the left she holds a flower.

Some Other Subjects

A series of tableaux that is peculiarly attractive may be arranged of the various subjects relating to the "Nine Muses," or a composite group could be given under the head of "Progress," showing scene after scene, either simple or elaborate, indicating the strides made in various branches of industry and art from the time that marked their first discovery.

To begin with, America, surrounded by the various peoples of the new world, could be disclosed, the single figure being that of a young girl draped in stars and stripes with the well-known, liberty-cap upon her flowing tresses. While the costumes and setting for every scene may be simple, they should be carried out as gracefully as possible, as detail counts for much in entertainments of this sort.

If the muses are chosen, their single figures or small groups are better than any number of people in one scene. Poetry, Music, Dancing, and Art may be represented with two or three figures if preferred, and the purely classical treatment need not be adhered to so long as the subject is shown in its true light. For instance, Dancing could be just as artistically depicted by young people in costumes of the Orient, or in more civilized garb, instead of the simple hanging folds that draped the Greek goddess.

These pictures need little in the way of properties to make up a delightful *ensemble*. An idea which is both artistic and instructive is to illustrate by living pictures a complete poem or story in prose. In doing this the best in literature becomes a part

of those who are called upon to take a place in it, and, though they could not remember the lines ten minutes after they were spoken, the story without words will live long in their memory.

A tableau club could be formed, and once a month during the winter some play of Shakespeare, or one of the dramatic poems of some other standard author, could be represented in a series of tableaux.

Advantages Derived

All copies of good pictures make fine tableaux. Mythology and history, likewise, furnish many subjects; in fact, the choice is unlimited, and though given purely in the spirit of amusement, still lessons are unconsciously taught, for underlying all the fun is a substratum of instruction that leaves its mark. Subjects, costumes, manners, and customs of ancient days, and the best in literature and art, can all be impressed on the mind in this pleasant way. To the timid no entertainment appeals so strongly, for there are no lines to be earnestly studied and then forgotten in a moment of stage fright, just when **you** had hoped to distinguish yourself before your friends. All that you need to do is to silently lend yourself and your thoughts to the spirit of the pictures, and your tableaux will be successful.

Etiquette of Evening Parties

From *Home Games and Parties*, by Mrs. Hamilton Mott, 1898

There are no iron-clad rules with regard to party etiquette; yet there are certain usual forms observed in good society about which no one can well afford to be ignorant. These forms are not mere conventionalities. They are, like the accepted rules of a well- ordered home, helps to both entertainer and guest.

When printed invitations are issued to the effect that "Mr. and Mrs. A.—will receive their friends on Friday evening, December 8, at nine: residence, 12 H Avenue," those who are invited understand perfectly well that full evening dress, flowers, gloves, and carriages are "the proper thing." In case the invitation cannot be accepted, "regrets" must be sent; otherwise a favorable answer is understood. Such a reception no persons except those named upon the envelope are expected to attend.

Invitations to an "At Home" are usually the ordinary engraved visiting card of the hostess, to which she adds in writing "At Home Friday evening, December 8, from 8 to 10." These, enclosed in dainty white envelopes, are sent out at least one week in advance of the evening named. An "At Home" gives unlimited liberty of dress, ranging from a street costume with bonnet and dark gloves, to full—though quiet—evening toilette. After six o'clock evening dress is the rule for gentlemen. The hostess receives in full toilette, assisted by ladies similarly dressed.

To a party of twenty guests, or fewer, the hostess writes personal notes, which may be sent as late as the day preceding the event, though three or four days earlier assures the guest that he or she has not been taken up at the last moment to fill the place of some one who has declined. "Very Bohemian," advises the person invited that the matter of dress is not important. To such a party a visiting friend may be taken.

The quality and style of stationery are important items. No refined lady will use that which is either cheap or showy. The best is never too good. That which is plain, with no ornamentation, except, perhaps, a monogram, without gilt edge, yet of finest texture and dainty pattern, is always to be preferred. It costs less than the "latest novelties," which often tempt the taste and purse. But let no delusion of *style* lead a hostess to send out other than pearl, cream, or the delicate mode tints, except when a "color tea," or something out of the conventional line of parties, is attempted.

Who shall be invited is always a question more or less perplexing to hostesses. As a rule it is well to consider whether or not one's guests would be congenial. For a formal reception, or an "At Home," it matters not so much how many kinds of people are brought together. Courtesy to host and hostess requires that for the evening, at least, there shall be cordial exchange of civilities; and there is little danger of dullness, since everybody is sure to find somebody with whom to be social.

Special entertainment is not required for a formal reception. Orchestral music is usually furnished. To arrive; to address the hostess and host; to be presented to new people; to pass through the rooms greeting friends and acquaintances here and there; to test the skill of the caterer, then to make one's adieux, is the leaven of conventional routine at large receptions. Musical and literary members, for the purpose of bringing out some promising young artists, are often introduced. It is always in good taste, and certainly a kindly courtesy, to thank and commend those who have contributed entertainment worthy of praise.

Smaller parties may be entertained with music and readings. The hostess is fortunate if among her invited guests there are amateurs who are willing to assist in this way. Novelty parties, such as "Color Teas," Frost, Harlequin, or Pantomime parties; tableaux, which reproduce pictures familiar to the company; living statuary, in color or white; guessing tableaux or amateur theatricals, though involving considerable previous preparation, carry the evening's enjoyment along with very little danger of failure.

For children's parties there is no end of pretty novelties. Among them are marches led by some older young people; familiar stories represented by callisthenic exercises; acting verbs; *tableaux vivants* grouped from illustrated copies of such familiar books as "Alice in Wonderland," "Little Lord Fauntleroy," or, even "Mother Goose;" ring games around the favor tree, etc., are all charming diversions.

In a word, the etiquette of evening parties consists in obeying that quick sense of kindliness which always prompts those receiving to do all in their power for the happiness of their guests; and for the guest to divine the time and place and how to assist their host and hostess so to direct the evening that all may spend it happily and in proper fashion.

Light Refreshments for Evening Companies

From *Home Games and Parties*, by Mrs. Hamilton Mott, 1898

For the unexpected guests the tea or chocolate table must do full duty. Those who entertain a great deal should keep on hand a few boxes of crackers and wafers, a small assortment of potted or devilled meats, olives, caviar, anchovies, and sardines. These being put up in small boxes keep well. Where the means are limited the potted meats, mock *pâté de foie gras* and dainty conserved sweets may be prepared at home at a nominal cost. The art of seasoning counts more in such dishes than the money spent.

Among the best and most sightly wafers to serve with tea are butter thins, Roquefort biscuits, five o'clock teas, outing biscuits, and fairy wafers. The latter come in three colors,—chocolate (brown), vanilla (white), and rose (pink).

The spiced or molasses wafers, fairy cakes, and raglets seem most appropriate to serve with chocolate or cocoa. When means and convenience will allow, these may be purchased, but they may be made at home. If thoroughly baked they will keep for an indefinite time.

Preliminary Preparations for Serving.

When there is but one, or, perhaps, no servant, arrange the table immediately after the evening meal. Decorate it with flowers or fruit, whichever is most available. Flowers are, of course, to be preferred. The plates required may be piled with a folded napkin between each, and placed at one end of the table. At the other end arrange the tea service.

Dishes of bonbons, almonds, and olives may be at once placed. If the ices are to be served in the dining-room, place the service on the sideboard or side table. Place the knives, forks, spoons, and glasses in groups.

The sandwiches may be made and placed between damp napkins in a tin or other box. The salads may be an ready to put together. Aspic forms may be turned out on lettuce leaves and placed in the cold. The wafers and cakes may also be arranged ready for serving.

Where there is not a five o'clock tea-kettle, fill the one in the kitchen with cold water and place it to slowly heat. At the moment it is wanted a little greater heat will at once bring the water to the boiling pointy and then the tea, coffee, and chocolate may be quickly prepared.

Five Simple Menus for Small Parties

Thin Bread and Batter
Chicken Salad   Coffee
Ice Cream and Sponge Cake

Chicken Sandwiches   Coffee
Tomato Aspic on Lettuce with Mayonnaise
Ices   Fancy Cakes

Caviar Sandwiches   Olives

Tongue in Aspic   Bread and Butter

Coffee

Charlotte with Lady-Fingers

Boston Brown-Bread and Butter

Oyster Salad   Coffee

Lemon Jelly   Sunshine Cake

Chicken and Nut Salad

Crescents   Coffee

Neapolitan Ice Cream   Fairy Wafers

For occasions where the number of guests and the formality of the occasion demand an elaborate arrangement of the table, a little greater variety may be served. The present fashion, however, tends to great simplicity in serving refreshments which follow closely the dinner hour.

Chicken in aspic on lettuce leaves with mayonnaise dressing, and tongue, braised and garnished with aspic and olives, are both sightly and appetizing. Boned chickens or boned birds may be sliced, and served with bread and butter and a celery salad. One hot dish, such as an oyster fricassee, creamed sweetbreads, lobster *à la* Newberg, creamed chicken, or lobster *à la* Bordelaise, or terrapin, may precede the salad, making, with a sweet, three courses. Serve these hot dishes on separate plates, in shells or paper cases. The salad may be served on the same plate at the same time.

With any of these dishes thin white or brown bread and butter, rasped rolls, plain bread, rolls, biscuit, or sandwiches of any sort, should be served.

Moulded Lobster in Aspic

Cover half a box of gelatine with half a cup of cold water and allow it to soak for half an hour.

Put into a saucepan a sliced small carrot, a slice of onion, a few celery tops, a bay leaf, and one pint of cold water. Bring slowly to a boil; add a teaspoonful of beef extract, a half teaspoonful of salt, a dash of cayenne, the juice of half a lemon, and the gelatine. Mix and strain. Put a layer of this in small moulds or egg-cups. When hard, fill with bits of boiled lobster. Pour over sufficient of the aspic to cover. Stand aside on the ice for several hours. Serve on lettuce leaves with mayonnaise dressing.

Tomato Aspic and Egyptian Salad

For twelve people one can of tomatoes will be required. Strain, and put them in a saucepan with one slice of onion, two bay leaves, a few celery tops, a teaspoonful of salt, half a teaspoonful of paprika or a dash of cayenne. Bring to boiling-point and add three-quarters of a box of gelatine, which has been soaked in half a cup of cold water for half an hour. Mix until dissolved; add the juice of half a lemon and strain again. Pour into egg-cups or small fancy moulds. Stand aside on ice for four or five hours. When it is time to serve them, dip each mould quickly into boiling water, and turn its contents out on a lettuce leaf. Serve as you would a whole tomato with mayonnaise dressing.

To make an Egyptian salad, boil until tender one three-pound chicken. When cold remove the meat from the bones (rejecting the skin) and cut it into half-inch cubes. Wash a pair of sweetbreads in cold water, put them in boiling water; add two bay leaves, one slice of onion, and four cloves. Boil slowly for half an hour. When cold pick into pieces, rejecting the membrane. Mix with the chicken, then add a quarter of a pound of almonds that have been blanched, and slightly browned in the oven, half a pint of pine nuts, washed and slightly browned. At serving time mix with these a quart of celery cut into small pieces, two teaspoonfuls of salt, half a teaspoonful of paprika or white pepper, half a teaspoonful of curry powder and the juice of two lemons. Mix thoroughly with a pint of mayonnaise dressing and serve on lettuce leaves.

Walnut Sandwiches to Serve with Salad

Shell half a pound of English walnuts. Put the kernels into a pint of boiling water; boil for a minute. Drain, and cover with stock; add a bay leaf, a few celery tops, and a slice of onion; cook gently for twenty minutes; drain and skim; chop fine; add half a teaspoonful of salt and a dash of cayenne. Spread between thin slices of buttered bread and cut in any shape preferred. Serve these with terrapin, lobster *à la* Newberg, duck salad or mock terrapin, which, by the way, makes, a very satisfactory and inexpensive hot dish for an evening party supper.

Mock Terrapin

This makes an inexpensive and very appetizing dish for an evening supper. For twelve persons a pair of ducks and one pound of calf's liver will be required. Clean the ducks, wash the liver, and place them together in a kettle; add two cloves of garlic, one small onion, two stalks of celery, four cloves; cover with boiling water and cook slowly until tender. Take out to cool. When cold cut both into dice. At serving time mash the hard-boiled yolks of six eggs to a smooth paste, adding gradually half a pint of thick cream. Put a quarter of a pound of butter into a saucepan; add a tablespoonful of flour; mix, and add the cream and eggs. Stir constantly until it reaches the boiling point; add half a cap of milk, bring again to a boil; add meat, a teaspoonful of salt, a dash of cayenne, a little white pepper, and just a suspicion of mace. Serve hot.

Celery Rolls Served with Chicken

These may be served alone or as an accompaniment to boned or sliced cold chicken or turkey. Select one dozen small rolls, out from the top a round piece the size of a silver dollar, and scoop out the soft part. When ready to serve, fill with the following mixture: Chop very fine sufficient celery to make a pint and a half. Dust over it a teaspoonful of salt, a salt-spoonful of pepper, a tablespoonful of grated onion, two tablespoonfuls of tomato ketchup, a teaspoonful of Worcestershire, sauce, four tablespoonfuls of olive oil, and one teaspoonful of lemon juice. The tilling may be varied by mixing the seasoned celery with mayonnaise.

Sandwiches of All Sorts and Shapes

The appropriate winter sandwiches are chicken, tongue, ham, beef, mutton, duck, celery, caviar, anchovy, and Indian.

Sweet sandwiches are sometimes served, instead of wafers or bread and butter, with tea or cocoa. They are made from conserved fruits, such as cherries, pineapple, gages, citron, sultanas, figs, dates, and angelicas. The fruits may be used separately or mixed, care being taken to use such as blend in flavors. For instance, cherries, pineapple, and gages, or cherries and figs, angelicas and cherries.

Fruit sandwiches are, as a rule, made from bread, and cut either into small rounds the size of a silver dollar, small crescents, or strips which are called fruit fingers. The crescents may be cut with a round cutter and then cut in half. If the slices are small it is more economical to serve the rounds and crescents at the same time, as the latter suggest themselves by the edges of the first. The fruits must be chopped fine, and slightly moistened with orange juice or a little syrup, and spread in a thin layer on the bread or crackers. Do not cover with a second slice. Nut sandwiches are best served with meat salads; walnuts, pine nuts, or almonds being best with chicken or turkey, and walnut sandwiches alone with duck salad.

Chicken Sandwiches and Tongue Fingers

Chop cold, cooked chicken very fine. Pound until smooth, adding gradually enough thick sweet cream to make a paste. To each pint add a teaspoonful of salt, a dash of pepper, a teaspoonful of onion, and a tablespoonful of lemon juice. This may be made in the early part of the day, and placed in the cold, and later spread on rounds or squares of bread.

Tongue fingers are made by chopping half a pound of cold, cooked salt tongue very fine. Rub to a paste, adding two tablespoonfuls of olive oil and two of lemon juice, a dash of cayenne, and a few drops of onion juice. Cut the end crust from a square loaf of bread, butter the top and cut off a thin slice. Trim off the crusts, and then cut a second slice. Spread on one a layer of the tongue mixture; put over it the other slice; press them together lightly, and then with a sharp knife cut into strips one inch wide.

Touraine Sweets and Chocolates

Cut slices of whole wheat bread into rounds about three inches in diameter. Chop a quarter of a pound of conserved pineapple fine; boil together for a moment four tablespoonfuls of sugar and three of water. When cool add the juice of half an orange, and then mix it with the pineapple. Butter the bread, and then cover over with the fruit. Press it down. Cut angelicas into rings, halve them, and press around the edges of the bread, forming a scallop border. Put a conserved cherry in the centre, and dish on a handsome round cut-glass or china plate.

Touraine chocolates are also made from whole wheat bread. Butter the loaf, cut off the slice, and then cut it into strips an inch wide and the length of the slice. Cover each strip with melted sweet chocolate; dust over at once chopped almonds, walnuts, or pistachio nuts. Stand aside for an hour or so to harden.

Fairy Wafers and Sweet Raglets

Beat half a pound of butter to a cream, adding gradually half a pound of granulated sugar. Dissolve half a teaspoonful of baking soda in two tablespoonfuls of warm water, and add it to the sugar; then add one tablespoonful of ginger, half a pint of milk; mix, and work in gradually one quart of sifted pastry flour. Spread the mixture in a very thin layer on baking sheets which have been lightly greased, and bake in a moderate oven. Cut into squares and roll while hot, or they may be cut into small strips.

Raglets must be made and used the same day. Put two ounces of butter in half a pint of water over the fire. When boiling, stir in hastily half a pint of pastry flour; beat until smooth. Take from the fire, and when cool break into the mixture one egg; beat a moment, add a second egg, and so continue until four eggs have been used. Beat thoroughly; fill the mixture into a pastry bag; press it in curious shapes into hot fat, a little at a time. When sufficiently brown, roll the raglets in powdered sugar and cinnamon.

Fancy Sandwiches of All Kinds

Fancy sandwiches of all kinds may be served with coffee. Thin bread and butter, both white and brown, may also be served. Salads, such as shrimp, lobster, chicken, celery, tomato, or Egyptian, served with thin bread and butter and coffee, are always in order. A lemon, orange, or fruit jelly with sponge or sunshine cake may form the sweet.

One thing the hostess should bear in mind when serving refreshments, and that is that thin bread and butter or plain cake, nicely served with a cup of good chocolate or coffee, is better than a great variety of dishes poorly prepared and served.

Appendix 1: Trees, Stars, and Birds

Becoming Acquainted with Trees

From *Trees, Stars, and Birds: A Book of Outdoor Science* by Edwin Lincoln Moseley, 1919

Trees have a fascination for us that abides as long as we live. The coming of the leaves on the bare branches is one of the most pleasing signs of spring; the deep green of the summer foliage is restful to the eyes; the red and gold of the autumn woods is one of the most splendid sights of nature; and even in winter the play of shadows and colors in a woodland is beautiful to behold. In the early history of our country trees were so plentiful that they were destroyed to get them out of the way. Now millions of them are planted every year. We like them about us because they are pleasing to our eyes and afford a source of interest and healthful enjoyment to our minds.

But trees are useful as well as beautiful. They shade us from the summer's sun and help to break the force of the winter winds. Their fruits and seeds are a most important source of food for men and animals, and, above all, they furnish us wood, without which civilized life would not be possible. Much of the material for our houses and vehicles is wood; the paper of the book you are reading is made from wood; your pencil, chair, and desk are mostly wood; and it is probable that in any household fifty different articles could be found that are made wholly or in part from the products of trees. Millions of persons are engaged in making these articles and in procuring and preparing the necessary materials. A knowledge of trees and woods is, therefore, not only satisfying to our minds, but useful in every kind of manual work. Few subjects that we study have more practical value than trees and the woods that come from them.

Jesse E. Hyde

Fig. 2. A sugar maple in summer.

Studying trees by seeing and thinking. The following pages will help you to become acquainted with some of the trees that are common over large parts of the United States and with others that are especially useful to us. But reading a book about trees is of little use, if you do not observe the trees themselves. Notice the buds, blossoms, and fruit, the shape of the tree and arrangement of its branches, the color of the bark, the peculiarities of the leaves, and whether any of these parts has a characteristic odor or taste. Try to answer the questions you will find in the various chapters by making the necessary observations yourself or by reflecting on what you have already observed or read. Perhaps some one at home will be interested in discussing these questions with you. If not, do the best you can in answering them alone. When they come up in class, you will learn what others think about them, but knowing this will be of little use to you unless you have thought about them yourself. Other questions as

Jesse E. Hyde

Fig. 3. The same tree in winter.

interesting and important as any of those in the book may suggest themselves to your mind. Try to answer these, too, for yourself before asking any one else about them.

How to make a collection. To learn to know the trees, their names, peculiarities, and uses, do not merely read about them, but look at them and take leaves and other parts to keep for further examination and for comparison with other trees. In gathering leaves for your collection, select those that have not been eaten by insects or damaged in other ways. Unless the leaves are very large, cut off a twig with several typical leaves attached. If you cannot press your specimens at once, you may prevent withering by keeping them inclosed in a box or laying them in a large magazine.

For pressing leaves, use absorbent paper like large sheets of blotting paper, or the soft felt paper that is used under carpets. If you cannot get either of these kinds of paper, place several thicknesses of newspapers between each two specimens. Spread out the leaves on a sheet of the absorbent paper in such a way that each leaf will lie flat and will not cover other leaves. It may be necessary to trim off some of them. Let at least one leaf of each specimen show its under side. Cover the first specimen with absorbent paper and upon this paper spread out another specimen, continuing in this way until you have put into the press all the good specimens you

have collected. With each specimen place a strip of paper telling where you found it, the date, and the name of the tree, if you know it. Then put the pile of papers and specimens where it will not be in the way and cover it with a board on which is placed a stone or some other convenient weight. For a few delicate specimens a weight of 15 or 20 pounds will suffice. Ordinarily a heavier weight will be better.

The day after you put the specimens in the press, change the drying sheets. If you use felt paper, one or two changes at intervals of a day or two will probably suffice for the leaves of most trees. If newspapers are used for "driers," they should be changed each day until the specimens are dry. In pressing delicate plant specimens it is easier to handle them if you lay each one in a folded sheet of thin paper before putting it into the press. You need not remove it from this thin paper when you change the drying sheets, or before you find time to mount the dry specimen.

The slat press. If you have the tools and materials, you can make a slat press, to which pressure is applied by means of a cord or by straps. Such a press is convenient to handle at home and may be carried to the woods. It makes better-looking specimens than a board press, because it is somewhat flexible and applies pressure along the edges as well as in the middle and thus keeps the tips of all the leaves flat.

Mounting specimens. To preserve the pressed spedmens so that they can be examined without

Figs. 4-5. A slat press for drying specimens of leaves and flowers.

risk of breaking, mount them on sheets of unruled stiff white paper. You can fasten them to the paper with glue, but you will find strips of gummed paper or linen more satisfactory for this purpose. These may be purchased from a botanical supply house or possibly at a printing office or stationer's. A neat label may be attached to the sheet. It should give the name of the tree, the place where it grows, the date when the specimen was collected, and the collector's name. Do not mount leaves from more than one kind of tree on the same sheet, as that would interfere with a systematic arrangement of the specimens. If the bark of the tree is peculiar and a thin piece can easily be obtained, attach it to the same sheet as the leaves.

All the sheets of closely related specimens, e.g., the different kinds of maples or oaks, should be placed together in a folder made of a larger sheet of strong manila paper, or a large-paged blank book may be used for mounting the specimens. A bookbinder will prepare suitable books at a small cost for each pupil, if enough of them can be ordered at one time; it is best to have the sheets removable, so as to make possible the insertion of specimens in their proper order. If a suitable book cannot be obtained, a pasteboard box may be used to hold the sheets, or they may be perforated and fastened together in book form by tying them with a shoestring or ribbons.

Fruit collections. The term "fruit" as used in botany means the part of the plant that contains the seed. It may be fleshy or dry, edible or quite unfit for food. From what part of the blossom does it develop? Frequently a tree can be most easily identified by its fruit, and when possible specimens of the fruit should be collected with the leaves. Fruits that are dry and thin may be attached to the same sheets as the leaves.

Have also a collection of fruits in a box. A strong paper box 3 or 4 inches deep and a foot or so in length may be divided into a score or more of compartments by partitions running both ways. It is best to have the partitions not more than half as high as the box; they are merely to keep the specimens from the same tree together, and apart from those of different trees. Some compartments should be larger than others, to accommodate cones and other large specimens. More than one box may well be used for the fruit collection; or, instead of using a box with partitions, you may sew the fruit specimens to a card or to the inside of a pasteboard box—say a suit box—that can be closed and put away.

Arrangement of specimens. Whatever method is used for keeping the specimens of leaves and fruit in place, they should be arranged according to some plan. Usually they are arranged according to their natural classification. Specimens from different kinds of oak, for instance, will be placed near each other, preceded or followed by beech and chestnut, which belong to the same family as the oak; likewise walnut and the different kinds of hickory will be associated.

School collections. The directions given above refer to individual collections. For use in the schoolroom, large cardboards can be prepared, with specimens of leaves or other parts or products of trees mounted on them. They should be arranged, not with a view to making a design or picture, but to facilitate a comparison of things that are related.

If you wish to preserve for a time the autumnal tints of the foliage, gather leaves that are free from blemishes and ragged edges, and press them for a day or so between blotters. Then dip them in barely melted paraffin and press them between papers with a hot iron. Leaves prepared in this way look very pretty mounted on green cardboard.

Collections of woods. In Europe so few kinds of wood are in common use that woodworkers soon learn to recognize the different kinds. But the number of woods in use in America is so large that even lumbermen, carpenters, and cabinet makers rarely are able to distinguish closely related kinds. They know red oak from white oak, but do not distinguish the various species that are sold under the name of red oak or of white oak.

To learn to recognize a dozen or more kinds of wood is easy. The best way to do this is to get samples from persons who know what they are, label them, and then find articles that are made of these different kinds of wood. Every pupil should have, either at home or in the schoolroom, a collection of this kind, and the school should have a larger collection. The samples can be obtained from various sources, some of which will be suggested by the uses of the wood given for the different species in this book. At a woodworking shop it is often possible to obtain small pieces of a dozen kinds, some of them in sufficient quantity for a class. By visiting more than one such shop quite a variety can be procured without any expense. If the manager is willing to have the whole class visit the factory at one time, much can be learned. You may send any specimens of wood concerning which you are doubtful to the United States Forest Products Laboratory, Madison, Wisconsin, for identification.

Many useful tree products besides wood and fruit are mentioned in the following chapters. A collection of them might be so arranged as to make an instructive exhibit in a schoolroom. Of course there are many trees not mentioned in this book that are just as interesting to those who live where they grow as any that are included here.

The Structure of a Tree

From *Trees, Stars, and Birds: A Book of Outdoor Science* by Edwin Lincoln Moseley, 1919

We are awed by the grandeur of a great tree; it is the largest and the oldest of living things. Its roots penetrate deep into the earth to anchor the tree in its place and to gather water and food materials from the soil. Its trunk and branches hold the crown of leaves up to the light. It is a living being like ourselves and also a structure that, like a tall building, must carry a great weight and withstand the force of the winds. And so well is this structure planned and built that generations of men and animals may come and go and even nations may rise and fall while a tree lives on and on. In nearly every part of the United States there are trees still standing that Indian children may have played under before the white man came, and some of the trees that are still growing in the Western states had already reached a large size before Julius Cæsar or Hannibal was born. One way in which a tree

Fig. 6. The "Boone Tree" near Jonesboro, Tennessee. On it was carved: "D. Boon cilied A BAR on the tree in year 1760." The tree was blown down in 1916. It was a beech about 90 feet tall.

U. S. Forest Service

differs from a person is that some of its parts are always young; for unlike ourselves, trees grow as long as they live.

Only part of a living tree alive. The outer bark of an old tree is dead and a great part of the wood is dead. But just as the dead mineral material that is found in the bones of men and animals is useful in supporting them, so the dead wood of a tree forms a skeleton and holds the tree in place; and as the dead outer layers of our skin protect the living tissues beneath, so the dead outer bark of a tree protects the living parts within. The dead parts, of course, do not grow, but they form a skeleton that is useful in supporting and protecting the tree. Each year a new set of leaves, twigs, and small roots are produced, and the part that has changed to wood and died is buried within the tree to aid in its support. You have seen trees with hollow trunks whose crowns remained thrifty. In such trees it is not the living part but the dead wood in the heart that has decayed; but a tree in this condition is more likely to be blown down than one whose trunk is sound throughout.

The living material of a tree. The living parts of a tree, like the living parts of every other plant and animal, are composed of *cells*. In the young growing parts the cells are shaped like little boxes fitted together in an irregular manner. Each cell has a wall about it, and the inside of the cell is composed of living material called *protoplasm*, which in appearance is something like raw white of egg. Besides the protoplasm there is usually watery sap and often starch or other food material stored in a

Fig. 7. Cells from a moss leaf.

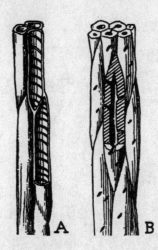

Fig. 8. Tracheids from a basswood tree (A), and wood fibers from a hard maple (B).

plant cell, but only the protoplasm is alive. Although most cells are too small to be seen with the naked eye, the cells in such material as the thin leaf of a moss or the skin from the bulb of an onion may easily be seen with a compound microscope. A tree, therefore, though it appears to be but a single thing, is in reality made of many small parts. A leaf is like a great structure built up of many hundreds of little boxes, and all the other living parts of a tree are, in the same way, built of many parts.

How the wood is formed in a tree. The cells in the tip of a growing shoot or root of a tree are all alike, but as they grow older great changes take place in many of them. Some of them grow wider and at the same time become greatly elongated. Then the cell walls are thickened by woody material being laid down on the inside of them. Finally, the end walls are absorbed, so that each cell is connected with the one above and below to form a long tube. The living matter in the cells then dies, leaving long, empty vessels, sometimes several inches or even several feet in length, made of cells joined end to end within the plant. These vessels are called *tracheæ* (singular, *trachea*). Through them water flows up to the leaves. In the cut end of a grapevine, in the root of a willow, and in many woods these large vessels are plainly visible as open pores. Is it possible to draw air through them?

Others of the cells become changed into *tracheids*. These have thicker walls than the tracheæ,

and the end walls are not absorbed. They do not, therefore, form long open vessels in the tree, and the water makes its way from tracheid to tracheid by passing through thin places in the walls. The tracheids conduct water more slowly than do the much larger tracheæ that have no cross walls, but they give more strength to the wood.

A third element that is prominent in wood, especially in hard woods, is the *wood fibers*. These are formed by groups of cells elongating and forming slender fibers with pointed ends and thick walls. These fibers are much like the tracheids, but they are smaller and have walls so thick that the spaces within them are sometimes almost closed. They do not conduct water, but when the protoplasm in them dies they stand in a tree like bundles of little, tightly sealed tubes filled with air. The function of the wood fibers is to give strength to the wood; their thick walls make it difficult to crush or break them. Oak wood has in it dense bundles of these fibers, and other hard and heavy woods also are richly supplied with them.

It should be understood also that in all woods many of the cells do not change into vessels or fibers, but retain their thin walls, and except in the older wood remain alive. They are called *parenchyma* cells. The pith of a tree is composed of cells of this kind, and in a freshly cut stump or log strands of these cells, called *medullary rays,* or pith rays, may be seen running out from the center to the bark. Cells of this

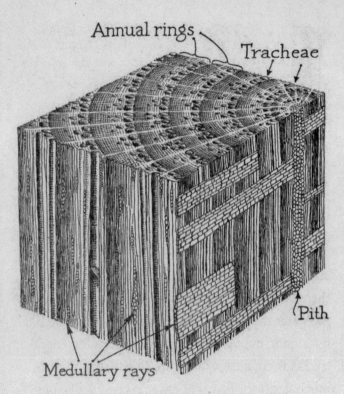

Annual rings

Tracheae

Pith

Medullary rays

Fig. 9. The structure of wood (diagrammatic).

kind may also be scattered through the wood; or they may lie in groups or run in chains, crosswise or up and down, in the wood, making connections with each other and with the living portions of the bark. These living cells are found in the wood of the roots as well as in the trunks and branches of trees. They make up a considerable part of many woods, sometimes as much as a quarter of the whole, and along with the tracheæ are the weakest elements in the wood. If the bark were hewed from a pine, it is estimated that the ends of 15,000 fine rays would be exposed on each square inch of surface. In oaks some of the rays are an inch, and in some species of oak even 4 or 5 inches, in height, and may be seen as light-colored bands running through the wood; but for each large ray that you see in a piece of oak there are perhaps one hundred too small to be seen without a lens.

These four elements are found arranged in various ways and in different proportions in all our hard woods. The woods of pines, cedars, firs, and other evergreens are composed of tracheids and parenchyma cells. They lack the large open vessels and the dense bundles of wood fibers and are therefore very even in texture.

How a tree grows in height. In the tip of a tender root or shoot each cell is growing; it increases in size by taking in food and out of this food building up more protoplasm. After the cell reaches a certain size, a partition is built across it which divides it into two cells. In like manner the two may become four, and so on until a large number of cells have been formed. This multiplication of cells and the increase in size of the cells as they become old cause growth.[1] The trunk of a tree is built upward, and the branches and roots increase in length in this way. New material is built on the top of the trunk, and added to the tips of the branches and roots by the multiplication of the cells in these parts.

Proof of where the trunk lengthens. It is said that if two nails are driven into a living tree trunk, one 6 feet above the other, they will remain 6 feet apart, no matter how long the tree grows. Driving nails into a trunk is not good for the tree or for the saw that may sometime cut it into lumber. Without driving in nails or waiting for years to see the result, you can decide about the lengthening of a trunk by examining trees that have been used as posts for a wire fence. You may find some in which the wire and staples have been covered by years of growth. Are the wires farther apart and higher above the ground than where they were fastened to dead posts? How do you account for the fact that on old trees the distance from the ground to the lowest limbs is so much greater than on young trees?

---

[1]In older plant cells there is usually in the center of the cell a large amount of water ("cell sap") in which mineral matter and certain food materials are dissolved. The taking in of this water stretches the cell and greatly enlarges it,—sometimes to several hundred times the size it has before the absorbing of the water begins. It is this pumping of water into the young shoots that causes the young branches of trees to push out so rapidly in the spring.

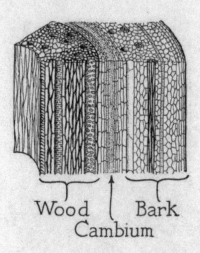

Fig. 10. The cambium is a growing layer between the wood and the bark.

Wood | Bark
Cambium

Where is the growth in a tree, that causes the trunk to become longer?

Mark off with ink the first foot of the end of a rapidly growing vine or other shoot into inch spaces. Watch the plant for a number of days. Where do the marks become separated most widely?

How a tree grows in diameter. A tree increases in diameter through the growth of the *cambium*. This is a layer of growing cells just inside the bark. Each year the cells of the cambium multiply; during the growing season they are constantly being divided by longitudinal partitions which cut off layers of cells on both the inside and outside of the cambium. On the outside this forms a thin layer of tissues in the inner part of the bark; inside the cambium a new layer of wood is laid down. Thus each year a sheet of wood is laid upon the tree from the outside. This causes the tree to increase in diameter.

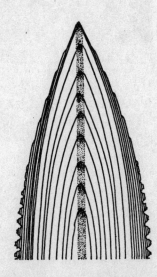

Fig. 11. Diagram showing the structure of a tree. The dotted part in the center represents the pith. The diagram is of course much wider in proportion to its length than is the trunk of a tree.

If you could remove from a tree the layer of wood that is added in a single year, what shape would it have? Do the layers of wood that were formed when the tree was young reach to the top of the tree? Do you understand that if you could begin with the outermost and remove the layers of wood one by one from the trunk of an unbranched tree, you would take off a series of thin-walled hollow columns which taper to a point above and which in the tree fit over one another? The column which grew last year incloses the one that grew the year before, and the columns that will grow in the years to come will be fitted about those that are now standing in place.

Springwood and summerwood. When a pine tree begins its growth in the spring, comparatively large vessels with thin walls are formed. Later in the summer, as growth becomes slower, the vessels formed are smaller and have thicker walls; the openings in them are much smaller than the openings in the springwood. We have in the tree, therefore, alternating layers of light springwood and of denser summerwood. This causes the appearance of rings in the wood, which you have often seen. In different kinds of trees there are often differences in the springwood and summerwood.

The bark of a tree. The inner cells of the bark of a tree are alive, and as the tree increases in size the bark grows by the multiplication of these cells. Thus the bark increases in thickness year by year, unless at the same time the outer layers are scaling off and falling away. Why are the outer layers of bark on an old oak or elm furrowed and broken? Why is the bark of an oak or elm rougher than the bark of a sycamore **or** birch of the same size?

Cork and how it is formed. In the bark of trees the outer cells become changed into cork. This is done by thickening the cell walls with a waxlike material, after which the protoplasm in the cells dies. The corky layer of cells thus formed protects the tree from drying and also keeps out fungi that would otherwise attack the tree and cause decay. An idea of the great usefulness of the cork may be gained by noting what happens to an Irish potato when the thin, corky layer on its surface is broken or removed. When this is injured, decay very readily sets in, and a peeled potato loses water sixty times as fast as one that has its protective coat. In the cork oak the corky layer is of great thickness and is removed from the tree in large slabs. Examine the stoppers of bottles and see if you can find evidences of annual rings in them. Can you explain why a cork does not become water-soaked as a piece of wood does?

Vessels and fibers in the bark. The inner part of the bark is a layer of tissues consisting of vessels for conducting food, cells in which food is stored, and long, slender, and strong fibers. The latter are called *bast fibers* and are very abundant in some trees. Why do beetles and borers often feed on this layer of tissues in a tree? Will the roots of a tree die if the bark on the trunk is cut all around it? Why?

Telling the age of trees. On the top of a stump or the end of a log you can often count the rings. To determine the age of the tree, do you count the springwood and summerwood as representing two years or one? In exceptional cases, as when a drought divides the growing season into two parts, two fairly distinct rings may form in one year, but generally you can tell the age of a tree quite closely by counting the number of rings. If the section whose rings you are counting was not made near the ground, you must make allowance for the time it took for the tree to attain that height.

Are the annual rings all of equal thickness in the same stump? Are there places where you can count twice as many to the inch as in other places? What may have caused the tree to grow more in some years than in others? Can you think of a way to test the correctness of your explanation? How could you find out, without asking any one to tell you and without reading about it, whether a certain kind of tree grows fast or slowly? On the stump or

Fig. 12.   The monarch oak, the patriarch of the trees,
Shoots rising up, and spreads by slow degrees.
Three centuries he grows, and there he stays
Supreme in state; and in three more decays.

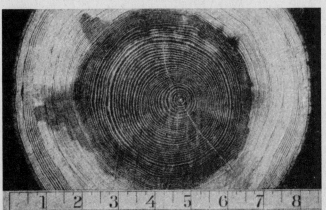

Fig. 13.   Section through a white ash almost 100 years old. It grew in a thick forest, but 12 years before it was cut some of the trees about it were blown down by a severe storm. Study the rings and see what you can learn of the life of the tree from them.

other section of a tree or of a branch, is the same ring uniform in thickness all the way round? How do you account for this? Frequently disputes about the ownership of land have been decided by the age of trees and by counting the rings to find how many years ago a certain mark was placed on a tree by a surveyor.

You will find it interesting to fix as nearly as possible the date when some large tree first began to grow. If you are careful, you will probably come near the actual date. Having done this, try to form a mental picture or give a description of the surrounding country when this tree was a young sapling. Regarding the tree as an individual which has suffered and enjoyed many experiences, you might write a story of its life, an imaginary autobiography, telling what it has seen and done.

Identifying Trees

From Trees, Stars, and Birds: A Book of Outdoor Science by Edwin Lincoln Moseley, 1919

Maples

Maple trees may be found in most parts of the United States and southern Canada. The larger kinds are widely planted for shade, and smaller varieties with cut leaves or richly colored foliage are often used for ornamental purposes in parks and on lawns. Some maples produce wood that is hard and handsome, and the leaves of many kinds show beautiful autumn coloration.

The blossoms of the maple are small, but they abound in honey and are very attractive to bees. In spring or early summer the peculiar key fruit is produced (Fig. 17). Among children, who like to eat them, these are known as "chickens." At the base of each wing is a seed. Have you ever noticed it? Are the leaves on one branch sometimes more highly colored than those on the rest of the tree? Will this branch show the same peculiarity year after year?

Making maple sugar. You have eaten maple sugar or maple sirup. It is made usually from sap of the sugar maple, occasionally from that of other maples. Good sugar may be obtained also from hickory or birch sap.

The first warm days in February or March start the sap flowing. Then the tree is tapped—that is, a hole is bored through the bark into the wood—and a spile, or little spout, is inserted so that the sap will flow along it and be caught in a bucket instead of trickling down the trunk of the tree. The rise of the sap in early spring is due partly to freezing and thawing; therefore a succession of warm days and

Fig. 14. Tapping the tree.

cold nights is necessary for a continuous flow. Later in the spring the sap becomes watery and bitter and is not suitable for sugar making. From 25 to 50 pounds of maple sap must be boiled down to obtain 1 pound of sugar.

A group, or orchard, of sugar maples is called a "sugar bush." The place where the sugar is made is called a "sugar camp." Oftentimes one or more sheds are built in the woods to accommodate those who gather the sap and keep up the fires under the kettle or great pans that are used in evaporating the water from the sap. Boys enjoy the work of sugar making and often stay in the camps at night. Nevertheless, much labor is required to produce a gallon of sirup or a few pounds of sugar. Can you think of three reasons why genuine maple sugar is expensive?

The maple-sugar industry has become so important in some of the Northern states and

U.S. Forest Service

Fig. 15. Collection the sap.

R. E. Horsey

Fig. 16. Silver map in winter.

Canada that those who engage in it make use of improved evaporators. These are broad, shallow pans with a number of partitions that do not reach entirely across the pan. The openings left between these partitions and the sides of the pan alternate, so that the sap in flowing around the partitions goes from one side of the evaporator to the other. As water is continually being driven off by the fire under the pan, what was at first thin sap has become thick sirup by the time it reaches the farther end of the evaporator. This sirup may be converted into sugar by driving off still more water. To test the boiled sap, a small amount is stirred and cooled in a saucer. If it granulates and adheres to the spoon and saucer, evaporation has gone on long enough, and the hot sirup is poured into molds to form cakes of sugar of the desired shape.

Maple sugar, like that made from sugar cane, is darker than ordinary brown sugar, unless the impurities are removed. To do this milk or beaten eggs are stirred into the boiling maple sap. This causes most of the coloring matter to rise to the top and mingle with the froth, which is then skimmed off. Those who live near sugar bushes enjoy making and eating maple wax. This is formed by letting the hot sirup fall upon snow or ice.

The sugar made by the leaves of the trees. The leaves are the food-making organs of a plant, and the sugar that is obtained from maple sap in the spring was made the summer before by the leaves of the tree. As the sugar is manufactured it passes down from the leaves into the trunk and roots of the tree, and is stored in the living cells of these parts in the form of starch. Then when food is needed in the spring to enable the buds to grow and expand into blossoms and leaves, and to produce the seeds, the starch is changed back to sugar, which is dissolved out of the storage cells and carried upward in the sap.

The sugar that is manufactured by the leaves is made from water, which is absorbed by the roots and passed up through the vessels of the wood, and from carbon dioxid, a gas that is taken in from the air. In the leaves these are united to form sugar. Leaves cannot do this work without light; when the sun shines on them it supplies the energy for the process.

Uses of the wood of the maple. The sugar maple is called also "hard maple." Try to cut a piece across the grain with a knife or saw and see whether it is the hardest wood you have. Hardwood floors are often made of maple, the pieces of which have been planed and matched with tongue and groove. Maple wood is used for this purpose because it has no soft places to wear away and leave the floor uneven or splintered.

Fig. 17. Leaves and fruit of silver maple (A) and red maple (B).

"Bird's-eye maple" is an ornamental wood obtained from certain sugar-maple trees of the same species as those whose wood is straight-grained. "Curly maple" is found in this species as well as in the soft maples.

Until a tree is cut it is seldom possible to tell whether its wood will show these peculiarities.

Have you seen maple furniture? Try to find examples of bird's-eye maple and of curly maple. Tool handles, rulers, butcher's blocks, piano actions, and the backs and sides of violins often are made of hard maple. This wood is used also for shoe lasts and pegs, croquet balls and mallets, for various implements, and in the construction of machinery, cars, and automobiles. It has a fine and even grain, polishes well, and is heavy, hard, strong, and elastic. Which of these properties are most needed in a wood used for each of the purposes mentioned?

The sugar maple as a shade tree. The sugar maple is one of the very best of our shade trees. It is well shaped, affords dense shade in summer, and in autumn becomes beautiful because of the rich and varied colors of its foliage. In the spring its blossoms unfold with the leaves. It grows more slowly than the soft maples, but it requires less moisture and is more useful and durable.

Red and silver maples. The red maple and silver maple are both soft maples. They are extensively planted for shade, but like the sugar maple they grow wild also in all our Eastern states, and in southeastern Canada, and as far west as Kansas. You will not find it easy to distinguish these maples at all times from each other or from other maples. In autumn the leaves of the red maple turn crimson, and where this species abounds it adds much to the beauty of the woods at that season. Its blossoms, which are red, open before the leaves.

The silver maple, also called "white maple," grows larger than the red maple. It is one of the most common of shade trees, although not always known by its correct name. The leaves are pale underneath, but not so white as those of the white poplar. Its blossoms open in advance of its leaves, before most kinds of trees show signs of life.

Experience has shown that the silver maple, in spite of its rapid growth, is a poor tree for street planting. Many kinds of insects eat the foliage or bore into the trunk. The breaking of its limbs causes much trouble. In the living tree the wood is quite subject to decay. When the tree is cut down, even the wood that is still sound is not very valuable, but both silver maple and red maple are now used for woodenware and flooring.

The Norway maple. Of late years the Norway maple has been planted in many cities in the United States. Its flowers are greenish yellow; its leaves are large and remain green until late in autumn. The leafstalks contain a milky juice. This tree is remarkably free from insects and has proved a very satisfactory shade tree.

Fig. 18. Leaves and fruit of silver maple (C) and Norway maple (D).

Maple leaves and their arrangement. Notice that the leaves of different kinds of maples differ a little in shape. All have, however, the main veins diverging from the leafstalk, whereas elm leaves have a midrib with veins coming off on each side. The former arrangement is called *palmate* (palmlike); the latter is *pinnate* (featherlike). Find other examples of palmate and of pinnate leaves. Which is wider in comparison with its length, a palmate or a pinnate leaf?

The maples have the leaves and twigs *opposite* each other on the stem, as contrasted with the *alternate* leaves and twigs of the elm (Fig. 23). Find other examples of opposite and alternate leaves.

The ash-leaved maple. This tree, more commonly called the "box elder," is a maple, as its fruit shows. It differs from the other maples, however, in having *compound* instead of *simple* leaves; that is, its leaves are cut into a number of leaflets instead of being all in one piece. In ordinary locations it is not so desirable a shade tree as some of the other maples, but it grows rapidly and may be planted in sandy or gravelly soil, where most other trees do not thrive. The box elder is distinguished from other trees with opposite leaves by the green bark of the young shoots. This tree is rare east of the Appalachians, but can be found in most parts of the United States with the exception of the states in the northwestern portion.

Fig. 19. Leaves and fruit of the ash-leaved maple or "box elder." This maple, unlike the other members of the family, has compound leaves.

The maple family. Nearly one hundred species of maples are known in the wild state, most of them growing in the north temperate zone. Some are found on mountains, others on ground that is low and wet. Most species thrive best in rich, moist soil. They differ greatly in size; some of the Japanese species, which are cultivated in this country on account of the rich colors of the finely divided foliage, seem like dwarfs when compared with our great sugar maples, which tower to a height of 100 feet.

Considering their wide distribution, the great number that have been planted, and the variety of uses made of them, we may well give maples a prominent place among important trees.

Maple seeds dispersed by the wind. Out of doors, when the wind is blowing, drop a maple seed from a height of several yards and see whether it falls straight down. Does it acquire a whirling motion? Does this retard its descent? Is it better for the seeds of a maple to fall close to the tree or to be carried to distant places? Why? Are seeds more likely to get loose from the tree on still days or windy days? How far do you suppose the wind carries them? Name different kinds of trees with winged fruits; name some kinds whose seeds have cottonlike appendages that enable them to be carried through the air. Have you seen young maples pushing up in lawns or along fences?

Leaves and light. Examine Figure 18. The stalk of one leaf has lengthened and pushed the leaf out to the light, past the other leaves on the tip of the branch. Almost any maple tree will show this interesting leaf arrangement on dozens of its twigs.

Study the plants that are growing about you and note that leaves always seek the light. When a vine grows on a wall, each leaf fits itself into its space as best it can to receive the light. Note the arrangement of the leaves on a plantain or a dandelion. Do the upper leaves grow so that they will not cover the lower ones, or must the lower

Fig. 20. White birches.

U.S. Forest Service

Fig. 21. River birches.

U.S. Forest Service

leaves take care of themselves? Does each leaf on a tree grow as it pleases, or is there some outside directing force that causes each one to take its proper place?

Birches

Because of their grace and beauty birches are a favorite subject for landscape artists and photographers, and they are frequently planted in parks and on lawns. The white and the paper birch are the species of birch most frequently planted for ornamental purposes. They are especially effective when placed among evergreens, because of the contrast in colors. Many of the white birches have slender, drooping branchlets with deeply cut leaves that might be taken for those of some varieties of maples. White birch grows wild in Europe and Canada and to some extent in our Northern states, but with us the paper birch is more common. Where a forest of spruce or of certain species of pine—as white pine—has been burned, paper birch and aspens spring up. In the abundant sunlight of the open spaces these trees grow more rapidly than seedlings of the spruce or pine, and a forest of birch and aspen grows up in place of the evergreen forest.

Birch bark. The yellow birch has yellowish or silver-gray bark which has an aromatic odor. The bark of the white birch and paper birch is creamy or pinkish white and splits into paperlike layers. From birch bark the Indians made canoes, as well as boxes, buckets, baskets, kettles, and dishes. In making their canoes, they stitched together large plates of birch bark with the fibrous roots of white spruce, coating the seams with resin obtained from spruce and pine trees. If you can get a piece of the bark, see into how many layers you can split it.

In parts of northern Europe the bark of the white birch is used for shingles. Boats made from it are used on the Volga River. From it are made birch oil and birch tar. Russia leather has an aromatic odor due to the oil of birch bark used in tanning it. As the odor repels insects, this leather is valuable for binding books. A few such bindings in a bookcase are a safeguard against insect enemies, and this oil is said also to prevent damage to the books by mildew.

Birch wood. The wood of the white birch is used as a fuel for smoking hams and herrings, because of the flavor which it imparts. Being light colored, soft, and easily worked, it is used for making spoons, ladles, bowls, and fish casks. Spools, wooden shoes, ox yokes, chairs, and tables also are made of it. Charcoal made from it is burned in forges, and soot made from birch fires is used for making printer's ink.

The wood of the paper birch is used for fuel, shoe pegs, spools, and toys. The yellow birch and sweet birch yield wood that makes fine furniture and a good interior finish for houses. It is often stained dark red and varnished. It is then said to have a "mahogany finish." Few trees are useful for so many purposes as is the birch.

Birches in the far north. The paper birch grows in Newfoundland, in Labrador, about Great Slave Lake, and along the valley of the Yukon. Dwarf birches, which are mere shrubs, grow even farther north. They are common in Greenland and in the arctic barrens of America and Asia, beyond the northern limit of trees. In these frigid regions the birches have for companions several kinds of willows, only a few inches tall, crowberry, bearberry, and a number of other low shrubs, besides lichens, mosses, and, during the short summer season, many herbs with brightly colored blossoms.

Size of branches and size of leaves. Have you ever thought of any connection between the size of a tree's leaves and the coarseness or slenderness of its branches? Even in winter birch trees look quite different from ash or hickory, not merely in color but in the appearance of the branchlets. Can you explain the difference? Name several trees with slender branchlets and others with thick branchlets.

The function of the branches is to hold the leaves up to the light, and the number of branches required depends on the size of the leaves. Trees with small leaves, like birch, elm, and willow, have very numerous branchlets. Those with large leaves, like ash and hickory, do not require so many branchlets. The leaves themselves reach out to the light and fill up the spaces in the crown of the tree. Most palm trees, of which there are a thousand kinds in the tropics, do not branch at all, but they have immense leaves with long stalks to reach out to the light.

Breathing pores in the bark of small branches. On the twigs or small branches of a tree look for small oblong and elevated places on the bark. These are called *lenticels*. They are breathing pores through which the air can enter to reach the living inner portion of the bark and from which water vapor escapes. On birch and cherry trees the lenticels may be seen not only on the branches but even on the trunk. Here they have become elongated by the growth of the bark. Does their long axis extend across the tree, or up and down?

Lenticels are to be found on all trees. Where the bark is very thick, as it is on old oaks, they are at the bottom of the deep cracks.

Elms

In the wild state elms are common throughout most of the country. In many cities they are planted for shade more generally than any other kind of tree, for in deep soil they grow fast and make large, well-shaped trees. The elm is one of the first trees to show signs of life in the spring, and at this season it has a peculiarly graceful and airy appearance. The flowers do not attract much attention, although they appear before the leaves. The winged fruits soon develop and are blown away by the wind, some falling where the seed may grow into another great tree.

The American elm. Without the flowers or fruit, or even the leaves, an American elm may be

Fig. 22. Elm at Northampton, Massachusetts. It is 75 feet high, 18 feet in circumference, and has a spread of 125 feet.

Journal of Heredity

American Forestry

Fig. 23.　Leaves, flowers, and fruits of American elm.

distinguished from other trees. Its bark is dark and rough, with deep fissures. The trunk is short and divides into large branches before reaching the upper parts of the tree. The small branches or twigs are slender and the outer ones drooping, giving it a graceful appearance by which you can tell it at a considerable distance even in winter.

In the woods the American elm sometimes grows to be more than 100 feet tall, and in open places a large tree spreads over a wide area. There have been wellknown trees of this kind in the older cities of the Eastern states, such as the famous elm at Cambridge, Massachusetts, under which Washington took command of the Continental army, and the one at Philadelphia, under which William Penn signed a treaty with the Indians.

Notice the buttresses that are found at the bases of many large elms. What purpose do these serve, and why are they especially needed by the elm?

The wood of the elm. Elm wood is less prized than many other kinds of wood. It is heavy and solid, but difficult to work because it is very hard to split. This is because, as the wood fibers grow, the ends push past each other and become interlaced.

Because of its toughness, however, elm wood is useful for some purposes. The hubs of wheels and the handles and bands of baskets are made of it, and much elm is used for barrel hoops and crating.

Elm trees are subject to decay, and many of the old elms that were formerly so common in the woods contained large hollows high up in the trunk, or even in the limbs. These afforded nesting places for owls and homes for raccoons, porcupines, and squirrels. Many of the "bee trees," which were cut down simply to get the stores of honey the bees had placed in them, were elms.

The early settlers chopped down elms for still another purpose. Knowing that the buds and twigs are nutritious, they gave their cattle a chance to eat them, when other feed was scarce. The cattle would leave their barn feed to browse on the elm.

The slippery elm. The red elm, or slippery elm, has a fragrant and mucilaginous inner bark which children like to chew. Its leaves are larger and rougher than those of the American elm, and its wood, in contrast with that of the latter, is easy to split. Because it wears well and is pliable when steamed, it is sometimes used for making sleigh runners. It is also used for parts of agricultural implements. It is sometimes used locally for the framing of buildings. The slippery elm grows in deep, fertile soil on the banks of streams and on rich, rocky hillsides, throughout most of the eastern half of the United States.

Objections to elms as shade trees. The principal objection to the elm for planting is that its foliage is attacked by many kinds of insects. Caterpillars of the gypsy moth and tussock moth as well as the larvae of the elm-leaf beetle eat the leaves. In the streets of Eastern cities many elms have been ruined by insects. On this account it would be better not to plant so many elms. They should not be planted at all along ordinary city streets where houses are close to the sidewalk, for they need space to grow into their full beauty. Nor should they be planted where large quantities of soft coal are burned, for their rough leaves catch the soot, which, sticking fast, chokes up the breathing pores and in time kills the tree.

What beautiful bird selects the swaying branches of the elm from which to hang its nest? Why is the nest built so far out from the trunk of the tree?

Shapes of trees. The trunks of some kinds of trees divide into so many branches that in the upper part of the tree no trunk can be distinguished. Such trees are called *deliquescent*. In other kinds of trees the trunk extends to the top of the tree. These trees are called *excurrent*. The pine is an example of a tree of this kind.

Examine an elm tree. Is it of the deliquescent or excurrent type? Note that the lower branches are drooping, those midway up the tree are horizontal, and those in the top of the tree ascending. By this arrangement all the leaves are exposed to the light.

Position of leaves in the crown of a tree. If you stand under a young Norway maple or other tree that has a dense head of foliage, and look up, you may be surprised to see how scanty the foliage is except near the outside of the head. Such trees have a dense layer of leaves on the outer branches, and these cut off the light from the bases of the branches so that few or no leaves are found in the inner part of the crown. Other kinds of trees have open crowns; the outer branches stand apart so that the sunlight penetrates to the heart of the crown. Such trees have leaves near the trunk and on twigs springing from the bases of the large branches. To which of these types of trees does the elm belong?

The Ash

The ash belongs to the olive family. It is common in the wild state and is often planted for shade; yet many persons fail to recognize ash trees when they see them. The leaves of the ash are large and compound and bear some resemblance to the leaves of the walnut and hickory, but the leaves of these latter trees are arranged alternately on the branchlets, while those of the ash are opposite. Since young branches come from buds at the bases of leaves, the branches of the ash are also opposite, while those of the walnut and hickory are alternate. The fruit of the ash is winged and identifies the tree at once (Fig. 30).

To support the long and heavy leaves of the ash the branchlets must be large and strong. This gives to the ash in winter a stiff and naked appearance, very different from the graceful elm with its many slender, drooping twigs. The bark on the branches of most kinds of ash is somewhat tinged with red.

Species of ash. Black ash may be distinguished from other native species by its *sessile* leaflets; that is, each leaflet is attached to the common leafstalk

Fig. 24. American elm near Mumford, New York.

Fig. 30. Leaves and fruit of the white ash.

Fig. 31. Ash trees in a North Carolina forest.

Fig. 32. A white ash that grew in a forest. The other trees have only recently been cut away from around it.

U.S. Forest Service

without even a short stalk of its own. Blue ash may be recognized by its square branchlets. The branchlets and leafstalks of red ash are downy, those of the white ash smooth. Where only these four kinds grow, they can be distinguished in this way; but four other kinds grow in the eastern half of the United States, and several others farther west. The following points may prove helpful in recognizing the different kinds:

The inner bark of the blue ash will give a blue color to water. The bark on the branches of the red ash has a more decidedly reddish brown color than the bark of other species. Black ash has very dark-colored buds. White-ash leaves are usually whitish underneath. Green-ash leaves are brighter green than the leaves of other species. Pumpkin ash, which grows in the South, often has the base of the trunk bulging so that it is of a much greater diameter at a height of 4 feet than at a height of 12 feet. Water ash grows in Southern swamps. The Biltmore ash is found from Pennsylvania to Georgia, but was first distinguished from other kinds of ash at Biltmore, North Carolina.

The best kinds of ash for planting. The European ash is an attractive shade tree. A tree of

this kind was set out in Sandusky, Ohio, after the Civil War, where a quarry had been filled with earth. It now spreads about 80 feet and is the finest tree in the city. How did its location favor its rapid growth?

White ash also is a desirable tree for planting, though it does not give so dense a shade as some other trees. It grows fast, is straight and symmetrical, and has no serious insect enemies. Blue ash, which is much less common, also is recommended for planting, but it is more likely to be damaged by insects.

Properties and uses of ash wood. Since ash is strong, elastic, and not very heavy, it is a valuable wood for oars, bats, handles of hoes, rakes, and pitchforks, and for various parts of wagons, railway-car frames, and agricultural implements. White ash and blue ash

U.S. Forest Service

Fig. 33. A white ash that grew in the open. Note the difference in the trunk of this tree and that of the tree shown in Figure 32.

produce the best timber, when a high degree of strength and elasticity is required. By the elasticity of a wood is meant its power to spring back after it has been bent.

For ball bats and some other purposes second-growth trees are valued much more than those which formed part of the original forest. Which do you think grew faster? Contrary to what you might think, the more rapidly growing trees produce the tougher wood. This is because the wood is ring-porous, and the faster the tree grows the thicker the layers of firm summerwood will be and the farther apart the rings of weak, porous springwood will be placed.

The mountain ash. The foliage of the mountain ash somewhat resembles that of the true ash; but, as is shown by the flowers and fruit, it belongs to the family of the rose and apple and is not a relative of the ash. The streets of Toronto, Canada, are beautified by these trees, and they should be planted more frequently in the United States. They are found growing wild only where the climate is cool. Their scarlet fruits, which attract birds, make them ornamental all winter, and their foliage is admired in summer. The mountain ash has one serious disadvantage: it suffers much from the scale insects which attack members of the apple family.

Growth affected by light. Have you observed how a plant, when placed in a window, grows toward the source of light? Notice trees that are growing in open places, along streams, in the edge of a forest, and in a forest surrounded by other trees. Do the branches grow in such a way as to bring the leaves to the light? Why do forest trees have longer trunks than trees of the same kind that grow in the open?

Poplars

The leaves of poplars, especially those called aspens, quake in even a slight breeze. The sound they make has been compared to the patter of rain.

American Museum of Natural History

Fig. 34. The mountain ash
Decked with autumnal berries that outshine
spring's richest blossoms.
Yields a splendid show amid the leafy woods.
Wordsworth

Fig. 43. Leaves and catkins of aspen (left) and leaves of cottonwood (right).

Secure a leaf from a poplar and examine the leafstalk just below the blade of the leaf. Do you understand why the leaves of a poplar are stirred by even a light breeze?

The flowers of the poplar are borne in long, drooping *catkins* which appear in early spring. The staminate flowers are borne on one tree and the pistillate flowers on another tree; thus only certain trees produce seed. The small seeds are provided with tufts of fine white hairs. These are blown about by the wind, sometimes for long distances.

The cottonwood. The cottonwood, or necklace poplar, is found from Quebec to Florida and west to the Rocky Mountains. It produces as fruit little capsules strung along a curved stem like beads in a necklace. They mature and split open in the spring, and the seeds with their cottonlike tufts of hairs are scattered by the wind. They do not wait till the next spring to sprout, but like some maple seeds germinate at once.

As the cottonwood will grow where other trees do not thrive, it is very widely distributed. On recently formed sand spits in rivers and lakes the soil is too poor for any trees except cottonwood and willows, for it contains no humus, or vegetable mold, such as you can find in any woods where trees have grown and shed their leaves year after year.

Generally speaking, the cottonwood is likely to be short lived, but some cottonwood trees are more than a century old and are among the largest trees east of the Rocky Mountains.

The wood. Cotton-woods abound along streams in the plains where other trees are scarce. In such places people use the wood for fuel and for other purposes. Boards made of it warp badly, especially when exposed to moisture, and are inferior in both strength and durability to boards made from most other woods. The tree is a very rapid grower, sometimes increasing in diameter 10 inches in as many years. The wood is soft and light colored and is much used for paper pulp.

Objections to the cottonwood as a shade tree. The leaves of the cottonwood, being smooth, do not catch soot and dust like those of the elm. On this account and because of its rapid growth, this tree (especially the variety known as the Carolina poplar) has been planted along many city streets. Like many other things that are cheap, the cottonwood usually proves unsatisfactory. It is attacked by several kinds of insects and is likely to be short lived. It is not ornamental, and its capsules and cottony seeds—and in summer its leaves and twigs—litter the ground. Its roots, sometimes more than 100 feet long, in their search for water send

Fig. 44. Giant cottonwood near Shakopee, Minnesota. It is over 9 feet in diameter and 130 feet tall. Note the man near the base.

Fig. 45. Leaves of Lombardy poplar (left) and silver poplar (right).

H.B. Ayer

their rootlets into drains and obstruct the drainage; they have been known even to break through the cement linings of cisterns. Some cities have passed ordinances forbidding the planting of this tree.

Aspens. The American aspen is a small species of poplar with light-colored bark and soft, light wood. It is found through the cool portions of North America and grows in poor soil, often springing up extensively where woods have been burned. Beavers cut it down with their strong, sharp incisor teeth, using it to build their dams and lodges and eating for food the bark and water-soaked wood. Its wood, like that of other poplars, is much used for making paper. A similar species of aspen grows in Europe.

Lombardy poplar. The tree that is best known under the name of "poplar" is one which is not a native of this country but has been brought from Europe. It is called the *Lombardy poplar*. Its branches are ascending, so that the tree is like a spire and becomes very tall without spreading out. This variety is often prominent in French and Italian landscapes. Driveways that lead back from main thoroughfares to country mansions are often bordered by Lombardy poplars.

Silver poplar. The white or silver-leaf poplar, also from Europe, has quite a different habit from the Lombardy poplar, for its branches are spreading. Its leaf-stalks are only slightly flattened, and its leaves are cottony white on the under side. Some people incorrectly call it the "silver maple." It spreads by means of the roots, the sprouts which it sends up forming within a few years extensive thickets that are difficult to eradicate. On this account it is not a desirable tree to plant.

Root systems. The root system of poplars and most other trees is composed of many slender branches of nearly equal length. Such a system of roots is called a *fibrous root system*. On the other hand, an oak, a pine, or a walnut or other nut-bearing tree has a *tap root*; that is, it has one large root going down deep into the ground, with smaller

Fig. 46. A cottonwood seedling less than 1 year old. The roots have reached a length of from 3 to 4 feet.

roots branching off from the side. The radish and dandelion are examples of herbs with tap roots. Grasses, corn, and other grains have fibrous root systems.

The combined length of all the roots of so small a plant as a wheat plant has been found to be more than 1800 feet. It would be difficult to tell how far all the roots of a big cottonwood tree would reach if placed end to end. Figure 46 shows the roots of a cottonwood tree less than one year old. This tree grew in sandy soil. In arid parts of the Southwest the mesquite has been known to send its roots to a depth of 60 feet in search of water. In ordinary soils the roots of trees must remain nearer the surface, where they can get air as well as water. If the soil is not drained and water completely fills the spaces between the soil partides, the roots of most trees will die for lack of oxygen.

Fig. 47. Young Lombardy poplars.

Functions of roots. The roots of most trees do not serve, like those of the silver poplar, to reproduce the tree, but they have other very important functions. They anchor the tree in its place, and they gather from the soil and supply to the tree the water and mineral materials that it needs. Roots excrete substances which help to dissolve limestone and other mineral materials in the soil. In this way they secure more mineral matter for the tree. If the ground on one side of a tree is well watered and on the other side dry, the roots grow toward the water.

Oaks

Oaks are among the most common and useful of trees. Nearly three hundred kinds of oak are known, of which about fifty grow wild in the United States. There are probably few areas of the size of a county that contain more than ten species of oak, though in one piece of woodland thirteen different species have been found growing wild. Because of their abundance and the many valuable properties of their woods, oaks are the most important of all the hardwood trees of our forests.

Oak leaves. A collection of the leaves of the different oaks that grow near your home is easily made and will help you to know the trees. The leaves of most species are lobed, but the shape of the lobes is different in the different species. Look at Figures 55 and 56 or at specimens, and tell how a white-oak leaf differs from a red-oak leaf. Which species of oak have leaves that closely resemble each other? How can you tell them apart? Does any species of oak retain its leaves long after they have lost their green color?

Acorns. The acorns as well as the leaves of different kinds of oaks differ and should also be collected. Pin oaks have small and nearly hemispherical acorns, which in many cases are striped. Bur oaks have large acorns with deep, shaggy cups or cupules, and are therefore also called "mossy-cup" oaks. Red oaks have large acorns with shallow, saucerlike cupules. Which kinds of oaks have acorns that are good to eat? What birds eat them?

When the crop of acorns is abundant in parts of our Southern states, the hogs that run in the woods fatten on them. Cattle, deer, and squirrels also eat them. The Indians esteemed them as an article of food; in southern Europe the people boil and eat them, and we too should do this if we were not well supplied with better food.

Uses of oak bark and wood. In the bark of some kinds of oak a dark-colored substance called *tannin* is deposited very abundantly. This is used in tanning hides to make leather. Why are untanned hides less useful than leather for making shoes, harness, and other articles? Have you ever seen a piece of raw hide? Corks are made from the bark of an oak that grows in Spain and in northern Africa.

Fig. 55. Leaves and acorns of the white oak (A) and of the bur oak (B).

Fig. 56. Leaves and acorns of the red oak (C) and of the pin oak (D). The lobes in the leaves of the red oak point forward. In its near relative, the black oak, they point to the side.

Fig. 57. Giant white oak near Amelia, Virginia. It has a height of 118 feet and a spread of 128 feet.

Fig. 59. Live oak near Sutherland Springs, Texas. The branches are draped with Spanish moss.

Oak wood is heavy, hard, and strong; it has wide pith rays that give many of the boards a mottled appearance, and many of the species are very durable. For fuel how does oak compare with other kinds of wood? What properties of oak adapt it for floors? for the making of furniture? of wagons? of ships? What other things are made from it? Why? Verify by actual test all the properties of oak that you have named.

Galls. On some oak leaves and branches you will find peculiar growths which you might suppose to be fruits, if you did not know that the fruit of the oak is an acorn. These peculiar growths are **galls.** Some twenty-five kinds of galls have been found on white oaks alone. Open a gall and look for a tiny, wormlike creature. It is not a real worm, for, if you had not disturbed it, it would in time have developed into a gallfly. Indeed, it came from an egg laid by a gallfly and is the young of the fly. Like the caterpillar and grub, it is the larva stage,—the stage

which follows the egg of an insect and during which it eats a great deal and grows fast. The little gallfly lays an egg beneath the skin of the leaf or twig, and when this egg hatches, the larva feeds on the juices contained in the leaf or twig. The abnormal growth (the gall) which the plant makes around the larva serves to protect the young insect from other insects and from birds.

Some galls are quite pretty. A collection of a dozen or more kinds would form an interesting exhibit in a schoolroom. Black ink is made from copperas and certain oak galls called "nutgalls," combined with a little dextrin or gum arabic, which is added to make it adhere to the pen. In Hungary and the Balkan States certain oak galls are gathered and sold for tanning, and pyrogallic acid, which is used in photography, is made from them.

Fig. 58. Trunk of the same tree. The circumference is more than 15 feet at a height of 6 feet from the ground.

Fig. 60. Young pin oaks on Pennsylvania Avenue, Washington, D. C.

Oaks as shade trees. Besides the usefulness of their wood, bark, acorns, and galls, oaks are desirable as shade and ornamental trees. Oaks from the original forest, left standing after the land has become the site of a town or city, are often highly prized. The red oak is considered one of the best of all our shade trees. It is suitable for planting along broad streets. This species and the scarlet and pin oaks grow more rapidly than most of the other oaks. They are desirable as shade trees on account of their durability, symmetry, beauty of foliage, and comparative freedom from injury by insects or fungi.

Have you seen many large oak trees? How old do you suppose they are? How do live oaks get their name? Where do they grow? Which kind of oak do you consider the most valuable? Why?

Relatives of the oak. To the same family as the oak belong the beech and chestnut. All these trees produce staminate and pistillate flowers on the same tree. The flowers have no corolla, and the pistillate flowers are rarely noticed. They give rise to nuts which have no partition and contain but one seed. The seed or meat contains nourishment to start the growth of a new tree. Beechnuts, chestnuts, and acorns constitute a large part of the food of many birds and mammals.

Evergreens

The trees that we have studied up to this time are *deciduous*; that is, they shed their leaves in the autumn. But in many parts of the United States and Canada *evergreens* are more common than the trees that lose their leaves with the coming of the cold months. Each type of tree is best suited for life under certain conditions, and whether evergreens or deciduous trees are more common in any given region depends on the prevailing conditions of soil and climate.

Definition of an evergreen. While any plant that remains green throughout the winter is an evergreen, and while in many parts of the United States we have broad-leaved evergreen trees and shrubs like the magnolia, holly, and rhododendron, yet we commonly mean by an evergreen a tree or shrub with needle-shaped, awl-shaped, or scaly leaves. The pine, spruce, cedar, and fir are trees that belong to this group. They do not, however, retain the same leaves as long as they live. Under a pine or cedar tree the ground may be covered with fallen leaves, but they fall a few at a time and not all in a single season or year.

The deciduous tree. In the spring a deciduous tree spreads out a vast number of broad, thin leaves to the light. All leaves give off water, and it is estimated that a large birch tree must draw from the earth 100 gallons of water each day to prevent its leaves from withering and drying in the hot sun. The delicate, thin leaves of such a tree cannot endure cold, and in winter it is possible for the roots of a tree to secure only very small amounts of water from the frozen soil; so trees with broad, thin leaves drop them before the cold season comes. During the months when the air is warm and water is abundant they run a great food factory and store in their branches, stems, and roots the surplus food which they make. On this surplus they live through the winter, and from it they build in the spring their flowers, leaves, and young twigs. The working season of most deciduous trees is even shorter than we think, for the delicate leaves cannot appear until after the season of frost is over, and they fall from many trees as soon as the first frosts of autumn come.

On the other hand, the leaves on most evergreen trees are small, and they are tough and leathery so that they resist cold and drying. A tree of this kind does not have the great spread of leaf surface that a deciduous tree has. At no time can it manufacture food as rapidly as a deciduous tree does when it is in full leaf; yet the leaves of evergreens are able to build some food for the tree during the greater part of the year, whereas the trees that lose their leaves at the end of summer cannot add to their stock of nourishment until the following spring. In some locations the slower and steadier method of the evergreen succeeds better than the plan of rapid work for a shorter part of the year followed by the deciduous tree.

Where the deciduous and evergreen types succeed. In most parts of the temperate zone where the soil is deep and moist, as in rich river bottoms, and where the growing season is long and the air moist, the deciduous tree grows better than the evergreen. The abundant water supply and the low rate of evaporation from the leaves enable it to support a great crown of leaves, and the long growing season allows it to keep these leaves for so long a time that in the course of a summer it can manufacture more food than an evergreen can, even though it keeps its leaves during the whole year.

The evergreen, on the other hand, succeeds where the water supply is not so great, where evaporation is more intense, or where the winters are long and cold. In sandy soils and on steep and rocky mountain slopes; where the air is dry; and in the far north, it is the prevailing type of tree. Its small, tough leaves demand only a small amount of water, and by working through a longer season

they make more food for the tree than the leaves of a deciduous tree can produce in dry locations or during short summers. Do you think evergreens are not found in deep, moist soils because they will not grow in these locations, or because in such places the deciduous trees grow more rapidly and crowd them out?

In the moist tropics where there are no cold seasons the trees do not need to shed their leaves and are all evergreens. But these evergreens have broad leaves like our deciduous trees and differ in type from the evergreens of dry and cold regions. Just why the trees in many swamps are evergreens has not been fully explained, but one reason probably lies in the fact that under swamp conditions only a feeble root system can be developed.

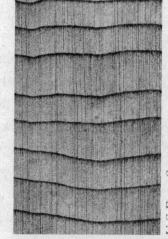

Fig. 69. Wood of arbor vitæ as seen through a microscope. The wood is light and, like that of other evergreens, is non-porous and uniform in texture.

Fig. 68. Cones from six different evergreens: (I) Blue spruce. (II) Norway spruce. (III) White spruce. (IV) Douglas fir. (V) Big Tree. (VI) Austrian pine.

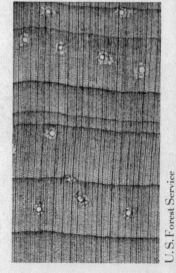

Fig. 70. Wood of the piñon, a species of western pine. In the pine there are resin ducts which appear as openings in the wood.

Conifers. Most of our evergreens produce cones and hence are called *conifers* or cone bearers. The cone *is* the fruit. The seeds are protected by the scales of *the* cone but are not inclosed in an ovary. Pollen from other flowers falls directly upon the ovules. The pollen is produced in great abundance and is carried by *the* wind. If the tree is surrounded by others of the same species, its chance of receiving pollen for its many ovules *is* greater. For this reason evergreen trees are not often found scattered in small numbers over a large area. You might travel a hundred miles without seeing a pine, spruce, or hemlock, excepting such as have been planted, but when you come to one you will probably see near it many others of the same species.

The coniferous trees of the United States and Canada all belong to the pine family. Among lumbermen their wood is spoken of as "soft wood," although that of the Georgia pine and some other kinds is hard. The wood of deciduous trees is called "hardwood," although that of some kinds of deciduous trees is soft. In the four chapters that follow will be found descriptions of our most important conifers. The wood that is furnished by these trees is a most important source of lumber. It is fine grained and easily worked, is light, and for its weight strong, and shrinks evenly when it is dried. The habit which these trees have of growing in large

U. S. Forest Service

Fig. 71.   Paper leaving the mill for a metropolitan daily. The paper in this photograph represents about one half the amount used by the newspaper each day. Much paper is made from spruce and other evergreens.

numbers together is also valuable to the lumberman. It enables him to get out a large amount of lumber of the same kind at one time.

Spruce and Fir

Spruce and fir resemble pines in having the branches arranged in whorls; that is, several branches grow in a circle at the same level. They differ from pines in having the leaves scattered on the branchlets instead of being arranged in clusters. They grow as forest trees in the northern parts of the United States and in our Western mountains, but spruce trees have been extensively planted in cemeteries and near dwellings in other parts of the country. Besides affording dense shade, these trees are ornamental and break the force of the wind. Many thousands of young spruce and fir trees are sold each year as Christmas trees. At the holiday season children who live hundreds of miles from the forests where these trees grow become familiar with them.

Kinds of spruce. The blue spruce from Colorado has foliage of a bluish color. From the main branches the longer branchlets droop. When not trimmed, the lowest branches are near the ground and the tree is shaped like a cone.

The Norway spruce sometimes grows two or three feet in one season and is the species most commonly found in cultivation. Its branches extend out almost horizontally from the trunk, curving up a little toward the ends. By its larger cones it is readily distinguished from the white, red, and black spruces, all of which grow in Canada and the Northern states. Other large species of spruce are found in the mountains of the West.

The cones and seeds of the spruce. The cones of both spruces and firs have much thinner scales than the cones of the pines. The cones of the spruce are drooping. In what part of the tree do they hang in greatest numbers? If you can get a full-grown cone

Fig. 80. Blue spruce in Highland Park, Rochester, New York.

R. E. Horsey

which has not yet lost its seed, take it home or to the schoolroom. After a time the scales will spread apart so that the winged seeds can drop out. When thrown in the air, do the seeds fall straight down? Why?

The wood of the spruce. In Europe masts and spars are often made from the tall, straight trunks of the Norway spruce. On account of its uniform grain the wood of this and other species of spruce is used for the sounding boards of musical instruments. The lumber is soft, white, and straight grained and, in proportion to its weight, has great strength. It is used for many purposes, and of recent years has come into great prominence because of the large amounts of it needed for the manufacture of airplanes. Much of the paper used in books and newspapers is made of spruce wood.

Firs. Different species of pine and spruce are often called "firs"; but the name "fir" is properly applied to evergreens that resemble spruces in general appearance, but have erect instead of drooping cones, and leaves that are not jointed at the base. The only true fir native to the northeastern part of the United States is the balsam fir, which grows also over much of Canada and in the mountains as far south as Virginia.

The leaves on this fir are blunt and flat, and not foursided like those of a spruce. On the horizontal branches they appear to be two-ranked instead of standing out all around the branch, as do the leaves of the spruce. Persons camping where fir trees are growing often make a bed of the boughs; but they avoid the spruce because its leaves (needles) are sharp and stand out all around the stem. The leaves of the fir last a long time; if undisturbed, they persist on the tree for 8 years.

Young balsam firs and Norway spruces look so much alike that it is difficult to tell them apart at a distance. But the bark of the fir, except on old trunks, is quite smooth, and on its surface are numerous blisters of a resinous substance called "balsam." These blisters distinguish the true firs from all other trees. The balsam which is obtained from the balsam fir is called "Canada balsam." It is used in fixing delicate specimens on glass slides for examination through a compound microscope. "Pine

U.S. Forest Service

Fig. 81. Alpine fir, Blackfeet National Forest, Montana.

Fig. 82. Douglas fir, Highland Park, Rochester, New York.

R. E. Horsey

Fig. 83. Red fir forest on Mount Shasta at an elevation of 5000 feet.

When the Douglas fir grows in open places, the lowest branches, like those of various spruces, touch the ground. It grows rapidly and is a handsome tree. In the moist, mild atmosphere of England it was found to thrive as soon as introduced, but in our Northeastern states the climate is too severe for it. It has been found recently that stock from the mountains of Colorado is perfectly hardy, so that the tree may now be successfully planted in various parts of this country.

The Pine

More of our lumber comes from the pine than from any other one tree, yet many people do not know a pine when they see one. Some think that all evergreens are pines.

Pine trees have slender leaves, called "needles," growing in clusters. When young, each cluster has a sheath of papery scales at its base. The cone scales of the pine are thicker than those of spruce or fir. Pines, like spruces and most other conifers, are excurrent trees. Many species have trunks that extend to a height of more than 100 feet, and some species to a height of more than 200 feet. They often grow in *pure stands*; that is, to the exclusion of other kinds of trees.

pillows," filled with the leaves of this tree, keep their fragrance for 2 or 3 years.

In the mountains of Tennessee, North Carolina, and Virginia a different species called "Fraser's fir" is found, and other large species of fir from which valuable lumber is obtained grow in the mountains of our Western states. Although abundant in the woods in cold regions, firs are not seen in cultivation as often as spruces.

The Douglas fir. The Douglas fir is also called "Douglas spruce," though it is neither a fir nor a spruce, but only a close relative of these trees. It is one of the most valuable trees of the whole country. It is widely distributed in the mountains of the West and along the coast of Oregon, Washington, and British Columbia, where it grows taller than any tree in the Eastern forests. In the interior of the continent it is not a remarkably large tree, but on the Pacific coast it frequently exceeds 250 feet in height and 10 feet in diameter. Ladders used by fire departments are made from its wood, for it is light, straight grained, and free from knots. Large quantities of this wood are used for building and other purposes. Many masts and flag-poles are made of it.

Fig. 84. Long-leaf pine forest near Ocilla, Georgia. Turpentine and rosin are being collected from the trees.

Products of pine trees. Tar, turpentine, and rosin are obtained from several species of pine. These materials have long been called "naval stores," but they are now used more extensively on land than in connection with ships. Pieces of pine stumps and roots are heated in retorts, ovens, or kilns, and the turpentine thus driven off as a vapor is condensed by cooling it and afterwards separated from the acids, wood alcohol, and other products that come from wood when it is heated without air. Tar requires more heat to change it to vapor, so that it collects in another part of the distilling apparatus. What is pine tar used for? What other kind of tar is there and how is it used?

When a small cavity is made in the trunk of a Georgia pine or of a western yellow pine, crude turpentine flows out. By distillation in large copper stills, oil or spirit of turpentine is derived from this. Rosin is left in the still. This is used in making the cheaper kinds of soap and varnish, and also in sealing wax and shoemaker's wax. What other uses has rosin? Turpentine is used largely in varnish and paint. What other uses has it?

Most frame houses are built chiefly of pine. Can you name other uses for the wood? What are the properties of the wood? How do these properties adapt it to its various uses? Do pines furnish any food?

What other uses have pine trees besides those already mentioned?

Species of pines. In the United States there are about thirty-six species of pines growing wild. The white pine formerly grew abundantly in parts of the Northern states from Maine to Minnesota and in southern Canada. It furnished a vast amount of good lumber, but the supply is now nearly exhausted, so that white pine of good grade brings a high price. Southern yellow pine has taken its place for many uses. It is a harder and heavier wood than white pine, and contains more resin, but it is likely to split along the annual rings when it is nailed. Test the cleavability of a piece of yellow pine by driving a nail through it near the end.

Fig. 86. Spray of Scotch pine, showing leaves and cone (A). Leaves of the white pine are shown at the left (B) and of the Georgia or long-leaf pine at the right (C).

In California, the sugar pine grows 200 feet tall and produces cones that may be 18 inches or more in length. Its seed or nut, the size of a navy bean, is edible, as are the seeds of several smaller species of pine, called "piñons," that grow in the Southwest. Another important pine is the western yellow pine, which is a valuable source of both lumber and turpentine.

Cones of the pine. By comparing the cones of such pines as grow in your vicinity you will find differences in form and size. The Scotch pine, which is often planted in this country, has cones about 2 inches long, while the cones of the white pine are usually from 4 to 6 inches in length and may reach a length of 11 inches. The cones of pines require 2 years for their development, while those of the

Fig. 85. White pine trees about 120 years old, St. Louis County, Minnesota. The trees are still growing in height.

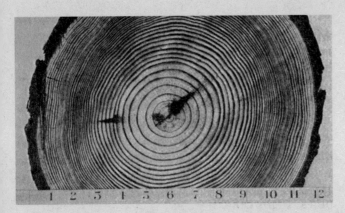

Fig. 87. Section from a 52-year-old short-leaf pine. The tree grew in a forest near Glenville, Arkansas, and was of average size.

spruce and fir require but 1 year. When the winged seeds at the base of the scales are mature, the scales spread apart enough to allow the seeds to fall out and be borne away by the wind. The seeds of these and other evergreens are not inclosed in an ovary, but grow at the base of the cone scales. See if you can find them.

Pine needles. The needles of the valuable Georgia pine, which is one species of yellow pine, are sometimes as much as 18 inches long and grow in clusters of three; those of the white pine are very slender, but shorter, and grow in fives; those of the Scotch pine are still shorter and are in twos, as are those of many of the native species.

Examine the leaves of a young pine seedling. Are they needle leaves or ordinary leaves, and are they on the ends of dwarf branches or attached to the sides of the stem? What inference can you draw as to the leaves of the ancestor of the pine?

Pollen of the pine. In spring the yellow pollen from the pine trees falls in such quantity that it is sometimes spoken of as a shower of sulfur. For seed production some of this pollen must fall on the young cones. You can see an advantage to these trees from growing in pure stands. Will a cornstalk growing by itself produce much grain?

Knowledge of the Star

From *Trees, Stars, and Birds: A Book of Outdoor Science* by Edwin Lincoln Moseley, 1919

Can you remember looking up into the sky when you were a little child and wondering about the stars? And did you learn to recite the familiar lines:

> Twinkle, twinkle, little star,
> How I wonder what you are!
> Up above the world so high,
> Like a diamond in the sky.

Are you now too old to wonder about the stars or to wander in imagination among the celestial spheres? Should you like to know where shooting stars come from, what they are, and what becomes of them? Are the other stars like them? Do people live on the stars? If they do, can they see the earth, and what would the earth look like from the stars?

The science of astronomy. The science which treats of the heavenly bodies is called *astronomy*.

Fig. 109. Yerkes Astronomical Observatory, Lake Geneva, Wisconsin.

It is interesting to study because it satisfies the spirit of wonder within us, our desire to know, which is the foundation of all science. It is also a most useful science. It enables us to determine directions and to keep accurate time. For thousands of years men have guided their course across the seas and over desert wastes by the stars, and by the use of astronomy explorers have found their way over unknown regions of the earth. Maps and surveys are based on observations on the stars. The surveyor who marks out the line of a railroad or the boundaries of a farm is using knowledge gained from study of the heavenly bodies.

Time measured by the movements of the heavenly bodies. If your clock gained 5 minutes a day, would it matter, provided that every other clock and watch did the same? People could keep appointments because their timepieces would agree. School would begin each morning when the clock pointed to nine o'clock. But after a few weeks a clock gaining 5 minutes a day would point to nine o'clock before sunrise. A little reflection will show that the length of a day is not determined by our clocks and watches, but that our timepieces must be made to conform to the actual length that the day has. Likewise the length of a year does not depend on any human law or decree. We might agree to call 360 days a year. If we did, after a while Christmas would come in summer and the Fourth of July in winter. Like the day, the year has its own length. What determines the length of a day and of a year?

Fitting the calendar to the year. In the early history of the world much confusion arose because of the lack of a calendar, but before the beginning of the Christian era, Julius Cæsar, by the advice of the astronomer Sosigenes, decreed that the calendar year should be 365¼ days, every fourth year containing 366 days and the others 365 days. The actual length of a year is almost 365¼ days, but in 16 centuries the difference between the true length and 365¼ days caused the seasons to shift in reference to the calendar 10 days. To remedy this, Pope Gregory in 1582 decreed that the day following October 4 should that year be called October 15, thus making up the 10 days. He further decreed that the last year of each century should not be a leap year unless divisible by 400. Thus 1700, 1800, and 1900 were not leap years, although they are divisible by 4, but the year 2000 will be a leap year. This arrangement so nearly approximates the length of the real year that in 4000 years the seasons will shift not more than 1 day.

Astronomy the oldest of the sciences.
When the ancient Assyrians and Egyptians went on a journey, they often traveled at night, for the day was hot. They did not ride on a railroad train or along a highway with a fence on either side, but guided their courses by the stars. They had no electric or gas lights or such lamps as ours, and so the light of the moon was more important to them than it is to us. Whether on a journey or at home, they often spent much of the night with no roof over them but the great vault of heaven, and clouds or mist rarely obscured the stars. These ancient peoples, therefore, had many opportunities for observing the heavenly bodies, and although they possessed no telescopes they learned more about astronomy than most persons nowadays know. They knew what bright stars and what groups of stars could be seen in the east at a certain season. They could compute when the moon would rise, when there would be a

new moon, and when an eclipse. They knew the polestar and that it is always in the north, and from their knowledge of astronomy they knew the directions and how to guide themselves across uncharted wastes.

How to know the heavenly bodies. Some fields of study are too wide to be passed over in a short time. They are rich enough for us to visit again and again. Only in this way can we see and appreciate the treasures that are there stored. We cannot become well acquainted with more than a few kinds of trees or birds in a single month. We may come to know them better as long as we have health to enjoy life. The same is true of the stars. The student might read the chapters in this book on the stars in an hour or two. It would be more profitable for him to read them a little at a time. The stars cannot all be seen to advantage at any one season. To study them most conveniently one should look at them night after night through the different months of the year.

It would be well to begin the study of the stars and constellations sometime in the fall, when a clear sky permits them to be well seen, and to take them up again every week or two for several months and perhaps again the next year. In this way, little by little you will acquire an acquaintance with some of the brightest stars and most conspicuous constellations, and this will continue to be a source of pleasure to you in after years.

Reasoning as well as observation required in astronomy. By looking through a telescope you could see many stars too faint to be seen with the naked eye, but even the brightest stars would appear as points of light, just as they do when seen without a telescope. How, then, do we know that some of them are very large? Science has revealed to us many wonderful things in the heavens which the ancients did not know. Telescopes and other instruments are very useful to the astronomers, but what is seen by means of them would not afford much knowledge about the heavenly bodies if the astronomers did not reason correctly from the facts that they gather. The scientific method requires not only careful observations but also careful reasoning.

The questions that are asked in the chapters that treat of the heavenly bodies are intended to guide you in your thinking. Many of them may seem difficult to young pupils. Older students, even, will be puzzled to find correct answers to some of them. It would be well to give some attention to them early in your study, so that, as opportunity occurs for observing the heavens, some of them at least may be answered without the aid of teachers or of books.

The Universe and Solar System

From *Trees, Stars, and Birds: A Book of Outdoor Science* by Edwin Lincoln Moseley, 1919

Lying with your back upon the earth and looking up into the blue sky, did you ever wonder what there might be far away in space? Is there a wall that bounds it all? If there is, what is beyond that wall? If not, how far does space extend? Are there other suns, larger, hotter, and more brilliant than our own? Are there great heavenly bodies, thousands of times as large as the earth, which no one on the earth has ever seen? Far out in space are there other worlds like ours on which beings like ourselves could live?

The earth, with everything on it, and all the heavenly bodies, seen and unseen, make up the *universe*. In every direction it stretches away through limitless space, a vast collection of giant bodies that the imagination can hardly picture. When we stand forth under the sky at night and think of

Clusters and beds of worlds and beelike swarms
Of stars and starry streams,

sweeping on and on through space, we are awed by the majesty of the spectacle before our eyes.

The stars. What are the twinkling points of light which our eyes behold in whatever direction we look on a clear night? They are great blazing suns, set here and there at vast distances through space. We do not see that they are farther from us than the clouds, except when a drifting cloud hides them from our view. Yet the clouds are only a short distance from us, floating in the air above us, while the stars are out in space so far away that even were we able to fly with the swiftness of a nighthawk we

could not reach them in a thousand years. The sun is a star, no larger or brighter than thousands of others; but it is much nearer to us, and that is why it gives us so much more heat and light and seems so much larger than the other stars.

The solar system. The earth and seven other worlds or planets, some smaller than the earth, others larger, revolve around the sun (Fig. 108). These are the *major* planets. The sun controls the motion of several hundred *minor* planets, which are of much smaller size also, as well as the movements of various comets and a host of meteors. Some of the major planets are attended by satellites that revolve around them as they themselves revolve around the sun. The moon is the earth's satellite, and some other planets have several moons or satellites.

The sun and all the bodies that revolve around it—the planets with their satellites, the minor planets, and the comets and meteors—constitute the *solar system;* that is, the system of the sun. Whether, like the sun, the other stars have smaller bodies revolving about them we cannot tell. They are so far away that at such distances bodies like our earth would be invisible to us. Yet it would seem reasonable to believe that each star is the controlling center of a great system of worlds like our own.

The vastness of the universe. The earth on which we live is so large that none of us will ever see more than a small part of its surface, and the vast mass of matter that lies deep in the earth's interior has never been seen by human eye. Yet the earth is but a small member of our solar system, and our entire solar system is so small a part of the whole universe that blotting it out of existence would be only like wiping a speck of star dust from the sky. Well has the poet Emerson said: "If the stars should appear one night in a thousand years, how would men believe and adore; and preserve for many generations the remembrance of the city of God which had been shown."

The work of astronomers. In the vast voids of space between the heavenly bodies there is no air, and across them no sounds can pass. In them all is darkness and silence, and there the cold is of an intensity not known on earth. Nothing comes to us across this space except waves of light and heat and the mysterious force of gravitation, which all material bodies exert on each other. Yet from the information gained from these sources, astronomers have measured the distances to some of the stars, learned that certain of them are young and others old, and calculated the weights of the sun, moon, and many other heavenly bodies. By countless observations and by careful thought and long computations they have learned the secrets of the universe and have built them into a system so wonderful and so complete that of it the philosopher Laplace has said: "Contemplated as one grand whole, astronomy is the most beautiful monument of the human mind, the noblest record of its intelligence."

Determining the Distances to the Heavenly Bodies

From Trees, Stars, and Birds: A Book of Outdoor Science by Edwin Lincoln Moseley, 1919

A baby reaches for the moon and a dog barks at it. Apparently they think it is near them. Can you tell merely by looking at it whether it is near or far away? Have you ever mistaken a town clock at night or some other artificial light for the moon and are you sure that the moon is farther away than objects on the earth? Doubtless you have read about the great distances of the sun, moon, and other heavenly bodies from the earth, and perhaps you have wondered how it is possible to learn the distance to an object that no one has ever been able to reach. Astronomers and surveyors do this in a rather simple way.

Determining distances without measuring them. A surveyor can find the distance to a tree on the other side of a river without crossing the river. On his own side of the river he drives two stakes and then carefully measures the distance between them. Then with his instruments he sights at the tree from each stake, measuring the angles that lines from each stake to the tree make with a line connecting the two

stakes. The two stakes and the tree form a triangle of which he knows the length of one side and the size of two angles. By his knowledge of trigonometry he is then able to calculate the length of the other sides of the triangle and thus find the distance from either of the stakes to the tree. By examining Figure no you will note that the farther away the tree is the larger are the angles at the two stakes.

Finding the distances to the heavenly bodies. Astronomers use the method of the surveyor in finding the distances to the heavenly bodies. Two observers can sight their instruments on the moon from different points on the earth's surface and find the angles which the lines to the moon make with a line connecting the two points on the surface of the earth. They know the distance apart of the observers on the surface of the earth, and they can then calculate the length of the lines which extend to the moon (Fig. 111).

In measuring the distance to fixed stars, which are very distant from us, astronomers take observations at different times of the year and use the distance of the earth from the sun as one side of the triangle. Figure 112 will help to make clear how this is done.

Distances to some heavenly bodies. Suppose that Romulus and Remus, the traditional founders of Rome, had started from Italy in 753 B.C. in an airplane that would carry them 125 miles an hour. In 2 days they might have reached North America, and on the third they would have crossed the continent and reached the Pacific Ocean. Keeping on around

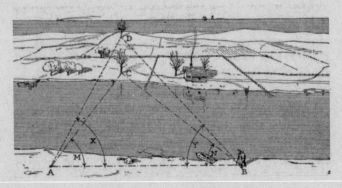

Fig. 110. Determining distances to objects without measuring them.

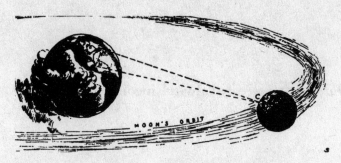

Fig. 111. How the distance to the moon is measured. If the astronomer knows the length of the line AB and the size of the angles M and N, he can compute the distance to the point C.

the world they would have arrived at their native land in about a week from the time they started. Suppose them to start again on a journey, this time to the moon, traveling at the same high rate of speed. The journey would have required about 80 days, and if they had started back to the earth at once it would have been more than 5 months before they reached their home again.

Suppose they had then set out for the sun. They would have taken 85 years to reach it and would have grown quite old before they arrived. If, not content with seeing so much of the universe, they had kept on through space, directing their swift flight toward the great planet Jupiter, the journey from the sun to Jupiter would have required 441 years; for Jupiter is more than 5 times as far from the sun as we are.

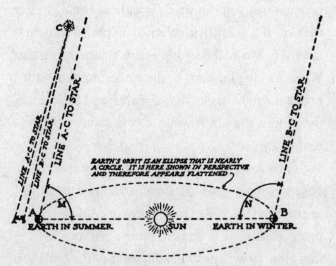

Fig. 112. How the distance to a star is measured.

If they had arrived at Jupiter in 227 B.C., and that same year had directed their course toward the orbit of Neptune, the most distant of all the worlds that revolve around the sun, they would not have reached the path of that planet until the year 1879.

Suppose Neptune in 1879 to have been on the opposite side of his orbit from the point where Romulus and Remus arrived, and that they had set out to meet him, traveling still at the rate of 125 miles an hour, or 3000 miles a day. Neptune is the slowest of all the planets; nevertheless, he moves along his path at a speed of about 200 miles a minute, which is farther than Romulus and Remus are flying in an hour. Although Neptune and our voyagers through space were moving toward each other with such high speed, yet some 80 years would elapse before they would meet.

Within your lifetime let Romulus and Remus bid adieu to Neptune and set out for Alpha Centauri, the star that is nearest to our solar system. Their journeys made among the planets have occupied nearly 27 centuries. 7000 times 27 centuries would be required to reach Alpha Centauri, the nearest star. Many of the stars are hundreds of times as far away as Alpha Centauri. Only a few of them are within 400 trillion miles of the earth. Most of them are many times this distance from us, but it is believed that none are so far away as 1000 times this distance.

Some problems to be explained. Riding along a straight road in the country at night, did you ever notice a light in some house to your right or left, and, after riding for some minutes more, notice that it was still in nearly the same direction? Was the house near the road or far from it? Did you ever go along a city street and notice when you came to a cross street that the moon was right down that street? Going on another block, you saw the moon again right over another cross street, and so on, block after block. Was the moon following you? What other explanation can you give?

Birds

From *Trees, Stars, and Birds: A Book of Outdoor Science* by Edwin Lincoln Moseley, 1919

Birds and insects come to our notice oftener than most other creatures. Their rapid movements and bright colors or the sounds they make attract our attention. Some of our common insects spread diseases among us, and many of them destroy our crops; in the United States they take each year one tenth of all the farmer's produce and cause a loss of more than a billion dollars. Birds are the natural enemies of the insect world,—the balance nature

Fig. 158. Birds are the natural enemies of insects.

Fig. 159. Small birds rear their young almost entirely on insect food. The illustration shows a black-throated gray warbler feeding its young.

has provided to hold insects in check. Almost all birds feed their young on bugs, flies, and worms, and many birds throughout their whole lives eat little other food. Indeed, if it were not for the work of the birds, insects would overrun the earth; in the stomach of one martin nearly 2000 mosquitoes were found. Whether birds are harmful or beneficial you can judge after you have watched the feeding habits of a score or more of different kinds.

Birds may be studied both in town and country; in some city parks more than a hundred kinds have been seen. Wherever you find a variety of trees and shrubs you are likely to find a number of birds, if they are safe from enemies there. Look for them in orchards, pastures, and along the borders of ponds and brooks. You will find them at all seasons, but the best time to see them is when the leaves are developing on the trees.

To get a good view of a bird, take such a position that you can watch it without having to face the sun. If it is easily frightened, do not go straight toward it, but walk steadily as if you were going past. When looking for birds in the woods, walk quietly, notice the motion of twigs or leaves, and listen to the various sounds. A windy day is unfavorable for bird study.

In a good locality for birds you may succeed in observing them if you sit down and allow the birds to come to you. If you have opera or field glasses, practice using them so as to bring a bird quickly into clear view. Try mimicking some of the birds you hear; you may succeed in calling them to you.

Finley & Bohlman

Fig. 160. A call for insect food.

When you see an unfamiliar bird, make notes that will help you to identify it in a museum or by the use of a bird book. Compare its size with that of some common bird. Notice whether its bill is slender and straight, whether its wings and tail are short, any color markings you are able to see, and how it is getting food. Do not stop to make notes until you have watched the bird for some minutes or have lost track of it.

A notebook will be useful also in keeping a list of the birds you see and various things you notice about their habits. Record the date, weather, locality where found, and any observations that interest you. If the notes you make outside are written up more carefully after you return home and before you go on another trip, they will be interesting and useful to you at various times, perhaps for years to come.

The birds described in the following pages are those that are most likely to be seen in the eastern and, middle parts of the United States and Canada. However, not many of them may be seen at all seasons, and it is better to study each kind when it can be observed than to follow invariably the order in the book, where they are arranged according to their relationships to one another. It is not important to study every bird that is mentioned in the book. If you answer half the questions by means of your own observation, you will have acquired some real knowledge of birds.

Making Grounds Attractive to Birds

From *Trees, Stars, and Birds: A Book of Outdoor Science* by Edwin Lincoln Moseley, 1919

Within the last few years appreciation of birds has led to efforts to protect them and enable them to increase in number. The United States Government has given the birds about seventy islands, lakes, and other bird reserves, for their exclusive use, so that they may rear their young unmolested, and the National Association of Audubon Societies guards with paid agents over one hundred of the most important breeding colonies of birds in the United States. In addition, private citizens have appropriated large tracts of land for the use of wild birds, and the grounds about thousands of homes have been made more pleasant by making them attractive to the feathered songsters.

Houses, food, drink, and safety for birds. even in small yards, boxes or houses can be put up for birds to occupy, sheltered feeding places can be provided and stocked with food in winter, and water supplied in dry seasons. A fountain with a shallow bowl where birds may drink and bathe will attract a great many, which may then be watched while they are having a good time. However, none of these things will be of much use if the birds are allowed to be killed by cats or driven off by English sparrows. Families that are unwilling to dispense with cats sometimes provide them with collar and bell to give the birds warning of the enemy's approach.

R. E. Horsey

Fig. 243. A robin in a bird bath.

Planting trees and shrubs for birds. Where room permits, grounds may be beautified and at the same time made more attractive to birds by planting a variety of trees, shrubs, and vines. Smoothly trimmed hedges and stiff trees of a formal garden are not so attractive to them as untrained bushes and tangled thickets. Seclusion from real or imaginary foes, protection from wind and storm, as well as a supply of food and water, are advantages the birds derive from trees and shrubbery of the right sort.

The choice of the trees and shrubs to be planted must be determined partly by the climate. There are wild plants in every part of America whose fruit is relished by birds as much as is the fruit of cultivated varieties.

The planting of some of these wild varieties on the borders of orchards and vineyards oftentimes serves to protect the cultivated fruit. If selected for

Joseph H. Dodson

Fig. 242. Grounds that are attractive to birds.

Fig. 244. Making bird houses.

R. E. Horsey

frost grape, roses, and in the South, the magnolia, chinaberry, and holly. The mulberries, service berries, redberried elder, European bird cherry, and mahaleb cherry ripen in the spring or early in the summer. Some of the best of the fruits that ripen later are the elder, wild cherry, chokecherry, the flowering dogwood and other cornels, the black haw and other viburnums, the Virginia creeper, and the climbing bittersweet. Some foreign species that may be obtained from nurseries are very fine for birds. Among these are honeysuckles of different kinds, especially the Tartarian, honeysuckle, the hawthorn, the larch, the Japanese rose, and the Japanese flowering crab. Old apple trees, cherry trees, and blackberry, raspberry, currant, and other bushes whose fruit we prize are of use to the birds.

this purpose, the wild fruit should ripen at the same time as that which is to be saved. For the sake of the birds, various plants can be grown whose fruit ripens at different seasons. A number of kinds are useful to supply food in winter.

Of plants that retain their fruit a long time, some of the best are the juniper, sumach, mountain ash,

Dimensions of Nesting Boxes
As given in Farmers' Bulletin 609, U. S. Department of Agriculture

Species	Floor of Cavity	Depth of Cavity	Entrance Above Floor	Diameter of Entrance B	Height Above Ground
	Inches	*Inches*	*Inches*	*Inches*	*Feet*
Bluebird	5 by 5	8	6	1½	5 to 10
Robin	6 by 8	8	*	*	6 to 15
Chickadee	4 by 4	8 to 10	8	1⅛	6 to 15
Tufted titmouse	4 by 4	8 to 10	8	1¼	6 to 15
White-breasted nuthatch	4 by 4	8 to 10	8	1¼	12 to 20
House wren	4 by 4	6 to 8	1 to 6	⅞	6 to 10
Bewick wren	4 by 4	6 to 8	1 to 6	1	6 to 10
Carolina wren	4 by 4	6 to 8	1 to 6	1⅛	6 to 10
Dipper	6 by 6	6	1	3	1 to 3
Violet-green swallow	5 by 5	6	1 to 6	1½	10 to 15
Tree swallow	5 by 5	6	1 to 6	1½	10 to 15
Barn swallow	6 by 6	6	*	*	8 to 12
Martin	6 by 6	6	1	2½	15 to 20

Song sparrow	6 by 6	6	†	†	1 to 3
House finch	6 by 6	6	4	2	8 to 12
Phœbe	6 by 6	6	–	*	8 to 12
Crested flycatcher	6 by 6	8 to 10	8	2	8 to 20
Flicker	7 by 7	16 to 18	16	2½	6 to 20
Red-headed woodpecker	6 by 6	12 to 15	12	2	12 to 20
Golden-fronted woodpecker	6 by 6	12 to 15	12	2	12 to 20
Hairy woodpecker	6 by 6	12 to 15	12	1½	12 to 20
Downy woodpecker	4 by 4	8 to 10	8	1¼	6 to 20
Screech owl	8 by 8	12 to 15	12	3	10 to 30
Sparrow hawk	8 by 8	12 to 15	12	3	10 to 30
Saw-whet owl	6 by 6	10 to 12	10	2½	12 to 20
Bam owl	10 by 18	15 to 18	4	6	12 to 18
Wood duck	10 by 18	10 to 15	3	6	4 to 20

*One or more sides open.
†All sides open.

Identifying Common Birds

From *Fifty Common Birds of Farm and Orchard* by Henry W. Henshaw, 1913

Bluebird (Sialia sialis)

Length,*about 6½ inches.

Range: Breeds in the United States (west to Arizona, Colorado, Wyoming, and Montana), southern Canada, Mexico, and Guatemala; winters in the southern half of the eastern United States and south to Guatemala.

Habits and economic status: The bluebird is one of the most familiar tenants of the farm and dooryard. Everywhere it is hailed as the harbinger of spring, and wherever it chooses to reside it is sure of a warm welcome. This bird, like the robin, phoebe, house wren, and some swallows, is very domestic in its habits. Its favorite nesting sites are crannies in the farm buildings or boxes made for its use or natural cavities in old apple trees. For rent the bird pays amply by destroying insects, and it takes no toll from the farm crop. The bluebird's diet consists of 68 per cent of insects to 32 per cent of vegetable matter. The largest items of insect food are grasshoppers first and beetles next, while caterpillars stand third. All of these are harmful except a few of the beetles. The vegetable food consists chiefly of fruit pulp, only an insignificant portion of which is of cultivated varieties. Among wild fruits elderberries are the favorite. From the above it will be seen that the bluebird does no essential harm, but on the contrary eats many harmful and annoying insects.

Robin (Planesticus migratorius)

Length, 10 inches.

Range: Breeds in the United States (except the Gulf States), Canada, Alaska, and Mexico; winters in most of the United States and south to Guatemala.

Habits and economic status: In the North and some parts of the West the robin is among the most cherished of our native birds. Should it ever become rare where now common, its joyous summer song and familiar presence will be sadly missed in many a homestead. The robin is an omnivorous feeder, and its food includes many orders of insects, with no very pronounced preference for any. It is very fond of earthworms, but its real economic status is determined by the vegetable food, which amounts to about 58 per cent of all. The principal item is fruit, which forms more than 51 per cent of the total food. The fact that in the examination of over 1,200 stomachs the percentage of wild fruit was found to be 5 times that of the cultivated varieties suggests that berry-bearing shrubs, if planted near the

*Measured from tip of bill to tip of tall.

orchard, will serve to protect more valuable fruits. In California in certain years it has been possible to save the olive crop from hungry robins only by the most strenuous exertions and considerable expense. The bird's general usefulness is such, however, that all reasonable means of protecting orchard fruit should be tried before killing the birds.

Russet-Backed Thrush (Hylocichla ustulata)

Length, 7¼ inches. Among thrushes having the top of head and tail nearly the same color . as the back, this one is distinguished by its tawny eye-ring and cheeks. The Pacific coast subspecies is russet brown above, while the other subspecies is the olive-backed thrush. The remarks below apply to the species as a whole.

Range: Breeds in the forested parts of Alaska and Canada and south to California, Colorado, Michigan, New York, West Virginia (mountains), and Maine; winters from Mexico to South America.

Habits and economic status: This is one of a small group of thrushes the members of which are by many ranked first among American songbirds. The several members resemble one another in size, plumage, and habits. While this thrush is very fond of fruit, its partiality for the neighborhood of streams keeps it from frequenting orchards far from water. It is most troublesome during the cherry season, when the young are in the nest. From this it might be inferred that the young are fed on fruit, but such is not the case. The adults eat fruit, but the nestlings, as usual, are fed mostly upon insects. Beetles constitute the largest item of animal food,

and ants come next. Many caterpillars also are eaten. The great bulk of vegetable food consists of fruit, of which two-fifths is of cultivated varieties. Where these birds live in or near gardens or orchards, they may do considerable damage, but they are too valuable as insect destroyers to be killed if the fruit can be protected in any other way. (See Biol. Surv. Bul. 30, pp. 86–92.)

Ruby-Crowned Kinglet (Regulus calendula)

Length, about 4¼ inches. Olive green above, soiled whitish below, concealed feathers on head (crest) bright red.

Range: Breeds in southern Canada, southern Alaska, and the higher mountains of the western United States; winters in much of the United States and south to Guatemala.

Habits and economic status: In habits and haunts this tiny sprite resembles a chickadee. It is an active, nervous little creature, flitting hither and yon in search of food, and in spring stopping only long enough to utter its beautiful song, surprisingly loud for the size of the musician. Three-fourths of its food consists of wasps, bugs, and flies. Beetles are the only other item of importance (12 per cent). The bugs eaten by the kinglet are mostly small, but, happily, they are the most harmful kinds. Treehoppers, leafhoppers, and jumping plant lice are pests and often do great harm to trees and smaller plants, while plant lice and scale insects are the worst scourges of the fruit grower—in fact, the prevalence of the latter has almost risen to the magnitude of a national peril. It is these small and seemingly insignificant birds that most successfully attack and hold in check these insidious foes of horticulture. The vegetable food consists of seeds of poison ivy, or poison oak, a few weed seeds, and a few small fruits, mostly elderberries. (See Biol. Surv. Bul. 30, pp. 81–84.)

Chickadee (Penthestes atricapillus)

Length, about 5¼ inches.

Range: Resident in the United States (except the southern half east of the plains), Canada, and Alaska.

Habits and economic status: Because of its delightful notes, its confiding ways, and its fearlessness, the chickadee is one of our best-known birds. It responds to encouragement, and by hanging within its reach a constant supply of suet the chickadee can be made a regular visitor to the garden and orchard. Though insignificant in size, titmice are feu: from being so from the economic standpoint, owing to their numbers and activity. While one locality is being scrutinized for food by a larger bird, 10 are being searched by the smaller species. The chickadee's food is made up of insects and vegetable matter in the proportion of 7 of the former to 3 of the latter. Moths and caterpillars are favorites and form about one-third of the whole. Beetles, ants, wasps, bugs, flies, grasshoppers, and spiders make up the rest. The vegetable food is composed of seeds, largely those of pines, with a few of the poison ivy and some weeds. There are few more useful birds than the chickadees.

White-Breasted Nuthatch (Sitta carolinensis)

Length, 6 inches. White below, above gray, with a black head.

Range: Resident in the United States, southern Canada, and Mexico.

Habits and economic status: This bird might readily be mistaken by a careless observer for a small woodpecker, but its note, an oft-repeated *yank*, is very unwoodpecker-like, and, unlike either woodpeckers or creepers, it climbs downward as easily as upward and seems to set the laws of gravity at defiance. The name was suggested by the habit of wedging nuts, especially beechnuts, in the crevices of bark so as to break them open by blows from the sharp, strong bill. The nuthatch gets its living from the trunks and branches of trees, over which it creeps from daylight to dark. Insects and spiders constitute a little more than 50 per cent of its food. The largest items of these are beetles, moths, and caterpillars, with ants and wasps. The animal food is all in the bird's favor except a few ladybird beetles. More than half of the vegetable food consists of mast, i.e., acorns and other nuts or large seeds. One-tenth of the food is grain, mostly waste corn. The nuthatch does no injury, so far as known, and much good.

Brown Creeper (Certhia familiaris americana and other subspecies)

Length, 5½ inches.

Range: Breeds from Nebraska, Indiana, North Carolina (mountains), and Massachusetts north to southern Canada, also in the mountains of the western United States, north to Alaska, south to Nicaragua; winters over most of its range.

Habits and economic status: Rarely indeed is the creeper seen at rest. It appears to spend its life in an incessant scramble over the trunks and branches of trees, from which it gets all its food. It is protectively colored so as to be practically invisible to its enemies and, though delicately built, possesses amazingly strong claws and feet. Its tiny eyes are sharp enough to detect insects so small that most other species pass them by, and altogether the creeper fills a unique place in the ranks of our insect destroyers.

The food consists of minute insects and insects' eggs, also cocoons of tineid moths, small wasps, ants, and bugs, especially scales and plant lice, with some small caterpillars. As the creeper remains in the United States throughout the year, it naturally secures hibernating insects and insects' eggs, as well as spiders and spiders' eggs, that are missed by the summer birds. On its bill of fare we find no product of husbandry nor any useful insects.

connected with country and suburban life. Its tiny body, long bill, sharp eyes, and strong feet peculiarly adapt it for creeping into all sorts of nooks and crannies where lurk the insects it feeds on. A cavity in a fence post, a hole in a tree, or a box will be welcomed alike by this busybody as a nesting site; but since the advent of the quarrelsome English sparrow such domiciles are at a premium and the wren's eggs and family are safe only in cavities having entrances too small to admit the sparrow. Hence it behooves the farmer's boy to provide boxes the entrances to which are about an inch in diameter, nailing these under gables of barns and outhouses or in orchard trees. In this way the numbers of this useful bird can be increased, greatly to the advantage of the farmer. Grasshoppers, beetles, caterpillars, bugs, and spiders are the principal elements of its food. Cutworms, weevils, ticks, and plant lice are among the injurious forms eaten. The nestlings of house wrens consume great quantities of insects. (See Yearbook U. S. Dept. Agric. 1895, pp. 416–418, and Biol. Survey Bul. 30, pp. 60–62.)

House Wren (Troglodytes aëdon)

Length, 4½ inches. The only one of our wrens with wholly whitish under-parts that lacks a light line over the eye.

Range: Breeds throughout the United States (except the South Atlantic and Gulf States) and southern Canada; winters in the southern United States and Mexico.

Habits and economic status: The rich, bubbling song of the familiar little house wren is one of the sweetest associations

Brown Thrasher (Toxostoma rufum)

Length, about 11 inches. Brownish red above, heavily streaked with black below.

Range: Breeds from the Gulf States to southern Canada and west to Colorado, Wyoming, and Montana; winters in the southern half of the eastern United States.

Habits and economic status: The brown thrasher is more retiring than either the mocking bird or catbird, but like them is a splendid singer. Not infrequently, indeed, its song is taken for that of its more famed cousin, the mocking bird. It is partial to thickets and

gets much of its food from the ground. Its search for this is usually accompanied by much scratching and scattering of leaves; whence its common name. Its call note is a sharp sound like the smacking of lips, which is useful in identifying this long-tailed, thicket-haunting bird, which does not much relish close scrutiny. The brown thrasher is not so fond of fruit as the catbird and mocker, but devours a much larger percentage of animal food. Beetles form one-half of the animal food, grasshoppers and crickets one-fifth, caterpillars, including cutworms, somewhat less than one-fifth, and bugs, spiders, and millipede comprise most of the remainder. The brown thrasher feeds on such coleopterous pests as wire-worms, May beetles, rice weevils, rose beetles, and figeaters. By its destruction of these and other insects, which constitute more than 60 per cent of its food, the thrasher much more than compensates for that portion (about one-tenth) of its diet derived from cultivated crops. (See Yearbook U. S. Dept. Agric. 1895, pp. 411–415.)

Catbird (Dumetella carolinensis)

Length, about 9 inches. The slaty gray plumage and black cap and tail are distinctive.

Range: Breeds throughout the United States west to New Mexico, Utah, Oregon, and Washington, and in southern Canada; winters from the Gulf States to Panama.

Habits and economic status: In many localities the catbird is one of the commonest birds. Tangled growths are its favorite nesting places and retreats, but berry patches and ornamental shrubbery are not

disdained. Hence the bird is a familiar dooryard visitor. The bird has a fine song, unfortunately marred by occasional cat calls. With habits similar to those of the mocking bird and a song almost as varied, the catbird has never secured a similar place in popular favor. Half of its food consists of fruit, and the cultivated crops most often injured are cherries, strawberries, raspberries, and blackberries. Beetles, ants, crickets, and grasshoppers are the most important element of its animal food. The bird is known to attack a few pests, as cutworms, leaf beetles, clover-root curculio, and the periodical cicada, but the good it does in this way probably does not pay for the fruit it steals. The extent to which it should be protected may perhaps be left to the individual cultivator; that is, it should be made lawful to destroy catbirds that are doing manifest damage to crops. (See Yearbook U. S. Dept. Agric. 1895, pp. 406–411.)

Mocking Bird (Mimua polyglottos)

Length, 10 inches. Most easily distinguished from the similarly colored loggerhead shrike (see p. 16) by the absence of a conspicuous black stripe through the eye.

Range: Resident from southern Mexico north to California, Wyoming, Iowa, Ohio, and Maryland; casual farther north.

Habits and economic status: Because of its incomparable medleys and imitative powers, the mocking bird is the most renowned singer of the Western Hemisphere. Even in confinement it is a masterly performer, and formerly thousands were trapped and sold for cage birds, but this reprehensible practice has been largely stopped by protective laws. It is not surprising, therefore, that the mocking bird should receive protection principally because of its ability as a songster and its preference for the vicinity of dwellings. Its place in the affections of the South is similar to that occupied by the robin in the North. It is well that this is true, for the bird appears not to earn protection from a strictly economic standpoint. About half of its diet consists of fruit, and many cultivated varieties are attacked, such as oranges, grapes, figs, strawberries, blackberries, and raspberries. Somewhat less than a fourth of the food is animal matter, and grasshoppers are the largest single element. The bird is fond of cotton worms, and is known to feed also on the chinch bug; rice weevil, and boll worm. It is unfortunate that it does not feed on injurious insects to an extent sufficient to offset its depredations on fruit. (See Yearbook U. S. Dept. Agric. 1895, pp. 415–416, and Biol. Survey Bul. 30, pp. 52–56.)

Myrtle Warbler (Dendroica coronate)

Length, 5½ inches. The similarly colored Audubon's warbler has a yellow throat instead of a white one.

Range: Breeds throughout most of the forested area of Canada and south to Minnesota, Michigan, New York, and Massachusetts; winters in the southern two-thirds of the United States and south to Panama.

Habits and economic status: This member of our beautiful wood warbler family, a family peculiar to America, has the characteristic voice, coloration, and habits of its kind. Trim of form and graceful of motion, when seeking food it combines the methods of the wrens,

creepers, and flycatchers. It breeds only in the northern parts of the eastern United States, but in migration it occurs in every patch of woodland and is so numerous that it is familiar to every observer. Its place is taken in the West by Audubon's warbler. More than three-fourths of the food of the myrtle warbler consists of insects, practically all of them harmful. It is made up of small beetles, including some weevils, with many ants and wasps. This bird is so small and nimble that it successfully attacks insects too minute to be prey for larger birds. Scales and plant lice form a very considerable part of its diet. Flies are the largest item of food; in fact, only a few flycatchers and swallows eat as many flies as this bird. The vegetable food (22 per cent) is made up of fruit and the seeds of poison oak or ivy, also the seeds of pine and of the bayberry.

Loggerhead Shrike (Lanius ludovicianus)

Length, about 9 inches. A gray, black, and white bird, distinguished from the somewhat similarly colored mocking bird by the black stripe on side of head.

Range: Breeds throughout the United States, Mexico, and southern Canada; winters in the southern half of the United States and in Mexico.

Habits and economic status: The loggerhead shrike, or southern butcher bird, is common throughout its ranee and is sometimes called "French mocking bird" from a superficial resemblance and not from its notes, which are harsh and unmusical. The shrike is naturally an insectivorous bird which has extended its hill of fare to include small

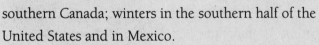

mammals, birds. and reptiles. Its hooked beak is well adapted to tearing its prey, while to make amends for the lack of talons it has hit upon the plan of forcing its victim, if too large to swallow, into the fork of a bush or tree, where it can tear it asunder. Insects, especially grasshoppers, constitute the larger part of its food, though beetles, moths, caterpillars, ants, wasps, and a few spiders also are taken. While the butcher bird occasionally catches small birds, its principal vertebrate food is small mammals, as field mice, shrews, and moles, and when possible it obtains lizards. It habitually impales its surplus prey on a thorn, sharp twig, or barb of a wire fence. (See Biol. Survey Bul. 9, pp. 20–24, and Bul. 30, pp. 33–38.)

Barn Swallow (Hirundo erythrogastra)

Length, about 7 inches. Distinguished among our swallows by deeply forked tail.

Range: Breeds throughout the United States (except the South Atlantic and Gulf States) and most of Canada; winters in South America.

Habits and economic status: This is one of the most familiar birds of the farm and one of the greatest insect destroyers. From daylight todark on tireless wings it seeks its prey, and the insects destroyed are countless. Its favorite nesting site is a barn rafter, upon which it sticks its mud basket. Most modern barns are so tightly constructed that swallows can not gain entrance, and in New England and some other parts of the country barn swallows are much less numerous than formerly. Farmers can easily provide for the entrance and exit of the birds and so add materially to their numbers. It may be well to add that the parasites that sometimes infest

the nests of swallows are not the ones the careful housewife dreads, and no fear need be felt of the infestation spreading to the houses. Insects taken on the wing constitute the almost exclusive diet of the barn swallow. More than one-third of the whole consists of flies, including unfortunately some useful parasitic species. Beetles stand next in order and consist of a few weevils and many of the small dung beetles of the May beetle family that swarm over the pastures in the late afternoon. Ants amount to more than one-fifth of the whole food, while wasps and bees are well represented.

Purple Martin (Progne subis)

Length, about 8 inches.

Range: Breeds throughout the United States and southern Canada, south to central Mexico; winters in South America.

Habits and economic status: This is the largest as it is one of the most beautiful of the swallow tribe. It formerly built its nests in cavities of trees, as it still does in wild districts, but learning that man was a friend it soon adopted domestic habits. Its presence about the farm can often be secured by erecting houses suitable for nesting sites and protecting them from usurpation by the English sparrow, and every effort should be made to increase the number of colonies of this very useful bird. The boxes should be at a reasonable height, say 15 feet from the ground, and made inaccessible to cats. A colony of these birds on a farm makes great inroads upon the insect population, as the birds not only themselves feed upon

insects but rear their young upon the same diet. Fifty years ago in New England it was not uncommon to see colonies of 50 pairs of martins, but most of them have now vanished for no apparent reason except that the martin houses have decayed and have not been renewed. More than three-fourths of this bird's food consists of wasps, bugs, and beetles, their importance being in the order given. The beetles include several species or harmful weevils, as the clover-leaf weevils and the nut weevils. Besides these are many crane flies, moths, May flies, and dragonflies.

Black-Headed Grosbeak (Zamelodia melanocephala)

Length, about 8¼ inches.

Range: Breeds from the Pacific coast to Nebraska and the Dakotas, and from southern Canada to southern Mexico; winters in Mexico.

Habits and economic status: The black-headed grosbeak takes the place in the West of the rosebreast in the East, and like it is a fine songster. Like it also the blackhead readily resorts to orchards and gardens and is common in agricultural districts. The bird has a very powerful bill and easily crushes or cuts into the firmest fruit. It feeds upon cherries, apricots, and other fruits, and also does some damage to green peas and beans, but it is so active a foe of certain horticultural pests that we can afford to overlook its faults. Several kinds of scale insects are freely eaten, and one, the black olive scale, constitutes a fifth of the total food. In May many cankerworms and codling moths are consumed, and almost a sixth of the bird's seasonal

food consists of flower beetles, which do incalculable damage to cultivated flowers and to ripe fruit. For each quart of fruit consumed by the black-headed grosbeak it destroys in actual bulk more than 1½ quarts of black olive scales and 1 quart of flower beetles, besides a generous quantity of codling-moth pupae and cankerworms. It is obvious that such work as this pays many times over for the fruit destroyed. (See Biol. Survey Bul. 32, pp. 60–77.)

Rose-Breasted Grosbeak (Zamelodia ludoviciana)

Length, 8 inches.

Range: Breeds from Kansas, Ohio, Georgia (mountains), and New Jersey, north to southern Canada; winters from Mexico to South America.

Habits and economic status: This beautiful grosbeak is noted for its clear, melodious notes, which are poured forth in generous measure. The rosebreast sings even at midday during summer, when the intense heat has silenced almost every other songster. Its beautiful plumage and sweet song are not its sole claim on our favor, for few birds are more beneficial to agriculture. The rosebreast eats some green peas and does some damage to fruit. But this mischief is much more than balanced by the destruction of insect pests. The bird is so fond of the Colorado potato beetle that it has earned the name of "potato-bug bird," and no less than a tenth of the total food of the rosebreasts examined consists of potato beetles—evidence that the bird is one of the most important enemies of the pest. It vigorously attacks cucumber beetles and many of the scale insects. It proved an active enemy of the Rocky Mountain locust during that insect's ruinous invasions, and among the other pests it consumes are the spring and fall cankerworms, orchard and forest tent caterpillars, tussock, gipsy, and brown-tail moths, plum curculio, army worm, and chinch bug. In fact, not one of our birds has a better record. (See Biol. Survey Bul. 32, pp. 33–59.)

Song Sparrow (Melospiza melodia)

Length, about 6¼ inches. The heavily spotted breast with heavy central blotch is characteristic.

Range: Breeds in the United States (except the South Atlantic and Gulf States), southern Canada, southern Alaska, and Mexico; winters in Alaska and most of the United States southward.

Habits and economic status: Like the familiar little "chippy," the song sparrow is one of our most domestic species, and builds its nest in hedges or in garden shrubbery close to houses, whenever it is reasonably safe from the house cat, which, however, takes heavy toll of the nestlings. It is a true harbinger of spring, and its delightful little song is trilled forth from the top of some green shrub in early March and April, before most of our other songsters have thought of leaving the sunny south. Song' sparrows vary much in habits, as well as in size and coloration. Some forms live along streams bordered by deserts, others in swamps among bulrushes and tules, others in timbered regions, others on rocky barren hillsides, and still others in rich, fertile valleys. With such a variety of habitat, the food of the species naturally varies considerably. About three-fourths of its diet consists of the seeds of noxious weeds and

one-fourth of insects. Of these, beetles, especially weevils, constitute the major portion. Ants, wasps, bugs (including the black olive scale), and caterpillars are also eaten. Grasshoppers are taken by the eastern birds, but not by the western ones. (See Biol. Survey Bul. 15, pp. 82–86.)

Chipping Sparrow (Spizella passerina)

Length, about 5¼ inches. Distinguished by the chestnut crown, black line through eye, and black bill.

Range: Breeds throughout the United States, south to Nicaragua, and north to southern Canada; winters in the southern United States and southward.

Habits and economic status: The chipping sparrow is very friendly and domestic, and often builds its nest in gardens and orchards or in the shrubbery close to dwellings. Its gentle and confiding ways endear it to all bird lovers. It is one of the most insectivorous of all the sparrows. Its diet consists of about 42 per cent of insects and spiders and 58 per cent of vegetable matter. The animal food consists largely of caterpillars, of which it feeds a great many to its young. Besides these, it eats beetles, including many weevils, of which one stomach contained 30. It also eats ants, wasps, and bugs. Among the latter are plant lice and black olive scales. The vegetable food is practically all weed seed. A nest with 4 young of this species was watched at different hours on 4 days. In the 7 hours of observation 119 feedings were noted, or an average of 17 feedings per hour, or 4¼ feedings per hour to each nestling. This would give for a day of 14 hours at least 238 insects eaten by the brood. (See Biol. Survey Bul. 15, pp. 76–78.)

White-Crowned Sparrow (Zonotrichia leucophrys)

Length, 7 inches. The only similar sparrow, the white-throat, has a yellow spot in front of eye.

Range: Breeds in Canada, the mountains of New Mexico, Colorado, Wyoming, and Montana, and thence to the Pacific coast; winters in the southern half of the United States and in northern Mexico.

Habits and economic status: This beautiful sparrow is much more numerous in the western than in the eastern States, where, indeed, it is rather rare. In the East it is shy and retiring, but it is much bolder and more conspicuous in the far West and there often frequents gardens and parks. Like most . of its family it is a seed eater by preference, and insects comprise very little more than 7 per cent of its diet. Caterpillars are the largest item, with some beetles, a few ants and wasps, and some bugs, among which are black olive scales. The great bulk of the food, however, consists of weed seeds, which amount to 74 per cent of the whole. In California this bird is accused of eating the buds and blossoms of fruit trees, but buds or blossoms were found in only 30 out of 516 stomachs, and probably it is only under exceptional circumstances that it does any damage in this way. Evidently neither the farmer nor the fruit grower has much to fear from the whitecrowned sparrow. The little fruit it eats is mostly wild, and the grain eaten is waste or volunteer. (See Biol. Survey Bul. 34, pp. 75–77.)

English Sparrow (Passer domesticus)

Length, about 6¼ inches. Its incessant chattering, quarrelsome disposition, and abundance and familiarity about human habitations distinguish it from our native sparrows.

Range: Resident throughout the United States and southern Canada.

Habits and economic status: Almost universally condemned since its introduction into the United States, the English sparrow has not only held its own, but has ever increased in numbers and extended its range in spite of all opposition. Its habit of driving out or even killing more beneficial species and the defiling of buildings by its droppings and by its own unsightly structures, are serious objections to this sparrow. ' Moreover, in rural districts, it is destructive to grain, fruit, peas, beans, and other vegetables. On the other hand, the bird feeds to some extent on a large number of insect pests, and this fact points to the need of a new investigation of the present economic status of the species, especially as it promises to be of service in holding in check the newly introduced alfalfa weevil, which threatens the alfalfa industry in Utah and neighboring States. In cities most of the food of the English sparrow is waste material secured from the streets.

Crow Blackbird (Quiscalus quiscula)

Length, 12 inches. Shorter by at least 3 inches than the other grackles with trough-shaped tails. Black, with purplish, bluish, and bronze reflections.

Range: Breeds throughout the United States west to Texas, Colorado, and Montana, and in southern Canada; winters in the southern half of the breeding range.

Habits and economic status: This blackbird is a beautiful species, and is well known from its habit of congregating in city parks and nesting there year after year. Like other species which habitually assemble in great flocks, it is capable of inflicting much damage on any crop it attacks, and where

it is harmful a judicious reduction of numbers is probably sound policy.

It shares with the crow and blue jay the evil habit of pillaging the nests of small birds of eggs and young. Nevertheless it does much good by destroying insect pests, especially white grubs, weevils, grasshoppers, and caterpillars. Among the caterpillars are army worms and other cutworms. When blackbirds gather in large flocks, as in the Mississippi Valley, they may greatly damage grain, either when first sown or when in the milk. In winter they subsist mostly on weed seed and waste grain. (See Biol. Surv. Bul. 13, pp. 53–70.)

Brewer's Blackbird (Euphagus cyanocephalus)

Length, 10 inches. Its glossy purplish head distinguishes it from other blackbirds that do not show in flight a trough-shaped tail.

Range: Breeds in the West, east to Texas, Kansas, and Minnesota, and north to southern Canada; winters over most of the United States breeding range, south to Guatemala.

Habits and economic status: Very numerous in the West and in fall gathers in immense flocks, especially about barnyards and corrals. During the cherry season in California Brewer's blackbird is much, in the orchards. In one case they were seen to eat freely of cherries, but when a neighboring fruit raiser began to plow his orchard almost every blackbird in the vicinity was upon the newly opened ground and close at the plowman's heels in its eagerness to get the insects exposed by the plow. Caterpillars and pupæ form the largest item of animal food (about 12 per cent). Many of these are cutworms, and cotton bollworms or corn earworms were found in 10 stomachs and codling-moth pupae in 11. Beetles constitute over 11 per cent of the food. The vegetable food is practically contained in three items—grain, fruit, and weed seeds. Grain, mostly oats, amounts to 54 per cent; fruit, largely cherries, 4 per cent; and weed seeds, not quite 9 per cent. The grain is probably mostly wild, volunteer, or waste, so that the bird does most damage by eating fruit. (See Biol. Surv. Bul. 34, pp. 59–65.)

Bullock's Oriole (Icterus bullocki)

Length, about 8 inches. Our only oriole with top of head and throat black and cheeks orange.

Range: Breeds from South Dakota, Nebraska, and Kansas to the Pacific Ocean and from southern Canada to northern Mexico; winters in Mexico.

Habits and economic status: In the West this bird takes the place occupied in the East by the Baltimore oriole. In food, nesting habits, and song the birds are similar. Both are migratory and remain on their summer range only some five or six months. They take kindly to orchards, gardens, and the vicinity of farm buildings and often live in villages and city parks. Then* diet is largely made up of insects that infest orchards and gardens. When fruit trees are in bloom they are constantly busy among the blossoms and save many of them from destruction. In the food of Bullock's oriole beetles amount to 35 per cent and nearly all are harmful. Many of these are weevils, some of which live upon acorns and other nuts. Ants and wasps amount to 15 per cent of the diet. The black olive scale was found in 45 of the 162 stomachs examined. Caterpillars, with a few moths and pupae, are the largest item of food and amount to over 41 per cent. Among these were codling-moth larvae. The vegetable food is practically all fruit (19 per cent) and in cherry season consists largely of that fruit. Eating small fruits is the bird's worst trait, but it will do harm in this way only when very numerous. (See Biol. Surv. Bul. 34, pp. 68–71.)

weeds, with near-by water, furnish the conditions best suited to the meadowlark's taste. The song of the western bird is loud, clear, and melodious. That of its eastern relative is feebler and loses much by comparison. In many localities the meadowlark is classed and shot as a game bird. From the farmer's standpoint this is a mistake, since its value as an insect eater is far greater than as an object of pursuit by the sportsman. Both the boll weevil, the foe of the cotton grower, and the alfalfa weevil are among the beetles it habitually eats. Twenty-five per cent of the diet of this bird is beetles, half of which are predaceous ground beetles, accounted useful insects, and one-fifth are destructive weevils. Caterpillars form 11 per cent of the food and are eaten in every month in the year. Among these are many cutworms and the well-known army worm. Grasshoppers are favorite food and are eaten in every month and almost every day. The vegetable food (24 per cent of the whole) consists of grain and weed seeds. (See Yearbook U. S. Dept. Agr. 1895, pp. 420–426.)

Meadowlarks (Sturnella magna and Sturnella neglecta)

Length, about 10¾ inches.

Range: Breed generally in the United States, southern Canada, and Mexico to Costa Rica: winter from the Ohio and Potomac Valleys and British Columbia southward.

Habits and economic status: Our two meadow-larks,

though differing much in song, resemble each other closely in plumage and habits. Grassy plains and uplands covered with a thick growth of grass or

Red-Winged Blackbird (Agelaius phœniceus)

Length, about 9¼ inches.

Range: Breeds in Mexico and North America south of the Barren Grounds; winters in southern half of United States and south to Costa Rica.

Habits and economic status: The prairies of the upper Mississippi Valley, with

their numerous sloughs and ponds, furnish ideal nesting places for redwings, and consequently this region has become the great breeding ground for the species. These prairies pour forth the vast flocks that play havoc with grain-fields. East of the Appalachian Range, marshes on the shores of lakes, rivers, and estuaries are the only available breeding sites and, as these are comparatively few and small, the species is much less abundant than in the West. Redwings are eminently gregarious, living in flocks and breeding in communities. The food of the redwing consists of 27 per cent animal matter and 73 per cent vegetable. Insects constitute practically one-fourth of the food. Beetles (largely weevils, a most harmful group) amount to 10 per cent. Grasshoppers are eaten in every month and amount to about 5 per cent. Caterpillars (among them the injurious army worm) are eaten at all seasons and aggregate 6 per cent. Ante, wasps, bugs, flies, dragonflies, ana spiders also are eaten. The vegetable food consists of seeds, including grain, of which oats is the favorite, and some small fruits. When in large flocks this bird is capable of doing great harm to grain. (See Biol. Survey Bul. 13, pp. 33–34.)

Bobolink (Dolichonyx oryzivorus)

Length, about 7 inches.

Range: Breeds from Ohio northeast to Nova Scotia, north to Manitoba, and northwest to British Columbia; winters in South America.

Habits and economic status: When American writers awoke to the beauty and attractiveness of our native birds, among the first to be enshrined in song and story was the bobolink. Few species show such striking contrasts

in the color of the sexes, and few have songs more unique and whimsical. In its northern home the bird is loved for its beauty and its rich melody; in the South it earns deserved hatred by its destructiveness. Bobolinks reach the southeastern coast of the United States the last half of April just as rice is sprouting and at once begin to pull up and devour the sprouting kernels. Soon they move on to their northern breeding grounds, where they feed upon insects, weed seeds, and a little grain. When the young are well on the wing, they gather in flocks with the parent birds and gradually move southward, being then generally known as reed birds. They reach the rice fields of the Carolinas about August 20, when the rice is in the milk. Then until the birds depart for South America planters and birds fight for the crop, and in spite of constant watchfulness and innumerable devices for scaring the birds a loss of 10 per cent of the rice is the usual result. (See Biol. Survey Bul. 13, pp. 12–22.)

Common Crow (Corvus brachyrhynchos)

Length, 19 inches.

Range: Breeds throughout the United States and most of Canada; winters generally in the United States.

Habits and economic status: The general habits of the crow are universally known. Its ability to commit such misdeeds as pulling corn and stealing eggs and fruit and to get away unscathed is lime short of marvelous. Much of the crow's success in life is due to cooperation, and the social instinct of

the species has its highest expression in the winter roosts, which are sometimes frequented by hundreds of thousands of crows. From these roosts daily flights of many miles are made in search of food. Injury to sprouting corn is the most frequent complaint against this species, but by coating the seed grain with coal tar most of this damage may be prevented. Losses of poultry and eggs may be averted by proper housing and the judicious use of wire netting. The insect food of the crow includes wireworms, cutworms, white grubs, and grasshoppers, and during outbreaks of these insects the crow renders good service. The bird is also an efficient scavenger. But chiefly because of its destruction of beneficial wild birds and their eggs the crow must be classed as a criminal, and a reduction in its numbers in localities where it is seriously destructive is justifiable.

California Jay (Aphelocoma californica)

Length, 12 inches. Distinguished from other jays within its range by its decidedly whitish underparts and brown patch on the back.

Range: Resident in California, north to southern Washington, and south to southern Lower California.

Habits and economic status: This jay has the same general traits of character as the eastern blue jay. He is the same noisy, rollicking fellow and occupies a corresponding position in bird society. Robbing the nests of smaller birds is a favorite pastime, and he is a persistent spy upon domestic fowls and well knows the meaning

of the cackle of a hen. Not only does he steal eggs but he kills young chicks. The insect food of this jay constitutes about one-tenth of its annual sustenance. The inclusion of grasshoppers and caterpillars makes this part of the bird's food in its favor. But the remainder of its animal diet includes altogether too large a proportion of beneficial birds and their eggs, and in this respect it appears to be worse than its eastern relative, the blue jay. While its vegetable food is composed largely of mast, at times its liking for cultivated fruit and grain makes it a most unwelcome visitor to the orchard and farm. In conclusion it may be said that over much of its range this jay is too abundant for the best interests of agriculture and horticulture. (See Biol. Survey Bul. 34, pp. 50–56.)

Blue Jay (Cyanocitta Cristata)

Length, 11½ inches. The brilliant blue of the wings and tail combined with the black crescent of the upper breast and the crested head distinguish this species.

Range: Resident in the eastern United States and southern Canada, west to the Dakotas, Colorado, and Texas.

Habits and economic status: The blue jay is of a dual nature. Cautious and silent in the vicinity of its nest, away from it it is bold and noisy. Sly in the commission of mischief, it is ever ready to scream "thief" at the slightest disturbance. As usual in such cases, its remarks are applicable to none more than itself, a fact neighboring nest holders know to their sorrow, for during the breeding season the jay lays heavy toll upon the eggs

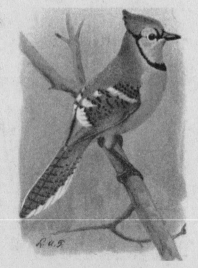

and young of other birds, and in doing so deprives us of the services of species more beneficial than itself. Approximately three-fourths of the annual food of the blue jay is vegetable matter, the greater part of which is composed of mast, i. e., acorns, chestnuts, beechnuts, and the like. Corn is the principal cultivated crop upon which this bird feeds, but stomach analysis indicates that most of the corn taken is waste grain. Such noxious insects as wood-boring beetles, grasshoppers, eggs of various caterpillars, and scale insects constitute about one-fifth of its food.

Horned Lark (Otocoris alpestris)

Length, about 7¾ inches. The black mark across the breast and the small, pointed tufts of dark feathers above and behind the eyes distinguish the bird.

Range: Breeds throughout the United States (except the South Atlantic and Gulf States) and Canada; winters in all the United States except Florida.

Habits and economic status: Horned larks frequent the open country, especially the plains and deserts. They associate m large flocks, are hardy, apparently delighting in exposed situations in winter, and often nest before snow disappears. The flight is irregular and hesitating, but in the breeding season the males ascend high in air, singing as they go, and pitch to the ground in one thrilling dive. The preference of horned larks is for vegetable food, and about one-sixth of this is grain, chiefly waste. Some sprouting grain is nulled, but drilled grain is safe from injury. California horned larks take much more grain than the eastern birds, specializing on oats, but this is accounted for by the fact that oats grow wild over much of the State. Weed seeds are the largest single element of food. The insect food, about 20 per cent of the whole, includes such pests as May beetles and their larvæ (white grubs), leaf beetles, clover-leaf and clover-root weevils, the potato-stalk borer, nut Weevils, billbugs, and the chinch bug. Grasshoppers are a favorite food, and cutworms are freely eaten. The horned larks, on the whole, may be considered useful birds. (See Biol. Survey Bui. 23.)

Arkansas Kingbird (Tyrannus verticalis)

Length, 9 inches. The white edge of the feather on each side of the tail distinguishes this from all other flycatchers except the gray and salmon-colored scissortail of Texas.

Range: Breeds from Minnesota, Kansas, and Texas to the Pacific Ocean and from northern Mexico to southern Canada; winters from Mexico to Guatemala.

Habits and economic status: The Arkansas kingbird is not so domestic as its eastern relative and seems to prefer the hill country with scattered oaks rather than the orchard or the vicinity of ranch buildings, but it sometimes places its rude and conspicuous nest in trees on village streets. The bird's yearly food is composed of 87 per cent animal matter and 13 per cent vegetable. The animal food is composed almost entirely of insects. Like the eastern species, it has been accused of destroying honeybees to a harmful extent, and remains of

honeybees were found to constitute 5 per cent of the food of the individuals examined, but nearly all those eaten were drones. Bees and wasps, in general, are the biggest item of food (38 per cent), grasshoppers and crickets stand next (20 per cent), and beetles, mostly of noxious species, constitute 14 per cent of the food. The vegetable food consists mostly of fruit, such as the elder and other berries, with a few seeds. This bird should be strictly preserved. (See Biol. Survey Bul. 34, pp. 32–34, and Bul. 44, pp. 19–22.)

Kingbird (Tyrannus tyrannus)

Length, about 8½ inches. The white lower surface and white-tipped tail distinguish this flycatcher.

Range: Breeds throughout the United States (except the southwestern part) and southern Canada; winters from Mexico to South America.

Habits and economic status: The kingbird is a pronounced enemy of hawks and crows, which it vigorously attacks at every opportunity, thereby affording efficient protection to near-by poultry yards and young chickens at large. It loves the open country and is especially fond of orchards and trees about farm buildings. No less than 85 per cent of its food consists of insects, mostly of a harmful nature. It eats the common rose chafer or rose bug, and more remarkable still it devours blister beetles freely. The bird has been accused of eating honeybees to an injurious extent, but there is little ground for the accusation, as appears from the fact that examination of 634 stomachs showed only 61 bees in 22 stomachs.

Of these 51 were useless drones. On the other hand, it devours robber flies, which catch and destroy honeybees. Grasshoppers and crickets, with a few bugs and some cutworms, and a few other insects, make up the rest of the animal food. The vegetable food consists of fruit and a few seeds. The kingbird deserves full protection. (See Biol. Surv. Bul. 44, pp. 11–19.)

Nighthawk (Chordeiles virginianus)

Length, 10 inches. Not to be confused with the whippoorwill. The latter lives in woodland and is chiefly nocturnal. The nighthawk often flies by day, when the white bar across the wing and its nasal cry are distinguishing.

Range: Breeds throughout most of the United States and Canada; winters in South America.

Habits and economic status: The skillful evolutions of a company of night-hawks as the birds gracefully cleave the air in intersecting circles is a sight to be remembered. So expert are they on the wing that no insect is safe from them, even the swift dragonfly being captured with ease. Unfortunately their erratic flight tempts men to use them for targets, and this inexcusable practice is seriously diminishing their numbers, which is deplorable, since no birds are more useful. This species makes no nest, but lays its two spotted eggs on the bare ground, sometimes on the gravel roof of the city house. The night-hawk is a voracious feeder and is almost exclusively insectivorous. Some stomachs contained from 30 to 50 different kinds of insects, and more than 600 kinds have been identified from the stomachs thus far examined. From 500 to 1,000 ants are often found in a stomach. Several species of mosquitoes, including *Anopheles,* the transmitter of malaria, are eaten. Other well-known pests destroyed by the nighthawk are the Colorado potato beetle, cucumber beetles, chestnut, rice, clover-leaf and cotton-boll weevils, billbugs, bark beetles, squash bugs, and moths of the cotton worm.

Flicker (Colaptes auratus)

Length, 13 inches. The yellow under surface of the wing, yellow tail shafts, and white rump are characteristic.

Range: Breeds in the eastern United States west to the plains and in the forested parts of Canada and Alaska; winters in most of the eastern United States.

Habits and economic status: The flicker inhabits the open country rather than the forest and delights in park-like regions where trees are numerous and scattered. It nests in any large cavity in a tree and readily appropriates an artificial box. It is possible, therefore, to insure the presence of this useful bird about the farm and to increase its numbers. It is the most terrestrial of our woodpeckers and procures much of its food from the ground. The largest item of animal food is ants, of which the flicker eats more than any other common bird. Ants were found in 524 of the 684 stomachs examined and 98 stomachs contained no other food. One stomach contained over 5,000 and two others held over 3,000 each. While bugs are not largely eaten by the flicker, one stomach contained 17 chinch bugs. Wild fruits are next to ants in importance in the flicker's dietary. Of these sour gum and wild black cherry stand at the head. The food habits of this bird are such as to recommend it to complete protection. (See Biol. Survey Bul. 37, pp. 52–58.)

Yellow-Bellied Sapsucker (Sphyrapicus varius)

Length, about 8½ inches. Only woodpecker having top of head from base of

bill red, combined with a black patch on breast.

Range: Breeds in northern half of the United States and southern half of Canada; winters in most of the States and south to Costa Rica.

Habits and economic status: The yellow-bellied sapsucker is rather silent and suspicious and generally manages to have a tree between himself and the observer. Hence the bird is much better known by its works than its appearance. The regular girdles of holes made by this bird are common on a great variety of trees; in all about 250 kinds are known to be attacked. Occasionally young trees are killed outright, but more loss is caused by stains and other blemishes in the wood which result from sapsucker punctures. These blemishes, which are known as bird pecks, are especially numerous in hickory, oak, cypress, and yellow poplar. Defects due to sapsucker work cause an annual loss to the lumber industry estimated at $1,250,000. The food of the yellow-bellied sapsucker is about half animal and half vegetable. Its fondness for ants counts slightly in its favor. It eats also wasps, beetles (including, however, very-few wood-boring species), bugs, and spiders. The two principal components of the vegetable food are wild fruits of no importance and cambium (the layer just beneath the bark of trees). In securing the cambium the bird does the damage above described.

The yellow-bellied sapsucker, unlike other woodpeckers, thus does comparatively little good and much harm. (See Biol. Survey Bul. 39.)

Downy Woodpecker (Dryobates pobescens)

Length, 6 inches. Our smallest woodpecker; spotted with black and white. Dark bars on the outer tail feathers distinguish it from the similarly colored but larger hairy woodpecker.

Range: Resident in the United States and the forested parts of Canada and Alaska.

Habits and economic status: This woodpecker is commonly distributed, living in woodland tracts, orchards, and gardens. The bird has several characteristic notes, and, like the hairy woodpecker, is fond of beating on a dry resonant tree branch a tattoo which to appreciative ears has the quality of woodland music. In a hole excavated in a dead branch the downy woodpecker lays four to six eggs. This and the hairy woodpecker are among our most valuable allies, their food consisting of some of the worst foes of orchard and woodland, which the woodpeckers are especially equipped to dig out of dead and living wood. In the examination of 723 stomachs of this bird, animal food, mostly insects, was found to constitute 76 per cent of the diet and vegetable matter 24 per cent. The animal food consists largely of beetles that bore into timber or burrow under the bark. Caterpillars amount to 16 per cent of the food and include many especially harmful species. Grasshopper eggs are freely eaten. The vegetable food of the

downy woodpecker consists of small fruit and seeds, mostly of wild species. It distributes seeds of poison ivy, or poison oak, which is about the only fault of this very useful bird. (See Biol. Survey Bul. 37, pp. 17–22.)

Yellow-Billed Cuckoo (Coccyzus americanus)

Length, about 12 inches. The yellow lower part of the bill distinguishes this bird from its near relative, the black-billed cuckoo.

Range: Breeds generally in the United States and southern Canada; winters in South America.

Habits and economic status: This bird lives on the edges of woodland, in groves, orchards, parks, and even in shaded village streets. It is sometimes known as rain crow, because its very characteristic notes are supposed to foretell rain. The cuckoo has sly, furtive ways as it moves among the bushes or flits from tree to tree, and is much more often seen than heard. Unlike its European relative, it does not lay its eggs in other birds' nests, but builds a nest of its own. This is, however, a rather crude and shabby affair—hardly more than a platform of twigs sufficient to hold the greenish eggs. The cuckoo is extremely useful because of its insectivorous habits, especially as it shows a marked preference for the hairy caterpillars, which few birds eat. One stomach that was examined contained 250 American tent caterpillars; another, 217 fall webworms. In places where tent caterpillars are abundant they seem to constitute a large portion of the food of this and the black-billed cuckoo.

Screech Owl (Otus asio)

Length, about 8 inches. Our smallest owl with ear tufts. There are two distinct phases of plumage, one grayish and the other bright rufous.

Range: Resident throughout the United States, southern Canada, and northern Mexico.

Habits and economic status: The little screech owl inhabits orchards, groves, and thickets, and hunts for its prey in such places as well as along hedgerows and in the open. During warm shells in winter it forages quite extensively and stores up in some hollow tree considerable quantities of food for use during inclement weather. Such larders frequently contain enough mice or other prey to bridge over a period of a week or more. With the exception of the burrowing owl it is probably the most insectivorous of the nocturnal birds of prey. It feeds also upon small mammals, birds, reptiles, batrachians, fish, spiders, crawfish, scorpions, and earthworms. Grasshoppers, crickets, ground-dwelling beetles, and caterpillars are its favorites among insects, as are field mice among mammals and sparrows among birds. Out of 324 stomachs examined, 169 were found to contain insects; 142, small mammals; 56, birds; and 15, crawfish. The screech owl should be encouraged to stay near barns and outhouses, as it will keep in check house mice and wood mice, which frequent such places. (See Biol. Survey Bul. 3, pp. 163–173.)

Barn Owl (Aluco pratincola)

Length, about 17 inches. Facial disk not circular as in our other owls; plumage above, pale

yellow; beneath, varying from silky white to pale bright tawny.

Range: Resident in Mexico, in the southern United States, and north to New York, Ohio, Nebraska, and California.

Habits and economic status: The barn owl, often called monkey-faced owl, is one of the most beneficial of the birds of prey, since it feeds almost exclusively on small mammals that injure farm produce, nursery, and orchard stock. It hunts principally in the open and consequently secures such mammals as pocket gophers, field mice, common rats, house mice, harvest mice, kangaroo rats, and cotton rats. It occasionally captures a few birds and insects. At least a half bushel of the remains of pocket gophers have been found in the nesting cavity of a pair of these birds. Remembering that a gopher has been known in a short time to girdle seven apricot trees worth $100 it is hard to overestimate the value of the service of a pair of barn owls. 1,247 pellets of the barn owl collected from the Smithsonian towers contained 3,100 skulls, of which 3,004, or 97 per cent, were of mammals; 92, or 3 per cent, of birds; and 4 were of frogs. The bulk consisted of 1,987 field mice, 656 house mice, and 210 common rats. The birds eaten were mainly sparrows and blackbirds. This valuable owl should be rigidly protected throughout its entire range. (See Biol. Survey Bul. 3, pp. 132–139.)

Sparrow Hawk (Falco sparverius)

Length, about 10 inches. This is one of the best known and handsomest, as well as the smallest, of North American hawks.

Range: Breeds throughout the United States, Canada, and northern Mexico; winters in the United States and south to Guatemala.

Habits and economic status: The sparrow hawk which is a true falcon, lives in the more open country and builds its nest in hollow trees. It is abundant in many parts of the West, where telegraph poles afford it convenient perching and feeding places. Its food consists of insects, small mammals, birds, spiders, and reptiles. Grasshoppers, crickets, and terrestrial beetles and caterpillars make up considerably more than half its subsistence, while field mice, house mice, and shrews cover fully 25 per cent of its annual supply. The balance of the food includes birds, reptiles, and spiders. Contrary to the usual habits of the species, some individuals during the breeding season capture nestling birds for food for their young and create considerable havoc among the songsters of the neighborhood. In agricultural districts when new ground is broken by the plow, they sometimes become very tame, even alighting for an instant under the horses in their endeavor to seize a worm or insect. Out of 410 stomachs examined, 314 were found to contain insects; 129, small mammals; and 70, small birds. This little falcon renders good service in destroying noxious insects and rodents and should be encouraged and protected. (See Biol. Survey Bul. 3, pp. 115–127.)

Red-Tailed Hawk (Buteo borealis)

Length, about 2 feet. One of our largest hawks; adults with tail reddish brown.

Range: Breeds in the United States, Mexico, Costa Rica, Canada, and Alaska; winters generally in the United States and south to Guatemala.

Habits and economic status: The red-tailed hawk, or "hen-hawk," as it is commonly called, is one of the best known

of all our birds of prey, and is a widely distributed species of great economic importance. Its habit of sitting on some prominent limb or pole in the open, or flying with measured wing beat over prairies and sparsely wooded areas on the lookout for its favorite prey, causes it to be noticed by the most indifferent observer. Although not as omnivorous as the red-shouldered hawk, it feeds on a variety of food, as small mammals, snakes, frogs, insects, birds, crawfish, centipedes, and even carrion. In regions where rattlesnakes abound it destroys considerable numbers of the reptiles. Although it feeds to a certain extent on poultry and birds, it is nevertheless entitled to general protection on account of the insistent warfare it wages against field mice and other small rodents and insects that are so destructive to young orchards, nursery stock, and farm produce. Out of 530 stomachs examined, 457, or 85 per cent, contained the remains of mammal pests such as field mice, pine mice, rabbits, several species of ground squirrels, pocket gophers, and cotton rats, and only 62 contained the remains of poultry or game birds. (See Biol. Survey Bul. 3, pp. 48–62.)

Cooper's Hawk (Accipiter cooperi)

Length, about 15 inches. Medium sized, with long tail and short wings, and without the white patch on rump which is characteristic of the marsh hawk.

Range: Breeds throughout most of the United States and southern Canada; winters from the United States to Costa Rica.

Habits and economic status: The Cooper's hawk, or "blue darter," as it is familiarly known throughout the South, is preeminently  a poultry- and bird-eating species, and its destructiveness in this direction is surpassed only by that of its larger congener, the goshawk, which occasionally in autumn and winter enters the United States from the North in great numbers. The almost universal prejudice against birds of prey is largely due to the activities of these two birds, assisted by a third, the sharp-shinned hawk, which in habits and appearance might well pass for a small Cooper's hawk. These birds usually approach under cover and drop upon unsuspecting victims, making great inroads upon poultry yards and game coverts favorably situated for this style of hunting. Out of 123 stomachs examined, 38 contained the remains of poultry and game birds, 66 the remains of other birds, and 12 the remains of mammals. Twenty-eight species of wild birds were identified in the above-mentioned material. This destructive hawk, together with its two near relatives, should be destroyed by every possible means. (See Biol. Survey Bul. 3, pp. 38–43.)

Mourning Dove (Zenaidura macroura)

Length, 12 inches. The dark spot on the side of the neck distinguishes this bird from all other native doves and pigeons except the white-winged dove. The latter has the upper third of wing white.

Range:, Breeds throughout the United States and in Mexico, Guatemala, and southern Canada; winters from the central United States to Panama.

Habits and economic status: The food of the mourning dove is practically all vegetable matter

(over 99 per cent), principally seeds of plants, including grain. Wheat, oats, rye, corn, barley, and buckwheat were found in 150 out of 237 stomachs, and constituted 32 per cent of the food. Three-fourths of this was waste grain picked up after harvest. The principal and almost constant diet is weed seeds, which are eaten throughout the year and constitute 64 per cent of the entire food. In one stomach were found 7,500 seeds of yellow wood sorrel, in another 6,400 seeds of barn grass or foxtail, and in a third 2,600 seeds of slender paspalum, 4,820 of orange hawk-weed, 950 of hoary vervain, 120 of Carolina cranesbill, 50 of yellow wood sorrel, 620 of panic grass, and 40 of various other weeds. None of these are useful, and most of them are troublesome weeds. The dove does not eat insects or other animal food. It should be protected in every possible way.

Ruffed Grouse (Bonasa umbellus)

Length, 17 inches. The broad black band near tip of tail distinguishes this from other grouse.

Range: Resident in the northern two-thirds of the United States and in the forested parts of Canada.

Habits and economic status: The ruffed grouse, the famed drummer and finest game bird of the northern woods, is usually wild and wary and under reasonable protection well withstands

the attacks of hunters. Moreover, when reduced in numbers, it responds to protection in a gratifying manner and has proved to be well adapted to propagation under artificial conditions. Wild fruits, mast, and browse make up the bulk of the vegetable food of this species. It is very fond of hazelnuts, beechnuts, chestnuts, and acorns, and it eats practically all kinds of wild berries and other fruits. Nearly 60 kinds of fruits have been identified from the stomach contents examined. Various weed seeds also are consumed. Slightly more than 10 per cent of the food consists of insects, about half being beetles. The most important pests devoured are the potato beetle, clover-root weevil, the pale-striped flea beetle, grapevine leaf-beetle, May beetles, grasshoppers, cotton worms, army worms, cutworms, the red-humped apple worm, and sawfly larvæ. While the economic record of the ruffed grouse is fairly commendable, it does not call for more stringent protection than is necessary to maintain the species in reasonable numbers. (See Biol. Survey Bul. 24, pp. 25–38.)

Bobwhite (Colinus virginianus)

Length, 10 inches. Known everywhere by the clear whistle that suggests its name.

Range: Resident in the United States east of the plains; introduced in many places m the West.

Habits and economic status: The bobwhite is loved by every dweller in the country and is better known to more hunters in the United States than any other game bird. It is no less appreciated on the table than in the field, and in many States has unquestionably been hunted too closely. Fortunately it seems to be practicable to propagate the

bird in captivity, and much is to be hoped for in this direction. Half the food* of this quail consists of weed seeds, almost a fourth of grain, and about a tenth of wild fruits. Although thus eating grain, the bird gets most of it from stubble. Fifteen per cent of the bobwhite's food is composed of insects, including several of the most serious pests of agriculture. It feeds freely upon Colorado potato beetles and chinch bugs; it devours also cucumber beetles, wire worms, billbugs, clover-leaf weevils, cotton-boll weevils, army worms, bollworms, cutworms, and Rocky Mountain locusts. Take it all in all, bobwhite is very useful to the farmer, and while it may not be necessary to remove it from the list of game birds every farmer should see that his own farm is not depleted by eager sportsmen. (See Biol. Survey Bul. 21, pp. 9–46.)

Killdeer (Oxyechus vociferus)

Length, 10 inches. Distinguished by its piercing and oftrepeated cry—*kildee.*

Range: Breeds throughout the United States and most of Canada; winters from central United States to South America.

Habits and economic status: The killdeer is one of the best known of the shorebird family. It often visits the farmyard and commonly nests in pastures or cornfields. It is rather suspicious, however, and on being approached takes flight with loud cries. It is noisy and restless, but fortunately most of its activities result in benefit to man. The food is of the same general nature as that of the upland plover, but is more varied. The killdeer feeds upon beetles, grasshoppers, caterpillars, ants, bugs, caddis flies, dragonflies, centipedes, spiders, ticks, oyster worms,

earthworms, snails, crabs, and other crustacea. Among the beetles consumed are such pests as the alfalfa weevil, cotton-boll weevil, clover-root weevil, clover-leaf weevil, pine weevil, billbugs, white grubs, wireworms, and leaf beetles. The bird also devours cotton worms, cotton cutworms, horseflies, mosquitoes, cattle ticks, and crawfish. One stomach contained hundreds of larvæ of the saltmarsh mosquito, one of the most troublesome species. The killdeer preys extensively upon insects that are annoying to man and injurious to his stock and crops, and this should be enough to remove it from the list of game birds and insure its protection.

Upland Plover (Bartramia longicauda)

Length, 12 inches. The only plainly colored shorebird which occurs east of the plains and inhabits exclusively dry fields and hillsides.

Range: Breeds from Oregon, Utah, Oklahoma, Indiana, and Virginia, north to Alaska; winters in South America.

Habits and economic status: This, the most terrestrial of our waders, is shy and wary, but it has the one weakness of not fearing men on horseback or in a vehicle. One of these methods of approach, therefore, is nearly always used by the sportsman, and, since the bird is highly prized, as a table delicacy, it has been minted to the verge of extermination. As the upland plover is strictly beneficial, it should no longer be classed as a game bird and allowed to be shot. Ninety-seven per cent of the food of this species consists of animal forms, chiefly of injurious and neutral species. The vegetable food is mainly weed seeds. Almost half of the total subsistence is made up of grasshoppers,

crickets, and weevils. Among the weevils eaten are the cotton-boll weevil, greater and lesser clover-leaf weevils, cowpea weevils, and billbugs. This bird devours also leaf beetles, wireworms, white grubs, army worms, cotton worms, cotton cutworms, sawfly larvæ, horseflies, and cattle ticks. In brief, it injures no crop, but consumes a host of the worst enemies of agriculture.

Black Tern (Hydrochelidon nigra surinamensis)

Length, 10 inches. In autumn occurs as a migrant on the east coast of the United States, and then is in white and gray plumage. During the breeding season it is confined to the ulterior, is chiefly black, and is the only dark tern occurring inland.

Range: Breeds from California, Colorado, Missouri, and Ohio, north to central Canada; winters from Mexico to South America; migrant in the eastern United States.

Habits and economic status: This tern, unlike most of its relatives, passes much of its life on fresh-water lakes and marshes of the interior. Its nests are placed among the tules and weeds, on floating vegetation, or on muskrat houses. It lays from 2 to 4 eggs. Its food is more varied than that of any other tern. So far as known it preys upon no food fishes, but feeds extensively upon such enemies of fish as dragonfly nymphs, fish-eating beetles, and crawfishes. Unlike most of its family, it devours a great variety of insects, many of which it catches as it flies. Dragon-flies, May flies, grasshoppers, predaceous diving beetles, scarabæid beetles, leaf beetles, gnats, and other flies are the principal kinds preyed upon. Fishes of little economic value, chiefly minnows and mummichogs, were found to compose only a little more than 19 per cent of the contents of 145 stomachs. The great consumption of insects by the black tern places it among the beneficial species worthy of protection.

Franklin's Gull (Larus franklini)

Length, 15 inches. During its residence in the United States Franklin's gull is practically confined to the interior and is the only inland gull with, black head and red bill.

Range: Breeds in the Dakotas, Iowa, Minnesota, and the neighboring parts of southern Canada; winters from the Gulf Coast to South America.

Habits and economic status: Nearly all of our gulls are coast-loving species and spend comparatively little of their time in fresh water, but Franklin's is a true inland gull. Extensive marshes bordering shallow lakes are its chosen breeding grounds, and as many such areas are being reclaimed for agricultural purposes it behooves the tillers of the soil to protect this valuable species. When undisturbed this gull becomes quite fearless and follows the plowman to gather the grubs and worms from the newly turned furrows. It lives almost exclusively upon insects, of which it consumes great quantities. Its hearty appetite is manifest from the contents of a few stomachs: A, 327 nymphs of dragonflies; B, 340 grasshoppers, 52 bugs, 3 beetles, 2 wasps, and 1 spider; C, 82 beetles, 87 bugs, 984 ants, 1 cricket, 1 grasshopper, and 2 spiders. About four-fifths of the total food is grasshoppers, a strong point m favor of this bird. Other injurious creatures eaten are billbugs, squash bugs, leaf-hoppers, click beetles (adults of wireworms), May beetles (adults of white grubs), and weevils. Franklin's gull is probably the most beneficial bird of its group.

Appendix 2: Animal Tracks

Badger

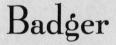

The west and Midwest, ranging from Canada to Mexico, is badger territory. When looking for badgers, keep an eye out not only for its tracks, but the holes that the animal digs along its trail in search for rodents. The badger's front feet are endowed with lengthy claws for that specific purpose, and those gigantic claws help indicate that it's a badger to which the trail belongs. Compared to the front ones, the badger's hind claws barely express themselves. Each foot has five toes that register in each track. The trail of the badger implies that it's a clumsy animal because of the double row, close together footprints. The hind feet toe-in a little and tend to touch the earlier tracks made by the forefeet.

Beaver

Found around water in much of the northern hemisphere, these animals leave obvious traces through their lumbering activities. Beavers are exceptional engineers, renowned for their dams, which are constructed with branches, sticks, mud, and roots, and also their lodges, which are mounds of mud and sticks, often reaching 20 feet in diameter and 4-6 feet in height. Other signs of beavers are in the water, too, like floating plant roots with teeth marks or even a straight, slow trail in water—a black arrowhead—which indicates that a beaver is swimming by. Alternatively, look on land for mud-pies, the romantic calling cards of male beavers, scented with drops of beaver castoreum. Beavers have 5 toes on both their front and hind

feet, although the latter set is webbed for swimming purposes, and this shows itself in their trails. Each toe has a claw, a characteristic that appears in the track. However, the claw on the second toe of the hind foot is split, which seldom registers. The beaver can use this odd toe as a comb. The beaver's tail is broad and flat and often drags in the trail, weaving from side to side.

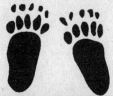

Black Bear

Black bears are the only bears that climb trees into adulthood, so they're commonly found in wooded sections of the arctic all the way down to Mexico. Their tracks are reminiscent of grizzly and giant brown bears' except for the much smaller size and claw marks. A black bear's hind foot measures about 6 inches and its claws are not nearly as large as a grizzly bear's. Often, the claws don't show up in the track at all. Black bears have five toes on both front and hind feet, and though the toe is well-developed in both places, it doesn't register. Black bears typically hibernate during winter, so their tracks are seldom seen in snow.

Bobcat

The bobcat, found in almost all the wooded sections of the United States, has tracks similar to a domestic cat, but larger. Bobcats also have a more complex palm and heel pad outline than other cats. It walks correctly, meaning the hind feet step into the marks made by the front feet, which helps the animal stalk its prey.

Brown Bear

The brown bear is the most massive meat eater living in the world today, weighing in at around 1200-1400 pounds. Tracks of brown bear hind feet measure an impressive 14-16 inches long. These animals make it a habit to step in tracks they have already made, meaning that the hind foot and front foot register, and so claw marks are generally not visible in their tracks. The fifth toe in both front and hind feet is well developed, but it also does not show up in the trail. Other signs of a brown bear, or any bear, for that matter, are gnawed and gouged trees acting as signposts or billboards, droppings, and logs that have been torn open. Brown bears are found along the Pacific coast, ranging from Alaska to British Columbia.

Cottontail Rabbit

This small, widespread animal is famous for its hopping, bounding movements. Rabbits place their hind feet in front of the tracks made by their forefeet; they are able to travel 10-15 ft in one bound. Cottontail rabbits are fast, but often resort to tricks to avoid their pursuers, like doubling back or leaping to the side. Often, they travel the same route every day, and they also do not stray too far from their home, not beyond an acre. They have 5 toes on their forefeet and 4 on their hind ones, although only 4 of the toes on the front foot make any impact in their track.

Coyote

Like cats, coyotes walk on their toes, and their tracks are similar to a wolf's, except smaller, although their prints are not as small as a fox's. A coyote's claws are always apparent in the trail, and the outer toes of the hind foot are larger than the inner toes. These animals are found in a variety of places, but especially in the prairies and open woodlands of North America. Their reach even stretches into Alaska.

Crow

Crows can be found almost anywhere except for deserts and pine forests. Because they are birds, the signs that identify them are sometimes more difficult to find. Their characteristic "caw-caw" bird call identifies them immediately, but if they are not in the vicinity, look for regurgitated pellets at the base of their roosting places. Composed of things that can't be digested, crow pellets will reflect their varied diet. If you happen to spot a nest, crows make 4-6 green-colored eggs that have brown spots.

Deer

The white-tailed deer is regularly found in the east, living in fields and woodlands that are close to communities. They have nimble cloven hoofs and their hind feet always step into the tracks made by the forefeet. The tracks of the doe are more petite and narrow than those of the buck, and her tracks will often face straight forward or inward, while his toes point out. A buck also spreads his feet more widely and drags them during rutting season. Other buck signs are pawed-up ground and trees and bushes scraped by antlers. A whitetail's track measures about 3 inches for a buck, 2½ inches for a doe, and ¾ inches for a fawn. A mule deer, native of the west and heaviest type of deer at 200 pounds, leaves tracks that are rounder in appearance than a whitetail, and when it bounds, the deer will produce a peculiar, close group of tracks that is much different from their eastern counterparts. A mule deer's track measures 3¼ inches long. The coast blacktail deer lives on the Pacific coast, ranging from Alaska to California. Their tracks resemble those of a mule deer, especially when bounding, but their walk is like any other. They weigh around 150 pounds.

Fox

A red fox can be found all over North America, but will more likely be in northern areas. They frequent mixed woodlands, open country, and especially farming areas. Like other members of the dog family, a fox has prominent claws, but their track itself is more delicate than the others. They leave little, widely spaced, pad marks, and that distinguishes them. They are also good trackers because their hind feet step into the tracks made by the forefeet, their trail often leading in a straight line. Another sign of a fox is digging; their holes are similar to the ones dug by skunks, although they are deeper and narrower. A gray fox is likely to be found in the south and resembles a dog more than a red fox; their tracks are somewhat smaller because the toes of a gray fox make a larger print. A desert fox can be found in Southwest and lower California, while a kit fox is only found in the prairies and grows to be about the size of a housecat—their tracks resemble a cat's, too, other than the claws. An arctic fox lives between the timberline and then northward as far as the land reaches. Their tracks are smaller than the red fox, and in the winter resemble little oval pads because they grow extra fur as protection.

Grizzly Bear

Inhabiting the west, the grizzly bear is known as the giant of the western mountains. Grizzly bears have excessively long claws that help them dig for burrowing animals. All 5 of their toes leave marks when they walk, and a grizzly's hind foot often measures about 12 inches. They are known to bury their kills with fresh dirt, and they also make use of bear trees as signposts and billboards to communicate with other bears.

Moose

Moose reside in the north: Canada and some of the northern areas in the United States. These animals have hoofs, although theirs are long and pointed because they are used as weapons. Measuring in at around 7 inches long, they may be the largest of the native ungulates. Their hoofs are easily distinguishable from those of a domestic cow. Other signs of moose, particularly bull moose, are twigs and branches broken down by antlers, pawed ground, and acrid smelling wallows.

Opossum

Found in the eastern United States, the Midwest, and Pacific coast, opossums live in any woodland habitats, farming areas, and even some urban areas. They climb trees, and their feet have evolved into resembling hands with thumbs rather than having claws; their hind feet is one of their distinguishing qualities, as is that each toe, other than the thumb, has claws. Opossums waddle when they walk, moving the feet of one side at the same time. Their tracks are normally not larger than 1¾ inches in width, and they are often spotted along streams.

Otter

Otters live from the northern timberline to southern South America always near water. There are many different species, but the Canadian otter is most common throughout Canada and the United States. Otters measure around 4-5 feet long and can usually be found in the water, searching for fish. Their water trail is quite distinctive because they swim quickly, leaving a zig-zag trail in the water. In winter, otters have to travel on land in order to find open water, and they leave a very characteristic trail: they bound, each one leaving a full-length, well defined imprint in the snow. Their padded footprints that can often be seen. Otters have 5 curled toes on both their fore and hind feet, but the 5th toe does not make an impression. Both feet leave a rounded track, but the hind foot is slightly longer. Otters can also be identified by their slides as they enjoy sliding down slippery mud banks which cuts down travel time.

Porcupine

Famous for its pricks, a porcupine is the size of a small dog and lives in forests or similarly brushy areas in the western and northern United States, spreading their influence as far as Canada and Alaska. Because they spend much of their time in trees, they have strong climbing claws on both their front and hind feet. The forefoot has 4 toes while the hind one has 5, and because porcupine do not hibernate, their tracks are visible in the snow. Look for teeth marks on evergreen trees or on axe handles or canoe paddles; porcupines love salt and will gnaw on salty leftovers.

Raccoon

Another tree climber, the raccoon's claws are very important in distinguishing its track. Raccoons have bare soles and toes that can be plainly seen from the impression they leave, 5 well developed toes that have claws on each foot, and hind feet that are longer than the forefeet. The forefoot measures about 3¼ inches while the hind is about an inch longer. When it walks, it steps upon the track of its forefoot with its hind foot. Other signs of a raccoon are its den which is usually found in a hollow tree and hairs that catch in wood and bark. They are found all over the United States.

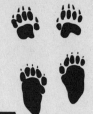

Skunk

T he easiest way to spot a skunk is by its smell thanks to their poison gas scent glands. They're located anywhere from the Hudson Bay in Canada south to Guatemala. Skunks are flat-footed with 5 toes on each foot, although their claws usually do not show on their hind foot. Their prints look somewhat similar to those of a small bear. When walking, skunks toe-in and place the fore and hind foot of the same side close together. Like foxes, skunks dig holes, although theirs are more shallow and round than the holes dug by foxes.

Squirrel

G ray squirrels populate the East: southern Canada to southern United States. These are animals that bound with hind legs that are longer than the fore. When running, squirrels pair their forefeet behind their hind feet, a nod to their tree climbing capabilities. Squirrels have 5 toes on their hind feet that clearly show up and 4 in the front; the thumb of the front has disappeared from their anatomy over the centuries. They have flat feet and walk on the palms and soles of their aforementioned feet. Fox squirrels are bigger and stockier than gray ones, and they live in eastern hardwood forests from the southern tip of the Great Lakes to southern United States. Red squirrels can be found in the northern United States and Canada. Traces of those squirrels can be seen even in winter; they only sleep during the darkest, most frigid days and dig tunnels in the snow otherwise.

Turkey

Turkeys are distinctly American, found in many open woodlands. They are the largest game bird, therefore their tracks are also the largest. Their middle toe curves slightly inward, which adds to their already toe-in imprints. Their stiff feathers on their wings can leave marks on the trail when they strut around.

Wolf

Wolves are found in the wilderness of the northern forests and tundra. They also appear in most other habitats, except deserts and high mountains. The tracks of a dog and wolf are so similar that many concede that there is not one reliable feature that will distinguish between the two. A wolf's tracks tend to be larger and also their suspicious, shy nature leads wolf to use every bit of cover as they approach an object, while dogs approach things openly. The inner toes of the hind foot of a wolf leave a larger track than do the outer toes.